I0800556

The Persecution and Murder of the Jews, 1933–1945

The Persecution and Murder of the European Jews by Nazi Germany, 1933–1945

Series edited on behalf of the German Federal Archives, the Leibniz Institute for Contemporary History (IfZ), and the Modern History Research Group at the Albert Ludwig University of Freiburg

In cooperation with Yad Vashem

Volume 4

Editorial and International Advisory Board
for the English edition (PMJ)
Nomi Halpern, Elizabeth Harvey, Susanne Heim, Ulrich Herbert, Michael Hollmann, Ingo Loose, Dan Michman, Dieter Pohl, Sybille Steinbacher, Alan E. Steinweis, Simone Walther-von Jena, Nikolaus Wachsmann, and Andreas Wirsching

German edition (VEJ) also edited by
Hans-Dieter Kreikamp, Horst Möller, and Hartmut Weber

The Persecution and Murder of the European Jews by Nazi Germany, 1933–1945

Volume 4

Poland September 1939–July 1941

Executive Editor
Klaus-Peter Friedrich
with Andrea Löw

English-language edition prepared by
Elizabeth Harvey, Russell Alt-Haaker, Johannes Gamm,
Georg Felix Harsch, Dorothy A. Mas, and Caroline Pearce

DE GRUYTER
OLDENBOURG

יד ושם
YAD VASHEM
THE WORLD HOLOCAUST
REMEMBRANCE CENTER

THE INTERNATIONAL INSTITUTE
FOR HOLOCAUST RESEARCH

ISBN 978-3-11-068737-8
e-ISBN (PDF) 978-3-11-068779-8
e-ISBN (EPUB) 978-3-11-068790-3

Library of Congress Control Number: 2022950742

Bibliographical information published by the Deutsche Nationalbibliothek
The Deutsche Nationalbibliothek lists this publication in the Deutsche Nationalbibliografie; detailed bibliographical information is available at http://dnb.dnb.de.

© 2023 Walter de Gruyter GmbH, Berlin/Boston
Typesetting: Meta Systems Publishing & Printservices GmbH, Wustermark
Cover and dust jacket: Frank Ortmann
Cartography: Peter Palm
Printing and binding: Beltz Grafische Betriebe GmbH, Bad Langensalza

www.degruyter.com

Contents

Foreword to the English Edition

The Persecution and Murder of the European Jews by Nazi Germany, 1933–1945 presents a broad range of primary sources in a scholarly edition. A total of sixteen English-language volumes will be published in this series, organized chronologically and according to region. The series places particular focus on the countries which had the highest Jewish populations before the outbreak of the Second World War, above all Poland and the occupied territories of the Soviet Union. The English-language edition (PMJ) reproduces all the materials in the German edition (VEJ) and has been adapted for an English-speaking readership. Apart from those originally written in English, all documents presented here have been translated from the language of the original source.

This volume, the fourth in the series, covers the persecution of Jews in occupied Poland in the period from the German invasion on 1 September 1939 up to the attack on the Soviet Union in summer 1941. The sources shed light on developments in the annexed territories of western and northern Poland and in the so-called General Government. Two further volumes document the persecution and murder of the Jews in Poland in the years up to 1945: volume 9 covers the General Government from August 1941 to 1945, and volume 10 deals with the annexed territories of Poland over the same period. While some documents in volumes 4, 9, and 10 mention Jews deported from elsewhere in Europe to the formerly Polish territories, the main focus in the three volumes is the fate of the Polish Jews.

The foreword to the first volume of the series details the criteria for the selection of the documents. These criteria can be summarized as follows. First, the sources used are written documents and, occasionally, transcribed audio recordings, dating from the period of Nazi rule between 1933 and 1945. The decision was taken not to include memoirs, reports, and judicial documents produced after 1945; however, the footnotes make extensive reference to such retrospective testimonies and historical accounts. Second, the documents shed light on the actions and reactions of people with differing backgrounds and convictions and in different places, and indicate their intentions as well as the frequently limited options available to them. The volumes include a variety of document types, such as official correspondence, private letters, diary entries, legal texts, newspaper articles, and reports of foreign observers.

The documents are ordered chronologically, meaning that the perspective switches frequently in the course of the volume. The diary entry of a young Jew portraying the humiliations inflicted by the German occupiers on the Jews in the aftermath of the invasion is followed later in the document sequence by a speech by Hitler outlining his plans for the ethnic reordering of Eastern Europe. A poster banning Jews from buying and selling textiles, and threatening prison or even the death penalty for those infringing the order, contrasts with a letter written by a Jewish dental assistant from Bromberg (Bydgoszcz) describing the desperate situation of Jews expelled from that city to Warsaw. Petitions written by Jews to the occupation authorities or to Jewish aid organizations are to be found along with appeals issued by the Polish underground or reports by representatives of the Polish Catholic Church.

The editors wish to thank the German Research Foundation (DFG) for its generous funding of the German- and English-language projects. The English-language volumes are produced in cooperation with the Yad Vashem International Institute for Holocaust Research, which provides important assistance in revising the introductions to the volumes. The editors are also grateful to the large number of specialists and private individuals who have provided them with advice and comments on sources and with information for the annotations, including biographical details for the people featured in the documents.

Kathleen Luft and Martin Pearce translated most of the German documents for this fourth volume in the series; additional translations from German were provided by David Hill, Jessica Spengler, and Nancy Twilley. Kathleen Luft also translated documents from Russian. George Szenderowicz and Jasper Tilbury translated the documents from Polish. Daria Chernysheva translated documents from French. Yad Vashem provided translations from Hebrew (by Ruchie Avital) and Yiddish (by Rebecca Wolpe). Rona Johnston Gordon, Alissa Jones Nelson, Merle Read, and Sarah Pybus provided proofreading and copy-editing services. Peter Palm created and Giles Bennett advised on the maps, and Frank Ortmann designed the book jacket. Lea von der Hude, Ashley Kirspel, Charlie Perris, Aliena Stürzer, and Aslihan Özcan contributed to this volume as student assistants. The following research associates and assistants contributed to the original German volume: Romina Becker, Giles Bennett, Natascha Butzke, Florian Danecke, Miriam Schelp, Remigius Stachowiak, and Gudrun Schroeter.

Despite all the care taken, occasional inaccuracies cannot be entirely avoided in a document collection on this scale. We would be grateful for any notifications to this effect. The address of the editorial board is: Leibniz Institute for Contemporary History, Edition 'The Persecution and Murder of the European Jews by Nazi Germany, 1933–1945', Finckensteinallee 85/87, 12205 Berlin, Germany.

Berlin/Munich/Freiburg/Klagenfurt/Jerusalem, December 2022

Editorial Preface

This document collection on the persecution and murder of the European Jews should be cited using the abbreviation PMJ. This citation style is also used in the work itself where there are cross references between the individual volumes. The documents are consecutively numbered, beginning anew with each volume. Accordingly, 'PMJ 1/200' refers to document number 200 in the first volume of this series. The individual documents are presented as follows: title (in bold type), header, document, footnotes.

The titles have been formulated by the editor(s) of the respective volume and provide information on the document's date of origin, its core message, author, and recipient(s). The header underneath the title is part of the document itself. It specifies the type of source (letter, draft law, minutes, and so on), the author's name, the source's origin, the file reference (where applicable), remarks indicating confidential or classified status, and other special features of the document. The location of ministries or other central agencies in Berlin at the time, for instance the Reich Security Main Office or the Chancellery of the Führer, is not cited. The header also contains details about the addressee and, where applicable, the date of the receipt stamp, and it concludes with the date of origin and a reference to the source's stage of processing, for instance 'draft', 'carbon copy', or 'copy'.

The header is followed by the document text. Salutations and valedictions are included, though signatures are only indicated in the header. Instances of emphasis by the author in the original document are retained. Irrespective of the type of emphasis used in the original source (for example, underlined, spaced, bold, capitalized, or italicized), they always appear in italics in the printed version. Where necessary, additional particulars on the document are to be found in the footnotes. To enhance readability, words missing in the original due to obvious mistakes have been added in square brackets. Additional contextual information that has no direct equivalent in the original but is required to understand the text has also been added in square brackets.

Abbreviations are explained in the List of Abbreviations. Uncommon abbreviations, primarily from private correspondence, are explained in a footnote upon first mention in a given document.

Handwritten additions in typewritten originals have been adopted by the editors without further indication insofar as they are formal corrections and most probably inserted by the author. If the additions significantly alter the content – either by mitigating or radicalizing it – this is mentioned in the footnotes, and, if known, the author of the addition(s) is given.

As a rule, the documents are reproduced here in full. Documents are only abridged in exceptional cases where the original source was overly long, or where, in the case of the written records of meetings, Nazi policies relating to the persecution of Jews were only addressed within a single part of the proceedings. Any such abridgements are indicated by an ellipsis in square brackets; the contents of the omitted text are outlined in a footnote.

Documents are presented in strict chronological order according to the date they were produced. There are a few exceptions: descriptive texts written soon after the period covered, but nonetheless retrospectively, are sometimes classified according to the date of the events portrayed rather than the date of writing. These include a Jewish eyewitness account written in Palestine in 1940 describing the first weeks and months of the German occupation in Poland (Doc. 13). Other instances are reports written in late 1940 and early 1941 for the underground archive of the Warsaw ghetto (Ringelblum archive, Oyneg Shabes) which describe developments in late 1939 (e.g. Doc. 47 and Doc. 48). The precise dating of documents is particularly difficult in the case of the reports collected for the underground archive. Where there is any uncertainty regarding the date the documents were written or whether they constitute originals or copies, reference is made in the footnotes.

The first footnote for each document, which is linked to the title, contains the location of the source and, insofar as it denotes an archive, the reference number, as well as the folio number(s) if available. Reference to copies of archival documents in research institutions and in the German Federal Archives in Berlin is always made if the original held at the location first mentioned was not consulted there. In the case of printed sources, for instance newspaper articles or legislative texts, this footnote contains standard bibliographical information. The documents in this series have been translated from the original sources. If the source has already been published in a document collection on National Socialism or on the persecution of the Jews, reference is made to its first publication, alongside the original location of the source. Where English-language versions of these sources are available, references to these are given and in some cases the published English version is reproduced, with acknowledgements. If a document has already been published in English translation but has been newly translated for this volume, this is indicated in a footnote.

The next footnote places the document into context and, where appropriate, mentions related discussions, the specific role of authors and recipients, and activities accompanying or immediately following its genesis. Subsequent footnotes provide additional information related to the document's subject matter and the persons relevant to the content. They refer to other – published or unpublished – sources that can place the document in its historical context.

The footnotes also point out individual features of the documents, for instance handwritten notes in the margin, underlining, or deletions, whether by the author or the recipient(s). Annotations and instructions for submission are referred to in the footnotes where the editors consider them to contain significant information. Where possible, the locations of the treaties, laws, and decrees cited in the source text are provided in the footnotes, while other documents are given with their archival reference number. If these details could not be ascertained, this is also noted.

Where biographical information is available on the senders and recipients of the documents, this is provided in the footnotes. The same applies to persons mentioned in the text if they play an active role in the events described. As a general rule, this information is given in the footnote inserted after the first mention of the name in question in the volume. Biographical information on a particular person can thus be retrieved easily via the index.

The short biographies draw on data found in reference works, scholarly literature, or the Central Database of Shoah Victims' Names established and run by Yad Vashem. In many cases additional information was retrieved by consulting personnel files and indexes, municipal and company archives, registry offices, restitution and denazification files, or specialists in the field. Indexes and files on persons from the Nazi era held in archives were also used, primarily those of the former Berlin Document Center and the Central Office of the Judicial Authorities of the Federal States for the Investigation of National Socialist Crimes (Zentrale Stelle der Landesjustizverwaltungen zur Aufklärung nationalsozialistischer Verbrechen) in Ludwigsburg, the latter now stored in the German Federal Archives. National archives and special archives on the Second World War and the persecution of the Jews in the respective countries were also consulted. Despite every effort, it has not always been possible to obtain complete biographical information. In such cases, the footnote in question contains only verified facts such as the year of birth. In some cases a year of death has been assumed, as indicated by a question mark immediately after it. Where a person could not be identified, there is no footnote reference.

As a rule, in the titles, footnotes, and introduction inverted commas are not placed around terms that were commonplace in Nazi Germany, such as Führer, Jewish Council, or Aryanization, but German-language terms expressing ideological concepts of race, such as *Mischling*, are placed in italics. The terms 'Jew' and 'Jewish' also require some comment. The personal identification of victims as Jews was not the defining factor in someone's persecution. Rather, the terms 'Jew' and 'Jewish' which were used as the basis for persecution were defined by the perpetrators on the basis of racial legislation. References in the documents to the 'Gestapo', an acronym of the German GEheime STAats-POlizei, and to the 'State Police' denote one and the same institution: the Secret State Police.

The glossary contains concise descriptions of key terms and concepts that are repeated on multiple occasions or are related to the events and developments described in the volume. All primary and secondary sources consulted are listed in the footnotes and bibliography.

Note on the translation

British English is used in all translations into English. Where a document was originally written in British or American English, the spelling, style, and punctuation of the original have been retained, with silent corrections of minor spelling or grammatical errors and insertions in square brackets to clarify the meaning if necessary.

The spelling, style, and punctuation of the translated documents broadly conform to the guidelines in *New Hart's Rules: The Oxford Style Guide* (2014). Accordingly, the ending -ize rather than -ise is preferred throughout.

SS, police, and certain other ranks are given in the original German, as are titles where there is no standard equivalent in English or where there may be confusion with contemporary usage. A table of military and police ranks is included as an appendix, along with English-language equivalents of these terms and an indication of their position in the National Socialist hierarchy. Administrative and other terms have been left in the original language where there is no satisfactory equivalent in English. These terms are either explained in a footnote or, if they appear on multiple occasions, in the glossary.

All laws and institutions are translated into English in the documents. In the introduction and footnotes, foreign-language terms and expressions are added in brackets after the translation where this is considered important for understanding or context. The original spelling of foreign organizations is retained in the footnotes. The titles of published works not in the English language are not translated unless the work in question is of contextual or substantial relevance. If a foreign-language word or phrase appears in a document, this is retained in the translated text and its meaning explained in a footnote or, if necessary, the glossary.

Where the documents translated from Polish from a specifically Christian perspective contain quotations from the Bible, the New King James Version (KJV) has been preferred, especially where the context is religious or ecclesiastical. For Bible quotations in documents written specifically from a Jewish perspective, the 1917 Jewish Publication Society (JPS) translation of the Tanakh (Hebrew Bible) has been used.

In order to avoid confusion between British and American English, dates are spelled out in the order day, month, and year. Foreign proper names are not italicized. Thus, names of institutions, organizations, and places are written in roman type in the footnotes, but legislation and conceptual terms are in italics.

In the titles, footnotes, and translated documents, place names are generally written according to the variant commonly used in scholarly literature on the period. This also applies to places that have since been renamed, so, for example, 'Danzig' not 'Gdańsk'. The modern English version of a place name is given where this is widely used, for example Warsaw or Cracow. In other cases, place names in the translated documents are given in either their Polish or their German form according to usage in the original source and the perspective of the writer. Both variants are included in the index. In editorial text and in sources written from a Jewish or Polish perspective, the Polish place names are used in the titles, headers, document text, and footnotes. In the case of Polish cities that were renamed following post-1945 border changes, the Polish place names that applied up to 1945 are used, also in the footnotes (thus Lwów, Łuck). In the translations of German official documents, newspapers, and letters, German place names are used throughout. In the titles of German documents that include a place name, the Polish place name is also given in brackets. In the footnotes to documents translated from German, the Polish place names are used in cases of general references to a town or city, but the German place names are used if they are part of a German title or function.

Diacritical marks in Polish are as a rule retained. However, they are not added if they do not appear in an originally German source. Nor are diacritics included in the names of concentration and extermination camps and ghettos, where diacritics have been removed in order to emphasize that these camps were established by the German National Socialist regime, hence Sobibor or Lodz. The ghetto in Łódź is referred to as the Lodz ghetto or the Litzmannstadt (Lodz) ghetto. The forms Lodz and Lodsch are retained where they occur in German documents as the Germanized form of Łódź (renamed Litzmannstadt in 1940). For Chelmno/Kulmhof, the German name is used.

Language-specific characters such as the German ß (*Eszett*) for ss have also been retained.

The YIVO conventions for romanizing words and names written in Yiddish with Hebrew characters are used in this volume. In some cases, the romanized form of a person's name in a text translated from Yiddish may differ in spelling from the same person's name appearing in a text translated from Polish, for example. This is due to the fact that a Jewish person's given name was Polonized one way during the period and region in question, while having been pronounced another way among Yiddish speakers, e.g. Izaak or Icchak vs. Yitskhok. In other instances, English-language equivalents of the names in question have also established themselves. Whenever possible, the different spellings and variations are provided in the footnote containing the individual's biographical information. Finally, Hebrew and Yiddish terms are described in the footnotes or glossary, along with any other words requiring explanation.

Two specific terminological issues can be noted in relation to this volume. The first relates to administrative divisions imposed by the German occupiers in the annexed territories of western and northern Poland and in the General Government. In western and northern Poland, parts of the conquered territories were annexed to the existing Prussian provinces of Silesia or East Prussia, while other parts constituted the new so-called Reichsgaue (Danzig-West Prussia and Wartheland). Below the level of the provinces or the new Reichsgaue, the administrative subdivisions were Regierungsbezirke, each headed by a Regierungspräsident. Below the Regierungsbezirk was the Kreis (plural: Kreise). Each Kreis was headed by a Landrat. In the General Government, administrative subdivisions were the four (from summer 1941: five) districts, below which were the Kreise. Each Kreis in the General Government was headed by a Kreishauptmann (plural: Kreishauptmänner or Kreishauptleute), or, in some larger cities, a Stadthauptmann. At the level below the Kreis in the General Government, Landkommissare and Stadtkommissare were appointed to assist in enacting the orders of the Kreishauptleute. While the German term Distrikt has been translated as district, the other terms have been left in German to avoid confusion. Polish terms related to the structures of authority operating under German rule at village or local level in the General Government have generally been left untranslated, as in the case of wójt (Polish local administrative official). Gmina, meaning a local authority, has been translated as community.

The use of terminology in relation to departments within the civil administration in the General Government (GG) may also be noted. At the level of the government of the GG in Cracow, responsibilities for different policy areas were assigned to Main Departments (Hauptabteilungen). The Hauptabteilungen at the level of the government of the GG had equivalent departments at the level of the districts. In the translated documents, the departments at the level of the GG are referred to as main departments in those cases where the distinction between GG-level and district-level departments needs to be emphasized. Otherwise, it should be clear from the context whether a GG-level department or a district-level department is being referred to.

The second issue is the challenge for translation posed by the euphemistic German terms associated with the forced displacement of the Jewish population both within the annexed territories and from the annexed territories to the General Government. These forcible expulsions, which are a major theme in the current volume, were referred to in German documents as 'resettlement' measures using both the terms *umsiedeln/Umsiedlung* and *aussiedeln/Aussiedlung*. The occupiers' use of the vocabulary of 'resettlement' in relation to the Jewish population overlapped with the use of the same terms for quite different operations during the period 1939 to summer 1941 to evict, displace, and transfer population groups within and to occupied Poland: these included expulsions of Poles from their homes in the annexed territories to the General Government, and the transfer of ethnic Germans from the Baltic states, Soviet-occupied eastern Poland, and Romania to the 'Greater German Reich', including the annexed territories of Poland. After the onset of systematic mass murder from summer 1941 (documented in volumes 9 and 10), German officials increasingly used 'resettlement' terminology to refer to the mass murder of the Jews, whether they were being removed to killing sites in the immediate vicinity or deported to extermination camps. In the present volume, the euphemistic terms *umsiedeln/Umsiedlung* and *aussiedeln/Aussiedlung* that are used in German official documents are as a rule translated as 'resettlement', but in document titles and footnotes the process involved is described as forced resettlement or expulsion.

Introduction

After Nazi Germany invaded Poland on 1 September 1939, around 2 million Polish Jews came under German control in a matter of weeks.[1] Five years later, when the occupiers were forced to leave Poland, less than 10 per cent of the pre-war Jewish population were still alive. Three volumes of this edition address the persecution of the Jews in Poland. This volume documents the persecution in the Polish territories under German occupation in the period from the invasion of Poland up to the attack on the Soviet Union in the summer of 1941. Volume 9 deals with the situation in the General Government from August 1941 to 1945; volume 10 focuses on conditions during the same period in the western and northern Polish territories incorporated into the German Reich.

The central themes of this volume are the terror unleashed by the SS/police and Wehrmacht immediately after the invasion, the humiliation of the Jewish population, the erosion and abolition of Jews' rights, their economic plundering, their forcible concentration and ghettoization, individual killings and massacres, and the rising mortality among the Jewish population. Documents detailing the actions of the occupation authorities – orders, regulations, announcements, activity reports, and minutes of meetings – reveal the scale of the onslaught on the Polish Jews. They also show how much confusion reigned, particularly during the first weeks after the invasion. The occupation of Poland meant that the number of Jews within the German sphere of control increased many times over. At the same time, the eastward expansion of the Reich appeared to open up new possibilities for a 'solution to the Jewish question'. Large-scale projects emerged for resettling Jews and other population groups, with the aim of restructuring the 'eastern territories' according to 'racial' principles. The deportations of Jews to the eastern part of the territories just occupied, together with the resettlement of ethnic Germans from the territories claimed by the Soviet Union, were meant to bring about the 'Germanization' of the annexed territories in western Poland. These various resettlement and deportation schemes, the obstacles they faced and the consequences that ensued, are documented in this volume, along with the aggressive anti-Jewish propaganda in the German-occupied regions.

After the outbreak of war, around 200,000 Polish Jews fled to the Soviet-occupied territories of eastern Poland in the hope of escaping persecution. Most, however, stayed where they were and tried to adjust, working out the options for eking out an existence and, later, for simply surviving. The sources published here – letters, diary entries, official and secret files, leaflets and other underground publications – convey the perplexity that prevailed among the Polish Jews, what they made of the situation and how they dealt with the threat to their livelihoods and safety. The documents bear witness to the ambivalent role of the Jewish councils installed by the Germans, and to the efforts made by Jewish organizations and individuals to organize daily life and find opportunities for self-help, as well as ways to resist. They show the varied reactions of the non-Jewish Poles, who were also subject to terror, to the persecution of the Jews. Furthermore, they

1 In what follows, the terms 'Jews' and 'Poles' are used, notwithstanding the fact that the Polish Jews were also Polish citizens and that not all of them considered themselves Jews.

shed light on the role of the Polish government in exile and indicate what news from occupied Poland found its way abroad.

By the end of the period of less than two years' duration documented here, the Polish Jews under German occupation had been visibly identified, deprived of their rights, and pauperized. A large proportion were imprisoned in overcrowded ghettos or in labour camps. Tens of thousands had already been murdered or had died of hunger or disease. In the summer of 1941, as the threshold to systematic mass murder was about to be crossed, the world of Polish Jewry, along with the culture it had created over centuries, lay in ruins.

Jews in Poland up to the First World War

> And there are those who believe that the name of the country also springs from a divine source: the language of Israel. For Israel said upon arriving there: po-lin, that is [in Hebrew]: here you will stay the night! And meant: let us lodge here until God causes the scattered of Israel to be gathered in again.[2]

For centuries Poland, which is extolled in this Jewish legend as a new homeland, was regarded as the centre of Jewish life, characterized by cultural and religious diversity. The Jewish communities there were largely autonomous. The presence of Jews in this region is documented as early as the eleventh century. After that time, increasing numbers of Ashkenazim – Jews from Central and Western Europe – came to the country, seeking to escape economic and occupational restrictions in their native countries or fleeing the pogroms that threatened them in Europe during the Crusades of 1096 and 1146–1147 and during the Black Death of 1348–1349.

The Polish rulers welcomed the immigration of Jews because they hoped that the new arrivals would help foster economic development. In the Statute of Kalisz, issued in 1264 by the Duke of Greater Poland, Bolesław the Pious (1221–1279), the Jewish settlers were therefore guaranteed freedom of economic activity, equal rights in civil proceedings, and the right to form their own communities. From then on, the Jews were subject to the ruler and thus to his laws and his protection. Until the partitioning of Poland in the late eighteenth century, these privileges – which were both broadened and extended in their territorial applicability to include Lithuania, from 1569 onwards part of the Polish-Lithuanian Commonwealth – were the basis for the legal position of the Polish Jews. The king and the aristocracy, on whose lands Jews lived, profited from the exis-

2 Shmuel J. Agnon, 'Polen – die Legende von der Ankunft', in S. J. Agnon and Ahron Eliasberg (eds.), *Das Buch von den polnischen Juden* (Berlin: Jüdischer Verlag, 1916), pp. 3–5, here pp. 4–5; Semen M. Dubnow, *History of the Jews in Russia and Poland, from the Earliest Times until the Present Day* (Philadelphia, PA: Jewish Publication Society of America, 1916); Heiko Haumann, *Geschichte der Ostjuden* (Munich: Deutscher Taschenbuch-Verlag, 1998); Antony Polonsky, *The Jews in Poland and Russia*, vol. 1: *1350 to 1881* (Oxford: Littman Library, 2009); Moshe Rosman, 'Poland before 1795', in Gershon David Hundert (ed.), *The YIVO Encyclopedia of Jews in Eastern Europe*, vol. 2 (New Haven, CT: Yale University Press, 2008), pp. 1381–1389; *Żydzi w dawnej Rzeczpospolitej: Materiały z konferencji 'Autonomia Żydów w Rzeczpospolitej Szlacheckiej'* (Wrocław, Warsaw and Cracow: Ossolineum, 1991).

tence of strong, protected Jewish communities because they yielded great economic advantages: the Jews boosted economic activity, paid high taxes, and granted loans on favourable terms. In addition, in the towns they were exempt from municipal jurisdiction. In royal disputes with the citizens of a town, Jews formed a useful counterweight favouring the king.

Under these conditions, a unique form of Jewish self-governance came into being. At the local level, the governing bodies of the communities managed political and religious affairs. They set the tax rates and collected the taxes, funded the Jewish court system, and operated religious institutions as well as welfare and educational establishments. The regional assemblies represented the next administrative level, and from 1581 the Council of Four Lands (Hebrew: Va'ad Arba' Aratzot) in Lublin formed the central authority for the entire Jewish population of Poland and Lithuania.[3]

For Polish Jewry this period was in many respects a 'golden age'. In 1534 the first Hebrew printing house was founded in Cracow. Every major city had a yeshiva, a school of higher instruction in the Talmud, as well as synagogue buildings. Poland became a new religious and cultural centre of European Jewry. Nonetheless, even in Poland the Jews were confronted with hostility and animosity: signs of this were evident from the thirteenth century onwards. At first it was representatives of the Catholic Church in particular who demanded that Jews be allowed to live only in separate neighbourhoods, and be visibly identified with a 'badge of shame', as well as barred from holding public office and from the financial sector. In the early modern period, anti-Jewish sentiment took hold among broader sections of the Polish population. From the fifteenth century onwards, Jews were accused with increasing frequency of committing ritual murder and desecrating the consecrated host. Christian merchants resented competition from Jewish traders, who often had extensive connections. In a number of cities violent assaults and forced expulsions of the local Jewish communities took place.[4]

The important economic role and the privileged legal position of the Polish Jews quickly led to their being caught up in social conflicts between the nobility and the peasantry. As tavern-keepers, traders, pedlars, administrators, tenants, and tax collectors, they acted as intermediaries between the nobles or landowners and the peasants, and between the towns and the countryside. This role increasingly became a fateful one for them, especially in the eastern part of the realm. In 1648, when peasant uprisings against the Polish manorial system broke out in Ukraine, the violence of the rebels under the leadership of the Cossack hetman Bohdan Chmielnicki (Bohdan Khmelnytsky) was directed primarily against the Jews, who were perceived as representatives of the hated Polish noble class. According to estimates, at least 13,000 Jews were killed in massacres. Among the survivors, great insecurity prevailed.

3 Rosman, 'Poland before 1795', pp. 1386–1388.

4 Maria Kłańska, 'Juden in Krakau und Kazimierz', in Maria Kłańska (ed.), *Jüdisches Städtebild Krakau* (Frankfurt am Main: Jüdischer Verlag, 1994), pp. 7–39; Anatol Leszczyński, *Sejm Żydów Korony 1623–1764* (Warsaw: Żydowski Instytut Historyczny, 1994); Haumann, *Geschichte der Ostjuden*, pp. 22–35; Gertrud Pickhan, 'Polen', in Wolfgang Benz (ed.), *Handbuch des Antisemitismus: Judenfeindschaft in Geschichte und Gegenwart*, vol. 1: *Länder und Regionen* (Munich: De Gruyter Saur, 2008), pp. 276–283; Eugene M. Avrutin, Jonathan Dekel-Chen, and Robert Weinberg (eds.), *Ritual Murder in Russia, Eastern Europe, and Beyond: New Histories of an Old Accusation* (Bloomington, IN: Indiana University Press, 2017).

This crisis, however, also helped engender a religious revival and new religious movements. The Hasidic movement (from Hasid = 'pious'), which emerged in the second half of the eighteenth century, gave a new expression to Jewish mysticism by linking piety with a life-affirming gaiety. Distinguished Hasidic scholars (tzaddikim) soon gathered large numbers of students around them. They maintained 'courts' of their own. During this period a specifically Eastern Jewish way of life took shape that combined the preservation of tradition and memory with a receptiveness to new influences.[5] That said, everyday life was largely defined by traditional customs and religious laws. Jewish life was organized in *kehillot* (communities; plural of *kehilla* in Hebrew) run by Jewish community councils. The language of daily life was East Yiddish: derived from Middle High German, on which its grammar is based, its vocabulary includes words from German, Hebrew, Aramaic, and the Slavonic languages spoken in the different regions where Jews settled.[6]

Between 1772 and 1795 Russia, the Habsburg monarchy, and Prussia divided up the Polish-Lithuanian 'republic of nobles' among themselves. The region in which most of the Jews lived came under Russian control: this was the Kingdom of Poland (as of 1815 also known as Congress Poland), whose territories formed a part of the Pale of Settlement created in 1791, stretching from Lithuania to the coast of the Black Sea. That was the only territory under Russian rule where Jews could settle permanently. Meanwhile, a large Jewish minority in Galicia came under the rule of the Habsburg monarchy.

In practice, the new political borders – at a time when passports and visas were prohibitively expensive, border guards were open to bribery, and smugglers with local knowledge were easy to find – did not prevent many Jews maintaining the old relationships. Nonetheless the partitions of Poland did affect the development of Polish Jewry. While the small numbers of Jews who lived in Prussia were largely assimilated into the German Jewish community and into German culture, the Polish Jews under Russian rule and in Galicia remained a separate ethnic group.

Now that the Jews had ceased to enjoy the protection of the Polish king and the nobles, each of the partitioning powers determined its own policy with respect to its Jewish minority. While emancipation was making headway in Western Europe, the process of obtaining legal equality was far slower for the Jews in divided Poland, where the progress of rights and freedoms depended on the partitioning power. Particularly in the Russian Pale of Settlement, some towns and cities retained the right to deny Jews entry until well into the late nineteenth century. Although the Edict of Toleration issued by Emperor Joseph II in 1789 granted the Galician Jews some freedoms, they obtained full equality only in 1867, when the constitution of the newly formed dual monarchy of Austria-Hungary was proclaimed. The Jews in the Province of Posen had been able to acquire Prussian citizenship from 1833 onwards, but, as everywhere in Prussia, there was no legal equality for Jews until 1869.

In Russia, Tsar Alexander II also relaxed some anti-Jewish regulations after 1856. He repealed some of the harsher decrees introduced by his father, such as the forced recruitment to the army (the so-called 'cantonist system'), and granted the right of residence

5 Haumann, *Geschichte der Ostjuden*, p. 58.

6 Dovid Katz, 'Yiddish', in Hundert (ed.), *YIVO Encyclopedia of Jews in Eastern Europe*, vol. 2, pp. 979–987.

throughout Russia to selected groups of 'useful' Jews: wealthy merchants (1859), university graduates (1861), certified craftsmen (1865), and medical staff of every category (including medical orderlies and midwives). The Jewish communities outside the Pale of Settlement rapidly expanded. Congress Poland, where the economy was flourishing and the most significant legal restrictions on Jews were temporarily lifted as early as 1862, attracted large numbers of Jews. The number of Jews in this area increased from 213,000 in 1816 to more than 1 million in the 1880s; their share of the total population grew from 8 per cent to 14.5 per cent during this time. After the assassination of the tsar in 1881, however, his successors took a more repressive course. The situation remained unchanged until the February Revolution of 1917. One of the first measures taken by the new Provisional Government was the cancellation of the hundreds of restrictions imposed on the Jews and the granting of full equality to the Jewish population.

In the Russian Empire, as in other countries, a rural exodus and urbanization had gone hand in hand with the onset of industrialization. Some cities with large Jewish populations, notably Łódź, Warsaw, Białystok, and Lwów, developed rapidly as a result of industrialization and the building of railways. This social change had profound consequences for the Jews. Some adopted modern ways, as Israel Singer describes in his novel *The Brothers Ashkenazi* (1936). Pioneers such as the textile manufacturer Izrael Poznański in Łódź, and the bankers and railway entrepreneurs Leopold Kronenberg and Jan Gotlib Bloch in Warsaw, became enormously successful. Some of them had been educated in German schools and universities, and a few of them had converted to Protestantism. But the majority of the Jews, who adhered to traditional ways of life and made a living as craftsmen and small-scale traders, became increasingly impoverished.

In Galicia economic development was uneven, with economic modernization limited to Cracow, Tarnów, Lwów, and a few other larger towns. Most Jews in Galicia lived in precarious conditions.[7] 'Only a small fraction of them', wrote the sociologist Arthur Ruppin, 'have a halfway stable and secure existence. The others live from hand to mouth and often have no idea at the start of the day where they will find the means to provide a midday meal for their families.'[8] This was the world of the shtetl. It was village or small-town life, traditional and predominantly shaped by the Jewish population. At the same time the shtetl was one of the places where Jews and Poles encountered one another, when the farmers from the surrounding area made their purchases there and in turn offered their goods for sale.[9]

The conflicts with the majority population intensified in the last quarter of the nineteenth century. A series of anti-Jewish pogroms occurred in the western part of the

7 Artur Eisenbach, *The Emancipation of the Jews in Poland, 1780–1870*, trans. Janina Dorosz (Oxford: Blackwell, 1991 [Polish edn, 1988]); François Guesnet, *Polnische Juden im 19. Jahrhundert: Lebensbedingungen, Rechtsnormen und Organisation im Wandel* (Cologne: Böhlau, 1998); Gershon C. Bacon, 'Poland from 1795 to 1939', in Hundert (ed.), *YIVO Encyclopaedia of Jews in Eastern Europe*, vol. 2, pp. 1390–1403, here p. 1393. On the history of the Russian Jews, see Salo W. Baron, *The Russian Jew under Tsars and Soviets* (New York: Macmillan, 1964).

8 Quotation translated from Arthur Ruppin, *Die Juden der Gegenwart: Eine sozialwissenschaftliche Studie*, 3rd edn (Berlin: Jüdischer Verlag, 1920), p. 48.

9 Eva Hoffman, *Shtetl: The Life and Death of a Small Town and the World of Polish Jews* (Boston: Houghton Mifflin, 1997); Steven T. Katz (ed.), *The Shtetl: New Evaluations* (New York: New York University Press, 2007); Bacon, 'Poland from 1795 to 1939', pp. 1394–1395.

Russian Empire, notably in Białystok in 1906.[10] The traditional hatred of Jews was increasingly overlaid by the trend towards national or ethnic exclusivity and political antisemitism. Even the Polish Socialist Party (Polska Partia Socjalistyczna, PPS), which included many Jews among its members, was not prepared to grant specific minority rights to the Jews. The Polish right-wing political movement National Democracy (Endecja for short) warned of a 'Jewish danger' and called for an anti-Jewish economic boycott in 1912.[11]

Economic hardship and social discrimination triggered a wave of emigration to the USA by Jews from Russia and Galicia – between 1881 and 1929 alone, more than 2½ million left their homelands.[12] Soon the majority of the Jews living in the Prussian Province of Posen also moved away, going either to other parts of Prussia, particularly to Berlin, or directly overseas.[13] Meanwhile, the idea of an Eastern Jewish nationality emerged among the Jews. Increasing numbers of Jews joined socialist and Zionist organizations. The largest socialist party, founded in Vilna in 1897, was the General Jewish Labour Bund (Algemeyner Yidisher Arbeterbund, for short: Bund) in Lithuania, Poland, and Russia. The Bund demanded national-cultural autonomy for Jews and other minorities in the Russian Empire. The non-socialist Folkspartay (People's Party), founded in 1905 by the historian Simon Dubnow, mainly representing the middle class, also demanded national-cultural autonomy and promoted Yiddish as the Jewish national language. Various Zionist groups, by contrast, advocated and promoted preparation for emigration to Palestine.[14] Meanwhile, Agudas Yisroel (Agudat Yisrael), founded in Kattowitz (Katowice) in 1912, became the principal party of the ultra-Orthodox Jews, both Hasidic and 'Misnagdic'. It was conservative in its political outlook and represented the interests of that part of the population whose daily life was determined by religion.[15]

After the beginning of the First World War, hundreds of thousands of Jews fled from their homes to avoid the hostilities, or were driven out and deported in 1915 when the

10 John D. Klier and Shlomo Lambroza (eds.), *Pogroms: Anti-Jewish Violence in Modern Russian History* (Cambridge: Cambridge University Press, 1992).

11 Frank Golczewski, *Polnisch-jüdische Beziehungen 1881–1922: Eine Studie zur Geschichte des Antisemitismus in Osteuropa* (Wiesbaden: Steiner, 1981); Heiko Haumann, 'Juden in der ländlichen Gesellschaft Galiziens am Ende des 19. und zu Beginn des 20. Jahrhunderts', in Andrea Löw, Kerstin Robusch, and Stefanie Walter (eds.), *Deutsche – Juden – Polen: Geschichte einer wechselvollen Beziehung im 20. Jahrhundert* (Frankfurt am Main: Campus, 2004), pp. 35–58, here p. 51.

12 Zvi Gitelman, 'Native Land, Promised Land, Golden Land: Jewish Emigration from Russia and Ukraine', *Harvard Ukrainian Studies*, vol. 22 (1998), pp. 137–163; O. V. Budnitskii (ed.), *Evreiskaia emigratsiia iz Rossii 1881–2005* (Moscow: Rosspen, 2008); Gur Alroey, 'Jewish migration, 19th century to present', in Immanuel Ness (ed.), *The Encyclopedia of Global Human Migration* (London: Wiley, 2013).

13 Cornelia Östreich, *'Des rauhen Winters ungeachtet …': Die Auswanderung Posener Juden nach Amerika im 19. Jahrhundert* (Hamburg: Dölling & Galitz, 1997).

14 Ezra Mendelsohn, *Zionism in Poland: The Formative Years, 1915–1926* (New Haven, CT: Yale University Press, 1981); Jolanta Żyndul, *Państwo w państwie? Autonomia narodowo-kulturalna w Europie Środkowowschodniej w XX wieku* (Warsaw: DiG, 2000); Joshua D. Zimmerman, *Poles, Jews, and the Politics of Nationality: The Bund and the Polish Socialist Party in Late Tsarist Russia, 1892–1914* (Madison, WI: University of Wisconsin Press, 2004).

15 Gershon C. Bacon, *The Politics of Tradition: Agudat Yisrael in Poland, 1916–1939* (Jerusalem: Hebrew University Magnes Press, 1996).

Russian army withdrew, because they were considered disloyal.[16] When the Polish state was re-established in 1918, many Jews hoped for a return to the ideals of the multi-ethnic, tolerant Polish-Lithuanian 'republic of nobles', whereas many Poles favoured an ethnically homogeneous nation state.

Jews in the Second Polish Republic

In the newly established Poland, more than a third of the population belonged to a national minority – Ukrainian, Jewish, German, Lithuanian, or Byelorussian. According to the 1931 census, approximately 3.1 million people, around 10 per cent of the population, professed the Jewish religion. Jews constituted the second-largest minority after the Ukrainians (5 million), outnumbering the Germans (around 1 million). The key areas of Jewish settlement were unevenly distributed. Many Jews had already left the formerly Prussian territory by the mid 1920s, so that the Jewish share of the population there was correspondingly small. But some voivodeships (administrative regions) in central and eastern Poland, especially in the areas awarded to Poland by the Peace of Riga signed by Poland and Soviet Russia in 1921, had much greater concentrations of Jewish inhabitants. In *shtetlekh* (the term used in Yiddish for small towns of several thousand residents with a dominant Jewish population), Jews sometimes constituted a large majority, especially in the Kresy, the regions east of the Curzon line.[17]

When the Second Republic was founded, the boundaries of Poland had not yet been conclusively defined, and the Jewish population at times found itself caught between the camps of the rival states. To the Jews in the region around Vilna, the Lithuanian leadership held out the prospect of full national minority rights, but in 1919 the territory was awarded to Poland. During the period 1918–1920, when Poland was at war with the West Ukrainian People's Republic and with Soviet Russia, pogroms broke out. It has been estimated that between 1918 and 1921 over 100,000 Jews across the region were killed by soldiers and civilians of the warring parties.[18] This estimate includes victims in the Polish and Ukrainian territories within and outside the new Polish borders. Not least in reaction to that violence, the victorious Western powers pressed successfully for a Minorities Protection Treaty in Poland, containing two clauses that concerned Jews alone: protection of the Sabbath and state funding for Jewish schools (which the Polish state later withheld).[19]

16 Frank M. Schuster, *Zwischen allen Fronten: Osteuropäische Juden während des Ersten Weltkrieges (1914–1919)* (Cologne: Böhlau, 2004).

17 Joseph Marcus, *Social and Political History of the Jews in Poland, 1919–1939* (Berlin: De Gruyter, 1983); Ezra Mendelsohn, *The Jews of East Central Europe between the World Wars* (Bloomington, IN: Indiana University Press, 1987); Bacon, 'Poland from 1795 to 1939', p. 1399.

18 Jeffrey Veidlinger, *In the Midst of Civilized Europe: The Pogroms of 1918–1921 and the Onset of the Holocaust* (New York: Metropolitan Books, 2021), p. 5.

19 William W. Hagen, *Anti-Jewish Violence in Poland, 1914–1920* (Cambridge: Cambridge University Press, 2018); Eva Reder, *Antijüdische Pogrome in Polen im 20. Jahrhundert: Gewaltausbrüche im Schatten der Staatsbildung 1918–1920 und 1945–1946* (Marburg: Herder-Institut, 2019); Carole Fink, *Defending the Rights of Others: The Great Powers, the Jews, and International Minority Protection, 1878–1938* (Cambridge: Cambridge University Press, 2004).

The Polish constitution of March 1921 gave Jews the same legal rights as other citizens. They were subject, however, to numerous forms of discrimination in practice and increasing antisemitism. Prejudice against Jews served as an outlet for economic insecurities and domestic political power struggles, with the added influence of the Catholic religious anti-Jewish tradition. The conflict between Polish nationalist ambitions to achieve ethnic homogeneity and Jewish efforts to obtain cultural autonomy was thus firmly established in the Second Polish Republic. An increasingly aggressive antisemitism became an integral component of Polish ethno-nationalism.[20]

'The idea of "Jewish nationalism"', Joseph Roth wrote in 1927,

> is very much alive in the East. Even people who themselves have little truck with the language, culture, and religion of their forefathers claim membership of the 'Jewish nation' on the basis of being a 'national minority' in a foreign country, striving for their rights as citizens and nationals. Some look toward a future in Palestine, and some, rightly believing that the earth belongs to everyone who treats it with respect, have no national aspirations. (But in either case Jews are unable to extinguish the primitive hatred that burns so corrosively in their host-people for what they see as a dangerous number of foreigners.)[21]

This summarizes briefly and aptly various currents within Polish Jewry. In the 1920s and 1930s the visibility and profile of the different currents were accentuated as Jewish parties were elected to the Sejm and to town councils. In the early interwar period the Jewish representatives in the Sejm cooperated with other minorities and established the Minorities Bloc; later on, the cooperation dwindled. In 1927, in an act that was intended to counter the attempt by various Jewish political parties to turn the kehillot into units of an autonomous Jewish minority, the Polish government enacted a uniform code regulating the kehillot specifically as Jewish religious communities. According to this law, each community had its council and they were part of the Religious Council of Jewish Communities, the overarching organization in which rabbis were a third of the members.[22] These communities were thus official organizations – as was the case in Central and Western Europe – whose tasks were focused on religious life. Nevertheless, they also functioned to a considerable extent as the forum of Jewish politics. This became clear when in 1936 the Bund dropped its boycott of kehilla elections and won majorities in many Jewish community councils.

Jewish political parties offered radically different solutions to the dilemmas facing the Jewish minority. The Zionists advocated emigration to Palestine. In the Polish state, they argued, Jews would always remain an alien element – a predominantly urban group in a country that was largely rural in character, and, moreover, a group that clearly stood out from its surroundings because of its faith, its language, and its customs. A minority of the Jews, however, identified with Polish culture and believed in the possibility of

20 Agnieszka Pufelska, *Die 'Judäo-Kommune': Ein Feindbild in Polen. Das polnische Selbstverständnis im Schatten des Antisemitismus 1939–1948* (Paderborn: Ferdinand Schöningh, 2007), pp. 46–47.

21 Joseph Roth, *The Wandering Jews*, trans. Michael Hofmann (London: Granta Books, 2001 [German edn, 1927]), p. 9.

22 Celia S. Heller, *On the Edge of Destruction: Jews of Poland between the Two World Wars* (New York: Columbia University Press, 1977), pp. 162–168; Mendelsohn, *Jews of East Central Europe*, p. 39.

integration, although even the proponents of assimilation could not ignore the fact that this path was in danger of coming to nought. The representatives of the Bund, by contrast, advocated a pluralistic, multi-ethnic Poland. Others sought to overcome the exclusion of the Jews by espousing the transnational goals of communism and joining the Communist Party of Poland, which was later forcibly dissolved by Stalin in 1938.[23] The Orthodox party Agudas Yisroel, which viewed support for the government as offering the best odds for defusing the tense situation, built up relatively good relationships with the authoritarian regime of Józef Piłsudski after he came to power in 1926 for the second time, through a *coup d'état*.

The enormous political and cultural diversity of Jewish political life was also reflected in the remarkable flourishing of the Jewish press: newspapers were published in Yiddish, Polish, and Hebrew, with twenty-two daily newspapers appearing alongside numerous weeklies, monthly magazines, and academic and literary journals. This was an important basis for the underground press during the German occupation. Meanwhile, there was among Jews a high degree of popular participation in politics, and younger Jews were extensively involved in political activism: in fact, every Jewish party had a youth movement affiliated with it. Young people's energies were also directed towards education, which appeared to many as the only realistic path to upward mobility. New educational opportunities and research centres burgeoned in this period. From 1925 Jewish scholars carried out research on Yiddish language and literature and on Jewish history in Eastern Europe at the newly founded Yiddish (Jewish) Research Institute (Yidisher Visnshaftlekher Institut, YIVO), which had its headquarters in Vilna and branches in Berlin, Warsaw, and New York. Vilna was also home to the largest Jewish library in Europe. In Warsaw, Jewish historians founded the Institute for Jewish Studies in 1928; Samuel Majer Bałaban and Mojżesz Schorr were among the institution's directors.[24]

The Polish capital was the intellectual and cultural centre of Polish Jewry. Several Yiddish daily newspapers were published there, and the life of distinguished artists and actors also centred on the city. Around 350,000 Jews lived in Warsaw – 'half as many as in all of Germany', as the German writer Alfred Döblin noted during a trip to Poland in 1924. With amazement, he described Nalewki Street, the 'main artery of the Jewish district': 'everything [is] filled and teeming with Jews. [...] I enter a [courtyard]; it is rectangular and, like a marketplace, full of loud people, Jews, mostly in caftans. Large

23 Marcus, *Social and Political History*, p. 289; Gertrud Pickhan, *'Gegen den Strom': Der Allgemeine Jüdische Arbeiterbund 'Bund' in Polen 1918–1939* (Stuttgart: Deutsche Verlagsanstalt, 2001), pp. 263–279, 325; Jack Jacobs (ed.), *Jewish Politics in Eastern Europe: The Bund at 100* (Basingstoke: Palgrave, 2001); Katrin Steffen, *Jüdische Polonität: Ethnizität und Nation im Spiegel der polnischsprachigen jüdischen Presse 1918–1939* (Göttingen: Vandenhoeck & Ruprecht, 2004).

24 Artur Eisenbach, 'Jewish Historiography in Interwar Poland', in Yisrael Gutman et al. (eds.), *The Jews of Poland between Two World Wars* (Hanover, NH: University Press of New England, 1989), pp. 453–493; Bacon, 'Poland from 1795 to 1939', pp. 1401–1403; Moyshe Kligsberg, 'Die jüdische Jugendbewegung in Polen zwischen den Weltkriegen: Eine soziologische Studie', *Osteuropa*, vol. 58, nos. 8–10 (2008), pp. 131–146; Moyshe Kligsberg, 'Di yidishe yugnt-bavegung in Poyln tsvishn beyde velt-milkhomes (a sotsyologishe shtudye)', in Joshua A. Fishman (ed.), *Studies on Polish Jewry, 1919–1939: The Interplay of Social, Economic and Political Factors in the Struggle of a Minority for Its Existence* (New York: YIVO Institute for Jewish Research, 1974), pp. 137–228; Cecile Esther Kuznitz, *YIVO and the Making of Modern Jewish Culture: Scholarship for the Yiddish Nation* (Cambridge: Cambridge University Press, 2014).

shops line this Nalewki Street. Brightly coloured signs by the dozen advertise: pelts, furs, ladies' suits, hats, suitcases.' But Döblin also noted: 'I read strange names: Waiselfisch, Klopfherd, Blumenkranz, Brandwain, Farsztandig, Goldkopf, Gelbfisch, Gutbesztand. Mocking names have been foisted on these members of the ostracized people.'[25]

Piłsudski, the charismatic head of state, died in 1935. His death would have far-reaching consequences for the Polish Jews. A short time earlier, in September 1934, Foreign Minister Józef Beck had already abrogated the Minorities Protection Treaty, and the new constitution that came into force in April 1935 further weakened the position of the minorities. When Piłsudski died, the government lost its unifying figure. Now it sought a connection to the National Democracy movement as well as to more radical right-wing groups. In this process, antisemitism sometimes functioned as a useful binding agent. The Polish right, for example, made frequent use of the stereotype of 'Judeo-Communism' (*żydokomuna*), according to which the Jews, as supposed initiators and standard-bearers of the Bolshevik movement, represented a threat to the Polish nation. In addition, under the influence of the anti-Jewish policy in Nazi Germany, far-right groups broke away from the main right-wing movement. In veritable crusades these splinter groups advocated eliminating Jews from the crisis-ridden economy, as well as bringing about 'de-Jewification' (*odżydzenie*) of Polish society. Radical right-wing subgroups of the National Democrats increasingly organized violent riots and pogroms, including the violent incidents in Przytyk on 9 March 1936. Overall, at least fourteen Jews were killed and approximately 2,000 injured between 1935 and 1937.[26] In response to these excesses, the Bund made efforts to defend Jews in the streets, and other Jewish political movements also started to train their members in self-defence.

From 1937 a new alliance of parties close to the government moved into the vacuum left by Piłsudski's death: the Camp of National Unity (Obóz Zjednoczenia Narodowego, OZN), which openly agitated against the Jews. The Polish government now pursued a policy intended to induce as many Jews as possible to emigrate. In this context it even examined the possibility of using Madagascar as a suitable destination for initially 25,000 Jewish emigrants, and sought to reach an agreement to this effect with the French colonial power. Of great symbolic significance for both the Jewish minority and the majority society was a law enacted as early as April 1936 that prohibited the ritual slaughter of livestock. Officially passed in the interests of hygiene and animal welfare, the measure

25 Alfred Döblin, *Reise in Polen* (Berlin: Fischer, 1926), pp. 77–79; Dietz Bering, *The Stigma of Names: Antisemitism in German Daily Life, 1812–1933*, trans. Neville Plaice (Ann Arbor, MI: University of Michigan Press, 1992 [German edn, 1987]); Gabriela Zalewska, *Ludność żydowska w Warszawie w okresie międzywojennym* (Warsaw: Wydawnictwo Naukowe PWN, 1996); Marci Shore, *Caviar and Ashes: A Warsaw Generation's Life and Death in Marxism, 1918–1968* (New Haven, CT: Yale University Press, 2006).

26 Dietrich Beyrau, 'Antisemitismus und Judentum in Polen, 1918–1939', *Geschichte und Gesellschaft*, vol. 8, no. 2 (1982), pp. 205–232; Jolanta Żyndul, *Zajścia antyżydowskie w Polsce w latach 1935–1937* (Warsaw: Fundacja im. K. Kelles-Krauza, 1994), pp. 54–55; Klaus-Peter Friedrich, 'Juden und jüdisch-polnische Beziehungen in der Zweiten Polnischen Republik (1918–1939)', *Zeitschrift für Ostmitteleuropa-Forschung*, vol. 46, no. 4 (1997), pp. 535–560; André W. M. Gerrits, *The Myth of Jewish Communism: A Historical Interpretation* (New York: Peter Lang, 2009); Kamil Kijek, Artur Markowski and Konrad Zieliński (eds.), *Pogromy Żydów na ziemiach polskich w XIX i XX wieku*, vol. 2: *Studia przypadków (do 1939 roku)* (Warsaw: Polska Akademia Nauk, 2019); Antony Polonsky, 'Przytyk Pogrom', in Hundert (ed.), *YIVO Encyclopedia of Jews in Eastern Europe*, vol. 2, pp. 1482–1483.

imposed a restriction on an essential aspect of Jewish life and denounced Jewish rituals as barbaric. The situation of Jewish tradesmen who kept Shabbat as a day of rest had already been made difficult in 1919 by the introduction of a mandatory observance of Sunday as a day of rest, but now the Jewish labourers and white-collar workers employed in government enterprises also came under pressure. Many Jewish employees were dismissed and replaced with Poles.[27]

Polish antisemites, as these examples demonstrate, increasingly looked to Germany as a model.[28] They found support in such major social institutions as the universities and the Catholic Church, to which most of the Polish majority population belonged. At the universities, for example, student groups in the mid 1930s forced the adoption of an upper limit on the percentage of Jewish students, and demanded that Jews henceforth be allowed to sit only on so-called ghetto benches in the lecture halls.[29] In the Catholic Church, which had close ties to the Polish national movement, many bishops and a large portion of the clergy were sympathetic to National Democracy. When an anti-Jewish economic boycott was declared in 1936, the Church was among its advocates.[30]

The developments in Germany were monitored and reported by the Jewish press, and Polish Jewry responded to them in various ways, among them an attempt, which started shortly after the 1 April 1933 anti-Jewish boycott in Germany, to organize a boycott of Nazi Germany. The Polish government put an end to this boycott in 1935.[31] However, the main concern of Polish Jews was their own situation in Poland. Within the Jewish minority there was growing insecurity. More and more businessmen gave up their enterprises, which were taken over by Polish owners. While the proportion of Jews in certain sectors such as garment-making and shopkeeping remained high, artisans and shopkeepers could often barely support themselves on their earnings. Many self-employed professionals also found themselves economically and socially marginalized. By the end of the 1930s a quarter of all Jews were dependent on welfare.[32] In reaction to the growing poverty, Jewish communities developed an extensive network of welfare institutions, and private sponsors created self-help organizations. As a result of these developments, Agudas Yisroel lost support, and the Bund became more popular instead.

27 Magnus Brechtken, *'Madagaskar für die Juden': Antisemitische Idee und politische Praxis 1885–1945* (Munich: R. Oldenbourg, 1997); Grzegorz Krzywiec, 'The Balance of Polish Political Antisemitism: Between "National Revolution", Economic Crisis, and the Transformation of the Polish Public Sphere in the 1930s', in Frank Bajohr and Dieter Pohl (eds.), *Right-Wing Politics and the Rise of Antisemitism in Europe, 1935–1941* (Göttingen: Wallstein, 2019), pp. 61–80.

28 Albert S. Kotowski, *Hitlers Bewegung im Urteil der polnischen Nationaldemokratie* (Wiesbaden: Harrassowitz, 2000); Michał Musielak, *Nazizm w interpretacjach polskiej myśli politycznej okresu międzywojennego* (Poznań: Wydawnictwo Poznańskie, 1997).

29 Monika Natkowska, *Numerus clausus, getto ławkowe, numerus nullus, 'paragraf aryjski': Antysemityzm na Uniwersytecie Warszawskim 1931–1939* (Warsaw: Żydowski Instytut Historyczny, 1999); Szymon Rudnicki, 'From "Numerus Clausus" to "Numerus Nullus"', in Antony Polonsky (ed.), *From* Shtetl *to Socialism: Studies from Polin* (London: Littman Library of Jewish Civilization, 1993), pp. 359–381.

30 Ronald Modras, *The Catholic Church and Antisemitism: Poland, 1933–1939* (Chur: Harwood Academic Publishers, 1994); Viktoria Pollmann, *Untermieter im christlichen Haus: Die Kirche und die 'jüdische Frage' in Polen anhand der Bistumspresse der Metropolie Krakau 1926–1939* (Wiesbaden: Harrassowitz, 2001).

31 Pickhan, *'Gegen den Strom'*, pp. 294–297.

32 Mendelsohn, *Jews of East Central Europe*, pp. 73–74.

It tried hard to establish close ties to the Polish socialists, whose positions were closest to the Bund's own goals. In any case, opponents of the intensifying antisemitic rhetoric and policies were most likely to be found on the left wing of the political spectrum in Polish society.[33] More than 400,000 Jews opted for emigration as a solution during the 1920s and 1930s; approximately a quarter went to Palestine. In the mid 1930s, however, the British administration responsible for the Mandate for Palestine introduced increasingly harsh restrictions on Jewish immigration. The United States tightened up its immigration regulations as well.

Developments in the German Reich and the German–Polish conflict gave additional cause for concern. The situation escalated in the spring of 1938. On 31 March 1938 the Polish government issued legislation that, for all practical purposes, was directed against Jews: the Law on Deprivation of Citizenship. According to this law, persons who had been resident in a foreign country for more than five years could have their citizenship withdrawn. The citizenship law was followed in October 1938 by a decree stipulating that passports issued in another country entitled the holders to enter Poland only if the documents bore a stamp of approval from the appropriate Polish consulate. This provision was intended to prevent, above all, the return of Polish Jews living in Germany. During the night of 28 October 1938, just before the law came into force, the German police deported approximately 17,000 Jews who were registered in the Reich and held Polish passports. They were taken to the border and forced to cross into Polish territory. The Polish border guards initially would not let about half of them enter the country, and as a result they wandered around in the no man's land between the two borders for days. Temporary camps were subsequently set up; the largest of them remained in existence in Zbąszyń (Neu-Bentschen) until the summer of 1939.[34]

The Path to War

Relations between the German Reich and the Second Polish Republic were fraught from the outset, primarily because of Germany's refusal to accept the border with its neighbour to the east that had been established by the Treaty of Versailles. German resentment derived not least from the fact that some regions with a German majority had been awarded to Poland. Meanwhile, the so-called Polish Corridor – a land bridge between central Poland and the Baltic coast near Danzig – now separated the Province of East Prussia from the rest of the Reich's territory. The demand for a revision of the eastern

33 Robert Moses Shapiro, *The Polish Kehile Elections of 1936: A Revolution Re-examined* (New York: Holocaust Studies Program, Yeshiva University, 1988); Pickhan, *'Gegen den Strom'*, pp. 314–318.

34 Sybil Milton, 'The Expulsion of Polish Jews from Germany, October 1938 to July 1939', *Leo Baeck Yearbook*, vol. 29 (1984), pp. 169–199; Trude Maurer, 'The Background for Kristallnacht: The Expulsion of Polish Jews', in Walter Pehle (ed.), *November 1938: From 'Reichskristallnacht' to Genocide*, trans. William Templer (New York: Berg, 1990 [German edn, 1988]), pp. 44–72; Jerzy Tomaszewski, *Preludium Zagłady: Wygnanie Żydów polskich z Niemiec w 1938 r.* (Warsaw: Wydawnictwo Naukowe PWN, 1998); Ingo Loose, '"Thus Ends … the Golden Age of Jewry in Germany": The Reactions to the November Pogrom in the Jewish Press in Poland in 1938/39', in Andreas Nachama, Uwe Neumärker, and Hermann Simon (eds.), *Fire! Anti-Jewish Terror on 'Kristallnacht' in November 1938*, trans. Adam Blauhut et al. (Berlin: Topography of Terror, 2008 [German edn, 2008]), pp. 128–135. See also PMJ 2/112, 113, 118, and 203.

border was one of the key objectives of German foreign policy during the Weimar Republic. Violent unrest in the border areas – disturbances that Berlin characterized as an 'ethnic struggle' (*Volkstumskampf*) – continued until 1921 and remained thereafter a source of friction between the two countries. Up to the end of the Weimar Republic, German policy remained focused on weakening Poland economically and supporting the German minority there. Most political observers were therefore surprised when Hitler, after coming to power in 1933, initially refrained from adopting a course of confrontation with Poland. Instead he gambled on gaining the support of the authoritarian and anti-Bolshevik Polish government as a junior partner for his expansion plans regarding the Soviet Union. In 1934 the Non-Aggression Pact, the Agreement for 'Cooperation in the Shaping of Public Opinion', and an economic agreement contributed to an easing of tension between the two states.[35] The Soviet Union was regarded as a common enemy, and Hitler hinted at territorial gains for Poland if the latter were to support the planned German campaign of conquest in the East.[36]

With Hitler on a clear trajectory towards war from 1937 onwards, German academics developed scenarios for a reshaping of Europe in which the German-speaking minorities in Eastern Europe played a key role. The *Ostforscher*, or 'Eastern specialists', declared the areas settled by these minorities to be German *Volksboden*, 'ethnic terrain', which should be incorporated into the Reich. Concepts of this sort formed the basis for expansion plans that were to be carried out jointly with Poland or, alternatively, against Poland.[37] In the summer of 1937, for example, Theodor Oberländer, head of the Institute for Eastern European Economics at the University of Königsberg, gave a lecture on the 'struggle for the outpost' ('Kampf um das Vorfeld'). In it he advocated exploiting the antagonisms between the ethnic groups in East Central Europe in order to construct a German hegemonic order, and redirecting the 'ethnic struggle' of the Poles, so far waged against the Germans, towards Jews and Russians.[38]

The Jews of Eastern Europe had a prominent place in the thinking of the German planners, who incorporated into their blueprints popular stereotypes of the so-called Eastern Jews and linked them to antisemitic agitation from the days of the Weimar Republic. During the interwar period around 150,000 Jews from Eastern Europe and East Central Europe lived in Germany, and their culture, customs, and practices, unfamiliar in part to Germans, often acted as an irritant for both Jews and non-Jews there.[39] The radical nationalist right directed its agitation efforts against these immigrants wherever

35 Marian Wojciechowski, *Die polnisch-deutschen Beziehungen 1933–1938*, trans. Norbert Damerau (Leiden: Brill, 1971 [Polish edn, 1965]).

36 Carsten Roschke, *Der umworbene 'Urfeind': Polen in der nationalsozialistischen Propaganda 1934–1939* (Marburg: Tectum, 2000).

37 Michael Burleigh, *Germany Turns Eastwards: A Study of Ostforschung in the Third Reich* (New York: Cambridge University Press, 1988); Michael Fahlbusch, *Wissenschaft im Dienst der nationalsozialistischen Politik? Die 'Volksdeutschen Forschungsgemeinschaften' von 1931–1945* (Baden-Baden: Nomos, 1999); Ingo Haar, *Historiker im Nationalsozialismus: Die deutsche Geschichtswissenschaft und der 'Volkstumskampf' im Osten* (Göttingen: Vandenhoeck & Ruprecht, 2000), pp. 307–311; Eduard Mühle, *Für Volk und deutschen Osten: Der Historiker Hermann Aubin und die deutsche Ostforschung* (Düsseldorf: Droste, 2005).

38 See PMJ 1/284.

39 Salomon Adler-Rudel, *Ostjuden in Deutschland 1880–1940: Zugleich eine Geschichte der Organisationen, die sie betreuten* (Tübingen: Mohr, 1959); Trude Maurer, *Ostjuden in Deutschland 1918–1933* (Hamburg: H. Christians, 1986).

possible, and had called for their deportation or even internment at the height of the inflation crisis in 1923. The first anti-Jewish excesses took place that same year, in Berlin's Scheunenviertel, a neighbourhood with numerous Eastern Jewish inhabitants.[40]

In the late 1930s the German 'Eastern specialists' observed with keen interest every antisemitic measure of the Polish government, and discussed its plans for the forcible emigration of the Jewish minority.[41] In mid 1939 the Königsberg historian Werner Conze recommended the 'de-Jewification of the cities and market towns', especially in Polish Galicia. Because he blamed 'overpopulation' for 'the Bolshevik seizure of power', he thought that driving out the Jews might help to counteract dangerous revolutionary unrest.[42] Even more extreme in his views regarding the *Ostjuden* (East European Jews) was the leading antisemitic expert Peter-Heinz Seraphim. In September 1938 he published a 736-page book in which he analysed numerous aspects of the Jewish population in Eastern Europe, pointing to 'the Ghetto', that is, the densely populated poor Jewish neighbourhoods in Eastern European cities, as 'the basis from which the Jewish expansion stems [...] this is where the Jewish essence is moulded in its specific form as it is found in Eastern Europe, in order to exert from here, from the centres of business, an influence on the surroundings and on the nations among whom the Jews live'.[43] Not only scholars analysed Polish Jewry in the period preceding the invasion: the self-styled experts on Jewish affairs in the SD (Sicherheitsdienst, Security Service of the SS) did so too. On 7 May 1939 some of them 'discussed the possibilities for contacts in Poland' and 'noted that it is important to find people in Poland who can provide accurate information for a thorough registration of the Jews in Poland'.[44] The radical transformation of the neighbouring country that Conze and others were contemplating was by that time just around the corner.

The German Invasion of Poland

In the wake of the Munich Agreement of 30 September 1938, which had enabled Germany to annex the Sudetenland, Hitler also confronted the Polish government with his demands. These included an extraterritorial road and rail connection running through the Polish Corridor to East Prussia, the reincorporation of Danzig into the Reich, and the accession of Poland to the Anti-Comintern Pact. Poland was to become a junior

40 Dirk Walter, *Antisemitische Kriminalität und Gewalt: Judenfeindschaft in der Weimarer Republik* (Bonn: Dietz, 1999), p. 151.

41 Gerhard F. Volkmer, 'Die deutsche Forschung zu Osteuropa und zum osteuropäischen Judentum in den Jahren 1933–1945', *Forschungen zur osteuropäischen Geschichte*, vol. 42 (1989), pp. 109–214.

42 Werner Conze, 'Die ländliche Überbevölkerung in Polen' (text for the planned International Congress of Sociologists in 1940), cited in Götz Aly and Susanne Heim, *Architects of Annihilation: Auschwitz and the Logic of Destruction*, trans. Allan Blunden (London: Phoenix, 2003 [German edn, 1991]), p. 58.

43 Peter-Heinz Seraphim, *Das Judentum im osteuropäischen Raum* ([Essen]: Essener Verlagsanstalt, 1938), p. 355. On Seraphim, see Hans-Christian Petersen, *Bevölkerungsökonomie, Ostforschung, Politik: Eine biographische Studie zu Peter-Heinz Seraphim (1902–1979)* (Osnabrück: fibre, 2007); Alan Steinweis, *Studying the Jew: Scholarly Antisemitism in Nazi Germany* (Cambridge, MA: Harvard University Press, 2006), pp. 142–151.

44 Vermerk, II 112 (Hagen) to SS-Untersturmführer Augsburg of II P, 9 May 1939, BArch, R 58/954, fols. 179–180. See Ian Kershaw, *Hitler, 1936–1945: Nemesis* (London: Penguin, 2000), p. 910, n. 75; Dan Michman, 'Why Did Heydrich Write the Schnellbrief? A Remark on the Reason and on Its Significance', *Yad Vashem Studies*, vol. 32 (2004), pp. 433–447, here pp. 439–440.

partner and simultaneously a staging area for the war against the Soviet Union. In exchange Hitler pledged to extend the Non-Aggression Pact and to guarantee Poland's borders. The Polish government refused to agree to these terms. In early April 1939 Hitler responded by ordering preparations to be made for the attack on Poland (codenamed *Fall Weiß*, 'Case White'), and that same month he withdrew from the Non-Aggression Pact. Within a few months the Reich had reached agreement with a new ally. The German–Soviet pact that foreign ministers Joachim von Ribbentrop and Vyacheslav Mikhaylovich Molotov signed on 23 August 1939 contained a secret addendum, often referred to as the 'secret protocol', in which the two parties agreed to divide Poland between them. The previous day, at Obersalzberg, Hitler had made clear to his top generals how he envisaged the war that was on the horizon: 'Destruction of Poland as priority. Aim is to eliminate the vital forces, not to reach a specific line. [...] Hearts must be closed to compassion. Brutal course of action. 80 million people must obtain justice. Their existence must be ensured. The stronger is right. Maximum severity.'[45]

In the early hours of 1 September 1939 the German Wehrmacht invaded Poland without a declaration of war. In response Britain and France declared war on the German Reich on 3 September, but at that point the Allies did not take any immediate military action. The Polish army did not stand a chance on its own against the formidably armed German Wehrmacht, especially after the Red Army invaded Poland from the east on 17 September. That same day the Polish government fled to Romania. Warsaw capitulated on 27 September, and the remaining Polish troops surrendered on 6 October. The German–Soviet Boundary and Friendship Treaty of 28 September 1939 established the demarcation line.[46] About half of Poland's territory, in which two thirds of the approximately 3.3 million Jews lived, came under German occupation.[47]

45 *Trial of the Major War Criminals before the International Military Tribunal*, vol. 26 (Nuremberg: Secretariat of the Tribunal, 1947), pp. 523–524. The exact wording cannot be reconstructed with absolute certainty: see Winfried Baumgart, 'Zur Ansprache Hitlers vor den Führern der Wehrmacht am 22. August 1939: Eine quellenkritische Untersuchung', *Vierteljahrshefte für Zeitgeschichte*, vol. 16, no. 2 (1968), pp. 120–149; Christopher R. Browning, *The Origins of the Final Solution: The Evolution of Nazi Jewish Policy, September 1939 – March 1942* (Lincoln: University of Nebraska Press; Jerusalem: Yad Vashem, 2004), p. 15.

46 Horst Rohde, 'Hitlers erster "Blitzkrieg" und seine Auswirkungen auf Nordosteuropa', in Klaus A. Maier, Horst Rohde, Bernd Stegemann, and Hans Umbreit, *Das Deutsche Reich und der Zweite Weltkrieg*, vol. 2: *Die Errichtung der Hegemonie auf dem europäischen Kontinent* (Stuttgart: DVA, 1979), pp. 79–158; Gerhard L. Weinberg, *A World at Arms: A Global History of World War II*, 2nd edn (New York: Cambridge University Press, 2005), pp. 48–62; Rolf-Dieter Müller, *Der Zweite Weltkrieg 1939–1945* (Stuttgart: Klett-Cotta, 2004), pp. 65–66; Jochen Böhler, *Der Überfall: Deutschlands Krieg gegen Polen* (Frankfurt am Main: Eichborn, 2009); Richard Evans, *The Third Reich at War: How the Nazis Led Germany from Conquest to Disaster* (London: Penguin, 2009), pp. 5–9.

47 According to the extrapolation of Polish statisticians: Główny Urząd Statystyczny Rzeczypospolitej Polskiej, *Mały rocznik statystyczny Polski, wrzesień 1939 – czerwiec 1941* (Warsaw: Zakład Wydawnictw Statystycznych, 1990 [English edn, 1941]), p. 10. On the German occupation, see especially Martin Broszat, *Nationalsozialistische Polenpolitik 1939–1945* (Stuttgart: DVA, 1961); Czesław Madajczyk, *Polityka III Rzeszy w okupowanej Polsce* (Warsaw: Państwowe Wydawnictwo Naukowe, 1970); Włodzimierz Bonusiak, *Polska podczas II wojny światowej* (Rzeszów: Wydawn. Wyższej Szkoły Pedagogicznej, 1995); Jacek Andrzej Młynarczyk (ed.), *Polen unter deutscher und sowjetischer Besatzung 1939–1945* (Osnabrück: fibre, 2009); Martin Winstone, *The Dark Heart of Hitler's Europe: Nazi Rule in Poland under the General Government* (London: Tauris, 2015); Joanna Urbanek, *Everyday Life in the Shadow of Terror: German Occupation in Poland, 1939–1945*, trans. Katarzyna Gucio (Gdańsk: Muzeum II Wojny Światowej, 2015 [Polish edn, 2014]).

On 1 September 1939, the first day of the war, Chaim Kaplan, a Jewish teacher in Warsaw, noted in his diary: 'We are witnessing the dawn of a new era in the history of the world. This war will indeed bring destruction upon human civilization.' And in another passage: 'Wherever Hitler goes, there is no hope for the Jewish people.'[48] The violence with which the Wehrmacht and the Einsatzgruppen overwhelmed the country did indeed target Jews from the outset. At the same time, the German troops also – and, at the beginning of the war, primarily – took action against Poles, in line with the guiding principle stated by Hitler: the destruction of the Polish nation. The onslaught against the resident population of Poland was underpinned by aggressive propaganda depicting the war as one between superior and inferior peoples. Such portrayals ridiculed and demonized both non-Jewish and Jewish Poles. From German soldiers' diaries and letters, it seems that in practice their curious gaze was drawn particularly to the sight of 'exotic-looking' Eastern Jews, known previously to many only from antisemitic caricatures. Some expressed their aversion in stereotypical descriptions: 'In Bircza we realized the need for a radical solution to the Jewish question. One could see there how these beasts in human form live. In their beards and caftans, with their fiendish grimaces, they made a repellent impression on us. Anyone who was not yet a radical opponent of the Jews inevitably became one here.'[49]

Alongside the Wehrmacht, SS and police formations took part in the invasion of Poland – seven Einsatzgruppen, approximately 2,700 men strong. They were meant to crack down on all Poles who were classified as particularly hostile, primarily activists from the western regions who had, for instance, been involved in the 'ethnic struggle' in Upper Silesia. Increasingly, however, these ideological warriors took aim at the entire Polish elite. The SD had already set up its own Central Office II 2 P (Poland) in May 1939, and files were compiled there on individuals who were considered enemies of the Reich, including many leaders of Jewish organizations (Doc. 2). A *Sonderfahndungsbuch*, or 'special wanted arrest list', listed 61,000 Polish citizens against whom action was to be taken in the event of war. The 'Einsatzgruppe for special assignments' that was created on 3 September 1939 and commanded by Udo von Woyrsch received its instructions from Himmler: 'disarming and overpowering of the Polish bandit groups, executions'.[50] Charged with taking action against 'all enemies of the Reich and anti-German elements',

48 *Scroll of Agony: The Warsaw Diary of Chaim A. Kaplan*, ed. and trans. Abraham I. Katsh (New York, Macmillan: 1965), pp. 1–2.

49 Jochen Böhler, *Auftakt zum Vernichtungskrieg: Die Wehrmacht in Polen 1939* (Frankfurt am Main: Fischer, 2006), p. 48: Gefr. [Private] G., 'Erinnerung an den PF' [Memories of the Poland Campaign].

50 'Richtlinien für den auswärtigen Einsatz der Sicherheitspolizei und des SD' (no date), BArch, R 58/241; letter from the RFSS [Reichsführer-SS] to Udo von Woyrsch, dated 7 Sept. 1939, cited in Jürgen Matthäus, Jochen Böhler, and Klaus-Michael Mallmann (eds.), *War, Pacification, and Mass Murder, 1939: The Einsatzgruppen in Poland*, trans. Kathleen Luft et al. (Lanham, MD: Rowman & Littlefield, 2014 [German edn, 2008]), pp. 32–36; Helmut Krausnick and Hans-Heinrich Wilhelm, *Die Truppe des Weltanschauungskrieges: Die Einsatzgruppen der Sicherheitspolizei und des SD 1938–1942* (Stuttgart: DVA, 1981), pp. 32–42; Ulrich Herbert, *Best: Biographische Studien über Radikalismus, Weltanschauung und Vernunft 1903–1989* (Munich: C. H. Beck, 2016), p. 259; Dorothee Weitbrecht, *Der Exekutionsauftrag der Einsatzgruppen in Polen* (Filderstadt: Markstein, 2001); Michael Wildt, *An Uncompromising Generation: The Nazi Leadership of the Reich Security Main Office*, trans. Tom Lampert (Madison, WI: University of Wisconsin Press, 2009 [German edn,

a task open to all kinds of interpretation, the Einsatzgruppen murdered during their operations around 10,000 members of the Polish intelligentsia, clergy, and aristocracy, as well as Jews.

From the outset the Wehrmacht units, Einsatzgruppen, Order Police, and Waffen-SS took brutal measures against prisoners of war and the civilian population. They deported tens of thousands of Poles and Jews who were of military service age to camps in the Reich, or interned them in the conquered territory. Mere suspicion of resistance was sufficient reason for the Germans to carry out mass shootings, and the nervous troops sensed partisan activity almost everywhere. By the end of October the Wehrmacht, the SS, and the German police had executed at least 16,000 civilians and more than 1,000 captured members of the Polish army.[51] The Einsatzgruppen frequently received active support from members of the German minority in Poland, who knew the places and the locals well and spontaneously formed militias as early as the first days of September 1939. Subsequently, on Himmler's instructions, these forces became centrally organized as the Volksdeutscher Selbstschutz ('Ethnic German Self-Protection').

Tensions were further fuelled by anti-German riots. These notably included the physical attacks and murders that took place in Bydgoszcz (Bromberg) on 3 September 1939, which resulted in probably around 360 deaths. The 'Bromberg Bloody Sunday' led to brutal acts of retribution, and Nazi propagandists seized on the events. Soon there were reports that Poles had murdered 58,000 ethnic Germans during the days that followed the German invasion. Members of the Selbstschutz now began to take an active part in German acts of terror. During these events, around 3,000 murders were committed in the area of Bydgoszcz, with victims including both Jews and Poles. In addition, from the first days of the war onwards, Jewish men and women became the target of indiscriminate humiliation, violence, looting, and rape. German soldiers and policemen cut off the beards of Orthodox Jews and, to the amusement of any colleagues from their units who were present, forced Jews to do meaningless and unpleasant tasks or to perform gymnastic exercises. Often members of the German minority or Poles participated in the harassment and abuse, or took advantage of the unclear situation to enrich themselves. In this atmosphere, antisemitic violence increased. Jews were fair game.

In Łódź on 12 September 1939, Dawid Sierakowiak described in his diary how a group of Jews had been forced to interrupt their work and strip naked. Some Germans told the men, who had been made to stand facing the wall, that they would now be shot, and raised their rifles to their shoulders. The Germans did this several times, without actually

2003]). On the SS units in the war against Poland, see Martin Cüppers, *Wegbereiter der Shoah: Die Waffen-SS, der Kommandostab Reichsführer-SS und die Judenvernichtung 1939–1945* (Darmstadt: WBG, 2005), pp. 33–60.

51 Irena Sroka, *Górny Śląsk i Zagłębie Dąbrowskie pod okupacyjnym zarządem wojskowym* (Katowice: Śląski Instytut Naukowy, 1975), p. 198; Tatiana Berenstein and Adam Rutkowski, 'Prześladowania ludności żydowskiej w okresie hitlerowskiej administracji wojskowej na okupowanych ziemiach polskich (1.IX.1939 – 25.X.1939)', *Biuletyn Żydowskiego Instytutu Historycznego*, no. 38 (1961), pp. 3–38, and no. 39 (1961), pp. 63–87, here pp. 63–72; Czesław Łuczak, *Pod niemieckim jarzmem (Kraj Warty 1939–1945)* (Poznań: PSO, 1996), pp. 16–19; Hans-Jürgen Bömelburg and Bogdan Musiał, 'Die deutsche Besatzungspolitik in Polen 1939–1945', in Włodzimierz Borodziej and Klaus Ziemer (eds.), *Deutsch-polnische Beziehungen 1939–1945–1949: Eine Einführung* (Osnabrück: fibre, 2000), pp. 43–111; Alexander B. Rossino, *Hitler Strikes Poland: Blitzkrieg, Ideology, and Atrocity* (Lawrence, KS: University Press of Kansas, 2003), p. 86.

firing their weapons – physically, at least, no one was harmed that day.[52] Marcel Reich-Ranicki described in his autobiography the first weeks of the occupation in Warsaw: 'Frequently the Jews – and Jewesses – picked up in the street were taken to a German office building which needed cleaning. If no rags were available for mopping the floor, the Jewish women, especially the prettier ones, were ordered to take off their knickers. These were then used as rags. For the soldiers this was tremendous fun.'[53]

The 'Einsatzgruppe for special tasks', on its journey from Upper Silesia to Western Galicia, killed several hundred Jews before organizing a massacre in Przemyśl that claimed the lives of 500 to 600 Jews between 16 and 19 September.[54] More than 500 Jewish inhabitants were killed on 9 September in an arson attack on the synagogue in Będzin in East Upper Silesia.[55] In Chmielnik, near Kielce, German soldiers locked around fifty Jews in the synagogue and set it on fire.

In addition to these killings, as many as 20,000 Jewish civilians perished and around 32,000 Jewish officers and men lost their lives in the fighting. Approximately 50,000 to 60,000 Jewish soldiers in the Polish army were captured. The Wehrmacht segregated the Jewish prisoners of war within the prisoner-of-war camps, and the mortality rate among them was higher than average. Wilm Hosenfeld was the commander of a prisoner-of-war camp in Pabianice, near Łódź. In a letter to his wife on 16 September 1939, he said that thousands of prisoners were arriving every day and, as a result, hardships could not be avoided. However, he expressed disapproval: 'The Jews' lot is not to be envied. I am outraged at the rough treatment. The locals stand and watch complacently: according to them, the Jews have exploited them in every way possible and enriched themselves at their expense. The rich J[ews], however, have run away, and the poor Jews must suffer for it.' By March 1940 the Wehrmacht released most Jewish soldiers and sent them to the General Government. A small number of Jewish officers remained in captivity until the end of the war; most of them survived.[56] Jewish prisoners of war whose homes were

52 *The Diary of Dawid Sierakowiak: Five Notebooks from the Łódź Ghetto*, ed. Alan Adelson, trans. Kamil Turowski (New York and Oxford: Oxford University Press, 1996 [Polish edn, 1960]), pp. 37–38 (12 Sept. 1939). The incident he reported had taken place in Chmielnik: see Sara Bender, 'Die Juden von Chmielnik unter deutscher Besatzung (1939–1943)', in Christoph Dieckmann and Babette Quinkert (eds.), *Im Ghetto 1939–1945: Neue Forschungen zu Alltag und Umfeld* (Göttingen: Wallstein, 2009), pp. 74–96, here p. 77.

53 Marcel Reich-Ranicki, *The Author of Himself: The Life of Marcel Reich-Ranicki*, trans. Ewald Osers (London: Phoenix, 2002 [German edn, 1999]), p. 125.

54 Bömelburg and Musiał, 'Die deutsche Besatzungspolitik', p. 48; Rossino, *Hitler Strikes Poland*, pp. 96–98; Matthäus, Böhler, and Mallmann (eds.), *War, Pacification, and Mass Murder*, pp. 93–94; Böhler, *Der Überfall*, pp. 199–207.

55 Christian Jansen and Arno Weckbecker, *Der 'Volksdeutsche Selbstschutz' in Polen 1939/40* (Munich: Oldenbourg, 1992); Böhler, *Auftakt zum Vernichtungskrieg*, p. 136; Tomasz Chinciński and Paweł Machcewicz (eds.), *Bydgoszcz 3–4 września 1939: Studia i dokumenty, Einsatzgruppen* (Warsaw: Instytut Pamięci Narodowej, 2008), p. 56; Böhler, *Der Überfall*, pp. 117–120; Mary Fulbrook, *A Small Town Near Auschwitz: Ordinary Nazis and the Holocaust* (Oxford: Oxford University Press, 2012), pp. 49–54.

56 Wilm Hosenfeld, *'Ich versuche jeden zu retten': Das Leben eines deutschen Offiziers in Briefen und Tagebüchern*, ed. Thomas Vogel (Munich: DVA, 2004), p. 250; Shmuel Krakowski, 'The Fate of Jewish POWs of the Soviet and Polish Armies', in Asher Cohen, Yehoyakim Cochavi, and Yoav Gelber (eds.), *The Shoah and the War* (New York: Peter Lang, 1992), pp. 233–244; Böhler, *Auftakt zum Vernichtungskrieg*, pp. 176–180.

in the Soviet zone were handed over to the SS – several thousand ended up in the Lipowa 7 camp in Lublin. There were also forced marches of about 8,000 Jewish prisoners of war between the end of 1939 and the first months of 1941, mainly to Lublin, Włodawa, and Biała-Podlaska; a considerable number of them perished during those marches.[57]

In October 1939 the SS and police began to murder psychiatric patients in the annexed territories. These murders took place at a time when the regime had embarked on the murder of the mentally and physically disabled in the Old Reich. In November 1939 a large number of patients, probably the majority of the approximately 870 Polish and 30 Jewish patients of the Owińska hospital for the mentally ill near Poznań, were shot in the surrounding woods. Later, more patients were killed with poison gas. Between January and April 1940 the so-called Sonderkommando Lange was active in the region, which had been incorporated into the Reich as the Reichsgau Wartheland (Warthegau). This 'special commando' moved from one psychiatric hospital to the next, murdering patients; among its victims were at least 183 Jews. At the end of October 1940, near Kalisz, 290 Jewish residents of a care home for the elderly were murdered. Herbert Lange and his colleagues continued the killing until the summer of 1941, sparing only a few of the Polish patients while murdering all the Jews. In autumn of the same year, Lange set up an extermination camp for Jews in Kulmhof (Chelmno) – a process which clearly shows the connection between murdering the sick and murdering the Jews.[58]

The Wehrmacht, which initially exercised executive authority in the occupied territory, was involved to a significant degree in these crimes against the Polish population. The Wehrmacht leadership initially approved the murders, expecting them to result in a lasting 'pacification' of the conquered area.[59] The commander-in-chief of the army, Walther von Brauchitsch, informed his subordinates on 21 September 1939 that the Einsatzgruppen were performing 'certain ethnopolitical [*volkspolitisch*] tasks'.[60] Only infrequently did dissent arise within the military leadership at this early stage, as in the cases of a few army generals such as Georg von Küchler and Joachim Lemelsen. Generaloberst Günther von Kluge, commander of the 4th Army, expressed outrage at the 'shootings of Polish nationals and Jews' and at the 'plan to create a Jewish reservation in Lublin'. Such objections to the crimes committed in Poland must also be seen in the context of the rivalries between the Wehrmacht and the SS. In isolated cases the military courts

57 David Silberklang, *Gates of Tears: The Holocaust in the Lublin District* (Jerusalem: Yad Vashem, 2013), pp. 90–92.

58 Volker Rieß, *Die Anfänge der Vernichtung 'lebensunwerten Lebens' in den Reichsgauen Danzig-Westpreußen und Wartheland 1939/40* (Frankfurt am Main: Peter Lang, 1995); Zdzisław Jaroszewski (ed.), *Zagłada chorych psychicznie w Polsce 1939–1945 / Die Ermordung der Geisteskranken in Polen 1939–1945* (Warsaw: PWN, 1993); Ingo Loose, 'Eksterminacja chorych w Kraju Warty: Stan badań i kontrowersje', in Michał Musielak and Katarzyna B. Głodowska (eds.), *Medycyna w cieniu nazizmu / Medicine in the Shadow of Nazism* (Poznań: Wydawnictwo Naukowe Uniwersytetu Medycznego im. Karola Marcinkowskiego w Poznaniu, 2015), pp. 155–167; Henry Friedlander, *The Origins of Nazi Genocide: From Euthanasia to the Final Solution* (Chapel Hill, NC: University of North Carolina Press, 1995); Michael Alberti, *Die Verfolgung und Vernichtung der Juden im Reichsgau Wartheland 1939–1945* (Wiesbaden: Harrassowitz, 2006), pp. 325–336.

59 Hans Umbreit, *Deutsche Militärverwaltungen 1938/39: Die militärische Besetzung der Tschechoslowakei und Polens* (Stuttgart: DVA, 1977), p. 206.

60 BArch-MA, RH 20-14/178. Published in Matthäus, Böhler, and Mallmann (eds.), *War, Pacification, and Mass Murder*, pp. 130–131.

took action against the perpetrators.[61] But on 4 October 1939 Hitler granted amnesty to German personnel for acts that had been committed 'out of bitterness due to the atrocities committed by the Poles'. The amnesty prevented almost all punishment of their early war crimes. Members of the SS and police were exempted from regular judicial prosecution and placed under special jurisdiction.[62]

Flee or Stay?

In light of the persecution of the Jews in the German Reich, the Polish Jews viewed the invasion by German troops with great concern. Nonetheless, no one had expected violence on such a scale, especially as many remembered the occupation during the First World War. At that time the Germans had displayed a degree of antisemitic prejudice but in practice had shown themselves to be relatively tolerant and fair overall towards the Jews. The events of the first few days of the invasion were horrifying. Above all, those young men who had been politically active decided to flee eastward and attempted to reach Soviet-occupied territory, Romania, or Hungary. Within the larger flight of Polish citizens from the German occupiers, ultimately reaching an estimated 800,000, Jews were a significant component. There was also a brief Soviet occupation of the southern and eastern parts of District Lublin, which had followed a brief German occupation. Thousands of Jews fled with the Soviets when they retreated over the new demarcation line.

Thomas T. Blatt, a native of Izbica near Lublin, later recalled: 'We didn't know what to do. Some Jews suggested fleeing toward the east, whilst others said that the Germans were only people too, after all, and they would empathize with the civilians and do them no harm. Still others moved on further, intending to cross the Bug and side with the Soviets.'[63] This could be done with relative ease at first, but from mid October 1939 onwards Soviet border guards turned away the refugees and sent them back under threat of violence. On the other side of the demarcation line, however, stood the German sentries. One woman, who had fled from Jarosław, described the terrifying situation:

> We reached the San river in the morning of our third day on the run. Gestapo men stood on the bank and forced the people onto the boat, or more accurately the raft made of two wobbly boards, from which women and children fell into the San. All around we could see those who had drowned during the preceding days; near the riverbank, women stood in the water, holding their children on their shoulders and calling for help; the Gestapo men responded by shooting them.[64]

61 Beate Kosmala, 'Der deutsche Überfall auf Polen: Vorgeschichte und Kampfhandlungen', in Borodziej and Ziemer (eds.), *Deutsch-polnische Beziehungen*, pp. 19–41, here p. 38; Matthäus, Böhler, and Mallmann (eds.), *War, Pacification and Mass Murder*, pp. 29–30.

62 Jürgen Förster, 'Wehrmacht, Krieg und Holocaust', in Rolf-Dieter Müller and Hans-Erich Volkmann (eds.), *Die Wehrmacht: Mythos und Realität* (Munich: Oldenbourg, 1999), pp. 948–963, here p. 952.

63 Thomas T. Blatt, *From the Ashes of Sobibor: A Story of Survival* (Evanston, IL: Northwestern University Press, 1997), p. 11.

64 Statement of Róża Wagner, 1945, in Michał M. Borwicz, Nella Rost, and Józef Wulf (eds.), *Dokumenty zbrodni i męczeństwa* (Cracow: Wojewódzka Żydowska Komisja Historyczna w Krakowie, 1945), p. 143 (translated from Polish).

At first, many Jews in the eastern voivodeships were grateful for the invasion by the Red Army and believed this would protect them from Nazi persecution. Calel Perechodnik mentions this in his memoir, written in a Warsaw bunker in 1943: 'The first feeling was that of immense happiness. This is nothing to be surprised at. From one side there was the German invader, proclaiming slogans of merciless destruction and murder of all Jews; from the other side, the Bolshevik, proclaiming slogans that for him all people were equal under the law.'[65] An estimated 200,000 to 300,000 refugees joined the Jews already living in the region. Younger people in particular seized the opportunity to integrate into the Soviet system, which was new to them. During the early phase, the Soviet occupying power dismissed and persecuted large numbers of Polish office holders and replaced them with Jews, including local resident Jews, as the latter were often well educated. Unemployed Jews were given jobs in the eastern part of Byelorussia or in the mining district in eastern Ukraine.[66] Nevertheless, most of the refugees decided against becoming Soviet citizens. Meanwhile, the Soviet secret police, the NKVD, were often suspicious of incoming refugees from the West, whether Poles or Jews. They regarded them as a security risk and hence deported many of them to the eastern part of the Soviet Union. Many of the deportees were ultimately sent to Siberia, especially around the area of Tomsk, and later to Kyrgyzstan and Kazakhstan.

The majority of the Jews in German-occupied Poland, however, remained in their home towns or left them only briefly and returned after the fighting was over. Leon Zelman described the mood in his milieu in Łódź: 'Here and there, you heard of a Jew who had taken his own life in despair. Others left their belongings behind and fled eastward at the last minute. Those who stayed behind shook their heads: Why give up hope, why put yourself in such danger? The hardships would be eased, things would not work without us, somehow we would get through.'[67]

The Administration of the Occupied Territories

To end the phase of military administration as quickly as possible and to embark on the planned measures of ethnic restructuring, Hitler signed a decree on 12 October 1939 on the integration and administration of the conquered eastern territories. As of 26 October, the German Reich annexed the western Polish territories. These included regions that Germany had been forced to cede in 1919: East Upper Silesia, West Prussia, and

65 Calek Perechodnik, *Spowiedź*, ed. David Engel (Warsaw: Ośrodek KARTA and Żydowski Instytut Historyczny, 2016); an earlier, heavily edited version is available in English translation: Calel Perechodnik, *Am I a Murderer? Testament of a Jewish Ghetto Policeman*, ed. and trans. Frank Fox (Boulder, CO: Westview, 1996), p. 2.

66 Sławomir Kalbarczyk, 'Żydzi polscy wśród ofiar zbrodni sowieckich w latach 1939–1941', *Pamięć i Sprawiedliwość*, vol. 40 (1997/98), pp. 173–194; Albin Głowacki, *Sowieci wobec Polaków na ziemiach wschodnich II Rzeczypospolitej 1939–1941* (Łódź: Wydawnictwo Uniwersytetu Łódzkiego, 1998), pp. 376–379; Marek Wierzbicki, *Polacy i Żydzi w zaborze sowieckim: Stosunki polsko-żydowskie na ziemiach północno-wschodnich II RP pod okupacją sowiecką (1939–1941)* (Warsaw: Stowarzyszenie Kulturalne 'Fronda', 2001); Andrzej Żbikowski, *U genezy Jedwabnego: Żydzi na Kresach Północno-Wschodnich II Rzeczypospolitej, wrzesień 1939 – lipiec 1941* (Warsaw: Żydowski Instytut Historyczny, 2006).

67 Leon Zelman, *After Survival: One Man's Mission in the Cause of Memory* (New York: Holmes & Meier, 1998), p. 21.

the Province of Posen. However, the area around Łódź and territories east of the Polish voivodeship of Silesia (Śląsk) were also incorporated into the Reich, as was Kreis Zichenau (Ciechanów), which was incorporated into East Prussia. In the north the Reichsgau Danzig-West Prussia was established, in the centre the Reichsgau Wartheland was formed, and East Upper Silesia became part of the Province of Silesia. The great majority of the almost 10 million inhabitants of the annexed territories, including 500,000 to 550,000 Jews, did not see themselves as Germans.

While the incorporated western Polish territories were designated from the very start for complete integration into the Reich, and thus 'Germanization', the Germans saw the rest of German-occupied Poland as a sketchily defined colonial borderland into which 'undesirable elements' from the now expanded Reich territory could be moved. It was intended to serve as a pool of cheap labour and as a staging area for a war against the Soviet Union. At the lower and middle tiers of administration, pre-war non-Jewish staff remained largely in place throughout the war, but the Germans had no intention of preserving any form of autonomous Polish statehood. These aims were explained by Hitler on 17 October 1939 at a meeting in the Reich Chancellery, during which he informed Wilhelm Keitel, the Chief of the Wehrmacht High Command (OKW), of the end of the military administration and the establishment of the 'General Government of the Occupied Polish Territories'. This territory, known after mid 1940 simply as the 'General Government', had a population of 12 million, including approximately 1.5 million Jews.[68]

Hitler gave the post of governor general to the top Nazi lawyer Hans Frank, his former legal advisor, who reported directly to him. Frank's deputy until May 1940 was the Austrian Arthur Seyss-Inquart, who had played an important role in the 1938 annexation of Austria and would become the Reich Commissioner for the Occupied Dutch Territories in May 1940. The post of deputy was then taken over by Josef Bühler, who also headed the so-called government of the GG from the summer of 1940. When posts in the incorporated territories were being filled, NSDAP leaders from Danzig had a good chance of being selected on the basis of their contribution to the anti-Polish 'ethnic struggle'. In the north, Gauleiter Albert Forster, based in Danzig, was able to vastly increase the territory under his control through the creation of the new Reichsgau Danzig-West Prussia. His former deputy and rival Arthur Greiser made a career leap when he became the new Gauleiter and Reichsstatthalter of the Warthegau. Finally, in the south, the Silesian Gauleiter Josef Wagner was given additional territory in the east. When this large Gau was divided in January 1941, occupied Polish Silesia became part of the Province of Upper Silesia under Fritz Bracht. Erich Koch, the Gauleiter of East Prussia since 1928, meanwhile controlled Regierungsbezirk Zichenau. All these men were avowed antisemites and united by their brutal lust for power. These Gauleiter in the new Reichsgaue and in the territories annexed to existing provinces in the so-called Old Reich now faced responsibilities that were completely different from those of their colleagues in the Old Reich. At the forefront was the radical transformation of entire regions, including deportation and mass murder.[69]

68 Bömelburg and Musiał, 'Die deutsche Besatzungspolitik', pp. 49–52, 71–72.

69 Wolf Gruner and Jörg Osterloh (eds.), *The Greater German Reich and the Jews: Nazi Persecution Policies in the Annexed Territories, 1935–1945*, trans. Bernard Heise (New York and Oxford: Berghahn, 2015 [German edn, 2010]), including chapters by Wolfgang Gippert on Danzig-West Prus-

While the occupied territories that had been incorporated into the Reich were divided into Regierungsbezirke, the General Government was split into four districts (Cracow, Lublin, Radom, Warsaw), run by district governors. Cracow was chosen as the seat of government, in order to erase the political and symbolic importance of Warsaw as the Polish capital. Below the districts, the Kreise and the bigger cities formed the crucial framework of German domination, presided over by Kreishauptleute and Stadthauptleute, who were endowed with considerable autonomy and authority. They set out to exploit their territories in the interests of Germany and had few scruples in applying repressive measures. At the local level, a largely powerless Polish administration with local mayors and village officials was left in place.[70]

Almost every part of the civil administration concerned itself with the 'Jewish question', especially the Interior Administration, Labour, Economic Affairs, Finance, and Food and Agriculture Departments. But it was the Population and Welfare Division within the Interior Administration Department that wielded particularly crucial influence on the fate of the Jews. This division had been set up within the government in Cracow in late 1939 by Fritz Arlt, previously head of the Racial Policy Office in Breslau. In May 1941 Arlt was succeeded in this office by his former deputy, Lothar Weirauch.[71]

The SS and police played a far greater role in occupied Poland than in the Reich. Heinrich Himmler, using the far-reaching latitude given to him in his new role as Reich Commissioner for the Strengthening of Germandom (Doc. 25), was able to consolidate the various branches of his empire – the Security Police, Order Police, and Waffen-SS – to a greater extent than in the Reich. Once military operations were at an end, the Einsatzgruppen were converted into permanent offices. All units were subordinated to the Higher SS and Police Leaders (HSSPF): Friedrich-Wilhelm Krüger in the General Government, Wilhelm Koppe in the Warthegau, and Richard Hildebrandt in Danzig-West Prussia, whose significance increased substantially as a result. The annexed territories in Upper Silesia and East Prussia were assigned to the HSSPF in Breslau (Erich von dem Bach-Zelewski) and Königsberg (Wilhelm Redieß) respectively. In addition, Himmler

sia, Ingo Loose on Wartheland, Andreas Schulz on Zichenau, and Sybille Steinbacher on East Upper Silesia; Dieter Pohl, 'Die Reichsgaue Danzig-Westpreußen und Wartheland: Koloniale Verwaltung oder Modell für die zukünftige Gauverwaltung?', in Jürgen John, Horst Möller, and Thomas Schaarschmidt (eds.), *Die NS-Gaue: Regionale Mittelinstanzen im zentralistischen 'Führerstaat'* (Munich: Oldenbourg, 2007), pp. 395–405, here p. 396; Edward Serwański, *Wielkopolska w cieniu swastyki* (Warsaw: Pax, 1970); Włodzimierz Jastrzębski and Jan Sziling, *Okupacja hitlerowska na Pomorzu Gdańskim w latach 1939–1945* (Gdańsk: Wydawnictwo Morskie, 1979); Łuczak, *Pod niemieckim jarzmem*, pp. 16–19; Catherine Epstein, *Model Nazi: Arthur Greiser and the Occupation of Western Poland* (Oxford: Oxford University Press, 2010); Ryszard Kaczmarek, *Górny Śląsk podczas II wojny światowej: Między utopią niemieckiej wspólnoty narodowej a rzeczywistością okupacji na terenach wcielonych do Trzeciej Rzeszy* (Katowice: Wydawnictwo Uniwersytetu Śląskiego, 2006); Ralf Meindl, *Ostpreußens Gauleiter: Erich Koch – eine politische Biographie* (Osnabrück: fibre, 2007).

70 Werner Präg and Wolfgang Jacobmeyer (eds.), *Diensttagebuch des deutschen Generalgouverneurs in Polen 1939–1945* (Stuttgart: DVA, 1975); Bogdan Musiał, *Deutsche Zivilverwaltung und Judenverfolgung im Generalgouvernement: Eine Fallstudie zum Distrikt Lublin 1939–1944* (Wiesbaden: Harrassowitz, 1999); Markus Roth, *Herrenmenschen: Die deutschen Kreishauptleute im besetzten Polen – Karrierewege, Herrschaftspraxis und Nachgeschichte* (Göttingen: Wallstein, 2009).

71 Aly and Heim, *Architects of Annihilation*, pp. 131–138; Musiał, *Deutsche Zivilverwaltung*, pp. 96–100.

installed an SS and Police Leader (SSPF) in each of the four districts of the General Government.[72]

Although there were conflicts between the police and the civil administration over spheres of authority and resources, there was far-reaching consensus when it came to the treatment of the local population. The occupiers regarded themselves as members of the 'master race' and behaved accordingly. Especially in the incorporated territories, the humiliation and maltreatment of Jews and the discrimination against the Polish population became routine. Many of the officials now deployed in the East also viewed their new job as an opportunity to enrich themselves or otherwise turn their position to their advantage. This was all the more the case as a number of offices in the Reich had dispatched officials with questionable records to occupied Poland, and quite a few individuals who had failed in business in Germany now tried their luck there.[73]

Expulsion

One of the central aims of German policy in occupied Poland was the Germanization of the incorporated territories, and the regime promptly began to implement this plan. In the process it was able to draw on a long tradition of 'nationhood projects' dating back to the First World War, and on the experience of earlier expulsion operations. Even though the self-styled experts on population and spatial planning had been discussing ethnic restructuring in Poland since 1937, concrete planning for deportations began only after the country had been conquered. The plans were developed in the context of the Nazis' overall policies for resettlement and deportation which Hitler had set in motion with the border changes from 1938 onwards.[74] In addition to the Jewish refugees and expellees from the German sphere of control, tens of thousands of Czechs had already been forced to leave the annexed Sudetenland. Slovakia, officially autonomous, had also endeavoured to deport Jews when it was forced to cede territories to Hungary in 1938.

From September 1939 onwards, however, forced displacement projects began on an entirely new scale. On 6 October, Hitler announced in the Reichstag a 'reordering of ethnographic conditions' in the territories within the German sphere of influence (Doc. 17). This included, to begin with, the German–Soviet population exchange that had been agreed upon with Stalin at the end of September. The German-speaking minorities who had just come under Soviet rule, together with those in territories that were expected to fall to Soviet control in the foreseeable future, were to be relocated to the

72 Ruth Bettina Birn, *Die Höheren SS- und Polizeiführer: Himmlers Vertreter im Reich und in den besetzten Gebieten* (Düsseldorf: Droste, 1986); Peter Longerich, *Heinrich Himmler: A Life*, trans. Jeremy Noakes and Leslie Sharpe (Oxford: Oxford University Press, 2012 [German edn, 2008]), pp. 437–439.

73 Musiał, *Deutsche Zivilverwaltung*, pp. 80–86; Roth, *Herrenmenschen*; Stephan Lehnstaedt, *Okkupation im Osten: Besatzeralltag in Warschau und Minsk 1939–1944* (Munich: Oldenbourg, 2010).

74 Götz Aly, *'Final Solution': Nazi Population Policy and the Murder of the European Jews*, trans. Belinda Cooper and Allison Brown (London: Arnold; New York: Oxford University Press, 1999 [German edn, 1995]); Isabel Heinemann, *'Rasse, Siedlung, deutsches Blut': Das Rasse- und Siedlungshauptamt der SS und die rassenpolitische Neuordnung Europas* (Göttingen: Wallstein, 2003); Alexa Stiller, *Völkische Politik: Praktiken der Exklusion und Inklusion in polnischen, französischen und slowenischen Annexionsgebieten 1939–1945* (Göttingen: Wallstein, 2021).

Reich. At the same time, Hitler planned to extend the 'German living space' to western Poland. Hitler called upon high-ranking Party officials and military officers to engage in 'a rigorous ethnic struggle that is subject to no legal restrictions'. Large groups within the population, he stated, must be forcibly driven eastwards, and the present territory of the Reich should be 'cleansed of Jews, Poles, and riffraff'.[75]

The idea of carrying out this 'cleansing' by creating a reservation in the eastern part of the occupied territory was already under discussion at the top level of the Security Police while military operations were still under way. Reinhard Heydrich, Chief of the Security Police and the SD, issued instructions to the Einsatzgruppen in an express letter on 21 September 1939, directing them to force the Jewish population in western Poland to move from rural areas to places more conveniently located with regard to transport facilities, and to concentrate the Jews there (Doc. 12).[76] By the next day he already spoke of a 'Jewish state under German administration, near Cracow'.[77] At one of the first top-level conferences of his new government agency, the Reich Security Main Office (Reichssicherheitshauptamt, RSHA), it was then said that the intention was to create a 'Reich ghetto', 'to the east of Warsaw and around Lublin', in which 'all the political and Jewish elements to be resettled from future German Gaue must be placed'.[78]

Heydrich's men soon set about making this plan a reality. Gestapo Chief Heinrich Müller tasked Adolf Eichmann, the head of the Resettlement Section at the Reich Security Main Office, with the deportation of 70,000 to 80,000 Jews from East Upper Silesia (Doc. 18). In mid October 1939 Eichmann decided to add to the list of places from which Jews would be deported and to send the transports to an area near the small town of Nisko, on the San river, in the western part of the Lublin region. Between 18 and 26 October he had around 5,000 Jews in total from Vienna, Mährisch-Ostrau (Moravská Ostrava) in the Protectorate of Bohemia and Moravia, and Kattowitz deported to that area, although no preparations of any kind had been made to receive them. Müller then called a halt to the deportation programme, saying that it required 'central management', and announced on 21 December that Himmler had suspended the deportations 'until further notice'. The priority at this point was the massive relocations of the population in the western Polish territories, discussed below.[79] Many of the Jews who had been deported by then either fled across the German–Soviet demarcation line or made their way to

75 Hitler's remarks to OKW Chief Keitel on 17 October 1939 in Franz Halder, *Kriegstagebuch: Tägliche Aufzeichnungen des Chefs des Generalstabes des Heeres 1939–1942*, vol. 2: *Von der geplanten Landung in England bis zum Beginn des Ostfeldzuges (1.7.1940–21.6.1941)*, ed. Hans-Adolf Jacobsen and Alfred Philippi (Stuttgart: W. Kohlhammer, 1963), p. 107.

76 Michman, 'Why Did Heydrich Write the Schnellbrief?'

77 Seev Goshen, 'Eichmann und die Nisko-Aktion im Oktober 1939: Eine Fallstudie zur NS-Judenpolitik in der letzten Etappe vor der "Endlösung"', *Vierteljahrshefte für Zeitgeschichte*, vol. 29, no. 1 (1981), pp. 74–96, here p. 79.

78 'Protokoll der Amtschefbesprechung vom 29.9.1939', BArch, R 58/825, fols. 36–37.

79 Goshen, 'Eichmann und die Nisko-Aktion'; Jonny Moser, 'Nisko: The First Experiment in Deportation', *Simon Wiesenthal Center Annual*, vol. 2 (1985), pp. 1–30; Wolf Gruner, 'Von der Kollektivausweisung zur Deportation der Juden aus Deutschland (1938–1945): Neue Perspektiven und Dokumente', in Birthe Kundrus and Beate Meyer (eds.), *Die Deportation der Juden aus Deutschland: Pläne – Praxis – Reaktionen 1938–1945* (Göttingen: Wallstein, 2004), pp. 21–62; Longerich, *Heinrich Himmler*, p. 441; Jonny Moser, *Nisko: Die ersten Judendeportationen* (Vienna: Steinbauer, 2012).

neighbouring localities. When the camp near Nisko was closed in April 1940, the approximately 500 remaining inmates were sent back to Vienna or Mährisch-Ostrau.[80]

Governor General Frank had occasionally declared his willingness to accept into his domain the 'Jews from the Reich, Vienna, from everywhere'. He explained to his Kreishauptleute and Stadthauptleute that it was necessary to make the General Government into 'a large concentration area' for Jews. At the same time, he factored in their gradual demise:

> Give the Jews short shrift. It'll be a pleasure to be able to tackle the Jewish race physically at last, for a start. The more of them die, the better; to strike him [the Jew] is a victory for our Reich. The Jews should be made to feel that we have arrived. We want to put ½ to ¾ of all the Jews east of the Vistula.[81]

There, in a region that was never clearly delineated, a so-called Jewish reservation was supposed to be created (Doc. 65). But by March 1940 Hitler had already backed away from the idea of a reservation,[82] and the Wehrmacht had also come out against a concentration of the Jewish population in the territory adjoining the Soviet Union. In light of these developments, Himmler instructed the SS and police leadership in the annexed territories to regard, in future, not only the region around Lublin but the entire General Government as a 'reservoir for all those who are racially unsuitable for Germany'.[83]

That was actually how Himmler, as Reich Commissioner for the Strengthening of Germandom, had seen the General Government all along. By mid October 1939 a Central Immigration Office (Einwandererzentralstelle, EWZ) had already been established on Heydrich's orders. This organization, which from January 1940 had set up its headquarters in Łódź together with several branch offices, carried out the screening and settling of incoming population groups that were of German descent.[84] The Central Resettlement Office (Umwandererzentralstelle, UWZ) in Posen (Poznań), which also set up branch offices, was responsible for the expulsion of Jews and Poles.[85] As a first step

80 Browning, *Origins of the Final Solution*, pp. 41–42.

81 'Protokoll der Besprechung Hans Franks mit den Kreis- und Stadthauptmännern des Distrikts Radom am 25. November 1939', published in Tatiana Berenstein, Artur Eisenbach, Bernard Mark, and Adam Rutkowski (eds.), *Faschismus – Getto – Massenmord: Dokumentation über Ausrottung und Widerstand der Juden in Polen während des zweiten Weltkrieges* ([East] Berlin: Rütten & Loening, 1960), p. 46.

82 So Hitler told Colin Ross on 12 March 1940, in *Akten zur deutschen auswärtigen Politik*, series D: *1937–1945*, vol. 8/1: *Die Kriegsjahre: 4. September 1939 bis 18. März 1940* (Baden-Baden: Imprimerie Nationale, 1961), pp. 716–717.

83 Himmler's letter of 20 May 1940, in Kurt Pätzold (ed.), *Verfolgung, Vertreibung, Vernichtung: Dokumente des faschistischen Antisemitismus 1933 bis 1942* (Frankfurt am Main: Röderberg, 1984), p. 264.

84 Andreas Strippel, *NS-Volkstumspolitik und die Neuordnung Europas: Rassenpolitische Selektion der Einwandererzentralstelle des Chefs der Sicherheitspolizei und des SD 1939–1945* (Paderborn: Schöningh, 2011).

85 Robert Lewis Koehl, *RKFDV: German Resettlement and Population Policy, 1939–1945. A History of the Reich Commission for the Strengthening of Germandom* (Cambridge, MA: Harvard University Press, 1957); Heinemann, *'Rasse, Siedlung, deutsches Blut'*; Alexa Stiller, 'Reichskommissar für die Festigung deutschen Volkstums', in Ingo Haar and Michael Fahlbusch (eds.), *Handbuch der völkischen Wissenschaften* (Munich: Saur, 2008), pp. 531–540; Stiller, *Völkische Politik*.

Himmler directed the SS and police to begin removing the Jewish population and the 'undesirable' Poles to the General Government (Doc. 25).

Leading *Ostforscher* provided intellectual backing. On 7 October 1939 Theodor Schieder summarized the guidelines in a draft memorandum. The German ethnic group and the Polish one, he wrote, were to be separated from one another through 'population transfers on the largest possible scale'. Schieder proposed that German resettlers from Eastern Europe be settled in the annexed provinces and that, in turn, the Poles living there be expropriated en masse and relocated. Space was to be made for them elsewhere in the occupied territory. Schieder noted, however, that the 'development of a healthy ethnic order' required the 'de-Jewification of the remainder of Poland (*Restpolen*)'.[86] Otherwise, 'the degradation of the Polish racial corpus may become the focus of new and dangerous unrest'.[87] The recommendations of the Party's race strategists were similarly radical. In order to Germanize the annexed territories, asserted Erhard Wetzel and Gerhard Hecht of the Racial Policy Office of the NSDAP in a memorandum dated 25 November 1939, most 'ethnic Poles' and the Jews must be deported 'ruthlessly and as swiftly as possible [...] to the remainder of Poland'.[88]

The first six months of the German occupation were characterized by gargantuan planning and the partial failure of these plans. The Reich Commissariat for the Strengthening of Germandom (RKF) and the Security Police kept developing new resettlement projects, each replacing and partially revising the previous one. On 30 October 1939 Himmler announced the deportation of all Jews and an as yet unspecified section of the Polish population, approximately 1 million residents in total, from the incorporated territories to the General Government.[89] One month later his subordinate Heydrich had developed the so-called first *Nahplan* ('short-range plan'), on the basis of which more than 87,000 persons were deported from the Warthegau to the General Government between 1 and 17 December. Because the measures primarily targeted people living in towns and cities, the deportations affected sizeable numbers of Jews, around 60,000. The deportees were to make room for the Germans resettled there from the Baltic region and from the Ukrainian–Polish region of Volhynia.[90]

As early as 13 December 1939 a second *Nahplan* was issued. It envisaged the deportation of an additional 220,000 persons – alternatively, in a stepped-up version, 600,000 persons – this time almost exclusively Jews (Doc. 66). Meanwhile, deportations under the first *Nahplan* continued. The victims were usually given only twenty-four hours to prepare for their departure, and were allowed to take only a small amount of

86 The term 'Restpolen' was used to refer to the General Government.

87 'Vorläufer des "Generalplans Ost": Eine Dokumentation über Theodor Schieders Polendenkschrift vom 7. Oktober 1939', ed. Angelika Ebbinghaus and Karl Heinz Roth, *1999: Zeitschrift für Sozialgeschichte des 20. und 21. Jahrhunderts*, vol. 7, no. 1 (1992), pp. 62–94 (memorandum pp. 84–91).

88 'Denkschrift zur "Frage der Behandlung der Bevölkerung der ehemaligen polnischen Gebiete nach rassenpolitischen Gesichtspunkten"', in Karol Marian Pospieszalski (ed.), *Documenta Occupationis*, vol. 5: *Hitlerowskie 'prawo' okupacyjne w Polsce: Wybór dokumentów*, part 1: *Ziemie 'wcielone'* (Poznań: Wydawnictwo Instytutu Zachodniego, 1952), pp. 2–28, here pp. 19, 27.

89 Berenstein et al. (eds.), *Faschismus – Getto – Massenmord*, pp. 42–43; Phillip T. Rutherford, *Prelude to the Final Solution: The Nazi Program for Deporting Ethnic Poles, 1939–1941* (Lawrence, KS: University Press of Kansas, 2007); Maria Rutowska, *Wysiedlenia ludności polskiej z Kraju Warty do Generalnego Gubernatorstwa 1939–1941* (Poznań: Instytut Zachodni, 2003).

90 Browning, *Origins of the Final Solution*, pp. 47–50.

luggage with them. Many did not survive the transport in the frequently unheated goods wagons. The journey by train was often followed by lengthy marches on foot to the destinations. After open criticism was voiced, even among the occupation officials, of the fact that tens of thousands of people were being sent in goods wagons in midwinter, under appalling conditions, without food and heat, on a journey lasting for days, an agreement on certain minimum standards was reached at the Reich Security Main Office. The deportees were allowed to take 100 złoty with them, they were to be given food for ten days, and, in particularly cold weather, women and children were to travel in passenger coaches (Doc. 71).

To free up housing and jobs more quickly for the Baltic German resettlers, Heydrich put in place an 'intermediate plan' ahead of the second *Nahplan*. Between 7 February and 15 March 1940 the deportation trains took more than 42,000 persons, almost all of them Poles, to the General Government. In addition, in January 1940 Himmler's RKF had drawn up an initial comprehensive 'general plan' for all intended large-scale relocations from annexed western Poland. Over the long term no fewer than 3.4 million Poles were to be expelled from the territory, and the entire Jewish population was to be deported even sooner, namely by the spring of 1940.[91]

Before long, however, economic considerations increasingly came to the fore. The Plenipotentiary for the Four-Year Plan, Hermann Göring, urged the occupation authorities on 12 February 1940 to pay more attention to the requirements of the wartime economy. The 'Ostgaue', he said, needed to increase agricultural production and supply the Reich with manpower on a grand scale. That meant deportations from the annexed territories of Poland to the west, not to the General Government. Meanwhile, because people who were considered 'racially valuable' had also been caught up in the previous deportations to the General Government, Himmler now pushed for vetting by the Race and Settlement Main Office when further selections for such deportations were made.[92]

The chief reason for the failure of the deportation programme was that the German authorities in the General Government, a territory which had been left in ruins by the wartime devastation, were neither willing nor able to deal with a mass influx of impoverished people. Moreover, the decision to assign the city of Łódź and its environs, where around 250,000 Jews lived, to the Warthegau rather than to the General Government implied a drastic increase in potential deportations. Meanwhile, Frank had started complaining that officials in Berlin were 'increasingly viewing the terrain of the General Government east of the Vistula as a kind of reservation for Jews'. In early March 1940 he expected that the resettlement operations would be reduced and would include, at most, 'around 100[,000]–120,000 Poles, around 30,000 Gypsies, and, from the Reich, a number of Jews to be determined as one may see fit'.[93]

In the meantime, the deportation of the Jews living in the German Reich – a measure halted in November 1939 – had been resumed by the Gestapo in February 1940. This was also prompted by the wish to free up housing space for Baltic Germans. The deport-

91 Rolf-Dieter Müller, *Hitlers Ostkrieg und die deutsche Siedlungspolitik: Die Zusammenarbeit von Wehrmacht, Wirtschaft und SS* (Frankfurt am Main: Fischer, 1991), pp. 130–138.

92 Aly, '*Final Solution*', pp. 59–63; Longerich, *Heinrich Himmler*, pp. 434–436, 445–450.

93 Präg and Jacobmeyer (eds.), *Diensttagebuch des deutschen Generalgouverneurs*, pp. 146–147 (4 March 1940).

ation of approximately 1,000 Jews from Stettin and around 160 persons from Schneidemühl to District Lublin in March 1940 caused a considerable sensation abroad, much to the displeasure of the Reich Foreign Office.[94] On 24 March, Göring, in his capacity as chairman of the Ministerial Council for the Defence of the Reich, prohibited further deportations for the time being.[95]

Including the deportations undertaken on the basis of the intermediate plan, a total of 110,000 Jews and Poles had been deported by mid March 1940 from the incorporated territories, primarily to the neighbouring districts Radom and Warsaw.[96] On 1 April 1940 – significantly later than planned – deportations based on the second *Nahplan* were set in motion. This time Poles made up the vast majority of the deportees. In the autumn of 1940 another sizeable number of Poles were moved from the Warthegau into the General Government, to make room for ethnic Germans arriving from Bukovina and Bessarabia, but also to create military training areas for the Wehrmacht. Simultaneously, the Vienna Gauleitung in particular pressed for the deportation of 'its' Jews, which had begun in the autumn of 1939, to be resumed.

In January 1941 Heydrich therefore presented the third *Nahplan*, which envisaged the deportation of 771,000 persons, mostly Poles from the annexed territories, but also 60,000 Jews from Vienna, to the General Government. This project never progressed beyond its initial stages either, but, beginning on 5 February 1941, the police deported around 25,000 Poles from the incorporated territories and 5,000 Jews from Vienna. In his diary Chaim Kaplan described the circumstances of these deportations:

> The exiles were driven out of their beds before dawn, and the Führer's minions did not let them take money, belongings or food, threatening all the while to shoot them. Before they left on their exile, a search was made of their pockets and of all the hidden places in their clothes and bodies. Without a penny in their pockets or a covering for the women, children, old people and invalids – sometimes without shoes on their feet or staffs in their hands – they were forced to leave their homes and possessions and the graves of their ancestors, and go – whither? And in terrible, fierce, unbearable cold![97]

On 15 March 1941 Gestapo chief Müller instructed Eichmann, the resettlement specialist at the Reich Security Main Office, to halt the deportations. Priorities had shifted: in the General Government the Wehrmacht was beginning to concentrate troops in

94 The transport from Schneidemühl did not reach its destination but was stopped near Posen. After that, the deportees were taken to Neuendorf and to a country estate near Radinkendorf in Brandenburg: Alfred Gottwaldt and Diana Schulle, *Die 'Judendeportationen' aus dem Deutschen Reich 1941–1945: Eine kommentierte Chronologie* (Wiesbaden: Marix, 2005), p. 35.

95 Pätzold, *Verfolgung, Vertreibung, Vernichtung*, p. 262; Christopher R. Browning, *The Final Solution and the German Foreign Office: A Study of Referat D III of Abteilung Deutschland, 1940–43* (New York: Holmes & Meier, 1978), pp. 21–22.

96 Czesław Łuczak, *Polityka ludnościowa i ekonomiczna hitlerowskich Niemiec w okupowanej Polsce* (Poznań: Wydawnictwo Poznańskie, 1979), pp. 127–128. On Radom, see Robert Seidel, *Deutsche Besatzungspolitik in Polen: Der Distrikt Radom 1939–1945* (Paderborn: Schöningh, 2006), pp. 270–273; Jacek Andrzej Młynarczyk, *Judenmord in Zentralpolen: Der Distrikt Radom im Generalgouvernement 1939–1945* (Darmstadt: WBG, 2007), pp. 67–70, 97–100.

97 Kaplan, *Scroll of Agony*, p. 219 (31 Jan. 1941).

preparation for the invasion of the Soviet Union. The Central Resettlement Office, working together with the SS and police and the occupation administration, had by then organized mass deportations of inhabitants of the annexed territories to the territory of the General Government – 365,000 persons,[98] according to official statements, and around 460,000, according to later estimates. Among these deportees were approximately 60,000 Jews. Tens of thousands fell victim to *wilde Vertreibungen* ('wild expulsions', uncoordinated and chaotic), as in Danzig-West Prussia, or fled eastward.[99]

At their destinations the expelled Jews found neither appropriate housing nor sufficient food. The Jewish communities tried to help them, but in this effort they received almost no support from the local occupation authorities, who did not welcome the deportees and sent them on their way whenever possible. The Jewish refugees were almost destitute, and thus unable to draw on reserves for the longer term. They were the weakest link within the Jewish community in the General Government and were among the first victims when the systematic mass murder operations in this territory began in 1942.[100]

By the spring of 1941 the Jewish population had been expelled from most of the Polish territories near the old borders of the Reich. However, 400,000 to 450,000 Jews still remained in the eastern half of the new Reich provinces, with more than 250,000 of them in the Warthegau alone. Regierungsbezirk Zichenau still had more than 40,000 Jewish inhabitants, and 100,000 Jews still lived in the Oststreifen ('Eastern Strip'), the most easterly part of the territory annexed to Silesia. Some of the latter were conscripted for forced labour.[101] The Nazi leadership's original plan to remove all Jews from the incorporated territories had failed. And the scheme meanwhile under discussion in the summer of 1940 – to deport all of Europe's Jews to Madagascar – was not seriously pursued any further, even though the idea continued to surface sporadically thereafter.[102] This plan was abandoned mainly on the grounds that it was not viable even after the military victory over France was concluded on 22 June, because Germany did not control the sea routes. The conflicting goals evident in the implementation of the early resettlement programmes determined the further course of action as well. A 'territorial final solution' was repeatedly discussed and attempted, but in the end it seemed impossible to realize. Bureaucratic resistance in the reception areas was too great, and the consequences for the societies there seemed too serious. These experiences increased the willingness of the occupation authorities to resort to even more brutal methods in 1941.

98 According to Himmler's report as RKF dated 20 Jan. 1943, BArch, R 43 II/1411a, fols. 405–415.

99 Łuczak, *Polityka ludnościowa*, p. 128; Alberti, *Die Verfolgung*, p. 144; Alexandra Pulvermacher, 'Early Deportations of Jews in Occupied Poland (October 1939 – June 1940)', *Holocaust and Genocide Studies*, vol. 36, no. 2 (2022), pp. 125–153.

100 Lea Prais, *Displaced Persons at Home: Refugees in the Fabric of Jewish Life in Warsaw, September 1939 – July 1942*, trans. Naftali Greenwood (Jerusalem: Yad Vashem, 2015).

101 *Trial of the Major War Criminals before the International Military Tribunal*, vol. 36 (Nuremberg: Secretariat of the Tribunal, 1949), pp. 299–307; Sybille Steinbacher, 'East Upper Silesia', in Gruner and Osterloh (eds.), *The Greater German Reich and the Jews*, pp. 239–266.

102 Brechtken, *'Madagaskar für die Juden'*, pp. 274–283.

Visible Identification and Plunder

While the authorities in the Old Reich debated, vigorously and at length, individual anti-Jewish measures and their domestic political and diplomatic repercussions, the German occupiers in Poland were untroubled by such scruples. Discriminatory regulations, humiliation, and physical violence defined Jewish everyday life even after the military operations were over, and the anti-Jewish operations undertaken by the military administration and those of the civil administration frequently merged seamlessly into each other.

The occupiers quickly introduced the visible identification of the Jewish population, a measure that was only introduced in the Reich in September 1941 and elsewhere, such as in Western Europe, even later. The main aim behind this was to ensure that acculturated and assimilated Jews, most of whom lived in the cities, could be easily identified. From late October 1939 onwards, Jews in parts of the Warthegau had to wear a special badge on their clothing, and as of December 1939 those in the General Government were required to wear a white armband with a blue Star of David.[103] In some places these mandatory measures had been practised even before corresponding regulations were issued, indicating a degree of local initiative in the process (Doc. 8). The Jews had now been made visibly distinct from the Poles in public. In Cracow, Halina Nelken noted in her diary:

> The Germans have issued a most hideous ordinance. From now on, all Jews have to wear a blue Star of David on the right arm. [...] One of the girls in our group, Anka, said she is ashamed, that she is never going to wear this armband, that she does not look Jewish. I also do not look Jewish. [...] However, I'll probably wear the armband. If everyone has to, everyone must.[104]

The visible identification made it easier for the police to monitor compliance with the curfews, which were especially restrictive for Jews, and with the numerous prohibitions that denied Jews access to certain streets, squares, whole neighbourhoods, and even extensive administrative districts. It also affected contacts and relationships between Jews and their Christian neighbours.

The occupiers simultaneously set about seizing Jewish property as they pleased. Jews were not safe from robbery anywhere. Meyer Wolf Liebermann, who owned a shop in Łódź, described this state of affairs quite matter-of-factly in a post-war testimony: 'When the Germans came to Litzmannstadt, they started to requisition quilts, and kept it up until I had nothing left.'[105] These uncoordinated acts of plunder soon began to give way to more concerted measures of dispossession, first in the annexed territories, where the majority of Poland's industrial firms were located and where Germans were scheduled to settle over the long term. Robbery was now replaced by systematic confiscation of the

103 Regulation on the Visible Identification of Jews in the General Government (23 Nov. 1939), *VOBl-GG* 1939, no. 8, 30 Nov. 1939, p. 61.

104 Halina Nelken, *And Yet, I Am Here!*, trans. Halina Nelken with Alicia Nitecki (Amherst, MA: University of Massachusetts Press, 1999 [Polish edn, 1987]), p. 59 (entry for 8 Dec. 1939).

105 Report: Meyer Wolf Liebermann (August 1945), AŻIH, 301/4935, fol. 1 (quotation translated from German).

property owned by the Polish state and the Church, by the Poles who had fled or been deported, and by the Jews (Doc. 44). Large amounts of the stolen goods went to the German resettlers in western Poland.[106]

The takeover of Jewish real estate was initiated by the Race and Settlement Main Office as early as 2 September 1939.[107] A few days later Hans Frank, as chief of the civil administration for the military commander in Poland, prohibited any selling of Jewish assets in the occupied territory (Doc. 4). Jewish shop owners were required to place special signs in their display windows (Doc. 8), which made looting easier. Numerous shops and businesses that had been closed during the military operations were not allowed to reopen. By requiring 'contributions' in the form of cash or tangible assets, the conquerors quickly ensured that the coffers of the occupation administration would be full.[108]

The Jews first lost the right to dispose of their own belongings. Numerous specific provisions imposed restrictions upon Jewish businesses and prohibited 'price gouging' and 'illicit trade'. In November 1939 the occupiers blocked the bank accounts owned by Jews; the account holders were allowed to have only modest sums at their disposal. In addition, discriminatory taxes were introduced, and Jews were required to fully disclose their financial circumstances (Doc. 64). At the end of 1939 Jews were excluded from receiving benefits from pension and insurance funds; they had to yield all their claims to the Reichsbank.[109]

On 19 October 1939 Göring ordered the establishment of the Main Trustee Office East for the purpose of registering Polish state assets and private property. It evolved into the chief instrument of economic plunder in the incorporated territories.[110] The head office in Berlin and its branches in Danzig, Posen, Kattowitz, and Zichenau managed the confiscated assets that were classified as Jewish. In the territories of western Poland, Jews lost almost all their significant possessions.[111]

In the General Government, where a separate trustee agency had been in operation since 15 November 1939, the occupiers only gradually forced the handover or closing down of the Jewish-owned commercial and craft businesses, primarily because the Jews there played a particularly important role in economic life. The municipal administrations usually took possession of the real estate. In addition, 'the owner's right of disposal' with regard to furnishings from Jewish homes was 'revoked'.[112] These items often found

106 Aly, *'Final Solution'*, pp. 105–113.

107 Kazimierz Radziwończyk, '"Akcja Tannenberg" grup operacyjnych *Sipo* i *SD* w Polsce jesienią 1939 r.', *Przegląd Zachodni*, vol. 22, no. 5 (1966), pp. 94–118, here pp. 97–98.

108 Andrzej Dmitrzak, *Hitlerowskie kontrybucje w okupowanej Polsce 1939–1945* (Poznań: Wydawnictwo Naukowe UAM, 1983).

109 Itamar Levin, *Walls Around: The Plunder of Warsaw Jewry during World War II and Its Aftermath*, trans. Rachel Neiman (Westport, CT: Praeger, 2004 [Hebrew edn, 2003]); Ingo Loose, *Kredite für NS-Verbrechen: Die deutschen Kreditinstitute in Polen und die Ausraubung der polnischen und jüdischen Bevölkerung 1939–1945* (Munich: Oldenbourg, 2007).

110 Werner Röhr, Elke Heckert, and Wolfgang Schumann (eds.), *Nacht über Europa*, vol. 2: *Die faschistische Okkupationspolitik in Polen (1939–1945)* (Cologne: Pahl-Rugenstein, 1989), pp. 132–133.

111 Jeanne Dingell, *Zur Tätigkeit der Haupttreuhandstelle Ost, Treuhandstelle Posen 1939–1945* (Frankfurt am Main: Peter Lang, 2003); Bernhard Rosenkötter, *Treuhandpolitik: Die 'Haupttreuhandstelle Ost' und der Raub polnischer Vermögen 1939–1945* (Essen: Klartext, 2003), pp. 158–159.

their way into the residences of German occupation personnel, ethnic Germans and resettlers, and Poles enriched themselves as well.[113]

The drive to expropriate the Jews had devastating consequences for those affected. Because most Jewish owners lost their businesses, the majority of the Jewish population became unemployed and now faced a daily struggle for their own survival and that of their families.

Jewish Councils and Jewish Social Self-Help

Prompted by officials in the SS who were in charge of Jewish affairs, the German occupation authorities ordered that so-called Jewish councils and councils of elders be established to organize Jewish life and implement German directives. On 21 September 1939 Heydrich officially ordered the formation of these organizations in his express letter to the heads of the Einsatzgruppen. They were to consist of up to twenty-four rabbis and other respected men; the Jewish council was to be 'made *fully responsible*, in the strict sense of the term, for the prompt and exact implementation of all orders issued so far and in the future' (Doc. 12). In practice, a considerable number of Jewish elders and councils had already been appointed from 6 September 1939 onwards.[114] Many more were established after 21 September, while the military administration was still in charge. After Hans Frank was appointed governor general, he issued a central directive for the General Government in November 1939. The Jewish councils in Poland were envisaged as local and in some cases as regional bodies following the pre-war precedents of Vienna and Prague, but not as entities operating at a supra-regional level on the lines of the Reich Association of Jews in Germany.[115] In Warsaw the Gestapo appointed a Jewish council on 7 October 1939, headed by the engineer Adam Czerniaków, who had been approached three days earlier by the Einsatzgruppe.[116] In Łódź, which was renamed

112 'Rundschreiben des Amtschefs im Amt des GG, Bühler', dated 8 August 1940, AIPN, Deutsche Strafanstalt Reichshof 110/2, fol. 5.

113 Jan Grabowski and Dariusz Libionka (eds.), *Klucze i kasa: O mieniu żydowskim w Polsce pod okupacją niemiecką i we wczesnych latach powojennych 1939–1950* (Warsaw: Stowarzyszenie Centrum Badań nad Zagładą Żydów, 2014).

114 This was the case in Kępno, Grudziądz, Sosnowiec, Katowice, Piotrków Trybunalski, Łódź, Cracow, Częstochowa, Konopisko, Maków Mazowiecki, Raciąż, Przasnysz, Ciechanów, and Będzin.

115 Isaiah Trunk, *Judenrat: The Jewish Councils in Eastern Europe under Nazi Occupation* (New York: Macmillan, 1972); Aharon Weiss, 'Jewish Leadership in Occupied Poland – Postures and Attitudes', *Yad Vashem Studies*, vol. 12 (1977), pp. 335–365; Dan Michman, 'Reevaluating the Emergence, Function, and Form of the Jewish Councils Phenomenon', in *Ghettos, 1939–1945: New Research and Perspectives on Definition, Daily Life, and Survival. Symposium Presentations* (Washington, DC: United States Holocaust Memorial Museum Center for Advanced Holocaust Studies, 2005), pp. 67–84.

116 Dan Michman, 'O okolicznościach ustanowienia warszawskiego Judenratu: Nowy punkt widzenia', *Kwartalnik Historii Żydów / Jewish History Quarterly*, vol. 221, no. 1 (2007), pp. 33–41; Aldona Podolska, *Służba Porządkowa w getcie warszawskim w latach 1940–1943* (Warsaw: Wydawnictwo Fundacji 'Historia pro Futuro', 1996); Barbara Engelking and Jacek Leociak, *The Warsaw Ghetto: A Guide to the Perished City*, trans. Emma Harris (New Haven, CT, and London: Yale University Press, 2009 [Polish edn, 2001]), pp. 136–218. See also the biography by Marcin Urynowicz, *Adam Czerniaków 1880–1942: Prezes getta warszawskiego* (Warsaw: Instytut Pamięci Narodowej, 2009).

'Litzmannstadt' in April 1940, a first 'head of the community' was appointed on 12 September 1939; his name was Lezer Plywacki. A month later, on 13 October, the German Stadtkommissar Albert Leister named 63-year-old Mordechai Chaim Rumkowski to serve as 'Jewish elder', and tasked him with forming an advisory board (*Beirat*).[117]

Approximately 400 Jewish councils were appointed in occupied Poland. Some of them represented only a few hundred Jews, whereas others, as in Warsaw, represented more than 450,000 persons. In the larger cities the Jewish councils, with the help of tax money, levies, fees, and funds released from confiscated Jewish holdings, created extensive administrations that organized Jewish life largely autonomously. The Jewish councils were responsible for registration matters, allocating living quarters and food, social welfare and medical care, refugee relief, education, supplying and remunerating forced labourers, and constructing the ghetto walls. Many Jewish councils, however, first had to look after the expellees who arrived as a result of the various resettlement projects in the cities. The Jewish Order Service, a sort of police force, was responsible for guarding the perimeter walls or fences of ghettos, keeping smuggling under control, and generally maintaining public order.[118]

When Adam Czerniaków became chairman of the Jewish Community in Warsaw, he believed that he was taking on 'a historic role in beleaguered Warsaw', and vowed in his diary: 'I will try to live up to it.'[119] This would turn out to be an impossible aspiration. After he had tried for almost three years to mitigate the cruellest orders issued by the occupiers concerning the Jews who were locked in the ghetto, Czerniaków took his own life on 23 July 1942 after he was ordered to make arrangements for the deportation of orphaned children.

Among Jews, opinions differed considerably about the actions taken by the Jewish councils. Particular criticisms were levelled at Moshe Merin in Sosnowitz (Sosnowiec)[120] and Mordechai Chaim Rumkowski in Litzmannstadt (Łódź), who exercised considerable latitude in internal matters and who were controversial on account of their autocratic behaviour. However, they were largely powerless against the German administration.[121] Adam Czerniaków in Warsaw cultivated a less autocratic style, yet corruption spread, and he too had many detractors among the Jewish population. Attitudes in other places varied, depending on the character of the chairmen and members of the Jewish

117 Alter Shnur, '"Min Hametzar" – The Diary of Alter Shnur', *Dapim Leheker Hashoah Vehamered*, vol. 1 (April 1951 [Hebrew]), p. 118; Andrea Löw, *Juden im Getto Litzmannstadt: Lebensbedingungen, Selbstwahrnehmung, Verhalten* (Göttingen: Wallstein, 2006), pp. 72–75, 99–116.

118 Podolska, *Służba Porządkow*; Löw, *Juden im Getto Litzmannstadt*, pp. 72–75, 99–116; Andrea Löw, 'Ordnungsdienst im Getto Litzmannstadt', in Paweł Samuś and Wiesław Puś (eds.), *Fenomen getta łódzkiego 1940–1944* (Łódź: Wydawnictwo Uniwersytetu Łódzkiego, 2006), pp. 155–167; Engelking and Leociak, *Warsaw Ghetto*, pp. 136–218.

119 *The Warsaw Diary of Adam Czerniakow: Prelude to Doom*, ed. Raul Hilberg, Stanislaw Staron, and Josef Kermisz, trans. Stanislaw Staron and the Staff of Yad Vashem (Chicago: Ivan R. Dee, 1999), p. 76 (entry for 23 Sept. 1939).

120 Aleksandra Namysło, 'Wpływ kierownictwa Centrali Żydowskich Rad Starszych Wschodniego Górnego Śląska na postawy i zachowania Żydów wobec rzeczywistości okupacyjnej', in Aleksandra Namysło (ed.), *Zagłada Żydów na polskich terenach wcielonych do Rzeszy* (Warsaw: Instytut Pamięci Narodowej, 2008), pp. 176–185.

121 Löw, *Juden im Getto Litzmannstadt*; Michal Unger, *Reassessment of the Image of Mordechai Chaim Rumkowski*, trans. Naftali Greenwood (Jerusalem: Yad Vashem, 2008).

councils. While the German occupiers, as has already been emphasized, set up the Jewish councils to control Jewish communities, the councils not only dealt with tasks assigned to them by the Germans, but were involved in running much of daily life. In effect they became the boards of the respective communities, replacing the pre-war Jewish community boards. That opinions about the Jewish councils differed so greatly was partly due to these different dimensions of their role and how they played out in different places.[122]

Members of Jewish councils that failed to cooperate with the occupation authorities were arrested, and some were murdered. In Cracow the German administration removed two successive chairmen from office and had them arrested or deported and murdered before appointing Dawid Gutter, a chairman known for his ruthless behaviour towards the Jewish population.[123]

Over time the Jewish councils faced growing opposition. Where there was a well-organized underground, usually composed of political parties or youth movements, the opposition came primarily from that quarter, sometimes focused especially on the issue of equitable food distribution. In some cities committees of the Jewish Social Self-Help (JSS, Żydowska Samopomoc Społeczna), which looked after the impoverished population, acted as a counterbalance to the Jewish councils.[124] As early as 14 September 1939 a central coordinating committee for the Jewish welfare organizations in the General Government was constituted, but it was not officially recognized by the occupation authorities. However, in late May 1940 they granted recognition to the Chief Welfare Council (Naczelna Rada Opiekuńcza, NRO), in which the JSS and the Polish and Ukrainian Central Welfare Councils were combined. As of July 1940 all the independent Jewish social welfare organizations of the JSS were put under the control of the JSS chairman, Michał Weichert.

Through the aid committees of the JSS in the larger towns, relief supplies and food were distributed to the branches, or *delegatury*, in the smaller localities. These branches set up soup kitchens and hospitals, became involved in the care of children and the elderly, and also gave financial support to those who were particularly destitute, such as refugees and those forcibly resettled, who were on their own in unfamiliar surroundings.[125] Initially the German civil administration refused to fund Jewish welfare, so aid was dependent on contributions and relief supplies from abroad, in particular on the

122 Trunk, *Judenrat*, pp. 368–387, 451–474, 528–585; Dan Diner, *Beyond the Conceivable: Studies on Germany, Nazism, and the Holocaust* (Berkeley, CA: University of California Press, 2000), pp. 117–137.

123 Trunk, *Judenrat*; Andrea Löw and Markus Roth, *Juden in Krakau unter deutscher Besatzung 1939–1945* (Göttingen: Wallstein, 2011), pp. 140–141.

124 Silberklang, *Gates of Tears*, pp. 204–209.

125 Michał Weichert, *Yidishe aleynhilf* (Tel Aviv: Menoyre, 1962); Aleksandra Bańkowska and Maria Ferenc Piotrowska (eds.), *Archiwum Ringelbluma: Konspiracyjne archiwum getta warszawy*, vol. 27: *Żydowska Samopomoc Społeczna w Warszawie (1939–1943)* (Warsaw: Wydawnictwo Naukowe PWN, 2017); Ruta Sakowska, 'Instytucje pomocy społecznej w getcie warszawskim: Struktura organizacyjna 1940–1942', in Krzysztof Dunin-Wąsowicz, Janina Kaźmierska, and Barbara Winnicka (eds.), *Warszawa lat wojny i okupacji 1939–1944*, vol. 2 (Warsaw: Państwowe Wydawnictwo Naukowe, 1972), pp. 119–137; Tatiana Brustin-Berenstein, 'Jüdische Soziale Selbsthilfe', in Götz Aly (ed.), *Arbeitsmarkt und Sondererlaß: Menschenverwertung, Rassenpolitik und Arbeitsamt* (Berlin: Rotbuch, 1990), pp. 156–174; Andrea Löw, 'Zwischen Untergang und Selbsthilfe: Juden im Kreis Radzyń während des Zweiten Weltkrieges', *Zeitschrift für Geschichtswissenschaft*, vol. 53, no. 8 (2005), pp. 716–735.

support of the American Jewish Joint Distribution Committee (Joint or JDC). But the Relief Committee for the War-Stricken Jewish Population (RELICO) in Geneva, the International Committee of the Red Cross (ICRC), and the Relief Effort for Jews in Need in Poland (Hilfsaktion für notleidende Juden in Polen, HAFIP) in Zurich also sent relief supplies into occupied Poland. The JDC soon confined its activities to the General Government. Additional sources of income for the JSS were donations, levies upon the Jewish councils, and eventually contributions from the German administration as well: 17 per cent of the money allocated to the Chief Welfare Council by the Population and Welfare Division in the General Government actually went to the JSS. To generate additional income, the local *delegatury* organized cultural events and lotteries.[126]

Despite its many and varied efforts to support those in need, the JSS was also not uncontroversial and was occasionally accused of collaboration. The JSS executive committee, however, defended its stance: 'In view of the ever-worsening situation of the Jewish population, it was unanimously decided to take full advantage of the opportunity presented for providing aid in compliance with the law.'[127]

Forced Labour

The occupiers had their eye on the exploitation of Jewish labour from the outset. Jews were forced to work for German institutions and individuals from the very first days of the war, and were rounded up arbitrarily for this purpose. They received meagre pay or nothing at all. Members of the police or the Wehrmacht compelled Jews to work in forestry or agriculture, for example, or made them work as cleaners in barracks and private residences. They frequently humiliated or harassed the Jews in the course of this work (Docs. 6, 16).[128] The Germans repeatedly organized raids in order to round up workers at random.

126 Yehuda Bauer, *American Jewry and the Holocaust: The American Jewish Joint Distribution Committee, 1939–1945* (Jerusalem: Institute of Contemporary Jewry, Hebrew University; Detroit, MI: Wayne State University Press, 1981), pp. 67–106; Raya Cohen, *The Story of Witnesses to Destruction: Jewish Emissaries in Switzerland, 1939–1942* (Tel Aviv: Am Oved, 1999 [Hebrew]); Raya Cohen, 'The Lost Honour of the Bystanders? The Case of Jewish Emissaries in Switzerland', in David Cesarani and Paul A. Levine (eds.), *'Bystanders' to the Holocaust: A Re-evaluation* (London: Taylor & Francis, 2002), pp. 146–170; Löw, 'Zwischen Untergang und Selbsthilfe', p. 730; Młynarczyk, *Judenmord in Zentralpolen*, pp. 196–212.

127 'Kurzer Bericht ueber die Taetigkeit der J.S.S., spaeter J.U.S. 1939–1944', YIVO, RG 532, box 2, fol. 3; Hans-Jürgen Bömelburg, 'Der Kollaborationsvorwurf in der polnischen und jüdischen Öffentlichkeit nach 1945 – das Beispiel Michał Weichert', in Joachim Tauber (ed.), *'Kollaboration' in Nordosteuropa: Erscheinungsformen und Deutungen im 20. Jahrhundert* (Wiesbaden: Harrassowitz, 2006), pp. 250–288.

128 Christopher R. Browning, *Nazi Policy, Jewish Workers, German Killers* (Cambridge and New York: Cambridge University Press, 2000), pp. 60–87; Wolf Gruner, *Jewish Forced Labor Under the Nazis: Economic Needs and Racial Aims, 1938–1944*, trans. Kathleen M. Dell'Orto (Cambridge: Cambridge University Press, 2006), pp. 177–213, 230–275. On the Warthegau, Berenstein and Rutkowski, 'Prześladowania ludności żydowskiej', pp. 78–87; Anna Ziółkowska, *Obozy pracy przymusowej dla Żydów w Wielkopolsce w latach okupacji hitlerowskiej (1941–1943)* (Poznań: Wydawnictwo Poznańskie, 2005). On the General Government, Witold Mędykowski, *Macht Arbeit Frei? German Economic Policy and Forced Labor of Jews in the General Government, 1939–1943* (Boston: Academic Studies Press, 2018).

Halina Birenbaum, who lived in the Warsaw ghetto as a schoolgirl and survived the Majdanek, Auschwitz, and Ravensbrück concentration camps, later wrote a memoir in Israel in which she described the situation in Warsaw during the first weeks of the occupation:

> Many did not return from this work – they were killed by bullets or died as a result of beatings and floggings. But those who did come back, witnesses and victims of the brutal torments inflicted by the Nazis, aroused an indescribable fear with their tales. [...] Lorries suddenly appeared at the end of the crowded street, and the passers-by took to their heels. 'Stop!' the Germans shouted; they grabbed the men, hanging on to them tightly, and loaded them onto the lorries, shoving and battering them all the while.[129]

To prevent at least the ill-treatment during the roundups, many Jewish councils soon suggested that they themselves organize the 'recruitment' for forced labour.

On 26 October 1939 Governor General Frank introduced forced labour for the Jews in the General Government (Doc. 27), and at the end of the year Higher SS and Police Leader Krüger spelled out the details of the measure more precisely (Doc. 58). At the beginning of 1940 the labour administration assumed responsibility for supplying and deploying Jews as forced labourers, while the SS and police officially remained in charge only of guarding the labour camps. New large-scale projects were to be carried out with the help of the forced labourers: Heydrich proposed concentrating hundreds of thousands of Jews from western Poland in gigantic camps in the eastern part of the General Government, so that they could be used to build defence barriers and border fortifications (Doc. 82). Especially in District Lublin, many forced labour camps were created in 1940 for the civil administration's land improvement projects. But it was above all the Lublin SS and Police Leader Odilo Globocnik, acting largely independently of the civil administration, who operated camps for the purpose of building an 'Eastern Wall' along the demarcation line that marked off the General Government from Soviet-occupied territory.[130]

In mid 1940 more than 20,000 Jewish men were working in the District Lublin camps. They came not only from the region, but also from Districts Warsaw and Radom. The main camp, which at times held as many as 2,500 prisoners, was located in Bełżec. The forced labourers, herded together in the most primitive housing and without adequate rations, did extremely taxing work from early morning until evening, and many of them fell ill. Jewish physicians inspected their living quarters in September 1940:

> The rooms are completely unsuited to house such numbers. They are dark and dirty. The rate of infestation with lice is very high. Around 30 per cent of the workers have no shoes, trousers, or shirts. They all sleep on the floor, without any straw. The roofs are in disrepair everywhere, there are no windowpanes, and it is appallingly

129 Halina Birenbaum, *Hope Is the Last to Die: A Personal Documentation of Nazi Terror*, trans. David Welsh (New York: Twayne, 1971 [Polish edn, 1967]), pp. 4–5.

130 Frank Grelka, 'Rural Hubs of Early Destruction: The Waterworks' Camps in the Lublin District, 1940–1942', *Yad Vashem Studies*, vol. 45, no. 2 (2017), pp. 39–67.

> cramped. […] To make things worse, there is no soap, and it is even difficult to get water. The sick lie and sleep together with the healthy. During the night, no one is allowed to leave the barracks, so all calls of nature must be answered then and there. Given these conditions it is no surprise that there are numerous cases of illness.[131]

Even the District Governor of Cracow, Otto Wächter, commented in a situation report at the end of 1940 that the poor physical condition of the Jews made their deployment as labour difficult, if not altogether impossible. Many companies refused to employ Jews for this reason.[132] The project soon proved pointless from a military perspective, because preparations for war against the Soviet Union began as early as the autumn of 1940.

Overall, more than 100 forced labour camps for Jews were set up in the General Government alone in 1940, and in all of German-occupied Poland the number was much higher. In the Warthegau, 187 such camps have been identified.[133] Most of them existed only for a short time and gradually ceased activity. Over the course of 1941, the number of camps increased once again.[134] In September 1940 the SS began building a second large network of camps. Himmler assigned the task of organizing Jewish forced labourers in East Upper Silesia to Albrecht Schmelt, the chief of police in Breslau (Doc. 189). After plans to deport the Jews out of the region had largely foundered, the aim was now to make maximum use of their labour power within the region. Schmelt set up an office of his own, which exercised virtually exclusive authority over the Jewish forced labourers. The plan was to use these Jews to extend the motorway from Breslau to Cracow, but they were also to be a supply of labour for company-run camps and in munitions plants. The central Jewish Council for East Upper Silesia, headed by Moshe Merin, had to establish a Section for Labour Deployment, which was responsible for recruiting the workforce with the help of the Jewish Order Service. Schmelt soon had camps set up in Lower Silesia and the Sudetenland as well. By the autumn of 1941 some 17,000 Jewish men and women were deployed under Schmelt's supervision, approximately half of them in the so-called motorway camps, where they had to perform hard physical labour twelve hours a day, seven days a week. Conditions were insanitary and the treatment of the workers appalling. The meagre wages went to the Jewish Council in Sosnowiec, which used the money to fund welfare measures. Conditions were substantially better for the Jews who worked in the Wehrmacht's manufacturing plants in

131 'Beilage zum Bericht des Referates Arbeitslager beim Judenrat Warschau, Ende 1940', in Berenstein et al. (eds.), *Faschismus – Getto – Massenmord*, p. 221 (translated from Polish).

132 'Lagebericht des Gouverneurs des Distrikts Krakau vom 18.12.1940', BArch, R 52 III/16, fol. 26.

133 Mario Wenzel, 'Zwangsarbeitslager für Juden in den besetzten polnischen und sowjetischen Gebieten', in Wolfgang Benz and Barbara Distel (eds.), *Der Ort des Terrors: Geschichte der nationalsozialistischen Konzentrationslager*, vol. 9 (Munich: C. H. Beck, 2009), pp. 124–154, here p. 127.

134 Józef Marszałek, *Obozy pracy w Generalnym Gubernatorstwie w latach 1939–1945* (Lublin: Państwowe Muzeum na Majdanku, 1998), p. 14, counts 115 forced labour camps for Jews in the General Government for 1940 alone, and even more – 209 – for 1941. 'Bericht des Vorstands der Jüdischen Sozialen Selbsthilfe an die Regierung des GG über die Lage der Juden in den NS-Arbeitslagern', in Tatiana Berenstein, Artur Eisenbach, and Adam Rutkowski (eds.), *Eksterminacja Żydów na ziemiach polskich w okresie okupacji hitlerowskiej: zbiór dokumentów* (Warsaw: Żydowski Instytut Historyczny, 1957), pp. 225–228; Czesław Pilichowski (ed.), *Obozy hitlerowskie na ziemiach polskich 1939–1945: Informator encyklopedyczny* (Warsaw: Państwowe Wydawnictwo Naukowe, 1979).

Będzin and Sosnowiec and elsewhere, and were permitted to stay in their homes with their families.[135]

In the larger towns the Jewish councils were heavily involved in organizing the deployment of labour. In Lublin, from early 1940, the Jewish Council had its own separate employment office. This office had to record in a card index the names of the Jews in the community who were fit for work and make 1,000 men available to the German authorities every day for forced labour. In August 1940 the labour battalions deployed by the Warsaw Jewish Council totalled 10,600 persons. In Litzmannstadt, volunteers were initially recruited for building motorways in the Reich, a project for which Fritz Todt, the Inspector General for German Roadways, was allowed to utilize Polish Jews from the end of 1940 onwards. Later, the Jewish elder of Litzmannstadt sent primarily Jews who had violated the ghetto rules to the camps. In the Reichsgau Wartheland, to which Litzmannstadt belonged, the civil administration was responsible for the labour deployment of the Jewish population throughout the occupation period.[136]

Concentration and Ghettoization

In the 1930s the term 'ghetto' in Jewish and non-Jewish discourse – echoing the term that had originated in sixteenth-century Italy to refer to a Jewish neighbourhood – came to mean, especially in Poland, a densely populated, poor Jewish neighbourhood. As they moved through Poland the German invaders encountered such neighbourhoods, and before long the German authorities began to control and dictate where Jews were allowed to reside. While the resulting processes of concentration and ghettoization are sometimes assumed to be identical, a distinction can be drawn between the two phenomena in terms of the decision-making process. The idea of concentrating Jews in certain towns and cities stemmed from policies formulated at a higher level, while the restriction of Jews to certain neighbourhoods in cities – usually the already densely populated poor ones dating from the pre-war period – resulted primarily from local ad hoc decisions. These were thus essentially two different developments. The imposed ghetto phenomenon spread gradually and not systematically, and the number of ghettos imposed had only reached a few dozen by the spring of 1941; the majority of the ghettos in Poland were established after that time.[137]

135 Alfred Konieczny, 'Die Zwangsarbeit der Juden in Schlesien im Rahmen der "Organisation Schmelt"', in Götz Aly, Susanne Heim, and Miroslav Kárný (eds.), *Sozialpolitik und Judenvernichtung: Gibt es eine Ökonomie der Endlösung?* (Berlin: Rotbuch, 1987), pp. 91–110; Sybille Steinbacher, *'Musterstadt' Auschwitz: Germanisierungspolitik und Judenmord in Ostoberschlesien* (Munich: Saur, 2000), pp. 138–153; Aleksandra Namysło, *Zagłada Żydów Zagłębiowskich* (Będzin: Instytut Pamięci Narodowej, 2004); Gruner, *Jewish Forced Labor*, pp. 196–229; Andrea Rudorff, 'Arbeit und Vernichtung *reconsidered*: Die Lager der Organisation Schmelt für polnische Jüdinnen und Juden aus dem annektierten Teil Oberschlesiens', *Sozial.Geschichte Online*, vol. 7 (2012), pp. 10–39.

136 Jakub Poznański, *Pamiętnik z getta łódzkiego*, ed. Horacy Safrin (Łódź: Wydawnictwo Łódzkie, 1960), p. 39; Nachman Blumental (ed.), *Te'udot mi-geto lublin – yudenrat le-lo derekh / Documents from Lublin Ghetto: Judenrat without Direction* (Jerusalem: Yad Vashem, 1967 [Hebrew]); Gruner, *Jewish Forced Labor*, pp. 177–212.

137 Dan Michman, *The Emergence of Jewish Ghettos during the Holocaust*, trans. Lenn J. Schramm (Cambridge: Cambridge University Press, 2011), pp. 61–89.

Because Heydrich assumed in September 1939 that the Jews would soon be expelled and sent eastward, he sent out an express letter directing that the Jewish population should be concentrated in cities with good rail connections. It soon became apparent, however, that the deportation projects were not feasible. By the end of 1939 some of those in charge were already discussing proposals for isolating the Jews *in situ* by forcing them to reside in designated areas of towns and cities. But because this measure was not mandated by general directive – either in the incorporated territories or in the General Government – in practice there were wide variations from place to place. By creating self-contained Jewish residential districts, known as ghettos, the local German authorities pursued several objectives. First and foremost, the Jewish population was to be concentrated and isolated from the Poles so that the Jews could be quickly deported, should the occasion arise. But often other reasons were given as well. The German authorities and the Nazi press claimed that the Jews were dirty and therefore 'plague carriers', and that they consequently had to be kept segregated to protect the German and Polish population from contagious diseases. Another pretext was the assertion that it was Jews who fuelled black-market activity and that concentrating them in ghettos would enable them to be more tightly controlled. A further allegation was that there were known to be many spies among them, so the ghettos needed to be created for security reasons.[138]

The first ghettos were established in late 1939 in two smaller towns in the area around Radom, namely in Piotrków-Trybunalski at the end of October and in Radomsko at the end of December. There, members of the civil administration had seized the initiative apparently because they were unwilling to wait for the implementation of the large resettlement projects and because the Soviet Union was closing its borders to refugees.[139] In the Reichsgau Wartheland, the failure of deportation projects also prompted Regierungspräsident Friedrich Uebelhoer at the end of 1939 to begin preparations for the establishment of a ghetto in Łódź. But, he declared:

> It goes without saying that the establishment of the ghetto is only a transitional measure. I reserve the right to determine when and by what means the ghetto – and with it the city of Lodsch – will be cleansed of Jews. In any event, the ultimate goal must be to cauterize this plague boil completely (Doc. 54).

In February 1940 the Jews began moving into the area allocated to them in the northern part of the city. The Jewish population in Łódź had shrunk considerably as a result of Jews' flight early in the war, but had grown again with the influx of Jews in 1940 from various places. The ghetto was sealed off on 30 April. From then on, almost 160,000 people were

138 Raul Hilberg, *The Destruction of the European Jews*, vol. 1 (New Haven, CT: Yale University Press, 2003), pp. 191–192, 215; Christoph Dieckmann and Babette Quinkert, 'Einleitung', in Dieckmann and Quinkert (eds.), *Im Ghetto*, pp. 9–29. On the historiography, see Guy Miron and Shlomit Shulhani (eds.), *The Yad Vashem Encyclopedia of the Ghettos during the Holocaust* (Jerusalem: Yad Vashem, 2009); Martin Dean and Mel Hecker (eds.), *United States Holocaust Memorial Museum Encyclopedia of Camps and Ghettos, 1933–1945*, vol. 2: *Ghettos in German-Occupied Eastern Europe* (Bloomington, IN: Indiana University Press, 2012); Dieter Pohl, 'Ghettos im Holocaust: Zum Stand der historischen Forschung', in Jürgen Zarusky (ed.), *Ghettorenten: Entschädigungspolitik, Rechtsprechung und historische Forschung* (Munich: Oldenbourg, 2010), pp. 39–50.

139 Młynarczyk, *Judenmord in Zentralpolen*, pp. 112–113.

forced to live in an area that was far too small, totalling around 4 square kilometres. This resulted in intense overcrowding. Łódź/Litzmannstadt thus became the town with the largest Jewish population in the territory of the Reich.

Of all the ghettos in occupied Poland, the one in Litzmannstadt survived the longest: the Germans did not liquidate it until the summer of 1944. In addition to the Reich governor's office, the German ghetto administration, headed by the Bremen businessman Hans Biebow, had primary responsibility for decision-making. Both authorities, motivated by concern for their own financial interests, sought to 'increase the productivity' of those imprisoned in the ghetto. It was Biebow's ambition to keep the ghetto from becoming a subsidized undertaking. Even before the ghetto was sealed off, Jewish elder Mordechai Chaim Rumkowski had approached the administration to suggest ways in which the ghetto could be funded through the labour of its inhabitants. Rumkowski's initiative stemmed from the fact that Łódź had been the textile capital of Eastern Europe before the war, and Jews were a significant part of the skilled workers in this trade. In accordance with his motto 'Work is our only path', Rumkowski built up an extensive industry in which men, women, and children produced goods, above all clothing and footwear, for the Wehrmacht and for German firms.[140]

The establishment of the ghetto was a less straightforward process in Warsaw, where a lack of uniform guidelines led to much improvisation. The former Polish capital, with a population of around 400,000 Jews, had the second-largest Jewish community in the world after New York, and numbers rose further after the war began as expellees and refugees sought shelter there.[141] Initially, the Jewish Council was able to intervene with the Stadtkommandant and head off the call made by the Gestapo on 4 November 1939 for the immediate establishment of a ghetto. But Governor General Hans Frank and the district governor of Warsaw, Ludwig Fischer, were in agreement that 'a special ghetto for the Jews must be created' in Warsaw.[142] Initially, an area with mostly Jewish residents in the northern part of the inner city was designated a 'quarantined area' and marked out with warning signs and barbed wire.[143] At the end of March 1940, when gangs of youths

140 Isaiah Trunk, *Łódź Ghetto: A History*, ed. and trans. Robert Moses Shapiro (Bloomington, IN: Indiana University Press, 2006 [Yiddish edn, 1962]); Icchak (Henryk) Rubin, *Żydzi w Łodzi pod niemiecką okupacją 1939–1945* (London: Kontra, 1988); Michal Unger, *Lodz: Aharon ha-getaot be-polin* (Jerusalem: Yad Vashem, 2005); Löw, *Juden im Getto Litzmannstadt*; Gordon J. Horwitz, *Ghettostadt: Łódź and the Making of a Nazi City* (Cambridge, MA: Belknap Press of Harvard University Press, 2008); Peter Klein, *Die 'Gettoverwaltung Litzmannstadt' 1940–1944: Eine Dienststelle im Spannungsfeld von Kommunalbürokratie und staatlicher Verfolgungspolitik* (Hamburg: Hamburger Edition, 2009); Monika Polit, *Mordechaj Chaim Rumkowski – Wahrheit und Legende: 'Meine jüdische Seele fürchtet den Tag des Gerichts nicht'*, trans. Jürgen Hensel, Heidemarie Petersen, and Małgorzata Sparenberg (Osnabrück: fibre, 2017 [Polish edn, 2012]).

141 Yisrael Gutman, *The Jews of Warsaw, 1939–1943: Ghetto, Underground, Revolt*, trans. Ina Friedman (Bloomington, IN: Indiana University Press, 1982 [Hebrew edn, 1977]); Ruta Sakowska, *Ludzie z dzielnicy zamkniętej: Z dziejów Żydów w Warszawie w latach okupacji hitlerowskiej październik 1939 – marzec 1943*, 2nd edn (Warsaw: Wydawnictwo Naukowe PWN, 1993); Engelking and Leociak, *Warsaw Ghetto*, pp. 47–51; Browning, *Origins of the Final Solution*, p. 121; Prais, *Displaced Persons*, pp. 429–433.

142 Präg and Jacobmeyer (eds.), *Diensttagebuch des deutschen Generalgouverneurs*, p. 59 (7 Nov. 1939).

143 Klaus-Peter Friedrich, 'Rassistische Seuchenprävention als Voraussetzung nationalsozialistischer Vernichtungspolitik: Vom Warschauer "Seuchensperrgebiet" zu den "Getto"-Mauern (1939/40)', *Zeitschrift für Geschichtswissenschaft*, vol. 53, no. 7 (2005), pp. 609–636.

repeatedly attacked Warsaw Jews – whether this violence was tolerated or provoked by the German occupation authorities is unclear – the Jewish Council was instructed to put a wall 2 to 3 metres high around the area. Jews had to pay for the wall and also build it.[144]

Bans on Jews residing in or entering numerous streets and entire neighbourhoods increasingly constricted the space in which Jews could lead their lives. Finally, on 12 September 1940, Frank announced that 'the ghetto in Warsaw is being closed off, above all because it has become clear that the threat posed by 500,000 Jews is such that they must be stopped from traipsing around'.[145] In the autumn of 1940 approximately 113,000 Poles were forced to move out of the ghetto area, while 138,000 Jews had to move in. In mid November the ghetto was sealed off, and German and Polish policemen were posted to guard the gates in the surrounding wall.[146] Inside the ghetto the German occupiers made the Jewish Order Service responsible for maintaining public order. Approximately 400,000 persons were crowded together in an area of 4 square kilometres: this meant that 30 per cent of Warsaw's inhabitants were living in 2.4 per cent of the urban area. Six to seven persons on average lived in each room, and thousands had to live in emergency shelters or were homeless. Despite all the efforts of the Jewish administration and the ghetto inhabitants, many were unable to find work. At the end of 1940, only 12 to 16 per cent of the ghetto inmates had found employment in commerce and industry. Around 6,000 worked for the administration of the Jewish Council, and 2,000 were in the Order Service (Doc. 162).[147]

Far too little food found its way into the sealed ghetto. People were starving, and infectious diseases spread quickly. Sophie Leviathan described the situation: 'On the street [...] lie hundreds of beggars in tattered clothing, children dressed in rags cry for a bit of bread, women collapse in the street, enfeebled by hunger. Anyone who goes without food for so long gets swollen legs, a puffy face, can no longer walk. Anyone lying in the street for long will not get up again.'[148] The authorities of District Warsaw exacerbated the situation still further in early 1941, when they ordered the Jews from all the Kreise west of Warsaw to be transferred into the ghetto. As part of the third *Nahplan*, Poles were to be expelled from the Warthegau and taken to these regions, in order to free up space in turn for ethnic Germans resettled in the Warthegau from Bukovina and Bessarabia. As a result around 50,000 Jews had to leave their homes and move into the ghetto, most of them with no chance of obtaining housing and jobs. As a general rule, they were housed at improvised 'points' and were completely dependent on welfare. Overcrowding became even worse when in March 1941 deportation trains from Vienna

144 Tomasz Szarota, *On the Threshold of the Holocaust: Anti-Jewish Riots and Pogroms in Occupied Europe, Warsaw – Paris – The Hague – Amsterdam – Antwerp – Kaunas*, trans. Tristan Korecki (Frankfurt am Main: Peter Lang, 2015 [Polish edn, 2000]), pp. 23–65.

145 Präg and Jacobmeyer (eds.), *Diensttagebuch des deutschen Generalgouverneurs*, p. 281.

146 On the Polish 'Blue Police', see Jan Grabowski, *Na posterunku: Udział polskiej policji granatowej i kryminalnej w zagładzie Żydów* (Wołowiec: Czarne, 2020).

147 Gutman, *Jews of Warsaw*, pp. 74, 83–84.

148 Report: Sophie Leviathan (May 1945), AŻIH, 302/231, fol. 32. See Miriam Offer, *White Coats in the Ghetto: Jewish Medicine in Poland during the Holocaust*, trans. Naftali Greenwood (Jerusalem: Yad Vashem, 2020 [Hebrew edn, 2015]).

and Danzig arrived in the ghetto, where 445,000 persons were now crowded together in the tightest of spaces.[149]

For the Cracow Jews, the establishment of a ghetto in March 1941 meant that they had to leave Kazimierz, the old Jewish quarter, as well as other parts of the city, and move to Podgórze on the other side of the Vistula. Before the war, 3,000 persons had lived in the approximately 320 buildings in this neighbourhood, but now there were 15,000 residents.[150]

As there were no uniform directives, the hundreds of ghettos in occupied Poland differed substantially from each other, both with regard to the time when they were cordoned off, if they were cordoned off at all – there were many so-called 'open ghettos' – and in terms of their respective configurations. In District Cracow and District Radom, and in the city of Lublin, ghettoization did not take place until the spring of 1941, in the course of the preparations for war against the Soviet Union. The measure was motivated not least by the prospect of using the residences freed up by evicting Jews as quarters for billeting German soldiers. Meanwhile, in a number of places there was no clear drive to create sealed-off ghettos. In the heavily industrialized region of Upper Silesia, in the rural Regierungsbezirk Zichenau, in many localities in the eastern Warthegau, and in smaller localities in the General Government, Jews frequently continued to live in the places where they had made their homes before the war. There, and even more so in the smaller ghettos in the countryside, the Jewish neighbourhoods were often not fully sealed off, owing to the shortage of building supplies. In many places the lack of personnel meant that the ghettos could not be completely isolated. By contrast, in Litzmannstadt the German guards around the ghetto enclosure had been under orders since the spring of 1940 to shoot at anyone trying to escape. In Warsaw, District Governor Ludwig Fischer also recommended in December 1940 that leaving the ghetto 'illegally' should be prohibited under penalty of death (Doc. 211), though the Governor General did not issue an order to this effect until the autumn of 1941.

Daily Life and the Reactions of the Jewish Population

The Jewish communities did whatever they could under the circumstances to alleviate the situation. Continually confronted with new demands and prohibitions by the occupiers, and facing sudden influxes of impoverished refugees who abruptly descended upon the Jewish communities as a result of resettlement operations,[151] the JSS and those in charge in the Jewish communities undertook an increasingly desperate search for outside sources of aid and ways of organizing self-help (Doc. 216). They negotiated with the authorities and with the JDC, and appealed for solidarity within the communities. They set up homes for orphans and the elderly, soup kitchens, hospitals, and disinfection facilities, but they had less and less room for manoeuvre.

149 Aly, *'Final Solution'*, pp. 149–153; Barbara Engelking, Jacek Leociak, and Dariusz Libionka (eds.), *Prowincja noc: Życie i zagłada Żydów w dystrykcie warszawskim* (Warsaw: Wydawnictwo Instytutu Filozofii i Socjologii PAN, 2007), pp. 223–267.

150 Aleksander Biberstein, *Zagłada Żydów w Krakowie* (Cracow: Wydawnictwo Literackie, 1985), p. 56.

151 Prais, *Displaced Persons*, pp. 199–203.

The overall impact of German occupation policies on Poland's Jews was clear: in Christopher Browning's words, 'Ruthless expropriation and exploitation of labour combined with a totally inadequate food supply, terrible overcrowding in poor housing, and utterly inadequate sanitation and medical care turned Polish Jewry into a starving, disease-ridden, impoverished community'.[152] In the hierarchy of supply specified by the Germans, the Jews were at the very bottom. Food and fuel could only rarely be obtained in sufficient quantities, and the shortage had particularly fateful consequences when the ghetto inmates had scarcely any contacts with the outside world. Especially in the large and overcrowded ghettos of Litzmannstadt and Warsaw, around a quarter of the inhabitants (approximately 45,000 and 100,000 persons, respectively) starved to death or died of illnesses such as typhus, tuberculosis, and gastrointestinal diseases. In every Jewish community, elderly persons and small children accounted for a disproportionately high share of the deaths. In Warsaw the writer Leyb Goldin described the perpetual hunger in the summer of 1941:

> Food, food … Now it's not coming from my stomach, but from my palate, my temples. If only I had half of a quarter-loaf of bread, at least a piece of crust, even if it's burned, black, charred. I slowly get myself out of bed, a ladle of water is soothing, lessens my hunger for a moment. You head back to bed and fall into it. Your legs refuse to work, are swollen. They hurt. But you don't complain. How many months has it been now since you got out of the habit of complaining, even when it hurts.[153]

Over time, almost everything was in short supply: clothing, shoes, soap, medicines. Anyone who could tried to procure the essentials through smuggling, bribery, or black-market transactions.

Jewish communities in occupied Poland also sought to organize aspects of daily life beyond the sphere of essential physical needs. Religious observance was a central concern: on the eve of the German occupation, about a third of Polish Jewry was religiously observant (that is, belonged to the various Orthodox groupings), and religious life continued everywhere. Religious observance faced considerable obstacles. Forced labour (often deliberately set to be carried out on the Sabbath and the holidays), food shortages, and restrictions on mobility all reduced the Jews' capacity to adhere strictly to all halakhic rulings, to hold regular services, or to continue traditional religious learning practices. Even so, they were maintained.[154]

152 Browning, *Origins of the Final Solution*, p. 167.

153 Cited in Ruta Sakowska, *Die zweite Etappe ist der Tod: NS-Ausrottungspolitik gegen die polnischen Juden, gesehen mit den Augen der Opfer* (Berlin: Hentrich, 1993), pp. 122–137, here p. 125. On the conditions, see also Andrea Löw, 'Arbeit, Lohn, Essen: Überlebensbedingungen im Ghetto', in Zarusky (ed.), *Ghettorenten*, pp. 65–78; Gustavo Corni, *Hitler's Ghettos: Voices from a Beleaguered Society, 1939–1944*, trans. Nicola Rudge Iannelli (London: Arnold, 2002 [Italian edn, 2001]).

154 Shimon Huberband, *Kiddush Hashem: Jewish Religious and Cultural Life in Poland during the Holocaust*, ed. Jeffrey S. Gurock and Robert S. Hirt, trans. David E. Fishman (Hoboken, NJ: Ktav, 1987); Havi Dreifuss, '"The Work of My Hands is Drowning in the Sea, and You Would Offer Me Song?!": Orthodox Behavior and Leadership in Warsaw during the Holocaust', in Glenn Dynner and François Guesnet (eds.), *Warsaw: The Jewish Metropolis. Essays in Honor of the 75th Birthday of Professor Antony Polonsky* (Leiden and Boston: Brill, 2015), pp. 467–495; Dan Michman, *Holocaust Historiography: A Jewish Perspective. Conceptualizations, Terminology, Approaches and Fundamental Issues* (London: Vallentine Mitchell, 2003), pp. 251–284.

While there was limited scope in smaller communities for wider cultural life, in the Warsaw ghetto and other larger Jewish communities artistic, political, and educational activities helped create an intellectual world that offered an alternative to the destructive conditions.[155] Jewish musicians sought to get their instruments into the ghetto and play them there in private circles. In some larger cities, there were drama groups and classical orchestras. Political youth organizations, the Zionists in particular, offered courses on Palestine or Jewish history, and organized Hebrew lessons to prepare the young people in the ghetto for later emigration to Palestine. In underground work it was the youth organizations that set the tone in any case – groups such as the leftist Zionist associations Dror, Gordonia, and Hashomer Hatzair, the revisionist Zionist Betar, and the Bund, with its youth association Tsukunft. This was because most of the leaders of the Jewish political parties had fled eastward. In Warsaw, Jewish political groups and youth associations published underground newspapers from mid 1940. Although the papers were distributed in small numbers, this underground press was an important tool for disseminating information and providing a discussion forum for those who were cut off from the outside world.[156]

Then there were those who set out to document what was taking place – and also to shape how these events would be remembered. Again, it was in the larger Jewish communities that there was most scope for such efforts. A great many people kept private diaries and wrote chronicles, and archives were established in the Warsaw and Litzmannstadt ghettos. The central figure in the creation of the Warsaw underground archive was Emanuel Ringelblum. Born in Galicia in 1900, the historian was one of the scholars who, in the 1930s, had recorded everyday life in the Polish shtetls as part of a large project inspired by YIVO. Under different circumstances in the ghetto, Ringelblum and his colleagues used the methods of social and economic history they had developed earlier, as well as the practice of working with non-professional interviewers. The members of the group working on the secret archives made notes of their own and collected records in order to document every aspect of Jewish life under German occupation, especially the fates of individuals. Two of the three parts of the hidden archives were found after the war. To this day, they represent the most significant collection of sources on the history of the Polish Jews during the Second World War.[157] In the Litzmannstadt

155 Löw, *Juden im Getto Litzmannstadt*, pp. 72–75 and 99–116; Engelking and Leociak, *Warsaw Ghetto*, pp. 136–218; Reich-Ranicki, *The Author of Himself*, pp. 153–160.

156 Daniel Blatman, *For Our Freedom and Yours: The Jewish Labour Bund in Poland, 1939–1949*, trans. Naftali Greenwood (London: Vallentine Mitchell, 2003 [Hebrew edn, 1996]); Daniel Blatman, *En direct du ghetto: La presse clandestine juive dans le ghetto de Varsovie 1940–1945*, trans. Nelly Hansson (Paris: Cerf, 2005 [Hebrew edn, 2002]); Joseph Kermish et al. (eds.), *Ittonut ha-mahteret ha-yehudut be-Warsha*, 6 vols. (Jerusalem: Yad Vashem, 1979–1997); Tikva Fatal-Knaani (ed.), *The Jewish Underground Press in Warsaw*, vols. 1–3, trans. Shulamit Berman, Sandy Bloom, Moshe Devere, and Naftali Greenwood (Jerusalem: Yad Vashem, 2017–2020); Gutman, *Jews of Warsaw*, pp. 122–144.

157 Samuel D. Kassow, *Who Will Write Our History? Rediscovering a Hidden Archive from the Warsaw Ghetto* (New York: Vintage Books, 2009). Numerous excerpts from the documents are contained in Joseph Kermish (ed.), *To Live with Honor and Die with Honor! Selected Documents from the Warsaw Ghetto Underground Archives 'O.S.' ('Oneg Shabbath')* (Jerusalem: Yad Vashem, 1986); Ruta Sakowska et al. (eds.), *Archiwum Ringelbluma: Konspiracyjne archiwum getta warszawy* (Warsaw: Wydawnictwo Naukowe PWN, 1997–); Israel Gutman (ed.), *Emanuel Ringelblum: The Man and the Historian*, trans. Chaya Naor (Jerusalem: Yad Vashem, 2010).

ghetto, archives were established within the Jewish administration. Writers and journalists created an extensive chronicle in which they documented, day by day and in minute detail, what was happening in the ghetto (Doc. 222).[158]

The dwindling prospects of earning a living, the hunger and cold, the overcrowded conditions, and the loss of almost all privacy frequently made life unbearable. The young Lucjan Orenbach described this situation in a letter to a friend in early 1941:

> All of us here are alive and yet not alive. Sometimes I no longer know whether I'm alive or not. Is it *me* or is it not me? Sometimes you have to repeat to yourself a hundred times: I'm alive, you're alive, he's alive. You forget that you *exist*. (Doc. 242).

The traditionally close Jewish family ties were also put under great strain. Many families had to look after seriously ill family members, and were faced with the loss of relatives, whether through deportation and imprisonment or through death in the ghetto or in a camp. Fathers were often absent, having been recruited for forced labour, and a shift in authority occurred within the families, which were increasingly held together by the mother. The knowledge that parents could no longer provide for or protect their children also affected relationships. When family structures broke down, new frameworks had to take their place. But if belonging to a family or to another community offered no support, even young and initially healthy people could scarcely continue to withstand the constant pressure of persecution, humiliation, and physical abuse.

Reactions to the Persecution of the Polish Jews

The relationship between the Jews and the Christian population in Poland was ambivalent. Following the headlong flight of the government and the swift military defeat, Polish society was initially leaderless and disoriented. The scale of the violence in the first few days of the war, the repressive measures, and the widespread destruction demoralized and unsettled broad sections of the population. Faced with the consequences of the war, roundups, and a brutal occupation regime, the Poles were largely preoccupied with their own worries. Rumours spread from the Soviet-occupied parts of the country about the Jews' allegedly anti-Polish attitude and their supposedly favourable view of Soviet communism. The stereotype of 'Judeo-communism' acquired renewed resonance. Many Poles felt surrounded by enemies and forsaken by their British and French allies.

Among the Jews the impression very quickly formed that parts of the Polish population endorsed the occupiers' antisemitic brutality, while the masses regarded the abuses with indifference. The Jewish underground press, on the other hand, initially emphasized the compassionate attitude of the Poles (Doc. 258), and the Bund in particular underscored the common bond with Poland. But many ghetto inmates viewed the attitude of the people on the other side of the walls with growing disappointment, particularly when Poles and

158 Lucjan Dobroszycki, *The Chronicle of the Łódź Ghetto, 1941–1944*, trans. Richard Lourie, Joachim Neugroschel, et al. (New Haven, CT, and London: Yale University Press, 1984); complete unabridged edition: Julian Baranowski et al. (eds.), *Kronika getta łódzkiego / Litzmannstadt Getto 1941–1944*, 5 vols. (Łódź: Wydawnictwo Uniwersytetu Łódzkiego, 2009).

ethnic Germans took advantage of the Jews' plight to enrich themselves with Jewish belongings, or when they benefited from the persecution by denouncing someone.[159]

Meanwhile, the occupiers drove a wedge between Poles and Jews with measures such as visible identification, the erosion and destruction of economic contacts, and the segregation and isolation of the Jews, whether through locking them up in a closed ghetto or through other restrictions on freedom of movement.

The 'de-Jewification' of the economy and of society – something that Polish nationalist groups had demanded for years – now commenced, although under circumstances that were entirely different from those that these groups had imagined. Emanuel Ringelblum described how Polish antisemites worked together with German soldiers, police, and ethnic Germans when it came to identifying Jews and Jewish businesses, and how Poles took their cue from the brutality of the German occupiers towards the Jewish population.[160]

In their underground publications, members of the Polish far right were already dreaming in wartime about inducing their Jewish fellow countrymen to emigrate en masse after the end of the war (Doc. 318).[161] Anyone who was unwilling to go that far could nonetheless benefit from the persecution. In the General Government, non-Jews were presented with an opportunity to profit from so-called Aryanization by taking over homes and inventories and by acquiring valuables and furnishings at favourable prices. In many cases they could also take the jobs of Jews who had been dismissed. The American historian Jan T. Gross coined the term 'opportunistic complicity' to describe such behaviour.[162]

However, there were also a great many Poles who, at their own peril, helped their Jewish neighbours or friends (Doc. 306). They participated – sometimes also for pay – in smuggling food or other commodities into the ghettos, and they also sold food and other commodities to the Jews in localities without ghettos or where the ghetto was

159 Havi Ben-Sasson, '"Chcemy wierzyć w inną Polskę": Stosunki żydowsko-polskie w podziemnej prasie żydowskiej getta warszawskiego', *Zagłada Żydów: Studia i materiały*, vol. 1 (2005), pp. 96–113; Havi Dreifuss (Ben-Sasson), *Relations between Jews and Poles during the Holocaust: The Jewish Perspective*, trans. Ora Cummings (Jerusalem: Yad Vashem, 2017 [Hebrew edn, 2009]); Monika Rice, 'Envisioning Poles: Polish-Jewish Relations at the Beginning of the German Occupation', *Yad Vashem Studies*, vol. 46, no. 1 (2018), pp. 11–40.

160 Emanuel Ringelblum, *Polish-Jewish Relations during the Second World War*, ed. Joseph Kermish and Shmuel Krakowski, trans. Dafna Allon, Danuta Dabrowska, and Dana Keren (New York: Howard Fertig, 1976 [Polish edn, 1958–1959]), pp. 40–45, 51–55.

161 Klaus-Peter Friedrich, *Der nationalsozialistische Judenmord und das polnisch-jüdische Verhältnis im Diskurs der polnischen Untergrundpresse (1942–1944)* (Marburg: Herder-Institut, 2006).

162 Jan T. Gross, *Fear: Anti-Semitism in Poland after Auschwitz. An Essay in Historical Interpretation* (New York: Random House, 2007), p. 249; Yisrael Gutman and Shmuel Krakowski, *Unequal Victims: Poles and Jews during World War II*, trans. from Hebrew and Polish by Ted Gorelick and Witold Jedlicki (New York: Holocaust Library, 1987); Joshua D. Zimmerman (ed.), *Contested Memories: Poles and Jews during the Holocaust and Its Aftermath* (New Brunswick, NJ: Rutgers University Press, 2003); Lars Jockheck, *Propaganda im Generalgouvernement: Die NS-Besatzungspresse für Deutsche und Polen 1939–1945* (Osnabrück: fibre, 2006); Andrzej Żbikowski (ed.), *Polacy i Żydzi pod okupacją niemiecką 1939–1945: Studia i materiały* (Warsaw: Instytut Pamięci Narodowej, 2006); Młynarczyk, *Judenmord in Zentralpolen*, pp. 228–243; Jan Grabowski, 'German Anti-Jewish Propaganda in the Generalgouvernement, 1939–1945: Inciting Hate through Posters, Films, and Exhibitions', *Holocaust and Genocide Studies*, vol. 23, no. 3 (2009), pp. 381–412.

'open'. Other Poles, who came into contact with Jewish forced labourers deployed outside the ghetto, slipped them bread or vegetables in an effort to support them at least in some small way. Even this modest assistance could place the donor in mortal danger.

The helpers had little backing. The Polish Roman Catholic Church did not speak out against the persecution of the Jews. One reason for its silence was that the Church itself was under intense pressure. The occupiers, viewing the Church as the upholder of Polish national traditions, were merciless in their persecution of Polish bishops and priests; many of them were shot for subversive activities or lost their lives in concentration camps. Another reason was that notions rooted in anti-Judaism continued to exist in sections of the clergy. As a result the Church scarcely used the little leeway it still had to work against the persecution of the Jews before the German authorities made the decision to embark on mass murder. In the General Government the bishops' conferences did not discuss the Jews' situation. Most Church representatives who had gone into exile, however, condemned the crimes against the Jews.[163]

The political-military resistance groups, which had begun to organize at the end of 1939, likewise had only a rudimentary notion of the extreme danger in which the Jewish population found itself. Even the underground organizations that were associated with the government in exile did not fully support the idea of a Polish nation that included the Jews as citizens with equal rights. By contrast, communist and left-wing socialist groups, as well as groups close to the PPS, often expressed solidarity with the Jews.

Meanwhile, the Polish statesmen in exile – first from Paris, then from Angers, and finally from London from mid 1940 – kept a close eye on developments within the national minorities. They clearly recalled the experiences of the First World War, when the Central Powers had tried to play off the Jews and the Poles against each other. Their close attention to the 'Jewish question' was, however, also rooted in the knowledge that cultivating a good relationship with Jewish organizations was important in the eyes of Britain and the United States as Allied powers. This forced the Poles to pay greater heed, in part for tactical reasons, to the views of Jewish representatives.

These representatives, especially the World Jewish Congress, were wary of Poland and expected the government in exile to distance itself unequivocally from the antisemitic machinations of the immediate pre-war period. But both right-wing and left-wing parties were represented in the exile parliament – the National Council of Poland, which supported the government in exile under Prime Minister Władysław Sikorski – and consequently the controversies of the pre-war era continued. Moreover, the statesmen in exile feared that official statements construed as 'pro-Jewish' would be met with hostility or incomprehension within the occupied country itself. Indeed, the Polish government, provided with detailed reports by couriers such as Jan Karski, was well informed early on about the specific and appalling plight of the Jews (Doc. 90), but it perceived this crisis merely as a single element of a policy of repression that was aimed primarily at the

163 Jonathan Huener, *The Polish Catholic Church under German Occupation: The Reichsgau Wartheland, 1939–1945* (Bloomington, IN: Indiana University Press, 2021); Dariusz Libionka, 'Antisemitism, anti-Judaism and the Polish Catholic Clergy during the Second World War, 1939–1945', in Robert Blobaum (ed.), *Antisemitism and Its Opponents in Modern Poland* (Ithaca, NY: Cornell University Press, 2005), pp. 233–264; cf. the relevant special issue of the journal *Zagłada Żydów: Studia i Materiały*, 5 (2009).

Poles.[164] During this period, Jewish interests were represented in the National Council solely by the Zionist politician Ignacy Schwarzbart (Doc. 208).[165]

The Jewish organizations abroad were well informed about the events in Poland. The World Jewish Congress, which maintained offices in Paris (until mid 1940) and Geneva, received the reports of refugees from occupied Poland. In addition the British press, as well as the embassy officials and journalists from neutral countries, kept the international public informed about the events in Poland. And finally, even after the onset of the war, postal communication between Jews in Poland and correspondents abroad was still possible, even though the post was slow and subject to censorship.

The reports made little impact, however. Jewish organizations in the United States did try to alert the public by publishing reports about the crimes committed under the occupation (Doc. 80). But compared to the extensive reporting in 1938 on the fate of the Jews in Germany, the topic now receded into the background. In the Soviet Union the press had until the summer of 1939 continued to report quite extensively on the persecution of the Jews. After the Molotov–Ribbentrop Pact it was silenced. Information about the situation in German-occupied Poland could now be acquired only from the oral accounts given by Jewish refugees. As a result, the Jewish minority in eastern Poland remained largely unaware of what was going on in the western part of the country – and what danger it was in.[166]

On the Threshold of Mass Murder: Spring and Summer 1941

In spring 1941 the Nazi leadership and the Wehrmacht finalized their preparations for war against the Soviet Union, transforming the context within which the regime's anti-Jewish policies were decided.

Poland's Jews immediately felt the effect of the military preparations. To make room for the German troops, many Poles in the eastern part of the General Government were evicted from their homes. The homes of Jews were allocated to these Poles, and the Jews in turn were forced into ghettos, which were set up in March 1941 in Lublin, Cracow, and District Radom. At the same time, conditions in the existing ghettos were deteriorating. In the dangerously overcrowded Warsaw ghetto, epidemic typhus was raging, with thousands dying every month. There and in other large ghettos, hundreds of thousands faced imminent death from starvation.

164 See for instance 'Part III: The Persecution of the Jews and the Ghettoes', in Polish Ministry of Information [in Exile], *The German New Order in Poland* (London: Hutchinson, January 1942), pp. 213–248.

165 David Engel, *In the Shadow of Auschwitz: The Polish Government-in-Exile and the Jews, 1939–1942* (Chapel Hill, NC: University of North Carolina Press, 1987); Dariusz Stola, *Nadzieja i zagłada: Ignacy Schwarzbart – Żydowski przedstawiciel w Radzie Narodowej RP (1940–1945)* (Warsaw: Oficyna Naukowa, 1995).

166 Bernard Wasserstein, *Britain and the Jews of Europe, 1939–1945* (London: Institute of Jewish Affairs, 1979); David S. Wyman, *The Abandonment of the Jews: America and the Holocaust, 1941–1945* (New York: Pantheon, 1984); Deborah E. Lipstadt, *Beyond Belief: The American Press and the Coming of the Holocaust, 1933–1945* (New York: Free Press, 1986); Richard Breitman and Allan J. Lichtman, *FDR and the Jews* (Cambridge, MA, and London: Belknap Press of Harvard University Press, 2013), pp. 161–187.

Jews in Poland were thus dying en masse from disease and starvation long before the death squads entered eastern Poland in June 1941. The occupiers then used the 'untenable conditions', which they themselves had brought about and nonetheless repeatedly deplored, as a pretext to press for radical action. The sealing and undersupplying of the ghettos had led to the spread of many diseases, so the German authorities demanded that drastic steps be taken against the Jews as carriers of epidemics. As a result of the starvation in the ghettos, there was increased contraband trade and black-market dealings, which German officials sought to eradicate. Contrary to its original plans, the German administration also found itself compelled to provide for those enclosed in the ghetto. Against this backdrop, Nazi efficiency experts appeared on the scene. They concluded that the Warsaw ghetto in particular was unprofitable. Consultants from the Reich Auditing Office (for the Litzmannstadt ghetto) and from the Reich Board for Economic Efficiency (for the Warsaw ghetto) calculated that the German authorities would have to subsidize these two segregated areas to the tune of 50 million Reichsmarks per annum unless more Jews were brought into the labour force and the regulations sealing off the ghetto were relaxed.[167]

With tthe prospect of a victory over the Soviet Union, new perspectives opened up for the German officials in occupied Poland. At the beginning of 1941 Hans Frank had declared that whether the Jews 'go to Madagascar or somewhere else is of no interest to us. We are clear in our minds that this mishmash of Asiatic progeny had best traipse back to Asia, where they came from.'[168] At a lunch Frank had with Hitler on 17 March 1941, the Führer had assured him that the General Government would be the first region 'to be made completely free of Jews'.[169] On 20 June 1941, two days before the attack on the Soviet Union, Goebbels reported on a meeting with Hitler and Frank, at which the latter had spoken of his hopes for the territory under his control: 'Dr Franck [*sic*] talks about the General Government. People there are already looking forward to being able to deport the Jews. Jewry in Poland is in an advanced state of decay.'[170] Those in authority in occupied Poland still assumed that a 'final solution to the Jewish question' meant the deportation of the Jews. To what destination, however, continued to be unclear – perhaps to the Pripyat Marshes, which adjoined the General Government, or to the Arctic regions of northern Russia.

In March 1941, however, the political and military leadership had also drawn up the orders that sanctioned mass murder during the campaign. By means of the Commissar Order issued by the Wehrmacht High Command on 6 June 1941 and a decree suspending legal protection for the population, the Wehrmacht scrapped the restraints enshrined in the laws of war even before the invasion. New Einsatzgruppen of the Security Police and the SD were to follow in the wake of the invading troops and systematically murder the Soviet elite, Jews in particular. Even during the planning phase, the signs were clear:

167 The expert opinions are published in Susanne Heim and Götz Aly (eds.), *Bevölkerungsstruktur und Massenmord: Neue Dokumente zur deutschen Politik der Jahre 1938–1945* (Berlin: Rotbuch, 1991), pp. 44–73 and 84–138; Aly, *'Final Solution'*, pp. 206–209.

168 Präg and Jacobmeyer (eds.), *Diensttagebuch des deutschen Generalgouverneurs*, pp. 330–331 (22 Jan. 1941).

169 Ibid., p. 361 (19 April 1941).

170 *Die Tagebücher von Joseph Goebbels*, part 1: *Aufzeichnungen 1923–1941*, vol. 9: *Dezember 1940–Juli 1941*, ed. Elke Fröhlich (Munich: Saur, 1998), pp. 389–390.

this war of extermination would entail a further dramatic radicalization of anti-Jewish policy. This was inevitable because even more Jews now came under German control, but above all because the Nazi leadership identified the Soviet Jews with Bolshevism, which was anathema to the Nazis. The Jews were the main ideological enemy, no longer to be 'merely' driven out, but to be exterminated.

Following the invasion of the Soviet Union, German occupation officials in Poland addressed once again the question of the future treatment of the Jews. On 16 July 1941 Rolf-Heinz Höppner, chief of the SD head office in Posen and director of the local Central Resettlement Office, notified Adolf Eichmann of a discussion held in Posen in which the question had been raised whether the 'most humane solution' might not be 'to use some fast-acting means to finish off the Jews who are not fit for work' (Doc. 314). The Sonderkommando Lange at the Gestapo office in Posen had already gained experience with such means in its actions against the psychiatric patients in the Reichsgau Wartheland and in East Prussia. Only two days later, on 18 July, Reichsstatthalter Arthur Greiser met with Hitler and may have made these suggestions, too, part of the discussion. In any event, the Gauleiter believed he had sufficient backing to order the establishment of the Kulmhof (Chelmno) extermination camp some months later.[171] From the end of July, when it began to seem that the war against the Soviet Union might last longer than originally planned, and the deportation of the Jews therefore receded into the distance again, internal discussions intensified about murdering the Jews in the entire German sphere of influence. These discussions took place both in Berlin and in the occupied territories.

The Jews imprisoned in the ghettos knew nothing of these deliberations. Chaim Kaplan in Warsaw had admittedly confided to his diary as early as March 1941:

> As to the outside, we are afraid of what is coming. Today the radio announced, quoting TASS, that Stalin is mobilizing his forces. In whispers we hear of the 'eve of war' between two comrades who embraced one another up until now. In the event of a war with Russia – which for my own part I do not believe in – we are lost. With plutocracy and communism in a partnership to fight Nazism, the Jews will immediately be the target of revenge.[172]

But for many Jews the German invasion of the Soviet Union raised hopes for a speedy end to the war and thus their liberation. Halina Nelken in Cracow noted in her diary on the day of the German invasion:

> A new war, with Russia. Everyone is pleased, even pessimists like our neighbours. People say this is the only salvation because either Russia will break them, or – and God forbid! – they will conquer Russia, and in either case the war will end more quickly, and that is our only hope. As yet no one has ever conquered Russia, not even Napoleon, so perhaps the Germans will finally get what they deserve.[173]

171 This was pointed out by Klein in his detailed analysis of the file note: Klein, *Die 'Gettoverwaltung Litzmannstadt'*, pp. 336–352.
172 Kaplan, *Scroll of Agony*, p. 235 (13 March 1941).
173 Nelken, *And Yet, I Am Here!*, p. 83 (22 June 1941).

In the Litzmannstadt ghetto Dawid Sierakowiak wrote the following day: 'The entire ghetto is buzzing like one big beehive. Everyone feels that a chance for liberation is finally possible.'[174] But the rapid advance of the Wehrmacht in the East demonstrated that the situation was becoming worse rather than better. Only one week later, on 30 June 1941, Sierakowiak wrote resignedly: 'Yesterday's news turns out to be unfortunately true. According to today's newspaper, the Germans have captured Kovno, Dyneburg, Vilna, Grodno, Białystok and Brześć on the Bug. [...] [A]fter a week's revival, I have been like a corpse again since yesterday.'[175] Soon after that, members of the Einsatzgruppen in the East began shooting Jewish men, women, and children indiscriminately.

174 *Diary of Dawid Sierakowiak*, p. 105 (23 June 1941).
175 Ibid., p. 108 (30 June 1941).

List of Documents

140 *Gazeta Żydowska*, 23 July 1940: report on the situation of the Jewish population in Warsaw since September 1939

141 On 24 July 1940 the Selbstschutz in Lublin cautions the Jewish population against gatherings and demonstrations

142 On 25 July 1940 the Labour Department of the General Government issues instructions for the deployment of Jewish forced labourers from Cracow

143 On 25 July 1940 the National Socialist People's Welfare Organization in Schroda describes the confiscation of goods from Jewish shops to benefit ethnic Germans in September 1939

144 On 28 July 1940 Jewish representatives report to the American embassy in Berlin on the persecution of Jews in western Poland

145 On 31 July 1940 Reichsstatthalter Greiser discusses the resettlement of the Jewish population with the GG government in Cracow

146 On 1 August 1940 the personnel office in District Cracow warns Reich German employees against using the services of Jewish artisans

147 *Szaniec*, 1 August 1940: a Polish underground newspaper comments on German policies towards the Jews

148 On 2 August 1940 an anonymous informer alleges that the Jewish Council in Lublin gives preferential treatment to the well-to-do

149 *Dror*, August 1940: Tuwia Borzykowski sets out an agenda for Jewish youth work

150 Between 2 and 5 August 1940 the chairman of the Warsaw Jewish Council describes the increasing restrictions on the Jewish population

151 Between 5 and 12 August 1940 the physician Zygmunt Klukowski describes the persecution of the Jews in Szczebrzeszyn

152 *Gazeta Żydowska*, 6 August 1940: article on the situation of the Jewish Community in Oświęcim

153 On 8 August 1940 the employment office in Neu-Sandez (Nowy Sącz) in the General Government orders the Jewish Council in Mszana Dolna to set up a forced labour camp

154 On 9 August 1940 the Chełm employment office calls for all Jewish forced labourers to be paid

155 On 12 August 1940 the head of the Main Trustee Office East decrees how confiscated and temporarily administered assets should be exploited

156 On 12 August 1940 the chairman of the Polish Central Welfare Council criticizes the circumstances under which Jews are expelled from Cracow

157 On 12 August 1940 the Jewish elder in the Litzmannstadt (Lodz) ghetto calls for public peace and order to be maintained

158 On 13 August 1940 a physician describes how the Gestapo robbed Jews in Warsaw in the winter of 1939/1940

159 On 14 August 1940 the teacher Chaim Kaplan describes the gruelling situation of Jews in Warsaw

DOCUMENTS

DOC. 1

Nowe Życie, 30 April 1939: in a May Day appeal, the Bund warns of the threat to Poland and Polish Jews posed by Nazi Germany[1]

Long live the First of May!

Below we quote the First of May appeal from the Bund's Central Committee,[2] to some extent abridged and partly summarized (sections cited literally are in quotation marks).

> 'Amidst the thunder and lightning of the oncoming storm, the working class will celebrate the First of May this year. This will be the 50th consecutive *May Day*. The founders of the Socialist International proclaimed the First of May as a day of struggle against capitalist exploitation and nationalist hatred and war. And at the same time, as a celebration of the brotherhood of the people, the unity of all working people of the world, and as a day of longing for a socialist system …'

The appeal goes on to describe the world's present situation and the latest fascist violence, concluding:

> 'Fascist violence has shaken the world. It has become perfectly clear: no nation or country can be sure of its freedom and existence until the barbarity of fascism has been curbed; until then, states can be erased from the map and free countries converted into concentration camps.'
>
> '*All over the world, a mobilization of forces aiming to fight the criminal designs of fascism has begun.*'
>
> 'The working masses of the world are prepared to make any sacrifice necessary to repel the danger of fascism that is threatening them and their countries. The masses of Poland, who instinctively perceived the danger, also show this readiness and "clearly demonstrate their decision to *repel any attack by Nazism by any means for the sake of the unity and independence of their country.*"'
>
> 'Even some of our antisemites at home, not hiding their admiration for Nazism, declare that "Nazism is the vanguard of antisemitism."'
>
> 'As citizens of a country with which history has bound our fortunes for many centuries and which is now in grave danger, as socialists who detest all oppression and love freedom, and as Jews for whom a victory of fascism means physical extermination – we declare on behalf of the broadest masses of the Jewish population that we are ready to defend Poland against the dangers to its existence and independence

1 *Nowe Życie*, no. 8 (87), 30 April 1939, p. 1. Biblioteka Narodowa, P.36139. This document has been translated from Polish. *Nowe Życie*, the party organ of the socialist General Jewish Labour Bund in Lithuania, Poland, and Russia (Algemeyner Yidisher Arbeter Bund in Lite, Poyln un Rusland; known as the Bund), was published fortnightly in Warsaw.

2 The Bund, founded in Vilna in 1897, argued for the national and cultural autonomy of Jews in Poland and was in competition with the Zionist parties, which espoused emigration to Palestine. The Bund, which worked together with the Polish Socialist Party (PPS), became the most influential Jewish party in Poland in the mid 1930s. From 1939 members of the Bund worked in the underground. In 1943 they played a leading part in the Warsaw Ghetto Uprising. The party was re-established in 1944 and banned in Poland in 1950.

by all available means and at the cost of the greatest sacrifice – shoulder to shoulder with the Polish masses.'

'We have always demanded and will continue to demand all rights for the Jewish masses, but we are also aware of our duties.'

The appeal expresses our feelings for the freedom fighters in Spain and in all other countries, acknowledges the solidarity of Jewish working masses with the Polish working masses, and concludes with a call by the masses of Jewish workers to honour the First of May in accordance with the resolutions of the Bund, quoting the slogans:

'Against the danger of a Nazi attack – for the defence of an independent Poland!
'Against fascist reaction, nationalism, and antisemitism – for democracy!
'Against capitalist exploitation – for socialism!'

DOC. 2

On 7 May 1939 the SS Security Service makes plans to establish an information system for registering Polish Jews and the Polish elite[1]

Memorandum (marked 'secret Reich matter') by SD II 112[2] (Hg[3]/Pi), unsigned, dated 9 May 1939

Re: contacts with Poland
1) Memorandum:
II 112 held a meeting with SS-Untersturmführer Augsburg[4] on 7 May about establishing contacts in Poland. II 112 made the point that it was a matter of knowing people in Poland who would be able to provide accurate information for the complete registration of Polish Jewry.

SS-Untersturmführer Augsburg pointed out that he felt the head of the German People's Association in Poland,[5] Wolff,[6] was the right man for this. Augsburg knew him

1 BArch, R 58/954, fols. 179–178. This document has been translated from German.
2 The SD's section for Jewish affairs had been known as II 112 since early 1936.
3 Herbert Hagen (1913–1999), commercial employee; joined the SS in 1933 and the NSDAP in 1937; employed at SD headquarters from 1934; head of SD Department II 112, 1937–1939; active for the SD in France, 1940–1944; private secretary to the Higher SS and Police Leader in France, 1942–1944; then commander of an Einsatzkommando in Carinthia; interned, 1945–1948; worked as a company manager in Warstein after the war; sentenced to life imprisonment in Paris in absentia in 1955; sentenced to twelve years in prison by the Cologne Regional Court in 1980; released in 1984.
4 Dr Emil Augsburg (1904–1981), interpreter and translator; employed by the SD from 1936; joined the NSDAP in 1937 and the SS in 1938; worked at the SD's Wannsee Institute as head of its department for culture and nationalities from 1937; expert on Poland at the Reich Security Main Office (RSHA) (Office VII and Central Office II P) from 1939; member of Einsatzgruppe B's Advance Commando Moscow in mid 1941; became an informant for the US Counterintelligence Corps in 1946; held a high-ranking position in the Gehlen Organization, the precursor of the Federal Intelligence Service (Bundesnachrichtendienst) from 1950.
5 The German People's Association in Poland (Deutscher Volksverband in Polen) was a conservative-nationalist party founded in 1924 to represent the interests of the German ethnic minority in central Poland. It held seats on the municipal council in Łódź.

personally and would vouch for him. Over the last few years Wolff had turned an organization with 35,000 members into one with 350,000 members, despite constant surveillance by the Polish secret police. Its members are absolutely reliable and have access to all the documents that would be required in case of an intervention. Wolff [...][7]
2) All departments must at all times keep the Central Office[8] abreast of all relevant processes for the purpose of information and potential evaluations.

The Central Office maintains a central card index organized by regional (Bezirke and municipalities) and personal (individuals, associations of individuals, institutes) categories.[9] Since this card index will have to be made available to a potential Einsatzkommando, the officials in charge of Polish affairs in the individual departments will for their part establish corresponding card indexes for the areas in which they are working. These card indexes will remain at the main departments or in a central office based at the SD Main Office when operations are under way.

SS-Untersturmführer Augsburg will be put in charge of Polish Affairs at the Eastern Institute (Wannsee)[10] and act as the liaison officer for Central Office II P of the SD Main Office.

6 Ludwig Wolff (1908–1988), teacher; born and grew up near Łódź; studied in Germany; youth secretary of the Łódź-based German School and Education Association for the Central Polish Territories from 1934; chairman of the German People's Association in Poland, May 1938–1939; detained in Poland in August 1939; joined the NSDAP and the SS in 1939; NSDAP Kreisleiter in Łódź, 1940–1942; taught National Socialist ideology on Waffen-SS training courses in 1944, then transferred to the SS Main Office; lived in West Germany after the war; active in the Landsmannschaft Weichsel-Warthe expellee organization; worked for the Gehlen Organization and later the Federal Intelligence Service until his retirement in 1973.

7 At least one page is missing from the original.

8 Central Office II P (Zentralstelle II P) at the SD was the office in charge of compiling the Special Wanted Arrest List (*Sonderfahndungsbuch*) for Poland between 1937 and 1939. This was a list of prominent members of Polish civil society who were to be arrested after the invasion of Poland.

9 The SD had been intensively preparing for its deployment to Poland since 1937. The persecution of the Polish elite was planned under the code name 'Operation Tannenberg'. The SD used the card index mentioned in this memorandum to draw up the Special Wanted Arrest List for Poland, which included about 61,000 names by August 1939.

10 The Wannsee Institute was established in 1937 as an SD research institution and provided the Einsatzgruppen with reports on Eastern Europe as well as specialized personnel with local cultural expertise.

DOC. 3

Illustrierter Beobachter, 3 August 1939: a photo story vilifies Polish Jews[1]

The centre of Europe's epidemic: the Polish ghetto (facsimile)

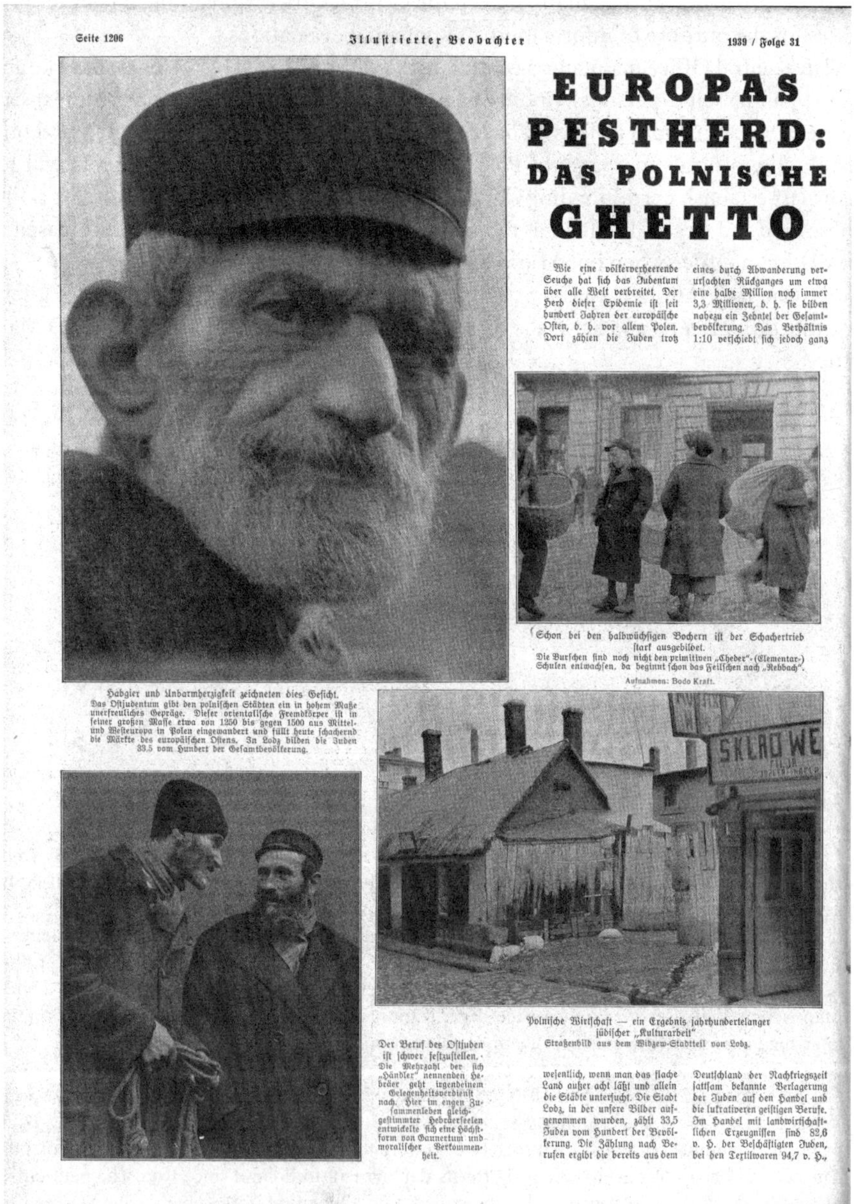
Seite 1206 Illustrierter Beobachter 1939 / Folge 31

EUROPAS PESTHERD: DAS POLNISCHE GHETTO

Wie eine völkerverheerende Seuche hat sich das Judentum über alle Welt verbreitet. Der Herd dieser Epidemie ist seit hundert Jahren der europäische Osten, d. h. vor allem Polen. Dort zählen die Juden trotz eines durch Abwanderung verursachten Rückganges um etwa eine halbe Million noch immer 3,3 Millionen, d. h. sie bilden nahezu ein Zehntel der Gesamtbevölkerung. Das Verhältnis 1:10 verschiebt sich jedoch ganz wesentlich, wenn man das flache Land außer acht läßt und allein die Städte untersucht. Die Stadt Lodz, in der unsere Bilder aufgenommen wurden, zählt 33,5 Juden vom Hundert der Bevölkerung. Die Zählung nach Berufen ergibt die bereits aus dem Deutschland der Nachkriegszeit sattsam bekannte Verlagerung der Juden auf den Handel und die lukrativeren geistigen Berufe. Im Handel mit landwirtschaftlichen Erzeugnissen sind 82,6 v. H. der Beschäftigten Juden, bei den Textilwaren 94,7 v. H.,

Habgier und Unbarmherzigkeit zeichneten dies Gesicht.
Das Ostjudentum gibt den polnischen Städten ein in hohem Maße unerfreuliches Gepräge. Dieser orientalische Fremdkörper ist in seiner großen Masse etwa von 1250 bis gegen 1500 aus Mittel- und Westeuropa in Polen eingewandert und füllt heute schachernd die Märkte des europäischen Ostens. In Lodz bilden die Juden 33,5 vom Hundert der Gesamtbevölkerung.

Schon bei den halbwüchsigen Bochern ist der Schachertrieb stark ausgebildet.
Die Burschen sind noch nicht den primitiven „Cheder"-(Elementar-)Schulen entwachsen, da beginnt schon das Feilschen nach „Rebbach".

Aufnahmen: Bodo Kraft.

Polnische Wirtschaft — ein Ergebnis jahrhundertelanger jüdischer „Kulturarbeit"
Straßenbild aus dem Widzew-Stadtteil von Lodz.

Der Beruf des Ostjuden ist schwer festzustellen.
Die Mehrzahl der sich „Händler" nennenden Hebräer geht irgendeinem Gelegenheitsverdienst nach. Hier im engen Zusammenleben gleichgestimmter Hebräerseelen entwickelte sich eine Höchstform von Gaunertum und moralischer Verkommenheit.

1 *Illustrierter Beobachter*, no. 31, 3. August 1939, pp. 1206–1207. The *Illustrierter Beobachter* was an NSDAP weekly pictorial magazine published by Franz Eher Nachfolger, Munich, from 1926 to 1945. This document has been translated from German.

1939 / Folge 31 Illustrierter Beobachter Seite 1207

bei der Handelsgruppe Leder und Pelze 95,6 v. H. In Lodz und Warschau sind dagegen unter den Arbeitern in der Großindustrie nur 3 bis 4 v. H. Juden zu ermitteln.

Vor dem Kriege waren wiederum 40 v. H aller Anwälte Juden; 1935 ist die Zahl der jüdischen Anwälte auf 55 v. H. gewachsen; die Zahl der jüdischen Anwaltsreferendare betrug in Lodz 64 v. H. der Gesamtzahl, in Warschau (1936) gar 80 v. H. In Lodz sind 66,7 aller Ärzte Juden. Die Polen haben z. Z. Burgfrieden mit den Juden geschlossen. Ein schlechtes Geschäft!

In Schmutz und Lumpen.
Aber die „Armut" ist in den meisten Fällen nur die Tarnkappe stillgehäufter Gewinne.

Die Hauptstraße der Lodzer Altstadt wimmelt von Hebräern.
Während die Gesamtzahl der Juden Polens infolge Auswanderung gesunken ist, stieg die Zahl der Juden von 1910 bis 1931 in den Städten: in Warschau um 10, in Lodz um 4 v. H.

Diesen speckigen Kaftanjuden öffnete Deutschland 1918 willig Tür und Tor …
… und als Iwan Baruch Kutisker, Judko Barmat, Sklarz und Sklarek spielten sie bald darauf bei uns den Herrn.

Das Holz, aus dem die Radek-Sobelsohns geschnitzt sind.

Jüdischer Kramladen in Lodz.
Der Handel mit Lebensmitteln ist zu 80 v. H. in jüdischen Händen, so daß dem Nichtjuden meist keine Wahl bleibt, auch wenn ihn der Ekel schüttelt.

[Page 1] [Top right under headline and bottom right; continued in top-left corner on p. 2]

Jewry has spread across the whole world like a plague, devastating entire nations. And Europe's East, i.e. especially Poland, has been the centre of this epidemic for a hundred years. Despite a reduction in numbers due to the emigration of approximately half a million, the Jews there still number 3.3 million, which means they make up almost one tenth of the overall population. However, this ratio of 1:10 changes significantly if we discount the countryside and only look at the towns and cities. In the city of Lodz, where these pictures were taken, 33.5 out of every 100 inhabitants are Jews. If we list them by profession, we can find the same concentration of Jews in business and the more lucrative intellectual professions. In the sale and distribution of foodstuffs, 82.6 per cent of those involved in the business are Jews, and they constitute 94.7 per cent of those employed in the textile business, [page 2] and 96.7 per cent in the leather and fur business. By contrast, only 3 to 4 per cent of workers with big industrial companies in Lodz and Warsaw were found to be Jews. By the same token, 40 per cent of all lawyers were Jews before the war. In 1935, the proportion of Jewish lawyers rose to 55 per cent; the proportion of Jews among the total number of trainee lawyers in Lodz was 64 per cent, and in Warsaw (1936) it was as high as 80 per cent. In Lodz, 66.7 per cent of all physicians are Jews. The Poles have currently declared a truce with the Jews. A bad deal!

[Caption underneath top-right photograph, page 1]
The drive to haggle is very strong even in the adolescent bokhers.[2] The boys are not yet out of their primitive 'kheyder' (primary) school and are already out bargaining, trying to make a profit.[3] Photographs by Bodo Kraft.

[Caption underneath top-left portrait photograph, page 1]
This is a face marked by avarice and ruthlessness. Eastern Jewry has left a highly unpleasant imprint on the Polish towns and cities. The vast majority of these oriental contaminants migrated to Poland from Central and Western Europe between 1250 and 1500, and today they fill the markets of Eastern Europe with their haggling and bargaining. In Lodz, the Jews make up 33.5 per cent of the total population.

[Caption underneath bottom-right photograph, page 1]
Polnische Wirtschaft[4] – a result of centuries of Jewish 'cultural contributions'. A street scene from the Widzew quarter of Lodz.

[Caption next to bottom-left photograph, page 1]
It is difficult to establish what line of work the Ostjude is in. Most of the Hebrews who call themselves 'salesmen' in reality only occasionally perform any kind of casual work. Like-minded Hebrew souls living together at close quarters has led to the development of the highest form of idleness and moral depravity here.

2 Yiddish for 'young man'.

3 The German uses a version of the word 'Reibach' in this sentence, an antisemitically charged term that describes morally questionable profit. It comes from the Hebrew word for 'profit' – 'revekh' – which entered the German lexicon via Yiddish and only acquired its antisemitic overtones in its German usage.

4 Literally 'Polish conditions' or 'Polish business': German pejorative expression for a disorderly state of affairs, a shambles.

[Caption underneath centre-left photograph, page 2]
Dressed in dirty rags. But in most cases, this 'poverty' is only camouflage for secretly hoarded profit.

[Caption underneath top-right photograph, page 2]
The main street in Lodz's old town is teeming with Hebrews. While the total number of Jews in Poland has declined due to emigration, the number of Jews in the cities rose by 10 per cent in Warsaw and 4 per cent in Lodz between 1910 and 1931.

[Caption underneath bottom-left photograph, page 2]
In 1918, Germany willingly threw open its doors to this greasy kaftaned Jew … … and soon afterwards, they began lording it over us under the names of Iwan Baruch Kutisker,[5] Judko Barmat,[6] Sklarz or Sklarek.[7]

[Caption underneath bottom-centre photograph, page 2]
This is what the Radek-Sobelsohns[8] are made of.

[Caption underneath bottom-right photograph, page 2]
A Jewish corner shop in Lodz. Eighty per cent of the grocery business is in Jewish hands. This means that non-Jews, even if they find the conditions repellent, usually have little choice.

5 Iwan Baruch Kutisker (1873–1927), Jewish businessman involved in a high-profile corruption and financial scandal in Berlin in the 1920s.

6 Julius Barmat (1887–1938), Jewish businessman involved in a high-profile corruption and financial scandal in Germany in the 1920s. Both Kutisker and Barmat had bribed officials in return for fraudulent state contracts and loans. The two scandals were conflated by right-wing politicians and the right-wing press as the Barmat scandal, which became a byword in antisemitic propaganda for 'fraudulent Jewish business practices'.

7 The Jewish Sklarek brothers – Max, Leo, and Willi – were involved in another prominent corruption and fraud scandal that was widely publicized and which the Nazis used for antisemitic propaganda in the last years of the Weimar Republic.

8 Karl Radek, born Karol Sobelsohn (1885–1939), politician and journalist; active in the Polish and German social democratic movement, later the German Communist Party, and then as a Comintern secretary in the Soviet Union; expelled from the Party in 1929 and later readmitted; fell victim to the 1937 purge and was subsequently a defendant in the second Moscow show trial; sentenced to ten years of penal labour; perished in a Soviet labour camp.

DOC. 4

On 6 September 1939 the Chief of the Civil Administration for the Military Commander prohibits the sale of Jewish assets in the occupied territory[1]

Regulation issued by the Chief of the Civil Administration[2] for the Military Commander, unsigned,[3] dated 6 September 1939

Regulation
on the Prohibition of the Removal and Transfer of Jewish Movable and Immovable Assets in the Territories Occupied by German Troops
On the basis of the executive powers conferred on me, I hereby order the following for my area of responsibility:
§ 1
The removal, sale, leasing, donation, and any mortgaging of movable and immovable assets that are found wholly or partially under Jewish ownership shall be prohibited.
§ 2
This also applies to legal transactions which give rise to obligations that relate to the legal transactions referred to in § 1.
§ 3
All legal transactions within the meaning of § 1 and § 2 concluded after 1 September 1939 shall be invalid.
§ 4
In justified cases, an exemption from the provisions set out in §§ 1–3 may be granted. This shall be the responsibility of the Chief of the Civil Administration and/or the German agencies authorized by him.
§ 5
Contraventions and/or evasions of this regulation shall be severely punished.
§ 6
This regulation shall come into force with retrospective effect from 1 September 1939. It shall apply until such time as it has been repealed by a subsequent regulation.

1 *VOBl-CdZ Krakau*, no. 1, 12 Sept. 1939. Published in Tatiana Berenstein et al. (eds.), *Faschismus – Getto – Massenmord: Dokumentation über Ausrottung und Widerstand der Juden in Polen während des Zweiten Weltkrieges* ([East] Berlin: Rütten & Loening, 1960), p. 165. This document has been translated from German.

2 During the early days of the war, the chiefs of the civil administration (CdZ) at the high commands of the five attacking German armies were in charge of local administration in the occupied Polish territories. This lasted from the beginning of the occupation until Germany annexed the western Polish territories on 8 Oct. 1939 and ended the military administration in the General Government on 25 Oct. 1939. The CdZ's responsibilities included maintaining order and security, ensuring supplies for the population, maintaining a functioning economy, and preparing the transfer of these territories to a civil administration.

3 The office was held by Hans Frank (1900–1946), lawyer; member of the Epp Freikorps in 1919; participated in Hitler's Beer Hall Putsch in 1923; joined the SA and the NSDAP in 1923; acted as Hitler's legal advisor in 1926; founded the National Socialist Association of Lawyers in 1928; head of the NSDAP's Legal Office, 1933–1942; Bavarian minister of justice, 1933–1934; Reich minister without portfolio, 1934–1945; in Sept. 1939 simultaneously Chief of the Civil Administration for the Whole Occupied Polish Territory, then Governor General; sentenced to death in Nuremberg and executed in 1946.

Undisclosed location, 6 September 1939

On behalf of the Commander-in-Chief:
The Chief of the Civil Administration

DOC. 5
In diary entries for 7 to 9 September 1939, a Wehrmacht soldier describes the invasion of Poland[1]

Handwritten diary of a Wehrmacht soldier,[2] entries for 7 to 9 September 1939

Thursday, 7 September
5.45 a.m.: Set off through properly Polish territory.[3] Dusty and dirty roads. Dilapidated houses. Filthy population. Straggling villages. One big wasteland. Worse than Neuhammer. Minefields. Marched through Siewierz (town) with a break. On through Poremba to *Zawiercie*. A backwater teeming with Jews.

Obstreperous locals. Billeted in a school. Wrote to Käte and Annemarie.

Friday, 8 September
3 a.m.: Reveille. 5 a.m.: Set off through *Zawiercie. The kaftaned Polish Jews scurry out of their holes like rats. Insurgent activity grows. German soldiers are shot in the marching column by Polish Jews. As reprisals, ten Polish civilians are shot and 2,000 taken prisoner for each one.* The area becomes slightly more populated and mountainous. Otherwise nothing but sun, dust, pines, and sand. The trees along the roads look as if they are covered in white frost. Polish roadblocks and destroyed bridges en route. The civilian population is slowly returning to their villages. We march via Rodaki, Olkusz to Lgota. It has been announced that we will be posted to Cracow as occupation forces. Billeted in an empty house. Polish field kitchen en route.

Saturday, 9 September
6 a.m.: Set off from Lgota. Scorching hot day. Poor roads. The landscape gets prettier. Hilly area. Traces of the war can now also be seen from time to time. These include a village half-destroyed and burned down by an aerial attack. Horses and men getting ever more exhausted. Lots of vehicles have to be brought up from the rear. We march via Olkusz to Tomaszowice.[4] Good billeting, together with the staff, on an old Austrian estate. The people there completely misinformed about the situation at the border. Interesting disagreement between two Polish cousins. Poland is reported to have offered peace. Ever more Jews among the locals.

1 AAN, 1335/214/XIII-6, fols. 24a r–26v. This document has been translated from German.
2 Probably Willy Herzog (b. 1909); lived in Neuhammer, Silesia, before the war. The diary contains entries from 17 Dec. 1938 to early Jan. 1940.
3 The author marched eastward through East Upper Silesia, then southward towards Cracow.
4 A village that has now been absorbed into Wielka Wieś, north-west of Cracow.

DOC. 6

On 9 September 1939 a member of the Jewish youth movement describes violent attacks on Jews in Łódź[1]

Handwritten diary by Yarden,[2] entry for 9 September 1939

9 September 1939
With bared teeth and hungry for prey, the wolf has shed its sheep's clothing. They lie in wait for us on street corners, our neighbours of days past, the German residents of Łódź,[3] sobered up from the intoxication of the revelries.[4] The time for action has come. The eyes of the bloodthirsty beast vigilantly survey all those passing by.

'Jude!'[5] a wild voice suddenly snarls. The wretched victim buckles instantly, powerless under a hail of heavy blows. Thugs armed with scissors run wild through the streets of the city. They have been granted the honour of proving to the liberating army that they have learned their master's lessons well. They murderously lunge at the Jewish passers-by, sparing neither the elderly nor the frail, cutting off beards, pulling out hair until blood flows, and laughing all the while, their faces beaming with delight. This is their national duty, which they will fulfil perfectly for the glory of their nation!

The Jews of Łódź are stunned. Fear has injected its venom into their hearts. It is dangerous to venture outside. It took only a few hours for the Nazi drug to poison the lives of tens of thousands of people. What will happen next? How will we endure?

Our neighbour B. was seized and taken to work at the office of the central administration. After scrubbing the floor, he was ordered to wipe it dry with his jacket. When he hesitated, astounded by this strange request, he was brutally flung to the floor, the soldiers' strong arms then dragging him the length and breadth of the room. After his clothes had absorbed enough of the floor's filthy water, they stood him up on his feet, muddy and foul, shaved a strip of hair down the centre of his head, and, in this state, they cast him out.

Had I not seen him with my own eyes when he came home, had I not heard from him how these citizens of a nation of 'great culture and civilization' had abused him, I would never have believed that human hands were capable of something like that. But, once again, reality, that old jester, can celebrate a great success. From time to time, he bares his rotten teeth before us in obscene laughter. With his satanic claws, he pierces the fabric of our lofty dream, tears it to shreds, and sniggers: Here is the reality! Yet how terrible is the realization that we must live in a reality created by Satan, without recourse to a judge or a trial, without protest.

1 Moreshet Archive, D.1.332. Published in *Al masu'ot polin* [Signals from Poland] (Merhavya: Hakibutz Ha'artzi Hashomer Hatzair, 1940), pp. 24–27. This document has been translated from Hebrew.

2 Yarden was a member of the Hashomer Hatzair Zionist youth organization in Łódź. The diary consists of four copybooks, which were later discovered in Vilna. They contain accounts of the writer's experiences in various Polish towns during the first months of the German occupation. The diarist was never identified. See Alexandra Zapruder (ed.), *Salvaged Pages: Young Writers' Diaries of the Holocaust* (New Haven, CT: Yale University Press, 2002), p. 443.

3 In the 1930s the industrial city of Łódź was the second largest city in Poland, with over 600,000 inhabitants; 59 per cent of the population were Poles, 32 per cent were Jews, and 9 per cent listed German as their native language.

4 This passage refers to the celebrations that occurred after the German troops had occupied Łódź.

5 German in the original: 'Jew'.

DOC. 7

On 12 September 1939 the Quartermaster General of the German army gives orders for the Jewish population to be expelled from East Upper Silesia eastwards across the San river[1]

Teletype message from the chief of staff of the Army Quartermaster General,[2] signature illegible, to Army Group South, dated 12 September 1939[3]

The Jews in East Upper Silesia are to be deported eastwards across the San river. The operation must begin immediately.[4] East Upper Silesian territory is defined in Order OKH Gen Qu No. 697/39 G. (QU 2) dated 11 September.
For the Quartermaster General
The Chief of Staff

DOC. 8

On 13 September 1939 the German local military commander in Rzeszów orders Jewish shops to be visibly identified as such and Aryanized[1]

Announcement by the German local military commander of Rzeszów, signed Captain Lorenz,[2] dated 13 September 1939 (poster)[3]

A board with the words 'Shop is open 8–12 and 3–6' must be displayed at every shop.

A board proclaiming 'Aryan business' or 'Jewish business' must be displayed at every shop.

Additionally, every shop must display an announcement of the conditions of sale for its wares. The forms can be obtained from the town hall at a price of 10 gr.[4] per item.

The Citizens' Committee will appoint Aryan administrators for all Jewish businesses, to be paid by the owner.

Retired civil servants and civil servants of all categories are called upon to report to the Citizens' Committee to take over the administration of the businesses.

Businesses owned by Jews who have left town will be put under Aryan administration. The administrators must pay the money they received for goods previously bought by the business owner to the office of the Citizens' Committee.

1 Copy in IfZ-Archives, NOKW-0129. This document has been translated from German.
2 The chief of staff was Eduard Wagner (1894–1944), career officer; member of the Epp Freikorps; artillery general; army quartermaster general from Oct. 1940; committed suicide after the attempt to assassinate Hitler on 20 July 1944.
3 The original contains handwritten annotations.
4 The deportations were carried out on a limited scale. Some weeks later, in October 1939, more than 5000 Jews in total were deported from Vienna, Moravská Ostrava, and Katowice to Zarzecze near Nisko on the San river: see PMJ 3, p. 39, and Doc. 42.

1 Muzeum Okręgowe w Rzeszowie, MRR 1006. Copy in YVA, M-54/20. This document has been translated from German.
2 Following the arrival of German troops in Rzeszów (9 Sept. 1939), Alfred Lorenz was the town's local commander for several days.
3 In Polish and German.
4 Groszy: in Polish currency there are 100 groszy in 1 złoty.

DOC. 9

New York Times, 13 September 1939: article on the Nazi persecution of Jews in Poland and German plans for mass expulsions[1]

Nazis Hint 'Purge' of Jews in Poland. 'Special Report' From Invaded Region Discusses Possible Solution of Problem. Group Europe's Largest. 3,000,000 Population Involved – 'Removal' From Europe Viewed as Benefit.

Wireless to *the New York Times*
Berlin, Sept. 12 – First intimations that a 'solution of the Jewish problem' in Poland is on the German-Polish agenda are revealed in a 'special report' of the official German News Bureau[2] that emanates from Polish territory now occupied by German military, somewhere in East Silesia.[3]

In view of the world refugee problem and the individual suffering created in the last six years by Germany's determination to rid her borders of Jews, the implications of the 'solution of the Jewish problem in Poland', were it carried out on the German model, are ominous.

Where Germany and Austria together had a total of 750,000 Jews,[4] the Jewish population of Poland, at about 3,000,000, is the largest of any European nation and the second largest in the world.

'Solution' Offered to Poland
In addition to proposing prevention of a second 'invasion' of Polish Jews into Germany, this 'special report' contains a 'solution of the Jewish problem in Poland that can contribute considerably to create ordered relations between the German and the Polish people.' It was Polish Jews, primarily, after the advent of National Socialism, 'who agitated the whole world against Germanism', the report continues.

Then in explanation of the alleged attack against 'Germanism' in Poland – given by Chancellor Hitler as the reason for Germany's present military activities – this 'special report' alleges that the 'rage' which broke out from time to time in Poland against the Jews extended to 'Germanism' because 'the Jews, as a result of their knowledge of the German language – paradoxically as it may sound – were regarded by the primitive Polish peasants as unquestioned Germans.'

As a possible solution of this question, 'purge' is indicated by the Official News Bureau, which continues:

'Removal of the Polish Jewish population from the European domain would furthermore, in the long view, definitely bring a solution of the Jewish question in Europe nearer. For this is just the Jewry which, through its high birth rate and in spite of all existing

1 *New York Times*, no. 29 817, 13 Sept. 1939, p. 5. The daily newspaper was founded in 1851 and is still in circulation today.
2 German newspapers also published this 'special report'. See 'Nie wieder polnische Juden nach Deutschland', in *Soldatenzeitung*, no. 12, 9 Sept. 1939, p. 2.
3 This refers to East Upper Silesia, which had belonged to Poland before the war. See Docs. 7 and 110.
4 This number refers to the Jewish population in 1933.

differences between the two groups, has continually established the large numbers of Western Jewry, whose birth rate is small.'

How, however, the 'removal' of Jews from Poland without their extermination can halt the alleged 'strengthening' of Western Jewry is not explained.

Polish Jews Ridiculed

National Socialism's antisemitic campaign was directed against Jews who emigrated from Poland immediately following the World War and who, it is claimed here, enriched themselves during the German post-war inflation at the expense of the German people. The 'Eastern Jew' is constantly held up to greatest ridicule here, and so this 'special report' begins with hardly flattering descriptions of the dress, appearance and mannerisms of the Jews encountered by the German Army as it advances further east in Poland, as well as a resumé of the role allegedly played in the last war against Germany by Polish Jews.

It asserts that during the present military campaign Jews have servilely attempted to strike up friendships with German soldiers and have approached them with open arms. One Jew is said to have told the Germans he felt himself German at heart and had prayed the Germans would soon come so 'prosperous times would begin.'

'The answer given to him,' the special report continues, 'was certainly very clear, with the result the son of Israel preferred to beat it as quickly as possible.'

Jews are accused of having plundered Polish towns and villages without regard for the watchfulness of the German soldiers and field police, who, the 'special report' continues, 'caught many of them, inflicting the punishment they deserved.' Looting in territory under martial law is punished by death.

Polish Jewish women whose husbands were arrested at the scenes of their alleged plundering are 'accused of having endeavored to entice German guards into setting their husbands free.'

Before all others, the report says, Jewish dwellings were searched for weapons and ammunition.

An official news agency dispatch dated Koenigsberg alleges that in Northern Poland Jewish shops were raided by Polish women shouting, 'The Jews are the cause of our misfortune. They inveigled our men into war.'

The German field police, however, it is added, soon restored order.

DOC. 10

Shortly after 13 September 1939 the Kattowitz (Katowice) branch of Dresdner Bank presents a list of Jewish businesses that could be Aryanized[1]

List drawn up by Dresdner Bank, Kattowitz branch, undated[2]

Jewish firms that have worked with us and could potentially be Aryanized:

Name of firm	Sector
Adler i Panofski, Sohrau	iron foundry
Aufrecht, Ruda	timber merchant
Badewitz, D., Kattowitz	animal gut supplier
Czwiklitzer, D., Kattowitz	soap factory
Fuchs, S., Kattowitz	timber merchants
Mrachacz i Schutz, Kattowitz[3]	ironmongers
Nacks successor, Kattowitz	plumbing and drainage supplies
'POLPAP', Schwientochlowitz	paper factory
Szleszyngier, J. M., Bendzin	hemp rope factory
Weichmann, Max, Kattowitz[4]	hulling mill
Fiedler and Glaser, Kattowitz	mill
Zakłady Przemysłu Metalowych Bracia Szajn Spółka Akcyjna, Bendzin	iron and metal factory
J. D. Potoka i Synowie, Bendzin-Małabodz	oils, fats etc.
'Wholworth'[5] Spółka Akcyjna, Kattowitz	department store

1 APK, 320/121, fol. 293. Published in Ingo Loose, *Kredite für NS-Verbrechen: Die deutschen Kreditinstitute in Polen und die Ausraubung der polnischen und jüdischen Bevölkerung 1939–1945* (Munich: Oldenbourg, 2007), pp. 146–147. This document has been translated from German.

2 The Dresdner Bank branch in Katowice had been dissolved in 1938 and officially resumed business on 13 Sept. 1939. There is no covering letter for this list, which was found in a folder of materials on internal processes during the phase shortly after the branch reopened.

3 The original contains handwritten question marks on the left side.

4 The original contains handwritten question marks on the left side.

5 Correctly: Woolworth.

DOC. 11

On 15 September 1939 the Chief of the Civil Administration in Kattowitz (Katowice) prohibits Jewish refugees from returning to their homes[1]

Letter from the Chief of the Civil Administration[2] for Border Force Section Commando 3, signed p.p. Count Matuschka,[3] Kattowitz, dated 15 September 1939 (copy)

Re: *repatriation of refugees*

Some of the inhabitants who have fled into the Polish interior can be expected to return in the near future. In principle, persons who reside or work within the border that was expanded under the Announcement Concerning the Customs and Police Border of 12 September 1939, *Verordnungsblatt* no. 4, shall be permitted to return.[4]

Only Jews and unreliable elements will be denied permission to cross. The following therefore applies only to those persons who will be permitted to return:

Entry will only be permissible via customs roads.

Returning migrants will be registered in lists by the respective border customs offices. These lists will contain the following information:

1) first name and surname,
2) date and place of birth (Kreis),
3) occupation,
4) last place of residence (place of origin in the occupied territory),
5) destination.

Separate lists will be kept for each Kreis from which the returning migrants originate.

The border customs offices must forward the lists as soon as possible in accordance with the instructions given by the Bezirk customs commissioner and/or the head of the customs office. As for forwarding the lists to the Landräte and mayors, which is currently only possible through the courier service, the chief of police in Kattowitz needs to communicate with the different branches of the customs administration involved.

The above instructions apply to the following customs offices together with their sub-offices, the Bezirk border customs commissioners:

1 GStAPK, XVII. HA Ost 4, Reg Katowice/3, fol. 141r–v. This document has been translated from German.

2 Otto Fitzner (1888–1945), director of a mining business; member of a Freikorps after 1918; technical director of the Georg von Giesches Erben mining company; joined the NSDAP and the SA in 1931; became head of the Silesia Chamber of Economics and president of the Breslau Chamber of Industry and Commerce in 1935; special representative of the Gauleiter of Silesia and chief of the civil administration for the territory occupied by Border Force Section Commando 3 in Kattowitz from Sept. 1939; Gau economic advisor in Lower Silesia from 1941.

3 Count Michael von Matuschka (1888–1944), lawyer; elected to the Prussian Landtag for the Centre Party in 1932; Landrat of Oppeln, 1923–1933; subsequently worked in the Prussian Ministry of the Interior and the office of the Lower Silesian Oberpräsident; appointed chief of the civil administration for Border Force Section Commando 3 in 1939; became Oberregierungsrat and head of the Trustee Office of the Oberpräsident in Kattowitz in 1941; executed in connection with the attempt to assassinate Hitler on 20 July 1944.

4 Despite the annexation of the western Polish territories, the old Reich border continued to exist until 1941 as a 'police border'.

Kreuzburg (Upper Silesia) *Central Customs Office* with the Bezirk customs commissioner in Lissau.

Beuthen (Upper Silesia) *Central Customs Office* with the Bezirk customs commissioners in Woischnik, Tarnowitz, and Myslowitz.

Pless *Central Customs Office* with the Bezirk customs commissioners in Neuberun, Pless, Schwarzwasser, and Groß-Gorschütz.

The Kreis police departments in charge of the returning migrants' places of origin which will receive the lists via the offices of the customs administration are requested to check returning migrants' personal details and to contact the Kreis police authorities of the destinations stated on the list so that it can be determined whether the returning migrants have actually travelled to the places stated.

It is likely that some returning migrants will also attempt to avoid the customs roads when they return. Particular attention must be paid to the registration and vetting of such returning migrants.

DOC. 12

On 21 September 1939 the Chief of the Security Police sends guidelines on the treatment of Jews to the Einsatzgruppen in Poland[1]

Express letter (marked 'secret') from Chief of the Security Police Heydrich[2] (PP [II] – 288/39 geh.), Berlin, to the commanders of the Security Police Einsatzgruppen in Poland, dated 21 September 1939 (copy)[3]

Re: the Jewish question in the occupied territory

I am writing in reference to the meeting that took place today in Berlin[4] and want to draw your attention once again to the fact that the *planned overall measures* (i.e. their end goal) are to be kept *top secret.*

A distinction must be made between

(1) the end goal (which will demand longer periods of time) and

(2) the stages in which this end goal can be attained (which will be implemented in the short term).

1 BArch, R 58/954. Published in Klaus-Jürgen Müller, *Das Heer und Hitler: Armee und nationalsozialistisches Regime 1933–1940* (Stuttgart: DVA, 1969), pp. 668–671. This document has been translated from German.

2 Reinhard Heydrich (1904–1942), career officer; served in the navy, 1922–1931; joined the NSDAP and the SS in 1931; head of the SD from 1932; head of the Gestapo Central Office, the Gestapo office in Berlin (which was initially only in charge of Prussia), from 1934; Chief of the Security Police and the SD, 1936–1942; head of the Reich Security Main Office (RSHA), 1939–1942; simultaneously Deputy Reich Protector of Bohemia and Moravia from Sept. 1941; died in Prague on 4 June 1942 following an assassination attempt.

3 The original contains handwritten notes.

4 At this meeting of senior officials and Einsatzgruppen commanders, Heydrich gave orders for the Jews in the conquered territory to be concentrated in towns within three to four weeks. Furthermore, Jews were to be expelled from Reich territory within a year, 'including from the former eastern Prussian provinces that are to be annexed': minutes of the meeting of 27 Sept. 1939 in Tatiana Berenstein and Adam Rutkowski, 'Dokument o konferencji w Urzędzie Policji Bezpieczeństwa z 21 IX 1939 r.', *BŻIH*, no. 49 (1964), pp. 68–73, here p. 71.

The planned measures will require the most rigorous preparation, both technically and economically.

It goes without saying that the tasks at hand cannot be defined in every detail from here. At the same time, the instructions and guidelines below have been set out to prompt the commanders of the Einsatzgruppen to duly consider practical aspects.

I.

The first preliminary measure on the way to the end goal will be to concentrate the Jews from the countryside in the larger towns and cities.

This is to be implemented swiftly.

A distinction must be made in this respect between

(1) the territories of Danzig and West Prussia, Posen, East Upper Silesia, and

(2) the other occupied territories.[5]

If possible, the territory mentioned in *(1)* is to be cleared of Jews; at the least, however, the aim must be to designate at most a few towns where Jews are concentrated.

In order to facilitate the subsequent measures, as few concentration points as possible should be specified in the territories mentioned in *(2)*. It should be borne in mind that only towns that are either railway junctions or which are at least located on railway lines may be designated as concentration points.

As a basic principle, Jewish communities with *fewer than 500 persons* must be dissolved and the Jews must be taken to the nearest town serving as a concentration point.

This decree does not apply to the territory assigned to Einsatzgruppe I, located east of Cracow, which is roughly delimited by *Polanico*,[6] *Jaroslaw*, the new demarcation line,[7] and the former Slovak–Polish border. Only a provisional census of the Jews is to be carried out in this territory.[8] In addition, the Jewish councils of elders discussed below must be established.

II.

Jewish councils of elders

1. A Jewish Council of Elders must be established in every Jewish community. Wherever possible, the Council is to be made up of the remaining prominent individuals and rabbis. The Council of Elders should comprise no more than 24 male Jews (depending on the size of the Jewish community).

   The Council shall be held *fully responsible* in a literal sense for the precise and punctual execution of all instructions that have been issued or have yet to be issued.
2. The councils are to be given notice that the harshest measures will be imposed if such instructions are sabotaged.
3. The Jewish councils must carry out a preliminary census of the Jews in their local areas – if possible broken down by sex (age groups) (a) up to 16 years, (b) from 16

5 A distinction is already being made here between the territories that are to be annexed and what was later to become the General Government.

6 This most likely refers to Połaniec, where the Wisłoka river flows into the Vistula.

7 A reference to the border between the German and Soviet spheres of interest, which was defined on 28 Sept. 1939.

8 According to a vaguely formulated German plan, a 'Jewish reservation' was to be established in this territory in the south of Poland.

to 20 years, and (c) over 20 years, and by the principal professions and trades – and report the results at the earliest possible opportunity.

4. The councils of elders must be notified of the dates and deadlines for removal, the options for removal, and finally the roads to be used for removal. They shall then be made personally responsible for the removal of the Jews from the countryside.

   The justification to be given for the concentration of Jews in the towns will be that Jews participated heavily in franc-tireur attacks and looting.

5. The councils of elders in the towns where Jews have been concentrated shall be made responsible for suitably housing the Jews who move in from the countryside.

   For general policing reasons, the concentration of Jews in towns will probably require orders to the effect that certain parts of these towns will be completely off-limits to Jews, and that they will not be allowed, for example, to leave the ghetto, to leave the house after a particular time in the evening, etc. However, such orders will be subject to consideration of economic necessities.

6. The councils of elders shall also be made responsible for the necessary supply of food and drink to Jews when they are being transported to the towns.

   No objections are to be made if migrating Jews take their movable goods with them, provided this is actually technically possible.

7. Jews who fail to comply with the order to resettle in the towns are to be granted a brief grace period in justified cases. They are to be given notice of the harshest punishment if they should fail to comply with this deadline as well.

III.

As a basic principle, all requisite measures must always be taken in the closest possible consultation and collaboration with the German civil administrative authorities and the local military authorities in charge.

When these measures are implemented, care must be taken that the economic takeover of the occupied territories is not jeopardized.

1. The needs of the army must be taken into particular consideration.[9]

   It will hardly be possible, for example, to avoid leaving behind Jewish traders here and there who absolutely have to stay behind to provision the troops in the absence of other options. In such cases, however, the immediate Aryanization of these enterprises must be pursued, in consultation with the local German authorities in charge, and the emigration of the Jews is to be achieved at a later date.

2. When it comes to safeguarding German economic interests in the occupied territories, it goes without saying that Jewish industrial sectors and enterprises that are vitally important, important for the war effort, or important for the Four-Year Plan will have to be kept going for the time being.

9 This decree by Heydrich was partially repealed by Army High Command on 30 Sept. 1939. See Heydrich to the Einsatzgruppen, 30 Sept. 1939, in Kazimierz Radziwończyk, '"Akcja Tannenberg" grup operacyjnych *Sipo* i *SD* w Polsce jesienią 1939 r.', *Przegląd Zachodni*, vol. 22, no. 5 (1966), pp. 94–118, here p. 114. The consequences of its repeal are unclear. On this issue, the Army Quartermaster General stated in a letter to 8th Army Command dated 1 Oct. 1939, 'The order of 21 September 1939 will only be implemented at a later point in time': IfZ-Archives, MA 113/6 (WB 2752).

Immediate Aryanization should be pursued in these cases as well, and the emigration of the Jews must be achieved at a later date.

3. Finally, the food situation in the occupied territories must also be considered. If possible, land owned by Jewish settlers must be placed under the temporary management of neighbouring German or even Polish farmers to ensure that the harvest is brought in or the fields are replanted. This important question must be discussed with the chief of the civil administration's agricultural officer.
4. In all cases in which it is possible to reconcile the interests of the Security Police on the one hand and the German civil administration on the other, a report is to be made to me by the most expeditious channels prior to the implementation of the respective measures, and my decision is to be awaited.[10]

IV.

The commanders of the Einsatzgruppen are to report to me regularly on the following matters:

1. Statistical overview of the Jews in their areas (if possible using the categories given above). In these overviews, the numbers of Jews who have been made to leave the countryside and those who were already in the towns should be listed separately.
2. Names of towns that have been designated as concentration points.
3. The deadlines set for the Jews' departure for the towns.
4. Overview of all Jewish industrial sectors and enterprises that are vitally important, important for the war effort, or important for the Four-Year Plan in their areas.

   If possible, the reports should include information on the following:

   (a) Nature of the enterprises (also stating if and how they can be converted into enterprises that are of truly vital importance, important for the war effort, or important for the Four-Year Plan).

   (b) Which of these enterprises are to be Aryanized as a matter of priority (in order to rule out the possibility of them incurring damage).

   How should the Aryanization be implemented? Germans or Poles? (This depends on the importance of the enterprise.)

   (c) How many Jews are employed in these enterprises (including management positions).

   Could operations be easily maintained following the deportation of the Jews, or would maintaining the operations require the allocation of German and/or Polish workers? In what numbers?

   Where Polish workers have to be used, care must be taken that they are brought in above all from previously German provinces, so that the Polish presence there is thinned out. These questions can only be addressed by involving the German employment offices that have been established.

V.

In order to achieve the goals that have been set, I expect absolute commitment from all members of the Security Police and the Security Service.

10 As in the original, though logic would suggest that reporting to the Security Police for a decision would have been necessary where it had not been possible to reconcile the interests of the Security Police and the civil administration.

Commanders of Einsatzgruppen in neighbouring territories must immediately establish contact with one another to ensure that the territories under consideration are fully covered.

VI.

Copies of this decree have been forwarded to the Army High Command, the Plenipotentiary for the Four-Year Plan (attn State Secretary *Neumann*),[11] the Reich Ministry of the Interior (attn State Secretary *Stuckart*),[12] the Reich Ministry of Food, the Reich Ministry of Economics (attn State Secretary *Landfried*),[13] and the chiefs of the civil administration of the occupied territories.

DOC. 13

A Jewish eyewitness gives an account from Palestine of how the Germans persecuted the Jews in Włocławek in September 1939[1]

Transcript of a statement made by Mrs M. P. of Włocławek before the United Aid Committee of Polish Jews[2] in Jerusalem, dated 7 June 1940

The liquidation of the Jewish Community of Włocławek

Appearing before us is Mrs M. P. from Włocławek who now lives in Jerusalem and testified as follows:

A few days after they entered Włocławek,[3] on the eve of Yom Kippur,[4] the Germans entered a private home where Jews had gathered to pray. They ordered those present to

11 Erich Neumann (1892–1951), lawyer and economist; member of the German National People's Party (DNVP); worked in the Prussian Ministry of the Interior from 1920 and in the Prussian Ministry of State from 1932; joined the NSDAP in 1933 and the SS in 1934; head of the Foreign Currency Business Group of the Plenipotentiary for the Four-Year Plan, 1936–1942; state secretary from 1938; attended the Wannsee Conference in 1942; managing director of Deutsches Kalisyndikat GmbH from 1942; interned, 1945–1948.

12 Wilhelm Stuckart (1902–1953), lawyer; joined the NSDAP in 1922 and the SS in 1936; member of the Epp Freikorps; became leader of the National Socialist Association of Lawyers in Gau Pomerania in 1932; state secretary in the Prussian Ministry of Education from June 1933; state secretary in the Reich Ministry of the Interior (responsible for Department I: Constitution and Legislation) from 1935; attended the Wannsee Conference in 1942; interned, 1945–1949; found guilty of war crimes at the Nuremberg Ministries Trial in 1949; sentenced to the exact time he had spent on remand and subsequently released; classified as a 'follower' (*Mitläufer*) in denazification proceedings in 1950.

13 Friedrich Landfried (1884–1952), lawyer and financial expert; state secretary in the Prussian Ministry of Finance, 1933–1943; simultaneously state secretary in the Reich Ministry of Defence; member of the General Council of the Four-Year Plan, 1939–1943; deputy chairman of the supervisory board of Reichswerke Hermann Göring AG until 1942; interned in 1945.

1 The original has been lost. Published in Benjamin Mintz and Israel Klausner (eds.), *Sefer Hazeva'ot: Te'udot Eduyot Vedinim Veḥeshbonot Al Sho'at Hayehudim Bemilḥemet Ha'olam Hasheniya* [Book of the Horrors] (Jerusalem: R. Mas, 1945), p. 6. This document has been translated from Hebrew.

2 This presumably refers to the Committee of Four, appointed by the executive of the Jewish Agency in Jerusalem at the end of 1939. The committee members were Izaak Grünbaum, Emil Schmorak, Elijahu Dobkin, and Rabbi Moshe Shapiro. Grünbaum, a native of Poland, tasked the last president of the Zionist Organization in Poland, Apolinary Hartglas (1883–1953), with collecting statements from survivors. Hartglas had come to Palestine after fleeing Warsaw in early 1940.

leave the building and run. Then they ordered them to 'Halt!', but several Jews did not hear the order and kept running, whereupon the Germans opened fire and killed five or six Jews. On that Yom Kippur, the Germans set fire to the two large synagogues. The fire also spread to a number of private houses. The Jews threw their belongings outside, where they were then looted by the Polish mob. Most of the fires were started by SS men. The Jews tried to save the burning houses. Then the Germans took all the men who were in one house, 26 in all, and forced them to sign statements that they had set the buildings on fire. After taking these statements, the Germans informed the prisoners that they would be sentenced to death for arson and that they could not be saved unless they paid a ransom of 250,000 złoty. The Jewish population of Włocławek raised the required sum and the prisoners were released. Then the Germans started raiding the houses. They caught about 350 Jews, some of whom they took to a barracks and others to the Mühsam factory.[5] From there, they were taken to work every day, but they were given no food. Only their families were allowed to provide them with food. After extensive petitioning and effort, the prisoners were occasionally given special permission to return home for a short while to wash and change their clothes, to eat, etc. The seizure of these 350 prisoners for regular work was by no means the end of the practice of abducting Jews from the streets for forced labour. Then there was the Jewish Council, which was established to replace the previous Community administration. The Council's activities were limited to carrying out the orders of the German administration and providing a certain number of Jewish workers each day to meet the Germans' demand. Those seized and taken off were mercilessly beaten and abused by the Germans. One incident will serve to illustrate how they treated the Jews at work: one of these Jews, Jacob Hayman, 52 years old and too weak for physical labour, was beaten and stabbed with daggers while working. He died from his injuries a few days after he returned home. In October the Germans declared that the Jews had to attach a yellow badge to the back of their clothing and that they could no longer walk on the pavement, only in the middle of the road. Shortly after they had collected the ransom for the alleged arsonists in the amount of 250,000 złoty, the Germans set a new fine of 500,000 złoty for every alleged violation of the prohibition on using the pavement. The schools were also closed.

A few days after entering the city, the Germans closed and confiscated all Jewish factories and shops. The Jews were required to register all their property. Jews were not permitted to have more than 200 złoty at home (2,000 in Warsaw).[6] There were many instances of physical attacks on Jews. They were beaten not only under any pretext during forced labour, but also for no reason at all. People would simply walk up to Jews in the street, shout 'Żyd'[7] and begin to beat them. Those who had previously applied were given permits to leave the city for a short time. To receive a permit, the applicants had to stand in three lines: ethnic Germans (Volksdeutsche) received the travel permits for

3 The Wehrmacht occupied the city on 14 Sept. 1939.

4 In 1939 the eve of Yom Kippur fell on 22 Sept.

5 Engineering works, including an iron foundry, founded in 1884 by Jewish businessman Hugo Mühsam.

6 The prohibition on possessing more than 2,000 złoty in cash was imposed in the General Government on 20 Nov. 1939 (*VOBl-GG* 1939, no. 7, 20 Nov. 1939, pp. 57–58) and in the Warthegau on 18 Nov. 1939. See Doc. 40.

7 Polish in the original: 'Jew'.

free, Poles had to pay 1 złoty, and Jews 10 złoty. Jewish women were also seized for forced labour, but such cases were rare and their work was not hard. They were treated 'mercifully' at work, i.e. they were not harmed except for slaps across the face. But they were forced to scrub floors wearing only the undergarments that they had on. However, not all Jewish women were safe from maltreatment. The Germans would break into Jewish apartments at night, under the pretence of searching them, and force women to strip naked. This is what happened to Mrs S., a woman of social standing, who was forced to dance and jump naked before the Germans. There were numerous similar cases.

The Polish population also suffers under the Germans. The first arrests made after the Germans had entered the city were of members of the Polish intelligentsia and priests. All these prisoners were sent to Germany for labour, somewhere near Königsberg. There has been no news from there since December. Many members of the Polish intelligentsia were shot, including Mayor Mystkowski.[8] The town was almost completely emptied of its intelligentsia. Polish craftsmen and labourers were removed from the city. The districts where they lived were set on fire, and many of them were imprisoned and sent to Germany for work. Only a few faint signs of the city's Polish character remain. Some of the local Germans have declared themselves ethnic Germans, and abuse and harass both Poles and Jews. They serve as a kind of auxiliary guard for the German authorities and are the driving force behind the violence. The Poles treated the Jews fairly. Some of them came to the Jews of their own accord and offered to protect them or their belongings in their homes. The Germans also shut down and seized factories and shops belonging to Poles.

DOC. 14

On 25 and 26 September 1939 Higher SS and Police Leader Krüger describes the German invasion of the western Polish territories and his arrival in Lodz (Łódź)[1]

Handwritten diary of Higher SS and Police Leader Friedrich-Wilhelm Krüger,[2] entries for 25–26 September 1939

25 September: I set out from the office at about 8.30 a.m. with two cars, two motorcycles with sidecars, and eight men. Travelled via Küstrin–Schwerin. Because the motorcycles broke down, we only passed the old border at around 12.30 p.m. and arrived in Posen at

8 Witold Mystkowski (1896–1939), accountant; from 1927 lived in Włocławek, where he was the mayor from 1935 to 1939.

1 HIA, Fr. W. Krüger Collection. Copy in IfZ-Archives, F 157. The diary covers the period from 2 Oct. 1938 to 8 Oct. 1939. This document has been translated from German.

2 Friedrich-Wilhelm Krüger (1894–1945), office clerk; member of Freikorps Lützow, 1919–1920; joined the NSDAP in 1929 and the SS in 1931; worked on the Reichsführer-SS's staff in 1935; worked at the SS Main Office from 1936; Higher SS and Police Leader under the Lodz military commander in Sept. 1939; Higher SS and Police Leader East for the General Government in Cracow and Plenipotentiary of the Reich Commissioner for the Strengthening of Germandom (RKF) from Oct. 1939; additionally state secretary responsible for security in the General Government from May 1942; served in the war, Nov. 1943–1945; committed suicide at the end of the war.

roughly 3.30 p.m. On the way we became acquainted with the whole madness of war. Since no fighting had taken place in this part of Poland, the Poles in retreat had contented themselves with abducting ethnic Germans and taking them off into the interior of the country or murdering them and burning down their farmsteads. They had blown up all the bridges, which the Labour Service[3] or engineer corps were busy rebuilding during our journey. The return of the Polish peasants made a distressing impression as they returned on foot along the roads to their home villages on the most wretched horse-drawn carts, with their whole families lying among straw and bedding. Ragged, hollow-eyed, and starving, they trudged alongside the emaciated horses, some with shoes on and some without, in stockings or barefoot. A picture of misery! We encountered the first Polish prisoners, Polish railway officials, as they passed us going in the opposite direction. – Posen itself displayed in its architecture its character as a German city. Of the 250,000 inhabitants, only approximately 6,000 are ethnic Germans. We established our quarters in the dirty Hotel Monopol. I visited the police headquarters, the chief of the local Order and Security Police and the Chief of the Civil Administration, Senate President Greiser,[4] and ordered that quarters be prepared for the civil governor, Reich Minister Frank, and myself. – Since the motorcycles were in need of repair, I left the two riders, Jung and Kappe, behind in Posen and set out on *26 September* with only the two cars. I took Schulz, Brantenaer, the two drivers, Dauss, and the interpreter with me. When we were driving out of Posen in the morning, the makeshift pontoon bridge replacing the big bridge over the Warta had broken the night before, due to being overloaded with vehicles. We therefore crossed the river on a car ferry. Travelled eastwards as far as Konin, then we turned off south via Kalisz, Sieradz, Zdunska Wola, Lask to Lodz. With their dust and potholes, the roads themselves were no match for German standards. As we travelled, there were once again endless columns of peasants coming back, returning home from the forests after terrible weeks. We reached Lodz at about 4 p.m. At the city hall I called on the chief of the Order Police deployed there, who gave me a quick briefing; then I set up my quarters with my staff in a Jewish villa at 4 Swientokrzyskastraße, where SS-Gruppenführer Panke[5] had been living until then. – With its approximately 670,000 inhabitants, of whom 370,000 are Jews, 80,000 are ethnic Germans, and 220,000 are Poles, Lodz is probably the most unpleasant and also the dirtiest city on the entire European continent. The people seem to have a special affinity

3 The Reich Labour Service (Reichsarbeitsdienst, RAD).

4 Arthur Greiser (1897–1946), sales agent; member of Border Force East, 1919–1921; co-founder of the Stahlhelm militia in Danzig in 1924; his independent sales agency went bankrupt in 1928; joined the NSDAP and the SA in 1929; joined the SS in 1931; Gaugeschäftsführer (director of Gau affairs) under Gauleiter Forster in Danzig from 1930; appointed minister of the interior in Danzig in 1933; elected president of the Danzig Senate in 1934; chief of the civil administration in the Posen Militärbezirk, Sept. 1939; subsequently Gauleiter and Reichsstatthalter in Reichsgau Wartheland; sentenced to death and executed in Poland in 1946.

5 Correctly: Günther Pancke (1899–1973), farmer; served with the Border Force in West Prussia, 1918–1920; subsequently lived in Argentina; joined the NSDAP in 1930 and the SS in 1931; became head of the Race and Settlement Main Office (RuSHA) in 1938; Higher SS and Police Leader Centre in Braunschweig, 1940–1943; Higher SS and Police Leader in Denmark, 1943–1945; sentenced to 20 years in prison in Copenhagen in 1948; pardoned in 1953.

with filth. – I first had SS-Oberführer Langleist[6] brief me on the situation. He returned to Germany early the next morning, and I ate in the evening at the Grand Hotel, the headquarters of the commander of 8th Army Command, with General Blaskowitz.[7]

DOC. 15
On 29 September 1939 Alfred Rosenberg writes about Hitler's plans for reordering East-Central Europe[1]

Diary of Alfred Rosenberg,[2] entry for 29 September 1939

29 September
The Führer called me to the Reich Chancellery at 4 o'clock today to discuss de R.'s[3] proposal. He first spent an hour describing just the campaign in Poland. He said the army today is in an incomparably better state than that of 1914, a quite different bond between the leadership and the troops: the generals with the rank and file, the same food for all, the generals out ahead at the front. When he saw the battalions parading past, as he did on the San, [he thought to himself that] there would never be a human breed like this again. The Poles: a thin Germanic stratum, terrible stock below. The Jews, the most repulsive thing that could ever be imagined. The cities covered in dirt. He said he had learned a great deal during the last few weeks. Above all, if Poland had ruled over the old parts of the Reich for another couple of decades, everything would have become lice-infested and run-down; only a decisive ruler's hand could govern there now. He wants to divide the now defined territory into three strips: 1. Between the Vistula and the Bug: the whole of Jewry (including the Jews from the Reich) and all elements that

6 Walter Langleist (1893–1946), mechanic; joined the NSDAP in 1930 and the SS in 1931; SS-Standortführer in Stettin in 1939; commander of the Selbstschutz militia in Bydgoszcz in Sept. 1939; attended a training course at Buchenwald in 1941; commander of the guard squad at Majdanek concentration camp, 1942–1943; subsequently commander of the guard squad at Dachau concentration camp, and then commandant of the Dachau satellite camps Kaufering and Mühldorf; sentenced to death and executed in 1946.

7 Johannes Blaskowitz (1883–1948), career officer; appointed general and commander of the 8th Army in the war against Poland in Sept. 1939; Commander-in-Chief East, Oct. 1939–May 1940; defendant at the Wehrmacht High Command trial in 1948; committed suicide while on remand.

1 USHMM, The Alfred Rosenberg Diary. Published in *The Political Diary of Alfred Rosenberg and the Onset of the Holocaust*, ed. Jürgen Matthäus and Frank Bajohr, trans. Kathleen Luft and Jan Lambertz (Lanham, MD: Rowman & Littlefield, 2015 (German edn, 2015]), pp. 165–167. This document has been newly translated from German.

2 Alfred Rosenberg (1893–1946), architect and journalist; born in Tallinn, grew up in Riga; studied in Moscow until 1918; joined the German Workers' Party (precursor of the NSDAP) in 1919; editor-in-chief of *Völkischer Beobachter* from 1923; head of the Foreign Policy Office of the NSDAP from 1933; appointed Führer's Plenipotentiary for the Supervision of the Entire Intellectual and Ideological Training and Schooling of the NSDAP in 1934; editor of the *Völkischer Beobachter* from 1938; Reich Minister for the Occupied Eastern Territories, 1941–1945; sentenced to death at the Nuremberg Trials and executed in 1946.

3 Presumably Baron William de Ropp, born Sylvester Wilhelm (William) Gotthard (1886–1974); British citizen; London-based agent for the Foreign Policy Office of the NSDAP. His proposal probably concerned a mediation mission intended to end the war.

are in whatever way unreliable. On the Vistula, an impregnable eastern wall – even stronger than in the West. 2. Along the previous border, a broad swathe of Germanization and colonization. He believes the whole Volk faces a great task there: creating a German granary, a strong class of farmers, resettling good Germans from all over the world. 3. In between, a Polish 'state entity'. Only time will tell whether the zone of settlements can be expanded in a few decades.

The Führer then described individual battles, e.g. a division in Blaskowitz's army, 45 kilometres [of marching], and after two hours into battle with indomitable energy. Then the militia[4] against the Polish elite troops near Gdingen.

With Moscow: he had thought about this a great deal. He would not have been able to prevent some locations being seized (ports in Estonia) if Stalin had gone with England. He had chosen the lesser evil and gained a massive strategic advantage. The Russian officers. A general who had been sent to him: capable at most of commanding a battery in the German army. Stalin has wiped out the elite, he is afraid of a war. He is just as afraid of a defeated army as he is of a victorious one. Nonetheless, the bulk of the infantry was solid; it was not necessary to fear the Russians as sailors.

As far as de R.'s proposal is concerned: [Hitler] will give him free passage and receive him! [De R.] should ask his own government whether it will permit him to make the journey.

Apart from this, the Führer will now propose a great peace conference; to that end, armistice, demobilization, settlement of all issues in a fair, reasonable manner.

Whether he would potentially want to conduct the war offensively to the west? – Of course, the Maginot Line no longer holds any terrors. If the English do not want peace, he would attack them with all of his resources and annihilate them. – In the war with Poland, in other words, a state with 34 million inhabitants, one would have had to reckon with losses of 100,000–200,000 dead. He said we had now suffered 8,000 dead and 30,000–35,000 wounded – evidence that it had been right to strike now. In five years' time, Poland would have been perfected and reconstructed, and not so easy to occupy.

The Führer went on to describe individual battles in great detail, said I should now go there as well.

Had a card sent immediately afterwards to R. in Montreux, informing him that the excursion would take place. Dispatched Harder[5] to get R. to Berlin.

Time will tell whether he will be able to mobilize forces in the British Air Ministry against the Churchills.

4 A reference to the ethnic German militias formed after the German invasion of Poland, which later became known as the Selbstschutz.

5 Presumably Baron Hermann von Harder und von Harmhove (1897–1983), businessman; co-owner of Harder & de Voss; joined the Foreign Policy Office of the NSDAP in 1935, and worked in the Middle East and Romania; responsible for the deployment of European volunteers in the occupied eastern territories in 1942.

DOC. 16

On 3 and 4 October 1939 the teenager Dawid Sierakowiak describes Germans attacking Jews in Łódź[1]

Handwritten diary of Dawid Sierakowiak,[2] entries for 3 and 4 October 1939

Tuesday, 3 October, Łódź. Slowly and with difficulty people are getting used to the new circumstances and are beginning to return to their everyday business. While this is possible for clerks and a portion of the workers and shopkeepers, it is more difficult for Jews. Jews – business people, shop owners, private entrepreneurs, middlemen, merchants, etc. – are losing their livelihoods, to say nothing of the fact that they fear walking out of the door because of the labour roundups. Like most of our neighbours, for instance, they leap at occasional trade, so-called door-to-door selling. There is trade in stockings, bread, sugar, fabrics, etc. Everyone has something to sell; goods pass through the hands of dozens of middlemen, wholesalers, merchants, etc., but none of this protects the Jewish masses from rapid impoverishment. And my father has no work; he is simply suffocating at home. We no longer have any money either. One big fiasco!

Wednesday, 4 October, Łódź. I was also not spared the sad fate of my countrymen seized for work. As luck would have it, I let my old folks talk me into going to school via Wólczańska, which is a bit shorter. As I walked along yesterday, nothing but swastikas on all the houses of this street, many German cars, many soldiers, and Łódź Germans with swastikas. I somehow slipped through unnoticed, and today I dared to go the same way. Somewhere near Andrzeja, a pupil from a German grammar school with a proper club in his hand runs up to me and shouts: Komm arbeiten! In die Schule darfst du nicht gehen.[3] I did not resist because I knew that no identity card would help me here. He led me to some square where a dozen Jews were already busy at work picking up leaves from the ground (!). The sadistically inclined young man wanted at all costs to make me climb over a two-metre-high fence, but seeing that I wouldn't do it, he went away. The work on the square was led by a soldier, also armed with a club, who swore at me and ordered me to fill in puddles with sand. Never in my life have I suffered such humiliation as when, through the courtyard gate, I saw the cheerful grins on the silly faces of passers-by laughing at others' misfortune. Oh, what a stupid lot you are, rude and abysmally stupid! It is not us who should be ashamed, but rather our tormentors. Humiliation inflicted by force is not humiliation! But anger and helpless rage tear a man apart when forced to do this stupid, disgraceful work fraught with maltreatment. There is only one thing left: revenge! After about half an hour of work, a soldier summoned all the Jews, some of whom had their caps turned back to front for 'laughs', and after having us line

1 USHMM, RG 10 247. Diary written by Dawid Sierakowiak from 28 June 1939. The entire diary has been published in English translation in *The Diary of Dawid Sierakowiak: Five Notebooks from the Łódź Ghetto*, ed. Alan Adelson, trans. Kamil Turowski (New York and Oxford: Oxford University Press, 1996 [Polish edn, 1960]). This document has been newly translated from Polish.

2 Dawid Sierakowiak (1924–1943); already kept a diary before Sept. 1939 and in seven notebooks described the events in Łódź and in the Łódź ghetto (two notebooks were lost in 1945). The diary ends in April 1943; the author died of tuberculosis three months later.

3 German in the original: 'Come and work! You are not allowed to go to school.'

up in a single file, he told one of them to return the spades and me to go home. What generosity! I got to school halfway through the first lesson, late for the first time since attending grammar school. The teachers are at their wits' end – 'for reasons independent of the Jews'. I returned the old way via Kiliński, and at home mother was horrified when she heard about my labour. Father no longer insisted on the shorter route via Wólczańska. In the evening we learnt that one of the Germans living on our street has his 'eye' on the Jews from the ZUS[4] tenement building and is 'taking care of them'. This has completely upset my poor anxious parents. Meanwhile it was announced at school that pupils who do not pay a certain sum of money will be prohibited from entering the school. We shall see what happens to me.

DOC. 17
On 6 October 1939 Hitler calls for the ethnic reordering of Eastern Europe[1]

Speech given by Adolf Hitler before the Reichstag, 6 October 1939

[…][2]
In one regard, however, Germany's determination is unalterable, namely to bring about peaceful, stable, and thus sustainable conditions in the eastern parts of our Reich as well. And in this respect in particular, German interests and desires are completely consonant with those of Soviet Russia. The two states are determined not to allow problematic situations to arise between them that might carry the seeds of domestic unrest and thus lead to external troubles, and which could perhaps adversely affect relations between the two great powers in some way. Germany and Soviet Russia have therefore drawn a clear border between their respective areas of interest with the determination that they will ensure peace and order in their respective parts, and prevent anything from happening which might be detrimental to the other partner.[3]

As far as the German sphere of interest is concerned, the goals and tasks resulting from the disintegration of the Polish state are the following:

1. Establishing a Reich border that does justice to the historical, ethnographic, and economic realities.
2. Pacifying the whole territory with the aim of establishing lasting law and order.
3. Fully guaranteeing the security not only of Reich territory, but also of the whole zone of interest.

4 Zakład Ubezpieczeń Społecznych: Social Insurance Institution.

1 Stenographisches Protokoll der 4. Sitzung vom 6.10.1939, *Verhandlungen des Reichstags: IV. Wahlperiode 1939*, vol. 460 (Berlin: Verlag der Reichsdruckerei, 1939), pp. 51–63, here pp. 56–57 and 60–61. This document has been translated from German.

2 Hitler first discussed the course of the war, condemned Polish policy on ethnic minorities and Polish plans for the annexation of German territories, and then turned to the 'new pact of friendship and interests' with the Soviet Union. He denied that Germany was seeking to expand into Ukraine or as far as the Urals.

3 This refers to the treaties the German Reich had concluded with the Soviet Union on 23 August and 28 Sept. 1939.

4. Reordering and reconstructing economic life, commerce, and thus cultural and civilizational development as well.
5. The most important task, however, is a reordering of ethnographic conditions, which means resettling different nationalities so that, at the conclusion of this development, there are better dividing lines than is the case today. In this sense, however, it is not a problem that is limited to this area, but rather a task that has far wider implications, as the whole east and south-east of Europe are partly filled with unsustainable fragments of German ethnicity. It is precisely these that are a reason for and cause of continued international friction. In the age of the nationality principle and the racial idea, it is utopian to believe that these members of a superior race could easily be assimilated. As a result, one of the tasks for a far-sighted ordering of European life is to carry out resettlements as a way of eliminating at least some of the problems that have led to conflict in Europe.

Germany and the Union of Soviet Republics have agreed to provide mutual support in doing this.[4]

The German Reich government will never permit the Polish rump state that is being created to become any kind of disruptive element for the Reich itself, or even a source of discord between the German Reich and Soviet Russia.

If Germany and Soviet Russia take on this task of renovation, both states would then justifiably be able to point out that the attempt to resolve this problem with the methods of Versailles has been a complete failure.

[…][5]

Why should war now take place in the West? For the restoration of Poland? The Poland of the Versailles Treaty will never rise again! This is guaranteed by two of the largest states in the world. The final shape of this area, the question of the re-establishment of a Polish state, are problems that will not be resolved by war in the West, but exclusively by Russia in one case and by Germany in the other. Moreover, any exclusion of these two powers in the territories in question would not create a new state, but total chaos. The problems that must be resolved there will not be resolved at the conference table or in editorial offices, but by decades of work. After all, it is not enough for a few statesmen who ultimately have no interest in the fate of those concerned in the first place to sit down together and make decisions; rather, it is necessary for someone who is himself involved in the life of these territories to take on the work of restoring genuinely lasting conditions. There has been no evidence of the Western democracies' capacity to

4 See the secret protocol to the German–Soviet Non-Aggression Pact, signed in Moscow on 28 Sept. 1939: 'Vereinbarung der Deutschen Reichsregierung und der Regierung der UdSSR über die Umsiedlung der ukrainischen und weißrussischen Bevölkerung aus dem zur Interessenzone des Deutschen Reiches gehörenden Gebiet', *Akten zur deutschen auswärtigen Politik 1918–1945*, series D: *1937–1945*, vol. 8/1: *Die Kriegsjahre: 4. September 1939 bis 18. März 1940* (Baden-Baden: Imprimerie Nationale, 1961), p. 128. Published in English in Jeremy Noakes and Geoffrey Pridham (eds.), *Nazism 1919–1945*, vol. 3: *Foreign Policy, War and Racial Extermination: A Documentary Reader* (Liverpool: Liverpool University Press, 2001), pp. 135–136.

5 Hitler subsequently criticized the peace settlement enshrined in the Treaty of Versailles. He argued for the expansion of German Lebensraum ('living space'), but he also gave assurances that Germany did not harbour any aggressive intentions towards its small neighbouring states. Hitler then boasted of having defused the German–French conflict and commented on the prospects of war in the West.

create such ordered conditions, at least in recent times. The example of Palestine shows that it would be better to deal with the tasks at hand and to resolve them sensibly than to meddle in problems that lie within other nations' spheres of life and interest, and which will definitely be mastered better by those nations. Certainly Germany has not only ensured law and order in its Protectorate of Bohemia and Moravia, but has above all also laid the foundations for new economic prosperity and for ever-closer understanding between both nations. England will have a lot more to do before it can point to similar results in its Palestinian protectorate.

Incidentally, we know perfectly well that it would be senseless to annihilate millions of human lives and to destroy hundreds of billions in assets potentially in order to re-establish a construct that all non-Poles described as a stillbirth at the time it was created. What other reason can there be? Has Germany made any demand of England that threatens the British Empire, for instance, or calls its existence into question? No, on the contrary! Germany has not addressed such a demand to either France or England.

But if this war is really only to be waged in order to give Germany a new regime – in other words, in order to dismember the current Reich again and thereby create a new Versailles – millions of people would be sacrificed pointlessly, for neither will the German Reich break up, nor will a second Versailles arise.

But even if this were to happen after a three- or four- or eight-year war, this second Versailles would only again become a source of new conflicts in the ensuing period. In any case, however, a settlement of the world's problems without consideration of the vital interests of its strongest nations will not end one jot differently in five or ten years than that attempt of 20 years ago did today. No, this war in the West will not sort out any problems, except for the ruined finances of a few armaments industrialists and newspaper owners or other international war profiteers.

Two problems are up for discussion today:

1. Settling the questions raised by the way Poland has fallen apart, and
2. the problem of resolving the international concerns that are making the lives of the nations more difficult politically and economically.

Now what are the Reich government's aims when it comes to ordering relations in the area that is recognized as the German sphere of influence to the west of the German–Soviet Russian demarcation line?

1. Creating a Reich border that – as has previously been emphasized – aligns with historical, ethnographic, and economic conditions;
2. ordering the entire area by nationalities, i.e. a solution to those minority questions that affect not only this area, but almost all the southern and south-eastern European states as well;
3. in this context, attempting to order and settle the Jewish problem;
4. reconstructing commercial and economic life for the benefit of all the people who live in this area;
5. guaranteeing the security of this whole territory; and
6. forming a Polish state, the structure and leadership of which will guarantee that it will constitute neither a new source of conflagration against the German Reich nor a hub of intrigue against Germany and Russia.

In addition, an attempt must be made to eliminate or at least alleviate the effects of the war, i.e. to ease the enormous suffering that currently exists by means of practical aid.

These tasks can – as has already been emphasized – certainly be discussed, but never resolved, at a conference table. If Europe is at all concerned with peace and tranquillity, the European states should be grateful that Russia and Germany are now prepared to turn this trouble spot into an area of peaceful development, and that the two countries are taking on the responsibility for this and are also making the sacrifices this involves. Because this task cannot be conceived in imperialist terms, it means an engagement of 50 to 100 years for the German Reich. The justification for this German work lies in the political ordering of this territory, as well as in its economic development. In the end, however, both will benefit the whole of Europe.

[...][6]

DOC. 18

On 6 October 1939 the chief of the Gestapo authorizes Eichmann to deport Jews from Bezirk Kattowitz to the East[1]

Memorandum by RSHA IV D 4, Eichmann[2] (Mährisch-Ostrau Central Office receipt stamp:[3] 8 October 1939), dated 6 October 1939

During a consultation with SS-Oberführer Müller[4] on 6 October 1939, SS-Oberführer Müller gave the following orders:

1) Contact is to be made with the office of Gauleiter Wagner – Kattowitz.[5] Discussion with this office concerning the deportation of 70,000–80,000 Jews from Bezirk Kattowitz.

6 In the rest of his speech, Hitler called for a German colonial empire and a 'new order for the markets'. He warned France and Britain against continuing the war.

1 NAP, 101-653-1. Copy in Documentation Centre of Austrian Resistance, 17 072/a. This document has been translated from German.

2 Adolf Eichmann (1906–1962), sales agent; joined the NSDAP and the SS in 1932; worked at the SD Main Office, 1934–1938; headed the Central Office for Jewish Emigration from summer 1938, first in Vienna and then also in Prague from March 1939; head of the Clearance of the Annexed Eastern Provinces Section at the Reich Security Main Office (RSHA) from Dec. 1939; then head of Section IV D 4 (Clearance Activities and Reich Central Office for Jewish Emigration); head of Section IV B 4 (Jewish Affairs, Clearance Activities) from at least March 1941; attended the Wannsee Conference in 1942; detained in 1945; escaped in 1946; lived under a false identity in Argentina, 1950–1960; abducted in 1960 to Israel, where he was sentenced to death in 1961 and executed in 1962.

3 In Oct. 1939 approximately 900 Jews were deported from Moravská Ostrava (Mährisch Ostrau) to a camp near Nisko on the San river: see Doc. 42. The Central Office for Jewish Emigration had a branch office in Moravská Ostrava for a brief period in autumn 1939.

4 Heinrich Müller (1900–1945), aircraft mechanic; worked at Munich Police Headquarters from 1919; joined the SS and the SD in 1934; transferred to the Gestapo Central Office Berlin; deputy chief of the Political Police Office in the Main Office of the Security Police from 1936; joined the NSDAP in 1938; chief executive of the Reich Central Office for Jewish Emigration from 1939; head of Office IV (Gestapo) of the RSHA from Oct. 1939; attended the Wannsee Conference in 1942; died at the end of the war.

5 Josef Wagner (1899–1945), teacher; joined the NSDAP in 1922; became Gauleiter of Westphalia in 1928 and of Westphalia-South in 1931; Gauleiter of Silesia and simultaneously Oberpräsident and Reich Defence Commissioner, 1935–1940; dismissed from all offices for reasons unknown in Nov. 1941; expelled from the NSDAP by Hitler in 1942; probably murdered in Gestapo detention at the end of the war.

Initially, these Jews are to be deported eastwards over the Vistula. At the same time, Jews from the Mährisch-Ostrau area can also be deported. The same applies to all Jewish immigrants from Poland who have sought refuge there in connection with recent events.

The primary purpose of this exercise is to gain enough experience to make it possible to implement the evacuation of larger masses on the basis of this experience.

2) Reports are to be sent to SS-Oberführer Müller by teletype on a daily basis.

DOC. 19

On 6 October 1939 the head of Einsatzgruppe IV reports on the persecution of Jews in Warsaw[1]

Report by the head of Einsatzgruppe IV of the Security Police, signed Beutel,[2] dated 6 October 1939 (copy)

Transcript

Terrible plight, population is intimidated, ethnic Germans relate that during the bombing of Warsaw, the junior officers of the air-raid warden service still came to them in the cellars and told them lies about how the situation in Warsaw was still nowhere near as bad as the one in Berlin, that the English and French had already invaded Germany, and Generalissimo Ryds-Schmigly[3] was already advancing towards the gates of Warsaw. Even on 4 October 1939 there were residents in the cellars who were still scared and did not dare to venture out.

According to various investigations, Warsaw remained a completely undamaged city up until 26 September, apart from a few military buildings.

The number of Germans said to have been living in Warsaw is 2,500–3,000, of whom approximately 500 could be regarded as ethnic Germans. According to the investigations carried out so far, about 10 per cent of these Germans are still in Warsaw, and only very few among them can be seen as reliable.

The profiteering and the hoarding of food, which the Jews have been engaged in thus far, are very widespread and must be combated through public announcements containing harsh threats.

1 APŁ, 175/41, fols. 40–43. A second, shorter version of this document (not used here), entitled 'Report on the Activities of Security Police Einsatzgruppe IV', has been published in Mirosław Cygański, 'Z akt szefa zarządu cywilnego przy dowództwie 8 armii niemieckiej, październik 1939 r.', *Najnowsze Dzieje Polski*, vol. 3 (Warsaw: Państwowe Wydawnictwo Naukowe, 1959), pp. 224–230, here pp. 225–226. This document has been translated from German.

2 Lothar Beutel (1902–1986), pharmacist; joined the NSDAP in 1929 and the SS in 1930; worked full-time for the SD from 1932 and held leading roles in Saxony and Munich; commander of Einsatzgruppe IV in Poland in 1939, then commander of the Security Police and the SD in Lublin until 23 Oct. 1939; posted temporarily to a Waffen-SS penal company for embezzlement; prisoner of war in the Soviet Union, 1945–1955; subsequently lived in Berlin.

3 Correctly: Edward Rydz-Śmigły, born Rydz (1886–1941), career officer; inspector general of the Polish Armed Forces, 1935–1939; made Marshal of Poland in 1936; fled to Romania in Sept. 1939; interned in Romania; fled to Hungary in 1940; returned to Warsaw under a false name in 1941; died shortly thereafter.

On 8 September 1939, at the instruction of the judicial administration, the prisoners were released from the prisons here in the direction of Siedlce–Brest, allegedly under the leadership of an officer from Warsaw. The Einsatzgruppe is searching for them.

The well-known Jewish *Samenhof* family, one of the leading families in Warsaw, was detained and interrogated about the Jewish elite.[4] House searches have yielded no results so far.

The well-known Jew *Landau* has fled to Paris via London and has taken valuables with him. His managing director stayed here and is being interrogated.

German soldiers' pay books have been found in the building of the Polish border force, which means they must have been interrogated. In addition, the entire Polish border force's membership list has been located and secured.

It is interesting that the Pole will openly oppose the Jew and is delighted by any measures taken against Jews.

As in other cities in Poland, investigations into the German banknotes that are not legal tender but which were brought into circulation have so far been fruitless.

The Association for Nationalities Questions at 4 Chlonowastraße yielded valuable material from its files.

The Archbishop of Warsaw's correspondence with the Nuncio has been secured – as have the files of Catholic associations, and the files and institutions of the Caritas organizations.

Under the Poles, Warsaw was divided into 25 police commissariats, with Commissariats II, III, IV, and VI described as out-and-out ghetto areas. According to one list, 374,000 Jews are supposed to have been counted on 31 December 1938 (out of a population of 1,196,000 residents and with 18,772 residential buildings).

The Polish Criminal Police, led by a Lieutenant Colonel Wasilewski,[5] still has approximately 360 officers today who are deployed to do minor tasks under the supervision of the Einsatzgruppe.

Investigations at the Citadel did not confirm the fear that ethnic Germans who had been kidnapped and taken there had been maltreated and murdered.

Given the lack of light and other opportunities for monitoring, letting Jews keep road vehicles involves a constant danger that weapons and assets will be moved and smuggled out across the Romanian border as a result. The confiscation of Jewish cars is therefore a necessity.

When the Polish Ministry of the Interior was searched, 4,000,000 lead bullets packed in 200 crates of 20,000 each were found. They will be delivered to the Stadtkommandant's office.

The Jews will be registered in accordance with the guidelines issued by the Reichsführer-SS and the Chief of the German Police,[6] which state that a Council of Elders consist-

4 This refers to the family of the physician and inventor of Esperanto, Lejser Samenhof, also known as Ludwik Lejzer or Leyzer Zamenhof (1859–1917); his son Adam was detained in 1939 and shot dead in Jan. 1940; his daughters Zofia and Lidia Zamenhof and his sister Ida were confined in the Warsaw ghetto and murdered in Treblinka in 1942.

5 Stanisław Wasilewski (1907–1990), officer in the Polish State Police; head of the investigative branch in Warsaw, 1934–1939; police lieutenant colonel in the General Government and liaison officer for the Criminal Police Directorate in Warsaw from 1939; simultaneously deputy head of the Home Army's State Security Corps in 1942.

ing of 24 prominent Jews be appointed by the Einsatzgruppe. This council will be made fully responsible for the implementation of instructions from the Einsatzgruppe, charged with conducting a census of Jews broken down by age groups and sex, and will make its own proposals for registering the Jews in the ghettos. The Einsatzgruppe will get in touch with the military authorities and the Chief of the Civil Administration about this. The Stadtkommandant has already been informed.

The Jewish Religious Community, its president, and its secretary have been seized, along with the Jewish Museum.[7]

The Grand Master of the Polish National Grand Lodge, Prof. Wolfke,[8] is being interrogated thoroughly, in addition to being called upon to report on the current state of hygiene in Warsaw, a topic he is very familiar with. At the same time, the state of the field hospitals occupied by Polish patients is being checked to ascertain the health situation.

According to still-unconfirmed information, a whispering campaign is being conducted to persuade young Polish people not to surrender their weapons, but to bury them in gardens. Furthermore, according to unverified information, at night underground radio stations in Warsaw are telling the population to hold out because a new Polish government has already been formed in Paris.

It has been observed that the citizens' militia entrusted with the distribution of foodstuffs is distributing them improperly and always serves itself first. Armed Jews comprise 25–30 per cent of the citizens' militia. The investigations are ongoing.

Six hundred ethnic Germans were said to have been abducted from Pomerelia and taken to a prison here. The matter will be discussed further. The prison director has been detained due to insolent behaviour and making patently untrue statements. Since some 30,000–40,000 civilian prisoners[9] will be released from the Reich into Poland, they will be fingerprinted, photographed, and placed under Criminal Police surveillance.

According to information from the head of the Polish Criminal Police, Lieutenant Colonel Wasilewski, the head of the Kommenta glowna,[10] Brigadier General Zamorski,[11] has escaped to Brest-Litovsk with all the important police files, and from there to Volhynia. The half-Jew Dr Nagler[12] and the internationally well-known detective Jakubiecz[13] are

6 See Section II of Heydrich's express letter: Doc. 12.

7 Probably the Mathias Berson Museum of Jewish Antiquities, which had survived the fighting unscathed. See Doc. 321, fn. 74.

8 Dr Mieczysław Wolfke (1883–1947), physicist; employed at Carl-Zeiss-Werke in Jena from 1907; became a lecturer at Karlsruhe Institute of Technology in 1912; conducted postdoctoral research at the Swiss Federal Institute of Technology, Zurich; professor of physics at Warsaw University from 1920; detained with his son in Nov. 1939; appointed lecturer at the State Higher Technical School in Warsaw in 1942; also active in the clandestine education system; lived in Zurich after the war.

9 These civilians had been detained and deported to Reich territory when the Wehrmacht advanced in Sept. 1939.

10 Correctly: Komenda Główna, meaning 'High Command'.

11 Józef Zamorski Kordian (1890–1983), career officer; served in the Polish Legions, then in the Polish army, 1914–1917; deputy chief of the general staff, 1928–1935; chief of the Polish State Police, 1935–1939; interned in Romania in 1939; exiled to Palestine, 1940–1942; lived in Britain after the war.

12 Dr Leon Nagler (1884–1939), lawyer; served as an officer in the Austro-Hungarian army during the First World War; employed in the Polish Ministry for Military Affairs from 1919; subsequently a police officer; head of the Inspectorate of the High Command of the Polish State Police, 1936–1939.

13 Presumably Józef Jakubiec, criminologist and police officer; head of the Central Investigation Service and Department IV (Fingerprinting) in the High Command of the Polish State Police.

supposed to have accompanied him. Another account says that, following a short trip to his estate near Grodno, Z. has returned to Warsaw, where he has told people he will escape to Romania with the government.

A collection of art, porcelain, and paintings has been secured not far from Warsaw.

The files of the Ukrainian academic institute have been secured.

The investigations carried out to date have found that the Ministry of Finance, the Voivodeship, the University, the Institute for Nationalities Research,[14] the Polish Institute for Foreign Cooperation, and the Institute for Research on Modern Polish History have been destroyed and/or largely gutted by fire.

The central building of the Polish Teachers' Association has been secured and identified as the centre of Polish chauvinism and anti-German agitation.

The leader of the communist youth organization, the Polish student Rosenkwiat, has been arrested.

Two convicted murderers of ethnic Germans have been arrested.

The well-known bishop of the Protestant Church of the Augsburg Confession, *Bursche*,[15] a well-known anti-German agitator, has fled to Lublin with all of his files. He has been put on thc wanted list.

The University's vice chancellor,[16] a well-known leader of the Polish intelligentsia, is currently being interrogated by the Einsatzgruppe.

DOC. 20

Manchester Guardian, 7 October 1939: article on Jewish and Christian clergy as early victims of the German invasion[1]

Victims of the Germans. Many Rabbis.

From our Former Warsaw Correspondent

Unconfirmed reports from Warsaw received in Jewish quarters in London state that the Chief Rabbi of Warsaw, Professor Moses Shorr, was shot by the Nazis shortly after they entered the capital.[2] Rabbi Shorr was for many years the chief spiritual figure of Polish Jewry and a professor in the University of Warsaw.

14 Presumably the Institute for the Study of Nationalities, which existed from 1921 to 1939.

15 Dr Julius Bursche (1862–1942), theologian; bishop of the Protestant Church of the Augsburg Confession in Poland; arrested during the German occupation; died in detention.

16 Probably Dr Włodzimierz Antoniewicz (1893–1973), archaeologist; studied in Vienna; worked at the University of Warsaw from 1920; vice chancellor of the University of Warsaw, 1936–1939; worked as a manual labourer during the German occupation; subsequently a professor at the University of Warsaw again until 1963.

1 *Manchester Guardian*, 7 Oct. 1939. Founded as a weekly in 1821 in Manchester; in the 1930s a major daily newspaper with a nationwide British readership.

2 Schorr actually died later in Soviet captivity. Moses (Mojżesz) Schorr (1874–1941), historian, rabbi, and linguist; studied in Vienna, Berlin, and Lwów, where he became a professor in 1910; rabbi at the Great Synagogue in Warsaw in 1918; professor in Warsaw in 1926; co-founder of the Institute for Jewish Studies in 1928; named a senator by the president of Poland in 1935; in early Sept. 1939 fled to eastern Poland (which was under Soviet rule), where he was sentenced to five years of forced labour.

It is feared that Archbishop Count Szeptycki[3] has been arrested in Lwow by the Russians. He was not only the religious but also the political leader of the Ukrainians in Southern Poland. Born in a well-known family of Polish nobility, he devoted all his life to the cause of the Ukrainians in Poland, championing their rights with great vigour and devotion.

To the great credit of the Christian and Jewish spiritual leaders it should be stated that in spite of the German and Russian invasions, they stayed at their posts.[4] Even German Catholic priests in Western Poland who had opposed the Nazi regime openly for many years refused to leave their parishes. As a result, many of the Christian clergymen fell victims to the Russians and a large number of Jewish rabbis were the first victims of the Germans.

It should be recorded that the Jewish quarter in Warsaw, which is densely populated, suffered greater losses in life than the non-Jewish districts. German shelling was for days particularly directed against the Jewish districts of Nalewki, Nowolipki, and other streets in the Jewish area, where most of the 330,000 Jews in the Polish capital lived. Even the ruins of Jewish houses in those districts were continuously kept under German shell fire.

DOC. 21
On 12 October 1939 the Chief of the Civil Administration in Cracow orders financial institutions to provide information on their Jewish clients[1]

Regulation issued by the Chief of the Civil Administration, signed on behalf of the commander-in-chief: Chief of the Civil Administration Dill,[2] Cracow, 12 October 1939

Regulation on Measures to Combat the Jews' Unreliability in Paying Taxes
In view of the unreliability of Jews in paying their taxes, and based on the executive powers conferred on me within my area of responsibility, I hereby order the following:
§ 1
(1) The duty of banks to uphold confidentiality in their dealings with the tax authorities (Article 60, § 4 Ordynacja podatkowa)[3] shall be repealed insofar as these relate to investigations into Jews and Jewish firms.

3 Andrei Sheptytskyi, born Roman Maria Aleksander Count Szeptycki (1865–1944), metropolitan of the Greek Catholic Church in Lwów.
4 This cannot be said of the primate of the Roman Catholic Church in Poland, Cardinal August Hlond (1881–1948), who fled the country in Sept. 1939 and spent the war years in exile in Italy and France.

1 *VOBl-CdZ Krakau*, no. 6, 12 Oct. 1939; AIPN, GK 196/333 (NTN 333), fol. 8. This document has been translated from German.
2 Dr Gottlob Dill (1885–1968), lawyer; joined the NSDAP in 1932 and the SS in 1939; undersecretary in the Württemberg Ministry of the Interior; deputy minister of the interior with responsibility for policing from 1938; transferred to the SD in August 1939; subsequently Chief of the Civil Administration in Cracow.
3 The Polish tax regulations.

(2) All financial institutions of any kind, bankers, and moneylenders will be obliged to provide officials from the Reich Financial Authorities and former Polish tax administration staff who present the required identification documents with any information requested about their commercial relationships with Jews and Jewish firms, and to disclose the relevant accounts, receipts, and correspondence. The aforementioned identification documents shall be issued by the representative of the Reich Financial Authorities for Property and Trade Taxes to the chief of the administration in the Cracow Militärbezirk.

§ 2

At the special request of the representative of the Reich Financial Authorities referred to in § 1(2), financial institutions, bankers, and moneylenders shall be obliged to submit a list of all of their clients to him for the purpose of ascertaining which Jews and Jewish firms are among them.

§ 3

Jewish firms are defined as all businesses that are either wholly or more than 50 per cent in Jewish hands, or are operated with Jewish money.

§ 4

Contraventions and/or evasions of the obligations stipulated in § 1(2) and § 2 of this regulation shall be punished with a fine of up to 10,000 Reichsmarks (20,000 zloty).

§ 5

This regulation shall come into force with immediate effect.

DOC. 22

On 15 October 1939 the refugee Artur Szlifersztejn describes his life in the Soviet-occupied part of Poland[1]

Letter from Artur Szlifersztejn[2] from Vilna to Joseph Stein[3] in Brooklyn, dated 15 October 1939

My beloved Józek,

I am currently in Vilna at our representative's. I came here from Białystok to collect a few hundred złoty from our clients. Tomorrow I'm returning to Białystok, where I'll be staying with (Dawid's) Lutek and (Edek's) Ludwik.[4] I left Warsaw with them on 7 September 1939, one week after the war began. In two days the Soviets will hand over Vilna to Lithuania, and I therefore expect this letter to reach you – but only God knows when.

1 USHMM, RG 10 248. This document has been translated from Polish.

2 Artur (Artek) Szlifersztejn lived in Lwów from 1940; later correspondence with his brother Józef (Józek) Szlifersztejn dwelt on his attempt to emigrate to the USA, which failed in the end. Artur is thought to have died during the war.

3 Joseph Stein was born in Warsaw in 1906 as Józef Szlifersztejn. He emigrated to New York before 1939, together with his wife, Tola, and daughter Danuta.

4 Artur Szlifersztejn's two nephews were the sons of his brothers Dawid and Edward (Edek). Dawid's son Lucjan (Lutek), who later called himself Lawrence, fled first to Łuck, and in summer 1941 continued farther east. The Soviet authorities put him in a labour camp in Sverdlovsk, from where he was later drafted into the Red Army. In 1951 he reached the United States via Sweden and Cuba.

I am writing because I understand very well how much you suffer when you read in the press about what has happened here.

Unfortunately, at this moment I'm not yet able to write anything comforting. Everyone except for me and our two oldest nephews on my brother's side has remained in Warsaw, and I hope to receive news from them in just a few days' time. An acquaintance went to Warsaw; he should also be back with news soon. Just like you, I think about them all the time and live with the hope that nothing bad has happened to them.

I too have suffered a lot under the Germans. It can hardly be described in a letter. We have been taken prisoner – as a civilian population. And when we were in Łuków, they simply ordered all men to leave their apartments, created groups of four, and chased us through the entire night to another town and – and after a day's stay – on to the second town. Thanks to our presence of mind, we managed to escape and free ourselves from the clutches of these executioners. Words cannot describe the bestiality of the Germans. We sighed with relief when we saw the first red flag. Everything up to the Bug river – all the way to Lwów – has been taken by the Soviets and everything farther west by the Germans. They defeated the Polish army in just a few weeks. Unbelievable, but true. Poland in a political sense no longer exists. The Ludwiks and I will stay within the borders of Soviet Russia. The Germans have tormented us too much for us to entertain the desire to return. I am not making any plans. I don't know what awaits us. All I know is that we are being treated as humans, and that is what we all longed for.

Perhaps sometime, down the road, once there is peace and it is possible to move about freely, I will want to see you in return for everything I have been through and spend the remainder of my modest life with you. I know that these are premature dreams.

A lot of time will have to pass before I see you again, but you become tougher and more resilient in suffering. I will make an effort to write to you as soon as I hear from Warsaw.

Beloved Józek! I implore you not to worry. The year 1939 has brought us great misfortune, but perhaps in the end the sun will shine for us. The living shall not lose hope. I admit that I have been saved by a miracle, so I believe that, since I've not died yet, I will survive. I am pleased that at least one of us did not have to go through these horrors. The Jewish people are indestructible. If some want to exterminate them in Europe, there will always remain some in England and in America and in the remaining countries unaffected by the plague of Nazism. Perhaps with time, once freedom comes, the refugees will be able to emigrate to the USA despite the quotas.[5]

But that is all a long way off.

In Białystok there are about 100,000 refugees.[6] Several of our acquaintances are among them, including Bolek Senator, who escaped with his wife and child, but 98 per cent are men, because it was impossible to take women and children along the unsafe route. They would hardly have survived the arduous journey. We covered about 350 kilometres on foot, and that under tough conditions, constantly under machine-gun fire and bombs being dropped from aircraft. We walked at night for the most part, and during

5 Immigration quotas introduced in the USA in 1921 drastically limited the number of Jewish and other immigrants, especially from Eastern Europe.

6 Polish citizens who had fled east beginning on 1 Sept. 1939.

the day we slept in peasants' barns. We now have peace in the area that was taken by the army of the USSR. We are staying with acquaintances in Białystok. For the time being, our sustenance doesn't cost anything, and we're waiting for things to settle down. I still have some money, and whatever happens to all – will also happen to me.

Heniek L. was lucky to get away. I knew I would not make it back in time. Unfortunately, they have cancelled my visa. I would not have made it in any case, because the next ship was scheduled for 4 September, four days after the Teutons started the war.

Dearest Józek, I hope you're all well. If you see Heniek L., give him and his wife my regards. Tell him that [...][7] is in Równe – my bitter rival Michał Zyst is there as well. We are all in the same boat today.

I have heard nothing from the Zylbermans and I do not know where they are, but I assume that they too have left Warsaw.

My current address is

Ch. Kustin, Białystok, 1 Marsz. Piłsudskiego, for A. Szlifen.

Write to me at the same time to this address:

E. Lubliński, Vilna (18 Wielka), Lithuania, PO Box 38, for A. Szlifen.

Because Vilna will belong to Lithuania, which is not involved in the war,[8] I might get a letter sooner through Mr Lubliński, with whom I am in touch.

I send everyone warm regards, especially Tola. Thank her for the letter. I never wrote back because of all the nervousness in the days leading up to the war.

She will probably forgive me.

Give little Danuta a kiss from me. I am pleased that you managed to send a present for her, and by the way, thank you for sending me the toiletry bag, which stayed behind in Warsaw – like everything else.

I give you a warm kiss and once again beg you to keep your spirits up. Do not lose hope – just as I am not losing hope – that we'll see each other again, and then we'll tell each other everything.

Your loving

7 Illegible word.

8 This refers to Lithuania's neutrality at that stage of the war. The transfer of Vilna to Lithuania was anticipated in the secret protocol to the Ribbentrop-Molotov pact of August 1939 and confirmed in October 1939.

DOC. 23

On 16 October 1939 the German legation in Bucharest reports on the situation in Soviet-occupied Eastern Galicia[1]

Report by the German legation in Bucharest, signed Fabricius,[2] copy Pol V 9841, log no. 5758/59 – I A 37, to Wehrmacht High Command, Foreign/Counter-Intelligence, Reich Ministry of Public Enlightenment and Propaganda, Reichsführer-SS, and Ethnic German Liaison Office, dated 16 October 1939 (copy)[3]

Re: mood of the Ukrainians in Eastern Galicia, communist terror
According to reliable reports that the legation and the Czernowitz consulate have received from the territories of Eastern Galicia occupied by the Russian army, the initially enthusiastic mood of the Ukrainians, who welcomed the Russian army with joyful celebrations in many places, has given way to a dejected and despairing mood. Their enthusiasm about the arrival of the Russians can be explained if we think of the bloody violence perpetrated by the Poles shortly before the collapse and the oppressive policies they pursued over the last few years. The Russian troops were immediately followed by the Russian administration with its police units. The Russian administration apparently thinks its main task is to annihilate the country's already small politically mature elite. At any rate, it seems that most of the better-known leaders have been killed or deported to Siberia. In the majority of cases, shady characters have been put in charge of local administration, many of them Jews. Big businesses and large estates have already been nationalized. Smaller enterprises have been left in the hands of their current owners and managers for the time being, because the new administration is overstretched. Attempts to join the Communist Party, also those undertaken by poorer elements, have failed; the Party leadership only admitted people who had openly professed their support for the communist idea in the past. Jews make up the largest percentage of this group. The Lemberg radio station, which disseminates pure communist ideas, is said to be exclusively in the hands of Jews. At present, the radio station primarily broadcasts propaganda for the forthcoming list elections, in which Jews, alongside politically unknown Ukrainians, will be elected, but certainly not a single one of the previous leaders.[4]

1 TsDAVOV, Central State Archive of the Highest Organs of Government and Administration of Ukraine, Kyiv, R/3676/4/133. This document has been translated from German.
2 Dr Wilhelm Fabricius (1882–1964), lawyer and diplomat; served in the German Foreign Service from 1910; posted to Cairo, Constantinople, Thessaloniki, and Zurich; envoy to Bucharest, 1936–1941; thereafter forced into partial retirement and given a temporary post in the Trade Policy Department of the Reich Foreign Office.
3 The original contains handwritten notes and underlining.
4 On 22 Oct. 1939 manipulated elections for the western Byelorussian and western Ukrainian national assemblies were held in Soviet-occupied territory. Jews were under-represented among the candidates relative to their proportion, while Byelorussians and Ukrainians were over-represented.

People in Ukraine do not expect to see any change in this state of affairs as long as Kaganovich's[5] influence over Stalin – and therefore the Soviet Russian state leadership – continues. This is because Jewry, as the sworn enemy of a nationally conscious Ukrainian culture, has the leadership under their control through Kaganovich. In this respect, it is important to know that the bulk of the Ukrainian peasantry in Eastern Galicia are still inclined to listen to a Jew as their leader, because they have become accustomed to this state of affairs over centuries. Even previously, the number of educated Ukrainians in Eastern Galicia was too small for them to play any decisive role in shaping their nation's life. At least now the farmers increasingly seem to realize that the Jew is the real enemy of a happier future for the Ukrainian people and that, like every other nation, they will ultimately only be able to achieve freedom through their own efforts.

The Ukrainian nation's hope is that the last Jews will disappear from the Kremlin over the course of the Russian-German cooperation, and Jewish supremacy in Ukraine will collapse as a consequence. The more politically flexible and more energetic Ukrainians hope they can deal with Greater Russia ideology alone, whether in a federal state under Russia or in a future independent Ukraine.

DOC. 24

On 18 October 1939 the commander-in-chief of Border Force Section Commando Centre bans Jews from dealing in textiles and leather[1]

Regulation issued by the commander-in-chief of Border Force Section Commando Centre, unsigned, dated 18 October 1939 (poster)

Regulation against Jewish Hoarders of Textiles and Leather, 18 October 1939
Substantial abuses in the sale of textiles of all kinds (raw materials, semi-finished products, finished goods) as well as leather and leather goods cause me to decree as follows, with immediate effect, for the administrative district of the chief of administration in the Lodz Militärbezirk[2] – with the exclusion of the territory east of the Vistula:

§ 1

1. *Jews are prohibited from dealing in textiles* of all kinds (raw materials, semi-finished products, finished goods), leather, and leather goods.

5 Lazar Moiseyevich Kaganovich, born Kogan (1893–1991), politician; held leading positions in the Communist Party of the Soviet Union (CPSU) Central Committee, 1922–1925 and 1928–1930; secretary general of the Ukrainian Communist Party, 1925–1928; head of the Moscow Party Organization, 1930–1935; member of the CPSU Politburo, 1930–1957; member of the State Defence Committee, 1942–1945; first secretary of the Ukrainian Party Organization, 1946–1947.

1 AIPN, GK 196/309 (NTN 309), fol. 10. Poster in German and Polish. This document has been translated from German.

2 On 13 Oct. 1939 the Chief of the Lodz Civil Administration had issued the 'Regulation on the Registration of Textile Raw Materials' and appointed a trustee to take charge of this: Karol Marian Pospieszalski (ed.), *Documenta Occupationis*, vol. 5: *Hitlerowskie 'prawo' okupacyjne w Polsce: Wybór dokumentów*, part 1: *Ziemie 'wcielone'* (Poznań: Wydawnictwo Instytutu Zachodniego, 1952), pp. 67–68.

2. Textile factories in Jewish hands may *only deliver to non-Jewish customers*. Retail textile shops owned by such textile factories may only sell goods to non-Jewish customers.
3. This trade prohibition also applies to non-Jews who conclude transactions on behalf of Jews, or for accounts belonging to Jews, or as fronts for Jews. This excludes persons who are acting on behalf of the chief of administration in the Lodz Militärbezirk or an office designated by him.

§ 2

The provision of *leather* to Jewish cobblers is permissible if they require the leather for purposes of repair (resoling etc.). The *manufacture of footwear and leather goods by Jewish cobblers is prohibited.*

§ 3

All Jewish shops selling textiles and leather must take an inventory immediately and submit it within one week. In the cities of Lodz and Warsaw, it must be submitted to the chief of police, and elsewhere to the Landrat or Stadtkommissar in charge.

§ 4

1. Jews are prohibited from purchasing textile goods and leather goods, as well as leather of any sort.
2. Exceptions are permissible for the purpose of meeting the most urgent personal needs. The details of putting this into effect are governed by the implementing regulation.

§ 5

Trade in textile waste and rags does not fall within the scope of this regulation.

§ 6

The chief of administration is authorized to issue the detailed implementing regulations.[3]

§ 7

Any breach of this regulation – including incorrect or incomplete information provided in fulfilment of § 3 – will be punishable by an unlimited punitive fine, imprisonment, or both, and in particularly serious cases by the death penalty.

3 In his implementing regulations of 18 Oct. 1939, the chief of administration in the Lodz Militärbezirk ordered that the sale of textiles and leather goods by German employees in non-Jewish shops was to remain unaffected by the ban in § 1 of the regulation for the time being; he further ordered that the inventory to be taken in accordance with § 3 had to contain a precise description of the goods, the quantity, the purchase price, and the retail price, and also had to include a legally binding signature: AIPN, GK 196/309 (NTN 309), fol. 10.

DOC. 25

In late October 1939 the Reich Commissioner for the Strengthening of Germandom formulates his primary goals[1]

Directive issued by the Reich Commissioner for the Strengthening of Germandom,[2] signed SS-Obersturmbannführer Creutz,[3] undated, issued after 19 October 1939 (copy)

General directives and guidelines issued by the Reich Commissioner for the Strengthening of Germandom

I. The first phase of our work has to be concerned with the following issues:

1. Expelling approximately 550,000 Jews, as well as the leading anti-German Poles and the Polish intelligentsia, across the border of the German Reich into the Polish General Government, starting with Danzig and Posen. The Jews must be taken to the territory east of the Vistula, between the Vistula and the Bug.
2. Confiscating the land owned by the former Polish state, the expelled Polish intelligentsia, and all the Poles shot or expelled due to hostile activities. This land will be confiscated on the basis of the Decree of the Führer and Reich Chancellor on the Strengthening of Germandom of 7 October 1939, section 5,[4] in consultation with the Main Trustee Office East, which was established on the basis of a decree by Field Marshal Göring on 19 October 1939.[5] This property must be transferred to the German Reich and placed at the disposal of the Reich Commissioner for the Strengthening of Germandom.
3. Carrying out a census in the newly acquired territories on a particular date, sometime in December.
4. Planning for rural and urban settlements, to be completed by the spring.
5. Registering restitution claims made by Germans driven out of Posen and West Prussia, and examining those claims.
6. Provisionally housing the ethnic Germans who will be coming in from the Baltic countries and Volhynia[6] within a few weeks.

II. In due time, the planned and systematic settlement of urban and rural areas, which will take many years, perhaps decades.

1 BArch, R 49/4, fol. 43. This document has been translated from German.

2 Reichsführer-SS Heinrich Himmler acted as Reich Commissioner after Hitler put him in charge of 'Strengthening Germandom' in a decree dated 7 Oct. 1939. The decree aimed to implement the programme for transforming the ethnic population make-up in the 'German sphere of interest' that Hitler had outlined in the Reichstag the previous day.

3 Rudolf Creutz (1896–1970), sales clerk; joined the NSDAP and the SS in 1933; worked full-time for the SS from 1934; deputy head of the Staff Main Office of the Reich Commissioner for the Strengthening of Germandom from 1939; leading official in the Resettlement/Volkstum section and the Labour Deployment section; sentenced to 15 years in prison in 1948, and released in 1955.

4 Decree on the Strengthening of Germandom, *Reichsgesetzblatt* I, 1939, p. 467. This decree authorized the expropriation of plots of land so that Germans who had been living outside Germany could settle; a provision was made for the expropriated parties to receive financial compensation.

5 Göring's Decree on the Main Trustee Office East of 19 Oct. 1939 was published on 1 Nov. 1939: *Deutscher Reichsanzeiger*, 1939, no. 260. On the Main Trustee Office East, see the Introduction, p. 46.

6 Tens of thousands of descendants of German settlers and colonists were living both in the Baltic states and in Volhynia. In the Baltic states they mainly lived in urban areas, while in Volhynia they tended to be farmers; they were all relocated from Latvia, Estonia, and the Soviet-occupied part of Poland in 1939 and 1940, and most of them were resettled in the annexed western Polish territories. See Doc. 34.

DOC. 26

On 23 October 1939 the Chief of the Security Police and the SD requests information on the number of Jews in Polish towns with populations over 20,000[1]

Express letter from the Chief of the Security Police and the SD (IV/II 0–134/39, entry book no. 459/39), signed Deumling,[2] to Einsatzgruppe I in Cracow, Einsatzgruppe II/III in Lodz, Einsatzgruppe IV in Warsaw, Einsatzgruppe VI in Posen, Gestapo Office in Kattowitz, and Einsatzkommando 16 in Danzig, dated 23 October 1939[3]

Re: Jewish population
I request a prompt report on how many Jews there are in the individual towns with populations of more than 20,000 under your jurisdiction; if possible, the number of Germans should also be given. Furthermore, it must be reported in which towns Jewish councils of elders have been appointed.

DOC. 27

On 26 October 1939 the Governor General for the Occupied Polish Territories orders the introduction of forced labour for the Jewish population[1]

Regulation on the Introduction of Forced Labour for the Jewish Population in the General Government dated 26 October 1939

On the basis of § 5(1) of the decree of the Führer and Reich Chancellor on the administration of the occupied Polish territories of 12 October 1939,[2] I hereby order that:
§ 1
Forced labour shall be introduced with immediate effect for Jews resident in the General Government. For this purpose, Jews will be assembled into forced-labour detachments.[3]
§ 2
The requisite provisions for the implementation of this regulation shall be issued by the Higher SS and Police Leader. He can designate territories east of the Vistula in which this regulation shall not be implemented.[4]

1 AIPN, GK 68/104, fol. 3. This document has been translated from German.
2 Dr Joachim Deumling (1910–2007), lawyer; joined the NSDAP in 1933 and the SS in 1938; employed by Hanover State Police Office in 1936; deputy head of Oppeln State Police Office in 1937; at Reich Security Main Office (RSHA), Section IV (II O) in 1939; promoted to Oberregierungsrat in Section IV D 2 with responsibility for the General Government in July 1941; appointed head of an Einsatzkommando in Croatia in 1943; after the war, lived in West Germany under an assumed name; fled to Egypt in 1954; company lawyer in Brackwede after 1956.
3 The original contains a Gestapo stamp.

1 *VOBl-GG*, no. 1, 26 Oct. 1939, pp. 6–7. This document has been translated from German.
2 On 12 Oct. 1939 Hitler gave the territories of German-occupied central and southern Poland the designation 'General Government of the Occupied Polish Territories'. He appointed Hans Frank as Governor General: *Reichsgesetzblatt* I, 1939, p. 2077.
3 See Doc. 58.
4 This provision was part of the plan to establish a 'reservation' to the east of Cracow in which the Jewish population from other parts of German-occupied Poland was to be concentrated.

DOC. 28

On 28 October 1939 a special court sentences Chascill Trojanowski to one year of penal servitude for illegal trading in textiles[1]

Letter from the prosecuting counsel of the Special Court of Upper Silesia Military Area, CdZ, S 107/39, signed by order by the head of the court registry, Marek, to the Chief of the Civil Administration in Kattowitz, dated 28 October 1939 (copy)[2]

A copy of the verdict delivered on 11 October 1939 in the criminal case against *Trojanowski* is forwarded for your information.

In the name of the German people:

In the criminal case against the Jew Chascill *Trojanowski* of 52 Malachowskiego, Bendzin, born 20 August 1914 in Lowicz, single, for infringement of the Regulation of the Chief of the Civil Administration, Border Force Section Commando 3, of 13 September 1939, the Special Court of Border Force Section Commando 3 – Chief of the Civil Administration – in Kattowitz, during its session on 11 October 1939, attended by:

Landgerichtsdirektor *Seehafer*[3] as presiding judge,

Landgerichtsrat *Herrman*,

Landgerichtsrat *Roederer*[4] as associate judges,

Public Prosecutor *Zippel*[5] as the official representing the Public Prosecution Office,

Officer of the Court Marek as registry clerk,

delivered the following decision:

The accused is sentenced to one year of penal servitude and must bear the costs of these proceedings concerned with the infringement of the Regulation of the Chief of the Civil Administration of Border Force Section Commando 3 of 13 September 1939.

Grounds

On 26 September 1939 the Jew *Chascill Trojanowski* offered men's and children's socks for sale in the streets of Bendzin without collecting ration coupons. Following his arrest, he admitted at the police station that he had already sold several pairs of socks. He claims to have acted out of hardship, intending to buy himself bread and potatoes. Since the socks came from his previous year's stock, he claims to have believed he was allowed to sell them. His statement that he had not known he was not allowed to sell them is implausible, because the relevant Regulation of the Chief of the Civil Administration in Kattowitz of 13 September 1939 concerning the Introduction of Ration Coupons for Tex-

1 GStAPK, XVII. HA Ost 4, Reg Kattowitz/6. This document has been translated from German.
2 The letter contains handwritten initials.
3 Probably Dr Hugo Paul Seehafer, lawyer; obtained a PhD from Breslau University in 1926. Landgerichtsdirektor is a rank equivalent to director of a regional court.
4 Probably Dr Heinz Roederer, lawyer; obtained a PhD in criminal law from Breslau University in 1923. Landgerichtsrat is a judicial rank within a regional court.
5 Probably Dr Georg Zippel (b. 1895), lawyer; joined the NSDAP in 1933; Landgerichtsdirektor (rank equivalent to director of a regional court) at the Special Court in Lublin in 1940, then a deputy judge at the People's Court in Berlin; appointed judge (Kammergerichtsrat) in the 3rd Senate of the People's Court in 1943; worked as a lawyer in Bonn after the war; became chairman of the Association of Displaced Civil Servants in the German Civil Service Federation in 1964.

tiles and Footwear[6] came into force on 17 September 1939 according to § 5 of this Regulation and, as everywhere in the territory occupied by Border Force Section Commando 3, had previously been made public on posters, including in Bendzin. It is clearly evident without further explanation that Bendzin's Jewish population is especially interested in regulations concerning trade and/or the impermissibility of trade under certain conditions. The accused was subject to punishment under § 1(1) of the aforementioned regulation pursuant to § 3 of the regulation.

This case cannot count as a minor infringement because, with truly Jewish insolence, the accused has disregarded the provisions of a regulation promulgated for the general welfare of the people. Consequently, it was essential as a matter of principle to impose a penalty of penal servitude as originally threatened in order to heighten awareness of the German regulations. Since this was the defendant's first offence of this nature and he may also not have been in a favourable situation economically, the statutory minimum punishment of one year of penal servitude appeared sufficient.

The decision with respect to costs is based on § 465 of the Code of Criminal Procedure.

DOC. 29

On 29 October 1939 the Kreishauptmann in Konsk (Końskie) reports on the first weeks of the German occupation[1]

Situation report by the acting Landrat [Kreishauptmann] in Konsk[2] to the Governor of District Radom, dated 29 October 1939[3]

Situation report no. 7[4]

I. Food situation

The bread supply in the town of Konsk and the iron industry areas to the east of the town has now collapsed. Most of the population has not received any bread for five days. I have allocated 200 grams per person per day to the remaining residents. It goes without saying that I have only issued flour to Polish bakers, not to Jewish bakers. As for the crisis in the iron industry towns in the eastern part of the Kreis, please allow me to refer you to the report by the local commandant in Staporkow.[5]

In response to the fuss they have been making, I have ordered the Jewish special administration to inform the Jews that their hunger is a consequence of the war that the Jews around the world started. I told them the English Jews in particular had not been

6 On regulations prohibiting Jews from dealing in textiles and leather, see also Doc. 24.

1 BArch, R 102/III/2, fols. 1–13 (147–159). This document has been translated from German.
2 The Kreis came under the authority of Dr Heinz Gustav Albrecht (1902–1980), lawyer; joined the SA in 1933 and the NSDAP in 1937; Oberregierungsrat in Stade, then in Hildesheim, 1935–1937; Landrat in Konsk, Sept. 1939 – August 1941, then in Stanislau (Stanisławów) until Sept. 1944; served in the war from Feb. 1945; interned, 1945–1946; Oberregierungsrat and department head in the office of the Regierungspräsident in Hildesheim from 1949; headed the Hildesheim branch of the Lower Saxony expellee reparations office (Lastenausgleichsamt).
3 The original bears the stamp of the official authority in charge of Kreis Konsk.
4 Handwritten note on the left: 'Nine enclosures'. Only Enclosure 7, the situation report, is on file.
5 Polish spelling: Stąporkow. A small town located to the east of Końskie.

ashamed to cold-bloodedly allow several hundred thousand German women and children to perish of hunger during the 1914–1918 World War. The English wanted to do the same again in this war. However, this time the opposite is going to happen: we will make the Jews living under German rule feel the consequences of the English blockade first. We have enough bread for the Germans in Germany. Moreover, our economic treaties with Russia will also gradually have a beneficial effect on the misguided Poles. If people now start to go hungry in Kreis Konsk, I will ensure that the Jews starve first, before the Poles. The Jews are free to write a letter to Chamberlain in which they describe their difficulties truthfully and draw his attention to my measures, with the request to lift the English blockade of Germany. I will present this letter to my government with the request for it to be forwarded via the German Foreign Office. So far I have not received any such letter, nor have I become aware of any Jews dying of starvation. On the contrary, in spite of the flour shortage, sweet pastries were still available in the Jewish shops for 20–30 groszy. Since the Kreis hospital had been without flour and bread for its 80 patients for two days, I seized all the pastries, paid for at 10 groszy apiece, and allocated them to the hospital. Furthermore, I banned the baking of cakes and ordered the flour to be delivered to our purchasing and sales cooperative. Wheat flour is to be reserved for people with verified stomach complaints, particularly those in the Kreis hospital (cf. Enclosure 1).

Despite my report to Army Command on 15 October, the prisoner-of-war camp has still not been relocated and still receives its food supply from the Kreis. On the other hand, the military seems to have abandoned the plan to increase the number of prisoners there to over 2,000 and to expand the camp further. At least the regimental staff of the territorial troops, which had been moved here for that reason, has been posted elsewhere.

The local 1,600-strong construction battalion received the order yesterday to stay here for another four weeks.

In the coming days, 10,000 Poles are due to arrive from Pomerelia and West Prussia. Having made inquiries of the acting Wojts,[6] I have informed the Security Service that the Kreis is able to take in a maximum of 2,000.

I would like to express my thanks to you for allocating parts of the Kreis Grojec surplus to us to harvest. After many futile attempts, including at the vehicle pool in Opole, which eventually offered me a ten-year-old, 2.5-tonne Ford that, judging from the result of the test drive I was initially refused, would not have made it here, I finally succeeded through my Wojts in getting two lorries with carrying capacities of 1.5 tonnes and 4 tonnes, which had originally been based here, back from Kreis Kielce. The small truck has been deployed to coax corn out of farmers in the Kreis, paying them the guide price and delivering to them small quantities of sugar. The large truck travelled with a threshing detachment of 15 men to Kreis Grojec on the 26th of this month in order to thresh the corn ricks assigned by the Bezirk agriculture officer and bring the corn here. It returned for the first time on the 28th of the month with 2 tonnes of corn. This small amount was due to the poor weather and the inexperience of the threshing detachment sent by the employment office. The overseer has put together a better threshing detachment in Grojec and will continue

6 Correctly: 'wójtowie', plural of 'wójt', Polish term for a local administrative official.

threshing there. After its first journey, the lorry already had to go to the repair workshop I set up provisionally. The failure to comply with my request for operational resources to be increased by 15,000 Reichsmarks will presumably have disastrous effects, as it will not be possible to buy the lorry the representative of the Reich Trustee wanted to procure for me in Kattowitz for the iron ore mines here. *I now wish to request urgently that the new truck earmarked for me there be delivered to me immediately.*

According to the enclosed record card from the Association for the Study of Agricultural Law and Economics, Berlin, which was passed on to me by Regierungsrat Schmidt, [who is] Regierungspräsident Rüdiger's adjutant, for correction to reflect the current situation, Kreis Konsk *already had a shortfall necessitating additional deliveries of about 144,000 tonnes of bread cereals and about 290 tonnes of meat in the years 1931–1935 and 1938.* And that was in the middle of peacetime! Four armies have marched through the Kreis since: the retreating Polish army, the pursuing German army, the army ordered to the west, and the occupation army. Add to that the necessity to feed 2,000–8,000 prisoners of war and two construction battalions with 3,200 men. In the near future, 2,000–10,000 Poles from the western territories of the Reich are expected to arrive. If, as my regional agricultural officer informed me this morning, the allocation of goods from Kreis Grojec, which has a surplus, is now being wholly or partially discontinued due to the emergency in Warsaw, it will no longer be possible to prevent the outbreak of severe unrest in Kreis Konsk.

I am continuing to fight profiteering and the buying up of foodstuffs by traders from outside the Kreis with the 14 gendarmes I have left. I am also trying to involve the Wojts I have appointed on an acting basis and the Polish auxiliary police force that is being established. Please see Enclosures 2 and 3 for the details. Please support me by also ensuring that the other Landräte and mayors, and above all the military agencies, are obliged to adhere to the maximum prices set in Radom. Haphazard ventures into other Kreise and a just as haphazard pricing of goods above the upper limit will irresponsibly exacerbate privation in the days to come. In my opinion, we will only get through the winter without hunger riots and epidemics if coordinated action to even out conditions in the surplus and shortage areas is undertaken and implemented from above. I believe that if the food shortage forces us to do this, flour and bread rations will also have to be reduced to 200 grams per person per day in the surplus areas so that the shortage areas can receive this subsistence amount as well. If the prescribed prices are not adhered to, it will no longer be possible to curb wages either, and rising wages will in turn drive up prices further. Both in the interest of maintaining public security and order, and in the interest of German prestige, it is unacceptable, in my opinion, for a local commandant to issue passes to Jews in exchange for a 10-zloty administrative charge and to instruct them to buy up the last foodstuffs from neighbouring crisis areas in Kreis Konsk. This is what the local commander did in Szydlowiec, Kreis Radom, on the eastern border of my own Kreis. I enclose a copy of my letter to him (Enclosure 4). Please once again emphatically remind the local commandant and all other agencies to follow Daily Order 17 IV, 2.[7]

I am making efforts to increase production in the main industry in this Kreis, the iron industry, as rapidly as possible. In the process, I am also continuing the production

7 This could not be found.

of what are known as 'Russian items' (iron pots and cheap iron ovens that only last one winter) in order to potentially bring in Russian foodstuffs by exporting a large consignment [of these items] to Russia, with which there are convenient transport links. *I would be grateful if you could inform me of the agency in charge of such barter trading.*

Feeding the entire population of Konsk with six soup kitchens, which I announced in my last situation report, has proved to be impossible. Given the shortages of means of transport and financial resources, it was impossible to assemble the necessary quantities of food. In addition, the monotony of the food would provoke dissatisfaction and, when it comes to the use of supplies, the Polish staff would succumb to temptation, put aside some of the stock for themselves and their relatives, and sell some at inflated prices on the black market. Supervision is not possible due to the lack of personnel. In addition, all criticism of the food would be directed exclusively at the German administration. I have therefore only set up three soup kitchens: one at the railway station for the reception of refugees who are unfit to be transported, one for impoverished Poles, and a small one in a Jewish school for starving Jews. The kitchens are to be managed by the Poles and the Jews themselves as soon as the need for this becomes indisputable for security reasons.

II. Public security

The general security situation in the Kreis is illustrated by two incidents that happened yesterday and during the night. Yesterday, a German sentry from the territorial company at Staporkow, about 13 kilometres east of Konsk, was held up in broad daylight and ordered to show his identity papers by two Polish officers on horseback and two Polish soldiers, who were all heavily armed. The Poles then told him to leave immediately, because the Germans no longer have any business being in the country. It was probably only because the sentry was able to speak Polish that he got away with his life. I was given this account of the incident by Räder, the leader of the local construction battalion. I regard Räder as a sensible person. Furthermore, an exchange of fire with armed Poles took place during the night at Ruda Maleniecka, approximately 20 kilometres west of Konsk, while the moon was at its brightest, as I have also been informed by Räder, some of whose men are stationed at Ruda Maleniecka. The military authorities have taken up the pursuit of the culprits.

Since it is virtually impossible to find weapons buried in the extensive forests in the Kreis and I do not have even a minimal police force in the area any more since the withdrawal of 72 auxiliary police officers, it is certainly possible that the starving population could be armed by the scattered remnants who are still roaming the forests. Every mistake made by the administration, particularly in its efforts to provide the population with food, may lead to greater disruptions to public security within a short period. One such mistake is to withhold lorries. I find it irresponsible that the civil administration has not received any trucks with which to carry out its most important transports in the occupied territories, while military lorries have been standing in Neiße for nine weeks without their engines being turned on even once. I therefore urgently request that vigorous action be taken against such organizational mistakes. What is at stake is not the private security of individual Germans, but rather the preservation of the few German officials and soldiers in Poland as a fighting force in the hands of the Führer against opponents who have so far only been overcome militarily.

Furthermore, I would like to request once again that the strictest orders be issued to the military units in order to prevent the troops from irresponsibly encroaching on economic life. Time and again, individual acts of the following kind come to my attention: the grain left on the Falkow estate needs to be threshed, but this is not possible, as the Panzer troops have taken the two drive belts for the threshing machines with them.

I had the Governor General's announcement put up today in the Kreis seat while the churches were holding their services. The population read it eagerly. The so-called intelligentsia are said to have found the tone a bit harsh, but the most upright among them have indicated that the accusations against the former intelligentsia clique certainly hit the nail on the head. The Jews are puzzling over whether 'Jewish exploiters' refers to particular individuals who have already been identified by the German police, or whether it refers to the Jewish community as a whole.[8]

III. Trade and industry

After I successfully procured some of the most important tools in Oppeln, the three iron foundries in Konsk itself have resumed production under the overall management of the energetic Hauptmann Keller, the commander of the 4th Territorial Company (cf. the beginning of my 6th situation report).[9] One hundred and eighty men are back at work at the Aryan foundry Herzfeld & Victorius. Iron is being cast there again. One hundred and fifty men are back at work at the formerly Jewish Neptun foundry, which I placed under an Aryan trustee, and 40 men are still engaged in the clean-up work at the Kronenblum foundry, which has also been placed under an Aryan trustee and sustained the worst damage in the aerial attacks. It was possible to bring these businesses back into operation without taking out any loans by selling off their remaining warehouse stock. Salaries and wages have been paid in full for the period during which the workers have been working under German rule. Under Polish rule, unskilled workers' wages were three zloty a day. I initially had to retain these rates. However, the workers have not been able to get by on this due to the rising cost of living (agricultural prices raised by the authorities to support farming) and have grown embittered on account of the high wages of the Polish railway workers who are working nearby. I have therefore conceded a wage increase of 10 per cent and have promised to establish a factory canteen with cheap food for the workers. I have written the enclosed letter to the Kamienna Reich Railway operations office, which is responsible for this matter, calling for cuts to the track workers' wages, which are too high in relative terms (Enclosure 6).

As there is already talk of the territorial battalion being withdrawn, I repeat the request made in my 5th situation report, at the top of page 7, for a technically and commercially trained German expert to be sent to me, possibly from the Kattowitz Friedenshütte ironworks. In addition to the enormous amount of administrative work we have, it is impossible for me and my staff to exercise the necessary oversight of the Polish trustees

8 In his announcement of 26 Oct. 1939 on the occasion of the 'establishment of the General Government', Governor General Frank addressed 'Polish men and women!' and promised that, 'Under just rule, everyone will earn their bread with labour. By contrast, there will no longer be any room for political agitators, racketeers, and Jewish exploiters in a territory that finds itself under German authority': *VOBl-GG* 1939, no. 1, 26 Oct. 1939, pp. 1–2.

9 This is not on file.

I have appointed. But given the Poles' dubious moral concepts and the major assets located at the iron foundries, the enterprises must be monitored daily to prevent large-scale swindling and dishonest dealing.

The iron mines at Staporkow, Nieklan, and Chlewiska have resumed operations again under the overall supervision of the Swedish engineer Absolon,[10] appointed by Reich Trustee Wagner[11] in Breslau. In the absence of another expert, I have entrusted him with the overall supervision of the smaller ironmaking businesses. Since he has Polish nationality and is in charge of all the ironmaking enterprises in the eastern part of the Kreis, expert oversight by a Reich German would be necessary here as well.

III.[12] *Kreis savings bank*

I reopened the Kreis savings bank on 16 October. I have appointed Sergeant Major Schneider from the 4th Territorial Company, a bank manager in Birkenfeld in civilian life, as its acting manager. The Polish manager and the Polish staff have resumed work under his leadership. Developments over the first two weeks warrant a certain degree of hope.

1) Non-interest-bearing overnight deposits paid in by the three iron foundries (revenues from the sale of manufactured goods): 52,124 zloty.

These deposits are mostly required for procuring the tools completely lost in the war.

2) 34 Jewish savings accounts: 13,500 zloty.

3) commercial bills collected: 3,700 zloty.

4) interest collected on commercial bills: 250 zloty.

Liabilities:

Among the liabilities, the 182,000 deposit account balances of small savers, most of whom are in need, should be mentioned. I intend to make repayments of approximately 40 zloty a week to the small savers as soon as the bank bill loans collected have reached the sum of 10,000 zloty.

I have set up paying-in offices for the Kreis savings bank at the 16 local authority offices in the Kreis and ordered the Wojts to settle their accounts with the main branch in Konsk on the 15th and 1st of each month.

IV. The Jewish question

In order to prevent my administration from being harassed by Jews, I have established a Jewish special administration and forbidden all Jews to visit the Landrat's office, the town hall, and the other authorities. I enclose a copy of my announcement (Enclosure 7). The special administration is functioning after a fashion. It has punctually met the following requirements: 250 Jews to be supplied every day for labour service under the supervision of the construction battalion, lists to be drafted for the SS, and various lesser

10 Bruno(n) Absolon (1892–1940), mining engineer; attended the German secondary school in Teschen (Česky Těšin) until 1912; served in the Austro-Hungarian army; manager of various ironworks after 1918; appointed by the occupation authorities as head of the 'Pokój' group in 1939; detained by the Gestapo in 1940 for cooperating with the Polish resistance (Union of Armed Struggle, ZWZ) and shot dead in a summary execution.

11 It is not clear who is being referred to. The Reich Trustee of Labour in Breslau was Walter Schuhmann. Josef Wagner was Gauleiter in Silesia.

12 Numbering as in the original.

tasks. However, the chairman Rozen has been temporarily overwhelmed by the avalanche of petitions from his fellow Jews. His deputy has asked me to place a detention cell at his disposal for recalcitrant Jews, particularly the work-shy. As two cells have remained in good order at the burned-out starosta building, I have allocated them to him.

V. Administrative structure

1. Konsk town

I have appointed Dünnebeil,[13] the town clerk transferred from Stadtilm for the post of town commissioner, as acting mayor of the Kreis seat because the acting Polish mayor I had initially appointed was not up to the job due to his age. I have made him honorary town elder. Dünnebeil thinks he would be able to cope better with the work if the mayor in Stadtilm (Thuringia) were to assign Reinhard Riemer, an administrator with whom he has worked well before, to him to run his office. He is making successful efforts to bring order to the conditions in the town, in line with German expectations. I will submit a special report on Riemer's transfer to the Reich Minister of the Interior.

2. State administration at Kreis level

It is impossible for me to perform further administrative tasks, such as running the school administration, administrative police, and similar tasks, and the Aryanization in particular, with the German administrative personnel that have been allocated to me: one senior clerical officer, one higher clerical officer, one interpreter, and one clerk, although they are all doing as much as they can. I therefore urgently request that, like other Landräte, I also have another state clerical officer assigned to me. I believe the size and difficulty of the Kreis justify this request. At the same time, however, I request that the operating funds I receive as a Landrat are topped up, because otherwise I will not be able to pay their salaries.

3. Communal administration within the Kreis

So far I have only provisionally appointed a Kreis delegate – the retired Polish justice of the peace von Koraszewski, who has been released from his duties as alderman of the town administration – and the Kreis highways department of the municipal administration. It appears urgently necessary to appoint a municipal treasurer and a welfare officer. I have informed the other former officials of the communal administration within the Kreis that I will only be able to give them jobs again, at 50 per cent of their previous salaries, if there are particularly urgent administrative tasks to be done and tax revenues are available to pay for them. I have urged them to look at the Jewish shops in the Kreis seat as discreetly as possible to see which of them they would wish to run in the future as Aryan trustees. I hope to be able to keep their heads above water in this way and to obtain the Aryans we are missing for the large number of Jewish shops. I intend to entrust the Aryanization itself to the clerk of the administrative detachment, Schneider, who is a clerk in the loans department of Deutsche Bank in Berlin, and to use him exclusively for drafting confidential reports in the service of the Landrat's office.

After initially detaining them, I have released the Poles who were responsible for the administration of the Kreis finances, on the condition that they report twice a day to the gendarmerie, and I will try to bring back what remains of the assets of the Kreis as soon

13 Hugo Dünnebeil (b. 1900).

as my concern for the food situation and the work of bringing in foodstuffs allows me some freedom of action.

In emergency cases, I have been making small support payments from my own private funds. Since these are not adequate, I request that, if possible, a loan of several thousand zloty be placed at my disposal, in anticipation of the revenues from Kreis taxes levied at communal level, in order to fund the Kreis welfare office and the most essential officials' salaries. The Kreis savings bank's funds have been completely exhausted as a result of granting short-term loans to the 'Kreis provisioning office' for the purchase of sugar, salt, petroleum, window glass, and leather. [...][14]

DOC. 30

The Jewish activist Ber Fisz describes the situation in Gdynia from September 1939 until the expulsion of the Jewish population in October 1939[1]

Report by Ber Fisz[2] for the underground archive of the Warsaw ghetto, written after October 1939

Gdynia

The Jewish population of Gdynia numbered 3,500 souls in 1937/1938. When war broke out, it numbered only approximately 2,000, because, in an effort to de-Jewify Gdynia, the Polish authorities expelled them en masse from May 1938 onwards on the basis of the law on the protection of border areas.[3]

Most of these 2,000 Jews, predominantly women with children, left Gdynia one week before war broke out and moved farther inland. Several hundred people left at the very last moment, so that at the start of hostilities there were only 700–800 Jews in the city, who were joined by another 200 from outlying areas, i.e. from Wejherowo, Puck, and Kartuzy. The latter had been evacuated from towns as the Germans approached.

Nearly all the wealthier Jews, i.e. company owners, managers, and senior employees of major firms, left Gdynia and only the proletariat (blue- and white-collar workers and craftsmen) remained.

The latter were left practically without any livelihoods, so they needed to be taken care of. It was very difficult, because there was no one from whom to raise the necessary funds, especially because the Polish authorities had requisitioned virtually all the food warehouses whose owners had left.

However, the three remaining members of the Jewish Community administration, chaired by the present author, formed an aid committee, collected a considerable quan-

14 In sections VI to XI, Albrecht reported on tax revenues, mayors' assemblies, the state forestry administration, the notary's office, the appointment of the Kreis veterinary officer, and the Kreis chimney sweep.

1 AŻIH, Ring I/740 (16). This document has been translated from Polish.

2 Ber Fisz, also Bernard Fisch (1885–1941), merchant; member of the Poale Zion party; in Gdynia from 1932; director of the Colonial trading company; founder of a Jewish fishery cooperative, 1935; chairman of the Zionist Union in Gdynia, 1938; in Warsaw from Oct. 1939; in the Warsaw ghetto deputy chairman of the Central Refugee Committee and employee of the American Jewish Joint Distribution Committee (JDC); thought to have died in Rzeszów in 1941.

3 In Sept. 1938 the Polish Republic began resettling Jews away from territories close to the border.

tity of various foodstuffs such as rice, flour, coffee, tea, cocoa, herring, etc., from the firms Łuszczarnia Ryżu,[4] Józef Fetter SA., Colonial GmbH (Fish), Nordia-Have (Krakowski and Klein), J. Bankier, and others, and gradually distributed them to all those in need.

This state of affairs lasted until 14 September, i.e. until the Germans marched in. At 5 a.m. that day, the Germans took over the city and seized power. At 7 a.m. patrols went through the streets and ordered all men out of their homes. They were led to the big square in front of the administration headquarters. There, German nationals were inspected and the so-called Volksdeutsche[5] were released on the spot. The infirm and the sick, as well as youngsters below the age of 15 and the elderly over the age of 60, were also told to go home. All the rest were detained and taken to various assembly points such as churches, schools, cinemas, barracks, parks, etc., where their personal data was checked to see if they appear on a blacklist (printed book)[6] of Polish national activists and members of various patriotic organizations, etc. Afterwards, they were gradually released, several thousand each day, or were sent to prison. This lasted six days.

Anyone who was unfortunate enough to be called to the desk for verification by that time (Jews were usually not called) was detained. Several thousand such people were detained (including approximately 150 Jews) and sent to a camp in Gdańsk, from where they were sent to various places of forced labour (agricultural work, road work, etc.). Not a single Jew returned from there and they disappeared without a trace. In such cases, when relatives turn to the Red Cross for information, they usually receive the standard reply that the camp inmate in question has died.

Although it was unpleasant to stay in churches, cinemas, etc. because one sat there for entire days and nights in filthy, stuffy, smelly rooms, there was no particular bullying, with the exception of sporadic cases of maltreatment. There was one case where a boy, a halutz[7] from the 'Gordonia' kibbutz, was shot dead for no reason or for no apparent reason or by accident. They did not give us food, but the Polish Red Cross distributed 1.5 kg of bread with butter and one egg to everyone. In addition, relatives were allowed to bring food and tea.

Anti-Jewish regulations were introduced on the very day the Germans marched in, namely: 1) Jewish businesses are to remain closed, 2) Jews are not to be paid sums of more than 400 złoty (they are to be deposited into blocked bank accounts instead), 3) Jews may not have more than 2,000 złoty in total, 4) Jews must submit lists of assets, 5) Jews aged 15–50 must report daily to the local German police headquarters, 6) associations and institutions must submit lists of assets, etc.[8]

The premises of the Jewish Community and house of prayer were sealed only after they had been ransacked and the Torah scrolls destroyed.

The Jews remained in Gdynia until the entire Polish population had been resettled, i.e. until 17 October 1939. Throughout this period the Jews hardly ventured onto the streets for fear of being attacked or rounded up for forced labour, such as for repairs of

4 English: rice mill.

5 German in the original: 'ethnic Germans'.

6 On the Special Wanted Arrest List for Poland (*Sonderfahndungsbuch Polen*) compiled by the Security Police, see Doc. 2, fn. 8, and Introduction, p. 30.

7 Hebrew: 'pioneer'.

8 See Doc. 4.

the main road in Orłowo,[9] where they were mistreated. Even 70-year-olds, if caught, had to go and perform hard labour. When roundups on streets became less successful, people who had to register daily with the authorities were ordered to report for forced labour the following day.

Official and unofficial searches of homes were performed and thefts occurred. It must be said that when robberies were reported to the police, the latter tried to find the perpetrators, punish them, and make them pay for the losses, if possible.

Only one week before the resettlement, the chief of police summoned the vice chairman of the Jewish Community and ordered him to present a list of all the Jews in Gdynia and to appoint, pending approval, a Council of Elders consisting of twelve respected citizens, which he did.

Meanwhile it became known that a general resettlement would soon take place. At the same time, individual permits to travel farther inland began to be issued.[10]

From then on, thousands of people (Poles and Jews) queued in front of the police headquarters from 5 a.m. to 6 p.m. in order to obtain a permit for departure. They were allowed to take only 50 kg of hand luggage and cash in an amount determined by the Devisenschutzkommando.[11]

Many Jews left this way, including the present author, having previously obtained a special permit. The rest left on a transport several days later, in goods wagons, eighty people per wagon, taking a roundabout route via Berlin [and] Wrocław to Częstochowa and Kielce, during which they were en route for eight days without food or fresh air.

Temporary administrators kept on several Jews as experts in certain businesses for another few weeks.

DOC. 31

On 2 November 1939 Goebbels writes about his trip to conquered Poland[1]

Diary of Joseph Goebbels, entry for 2 November 1939

2 November 1939 (Thursday)
Tuesday: Left by aeroplane in the morning. Arrived in Lodz around 1[1] o'clock. Got loads done on the flight. Our Jerry letter has made a big splash.[2]

Lodz: Seyss-Inquart[3] picks me up and gives me a short report. A thousand questions and problems. Lodz itself is a hideous city.

9 Adlershorst, village near Gdynia, now incorporated as part of the city.

10 On 8 Oct. 1939 the German Reich annexed the Polish coastal area and its hinterlands as part of the 'incorporated territories'. Anyone who wished to travel from Gdynia across the new border into the rest of the territory occupied by Germany now required official permission.

11 German in the original: 'Foreign Exchange Protection Commando'. According to § 4 of the directive of the Chief of the Civil Administration attached to the 14th Army Command, War Economy Department, dated 18 Sept. 1939, the export of more than 10 Reichsmarks in 'domestic or foreign currency […] from the occupied territory' was prohibited: APKr, 33, SMKr/62.

1 Diaries of Joseph Goebbels, from 9 Sept. 1939 to 15 May 1940; RGVA, literary estate of Goebbels, fond 1477. Published in *Die Tagebücher von Joseph Goebbels*, part 1: *Aufzeichnungen 1923–1941*, vol. 7: *Juli 1939 – März 1940*, ed. Elke Fröhlich (Munich: Saur, 1998), pp. 177–179. This document has been translated from German.

Discussion with Frank. The situation in Poland is still very difficult. We agree: Polish cultural life is not to be encouraged for the time being, because cultural life functions as an alternate venue for renascent Polish nationalism. But we do want to promote German cultural life for our people. I will allocate all available funds for this purpose.

Drive through the ghetto. We get out and look at everything in detail. It is indescribable. These are no longer human beings, these are animals. Ours is therefore not a humanitarian task, but rather a surgical one. One must make incisions here, and quite radical ones at that. Otherwise Europe will perish from the Jewish disease.

Drive over Polish roads. This is already Asia. We will have a lot to do in order to Germanize this territory.

Long discussion with my staff. We establish which paths need to be taken now. Radical action against the Poles and strongest protection of Germanhood.

Evening at Frank's. He describes his difficulties to me, above all with the Wehrmacht, whose policy is not völkisch,[4] but rather diluted and bourgeois. But Frank will prevail.

Palavered a long time after that. Touched on a thousand problems. One never comes to the end here. The country is oppressively bleak.

I sleep for only a couple of hours.

Wednesday: Molotov has spoken.[5] Very strongly in our favour. Harshly against Roosevelt, warning given to Finland and to Turkey. We can be satisfied with this speech. But it did not change the situation at all.

Drive to Warsaw. Through the battlefields, past villages and towns that have been completely shot to pieces. A scene of devastation.

Warsaw: This is hell. A demolished city. Our bombs and shells have done a thorough job. No building is undamaged. The population is lethargic and gloomy. People creep through the streets like insects. It is repellent and hard to describe.

At the Citadel. Everything here has been destroyed. Not a stone left standing. This is where Polish nationalism endured its most difficult years. We must wipe it out completely, or else it will rise up again one day.

In the Blank Palace,[6] a short midday break. I receive reports on the situation in the city, which is almost hopeless. The Polish people have their agitators to thank for that.

2 Presumably the bogus letter created by the German propaganda apparatus, supposedly written by a Czech Jew called 'Jaro' from the UK to a 'Dr Zdenek Thon, Prague 12'. It appeared in the German press on 31 Oct. 1939 (the version in the *Völkischer Beobachter*, North German edition, also included a photo of the bogus letter).

3 Arthur Seyss-Inquart (1892–1946), Austrian lawyer; in contact with the NSDAP from 1931; joined the NSDAP and the SS in 1938; appointed minister of the interior in Austria in Feb. 1938 under pressure from Hitler; briefly served as chancellor of Austria and Reichsstatthalter after the Anschluss in March 1938; deputy to Governor General Frank in Poland, Oct. 1939 – May 1940, then Reich commissioner in the Netherlands; sentenced to death at the Nuremberg Trials and executed in 1946.

4 Roughly: ethno-nationalist; term centred around a racial ideology and a key element of National Socialism.

5 Vyacheslav Mikhaylovich Molotov, born Skryabin (1890–1986), politician; member of the Central Committee from 1921 and the CPSU Politburo from 1926; premier of the USSR, 1930–1941; Soviet foreign minister, 1939–1949 and 1953–1956. On 31 Oct. 1939 Molotov gave a foreign policy speech at the Fifth Extraordinary Session of the Supreme Soviet of the USSR, in which he extolled the non-aggression pact with Germany and harshly criticized the Western powers.

6 On the Blank Palace, see Doc. 98, fn. 3.

Visit to the Belvedere Palace. Here Poland's Marshal lived and worked.[7] His death chamber and the bed in which he died. Possible to learn here what one is in for when the Polish intelligentsia is given the scope to develop freely.

But otherwise this visit to the palace turned out to be utterly pointless.

Another drive through the city. A horrific place.

We are all glad when we are able to fly back. Departure from Warsaw at 2 o'clock and back in Berlin just as darkness falls.

Briefly told Magda[8] about my experiences. She is overjoyed that I am back. And the children are very happy too.

Then straight to work. A great deal has piled up in these two days.

Molotov's speech is the big topic. Finland is baulking and threatening to leave the table. But that will not help it. London is simply claiming this speech for itself, despite the harsh diatribes against England. But that is the typical British bluff. London, at this moment, is publishing a White Paper about our concentration camps which is causing a great stir.[9] We will respond with a White Paper about English colonial policy.[10] Never defend, always attack.

In Rome, a changing of the guard: Alfieri and Starace have resigned. They are replaced by Pavolini and Muti.[11] Otherwise a number of other changes as well. Is it merely a change of personnel, or also a change of course? That is the claim being made in England and France. But I can't believe it. Well, we'll see. I am sorry about Alfieri. He was so useful to us.

New newsreel completed. Turned out splendidly. The Führer also likes it very much. Then new rushes from our film about Jews,[12] which are also very effective. Also saw a UFA propaganda film about air-raid precautions. It takes a humorous approach and with great success at that. Looked at the screenplay for the Poland film[13] and made considerable edits and revisions. The work just goes on and on, and I take enormous delight in it.

In the evening I talked to Magda about Harald.[14] He is giving us some cause for concern.

7 Józef Piłsudski.

8 Goebbels's wife Magda (1901–1945), née Behrend, formerly married to Günther Quandt.

9 *Papers Concerning the Treatment of German Nationals in Germany, 1938–1939* (London: His Majesty's Stationery Office, 1939). See also PMJ 2/52.

10 This paper was never published.

11 Edoardo 'Dino' Alfieri (1886–1966), minister of popular culture, envoy to the Holy See in Nov. 1939 and ambassador to Berlin, 1940–1943; Achille Starace (1889–1945), party secretary of the National Fascist Party of Italy (PNF), then leader of the paramilitary militia MVSN; Alessandro Pavolini (1903–1945), president of the Confederation of Professionals and Artists, then minister of popular culture; Ettore Muti (1902–1943), militia officer, then PNF party secretary. Muti replaced Starace as secretary of the PNF in Oct. 1939, while Pavolini took the place of the previous minister of popular culture, Alfieri.

12 Goebbels himself conceptualized and produced the propaganda film *The Eternal Jew*, directed by Fritz Hippler. After a screening for high-ranking Nazi leaders in Sept. 1940, it was shown in approximately half of Germany's cinemas in Dec. 1940 and Jan. 1941. See also PMJ 12/243.

13 *Feldzug in Polen*, a propaganda film directed by Fritz Hippler, which played in German cinemas from Feb. 1940.

14 Harald Quandt (1921–1967), Magda Goebbels's son from her first marriage to the industrialist Günther Quandt.

DOC. 32

On 5 November 1939 the Justice Department in District Cracow demands that Jewish employees be dismissed[1]

Letter from the head of the Justice Department, District Cracow, signed Landgerichtsrat Dr Mnich,[2] to the head of the Court of Appeal in Cracow, dated 5 November 1939 (copy)

Enclosed please find a written compilation of the directives that I issued to you verbally during the establishment of the courts.[3]

I request that a copy be sent to the local notaries' association and the lawyers' association for their information and careful attention.

Should a judge, notary, or other official of the Jewish race by any chance still be employed, I request that he be instructed to cease his activities immediately.

Jews must be defined on the basis of race. This means that a baptized Jew must still be regarded as a Jew.

I request that I be informed by 20 November that no Jewish officials are working for the authorities any more, and no Jewish notaries either.[4]

DOC. 33

New York Times, 6 November 1939: article on the persecution of Jews and the threat of famine in occupied Poland[1]

Jews Said to Face Famine in Poland; 1,500,000 in the German-Held Areas Are Reported to Have Been Condemned to Starve. Flight to Soviet Barred. Thousands Camp in Fields at Frontier Because Russians Have Closed Boundary.

Wireless to *the New York Times*

Paris, Nov. 5 – The Jews' plight in the German-occupied part of Poland is worse than in the Reich, judging from the steady flow of allegations of Nazi brutality and persecution reaching the Polish Government and Jewish relief organizations here.

Reports from German Poland include the following:

About 1,500,000 Jews remaining in that area are condemned by the Nazis to starvation. Confiscation of property of Jews, begun in Lodz and other West Poland towns, is now proceeding on a large scale in Warsaw.

1 AIPN, GK 196/309 (NTN 309), fol. 1. This document has been translated from German.

2 Presumably Dr Johannes Mnich (b. 1896), who was awarded a PhD in law from Breslau University in 1922.

3 The enclosed 'Guidelines for the Resumption of Work in Polish Courts' state that Jewish judges, public officials, and notaries would not be allowed 'to take up their work again': AIPN, GK 196/309 (NTN 309), fols. 2–3.

4 On 23 July 1940 the Justice Department once again asked the head of the appellate court in Cracow whether there were 'any Jews, Jewish Mischlinge, or persons intermarried with Jews among the court's legal experts and interpreters' and demanded that 'Jews and half-Jews, as well as persons married to Jews' should 'be discharged immediately': AIPN, GK 196/309 (NTN 309), fol. 34.

1 *New York Times*, no. 29 871, 6 Nov. 1939, p. 7.

The Jews' wholesale businesses have been taken over by Nazi commissioners. Many profitable trades are prohibited to Jews, who are permitted to retain a maximum of only $400. On the pretext of searching for arms Nazis raid Jews' homes and seize property.

Funds of Jewish religious groups have been confiscated and hospitals and schools have been requisitioned. Only the joint commission[2] is allowed to distribute food among Jews who are chased from lines in front of food stores. Bread ration cards are not given to Jews.

A 'specialist' from the Dachau concentration camp has arrived in Warsaw to set up a concentration camp for Jews.

In the provinces the situation is worse. Pogroms are reported from Kaluszyn, with fifty victims; Lukow, where thirty Poles and thirty Jews were executed;[3] and Pultusk, where one Jew in each house on one of the streets was executed for alleged shooting at German soldiers.[4]

In one village the Catholic priest saved the lives of many Jews, offering himself as a hostage guaranteeing the 'contribution' of $4,000 demanded from the Jews.

In Lodz all Jews in the principal street were told to evacuate, leaving their homes in perfect order. Germans from the Baltic States will be settled there. The Jews were told to flee to Soviet-occupied Poland but thousands who were driven eastward were barred by Russians, distrustful of the Nazis, who are allowing no one to cross the German–Soviet border.

The situation is aggravated by the fact that Polish Jews who had lived in Czecho-Slovakia were expelled to Poland. Jews are being removed from Silesia and other western provinces. The transfer of adult males has begun. Women and children will be transported separately.

Thousands of Polish refugees who fled to Lwow from the west are being encouraged by the Russians to go back to the German area. The Nazis bar them and the Soviet does not allow them to return. On both sides of the demarcation line thousands camp in the fields.

2 The American Jewish Joint Distribution Committee (JDC).

3 On 19 Sept. 1939 the German occupying forces in Łuków killed dozens of people and burned 25 houses to the ground.

4 Pułtusk was taken by the Germans on 7 Sept. 1939. On 11 Sept. 1939 the SS shot and killed at least 10 Jews and displaced approximately 300 people.

DOC. 34

On 11 November 1939 the Higher SS and Police Leader in Posen (Poznań) orders the formation of a special staff for the deportation of Poles and Jews[1]

Order (marked 'secret') from the Higher SS and Police Leader in Posen, Wilhelm Koppe,[2] dated 11 November 1939 (copy)

Re: settlement of Baltic Germans and Germans from Volhynia, and evacuation of Jews and Poles

1. The Reichsführer-SS has named me authorized representative of the Reich Commissioner for the Strengthening of Germandom for the region of the Reichsgau Wartheland.
2. To perform the tasks set for me, I have formed the following staffs:
   a) Staff for the housing and occupational placement of Baltic and Volhynian Germans.
   Head: Reichsamtsleiter Dr Derichsweiler[3]
   Deputy: Reichsamtsleiter Weber
   Office: Posen, 5 Reichsring, II
   b) Staff for the evacuation and deportation of the Poles and Jews to the General Government.
   Head: SS-Sturmbannführer Rapp[4]
   Office: Posen, 15 Kaiserring
3. The Party and state offices involved in the aforementioned tasks will be requested by the heads of the aforementioned staffs to allocate a suitable employee, if they have not yet done so.
4. The Reichsführer-SS and Reich Commissioner for the Strengthening of Germandom expect all the offices in question to demonstrate the urgently needed interest in the great historical task of strengthening Germandom in the Reichsgau Wartheland, and to give all possible and conceivable support to the staffs appointed by me.

1 BArch, R 70 Polen/198, fol. 1. This document has been translated from German.

2 Wilhelm Koppe (1896–1975), wholesale clerk; joined the NSDAP in 1930, the SA in 1931, and the SS in 1932; promoted to SS-Führer in Danzig in 1934; became deputy leader of the SS Main District East in 1935; SS-Gruppenführer and head of the Elbe SS Main District in Dresden in 1936; then Inspector of the Security Police and the SD in Leipzig; worked in the SD Main Office in 1938; Higher SS and Police Leader Warthe in Posen, Oct. 1939–1943; simultaneously representative of the Reich Commissioner for the Strengthening of Germandom (RKF); Higher SS and Police Leader for the General Government, 1943–1945; managed a chocolate factory in Bonn under an assumed name after the war.

3 Dr Albert Derichsweiler (1909–1997), lawyer; joined the NSDAP and the SA in 1930; head of the National Socialist German Students' League, 1934–1936; Reichsamtsleiter and head of the staff responsible for the housing and occupational placement of resettled Germans in Reichsgau Wartheland in Nov. 1939; local and state politician for the Deutsche Partei and later the FDP in Hesse after the war.

4 Dr Albert Rapp (1908–1975), lawyer; joined the NSDAP in 1931, the SA in 1932, and the SS in 1936; member of the SD from 1936; department head in the SD for the Karlsruhe district in 1937, then in Berlin; member of Einsatzgruppe VI in Poland in 1939, then head of the SD Posen Main District until 1941; simultaneously head of the 'evacuation staff', then of the Central Resettlement Office (UWZ); head of Sonderkommando 7a in the Soviet Union in 1942; sentenced to life in prison in 1965.

DOC. 35
Dawid Sierakowiak describes the anti-Jewish terror in Łódź between 12 and 18 November 1939[1]

Handwritten diary of Dawid Sierakowiak, entries for 12 to 18 November 1939

Sunday, 12 November, Łódź. I stayed at home all day and before the evening I went to the Hamers'.[2] As everywhere else, various rumours were discussed here, too. There is talk of disagreement between the Germans and the Russians and about Russian demands (the 1914 border).[3] It all seems like idle talk. Jewish primary schools, which have been taken over by the local communities, are to teach German and Hebrew. Nothing new with us for now. The Jews have been expelled from all Polish grammar schools, both state-owned and private. Two grammar schools, the Orzeszkowa school (for girls) and the state school (for boys), the overwhelming majority of whose pupils are Jewish, are being converted to Jewish schools (Christians are being expelled). What a paradox! New Jewish grammar schools are formed under German rule. But they do not exist yet. Tomorrow we might get back the English tests we took last week.

Monday, 13 November, Łódź. Lessons are becoming irregular again. Changes to the schedule, fewer lessons per day, several teachers absent. Salary payments are drying up again. There is talk of a Russian ultimatum to Germany etc. It seems that these are just comforting words. The gentlemen[4] will always come to an agreement and crush us. Julek, cousin Rózia's fiancé, left today. He left for Warsaw for now. From there, he intends to get himself to Russia. Perhaps he will make it. He was a well-known left-wing activist.

Tuesday, 14 November, Łódź. There is nothing new. The rumours intensify. Classes are still irregular.

Wednesday, 15 November, Łódź. A synagogue was burned down. The barbarian methods of destroying the world are beginning to work. Apparently, 25,000,000 złoty have been demanded to end the terror. The Community does not have it, so it did not pay. A second synagogue on Wolborska is apparently being burned down! Something about the Germans is not quite right. Yesterday they began to loot in a horrible and chaotic way. They are taking everything: furniture, clothes, linen, food. Poles and Jews have until tomorrow to turn in all spades and pickaxes. An order drafting the Łódź Germans aged 18 to 45 into the Selbstschutz was issued today. The army is leaving the city, no one knows where for, so someone has to remain in the city. But this will affect us most of all,

1 USHMM, RG 10 247, Diary written by Dawid Sierakowiak from 28 June 1939. This document has been translated from Polish.

2 Family in the neighbouring apartment. Dawid Sierakowiak was friends with Dawid Hamer (1917–1942). See also Doc. 59.

3 This is evidently a reference to the unfounded rumour that the Soviet government had demanded the restoration of the 1914 state borders.

4 This refers to Hitler and Stalin.

because having anything to do with Łódź Germans is worse than facing a regiment of Germans from the Reich. Maybe they won't torment us for long. But who knows …

Thursday 16 November, Łódź. We are going back to the Middle Ages. The yellow patch is once again becoming part of Jewish clothing. An order was announced today that all Jews, regardless of age and sex, must wear a 'Jewish yellow' armband, 10 cm wide, on their right arm, just below the armpit. In addition, Jews are forbidden from leaving their flats between 5 p.m. and 8 a.m.[5] The armband is mandatory from the 18th, and the curfew already from today. Today we only had four lessons. I walked slower and covered my route in 50 minutes, reaching home 10 minutes before 5 p.m. The real Middle Ages! Yellow prison patches like in a ghetto, but it doesn't matter. We will survive this period for the sake of a good and sunny future.

Friday, 17 November, Łódź. The mood in the city is depressing. It is difficult to get used to the stigmatization. There is also fear of Jews with patches being provoked and harassed. A perfect opportunity for ridicule and taunts. I wonder how Poles will behave. Will they join the German mob? Or perhaps they too have understood the meaning of Jewish sacrifice? Perhaps they'll remember their priests who were forced to hammer away yesterday at the Kościuszko[6] statue on Wolność until the Germans, seeing their ineffectiveness, blew it up with dynamite? We'll see. At school we took a history test. Today Lipszyc gave me two pieces of leather for soles and heels. At least I will have something to walk in without getting completely soaked like today. Lipszyc himself is not richer than me, but he has a good quantity of leather, so he gave me some. The obligatory armbands have already been prepared at home.

Saturday, 18 November, Łódź. I haven't been out at all today. I already received the shoes repaired with iron heel plates and nails. Poles cast down their eyes at the sight of Jews with patches; our acquaintances comforted us that it won't be for long. The Germans are acting totally indifferently for now. Curfew hours for Poles and Germans were also changed today. They can only go out after 6 a.m. (previously 5 a.m.), but in return, they can stay out until 8.30 p.m. (8 p.m. until today). It doesn't matter. Then we'll just stay confined to our homes from 5 o'clock in the evening. Nothing matters. Times will change.

5 On 14 Nov. 1939 the Regierungspräsident in Kalisz, Friedrich Uebelhoer, had issued a decree that required the Jewish population to wear an armband 'in Jew-yellow colour' and imposed a curfew between 5 p.m. and 8 a.m.: Berenstein et al. (eds.), *Faschismus – Getto – Massenmord*, pp. 68–69.

6 Tadeusz Kościuszko (1746–1817), leader of the 1794 uprising against Russia.

DOC. 36

On 14 November 1939 Einsatzkommando 11 of the Security Police issues instructions to seize the property of the Jewish population prior to their expulsion[1]

Letter from Einsatzkommando 11, Ciechocinek Field Office (log no. 29/39), SS-Oberscharführer (signature illegible), to the mayor of Alexandrow (Aleksandrów Kujawski), dated 14 November 1939[2]

On the basis of precise instructions from Berlin,[3] I ask that you establish a Council of Elders within your Jewish community. The task of this council is to ensure that all Jews leave the municipality of Alexandrow for Warsaw within ten days, i.e. by 24 November 1939.

The Jews are only allowed to take the absolute essentials with them. Everything else will remain as and where it is and will be used for the benefit of the ethnic Germans. In particular, the Jews are to be prevented from taking valuables and an overabundance of clothes with them, especially new clothes. If the Jews are found to be in possession of such items, they are to be taken away and secured for the Gestapo, which will decide on their further use.

In addition, I ask that you provide a suitably large shop – or even several adjoining shops – for the establishment of a small department store where the Jewish goods can be offered for sale to the community.

A list of the names of the members of the Jewish Council of Elders must be submitted to me. The members of the Council of Elders will be the last to leave the community. They are liable with their property and their lives for the orderly management of the emigration.

One particular case forces me to point out that one administrative authority has not transferred to us the confiscated assets of the Jews in their entirety. I note that I have received very specific orders for such cases, and they have extremely severe consequences for the individual. I hope I will have no need to apply these orders in Kreis Nierschawa.[4]

1 AIPN, GK 67/2, fol. 1. Copy in USHMM, RG 15 004M. This document has been translated from German.

2 Parts of the original have been underlined by hand.

3 See Doc. 12.

4 Correctly: Nieszawa, to the south of Thorn, seat of the Kreis administration. The name of the Kreis (part of Reichsgau Wartheland) was subsequently Germanized as Kreis Nessau; in 1941 it was renamed Kreis Hermannsbad.

DOC. 37

On 15 November 1939 the teacher Chaim Kaplan from Warsaw writes about the mass escape of Jews across the German–Soviet demarcation line[1]

Handwritten diary of Chaim Kaplan,[2] entry for 15 November 1939

15 November 1939
There is no end to the flight! They flee to the Führer's 'friend',[3] who welcomes with open arms the persecuted Jews who were forced to leave their homeland by the persecutor's fury.

One has to admit that our sages' words were true: 'The Almighty prepares the remedy before the sickness.' Were it not for Soviet Russia, we would be choked to death. Polish Jewry has suffered complete and utter destruction. Tens of thousands of young Jews were left without means of sustenance. Every day sees a new decree. Every morning, a new calamity supplants the last horror, which the Jews are still trying to comprehend. It is terribly confusing to read all the orders, edicts, announcements, and notices that the conqueror publishes. We know in advance that they hold no good news for the Jews. We are always discriminated against: they feed the poor from public kitchens – except the Jews; they eliminate unemployment by means of providing necessary work – except for the Jews. The Jews are not taken into account. In every public position, the Jews have a special status. It is against them that the occupier is fighting. That is what a German general explicitly stated. Jewish youth has no present and no future, and it is fleeing for its very life. The escape is accomplished in various ways: on foot, by automobile, by train, in carts, and in all sorts of other vehicles. The border is open. There is no obstacle from the Soviet side.[4] And the Nazi conqueror has no established policy. One never knows what is prohibited and what is permitted. In some cases they may be lenient and in others strict for the exact same offence. This is understandable, for wherever there is arbitrariness and malice, there can be no consistent or specific policy. Moreover, what one authority permits, the other prohibits. Immediately after the occupation, the border was opened. They let anyone cross without a written permit, and whoever wanted to queue up for three days could even receive a permit that explicitly states that the bearer

1 USHMM, Collection 2 004 405, fols. 205–207. This document has been translated from Hebrew. Published in Chaim Kaplan, *Megillat yissurin: Yoman getto varshah* (Tel Aviv: Am Oved, 1966), pp. 82–84. An incomplete English translation can be found in *Scroll of Agony: The Warsaw Diary of Chaim A. Kaplan*, ed. and trans. Abraham I. Katsh (London: Hamilton, 1966), pp. 52–53.

2 Chaim Kaplan (1880–1942), Hebrew teacher; trained in the Mir yeshiva; studied pedagogy in Vilna; founder and later director of a grammar school with Hebrew as language of instruction in Warsaw in 1902; visited the USA in 1921; visited Palestine in 1936; murdered in Treblinka. Kaplan wrote a diary from 1933 that ends on 4 August 1942. He gave his records to Władysław Wójciek, who hid them. In 1952 Wójciek gave the part of the diary covering the period from late Dec. 1939 to April 1941 to the Jewish Historical Institute (AŻIH, 302/218). Wójciek later emigrated to the USA, where he sold another part of the manuscript that he had only later found again. Today the entries for August to Dec. 1939 and June to July 1942 are held at the USHMM; another part, covering the period from May 1941 to May 1942, is at the archive of the Moreshet Mordechai Anielevich Memorial Holocaust Study and Research Center (D.2.470) in Israel.

3 That is, to the Soviet Union.

4 A different picture emerges from other sources: see Docs. 33, 63, and 275.

is entitled to cross the border into Russia with his baggage and possessions, using any means of transportation. But all this is in writing. In reality, the route is perilous. According to the 'law', those crossing the border are permitted to take only 20 złoty with them. This is a sadistic law that cannot possibly be obeyed. As a result, people connive to smuggle out larger sums, and here many have failed. They have been assaulted and robbed en route, left naked and penniless. The border guards know that Jewish lives and money are public property, and they deal with those who cross in whatever way they like. People therefore prefer to cross without permission. They do not trust the conqueror's legalities. They feel safer when they cross secretly, as every refugee takes with him a larger sum of money than the 'law' permits. And so, word of the 'green border'[5] has spread among the refugees, and experts in border crossings earn tremendous sums through their 'profession'.

Those in the know estimate that over a million refugees have fled to Russia.[6] And no matter how the numbers swell, they are welcomed. But where will this large mass of people settle? Some skilled workers in certain trades have managed to get transferred to the Russian interior. But the majority either have some available cash and are well fed, or have nothing and are hungry and thirsty. As always, there are those who are successful and those who have no luck and suffer. Ultimately no blame can be put on Soviet Russia, which opened its gates to the Polish exiles and saved them from untold suffering. The Soviets condemn America and England, the wealthy democracies, for closing their gates and turning a deaf ear to the heartrending cries of the German refugees at the very hour of their most terrible distress. The Soviets, on the other hand, say, 'Come, we will give you work; just join us.'

The politics of sovereign friendship does not permit admonishing the Nazis so that they abandon their despicable practices towards the Jews. 'Jews' is a complex concept. Among them are the wealthy, whom they despise. The [wealthy] benefit from the work that they have others do in their name. The Nazis are hastening the much-desired proletarianization. Such [impoverished] men will not find themselves the objects of Soviet disdain. But the Jewish youth who yearn for work, for manual labour, for a life of creation and construction, and who are prepared to accept the authority of Stalinist Bolshevism – they are welcome guests. Tens of thousands of them are fleeing from the Nazi hell.

Here is what happened to us in a single day:

After much work and effort the schools, which exist only by a miracle, were opened. Because of the dearth of students, the teachers don't even earn enough for a dry crust of bread. One school of 300 students dwindled to 100; another, of 100, is down to 20. The teaching is not being done properly because of crushed spirits and insufficient pay. We earn as much as Hanina and his small measure of carobs.[7] Now even this has come to an end … Because of the contagious diseases spreading throughout the city, especially

5 A reference to the so-called grüne Grenze, an unmarked border.

6 It is estimated today that between 200,000 and 300,000 Jews fled from western Poland into Soviet-occupied territory. Among them were tens of thousands of persons displaced by the Germans.

7 Hanina ben Dosa was an ancient Jewish scholar and miracle-worker from the first century CE. It is said that he was extremely poor, and although the virtuous man provided for others through prayer and miracles, he himself was sustained by nothing more than a small amount of carob beans from week to week.

typhoid fever, all schools have been ordered to close. Now hunger and poverty await us, a hideous and degrading life.

It is a day of reckoning for Jewish prostitutes too. Just as a Jewish shoemaker is forbidden to make new shoes, Jewish women are forbidden to engage in … prostitution. The conqueror fears 'race defilement', and if prostitution as a profession were to be permitted to Jewish women, their soldiers might not be able to control their urges and stumble – heaven forbid! – with a non-Aryan harlot.

And proper Jewish women were also advised not to fraternize with the soldiers, otherwise they will be accused of sabotage and, according to Frank's most recent decree,[8] sentenced to death, no more and no less …

DOC. 38

Warschauer Zeitung, 16 November 1939: an inflammatory article against the Jews[1]

The Jews must help themselves. The proceeds of the 'religious tax' go to mitigate the appalling misery the rich Jews never concerned themselves with at all – this is how members of that race treat each other.

Cracow, 16 November
A committee has recently started working in the building of the Cracow Jewish Religious Community. The group, assembled by the *German* authority as a sort of self-administration, is made up of the thin upper stratum of Jewry that did not flee. Its purpose is to relieve at last the terrible distress of the ghetto population, suffering that has existed for years.

Because the majority of the rich Jews, even after the failed war experiment, knew how to get themselves and their ill-gotten wealth to safety, the German authorities were forced to make initial capital available to this Jewish welfare institution. Its further funding will be ensured through a *religious tax*. The German authority will supervise the collection of this tax from the well-to-do Jews.

Saved from starvation
This precautionary measure prevented a *catastrophe* in Cracow, which had been brewing since long before the collapse, as a result of the former Polish state's insane policies. When the German troops invaded, this catastrophe was just approaching its final, terrible act, which would have swept not only the tens of thousands of Jews but also the entire population of Cracow into a dreadful frenzy of starvation, crime, and disease.

The German authorities had no cause at all to shower compassion and welfare services upon the Jewish enemy in Poland, an enemy wrestled down only after many

8 This could not be found.

1 *Warschauer Zeitung*, no. 4, 16 Nov. 1939, p. 6. This document has been translated from German. The *Warschauer Zeitung* was published from Nov. 1939 to Dec. 1940 in an edition almost identical to the *Krakauer Zeitung*, and from Oct. 1941 to August 1944 as that paper's local edition. The *Krakauer Zeitung* was the daily newspaper for the German population in the General Government. It was also published as a military newspaper and, from 1941 to 1944, in a Lemberg (Lwów) edition.

sacrifices and fierce struggles on the part of the German population. But they did what every civilized nation would have had to do, at the very least: save tens of thousands of Jews in Europe from *starvation*, which, in its final stage, would have threatened friend and foe indiscriminately and mercilessly, with horrendous consequences. The rabble-rousers led by Rydz-Smigly and Beck[2] have often shouted across the border to Germany in an insolent and fatuous manner, claiming that Poland was the sole true civilized nation in Eastern Europe and was destined by fate to carry the concepts of freedom and culture – albeit by means of fire and sword – into the German space. But the *Germans* came in order to bring charity to Polish Jews, who were facing a famine that endangered one and all – aid that neither the Poles nor the Jews were able to give to their people or their racial comrades …

A living indictment

Anyone who realizes the monstrosity of this situation and wants to have it proven will find a living indictment in the building of the Cracow Jewish Religious Community. Three cliques are to blame: the wretched, lice-ridden, smarmy ghetto Jews; their racial comrades, dripping with money, in the Romanian villas; together with the insane Polish politicians.

The filthy ghetto is spread out in the immediate vicinity of the defiant, massive walls of the Cracow Fortress. Just as poverty and wealth and misery and splendour seemed to coexist well in Polish life, so too did the mighty fortress sit enthroned above malodorous huts and dilapidated homes. This is where Polish statesmen walked casually past shabby, wretched creatures and entered the ceremonial rooms of the castle without thinking twice.

Situated only a few minutes from Wawel Castle is the building of the Jewish Religious Community. From its entrance, foul-smelling vapours, the odours of unkempt human beings, waft towards us. Just now, a Jew laboriously lifts a crippled racial comrade up the stone steps.

The revolting ghetto

In the first room we enter, the pitiable figures move aside with the sort of obsequiousness only a Jew can display after a defeat. Everywhere in the building, one encounters dirty Jews, many of them dressed in rags, and a nauseating odour is emitted from all directions. The base world of the ghetto is reflected in the bloodless but dull-witted and dangerous faces. We understand why the German authority has closed off the centre of Cracow to these people.

The Jewish committee meets in the upper rooms. This is the group that the Germans first had to assemble and induce to do welfare work, as the Jews themselves would never have accomplished this due to their *apathy towards the fate of their own racial comrades and the utter lack of organizational talent among the Jews*. Perhaps for the first time,

2 Józef Beck (1894–1944), career officer; studied mechanical engineering in Lwów and foreign trade in Vienna; member of the Polish Legions and the Polish Military Organization (Polska Organizacja Wojskowa), 1914–1917; close associate of Piłsudski and, during the Polish–Soviet War, his chief of staff; military attaché in France, 1922–1923; minister of military affairs, 1926–1930; Polish foreign minister, 1932–1939; in 1939 fled to Romania, where he was interned.

former senior Jewish employees of the collapsed Polish state are now dealing with the misery of their fellow Jews from the ghetto. They now ensure that three kitchens, set up on a German initiative, are operating properly, and that the hospital, the orphanage, the home for the aged, and the delousing and bathing facilities are properly managed. What they themselves did not get done, indeed did not think possible, they now accomplish under German supervision. After four weeks in operation, the kitchens are already able to distribute more than 4,000 meals per day, and three tea-dispensing points hand out hot drinks.

When the religious tax is collected, however, the German hand must intervene forcefully to create order. The Jews find it difficult to get used to the idea that they must not just look after themselves, but share some of their assets with their poorer racial comrades. The baptized Jews, moaning and wailing, point to their Christian faith and try to free themselves from their obligation to provide support. They think that baptism also meant a change of race.

As everywhere among the people of Judah, they find the words 'give' and 'work' unappealing. Nonetheless, with the help of the Jews, it was possible to fill in all the air-raid trench shelters in the vicinity of the city of Cracow within two days. The spades that had produced blisters and calluses on many a soft Jewish hand accustomed only to haggling still lie in heaps in one of the Religious Community's rooms. One case we have been told about illustrates just how difficult this first instance of work may have been, especially for the rich Jews: a rich Jew appears as ordered at one of the worksites – he shows up in a car and with a driver, of course. The Jew, a paunchy man in the habit of giving orders rather than doing work, immediately instructs the driver to do the desired work in his stead. However, the Jew himself was made to do twice the work his driver did.

In the basement of the Religious Community, which serves as a lunchroom, half-starved Jews crowd around the tables, tightly packed, and wait for the soup that is being prepared in a dark adjoining room. In Germany, this room would be adequate at most to feed cattle, but these people do not demand the normal degree of cleanliness, either here or at home. Only a few of them stand out as a result of somewhat better-looking clothing. These few are Jews who, through their own fault, were expelled from Germany. They like to speak of 'Nazi Germany', whose realms must now seem like paradise to them.

With a deep sigh of relief back out in the open air, we leave the building of the Jewish Religious Community, where we experienced a world that we have overcome once and for all in Greater Germany. And in Cracow, too, it is already a world apart, one which – ordered and guarded by Germans – can never again overflow its bounds, impose upon others, and endanger the world around it. But this, too, would be nothing but pandemonium had a German authority not shown more humanity than these Jews' own *racial comrades* and the bygone 'civilized nation' of Poland ever did.

DOC. 39

The chairman of the Warsaw Jewish Council describes the harassment of the Jewish Community by the SS between 17 and 20 November 1939[1]

Handwritten diary of Adam Czerniaków,[2] entries for 17 to 20 November 1939

17 November 1939 – The SS agrees to the kitchens and baths. 300,000 złoty are to be collected for the labour battalion. I am summoned to the SS in the evening. A levy of 300,000 złoty by Monday.[3] Five of the hostages from the Council in jeopardy – lots to be drawn. A model of a Jewish gravestone on my desk. The Council is to meet at 10 a.m. tomorrow.

18 November 1939 – 8 a.m. with the SS about the levy, because I mentioned the difficulties with the bank. I've been given until Monday, 21 November 1939, for the levy. The ghetto has been postponed for a few months. The Community is to put up signposts at the boundaries of the ghetto that read, 'Achtung Seuchengefahr, Eintritt verboten.'[4] The transfer of the hospital, orphanages, and old people's home has been postponed until 31 December 1939. I'm to consult with Dr Schrempf about the transfer of the hospital.[5] With regard to the levy, I went to see Laschtoviczka[6] to obtain a list of blocked Jewish accounts. I received a fragmentary list with only the unblocked accounts.

19 November 1939 – Council meeting from the early morning. The whole day spent collecting money for the levy. After lunch, a meeting at the Red Cross with Delegate

1 YVA, O-33/1090. Published in Adam Czerniaków, *Adama Czerniakowa dziennik getta warszawskiego, 6 IX 1939–23 VII 1942*, ed. Marian Fuks (Warsaw: Państwowe Wydawnictwo Naukowe, 1983), pp. 62–63. The entire diary has been published in English translation in *The Warsaw Diary of Adam Czerniakow: Prelude to Doom*, ed. Raul Hilberg, Stanislaw Staron, and Joseph Kermisz, trans. Stanislaw Staron and the Staff of Yad Vashem (Chicago: Ivan R. Dee, 1999). This document has been newly translated from Polish.

2 Adam Czerniaków (1880–1942), engineer; studied chemistry in Warsaw and engineering in Dresden; teacher at a Jewish vocational school in Warsaw; city councillor in Warsaw; representative for Jewish craftsmen on the Jewish Community Council, 1927–1934; named head of the Jewish Religious Community by the mayor on 23 Sept. 1939 and chairman of the Warsaw Jewish Council by the Gestapo on 4 Oct. 1939; took his own life after the German authorities demanded that the Jewish Council make arrangements for the deportation of orphaned children.

3 On 13 Nov. 1939 a Jewish criminal just released from jail had shot dead a Polish police officer at 9 Nalewki Street. The Gestapo subsequently arrested 53 men from the building at this address and demanded 300,000 złoty for their release as 'atonement fine' (*Sühnegeld*) from the Jewish Community. The money was delivered, but the hostages still became victims of the first mass shooting in Warsaw on 22 Nov. 1939.

4 German in the original: 'Attention, risk of epidemic. Entry forbidden.'

5 Dr Kurt Schrempf (b. 1903), physician; public health officer in Kreis Birkenfeld from 1927; member of the NSDAP and the SA, and later member of the SS; head of the health office in the German municipal administration in Warsaw, Oct. 1939 – Feb. 1941.

6 Correctly: Dr Karl Laschtowiczka (1885–1973); representative of Austrian banks in Poland from 1923; head of the Finance Department of the City of Warsaw, Oct. 1939 – April 1940; deputy head of banking supervision in the General Government, June 1940–1945; Austrian ministry official after the war, and thereafter held leading positions in the Austrian business world.

Junod.[7] He promised support for Jews, medication, and food. Another meeting in the evening. I have collected approximately 260,000 złoty in cash and transfers from old and new blocked accounts. Another money collection tomorrow morning. Afterwards I have to take the levy to the SS. Baptisms![8] Architecture.

20 November 1939 – The census of Jews in Warsaw is complete. At 8 a.m. – the Community – the payment of the levy. At 11 a.m. I will take 40,000 złoty in cash as well as bank transfers in the amount of 260,000 złoty to the SS. Then to the Foreign Currency Office[9] for a permit. The 'ghetto' will be marked with signposts that read, 'Achtung Seuchengefahr, Eintritt verboten.'[10] Alongside these, the military authorities will put up signs banning soldiers from entering. Collecting money in the Community continues. I am to take over the hospital etc. A landlady refuses to reward those who saved her house from a fire. At 4 p.m. to the SS about the levy. At 5 p.m. another meeting with the SS on the same matter. From there to the Foreign Currency Office on Freta Street on the matter of cashing cheques. Meanwhile, I have neglected the office where I earn my daily bread.[11] What will I live on? – God only knows – especially as I do not wish to take anything from the Community, although I contribute to it (transportation costs and tips – a droshky is 4–5 złoty per ride). I go to bed at 9 p.m. and read. I wake up at 2 a.m. And so it goes until 5–6 a.m., when I get up. Shoes.

7 Dr Marcel Junod (1904–1961), Swiss physician; initially the only delegate for the International Committee of the Red Cross (ICRC) in Germany and in the occupied countries from Sept. 1939; with UNICEF in China after the war; professor of anaesthesiology in Geneva from 1950; vice president of the ICRC, 1959–1961.

8 Hoping to avoid persecution, over 200 Jews in Warsaw, mainly members of the liberal professions, converted to Christianity between Nov. 1939 and March 1940.

9 The foreign currency offices controlled the import and export of foreign currencies, bonds, etc. These offices were introduced with the currency regulation for the General Government dated 15 Nov. 1939: *VOBl-GG* 1939, no. 7, 20 Nov. 1939, pp. 44–51.

10 German in the original: 'Attention, risk of epidemic. Entry forbidden'.

11 Czerniaków worked for a foreign trade clearing house (Instytut Rozrachunkowy Zagranicznego Handlu), which he often called his 'office'.

DOC. 40

On 18 November 1939 the tax authorities in the Wartheland order Jewish assets to be frozen[1]

Directive no. 12 from the Reichsstatthalter in Posen, signed Reich Judge Dr Gebhard,[2] regional tax director in charge of implementation at the Foreign Currency Office, dated 18 November 1939

General Directive on Securing Jewish Assets and Anonymous Bank Deposits etc.
18 November 1939
Under § 5 of the Regulation on the Introduction of Legislation on Foreign Exchange Control and Monetary Transactions with Foreign Countries in the Eastern Territories Incorporated into the German Reich of 17 November 1939,[3] and in consultation with the Reich Minister of Economics, the Foreign Exchange Investigation Office, and the Main Trustee Office East, I order as follows:

(1) Anonymous bank deposits (accounts), securities accounts, safe-deposit boxes, etc. at financial and credit institutions that have their headquarters in the incorporated eastern territories, with the exception of the territory of the former Free City of Danzig, are hereby frozen.

(2) The same applies to bank deposits (accounts), securities accounts, safe-deposit boxes, etc. at financial and credit institutions managed in the names of Jews or over which Jews have the right of disposition.

(3) Jews are required to consolidate their available bank deposits, safe-deposit boxes, and securities accounts at a bank without delay, by no later than 31 December 1939. Exceptions are permissible only with the authorization of the Foreign Currency Office.

(4) By debiting the assets frozen under (2) above, the financial and credit institutions may pay out up to 250 zloty per week to persons entitled to draw on the accounts or, for their benefit, to third persons.

For the purposes of the current requirements regarding commercial undertakings, the required sums can be debited to the blocked accounts and paid out without authorization, in the amount of the need proven to the bank or savings bank that manages the account.

(5) Payments in excess of 500 zloty may only be made to Jews if they are paid into an account with a financial or credit institution. In the calculation of the aforementioned sum, payments made with regard to the same debt within the calendar month are to be added together.

1 *VOBl des Reichsstatthalters im Reichsgau Wartheland*, no. 2, 15 Jan. 1940, p. 22. This document has been translated from German.

2 Dr Karl Gebhard (1883–1945), lawyer; worked for the Reich tax authorities from 1920; then with Thuringia's regional tax office; in Berlin from 1929; director of Thuringia's regional tax office in Rudolstadt, 1933–1935; then with the Cologne regional tax office; Reich judge at the Reich Fiscal Court in 1939 and simultaneously representative of the Reich Minister of Finance in the Posen Militärbezirk; acting regional tax director for Reichsgau Posen in Oct. 1939; regional tax director in Reichsgau Posen (later Reichsgau Wartheland), 1940–1945.

3 Under § 5, the foreign currency offices in the annexed territories could issue general directives for the purpose of 'securing' Jewish assets: *Reichsgesetzblatt* I, 1939, p. 2256.

(6) Jews are required to deposit any cash in their possession in an account with a financial or credit institution, if it is in excess of the amount of 2,000 zloty. The deposit must be made immediately after this directive comes into force or after the acquisition of these amounts. (4), para. 2 of this directive remains unaffected.

The same requirement applies to a Jew who owns such sums or exercises power of disposal over them through a trustee or in some other way. Moreover, it applies to anyone who, as a trustee, as an asset manager, or in some other way, controls cash belonging to a Jew.

(7) The Foreign Exchange Protection Commandos are in charge of unblocking assets that are affected by the preceding provisions. When the tasks of the Foreign Exchange Protection Commandos are handed over to the Customs Investigation Offices, this authority devolves on the Customs Investigation Office.

(8) This directive comes into force on 20 November 1939.

DOC. 41

Warschauer Zeitung, 19 November 1939: article about a Jewish neighbourhood in Warsaw being sealed off[1]

Warsaw ghetto now being sealed off. Jews now separated from the rest of the population by barricades. German soldiers prohibited from entering the Jewish quarter. Universal compulsory vaccination.

Report by the Krakauer and Warschauer Zeitung[2]
Warsaw, 19 November
The Jews of Warsaw, who have always been a heavy burden on the city, particularly in moral and hygienic terms, will henceforth be able to lead a strictly separate life of their own. In accordance with a regulation issued by the governor, the Warsaw Jewish quarter is being closed off with barricades. The goal is to strictly separate the ghetto from the rest of Warsaw's population. German soldiers are forbidden from entering the Jewish quarter.

This new provision is the answer to the wishes of the majority of the population of Warsaw. Particularly in the past weeks and months, the true, inferior character of the Jews in Warsaw has become shamefully apparent. Unscrupulously and with tremendous rapacity, these parasites took advantage of the *suffering* that the Polish government brought upon the people, and the population of Warsaw in particular, and they enriched themselves. What that inevitably meant for the Varsovians is clear from the number of Jews living in the city: Warsaw has 300,000 to 400,000 *sons of Israel.*

It was a dismal spectacle to behold these characters whose personal hygiene leaves much to be desired, and whose faces belie their inferiority – haggling and trading in every street, all the way to the back courtyards. They made use of everything imaginable to *amass usurious profits*, from a pair of braces all the way to a loaf of onion bread and a cat. Precious jewels were found in the hands of the Jews, as well as thousands of other things that could be recognized at first glance as looted goods.

1 *Warschauer Zeitung*, no. 7, 19 Nov. 1939, p. 5. This document has been translated from German.
2 A Polish version appeared in the Cracow daily *Goniec Krakowski*, no. 20, 20 Nov. 1939, p. 2.

In future, the activities of those elements who are now selling the property that was looted from the vacant or damaged homes of the Warsaw population will also be stopped. *In accordance with a further regulation issued by the Governor, all looted goods are to be confiscated.*[3] The items offered for sale in the streets are being examined to determine their origin. We can rest assured that an ignoble state of affairs will soon come to an end.

Life in Warsaw is slowly regaining its normal appearance. Electricity and water are available again, and in some neighbourhoods, even gas. The tram service has been almost completely restored in the suburbs, and the trains connecting Warsaw to Posen and to Cracow are running again. One tiny detail in this larger mosaic: the last grave has disappeared from Pilsudski Square.[4]

Another regulation is important to the population: compulsory vaccination has been introduced for everyone in Warsaw, including the German officers, civil servants, and public employees, as well as all sections of the Polish population.[5] This measure of public hygiene and disease prevention demonstrates just how conscientious the German leadership is.

DOC. 42

On 22 November 1939 the Geneva office of the World Jewish Congress reports on a Jewish reservation near Lublin and on relief efforts in Poland and Hungary[1]

Report by the Geneva representative office of the World Jewish Congress,[2] unsigned, dated 22 November 1939

Report on the situation of the Polish refugees in Hungary and on the establishment of the reservation for the Jewish population of Greater Germany and the protectorates south-east of Lublin

This is not an eyewitness report, at least as far as the situation of the Jewish population in Poland is concerned. The notes were made after conversations with prominent Jews from the Jewish communities of Budapest and Berlin, and are based on information from the English Society of Friends in Budapest and the American Quaker Society in Berlin.[3]

3 This could not be verified.
4 From early Oct. 1939 the victims of the siege of Warsaw, initially buried in squares and streets, were reinterred in cemeteries.
5 On 30 Oct. 1939 the head of the Health Department in District Warsaw, Oberstabsarzt (military medical officer) Prof. Richter, announced that vaccinations were to be carried out as part of the 'battle against disease': *Amtsblatt des Chefs des Distrikts Warschau*, no. 1, 22 Nov. 1939, pp. 19–20. Vaccination against typhoid fever was not ordered by District Governor Ludwig Fischer until 2 Dec. 1940: *Amtsblatt des Chefs des Distrikts Warschau*, no. 12, 28 Dec. 1940, p. 177.

1 CZA, C 3/7–14, fols. 257–260. Copy in USHMM, RG 68 045M, reel 2. This document has been translated from German.
2 The World Jewish Congress (WJC) was founded in Geneva – the seat of the League of Nations – in August 1936 by Nahum Goldmann and representatives from 32 countries as an international federation of Jewish communities and organizations.

The removal and resettlement of Jews in south-eastern Poland

The following report is based on statements by German or Polish persons of note, which have been fully confirmed by reports from well-known Jewish individuals in Hungary.

The territory that is planned to serve as a reservation for the Jewish population of the Old Reich, Austria, the Protectorate, and Poland is said to cover an area of approximately 800 to 1,000 (?) square kilometres south-east of Lublin. Two rivers, the San and the Vistula, form the natural border in the west, and in the east this territory borders on Russia. In the coming days, a map will reportedly be issued by the German government, on which this more or less clearly outlined part of Poland will be labelled Judea. The Russian border[4] and certain regions along the banks of the San have already been 're-inforced' with strong 'barbed-wire snares' to make it impossible for the Jewish population to flee to Russia. However, it has recently been reported that an escape to Russia by several thousand Viennese Jews who had been deported to Lublin was prompted and facilitated by the Russian military authority.[5] For the past three weeks, the Polish population and the German minority have been systematically evacuated from this region. The Polish population will be resettled in the area around Warsaw, and the German population in the old Polish Corridor region and in the area around Posen.[6]

The resettlement of the Jews – in the most barren part of Poland (mostly marshes and swamplands) – will be implemented in four phases:

1 By the end of October, the Jewish population of the Polish Corridor and the cities of Gdynia, Posen, Graudenz, and Kattowitz had already been evacuated. They were placed in several so-called retraining camps in the Nisko region. Several hundred persons were put up in evacuated and largely destroyed Polish villages. The majority, however, first had to clear woodland and are now reportedly housed in huts that they knocked together themselves. Bread and potatoes are said to be their only food. The camps are thus nothing other than concentration camps surrounded by barbed wire and guarded by SS formations.

2 The first phase of the removal of the Jews from the German cities of Poland will now be followed by the *deportation of the Jews from Vienna*, or from all of Austria. Approximately 55,000 Jews are to be removed from Vienna alone in the coming months. It was envisaged that one transport carrying at least 2,000 men, women, and children would depart every week.

According to the latest reports, however, the Jewish Community of Vienna found it [im]possible to put together a train carrying 1,400 people, because many Jews had preferred to flee to Slovakia or take their own lives rather than be forced into exile.

3 As part of a third phase, all Jews – approximately 160,000 people in all – are to be moved out of the Protectorate of Bohemia and Moravia. These transports have also been under way since early November. According to statements made by individuals

3 The Religious Society of Friends (Quakers) is a religious community that was founded in the mid-seventeenth century. After the end of the First World War, Quakers became involved in poor relief and social welfare in various locations around Europe.

4 A reference to the demarcation line between the German and Soviet areas of occupation.

5 In the initial days and weeks of the Soviet occupation of eastern Poland, the Soviet authorities did not hinder Jewish refugees seeking to cross into Soviet-occupied territory.

6 The information in this document does not always fully reflect the actual measures taken by the German occupiers.

(as is more or less confirmed, incidentally, by an article published on 18 November in the *Neue Zürcher Zeitung*[7]), a train carrying Jews from Mährisch-Ostrau (around 2,000) reportedly arrived in the vicinity of Nisko; once there, everyone on the transport was put out in the open, and men, women, and children were abandoned to their fate, after the little money they had was taken from them.

4 The fourth phase concerns the Jews from the Old Reich (approximately 200,000 people). As of 10 November, however, the Reich Representation of German Jews[8] has not yet been asked to put these transports together.

The *Central Office* for all of these transports is located in *Mährisch-Ostrau*, under the leadership of a certain Eichmann from the Gestapo.[9] The Jewish communities of all four resettlement regions are charged with putting together and funding the transports. If enough people do not volunteer for deportation, Jews will be arrested in the street and taken into custody. Officially, every Jew is allowed to take along a maximum sum of 300 marks (600 Kc.).[10] Individual assets left behind, such as real estate, shops, furniture, etc., must be forcibly liquidated by the Religious Community.[11] (See the enclosed text of the regulation of the Jewish Community in Mährisch-Ostrau.[12]) The entire process of removing the Jews and resettling them in these regions is to be completed by 1 April 1940. In addition, all Polish Jews (approximately 1½ million) must be removed from the rest of Poland and transported to this region by this date. The resettlement of all Jews from the Greater Reich[13] and its protectorates to south-eastern Poland is said to have been decided at the last meeting between Ribbentropp[14] and Molotov.[15] The aim, however, is not to establish a self-determined Jewish state, but rather to deport all Jews to a reservation that is completely cut off from the world around it and under the heaviest possible guard. After the establishment of a Polish rump state or protectorate, with Warsaw as its capital,[16] the Polish administration will be put in charge of guarding the reservation. But because all assistance for the Jewish population is already now being forbidden by the German government, one can readily imagine that the elderly, women, and children in this region are to be abandoned to a slow death from starvation.

Supplementary information with regard to the reports about Warsaw

The Jewish population in Warsaw has grown from 300,000 before the war to approximately 500,000 persons. The mortality rate among this population is said to have in-

7 'Die deutsche Herrschaft in Polen', *Neue Zürcher Zeitung* (morning edition), no. 1964, 18 Nov. 1939, p. 1.

8 This was the former name of the organization, which had been renamed Reich Representation of Jews in Germany (Reichsvereinigung der Juden in Deutschland) in 1935 and Reich Association (Reichsvereinigung der Juden in Deutschland) in 1939.

9 The Central Office for Jewish Emigration, headed by Eichmann until late 1939, had a branch office in Mährisch Ostrau (Moravská Ostrava) for a brief period in autumn 1939.

10 Czech korunas.

11 Note in the original: the proceeds are to be used for the 'general public welfare'.

12 This is not included in the file.

13 Presumably: the Greater German Reich.

14 Correctly: Joachim von Ribbentrop.

15 Such plans were probably not part of the negotiations.

16 This refers to the setting up of the General Government for the Occupied Polish Territories in late October 1939. The capital was Cracow.

creased from 10 (before the war) to 80 per day. Approximately 80 per cent of the Jewish population of Warsaw is in need of support. According to a conservative estimate, approximately 25,000 to 30,000 corpses are still buried beneath the ruins of Warsaw today. Because the water pipes are operational in only a very few neighbourhoods, epidemics are said to have broken out in the last few week[s], especially in the Jewish quarter, which is completely isolated from the rest of Warsaw (scattered cases of cholera and typhus).

According to information from German military personnel, villages inhabited mainly by Jews in the area around Warsaw and Lodz have been completely levelled. Jewish shops in Warsaw were already looted by the Polish population during the siege; today, Jews are forbidden to engage in any business activity.

Relief efforts

1. The *first relief efforts* were provided while the war was still going on, by the Hilfszug Bayern, but only for the members of the German minority. Poles and Jews were excluded from this relief effort.[17]
2. *Since the end of the war, the American Joint [JDC]* in Warsaw is said to have provided up to 12,000 meals daily [in] approximately 50 kitchens. (This number is to be increased to 50,000 per day.) In addition, clothing and medicines (approximately 15,000 parcels) were distributed by the end of October. According to the latest reports, however, a shortage particularly of warm clothing, medicines, condensed milk, etc. is making itself felt. In addition, members of the Jewish population are to receive absolutely no window glass for their devastated homes. (All window glass still available was requisitioned by the German administrative authority.)
3. *The American Society of Friends* has been in negotiations with the German government offices for around three weeks, trying to organize a relief effort especially for women and children in Poland. At first, the German government wanted the Quakers' entire effort to go through the National Socialist People's Welfare Organization. The Quakers, of course, took issue with this suggestion. Now, however, the negotiations have progressed to the point where the American Quakers can organize a direct, *independent relief* effort for the *Polish* population. The German government forbade the provision of support for the Jews in Poland. On the day of my departure from Berlin, however, the Quakers supposedly obtained permission for a *Jewish* relief programme now too. Only the members of the German minority are excluded, who receive assistance directly from the National Socialist People's Welfare Organization.

   But the American Quakers' aid organization for the Polish and Jewish population of Poland will not be set up until late November, after the arrival of the delegate from the Quaker Society in New York, Edgar Rhods.[18] It is supposed to mainly concern shipments of medicines and clothing, as well as milk for mothers and children. In

17 The Hilfszug Bayern was a mobile soup kitchen unit that was deployed for large-scale events or catastrophes. The NSDAP organization behind it, which had been established in 1933, was used for propaganda purposes abroad on a number of occasions in 1938 and 1939. After the Wehrmacht entered Warsaw, the Hilfszug Bayern, contrary to the statement in the document, initially also assisted the Polish civilian population in the destroyed residential quarters.

18 Correctly: Joseph Edgar Rhoads (1883–1981), chemist and entrepreneur from Wilmington, Delaware.

addition, plans call for organizing a service in Berlin for the exchange of letters, parcels, and cash remittances between relatives and friends living abroad and the Polish-Jewish population in Poland. This entire Quaker relief effort will be funded mainly by the Commission of Polish Relief in New York City.[19]

4. *With regard to a relief effort to be organized by the Red Cross,* information can be provided only after the return of the American Red Cross delegates from Warsaw or Berlin. Here, too, it will probably concern the shipment of medicines and other medical supplies in particular.

In my opinion, a relief effort for the Jews in Poland can be organized effectively only in cooperation with the American Society of Friends in Berlin. The *American Joint [JDC]* in Warsaw could possibly be supported by the delivery of warm clothing, medicines, food, etc. One can assume that a *direct relief effort* on the part of Jewish committees abroad to aid the Jews of Poland is utterly impossible, given the present attitude of the German government offices towards the Jewish problem.

Hungary

Since the collapse of the Polish state, there have been approximately 50,000 Polish refugees in Hungary. Approximately 45,000–50,000 of them are military personnel, and the rest are civilians. The total number of Jewish refugees is estimated at approximately 3,000–4,000. However, this number is probably too low, because many soldiers are unwilling to acknowledge that they are members of the Jewish race, out of fear of reprisals. But it must be said, particularly in this context, that the Hungarian government has thus far drawn no distinction between Jewish and non-Jewish refugees. All the military refugees were quartered in 40 camps. Besides board and lodging, the rank and file are given 50 fillér, the officers 2 pengő.[20] The whole organization is a massive burden on state finances. The Red Cross and Quaker organizations are reportedly due to step in and help from now on by providing money and sending medicines.

According to the president of the Hungarian Red Cross,[21] it is especially difficult these days to procure enough bandages, as the Hungarian Red Cross has now been in permanent mobilization status for a year and a half and must make all its resources available to the Hungarian military.

The majority of the Polish refugees, however, would like to be transported as soon as possible to the part of Poland that is under Russian control. The Jewish Religious Community in Budapest is trying to obtain entry permits to Palestine for the Jewish refugees. A few transports were successfully taken across the Palestinian border *illegally.* According to the director of the religious community,[22] it is reportedly impossible to obtain an entry permit to Hungary for Jewish refugees from Vienna at present.

19 Correctly: Commission for Polish Relief. It was created at the instigation of former US president Herbert Hoover (1874–1964) and, in collaboration with the American Red Cross, provided substantial assistance to the Polish population, in the form of food and clothing, until the end of 1940.

20 The pengő was Hungary's currency from 1927 to 1946. One pengő consisted of 100 fillér.

21 The president of the Hungarian Red Cross was Baroness Gizella Apor (1886–1971).

22 The long-time chairman of the Jewish Community of Pest was Samu Stern (1874–1947), banker, simultaneously chairman of the central organization of the reform-oriented (Neolog) communities in Hungary; opposed Zionism; chairman of the Budapest Jewish Council after the German occupation of Hungary in 1944.

DOC. 43

On 23 November 1939 the commanding general of the Posen (Poznań) military district complains about conflicts between the Wehrmacht and the SS in the Wartheland[1]

Report (marked 'secret') by Walter Petzel,[2] of Military District Command XXI, Posen, for the senior commander of the replacement army in Posen, dated 23 November 1939 (copy)

The Warthegau must be regarded as pacified. Repeated rumours of rebellion have not been confirmed in any instance. The reason for this is not a change in the mood of the Polish population, but rather their realization that resistance is futile. That said, it is evident that the large number of released prisoners and miscellaneous demobilized Polish soldiers now pose a threat which requires constant vigilance, especially as a great many officers have not yet been captured. Suppression of this threat is possible only through the military occupation of the country in the present form; the civilian administration is completely incapable of accomplishing this with the available police forces.

The extensive reconstruction work in every area is not assisted by the intervention of SS formations on 'special ethnopolitical missions', which are not answerable to the Reichsstatthalter[3] in the performance of these tasks. What we see here is a tendency to intervene decisively in all administrative areas beyond the scope of these tasks and to create a 'state within a state'. This development cannot fail to have an effect on the troops, who are outraged at the ways in which these missions are carried out. As a result, by generalizing on the basis of such cases, they become set against the administration and the Party. I will eliminate the danger of serious conflicts by issuing strict orders. It cannot be denied that this presents a great challenge to troop discipline.

In almost all the larger towns, the aforementioned organizations have carried out public shootings. The selection process for these varied greatly and was often incomprehensible, and in many cases the implementation was a disgrace.

In some Kreise, all the Polish landowners have been arrested and interned with their families. Arrests were almost always accompanied by looting.

In the cities, evacuations were carried out, during which residential blocks were emptied at random and the inhabitants loaded onto lorries at night and taken to concentration camps. Here, too, looting was a constant occurrence. Housing and rations in the camps were such that the corps physician feared an outbreak of disease and thus a danger to the troops. In response to my appeal, these issues are now being rectified.

In several cities, operations against Jews were carried out which degenerated into the gravest excesses. In Turek on 30 October 1939, three SS vehicles under the command of a senior SS officer drove through the streets, and the people in the street were randomly beaten about the head with bullwhips and other long whips. Ethnic Germans were also

1 BArch, NL 104/3. Published in *Trial of the Major War Criminals before the International Military Tribunal*, vol. 35 (Nuremberg: Secretariat of the Tribunal, 1949), pp. 88–91. This document has been translated from German.

2 Walter Petzel (1883–1965), career officer; commander of the Wehrmacht's 1st Army Corps from 1 Sept. 1939; artillery general from 1 Oct. 1939; commanding general and commander of Military District XXI in Posen, 1939–1945.

3 Arthur Greiser.

among the victims. In the end, a number of Jews were driven into the synagogue, where they were made to sing as they crawled through the pews, while being beaten the entire time by SS men with whips. Then they were forced to drop their trousers so their naked buttocks could be beaten. One Jew, who had soiled himself in fear, was forced to smear his faeces onto the faces of the other Jews.

In Lodz it has become known confidentially that SS-Oberführer Mehlhorn[4] issued the following directives:

(1) From 9 November unemployment benefits will no longer be paid to Poles and Jews; only compulsory labour is remunerated. (Measure already confirmed.)
(2) From 9 November Jews and Poles will be excluded from the allocation of rationed foodstuffs and coal.
(3) Provocation is to be used to create unrest and trigger incidents in order to facilitate the ethnopolitical work.
(4) The fire brigade is to be reinforced immediately to prevent accidental fires in Jewish and Polish residential neighbourhoods and factories from getting out of control and spreading to other properties.

(The measures pertaining to (2) and (4) have not yet been confirmed.) While the Reichsstatthalter invariably stresses the Wehrmacht's merits in speeches and announcements, a tendency to the contrary is apparent on the part of the offices and institutions mentioned above, which seek to belittle and disparage the Wehrmacht's achievements. A particularly blatant case of this has been reported to me from a victory celebration at Ostrowo[5] on 5 November 1939. Reich Orator Bachmann[6] was the speaker there. He did not mention the Wehrmacht at all as far as the Polish campaign was concerned. He mentioned the Wehrmacht only in a single sentence, which dealt with the war against England.

When giving the number of soldiers killed in action, he mentioned only the murdered ethnic Germans; the fallen soldiers were not commemorated with a single word.

The ethnic Germans received recognition, and the audience inevitably gained the impression that the Wehrmacht had not actually been involved in the liberation. This impression became all the stronger when the speaker stated that it had not been a war against Poland at all. Rather, he said that the Führer had merely ensured that the Poles were stripped of the weapons delivered to them by England and France, arms which they would not have known how to use anyway.

One gained the impression that what mattered to the speaker was simply preventing the German population from developing any sort of respect for the army.

4 Dr Herbert Mehlhorn (1903–1968), lawyer; joined the NSDAP and the SA in 1931, and the SS in 1933; chief of staff and deputy head of the Gestapo in Saxony, 1933–1935; head of the Central Department of the SD Main Office at the Gestapo Central Office in Berlin from 1935; head of Central Office I/1 at the SD Main Office; deputy chief of the civil administration in Poznań in Sept. 1939; head of the Reichsstatthalter's Administration Department, senior official in charge of all 'Jewish questions' in the Warthegau from Sept. 1941; Regierungspräsident in Opole in 1944; thereafter a corporate lawyer in Oberndorf/Neckar.

5 Ostrów Wielkopolski: a small town south-west of Kalisz.

6 Presumably Hans Bachmann of the Gau Thuringia Press Department. 'Reich orator' (Reichsredner) was an official function in the NSDAP for Party officials who were deemed especially proficient as speakers or propagandists.

The speech, which was witnessed by the honour guard present at the ceremony, did not fail to make the corresponding impression on the troops.

As the military commander of Posen has already reported to the OKH, the troops are very keenly aware of the incongruity between their service pay and the far greater daily allowances of the other formations.

The facts noted here involve areas that are largely beyond the Reichsstatthalter's direct influence. Corrective action concerning these matters could be taken only by higher offices. I believe I do not err in my assumption that such action would lend welcome assistance to the Reichsstatthalter in his resolute reconstruction work, which he is undertaking with vigour and vigilance.

DOC. 44

On 23 November 1939 representatives of several German agencies and authorities in the Wartheland discuss the plundering of the Jewish and Polish populations[1]

Record of the discussion led by SS-Sturmbannführer Rapp in the office of the Higher SS and Police Leader in Posen, dated 25 November 1939[2]

Minutes
of the discussion led by SS-Sturmbannführer Rapp on 23 November 1939 – 4 p.m. – concerning the treatment of the Jewish and Polish assets that have been confiscated and forfeited to the Reich in the course of the evacuation measures.

SS-Sturmbannführer *Rapp* began by outlining the political objective and the current status of the evacuation measures. He explained that the point is to deport all Jews from the Reichsgau 'Wartheland', as well as those Poles who might constitute a threat to the dominance of Germandom because of their Polish nationalist attitude or their intellectual influence.

In connection with the evacuation, quite a number of grave economic problems have surfaced, which the discussion today was meant to help resolve. Foremost among these was the registration, conservation, and safeguarding of the confiscated assets.

Dr *Beyer*[3] first pointed out that the economic authorities must know, in good time, the names of the persons slated for evacuation, as the planning of the replacement and

1 AIPN, GK 68/107, fols. 10–14. Copy in USHMM, RG 15 015M, reel 2. This document has been translated from German.

2 Added to the first page of the original: 'Distribution list: present: SS-Sturmbannführer Rapp and staff; Reichsstatthalter's Economics Department: Oberregierungsrat Haßmann, Dr Beyer; Main Trustee Office East: Bank Director Ratzmann; regional tax authority: Oberfinanzrat Rose; land office: SS-Standartenführer Hammer; Urban Police: Major Hagelstein; Security Police: SS-Untersturmführer Wiebeck; staff of SS-Gruppenführer Koppe: SS-Obersturmführer Massury; Gau commissioner's office for immigration: Reichsamtsleiter Weber; Chamber of Industry and Commerce: Dr Karsten, Dr Tomaschewski; Foreign Exchange Protection Commando: SS-Untersturmführer Geisler; Trustee of Labour: SS-Untersturmführer Kendzia; president of the German Resettlement Trustee Company: Dr Bang.'

3 In Jan. 1940 Dr Beyer was the head of the trustee branch office in Łódź and, in this function, also chairman of the advisory committee of the Łódź office of the Main Trustee Office East's real estate section.

the orderly registration of the assets depended upon this. SS-Sturmbannführer Rapp promised to inform the relevant authorities in a timely manner.

Bank Director *Ratzmann*[4] stated that the Main Trustee Office East was founded for the purpose of registering and accepting in trust all assets that become available. Trustees are placed in the businesses, the homes are taken over by the cities, and the bank accounts are blocked. In this way, conservation of the assets is largely ensured.

In a discussion of liabilities and possible claims for compensation, Dr *Beyer* next put up for debate the question of whether a large, combined fund should be created, or whether the individual assets must continue to be linked to the previous owner in order to facilitate the subsequent reconstruction of economic life. The discussion ultimately produced unanimous agreement that special administration of the separate assets is necessary to a degree. It was agreed that the economic authorities concerned will create a form that must be filled out by the evacuated Poles and Jews, along the lines of the income tax declaration for Reich Germans. SS-Sturmbannführer Rapp pointed out that the procedure must be made as simple as possible, because otherwise the implementation of the evacuation measures within the designated time period would be at risk.

Next the discussion turned to the question of how the political measure of evacuation could be balanced with the needs of the economy. The deportation operation must not cause any disturbance to economic life. SS-Sturmbannführer Rapp pointed out that his office's card index could be used and asked the business and industry representatives to supply, on an ongoing basis, the names of those who cannot currently be removed from the economic process. Dr Karsten emphasized that the appointment of trustees generally causes no difficulties.

SS-Sturmbannführer *Rapp* suggested that, if necessary, individual instructions should be given to the Landräte with regard to evacuation-related issues, or that the economic authorities at local level should be involved.

Next SS-Sturmbannführer *Rapp* asked Oberfinanzrat *Rose*[5] from the regional tax authority to inform him whether and to what extent the wealth of the Poles and Jews could already be assessed at this point. Oberfinanzrat Rose replied that a comprehensive view is difficult, as Poland did not levy a tax on assets. A broad-brush estimate will require at least four weeks.

Oberregierungsrat *Haßmann* raised the question of whether the decision on who is economically dispensable and who is not can be left to the Landräte. In his opinion, a central office must decide on expendability or indispensability, because the pros and cons of the various interests can only be weighed in this way. He noted that it is necessary to make the list for every evacuation operation in the Kreise available to the economic

4 Hugo Ratzmann (1898–1960), bank director; joined the NSDAP in 1933; managing director of Hardy & Co. Bank in Berlin from 1936; head of banking oversight in the civil administration for the military commander in Poznań in 1939; head of the trustee office in Poznań from Dec. 1939 to Feb. 1941; again managing director of Hardy Bank from March 1941; thereafter head of Hermann Lampe Bank in Bielefeld.

5 Oskar Rose (b. 1910), lawyer; worked for the Reich tax administration, first with the regional tax authority in Pomerania; senior tax officer with the regional tax authority in Poznań from late 1939; between 1945 and 1960 personnel manager for various tax authorities in Westphalia and the Rhineland; appointed president of the regional tax authority in 1966; head of the Regional Property and Construction Department in Münster from 1971.

authorities concerned for prior approval. SS-Sturmbannführer Rapp expressed reservations concerning this centralization and pointed out that this would result in an added burden on the Landrat.

The group of offices interested in the economic side effects of the evacuation measures was hereupon identified: the Economics Department of the Reichsstatthalter, the Main Trustee Office East, the regional tax authority, the Trustee of Labour, the land office, the Chamber of Industry and Commerce, the Chamber of Crafts. If questions arise that touch on other offices' areas of responsibility, then these offices are to be involved.

Finally, there was a discussion of individual measures intended to prevent the disorderly loss of confiscated assets: the threat of death sentences for looters, taking inventory in homes and offices, a ban on purchasing from Poles unless they run businesses, and threats of punishment for removing or keeping items subject to confiscation.

DOC. 45

On 24 November 1939 the Higher SS and Police Leader in Posen (Poznań) orders the Jewish councils to cooperate in the mass expulsion from the Wartheland[1]

Letter (marked 'secret') from the Higher SS and Police Leader in Posen, signed Rapp, dated 24 November 1939

Re: deportation of Jews from the Reichsgau Wartheland
Enclosures: 1
To my decree of 12 November 1939,[2] I am adding the requirement that the Jewish councils of elders or Community executive boards must be involved in and be made accountable for the deportation of Jews. The list of the councils of elders appointed by the Security Service is enclosed with this letter.[3]

The local State Police offices and SD offices are to be apprised of the deportation operation in a timely manner.

Using temporary holding camps to house the Jews scheduled for deportation is out of the question. Instead, the Jewish Community executive boards are to be given the order approximately 24 hours before the scheduled departure of the transport to ensure that the selected number of Jews are present. The Community executive boards are to be held personally liable for the proper implementation of the operation. Because of the risk that assets may be carried off, I consider it inadvisable to announce the departure date at an earlier time.

In terms of practicality, the Jews must be assembled several hours before the departure of the train in an enclosed room or courtyard (school), so that there is sufficient time to search their clothing and suitcases for objects that may not be taken along. Before

1 BArch, R 75/3b, fols. 617–618. This document has been translated from German.
2 On 12 Nov. 1939 Wilhelm Koppe, the Higher SS and Police Leader (HSSPF) in Poznań, had issued detailed instructions to expel 100,000 Jews and 200,000 Poles from Reichsgau Posen (later renamed Reichsgau Wartheland) and send them to the East between 15 Nov. 1939 and 28 Feb. 1940: circular letter from the HSSPF Posen, 12 Nov. 1939, BArch, R 49/3033, fols. 2–5. Published in Berenstein et al. (eds.), *Faschismus – Getto – Massenmord*, pp. 43–46.
3 None of the lists mentioned in the document are included in the file.

the search, the Jews must be ordered to voluntarily surrender all prohibited items under threat of the harshest penalties.

It must be ensured that sufficient personnel – including female personnel – are on hand to conduct the search.

Also to be regarded as Jews are all Mischlinge with two or more Jewish grandparents, that is, half-Jews. Aryan wives of Jews, if these wives are of German ethnic origin, must be informed of the possibility of obtaining a divorce. If they are unwilling to part from their family permanently, they are likewise to be deported.

To prevent the transport of the Jews from being delayed by the preparation of the list of deportees, the councils of elders are to be asked forthwith to submit the list of local Jewish residents, in multiple copies, without delay. Furthermore, they are to be asked to provide a list of the Jews who have left since 1 September 1939.

DOC. 46
On 28 November 1939 Governor General Frank orders the formation of Jewish councils[1]

Regulation on the Appointment of Jewish Councils

On the basis of § 5(1) of the Führer and Reich Chancellor's Decree on the Administration of the Occupied Polish Territories of 12 October 1939 (*Reichsgesetzblatt* I, p. 2077), I hereby order that:

§ 1

An agency representing the Jews must be created in every community.

§ 2

This representative body of the Jews, known as the Jewish Council, will consist of 12 Jews in communities with up to 10,000 residents and of 24 Jews in communities with more than 10,000 residents. These Jews must be drawn from the local population. The Jewish Council is to be elected by the Jews of the community. If a member of the Jewish Council withdraws, a new member must be elected immediately.

§ 3

The Jewish Council will elect, from among its members, a chairman and a deputy.

§ 4

(1) After these elections, which must have taken place by 31 December 1939 at the latest, the Kreishauptmann – in the Stadtkreise,[2] the Stadthauptmann – in charge must be informed of the composition of the Jewish Council.

(2) The Kreishauptmann (Stadthauptmann) will decide whether the reported composition of the Jewish Council is to be approved. He can order a different composition.

§ 5

The Jewish Council is required to take orders from German offices through its chairman or his deputy. The Council is liable for the complete and conscientious implementation

1 *VOBl-GG* 1939, no. 9, 6 Dec. 1939, pp. 72–73. Published in Berenstein et al. (eds.), *Faschismus – Getto – Massenmord*, p. 71. This document has been translated from German.

2 Municipal Kreise. Stadtkreise in the Generalgouvernement were headed by a Stadthauptmann.

of such orders. All Jews must obey the instructions issued by the Council for the purpose of carrying out these German orders.

Cracow, 28 November 1939
The Governor General for the Occupied Polish Territories
Frank

DOC. 47

Anonymous report on developments in Kalisz in the Wartheland under German occupation up to November 1939[1]

Handwritten report for the underground archive of the Warsaw ghetto, written on 2 August 1941

III.[2] *Jews in Kalisz from September to November 1939*

Anti-Jewish policies became increasingly evident in Kalisz in early October. Up until then, the situation of the Jews in Kalisz had been bearable. After returning from their wanderings,[3] they had resumed their old activities, started up workshops, opened shops, and business was almost as usual. Due to the masses of German soldiers passing through Kalisz, shops began to thrive, especially pastry shops and restaurants. Jewish bakers and confectioners had a lot of work and made a good living.

However, the city became increasingly German. All Polish signs were removed and replaced with German ones, and the streets were given German names, such as Friedrichstr. (Aleje Piłsudskiej), Rathausplatz (pl. 11 List[opada]),[4] Feuerwehrstr. (Kanonicka), Poststr. (6 Sierpnia)[5] etc. Likenesses of Hitler appeared in display windows. Nazi swastikas fluttered everywhere. The Polish population was able to adapt to the new conditions very quickly; many were eager to show the Germans that they were one step ahead in some ways. In addition to swastikas and portraits of Hitler and Göring, many shop windows now displayed, in place of the previous signs reading 'Christian firm', signs reading 'Arische Firma' and 'Juden Zutritt verboten'.[6] Also, as early as 10 September, an old Endek[7]

1 AŻIH, Ring I/783 (825). Published in English translation in *The Kalish Book*, ed. I. M. Lask (Tel Aviv: Societies of Former Residents of Kalish and the Vicinity in Israel and U.S.A., 1968), pp. 284–287. This document has been translated from Polish.
2 The report is part of three texts filed together, the first sections of which are entitled 'Report of a Kaliszer from 1939' and 'Part II, Sept. 1939. Koło' (19 July 1941). The third text, dated 2 August 1941 and printed here, is the final draft of a report that was probably composed earlier. The author is likely to have been Nusen Aron Koniński (d. 1942), teacher; member of the Poale Zion party and the Association of Primary School Teachers; lived in Kalisz before the war; head of the boarding school at 18 Mylna and contributor to the underground archive of the Warsaw ghetto; on 8 August 1942 deported with his wife and his pupils to Treblinka, where he was murdered.
3 This is a reference to the flight of Jews when German troops entered Kalisz in early Sept. 1939 and their return soon after, when the situation appeared to have settled down.
4 11 November Square (11 Listopada), named in remembrance of 11 Nov. 1918, when Poland regained its independence.
5 6 August Street (6 Sierpnia), named in remembrance of 6 August 1914, when Polish volunteer forces under Piłsudski crossed the Russian border on their own initiative and thus, from the Polish national perspective, planted the seed from which the Polish army would grow again.
6 German in the original: 'Aryan firm' and 'Off limits to Jews'.
7 Reference to the Narodowa Demokracja (ND) movement founded by Roman Dmowski.

pre-election banner reading 'Kalisz without Jews'[8] mysteriously appeared across the whole width of the street at the junction of Kanonicka and 6 Sierpnia. This is how Poles demonstrated to the Germans their attitude towards the Jewish population. The following incident, which occurred in Kalisz repeatedly, is characteristic of Poles' attitude towards Jews. Many Polish men and women, mainly from the working class, maids, and servants, got acquainted with German soldiers and exploited these acquaintances by going with the Germans to Jewish shops (e.g. Siemiatycki's[9]) and forced the shops to give them various goods for free or for a ridiculously low price. There were also incidents of Polish women, domestic helps in Jewish households, bringing gendarmes to their employers, and forcing them to pay rather high sums as alleged compensation or a settling of debts. That is how Polish–Jewish relations unfolded before the eyes of the German occupier. It would be a crude exaggeration to claim that such things caused the hostile German policies towards the Jews. But they may have contributed to a quicker introduction of anti-Jewish regulations by the German authorities.

Immediately after the Germans took Kalisz, they arrested numerous Jews and Poles who had remained in the city. These Jews returned 5–6 weeks later and reported (Weingart from 28 Górnośląska, owner of an oil mill, was one of them[10]) that they had been taken to various German cities and paraded before the population with the words: 'Das sind die jüdischen Schweine die zu den deutschen Soldaten geschossen haben.'[11] In addition, soon after the Germans had marched in, German soldiers went around Polish and Jewish shops and confiscated various goods, primarily cotton goods. The stores of Siemiatycki, Sender, Braun and Frydlender, Gerszt, Hejszerek, and Naparstek were affected by the first confiscations. Gradually, regulations were issued that applied only to the Jews. It was ordered that Nazi flags be removed from all Jewish homes. German officers then went specifically to Jewish shops and confiscated goods en masse, took furniture from apartments. Many Jews were ordered to vacate their shops and homes within hours, even minutes, and German or Polish families were housed in them. The city was transformed within a matter of days. Numerous Jewish shops were closed, many were emptied of their goods, while other shops were taken over by new owners, mainly Germans. For example, Maria Hoffmann took over Herszkowicz's grocery store 'Golden Horn'; Siemiatycki's factory store was acquired by the Kurz firm, Sender's storehouse by the Miller brothers, and Perl's warehouse by Rymanowicz.

The appearance of Kalisz's Jewry also changed. Before the war, the Jewish population in Kalisz included a very large Orthodox group. There were many Jews in Kalisz who had beards and sidelocks, wore kapotes and traditional Jewish caps. This garb now disappeared almost completely. Not a single Jew with a Jewish cap could be seen in the streets; all wore hats or flat caps. Given the numerous cases in which German soldiers had cut off Jews' beards and sidelocks, these too had largely disappeared. The Jews shortened their beards and tried to make them less noticeable, in any case.

One day the Germans inspected all Jewish shops and ordered that signs reading 'Jude',[12] at the prescribed height of no less than 20 cm, be prominently displayed.

8 Before the Second World War, the National Party (SN) linked to Narodowa Demokracja led numerous anti-Jewish initiatives. It was particularly strong in western Poland.

9 Leon Siemiatycki, merchant; chairman of the board of directors of the Jewish Commercial Bank.

10 Probably Jakob Weingart (1889–1942); merchant in Kalisz until 1939, then lived in Warsaw.

11 German in the original: 'These are the Jewish pigs who shot at the German soldiers.'

On 10 October a Jewish Council of Elders was appointed in Kalisz by order of the German authorities. None of the former representatives of the Jewish Community were in Kalisz. On Saturday, 2 September, at 2 p.m., the rabbi of Kalisz, Mendel Alter,[13] left the city and went to Łódź by car, and then never returned to Kalisz. Former representatives of the Community, Heber[14] and Rozenblum, also left for Łódź. Jewish Kalisz was left without its representatives. Given the lack of more suitable people, the starosta of Kalisz[15] summoned Hahn,[16] the cantor at the new synagogue, regarding him as the only person with a certain social standing before the war. He appointed him 'den Ältesten der Juden', and instructed that he form an 'Ältestenrat'[17] composed of 25 members that would represent the Jewish Community of Kalisz to the Germans and ensure that all German decrees relating to Jews were fully obeyed and adhered to. The Council members were liable for this to the Germans with their lives and property.

Within the next two days, the following people were appointed to the Ältestenrat: Hahn – cantor; engineer Cukier[18] – manufacturer; Leon Rynek – manufacturer; Zajdel – merchant; Lewkowicz – president of the Jewish bank and of the Jewish grammar school; Kacinel,[19] lawyer; Perkal, lawyer – president of ORT and TOZ; Dr Płocki;[20] Mojżesz Szlumper[21] – former city councillor and Poale Zion-Left activist;[22] Michał Ajzenberg[23] – former city councillor, Bund activist; Dawid Herman; Luzer Mitz – Bund activist, chairman of the tailors' union; Leon Siemiatycki – president of the Jewish bank; Rzepkowicz – a board member of the bank; Wiśniewski[24] – manufacturer; Arkusz,[25] secretary of the Union of Jewish Craftsmen; Dr Lubelski;[26] Dr Seid.[27]

12 German in the original: 'Jew'.
13 Menachem Mendel Alter (1877–1942), Hasidic rabbi in Kalisz; brother of Rabbi Abraham Mordecai Alter (popularly known as the Gerer rebbe); chairman of the Association of Rabbis in Poland from 1924; wanted by the German authorities, he went into hiding for a time and then fled to Warsaw; murdered in Treblinka.
14 Josef Mosze Heber was the chairman of the Jewish Community.
15 Hermann Marggraf (b. 1887); joined the NSDAP in 1930; head of the NSDAP Gau office and Landrat in Heiligenstadt from 1938; acting Landrat in Kalisz from late 1939.
16 On 10 Oct. the Landrat ordered Gerszon Hahn, the cantor of the synagogue on Krótka Street, to set up a Council of Elders.
17 German in the original: 'the Jewish elder' and 'Council of elders'.
18 Stefan Cukier, engineer; factory owner in Kalisz.
19 Moryc Kacynel.
20 Dr Juda Płocki.
21 Dr Mosze Szlumper; local Bund politician and member of the city council.
22 The Zionist-Marxist workers' party Poale Zion (Workers of Zion) split into two independent parties (Poale Zion-Left and Poale Zion-Right) in 1920. The Poale Zion-Left sympathized with the Bolshevik revolution in Russia. It promoted the Yiddish language and was an important influence on leading Jewish intellectuals in Poland. During the German occupation, many of its members worked for the underground archive or were politically and culturally active in the Warsaw ghetto.
23 Michał Ajzenberg, factory owner in Kalisz.
24 Izydor Wiśniewski, factory owner in Kalisz.
25 Ben-Cijon (also Samuel) Arkusz (b. 1899); secretary of the Union of Jewish Craftsmen in Kalisz; lived in Łódź from 1940.
26 Dr Rafał Lubelski.
27 Dr Dawid Seid (1892–1942), gynaecologist; chairman of Hashomer Hatzair in Kalisz, his birthplace; expelled from Kalisz in late 1939; thereafter lived in Warsaw, then in Łosice.

Considering the absence of many of those who were active in society, this group of members can be said to have been generally rather good. The Council of Elders officiated in the Community's former premises on Kanonicka. Hahn was the president,[28] Herman was the secretary, later Arkusz.

Around 15 October the Council received its first task when it was given three days to conduct an accurate census of the Jewish population, their property, sums of money exceeding 2,000 złoty, and jewellery. The lawyer Kacinel took on the census; 15–20 people worked with him non-stop, day and night, in shifts, for ten days. It's worth mentioning that, during this time, the Germans provided the Community with typewriters for the nights. The census recorded over 20,000 Jews.

The Germans turned to the Council with various kinds of demands, such as the delivery of 50 sets of bed linen within four hours. Because goods of this type had been confiscated and removed from Jewish shops long ago, the linen was collected from private Jewish homes. It was collected by Jews, employees of the Council. There were cases in which some households refused to hand over these items and those carrying out the collection (e.g. Mr Górny[29]) had to then drag out the linen by force. The Germans often demanded money from the Council. The Ältestenrat therefore imposed on the more affluent Jews a community tax, which met these demands. Councillors Cukier, Kacinel, and Szlumper attended to the finances.

The Council's main task was the Labour Section. The Germans announced that they would not round up Jews in the streets for labour; instead, they would inform the Council every day of their demand for a specified number of workers, which the Council was obliged to supply. The Council was obliged to comply only with demands from senior army authorities and the Gestapo. The Labour Section provided the Germans with an average of 150–200 workers per day, in exceptional cases (e.g. when troops passed though the city) with 400 workers. The Labour Section sent out summonses to Jews ordering them to report for work two to three days per week. Those who did not want to report for work had to pay a fee of 2–3 złoty per each day of work. The monthly rate for them was 36 złoty. In addition to this, 50 groszy per day were charged for deferment and 1 złoty per day for a sick note (issued by physicians working for the Council). Many Jews bought themselves out of work, and therefore 60–70 per cent of the workers sent to the work sites by the Labour Section were substitutes, who were paid 2 złoty for each day of work. The section paid these workers out of the proceeds for sick leave and deferment, and gave the Council the surplus of 50–100 złoty per day.

Jewish workers were deployed at various German sites. The Germans used Jews to bury Poles who had been executed in the new Jewish cemetery. Jews also worked in the barracks in Piskorzew,[30] at the Holy Trinity hospital, at the city council, at the sappers' quarters in the school building on Polna, at the Verkehrspolizei[31] in the starosta's building, at the Hilfspolizei[32] in the social insurance building, at the gendarmerie at 23 Aleja, and at the

28 In fact, it was the lawyer Perkal who took on the leadership of the Jewish Council.

29 Probably Maks Górny; later one of the leaders of the labour battalion attached to the Jewish Council; imprisoned in a labour camp in 1941.

30 A neighbourhood in Kalisz.

31 German in the original: 'traffic police'.

32 German in the original: 'auxiliary police'.

Gestapo at 3 Jasna. Four Jewish workers were continuously engaged in removing or painting over Polish inscriptions and signs in the city. Ten workers were also always held in reserve at the Community building to meet the ad hoc demands frequently made of the Council by the authorities. Normally, however, demands were made one day in advance.

The Germans didn't pay the Jews for labour; only at some sites did they give the workers meals and bread. Their treatment of Jews at work varied. At some sites, German soldiers and Jews developed almost friendly relations; they gave the Jews cigarettes, talked freely, and offered them beer. At other sites, however, they beat the Jews as they worked, goaded them, and shoved them around. One day a German soldier stamped the foreheads of all the Jews working at the city hall with the word 'Schweine'[33] and ordered them not to wash it off for a whole week. He checked every day whether the writing was still visible on the foreheads.

A group of 25 Jews worked the land on an estate near Kalisz for three weeks, and the German soldiers there treated the Jewish workers much better than the owner of the estate did – a Volksdeutschka.[34]

The Labour Section's Council representative was Michał Ajzenberg, the technical head was Maks Górny, and working with him were Bordowicz, Karo, Winter, and Edelsztajn.

The Council also had a hospital ward, which was managed by Wiśniewski and Samuel Arkusz. In late October a ward for internal medicine and gynaecology was opened in the building of the old Jewish hospital. As there was no hospital equipment there of any kind, the Council bought 30 beds, and a minimum of bed linen was collected from among the Jewish population. A pharmacy was opened at the hospital, albeit very poorly stocked, as well as an outpatient clinic, which soon saw considerable activity. Dr Seid, Dr Lubelski, Dr Płocki, and Dr Gross-Schinaglowa[35] worked at the hospital and at the outpatient clinic.

The Council also developed certain social welfare activities. It maintained a home for the elderly and opened a canteen at the Talmud-Torah House. It was run by Mrs Marta Cwasowa. The canteen was open from late October for four weeks and provided 100 meals each day; some of them for 30 gr., some for 10 gr., and some for free. The canteen was financed by the Labour Section's takings. The mikvah[36] in Kalisz was periodically open during the Council's administration.

It is difficult to determine the attitude of the German authorities towards the Council with any certainty. On the one hand, the Germans recognized the Council as the official Jewish representation, and they turned to it with various demands, which the Council met completely. On the other hand, however, incidents occurred that attest to an entirely different attitude towards it. On one occasion, the Gestapo summoned two Council members (Herman and someone else). When they arrived at 11 a.m., they were locked in a separate room and held there until the evening. Nothing was done to them. One day the Germans came to the Community building and took ten Council members with them to the Gestapo. Among them was 80-year-old Dr Beatus, who happened to be in

33 German in the original: 'pigs'.
34 Mixed German-Polish term for an ethnic German woman.
35 Dr Debora Schinagel, née Gross (1910–1944); paediatrician in Kalisz; murdered in Auschwitz.
36 Jewish ritual bath.

the Community building at the time. The Germans 'trained' the whole group in the yard; they ordered the men to exercise, jump, and sand the floors, while at the same time severely beating them. Several Germans stood with cameras the entire time and photographed all these feats. On one occasion, the Germans came to the Community building and wrecked the place, destroyed railings and broke chairs.

The Germans turned the building of a Jewish grammar school into a hospital for wounded Polish prisoners of war. They did the same with the buildings of a Jewish primary school. The new synagogue remained closed and undamaged the entire time. The Germans temporarily housed Polish prisoners of war in the large synagogue and in the Talmud-Torah House.

There were numerous cases of Germans desecrating Jewish holy books. For instance, they entered the synagogue at 19 and 21 Ciasna, took the Torah scrolls, and burned them in the courtyard, ordering Jewish girls to dance around the fire. On Polish Army Street, German soldiers wrecked a synagogue and threw the Torah scrolls and Hebrew books that were there into the river. This was accompanied by beatings and shootings.

Under the pretence of carrying out a sanitary inspection of Jewish homes, German soldiers entered the home of one poor family and ordered the mother to undress her 17-year-old daughter and wash her in their presence.

In Kalisz the Germans killed Flinkier, a Jew, co-owner of a mill and former editor of the Jewish Kalisz newspaper. His maid, a Pole, had denounced him to the Germans for keeping a weapon in his home. He was arrested, but on the way to prison had an attack,[37] and the German soldiers shot him. In early November the Germans also shot a Polish priest on suspicion of possessing a firearm.[38] They ordered the Jews to bury his corpse in front of the gate to the Jewish cemetery.

In connection with the resettlement of Germans from the Baltic countries within the Reich, many of the better Polish and Jewish apartments were seized in early November. Those who were thrown out of their homes were allowed to take only a few things with them and they were all housed in the monastery on Stawiszyńska. The vacated apartments were promptly taken over by the numerous Baltic Germans who had been resettled to Kalisz. The Poles were gradually released from the monastery; some Jews were also allowed to leave, but the remainder were moved to the market hall, which had already previously been used in turn to house prisoners of war and horses for the army. Around 10 November the system for vacating apartments changed, insofar as the Germans now systematically sought out Jewish homes and assembled the Jewish population in the market hall. German gendarmes closed off the entire street, blocking off all its exits, ordered the occupants of all Jewish apartments to leave in a matter of minutes, and led them in groups to the hall. Every few minutes, Jewish families could be seen being escorted in groups through the city, carrying small bundles, rucksacks, or pillows. There was a lot of confusion among the Jews during the roundups. The gendarmes gave them so little time that everyone nervously grabbed what they could in the apartment and hardly anyone considered what would be needed most during the imminent journey.

37 Presumably a heart attack.

38 This is a reference to the execution of the priest Roman Pawłowski in Kalisz on 20 Oct. 1939.

Given the situation, anyone who could still escape from Kalisz did so, mainly to Warsaw. Many people even sneaked out of the hall and left for Warsaw by train. There were many among the escapees who intended to get not only to Warsaw, but from there also farther east – to cross the border and settle among the Soviets. That was the intention of many young people from Kalisz in particular, who had discontinued their education, lost their jobs and livelihoods, and intended to start a new life over there under normal conditions. Kalisz railway station was thus constantly full of departing people; hundreds of Jews left the city with every train, never again to return. More and more Jews assembled in the hall each day. The city became deserted. There were now only Christian caretakers in the homes previously occupied by Jews. The absence of over a quarter of the population significantly affected the look of Kalisz. While it was now evident to all that the Germans intended to radically rid Kalisz of Jews and resettle them away from the city, no one yet knew where.

On 16 November the Germans, headed by the city mayor[39] himself and the newly appointed Hauptmann,[40] went to the Council of Elders. With shouts of 'keine Juden mehr in Kalisch' and 'keine Gemeinde mehr',[41] they herded all the present Council members and officials to the hall, having first searched them and taken their money and jewellery. At the same time, the Germans broke open the Community's cash box and took 3,500 złoty.

Before the resettlement, around 20 November, an order was issued in Kalisz that limited the time Jews were permitted to be outside their homes. From that point on Jews were allowed to move about the city only between 8 a.m. and 5 p.m. This same order required Jews, regardless of age or sex, to wear a 10 cm wide 'Jewish yellow' (judengelbe Farbe[42]) armband on the right arm.

The Germans were to resettle all Jews from Kalisz within a short time, permitting only the ill and those convalescing to remain in the hospital. They also allowed Hahn, Wiśniewski, and Arkusz, as representatives of the Council, to stay. Apart from the hospital, in which about 200 people remained, including staff and their families, the Germans sent those who had not left of their own accord in goods trains to the Lublin area, Cracow, and Rzeszów. Residents from the home for the elderly were sent to Baczki near Lochów.

This is how the Germans emptied one of Poland's oldest Jewish communities of its Jews within a very short space of time, sending a mass of over 20,000 people into wandering and exile.

39 The author means the Stadtkommissar in office from Oct. 1939 to mid Jan. 1940, Walter Grabowski (1896–1945?), sales representative; joined the NSDAP and the SA in 1926; Kreisleiter in Schlawe in 1936 and in Greifenhagen, Pomerania, in 1939; employee of the Central Office for Relocating the Sick (the camouflage organization for the 'euthanasia' operation) from Nov. 1939; involved in the murder of the sick in Schneidemühl and Kościan; financial director from 1941; later director of the killing centre at Meseritz-Obrawalde.

40 German in the original: 'captain'; probably the local Wehrmacht commander.

41 German in the original: 'no more Jews in Kalisz' and 'no more Community'.

42 German in the original: 'Jewish yellow'. The German expression used in the regulation issued by the Regierungspräsident in Kalisz, Friedrich Uebelhoer, is added here in parentheses. See Doc. 35, fn. 5.

DOC. 48

Anonymous report on the expulsion of Jews from Poznań and the surrounding area to the General Government in November 1939[1]

Handwritten report for the underground archive of the Warsaw ghetto, written in late 1940 (copy)[2]

The resettlement of Poznań Jews to Kreis Sochaczew–Błonie

During the current war, Poznań Jews were the first to be subjected to homelessness brought on by evacuation and resettlement. This process is officially called being 'ausgebürgert',[3] i.e. losing citizenship rights. Even those who opted for Germany after the World War were resettled. The following places became 'judenrein':[4] Buk, Nowy-Tomyśl, Lwówek, Pniewy, Szamotuły, Grodzisk-Pozn.,[5] Wronki, Ryczywół, Klecko, Sieraków, Oborniki. Added to this transport were also Jews from Kowal and Lubień, a total of 1,300 (one thousand three hundred) souls. From these same places up to 3,000 Poles, party leaders, reputable craftsmen, and merchants were evacuated – a total of 80 per cent of the Polish population.[6]

On 4 November 1939 Gestapo men arrived. They went from house to house and announced to the Jews that, on 7 November, all Jews were to go to a central assembly point in Buk, in the synagogue and in the Catholic community building. They could take with them bed linen and winter clothing, as well as 200 zł. per family. The Jews from the aforementioned places remained in Buk for the whole month.

Episode from Grodzisk–Wkp.[7]

The assets of the Jewish Community were to be deposited with the gendarmerie. A member of the Community, Mr Glicensztejn, brought the Torah scrolls, as well as gold and silver objects. The Obermeister[8] ordered that the scrolls be placed on the floor. [Mr G.] asked for permission to place them on the table because they were sacred items. He was given permission to do so, but in another room. Mr G. was very frightened because that room was hermetically sealed and was once used to extract confessions. With tears in his eyes, he placed the scrolls on the table. Seeing this, the Obermeister closed the door, checked again to see whether it was properly locked, approached him, and seeing the tears in Mr G's eyes said, 'Weinen sie nicht, trösten Sie ihre Frau und Kinder, es wird so nicht bleiben.'[9] He said a warm goodbye and left.

1 AŻIH, Ring I/969 (1072). This document has been translated from Polish.
2 The document is probably by Bernard Kampelmacher, a teacher and contributor to the underground archive, who worked on a monograph about the town of Grodzisk Mazowiecki; died of typhus in the Warsaw ghetto.
3 German in the original: 'expatriated'.
4 German in the original: 'free of Jews'.
5 Grodzisk Poznański (now Grodzisk Wielkopolski): a town located south-west of Poznań.
6 This figure is almost certainly greatly inflated.
7 Grodzisk Wielkopolski; evidently, both names were common at the time.
8 German in the original here and in the following: 'police chief', referring to the local gendarmerie chief.
9 German in the original: 'Do not cry, comfort your wife and children; it will not remain like this.'

The resettled Jews in Buk lived in constant fear. They were not permitted to sleep at night. The service[10] and Sturmabteilung[11] of surrounding towns and villages, as well as various commissions, continued to check the number and condition of the resettled people. They lived off their own money and provisions that they had brought with them. There were constant reminders that anyone with foreign currency or more money than the permitted amount would be shot. The wealthier surrendered the money. The Oberpolizeimeister[12] allowed for a vat for communal cooking, opened an account with the butcher and a cooperative, which delivered supplies in return for the surrendered money. These supplies were used to cook good dinners. Another order followed: Polish currency is to be surrendered and exchanged for German marks. The cash was taken and everyone was told to come back in a few days, but a transport took place in the meantime and the money of those naive people was gone.

On 7 November ¼ kg of butter was issued per person and meat was cooked, but all the luggage, including bedding and linen, which had been initially permitted, was now withheld and would be sent on later. The military surrounded the road, and the Jews were herded into stinking wagons and, together with the sick and the old, taken to Grodzisk–Wkp. Several thousand Poles were already assembled there at the station. The escort was composed of the Selbstschutz and the SA. Here the intention was to separate the Poles from the Jews during the march to Südhof camp, 5 km from Grodzisk–Wkp. The Poles walked together with the Jews. It was raining heavily. The endless column moved through the town. The onlookers wept. High-voltage wire fences surrounded the grounds of the camp. Two of the expellees died in this barbed wire. They were buried in the Catholic cemetery in Grodzisk Pozn., because the Jewish one had been levelled. Leopold Kohn, a rich industrialist from Zbąszyn, also died in Südhof, in a dark corner of a barrack. Everyone was placed in unlit barracks, the Poles separated from the Jews. The Poles were given meals, and the Jews were not. Three days later the Stadtkomisarz[13] arrived. He never spoke to the Jews other than through an intermediary. He shouted: 'Heraus mit dem Judendreck.'[14] In half an hour everyone in the camp was ready to leave. There was another inspection at this point; some had their remaining money taken from them and were escorted by the SA to Młyniew.[15] The Jews were loaded into goods wagons, women with children separately; the Poles by contrast in carriages. The wagons were sealed with lead and supplied with buckets. They were to go to Volhynia. House owners from the Poznań area were promised similar properties in Volhynia. Promises!

They travelled for three days and three nights non-stop. They passed through some stations twice. They went through Kutno, Warsaw, and Otwock. Sometimes the train travelled at great speed, as if into an abyss. Twice they wanted to unload them, but the

10 Ethnic German auxiliary service.

11 German in the original: 'Storm Troopers'.

12 The local gendarmerie chief.

13 Polish version of the German original: Stadtkommissar. The Stadtkommissar was Richard Lissberg (1912–1996), businessman; joined the NSDAP in 1930; attended an NSDAP training academy (Ordensburg); Landkommissar in Grodzisk Maz. in early 1941; assigned to the commissioner for the Jewish quarter in Warsaw in June 1941; Landkommissar in Buczacz from August 1941; served in the war from May 1942; in Essen after the war.

14 German in the original: 'Out with the Jewish filth.'

15 Village near Grodzisk Wielkopolski, now part of the town.

local authorities refused. After three days the wagons were opened. It turned out that they were at Szymanów station, near Sochaczew. Here the escort took their leave and travelled back, together with the same wagons, while we were shown Niepokalanowo,[16] where we were to settle.

From then on, the Kreishauptmann[17] of Sochaczew assumed supervision of us. He was reasonably well disposed towards us. Straw was provided. On his orders we received food at a cheap price, seized from people passing through. The administrators of this settlement were monks, known before the war as great antisemites, publishers of the *Mały Dziennik*.[18] Common hardship now bound us together. They took pains to look after us, gave us warm food, provided iron stoves heated with sawdust, and there were even medical consultations and medicines. Next to arrive were Jews from Kowal and Lubień,[19] wearing yellow patches. They had been chased out with truncheons. The Poles ordered them to tear off the patches or they tore them off themselves.

Contact was established with the Joint [JDC]. Żychliński and Bartosz arrived. They brought tea, semolina for the children, and 2,000 złoty. A kitchen was set up. Winter approached, and it became necessary to leave 'Niepokalanowo'. The Joint sent a delegation to the towns of Błonie, Grodzisk,[20] Żyrardów, and Wiskitki. The city councils also receive orders from the Landraty[21] to accept the expellees.[22] Jewish councils provide assistance, aid committees are set up, and the expellees are given free apartments and warm food. Homes for the old and the sick are created. They are treated in clinics.

The Jews of Kreis Sochaczew-Błonie passed the hospitality test with flying colours. They frequently went without food in order to relieve the suffering of the homeless from the Poznań area. They can serve as an example to the Jews of Warsaw.

16 Correctly: Niepokalanów.

17 German in the original. Karl Adolf Pott (1906–1943), lawyer; joined the NSDAP in 1931 and the SS in 1941; acting mayor of Ratingen, 1933; assistant official in the Department for Local Government Affairs of the Prussian Ministry of the Interior, 1934; in the state governor's office in Münster, 1935–1937; deputy and acting Landrat in Zielenzig, 1937–1939; Kreishauptmann in Sochaczew, 1939–1942; served in the war, 1942–1943; killed in action in the Soviet Union.

18 The Catholic and antisemitic *Mały Dziennik* was edited by Father Maximilian Kolbe and appeared 1935–1939 in a high print run (130,000 copies on weekdays, 250,000 copies on weekends).

19 Towns in the east of the Wartheland, south of Włocławek.

20 Grodzisk Mazowiecki, about 30 km south-west of Warsaw.

21 German in the original. Correctly: 'Landräte'.

22 Change of tense in the original.

DOC. 49

In November 1939 the Jewish Religious Community in Rzeszów in District Cracow announces a directive requiring Jews to wear an armband[1]

Announcement from the Jewish Religious Community in Rzeszów (poster), undated (second half of November 1939)

To the Jewish population!
With effect from 1 December 1939, the Governor of District Cracow has ordered that all Jews over the age of 12 must wear visible identification when outside their homes.[2]

A Jew within the meaning of this directive is:

1) anyone who belongs, or has belonged, to the Mosaic religious community;
2) anyone whose father or mother belongs, or has belonged, to the Mosaic religious community.

As identification, an armband is to be worn on the upper part of the right sleeve of clothing and outer garments, displaying a blue Star of Zion on a white background, facing outwards. The white background must be at least 10 cm wide; the Star of Zion must be large enough for the opposite points to be at least 8 cm apart.

Jews who are in the district only temporarily are also subject to this directive for the period of their stay.

Jews who fail to comply with this requirement must expect severe punishment.

The armbands are available from the Jewish Religious Community, Rzeszow, 21 Ring, at the price of 50 pfennigs or 1 złoty apiece.

1 Muzeum Okręgowe w Rzeszowie, MRR 1047. Copy in YVA, M-54/20. Poster in German and Polish. This document has been translated from German.
2 The directive is dated 18 Nov. 1939: APKr, 33, SMKr/64.

DOC. 50

On 4 December 1939 the Governor of District Radom sets out the distribution of the transports of people expelled from western Poland to District Radom[1]

Letter from the Governor of District Radom in the General Government, p.p. signed Dr Krummacher,[2] to the Kreishauptmann in Busko, Dr Wilhelm Schäfer,[3] dated 4 December 1939[4]

1) Re: *resettlement*

Arrivals:

Kreis Radom:	Szydlowiec station	1,000 [Jews][5]
	Radom station	1,000
	to be housed in Przytik	
Kreis Kozienicza:	Garbatka station	1,000
	for the villages of Kozienice and Gniewoszow	
Kreis Ilza:	Wierzbnik station	1,000
Kreis Opatow:	Ostrowiec station	5,000
	for the villages of Ostrowiec, Opatow, Lagow, Iwanisza[6]	
	Jakubowice station	1,000
	for Ozärow[7]	
Kreis Sandomierz:	Dwikozy–Sandomierz station	1,000
	for Sandomierz	
Kreis Busko:	Jedrzejow station, with narrow-gauge railway to Chmielnik	1,000

1 AIPN, GK 639/37a, fols. 2–5. This document has been translated from German.

2 Dr Gottfried Adolf Krummacher (1892–1954), lawyer; served with Border Force East in 1919; joined the NSDAP in 1930; Landrat of Oberbergischer Kreis from 1933; briefly in charge of the Deutsches Frauenwerk (German Women's Work), 1933/34; leader of the German Christians movement in the Rhineland; temporarily pensioned off in 1935; chief of staff in District Radom from 1939. On 28 Nov. 1939 Krummacher had invited the representatives of various German authorities in District Radom to a meeting in Kielce on 30 Nov. 1939.

3 Dr Wilhelm Schäfer (1903–1979), lawyer; police chief in Ulm from 1931; joined the NSDAP and the SA in 1933; Landrat in Crailsheim, April 1935 – Sept. 1939; Kreishauptmann in Busko, 1939–1945; interned in 1945; employee and later company lawyer of a vinegar factory in Tübingen from 1946.

4 Distribution list: 1. Section heads (also financial, railway, postal, and judicial systems, regional road construction office, employment office); 2. Kreishauptleute and Stadtkommissare; 3. General Government; 4. SS and Police Leader, incl. gendarmerie and district commander of the Security Police and the SD; 5. Reichskreditkassen (branches of the special bank set up to facilitate transactions by the Wehrmacht) in Radom, Kielce, Petrikau, Tschenstochau; 6. NSV; 7. Special courts in Radom, Kielce, Tschenstochau, Petrikau; 8. Army Command XXXVI; 9. Ortskommandantur in Radom; 10. Oberfeldkommandantur 581 Moszczenica; 11. Oberfeldkommandantur 540 Kielce; 12. German forestry superintendents in Tschenstochau, Petrikau, Opoczno, Radom, Kielce North, Kielce South, Starachowice; 13. Radom local armaments inspectorate, 44 Traugutt-Staße. The original contains handwritten annotations and underlining.

5 Here and below, the expellees not specifically designated as Poles are Jews.

6 Correctly: Iwaniska.

7 Correctly: Ożarów.

Kreis Kielce:	Kielce station	2,000
	of these, half to Kielce, half to Checiny	
City of Tschenstochau:	Tschenstochau station	4,000 Poles
Kreis Radomsko:	Radomsko station	1,000 Poles
	Koniczpol[8] station	1,000 Poles
Kreis Wloszczowa:	Wloszczowa station	1,000 Poles
Kreis Jedrzejow:	Jedrzejow station	1,000 Poles
Kreis Petrikau:	Petrikau station	1,000 Poles
Kreis Rawa:[9]	Rogow station (District Warsaw), narrow-gauge railway to Royav–Biala–Rawa[10]	2,000 Poles
	of these, distributed	1,500 to Rawa 500 to Biala
City of Tomaschow:[11]	Tomaschow station	2,000 Poles
Kreis Opoczno:	Opoczno station	1,000 Poles

Whether additional transports will arrive and when the individual trains are likely to arrive has not been disclosed. At any rate, additional transports are to be expected.

2) Working committees for the care of the persons arriving – Polish ones for the Poles, Jewish ones for the Jews – should be formed immediately. These committees can operate under the auspices of the Red Cross. These working committees are to consult the organizations of the Polish Catholic and Protestant churches. The working committees are to be supervised and assisted. If serious emergencies are feared, such as the threat of epidemics, the German authorities can make limited funds available. The persons arriving are to be fed and then housed according to plans that must be drawn up in advance. The surrounding population must provide vehicles for transport. Provisional infirmaries for the sick must be set up by the Polish working committees, and they are to be staffed by Polish or Jewish physicians. Poles and Jews are to be kept separate in all instances. Arriving Jews should be kept together, so that they can be sent on elsewhere as soon as possible.
3) Segregated transports of Jews – exclusively or predominantly Jews – have not been registered for the district and must therefore be redirected if they do arrive. They are to be sent on to Brest Litowsk (transfer site for 'Ukrainians' to Russia) or taken across the pedestrian bridges over the Vistula from the neighbouring towns into District Lublin, as in Sandomierz, for example.
4) The relevant employment offices and the wojts[12] of the receiving municipalities are to be informed when transports arrive, so that the employment offices can begin working with the arrivals straight away.

Polish physicians with families are to be placed immediately, so that they can begin their work where they are needed.

Jewish physicians are to be placed provisionally in Jewish colonies. Skilled workers are to be supplied to the closest relevant firms and housed nearby.

8 Correctly: Koniecpol.
9 Rawa Mazowiecka.
10 Biała Rawska.
11 Tomaszów Mazowiecki.
12 Correctly: 'wójtowie', plural of 'wójt', Polish local administrative official.

5) The transports that have arrived so far and all additional arriving transports must be reported immediately to me by telephone, giving approximate figures for Poles and Jews separately, as well as their state of health, type of temporary housing, and final destination. It is to be anticipated that these transports, which are initially scheduled up to 15 December, will become a permanent feature. The population level will thus have to be increased by 30–40 per cent.

With the aid of forced labour and compulsory labour schemes, additional housing – if only in the most primitive form – will therefore have to be built in all the villages and towns that have been designated to house these persons. The idea is one-storey log cabins, made of unhewn logs, double-walled with a layer of earth between the walls as thermal insulation. Any additional work will have to be left to the inhabitants of these houses. This work must be done even in winter and kept on schedule by the Polish authorities with the aim of ensuring a normal housing distribution, first and foremost to prevent the spread of disease. However, under no circumstances must these additional housing facilities lead to increased billeting of troops etc. in rural localities, for example.

6) Regarding spring tillage, it is necessary to prepare for the expanded use of the available land in a way that will enable the new families to grow all the potatoes they need themselves. The same applies to growing vegetables. The Kreis agricultural officers will receive more detailed instructions on this matter. All fallow land must be included in this, and additional land must be cleared, if necessary. The newcomers must know where their fields are as soon as possible, so that they can take advantage of thaws to start preparing the land assigned to them as soon as possible. The subordinate Polish authorities are to be extensively involved and made responsible for planning and performing these tasks. Implementation should be monitored continuously, if necessary by specially appointed Polish supervisory officials.

7) At the same time, a special order (secret) will be issued to supplement my directives of 27 November concerning the expulsion of Jews.[13]

DOC. 51

On 4 December 1939 the World Jewish Congress's Executive Committee condemns the crimes against Jews in Poland[1]

Statement from the Executive Committee of the World Jewish Congress in Paris,[2] dated 4 December 1939 (carbon copy)

Communiqué

The Executive Committee of the World Jewish Congress, the major organization of Jews from all over the world, has just met in Paris to address the appalling situation of the Jews currently living under the control of the Nazi authorities, notably in Poland, where

13 This could not be found.

1 CZA, C 3/7–14, fol. 256. Copy in USHMM, RG 68 045M, reel 2. This document has been translated from French.

2 The headquarters of the World Jewish Congress was located in Paris until mid 1940.

the Jewish population is being treated with unheard-of cruelty and cold-heartedly left to die of starvation.

Moreover, the committee has learned of the inconceivable measures decreed by Hitler's government, with the intention of creating in the Lublin region of Poland a 'territory reserved for Jews' in which the Reich intends to forcibly concentrate all the Jews of Poland, Austria, Czechoslovakia, and Germany.

This project is already being implemented: thousands of Jews from the [Polish] Corridor, Gdynia, Poznań, Katowice, and other towns in Poland, Czechoslovakia, and Austria have already been transported like cattle towards this 'reservation'; they have been torn from their households and are only allowed to take a maximum of three hundred marks with them. They are currently deprived of everything, often without shelter and unable to provide for themselves. This is Hitlerism's most cynical effort at population resettlement thus far.

It should be added that one of the obvious goals of this measure is to create divisions between the Poles and those Jews who are citizens of other German-occupied countries by driving the former out of their lands, which have been transformed into concentration camps intended for the latter.

The Executive Committee of the World Jewish Congress formally protests against this act of barbarism. In particular, it indignantly rejects the Reich government's inadmissible claim to be able to resolve the Jewish question in the way it sees fit. The civilized world – drawing upon the enduring principles of human rights and the rights of nations – will undoubtedly consider the decisions taken by the current German government to be null and void.

In a letter addressed to His Excellency General Sikorski,[3] the Executive Committee has just informed the Polish government, which alone has legal sovereignty over the territory of Lublin, of the indignation provoked in Jewish communities all around the world by this latest act of Hitlerian barbarism, reiterating its sympathy in the face of the suffering endured by all Poles, irrespective of their race and belief.

3 Władysław Sikorski (1881–1943), career officer; chief of the Polish general staff, 1921–1922; Polish prime minister and minister of foreign affairs, 1922–1923; inspector general of the infantry, 1923–1924; minister of military affairs, 1924–1925; opponent of the Piłsudski and Sanacja governments from 1926; prime minister of the Polish government in exile in France and in Britain from Sept. 1939 to July 1943; also commander-in-chief of the Polish armed forces in exile from Nov. 1939; died in a plane crash off Gibraltar on 4 July 1943.

DOC. 52

On 7 December 1939 the Regierungspräsident in Marienwerder relays Himmler's ban on cutting off the beards of Jews[1]

Letter from the Regierungspräsident in Marienwerder (no. I 2489 P.4.),[2] signed Borchert, to the Landräte in the formerly Polish areas within the Regierungsbezirk West Prussia[3] (received by the Landrat in Kreis Briesen[4] on 11 December 1939) and the head of the gendarmerie regional division in Graudenz to be issued to the police administrative offices, dated 7 December 1939 (carbon copy)[5]

Order to the SS and police in the former Polish territory[6]
I hear that every now and then the beards of Jews are being cut off. Should this mischief have occurred anywhere, in future it must be strictly suppressed. First, such things do not help solve the Jewish question, and second, it is not our job to teach hygiene to the Jews.

To the senior commanders of the Order Police p.p.

1 AIPN, GK 82/5, fol. 21r–v. Copy in USHMM, RG 14 004M, reel 1. This document has been translated from German.

2 Otto von Keudell (1887–1972), lawyer; worked in the Prussian Ministry of the Interior and the Reich Ministry of the Interior; joined the NSDAP and the SS in 1933; Präsidialrat (official in charge) at the Reich Chamber of Fine Arts from Nov. 1933; Ministerialrat, head of the Department of Music and Fine Arts in the Reich Ministry of Public Enlightenment and Propaganda in 1935; Regierungspräsident in Marienwerder, 1936–1945.

3 The Regierungsbezirk West Prussia (seat of government: Marienwerder) was until Oct. 1939 part of the Prussian province of East Prussia. It was then incorporated into the new Reichsgau Danzig-West Prussia, enlarged through the addition of formerly Polish areas, and subsequently renamed Regierungsbezirk Marienwerder. The formerly Polish areas in Regierungsbezirk Marienwerder were Landkreise Briesen, Graudenz, Leipe, Neumark, Rippin, and Strasburg.

4 The Landrat in Kreis Briesen forwarded the order on 21 Dec. 1939 as a directive to the Urban Police in Briesen and Gollub and the head of the gendarmerie in the Kreis: AIPN, GK 82/5, fol. 21r–v.

5 The original contains official stamps of the chancellery of the Regierungspräsident of West Prussia.

6 Himmler's order as Reichsführer-SS (O-Kdo. O [1]1 no. 330/39) dated 17 Nov. 1939.

DOC. 53

On 9 December 1939 the chairman of the Warsaw Jewish Council describes the plight of the Jewish population[1]

Handwritten diary of Adam Czerniaków, entry for 9 December 1939

9 December 1939 – SS in the morning. I presented the case of a worker.[2] I was later ordered to employ Dr Nossig at the Community.[3] It was announced that Berlin would send new directives on emigration (the reservation?) in January.[4] Julek is ruined.[5] My wife is constantly crying.[6] Yesterday, on Zielna, I was rounded up for labour. Young Jews, like geese in a coop, driven off for labour. Ausweisy[7] helped: I was not taken for labour.

The Commissariat[8] summoned one of the Council members for labour. He had to find a substitute off the street for 8 złoty.

We were ordered to set up a new hospital with 500 beds. I have been summoned to see the Reichskommissar[9] (an official on Daniłowiczowska) about the hospital.[10]

The SS explained to me today that they are not our immediate superiors, but merely an executive body tasked with carrying out the orders of various authorities. They weighed in on the matter of the hospital. It was agreed that the city will cover the costs for December, but that we have to repay them as a loan.

I have 20,000 złoty in the Community coffers. Tomorrow, the workers' wages alone will amount to 40,000 złoty. What about the staff salaries due on the 15th? What will happen with the transfer of the hospital and orphanages?

1 YVA, O-33/1090. Published in Czerniaków, *Dziennik getta warszawskiego*, pp. 68–69. This document has been translated from Polish.
2 This probably refers to the murder of a forced labourer recruited by the Jewish Council.
3 Dr Alfred Nossig (1864–1943), author and sculptor; Zionist activist; lived in Berlin from 1900; founder of the General Jewish Colonization Organization in 1908; head of the culture and arts section of the Warsaw Jewish Council, 1940; killed by the Jewish Combat Organization (ŻOB) in Feb. 1943 as he was believed to be an informant for the German authorities.
4 See Doc. 42.
5 Julian Poznański (1880–1949), engineer; teacher at the Jewish Community's vocational school before the war.
6 Dr Felicja Czerniaków (1887–1950), educator; head teacher and employee at the Jewish Central Association for the Care of Orphans (CENTOS) before the war; left the ghetto in early August 1942 and found refuge with Poles on the 'Aryan side' of Warsaw.
7 German in the original. Correctly: Ausweise, 'identity cards'.
8 This presumably refers to the office of the Stadtpräsident.
9 German in the original: 'Reich commissioner'.
10 Czerniaków actually meant Stadtpräsident Oskar Dengel, whom he referred to using the title of Dengel's predecessor, Dr Helmut Otto, as Reich commissioner (for the city of Warsaw). Dr Oskar Dengel (1899–1964), lawyer; joined the NSDAP in 1931 and the SS in 1942; mayor of Würzburg, 1934–1939; Stadtpräsident of Warsaw, Nov. 1939 – March 1940; Stadtkommissar in Lille in 1940; deputy Regierungspräsident of Main-Franconia, 1941–1945; extradited after the war to Poland, where he was sentenced to five years in prison. He served his sentence until 1956.

DOC. 54

On 10 December 1939 the Regierungspräsident in Kalisz orders preparations for the establishment of the Lodz ghetto[1]

Circular letter (marked 'secret') from the Regierungspräsident in Kalisz, Uebelhoer,[2] to the local party and police offices, dated 10 December 1939[3]

Strictly confidential!
Establishment of a ghetto in the city of Lodsch
According to my assessment, approximately 320,000 Jews presently live in the city of Lodsch.[4] It will not be possible to evacuate them immediately. Extensive analyses of all the agencies potentially concerned have revealed that a consolidation of all the Jews in a closed-off ghetto will not be possible. For the time being, the Jewish question in the city of Lodsch must be resolved in the following manner:

1. The Jews living north of the line formed by Listopada/November-Straße, Freiheitsplatz, and Pomorska/Pommersche Straße are to be housed in a closed-off ghetto such that, first, the area required to form a German centre of power around Freiheitsplatz is cleansed of Jews and, second, the northern part of the city, inhabited almost exclusively by Jews, is included in this ghetto.
2. The Jews living in the remaining part of Lodsch who are fit for work are to be formed into work details, housed in military barracks, and guarded.

The preliminary work on and implementation of this plan are to be handled by a task force, to which the following authorities or agencies will delegate representatives:

1. NSDAP
2. Lodsch field office of the Regierungspräsident in Kalisch
3. Lodsch municipality (housing authority, construction office, public health authority, food supply office, etc.)
4. Order Police
5. Security Police
6. Death's Head Unit
7. Chamber of Industry and Commerce
8. Tax Office.

1 APŁ, 221/31866b, fols. 1–5, MF 15 065. Published in Artur Eisenbach (ed.), *Dokumenty i materiały do dziejów okupacji niemieckiej w Polsce,* vol. 3: *Getto łódzkie* (Warsaw: Centralna Żydowska Komisja Historyczna w Polsce, 1946), pp. 26–31. This document has been translated from German.

2 Friedrich Uebelhoer (1893–1945?), military officer; in the Freikorps Lettow-Vorbeck, 1919; joined the NSDAP in 1922 and the SS in 1935; dropped out of law school; NSDAP Kreisleiter in Naumburg an der Saale from 1931; head of the National Socialist People's Welfare (NSV) Gau office in Halle-Merseburg from 1933; mayor of Naumburg from 1934; Regierungspräsident in Kalisch (Kalisz) and in Litzmannstadt (Łódź) from Oct. 1939 to the end of 1942; suspended over a conflict with Himmler and Greiser, and transferred to Merseburg as Regierungspräsident in summer 1943; is thought to have died in 1945.

3 Distribution list: Reichsstatthalter in the Warthegau, NSDAP Bezirk Lodsch, Lodsch field office of the Regierungspräsident, Lodsch municipal administration, chief of police in Lodsch, Order Police, Security Police, Death's Head Unit, Chamber of Industry and Commerce, tax office, reserve, Regierungspräsident in Kalisch. The original contains handwritten annotations and notes.

4 In fact, there were just under 160,000 persons in the ghetto when it was sealed off in late April 1940.

I myself will chair this task force, and in my absence I will be represented by the head of my field office in Lodsch, Regierungsrat Dr Moser.[5] Kriminalrat Gans will be in charge of overall planning on the task force.[6] The offices listed above will supply the names of their representatives by 16 December 1939.

The proposals that I have received so far regarding the expansion of the ghetto are insufficient in my view. According to conservative estimates, some 220,000 Jews already live in the northern parts of the city, while approximately 100,000 more reside south of the line formed by Listopada/Novemberstraße, Freiheitsplatz, and Pomorska/Pommersche Straße. Those in the latter group who are not fit for work are likewise to be housed in the ghetto. The task force's first task is therefore to define the perimeters of the ghetto to be established and to resolve the ensuing issues, such as rerouting the roads running through it and tram lines, etc. In addition, it is necessary to immediately determine how many Germans and Poles still live in the area that is to become the ghetto and have to be relocated. New places of residence for these persons must be found and secured in order to ensure a smooth resettlement process. This process, which has to be undertaken before the ghetto is established, must be carried out by the Party and the municipal administration where Germans are concerned, but only by the municipal administration where Poles are concerned.

The following preparations must also be carried out:

1. Decisions on how to seal off the area (construction of road blocks, barricades in front of building façades and exits, etc.).
2. Establishing the procedures for guarding the boundaries of the ghetto.
3. Procuring the materials required to seal off the ghetto through the Lodsch municipal administration.
4. Making arrangements for healthcare for the Jews within the ghetto, i.e. supplying medicines and medical instruments (from Jewish ownership), especially to control epidemics (public health authority).
5. Preparing arrangements for the removal of bodily waste from the ghetto and the transport of corpses to the Jewish cemetery or the establishment of a cemetery within the ghetto (municipal administration).
6. Procuring the quantities of heating fuel required for the ghetto (municipal administration).

Once these preliminary tasks have been completed and sufficient guard units have been mustered, the establishment of the ghetto will take place at a stroke, on a day to be determined by me. This means that, at a certain hour, the ghetto's predetermined perimeter will be manned by the guard units designated for this purpose and the streets will be closed off with barbed-wire obstacles and other barriers. At the same time, Jewish workers who are to be recruited from within the ghetto will begin bricking up or

5 Dr Walter Moser (b. 1906), lawyer; joined the NSDAP and the SS in 1932; head of the Gestapo office in Braunschweig from 1933; head of the Municipalities Department in the Braunschweig Ministry of the Interior from 1934; head of the trustee office in Łódź, 1939–Dec. 1942; simultaneously head of the Łódź office of the Regierungspräsident in Kalisch, 1939–1940; deputy Regierungspräsident in Łódź; transferred to active duty in the Waffen-SS due to corruption, 1943–1944; corporate lawyer in Braunschweig after the war.

6 Presumably Karl Gans (b. 1893), acting head of the State Police office in Łódź in 1939.

otherwise blocking building façades. In the ghetto itself, a Jewish self-administration will be appointed immediately, consisting of the Jewish elder and a greatly expanded Community executive committee. This Council of Elders in the ghetto must perform the following tasks:

1. *Food supply section*

Setting up and maintaining communal kitchens.
Utilizing the foodstuffs available in the ghetto, which will be delivered by the municipal administration.
Distributing the fuels, which will be delivered by the municipal administration.

2. *Public health section*

Deploying physicians.
Supervising pharmacies.
Setting up one or more hospitals as well as epidemic wards.
Providing the requisite nursing staff.
Drinking-water supply.
Latrines and removal of bodily waste.
Funeral system.

3. *Accounting section*

Funding the foodstuffs delivered.

4. *Security section*

Establishing an order service.[7]
Establishing a fire brigade.

5. *Housing section*

Allocating the available rooms.
Constructing housing barracks.
Providing beds etc. for the ghetto residents.

6. *Registration section*

Registration of all persons living in the ghetto and monitoring of persons incoming and outgoing.

The Lodsch municipal food supply office will deliver the necessary food and fuel to points in the ghetto which are yet to be determined, and hand them over to the agents of the Jewish self-administration in the ghetto for utilization. The principle here must be that food and fuel may be paid for only with barter goods, such as textiles etc. This should allow us to extract all of the tangible assets that the Jews have stockpiled and hidden.

At the same time as or shortly after the ghetto is established, those Jews living outside the ghetto who are unfit for work will be moved into the ghetto (Security Police, Order Police, municipal administration). The homes in the rest of the city that have been vacated as a result of this relocation must be secured against unauthorized intrusions. The harshest punishments are to be used against Jews who engage in malicious destruction during their eviction from their homes. Supervision of the abandoned apartments is to be left to the individual administrators or caretakers, who are to be held responsible for

7 On the Jewish Order Service, see also Doc. 247.

this task, under the oversight of the relevant Order Police agencies. The municipal housing and real estate office will take over the management of these apartments and the furnishings they contain as soon as possible. The buildings and apartments that will no longer be used at all will be determined after their condition has been examined or after a decision has been taken regarding the city's replanning.

When combing the remaining parts of the city for Jews who are unfit for work and will therefore be moved to the ghetto at the same time as or shortly after the ghetto is established, the Jews living there who are fit for work must also be rounded up. They are to be formed into work details, housed in barracks designated in advance by the municipal administration and the Security Police, and placed under guard there. These Jews are earmarked for labour deployment in segregated groups. This deployment will initially consist in demolishing dilapidated buildings in the city centre. The municipal administration will make recommendations to me concerning the buildings to be demolished. These Jews will be fed by communal kitchens within the individual barrack blocks. The Lodsch food supply office will be in charge of ensuring the food supply for these Jews. It will also set the food rations for each individual Jew and ensure their needs are met for a period of three to four days.

It follows from the foregoing that the Jews first used for labour deployment will be those who live outside the ghetto. Jews in the labour barracks who become ill or unfit for work are to be transferred to the ghetto. The Jews living in the ghetto who are still fit for work are to perform the work that arises within the ghetto. I will later determine whether Jews who are able to work should be taken out of the ghetto and brought to the labour barracks.

It goes without saying that the establishment of the ghetto is only a transitional measure. I reserve the right to determine when and by what means the ghetto – and with it the city of Lodsch – will be cleansed of Jews. In any event, the ultimate goal must be to cauterize this plague boil completely.[8]

8 The Police Regulation on the Jews' Rights of Abode and Residence was issued by the police chief in Łódź, Johannes Schäfer, on 8 Feb. 1940, along with detailed implementing provisions; at the same time, he published a timetable for the eviction of the Jews in the *Lodscher Zeitung*, no. 40, 9 Feb. 1940, pp. 5–9.

DOC. 55

On 11 December 1939 the Higher SS and Police Leader in the General Government orders that the Jewish population be concentrated in designated residential districts[1]

First Implementing Regulation to the Regulation of 26 October 1939 on the Introduction of Forced Labour for the Jewish Population, dated 11 December 1939

On the basis of § 2 of the Regulation on the Introduction of Forced Labour for the Jewish Population in the General Government of 26 October 1939 (*Verordnungsblatt*, p. 6),[2] I decree as follows:

§ 1

From 1 January 1940 all Jews located in the General Government for the Occupied Polish Territories are forbidden to relocate their residence or their lodgings beyond the municipal boundary of their present residence, or to go beyond this municipal boundary by giving up their permanent residence or their lodgings and become itinerant without written permission from the local German administrative authority concerned.

§ 2

All Jews who move to or are resettled in the General Government must register with the mayor of their place of residence immediately after they have taken up lodgings in the General Government, but no later than 24 hours after entering the General Government, and inform the Jewish Council in their place of residence that they have moved into the area. The Jewish Council must keep a written record of the notification and present this record to the mayor each Monday, in exchange for written acknowledgement.

§ 3

All Jews named in § 2, once they have been housed, are subject to the provisions of § 1.

§ 4

All Jews in the General Government are forbidden to enter and use paths, streets, and open public spaces between 9 p.m. and 5 a.m. without written permission, limited as to time and place, from the local German authorities in charge. Directives from local German authorities that contain more far-reaching restrictions on movement are unaffected by this.

§ 5

The restrictions in § 4 do not apply in cases of public or personal emergency.

§ 6

Jews who contravene the provisions of § 1 to § 4 will be promptly transferred to severe, long-term forced labour. Punishment under other applicable regulations is unaffected by this.

§ 7

The provisions of § 1 to § 6 do not apply to Jews who verifiably invoke the right of resettlement to which they are entitled under the 'Agreement between the Government of the German Reich and the Government of the USSR on the Resettlement of the Ukrainian and Byelorussian Population out of the Territory of the German Reich's Zone of Interest'.[3]

1 *VOBl-GG* 1939, no. 13, 21 Dec. 1939, pp. 231–232. This document has been translated from German.
2 See Doc. 27.
3 See Doc. 17, fn. 4.

§ 8
The public announcement of this implementing regulation is the responsibility of the mayors, in accordance with instructions from the Kreishauptmann (Stadthauptmann). The Jewish councils are to be instructed by the mayors.
§ 9
This implementing regulation shall come into force with immediate effect.
Cracow, 11 December 1939
The Higher SS and Police Leader in the General Government for the Occupied Polish Territories
Krüger
SS-Obergruppenführer

DOC. 56
On 11 December 1939 the Governor of District Cracow prohibits Jewish children from attending school and orders the dismissal of Jewish teachers[1]

Directive issued by the Governor of District Cracow, signed Wächter,[2] dated 11 December 1939 (copy)

Directive no. 56.
1. All Jewish schools will be closed with immediate effect.
2. All Jewish children who have so far attended public or private schools must be expelled immediately.
3. All Jewish teachers, including Mischlinge of the first and second degrees, must be dismissed without notice immediately.
4. Whether and in what manner instruction for Jewish children will be arranged in future will be decided at a later date.
5. The first roll call of school officials deployed in the administrations of the Kreise will be held on Tuesday, 19 December 1939, at 10 a.m., in the Palais Potocki assembly chamber, 27 Ring. All information on the location, type, number of classes, number of pupils, and number of teachers of all schools in each Kreis must be brought along.

1 YVA, O-21/16/2, fol. 1. This document has been translated from German.
2 Dr Otto Freiherr von Wächter (1901–1949), lawyer; joined the SA in 1923, the NSDAP in 1930, and the SS in 1935; Gauamtsleiter (head of a Gau office) in Vienna and head of training with the NSDAP Landesleitung for Austria from 1931; state commissioner under Reichsstatthalter Seyss-Inquart from 1938; governor of District Cracow from 1939; governor of District Galicia from Jan. 1942; head of the military administration in Italy from 1944; lived in hiding in the Austrian mountains and later in the Vatican under an assumed name; died in Rome in 1949.

DOC. 57

On 11 December 1939 the Jewish Representative Body in Będzin orders Leon Żmigród to pay a levy[1]

Letter from the Jewish Representative Body in Będzin to Leon Żmigrod,[2] 24 Kołłątaja, dated 11 December 1939

In connection with the *second levy* imposed on the Jewish population of our town, we ask you to deposit 500 Reichsmarks at the Representation's cash office *today*, i.e. Monday, 11 December, no later than 6 p.m.

Should you fail to pay the aforementioned sum by the deadline stated above, which is final, you and your family are in danger of catastrophic consequences, not excluding placement in a *concentration camp*. We warn you once again that the aforementioned sanctions may follow automatically, even against the will of the Representation; you alone are liable.

DOC. 58

On 12 December 1939 the Higher SS and Police Leader in the General Government issues provisions on forced labour for the Jewish population[1]

Second Implementing Regulation to the Regulation of 26 October 1939 on the Introduction of Forced Labour for the Jewish Population in the General Government (registration provision), dated 12 December 1939

Under § 2 of the Regulation on the Introduction of Forced Labour for the Jewish Population in the General Government of 26 October 1939 (*Verordnungsblatt*, p. 6),[2] I decree:

§ 1

All Jews living in the territory of the General Government who are between the ages of 14 and 60 are subject to forced labour. As a rule, this obligation to perform labour will last two years; it will be extended if its educational purpose has not been achieved within this period of time.

§ 2

Those required to perform forced labour will be housed in camps and deployed for the utilization of their labour, if possible in accordance with any vocations learned. Those not fully fit for work will be deployed in keeping with their capacity for labour.

1 AŻIH, 212/19, fol. 1. Copy in USHMM, RG 15 060M, reel 2. This document has been translated from Polish.

2 Correctly: Leon Żmigród (1904–1942), businessman; lived in Katowice before the war; died in Sosnowiec.

1 *VOBl-GG* 1939, no. 13, 21 Dec. 1939, pp. 246–248. Published in Berenstein et al. (eds.), *Faschismus – Getto – Massenmord*, pp. 205–208. This document has been translated from German.

2 See Doc. 27.

§ 3
Initially, male Jews from the ages of 12 to 60 will be registered for forced labour. These persons will be summoned by a public notice issued by the mayors, in compliance with special instructions yet to be issued by the Kreishauptleute (or Stadthauptleute), to report via the Jewish Council in charge to be recorded in the registration card index. The mayors, in addition to the Jewish councils, will be responsible for the completeness and accuracy of the registration.

§ 4
Labour deployment will take place as specifically requisitioned by the German authorities.

§ 5
The Jews who have been called up for forced labour after being entered in the registration card index must appear punctually at the prescribed time and at the specified assembly point. Food for two days and two clean blankets must be brought along. Craftsmen and particularly owners of workshops must bring all the tools of their trade to the assembly point. The transport of the tools must be ensured, if necessary, by registering them in advance with the Jewish Council. Machinery required to perform a trade and their component parts owned by persons obligated to work will be subject to the discretionary power of the Forced Labour Service once the former have been called up.

§ 6
(1) Effective immediately, all Jews who are required to work are forbidden to sell, pawn, or otherwise dispose of any tools of their trade which are in their possession, including machinery and equipment, without written permission from the Kreishauptmann (Stadthauptmann). Furthermore, any removal or concealment of these trade tools is prohibited.
(2) Acquiring such tools is also prohibited without written permission from the Kreishauptmann (Stadthauptmann).

§ 7
(I) The following will be punishable by up to 10 years of penal servitude:
  (1) Any Jew required to work who
    (a) when ordered to enter his name in the forced labour registration card index fails to appear at the designated time at the place specified in the summons;
    (b) provides false or incomplete information about himself;
    (c) pretends to be unfit for work, or less fit than he actually is;
    (d) when called up for forced labour fails to bring along the tools of his trade that are in his possession, or disposes of these possessions in advance, in violation of the prohibition stated in § 6;
    (e) after he has been called up for forced labour fails to appear at the assembly point or otherwise attempts to evade the obligation to work.
  (2) Any member of the Jewish Council who
    (a) fails to carry out, promptly and meticulously, the registration of the Jews under § 3 after the pending special instructions from the Kreishauptleute (Stadthauptleute) have been issued;
    (b) helps any Jew to evade forced labour, in part or in full.

(3) Any person who
   (a) deliberately impedes the performance of forced labour, incites [others] to violations of this implementing provision, particularly to deceptions or attempts to deceive, or lends aid to such actions;
   (b) intentionally purchases or takes possession of the trade tools of a Jew who is required to work without receiving written permission from the Kreishauptmann (or Stadthauptmann) in charge.

(II) In addition to penal servitude, Jews can be sentenced to the confiscation of all of their assets.

(III) Offenders will be tried by the special court.

§ 8

This implementing provision is to be made public by the Jewish councils without delay, at the mayors' behest.

§ 9

The provisions of § 1 to § 5, § 6(1), and § 7(1) (a) to (e) do not apply to Jews who verifiably invoke the right of resettlement to which they are entitled under the 'Agreement between the Government of the German Reich and the Government of the USSR on the Resettlement of the Ukrainian and Byelorussian Population out of the Territory of the German Reich's Zone of Interest'.[3]

§ 10

This implementing provision shall come into force with immediate effect.
The provision under § 9 ceases to be effective on 2 March 1940.
The Higher SS and Police Leader in the General Government for the Occupied Polish Territories
Krüger
SS-Obergruppenführer

DOC. 59
Between 6 and 13 December 1939 Dawid Sierakowiak describes anti-Jewish terror in Łódź[1]

Handwritten diary of Dawid Sierakowiak, entries for 6 to 13 December 1939

Wednesday, 6 December, Łódź. The first Hanukkah candle was lit today. Given the lack of candles, Father lit some oil inside a hollowed-out potato with a wick made of twisted cotton wool. An original 'menorah'. All the Jews, our neighbours, are awaiting a new Hanukkah miracle. A new Hanukkah! Perhaps the fervent prayers of millions of Jews begging for their liberation will indeed be heard. We have a buyer for the cupboard and the sofa. He's giving us 130 złoty for the two pieces (they cost about 350 zł.). He is a German, but a very decent man known for his kindness to Jews. Father is therefore

3 See Doc. 17, fn. 4.

1 USHMM, RG 10 247. Diary written by Dawid Sierakowiak from 28 June 1939. This document has been translated from Polish.

trying to obtain a sales permit from the administration. I have applied for 'a permit to sell in order to pay rent'. They will probably approve this.

Thursday, 7 December, Łódź. Today I went to school at the appointed time. There were no lessons, but those present were registered. The rooms there are very nice, but not suitable for school use. After registration, I went to Herszkowicz's; Blaustein was there as well. We sat there until almost 4 p.m. At home I found out that the ZUS[2] administration has approved the sale of the cupboard and the sofa. Even so, Father is still restless; he gets worked up instantly. I wish everything were settled already. Everyone is surprised that there's been no news of Hitler lately. They say he's either dead or has been removed from power, etc. There is news of heavy defeats for the Germans in the air and at sea. An old Jewish saying: I need 'rachemim'![3]

Friday, 8 December, Łódź. We only had two lessons today because the cold has set in early. The old school identity cards are no longer valid, and there are no new ones. Today I had to pay 25 groszy for a ticket for the second time this year. The first time was in November, before the old school identity cards were extended. The cupboard has been taken away at last, and the rent has been paid in full up to 31 December of this year. Should Jews be allowed to continue living here, we will be able to sleep well and peacefully. Dozens of rumours are circulating throughout the city again. Good and bad. In any case, all just empty talk.

Saturday, 9 December, Łódź. Today we found out that Jews were badly beaten up on Reymont Square yesterday. Even children as young as three were being kicked on Nowo-Zarzewska. The Jews are now going through the stage of Messianic prophecies. The rabbi of Góra Kalwaria apparently said that liberation will occur on the sixth day of Hanukkah. My uncle says that very few soldiers and Germans can be seen on the streets. This search for consolation in little things is already getting on my nerves. It is better not to say anything. A rumour about a ceasefire spread in the evening. Apparently, to prevent the revolution that is brewing in Germany from spreading, England is demanding only the return of Austria, Czechoslovakia, and Poland, together with a contribution for Poland's reconstruction, allowing the present German government to remain. It seems Jews and Poles are forbidden to travel by train until the 11th. Why? No one knows.

Sunday, 10 December, Łódź. Many large buildings in the city centre have been 'cleansed' of Jews. There is talk of a large number of Jews being sent from Łódź to the Protectorate. Not very pleasant prospects. Today we received a message from our cousins who had left for Białystok. They are healthy there, but they still have no work.

Monday, 11 December, Łódź. School is coming to a standstill. There are no teachers, no lessons, literally nothing; everything is disappearing before our very eyes. In the evening we had two hours of lessons – and nervousness, which luckily turned out to be unfounded. In the evening Father went to our neighbour Hamer and comes back pale with news

2 Zakład Ubezpieczeń Społecznych: Social Insurance Institution.
3 Hebrew: 'mercy'.

that the expulsion of Jews from Łódź is to start at six o'clock today. All the neighbours are packing their rucksacks, bags, etc. We followed suit, and after a short while we were as good as ready. I declared that this is all empty talk and went to bed. Soon everyone else – more or less calmed down – did the same.

Tuesday, 12 December, Łódź. A lousy day. There are fewer and fewer teachers in school. No longer any desire to go at all any more due to the constant reading as a substitute for instruction and lessons ending early. On the way home I suddenly see a terrible scene on Kiliński. A Jew is walking along, and behind him a German dressed as a coachman who beats him on the back with a giant bar so hard that he staggers (the German, that is, while the Jew bends lower and lower, without turning around, so that he is not hit from the front). I began to tremble and I turned off onto Cegielniana as fast as I could and went to Frydrych, a friend from the first grammar school, where I stayed until late so that I could go home at the very last hour [before curfew], when the likelihood of being caught is down to a minimum. While there I read an order about exchanging the Jewish-yellow patches for the yellow, 10 cm wide 'Davidsterne'[4] to be worn on the right side of the chest and over the right shoulder blade.[5] The barbarity is intensifying. Soon they will have us running around with our noses painted red and wearing short trousers. The ingenuity of sadism – as we are aware – knows no bounds. New work in the evening: tearing off the armbands and sewing on the new decorations.

Wednesday, 13 December, Łódź. I was not allowed to go to school today. There was anxiety and fear again before dinner. An hour after Nadzia[6] went to school, Dadek Hamer comes and says that the Jews on Nowo-Zarzewska and Rzgowska are being taken to the vacated market halls to be then sent to the Lublin area. Of course, Father immediately imagines that they have caught Nadzia (whose school is on Nowo-Zarzewska), etc. Luckily, this all turned out to be empty talk and Nadzia returned safely. In the evening, however, terrible but true news arrives. There is massive panic in the city because the Jewish Community has announced that the Jews must leave Łódź. Apparently, over the next four days, anyone who wants to leave can leave and go wherever he wants (as long as it is not within the territory of the Reich). After that, the mass resettlement is going to begin. The Community is to give those without any money 50 złoty each for the departure and send them off today. Everyone is losing their heads. There are restrictions on rucksacks, bags, etc.

4 German in the original: 'Stars of David'.

5 Decree issued by the Regierungspräsident in Kalisz, Friedrich Uebelhoer, making it compulsory for the Jewish population to wear a yellow star as visible identification: Eisenbach (ed.), *Dokumenty i materiały*, vol. 3, p. 23.

6 Nadzia was Dawid Sierakowiak's younger sister.

DOC. 60

On 13 December 1939 the Gestapo office in Posen (Poznań) orders that Jews and Poles who return from the General Government to Reich territory must be shot[1]

Letter (marked 'secret') from the Gestapo office in Posen (B. no. 129/39 II/B-g), signed Bischoff,[2] to the Landrat in Schrimm,[3] dated 13 December 1939[4]

Re: dealing with Jews in German Reich territory in violation of the resettlement order
The Reichsführer-SS – Reich Security Main Office IV (II o) 2 – 288/39 g-1 – issued the following directive by decree on 29 November 1939:[5]

Jews and Poles[6] who have been resettled from German Reich territory to the General Government but are found in German Reich territory in breach of the resettlement order, even if they are in a different province, are to be summarily shot *on the spot.*

This order is to be communicated verbally to the elders of the Jewish communities, where they still exist.

Whenever such persons are found, they must be taken to the local Gestapo office *immediately.*

1 APP, 465/100, fol. 35. Published in Czesław Łuczak (ed.), *Documenta Occupationis*, vol. 8: *Wysiedlenia ludności polskiej na tzw. ziemiach wcielonych do Rzeszy 1939–1945* (Poznań: Wydawnictwo Instytutu Zachodniego, 1969), p. 17. This document has been translated from German.

2 Dr Helmut Bischoff (1908–1993), lawyer; joined the National Socialist German Students' League in 1929, the NSDAP in 1930, the SA in 1933, and the SS in 1935; head of the Gestapo offices in Liegnitz, Harburg-Wilhelmsburg, and Köslin; commander of Einsatzkommando 1 in Einsatzgruppe IV in Sept. 1939; then chief of the Gestapo office in Posen until 1941; then in Magdeburg; SD security officer in Mittelbau-Dora concentration camp from Dec. 1943; in Soviet captivity, 1946–1955; worked for the German Red Cross tracing service, 1957–1965.

3 Alfred Klostermann (1900–1945), teacher; joined the NSDAP in 1928 and the SS in 1938; NSDAP delegate in the Landtag of Hesse, 1931–1933; mayor of the small town of Schlitz in eastern Hesse; school administrator in the Ministry of Culture in Hesse and NSDAP Gau official in 1933; Landrat in Gießen, 1934–1937, in Groß-Gerau, 1937–1939, in Schrimm, 1939–1940, and in Alzey, 1941–1945; killed in action in 1945.

4 Himmler's order was conveyed to the gendarmerie offices in Kreis Schrimm on 3 Jan. 1940.

5 This could not be found. See also Doc. 109, fn. 7.

6 The three preceding words have been underlined by hand in the original.

DOC. 61

On 13 December 1939 the leader of the National Socialist Women's League in Kreis Teschen (Cieszyn) asks the mayor for furniture stolen from Jewish homes[1]

Letter from the Kreis leader of the National Socialist Women's League and German Women's Work, Marie Bless, to the mayor of Teschen, Koperberg,[2] dated 13 December 1939[3]

Dear Sir,

Following my letter of 8 December of this year, I hereby respectfully request permission to visit a few more Jewish apartments for the purpose of obtaining furniture. We will be moving into our new office in the old city hall starting next week and need to furnish the premises. We still lack several desks, chairs, etc., but in particular we also need antique[4] walnut chairs to go with the furniture from the Durst Jewish apartment[5] in Friedrichstraße.

I would be very grateful for a timely response.

Heil Hitler!

DOC. 62

On 16 December 1939 SS-Sturmbannführer Richter reports on the expulsion of Jews and Poles from Lodz (Łódź)[1]

Report by SS-Sturmbannführer Richter,[2] dated 16 December 1939[3]

Report on the evacuation of Poles and Jews carried out in Lodsch between 12 December and 16 December

In the city of Lodsch, the evacuation of a total of 15,000 Poles and Jews had been scheduled for December. Primarily politically suspicious or intellectual Poles were to be evacuated. Substantial difficulties occurred in registering these Poles in lists. According to the Security Service in Lodsch, the original lists, which were good, had been handed

1 APK, 124/10008, fol. 3. This document has been translated from German.
2 Wilhelm Koperberg, NSDAP member; trainee civil servant in Reichenbach (Silesia) in the late 1930s; mayor of Teschen (Cieszyn), Oct. 1939–1945.
3 The original contains handwritten annotations and underlining, as well as an official stamp of the NSDAP Kreisleitung in Teschen (Cieszyn).
4 In the original: kauk., meaning k.u.k. (*kaiserlich und königlich*, 'imperial and royal'), referring to the period style of the Habsburg Monarchy.
5 This may refer to Dawid Durst (1860–1942), who was expelled to Tarnów and perished there, or to his son Gustav Durst (1897–1942), who lived in Cieszyn, worked as a foreign-language teacher, and was forced into the ghetto in Zawiercie; he was murdered in Auschwitz.

1 AIPN, GK 68/218, fols. 27–35. Copy in USHMM, RG 15 015M, reel 3. This document has been translated from German.
2 Albert Richter (1897–1945?), police detective; head of the Gestapo office in the Litzmannstadt ghetto; deputy head of the 'Jewish desk', II B 4, later IV B 4, at the State Police office in Łódź; organized the deportations to the Kulmhof extermination camp, 1941–1942; was sent to the SS and police camp in Danzig-Matzkau following disciplinary proceedings in Jan. 1944; went missing.
3 The document contains several handwritten corrections and underlining.

over to what was then the Gestapo Einsatzgruppe. Only around 5,000 index cards were created there based on these lists. The Gestapo could no longer secure the other extensive lists. As a result, the Security Service was only able to draw up a very limited number of evacuation lists on time. When the lists were reviewed by the municipal administration, it turned out that they prominently featured ethnic Germans who had been identified as suspicious Poles. During the arrest operation, it also turned out that approximately one third of those who were to be apprehended had already left their homes. As a result, only around 2,600 Poles were arrested on the basis of the lists.

It was therefore necessary to resort to Jews to reach the required number of 15,000 persons. Negotiations were conducted with the Jewish Council of Elders in Lodsch with a view to having Jews who were willing to emigrate hand themselves in voluntarily at the camp in Radogosz.[4] So far, approximately 1,000 may have volunteered. Based on a consultation with the mayor[5] and the police chief, it was decided that the only practicable method was to surround city blocks in the Jewish quarter at night and then to clear them. The operation thus began at 8.30 p.m. on 14 December 1939, with 80 NSKK[6] deployed to cordon off the area and 650 members of the Urban Police to carry out the evacuation. It was surprisingly successful. During this operation, which continued until 4 a.m., an estimated 7,000 Jews were arrested and transported by tram to Radogosz camp and the concentration camp run by the State Police. As agreed, these Jews, with the exception of 500 who could no longer be removed by rail, were taken away the next day – that is, on 15 December 1939 – and transported to the [General] Government on three trains. Specifically, one train with 1,500 (according to my calculation 1,850) persons departed at 6 p.m., one train with 1,700 persons at 7.31 p.m., and one train with 2,406 persons at 11.05 p.m.

This evening – on 16 December – another evacuation will be carried out. In the course of this operation, 2,000 Jews are to be arrested and deported by train tomorrow, along with the 500 Jews still remaining in the camp.

The deployment of the Security Police and the collaboration with the Reich Railway worked extremely well. The Security Police had to handle nearly the whole process of conducting the evacuation, including the negotiations with the Reich Railway, single-handedly, as the Lodsch municipal administration failed completely.

I feel compelled to report below on the behaviour of the mayor of Lodsch, who was responsible for the evacuation:

With the exception of the aforementioned conversation between the mayor and the police chief in my presence, which took place on the platform at Kalisch train station,[7]

4 Correctly: Radogoszcz (Radegast), a northern suburb of Łódź. The Germans had set up a concentration camp for Poles and Jews in a former factory building there in autumn 1939. This camp was closed on 5 Jan. 1940, and some inmates were moved to the ghetto, others to the 'extended police prison in Radegast', which was located in a former textile factory. From there, many of the prisoners were taken to other concentration camps.

5 The Stadtkommissar was Franz Schiffer (1896–1940); first joined the NSDAP in 1927; rejoined the NSDAP and also joined the SA in 1932; Oberregierungsrat in the Reich Ministry of the Interior and NSDAP inspector in Gau Pomerania from 1935, as well as Landrat; with the Luftwaffe from Sept. 1939; thereafter Stadtkommissar and Landkommissar in Przemyśl; first Stadtkommissar, then mayor of Litzmannstadt, Nov. 1939 – May 1940; killed in action.

6 NSKK: Nationalsozialistisches Kraftfahrerkorps (National Socialist Motor Corps), the Party's paramilitary vehicle corps.

7 Łódź Kaliska: the largest train station in Łódź.

the mayor did not concern himself with the evacuation in the slightest, as far as I was able to tell. The mayor had put Oberinspektor Kloppmann in charge of implementing the evacuation. Kloppmann, as he emphasized to me several times, did not consider himself authorized to give any instructions to the police chief. But then Kloppmann was unable to reach the mayor at any time on 13 December 1939, for example. As the latter had previously told Kloppmann that he intended to ask Posen to postpone the evacuation until January, Kloppmann had no idea where he stood. The mayor lent Kloppmann no support, and his only vehicle was also taken from him. No other vehicle was available to either Kloppmann or his replacement, Dr Alsleben, because, according to both Kloppmann and Alsleben, the mayor had to transport wine … I also found it impossible, despite multiple attempts, to reach the mayor by telephone over the course of those days.

Oberinspektor Kloppmann had initially named a factory at 53 Kopernikus St. as the site where Jews were to voluntarily hand themselves in. This factory was in operation, and the proprietor had no inkling of the directive. When the Jews presented themselves there, the proprietor threw them out. As I discovered, this 'assembly area' consisted of a courtyard and a rundown, unenclosed basement room where the names were to be recorded on a list. Exactly where the body search was meant to take place, given the piercing cold, was unfathomable. In addition, it was impossible for the people to stand around outdoors with their children for hours in the cold and in driving snow. I therefore ordered that the registration and search of the Jews be conducted in the nearby guildhall of the butchers' guild.

This operation had already demonstrated a total lack of organization, but this shortcoming became even more disastrously obvious during the scheduled evacuation operation on 14 December 1939.

Although the evacuation was undertaken by order of the mayor, he had made almost no preparations. I must note explicitly that no one from the municipal administration – neither a representative of the mayor nor the mayor himself – concerned themselves with the execution of the police operation while it was being carried out, from 8.30 p.m. on 14 December 1939 until 4 a.m. on 15 December 1939. Even at midday on 15 December, the city administration was still of the opinion that 3,500 Jews had been arrested in the course of the operation, while the number of arrests was actually around 7,000. Until that time, the city administration had not even inquired about the operation's success. Above all, the city's job was to make arrangements for registering the Jews in lists and for their transport, which was supposed to take place the same day, on 15 December 1939. Here, too, the city showed a complete lack of interest and failed in every way. According to Oberinspektor Kloppmann, 20 men reported to the camp to register the Jews. Ten of them were sent home again for no discernible reason, although it was readily apparent that not even these 20 men would have been able to prepare the lists in time. Obviously the city had taken no notice at all of the presence of approximately 2,500 Jews in the second camp, because absolutely no provisions had been made for that location. As a result, only a fraction of the inmates in the first camp were recorded on the lists during the afternoon of 15 December 1939. I tried in vain to have Dr Alsleben, Oberinspektor Kloppmann's replacement, bring in enough typists in time. As a result, the vast majority of the Jews left for the [General] Government without having been recorded on the lists. The truth is that the passengers on the trains that departed on the previous days had indeed been registered in lists, but the city administration failed to distribute these lists to the persons in charge of the trains.

According to the arrangements made with the Reich Railway, which the city administration also had not taken care of, but which the Security Police and I had to make instead, the plan was for the Jews arrested in the operation on 14 December 1939 to be taken away on three transports on 15 December 1939. Once the operation got under way, it was impossible to stop it again, even after it turned out that the city had made no preparations of any kind. It was impossible for the very reason that the camps were so crowded that the inmates could no longer spend a single night there; moreover, the apartments, which had already been sealed, would have had to be opened up again, and that would have meant an intolerable loss of face for the German authorities. Above all, the departure had to take place because the inmates would simply have starved to death. The city's care of the inmates took the form of merely distributing bread, as I was informed by Oberinspektor Kloppmann and Dr Alsleben, but this, too, had to be acquired in great haste and only belatedly. Whether milk was handed out to infants is unknown to me. However, it is a fact that the children were not provided for in any way during the transport.

The transport of the Jews took place on 15 December 1939, predominantly in goods wagons, of which there were approximately 90. I repeatedly called the mayor's representatives' attention to the absence of straw on the previous trains. At this point, the city made the following provision: on the afternoon of 15 December 1939, the Police Leader responsible for loading the Jews onto the train at Kalisch train station informed me that 3 (three) carts with straw had appeared at the station, but for want of any agreements and instructions, the carts had left again and had vanished. As I was told today, 16 December 1939, by Dr Alsleben, these three loads of straw, which, let it be noted, were intended to suffice for 90 goods wagons, were being held somewhere at the Kalisch station, but the Reich Railway had refused to load the straw into the goods wagons. I pointed out that it was the city's responsibility, not that of the Reich Railway, to ensure that enough straw was provided for the goods wagons. As the transports on 15 December and 14 December had taken place at night in the piercing cold, the municipal administration's failure on this point is all the more consequential. Due to the inadequate provision of straw and food, it must be expected that not all the persons on the transports, especially the infants, will reach the destination station alive.

After I had noticed that no buckets or pails for the passengers had been placed in any of the goods wagons, including those on the previous days, I strongly rebuked Oberinspektor Kloppmann on 15 December 1939. His reply to me was that, according to the decree, the evacuees had to bring their own pails with them, and therefore the city did not have to make any provisions …

I repeatedly asked the police officers on duty whether the persons in charge of the transports had been provided with the necessary instructions, and every time the answer was affirmative. Where this was the case, however, these instructions were communicated to the transport officials by the police and not by the mayor, as it should have been done according to the decree.

I have repeatedly made the city aware that the departure times of the transport trains, the name of the destination station, and the occupancy figure must be communicated to Posen immediately by telephone and telegraph. Each time I was assured that this had been done. According to a message from the office in Posen, however, only the information for one train was sent there.

How little concern the city showed for the evacuation is best demonstrated by its inability even to state how many thousands of persons have been evacuated from Lodsch. According to the city, there were some 8,400 evacuees, while information from the police indicates that there were 9,600 to 9,900 …

The mayor of Lodsch bears full responsibility for the situations described above, while the police, Reich Railway, and Security Service came through in exemplary fashion and endeavoured, wherever possible, to make up for what the city had neglected to do.

DOC. 63

On 17 December 1939 the Soviet deputy commissioner for foreign affairs meets with the German ambassador to discuss the expulsions of Polish Jews to the Soviet-occupied part of Poland[1]

Record of conversation (marked 'secret') by the deputy people's commissioner for foreign affairs, signed V. Potemkin,[2] dated 17 December 1939

1. I asked Schulenburg[3] to come in so that I could inform him about a number of instances in which significant numbers of Jews – up to 5,000 or more – were forcibly transferred across the border into Soviet territory. I pointed out that when attempts are made to transfer these people back into German territory, German border guards open fire, killing dozens of people. I voiced my supposition that the German embassy had so far been unaware of these outrageous facts, as the embassy would otherwise undoubtedly have taken appropriate measures to stop the practice of forcibly transferring Jews into Soviet territory, which I had described. Given that this practice has not ceased and has even increased in scope at the present time, I made the request that the ambassador contact Berlin and ask the German command to issue orders from there to put a stop at once to the actions I indicated.

1 Archive of the Ministry of Foreign Affairs of the Russian Federation 06-1-7-72, fols. 112–114. Published in *Dokumenty vneshney politiki*, vol. 22/2 (Moscow: Mezhdunarodnyye otnosheniya, 1992), pp. 421–422. This document has been translated from Russian.

2 Vladimir P. Potemkin (1874–1946), teacher and diplomat; member of the School Policy Committee of the People's Commissariat for Public Education after 1917; fought in the Russian Civil War, 1919–1920; in diplomatic service from 1922; ambassador in Greece, Italy, and France consecutively from 1929; deputy commissioner of foreign affairs, 1937–1940; people's commissioner of education, 1940–1943.

3 Friedrich Werner Graf von der Schulenburg (1875–1944), diplomat; German envoy in Teheran in 1923 and in Bucharest in 1931; joined the NSDAP in 1934; ambassador in Moscow, 1934–1941; head of the Russia section in the Ministry of Foreign Affairs from July 1941; executed after the attempt to assassinate Hitler on 20 July 1944 because of his contacts with the Goerdeler Circle.

Schulenburg, displaying extreme outrage, declared that he would contact Berlin this very day and demand the termination of forcible transfers of Jews into Soviet territory.[4]

[…][5]

DOC. 64
On 18 December 1939 the Stadtpräsident of Warsaw orders that Jewish assets must be disclosed[1]

Directive on the Disclosure of Jewish Assets, issued by the Stadtpräsident of Warsaw[2]

§ 1

Based on § 1 of the Governor of District Warsaw's regulation of 17 November 1939,[3] the following assets must be registered:

(1) All physical assets and rights, as well as holdings of goods and valuables of any kind – regardless of the amount of the assets' value – if these were or are still owned or possessed by Jews on 1 October 1939, or have been since that date, in particular:
  (a) Businesses of any kind, with all their movable and immovable assets, including all property rights, such as patents and the like.
  (b) Buildings of any kind, provided they do not fall under (1); undeveloped sites with all associated material rights; plots of land that serve agriculture and forestry purposes, along with all livestock and equipment; as well as all material rights and appurtenances, such as grazing rights, routes for herding cattle, and the like. The registration requirement also applies to shares in such properties.
  (c) Mortgage receivables, stocks, and other share rights, as well as leasehold rights.

(2) All other items of property and valuables that are owned by or in the possession of Jews upon this regulation's entry into force, in particular deposits and credit institutions, notes receivable, securities, cash, home furnishings, and other articles for personal use and the like, if the total value of these assets for the persons living in a joint household (parents, grandparents, children, siblings) exceeds the amount of 2,000 złoty.

§ 2

The owners or their authorized representatives, official receivers, judicial oversight bodies, trustees of bankruptcy assets and dormant estates, trustees, and leaseholders are

4 Von der Schulenburg appealed to Wolf von Tirpitz in a telegram. See *The Ulrich von Hassell Diaries, 1938–1945: The Story of the Forces against Hitler inside Germany*, trans. Geoffrey Brooks (London: Frontline Books, 2011 [German edn, 1946/1988]), p. 69 (entry dated 11 Jan. 1940). Immediately afterwards, the envoy, von Wühlisch, went to see Governor General Frank and demanded that expulsions cease: unsigned note dated 20 Dec. 1939, *Akten zur deutschen auswärtigen Politik 1918–1945*, series D: *1937–1945* vol. 8/1: *Die Kriegsjahre: 4. September 1939 bis 18. März 1940* (Baden-Baden: Imprimerie Nationale, 1961), pp. 439–440.

5 The remaining six items have to do with military affairs.

1 *Amtsblatt des Chefs des Distrikts Warschau*, no. 1, 9 Jan. 1940, pp. 5–7, in German and Polish. This document has been translated from German.

2 This directive was issued before the general regulation for the General Government: see Doc. 81.

3 The Regulation of the Governor of District Warsaw on the Sale and Lease of Jewish Businesses in District Warsaw stipulated in § 1 that an official permit for these actions was required: *Amtsblatt des Chefs des Distrikts Warschau*, no. 1, 22 Nov. 1939, pp. 11–12.

required to register. In the event of the absence of these persons, the family members of the owners who share the joint household must register, or

(a) if businesses are concerned – the senior salaried employee,
(b) if real estate is concerned – it is the caretaker or concierge who makes the registrations, and in the event of their absence, the tenant of the apartment with the lowest sequence number,
(c) if property of another sort is concerned – the persons who possess or manage this property.

The legal or actual guardians of minors and persons declared legally incapable are under legal obligation to register on behalf of the latter.

§ 3

Anyone descended from two Jewish parents is regarded as a Jew within the meaning of this regulation. Mischlinge are regarded as Jews if they belonged to the Jewish Religious Community on 1 October 1939.

Legal entities are regarded as Jewish if there is even one Jew in their management bodies (supervisory board, board of directors, administration, board of trustees, and the like) or on their audit committee (in cases of companies that had no supervisory board), or if there was even one Jew in such bodies on 1 October 1939.

§ 4

The completed forms must be submitted in exchange for a receipt to the offices designated according to the property owner's residence (registered office of the legal entity) or according to the location of the municipal property or the business in Warsaw.

§ 5

The registration can only be completed on special forms. The place and time of sale of these forms will be announced separately by the Warsaw Chamber of Industry and Commerce.

§ 6

Jewish assets that have not been registered in the manner and within the time period outlined above, or that have knowingly been registered inaccurately, are subject to confiscation; in addition, the persons required to register the assets may be liable to fines or imprisonment.

Warsaw, 18 December 1939
The Stadtpräsident
(signed) Dr Dengel

DOC. 65

On 19 December 1939 the Reich Security Main Office discusses the establishment of a 'Jewish reservation' in Poland[1]

Memorandum on preparations for a meeting of office heads from Department II/II 112 of the Reich Security Main Office (RSHA), signed Dö.,[2] for the head of Office II at the RSHA,[3] dated 19 December 1939

Re: key points on the topic of Jewry for the meeting of office heads
Case file: circular letter dated 18 December 1939[4]
Final solution to the German Jewish problem
I. *Jewish reservation in Poland*
The question arises as to whether a Jewish reservation should be created in Poland, or whether the Jews should be housed in the future Government Poland.[5]

If plans call for creating a reservation, it would be necessary to consider whether the reservation should be administered by Jews or citizens of the German Reich. A Jewish administration would be preferable, as it would reduce the number of German administrative officials needed. Only the top posts would have to be staffed with Germans. In addition, it would have to be decided under whose authority this administration would be placed.

In our view, it would be useful to leave the administration under Security Police leadership until the resettlement of the Jews from Reich territory, the Ostmark, and Bohemia/Moravia has been completed.

II.
In this respect, a final decision would have to be made as to whether to continue the emigration of Jews with a view towards creating a reservation.

Moreover, a reservation would be a good lever from the standpoint of foreign policy for exerting pressure on the Western powers. Perhaps it would allow the question of the global solution to be raised at the conclusion of the war.

1 BArch, R 58/544, fol. 218r–v. This document has been translated from German.

2 Presumably Hans Döring (1901–1970), haulier; joined the NSDAP in 1928 and the SS in 1929; SS-Führer in Wiesbaden, 1929–1930, and thereafter in various other cities; chief of staff of the office of the Reich Commissioner for the Strengthening of Germandom (RKF) in Poznań, 1939–1941; on the staff of the Reichsführer-SS, 1942–1944; then on the staff of the Warthe SS Main District.

3 The head of Office II (Enemy Intelligence) at the Reich Security Main Office (RSHA) was Dr Franz Alfred Six (1909–1975), lawyer; joined the NSDAP in 1930, the SA in 1932, and the SS in 1935; in the SD from 1935; professor at the University of Königsberg in 1938 and the University of Berlin in 1939; commander of the Advance Commando Moscow, a unit of Einsatzgruppe B, in 1941; head of the Cultural Policy Department in the Reich Foreign Ministry in 1942; sentenced at Nuremberg to 20 years in prison in 1948; released in 1952; advertising consultant for Porsche-Diesel-Motorenbau in 1956.

4 This refers to an invitation to all RSHA departments to attend a meeting of office heads on 20 or 30 (date illegible) Dec. 1939, with the request to submit key points as a basis for discussion: BArch, R 58/544, fol. 218r–v.

5 This is a reference to the General Government.

DOC. 66

On 21 December 1939 the Chief of the Security Police and the SD announces that 600,000 Jews are to be expelled from the annexed territories of western Poland by the end of April 1940[1]

Letter from the Chief of the Security Police and the SD (C.d.S. – no. 12 743/39. IV/R Ech.[2]/Er.) to the Central Resettlement Office in Posen, dated 21 December 1939 (copy)

Second Nahplan[3]

The second Nahplan concerns the complete registration of all Jews regardless of age or gender in the eastern German Gaue[4] and their deportation to the General Government of Poland. Therefore, care must be taken to ensure that only Jews from the new eastern German Gaue are included in this operation. Jews from the Old Reich must not be included under any circumstances. Any outflow of individual Jews from the new eastern Gaue into the Old Reich, the Ostmark, and the Protectorate must also be prevented.

This concerns approximately *600,000 Jews*[5] who will be deported from the new eastern German Gaue by the end of April 1940. At the same time, owing to the small number of Jews living in West Prussia, approximately 10,000 Poles will also be deported from these regions. That will enable us to use the available rolling stock to full capacity. In addition, it will allow us to gain experience for subsequent transports of Poles.

The evacuation operation will have to scour the new eastern German Gaue, in a manner of speaking, proceeding from the north or west in the direction of the territory of the General Government of Poland. (When it comes to transports of Poles from West Prussia, the Poles living along the borders of the General Government will, for the sake of expediency, be the first to be deported.)

By order of the Higher SS and Police Leader, once again the inspectors of the Security Police and the SD will carry out the evacuation.

I. *Tasks of the inspectors of the Security Police and the SD in the eastern Gaue:*
   1. Registration of the persons involved.
   2. Confiscation of assets in accordance with the decree of the Plenipotentiary for the Four-Year Plan, St.M.Dev. 9547 of 19 October 1939,[6] and the decrees of the Reichsführer-SS in his capacity as Reich Commissioner for the Strengthening of Germandom, SIV1 no. 886/39–176– of 10 November 1939 and SIV1 no. 844 III/39–151 Sdb.P. of 16 December 1939.[7]

1 AIPN, GK 68/97, fols. 1–7. Copy in USHMM, RG 15 015M, reel 2. This document has been translated from German.
2 The Chief of the Security Police and the SD was Reinhard Heydrich. The letter was sent from his office and bears Adolf Eichmann's initials.
3 German for 'short-range plan'.
4 The annexed western Polish regions.
5 Underlined by hand.
6 This refers to Göring's decree on the establishment of the Main Trustee Office East (HTO): *VOBl-Warthegau* 1940, no. 5, 1 Nov. 1939, pp. 18–19.
7 Himmler's decree of 10 Nov. 1939 regulated the cooperation between his authorities and the HTO: Pospieszalski (ed.), *Documenta Occupationis*, vol. 5, part 1, pp. 205–207; on the decree of 16 Dec. 1939, see fn. 7 below.

3. Evacuation in consultation with the commanders of the Security Police and the SD in the General Government.

II. *Tasks of the Senior Commander of the Security Police and the SD in the General Government of Poland:*

1. Determining the terminal stations for the arriving transports in consultation with the inspectors of the Security Police and the SD in the eastern German Gaue.
2. Supervising the distribution of these transports by the Polish starostas and mayors. (It is left to your discretion, if opportunities exist, to put male Jews aged approximately 18–60 together in work details and deploy them appropriately.)

III. *Preliminary meeting with the relevant staff in Berlin:*

On 4 January 1940, at 11 a.m., a discussion will take place in the Reich Security Main Office, Section IV/R, Berlin W 62, 115/116 Kurfürstenstraße, to which the inspectors of the Security Police and the SD concerned and the Senior Commander of the Security Police and the SD in the General Government of Poland must send their staff members in charge of these issues.

The following material must be brought along:

1. By the staff of the inspectors in the eastern German Gaue:

   The numbers of Jews present in the individual regions and proposals concerning the loading stations.
2. By the staff of the Senior Commander of the Security Police and the SD in the General Government:

   The provisional distribution plan for the territory of the General Government and suggestions concerning the unloading stations.

After this meeting, the special section will prepare the evacuation plan, which will then serve as the basis for a final meeting.

Based on the final evacuation plan, the transport plan will then be prepared in consultation with the Reich Ministry of Transport and announced.

IV. *Guidelines for the evacuation:*

1. The councils of elders appointed by the Security Police and the SD must register the Jews without regard for age or gender:

   The local Jews are to be promptly registered by name on separate lists (multiple copies) according to gender and age group (up to 18 years of age; from 18 to 60; over 60).

   For now, the Nuremberg Laws should be applied to determine who is to be considered a Jew.
2. When the evacuation measures are carried out, it must be expected that individuals will try to prevent their deportation by filing appeals, and that businesses or public authorities will want to have a certain group of persons in their employ exempted from the evacuation. As a matter of principle, no deportation deferments are to be granted in view of the sufficient number of unemployed Poles available. Rather, care must be taken to ensure that the regions are completely cleared of Jews.
3. To facilitate the confiscation and recovery of assets, provided that these may not be taken along, it would be advisable to put wealthy Jews on later transports.

   This confiscation must not impede compliance with the evacuation deadline that has been set.

If necessary, wealthy Jews must appoint a non-Jewish representative who is fully informed of their financial circumstances and has general power of attorney.

Based on the decrees discussed under I, point 2., above, the registration and confiscation of assets must take place in consultation with the Main Trustee Office East or the trustee offices in Danzig, Posen, Zichenau, and Kattowitz. In consultation with the relevant trustee offices, the Landräte and mayors must initiate the confiscation and evaluation of the furniture owned by the Jews being evacuated (see Express Circular Decree of the RF, dated 16 December 1939, II 4[8]).

4. If possible, the following luggage should be taken along:

   one suitcase per Jew, with essential items of daily use, a complete set of clothing, one blanket per Jew (no duvets), food for approximately two weeks, personal documents.

   As no German money or other valuables may be taken along, złoty are to be made available for exchange in sufficient time before the transport's departure.

   The following items may not be taken along: securities, foreign currency, savings bank deposit books, etc., valuables of any kind (gold, silver, platinum), livestock.

   The secured valuables, foreign currency, cash, and other valuable items are to be dealt with in accordance with the decrees listed under I, point 2., above.
5. Before the train's departure, the Jews assigned to the transport will, for expediency's sake, be concentrated in suitably large rooms or halls located near the railway station. The Jews must report with their luggage and are to be searched before departure for weapons, ammunition, explosives, poison, foreign currency, jewellery, and excessive sums of money.
6. Since the census, everyone in the new eastern German Gaue has in their possession a copy of the census form. This is valid as a provisional identification document, which entitles the bearer to reside in this territory. These forms must be taken away from the Jews before their evacuation, which is tantamount to withdrawing their permission to continue residing there.
7. A Jewish transport team is to be set up in each case to ensure that the transport is properly carried out. This team must, of its own accord, appoint a steward for each wagon. These stewards will be responsible for maintaining order during the journey.
8. An appropriately equipped escort is to be assigned to each transport train. The leader of the escort must be given a list with the names of the Jews aboard the train. The Jewish transport team must prepare the list.
9. It is not specifically the German administrative and police authorities who are responsible for housing the Jews in the districts of the General Government, but

8 In the express circular decree by the Reichsführer-SS dated 16 Dec. 1939, which was not intended for publication and dealt with the confiscation of assets in the annexed eastern territories and the General Government, section II states that the HTO has appointed individuals who are authorized by the HTO 'or its trustee offices to undertake confiscations and to carry on their persons written credentials to that effect, equipped with an official seal': Karol Marian Pospieszalski (ed.), *Documenta Occupationis*, vol. 4: *Niemiecka lista narodowa w 'Kraju Warty': Wybór dokumentów* (Poznań: Wydawnictwo Instytutu Zachodniego, 1949), pp. 207–209.

rather the Polish starostas and mayors, who must be required to accept the respective number of Jews.

10. Given the shortage of rolling stock, compliance with the evacuation deadlines that have been set can be ensured only if the trains are available for further use immediately after their arrival. The trains must therefore be immediately returned after they reach their destination and have been emptied of Jews, disinfected, and sealed. The final evacuation can begin around 15 January 1940. From this time onwards, the Reich Transport Ministry will make rolling stock available for the evacuation of approximately 5,000 Jews per day from the eastern Gaue.

DOC. 67

On 26 December 1939 a German police captain reports on anti-Jewish rioting by 'Young Poles' in Tschenstochau (Częstochowa)[1]

Report by Urban Police Captain and Battalion Commander Bröschen, Police Battalion 72, in Tschenstochau (Częstochowa), to the Radom police regiment, the Stadtkommissar, and the Oberfeldkommandantur/Gestapo, dated 26 December 1939

Re: burning of the main synagogue in Tschenstochau, looting of Jewish shops, anti-Jewish demonstration by 'Young Poles'[2]

In the late afternoon and evening of 25 December 1939, Polish youths and children instigated an attack on the Jewish neighbourhoods north and east of the main avenue. The windows of Jewish homes and shops were broken with snowballs and also stones, resulting in approximately 600–900 broken windowpanes. The operation itself took place fairly unobtrusively. It began with Jews who were out in the streets being driven into their homes by Polish youths throwing snowballs, and later stones. The adult Poles openly sympathized with what the Polish youth were doing. It looks like the breaking of windowpanes was incited by this adult approval. The mood that resulted in this anti-Jewish behaviour is apparently due to the fact that Jewish shop owners took advantage of the pre-Christmas season in their pricing, and that the Jews themselves are increasing in numbers because of continued immigration into Tschenstochau.[3]

Around 7.30 p.m., soldiers from the 1st Company who were on leave in the city reported that Polish youths were pelting the Jews with snowballs and mocking them. At the same time, the guards at the *Narutowica School*[4] barracks reported a fiery glow from the west. The officer in charge of the company, Captain *Ambros*, immediately deployed the unit on standby and followed it. At the eastern end of Panny Mari [Avenue], a wooden kiosk was found in flames. At the site of the fire, news came from ethnic Germans that looting was in progress in Joselewicza-Berka. The troops who were immediately dispatched arrested 20 males, mostly adolescents, suspected of looting. Attempted looting was noted at a Jewish

1 APCz, 4/2, fol. 12r–v. This document has been translated from German.

2 This refers to organized Polish nationalist teenagers and young adults.

3 This influx was a result of the German policy of expulsion in the western Polish regions.

4 Correctly: Narutowicza.

bakery and a Jewish bicycle shop. After interrogations throughout the night, conducted by the officer in charge of the company, 19 of those who had been arrested were cleared of suspicion and released. There was evidence to implicate a 16-year-old unemployed engraver's apprentice, Stanislaw *Deregowski* of 3 Bor in Tschenstochau, in the looting of the bicycle shop, as a search of his residence turned up two new bicycle tyres. D. has confessed.

During the investigation at the looted Jewish shops, a police officer who had been dispatched to patrol the surrounding area – a man who speaks some Polish – informed Captain *Ambros* that the main synagogue had been set alight by Polish youths. According to the officer, when he approached, the culprits fled, calling out to each other that there was ammunition in the synagogue. Captain *Ambros* immediately ordered the synagogue residence to be cleared and cordoned off the danger zone. The fire in the interior of the synagogue, already quite advanced at several points, made it impossible to search for ammunition. In view of the explosion hazard, Captain *Ambros* also ordered the fire brigade, which he himself had alerted, to limit its activity strictly to securing the neighbouring buildings. Enquiries made in the surrounding area about the cause of the fire suggest that the perpetrators were 'Young Poles'. The language skills of one of the reservists from the 1st Company were sufficient to gather as much from the statements made by local residents.

I received the fire report around 8.45 p.m. and had the battalion alerted. The massive patrol force, deployed immediately, found no further indications of any new actions against the Jews. No unauthorized persons were found in the street after 9 p.m. Standing patrols safeguarded the Jewish shops affected by looting, and the increased patrol force was discontinued when the alert was lifted. The reinforced guard platoons no longer had any cause to intervene.

Two males arrested in the vicinity of the looting site were identified as Jews. They were placed in the police prison for failure to wear the prescribed armband. As it falls within their remit, the Gestapo office in Tschenstochau will be in charge of the further handling of this case.[5]

DOC. 68

In December 1939 the bank clerk Gerhard Schneider describes his impressions of Sosnowitz (Sosnowiec)[1]

Account by Gerhard Schneider[2] in the *Werkzeitschrift für die Betriebsgemeinschaft Commerz- und Privatbank*, Berlin, dated December 1939

[...][3]

3. *Sosnowitz.* Just outside the gates of Kattowitz, but in so-called Congress Poland,[4] lies the Dombrowa region[5] with the cities of Sosnowitz and Bendzin. Its ties to the Kattowitz industrial region (Sosnowitz is only 7 km from Kattowitz; a tram links the two cities)

5 In his report from the field office in Częstochowa, written on 26 Dec. 1939, SS-Hauptscharführer Dittmann also assumed that 'the instigators are to be sought among the groups of Young Poles': APCz, 4/2, fol. 13r–v.

1 *Der Arbeitskamerad: Werkzeitschrift für die Betriebsgemeinschaft Commerz- und Privatbank*, vol. 6, no. 12 (Dec. 1939), p. 200. This document has been translated from German.

soon made the establishment of a German bank branch an urgent necessity. On the advice of the Chief of the Civil Administration, our bank decided to set up a branch office in Sosnowitz. This decision was not made lightly. Sosnowitz may have 110,000 inhabitants, but most of them are Jews, and the rest are predominantly poor Polish workers. And it shows, too! At every turn, one finds material for the 'Stürmer'.[6] Should the editor-in-chief of this paper ever go there, he will be compelled to note with envy that even his pen could not describe this setting. The author of these lines cannot do so either, nor does he wish to be suspected of exaggeration. The passport photographs in one Jewish photo shop alone would provide material for the cover images for several years to come.

Under these circumstances, what does our bank branch look like? Well, from the outside it is still acceptable, as the rain occasionally washes off the grime, but inside it looks dreadful! The 'requisition' of the premises of the Bank Zwiazku Spolek Zarobkowych[7] (Bank of the Co-operative Societies Association) was relatively easy. After the Polish-speaking escort had responded to the concierge's greeting 'Co chcesz ty psie?' ('What do you want, you son of a bitch?') with appropriate words in the same language, rich in imagery, consensus on the measures to be taken was soon reached. Two unemployed men off the street helped to clean up; repeated heavy applications of soap and extremely vigorous scrubbing assuaged the doubts that had arisen concerning the nature of the floor covering in the bank's premises. But it was not possible to put all the bank's rooms in order according to our standards in the short time available before the opening of our branch office. The space that was not needed therefore had to be screened off with a wooden wall. The conversation with the Polish carpenter who was fetched to build the wall revealed the 'Polish conditions'[8] more eloquently than a long essay could do. The wood, yes, only the Jew has that. The machine tools, yes, they needed to be hired from the Jew. And this was an independent craftsman!

The bank's files and account books were no longer on hand. From the many remnants left behind on tables, chairs, and the floor, it was possible to determine that the bank, despite everything, had been organized along 'modern' lines. The slip system for processing bills of exchange was in operation there, too, and the bank had to report to its head office to an extent that far outstrips our facilities. So the Poles could 'organize' too.

Our branch manager was permitted, pending further notice, to continue living in Beuthen or Kattowitz. A tram ride of 1.5–2 hours twice a day seemed easier to bear than permanent residence in Sosnowitz. The tram passed through German customs control.

2 Gerhard Schneider (b. 1913), bank clerk; trained at Commerz- und Privatbank in 1932; then worked as an accounts clerk at a branch in Berlin; joined the SS in 1934; left the bank in June 1941 at his own request.

3 The series 'Our new branch offices' dealt first with the branch in Katowice (no. 11, pp. 187–188) and then with the one in Bielsko-Biała (no. 12, pp. 199–200).

4 This refers to the territory of the Kingdom of Poland created in 1815 at the Congress of Vienna; it remained under the Russian tsar's rule until the First World War.

5 Dąbrowa Region, also Zagłębie Dąbrowskie/Dąbrowa Coal Basin.

6 Antisemitic weekly newspaper published by Julius Streicher from 1923 to 1945.

7 Correctly: Bank Związku Spółek Zarobkowych.

8 'Die polnischen Wirtschaftsverhältnisse': allusion to pejorative set phrase in German, 'polnische Wirtschaft' (literally Polish business, Polish conditions), meaning a disorderly state of affairs, a shambles.

Delightful scenes sometimes played out there. For example, the border official asked one Pole whether he was an Aryan. 'No', the Pole replied tearfully, 'I am a cobbler'. One of our Polish-speaking officials was able to clear up the misunderstanding quickly.

DOC. 69
A Warsaw Jew writes about manhunts and abuse between 19 October 1939 and 1 January 1940[1]

Fragment from the handwritten diary of an unidentified Jewish man, for the underground archive of the Warsaw ghetto, entries for 19 October 1939 to 1 January 1940 (2 copies)[2]

From a diary

19 October 1939[3]
At 2 p.m., while I was at my daughter's home, two G[erman] officers with revolvers in their hands came and ordered us to leave the apartment immediately. Under the threat of being shot we had to go out, leaving everything behind as it was. They wanted to shoot the mother of a three-month-old child, who begged them to let her take the child's clothes. We all left the apartment.

21 October 1939
On Nowogrodzka I was seized for forced labour. While being beaten, I was dragged to the post office, where I had to carry very heavy containers with bricks, mortar, and waste until blood shot from my nose, and I collapsed. After seven hours of hard labour I was freed, and I lay very ill in bed for five days. I was in my room for 14 days and suffered terribly, both physically and mentally. Only after that did I go out into the street again.

10 November 1939
Walking along Marszałkowska I was pulled into the gate of number 127 with another ten Jews, whereupon they gave us the honour of carrying heavy crates with canned goods from the fourth floor, while they beat us horribly with sticks. A few of us were bleeding. Miraculously, I came out alive. A few hours later they took most of us with them in a truck. It is not known what happened to them. I was among the lucky ones who were set free.

22 November 1939
At 12 p.m. they arrested approximately 300 Jews, with me among them. They took us to a site outside the city and ordered us to sing and dance a bit. Afterwards, we were ordered to dig the damp earth with our bare hands. We had to dig until our hands became swollen. Late in the evening they began beating us, took overcoats from many of us, and

1 AŻIH, Ring I/483 (1026). This document has been translated from Yiddish.
2 The entries have survived in two versions. This translation is based on the later, more legible, version.
3 Erroneously 1940 in the original.

chased us back into the city. We had to run hard and sing while doing so. When one of us did not sing, they beat us in a wild fury. Many of us returned home as cripples.

26 December 1939
As my friend Rosen was taking me to the Number 3 tram, we were rounded up and taken to 9 Kobulewska.[4] There was a barrack at the back, in the courtyard. They honoured us by having us get the heating stoves going. We had to put the burned ashes into bags and take them out like that. The work was not even that difficult, but the mental humiliation was unbearable. After the job was finished, they released us from the courtyard. They took 2 złoty from each of us, let us all go, and immediately captured other Jews. For them it was all about business. They made good money for themselves with the 2 złoty.

1 January 1940
Jews were beaten today. Walking on Franciszkańska, I noticed from afar that they were giving out brutal beatings with rifles. Seeking to avoid the blows, a few other Jews and I fled into a café and quickly ordered tea. Not five minutes had passed when eight men with revolvers in hand came in and beat us with murderous intent. I received a heavy blow to my head from a revolver and fell unconscious to the ground. They worked like this for approximately 20 minutes and then went back out into the street and continued their work of beating and torturing Jews there. I will not forget this day. I will remember this blow, since it left marks.

DOC. 70
Daily Herald, 2 January 1940: article on the shooting of 53 Jews in Warsaw[1]

Swaffer's[2] headlines. Poland's worst pogrom. Had to dig own graves.

When, last August, I visited Pilsudski's prison in the Warsaw fortress[3] I little dreamed that within a few weeks there would be enacted in the grounds a tragedy as brutal as any that made Tsardom hated across the world.

Although many pogroms have taken place since the Nazis thundered into Poland, the worst story comes from the capital, where there were 352,700 Jews. Today they are scattered.

After declaring that some of them had killed a policeman, the Germans rounded up 53 Jews and shot them in the fortress, after making them dig their own graves and forcing all but the last to be shot to do the burying.

4 Possibly a reference to Kąkolewska Street in Warsaw's Mokotów neighbourhood.

1 *Daily Herald*, 2 Jan. 1940. Copy in IfZ-Archives, MZA 1–132, 207 F1 Poland. The *Daily Herald* was a British leftist periodical that appeared from 1912 to 1964. In the 1930s it was for a time the daily newspaper with the highest circulation in the world.

2 Hannen Swaffer (1879–1962), journalist; worked for various newspapers; with the *Daily Herald* from 1931; member of the Labour Party.

3 Józef Piłsudski was held in Russian captivity in the Warsaw Citadel in 1905.

'As for you,' said the Nazis to the last lot, 'you will have the honour of being buried by German soldiers.'

Then, summoning its leaders, the Nazis imposed on the local Hebrew community a fine of 300,000 złoty and, when it was paid, declared, 'If there is the least Jewish provocation, 1,000 Jews will be executed.'[4]

Only M. Czerniakow, head of the community, and one other member of the Board of Deputies had the courage to inform the relatives of the executions.

The rest all went out, dreading to face them.

The scene that followed exceeded their worst fears.

'The names of the dead will be inscribed in the annals of the community as martyrs of the Jewish faith,' said Czerniakow.

His words were drowned in the wailings that went up – 'How long, O Lord, how long?'

Women fainted, men tore their clothes, and the weeping and shouting could be heard all along the street outside.

One of the men executed for the alleged murder was a harmless rabbi.

Three others were a father and two sons who had committed the unspeakable crime of chancing to be in a nearby house when the Nazis arrived.

DOC. 71

On 4 January 1940 SS commanders and representatives of various German administrative offices meet at the Reich Security Main Office to discuss the expulsions to the General Government[1]

Minutes of a meeting held at the Reich Security Main Office (RSHA) on 4 January 1940, taken by Franz Abromeit,[2] Danzig,[3] dated 8 January 1940

1. *Memorandum*

   A preparatory discussion concerning the evacuation of Jews and Poles in the eastern territories in the very near future took place in Berlin on 4 January 1940. The meeting was chaired by SS-Hauptsturmführer *Eichmann* of the Reich Security Main Office, Section IV.

4 The fine had actually been imposed prior to the mass shooting as an 'atonement fine' (*Sühnegeld*) for the killing of the police officer. The shooting took place even though the Jewish Community had paid the sum: see Doc. 39, fn. 3.

1 AIPN, GK 166/247/III, fols. 612–614. Published as a facsimile in Szymon Datner, Janusz Gumkowski, and Kazimierz Leszczyński, 'Wysiedlanie ludności z ziem polskich wcielonych do Rzeszy', *Biuletyn Głównej Komisji Badania Zbrodni Hitlerowskich w Polsce*, vol. 12 (1960), pp. 3–180, 3F–184F (pp. 37F–39F). This document has been translated from German.

2 Franz Abromeit (1907–1944?), retailer; joined the NSDAP in 1930 and the SS in 1932; worked for Eichmann; commander in the SD Main Office from 1937; at the Reich Security Main Office (RSHA) from 1939; involved in the expulsion of Poles and Jews from Danzig and West Prussia, 1939–1941; served in Croatia in 1942, and in 1944 in Hungary, where he went missing; declared dead in 1964.

3 The original contains handwritten underlining.

Attendees: officials dealing with these issues for the inspectors of the Security Police and the SD, including from the General Government, and the relevant officials from the RSHA, plus representatives from the economics, transport, and finance ministries, and the Trustee Office East.

2. At the beginning of the meeting, the responsible officials reported on the experience with evacuations which they had gained to date. (SS-Obersturmbannführer Tröger spoke for the Gau Danzig.[4])

   The official in charge in the General Government, SS-Hauptsturmführer Mohr,[5] highlighted in particular the difficulties that have arisen because the quota of persons to be evacuated – which was approved by the General Government – has been exceeded in several cases, making it extremely difficult to house the people over there. People had to sit in locked railway wagons for up to a week without being able to relieve themselves. In addition, one hundred people froze to death on one transport during the big cold spell. In order to prevent similar incidents in future, it was stressed that the quota stipulated by the General Government must be strictly observed.

3. By order of the Reichsführer-SS, the evacuation of all Jews from the previously Polish-occupied territories must be carried out as a matter of priority.[6]

   The relevant officials based with the inspectors of the Security Police and the SD for the North-East, the South-East, and the Warthegau gave the following figures concerning the immediate evacuation of Jews:

North-East –	30,000
South-East –	120,000–125,000
Warthegau (Lodsch) –	200,000

   In addition, the Warthegau wants to evacuate 80,000 Poles straight away to make room for ethnic Germans from Galicia and Volhynia. (To date, the Warthegau has already evacuated 87,000 Poles.) Gau Danzig gave a figure of 10,000 Poles and Jews for immediate evacuation in January. This has already been approved by the Gruppenführer.[7] (The main office received a teletype message that the number has changed to 10,000 Poles and 2,000 Jews.[8])

4. It has not yet been possible to announce the date for the start of the evacuation because
   a) the loading stations have not yet been specified with absolute certainty.
   b) the official in charge in the General Government has not yet been able to specify the individual terminuses for the evacuees.

4 Dr Rudolf Tröger (1905–1940), lawyer; head of the Gestapo in Danzig in 1939; commander of Einsatzkommando 16 in Poland; inspector of the Security Police and the SD in Reichsgau Danzig-West Prussia, 1939–1940; on active duty in France in 1940; killed in action.

5 Robert Mohr (1909–1989), lawyer; joined the NSDAP and the SS in 1933; Regierungsrat and personnel officer in the RSHA; attached to the Senior Commander of the Security Police in the General Government, 1939–1940; commander of Einsatzkommando 6 in the Soviet Union, Nov. 1941–Sept. 1942; head of the Gestapo in Darmstadt, 1942–1944; subsequently lived under a false name in Burg an der Wupper; sentenced to eight years in prison by the Wuppertal regional court in 1967.

6 See Doc. 25 and Himmler's Directive I/II as RKF of 30 Oct. 1939: Berenstein et al. (eds.), *Faschismus – Getto – Massenmord*, pp. 42–43.

7 Reinhard Heydrich.

8 Crossed out: 'to be evacuated'.

c) only when the aforementioned requirements have been met will Section IV draw up the final transport plan in consultation with the Reich Ministry of Transport and notify the inspectors accordingly. A long-term plan is going to be drawn up, which will be divided up into several short-range plans.

5. Based on the figures for immediate evacuation cited by the inspectors' officials in charge, a clearance plan will be drawn up by the Section IV staff. This will serve as the basis for a final meeting in Berlin, which the Gruppenführer also wishes to attend. The exact date of this meeting will be made known by teletype. However, the evacuation is not expected to begin before 25 January 1940.
6. The persons to be evacuated will be deported to Districts Cracow, Warsaw, Lublin, and Radom.
7. The discussion that took place among all the officials in charge of these matters allowed for the identification of several points that must be borne in mind during the evacuation.
   a) *Families of Polish prisoners of war are to be evacuated* if the conditions set out in the current guidelines are satisfied.
   b) By order of the RFSS, *every Jew* is permitted to take a sum of *up to 100 zloty* with him when he is evacuated. Where necessary, this is to be paid out to Jews without cash funds by the Jewish Council of Elders that has been set up.
   c) It is essential to ensure that no *sums in Reichsmarks are smuggled* across the border. Cooperation with the Customs Investigation Office will be necessary during the evacuation to make sure that this is enforced. The relevant State Police office will provide officers to search the persons to be evacuated (spot checks).
   d) The *escorts for the transports* will be provided by the police, and/or reliable *ethnic* Germans will be recruited. These escorts are to be specially advised to conduct themselves in a disciplined manner during the journey. Various incidents have made this necessary.
   e) In order to protect *women and children* from freezing to death during the journey when there is heavy frost, women and children will be transported in *passenger carriages* and men in goods wagons, if possible.
   f) Each of the persons to be evacuated must be given *provisions for ten days.* This can be handled in cooperation with the relevant officials of the NSV,[9] based on appropriate instructions.
   g) The *head of the transport* must be provided with a *list* of names for the journey which gives the personal details and occupations of the evacuees. This list must be given to the District Governor or his representative on arrival in the General Government.
   h) The *police and/or the Landräte* must inform the *Trustee Office* prior to every transport so that the agency can implement the confiscation of furniture.
   i) The Senior Commander of the Security Police and the SD in Cracow and SS-Hauptsturmführer Eichmann, RSHA Section IV, must be informed by teletype about every departing transport.

9 National Socialist People's Welfare Organization.

j) The RSHA has agreed with the Reich Ministry of Transport that every departing *transport* will comprise *1,000 persons*. This figure must be strictly observed in order to prevent difficulties with respect to housing these persons in the General Government, as has previously been the case.

RSHA Section IV wishes to make one member of staff and one orderly available to each of the inspectors of the Security Police and the SD to arrange the measures to be carried out during the evacuation.

DOC. 72
On 9 January 1940 the leader of the resistance organization Service for Poland's Victory reports on the situation of the Jews in occupied Poland[1]

Political and economic report from the organization Service for Poland's Victory (SZP)[2] by General Tokarzewski,[3] Warsaw, for General Sosnkowski,[4] Angers, dated 9 January 1940 (copy)

[…][5]
Issues of nationality in the entire territory of the Polish Republic
1. *Jews*
As a result of the country's invasion by the aggressors, the Jews in Poland have found themselves in various situations depending on the occupation. On German territory, they feel the effect of Nazi practices even more than the Polish population, whereas on Soviet territory they are strongly favoured. The result of this state of affairs is a substantial emigration of the Jewish population from west to east. In any case, this phenomenon is welcomed by the German authorities, who would like to see the migration of all Jews in order to acquire more space for concentrating the Poles in the General Government. The Germans turn a blind eye to Jews escaping via the unmarked border and limit themselves to robbing them of their money, gold, and valuables. However, they do not let in

1 SPP, 3.3.1.1.1, SZP, Meldunek no. 5, L.dz. 972/6, fol. 76. Published in Halina Czarnocka et al. (eds.), *Armia Krajowa w dokumentach 1939–1945*, vol. 1: *Wrzesień 1939 – czerwiec 1941* (London: Studium Polski Podziemnej, 1970), pp. 68–69. This document has been translated from Polish.

2 Służba Zwycięstwu Polski (SZP), a military resistance organization founded on 27 Sept. 1939. Following its recognition by the government in exile as part of the Polish armed forces, it was officially called the Union of Armed Struggle (ZWZ) from 13 Nov. 1939 and Home Army (ZWZ-AK) from 15 Feb. 1942.

3 Michał Karaszewicz-Tokarzewski (1893–1964), career officer; commander in various military districts and of various armies; co-founder and first head of the SZP; in Soviet captivity, March 1940 – August 1941, then officer in the Polish army established on the territory of the Soviet Union, which was subordinated to the Polish government in exile (Anders' Army) in London after the war.

4 Kazimierz Sosnkowski (1885–1969), career officer; Piłsudski's associate; army inspector; commander-in-chief of the ZWZ while in exile, Nov. 1939 – June 1940; minister without portfolio in the Polish government in exile until 1941; commander-in-chief of the Polish armed forces, July 1943 – Sept. 1944; in Canada after the war.

5 The complete 35-page report to the command of the secret military resistance includes the statutes of the SZP and a detailed description of the situation in Poland: SPP, 3.3.1.1.1, SZP, Meldunek no. 5, L.dz. 972/6, fols. 48–82.

Jews wanting to return from Soviet occupation. The establishment of a Jewish zone around Lublin, as announced in the German press, has not yet been realized. The establishment of a ghetto in Warsaw has also been abandoned due to bribes. The Jews are subject to all sorts of abuse from the Germans, all the more so because the requirement to wear emblems and display them in shops and offices visibly stigmatizes a Jewish individual or business. So-called non-Aryans are treated on a par with Jews. Anyone whose either parent ever belonged to the Jewish Community is considered a non-Aryan. The consequence of this policy is the total destruction of Jewish social life under German occupation. The most prominent Jewish activists have either already escaped to Soviet territory or plan to do so; the same applies to the intelligentsia in general. The Jews have waited a long time for the arrival of the Soviet troops, without ever stating any support for the Soviets or Communism, but merely because they hoped to improve their living conditions. Such hopes vanished with the Soviets' military setbacks.[6] Nevertheless, the Bolsheviks rely to a considerable extent on the Jewish population, from whom they are recruiting the entire militia and administration in Białystok, Brześć, Równe, and Lwów. Self-employed Jews are favoured, provided that they declare their support for Communism.

Nevertheless, it is the case that both the Zionists and the Bund affiliates are fighting the Soviet occupation, and the Bolsheviks have made numerous arrests among both parties. The prisoners are doing time alongside Poles, and a cordial coexistence among the prisoners has been observed. Despite this positive sign, it must be emphasized that there is increasing antisemitism among the Polish and Ukrainian populations. A pogrom with wide-scale participation after the end of the Soviet occupation cannot be ruled out. Regardless of the future Polish government's stance on the Jewish question, everything must be done to ensure that, at the time of the country's liberation, pogroms do not occur as, in the opinion of the West, these would harm Poland just as much as the similar but much weaker excesses at the beginning of independence.[7] [...][8]

6 The author is referring to the Red Army's attack on Finland on 30 Nov. 1939, which started the so-called Winter War.

7 Pogroms in East Galicia in 1918 had done lasting damage to Poland's reputation in Western Europe and the United States.

8 The report next addresses the mood among the Germans, Ukrainians, Byelorussians, and Lithuanians and the attitude of Slovaks and Czechs.

DOC. 73
On 10 January 1940 the chief of police in Lodz (Łódź) calls on all Germans to avoid the Jewish quarter[1]

Announcement by Johannes Schäfer, the German chief of police in Lodz,[2] published in the *Lodscher Zeitung*, 10 January 1940

As a result of poor hygienic conditions, the north of the city of Lodsch, particularly the part inhabited almost exclusively by Jews, represents a permanent source of infection, above all for typhoid fever, dysentery, and typhus, so that there is a danger of these diseases spreading.

Any unnecessary contact with this part of the city must therefore cease immediately.

All Germans, both Reich Germans and ethnic Germans, who do not live in the north of the city and do not work in the health service, e.g. as physicians, nurses, health supervisors, disinfectors, etc., are hereby urgently requested to avoid this part of the city under all circumstances. In addition, I expect the Polish population to limit visits to relatives or acquaintances living in the part of the city in question to those that are absolutely necessary.

The exclusion line delimiting the area of the city in question runs as follows, beginning in the north:

Goplanska, Zórawia, Zabia, Tokarzewskiego, Marysinska, Brzezinska, Franciszkanska, Północna, Pilsudskiego, Łódka, Nowomiejska, Podrzeczna, Stodolniana, Drewnowska, Rymarska, Lutomierska, Rybna, Limanowskiego, Lotnicza, Zgierska as far as its junction with Goplanska.[3]

The drinking water supply represents another danger to the population. I therefore forbid the drinking of unboiled water across the whole area of the city.

1 *Lodscher Zeitung*, 10 Jan. 1940, p. 9; Biblioteka Narodowa, P. 101 304. This German daily newspaper was at first called the *Deutsche Lodzer Zeitung*, from 12 Nov. to 31 Dec. 1939 the *Lodzer Zeitung*, then until 11 April 1940 the *Lodscher Zeitung*, after which it was the *Litzmannstädter Zeitung* until 1945. This document has been translated from German.

2 Johannes Schäfer (1903–1993), wholesaler; joined the NSDAP in 1926 and the SS in 1927; became SA commander in Halle an der Saale, 1930; attached to SS Main District Central, 1934; then commander of the 2nd SS Standarte in Frankfurt am Main; subsequently SS commander in Bochum; chief of police in Danzig, 1939; acting chief of police in Łódź, Oct. 1939 – June 1940; subsequently SS commander in Stettin; served in the Waffen-SS from 1943; initially an agricultural worker after the war, then worked as an insurance salesman in Cologne.

3 Street names as in the original.

DOC. 74

On 14 January 1940 the commander of an SS cavalry squadron in Chełm in the General Government describes how he ordered a mass murder[1]

Report by the commander of the 5th Squadron of the 1st SS Death's Head Cavalry Regiment in Chelm, signed SS-Obersturmführer and Squadron Commander Reichenwallner,[2] to the staff of the 1st SS Death's Head Cavalry Regiment in the General Government of Poland, Warsaw, dated 14 January 1940 (copy)

Re: operation on Saturday, 13 January 1940
Concerning: –
Enclosures: –
On Friday, 12 January 1940, at around 10 p.m., the commander of the Security Police in Kreis Chelm, SS-Untersturmführer *Rollfing*,[3] telephoned me and asked me to take over guard duty for a transport of Jews that would be arriving during the night. Approximately 600 Jews would be coming from Lublin and were to stay in the carriages until morning. I therefore assigned an NCO and 20 men, who took over guard duties from 2 a.m. (when the train arrived) until morning. At 7 a.m. the Gruppenführer who had been detailed to the train reported to me that the carriages were completely contaminated. I therefore went to the train and inspected the carriages there with the commander of the Security Police and the deputy Landrat.

We found that the carriages, some of which were second- and third-class express carriages, were overcrowded with Jews, that around 40 dead people who had not withstood the long transport were lying in the corridors of the carriages, and that some compartments were covered with vomit and soiled with excrement. As soon as I opened the door, the foul liquid flowed towards me, and we were in agreement that dysentery had broken out on this train. After long deliberations, we unanimously concluded that it would be a crime to release the infected, louse-ridden Jews in Kreis Chelm. We therefore gave orders for the train to be manned with German officers and shunted off into an area of woodland in the direction of Ruda, in order to shoot everyone on the train there.

Since the 5th Squadron only had a total of 500 rounds of infantry ammunition and the Wehrmacht could not spare any either, it was impossible for me to carry out this operation. The deputy Landrat therefore assigned eight members of the gendarmerie; in addition to this, I detailed one NCO and ten men to reinforce the gendarmerie. I was not able to take command of the operation myself because the governor, SS-Brigadeführer

1 BArch, RS 4/60. This document has been translated from German.
2 Wilhelm Reichenwallner (1910–1943), retailer; joined the NSDAP and the SS in 1931; instructor with the 17th SS Cavalry Regiment from 1934; took over the Aryanized Diamant shoe factory in Strausberg in 1939; commander of SS Cavalry Company 2/7 in 1940; found guilty of rape and sexual relations with Polish women; killed in action in the Soviet Union.
3 Correctly: Hermann Rohlfing (1910–1961), clerical assistant; employed as a clerk at the Minden local court in 1928; joined the SS in 1933 and the NSDAP in 1937; worked at the branch office of the commander of the Lublin Security Police in Chełm from 1940; later head of Sonderkommando 1005; responsible for the killing of prisoners in Lublin when the Red Army was approaching in 1944; head of the Criminal Police in Minden in 1960; died while on remand.

Schmitt,[4] had announced he would be visiting on this day, and I had been asked to accompany him on his inspection tour. I therefore had the men who had been detailed (one NCO, ten men) form up prior to the train's departure and informed them that this operation had to be carried out. However, since two units were involved, the gendarmerie and the SS, and since the gendarmerie was equipped with submachine guns, I expected that the assignment would have to be divided and, to be precise, that one detachment would first have to guard the rest of the people who would remain on the train, and the other detachment would have to carry out the shootings. Later the detachments would have to swap.

On my return from the inspection, it was reported to me at the railway station that one of my men had been shot and injured. I therefore asked the governor to excuse me from taking part in the inspection for the time being.

The injured SS man is SS Cavalryman Fritz *Klüter*, b. 13 June 1909 in Bad Lippspringe, resident in Bad Lippspringe, single, SS no. 214 190. After the accident at 1 p.m., he was transported back on the train, which arrived in Chelm at 3.10 p.m. In the meantime, I had ordered an operation to be performed at the base hospital immediately. The ambulance was already at the train as well. By chance, the battalion physician, SS-Untersturmführer Wickl, was here in Chelm and was able to be present at the operation, which began immediately. The operation was led by the chief staff surgeon[5] from the Chelm Base, Dr Lichtschlag,[6] who is also SS-Oberführer in Silesia.

The investigation into the accident has revealed the following. Gendarmerie officer *Bleichner* was in charge of the transport. Having arrived at the specified location, all the prisoners were taken out of the carriages and lined up to form a marching column. The first of the detainees were just about to be taken away when some of the prisoners attempted to escape. The wounded SS cavalryman Klüter was suddenly surrounded by prisoners and, according to gendarmerie officer *Bleichner*, who was standing nearby, Klüter shouted, 'I've been hit', and collapsed.

From the statements of the witnesses who were interviewed, my impression is that one of the prisoners must still have been in possession of a firearm because

1. K. had found himself in the middle of a mob, so it was impossible for a stray bullet to reach him.
2. according to the physicians, it was a point-blank shot, fired from a distance of 70 cm.

The bullet smashed through his rifle barrel at the level of the lock and penetrated his clothing, lodging in his lower abdomen. There was no exit wound. His small intestine was perforated three times. The bullet could not be found during the operation. Major Lichtschlag is of the opinion that this shot was definitely not an infantry round, but in

4 Correctly: Friedrich Schmidt (1902–1973), primary school teacher; head of the Artamanen Movement in 1924; joined the NSDAP in 1925 and the SS in 1934; deputy Gauleiter of Württemberg, 1933–1937; head of the NSDAP Main Training Office, 1937; district governor in Lublin, Oct. 1939; recalled to the Reich in early 1940; worked at the headquarters of SS Section East in April 1940; in Allied captivity from 1944; interned in Ludwigsburg; sentenced to 30 months in a labour camp in 1948; thereafter worked as a sales representative in Burghausen.

5 Oberstabsarzt: Wehrmacht medical officer with a rank equivalent to major.

6 Dr Walter Lichtschlag (1889–1969), surgeon; joined the NSDAP and the SS in 1931; physician in the SS Main District South-East in Breslau from 1935; interned in Ludwigsburg after the war; surgeon with his own practice in Heidelberg from 1948.

all probability a bullet from an old revolver, since the shot left a round hole the size of a one-mark piece. The aforementioned physician said the reason for the opinion that the bullet had been fired at a range of less than 1 metre was that the edges of the wound were burned.

According to the witnesses' statements, and in the physician's view, it is therefore probably fair to conclude that one of the prisoners was still in possession of an old gun and shot at SS Cavalryman Klüter. Moreover, it would have been easy for a prisoner to have got hold of a weapon because they had been given food by Jews at railway stations during the long transport.

DOC. 75
On 18 January 1940 the American legation in Kaunas reports on the flight of Jewish refugees from the Soviet Union into Lithuania and German-occupied Poland[1]

Report no. 568 from the American envoy in Kaunas, Bernard Gufler,[2] to the Secretary of State[3] in Washington (received on 6 Feb. 1940), dated 18 January 1940[4]

Re: reported deterioration of conditions in Soviet Poland, measures against Catholic organizations.
Confidential as to sources
Sir:

I have the honor to report that conditions are apparently deteriorating in Soviet Poland and that large numbers of Jews are reported to be smuggling themselves over the frontier not only into Lithuanian territory but also into German Poland. Relief workers from Vilna state that Jews who have entered that district from Soviet territory say that many others of their compatriots have gone over 'the Green Frontier'[5] to German Poland.

Unbelievable as this report may be at face value it is apparently true. Mr. Joseph Schapiro[6] of the staff of this office has just informed me that he made the acquaintance a few days ago of two Jews who have just arrived from Russian Poland. These persons informed him that they had intended to enter German Poland and had come over the Lithuanian border by accident. When he asked why they had wanted to put themselves within German jurisdiction, they replied, 'Better anything than the Soviets,' and added, 'It is better to be worked by Germans than starved to death by the Soviets.' There exists,

1 NARA, Department of State, Decimal File 860c.00/802, Poland Internal Affairs 1916–1944. Copy in NARA, M 1197 Roll 71/602.
2 Bernard Anthony Gufler (1903–1973), diplomat; vice consul in Riga, 1932; interim envoy in Kaunas, 1940.
3 Cordell Hull (1871–1955), lawyer and politician; member of the US House of Representatives, 1907–1931; US senator, 1931–1933; secretary of state, 1933–1944; awarded the Nobel Peace Prize, 1945.
4 The original contains handwritten administrative notes and numerous stamps: Received Department of State 1940 Feb 2 PM 2 07 Division of Communications and Records; Department of State A-M/C Feb 1[9] 1940 Assistant Secretary of State; Feb 20 1940 [initialled]; [illegible] Division Mar 5 1940 Department of State; Filed Mar 11 1940. A note at the end of the document reads: 'To the Department in quintuplicate; Copy to the Embassy at Moscow.'
5 A reference to the so-called Grüne Grenze, an unmarked border.
6 Joseph Schapiro filmed documentary evidence in eastern Poland.

they went on to say, an almost complete disorganization in all branches of life in Soviet Poland. They added that the Jews who have taken the opportunity to slip into German territory have also felt that it would be easier to get away from there to some overseas country than it would from the normally hermetically sealed Soviet Union.

This office has been informed by Dr. J. Robinzonas,[7] a prominent local attorney and one of the leaders of the Jewish minority, that, according to information current in local Jewish circles, the population of the cities of Soviet Poland is swollen to many times normal by refugees, many of whom are faced with immediate starvation. He said, for example, that it was reported that there are now 600,000 refugees in Lwow in addition to the normal population of that city.[8] The Soviets are, he said, deporting many people from Soviet Poland to the interior of Russia.

The Lithuanian Press[9] reports that arrests of members of the Catholic Action have been made by the Soviet police in Bialystok and Lida, both of which lie near the Lithuanian border. At the latter place the Polish Senator Malski is said to have been among those arrested.[10]

The Secretary of the French Legation informed me that he has heard from refugees that the churches are still open in Russian Poland but that conditions are steadily being made worse for them. He added that all convents had been dispersed and their members forbidden to wear religious habits. The Soviets also, he went on to say, require that all religious services be performed in the church premises with the result that the dying must be carried to the churches to receive the last sacraments.

DOC. 76

On 20 January 1940 Higher SS and Police Leader Krüger orders the Jewish councils in the General Government to provide Jews for forced labour[1]

Order to the Jewish councils issued by Krüger, Higher SS and Police Leader on the staff of the Governor General for the Occupied Polish Territories, dated 20 January 1940 (copy)

Order to the Jewish Councils Concerning the Registration and Mustering of Jews for Forced Labour.

It is the statutory duty of the Jewish councils to perform the following tasks. Chairmen and members of the Jewish councils shall be punished with up to ten years of penal

7 Dr Jacob Robinson, also Robinzonas (1889–1977), lawyer; member of the Lithuanian parliament; emigrated to the USA, 1940; director of the Institute for Jewish Affairs of the World Jewish Congress in New York, 1943; compiled reports on the persecution of Jews.

8 This figure is inflated: see Doc. 37, fn. 5.

9 Note in the original: 'A local private news agency. This source not confidential.'

10 Władysław Malski (1894–1940 or 1941), landowner and community leader; fought in the Polish Legion, 1929–1935; elected to the Sejm, 1935–1939; member of the Senate; arrested by the NKVD, Oct. 1939; imprisoned in Minsk in 1940.

1 AŻIH, 213/2, fols. 183a–d. Published in Karol Marian Pospieszalski (ed.), *Documenta Occupationis*, vol. 6: *Hitlerowskie 'prawo' okupacyjne w Polsce*, part 2: *Generalna Gubernia: Wybór dokumentów i próba syntezy* (Poznań: Wydawnictwo Instytutu Zachodniego, 1958), pp. 565–568. This document has been translated from German.

servitude and, where appropriate, the seizure of all their assets as well if they fail to fulfil this duty.

A. Registration

1. The Jewish councils must ensure that all Jews resident in the areas administered by the local Jewish councils are apprised in detail of all regulations and orders concerning forced labour previously issued and yet to be enacted in future, and do so immediately after they have been announced by the mayors.
2. Immediately upon receipt of the index cards for the registration card index, the Jewish councils must acknowledge receipt through the chairman and, when doing so, state the exact quantities and numbers of the index cards issued. The enclosed acknowledgement form must be filled out immediately and forwarded to the Kreishauptmann via the mayor.[2] With its acknowledgement, the Jewish Council simultaneously has to pay the sum of 20 groszy for each index card to the Kreishauptmann via the mayor. The Jewish councils may have this sum reimbursed by the registered Jews when the detachable sections stamped by the mayors are distributed (see item 10).
3. Index cards left over after the first registration must be stored carefully and used in their numerical sequence for the ongoing further registration of arriving Jews. Each set of cards must correspond exactly to the quantity of cards issued according to the registration list (see item 8).
4. Any need for additional cards must be reported immediately to the Kreishauptmann via the mayor; the prescribed acknowledgement of receipt of these additional cards must be issued as well.
5. Immediately after receiving the index cards, the Jewish councils must order all male Jews in their communities aged between 12 and 60 to report to them in person without delay. The Jewish councils are liable for ensuring that no Jew fails to report; baptized Jews must also be registered.
6. The index cards must be filled out by the members of the Jewish councils on the basis of personally questioning the Jews who report, accurately and in accordance with the regulations, in clearly legible script with a typewriter or, if no typewriter is available, in ink.

   The information must be provided in German. The Jewish councils themselves must ensure that suitable interpreters capable of writing good German are recruited.

   The credibility of the information provided by the Jews being registered in response to each individual question must be examined in detail by the Jewish Council, which will bear the responsibility. The Jewish Council's chairman may allocate the work to the individual members of the Jewish Council, but the entire Jewish Council will remain responsible for its correct and expeditious completion.
7. In particular, the following points must be observed when the index cards are filled out:

a) Only the card for the occupational group to which the registered person belongs must be used. Each of the six occupational groups has a particular colour. Cards for other occupational groups, if they are still available, may not be used under any circumstances if the cards for an occupational group have already been used up;

2 Not in the file.

instead, more of the missing cards must be ordered from the Kreishauptmann via the mayors immediately.

b) The entire index card must be completed, including the detachable lower section (date of registration); only the part with the thick border is not to be completed.

c) Where a person has several given names, only the name by which he is known must be given.

d) Information about a physical disability (infirmity or sickness) is to be recorded only if this disability reduces an individual's capacity to work or precludes him from working.

In cases of doubt, the accuracy of the information must be verified by a Jewish physician, who must record the results of his examination in written German. This physician must have been previously appointed as a member of the Jewish Council and, like its other members, will therefore be personally liable for his conduct. The physician's written expert opinion must be sent to the Kreishauptmann via the mayor with the index card.

e) Not all components must be given in the lists of tools at hand; rather, in the case of a small tailor's workshop, for example, the following information would be sufficient: tools for a small tailor's workshop. Machines at hand must always be listed, e.g. two sewing machines or three carpenter's benches, one lathe, etc. In the case of factories, it is sufficient to state the type and size of the enterprise. The Jewish Council will be fully responsible for checking the completeness and correctness of the information.

8. The Jewish Council must compile a list in duplicate for each Jew registered, which states his card index number and includes his name, occupation, and place of residence. A special list of the tools at hand must be drawn up in duplicate, stating their owners.

9. The completed index cards and copies of the two special lists in accordance with § 8 must be forwarded to the Kreishauptleute and/or Stadthauptleute via the mayors within the deadlines set by the Kreishauptleute and/or Stadthauptleute.

10. The lower, detachable sections of the index cards, which have been stamped by the mayors and returned, must be issued to the registered Jews, who are to be required to keep these sections for control purposes. In the case of minors, their parents or other parties responsible for their care, where necessary the Jewish Council itself, are obliged to keep the cards.

11. All registered Jews, carrying their identity cards, must attend the control assemblies ordered by the Kreishauptleute and/or Stadthauptleute. The Jewish councils bear the responsibility for ensuring that all Jews attend punctually.

12. Male Jews between the ages of 12 and 60 who arrive from other areas, particularly from the Warthegau and from Gau Danzig-West Prussia, must be registered immediately by the Jewish Council in the card index for forced labour if they or their representatives inform the Jewish Council that they have taken up residence pursuant to § 2 of the First Implementing Regulation of 11 December 1939.[3] In each case, the completed index cards must be delivered to the mayor on the following Monday, together with the written documents that prove the individuals have taken up

3 See Doc. 55.

residence, as prescribed in § 2 above. Once they have been stamped, the mayor shall return the detachable control sections to the Jewish Council for issue to the registered Jews.[4]

B. Mustering for labour service

1. When Jews are called up for forced labour service, the Jewish councils must ensure that the Jews obliged to report for labour service report punctually, are clean, have been deloused, and bring the following items with them for their personal use: two sleeping blankets, one spare set of work clothes, one coat, two pairs of shoes (boots if possible), three shirts, three pairs of underpants, three pairs of socks, one pair of gloves, two handkerchiefs, a comb and a brush, and one complete set of cutlery, as well as food and drink for two days. All items of clothing and equipment not worn or carried on the body must be carried in a laundry bag or suitcase labelled with the owner's name.

   The listed items of clothing and equipment as well as food and drink are to be procured for impoverished Jews using resources from Jewish funds. Light tools will be taken to the mustering point; heavy tools such as sewing machines, lathes, etc. are to be made ready for transport and must be separately reported to the office by the muster date.

2. For particular consideration: unemployed persons must be registered on the card for their particular occupation with the addition: 'unemployed', e.g. an unemployed bricklayer on a red card: 'bricklayer, unemployed'.

   The individual's most recent earnings from employment (hourly or weekly pay) must be noted on the back of the card at the bottom. Immediately after the muster date has been announced, the Jewish councils must report factories, shops, landholdings, and other assets, including rights of use (such as leases), owned by the Jews called up for forced labour to the Kreishauptleute and/or Stadthauptleute via the mayors, who must confirm the correctness of these reports. This[5] report must state how these assets are to be managed during the Jew's absence so that the office can ensure they are secured where necessary.

DOC. 77

On 22 January 1940 the Jewish Council in Bendzin (Będzin) asks the Trustee Office in Kattowitz to alleviate its funding difficulties[1]

Letter from the executive committee of the Jewish Representative Body in Bendzin (no. W-803/40, Sp./N.), signature illegible, to the Trustee Office in Kattowitz, dated 22 January 1940[2]

The executive committee of the Jewish Representative Body in Bendzin was established in accordance with a directive dated 28 October 1939[3] from the mayor of Bendzin, Mr Kowohl.[4]

4 Krüger later ordered that the card indexes of forced labourers be handed over to the relevant employment offices: see Doc. 125.

5 One line is missing from this version of the document, which is here supplemented with a different version of the same order: APL, 501/75, fols. 10–13 (fol. 13).

1 APK, 124/1397, fols. 12–13. This document has been translated from German.

As the only Jewish institution active in the city of Bendzin at present, we have been assigned to deal with those Jewish problems and affairs that previously fell within the remit of the municipal administration and the civil administrative bodies.

Within the scope of the functions entrusted to us, we are obliged to fund the complete budget for feeding the most impoverished members of the population; medical costs; support payments for redundant public officials,[5] workers, and teachers; support payments to families of reservists; the maintenance of the orphanage and the retirement home; and so on and so forth.

In addition, we have to pay taxes and fees to the local and state authorities regularly, either in cash or in kind.

The aforementioned expenditures, not including the taxes and fees payable to self-administrations and state institutions, will amount to 21,858.00 Reichsmarks in December 1939 and, according to the projected budget, 30,376.25 Reichsmarks in January 1940. To cover these expenditures, we have been authorized to levy fees on individuals and Jewish firms in the city of Bendzin.

In view of the Aryan management of some Jewish firms and the takeover of Jewish enterprises by trustees, our sources of income are diminishing from day to day. The trustees do not allow the firms under their management to pay fees to the executive committee of the Jewish Representative Body in Bendzin, not even in small amounts.

As a matter of procedure we venture to point out that, for the aforementioned reasons, 90 per cent of the firms that used to contribute to our budget to a very significant degree are no longer able to contribute to the fees paid to our institution at all.

In view of the fact that the current situation we have described is having very negative effects on the performance of the roles assigned to us by the mayor and is hindering the conscientious implementation of current orders from both local and state authorities, we herewith venture to address the following respectful request to the Trustee Office: according to the regulations in place in the Old Reich, the Jewish firms which have been transferred into Aryan hands have to cede 20 per cent of their assets to the Jewish Community, whereas firms that continue their economic activities under the administration of trustees pay 3 per cent of their turnover to the Jewish Community.

Since these rules have still not been applied to date in the territory of the city of Bendzin, we herewith venture to address the respectful request to the Trustee Office that the relevant norms in place in the Old Reich also enter into force in the territory of the city of Bendzin.

In addressing this letter to the Trustee Office, we venture to remark most respectfully that our only intention in doing so is the desire to be able to perform, as conscientiously as possible, the duties entrusted to us by both the mayor and the state authorities.

2 The original contains handwritten notes.

3 This could not be found. According to the *Bulletin*, a periodical published by the Statistical Department of the Head of the Councils of Elders of the Jewish Communities in East Upper Silesia, a Jewish Community committee was formed in Sosnowiec on 6 Sept. 1939 and took over the Community in Będzin 'in the first few days of November 1939': *Bulletin*, no. 1, 15 Sept. 1940, p. 1; AŻIH, Ring I/1016 (11), fol. 2.

4 Hans Kowohl (b. 1907), retailer; joined the NSDAP and the SA in 1928; became NSDAP Kreisleiter in Oppeln, 1930; mayor of Krappitz (Oppeln), 1933–1940; acting mayor of Będzin from Sept. 1939.

5 Jewish public officials who had been dismissed.

In the hope that the information we have cited in this letter will be favourably taken into consideration by the Trustee Office, for which we wish to express our gratitude most respectfully in advance, we remain,

with the highest esteem,[6]

DOC. 78
On 23 January 1940 the commander of the Urban Police in Lodz (Łódź) orders the confiscation of Jewish apartments[1]

Special order from the commander of the Urban Police in Lodz (S I a), signed Keuck,[2] to the deputy chief of police and his adjutant, the commander and his deputy, the Urban Police stations in Lodz, Section Command A 2, O.v.O[3] stations, and Battalions 44–3 and 31–1, dated 23 January 1940 (carbon copy)[4]

Special Order

Re: confiscation of Jewish apartments to house Baltic German families in Lodsch

A. *General provisions*

1. The number of Baltic Germans to be settled in Lodsch has been set at 15,000 persons. As these are families of four to five on average, only some of the apartments cleared on the Wiwecki housing estate[5] are suitable to house the Baltic Germans. The Office for the Settlement of Baltic Germans, Lodsch, 2 Moniuszki, headed by SS-Hauptsturmführer Scheve,[6] has established an evacuation staff to clear suitable Jewish apartments. The evacuation staff will work independently. It will select the apartments, confiscate them, and seal them. The listing of assets, completion of confiscation forms, delivery of assets to the city, etc. will be carried out exclusively by the staff of the Office for the Settlement of Baltic Germans. Several police officers will be attached to each evacuation squad simply to legalize its work. The evacuations will be carried out from 24 January 1940, mainly in the areas of Section Commands East and West. Plans call for the evacuation of approximately fifty families each day, including on Sundays.

6 Such requests were repeatedly addressed to the Trustee Office in Katowice by various Jewish councils. The agency forwarded these letters to the Main Trustee Office East in Berlin, which filed them.

1 AIPN, GK 68/218, fols. 36–37. This document has been translated from German.

2 Walter Keuck (1889–1972), police officer; with the police in Breslau from 1920; joined the NSDAP in 1933; deputy chief of police in Frankfurt am Main, 1937–1939; colonel and commander of the Urban Police in Łódź, then in Wuppertal, 1940–1942; senior commander of the Order Police in Magdeburg and Hanover, 1943–1945; in 1946 extradited to Poland, where he was sentenced to eight years in prison in 1948; sentence reduced to two and a half years on appeal; released in 1949.

3 The meaning of the abbreviation O.v.O. is not known.

4 The order was also sent to the Criminal Police, Departments II and III, the Office for the Settlement of Baltic Germans, and the mayor, for information only. Sections of the original have been underlined by hand.

5 Correctly: Mirecki housing estate (Polish: Osiedle Mireckiego). See also Doc. 79.

6 Correctly: Dr Robert Schefe (1909–1945?), lawyer; joined the NSDAP in 1932 and the SS in 1934; head of the Allenstein Gestapo office, 1938–1939; Regierungsrat and head of Einsatzkommando 2, Einsatzgruppe V, in Poland in 1939; initially deputy head, then head of the Gestapo office in Łódź, 1939–1942; subsequently head of Group A Criminal Policy and Prevention in the Reich Criminal Police Office; later declared dead.

2. The evacuated Jewish families will initially be housed in Lodsch. The northern part of the city that is under consideration as a ghetto has been designated to house them. A sketch with the boundaries of the ghetto has already been sent to Section Command North. Additionally, they will be housed with other Jewish families. If a Jewish family is not in a position to find housing on their own, the Jewish elder must ensure they are housed. However, they may be housed only in apartments that are located within the area of the ghetto perimeter.

B. *Measures*

1. Section Commands East and West will each provide twelve patrol officers to support the evacuation squads. The same officers are always to be deployed and are not to be used for any other duties for the duration of the evacuations. *Dress*: service uniform, steel helmet, pistol. Report for the first time on 24 January 1940, 9 a.m., at 2 Moniuszki, to SS-Hauptsturmführer Scheve.

   Task – The police reinforcements are primarily required to legalize the work of the evacuation squads. Additionally, they will have to take the evacuated Jewish families to police stations 5 and 6. The families are to be marched on foot, conveyed by tram, or conveyed by other vehicles. The Jews must pay for the vehicles. The commander of the evacuation squad will decide what the Jews are allowed to take with them.

   The evacuated Jews are mainly to be taken to police station 5.

2. The evacuated Jews will be housed by stations 5 and 6, pursuant to A(2). All the Jews who arrive there are to be registered on lists. Their new residence must be evident from the lists. It must be explained to the Jews that once they have been housed, they will be forbidden from changing their residence of their own accord.

   If they fail to comply, they will be transferred to a forced labour camp. Should evacuated Jews be able to find housing with other families within the perimeter of the ghetto on their own, this is to be permitted. In all other cases, the Jewish elder must be called in to house them.

   To reinforce stations 5 and 6, Police Battalion 44 must provide ten officers to each station daily until further notice – including on Sundays.

   Dress: service uniform, carbine, thirty rounds of ammunition.

   Report for the first time on 24 January 1940, 10.30 a.m., at the aforementioned stations.

   Section Command North will direct the deployment of the reinforcements. Following the conclusion of the daily evacuations, the officers are to be released to their regularly assigned stations.

C. *Special directives*

1. Neither the evacuated Jews nor the Jewish elder must become aware that the establishment of a ghetto is being considered in the part of the city mentioned in A(2). All officers deployed are to be instructed accordingly.
2. The Jewish elder or the representatives appointed by him are to be involved as much as possible in housing the evacuated Jews. No delays must occur in the housing process.
3. The reinforcements and patrol officers from Section Commands East and West are to be instructed to take provisions with them. The evacuations will be carried out until nightfall, without a break for lunch.

4. The relevant police stations in the areas where evacuations are carried out are to be informed by telephone by the assigned patrol officers. Section Command West must nominate one officer who will ascertain the number of dwellings cleared each day following the conclusion of the evacuations and report it to Section Command West. Section Command West must record the number of dwellings cleared each day in its daily reports. Section Command North shall similarly report the number of Jews evacuated and newly housed each day.
5. Any difficulties encountered in the process of housing the evacuated Jews must be dealt with. Section Command North must intervene to put an end to these difficulties on its own. In special cases, contact the Office for the Settlement of Baltic Germans – telephone 10 455.
6. The section commands will submit an interim report on the experience gained during the evacuations by 30 January 1940. A final report will be requested from the command in due course.[7]

DOC. 79
On 23 January 1940 the Higher SS and Police Leader in the Warthegau reports on the confiscation of Jewish apartments in Lodz (Łódź)[1]

Report by the Higher SS and Police Leader Warthe, Koppe, as representative of the Reich Commissioner for the Strengthening of Germandom, Office for the Settlement of Baltic Germans, Lodsch Branch Office (Sch/S, log no. 272/40), signed SS-Sturmbannführer Rapp, dated 23 January 1940 (carbon copy)

Daily Report Lodsch no. 2
Re: evacuations
According to the mayor of the city of Lodsch, it was possible to clear the city's Mirecki Estate, which had a total of 990 one-, two-, and three-room apartments, for the Baltic Germans. When the Baltic Germans arrived, it was revealed that, of these 990 apartments, 141 were unfurnished, others were occupied by ethnic German and Polish railway officials, and yet other apartments were unsuitable for the Baltic Germans. As a result, the evacuation of this estate, carried out by Rapp's staff, only made 220 apartments available that could be used for the Baltic Germans. In addition, some apartments could not be occupied until the rooms, water pipes, and lavatories had been repaired. Since the Baltic Germans were already on their way, it was an emergency. Recourse was therefore made to a file note dated 9 January 1940 by the Higher SS and Police Leader concerning the meeting of 8 January 1940 in Lodsch about the occupational placement and housing of Baltic Germans,[2] which stated that a number of better Jewish apartments would be cleared in order to give 3,000 Baltic German families suitable homes in Lodsch.

7 See Higher SS and Police Leader Koppe's progress report of 26 Jan. 1940 concerning the resettlement of Poles and Jews from Reichsgau Wartheland: BArch, R 75/5, fols. 1–8.

1 AIPN, GK 68/218, fols. 38–39. Copy in USHMM, RG 15 015M, reel 3. This document has been translated from German.

2 The memo is not in the file.

Since the municipal Resettlement and Billeting Office, with its limited staff of officials, was not in a position to carry out this urgent concentration of the Jews, we decided to take matters into our own hands. After SS-Hauptsturmführer Scheve[3] had consulted the Lodsch chief of police, SS-Brigadeführer Schäfer, the attached special order concerning the clearance of Jewish apartments to house Baltic German families in Lodsch was issued.[4] Six men from the Office for the Settlement of Baltic Germans were detailed to carry out the evacuation with six Selbstschutz people, who were joined by twenty-four police officers. Working tirelessly, the team mastered its task to my complete satisfaction within the brief period of three days.

The following dwellings were evacuated and re-allocated:

	Evacuated	*Re-allocated*	
		Estate	Jewish dwelling[s]
19 January 1940	230 (estate) 19 (Jewish dwellings)		
20 January 1940	21	86	–
21 January 1940	21	11	4
22 January 1940	24	22	4
23 January 1940	7	22	19
24 January 1940	77	15	15
	399	156	42

This means that a total of 399 apartments have been evacuated, and 198 of them have already been used to house Baltic Germans. The remainder, 201 dwellings, some of which on the estate will be ready to move into only in the next few days, will be allocated tomorrow.

The cash assets secured during the evacuation are handed over to the Office for Confiscated Assets on the same day, in exchange for a receipt. The quality and size of the apartment are noted on its key tag. The keys are handed over to the Housing Office in the Office for the Settlement of Baltic Germans, the apartments are registered on index cards, the new Baltic German occupant is specified, and the Postal and Information Unit of the Office for the Settlement of Baltic Germans is notified of the new address (see attached index cards).[5]

DOC. 80

New York Times, 23 January 1940: an article reports figures of murdered and displaced Jews in Poland[1]

Two Hundred and Fifty Thousand Jews Listed as Dead in Poland – Reports to Joint Distribution Committee Cover Period Since Opening of War – Heavy Toll in Epidemics – Economic Life Is 'Completely Strangled,' It Is Said, and Thousands Lack Shelter.

3 Correctly: Robert Schefe.

4 See Doc. 78.

5 Not in the file.

1 *New York Times*, no. 29 949, 23 Jan. 1940, p. 5.

More than 250,000 Jews have been wiped out in Poland by military operations, disease, and starvation since Sept. 1, according to an estimate released yesterday by the Joint Distribution Committee on the basis of reports it has received.[2] It added that 80 percent of the remaining 1,250,000 Jews in the German-occupied area[3] have been 'reduced to beggary.'

Typhus epidemics are raging in Warsaw, Lodz, and many other towns, and their virulence is augmented by the widespread starvation and exhaustion, the committee said. Economic life has been 'completely strangled,' and hundreds of thousands of families, uprooted from their homes, wander along open roads, seeking a shelter. Women, aged men, and children are 'subjected to countless indignities.'

Although the suffering from starvation, epidemics, pogroms, persecutions, and wholesale expulsions is most acute in the German-occupied territories, there is also great hardship in the Russian-occupied section, where 600,000[4] Jews have taken refuge, and among the refugees in the bordering countries, according to the report of the committee.

Twenty-Five Hundred Suicides Reported

In Nazi Poland 2,500 Jews are reported to have committed suicide, and their number is being increased daily, according to the committee, while 'many hundreds' have been summarily executed. Hundreds of others have been and still are being held for ransom, the report says. The wearing of a yellow arm band bearing a six-pointed star has been instituted in many cities.[5]

'Not the least of the hardships confronting the Jews of Poland are their fears for the future,' the report says. 'The institution of a ghetto in Warsaw, which would have crowded 350,000 people into a few square blocks, half of whose buildings were destroyed by bombardment or fire, was officially ordered, but has been delayed because of fear that epidemics might spread to the rest of Warsaw's population.

'The search for corpses in the debris of the bombed Jewish sections of Warsaw continues even today. Rumors that the Nuremberg racial laws are shortly to be introduced have added to the panic of Poland's Jews.'

The committee's statement confirmed previous reports that the German authorities have decreed that Lublin is to become the hub of a Jewish reservation where not only all of Poland's Jews but the Jews of old Germany, Austria, Bohemia–Moravia, and Slovakia are to be concentrated. At the end of 1939 more than 40,000 Jews had been dumped into Lublin, the committee said, and no organized help is permitted in behalf of these refugees.

The borders between the German- and Russian-occupied areas, as well as between the German area and Lithuania, are 'peppered with "no man's lands," where small groups

2 This figure is a considerable overestimate. Based on current estimates, 32,216 Jewish soldiers and officers died on the battlefield, and about 20,000 Jewish civilians perished as a result of the fighting; several thousand Poles and Jews were murdered by Germans by the end of 1939. The number of dead from epidemics and starvation was still comparatively low at this time.

3 This figure, in turn, is considerably lower than the actual number of remaining Jews.

4 For more on this overestimated figure, see Doc. 37, fn. 5.

5 From late 1939, Jews in parts of annexed western Poland were forced to wear a 10 cm yellow star visible on the front and back of their outer garments; the Jewish population in the General Government was forced to wear a white armband with a six-pointed blue star.

of Jews are huddled under conditions of the utmost misery, unable to advance or retreat,' the committee said. It praised the self-sacrifice and devotion the small Jewish communities of these districts were said to have shown in aiding the refugees.

Housing Conditions Bad
There are about 900,000 refugees in the Russian-occupied area of Poland, 70 percent of them Jewish, according to the information reaching the committee. Housing conditions were said to be especially bad, with 300,000 homeless refugees crowded into Lemberg, 120,000 in East Galicia and its Provinces, 100,000 in the cities of Rovno, Lutsk, and Kowal, and 60,000 in Bialystok.

Although food is distributed under government auspices in public soup kitchens in this area, the number of such stations is insufficient and it is difficult for a refugee to get the single meal a day to which he is entitled, according to the committee. There are severe shortages of warm clothing, shoes, medicine, and fuel, and there is a lack of medical attention for the numerous cases of typhoid.

The situation of the 25,000 Jewish war refugees in Lithuania, most of whom are located in Vilna, was said by the committee to be 'severe,' but the situation of several thousand other refugees in Rumania, Hungary, and Latvia 'has now been brought under control' with funds supplied by the joint distribution committee. The report told in detail of relief work done by the committee in the other stricken areas.

DOC. 81

On 24 January 1940 Governor General Frank orders the registration of Jewish assets[1]

Regulation on the Duty to Register Jewish Assets in the General Government

On the basis of § 5(1) of the Führer and Reich Chancellor's Decree on the Administration of the Occupied Polish Territories, 12 October 1939 (*Reichsgesetzblatt* I, p. 2077),[2] I hereby issue the following regulation:

§ 1

Duty to register assets

All Jewish assets must be registered. Registration is to be based on the assets' value on the day of this regulation's entry into force. The duty to register assets cannot be evaded by abusing forms and legal options offered by civil law.

§ 2

Jewish assets

(1) Jewish assets are defined as:

1. the assets of Jews, insofar as they held Polish nationality on 1 January 1939 or acquired Polish nationality after this point, and the assets of stateless Jews; here, the non-Jewish spouse of a Jew shall be treated as a Jew;

1 *VOBl-GG* I 1940, no. 7, 29 Jan. 1940, pp. 31–35. This document has been translated from German.
2 On 12 Oct. 1939 Hitler declared the central and southern parts of Poland as the General Government of the Occupied Polish Territories; he appointed Hans Frank as governor general.

2. the assets of partnerships if more than half of the partners or, in the case of limited partnerships, more than half of the personally liable partners are Jews;
3. the assets of incorporated companies in which Jews have capital holdings exceeding 25 per cent or had such holdings on 1 January 1939, or which have or had Jews on their management or supervisory boards after 1 January 1939, or over which there is decisive Jewish influence in some other way.

(2) Assets within the meaning of (1) comprise movable and immovable assets, including accounts receivable, capital holdings, rights, and other interests.

§ 3

Formal requirements and deadline for registration

The registration of the relevant assets according to § 1 must be submitted on official forms (enclosures I and II) by 1 March 1940 to the Kreishauptmann (Stadthauptmann) responsible for the place of residence of the person required to register assets, or for the legal domicile of the partnership or incorporated company required to register assets. The registration deadline may be extended for a brief period only in specially justified cases of exception. Decisions about such extensions shall be taken by the Kreishauptmann (Stadthauptmann) at his professional discretion. See enclosures I and II on pp. 33 and 34.

§ 4

Ownerless assets

Assets that have not been registered within the registration deadline shall be regarded as ownerless and, following the expiry of the registration deadline, are to be seized pursuant to § 8 of the Regulation on the Procedure for Confiscation of Private Assets (24 January 1940) (*Verordnungsblatt*[-GG] I, p. 23).

§ 5

Penalties

(1) Contraventions of this regulation and the provisions promulgated for its implementation shall be punishable by imprisonment and fines up to an unlimited amount or with either of these penalties, and in particularly severe cases by penal servitude.

Cracow, 24 January 1940

The Governor General for the Occupied Polish Territories

Frank

DOC. 82

On 30 January 1940 high-ranking SS officers meet in Berlin to discuss expelling Poles and Jews from the Warthegau and resettling Baltic and Volhynian Germans[1]

Memo on the meeting of the Chief of the Security Police and the SD, Heydrich, with representatives of the SS and other agencies[2] at the Reich Security Main Office (IV D 4[3] – III ES[4]), unsigned, dated 30 January 1940, for SS-Obersturmbannführer Tröger (IV D 4–888/40), sent on 19 February 1940 (received on 26 February 1940)[5]

Re: meeting on 30 January 1940
1) SS-Gruppenführer *Heydrich* announced that today's meeting was convened by order of the Reichsführer-SS so that all the agencies involved can settle on a uniform line regarding the implementation of the resettlement tasks ordered by the Führer. The clearances carried out to date have relocated approximately 87,000 Poles and Jews from the Warthegau to make room for the Baltic Germans who are to be settled there. In addition, there has been unmanaged 'illegal emigration'.

Based on comments made by Reich Minister Seyss-Inquart and SS-Obergruppenführer Krüger, SS-Gruppenführer Heydrich noted that the relevant agencies under the Governor General had raised no fundamental objections to the evacuation to the General Government. The complaints made so far have merely concerned the fact that the numbers originally set had not been observed, but rather exceeded, during previous evacuations. The objections presented ceased to be relevant when Section IV D 4 was established for the purpose of managing expulsions centrally.

It is considered a matter of priority to deport 40,000 Jews and Poles from the Warthegau to the General Government in order to create space for Baltic Germans.[6] The order given by the Reichsführer-SS, which includes the stipulation that no persons of German ancestry may be deported, regardless of their previous history, is accepted as a guideline for the selection process.

1 BArch, R 58/1032, fols. 35–43. This document has been translated from German.
2 Attended by Seyss-Inquart, Krüger, Koppe, Rediess, Hildebrandt, Greifelt, Creutz, Streckenbach, Mohr, Rasch, Wiegand, Damzog, Rapp, Tröger, Abromeit, Wächter, Lasch, Moder, Zech, Globocnik, Katzmann, Meisinger, Liphardt, Hahn, Huppenkothen, Schäfer, Knobloch, Dreier, Tanzmann, Bischof, Kubitz, Winkler, Galke, Pfennig, Fuchs, Best, Müller, Ohlendorf, Ehlich, Eichmann, Günther, Deumling, Dannecker, and Rajakowitsch.
3 Section IV D 4 (later IV B 4) dealt with the deportation of Jews and Poles. It was headed by Adolf Eichmann.
4 The head of Section III E S, Immigration and Settlement, from 31 Oct. 1939 was Dr Hans Ehlich (1901–1991), physician; joined the NSDAP in 1931 and the SS in 1934; Regierungsmedizinalrat (state medical officer) and racial specialist in the Health Department of the Saxon Ministry of the Interior from 1935; employed in the NSDAP's Racial Policy Office; appointed to the SD Main Office as head of the Race and National Health Section (II 213), 1937; served with Einsatzgruppe V in Poland, Sept. 1939; head of the RSHA Volkstum section (III B), 1939; played a leading role in General Plan East; interned by the British, 1945–1947; subsequently worked as a physician in Braunschweig.
5 The original contains handwritten underlining.
6 The Baltic Germans who were resettled in autumn 1939 were members of the German-speaking minority in Latvia and Estonia. Most of them were resettled to the Warthegau in 1939 as part of the agreements set out in the secret protocol of the Molotov–Ribbentrop Pact.

After this movement [of people], another improvised expulsion is to be undertaken in favour of the Volhynian Germans[7] due to be settled in the eastern Gaue. If we assume that the Volhynian German families have six to seven children on average, approximately 20,000 households will have to be resettled. The number of Poles to be expelled for this purpose must provisionally be assumed to be approximately 120,000. However, a slight reduction can be expected, insofar as some of the displaced Polish owners of farms will themselves be deployed as agricultural workers in the eastern Gaue or the Old Reich. If possible, Congress Poles[8] should be registered for this.

Based on this number, the General Government has until 15 February 1940 to state its intentions regarding their distribution to the unloading stations.[9] The date on which the implementation of this movement [of people] is to begin will be set later, and all the agencies involved will be notified in time.

The Warthegau and West Prussia–Danzig, Zichenau, and East Upper Silesia will have until the same date (15 February 1940) to compile statistical information on the Volhynian Germans who will arrive there for settlement and to calculate the numbers of Polish landowners to be cleared based on these numbers. They will then communicate the numbers to Section IV D 4.

IV D 4 will have to collate the numbers and draw up the expulsion plan. While the persons to be expelled in the interest of settling Volhynian Germans are almost exclusively part of the rural population, the persons expelled in the interests of the Baltic Germans were almost exclusively part of the urban population.

SS-Gruppenführer *Koppe* stated that the expulsion in favour of the Volhynian Germans has to be undertaken in such a way that agricultural operations are not interrupted. The Volhynian Germans are to be taken to the selected settlement destinations by lorry and exchanged for the previous Polish owners. The Poles will be gathered in camps and undergo selection there. Those who cannot be utilized in the eastern Gaue and the Old Reich will be slated for deportation to the General Government. Consequently, the exact number of those who are eligible for resettlement in the General Government can only be established after this selection process.

In addition, however, 4,000–5000 Poles and Jews who have already been evicted in favour of the Baltic Germans have been gathered in camps in the Warthegau. So far it has not been possible to deport them.

SS-Obergruppenführer *Krüger* mentioned that 60,000 refugees from Russia are expected to arrive in the General Government and will also have to be housed there.[10]

7 The Volhynian Germans who were resettled in winter 1939/40 came from that part of Volhynia which was part of eastern Poland and which was occupied in Sept. 1939 by the Soviet Union. Like the Baltic Germans, they were also resettled following the Molotov–Ribbentrop Pact.

8 Poles from the part of Poland formerly under Russian rule who had settled after 1918 in the formerly German-ruled territories of western Poland.

9 This is a reference to the train stations where incoming expellees would disembark.

10 In the course of the population exchange across the demarcation line, it was expected that 60,000 returnees from the Soviet Union and 15,000 Poles and/or Ukrainians with Polish citizenship would resettle in the Soviet Union: see Doc. 83. In the end, the number of people who wanted to move westward was far higher: see Doc. 115.

2) SS-Gruppenführer Heydrich announced the following basic directives issued by the Reichsführer-SS:

Neither ethnic Germans nor persons of German ancestry may be deported, nor any Kashubs,[11] Masurians,[12] or similar ethnic groups; the latter on the grounds that these groups' behaviour has been pro-German and they have been racially entwined with the German people. However, the Reichsführer-SS does not want a Kashubian or a Masurian question to be raised because of this. When deportations are carried out, the official line should be that the German provinces must be cleansed of their alien population. This will leave open the possibility of deporting utterly inferior Kashubs etc., as well as pursuing racial screening at a later date.

On the general Polish question, it has been decreed that no selection process according to race has to be carried out at this point when selecting agricultural workers. This is because it might confuse the German population if a distinction were to be made between good and bad Poles among the masses that will be taken to the Old Reich. As far as the labour deployment of Poles in the Reich is concerned, attention must be paid to an appropriate proportional distribution of the sexes. According to the latest findings, a total of 800,000 to 1,000,000 Poles are being deployed to Reich territory, in addition to the prisoners of war. The selection is being handled by the employment offices. Some of these Poles are to be brought in from the eastern Gaue. In the course of the preparations, it was noted that the local agencies in the eastern Gaue were declaring these Poles indispensable because they were required there. For example, the Warthegau stated that it could only spare 20,000, while the Gau West Prussia–Danzig wanted to make only 8,000 available. It is therefore necessary to register without exception all Poles in the eastern Gaue who could potentially be considered for agricultural labour.

Exceptions to the basic prohibition against racial selection in the course of the deployment of agricultural workers [to the Reich] can only be considered where entire Polish families of farm labourers are designated for evacuation. Racially desirable elements may be left in Reich territory.

3) Following the two mass movements of

(a) 40,000 Poles and Jews for the benefit of Baltic Germans, and

(b) approximately 120,000 Poles for the benefit of Volhynian Germans,

the deportation of all Jews in the new eastern Gaue and 30,000 Gypsies from Reich territory to the General Government is to be carried out as the last mass movement [of people]. Since it has been decided that the expulsion of 120,000 Poles will commence around March 1940, the evacuation of Jews and Gypsies will have to be postponed until the operations mentioned above have been completed. In any case, however, the General Government is to provide notification of the distribution ratios so that planning can commence.

SS-Obergruppenführer Krüger stated that military training grounds of significant size have to be made available to the Wehrmacht, the Luftwaffe, and the SS in the [General] Government, which would require the resettlement of approximately 100,000 to 120,000 people within the [General] Government. It would therefore be desirable that

11 A Western Slavic ethnic group in the Danzig region.

12 Originally a Slavic ethnic group in East Prussia which converted to Protestantism at an early date and spoke a Polish dialect until the early twentieth century.

this is kept in mind when clearances to the General Government are carried out, in order to avoid resettling people twice. On this issue, SS-Gruppenführer Heydrich remarked that the construction of the wall[13] and other projects in the East will probably provide opportunities to assemble several hundred thousand Jews in forced labour camps. Their families could then be brought in, together with the other Jewish families who are already in the General Government, and this should resolve the problem touched upon earlier. SS-Obergruppenführer Krüger also mentioned that ethnic Germans (mainly peasant elements) would be relocated from the General Government and brought to the Reich. On this point, SS-Brigadeführer Greifelt remarked that the Reichsführer-SS has made plans for this question to be resolved in the longer term.

SS-Gruppenführer Heydrich announced that, following the three mass movements discussed earlier, the relocation offices will perform a racial selection in the eastern Gaue. Some of the Poles will be dispersed to the Old Reich with their families.

In mid February 1940, 1,000 Jews from Stettin whose apartments are urgently required for the war effort will be cleared and also deported to the General Government.

SS-Gruppenführer Seyss-Inquart reiterated the numbers the General Government will have to absorb in the immediate future: 40,000 Jews and Poles, 20,000 Poles and all the Jews in the new eastern Gaue, and 30,000 Gypsies from the Old Reich and the Ostmark. He mentioned the transport difficulties this could cause for the Reich Railway and finally the poor food situation in the General Government, which will not improve before the next harvest. As a result, the Reich will have to continue to provide aid. Reich Minister Seyss-Inquart asked SS-Gruppenführer Heydrich to support him in this matter if it should be necessary to procure more food aid for the General Government. SS-Brigadeführer Wächter requested assurance that evacuees coming from territories where the food situation is considerably better than in the General Government will be supplied with appropriate foodstuffs.

With regard to the transport difficulties mentioned by Reich Minister Seyss-Inquart, SS-Gruppenführer Heydrich commented that they have been included in the planning, insofar as all transport movements will be managed centrally by the Reich Ministry of Transport, so that wasteful deployments of rolling stock will be avoided.

Finally, SS-Gruppenführer Heydrich highlighted the fact that it is particularly important for the trustee offices in charge to be notified in good time of the persons to be evacuated – especially with regard to urban populations – so that their assets can be secured.

Following this meeting, which lasted from 11.30 a.m. to 1.15 p.m., relevant officials working for the inspectors in the new eastern Gaue and for the Senior Commander of the Security Police and the SD in the General Government met with III ES and IV D 4 to discuss specific issues.

13 There was a plan to build fortifications close to the General Government's eastern border.

DOC. 83

On 1 February 1940 the government of the GG gives an overview of the planned forced resettlement of approximately 1.6 million people[1]

Memorandum from the Office of the Governor General, Interior Administration Department (Dr S.[2]/Pi.), unsigned, dated 1 February 1940

Overview of resettlements in the General Government

A. From the German eastern territories to the General Government:

40,000 Poles and Jews[3]	
1,000 Poles and Jews	from 15 February 1940
120,000 Poles and Jews	from 1 March 1940
450,000 Jews	from 1 May 1940
30,000 Gypsies	from 1 May 1940

B. From the General Government to Germany:

780,000 agricultural workers	from 1 March 1940
60,000 ethnic Germans	from 1 April 1940

C. Resettlement from Russia to Poland and vice versa:

60,000 Poles from Russia	from 15 February 1940
15,000 Poles to Russia	from 15 February 1940

D. Internal resettlements due to the establishment of military training grounds:
120,000 Poles

Total: approximately 1.6 million people

1 APL, 498/133, fol. 1. This document has been translated from German.

2 Dr Friedrich Wilhelm Siebert (1903–1966), lawyer; joined the NSDAP in 1931 and the SS in 1935; mayor of Lindau in 1933, then Landrat in Bad Kissingen in 1939; head of the Interior Administration Department in the General Government from Oct. 1939; department head in the Bavarian State Ministry of Finance, Sept. 1940; once again head of the Interior Administration Department in the General Government, Feb. 1942; found guilty of war crimes in Cracow, 1948; released from prison, 1956; deputy mayor of Prien am Chiemsee, 1960–1966.

3 This number presumably refers to the Poles and Jews who had already been deported to the General Government at the time of the report.

DOC. 84

On 1 February 1940 the Kreishauptmann in Busko draws attention to the acute housing shortage in his Kreis[1]

Letter from the Kreishauptmann in Busko, Dr Wilhelm Schäfer, to the District Governor of Radom, Labour/Settlement Affairs Department (VII no. 1901/2), dated 1 February 1940 (carbon copy)[2]

Re: housing and settlement affairs – resettlement of Poles and Jews from Reich territory
Kreis Busko is already heavily overcrowded. Approximately 4,000–5,000 resettled persons have arrived here. On average, the occupancy rate in the apartments is approximately six to eight persons per room. However, there are also rooms occupied by ten to twenty persons. There are almost no vacant apartments available. Further housing space could be created only by cramming Jews together in the synagogue or in other Jewish apartments. Difficulties in the implementation of the resettlement operation are being caused primarily by the fact that, in many cases, the people who are arriving here are mainly from urban areas and cannot easily make a living in the rural communities. The burden placed on thc municipalities by the welfare expenditure for these people is so great that it can no longer be covered by the incoming tax revenues. The question of funding needs to be clarified urgently.[3]

1 AIPN, GK 639/37a, fol. 10. This document has been translated from German.

2 The letter is the Kreishauptmann's reply to a circular from the district government's Labour/Settlement Affairs Department of 15 Jan. 1940, which asked 'what population numbers can still be housed in the apartments available at the moment'. On 17 Jan. 1940 the District Governor informed the Kreishauptmann that '14,000 Jews and Poles' would be taken to the Kreis 'from the eastern Gaue of the Reich on railway transports of approximately 1,000 persons each' and ordered him to 'immediately draw up a distribution plan' for these people: AIPN, GK 639/37a, fols. 7–8.

3 Handwritten note in pencil in the bottom margin: 'I BuF 501/1'. The Population and Welfare Division (BuF) in the General Government's Interior Administration Department and in the corresponding departments in the district and Kreis administrations was in charge of population policy. The BuF was responsible for the treatment of individual ethnic groups in the General Government: this included measures regarding the Jews expelled from western Poland and deportations within the General Government. It also supervised the Jewish population's voluntary welfare organizations.

DOC. 85

On 1 February 1940 the medical officer Dr Walter Schultz writes a memorandum on why a ghetto needs to be created in Lodz (Łódź)[1]

Memorandum by Dr Walter Schultz,[2] dated 1 February 1940 (draft)[3]

Memorandum on the necessity of the establishment of a ghetto in Lodsch
The disease-control situation in the city of Lodsch, that is to say the frequent occurrence of typhus caused by wartime conditions, makes drastic measures necessary in order to limit the disease to its source. According to investigations that have been carried out, typhus started spreading from the northern part of the city, where almost exclusively Jews have been living in the most primitive hygienic conditions for a very long time. Given that race's lack of any sense of cleanliness, it did not come as a surprise that dwellings and people were generally infested with lice. No wonder that as a result of the great density of the Jewish population, contagious diseases had already spread rapidly from that district to all parts of the city through the unrestrained movement of Jews. The lice-ridden Jew mingling unhindered with the rest of the population is a danger to the general population because it opens up the whole city to the uncontrollable spread of infection. In view of the primitive living conditions and the uncultured nature of the bulk of the Jews, never mind the question of costs, it is impossible to combat and block the sources of infection by delousing persons, dwellings, and tenements every time. Even if dwellings and entire streets were deloused, supposedly contained sources of infection could spring up once again in areas that had previously been sanitized, because of the Jews' dealings with one another and the rest of the population. Given this situation, the sole remaining disease-control measure that holds out any promise of success is to ensure that all contact with Jews is avoided at all costs, because, as far as we know, this is the only way to rule out the transmission of lice. For these reasons, the idea of a ghetto has become an undeniable necessity. The practical conclusion drawn from this was to restrict the right to live in other peoples' properties and the right of residence *for all* Jews living in Lodsch to the aforementioned district in the north, so that all the channels for contagious disease that are known to scientists are hermetically sealed.

The area of the city assigned to the Jews to live in, once all the Germans and Poles who previously resided there had been evacuated, deloused, and then settled elsewhere, was surrounded on all sides by strong fortifications (fences, wire barriers, walls, etc.) with guard towers. This made it impossible for ghetto residents to escape clandestinely. It is absolutely necessary for the police to guard the ghetto boundaries at all times {in order to prevent conditions like those in Warsaw from arising. Due to a shortage of the

1 APŁ, 221/31866b, fols. 37–41. Copy in USHMM, RG 05 008M, reel 6. This document has been translated from German.

2 Dr Walter Schultz (1899–1940), physician; medical officer at the public health office in Rummelsburg (Pomerania) from 1939; became a public health officer in Łódź in Jan. 1940 in order to carry out a special mission within the public health authority there, presumably in connection with the establishment of the ghetto.

3 The original German text was drafted in the present and perfect tenses and changed into the simple past and pluperfect by hand. Brackets inserted by hand in the original are represented here with curly brackets.

necessary guards, roads that lead to the ghetto have been blocked off there with wire barriers, and no-entry signs have been put up. Some of these barriers have been trodden down, however, and others have been removed in some other way, such that the ghetto residents can continue their uninhibited dealings with the rest of the population. If these measures, imperfect as they are from a disease-control standpoint, have already helped to contain the spread of disease there, this can only be attributed to pure chance. These protective measures are also primarily said to have been implemented for the members of the Wehrmacht and the police, who are forbidden to enter the ghetto when off duty. However, since the rest of the population frequents the ghetto in spite of the no-entry signs and wire barriers that have been put up, the ban on the military and the police using those streets is only of limited value. At any rate, fully secure measures to control the spread of disease will not be achieved in this manner.}

An increase in morbidity had to be expected for the reasons mentioned earlier when the rest of the Jews living in Lodsch moved into the ghetto. In order to counteract this potential hazard – which threatens the guard details in particular – an exclusion zone had to be created along the ghetto perimeter, which the residents were prohibited from entering on pain of the strictest punishment, in certain cases including the death penalty. The establishment of a hospital for infectious diseases in the ghetto with at least 300 to 350 beds was the most crucial requirement for efforts to combat contagious disease in the ghetto. {While the Jewish hospital in Warsaw is located outside the ghetto}, it must nevertheless be insisted upon that the hospitals for the Jewish population be located in the ghetto itself, in order to avoid the spread of disease to other parts of the city as a result of hospital transports that may be necessary.[4] Consequently, a hospital of sufficient size for the treatment of ghetto residents' non-infectious diseases must also be available. These requirements are satisfied in Lodsch. In view of the expected increase in the number of cases, medical care for ghetto residents must be organized and provided by Jewish physicians. The number of physicians available here, 94, is barely sufficient {but will have to suffice if need be}. Essential equipment, in given cases, is to be supplied to the physicians by the Jewish hospitals. The physicians must also take care of selecting and training Jewish nursing staff. The supply of medicines from four Jewish pharmacies in the ghetto has also been guaranteed. Other medicines must be purchased wholesale on payment in cash. The same applies to disinfectants. {Since the ghetto in Warsaw still does not constitute a self-contained area, as mentioned, a system for providing medical care and procuring medicines has not yet been created there either. It will also be necessary to arrive at an arrangement of this kind there if the new ghetto planned near Praga in the north of the city is established. As the development in Warsaw has shown, the increase of the already well-known problems in the ghetto also requires particular attention.} Here it is primarily the housing conditions and their problems, i.e. drinking-water supply and faeces disposal, that are an issue. For example, it is not uncommon for three to five or even seven families to be living in one room there. Apartment blocks that previously had up to 100 residents now have 800 to 1,000 or even more. {Similar conditions must also be expected in Lodsch.} Given this situation, it is clear that the

4 On 5 Jan. 1940 the public health office had instructed the Jewish elder to establish a hospital for infectious diseases on Wesoła immediately and to construct a barrier around it: APŁ, 221/31866b, fol. 19.

latrines will have to be expanded significantly, and in view of the considerable amount of faeces that will accumulate every day, the cesspits will have to be emptied regularly and systematically. {In view of the urgency to establish the ghetto, a system for faeces disposal must be put into place that is neither costly nor demands lengthy preparations, but which offers at the same time sufficient protection against the spread of infectious diseases. Therefore, with all these issues in mind, only cesspits that are of sufficiently large dimensions from the outset can be considered – in line with the number of residents in each building. The emptying of the pits will have to be entrusted to a business that has reliable, experienced workers and suitable vehicles. These workers will have to be disinfected on a regular basis. In view of their unreliability, it is not advisable to enlist Jews for the disposal of excrement. With a procedure of this kind, there will also be no need for controls of other kinds, as are still necessary in Warsaw, for example. In contrast to the situation in Warsaw, the water supply to the ghetto must still be discussed. Although the water supply in Warsaw was also causing considerable difficulties three to four months ago, those difficulties have been remedied by restoring the pipe network or, where this was not possible, by installing standpipes.} However, the ghetto in Lodsch contains only local boreholes, which not only do not produce much water, but are also primitively constructed and constitute health hazards in some cases. It is not uncommon for these boreholes to be contaminated by surface water or underground inflows. {This water may be useful for industrial purposes – even if this means disregarding possible objections. Furthermore, since the transportation of drinking water by road creates technical difficulties and is not a satisfactory solution from a disease-control standpoint either, there remains no other option than to install dead-end mains with standpipes on the ghetto's perimeter, creating connections to the city water-pipe network. Even if the network is fed with firefighting water to begin with and the water cannot be used for drinking purposes until it has been boiled, this is the only way it will be possible to organize a sufficient water supply without bringing the water in by road, until the city waterworks have been put into operation.}

{As for the question of opportunities for paid employment in the ghetto, the conditions in Warsaw cannot be compared with the conditions here in the future ghetto, since in Warsaw the Jews are still allowed to trade on the street, for example, and there are also other opportunities for earning a living in other parts of the city. By contrast, the question of how food will be obtained in Lodsch requires some attention. It remains to be seen how this will eventually be accomplished (bartering textile items or other valuables for food). Particular care must be taken in this regard to ensure that all goods that could encourage the spread of lice have been deloused when they leave the ghetto. It goes without saying that the necessary caution must be exercised in dealings with representatives of the Jewish Community, which are to be limited to what is absolutely necessary. Contact must be avoided at all costs. It will be necessary to create suitable premises where delivered goods can be passed through into the ghetto.}

Finally, as for burials, it goes without saying that the cemetery will be located inside the ghetto in order to prevent, in cases of death from disease, any spread of disease as a result of corpses being transported through other parts of the city. This point has also been considered in Lodsch. The Jewish cemetery {at the former Jewish mental asylum} is designated as a burial ground. {The graves available there, most of which are in disrepair, are to be excavated and/or levelled.}

It is feasible that typhus can be contained at its source in Lodsch and that the general population can be protected against the spread of the disease, but only if the disease-control principle of complete isolation is not violated under any circumstances in accordance with the criteria discussed above as far as humanly and medically possible.

DOC. 86
On 3 February 1940 a Warsaw Jew describes how he was abducted and robbed by two German soldiers[1]

Fragment of a handwritten diary (author unidentified) for the underground archive of the Warsaw ghetto, entry for 3 February 1940 (2 copies)[2]

From a diary

3 February 1940
I returned at 8.30 [p.m.] and was already standing at the gate to the courtyard where I live when two German airmen appeared suddenly out of nowhere. 'Where are you going?' they ask. I reply that this is the gate to the courtyard where I live and I am going home. 'No!' they shout, 'you must come with us to headquarters.' None of my pleading helps and I have to go with them. There was no one on the street, since Jews are permitted to be out only until 9 o'clock.[3] I went in fear for my life. They evidently did not know themselves where they were taking me. Threatening to shoot me, they took me two kilometres outside the city. There they stopped and searched me. They took everything from me, including my overcoat, and then they ordered me to run home quickly and bring more money. They gave me ten minutes to do so. I ran in mortal fear, as I was at risk of being shot if the police spotted me on the street after curfew. No one noticed me and I arrived home safely.

DOC. 87
On 3 February 1940 a Polish teacher writes about the help given by Christian Poles to Jews across the fence surrounding the so-called epidemic containment zone in Warsaw[1]

Diary of Franciszka Reizer,[2] entry for 3 February 1940

Several boys from Albigowa were in Warsaw. They saw the Jewish ghetto closed off from Leszno Street and Bankowy Square. It is fenced off from the city by a 3-metre-high wooden fence. Knots have fallen out of it.[3] Nevertheless, the German gendarmerie

1 AŻIH, Ring I/483 (1026). This document has been translated from Yiddish. It is the continuation of Doc. 69.
2 The entry has survived in two versions. This translation is based on the later, more legible, one.
3 See Doc. 55.

1 The location of the original document is unknown. Published in Franciszka Reizer, *Dzienniki 1939–1944* (Warsaw: Ludowa Spółdzielnia Wydawnicza, 1984), p. 38. This is possibly a revised excerpt from a longer entry. This document has been translated from Polish.

patrols the perimeter. When there is no German nearby, people come up to the fence, look inside through those holes, and throw the unfortunates something to eat over the fence. Nothing can be heard all around, as if the people there had died. Through one of these knotholes our people saw a Jewish policeman dressed in a blue uniform with a yellow armband on the sleeve. He was armed with a truncheon. So the Germans have set them up with their own organization for the maintenance of public order. One of our boys – Janek Bartman – threw a few apples over the fence, reinette apples from Albigowa.

DOC. 88

On 15 and 16 February 1940 the dental assistant Ruth Goldbarth describes the reception Jews received in Warsaw after their expulsion from Bromberg (Bydgoszcz)[1]

Letter from Ruth Goldbarth[2] in Warsaw to her friend Edith Blau[3] in Minden (Westphalia), dated 15 and 16 February 1940

10[4]

My dearest Edith,

I really wanted to put off answering your letter dated the ninth [Feb. 1940] until tomorrow, but I have a couple of minutes of peace and quiet just now and I miss you so very much – I just have to write today. Where do I start, where do I stop? I look at your little picture: Edith, quite the lady in spite of the 'factory girl' look, so comfortable, surrounded by an atmosphere of peace, order, and a certain prosperity, just as we all knew it, and yet all of that is so far away today, almost no longer a reality. 'Net curtains, flowers on the table,' Dorlein[5] says, 'in short sleeves, these days!' It all looks so nice and peaceful. Do I have any right at all to tell you about us then? About all the sad things

2 Franciszka Reizer, née Dudzińska, Polish teacher from East Upper Silesia. During the occupation of Albigowa, a town south of Łańcut in the south-east of Poland, she worked in the illegal school system.

3 The author means that knotholes were enlarged to make peepholes.

1 USHMM, RG 10 250*03, WA 005, fols. 1–4. Ruth Goldbarth's correspondence with her friend Edith Blau and Blau's relatives in Minden from 1940 to 1942 amounts to approximately 100 letters. This document has been translated from German.

2 Ruth Goldbarth (1921–1942) grew up in an assimilated Jewish family in Bromberg (Bydgoszcz), where she was raised speaking German and Polish. In Sept. 1939 German units kidnapped Ruth's father, Rudolf, a dentist, and held him as a civilian prisoner; he was not released until mid Dec. 1939. The family was forced to move to the General Government on 1 Jan. 1940; in Warsaw, Ruth worked as an assistant at her father's practice. She is thought to have been deported to Treblinka in summer 1942 and murdered there.

3 Edith Brandon, née Blau (b. 1921), was from Danzig; her parents settled in Bydgoszcz at the end of the 1930s. On 20 Dec. 1939 Blau went to stay with relatives in Minden, from where she was deported to Riga on 13 Dec. 1941; she was subsequently imprisoned in several camps. After the war ended, she initially returned to Minden, and then settled in London.

4 Ruth Goldbarth numbered her letters to Edith Blau.

5 Dorlein or Dorli is Ruth Goldbarth's younger sister, Dorothea Charlotte (1924–1942); like her sister Ruth, she was probably deported to Treblinka in summer 1942 and murdered there.

one sees and hears every day? Do we not have to protect outsiders as long as possible? And you of all people, you are such a sensitive person, who sympathizes and feels everything. Edith, we have become callous here, empty and indifferent – because otherwise we simply couldn't bear it, but all of you … And yet, what I experienced a few days ago literally pulled the rug from under my feet. On Tuesday morning a messenger arrives from the Community with a slip of paper for me: I am to go there straight away. Signed by Helmut Jachmann (who has been employed there for six months).[6] I drop everything and run off. He meets me at the entrance and goes down to the basement with me without a word. The first thing I see is – Sonja and little Ester tumbling at my feet. And then people are shouting at me from all sides: 'Ruth, Ruth, Miss G.,' I look around: lots of familiar faces, the two old Neumann ladies, Mrs Ch. with her mother and children – the last 48 from our home town. And in such a state, indescribable! Without a penny, without underwear or clothes, starving, freezing, completely soaked to the skin, exhausted, and in the depths of despair. It was awful! First of all, the sick needed to be cared for. We therefore took Miss Jenny and old Mrs Ch. to the Jachmanns, brought Edith Ch. and the children to our apartment, and then we did what we could to get Miss Lise U., who had an inflamed gallbladder and a high fever; Mrs Kamnitzer, who had the flu; and the others into hospital. But for all our efforts we could get only one bed. This was given to Miss U. as the most severely ill (incidentally, she is still a patient there at the moment, with suspected typhoid fever; her physician is Dr Kerz).[7] The whole B.[8] colony was alerted, but there is nothing anyone can do to help. Can anyone get food, clothing, somewhere to live for 48 people? Who still has money these days? Edith, you cannot imagine how terrible it is to feel this powerless. I haven't had any time at all to think these last five days. Fortunately, we've now found a room for Mrs Ch., who's still living with us (everyone has terrible colds; one of her children is in bed with a temperature). They'll be moving tomorrow. The others are still at the Community. In the next few days they'll go to a point.[9] That's all we've been able to do. A thousand people are arriving every day; it's the same for all of them! And 100,000 are expected by April. What will that be like? Where will all of these people be put up, what are they to live on? The Viennese are expected, as well as people from the Reich. I certainly don't want to scare you, my little one, but – prepare yourself for all eventualities! We're all in such a gloomy mood here, so downcast; I've lost all courage and hope. We won't get through it. Dita, I don't want to give in, I don't want to give up on myself and us all, but this is too much for me now!

16 February
Herr Weyn.[10] has just been to see us. For the last time. He has been denied the permit. This is so sad for us. He is such a lovely fellow. Really, when we said farewell, the tears rolled down my face. I just can't control myself any longer. It was all a bit much at once

6 Helmut Jachmann (1910–1942?), originally from Bydgoszcz; thought to have perished in the Warsaw ghetto in 1942.
7 Dr Adolph (also Abram) Kerz (b. 1898 or 1900), physician; originally from Gorlice; lived in Bydgoszcz before the war; worked at the hospital on Stawki Street in the Warsaw ghetto; perished in the ghetto.
8 Here and throughout the remainder of the text: Bromberg.
9 An emergency shelter.

the other day. And on top of that I have a constant headache. And the people who have been billeted with us! As much as I am sorry for them and as terrible as it all is, Mrs Ch. does get on your nerves! She's so daft, so impractical! She doesn't sort out anything for herself, everything has to be done for her. She hasn't learned yet. It is not even that neither she nor her children ever think of helping with the tidying or drying the dishes – but she really could have shown some interest in her room at some point! She talks constantly of her misfortune and doesn't understand that everything isn't going to fall into her lap as the poor victim wherever she goes. 'I've been driven from my home, after all,' and 'Help must at least be found for me.' As if she were the only person in a bad situation, the only person who has been relocated, or who's suffered injustice. Is it possible to be so blind to everything? Seeing only your own situation and never the plight of anyone else? Or have I become so intolerant? I don't actually know any more. Oh, what an existence! It doesn't bear thinking about! – My little one, what a lot of dashing about and bother you have gone to. It really isn't necessary. It is really not the end of the world that you didn't get the fountain pen, particularly because Dorli already has one after all. So don't send one, and many thanks for the running around you have done on that account. The bread hasn't arrived yet. It'll be in a fine state. Mind you, it can never be old enough for Dad in any case. But if it is so much bother for you to get hold of it, it really isn't worth it! The calendar for Dorli cost 2.30 złoty because it was sent as a small parcel. You would have been better off sending it as a letter or printed matter, that would have cost only 10 or 20 groszy. You also wrote at one point that you'd sent a *Filmwelt*[11] for Dorli; that hasn't arrived yet either. But I am only writing this to keep you up to date; it is not supposed to be a subtle hint – on the contrary! The Walters very often get all kinds of magazines, so we have been well supplied in that respect. – Today you're finally getting the long-promised picture. It is not thrillingly beautiful, alas! I did the drawings a long time ago. Hopefully you will be able to make sense of them. I am just in the middle of unpicking an old jumper and will turn it into that one with stripes in three colours for myself and Dorli. The one I made has turned out really pretty. You ask how much I earn: 20–25 złoty per jumper privately, 15–18 złoty from shops. But at the moment I don't have anything to do, which is to say I haven't taken any orders. I've not been working with Hanka for a long time now. She's moved away and lives too far off now. She also knits more tightly. Thirdly, she isn't punctual, even though she actually has more time.

What's the situation with your residence permit? Have you received a decision yet? Dear God, you won't believe how afraid I am for you. I'm just glad Uncle Bubi[12] is there; he'll know what to do and how to help you. And maybe the danger won't be so great for you as a factory worker either. – There I am, talking about it again. It's terrible, again and again my thoughts end up at the same place; it's a real psychosis! – Incidentally, you

10 Weynerowski, a businessman, held a permit to enter the ghetto because he owned a factory there. He repeatedly took Ruth's letters outside the ghetto to post them. On 1 April 1941 Ruth wrote to her friend that he would no longer be coming: USHMM, RG 10 250*03, WA 005, fol. 3.

11 *Filmwelt*: a weekly film and photography magazine published in Berlin from 1929 until the post-war period.

12 Edith's uncle Hermann (known as Bubi) Bradtmüller, the brother-in-law of Edith's mother, Meta (née Samuel), who was originally from Minden; Meta and Edith lived with Bradtmüller, his wife Frieda, and their son Hans in 1940–1941.

remember I wrote to you about the concert I went to given by young performers? It began very nicely, but ended badly. What happened was Adi[13] turned up and took most of the men and some of the women in the audience with him. Yes, those are the delights you always have to be prepared for.

Paul has also been back now for a couple of days. My father's been to see him twice. It was quite a hassle, but Maniek Radomski,[14] Boria's boss,[15] managed to do it. Just imagine: Erika's having a baby in two weeks. That's something, isn't it? She is desperately unhappy, but there's nothing more to be done about it now. I can hardly imagine it. Just think, Erika with the 13-year-old boy, and all the rest! It's incredible. – Paul will probably stay here until the end of February, but then he won't come back again. He already has a furnished apartment at his relatives' house in B. All of his Berlin relatives' children are there. – Only a card from Aga,[16] but at least we know she's still there. – But that's enough for now – Little Ruth has to go to bed. Farewell my little darling! Please return the *small* photo![17]

Lots of love and kisses,
Ruth

DOC. 89

On 27 February 1940 a member of the German occupying forces describes a conflict over the treatment of Jews[1]

Report (signed Cz)[2] submitted to SS-Untersturmführer Hofbauer[3] in Lublin, dated 27 February 1940

Report about Annopol[4] (Jewish question)
If the phosphorite mines[5] at Annopol are to be put into operation, it will first be necessary to build an approximately 1.5 km long approach road from Nowa Wiec[6] to the main

13 Code word for the SS or police.
14 Probably Eliahu Mordechai Radomski (b. 1925), a student from Łódź who lived in Warsaw; perished in the Warsaw ghetto.
15 Boria F., a member of the Jewish Order Service with whom Ruth was in contact.
16 Aga[ta] was a Polish friend from Warsaw with whom Ruth corresponded and who sent her packages. In later letters 'Aga' is occasionally used as a synonym for the Poles on the 'Aryan side'.
17 Apart from letters, Ruth and Edith also exchanged current photographs.

1 APL, 498/746, fols. 12–13. This document has been translated from German.
2 Probably Max Czichotzki, later Runhof (1916–2000), retailer; ethnic German from Bydgoszcz; member of Globocnik's staff; shop owner in Wiesbaden after the war.
3 Dr Karl Hofbauer (b. 1911), lawyer; received a PhD from the University of Vienna in 1934; lecturer in international law in Vienna, 1938–1939; simultaneously head of a department at the SD in Vienna; joined the SS in 1939; official in charge of Jewish affairs for Lublin SS and Police Leader, Dec. 1939–August 1940; with the Waffen-SS from Nov. 1941; lawyer, military court of the Leibstandarte-SS Adolf Hitler from Oct. 1943; worked at the SS Business and Administration Main Office in Berlin from July 1944.
4 A small town near the Vistula in Kreis Janów Lubelski.
5 The briefing that comes next in the file, presumably written by the same author, states that the mine was 'under Jewish ownership' and that the exploitation of the phosphorite bed was 'absolutely in the interests of the military economy': APL, 498/746, fol. 14.
6 Correctly: Nowa Wieś.

Krasnik–Annopol road. Stones for this should be taken from the quarries located in the immediate vicinity, which are also important for further road-building.

Jews will then be needed to crush and sieve the phosphate minerals, and load the trains.

According to the local commandant, Lieutenant Libowski, few Jewish workers can be recruited from the town of Annopol, because they supposedly have to work for the local commandant's office. According to Rembalski, the enterprise's acting manager, who has been appointed by the Cracow Mining Office – and I could not help noticing this as well – the lieutenant holds peculiar views as far as the Jewish question is concerned. He demands that the Jews be regularly paid for the work they do. When I showed him *Amtsblatt* no. 1 of 1940, Directive 12, § 1,[7] he said that, although he was familiar with this directive, he had not yet received any implementing regulations for it.

Furthermore, he demanded that we feed the Jews from Annopol who will be provided for the construction of the road.

Rembalski recounted the following incident: a Jew functionary was beaten up by four to six other Jews, whom the functionary had reported for not turning up to work and who had been punished for this with two days' detention. These rascals were not punished for the beating.

R. wanted to confiscate a cupboard and a table that belonged to a Jew and were not being used. The Jew did not agree to this and complained to the lieutenant. The lieutenant forbade the confiscation, stating that the items would have to be paid for.

As a result of incidents of this kind, the Jews have become cocky and slandered the administrator appointed by Cracow, who has an ethnic German identity card, claiming he was a Pole.[8] As a result, the lieutenant refused to deliver the mail for R. or to let him use the telephone. Only in response to my request and in my presence was he allowed to do so.

During the discussion, the lieutenant was so kind as to give a dressing-down to Mr Ebert and myself in the corridor of an apartment building where we went to see him. Apart from Mr Ebert and myself, the Landrat of Janow[9] was also there. In no way did he intervene decisively in the discussion, and he had evidently resigned himself to the lieutenant's attitude.

7 The Second Implementing Regulation to the Regulation of 26 Oct. 1939 on the Introduction of Forced Labour for the Jewish Population of the General Government, *Amtsblatt des Chefs des Distrikts Lublin*, no. 1, 31 Jan. 1940, pp. 4–5. See Doc. 58.

8 Rembalski.

9 Otto Strößenreuther (1906–1990), lawyer; joined the NSDAP and the SA in 1933; Regierungsrat in Kraśnik and Landrat/Kreishauptmann in Janów Lubelski, Oct. 1939 – Sept. 1940; worked in the Reich Ministry of Aviation, 1940–1941; subsequently worked in the Luftwaffe administration; judge at the Higher Administrative Court in Munich after the war; thereafter Ministerialrat in the Bavarian State Ministry of Education and Cultural Affairs.

DOC. 90

In February 1940 Jan Kozielewski (known as Karski) gives an account of the situation in occupied Poland[1]

Report by Jan Kozielewski[2] (diary no. 2013/K) for the Polish government's minister of the interior, Stanisław Kot,[3] in Angers[4] (received on 8 March 1940), dated February 1940[5]

[...][6] IV. *The Jewish question in the country*

1) Introduction
2) The situation of the Jews in the territories annexed by the Third Reich
3) The conditions in the General Government
4) Examples illustrating the living conditions of the Jews under the German occupation
5) The situation of Jews in the territories occupied by the USSR
6) Jews – Occupiers – Poles
   a) Under German occupation
   b) Under Bolshevik occupation
7) The Jewish question as an element of German domestic policy in the Polish territories
8) The present danger posed by the Jewish question
9) Conclusions

1 HIA, Polish Government Collection, box 921, N/55 – Żydzi, fols. 1–11. The report has survived in two versions, the original and a second, revised version drawn up by Kozielewski on instructions from Minister Kot; changes are noted in fols. 6a and 9a–11a. Published with the changes in Artur Eisenbach (ed.), 'Raport Jana Karskiego o sytuacji Żydów na okupowanych ziemiach polskich na początku 1940 r.', *Dzieje Najnowsze*, vol. 21, no. 2 (1989), pp. 179–199; in English translation, including the changes, in David Engel (ed.), 'An Early Account of Polish Jewry under Nazi and Soviet Occupation Presented to the Polish Government-in-Exile, February 1940', *Jewish Social Studies*, vol. 45, no. 1 (1983), pp. 1–16. This document has been newly translated from Polish.

2 Jan Kozielewski (1914–2000), lawyer and diplomat; studied law from 1935; thereafter undertook military and diplomatic training; in Soviet captivity in autumn 1939; fled to the General Government and from there to France in 1940; liaison between the Polish government in exile and the underground in occupied Poland; reported on the murder of Jews in Poland at meetings with Roosevelt and other figures in July 1943; historian in the USA after the war.

3 Dr Stanisław Kot (1885–1975), historian; studied in Germany and elsewhere; professor in Cracow, 1920–1933; politician in the Peasant Movement in 1933; fled to France in Sept. 1939; interior minister and deputy prime minister in the Polish government in exile; ambassador in the USSR, 1941–1942; minister of state with the Polish troops in the Middle East, 1942–1943; minister of information, 1943–1944; returned to Poland in July 1945; ambassador in Rome until 1947; thereafter lived in exile in Britain.

4 The Polish government in exile was formed in Paris in Sept. 1939 and resided in Angers from Nov. 1939, then in London following France's defeat.

5 At the top left of the first page, Kot has inserted a handwritten note for the minister of information and documentation, Stanisław Stroński: 'Minister Stroński, to be put to use. 24 Feb. 1940. Attention: caution advised – author is returning [to Poland]!' At the top right there is another handwritten note: 'Attention: pp. 6, 9, 10, 11 have different wording.'

6 The report is part of several analyses of the situation in occupied Poland that Jan Kozielewski wrote after his arrival in France.

The Jewish question in Poland under occupation
Introduction
I have never specifically studied the Jewish question in the country. My information mainly consists of generally known facts, observations of moods, and a few conversations with and about Jews.

The situation of the Jews in the territories annexed by the Third Reich
The situation facing the Jews in these territories is clear, uncomplicated, and easy to understand.

They are above the law, beyond the protection of the authorities. The official aim is to exterminate or to remove them by force, by law, and by means of propaganda.

The Jews are removed from these territories, their property is confiscated, the 'guilty' are imprisoned. The aim is to completely cleanse this area of the Jewish element.

The Jews there are almost completely deprived of their livelihoods; when they live they do so as if in secret, in fear, deprived of rights, because the German authorities and German society 'turn a blind eye to this sad fact'.

Everyone wears armbands or patches (just like in the General Government) identifying them as Jews – disregarding this requirement carries severe penalties.

As a matter of principle, they are not permitted to shop in Aryan stores, not even for basic necessities; as a matter of principle, they are not permitted to manufacture objects, articles, or goods, but at most to repair them etc. In the early evening they are no longer allowed to appear in the city; they are not allowed to travel without special permission; they are not allowed to walk down certain streets or even to visit cinemas, theatres, or cafés, nor are they allowed to enter most businesses and shops. Aryans are not allowed to greet Jews or to stop and talk to them. Jews are assigned to forced labour, special 'gymnastics classes' (strenuous exercises) and 'cleanliness classes' (a type of 'water torture') are organized for them, etc., etc. The Germans frequently impose levies on Jewish communities under every conceivable pretext – these levies usually run into the tens or hundreds of thousands of złoty.

A Jew is considered not only someone of the Mosaic faith, but anyone with [two] parents or one parent who once belonged to the Jewish Community.

In some cases (as in the territory of the General Government) the restrictions, regulations, and the prevailing mood with regard to the Jews also apply to the Polish population. Naturally the Jews derive silent pleasure from this, and the bitterness, disappointment, and sense of humiliation among the Polish population is all the greater.

The conditions in the General Government
All the Jews from the annexed territories are to be resettled in the General Government. The Germans assume that these 'originally German areas, which have been horribly Jewified by the Poles', will revert to being German without the Jews. In the General Government, the Jews resettled from the annexed territories are mainly located in Lublin and the surrounding area. This gives the impression that the Germans want to create a type of *Jewish reservation* there. Incidentally, some German dignitaries and part of the German press express themselves to this effect.

The situation of the Jews in General Government territory is basically similar (to the above), but is ultimately alleviated by the fact that: 1) there are more Jews here, 2) the

Jews can no longer be thrown out from here, 3) there is only a small German population in these areas, and so far the Polish population shows no inclination to apply the same methods to the Jews or to create the same atmosphere as the Germans do.

Nevertheless, the Jews wear armbands or patches here as well, and they are subject to the same regulations as in the annexed territories. The Germans realize that the Jews here are 'somewhat at home' and that they must remain here.

However, the Germans try to 'organize' the Jews appropriately, to teach them 'work', 'cleanliness', 'respect for the Nordic people' and for 'Aryans in general', to ruin them financially, and to restrict their sphere of life as much as possible. Forced physical labour for Jews is organized on a large scale, especially for the purpose of 'cleansing' Warsaw and other cities of rubble.

Examples illustrating the living conditions of the Jews under the German occupation
I cannot resist citing a few typical cases that will shed some light on the conditions and the atmosphere in which the Jews live in the territories occupied by the Germans.

I. Jews and the law
A member of a certain Polish institution arranged to meet up with two German soldiers. They went to the Old Town in Warsaw and openly robbed a Jewish jeweller. When the head of this institution (a Pole) found out about this, he dismissed the thief. The latter complained to the Gestapo. The Gestapo summoned the head of the institution. Dialogue:

– Why did you dismiss Mr X?

– Because he turned out to be a thief. He robbed a jeweller.

– We don't know anything about a robbery. He merely confiscated from a Jew certain items that he needed for his personal use, and he's allowed to do that.

– In our country, that is called robbery.

– And we call it confiscation. Please familiarize yourself with our customs as soon as possible. One can take anything from a Jew, because everything the Jews possess derives from legalized robbery. *For us it is important that the Polish population learns* that any Pole can go into any Jewish shop and throw the Jew out, and our law will protect him. Anyone who wants to can kill a Jew – and will not be convicted for it under our law.

This really happened and is completely accurate.

II. A pregnant Jewish woman
One day I went to the Gestapo for a permit. In comes a Jewish woman, intelligent, dressed in a fur coat, frightened. She is expecting a child. She asks for a permit for herself or for the physician, so that she or the physician can go out onto the street after 8 p.m., should the delivery occur at that time.

The secretary, a Volksdeutsch (woman),[7] replies:

– There is no need for a permit. We are not going to make it easier for you to give birth to Jews. 'The dogs are dying of hunger, [there is] so much poverty, and yet you still want to give birth to Jews? Heraus … heraus.'[8]

7 German in the original: 'ethnic German'.
8 German in the original: 'Get out … Get out.'

III. The camp for Jews near Bełżec

Near Bełżec (on the border with the Bolshevik occupied territories) the Germans have set up a camp for Jews. Most of the inmates are Jewish families who tried to make their way to the Bolshevik side illegally or who had been waiting for the Bolshevik–German border to be opened for an assumed and expected population exchange. The camp [inmates] number several thousand men, women, elderly, and children. Incidentally, almost all of them are poor. I saw this camp in early December 1939.

A great number of them spent all their time outside and also slept in the open. Many of them were without suitable clothing and blankets. While some of them slept, others waited their turn, because they lent each other their blankets. Those who were waiting stamped their feet and ran around so as not to freeze to death. A couple of hundred people, including children, women, and the elderly, run around for hours or run on the spot, because if they stop, they will freeze to death. After a few hours, they change places. They go to sleep, while hundreds of other people stamp their feet and run around. Everyone is frozen solid, desperate, apathetic, hungry. A horde of tortured animals – not human beings. This went on for weeks.

I watched this spectacle for an entire hour, standing there rooted to the spot, horrified, and dismayed. A nightmare, a terrible dream – unreal: little blue and red creatures, not human beings. I will never forget it. I have never seen anything worse in my entire life.

IV. Gymnastics and cleanliness lessons in Lublin

A crowd of several dozen people performs difficult and strenuous exercises. They are taught humiliating songs. Insults, kicks, and sneers from the German guards. The elderly faint. The young boys are stricken with mute animalistic horror. Then a bath in cold water (in December!). Some of the young men are forced to strip naked – jokes from the Germans, threatening remarks and gestures. The 'master race' is really a nation of heartless madmen filled with inhuman hatred.

V. At the 'Kercelak'[9] *in Warsaw*

I was at the Kercelak. A Jewish market stall. The owner, a Jew, frozen to the bone. A German soldier comes. He takes socks, a comb, soap, and wants to leave without paying. The Jew demands the money. The soldier pays no attention. The old man raises his voice. The frightened neighbours hold him back and try to calm him down, [they] fear for him. The old man cries, or rather howls: 'What can he do to me? What can he do to me? He can only kill me. Let him kill me, kill me. I've had enough. I can't take it any more'.

The German left without paying. As he left, he said, 'Verfluchte Juden'.[10]

The situation of the Jews in the territories occupied by the USSR

The situation facing the Jews in these territories is fundamentally different. After all, here no distinctions are made based on nationality or religion. 'Everyone is equal', and 'everyone finds work and is protected by the law'.

9 Colloquial term for the largest open-air market in Warsaw, which existed until 1942. Correctly: Plac Kercelego.

10 German in the original: 'damn Jews'.

The Jews are at home here; not only are they not subjected to humiliation or persecution, but thanks to their quick-wittedness and their ability to adapt to every new situation, they also enjoy certain political and economic privileges.

They join political cells, many of them occupy important political and administrative positions, and play a considerable role in trade unions, at universities, and above all in commerce, especially in usury, in profiteering, and in illegal enterprises (smuggling, trading in foreign currency and in spirits, shady deals, and shady brokering and procurement).

Their situation in these territories is in very many cases better than it was before the war, both economically and politically.

This is especially true for small traders, artisans, the proletariat, and the semi-educated. Under the Soviet system, more affluent and educated groups (homeowners, owners of larger businesses, factories, and shops, lawyers, physicians, engineers, etc.) are all subject to basically the same restrictions, constraints, or social exclusion as other nationalities.

Jews – Occupiers – Poles

(a) Under German occupation

When dealing with the Germans, the Jews are obedient, submissive, mistreated; they live in constant fear and terror.

There is no question of any *active effort* to defend their right to live and to work. They do everything the Germans order them to do – quietly, without grumbling, humbly.

There is not the slightest attempt to resist and certainly no organized resistance; at most there are isolated acts of desperation, nervous breakdowns.

Here a Jew will sooner commit suicide than oppose a German.

The patience, the subservience, the agony, the mood, and the conditions governing the lives of broad swathes of the poorer Jews living in the territories annexed by the Third Reich, and even in the General Government, often exceed any conception of human misfortune.

Their only response is to try to flee to the Bolshevik occupied territory or, more often, literally to hide from the light of day.

The Jews' relationship to the Poles is similar to their relationship to the Germans. There is a general feeling that they would be glad if the Poles showed understanding for them, since the same enemy is unfairly tormenting both peoples, after all. However, the majority of mainstream Polish society does not show this understanding.

Their stance towards the Jews is predominantly ruthless, often merciless. They often profit from the powers that the new situation gives them. In large part they take advantage of these powers, and often they even abuse them.

In a sense, this makes them similar to the Germans.[11]

11 In the second version of the report, the seven preceding sentences read completely differently: 'In very many cases, the Poles' relationship to the Jews has changed as a result of what is happening. In general, conversations emphasize the Germans' boundless bestiality towards this segment of the population living in the Polish territories. In many cases, the Poles *visibly* demonstrate their sympathy for the Jews. This is all the more singular because such a *visible* display can and frequently does end *badly* for whoever show kindness.'

(b) Under Bolshevik occupation
Polish society believes that the Jews are favourably disposed towards the Bolsheviks. The general opinion is that the Jews betrayed Poland and the Poles, that fundamentally they are communists, and that they defected to the communists with their banners flying.

Indeed, in most cities the Jews greeted the Bolsheviks with bouquets of red roses, speeches, declarations of loyalty, etc., etc.

Certain distinctions need to be made here, however.

Yes, the communist Jews naturally welcomed the Bolsheviks enthusiastically, regardless of their social class. The Jewish proletariat, the small tradesmen, the artisans, and everyone whose position had now structurally improved and who had previously suffered persecution, insults, excesses, etc. from the Polish population – all of these people were also positive, if not enthusiastic, about the new regime.

One can hardly blame them.

However, it is worse when they denounce Poles, ethnic Polish students, and political activists, for example; when they direct the work of the Bolshevik militia from behind their desks or are members of this militia; when they unlawfully slander the conditions in the former Poland. Unfortunately it must be said that such cases are very frequent, much more frequent than those indicating their loyalty to the Poles or their emotional attachment to Poland.

The intelligentsia, on the other hand, the wealthier and more educated Jewry – I have the impression (with numerous exceptions, of course, and not taking pretence into account) that they often think of Poland with a certain fondness, and that they would happily welcome a change in the current state of affairs – Poland's independence.

Of course, there is also a certain amount of calculation behind this.

Currently they are also experiencing major difficulties, if not social exclusion; their houses are confiscated, while shops, businesses, and factories are taken away as part of the so-called 'socialization' and transformed into a type of association or cooperative (in which the state's share and the taxes to the state are abnormally high), and they are deprived of a chance to earn a living and often even an appropriate level of subsistence.

On the other hand, there is a very deep-rooted conviction among them, as there is in society more generally, that the future Poland will be a democratic state, which will owe a great deal to international Jewry, among others, and will be partly dependent on the Jews, which is why it will not oppress them.

Thirdly, their Polish patriotism undoubtedly plays a certain role as well, although it is difficult to say to what extent.

For example, I know of an authentic case in which a Jew, a well-known lawyer from Lwów, Mr …, warned Poles of the danger posed by the GPU[12] and of looming legal trials, of communist lawyers; while his son, an academic (who incidentally was severely beaten by ethnic Polish students a year ago), honestly and certainly selflessly fought for various forms of financial support and assistance for the student association, and for the majority of places in the student dorms to go to Poles.

Basically, however, the bulk of the Jews here have created a situation in which the Poles regard them as devoted to the Bolsheviks and – this can be bluntly stated – are

12 Official designation of the Soviet secret police until 1934 (also OGPU). It was later also used to refer to the NKVD.

just waiting for the moment when they can take their revenge on the Jews. Basically, all the Poles are bitter and disappointed in the Jews and a huge majority (especially the youth, of course) are openly waiting for an opportunity for a 'bloody reckoning'.

The Jewish question as an element of German domestic policy in the Polish territories
The relationship between the Jews and the Poles under German occupation is a very important and extremely complex issue. It is much more important and much more complicated here than [it is] under Bolshevik occupation.

The Germans are trying to win over the Polish population at any price. Not the intelligentsia, not the upper classes, not the affluent and more enlightened landed gentry or the bourgeoisie, but the common people: peasants, workers, artisans, and the like.

They use methods that surpass each other in perfidy, mendacity, and ruthlessness.

The Germans keep stressing that they 'wish the Polish people no harm', that they 'need the Poles', that 'cooperation is in the interests of the Germans and the Poles', that they 'do not in the least intend to destroy or exterminate Polish ethnicity', etc., etc.

The Germans are striving to gain a reputation among the people as 'harsh, relentless, but fair'.

In a variety of ways, they try to ensure that the desperate, downhearted, and broken Polish people turn to Berlin.

They stress that 'the government of Piłsudski's successors has betrayed the Polish people'; that 'France and England have betrayed Poland once and will do so again in the future'; that 'the present sham government wants to rashly and senselessly cause harm and provoke a German reaction'; that 'the Germans are protecting the common people from exploitation by big businesses and the landed gentry'; that 'the Polish people must "unfortunately" pay the penalty for the deeds of the irresponsible former government'. They create artificial conflicts within society – and resolve them 'fairly' by accepting every petition from the common people and intervening (in minor matters, of course), almost always greatly exaggerating these interventions.

They try to take advantage of the resulting conflicts between the Polish police[13] or other rump authorities or their officials and broad swathes of society by usually taking 'the side of the common people'. Lastly … 'the Germans, only and finally they, will finally help the Poles to clear up [the matter of] the Jews'.[14]

Thus the Germans' relationship to the Jews quite obviously far exceeds the directives dictated by their official ideology and is *one of the elements of their domestic policy.*

13 Officially: Polish Police in the General Government (Policja Polska Generalnego Gubernatorstwa); this was a police force made up of Poles, also known as the Blue Police (Policja Granatowa) because of their dark blue uniforms. It was subordinate to the German Order Police and had to carry out tasks related to public order and discipline and to control the Polish population. It was also involved in enforcing anti-Jewish measures. It consisted mainly of police officers from the pre-war State Police (Policja Państwowa); in early 1940 it comprised 8,700 people, by late 1942 approximately 12,000, and in 1943 approximately 16,000.

14 In the second version of the report, the preceding paragraph reads completely differently: 'They try to win the most diverse conflicts in Polish society, and ultimately – probably without recognizing the fact that the majority of Polish society is not antisemitic – they expect to win their support by [saying that] … the Germans, only and finally they will help the Poles to clear up [the matter of] the Jews.'

They are trying:

1) to extract as much as they can from the Jews (money, supplies, means of production, workshops).
2) to purge the territories they have seized of Jews, at the expense of Jewifying the General Government.
3) to use the Jews as bait with which to earn the sympathy, recognition, and respect of broad swathes of the Polish population.

'After all, in the General Government, it is the Germans who are finally resolving the Jewish question, not only for themselves, but also in the interest of the Polish people' – this is how the Germans want society to perceive their actions.

There is much to suggest that this is indeed what they want.

In principle and in theory, they are not so concerned with oppressing Polish Jews in the General Government. After all, a Jew can still buy himself out of the requirement to wear an armband or a patch if he has a lot of money; he can still go over to the Bolshevik side if he pays; often he can even still get a passport if he pays a bribe. For example, the Germans did not expel the Jews from Zakopane (as they said they would) because the Jewish Community had bought itself out; they still do not imprison distinguished rabbis or other Jewish personages if they pay for their freedom; etc., etc.

Irrespective of this, however, they are not really resolving the Jewish question at all.[15]

Robbery, the 'psychological discharge of the master race', and the deception of the Polish people – these are their true aims.

One must admit that they are succeeding.

The Jews pay and pay and pay … and the Polish peasant, the worker, or a foolish, demoralized, semi-educated, poor wretch loudly comments: 'Well, they're finally teaching them a lesson', 'One must learn from them', 'That's the end of the Jews', 'There's no question, we must thank God that the Germans came and dealt with the Jews', etc.[16]

The present danger posed by the Jewish question

The German 'solution to the Jewish question', and I must state this in full awareness of my responsibility for what I am saying, is an important and rather dangerous tool in the hands of the Germans with which to 'morally pacify' broad swathes of Polish society.

Naturally it would be wrong to assume that this matter alone will bring them success and earn them society's respect.

The people hate their mortal enemy, but this question is creating a type of narrow footbridge on which the Germans and a large segment of Polish society can come together in *harmony.*

Of course, this footbridge is as narrow as the Germans' desire to underpin and reinforce it is great.

15 See Doc. 147.

16 In the second version of the report, the two preceding paragraphs again read completely differently: 'One must admit that they are only partly succeeding in this, while to some extent they also achieve an effect that is downright contrary to their intentions. The Jews pay and pay and pay … but more and more frequently and in ever-wider circles, the Polish population is loudly commenting: "This is too much now", "These are not human beings", "This must end with some sort of terrible punishment for the Germans".'

Moreover, this state of affairs threatens to demoralize broad swathes of society, a demoralization that could certainly cause major difficulties for future authorities in the laborious reconstruction of the Polish state – be that as it may, 'the lesson will not be in vain'.

Furthermore, the current state of affairs has led to a double division among the population of these territories. Firstly, a division between the Jews and the Poles in the struggle against the common mortal enemy; secondly, a division among the Poles, some of whom are contemptuous of and outraged by the Germans' barbaric methods (while being aware of the impending danger), while others observe them (and thus also the Germans) with interest and often with enthusiasm, resenting the former group for its 'indifference' to such an important question.[17]

Conclusions

I will not discuss a solution to this issue. One would have to study this issue seriously, to research it, and to devote a lot of time to it.

However, it is not difficult to draw certain conclusions, which are obvious, perceptible by everyone.

1) Everything the Germans want to do to the Polish people is harmful to them. Therefore, in principle, one should suspect that their way of resolving the Jewish question in the General Government, the way in which they manipulate the Polish people, and their ultimate goals pose a great danger to us. If we succumb to them in this matter, if we display the reactions they hope for and expect, then, if it suits them, this will be dangerous for us to precisely the same extent.
2) I do not know either how or by what means this can be approached, nor who could do it, nor to what extent (if it is possible at all). However, given the existence of three enemies (if the Jews must necessarily be regarded as enemies), would it not be possible to create, to a certain extent and degree, something like a front for the two weaker [enemies] against the stronger third, the mortal enemy, and to postpone the reckoning between these two for a later date?

17 In the second version of the report, this subsection reads: '*The "danger" of the Jewish question, according to Germans' expectations.* The German "solution to the Jewish question" – this must be stated in full awareness of the responsibility – according to their plans will be an important and dangerous tool in their hands to either win over or to "morally pacify" broad swathes of Polish society. Naturally it would be wrong to assume they expect that this matter alone will bring them success and earn them society's respect. They know that the Polish people hate their mortal enemy, but at the same time they are convinced that in the end this issue will create something like a narrow footbridge on which the Germans and a certain segment of Polish society will come together in harmony. They also know, or rather hope, that their methods with regard to the Jews are apt to demoralize broad swathes of the population, a demoralization that will certainly cause major difficulties for future authorities in the laborious reconstruction of the Polish state. They are also aware that the current state of affairs leads to a double division in the population of these territories: (1) to a division between Jews and Poles in the struggle against the common enemy; (2) to a division among the Poles, some of whom will be contemptuous of and outraged by the Germans' barbaric methods (while being aware of the impending danger), while others (according to German expectations, the great majority) are to observe these methods (and thus, of course, their originators!) with interest or enthusiasm, resenting the former group's "indifference on such an important question." At present it is difficult to say to what extent the Germans realize that this group is small and will become smaller with time.'

3) The creation of a united front would encounter major obstacles from broad swathes of Polish society, whose antisemitism has by no means abated.
4) Adopting a passive attitude towards the current state of affairs threatens to demoralize Polish society (especially the lower strata), with all the dangers that would arise from the *'agreement'*, even if partial, in many cases nevertheless sincere, of a significant number of Poles with the occupier.[18]

The Lithuanian occupation
I know too little about the Jewish question under Lithuanian occupation to be able to assume responsibility for commenting on it, even on such a modest scale as [I have done] above.

DOC. 91

On 1 March 1940 the Landrat in Bendzin (Będzin) reports on the economic impoverishment of the Jewish population and the relationship between Poles and Jews[1]

Letter from the Landrat in Bendzin[2] (L.I.A., 401/2 no. 50g) to the Regierungspräsident in Kattowitz, for the attention of Regierungsrat Kirchner[3] or his representative in office, dated 1 March 1940 (registered letter)

Concerning the order of 3 December 1939, I Pol no. 489/39
Re: situation report
A. *General political and policing situation*
I. *Political matters*
[...][4]
a) The mayor in Bendzin[5] reported that, at 7 p.m. on 28 February 1940, a Polish employee in the administration, Josef *Weitzik*, residing in Kasernenstraße, Bendzin, was attacked by two unknown assailants and shot dead with three bullets. After the assassination, the perpetrators fled to Dombrowa. According to the mayor, it is suspected that Weitzik was the victim of an act of revenge on account of his work in the Housing Office. W.'s job was to clear furniture from confiscated Polish and Jewish apartments, register it, and/or carry out removals.

18 In the second version of the report, points 2–4 are combined into two points. They read as follows: '(2) I do not know either how or by what means this could be approached, nor who could do it, nor to what extent. However, would it not be possible to create something like a common front for the two weaker partners – against the stronger and mortal enemy? The current situation in the Country encourages such reflections. (3) Adopting a passive attitude towards the current state of affairs would be harmful. Who knows to what extent German perfidy would influence the future attitudes of Polish society (especially its lower and broader strata) with regard to the Jewish question.'

1 GStA, XVII. HA Ost 4, Reg Kattowitz/14. This document has been translated from German.
2 Probably Dr Hans Grotjan, economist; deputy Landrat in Landkreis Unna from 1933 and Landrat there from 1937; acting Landrat in Bielsko from Sept. 1939.
3 Dr Kirchner was the head of the Section for National Minorities in Regierungsbezirk Kattowitz.
4 The report is 15 pages long. The Landrat initially discussed (1) the attitudes towards the occupying forces displayed by individual groups of the Polish population and (2) oppositional behaviour.
5 The mayor of Bendzin was Hans Kowohl.

b) Mayor Beier from Dombrowa has informed me by telephone that a police and a railway police officer were injured at 00:30 on 29 February 1940. The railway officer is in critical condition after being shot in the stomach.[6] The perpetrators got away without being identified. One criminal is said to have been shot dead just outside Bendzin. The Dombrowa police believe this was one of the perpetrators. Investigations are under way. Following this incident, roads were blocked and searches carried out throughout the night in individual parts of Dombrowa until 8 o'clock this morning. However, at the time of writing these operations have not yielded a positive result. The Urban Police section commander and the Security Service suspect that these were pre-planned, violent, and systematic acts of resistance that were carried out first in Sosnowitz, then in Bendzin, and now in Dombrowa. Mayor Beier also believes that these were planned operations. He specifically assumes that the intelligentsia in Dombrowa are supplying the funds for these operations and for paying these criminal elements, whom they then persuade to commit these crimes.

For the time being, I am not inclined to concur with these suspicions. Rather, I believe there were Polish criminal elements involved here who, in response to the incidents at Sosnowitz and Bendzin and at the slightest indication of disturbances, want to wipe out everything that may threaten their security.

Polish business owners and workers are hostile towards the Jews. This is caused by the Poles' view that the Jew is still economically and financially better off than the Poles, and that the Jew still has the means to satisfy his material needs. The Jews display a hostile attitude towards the Poles as well and cheat them whenever they can.

A smaller number of Poles and Jews have strong hopes for the Western powers' victory and openly declare that, as far as they are concerned, Poland's fate has not been decided yet. This demands the most vigilant surveillance and extreme reserve and caution in dealing with these persons. A member of the executive committee of the Jewish Representative Body in Bendzin said, 'I will not let myself be involved in drawing up any evacuation lists.'

According to a report received by the gendarmerie, Jan *Gonsior*, a former captain of the border company, residing in Sosnowitz on Lemberger Straße at the insurance building, Block 3, Apartment 47, has declared: 'I am waiting for a new uprising in order to take action again.' Former Polish military personnel have been seen at Gonsior's apartment almost daily, mainly on Saturday evenings and Sunday mornings. Gonsior allegedly has access to larger sums of money and is said to have brought the company funds from the Polish war with him.

The documents on this matter have been forwarded with a corresponding report to the State Police office in Kattowitz.

Stanislaus Sindak, a Pole presently in Romania, has asked to be issued a certificate of good conduct for his return to Bobrownicki, Kreis Bendzin. He has stated that if he is not issued the certificate, he will be forced to travel to France and fight against Germany, although this is not what he wants to do.[7] He claims he has a wife and children at home who see Germany as the fatherland that provides their daily bread.

6 Handwritten insertion here: 'died this morning at 5 a.m.'

7 The Polish government in exile in Angers was assembling its own troops to fight against Germany.

The Jewish problem has come increasingly to the fore in the towns. The number of Jews without a livelihood is constantly on the increase. They are faced with food and supply difficulties that could very easily result in the outbreak of epidemics. The spring weather will probably contribute heavily to the outbreak of diseases. According to the statement of the estimated budget for the Jewish Community in Bendzin for February 1940, sent to me by the executive committee of the Jewish Representative Body in Bendzin, the executive committee will have a deficit of 11,110.25 Reichsmarks. The committee has pointed out that it feels compelled to implement the following measures in the next few days:

a) abandoning the work of the Jewish soup kitchen, where almost 40 per cent of the Jewish population receive their midday meal free of charge,
b) stopping support payments to reservists' families,
c) no longer paying bills from physicians, pharmacies, and hospitals.

The executive committee of the Jewish Representative Body in Bendzin has sent an application to the Main Trustee Office East[8] in Kattowitz, asking to be allocated 3 per cent of the turnover of the Jewish firms that are being administered by trustees and 20 per cent of firms that have been transferred into Aryan hands.[9] Since, in my opinion, it is exclusively a matter for the Reich Trustee Office to decide on the request made by the Jewish Representative Body, I have not taken any action in relation to this issue for the time being.

In view of the aforementioned difficulties faced by the Jewish population which are increasing by the day, and because the housing situation is also becoming ever more acute for Reich German civil servants, employees, and workers, whose numbers are growing daily, it has become extremely urgent to settle the Jewish question in this region. I therefore request that you advocate vigorously for the evacuation measures against the Jews to be carried out in the very near future.

II. *Policing matters*

The following offences have been reported during the period under review and investigations are ongoing:

1 sexual offence,
11 cases of aggravated larceny,
1 case of robbery,
4 cases of petty theft,
2 cases of embezzlement,
3 cases of fraud,
8 cases of overcharging,
9 cases of clandestine trading and usury,
5 offences under the Reich Hunting Act,
1 case of unauthorized possession of firearms, and
1 case of animal cruelty.

At 6 a.m. on 7 February 1940 the butchers *Macinek* and *Nowakofski* were robbed of a total of 865 Reichsmarks by three armed robbers in the open fields at Golonog.

8 This is a reference to the Kattowitz Trustee Office, a branch of the Main Trustee Office East.
9 See Doc 77.

The Poles were found to be in possession of two radios, which were confiscated. Five counterfeit 5-mark coins and one counterfeit 2-mark coin were used for payment at the Flora Mine in Golonog, presumably by coal merchants from out of town.

In Wojkowice-Komorne, the trader Kowalik was arrested for clandestine trading with Jews. Police officer *Bormann* from Beuthen was arrested by the Criminal Police on suspicion of acting as an accessory in the same case. The following has been reported to me on this matter:

> During a raid carried out by the Kreis head of the gendarmerie at 4 p.m. on 7 February 1940, Urban Police officer Ludwig Bormann, born 24 November 1898 in Charlottental, was found in a state of intoxication at Kowalik's residence. Since Bormann was in no position to make his way back to his police station in his condition, and in order not to hand the Poles any opportunity to criticize a German officer, Bormann was taken to Beuthen by the Kreis head of the gendarmerie in his official car and handed over to the Urban Police. Bormann's station was informed, and he was picked up.

[...][10]

DOC. 92

On 6 March 1940 the historian Emanuel Ringelblum makes a record of reports of German violence against Polish Jews[1]

Handwritten diary of Emanuel Ringelblum,[2] entry for 6 March 1940

My dearest,[3]

Today, 6 March, I heard the following story: [...] Mr Velvele was forced to work on Dynasy Street: 'Du bist kein Mensch, du bist kein Tier, du bist Jude.'[4] Beaten for the following reason: he was ordered to throw a fountain pen on the ground; it was later taken away, but he was ordered to look for it. He lay in bed for several weeks.

Three members of the master race were committing rape at 2 Tłomackie; screams resounded all over the courtyard. The Gestapo is interested in race defilement, but there is fear of reporting such cases. 'Jewish swindle' [they mutter] at the sight of Itzikl's and Knepele's sign.[5] They came to remove beds from a hospital, but couldn't because of the

10 The report continues with remarks on the administration and economic development in the Landkreis.

1 Ringelblum, Notatki 1939–1941, AŻIH, Ring I/449 (507/1). This document has been translated from Yiddish and Hebrew. A somewhat different version is published in Yiddish in Emanuel Ringelblum, *Ksovim fun geto*, vol. 1: *Togbukh fun varshever geto, 1939–1942*, ed. Artur Eisenbach, Tatiana Berenstein, Bernard Mark, and Adam Rutkowski (Warsaw: Yidish bukh, 1961), pp. 91–94.

2 Dr Emanuel Ringelblum (1900–1944), teacher and historian; studied in Warsaw; member of the Poale Zion-Left party; worked as the representative of the American Jewish Joint Distribution Committee (JDC) in the Zbąszyn (Neu-Bentschen) refugee camp, 1938–1939; took part in the 21st Zionist Congress in Geneva in August 1939; founder and head of the underground archive of the Warsaw ghetto (Oyneg Shabes), 1940; in hiding until March 1944, when he was found and shot dead by the Germans. On the Poale Zion-Left party, see Doc. 47, fn. 18.

3 Ringelblum often disguised his diary entries as letters.

4 German in the original: 'You're not human, you're not an animal, you're a Jew.'

[reason mentioned] above.[6] Jews are not allowed to travel by tram in Łódź; in Cracow only on the rear platform according to the *Kurier Warszawski*.[7] Over 1,000 people deported from Łódź to Piotrków: 900 Poles and 600 Jews. Poles are forced into work deployments and taken away from there. Rumours that in both Warsaw and Cracow [Poles] are wearing Jewish armbands.[8] The tragedy of the prisoners of war from the Warthegau. More than 600 were sent on a transport. In Lublin the Community could not take them in – it had no civilian clothing. Sent farther on to Parczew. Those who stopped on the way were shot at. Walked in wooden shoes that fell off. Many wounded were shot dead. Then taken to two barns: in one of them over 200 people, led away in groups of 20 and killed. Out of 627 only 278 remained. More than 20 managed to escape. They killed three at a time with one bullet. In Parczew many wanted to take their own lives. *On the way, they wanted to revolt against the guards because there were [only] thirteen of them, but they were told that this would be a great misfortune for all the Jews in Poland.*[9] *During the journey, a cruel man among [the guards] killed people who passed by along the way, Zając and others. [The guards] were promised money, which made it possible to save the rest. The leader told them that he was doing this because they wanted to flee*[10] *the black guards.*[11] *When they got to Biała, he asked where the rest were, as if they didn't know. I heard that they went to an apartment to take various things: two soldiers: a Jew and a Pole.* Two hundred children died in an orphanage in Warsaw. *In the village of Naguszewo four peasants were killed because they went into the forest to collect wood.* A fine of 500 złoty in the same village for not providing a horse and cart. The caretaker went to a Jewish building in Warsaw with a Christian and demanded an apartment from the owner, and should he not receive one, he threatened them with them.[12] The Community demands 60 złoty as a bribe for [being released from] six days of work shovelling snow. *From the money that was in the bank in Feliks Frydman's city,*[13] *200,000 was taken for the Warsaw Community from a sum of 400,000. From a sum of 100,000 for the aliyah*[14] *that was available in the community, officers took 10,000 because according to them there is nothing one could do with the money.* Workers from the Community who were shovelling snow were seized for other work. No requirement to wear the armband for foreign Jews. An abundance of dollars; there is a lack of local currency to exchange for it.

5 This is a reference to a plaque that referred to the JDC. Itsikl is a reference to its representative Icchak Giterman; Knepele refers to Dawid Guzik (the Polish word guzik means 'button'; Knepele is its Yiddish diminutive ['little button']).

6 Presumably the Germans were still showing restraint at this point and left the beds in place because they were owned by the JDC.

7 *Nowy Kurier Warszawski*, the official Warsaw daily newspaper in Polish, which was published from 11 Oct. 1939 to 1944.

8 The first mass shootings took place in Warsaw in late 1939. A great many Poles were arrested during roundups, especially in the large cities, and sent to concentration camps. The younger ones were deported to Germany for forced labour. At the start of the occupation, some Poles therefore thought that the Jews were faring better, so a few started wearing the armbands required for Jews.

9 Text in italics here and below is in Hebrew in the original.

10 Illegible. Possibly: flee or escape.

11 This is a reference to the black uniforms worn by the SS.

12 This means: he threatened them with the Germans.

13 Warsaw.

14 Hebrew for 'ascent'; Jewish emigration to Palestine with the Zionist aim of establishing a Jewish homeland.

On 28 [February] many Poles rounded up *in their homes, on the streets, and in the cafés. They say that the Christians are wearing Jewish armbands. In Łódź a million in people's money*[15] *in a bank, half of which belongs to the Poles.* Sad news from Łódź: Rumkowski is throwing poor families out of their homes and is bringing in rich ones. Even so, entire families are returning to Łódź. They would rather die in the place they call home than roam around somewhere unfamiliar. Jews are taken from Łódź to the [General] Government for 10 marks. Every day thousands of Jewish captives arrive. The problem of clothing: they cannot wear military garb and have no civilian clothes. The interesting story about Elio,[16] the painter. He was forced to work with the tank division. He heated the stove well and was asked how he knew how to do that. 'I am a painter.' He was asked to paint. He is now painting his sixth subject, all higher ranking. He receives a fee of 150 per painting, with the painter's signature written on every picture, confirming [his work]. Good portraits.

On 26 February a registration regulation was issued.[17] *Rumours of brutality in the building of the Polish parliament. On the first day the acts of savagery took place in a special room, followed by exercises concerning the [best] way of grabbing sidelocks: with hands or with feet. If the face covering*[18] *falls off, then […].*[19] *The hands [of one victim] still felt warm. They did the killing by [giving blows] to the ears and the head. Two men were killed.*[20] *People return from there half insane. They work there for two weeks. While Jews are being killed, workers turn to face the wall. The majority of the workers are Christians […].*[21]

The [German's] fear of being good. If he talks to a Jew in a friendly and nice way and then sees another [German], he shouts, 'Get to it, quickly', and sends down another curse. The price of gold has fallen from 80 to 40, the dollar to a hundred. Polish lawyers who have Jewish wives or junior lawyers are disbarred.[22] Each one must sign that he has never appeared against them [the Germans]. Politicians and other well-known Polish figures are being disbarred. Only a couple of hundred Polish lawyers are left. A National Democratic lawyer who argued for the Aryan paragraph[23] is proud to have been struck off for having a Jewish junior lawyer. Two hundred Christian women were taken from cafés; *they returned raped. I heard that this has happened repeatedly in the streets of Warsaw.* Marszałkowska at night half empty. Jewish streets in the morning look like a Jewish shtetl. Jewish labour details from the Community head to work. Ghastly, starved faces, earn 3.50 złoty per day.

15 Meaning unclear. Possibly a reference to money that was collected for social welfare purposes.

16 Maksymilian Eliowicz (1890–1942), painter and sculptor; board member of the Society for the Promotion of Jewish Art (Towarzystwo Rozpowszechniania Sztuki Żydowskiej) in Płock in the 1930s; expelled in 1939 to Warsaw, from where he was deported to Treblinka and murdered in 1942.

17 On 23 Feb. 1940 Ringelblum had noted that an additional registration of Jews between the ages of 14 and 60 had been ordered. Those aged between 16 and 25 were to be registered first, on 1 March 1940. See also Doc. 162.

18 This means: if the sidelocks are torn off in the process.

19 Two words are illegible.

20 Ambiguous in the original: possibly 'did the killing'.

21 One word is illegible.

22 They were removed from the list of lawyers and thus banned from their profession.

23 Clause in the statutes of an organization, corporation or the civil service that reserved membership solely for Aryans.

DOC. 93

A Jewish soldier in the Polish army recalls his time as a soldier and prisoner of war between 24 September 1939 and 11 March 1940[1]

Handwritten account by Shmuel Zeldman, recorded by Sh. Sheynkinder,[2] copy typed by M. Bojman,[3] probably dating from the first half of 1941

To a military parade in Berlin

The narrator of the following war experiences is named Shmuel Zeldman, a Warsaw boy in the best sense of the word. A simple, carefree, good-natured young man. Employed in a timber yard by day and a bon vivant after work, able to enjoy himself on little money and someone who knows how to pass time. A lover of dance halls and sports: a card game, a schnapps – and why not? Social, political, and cultural life has never been of any concern to him. No one in the circles that he moves in pays any heed to such matters. The main thing is to have a couple of złoty in your pocket, a few good close friends, two or three pretty girls, and all your needs have been completely satisfied.

In March 1938 Zeldman was called up to serve 18 months in the Polish military. Zeldman was not afraid of military service; the physical examination did not cause him any grief, no defect was found. The blonde, ruddy-faced, and broad-shouldered young man was not afraid of the military and his Christian 'colleagues', who he had scrapped with on the sports field on more than one occasion. But he has no desire to go. For all young people of this kind, military service is a drastic experience, a transition from recklessness to seriousness, from play to purpose. A conscripted soldier is like a young married woman who has got the trysts and foolishness of her early girlhood years out of her head. The harsh military discipline leaves its mark on the rest of everyday life.

And so Zeldman left behind his friends and girls in Warsaw, the dance clubs and sports fields, and his youthful years, and went to Włocławek to serve in the 14th Infantry Regiment. The one and a half years of military service went by as it did for everyone, sometimes better, sometimes worse. But when it was almost time to go home, on the day he had been awaiting for weeks, something went awry on God's little earth.

A few weeks earlier the younger cohort had already been sent to Konojady Pomorskie to dig trenches. The older cohort kept watch in the barracks. On 24 August, however, the soldiers of the older cohort were also sent there and put up in tents in a local forest, where they spent a week comfortably, without knowing for what purpose they had been sent.

Early on 1 September, the sentry spotted a German aeroplane in the sky. Shots were fired at it, and it quickly disappeared. But soon a larger squadron of enemy planes came and duly bombed the camp. Naturally, the camp was quickly disbanded and the military was hastily transported by train to the German border.

Zeldman recounts: we were not able to leave the wagons, as the enemy opened heavy fire on us from all sides. The entire 14th Regiment, which was assembled in the train, scattered panic-stricken in search of cover from enemy bombs. Only after considerable

1 AŻIH, Ring I/1090 (458). This document has been translated from Yiddish.

2 Sh. Sheynkinder, also Sz. Szejnkinder, journalist; editor of the Yiddish daily newspaper *Der Moment* in the 1930s; helped compile the underground archive of the Warsaw ghetto from 1940; wrote a diary; thought to have been murdered in Treblinka in summer 1942.

3 M. Bojman, who contributed to the underground archive of the Warsaw ghetto.

time did those in charge manage to reassemble the regiment and put it on the march. When night fell, we were already on German soil, in Mełno. The mood was good. In the darkness of the night, we marched along a long, narrow street. It was quiet around us. We began joking about the enemy, and the officers assured us that tomorrow we would already be in Berlin, where Rydz-Śmigły would hold a parade.

Suddenly the quiet was torn by terrible gunfire from all sides. Shots came from above and below. The rat-tat-tat of machine guns drummed from every house, from every window. No one had expected it and terrible panic set in. Cries and moans could be heard all around, and at every step you came across dead bodies, riddled with bullet holes, that made it difficult to flee in the darkness. What happened on that long street in Mełno on that terrible night is simply indescribable. Each one of us ran back in panic and fear, anywhere but there. Quite a few of us fell on the way, pierced by a bullet. The retreat lasted the whole night, and when the day dawned, we were back in Polish territory, defeated and worn out.

We looked pitiful. Now only remnants were left of the entire regiment that, only five hours earlier, had been marching towards Berlin. We were all drenched in sweat and [gripped by] fear. Filthy and covered in dust, each one of us had ditched along the way everything he had had on his person to make it easier to escape. We looked at each other aghast, many of us realizing that comrades from the unit were missing and would no longer be joining us.

Dejected and in silence, we started the march back. On the way, we repeatedly came across defeated remnants of other units. These remnants merged and joined the army of General Bortnowski near Łódź.[4] There they brought a bit of order – as far as possible – to our ranks so that we might have the semblance of soldiers again. There was a fierce battle with the enemy near the town of Piątek-Sobota.[5] Both sides suffered heavy casualties, and as a result we had to retreat as far as the Bzura, where we arrived on 16 September and positioned ourselves near Kutno.[6] We remained stationed there for seven whole days. The incessant shooting rent the air continuously. But we, that is a few of my comrades and I, had no idea about what was happening there. We felt gnawing hunger, and every day we looked for food in the surrounding area. Several times in that process we crossed the Bzura and back. Once I was on patrol with another six men along the riverbank. We heard shots coming from a mill. Some Germans, probably also on patrol, had hidden in the windmill (wiatrak)[7] and began shooting at us, believing that we were coming for them. We stopped and threw a few hand grenades at the enemy which exploded. From a distance, we then called on them to surrender, but no one answered. We approached the windmill and, after throwing a few more grenades, we found three German soldiers who had shot themselves in the mouth. They had preferred to die rather than surrender to the enemy.

4 Władysław Bortnowski (1891–1966), career officer; general in the Polish armed forces; commanded the Pomorze Army (Pomeranian Army); prisoner of war in Germany, 1939–1945; later lived in Britain and the United States.

5 The villages of Piątek and Sobota, north of Łódź, are actually 15 km apart.

6 The battle of the Bzura (or battle of Kutno) was the largest battle during the German invasion of Poland. It began on the night of 8 Sept. 1939 following a Polish counteroffensive and lasted nine days.

7 Polish: 'windmill'. The author included the Yiddish word for windmill, followed by the Polish term in parentheses.

On the morning of 23 September, I learned that we would be retreating in the direction of Warsaw. I sat myself on a machine-gun wagon, wrapped myself in a blanket … and fell asleep. In the midst of sleep I heard a voice: 'Stehen bleiben! Hände hoch!'[8] A German soldier approached my wagon, looked at me under the blanket, and asked: 'Sind Sie verwundet?'[9] 'Yes', I answered. The German gestured with his hand as if to say: 'Go on, you will certainly not escape from us …' So the day passed and I travelled and slept an entire night too.

When I woke in the morning, I saw that I was among Germans who were standing around us, marvelling and offering us chocolate and cigarettes. As later became apparent, I was in the Kampinos wilderness, where the Germans were concentrating Polish prisoners. Various prisoners in larger and smaller groups streamed in over the course of the entire day. Finally, after more than 10,000 men had gathered, we were rounded up and sent in the morning to Żyrardów, where we were instructed to take up quarters in the open air on a large sports field.

We stayed in this 'camp' for two weeks. The Germans did not concern themselves with us at all. As a result, many of the Jewish soldiers suffered under their Polish comrades, who organized themselves into groups, just like convicts in prison cells, and forcibly took from the Jewish soldiers their blankets and coats, as well as shoes in good condition. Leaving the camp to its own devices led to severe demoralization among the prisoners. They were tormented even more by hunger. The townspeople even brought good things, but only in exchange for good money.

One fine, clear day the masses rebelled, broke through the fence, and fled into the town. The Germans fired after them and several prisoners fell. A portion went back, but many managed to make it to the town, change their clothes, and disappear. I too succeeded in getting to the town. I took refuge in a Jewish house and asked for civilian clothes to change into. However, they were clearly afraid of getting involved in dangerous affairs and I did not get any civilian clothes.

I went back out onto the street and bumped into other escapees, who were also in great danger. We didn't know what to do: keep running or go back? Meanwhile, rumours had spread that all the prisoners from Warsaw and the Warsaw voivodeship would be freed immediately. So we made the decision to go back to the camp.

There we encountered an entirely different situation. The German soldiers were running around with bayonets attached to their rifles or with revolvers in their hands, herding the Polish prisoners back and forth. We were not subjected to any special treatment, and we soon found ourselves amid a crowd of 40,000 people. 'Iron' discipline dominated the next eight days. A few hundred men were shot as responsible for the insurrection. The camp was liquidated after that. The whole herd was transferred to Ostrzeszów near Poznań, where we were put up in barracks. We spent two weeks there, during which time the Poles and Jews got along poorly. The Germans did not get involved in our affairs and were totally indifferent. After two weeks, we were taken to Brandenburg to a large prison camp.[10] There we were soon busy with building barracks, burning straw from the former camp, and the like. I was employed as coffee waiter in the guardroom. The behaviour of the Germans, mostly older people, was very correct. I also received enough to eat.

8 German in the original: 'Stay where you are! Hands up!'
9 German in the original: 'Are you wounded?'
10 This is probably a reference to Woldenberg camp in the Neumark region.

After four weeks of 'paradise', we were relocated again, this time to Frankfurt an der Oder. There the prisoners were divided up according to profession. Four other Jews and I were assigned to work in a sawmill in Guben. Every day at 8 a.m. a car came from there to the camp to take us to Guben in a convoy, and every day at 4 p.m. the same car took us back. The wage of 1.50 marks per day was only on paper, but we had plenty to eat. The wife of the mill's owner treated us very properly and so our life was not at all difficult. This state of affairs lasted until New Year.

In the New Year, the owner of the mill, Robert Yokel,[11] an air-force captain who 'worked' on the Western front, came home on leave. He negotiated [a deal] so that we could stay at the mill and would not need to go back to Frankfurt every day. We felt very good there. The people of Guben were very friendly towards us and we were often invited for a meal. In the homes we mainly met elderly women, old men, and children. We saw no young men or women at all.

On a certain day a messenger came from Frankfurt with the news that we were going to 'fahren nach Hause'.[12] We left everything behind and drove to the Frankfurt camp, where our things were even already packed. They gave us food for the journey and brought us to Szubin near Bydgoszcz by train, where we spent four weeks in the buildings of the correction facility. There we were under the supervision of Volksdeutsche,[13] with whom we communicated in Polish, of course. Their attitude towards us was one of real enmity. They systematically took the post and packages that were meant for us, they invented 'work' for us, and so on.

Finally, the long-awaited, happy day arrived. At night on 11 March 1940, we – approximately 800 Jewish prisoners – were loaded onto a transport train and taken to Warsaw. The Varsovians got off there, and the rest travelled on. And as we later found out, great suffering was inflicted on the Jewish prisoners in Biała Podłaska. We arrived in Warsaw unscathed. When I saw 'my' Warsaw for the first time after nearly 15 months, I wept. I had not anticipated such destruction.

DOC. 94

Warschauer Zeitung, 13 March 1940: Dietrich Redeker reports on the ghetto in Cracow and justifies the forced segregation of the Jewish population[1]

German order arrives in the ghetto: Jews are successfully trained to help each other. Self-administration by Jewish offices.

Special report by Dr Dietrich Redeker[2] in the Krakauer Zeitung *and the* Warschauer Zeitung

The German people in its entirety has decided to set itself apart from the Jews, to organize its life independently from the life of the Jewish people. It has taken this decision after centuries of appalling and terrible experiences, as it has become clear time and

11 This refers to Albert Juckel, who owned a sawmill in Guben, at 10 Friedrichstraße.

12 German in the original: 'go home'.

13 German in the original: 'ethnic Germans'.

1 *Warschauer Zeitung*, 13 March 1940, pp. 3–4. This document has been translated from German. See Doc. 38, fn 1.

again that the Jews, as a consequence of their inherited dispositions, have only ever brought misfortune to us Germans in all spheres of life, in their political, economic, and cultural activities. The Jewish people are too much at odds with the German people to retain any connection with them, even in the most marginal aspects of life.

First of all: Jews for themselves
The rapid conclusion of the Polish war and the German administrative work that subsequently began in the occupied Polish territories have made finding a solution to the problem of the Jews a matter of urgency, if only due to the strong presence of the Jewish element in the Polish population. In the General Government as well, the segregation of the Jews was implemented first and foremost as a matter of principle. This kept them away from Germans. However, this measure has also been an effective way to protect the Polish part of the population from further Jewish exploitation. Anyone who is familiar with the conditions in the General Government will also know how pleased the Poles in particular are with this radical solution to the problem.

Star of David and separate compartments
We have drawn all the necessary conclusions from this segregation of the peoples: hence the white armband with the blue Star of David, which all Jews over the age of 16[3] have to wear; hence the separate compartments on the trams; and hence the gradual push back to designated residential quarters the Jews are experiencing, where they will be completely among their own. But none of these steps amount to anti-Jewish atrocities. We are certainly not making a secret of it: we do not love the Jews, and we would even be glad if we did not have a Jewish problem to solve, but one will not find a single German who would want to solve the problem with pogroms. Yes, there have previously been such pogroms in the territory of the current General Government. Ask the Jews themselves. Back then – it was about two years ago – the outrage in the soul of the Polish nation led to excesses in almost all the larger Polish cities. Jews were hunted in the streets and beaten when they were caught.

... But no anti-Jewish atrocities
Such things would be completely unimaginable in the General Government. It should be borne in mind that the first thing the German police did in Cracow was to recapture a large number of convicts who – having been set free by the Poles before our troops' arrival – formed gangs that went round attacking Jewish shops and homes. But this is not the way we can counter the foreign propaganda about atrocities, which trots out from time to time the same old story about the persecution of Jews in Germany. For once, those who spread anti-German lies should take a look at the comprehensive welfare services that have been established by Germans or undertaken by Jews in response to German orders and are being carried out by them in a kind of self-administration.

2 Dr Dietrich Redeker (1911–1979), journalist; joined the NSDAP in 1930; studied history and journalism in Paris, Greifswald, and Berlin, 1932–1933; worked for the football magazine *Der Kicker* in Nuremberg in 1938; with the *Krakauer Zeitung*, Jan. 1940 – Nov. 1942; lived in Neustadt am Rübenberge and worked as an editor for the *Leinezeitung* after the war.

3 In fact, wearing the white armband with the blue star was obligatory for those above the age of 10: see Doc. 130.

They are to administer themselves
Here is the evidence: we took the trouble to visit all the offices, all the entities, all the facilities and institutions of the Jewish Community in Cracow. We familiarized ourselves with the work of the Jewish Welfare Office and the Section for labour deployment; we saw soup kitchens, bathhouses, shelters, and hospitals. We gained a comprehensive impression. The ghetto is also experiencing the blessings of orderly Jewish administration under the watch of, and in accordance with the advice of, experienced German officials. Imagine if all of these facilities were not there, facilities that were created only after the Germans' arrival; imagine if the Jews were left to themselves with their inadequate organizational skills, as was previously the case after the Jewish Religious Community's former executive committee had fled with the Polish rulers, taking the Community's funds with them. The Jews would rob each other, annihilate each other.

In the dirt of the ghetto
For hours on end we waded through the dirt of the Cracow ghetto. The filth crunched under our feet on wobbly staircases and decaying steps. We held onto wooden banisters that had been gnawed by woodworms or begun to rot because they had not been cared for properly, if at all. There is a sink with running water on the landing via which one enters several Jewish apartments. The tap just barely protrudes from a 3–4 cm thick crust of dirt; everything else has taken on the colour of the floor and the walls. Waste, potato peelings, and a piece of orange peel rot on the ground in a corner. People from these apartments walk past this every day. Forty, fifty, or even a hundred of them, but no one takes it away, sweeps it up. It just carries on rotting.

Most of the apartments are hardly any cleaner either. Mould, rot, and stale air make one involuntarily put a hand over one's nose. It is hard to bear. A table has just three legs. By chance, we see the fourth leg lying in a corner of the room. Six people inhabit this room, but they will leave the leg lying there because they have provisionally replaced it with a crate, the table is steady again, and one day they will shove the fourth leg into the oven as fuel. The torn, worn-out beds are not grey, they are actually black and covered with an unimaginably shiny layer of grease. One chokes with disgust. A filthy rag covers just half of the windowpanes, which cannot be seen through because they have not been cleaned. By using the imagination, one realizes that it must be the remains of a net curtain. A latrine is so filthy with dirt and excrement that the door no longer closes. One wonders how people can live like this.

None of this has anything to do with poverty. The layer of dust is almost finger-thick on the picture frame that hangs lopsidedly. No, this is not a sign of poverty. There is enough water, and with a few buckets of water the worst of the filth and dirt could be removed from the steps and corridors. But that would involve work, and it would demand an innate sense of cleanliness. If disease were to break out in these residential quarters one day, it would find countless victims in such an ideal breeding ground!

First measure: protection against contagious diseases
By chance I was witness to an operation to combat contagious diseases. All the Jewish physicians were called together at the Jewish Community building, and a German official entrusted with mentoring the Jews impressed upon them the strict measures that were to be taken to ward off the spread of disease. Today no apartment block in the Cracow ghetto

goes without regular inspection visits from a Jewish physician, who has to inspect health and sanitary conditions in the most exhaustive detail and report on them.

At first sight, the club chairs and heavy carpets in the rooms occupied by the executive committee at the Jewish Community building form a startlingly sharp contrast to the stinking, dilapidated hovels through which we have just been creeping. On the table is stationery headed *'Cracow Jewish Community'*. This is telling. A few months ago the name was still 'Cracow Jewish Religious Community'. In itself, this reflects the difference in the range of tasks the German authorities have assigned to this Jewish self-administrative body. The Jews are very proud of their work, of their self-administration, something they have never exercised to such a degree in the past. As a matter of principle, every Jew who has some kind of concern has to go to the Jewish Community building at 2 Skawinska. Only in rare cases when the Jewish offices do not feel they are competent to deal with a matter do they send applicants on to the relevant German authority with an accompanying letter.

Jewish offices with skilled Jewish personnel

It was not easy to set up a massive administrative machine, which must look after a total of 80,000 Jews today. At the outset, the new executive committee had to be appointed from a pool of suitable Jews. Then the individual offices were established and staffed with appropriate skilled personnel. The German city administration even gave the Jews a larger sum to get their whole administrative machine up and running. Today the Jewish Community organization – set up on the model of rigorous German organization – is in a position to ensure the well-being of its members to such an extent that no one needs to go hungry, that no one is homeless, that diseases are treated, but also that work is done!

In this respect, the Cracow Jewish Community administration can be called the most exemplary in the General Government. The people who emigrated from the liberated eastern territories – from Posen and Lodsch – made its work particularly difficult.[4] (The Cracow Jewish Community has expanded by 30 per cent since the war began.)

Everything begins with the card index

It goes without saying that the more prosperous among the Jews have primarily been called upon to support those without means. This is achieved firstly by what is known as the religion tax,[5] which is means-tested, and secondly by clothing collection schemes and by billeting immigrants in their residences. These kinds of socialist measures have always been unpopular among the wealthy Jews, but there is nothing for it now. Ultimately the entire Jewish community only benefits from them.

Any orderly administrative work begins with the registration of the persons to be administered. So a card index was created on the German model, and a census of the Jewish population was carried out. Since some of the Jews were still accustomed from the era of Polish chaos to being out and about without index cards, because this was probably more expedient in certain cases, a ruse was employed. The white armbands came in handy. News had spread rapidly among the Jews that it was dangerous to evade the law and be out in the streets without an armband. People therefore had to obtain

4 Refugees and deportees from the territories annexed by Germany.
5 See Doc. 38.

armbands. However, these were only available at the Jewish Community office, and anyone who picked up an armband there had to fill in a questionnaire beforehand, giving his surname, first names, parents, family status, place of residence, civil status, proof of identity, etc. Then he received a kind of identification card with his registration number, and from then on he even possessed a proper identity card. Thus a little order was imposed upon the heaving, jumbled masses in the ghetto.

Jewish employment office reports successes

Every German has a duty to work. Why should the Jews of all people get by without working, as long as they live in our state or in a territory under German administration? If you want to eat, you need to work. This is the principle which the German authorities have recommended that the Jewish Community administration put into practice. The head of the office that organizes labour deployments for the Jewish population is happy about the numbers rising daily. Over his desk hangs a diagram, very much on the German model. The curve that represents the amount of labour deployed has risen continually over the last few weeks. The ghetto is gradually getting used to what, for a Jew, is the most unpleasant aspect of life. However, all work is remunerated; the city pays the Jewish Community a sum that corresponds to the number of workers provided, the further distribution of which is in turn incumbent upon the Jews. Those who have no funds but are able to work have to work for their food vouchers and their cash support. Food in exchange for work: a novel idea for many Jews, but that is the way of the world, after all.

Food twice a day at seven soup kitchens

Food is distributed twice a day at Cracow's seven Jewish soup kitchens, in the morning and at midday. Of course this does not proceed without lots of fuss and a great commotion. It is 'just like Jewish school'.[6] Slurping, chomping figures sit before their plates at long tables. A nutritious, tasty lunch is prepared from pearl barley, potatoes, and bread.

One certainly notices something of the German influence in the kitchen: by ghetto standards, a surprising cleanliness prevails. I happened to witness the manager of this kitchen being praised for her work by a German official. At a second soup kitchen, however, a rebuke is in order. Waste lies around on the floor so that one has to be careful not to slip on it. The pots and cutlery are by no means impeccable. On the whole, however, a great deal has been achieved in a short time; a great deal of German work has been done, for which the Jews express sincere gratitude to the German administration. Today 8,000 portions of food are served twice a day at the seven kitchens, which means, in other words, that one-tenth of the Jewish population is fed at these public kitchens.

All run by Jews: hospital, shelters, bathhouses, etc.

But the arm of the Jewish welfare system extends further. It takes in new arrivals, sends them for delousing, for examinations, gives them roofs over their heads (a number of synagogues have been converted into night shelters for this purpose), provides them with food vouchers, ensures they have coal, and ensures they have clothing. Everywhere, however, Germans have laid the foundations for these comprehensive services; the relevant

6 'Wie in der Judenschule' ('like in a Jewish school/synagogue') was a common idiomatic expression in German used to describe a particularly chaotic and noisy situation.

offices have been set up by German agencies and are inspected by them. It is quite interesting to see all the facilities that fall under the Cracow Jewish Community's authority: in addition to the offices themselves, in which only Jewish officials and employees work, and apart from the soup kitchens that have already been mentioned, three bathhouses; forty-nine shelters, in which almost 4,000 people are housed, while the larger ones even have small infirmaries; not to mention the Jewish hospital, with its 110 beds; an orphanage; two other homes for the orphans of craftsmen; and one home for the elderly.

All this does indeed look very different from the 'reports' by the foreign atrocity propagandists. The order the German administration has introduced even in the ghetto is probably the best proof that we are not attempting to solve the Jewish problem with pogroms. At the same time, such order has been created out of nothing, and all this has been done in a country where war had only recently left deep scars.[7]

DOC. 95

On 18 March 1940 Josef Baumann, a Jew who had been expelled from Germany to Poland, asks the American Jewish Joint Distribution Committee for help in getting to Palestine[1]

Handwritten letter from Josef Baumann,[2] Cracow, to the American Jewish Joint Distribution Committee in Warsaw, dated 18 March 1940

To the esteemed American Joint Committee in Warsaw,

I am turning to you with an earnest request: I have three children in Palestine. I am in Cracow with my wife[3] with no livelihood, a complete stranger here. *I lived in Berlin from 1906 (33 years)* and was deported during an operation in October 1938.[4] And so I came to Zbąszyn,[5] where I was held in a camp by the Poles. After nine months I came to Cracow, where the Jewish Community is barely keeping me afloat. With consideration for my situation and the fact that we have three children in Eretz Yisrael, we beg you most sincerely to help us get to our children. We have been *registered here in Cracow* for a couple of weeks. The Palestine Office in Berlin would also be glad to help me so that we can get to our children, but being outside Reich borders is making our emigration much more difficult. Faced with this desperate situation we are in, I am writing to you, esteemed gentlemen, to help us. Please understand our request: we are parents whose

7 Photographs published with the article show a ticket for a meal served at soup kitchen no. 2, the Jewish employment office, a synagogue used as emergency housing, and a ward at Cracow Jewish hospital. One photograph is captioned: 'A typically filthy courtyard in the ghetto'. The photographs were taken by Redeker and the photographer Otto Rösner, who worked for the General Government's news service.

1 YVA, M-28/1, fol. 114. This document has been translated from German.
2 Josef Baumann (1890–1942?); born in Jarosław; lived in Berlin, 1906–1938; died in Zamość.
3 Frieda Baumann, née Langer (1892–1942?); lived in Berlin before the Second World War.
4 See Introduction, p. 26.
5 A reception camp for Jews with Polish citizenship who had been expelled from Germany to the Polish border in Oct. 1938 existed in Zbąszyń (Neu-Bentschen) in 1938/39: see PMJ 2/112, 113, and 118; on the situation in Zbąszyń, see PMJ 2/203.

three children are in Eretz, and these parents cannot bear the torment of not being able to see them.

We beg you once again to help us and to show understanding for our situation. We look forward to your esteemed reply and thank you most sincerely.

With admiration and grateful esteem,

I remain most respectfully yours,

DOC. 96

On 18 March 1940 a Polish teacher describes the plight of the Jews who are forced to sell personal belongings[1]

Diary of Franciszka Reizer, entry for 18 March 1940

Holy Week. Penitential service. A priest from Kosina[2] delivers the sermon. There is more patriotism in it than religion. In one of his lessons, for example, he kept talking about the attitude of a Pole today. And at the end he said, 'Someone has to tell you this. So I will tell you: Poland will be!' The listeners were seized with fear. People fell to their knees, and he began to sing: *Boże, coś Polskę …*[3]

Because the fate of the Jews is uncertain, they are getting rid of many things. They are selling them at low prices. The Poles are buying from them what they can. Mostly, though, items for everyday use. Sales transactions are made in secret. Often at dusk or late at night.

It did not work out well for Tomasz Ulman, for example, who was spotted carrying out a sewing machine from a Jew by a gendarme or blue policeman.[4] Ulman was summoned to the Gestapo and beaten. But they released him. Without the sewing machine, which was confiscated. The Germans forbid the Jews to sell anything and the Poles to buy from them.

1 The original could not be located. Published in Reizer, *Dzienniki 1939–1944*, p. 40. This may be an edited excerpt from a longer entry. This document has been translated from Polish.

2 A town in southern Poland, in the vicinity of Rzeszów.

3 Polish in the original: 'God save Poland.' The beginning of an old church hymn which was sung as an expression of patriotism during the occupation, when other songs were prohibited.

4 See Doc. 90, fn 13.

DOC. 97

On 21 March 1940 the mayor of Sosnowitz (Sosnowiec) raises objections to the Aryanization of shops[1]

Letter from the mayor of Sosnowitz (A I 794/40; B III 3138), Josef Schönwälder,[2] to the Trustee Office in Kattowitz, dated 21 March 1940[3]

There is repeated talk that the Trustee Office should hand over Jewish shops within the ghetto to ethnic Germans. I would like to make the following general comments on this matter:

1) Today, the Religious Community levies a special tax on those shops licensed only for Jews, which enables it to fulfil its welfare obligations towards Jews in need. The number of Jews in need is very large here, and the number of rich Jews small, as the latter have mostly fled. The financial position of the Religious Community is so bad at the moment that it already needs public funds for support. It is therefore of vital public interest that the shops licensed for Jews are not transferred into Aryan hands, but remain with the Religious Community instead.

Furthermore, I believe it is right that the taxes and charges hitherto paid to the Religious Community by Jewish shops under trusteeship continue to be paid. On the other hand, if the Trustee Office prohibits these taxes and charges from being paid to the Religious Community, funds from the public sector will in turn have to be spent on welfare support for the Jews. I still feel it would be better if these funds were to come from the businesses of the Jews themselves.

2) The evacuation of the Jews will be completed either this year or next year at the latest. Once this has occurred, the previous ghetto will be an area devoid of people. Germans will not be settled there, and Poles will also be prevented from taking up residence in the ghetto in large numbers. Settling Germans in the ghetto would be a degrading state of affairs and will not be permitted by the Party under any circumstances. German businesses that are set up in the ghetto now would therefore be subject to ruin later on. In addition, the shops would have to be moved again, so the shopkeepers would incur a great deal of expense.

I therefore request that German shops be set up only in streets and neighbourhoods in which those shops will also be able to stay in business in the future. As far as the inner city is concerned, this means Hauptstraße and Rathausstraße, where there are still empty shops, as well as the Pogon and Alt-Sosnowitz districts.

1 APK, 124/1397, fols. 47–48. This document has been translated from German.

2 Josef Schönwälder (1897–1972), stonemason and architect; joined the NSDAP in 1922 and the SS in 1934; deputy mayor and Kreisleiter in Breslau, and NSDAP Reich Orator (Reichsredner), 1933–1940; mayor of Sosnowitz, 1940–1943; mayor of Breslau, 1943–1945; lived in Wesel after the war.

3 The original contains handwritten underlining. At the end there are several handwritten notes from B III (signed Dt), dated 24 April 1940: 'Sent to Department A I with reference to the meeting today at Landrat Seifarth's office. We will answer item 2. With regard to Item 1, I will merely inform the mayor that a general solution to the question of support payments must be found expeditiously.' Handwritten memorandum from A I 794/40, dated 30 April 1940: 'Case file "Support Paid to Poles and Jews in Need", log no. 745/40.'

I would be grateful if you would soon inform me whether you are prepared to proceed in accordance with the above proposal. In any event, the city administration can no longer be involved in placing Germans in shops in the ghetto in future.

I must reject any responsibility for such mismanagement.

Heil Hitler,

DOC. 98
On 28 March 1940 the economist Ludwik Landau describes anti-Jewish riots in Warsaw[1]

Daily chronicle by Ludwik Landau,[2] entry for 28 March 1940

The matter of anti-Jewish riots in Warsaw has now come to the fore. They have assumed such great proportions that the Jewish population is again living in fear and is afraid of appearing on the streets, especially in the main Jewish districts. First and foremost, shops are being plundered – the windows smashed, equipment destroyed, and, above all, goods looted; but homes are also being plundered, and even more often, passers-by, identifiable by their armbands, are being beaten and robbed. All this is the work of gangs roaming the entire city, both in Jewish districts and in the city centre: on Franciszkańska, Leszno, and Marszałkowska streets, and in the Powiśle and Praga districts. The gangs sometimes number as many as 500 people, mainly teenagers and all kinds of scum. It is becoming increasingly clear that the Germans are staging these actions. Germans are generally seen openly taking photographs and filming. Sometimes a German vehicle arrives first, the film crew gets out, and only then does a gang of robbers appear. Polish police officers were also dragged into the operation. A police officer somewhere is said to have ordered a closed shop to be opened. Then he invited the crowd of onlookers to help themselves to whatever they wanted. At any rate, there have been no cases where the police intervened. The German police observed the operation calmly. A crowd of about 500 people heading towards Praga were not hindered as they went past the Blank Palace, the seat of the German mayor of Warsaw.[3]

The purpose of this operation is to set the Christian and Jewish populations against each other and to obtain material that would legitimize in the eyes of foreign countries Germans being on Polish territory – indeed, to put them on a pedestal – as the defenders

1 Ludwik Landau, 'Sytuacja w okupowanej Polsce – dzienniki, 1939[–1940], 1942–1944', AAN, 1349/231/V, pp. 387–388. Published in Ludwik Landau, *Kronika lat wojny i okupacji*, vol. 1: *Wrzesień 1939 – listopad 1940*, ed. Zbigniew Landau and Jerzy Tomaszewski (Warsaw: Państwowe Wydawnictwo Naukowe, 1962), pp. 370–371. This document has been translated from Polish.

2 Ludwik Landau (1902–1944), economist; activist with the Polish Socialist Party (PPS); worked at the Main Office of Statistics from 1923; recorded a daily chronicle of the German occupation of Poland, 1939–1944; worked in the financial administration of the Warsaw Jewish Council in 1940, then worked on the 'Aryan side'; also co-edited the socialist underground paper *Kronika Okupacji*, 1940–1942; arrested by the Gestapo in 1944 and murdered.

3 From 26 March 1940, this late baroque building on Plac Teatralny was the seat of the District Governor's representative for the City of Warsaw (later Stadthauptmann) Ludwig Leist and the German administration.

of law and order and as the avengers of the oppressed. The documents and films will serve this purpose. Jews asking the Germans for protection against assaults by the Polish Christian population is also meant to serve this purpose. The Germans have apparently issued secret instructions to Jewish communities to officially turn to them for help. Otherwise – the Germans warn – riots will increase in magnitude. What is more, these incidents are taking place not just in Warsaw, but also in various provincial cities.

The intentions of the Germans are clear, and the unceremonious way in which they are being pursued fits the typical conduct of the Nazis. However, it is unfortunate that they are so easy to carry out, given the foundations that had been prepared for years by the Endecja and, for several years, by the Sanacja governments. These factors have been exploited in the German operation. Apparently, the organizers of the gangs are the antisemitic 'Atak'[4] group and the group of Prof. Cybichowski and comrades[5] – former members of the National Radical Camp,[6] etc. Public reaction in the streets is also disappointing. Although a generally negative attitude towards the gangs seems to predominate, no one brings themselves to protest anywhere, most likely not only out of fear of the Germans.

As for the Jews, they are trying to defend themselves by organizing some kind of self-help, a militia – obviously unarmed – to protect the population and its property against assailants. But will that be enough? In the end, will the Jews not be compelled to turn to the Germans, just as they demand?

[...][7]

4 Atak ('Attack') was a Slavic ethnonationalist organization. In the late 1930s it advocated that non-Jewish stores and homes be identified as such with the 'Atak' symbol, an axe with the Christian cross as its handle. Atak's rallying cry was 'Gospodarczą Organizujmy Jedność!' (GOJ) – 'Let us organize economic unity!' See also Doc. 321.

5 Dr Zygmunt Cybichowski (1879–1946), lawyer; doctoral studies in Strasbourg, 1902; postdoctoral studies in Freiburg, 1911; professor in Lwów in 1913, and in Warsaw, 1919–1939; judge at the International Court of Arbitration in The Hague from 1923; in late 1939 on the board of the National Radical Organization (Narodowa Organizacja Radykalna), which sought to create a National Socialist Party in Poland.

6 Obóz Narodowo-Radykalny (ONR) was a far-right movement formed in April 1934 as a breakaway faction from the National Democratic milieu. It was banned by the Polish government in 1935 but continued its activities underground.

7 Further on, Landau wrote about his disappointment that a less heavy-handed occupation policy was not materializing. The occupiers had cut the bread rations for the Jewish population and were committing constant acts of violence against them. He wondered when the war would begin in Western Europe.

DOC. 99

In March 1940 the Polish government's representative in occupied Poland contemplates the post-war emigration of the Jewish population[1]

Memorandum (no. 223/XIX) by Roman Knoll,[2] foreign policy advisor in the government delegation, for the Polish prime minister, Sikorski (received on 4 September 1940), dated March 1940

[...][3] II.

Among its other aspects, the current conflict also has a Jewish facet. It is a Jewish war in the sense that the conflict has thrown into sharp relief the question of Jewry's existence and nature – [a question] in which the Jews are deeply interested. It [the conflict] must also involve settling the Jewish question by giving the Jewish people the opportunity to develop undisturbed under normalized conditions. Even Western international Jewry, which is assimilating but is still often set apart, has understood for several decades that equal rights for Jews are not the only or the most important problem for the Jews. This realization gave rise to Zionism, a Jewish trend towards a nation state, which, although it has tended to focus primarily on Palestine in the last twenty years and has achieved this aim with varying degrees of success, was not originally organically connected to the Palestinian territory. It was and still is a question of creating somewhere, wherever it is most suitable, a Jewish state for all Jews. It is clear to all Jews, and also to all European nations with a sizeable Jewish population, that the Jewish question can only be resolved by the withdrawal of the Jewish masses from the vast areas of the diaspora, and that the few remaining people of Jewish origin, whether assimilated or not, will then no longer pose a threat to the surrounding nations. Zionism's success is the starting point not only for the equality of the Jews under the law, as this has already been achieved in many European states, but also for a true, de facto equality.

Primarily the Jews are interested in the serious realization of Zionism, but this is no less true of the Poles, the Romanians, the Hungarians, and the Ukrainians, who harbour within their respective national body a distinct Jewish mass, which predominates in a particular social class and disturbs free circulation within the nation. So-called antisemitism is an ugly expression of these nations' natural tendency towards modern social development. The ghettos are a pathological phenomenon in modern societies. How-

1 AIP, Protokoły Rady Ministrów/15A/6, fols. 54–65, here part II, fols. 60–63. This document has been translated from Polish. Published in Dariusz Libionka, 'ZWZ-AK i Delegatura Rządu RP wobec eksterminacji Żydów polskich', in Andrzej Żbikowski (ed.), *Polacy i Żydzi pod okupacją niemiecką 1939–1945: Studia i materiały* (Warsaw: Instytut Pamięci Narodowej, 2006), pp. 15–207, here pp. 141–143.

2 Roman Knoll (1888–1946), lawyer and diplomat; participated in the war between Poland and Soviet Russia in 1920; thereafter section head in the Eastern Department of the Polish Foreign Ministry; involved in the peace negotiations in 1921; ambassador to Moscow, Ankara, Rome, and Berlin consecutively, 1921–1931; retired from office as an opponent of Foreign Minister Józef Beck; joined the underground in 1939; foreign policy advisor in the government delegation in 1940; delegation section head for foreign policy, 1943–1945.

3 In part I, Knoll first developed his thoughts on the Polish government's policy towards ethnic minorities and then presented his proposals for the demarcation of borders in Central and Eastern Europe after the war.

ever, when a large mass of foreign human material is poured into a different kind of national body, this automatically creates an inflammation for which neither party is to blame, but which is harmful to both. This has been the state of affairs for a long time. However, it has come to a head in connection with the persecutions of the Jews in Central European countries, and it has spun out of control entirely as a result of the situation in which the Jews find themselves in the Polish territories under German occupation and the radicalism of the Jewish movement in the territories under Soviet Russian occupation. The unstable and delicate balance of the situation has been shaken so severely and to such a great extent that a return to the status quo ante is absolutely impossible. It is impossible both physically and politically. The West may not realize it, but that is how it is. Under these conditions Zionism is no longer a distant future ideal, but becomes an immediate necessity. There is no longer the alternative between 'the old state of affairs and Zionism'; instead, the new alternative is – Zionism or extermination. The Jewish masses who have been uprooted have nowhere to go and nowhere to which they can return, and they cannot peacefully remain where they are. Such is the situation in the Polish territories, and this state of affairs cannot fail to affect the Jews' position in Hungary and in Romania, and will also have an impact on the situation that threatens the Jews in Ukraine in the event of its de-Sovietization. The great Jewish financiers in the West should be properly informed of this, and a national solidarity should be awakened in them, which could lead them to start caring not only about their own matters, but also – at last – about the fate of the fellow members of their tribe.

Palestine was not only an area in which to settle. For the Zionist cause it also represented the land of their forefathers – whether rightly or wrongly, as it is difficult to say what proportion of formerly begotten Jews, despite Ezra and Nehemiah,[4] was indeed of Palestinian or even generally of Syrian origin, not only due to the preservation[5] of tribal unity, but also as a result of proselytizing.[6] For the Jews, however, the land is inadequate, barren, far from their European homes, with an unsuitable climate, and above all it is not Jewish. England has already had enough trouble with the Palestine question. Until the conflict is brought to an end, it [England] must have completely free rein in its relations with the Muslim world, and this is only possible if Zionism detaches itself from Palestine and finds another territory on which to build a Jewish state. For the Jews who will have to be removed from the former diasporic territories after this conflict, Palestine is a fiction, and the very idea of such a solution would be tantamount to throwing down a gauntlet to the Arab world. Alongside Great Britain, both the Vatican and the Christian nations will also support non-Palestinian Zionism, because turning the Holy Land into an area of permanent Arab–Jewish conflict has become intolerable to the spiritual descendants of the Crusaders.

For us, for Poland, only a realistically attainable, sizeable, fertile piece of land, carved out of the partitioned Soviet Empire and close to us geographically, will help resolve our Jewish question. One can certainly imagine this area in the vast hinterland of Odessa,

4 According to the Bible (the Christian Old Testament), Ezra and Nehemiah attempted to prevent intermarriage between Jews and members of other tribes (mid fifth century BCE).
5 The author means 'dissolution'.
6 The conversion of pagans.

which would become a Jewish haven.[7] However, we need not specify its future contours or its political system. We can leave that to the Jews. Such a turn of events not only serves our main political objective – the emigration of the Jewish masses from Poland – but it is also of great tactical benefit. For one thing, it enables us to come forward with a positive rather than a negative Jewish programme, one which is not directed against the Jews, but in defence of the Jews. Then we would not appear to be antisemites who wish to harm our own minority, but would become chivalrous champions of Jewish rebirth. Secondly, our own rebirth would not be internally connected with an influx of Jews and with Jewish domination, but with a genuine, significant, orderly Jewish emigration. In this way we would give our weary masses optimism and could rally public opinion in favour of a uniform policy.

This work must be initiated by means of propaganda among the Hungarian and Romanian Jews. It would be best if we provoke the initiative from there, and we would then immediately take it into our hands. We should not allow ourselves any internal disputes about the feasibility of the aforementioned solution, which, regardless of whether it is realized, will give us colossal political advantages merely as a slogan. This matter must be pursued somewhat blindly, without unnecessary precision. But proclaiming the necessity of finding a national home for this run-down tribe somewhere other than in an area under dispute with the Arabs would be an act that should not be delayed.

[…][8]

DOC. 100

Szaniec, 1 April 1940: a Polish underground newspaper claims that the Germans treat the Jews better than they treat the Poles[1]

Care and caregivers

What does the 'gentler approach' towards us really look like, that one reads so much about in the occupation press lately in German and in Polish? In German, the occupiers affectionately stress their 'paternal care' and the authorities' efforts to ensure the 'welfare of the working people', and in Polish, such as in the reptile paper[2] *Nowy Kurier Warszawski*, one often reads 'missing' persons notices. On the streets of Warsaw, young women, girls, boys, and young men are constantly disappearing without a trace, as if into the wilderness. The reptile papers charge for these notices, while the relatives of the missing persons weep and pay. However, not one notice has had any effect so far. There is nothing

7 The Polish minister of the interior and deputy prime minister also advocated this position; see the minutes of a discussion between Stanisław Kot and Jewish representatives from London on 6 April 1940, during which Kot argued in favour of resettling the Jews from Poland to Ukraine: AZHRL, kol. Stanisława Kota 350, fols. 6–18.

8 In the following section, Knoll advocated annexing Lithuania to Poland and recommended that the Polish government insist on the return of all the territories seized from Poland in 1939.

1 *Szaniec*, no. 14, 1 April 1940, pp. 2–3. This document has been translated from Polish. *Szaniec* (Rampart) was the main publication of the radical right-wing Szaniec group and appeared from Dec. 1939 to Jan. 1945.

2 Term used in occupied Poland for 'gutter press'.

surprising about that. The 'missing' persons are the result of being hunted down like quarry by the occupiers in broad daylight, out in the open. At some point, Gestapo patrols and the blue police[3] (!) cordon off a section of a street at both ends, round up the encircled people into a group, load everyone onto trucks, and transport them to 'distribution points'. There, the hunted animals are divided up. The older specimens, no longer fit for use, are released again into the reservation, whereas the young and healthy are trafficked (that is the milder option …). Boys and men are sent deep into Germany for heavy labour, whereas the younger and prettier girls and women go to serve in mess halls and brothels, and the rest – in hospitals, as support staff in the army rear areas, and in billets.

These are not malicious inventions, but proven facts. We know people who have experienced this. We have seen it with our own eyes. We have reports and names.

There is also another manifestation of this 'care'. Employers have been forbidden to hire and to dismiss workers, while the latter in turn have been forbidden to change their workplace without permission from the 'Arbeitsämter'.[4] This is nothing more and nothing less than officially regulated slavery.

However, one has to be fair. There is an area where the Germans have indeed softened their approach. I mean the Jews. Their ruthlessness and threats notwithstanding, the occupiers have been treating the Jews much better than they have the Poles for some time now. There are indeed labour camps for Jews, but they are here, whereas Poles are taken deep into Reich territory. Every day we see on the streets Jewish soldiers who have been released from captivity, whereas our prisoners of war are still behind barbed wire, suffering from cold, hunger, and maltreatment. This should also not surprise us, for certainly no one is under the illusion that the Germans intend to settle the Jewish question in Poland. They want to destroy Poland, and the Jews may prove useful for this purpose.

We have survived more than one invasion of barbarians, and God grant we will also survive this 'care'. It is true that the world has not seen a wickeder and crueller barbarian than the German, but our inner strength, our awareness and resilience have also grown immeasurably since the time of the crusades of the Teutonic Knights, the raids of the Tartars and of Muscovite hordes onto Polish soil.

3 See Doc. 90, fn 13.
4 German in the original: 'employment offices'.

DOC. 101

On 5 April 1940 the Polish ambassador to the Vatican denounces German press reports alleging that Polish pogroms are targeting Jews[1]

Report from the Polish ambassador to the Vatican, Kazimierz Papée,[2] to the secretary of state at the Vatican, dated 5 April 1940

German propaganda is trying to damage relations between Catholics and Jews in Poland
In collaboration with a section of the press in neutral countries dependent on Germany, German propaganda is trying to poison relations between Christians and Jews in Poland. To that end, rumours are being circulated about 'pogroms' allegedly occurring in Poland.

It must first be noted that, under the current circumstances, no 'pogrom' could occur without the participation, however passive, of the occupiers.

We have also been informed by various entirely trustworthy sources that the Gestapo organized, paid for, and protected the activities of the groups that attempted to loot Jewish shops in Warsaw on Friday, 22 March. This looting was organized on Good Friday in order to confirm the German myth that Catholic Holy Week services are intended to incite hatred of Jews among the Christians.

The German press and its affiliates also circulated a report alleging that a 'pogrom' took place in Vilna on 24 March, i.e. on Easter Sunday. This is what that event actually amounted to, as reported by the reliably informed press in Vilna:

> Last Sunday, at around 3 o'clock in the afternoon, a group of thieves broke into the synagogue on 90 Wilkomierska Street. The watchman who spotted them put them to flight before they were able to force the locks of the room in which the devotional objects are kept.

1 Vatican Apostolic Archive, Affari Ecclesiastici Straordinari 3128/40. Published in Pierre Blet et al. (eds.), *Actes et documents du Saint Siège relatifs à la Seconde Guerre mondiale*, vol. 3: *Le Saint Siège et la situation religieuse en Pologne et dans les pays baltes 1939–1945*, part 1: *1939–1941* (Città del Vaticano: Libreria Editrice Vaticana, 1967), pp. 234–235. This document has been translated from French.

2 Dr Kazimierz Papée (1889–1979), lawyer; Polish envoy in Prague; later Poland's diplomatic representative to the Free City of Danzig; Polish ambassador to the Vatican, 1939–1958.

DOC. 102

On 6 April 1940 the official in charge of Jewish affairs in the General Government's Population and Welfare Division discusses the aims of his work[1]

Circular from the official in charge of Jewish affairs in the Interior Administration Department, Population and Welfare Division (BuF) (Az. VI Dr. Go/Mu, 2581/40), signed Heinrich Gottong,[2] to the governors of Districts Cracow, Lublin, Radom, and Warsaw, dated 6 April 1940 (copy)

Re: Jewish affairs

To ensure consistency in the handling of all Jewish affairs, we need to reach an agreement about the basis on which our future work will be built.

I am therefore writing to the officials in this field upon taking charge of my section for Jewish affairs in the Office of the Governor General and would like to briefly explain the attitude that it would be useful to take towards Jewry. This will also make clarify our goals *(see foundations of our work 1–9). These foundations of our work* are as follows:

1. Spatial segregation between Poles and Jews. Whether someone is a Jew or a non-Jew can only be decided on the basis of his racial identity and bloodline, and his affiliation with Judaism (through the marriage of a non-Jew to a Jew); membership in a religious community cannot be the only grounds.
2. A full Jew – on this point modifying the Nuremberg Laws – is defined as anyone who has two or more Jewish grandparents, or is married to a Jew and does not dissolve this bond.
3. As a matter of principle, Jews are to work and pay only for Jews, e.g. Jews alone are to be deployed to build Jewish settlements.
4. The Jews are to establish their own social insurance scheme and are neither to pay their contributions to a non-Jewish insurance provider nor make use of a non-Jewish system.
5. The assets and capital of such Jewish organizations are under the protection of the German administration. The same applies to the Jewish welfare system!
6. A possible transitional measure could be to allow Jews to use the Polish Red Cross's service if Jews have supported and funded this institution until now.
7. All measures must be directed towards the aim of eventually concentrating all the Jews in a particular territory and confining them to a Jewish area of settlement as an independent community under the supervision of the Reich.
8. Drafting a plan for resettling the 400,000 Jews who will arrive in the General Government after 1 May 1940.
9. Creating an archive on Jewry in Poland and Jewry as a whole (newspaper reports, regulations, acts, culture, races, healthcare, etc.).

1 APL, 498/891, fols. 52–55. This document has been translated from German.

2 Dr Heinrich Gottong (1912–1944), anthropologist; obtained a PhD under the racial theoreticians Hans F. K. Günther and Bruno K. Schultz; in charge of Jewish affairs in the Population and Welfare Division of the General Government's Interior Administration Department from March 1940; assistant in the Ethnopolitical Research Department of the Institute for German Eastern Research in Cracow from Oct. 1940; subsequently served in the war; went missing in action in Hungary in 1944.

If possible, please also answer the following questions on the circumstances in your district:

1. In which districts and Kreise are most Jews currently living, and what is their percentage of the overall population in these areas (enclose maps if possible)?
2. Which territories are economically the least valuable on account of their soil conditions? How large are they? Where are they located (map)?
3. Which territories are the least populated, how large are they, and how many people live there at the moment? Why are they so thinly populated? Which ethnic groups live there (figures!)? To what extent could the resettlement of non-Jewish ethnic groups be considered? Is the territory suitable to be designated as a purely Jewish colony?
4. What assets are still owned by Jews? Where are the Jewish assets located, and what do they consist of? What funds would still have to be provided for the resettlement of the 400,000 Jews who will arrive here after 1 May 1940?
5. What proposals are there on your part for housing the resettled persons? What work opportunities are there for the relocated persons in the individual districts (ideally in public service)? What temporary options for housing them – camps etc. – are still available at the moment?
6. What has been done so far to prevent infection or the spread of disease to non-Jews if possible? What are the health and hygiene conditions for the Jews in the General Government, and particularly in the crowded residential areas where close contact between Jews and non-Jews is unavoidable?

In addition, please send a report on all labour projects and forward an itemized list of all the steps that have been taken by your agency on all Jewish affairs to date.

Heil Hitler!

DOC. 103

Ostdeutscher Beobachter, 9 April 1940: article on the conversion of the Great Synagogue in Posen (Poznań) into an indoor swimming pool[1]

Posen indoor swimming pool already under construction. Conversion of former Synagogue into 25-metre pool

As our readers will know, the former synagogue on Fischmarkt is being converted into an *indoor swimming pool.* The work is already under way. While even small and medium-sized towns everywhere in the Reich were able to afford indoor swimming pools, even during the years of crisis and especially thereafter, a Polish local council, by contrast, did not feel any obligation towards its 272,000 residents, Posen's population until January 1939, to create such a facility. It should go without saying that the population of a city of 300,000 residents has an inalienable *right* to an indoor swimming pool. If the administration of the Gau capital is now taking steps to let the population enjoy this right, this is happening with the complete support of Gauleiter *Greiser.*

1 *Ostdeutscher Beobachter*, 9 April 1940, p. 6. The *Ostdeutscher Beobachter*, the regional edition of the *Völkischer Beobachter*, was published in Poznań from autumn 1939. This document has been translated from German.

Many plans before the indoor swimming pool was built

When the German administration took over, the question of what should become of the Jewish synagogue on Fischmarkt was raised. The original intention was to let these solid, unusually durable walls fall victim to the pickaxe. Upon closer examination of these demolition plans – which were incidentally quite *self-explanatory*, since a synagogue, even a former synagogue, has *no* place in a Gau capital! – it was concluded that its demolition would require an expenditure of approximately 100,000 marks. This then prompted further deliberations, in the course of which the conversion of the synagogue into a sports and gymnastics hall, a warehouse, an archive, or a library were examined. As so often in life, the best idea came at the end: we will turn it into an *indoor swimming pool!*

Full support from the Gauleiter

When initial studies then concluded that the structure was actually *perfectly suited* for this purpose, the city administration immediately set about *putting the project into practice.* Since certain issues still had to be clarified first, it also got in touch with Gauleiter Greiser. After examining the plan, he immediately gave it his *general approval* and also pledged his particular *support*, saying he would make issues with funding and the allocation of building materials a priority. These issues have now been resolved in a manner that is particularly favourable for the city, for which it is especially grateful to the Gauleiter.

What it will look like

The first indoor swimming pool in the Gau capital Posen will be an uncommonly decorative structure that will in no way be reminiscent of the purpose for which it was previously used. The large *dome* of the former synagogue will be *completely dismantled* and replaced with a clear roof design, on which a tower-like structure will come to stand. Of course the small round turrets that are still located in front of the synagogue today will also *disappear completely* and make way for *clearly structured side extensions* with high windows. The design of the gable will also have to undergo drastic alterations so that, once it has been completed, the building will look more like a theatre. The red brick walls that can still be seen today will also no longer be visible, as all the façades and frontages will be *plastered.*

A 25-metre swimming pool

As discussed briefly above, the inside space is exceptionally well suited for conversion into a swimming pool. It is possible to install a pool with a 25-metre-long *swimming lane* that meets sporting requirements, and this will be done. Broad *galleries* will lead around this pool, and it is not just the high glass windows, but also the coloured *tiles* due to be laid there that will give this high space an unusually light, friendly appearance, satisfying the most modern demands.

In detail, the layout of this first indoor swimming pool in Posen will be roughly as follows: swimmers will make their way through a *foyer* on the ground floor to the *changing rooms* located on the upper storey, which will of course be arranged with separate areas for women and men. After changing, swimmers will have to pass through the *shower rooms.* It will not be permissible nor possible to use the swimming pool without first using the showers. The swimming pool itself will also be given a *section for non-swimmers*, which is to be designed in such a way that it can be used for *sporting competitions* as well.

A second indoor swimming pool eventually
Nothing more needs to be said about the necessity of giving the 300,000 inhabitants of Posen an indoor swimming pool. We are thinking not just of sports training for our young people, who will then at last be able to have *compulsory swimming lessons* with their schools in the autumn and the winter as well. Nor are we thinking just of the need to provide the *Wehrmacht* with opportunities to engage in water sports in Posen. Rather, such an indoor swimming pool in Posen will represent an overall enrichment that will have a *favourable* impact in every respect. When we learn in this context that Posen will eventually get a *second* indoor swimming pool of *twice the size*, this brief indication shows what great value will be placed on the promotion of healthcare in Posen from now on.

Redesigning the Fischmarkt
The *Fischmarkt* will also undergo certain changes to its urban environment to reflect the monumental character of the indoor swimming pool. The pickaxe will also come into use in this respect and, at least initially, eliminate the most dilapidated of the ugly 'apartment buildings' that stand there, the majority of which date from the Polish period.

We can already be certain that the fact that Posen will be given an indoor swimming pool will elicit the most enthusiastic response among the population. Once the fresh, high-spirited pursuit of water sports has been taken up there, once young and old are able to swim and bathe *from morning until evening*, this building, constructed by swimming experts in accordance with the most modern standards, will be the object of so much gratitude that one will no longer need to spell this out.[2]

DOC. 104

On 12 April 1940 Governor General Hans Frank declares his intention to expel the Jewish population from Cracow[1]

Minutes of the meeting of department heads on 12 April 1940 (extract)

[…][2]
The matter of the *construction of buildings* in the General Government has to be addressed on a more substantial scale than hitherto in view of the problem of housing for public officials, employees, and military personnel, Frank said. He talked about this question yesterday with several generals and learned that, because of the difficulties on

2 Reichsstatthalter Greiser opened the swimming pool in Sept. 1942. The former synagogue was used as a swimming pool until 2010.

1 AIPN, GK 95, vol. 2. Copy in IfZ-Archives, Fb 105, vol. 4, fols. 805–807. Published in Werner Präg and Wolfgang Jacobmeyer (eds.), *Diensttagebuch des deutschen Generalgouverneurs in Polen 1939–1945* (Stuttgart: DVA, 1975), p. 165. This document has been translated from German.

the housing market, generals who commanded divisions were forced to live in buildings which, apart from the general, had only Jews as tenants. This is also the case incidentally for civil servants across all categories. This situation is completely unacceptable in the long term, he said. If the National Socialist Reich's authority is to be upheld, then it is unreasonable for the representatives of that Reich to be forced to encounter Jews when entering or leaving the buildings where they live, and for them to be exposed to the danger of catching a disease. He therefore intends to cleanse the city of Cracow of Jews by 1 November 1940, as far as this is possible, and to launch a major *operation to resettle the Jews.* The rationale for this operation is that it is absolutely intolerable for a city on which the Führer has bestowed the great honour of being the seat of a high Reich authority to have thousands and thousands of Jews creeping around and taking up living space. He said he is going to discuss with the Governor of District Cracow[3] whether such an operation would be possible. His idea is to let approximately 5,000 or at most 10,000 Jews who are urgently required as craftsmen stay in Cracow, but to have all the other Jews distributed across the General Government. The city of Cracow has to become the most Jew-free city in the General Government, he said. Only if this is done would there be any point in building it up as a German capital. There are so many Jews in Lublin that the few Germans there almost do not count. If the Reich really wants to bring 450,000 Jews into the General Government, he added, another 50,000 Jews from Cracow could also be housed in other parts of the General Government. He is therefore going to instruct Ministerialrat Wolsegger[4] to prepare measures for the evacuation of the Jews from Cracow in consultation with the Higher SS and Police Leader. He said he is willing to allow the Jews to take everything they own with them, with the exception of stolen goods, of course. The ghetto will then be cleaned up, at which point it will be possible to build clean German housing estates, where people can breathe German air. What is to be done with the Poles is a question for a later date; they will remain here for the time being at least.
[...][5]

2 Prior to this, Frank commented on statistical matters, archival questions, minority policies, NSDAP life in the General Government, and his plan to open the Institute for German Eastern Research on 20 April 1940, Hitler's birthday.

3 Dr Otto von Wächter.

4 Baron Ferdinand Wolsegger (1880–1959), lawyer; joined the NSDAP and the SA in 1938; worked in the Austrian Federal Ministry of the Interior and Education; dismissed for his National Socialist views in 1932; later Landrat and director of the Regional Government Office in Carinthia; Chief of Staff of District Cracow; head of the General Government Chancellery, Feb.–June 1942; subsequently Regierungspräsident in Carinthia; then deputy to the supreme commissioner for the Adriatic Coast, 1943–1945.

5 The rest of the meeting consisted of Frank discussing further options for housing Germans in Cracow.

DOC. 105

On 12 April 1940 Martha Israel, a housewife who was deported to the General Government, asks to be allowed to return to Stettin[1]

Handwritten letter (registered mail) from Martha Israel[2] in Piaski to the Kreishauptmann of Lublin-Land[3] (received on 15 April 1940), dated 12 April 1940[4]

I kindly ask that the following request be noted and forwarded to the agency in charge:

As I now realise, it was in contravention of the law that I was brought here as a full Aryan on the transport of Jews from Stettin.

I have been married to the businessman Walter Israel[5] (a disabled veteran) since 1912. This union resulted in a son (aged 26),[6] who was brought up Jewish. I never converted to Judaism. I was a member of the Lutheran Church until I was evacuated, and I also paid my church tax until the end of March 1940.

Three of my brothers are Party and/or SS and SA members. My brother Emil Hofmann from Cottbus wrote to tell me that my sick 74-year-old mother is asking for me. My husband and my son have consented to my return to Germany. My brother Emil Hofmann has agreed to provide for my needs in Germany.

I can return at any time to the house owned by my mother, Ida Hofmann, divorced Pieske, 16 Stolpische Str., Berlin N 118, or stay with my brother Emil Hofmann, 37 Schillerstr., Cottbus.

If a quick decision is taken about my return, Dr Lenz, the trustee, will defer his decision concerning the sale of my belongings.

I therefore ask you to approve my request for repatriation.

Most respectfully yours,

1 APL, 498/891, fols. 115–116. This document has been translated from German.
2 Martha Israel, née Pieske (1890–1940); originally from Bydgoszcz; deported to District Lublin with her husband in 1940, then lived in Dubeczno, near Włodawa; died on 30 Sept. 1940 in Lublin.
3 Emil Ziegenmeyer (1906–1991), lawyer; joined the NSDAP and the SA in 1931; instructor with the SA and the National Socialist Motor Vehicle Corps; administrative civil servant in Upper Silesia, East Prussia, and Breslau, 1936–1939; promoted to Regierungsrat in 1938; Kreishauptmann of Lublin-Land, Oct. 1939–June 1944; subsequently worked briefly in the Interior Administration Department of the General Government; served in the war, 1944–1945; relicensed to practise law in 1951; senior administrator in the city of Duisburg's legal office from 1956.
4 At the end there is a typewritten note by Ziegenmeyer: 'To the Kreishauptmann of Lublin-Land: 2171/40: Lublin, 17 April 1940. Original forwarded to the Governor of District Lublin.'
5 Walter Israel (b. 1888), businessman; originally from Bronisławowo; deported to District Lublin on 12 Feb. 1940, then lived in Dubeczno.
6 Martha Israel's son Heinz (b. 1914), manual labourer; lived with his parents at Dubeczno in 1940.

DOC. 106

On 14 April 1940 Michał Weichert summarizes his discussion with the deputy director of the Department of Food and Agriculture in District Warsaw[1]

Minutes from memory by Michał Weichert,[2] Warsaw, dated 14 April 1940

Minutes from a meeting with Mr Wenderoth, director of the Department of 'Landwirtschaft und Ernährung'[3] in District Warsaw,[4] on 12 April 1940
I handed Mr Wenderoth a letter I had received from Mr Heinrich[5] in Cracow and made clear from the start that I had not come on behalf of the Council of Elders of the Warsaw Community, which is seeking a permit to exchange rye flour for wheat flour. When I was in Cracow dealing with matters of social welfare, one question I raised was that of exchanging the flour, and I suggested an exchange in the ratio of 1 to 2 (1 kg of wheat flour in exchange for coupons for 2 kg of bread). With the approval of the Department of Landwirtschaft und Ernährung in District Warsaw, Mr Heinrich came to an agreement by telephone with the General Government's Department of Landwirtschaft und Ernährung. He then handed me a letter and recommended I report to Mr Wenderoth and refer to the telephone conversation, which I am now doing.

Mr Wenderoth informed me that a delegate from the Council of Elders of the Jewish Community has already been to see him on this matter. He has already declared his willingness for the exchange if he receives foreign currency for the flour. As he receives the flour from the Reich and has to pay for it in foreign currency himself, he cannot change his decision.

I replied that the Jews have no foreign currency.

– What do you mean, they do not have any? Mr Wenderoth interrupted – Who has it if not the Jews?

– As far as I know, possession of foreign currency is subject to severe punishment.

– I am releasing them from all criminal liability, Mr Wenderoth interrupted again.

– I do not understand, I continued, why this matter is being made so difficult for the Jews. They are not asking for anything special. They would normally receive their bread ration, but if they only want half the amount of flour for it, then the food supply will only benefit from this and not lose.

– What makes you so sure they would get a bread ration? interrupted Mr Wenderoth.

1 AŻIH, Ring II/118 (2), fols. 17–19. This document has been translated from Polish.

2 Michał (also Michael) Weichert (1890–1967), lawyer and theatre director; studied with Max Reinhardt, co-founder of the Yiddish-language Yung Teater; head of the Jewish Social Self-Help (JSS), then of the Jewish Aid Office (JUS) in Cracow, May 1940–1942; in hiding on the 'Aryan side', 1943–1945; charged with collaboration in connection with his activity in the JUS in 1945, and acquitted by the Polish special tribunal in Cracow in 1946; emigrated to Israel in 1957.

3 German in the original here and in the following: 'agriculture and food'.

4 At the time, Georg Wenderoth was not the director but rather the deputy director of the department.

5 Herbert Heinrich (b. 1915), economist; joined the NSDAP in 1934; sent to Cracow in Jan. 1940, and was head of the Voluntary Welfare and Jewish Affairs section in the Population and Welfare Division (BuF) within the Interior Administration Department of the General Government; served in the war from April 1942; head of the BuF Division in District Warsaw, late 1942 – late 1943; civil servant at the Federal Ministry of Defence in the 1950s.

– Because we have been getting it so far, I replied.
– I give it as long as I have it, Mr Wenderoth interjected, but if I no longer have any, then I won't give any. There is no wheat flour in the country, nor has there been any. We Germans have not eaten a single kilogramme of flour here in the country. We bring in everything from the Reich. So if we have to buy flour in the Reich for the Jews to make matzos, I must have foreign currency. I am prepared to accept not just foreign currency, but also gold and silver, and you probably won't deny that the Jews have more than enough gold and silver?
– I do not know, I replied, if the Jews have a lot of gold and silver. If they had it, they have probably sold most of it by now.
– If the Jews want to eat matzos, they have to pay for them, Mr Wenderoth interrupted again. I am prepared to accept silver 5 złoty coins. You won't deny that they are in circulation. I have a few myself, said Mr Wenderoth, and took a few silver 5 złoty coins out of a bag.
– And I have one such coin and am prepared to offer it right away, I replied, taking out a 5 złoty coin. But I doubt whether there are many of them in circulation.
– What is the Council of Elders for? asked Mr Wenderoth. Let it collect foreign currency, gold, and silver from the Jews. Let it show what it can do. I want to help you; I want to accommodate you. If I demand foreign currency, I do not do so out of malice. The whole of Poland does not even have 250 tonnes of wheat flour. You know what has happened to the stocks. I have to buy every single sack from the Reich, and I can't pay with Polish złoty in the Reich. Besides, it doesn't have to be foreign currency. It can also be German marks. As a financier, you understand this.
– I am not a financier, I answered.
– So you will understand this as a merchant.
– I am not a merchant, I answered.
– So, what are you then? he asked.
– There are Jews who are neither financiers nor merchants. I am a social welfare worker and I am not an expert in financial transactions. All I know is that a great wrong is being done to practising Jews. Blow after blow rain down on them. I and others like me can go without matzos, but for the more religious, it is God's severe punishment. This is not only a religious matter, but a psychological one as well. When a practising Jew is attacked and beaten in the street, rounded up for hard labour, ordered to build the walls of a ghetto, and forbidden to sell matzos – and all of this almost simultaneously – then it seems that the world is falling apart around him (dass die Welt über ihn zusammenschlägt).[6]
– And isn't the world falling apart around me when the Jews smuggle pork en masse every day? When all incidents of the smuggling of goods involve or have at least been instigated by Jews? Even if we catch a Pole smuggling goods, it turns out that a Jew lies at the root of the crime. Does the world not fall apart around me when your English minister forces us into war? Let him arrange foreign currency for you so you can eat matzos.
– Unfortunately, I replied, I have no influence over English politics. I cannot take responsibility either for the English minister of war or for Jews or Poles who smuggle goods.

6 German in the original.

My task is to care for the poorest people and it is in their interests that I have intervened. With permission from the relevant authorities, we were intending to tax matzos sold to Jews for the benefit of the people in our care. I have done everything I could to convince the gentlemen in Cracow, Warsaw, in the office of the German Stadtpräsident and that of the District Governor. Unfortunately, I have failed. My mission has ended. I bid you farewell.
– Come back again tomorrow. We will discuss this. I am prepared to agree that you pay half in Polish złoty and the other half with other methods of payment. I want to show you my goodwill.
– Thank you. I won't come back. I have nothing more to say. I shall inform the Council of Elders of the Jewish Community. I shall ask them to inform you of their decision. All I can say is that the matter is very urgent in view of the approaching holiday.
– And when does the holiday begin? asked Mr Wenderoth.
– 23 April, I replied. The baking must be finished by then. There are only a few days left.
– Things are not quite that bad, Mr Wenderoth replied. Matzos are being sold in the city. I have seen packets of matzos in shop windows myself. Thus there is no reason to worry that those who want to eat matzos won't be able to buy them.
– If you have seen packets of matzos in shop windows, you probably know the prices that are asked for them. Do you think many Jews in Warsaw can afford to pay such prices? I assume that the financial situation of the Jews is as known to you as it is to us?
The last two questions remained unanswered.
– Mahlzeit,[7] said Mr Wenderoth.
The meeting began at 1 p.m. and went on until 1.45 p.m., despite the office officially having a lunch break.[8]

DOC. 107

On 15 April 1940 the Jewish Council in Warsaw reports on the elimination of Jewish businesses under German occupation[1]

Report by JB dated 15 April 1940

Report on the decline of Jewish businesses in Warsaw

The assets of the population of the city of Warsaw were partially destroyed by the war, largely because manufacturing facilities (machines, equipment) and warehouses burned down. However, the Jewish population has been hit particularly hard by the destruction,

7 German in the original: mealtime greeting used to begin and end conversations in work contexts.
8 In a discussion with the district official Bauer on 19 April 1940, Weichert was able to secure the release of the flour: AŻIH, Ring II/118 (2), fol. 42.

1 Wydział Statystyczny, 'Biuletyn wewnętrzny (Biuletyn Wydziału Statystycznego Rady Żydowskiej w Warszawie)', no. 1, pp. 4–6 (3 May–4 Sept. 1940): AŻIH, Ring II/75 (133). Copy in USHMM, RG 15 073M, reel 1. This document has been translated from Polish. Published in Szymon Datner (ed.), 'Działalność warszawskiej "Gminy Wyznaniowej Żydowskiej" w dokumentach podziemnego archiwum getta warszawskiego ("Ring II")', *BŻIH*, no. 73 (1970), pp. 101–132, here pp. 106–108. In the period up to 10 March 1941, the Statistical Department of the Jewish Council published 14 issues of the bulletin from which this report was taken.

mainly because the authorities have taken over some of the businesses that survived the flames (putting them under administration by trustees, or confiscating them) and because Jews have been banned from specific types of production.

Amongst the Polish population, businesses have in part – largely spontaneously – adapted to the changed conditions; businesses dating from before the war have been brought in line with the requirements, and new businesses have been created. The Jewish community has little opportunity to make use of the current demand for particular types of business – businesses that have been destroyed have not been re-established, while those that have survived now have far fewer employees or have been liquidated altogether.

These facts emerge from a specially conducted survey. The survey encompassed a representative sample of some 500 larger businesses, namely those that before the war normally employed 20 or more people. They include medium and large industrial businesses, as well as businesses engaged in commerce, transport, services, and other sectors of economic activity. Among them were the following 200 Jewish businesses:

144 industrial businesses
27 commercial businesses
22 other businesses
193

which were analysed in detail. The number of employees before the war in the Jewish businesses that were surveyed totalled 9,400; of these approximately 7,800 were employed in industrial businesses, 800 in trade, and 800 in other businesses.

Taking stock of the 144 industrial businesses that were surveyed, the picture is one of extensive devastation. Apart from 18 uncertain cases, it was established that 94 businesses have been entirely liquidated and only 32 are in operation, but with a workforce that is 60 per cent smaller than before the war, in other words, they employ on average 2/5 of their former personnel.

If we assume that the number of employees in a business is a measure of its productive capacity, then these figures confirm the verdict stated above, for in this case there is no question of any improvement in productivity or any restructuring of production that would allow significant savings in personnel.

Classification by industry sector shows 41 businesses in the metalworking industry, 23 in the chemical industry, and 26 in the textile industry.

Table 1 – The fate of the Jewish businesses surveyed that normally employed 20 or more people

Type of business	Number of businesses	Of these Active	Liquidated	Undetermined
Total	193	38	131	24
Of which: industrial businesses	144	31	94	19
Among these: metalworking	41	6	31	4
Chemical	23	10	10	3
Textile	26	3	21	2
Commercial businesses	27	7	17	3
Other businesses	22	–	20	2

Commercial businesses are mainly wholesalers or large department stores. Of these, 7 are still in operation, but employing less than half of their former personnel; 17 have been completely liquidated, a few of which burned down; and the fate of 3 has not yet been determined. Other businesses include mainly gastronomy, film companies, schools, etc. In this category, apart from 2 businesses whose fate has not yet been determined, 20 have been completely liquidated.

The extent of the decline is also illustrated even more clearly in table 2.

Table 2 – Decline in employment in the Jewish businesses surveyed

Type of business	Total	Of businesses surveyed: Liquidated businesses /100	Businesses with a reduced workforce 75–99 %	50–74 %	25–49 %	10–24 %	Average reduction in workforce in %
Total businesses	100	78	6	8	6	2	89
Of which: industrial businesses	100	76	7	7	8	2	88
Among which: metalworking	100	84	0	8	5	3	88
Chemical	100	50	10	15	20	5	78
Textile	100	88	8	0	4	0	97
Commercial businesses	100	71	4	17	4	4	84
Other businesses	100	100	–	–	–	–	100

Among all types of businesses that have not been liquidated, employment has fallen in all sectors by at least half. Overall, employment has suffered a catastrophic decline. Thus, one can see that in textile businesses that employed 20 or more people before the war, the employment rate is only 3 per cent of what it was before the war; in metalworking businesses, it is 12 per cent; and in chemical businesses, it is 22 per cent. The larger industrial businesses that were surveyed have an average of 12 per cent of their pre-war employment rate whereas commercial businesses have an average of only 16 per cent.

By way of comparison, among 300 non-Jewish businesses, 22 can be identified as newly established, whereas not a single newly established Jewish businesses could be identified. Similarly, there has been a slight increase in employment in 6 non-Jewish businesses, while it has not risen in a single Jewish business. Taken together with the evidence already mentioned, these facts are indicative of the overall development of Jewish businesses.

Given that the selection of businesses was more or less representative, in other words, the businesses were chosen largely at random, the situation underlying the catastrophic figures given above clearly explains the current impoverishment of the prosperous sectors of Jewish society.

DOC. 108

On 17 April 1940 the Stadtkommissar in Tarnow (Tarnów) prohibits the Jewish population from watching the public celebrations for Hitler's birthday[1]

Directive issued by the Stadtkommissar in Tarnow, Kreishauptmannschaft Tarnow, Dr Eckert,[2] dated 17 April 1940

Directive
On the occasion of the birthday of the Führer and Reich Chancellor Adolf Hitler, I order the following:
1) On 20 April 1940 Jews are forbidden to set foot in the following streets and squares in Tarnow between 9 a.m. and 3 p.m.: Krakauer, Wall, Bernardiner, and Mark streets, Kasimirplatz, and Ring[platz].
2) Jews who are present in the buildings along the Ring on 20 April 1940 between 9 a.m. and 3 p.m. are forbidden to have the windows and street doors of the buildings along the Ring open during this time or even to look out at the Ring through the closed windows.
Failure to comply with this directive will result in severe punishment.

DOC. 109

On 16 April 1940 a Gestapo summary court in Zichenau (Ciechanów) sentences Moschek Eitelsberger to death for returning to his home town[1]

Trial record (marked 'secret') by the Gestapo, State Police office in Zichenau (Ciechanów), II 99/40g, II B V. No. 751/40, SS-Hauptsturmführer Pulmer,[2] SS-Untersturmführer Renner,[3] and SS-Untersturmführer Schenk,[4] dated 17 April 1940

Session
of the Gestapo summary court – Zichenau State Police office – in the office in Zichenau on 16 April 1940.
Presiding judge: Head of the Zichenau State Police office, SS-Hauptsturmführer Regierungsassessor Pulmer.

1 APKr-T, 1/6, fol. 425. Copy in USHMM, RG 15 020M, reel 11. Poster in German and Polish. This document has been translated from German.
2 Dr Reinhold Eckert (1902–1943), lawyer; joined the NSDAP in 1937; Regierungsrat and from Jan. 1940 Stadtkommissar in Tarnów; deputy Stadthauptmann of Cracow, Oct. 1940 – March 1943; acting Kreishauptmann in Ostrów Mazowiecka from March 1943; shot dead by Polish resistance fighters on 25 May 1943.

1 AIPN, GK 629/889, fol. 3r–v. Copy in BArch, R 70 Polen/107, fols. 497–498. This document has been translated from German.
2 Hartmut Pulmer (1908–1978), lawyer; joined the SS in 1933; with the SD from 1935; Gestapo officer from 1938; deputy head of the Tilsit State Police office; member of an Einsatzkommando in Poland in 1939; became head of the Ciechanów State Police office in Płock (later known as Schröttersburg) in Jan. 1940; worked for the commander of the Security Police in Rennes from Dec. 1942; became an Oberregierungsrat and commander of the Security Police in Nuremberg in 1944; lived under an assumed name after the war; sentenced to death in absentia in France in 1953.

Associate judges: SS-Untersturmführer and Kriminalkommissar Renner, SS-Untersturmführer and Kriminalsekretär Schenk.
Facts of the case: The Jew *Eitelsberg*,[5] first name: Moschek, b. 15 August 1908 in Neu-Hof,[6] most recently resident in Warsaw, currently staying in Neu-Hof, illegally and without permission returned to Reich territory after being deported to General Government territory in September 1939 and following the registration of Jews carried out on 10 October 1939. He was aware that return migration to Reich territory was prohibited. Despite this, he returned across the unmarked border illegally and has been staying with acquaintances in Neu-Hof for months without being registered. He made his living by smuggling.

Eitelsberg was arrested in Neu-Hof on 8 April 1940 by the Kreis Modlin-Neu-Hof police post of the Zichenau State Police office and was interrogated under caution on 10 April 1940.

Eitelsberg has confessed and admits to having returned to Reich territory in contravention of the ban. He confirmed the correctness of his transcribed testimony with his own signature.

On the basis of the Reich Security Main Office's decree of 29 November 1939[7] – IV (II. o)2 – 288/39-g-1 and the facts of the case that have been ascertained, the Jew *Eitelsberg* is hereby sentenced to death.[8]

DOC. 110

On 19 April 1940 the Gestapo office in Kattowitz (Katowice) writes to the Trustee Office in Kattowitz enquiring about funding for Jewish welfare activities[1]

Letter (very urgent) from the Gestapo, Kattowitz State Police office (II B – IO12/40), signature illegible, to the Kattowitz Trustee Office, Kattowitz, 44 Bernhardstr.,[2] dated 19 April 1940[3]

Re: evacuation of Jews
Case file: none
The Reichsführer-SS has ordered all Jews to be deported from the eastern territories[4] to the General Government.[5] However, their deportation is not expected to commence before the end of August this year. Since most of the Jews' assets have been confiscated

3 Rudolf Renner (1908–1981), Kriminalkommissar; member and later head of Department III under the commander of the Security Police in Płock.
4 Albert Schenk (1900–1945), police detective; senior detective in Płock.
5 Correctly: Moschek Eitelsberger (1908–1940).
6 A small town located north-east of Warsaw.
7 This could not be found. See also Doc. 60, fn. 5.
8 Eitelsberger was executed on 16 May 1940 at the Inspector of the Security Police's transit camp in Działdowo: BArch, R 70 Polen/107, fol. 498.

1 APK, 124/1397, fols. 67–68. This document has been translated from German.
2 The head of the Trustee Office in Kattowitz (Katowice) was Count Michael von Matuschka.
3 The original contains handwritten notes and underlining.
4 The western Polish territories annexed by Germany.
5 See Doc. 71.

by the Trustee Office, the roughly 100,000 Jews in Regierungsbezirk Kattowitz have gradually become impoverished and destitute. All the Jewish communities' funds have been exhausted. This state of affairs has already led to Jewish soup kitchens and welfare institutions having to be closed. In the interest of maintaining order and particularly of safeguarding the health of the Germans who live in the territory, it is absolutely essential that the Jewish soup kitchens and welfare facilities are kept running and sanitary facilities are maintained until the Jews are deported. Several outbreaks of epidemic disease have already been reported, which does not bode well for the future. The State Police does not have the funds at its disposal to prevent the worst danger. The assistance I have ordered the Jews themselves to organize, the provision of funds by the Reich Association of Jews, and so forth are of little practical significance. The payments (in zloty) promised to the Jews by foreign Jewish organizations are not being disbursed because it is not possible to obtain the approval of the relevant foreign currency offices. For instance, the Joint [JDC] in Warsaw has promised monthly support payments of 100,000 Reichsmarks for the Jews in East Upper Silesia. However, the Foreign Currency Office in Cracow has not approved the transfer of this sum as an offset payment.

To avert the worst danger, the additional sum of 100,000 Reichsmarks is urgently required each month until the deportation of the Jews from East Upper Silesia has been completed.

Please inform me as soon as possible whether your office can make funds available for the above-mentioned purpose out of the confiscated assets of Jews.

DOC. 111

On 25 April 1940 the shopkeeper Chana Goldblum in Kielce asks for the release of the keys and goods confiscated from her shop[1]

Letter from Chana Goldblum[2] to the Stadtkommissar in Kielce[3] (received on 26 April 1940), dated 25 April 1940[4]

Request

The undersigned would like to convey the following request to the Stadtkommissar:

On 24 April of this year, one of the officials from the town hall came to my shop and drew up an inventory of all the goods that were in stock.

I would like to respectfully point out that there are no foodstuffs in stock at my shop, but only a small quantity of assorted goods, to be precise: shoe polish, dyes, laundry blue, and the like.[5]

1 AIPN, GK 652/85, fol. 11r–v. This document has been translated from German.
2 The widow Chana Goldblum was the owner of a shop at 3 Bodzentyńska in Kielce.
3 Hubert (?) Rotter; member of the NSDAP and the SS; mayor of Radomsko, 1939–1940; later promoted to Sturmbannführer, senior commander of the SS and the Selbstschutz in Kielce, and Stadtkommissar there.
4 Two coloured fee stamps issued by the city administration in Kielce, worth 5 and 10 złoty, respectively, and dated 26 April 1940 are affixed to the left side of the document. The document contains handwritten underlining.
5 Handwritten note on the left: '? Not correct.'

This shop is the only possible way for me and my large family – which consists of ten individuals – to earn a living.

I would therefore most humbly like to ask the Stadtkommissar to kindly have the keys and goods released, and for permission for me to continue running the business, because I am an aged widow and do not receive any welfare.

In the hope that my request will be favourably received, I remain sincerely yours,[6]

DOC. 112

On 26 April 1940 the Urban Police Command in Kattowitz (Katowice) passes on the Gestapo order to expel the Jewish population from East Upper Silesia[1]

Letter (marked 'confidential! sealed!') from the Urban Police Command in Kattowitz (S. 1a. 6222/20.40), signed Scheer,[2] to the local Urban Police command posts, dated 26 April 1940[3]

Re: resettlement of Jews from the Old Silesian area[4] (not including Beuthen, Gleiwitz, and Hindenburg).

1) The Gestapo, Kattowitz State Police Office, have informed us of the following in their letter of 18 April 1940 – Department II. B – Special Section (Circular no. 3):

As part of the overall measures to evacuate the Jews, the first resettlement will, due to urgent reasons related to State Police operations, take place from the Old Silesian area. The Old Reich territories (Beuthen, Gleiwitz, and Hindenburg) will remain unaffected by these measures. To this end, the following steps are ordered:

The councils of elders of the Jewish communities have been charged with implementing the resettlement. The State Police local and auxiliary command posts merely have to supervise and guarantee the maintenance of order on the transports, in consultation with the Kreis and local police authorities.

The Jews will be transported on scheduled trains in special Reich Railway carriages. The largest pieces of luggage and the necessary furniture will be loaded separately in advance. All household goods, textiles, and pieces of furniture may be taken on the journey, provided they are necessary for the Jews' subsistence (non-distrainable effects). Pieces of furniture and fittings whose value exceeds the threshold below which effects are non-distrainable, or which have previously been confiscated by the Trustee Office, may not be taken on the journey.

6 Two handwritten notes dated 26 April 1940 are found on the reverse: 'I do not have a case file. As far as I remember, the Gestapo closed the shop and the goods were confiscated. Inventory was taken.' (Initials.) '1. The items' release is rejected because the shop has been closed by the Security Police and placed at the disposal of the Stadtkommissar. 2. File.' (Signature illegible.)

1 APK, 807/317, fols. 2–2a. This document has been translated from German.

2 Probably Josef Scheer (b. 1911), railway operations assistant; joined the SS in 1932 and the NSDAP in 1937; served with the police in Katowice, 1940–1943; worked in the SS Main Office, Office CI (General Construction Tasks) in 1944.

3 Sixty-nine copies of the directive were sent to Urban Police command posts I–VI.

4 The forcible resettlement within the Gau Upper Silesia was to take place from west to east, i.e. from the territories that had been German before 1918 to the 'Eastern strip' of East Upper Silesia bordering the General Government.

The councils of elders of the Jewish communities at the resettlement destinations are instructed to make preparations for receiving and housing the resettled Jews, and to ensure they are housed. The Landräte are requested to support and direct the resettlement. The following resettlement dates and destinations have been specified for the individual Jewish communities:

I. Lublinitz (60)[5] and Tarnowitz (75) on 10 May 1940 to Zawierzie;[6]
II. Rybnik (63), Pleß (34), Nikolai (72), and Königshütte (506) on 14 May 1940 to Trzebinia;
III. Kattowitz (829) and Myslowitz (178) on 15 May 1940 to Chrzanow;
IV. Teschen (32), Karwin (82), and Oderberg[7] (322) on 16 and 17 May 1940 to Zawierzie;
V. Bielitz (1,023) and Dziedzitz (46) on 20 and 21 May 1940 to Olkusz;
VI. The Jews from the towns and villages in Kreis Saybusch will have to resettle to Sucha during the period from 10 May to 15 May 1940.

The only persons who will remain temporarily exempted from the resettlement are the heads of the Jewish communities that are due to be dissolved and, depending on the size of the Jewish communities, one or two members of the councils of elders who will wind up their affairs. The provisional administration of the assets and land owned by these Jewish communities will be dealt with by the Landräte, pending decisions made by the Trustee Office in Kattowitz. A period of fourteen days is foreseen for the handover. The Jews who have remained behind must then organize their own resettlement to the places to which they have been assigned.

All Jews will have to resettle. Jews who live in mixed marriages will be exempt, provided the marriage has produced children. Jews who live in childless mixed marriages will have to resettle if the male spouse in the mixed marriage is a Jew.

2) All Urban Police command posts are to support this resettlement operation by all possible means.

5 The figures in brackets give the number of persons to be resettled from these places.

6 Correctly: Zawiercie.

7 The Czech part of Cieszyn (Český Těšín), Karviná, and Bohumín belonged to the formerly Czechoslovak territory of Zaolzie (Olsa region), which Poland had annexed with German acquiescence in 1938 under the Munich Agreement.

DOC. 113

On 26 April 1940 the tax inspector in Mielec puts forward a proposal for collecting expelled Jews' tax arrears[1]

Letter from the tax inspector in Mielec (Zu Fin. o 1005–24),[2] signature illegible, to the Office of the Governor General for the Occupied Polish Territories, Finance Department,[3] Cracow (received on 28 April 1940), dated 26 April 1940

Re: confiscation of private assets
In Kreis Tarnobrzeg, the Jews were deported in September 1939 from the towns of Tarnobrzeg and Rozwadów to the territories to the right of the San[4] by the Landrat with the assistance of the Gestapo. When this was done, the Jews' money was taken from them except for a small sum. Business owners had to leave all of their goods behind and were generally not allowed to take any of the furniture from their homes and only the most essential personal possessions with them. The goods and belongings left behind were then sold by the towns' mayors. Some of the household furniture and other items are also said to have been handed over to impoverished Poles affected by the war and to expellees from Posen for their use, free of charge. Some of the confiscated money and the proceeds from the confiscated goods, household fittings, and other items have been left with the mayors of Tarnobrzeg and Rozwadów to fund necessary expenditures; some of the funds have been used by the Landrat. I have not yet been able to ascertain the precise total revenue.

I have had separate itemized lists of the tax arrears owed by the expelled Jews drawn up for taxpayers who own properties and for taxpayers who only lived in rented accommodation. The tax arrears amount to 387,689.17 zloty.

The Landkommissar has agreed to note the sums obtained from the individual Jews on these itemized lists. I will then be in a position to ascertain what arrears are actually outstanding. The Kreishauptmann wishes to ensure that money from the confiscation is also received by the tax administration, because he would like the Kreis to have its share of the taxes as well.

A trustee has now been appointed to administer the property of deported Jews in Kreis Tarnobrzeg. As soon as he has concluded his preliminary work, he is to make current tax payments out of the revenues from the properties and, if possible, settle the arrears owed.

Once the Landkommissar has noted the amounts on the itemized lists of arrears and I am able to ascertain the actual arrears, the intention is then to have mortgages registered on the properties as securities for outstanding arrears.

1 AAN, 111/1020/3, fols. 438–439. This document has been translated from German.
2 Added by hand above: 'Fin. o 1005-45'.
3 The Finance Department was headed by Dr Alfred Spindler (1888–1948), lawyer; worked for the Reich Finance Authorities (Reichsfinanzverwaltung) from 1920; member of the DVP, then the DNVP, 1927–1933; joined the SA in 1933 and the NSDAP in 1937; Oberregierungsrat; appointed president of the Regional Finance Office (Oberfinanzpräsidium) in Munich in 1936; head of the tax authorities in the General Government, Dec. 1939–1941; subsequently worked again in the Reich; extradited to Poland after the war; died in prison.
4 The part of Poland annexed by the Soviet Union.

The same operation against the Jews as in Kreis Tarnobrzeg was carried out in Kreis Nisko in the towns of Nisko and Rudnik in September 1939. The tax arrears amount to 132,017.63 zloty. The Landkommissar has not yet been able to tell me how much the confiscation raised.

I have issued the same directives in Nisko as in Tarnobrzeg. A trustee has been appointed for the Jewish properties.

In Tarnobrzeg and Nisko, I asked the Landkommissar for each region to incorporate the sums collected into the itemized lists of arrears drawn up by the tax offices as soon as possible so that the matter can be dealt with.

I will notify you when the liquidation of the items has been concluded.[5]

DOC. 114

In spring 1940 the Jewish Council in Lublin reports on living conditions and on the provision of health and welfare services for the Jewish population[1]

Report on the activities of the Jewish welfare and health institutions in the city of Lublin, unsigned, circa April 1940 (copy)

(1) *Living conditions for the Jewish population*

As a city with poorly developed industry, located in the middle of a voivodeship with an agrarian character, Lublin has long been a place marked by poverty. The constant influx of the landless element from the villages further exacerbated the situation for the residents of Lublin. The majority of the Jewish population were employed in artisan trades, home production of goods, and small-scale trading. There were very few large merchants or industrialists. The aid work undertaken for the poor and unemployed Jewish population of Lublin was run by both the municipal and the Jewish aid committees, which were supported both by people in Lublin and by Jews abroad.

At present, however, in parallel with the increase in deprivation among the Jews (numerous refugees have come from many different places to Lublin), the opportunities to provide aid have shrunk to a minimum. Foreign sources have dried up completely, Jewish trade and craft production have come to a standstill, and Jewish society is so impoverished that it cannot now provide any effective material aid to the poverty-stricken Jewish masses. This state of affairs has meant that, despite the ongoing stabilization of conditions, the living conditions for the Jewish population have been growing steadily worse.

(2) *Housing conditions for the Jewish population*

The housing conditions in Lublin, just as in Poland's other cities, left much to be desired. As in other places, the Jewish population lived in worse conditions than other parts of

5 On 3 May 1940 the finance inspector in Mielec informed the Finance Department that it was not possible to determine whether the persons registered on the confiscation lists were identical with the persons included in the lists of tax arrears. In view of this, the finance inspector recommended 'writing off in full the arrears of the Jews who have not left any properties behind, and as far as other arrears are concerned, using the available properties' to settle these debts. The Finance Department agreed to this course of action: AAN, 111/1020/3, fols. 442–443.

1 APL, 498/891, fols. 36–41. This document has been translated from German.

society. At the same time as the Polish population was moving into newer and more healthily situated parts of the city, the Jewish population remained within the boundaries of the ghetto. The Jewish quarter has suffered substantially as a consequence of wartime military operations

The streets inhabited exclusively by Jews – Szambelańska, Bramowa, Juzuicka,[2] Olejna, the Market Square, and Nowa – have been almost completely destroyed. Parts of Lubartowska, the main street in the Jewish quarter, have also suffered.

The Jews have been removed from many streets in the city. They have been forced to look for places to live in the Jewish quarter, overcrowded as it already is. If one also takes into consideration the fact that several thousand refugees have arrived in Lublin, one can easily imagine the extent to which housing conditions have worsened for Lublin's Jews. Hundreds of families are living in the synagogues and prayer houses. In many private houses there are several families, or even up to ten or 15 families living together.

(3) *Jewish welfare facilities, their functional capacity, and their use by the population*
The following Jewish welfare institutions exist in Lublin:

(1) The Jewish Aid Committee
(2) The Refugee Committee
(3) Children's Welfare (Jewish Central Association for the Care of Orphans, CENTOS)
(4) The orphanage and the home for the elderly.

Institutions (1) and (2) were created to replace the many pre-war institutions that had been wound up. The institutions listed under (3) and (4) have continued their pre-war activities.

I. The Jewish Aid Committee was set up at the beginning of February last year. It raises its funds from voluntary monthly contributions paid by Lublin's Jews. Since its inception up until the fifth of this month, the Committee has collected approx. 15,000 złoty in cash and 1,007 items of clothing.

With the cash collected, food products have been purchased and distributed to the poorest section of the population. Over the course of six weeks, the following goods have been distributed: 10,560 kg of bread, 1,400 kg of flour, 2,454 kg of pearl barley, 126 kg of soap, 60 kg of oil, and 27 kg of olive oil. In addition, 931 items of clothing have been handed out, mostly to former prisoners of war. –

Two thousand three hundred families (approx. 8,400 persons) have applied to the Committee for the allocation of food, and food products have been distributed to 1,700 families (approx. 6,800 persons).

The Aid Committee could extend its activities far more broadly, but this is prevented by lack of funds. It should also be noted that the lowest monthly contribution to the Committee is barely 20 groszy.

II. The Refugee Aid Committee was set up in December 1939. The Committee has been mainly concerned with securing housing for the rapid influx of refugees. It has tried to put up the refugees in private houses. The Committee has succeeded in finding lodgings for approx. 5,000 persons in private homes. Forty-three

2 Correctly: Jezuicka, one of the streets in the western part of Lublin's Old Town.

assembly points have been organized for the purposes of housing the remaining refugees. One thousand four hundred persons have been housed at these assembly points, which the Committee has equipped with the most basic items, such as beds, bedding, etc.

As of 1 April this year, the Committee had distributed 60,087 kg of bread, 255,732 midday meals, and several hundred items of clothing, underwear, and footwear.

The number of midday meals served daily by the Committee's three kitchens recently reached 3,400.

A public health brigade consisting of 32 men and women has been set up for the purpose of overseeing the cleanliness of the refugees and the premises they inhabit. As of 1 April this year, medical assistance had been given in 1,161 cases. In 533 cases, the City Welfare Office provided medical assistance at the Committee's request. At the Committee's expense 2,259 persons visited bathhouses.

In exceptional cases, the Committee also awards monetary support payments. The assistance in the form of clothes distribution and for personal cleanliness provided by the Committee is inadequate. The shortage of items of clothing and soap, which are not to be had, even for money, impedes an expansion of this assistance. There are similar difficulties when it comes to procuring the necessary quantities of food, primarily meat, which makes the food provision operation more difficult.

III. Children's Welfare (CENTOS) is continuing its work providing food to Jewish children, which it was already doing before the outbreak of the war. At present, Children's Welfare maintains three kitchens and feeds 1,362 children aged from 5 to 13. The children receive two meals a day, a midday meal and a breakfast or supper. Four hundred and eighty registered children cannot be provided with food due to the shortage of funds and lack of appropriate premises. The children are under medical supervision. In addition, there are units in operation known as mobile health commissions, which carry out checks on the children's health and hygiene.

Children's Welfare owes its existence to support payments from the CENTOS central office. More than 27,000 złoty has been spent on the operation to feed children since January last year.

IV. The orphanage and the home for the elderly have been in existence for more than 50 years. At present, there are 66 children (36 girls and 30 boys) in the orphanage. There are eight elderly women and three elderly men in the home for the elderly.

Before the war broke out, the orphanage was maintained by the municipal administration and the Jewish Religious Community. Since the outbreak of the war, it has been maintained solely through support from Jewish circles.

The children in the orphanage receive food three times a day and are under medical supervision.

(4) *Jewish health institutions in Lublin*

The Jewish Hospital in Lublin has one hundred beds for patients and is intended for the general population. The following departments are currently in operation: internal and neurological, surgical, gynaecological and women's conditions, and a department for paediatrics.

The hospital accepts all conditions for treatment, with the exception of infectious diseases and mental illnesses.

The hospital has an X-ray and electrotherapy clinic, a pharmacy, a chemical laboratory, and a library of medical texts and editions.

The hospital's income is made up of the charges and fees paid either by patients themselves or by the offices and institutions at whose expense they are treated, subsidies from the Religious Community and other institutions, and donations from various corporations and private individuals.

The patients treated at the hospital are residents of Lublin and also of the city's immediate and wider environs, as well as elderly patients who have been expelled from the German Reich (Stettin etc.).[3]

The hospital's capacity does not exceed 100 patients. It has been overcrowded for the last few months, with patient numbers reaching 150–200. If one takes into consideration the fact that the Jewish Hospital is the only institution of its kind serving a wide area, and furthermore that Jews are allowed to use only this hospital, it is evident that there is a need to increase the hospital's capacity to at least 150 beds. This could be done all the more easily as the building is large enough to comfortably house this number.

Irrespective of this, additional barracks for patients need to be constructed in the hospital grounds.

The completion of the administrative building, the roof of which is already in place, is also urgently necessary, particularly since this will ease the pressure on the actual hospital building and increase its capacity.

Further shortages that could be eliminated if the necessary funds were available are:

(1) the shortage of beds, mattresses, and bedding;
(2) the shortage of adequate hospital garments;
(3) the shortage of dressings and bandages; and finally
(4) the catering difficulties caused by the prevailing food supply situation.

The Health Centre (Society for the Protection of the Health of the Jewish Population in Poland, TOZ) currently consists of the following departments:

(1) a section for public health information,
(2) an outpatient clinic,
(3) a dental clinic for adults and children,
(4) a unit offering maternity advice,
(5) a department for the preparation and distribution of milk for babies,
(6) an electrotherapy room,
(7) an anti-tuberculosis outpatient clinic.

In addition, until the outbreak of the war, the Health Centre ran a psycho-technical advice point, a summer camp and play scheme for children, and a programme providing food for children in schools, which is suspended at present due to the closure of the schools. The children are only being provided with cod liver oil.

The outpatient clinic receives around 150 patients a day, advises them, and dispenses medicines to them. It also carries out tests, X-rays, and vaccinations.

3 See Docs. 82 and 104.

A physician specially appointed for the purpose undertakes between 20 and 25 home visits a day.

The outpatient clinic's surgical department receives and treats 40 to 50 patients a day. It performs surgery that does not require hospital stays.

The assistance provided by the Health Centre is free of charge, and its budget is funded solely and exclusively by the Jewish Council.

(5) *The number of expellees, their housing, and employment*
The registration of refugees revealed a total number of 5,583 currently in Lublin. However, we can assume that the number is substantially greater, firstly because not all the refugees were registered, and secondly because no supplementary registration has been carried out since the conclusion of the first registration.

As mentioned above, the expellees have been put up in private homes. Many expellees stayed in Lublin only temporarily, on their way to the towns and villages in the vicinity. More precise data about their subsequent circumstances are not available.

The survey carried out among the refugees found that 65 per cent of them are craftsmen, the rest small-scale traders and persons with no specific occupation.

(6) *Enlistment and deployment of Jews for forced labour*
Jews were enlisted for forced labour almost immediately after the German army arrived in Lublin.

However, this work was not organized, and its performance caused serious disruption to the everyday lives of the Jews. Since the beginning of December 1939, the forced labour Jews perform has become regularized. All Jewish men aged from 16 to 60, approx. 12,000 persons, are enlisted for forced labour, which takes up to one to two days per week. The Jews enlisted for this work are called up and checked by the Jewish Council.

DOC. 115

On 3 May 1940 the Governor of District Cracow reports on Jewish refugees seeking to return to the General Government from the Soviet-occupied part of Poland[1]

Minutes of the meeting of the Governor of District Cracow, Wächter, with Governor General Frank and Reich Labour Service official Hinkel,[2] Cracow, dated 3 May 1940

[...][3]
Governor *Wächter* reported to the Governor General on his impressions of conditions in Lemberg, which he had gained on an official visit there, and described the *situation*

1 AIPN, GK 95, vol. 4. Copy in IfZ-Archives, Fb 105, vol. 5, fols. 1023–1024. Published in Präg and Jacobmeyer (eds.), *Diensttagebuch des deutschen Generalgouverneurs*, pp. 191–192. This document has been translated from German.

2 Heinrich Hinkel (1892–1950), businessman; joined the NSDAP in 1932; worked in the Reich Labour Service from 1933; posted to the General Government as the liaison officer for Reich Labour Service Leader Konstantin Hierl to organize the paramilitary Polish Construction Service (Baudienst) in April 1940; promoted to a sequence of ranks within the Reich Labour Service; extradited to Poland in 1945; died in prison there.

of the refugees seeking to enter the General Government from Russia: Thousands of people are thronging to cross the Soviet border at Brest-Litovsk and Przemyśl. Of approximately 18,000 refugees, 16,500 are Jews who are also waiting to be allowed into the General Government.[4] There have been some heart-rending scenes. In Lemberg, the Russians arrested all the owners of residential buildings, declared the residential buildings to be state property, and appointed trustees, mostly Jews, each of whom has to administer a block of buildings. In the last few days all the lawyers were arrested.

The *Governor General* asked Governor Wächter to submit a detailed report on this official visit to him.[5]

Governor *Wächter* then also reported on the parade of Soviet troops which was held on 1 May. What was interesting about this was that no modern weaponry had been on display. Overall, he was not particularly impressed by the parade. In front of each individual block of 80 men marched its commander, to his right a Soviet commissar. Incidentally, this Soviet commissar has the right to veto the orders given by commanding officers down to the company-commander level.

The *Governor General* summarized the results of the discussion as follows:

1. the General Government is expected to take in yet more Jews;
2. the Soviet government is evidently unwilling to release the ethnic Germans from Russia; the Reich Foreign Office must embark on negotiations with the government in Moscow on this matter;
3. Moscow apparently does not want to allow the German Commission in Lemberg to begin its work, but it is absolutely vital that the German side does not accept this. To date, 60,000 refugees have gathered in Lemberg. Under no circumstances can more be taken in; nonetheless the work there must continue.

[…][6]

3 Frank, Hinkel, and Wächter also discussed the functions and organization of the Polish Construction Service. Frank expressed his high regard for the Ukrainian minority in the General Government.

4 The Soviet authorities deported most Jewish refugees to the interior of the country in June 1940; only approximately 1,600 Jews were resettled in the General Government.

5 This could not be found, but see Doc. 118.

6 Discussion continued on the following topics: the activity of the Trustee Office, the collection of metals, ore mining and oil production, and the opening of an SS wholesale business in Warsaw for furs.

DOC. 116

On 8 May 1940 the official in charge of Jewish affairs for the SS and Police Leader in Lublin sets out guidelines for the deployment of Jewish forced labourers[1]

Letter from the official in charge of Jewish affairs for the SS and Police Leader in District Lublin, signature illegible,[2] to the Governor of District Lublin, Labour Department[3] (received on 9 May 1940), dated 8 May 1940[4]

Re: deployment of Jewish forced labourers
Enclosures: 1
This enclosure provides notification of directives that must be complied with when Jewish forced labourers are deployed.

Notification is provided of the following directives for the deployment of Jewish forced labourers:

I) *Supply of Jewish forced labourers*
Jewish forced labourers shall be made available to carry out public works projects and tasks undertaken for members of German agencies in District Lublin.

II) *Supervision of forced labourers*
Jewish forced labourers must be supervised during their work. They must be supervised in accordance with the following principles:

a) Except in the case of small work groups and tasks supervised by the employer himself (e.g. gardening work at an official residence supervised by the employer's own gardener, the cleaning of a residence, etc.), a Ukrainian overseer shall be provided who will be in charge of a work group of ten to twenty men. This overseer will be responsible for ensuring that the work is actually done. If a particular agency wishes to provide its own appropriately trained foreman instead, there is no need to appoint a Ukrainian.
b) Should several such work groups be deployed, their overall supervision will be undertaken by a dedicated supervision detail, which will be provided by the Selbstschutz.
c) The employer will be responsible for the remuneration, feeding, and accommodation – insofar as this is required – of the Ukrainian overseers.

III) *Submission of requests for forced labourers*
The following guidelines shall apply for the submission of requests for Jewish forced labourers:

A) Requests for large numbers for major work projects, where labourers cannot be drawn from the local Jewish population or who have to be housed in camps, must be addressed exclusively to the SS and Police Leader.

   The request must be submitted in good time. Depending on its type and scale, this should be done one to four weeks in advance.

1 APL, 498/745, fols. 20–22. This document has been translated from German.
2 The official in charge of Jewish affairs for the SS and Police Leader in Lublin was Dr Karl Hofbauer.
3 The Labour Department in District Lublin was headed by Oberregierungsrat Jache.
4 The original features an official stamp, Jache's and Hecht's initials, and handwritten notes. Hecht was employed in the labour administration in Lublin.

B)

1) Requests for forced labourers for smaller-scale work projects, where no housing in camps is needed and demand can be met locally, are to be sent to the following addresses:

For the city of Lublin
Kreis Lublin: to the SS and Selbstschutz Leader, attn. SS-Sturmbannführer *Dolp*,[5] Lipowa, tel. 31–61.

For Kreis

Janow Lubelski:	to the gendarmerie platoon in Janow Lubelski	
Pulawy:	to the gendarmerie platoon in Pulawy	
Radzyn:	to the Security Police branch in Lukow	
Biala Podlaska:	»	in Biala
Chelm:	»	in Chelm
Wlodawa:	»	in Wlodawa
Hrubieszow:	»	in Hrubieszow
Zamosz:	»	in Zamosz
Tomaszow:	»	in Tomaszow
Biłgoraj:	»	in Biłgoraj

2) Requests must be submitted by 12 on the previous day at the latest.
3) The employer must have the Jews picked up in good time by the guard detail or the foremen (see II). The Security Police office shall give notification of the place and time once the request is submitted.

IV) *Housing and feeding forced labourers*

1) Housing
   a) If large numbers of Jewish forced labourers are deployed at a single workplace, they should be housed in labour camps. The Selbstschutz is to arrange camp housing for them.
   b) Should forced labourers be drawn from the local Jewish population, dedicated housing will not be provided.
2) The Jewish Council in charge must ensure the Jewish forced labourers are provided with food at its own expense. The employers may provide additional food at their own expense.

V) *Procurement of tools and equipment*

Should the employer not be in a position to provide the necessary tools and equipment for forced labourers, the Jewish Council has to ensure their procurement.

Should it nevertheless not be possible to procure tools and equipment in sufficient quantities, they must be requested from the SS and Police Leader.

5 Hermann Dolp (b. 1889), mechanic; member of a Freikorps from 1920; joined the NSDAP and the SS in 1928; worked at Dachau concentration camp in 1934 and Sachsenhausen concentration camp in 1939; appointed head of the State Police in Kalisz in autumn 1939; removed from his post and demoted in Dec. 1939; became SS and Selbstschutz Leader in Lublin in 1940; additionally head of the camp on Lipowa Street, then head of Belzec labour camp for Jews; attached to the Higher SS and Police Leader East in May 1942, then the Higher SS and Police Leader North in Norway; served with a Latvian SS volunteer division in 1944.

DOC. 117

On 8 May 1940 an activist in the Jewish youth movement reports on the activities of the Hehalutz organization[1]

Report by Mordechai Orenstein[2] for the World Centre of Hehalutz, Geneva Office, 125 Rue de Lausanne, Geneva, dated 8 May 1940

Report on Halutz work in the German-occupied territories of Poland (based on a conversation with Ch. *Henig*,[3] secretary of the Poale Zion-Hitachduth,[4] World Union, in Poland over the last few months)
In Trieste on 26 April, I talked to Ch. *Henig*, who left Warsaw a week ago. From our conversation, which lasted several hours, the following picture of the situation in the German-occupied territories of Poland emerged.

Existence of the Halutz movement
The Halutz movement and most Halutz youth organizations exist and are working in a manner that is neither legal nor illegal. The official agencies seem to be informed of their existence and work. This work is unofficially tolerated. The work of Hehalutz, Hashomer Hatzair, and Hehalutz Hatzair-Freiheit[5] makes itself particularly felt. The Gordonia and the generally Zionist and religious youth associations are less prominent.

Organization
Local groups of Hehalutz and the above-mentioned youth organizations exist. Many of them are working well and systematically. The organizational foundations for their work have been transformed from the ground up. The practical preparation for official illegality has already been completed in that the organization is already based on cells of five people today. Merkazim[6] also exist unofficially for Hehalutz and the youth organizations. Three people work in the Merkaz Hehalutz: Frunka,[7] Civja,[8] and Zuckermann.[9] They correspond with the local groups; circulars are sent out. The local groups are also

1 YVA, M-20/86, fols. 114, 116–117. This document has been translated from German. Hehalutz is Hebrew for 'The Pioneer'.
2 Mordechai Orenstein, who later called himself Oren (1905–1981), journalist; activist in the Hashomer Hatzair (Young Guard) youth movement in Germany, then in Switzerland; emigrated to Israel, where he was a Mapam (United Workers' Party) official; in 1952 represented Mapam in Prague, where he was arrested on account of his Zionist activities and detained until 1956.
3 Chaim Henig, member of the Central Committee of the Poale Zion-Hitachduth party before the war; attended the 21st Zionist Congress in Geneva in August 1939, then returned to Poland; left Warsaw in April 1940 and went to Palestine.
4 The reformist wing of the Zionist-Marxist workers' party Poale Zion (Workers of Zion) joined the democratically oriented Second Socialist International; merged with the Zionist Socialists in 1925 to form the Jewish Socialist Workers' Party Poale Zion, and with Hitachduth (Association) in 1933.
5 This was the Dror/Frayheyt (Freedom) youth movement.
6 Hebrew in the original: central bodies that coordinated the local groups' activities (singular: 'merkaz').
7 Correctly: Frumka Płotnicka (1914–1943), Zionist activist; joined the Dror/Frayheyt youth movement in 1931; fled east from Warsaw in Sept. 1939; returned in mid Oct.; later liaised between the Hehalutz groups in the General Government; in Vilna in Jan. 1942, then Białystok, again in Warsaw, and from Dec. 1942 in Będzin; murdered there on 1 August 1943 during the last deportation.

visited by members of the central body. The local groups also hold internal meetings, which are attended by all the groups of five. In response to my question about whether efforts by Jewish institutions generally for the complete legalization of Halutz work have any prospect of success, Henig answered that he believes there would be prospects for success if a general Jewish representative body were to form and tackle this matter, as well as other issues. At a discussion between an improvised Jewish representative body and German agencies in Cracow, one of the German representatives reportedly commented that the German administration was interested in preparing the Jewish population for emigration. However, considering that the leaders among the higher classes of Polish Jews have left Poland, the prospects of an authoritative representative body for Polish Jewry emerging in the near future are poor.

Zionist and Jewish life

Almost all the bourgeois Zionist groups are in a depleted state. The departure of the leaders is taking its toll in a very tangible fashion. There is a certain coordinating framework for [the] joint work done by the Zionist associations. Most active among the Zionist groups is the Poale Zion-Hitachduth, World Union, but what has remained of Zionism, possessing the constructive dynamism and strength to continue the work and give it new momentum, is the Halutz movement, and particularly the youth organizations that support it. They are writing a new page of heroism and self-sacrifice in the history of Zionism and the Jewish people. Nothing is left of the 'Bund'.[10] The interests of the Jewish population in their dealings with the occupation administration are mainly represented by the religious communities. 'Hias'[11] has resumed its work again. The Palestine Office has reconstituted itself under the auspices of Hias. The Joint [JDC] plays an important role in the promotion of Jewish interests.

Jews and Poles

No change of any kind has taken place in the attitude of significant sections of the Polish population towards the Jews. There is still antisemitism. At Passover there was an outright anti-Jewish pogrom in Warsaw, which went on for eight days. Jews were killed, many dozens injured, hundreds were beaten. Not a single Pole (not even members of

8 Correctly: Cywia (Zivia) Lubetkin (1914–1976), Zionist activist; member of the executive committee of Dror/Frayheyt from 1938; initially in the Soviet-occupied part of Poland, then in the General Government in 1939; co-founder of the Jewish Combat Organization (ŻOB) and member of the Jewish National Committee (ŻKN) in 1942; participated in the Warsaw Ghetto Uprising in 1943; worked for Bricha (Escape), 1945–1946; lived in Palestine from 1946; co-founder of the Ghetto Fighters' House Museum (Beit Lohamei Hagetaot).

9 Correctly: Icchak Cukierman, also Yitzhak Zuckerman and Yitskhok Tsukerman (1915–1981); lived in the Soviet-occupied part of Poland, 1939–1940; leader of the Dror/Frayheyt youth movement in Warsaw from spring 1940; deputy leader of the ŻOB as well as intermediary between the ŻOB, the Home Army, and the communist People's Guard in 1942; involved in the rescue of survivors of the Warsaw Ghetto Uprising in 1943 on the 'Aryan side'; worked for Bricha in 1945; co-founder of the Ghetto Fighters' House Museum in Israel; married to Cywia Lubetkin.

10 Algemeyner Yidisher Arbeter Bund (General Jewish Labour Bund).

11 The Hebrew Sheltering and Immigrant Aid Society of America (HIAS) supported the emigration of Jews to the USA and Palestine.

the PPS)[12] openly raised his voice against the pogrom. The number of Jews who have died, been murdered, disappeared, or gone missing during the war and during the occupation (up to mid April) in Poland is estimated at 250,000. When I mentioned the figure of 80,000 as the estimate predominantly accepted abroad, Henig laughed bitterly. Thousands of families have been destroyed.

Hundreds of families have been split up between three territories: fathers are in Russian Poland, mothers in German Poland, children in Vilna, or vice versa. The majority of the Jews are starving and freezing (in winter).

The need for financial support

It will not be possible for Halutz work to continue without significant financial support from abroad. Polish Jewry is utterly impoverished. Ninety per cent of the Jews are eking out an existence thanks to public and philanthropic funding. The financial assistance from the Joint [JDC] is insufficient. If the Halutz movement and the Halutz youth organizations are to be up to their tasks, they will require two things: cultural and informational materials (World Centre of Hehalutz and world leaderships of the youth organizations), and systematic support from the Jewish National Fund aid institutions[13] and other financial schemes to support Polish Jewry. What is necessary is an immediate, one-off support payment of 1,000 dollars, in addition to which a monthly grant of 250 dollars and funding of the coming emigration will have to be secured. The Halutz Zionism that is defying the conditions in that severely tested part of Poland expects the most extensive and most rapid help from the Jewish people and the Zionist movement in order to ensure the survival of Zionism in western Poland.

DOC. 118

On 10 May 1940 a German resettlement commission describes its impressions of the situation and attitudes of the Jews in the Soviet-annexed part of Poland[1]

Report, unsigned, from a German resettlement commission, dated 10 May 1940[2]

The attitude of the *Jews*

Mention has already been made before on several occasions of the pronounced hostility shown towards the German resettlement commando by the Jewish population in the area from which resettlement was taking place.[3] The Jews' generally anti-German attitude was so strong that in the first weeks of our work in the resettlement area, it was

12 Polish Socialist Party (PPS).

13 The Jewish National Fund was set up in 1901 following an initiative from Theodor Herzl. Its main goal before the foundation of Israel was to buy, develop, and manage land in Ottoman and later in Mandate Palestine.

1 BArch, R 59/321 fols. 19–23. This document has been translated from German.

2 It is evident from the context in the file that this report was probably sent to the German main plenipotentiary of the commission's Department I in Łuck.

3 On the basis of the German–Soviet Border and Friendship Treaty of 28 Sept. 1939, the commission had made preparations for resettling the Germans living in western Volhynia, who arrived in the Warthegau in 1940 and were settled on Polish farms or housed in camps there.

simply impossible for individual members of the commando to make even the smallest trips in the towns and larger settlements without escorts to protect them. This was all the more the case because their uniforms made them easily identifiable. However, the eastern Polish Jews' hatred equally extended to the ethnic Germans who have now been resettled.

As has already been mentioned several times, the anti-German Jewish elements in the village and town soviets have caused the greatest difficulties for the resettlement work day in, day out. They have frequently been guilty of the most outrageous attacks on ethnic Germans. These attacks were stopped as soon as possible by the Soviet government representatives in response to German protests and, insofar as this was at all possible, restitution was made. However, it was not possible to ensure that no new attacks would be committed in the future.

The Jews in the resettlement area are the only section of the population that has welcomed the Bolshevik shake-up and derived benefits from it. If we consider that the mass of the eastern Polish Jews lived in greatest poverty and under the most primitive conditions, it is not surprising from a social standpoint that they have benefited from the devaluation of everything valuable, from the general expropriation at the expense of the whole population, without having done anything in exchange. As a result, the Jews are the only people who have voluntarily offered to assist the new Soviet system. They have become the administrators of state shops, state guest houses, etc. everywhere. They have been given posts as acting officials in all the businesses and all the administrative bodies. To a great extent, the city, town, and village soviets are recruited from their number, and above all the militia, the NKVD's[4] spies – in short, they can be found in droves wherever Soviet Bolshevism needs agents, spies, and informers to establish and maintain its rule.

Wherever we went in the towns, we ended up with the impression that we were not in a Russian but a Jewish country.

If we look at this generally anti-German, hate-filled attitude of the Jews and at how they are also the mainstays of the Bolshevik system, it is difficult to imagine that there will be any permanence to the German–Soviet reconciliation efforts.

Even if Jews are the sole beneficiaries of the new communist system, by no means all the Jews are satisfied with the shake-up. The prosperous Jews have been affected by the general expropriation just as much as everyone else who lives there. Of course, there is now no longer any freedom of commerce for the Jews either. There have been instances of individual Jews from the resettlement area making offers to the German resettlement commando to donate all of their foreign assets to the Reich unremunerated, in exchange for the opportunity to be resettled along with the ethnic Germans. The number of Jews in the overcrowded towns is in fact quite considerable, particularly as a great many refugees from the General Government have settled on Soviet territory. Only some of them have been able to find jobs in the new Soviet state apparatus or otherwise to derive any benefits from the new regime. There have been repeated incidents in which individual Jews approached members of the German resettlement commando in the streets of

4 People's Commissariat for Internal Affairs (NKVD): Soviet secret police.

Lutsk, saying they were Jews but wanted to ask whether it might not also be possible for them to make it over into German territory.

As mentioned before, an openly hostile attitude towards Germans could be found among the majority of these eastern Polish Jews. This was demonstrated by shouts of 'Nazi murderers', 'Damned Germans', and the like aimed at the members of the German resettlement commando from every street corner. It was only thanks to the strictest discipline enforced by the Einsatzkommando that serious incidents could be avoided and physical violence did not occur. However, it is characteristic of the Soviet government representatives, a large proportion of whom are themselves Jews, that they, in their capacity as special agents of the Commissariat for Internal Affairs, made clear efforts to ensure that we were protected without fail, threatening very energetic measures in order to curb this openly hostile attitude, and probably also carrying them out now and then as cautionary examples.

The NKVD's intervention was clearly noticeable. The insults soon became somewhat less frequent and then stopped altogether, even if the hostile attitude naturally remained. Later the Jews took to sending Jewish children into the fray to carry on the abuse. Despite this, however, there would be the odd Jew who found it impossible to refrain from approaching the members of the German commando on the street and shouting at them – quite unnecessarily – 'I am a Jew.' They evidently wanted to provoke us in this way. Jews were even detailed to guard our headquarters building in their capacity as civilian militiamen, with a red armband on their clothing. One of these Jewish militiamen took childish delight in the fact that he, a Jew, was being allowed to guard the German headquarters, and asked again and again what people would say about this in the Reich.

The Jews in the new Soviet territory still have their own newspapers in the Jewish language with Hebrew letters. Today, however, these newspapers are nothing more than imitations that mimic the official Soviet press exactly. They show hardly any Jewish touches. Important official Soviet government announcements are also displayed in the cities on posters in Jewish script, alongside Ukrainian and Polish.

Quite in contrast to the hate-filled, anti-German attitude of the eastern Polish Jews, the government representatives at the district and local headquarters, who were mostly Jews, proved to be thoroughly businesslike as our opposite numbers during the resettlement operation. All the entries made on the resettlement lists, the inventories, and above all the signing of every list of assets, as well as all the other measures concerning the transports of the people who were resettling, etc., all that could only be dealt with in the closest consultation and cooperation with the Soviet government's representatives, that is to say, with Jews in their capacity as senior officials of Soviet state authorities.

To make this point absolutely clear once again: there was a spiteful Jewish representative of a local soviet who was guilty of outrageous attacks on German colonists, e.g. driving them out of their houses to the nearest railway station without clothing and food, and telling them to scarper off to the Reich. As a result of the protest lodged by the German plenipotentiary, the Soviet government representative responsible for the resettlement ordered that such actions, which pose a grave threat to the resettlement operation, must immediately cease. An authorized Jewish government representative intervenes against the Jew from the local soviet, sees that restitution is made for the attacks as far as possible, and threatens his fellow Jew with the severest punishments if he takes it into his head to endanger the requisite good cooperation between the Germans and the Soviets in such a fashion ever again.

It has been possible to ascertain that the Jews from the local soviets who were responsible for such attacks have in fact been held accountable. It is therefore clear that the eastern Polish Jews and the Soviet officials from the Soviet Union can by no means be equated in terms of their conduct.

All too troublesome Jews from the overcrowded towns have been forcibly evacuated in large numbers to the interior of the Soviet Union for labour deployment by the Soviet authorities of the Commissariat for Internal Affairs. A large proportion of them have supposedly been deported to the coalmining areas.[5] The eastern Polish Jews do not receive any direct support or preferential treatment from the Soviet authorities in charge in the newly occupied territory. Although indirect preferential treatment can often be found in practice, this is explained by the Jews' attitude as particularly compliant and reliable Soviet citizens. Otherwise, however, anything that could push the Jewish question to the fore in public has been avoided by the Soviet authorities wherever possible.

Most of the Soviet government representatives in the evacuation system were Jews. But it was not merely in this body that Jews were to be found holding the majority of the leading posts; they are also everywhere in the Red Army as political commissars, as well as in the Commissariat for Internal Affairs as key officials in the Party and state apparatus.

The difference between the attitudes of the Jews from the interior of the Soviet Union and the Jews from the former eastern Polish territories is entirely explicable, because Soviet Bolshevism refuses to acknowledge the concept of a Jewish race at all. The Soviet government representatives no doubt felt themselves to be the most zealous representatives of Soviet Bolshevism and acted accordingly, but they did not particularly emphasize their Jewish racial characteristics. On the contrary, as equal citizens of the Soviet Union, they were now very proud to be the most loyal servants of a great state system. Now and then one of the non-Jewish government representatives may have expressed his displeasure with his Jewish comrades to us Germans, but I do not believe this was more than a careless turn of phrase that was merely dropped in to excuse an error of judgement and to emphasize that the cooperation between the German and Soviet agencies was particularly good. If we bear in mind that several particularly ugly, crippled Jewish women were regularly attached to the German delegation members (who held the rank of German diplomats) as protection, i.e. to observe and escort them on the many long-distance road journeys within the resettlement area, then it is hard to believe that the Soviet government representatives, given their unquestioned determination to maintain a good understanding with us, have even the slightest idea of racial differences. At any rate, the attitude of the Soviet officials and old Party people from the Soviet Union is that they are all citizens of the great 'Soviet family of nations', which refuses to acknowledge other racial and ethnic differences as well. Evidently the feeling of being first and foremost Soviet citizens has genuinely been strongly instilled in people's minds by Marxist propaganda during Bolshevism's twenty-year rule in the old territory of the Soviet Union, even among the Soviet Union's primitive nations.

5 A reference to the eastern Ukrainian Donets Basin (Donbass or Donbas).

The racially and ethnically conscious attitude of the population of the new Soviet sphere forms a stark contrast to this. For one thing, there is a pronounced feeling of race and belonging among the Jews themselves, and consequently pronounced, natural antisemitic sentiments can be found among the Ukrainians and Byelorussians. Bolshevism now has to get to grips with these new facts. It is apparent that these questions are indeed causing it a few concerns, as evidenced by a Soviet film which was shown in the cinemas during the period of resettlement. It has the following plot: a work-shy Jewish clan living off speculation is educated by the achievements of Bolshevik rule in the Soviet state and motivated to join in the task of building the workers' fatherland.

DOC. 119

On 10 May 1940 Lucjan Orenbach describes developments in Tomaszów Mazowiecki and his impressions from a trip to Warsaw[1]

Handwritten letter from Lucjan (Lutek) Orenbach[2] from Tomaszów Mazowiecki to his girlfriend, Edith Blau, in Minden, Westphalia, dated 10 May 1940

23.[3]
My beloved Edith,

I arrived from Warsaw the day before yesterday (Wednesday). We got a telegram from Mother that we must come immediately: in Tomaszów – ghetto[4] 'kaput'. You understand, what anxiety. We had to stay in Warsaw for another day because the bus was full. What should I write you here? Tragedy. Meanwhile we're still in the apartment, but soon we'll have to 'fort'[5] to a different street. Meanwhile, everything's in a terrible mess, pêle-mêle,[6] no one knows anything exactly. I can walk on every street because I have a 'bescheinigung'[7] (as a 'beamter'[8] of the Kultus-Gemeinde[9] here). All in all, everything's gone to hell. I don't care about anything any more. Until now I was in Tomaszów and had no idea about the wide world. Until Warsaw … Oh, Warsaw! How can I describe it? Sadness, sadness, sadness. When I saw the former capitale polonaise[10] I wanted to cry. I immediately had dark thoughts that it's not worth building or creating anything, that everything dissolves into air,[11] that everything is 'fumé'[12] and

1 USHMM, RG 10 250*06, TM 023. This document has been translated from Polish.
2 Lucjan (Lutek) Orenbach (1921–1942 or 1943); from 1939 in Tomaszów Mazowiecki; the circumstances of his death are unknown. Most Jews from Tomaszów were deported to Treblinka in Oct. 1942, while several hundred were sent to a labour camp in Bliżyn.
3 Orenbach numbered his letters to Edith.
4 The word is blacked out – possibly by the censor – but still legible.
5 German: 'away'.
6 French: 'higgledy-piggledy'.
7 German in the original. Correctly: 'Bescheinigung', certificate, attestation.
8 German in the original. Correctly: 'Beamter', civil servant, public official.
9 German in the original: 'Religious Community'.
10 French: 'Polish capital'.
11 Polish in the original: 'do luftu', playing on German 'Luft', air.
12 French. Correctly: 'fumée', smoke, in the sense of an illusion.

that one should not only live as well as possible, but not think about what will happen. That it's not worth being an artist, no, no, no … Mickiewicz[13] stands forlorn and seems to be crying … the Grand Theatre … Bogusławski,[14] the creator of Polish culture, just stands … And above all this, a beautiful blue sky and some kind of harsh, cold God, a godless God. To hell with it! … Sometimes I truly am Mephistopheles. Is this Warsaw, or only: Warsaw?[15]

Ruth[16] was happy. I had not even had time to say much when that damned telegram … Ruth told me a few things. She gets letters from Lol, Nusia, Bronka …[17] I'd like to write, but now there's this mess. Your letter came yesterday, it was wonderful! But more about that later. Right now I'll say a little more about Warsaw. One meets acquaintances at every turn. Everyone is pleased. But everyone has suffered some tragedy. What can one say. In Warsaw I lost the rest of my optimism.

We also visited Mrs Klara Segałowicz.[18] I must tell you a little about her. An interesting person. She's an old friend of my father's. When Father still performed on stage and directed, she was a little girl and even then displayed enormous artistic capabilities. She acted together with Father and my mother. Then Father stopped, and she joined the theatre in Warsaw. She must have had ten husbands. Now she's rich. Her husband is the director of the Joint [JDC], Mr Neustadt.[19] They have a villa and a car and everything – if only I were like that. Mrs Klara is slightly hysterical, a little mad like all artists, lives like a Hollywood star and … and we went there. Of course she was pleased and said she'll do anything she can for us. That's very nice of her but … that house gets on my damn nerves. The housekeeper – a Russian – rules the whole house. Her ladyship lies in bed, her spouse, the director, eats lunch. He's short, bald, ugly. Papa said he looks like Dr Mabuse.[20] They address each other as 'baby'. 'Honey, the car's arrived' … I sat in an armchair, smoked and kept quiet; this whole thing began to annoy me. She lies there like a countess, damn it, making a fool of herself with that old geezer. Suddenly from under the bedcovers (sic!) two doggies appear and start kissing their Lady on the lips. Yuk! Yuk! Damn! … She tells me I've grown (very nice!) and that she just can't understand it at all, that she addresses me as Mr Lutek, that I offer her a cigarette. Later it was very

13 The memorial to the Polish national poet Adam Mickiewicz (1798–1855).

14 The memorial to Wojciech Bogusławski (1757–1829) in front of the Teatr Wielki (Grand Theatre).

15 In the original, this word is written in fragmentary capital letters that appear damaged or in the process of dissolving.

16 Ruth Goldbarth.

17 These mutual friends had fled to the Soviet Union in 1939.

18 Klara Segałowicz, née Borodino (1896–1942), theatre and film actress in Poland; first marriage in the 1920s to the Yiddish-speaking writer Zusman Segałowicz (1884–1949); worked for the American Jewish Joint Distribution Committee (JDC), 1940–1942; arrested in July 1942 and shot in Warsaw's Pawiak prison.

19 Lejba (Leon) Neustadt (1883–1942), educator; lecturer at the Jewish teacher training college in Warsaw, Sept. 1919; worked for the JDC from 1919 as head of care for children and orphans within the Health Department, and concurrently deputy chairman of CENTOS; chairman of the coordinating committee of the Jewish Aid Associations, Sept. 1939; representative of the JDC in the General Government, then in the underground, 1939–1941; arrested with Klara Segałowicz in July 1942 and also shot in Pawiak prison.

20 This is a reference to the novel by Norbert Jacques *Dr. Mabuse, der Spieler* (Dr Mabuse the Gambler, 1921), which was filmed in 1922 by Fritz Lang and Thea von Harbou.

pleasant. The former director of the Vilna troupe (theatre in Vilna) came with his wife, also an artist.[21] They discussed the theatre with Father. I had to tell everyone about my excursion and everything …

I could have had a job with the Joint [JDC], but now it's not worth it. In the future we might go to Warsaw for good, but nothing is certain. What lousy, rotten luck I have! Mrs Klara said that a few months ago I could have gone to Eretz.[22] But now, kaput. What more can I say? Your letter was very optimistic and full of love. It cheered me up. I am beginning to believe less and less in this 'tomorrow', morgen, morgen …[23] When will it be? Perhaps never. You were merely my dream and that's it … What the hell! I don't care any more. If there is a 'tomorrow', it'll come, if not, then not. I'd like to see you just once more, just once, and then … to hell with it. To hell with everything, Tomaszów, and Warsaw, and the Joint and Shmoint,[24] and the mess I am in (those girls can kiss my a…) and me, and everything. Everything is green, the sky so clear, but so what when I don't care about anything. I feel like I am on St Helena.[25] But why should I spoil your mood when you were so jolly in your last letter. You have always kept my spirits up. But who will understand me … I don't even understand myself any more. I don't examine myself any more and I don't know what I want. I thought one can turn one's life into such poetry, that it's a kind of romance, I somehow shaped my own life. I thought that life and poetry, and … But here I see a damned mess, nothing but rubbish, that poetry is in books, that beauty is in pictures, that romances are in the theatre, but here there's this … this … Warsaw. It's green. But so what? Ordinary leaves. The sky is – well, just a sky. Where's the poetry, where's the beauty here? You'll say it was here last year. So it was. Because there was you, there was love, and everything seemed a pretty decoration. And then – this fate, this fate, this Schicksal,[26] the guy 'smashed us in the face' – you understand, really smashed us in the face and woke us up, and now I slowly open my eyes and we see, we see, this Warsaw and such people. Everyone is now Warsaw.

Well, I got carried away. But don't blame me for such a depressing letter. I think this will change. Maybe I'll regain my spirits. Maybe I'll start playing Indians and smoke a peace pipe, maybe I'll put on Papa's hat and sit on the sofa like on a horse and pretend I'm a cowboy, and catch Bela and kill her. I'll jump up a tree like Tarzan, at night I'll sleep in the garden and dance around the fire, maybe they'll shoot me and get it over with. Laugh a little, little one. The next letter will definitely be merrier. In the meantime, take care! I am sending a few photographs and waiting for yours. I kiss you as warmly as I can.

Your Lutek

21 The Vilna Troupe (Yiddish: Vilner trupe) was a theatre ensemble that performed in the 1920s and 1930s in Warsaw, as well as in other locations within and outside Poland. It was led by Mordechaj Mazo, who perished in the Warsaw ghetto in April 1943 along with his wife, the actress Estera Goldinberg.

22 Hebrew: 'land', a reference to Palestine.

23 German in the original: 'tomorrow'.

24 In Yiddish, duplications with the prefix 'shm' – as here with 'Joint – Shmoint' – are used as a means of expressing irony or ridicule.

25 The island in the south Atlantic to which Napoleon was banished in 1815 by the British.

26 German in the original: 'fate'.

Say hello to Mama.[27]

1. who, what? (There is) a beautiful letter
2. who, what? (There is no) beautiful letter
3. to whom, to what? (I peruse) the beautiful letter
4. who, what? (I see) a beautiful letter
5. I call – Oh beautiful letter!
6. with whom, with what? (I go) with a beautiful letter
7. about whom, about what? (I think) about a beautiful letter.[28]

PS. I've started to paint again. You have no idea how enjoyable it is. I've painted a portrait for my cousin. Barażyński said it is good.[29]

DOC. 120

On 20 May 1940 Area Command V of the Urban Police in Sosnowitz (Sosnowiec) recommends sending Jews who evade forced labour to a concentration camp[1]

Letter from Area Command V (S.Ak.V 1b/20.5.) of the Urban Police in Sosnowitz, unsigned,[2] to the Sosnowitz Gestapo, dated 20 May 1940 (draft)

In the original to the Gestapo *in Sosnowitz*, with the request for further action.

It is advisable to put the Jews named in the enclosure[3] in a concentration camp for several days, and to teach them that they have to carry out the directive issued by their Religious Community and have to show up to perform the required work.

The attempt to have Jews taken to their job sites by police officers was unsuccessful, because the Jews, who are well known for being thick-skinned, failed to appear again the next day. A tough crackdown is imperative in order to uphold the authority of the German administration.[4]

27 Edith Blau's mother, Meta Blau, née Samuel.
28 The last seven lines constitute a word-play based on the Polish declension of nouns and adjectives and can be translated into English only imperfectly.
29 Probably Henryk Barczyński, also Barciński (1896–1941?), painter and graphic artist; attended art school in Dresden, 1919–1926; in Berlin, then in Łódź, 1927–1933; left for Tomaszów when the war broke out; the circumstances of his death are unknown.

1 APK, 807/317, fol. 5. This document has been translated from German.
2 Various initials appear at the bottom of the draft.
3 This is not included in the file.
4 Handwritten addition: '1) Enclosure. 2) To be filed. Note on the letter above: the Jewish Religious Community complains that the 15 Jews [named] in the enclosure did not turn up to perform work, despite having been summoned.'

DOC. 121

On 30 May 1940 the administrative heads of the General Government discuss the next measures to be taken against the Jewish population[1]

Minutes of an official meeting of the government of the GG with district governors and police chiefs, signed Dr Schulte-Wissermann,[2] in Cracow, dated 30 May 1940

[...][3]

SS-Obergruppenführer Krüger went on to state that he would accede to the request that, in future, the Selbstschutz should no longer be deployed on its own, but solely in combination with the SS and the police. Incidentally, the Selbstschutz will be heavily reduced in numbers in those regions where the Wehrmacht is conducting recruitment activities.

With regard to Jewish forced labour, no final decision has yet been reached. Deployment of Jewish workers as forced labour makes practical sense only once it is clear that the movement of the Jewish population within the General Government has come to a halt.

It is clear that a centrally directed system is necessary, particularly with regard to implementing the forced labour of Jews. A central office must be created to record all Jews in a card index. The individual agencies – the Wehrmacht, the districts, the civil administration, the police, etc. – could then notify this central office of their requirements for Jewish manpower and would have these workers placed at their disposal by the central office. This would bring about the unified management of Jewish forced labour within the General Government.

Regarding the question of the Polish Construction Service,[4] it must be noted that there is a risk here that workers who are deployed with this Polish Construction Service will no longer report for work in the Reich. That would hinder the efforts to bring not only agricultural workers but also industrial workers into the Reich. With the establishment of the Polish Construction Service, a substantial proportion of Polish workers will become unavailable for our labour recruitment drive.

The head of the Labour Department[5] has asked that Jews be made available for employment as free workers. This request must be categorically denied, as it contradicts

1 AIPN, GK 95, vol. 9. Copy in IfZ-Archives, Fb 105, vol. 5, fols. 1284–1285, 1287–1290, 1294. Published in Präg and Jacobmeyer (eds.), *Diensttagebuch des deutschen Generalgouverneurs*, pp. 215–218. This document has been translated from German.

2 Dr Fritz Schulte-Wissermann (1902–1959), lawyer; joined the NSDAP in 1933; Regierungsrat in the office of the Koblenz provincial governor, then Oberregierungsrat in the Office of the Reich Commissioner for Price Setting, and later Ministerialrat, 1935–1938; head of the Department of Price Setting in the General Government from Dec. 1939; temporarily interned in summer 1945; practised law in Koblenz from 1948.

3 Among other matters, the official meeting agenda included the security situation, which was allegedly detrimentally affected by a personnel shortage in the police force. Zörner and Frank argued the case for excluding farmers and workers from repressive measures against the Polish population.

4 The so-called Baudienst was a paramilitary organization for Polish youth, established by the Germans in May 1940 and mostly active in District Cracow.

5 Dr Max Frauendorfer (1909–1989), lawyer; joined the NSDAP and the SS in 1928; administrative official in the NSDAP Reichsleitung in 1931; Reichsschulungsleiter (NSDAP head of training) in 1934; in the General Government from Sept. 1939; head of the Labour Department in the General

the regulation of the Governor General stipulating that Jews are to be used only for forced labour.
[...][6]

Brigadeführer Streckenbach[7] then stated his position on the question of the Jewish councils, saying that the Security Police is greatly interested in the Jewish question, for obvious reasons. That is also why the Jewish councils of elders were created. After the formal establishment of the councils of elders, officers – a few or even more, depending on the given situation – were sent to supervise the councils of elders in the larger towns. These officers have insight into the customs associated with the Jewish religion etc. This arrangement has proved very successful. However, the Security Police's management of the Jews has been increasingly inhibited by all kinds of political authorities and Party organizations making use of the council[s] of elders and the religious communities in a chaotic, ad hoc fashion. For example, workers have simply been requested willy-nilly. Likewise, rather arbitrary material demands have been made of the councils of elders, and in some cases sums of money have been demanded as well. A clear solution must be found for this issue. Above all, a decision must be made as to which entity will supervise the Jewish councils of elders: the Kreishauptmann, the District Governor, the Stadthauptmann, or the Security Police. Streckenbach said that if he endorses the latter entity, this was for objective reasons. Any information gleaned by the administrative authorities about matters concerning the Jews would, after all, have to be passed on to the Security Police, especially if executive action were then required. Experience also shows that the Security Service has an ongoing overview of the situation among the Jews. This does not mean that, by means of such an arrangement, the Security Police would seek to skim off the cream from the Jews, as it were, and arrogate everything to itself. The approach taken by the Security Police is mandated by the confiscation regulation. It also draws its income from the Reich and has no need to enrich itself; all the more so as, administratively speaking, there is no provision for recording any such acquisitions. All that being said, he would suggest that the decision be made in such a way that the Jewish councils of elders, and thereby the Jews in general, will be collectively placed under the oversight of the Security Police, and that everything the Jews request will be managed through this agency. After all, the number of Jews will increase even more if the Jews from the eastern provinces[8] arrive in the General Government. If the Jewish communities continue to be exploited, as they have been up to now, then one of these days millions of Jews will become a burden on the

Government administration, Nov. 1939 – Feb. 1943; Ministerialdirigent in 1941; served in the Wehrmacht, 1943–1945; director of an insurance company in Munich and deputy treasurer of the Christian Social Union (CSU) after the war.

6 The following passages dealt with financing the Selbstschutz units, tightening price controls, and providing better uniforms for Polish policemen.

7 Bruno Streckenbach (1902–1977), commercial clerk; joined the NSDAP and the SA in 1930, and the SS in 1931; Gestapo chief in Hamburg from 1933; head of Einsatzgruppe I in Poland in Sept. 1939; then senior commander of the Security Police and the SD in the General Government until Jan. 1941; head of the Personnel Office in the Reich Security Main Office (RSHA), June 1940–Jan. 1943; then with the Waffen-SS; in Soviet captivity from 1945; returned to Germany in 1955 and lived in Hamburg.

8 This refers to the western regions of Poland that were annexed by Germany.

General Government. After all, Streckenbach said, we cannot let them starve. The means at the Jews' disposal are quite modest, since there are no longer any rich Jews in the General Government, but mostly only a Jewish proletariat.

He would therefore be glad if the question of supervising the Jewish councils of elders and religious communities were to be decided categorically once and for all. The Security Police is certainly not pressing for this additional workload, but experience has shown that the method of dealing with this question thus far is not expedient.

As for the prison system, the conditions there are simply disastrous, particularly due to the overcrowding in the penal institutions. It is hoped, however, that this state of affairs can be changed in the foreseeable future. In addition, the make-up of the prison population is utterly chaotic. All the inmates – from the remand prisoner and the protective custody prisoner to the convict – are in one and the same prison. A separation must therefore be brought about in Poland.

[...][9]

Governor Dr Zörner[10] stated that, with regard to deploying Jewish labour, the same things are probably being experienced everywhere. In District Lublin, Jews are requested for work every day but are not made available in sufficient numbers; however, one can see them standing around in the streets in towns inhabited mainly by Jews. In his view, the authority of the civil administration must be decisive in this matter. The elements of the civil administration, in the form of the Kreishauptmänner, Kreiskommissare, etc. are in a much better position to enlist the Jews for labour with the help of the councils of elders due to their knowledge of the local conditions. In the southern area of District Lublin, 22 km of road is still lacking. And it is precisely the southern area that is the best part of the district. From the last harvest, for example, 80 tonnes of grain is still lying there and has not yet been taken away. Now, however, the Wehrmacht is trying to remove the grain on lorries. In light of all this, he said that he was particularly interested in this specific labour deployment of the Jews. For the time being, the SD does not come into consideration as the agency to perform this task, for the simple reason that it does not have sufficient personnel. As things stand, labour deployment on a large scale will not reach the point at which one can expect it to make a real difference before the autumn. Other than that, he recalled from his work in Cracow that Landrat Dr Siebert quite often turned to him in the matter of the Jewish councils, and he, Governor Dr Zörner, placed his officials at Siebert's disposal for performing this task. He stated that as an administrative official, he had to carry on arguing in favour of the civil administration remaining in charge of this matter for now.

Governor Dr Fischer[11] expressed agreement with the previous speaker's remarks. A few months ago in Warsaw, the SD had been in charge of labour deployment, but had then ceded implementation to the civil administration because the SD was so overburdened.

9 Streckenbach went on to advocate dividing the prisons in the General Government between the police and the judicial system, so that every sizeable town would have a police prison and a court prison.

10 Ernst Zörner (1895–1945?), shopkeeper; with the Border Force in Danzig in 1919; joined the NSDAP in 1925; city councillor and Landtag delegate in Braunschweig, 1928–1933; mayor of Dresden in 1933; Stadthauptmann of Cracow in 1939; governor of District Lublin from Feb. 1940; dismissed at the urging of the SS in April 1943; subsequently worked in Organization Todt; missing since 1945; declared dead in 1960.

Governor Dr Lasch[12] said that he had had no difficulties so far regarding the deployment of the Jews. The Selbstschutz supported the district administration's measures in every way.

[...][13]

[Hans Frank:] On the question of supervising the Jewish councils – whether this supervision should be carried out by the SD or by the Kreishauptmann – I want to point out the following: The police are the armed branch of the Reich leadership when it comes to keeping order internally. It has been clearly assigned the same function in the General Government as well. The police are not an end in itself, which means that the question of supervising the Jewish councils of elders can only be a pragmatic one. Just as in Germany, supervision in political matters is the responsibility of the Political Police; supervision of the Jewish councils of elders must also be performed by the organization that exists for that purpose, the Security Police and the SD. To make a different arrangement would be madness. But calling on the Jewish councils of elders with regard to the procurement of workers is a completely different matter. Clearly this involves a wide range of interested parties. There must be a central office in charge, and, according to the Regulation on the Introduction of Forced Labour for the Jewish Population, this central office is that of the Higher SS and Police Leader. The main task of the Jewish councils of elders is the implementation of forced labour for Jews. Other tasks are resettling Jews, feeding Jews, etc. In this matter, I am of the opinion that these tasks can be assigned to the Kreis- and Stadthauptleute until the obligation to work has been conclusively enforced, and that all requests for labour by any of the agencies should go through the Kreis- and Stadthauptleute, who will handle the deployment of the Jewish workers, of course in the closest possible cooperation with the Security Police and the SD. A final arrangement for this matter must still be found. By the next meeting, which is to take place around 15 June, I expect to receive final suggestions from the district governors as to how they view the labour deployment of the Jews. Until then, the current arrangement will remain in place. Then, from 1 July, the final arrangement for regulating Jewish labour deployment will come into force.

11 Dr Ludwig Fischer (1905–1947), lawyer; joined the NSDAP in 1926 and the SA in 1929; deputy head of the Legal Department of the NSDAP Reichsleitung in 1931; Regierungsrat and main department head of the Academy for German Law in 1933; chief of staff in the NSDAP Reich Legal Office in 1938; governor of District Warsaw from Oct. 1939; simultaneously acting governor of District Lublin in April/May 1943; sentenced to death by the People's Supreme Court in Warsaw and executed in 1947.

12 Dr Karl Lasch (1904–1942), economist and lawyer; joined the NSDAP in 1931; director of the Academy for German Law in 1934; head of the NSDAP Reich Legal Office in 1936; governor of District Radom, 1939–1941; governor of District Galicia, 1941–1942; arrested for corruption in May 1942; thought to have been shot without trial on Himmler's orders while on remand in prison.

13 In what follows, Wächter, Krüger, and Frank discussed the methods for obtaining more Polish forced labourers for deployment in Germany.

DOC. 122

On 6 and 7 June 1940 the Price Setting Department in the General Government calls for radical action against the Jews[1]

Plan for supplying the General Government of Poland with the most essential commodities at appropriate prices for the 1940/1941 fiscal year; General Supply Plan, Cracow, 28 May 1940, signed Dr Schulte-Wissermann, enclosure with the minutes of the government of the GG's meeting on economic matters, dated 6 and 7 June 1940[2]

[...][3]

F. Jewish question.

It would be a mistake to prepare a supply plan for an entire fiscal year without considering that the distribution of goods in the General Government before this war, and in large part until the present day, was and has been a task that was first and foremost usurped by the Jews. Even now the Jew will not be inclined to give up his position in distributing goods and making money. All efforts to force him out of this position with economic control measures will only be partially successful. Without employing radical measures against the Jews, it will be impossible to create a system that is not at risk of completely collapsing every day as a result of attacks by the Jews. Therefore, in addition to the ban on Jewish trade, measures must be added which restrict the Jews outwardly and thus prevent them from plying their trade. Whether it is decided in the process to enclose the Jews in the ghetto completely, as in Litzmannstadt, or to institute forced labour for the Jewish population, or even to combine the two approaches, must depend on local circumstances. In any event, it appears vital to carry out these measures speedily, so that the most important sources of Jewish clandestine trade will have been blocked by the end of the summer at the latest.

1 AIPN, GK 95, vol. 8. Copy in IfZ-Archives, Fb 105, vol. 6, fols. 1517–1518. This document has been translated from German.

2 The document is included among the ancillary papers for the meeting on economic matters on 6 and 7 June 1940 (IfZ-Archives, Fb 105, vol. 6, fols. 1507–1518).

3 Parts A to E of the supply plan contain suggestions for registration, streamlining, and control, as well as for trade in goods and monetary transactions with the German Reich: IfZ-Archives, Fb 105, vol. 6, fols. 1504–1517.

DOC. 123

On 7 June 1940 the SS and Selbstschutz leader in the Kielce area prohibits the unauthorized seizing of Jews in the streets for labour[1]

Letter from the SS and Selbstschutz leader in the Kielce area, signed Claasen (?),[2] to the SS Cavalry Regiment, dated 7 June 1940[3]

All offices are hereby once again informed that requests for Jewish workers are to be made only to the SS and Selbstschutz leader in the Kielce area.

Seizing Jews in the streets is prohibited, as is the seizure of trade tools, work equipment, and the like.

Requests for workers must be reviewed with regard to the number actually required, as it has repeatedly been found that the number requested is many times greater than that actually required.

The daily requests must be sent to the Selbstschutz office no later than 5 p.m. for the next day. For workplaces which make continual use of Jewish workers, the requests apply for only one week at a time and must be made no later than Saturday at 1 p.m. Selbstschutz office telephone: 1023.

The work lists must always be signed by the offices, and the working time must be filled in on the relevant form.

All irregularities must be reported immediately to the labour office or reported through the group overseer.

Adherence to these guidelines is requested, as the prompt delivery of workers can only be ensured in this manner.

1 Copy in BArch, RS 4/334. This document has been translated from German.
2 Presumably Kurt Claasen (1908–1945?), accountant; joined the NSDAP in 1931 and the SS in 1932; member of the 45th SS-Standarte, Jan. 1939 – Sept. 1942; leader of the ethnic German Selbstschutz in District Radom, 1939–1940; then worked for the Jewish affairs section at the office of the SS and Police Leader in Lublin, responsible for the deployment of forced labourers; in charge of transport during Operation Reinhard; vanished in 1945; declared dead in 1953.
3 Office stamp of the SS and Selbstschutz leader.

DOC. 124

On 10 June 1940 the Soviet secret police orders the mostly Jewish refugees in the Soviet-annexed part of Poland to be deported[1]

Order (marked 'top secret') from the People's Commissariat for Internal Affairs of the USSR[2] (no. 2372/B), unsigned, to the NKVD of the Byelorussian Socialist Republic (Comrade Serov)[3] and the Ukrainian Socialist Republic (Comrade Tsanava),[4] dated 10 June 1940

As the exchange of refugees between Germany and the USSR will be completed in the coming days, it is necessary to begin implementing the resolution by the Soviet of People's Commissars of the USSR dated 2 March 1940 no. 289-127ss[5] on the resettlement to the northern regions of the USSR of refugees who were not accepted by the German government.[6]

You have already been provided with guidelines for carrying out the resettlement of this group of refugees in directive no. 894/B by the NKVD of the USSR dated 7 March 1940.[7]

As an addition to this directive, I order the following:

1. From 10 to 20 June, a new registration campaign for the refugees who were not accepted by the Germans must be carried out. This repeat registration is to be carried out under the pretext that Soviet passports will be issued to all citizens residing in the western parts of Ukraine and Byelorussia, including those who did not receive passports in the prescribed period.
2. During the repeat registration, the refugees who want to leave for German territories and the registered individuals who do not belong to this group of refugees should be identified by means of the registration questionnaires you have been issued.
3. To make the work more efficient, the names of all those who have already left for Germany must be removed from the files and card indexes before the registration

1 FSB, 3-7-20, fols. 302–303. This document has been translated from Russian. Published in *Deportacje obywateli polskich z Zachodniej Ukrainy i Zachodniej Białorusi w 1940 roku*, ed. Wiktor Komogorow et al. (Warsaw: Instytut Pamięci Narodowej, 2003), pp. 566–568.

2 The People's Commissariat of Internal Affairs (NKVD) was under the authority of Lavrentiy P. Beria (1899–1953), politician; secretary of the Communist Party in Georgia, 1931–1938; people's commissar for internal affairs of the USSR, 1938–1945; briefly in power as member of 'troika' after death of Stalin in March 1953; arrested, and shot at the end of 1953.

3 Ivan A. Serov (1905–1990), politician and NKVD general; head of the NKVD of the Ukrainian SSR, 1939–1941; from July 1945 NKVD plenipotentiary of the Soviet Military Administration in Germany and its deputy chief of civilian affairs; first head of the KGB, 1954–1958.

4 Lavrentiy F. Tsanava (1900–1955), politician; held various positions in the Communist Party of the Georgian Soviet Socialist Republic (SSR); people's commissar for internal affairs of the Byelorussian SSR (BSSR), 1938–1941; minister for state security of the BSSR, 1943–1951; deputy minister for state security of the USSR, 1951/1952; arrested in 1953; died in prison.

5 GARF, R-9479-1-52, fols. 12–13.

6 Of those who fled eastwards, more than 90 per cent were Jewish refugees from the German-occupied part of Poland.

7 The directive required the secret police in Byelorussia and Ukraine to use a questionnaire to establish within fifteen days which refugees wanted to return to the German-occupied part of Poland: FSB, 3-7-13, fols. 68–69.

begins. The lists prepared by the refugee exchange commission with annotations made at the border checkpoints are to be used for this purpose.

4. The resettlement of refugees must be carried out on 29 June 1940 in accordance with the guidelines issued previously and drawing on your experience of resettling colonists, the families of victims of persecution, and prostitutes.[8]
5. On 23 June the number of persons who are to be resettled and are registered with you, the station where refugees will be loaded onto transports, the number of railway carriages needed and a list of people who are indispensable for the operation must be submitted by telegraph.
6. The plans for the operation must be submitted to Comrade Khrushchev and Comrade Ponomarenko,[9] and locally to the first secretaries of the district committees of the All-Union Communist Party.[10]

DOC. 125

On 13 June 1940 the Higher SS and Police Leader orders that responsibility for the administration of Jewish forced labour be transferred to the Labour Department of the General Government[1]

Letter (marked 'personal') from the Higher SS and Police Leader for the East, Department Z, signed Krüger, to the head of the Labour Department in the Office of the Governor General, Frauendorfer, Cracow, dated 13 June 1940[2]

Now that the police task of *registering* all Jews subject to forced labour in the General Government has been carried out, in accordance with the 2nd Implementing Regulation to the Regulation of 26 October 1939 on the Introduction of Forced Labour for the Jewish Population of 12 December 1939 (V. Bl. G. G. P. I, p. 246), and the manner of proceeding when *deploying* the Jewish forced labourers has also been regulated by general directives from the Higher SS and Police Leader,[3] it now proves necessary – given the increasing need for workers of all types, especially for public work schemes – to transfer to the Labour Department the task of organizing and allocating the manpower of the Jewish

8 A total of 141,000 Polish military settlers and civil servants from the pre-war period had already been deported in Feb. 1940; in April 1940 a further 61,000 persons, mainly relatives of those arrested, were also deported. On 28/29 June 1940, a total of 79,000 persons were deported, primarily to the Arkhangelsk, Sverdlovsk, and Novosibirsk regions.

9 Nikita S. Khrushchev (1894–1971); first secretary of the Communist Party in Ukraine, 1939–1947; first secretary of the CPSU, 1953–1964; chairman of the Soviet Union's council of ministers, 1958–1964. Panteleimon K. Ponomarenko (1902–1984), first secretary of the Communist Party in Byelorussia, 1938–1947.

10 Vsesoyuznaya Kommunisticheskaya partiya (bol'shevikov), the All-Union Communist Party (Bolsheviks), was the official Russian name of the Communist Party of the Soviet Union. The original contains an annotation: 'The executor is Comrade Merkulov'. Vsevolod M. Merkulov (1895–1953); head of the Main Administration for State Security in the NKVD, 1938–1941.

1 APL, 498/748, fol. 1r–v. This document has been translated from German.

2 The original contains handwritten underlining.

3 See Docs. 58 and 76.

population, not only by placing free labour, but also by applying the provisions on forced labour.

I therefore order, with immediate effect:

1) The central card index that records all Jews subject to forced labour, which was compiled in the office of the Higher SS and Police Leader, is to be handed over to the Labour Department. This department will ensure the appropriate distribution of this card index to the individual districts and Kreise (employment offices).
2) The ongoing registration of Jews who are to be added will be the responsibility of the Labour Department.
3) The selection and allocation of Jewish forced labourers to the individual work schemes (labour deployment) is henceforth also the responsibility of the Labour Department. It will control the working conditions, with a view to the best possible maintenance and utilization of the Jewish workforce.
4) In the event that various deployment options exist simultaneously, workers will be deployed for whichever work scheme is deemed most urgent in military or economic terms by the head of the Office for the Four-Year Plan in the General Government, after consultation with the offices concerned.[4]
5) Securing the implementation of the measures involved in registering and deploying Jewish forced labourers, as well as control of the residence and registration requirements for the Jews, will continue to fall within the range of duties of the Higher SS and Police Leader.
6) The correspondence that arose in the office of the Higher SS and Police Leader dealing with the registration and work deployment of the Jews will be handed over to the Labour Department, which will continue this correspondence.

A written record is to be prepared concerning the transfer of this correspondence, together with the collection of regulations and instructions, and concerning the transfer of the card index with its equipment. The Labour Department must initiate without delay the collection of any monies outstanding for the index cards delivered to the Jewish councils and ensure that these monies are collected by the Kreis- and Stadthauptleute and paid to the Finance Department.

4 The office existed from autumn 1939 until July 1940. It was headed by Dr Walter Emmerich (1895–1967), economist; university lecturer in Hamburg, 1930–1934; worked in the Hamburg economic administration, 1935–1940; joined the NSDAP in 1937; head of the Department of Economic Affairs of the General Government, April 1940–1945; interned in Neuengamme, 1945–1947; thereafter worked as a businessman in Hamburg.

DOC. 126

On 16 June 1940 the underground newspaper *Walka* complains about Jews allegedly being privileged and their being enlisted as informants[1]

'General Government' – Paradisus Judaeorum[2]

While the Polish population on the territory of the General Government is being hunted like wild animals and captured men and women are sent to Germany for hard labour – the Jews clearly enjoy privileges under the antisemitic German racists. An armband with the Star of David has become a symbol of protection against roundups. Jews are not being seized in the streets or taken away. The occupiers use them solely for local labour, whereby Jews are paid for labour in the cities. They receive 4 złoty per day and lunch. Considering that only impoverished Jews are employed for urban labour (rich Jews buy themselves out of labour) and that these impoverished Jews used to earn considerably less – the Jewish ghetto has no reason to complain about the occupation.

The occupation authorities have recently issued a secret memorandum about referring Jews for agricultural labour – but only within the country.[3] Jews are to take the place of Polish peasants and farm labourers who were sent to Germany. They are already being assigned to landed estates, estate farms, and larger farmsteads. The German memorandum instructs the landrats[4] and Arbeitsamts[5] that 'informants' are to be selected from among these Jews (who will be supervised by the Selbschutz).[6] These informants are to report on the state of agricultural output to the German authorities, in other words, denounce any attempts to circumvent German regulations on the requisitioning of agricultural produce. In order to double the zeal of these 'informants' and suitably turn them against the landowners, the landrats are simultaneously (privately) instructing the landowners to be harsh towards the Jews that have been assigned for labour.

Thus, the network of informants in Poland occupied by Nazi Germany relies on Jews. They are to become the mainstay of governments.

1 *Walka*, no. 10, 16 June 1940, p. 4. Biblioteka Narodowa, MF 56 522. This document has been translated from Polish. *Walka* was the central underground publication of Stronnictwo Narodowe, the main political party of the National Democratic (Endecja) movement, and appeared from 1940 to 1945.

2 The Latin expression alludes to an old saying to the effect that the Polish–Lithuanian Commonwealth had been 'a peasant's hell, an urbanite's purgatory, a nobleman's heaven, and a Jew's paradise'.

3 This memorandum could not be found. Jewish forced labourers were deployed from 1940 to 1941 for three tasks: the erection of fortifications on the eastern border of the General Government; road construction, especially in Districts Cracow and Lublin; and land development projects. The head of the Labour Department, Max Frauendorfer, applied, without success, for permission to deploy Jews in agriculture.

4 German in the original here and in the following. Correctly: 'Landräte'.

5 German in the original. Correctly: 'Arbeitsämter', employment offices.

6 German in the original. Correctly: 'Selbstschutz'.

DOC. 127

On 18 June 1940 the Jewish Council informs the Stadtkommissar in Tarnow (Tarnów) that Jewish residences have been looted and vandalized[1]

Letter from the Jewish Council in Tarnow (Zhl. 1837/40), two illegible signatures,[2] to the office of the Stadtkommissar in Tarnow[3] (received on 18 June 1940), dated 18 June 1940[4]

The Jewish Council established in Tarnow takes the liberty of making the following report.

On Sunday, 16 June 1940, between 3 and 4 p.m., military personnel under the leadership of a railway official forcibly entered several Jewish apartments on the Ringplatz and on Breitestr[aße] and badly damaged these residences.

Various Polish civilians took advantage of this opportunity to loot these apartments.

When news of these incidents reached the Jewish Council, our representative interceded with the gendarmerie platoon and also with the duty officer at the Stadtkommandant's office. As a result, several military patrols were sent to the crime scene, where order was soon restored.

In reporting these incidents herewith, we request that you kindly arrange for the looted items to be surrendered at the appropriate offices and for a more frequent dispatch of patrols for the purpose of maintaining order.

DOC. 128

On 24 June 1940 the SS Security Service proposes that the Jews be removed from the Litzmannstadt (Lodz) ghetto by sending them on a trek[1]

Report from Department III B 4 – II/213, Racial and National Health, in the police district of Litzmannstadt,[2] unsigned, dated 24 June 1940

Reports from the police district
Re: III B 4 – II/213 – Racial and National Health
The census of Jews recently conducted in the Litzmannstadt ghetto has resulted in a total number of *158,000*. This stands in contrast to all previous data and estimates, which ranged from 200,000 to 320,000.

1 APKr-T, 1/6, fol. 285r–v. Copy in USHMM, RG 15 020M, reel 8. This document has been translated from German.

2 The chairman of the Jewish Council was Artur Folkman, also spelled Volkman (1898–1945?), retailer.

3 The Stadtkommissar in Tarnów was Ernst Kundt (1897–1947), lawyer; studied in Prague; cofounder of the Sudeten German Party (SdP) in 1935; joined the NSDAP in 1939; Stadtkommandant in Tarnów, Sept.–Dec. 1939; Kreishauptmann in Tarnów from Jan. 1940; head of the Interior Administration of the General Government, Sept. 1940 – July 1941; then governor of District Radom until 1945; sentenced to death in Prague and executed in 1947.

4 The original contains an illegible handwritten note and official stamps.

1 AIPN, GK 68/129, fol. 3. Copy in USHMM, RG 15 015M, reel 2. The following folio, 4, is missing from the file, so it is not clear whether the document is complete. This document has been translated from German.

The result of this latest count is generally thought to be incorrect and untrue. It may be noted that there is a suspicion that the Jews have deliberately inflated the figure in order to obtain a larger quantity of foodstuffs etc.

It has been announced that 2 trains per day will be available to the Warthegau for deporting Jews to the General Government beginning in August 1940. One of these trains is to be reserved for the Litzmannstadt ghetto every day.

For a total of approximately 160,000 Jews (if one takes the figure from the latest count as a basis), the deportation from the Litzmannstadt ghetto would require a period of 200 days, = approximately 7 months (allowing for cancellations), as only 1,000 Jews can be deported on each transport. This would mean the deportation of the Jews from Litzmannstadt to the General Government would take from August 1940 to February 1941. The plan in this form is therefore considered unacceptable both from a public health and an economic perspective, particularly given that the winter period would then be imminent, and we would like to point out again the only possible way of deporting the Jews – namely, a Jewish trek.[3]

DOC. 129

On 27 June 1940 the Trustee Office in Posen (Poznań) reports on the confiscation of property[1]

Report by Section A I (Registration of Assets) of the Trustee Office in Posen, signed Hugo Ratzmann, dated 27 June 1940 (draft)[2]

Activity Report for Section A I

Section A I's area of responsibility has greatly expanded since mid June of this year, as a result of Section A IIa 'Trustee Matters' being incorporated into this section [A I]. In addition to Section A I's previous areas of work:

a) registration of all Polish and Jewish assets in the Warthegau,
b) confiscation of these assets,
c) maintenance of a card index on these assets and assessment of the card index for statistical and practical purposes,

there is a fresh roster of tasks for the newly incorporated group: appointment and dismissal of the temporary administrators and the district representatives, preliminary processing of applications for positions as temporary administrators, maintenance of the newly established card index of individuals.

2 In Office III, 'German Settlement Areas', B stood for 'Nationhood' (*Volkstum*) and 4 for 'Immigration and Resettlement'. Department II 213 was in charge of 'Racial and National Health'.

3 The letter was forwarded on 27 June 1940 by the head of the SD Main District and the Central Resettlement Office (UWZ) in Poznań, Höppner, to Section IV D 4 (Resettlement) at the RSHA, for information (log no. E. V/3), with the comment that the Higher SS and Police Leader in the Warthegau, Koppe, was 'extraordinarily interested […] in the measures planned': AIPN, GK 68/129, fol. 2.

1 APP, 759/79, fols. 184–186. This document has been translated from German.

2 The original contains handwritten deletions and underlining. The deleted passages were included in the translation.

With the transfer of the aforementioned department, an additional 9 colleagues have joined Section A I, so that it currently employs 60 persons altogether, including 24 working in the field.

1. *Registration of assets*

Section A I has attached the greatest importance to registering all Polish and Jewish assets as quickly as possible, regardless of whether such assets were in the possession of Polish citizens who fled or were evacuated, or whether the owners are still located in the Warthegau. In the first period, assets about which we were informed by mail were registered. Additional material for the registration process was obtained from the reports of the temporary administrators on the basis of a notice which the Posen Trustee Office placed in the main newspapers of the Warthegau on three occasions. Since these sources only capture a relatively small portion of the actual assets, registration squads began to be deployed at the beginning of March. These squads, each consisting of three men, visited 37 Kreise in the Warthegau (five more Kreise are the responsibility of the Litzmannstadt branch office, which undertakes its own registrations). By and large, the registration work was concluded by the end of June. The squads were instructed to record, firstly, the industrial, commercial, and craft businesses (including even the smallest craftsmen, as well as closed and abandoned properties) and, secondly, residential property and items of furniture. For this they used the familiar registration form, the back of which now has additional space for detailed information. The business assets have almost all been registered by now. The residential properties and the furniture have been recorded in part, while the rest of the registration forms are being completed on the basis of instructions issued by our registration squads to the local offices in charge (Landräte and mayors), and are still being sent in by our representatives in the Kreise.

Around 10,000 business assets (around 7,500 file cards have already been created) have been registered, as well as around 5,000 residential properties and items of furniture. –

We would emphasize that the work of the registration squads is not confined to systematic recording. Rather, these squads also do an extraordinary amount of additional tasks that include reconnaissance work, undertaking checks, and developing the new frameworks of operation.

If businesses are in the hands of temporary administrators, the squad members almost always have to provide a great deal of information concerning the handling of temporary administration, setting the salaries paid to the temporary administrators, opportunities for purchase and lease, payment of debts, dismissal of employees of Polish nationality, questions of bookkeeping, etc.

In a great many cases, insofar as the queries posed by the temporary administrators reveal an insufficient grasp of the work required of a temporary administrator, the visit also involves an inspection of the business. For example, in various instances the members of the registration squad observed that the temporary administrators are insufficiently involved in the running of the business, which they have frequently more or less left to the former Polish owner. In these instances, reports to that effect were made to the operating section[3] for the purpose of final clarification.

3 Operating sections of the Trustee Offices.

The work of shaping the new structures can be seen in the fact, for example, that the B-sections, like the Handelsaufbau Ost GmbH in Posen,[4] were notified about a number of businesses in favourable locations and with not inconsiderable turnover that could be taken over by a temporary administrator. In addition, suggestions for further planning were made and were forwarded to the respective offices for final consideration. In addition, the squads reported on the nature and the business situation of the particular Bezirk being registered, information that gave the sections concerned an overview of the possibilities for deploying temporary administrators etc. In this regard, we would like to point out the detailed reports prepared by each squad, which are supplied to every section.

2. *Confiscation*

The confiscation orders were issued primarily on the basis of:

a) requests from the operating sections,
b) reports by the registration squads,
c) requests from temporarily appointed administrators for confirmation of the confiscation and of their appointment.

At present, 70 to 100 confiscation orders on average are prepared and delivered daily. A decrease in this daily output is not anticipated in the coming weeks.

The employees of the confiscation department are furthermore responsible for inducting the temporary administrators in Posen into their new premises. Because of the personnel shortage, it was unfortunately not possible to comply with this requirement in every case. Currently five employees are available for this purpose. This staff is insufficient, however, because these employees also have to respond to many requests from the operating sections for assessments of the potential to use temporary administrators in businesses through clarification of the local business situation, the size of the firm, etc., and for safeguarding shops and goods when a risk of theft or damage to the existing economic asset is anticipated.

There was a substantial accumulation of keys to confiscated and closed shops, particularly due to the activity of Section A IV – closure of Jewish and Polish shops whose owners have been evacuated. Detailed information on this is not available because no statistics have been kept so far. The shops were assigned to the appropriate sections, which also undertook the evaluation in some cases (for example, of the goods in stock).

3. *Card index*

The following card indexes are maintained by Section A I:

1) The *properties index*, which contains all properties, divided into Group I: business assets, and Group II: residential properties and furniture.

   The cards in Group I are arranged by Regierungsbezirk, and within these alphabetically by Kreis; within the Kreise, in alphabetical order by locality; within these localities in alphabetical order by the business. Those in Group II are arranged by Regierungsbezirk, and within these alphabetically by Kreis; within the Kreise, in alphabetical order by locality; and within the localities by street and house number.

4 This company dealt with the Germanization of commercial and retail businesses in Poznań.

2) The *branches index*, with the business assets arranged by business sectors or categories of craft production; within these categories, it is divided into those with acting administrators, those that have been shut down, those that have not yet been assigned an administrator, and those still in Polish hands.
3) The *index of individuals*, with the temporary administrators subdivided as follows: deployed temporary administrators and liquidators; dismissed or rejected temporary administrators and liquidators; applicants.
4) The *central card index*, based on the record forms sent here from the Main Trustee Office East in Berlin. We will regularly send lists containing the information gathered here to Berlin and ask them to complete the forms.
5) The *collection of registration sheets* as the basis of the indexes, one copy of which will be passed on, in each case, to the Main Trustee Office East in Berlin and to the local operating sections in charge.

At present, the existing card indexes are in constant use not only by the sections within our organization; enquiries also come in daily from other agencies, such as the Chamber of Industry and Commerce, the Chamber of Crafts, Aufbau Ost GmbH,[5] banks, and the police.

A separate report will be submitted on the activity of the merged Section A IIa (appointment and dismissal of temporary administrators and Kreis representatives) and on the preliminary processing of applications for positions as temporary administrators.

DOC. 130

On 1 July 1940 the Section for Jewish Affairs in the General Government reports on its activity since the start of the occupation[1]

'Section for Jewish Affairs'[2] part of the report on 'establishing the administration in the General Government',[3] unsigned,[4] dated 1 July 1940

Section for Jewish Affairs

At present there are 1.6 million Jews resident in the territory of the General Government (GG). Previous official counts gave a figure of approximately 1.3 million. The share of each district in this total is as follows:

Cracow	with	200,000 Jews,	i.e.	5.3 %	of the population
Radom	with	310,000 Jews,	i.e.	10.4 %	of the population
Warsaw	with	540,000 Jews,	i.e.	17.4 %	of the population
Lublin	with	250,000 Jews,	i.e.	9.6 %	of the population
[total]		1,300,000		10.4 %	of the population

5 This refers to the Handelsaufbau Ost GmbH: see previous note.

1 BArch, R 52 II/247, fols. 190–192. Published in Berenstein et al. (eds.), *Faschismus – Getto – Massenmord*, pp. 86–88. This document has been translated from German.

2 The section was part of the Population and Welfare Division in the Interior Administration Department of the General Government.

Measures to control the Jews are based on the regulations and decrees of the Governor General and the head of the Interior Administration Department, as well as on the directives of the Higher SS and Police Leader for the East.

The first measure was the introduction of forced labour for the Jewish population. (*Verordnungsblatt GG* no. 1, 26 October 1939[5]). Simultaneously, the ban on ritual slaughter was issued and penal servitude was threatened in the event of violations.[6]

Furthermore, regulations on the abolition of tax exemption and tax concessions for Jewish corporations[7] came into force, in addition to the regulation on the visible identification of shops in the GG,[8] as well as the requirement for Jews of both sexes over the age of 10 to be visibly identified with a blue Star of Zion on a white armband.[9]

The decision was taken to appoint Jewish councils, which are to facilitate cooperation with the German administration.[10] The members are responsible for the following areas of activity: financial matters, economic activity, welfare, health services, labour deployment, emigration, etc. In all areas, moreover, efforts are being made to promote self-administration. For example, all welfare measures are already being carried out by the 'Jewish Social Self-Help', which has its headquarters in Cracow.

The First Implementing Regulation to the Regulation of 26 October 1939 on the Introduction of Forced Labour contains measures that facilitate an official registration of the Jewish population: the obligation to report when there is a change of residence and when moving into the General Government, certain restrictions on movement, and restrictions on the use of streets and public spaces at certain times.[11]

The Second Implementing Regulation[12] stipulates that all Jews from the age of 14 to the age of 60 are categorically subject to forced labour. Forced labour is generally of two

3 The earlier parts of the report deal with the 'Organization and Spatial Planning of the Territory', the 'Basic Principles of Church Policy in the GG', control of epidemic disease (epidemic typhus and typhus), and Jewish schools.

4 The person in charge was Dr Fritz Arlt (1912–2004), sociologist; joined the NSDAP and the SA in 1932, and the SS in 1937; head of the Office of Racial Policy for Gau Silesia from 1936; Gau representative there in 1938; head of the Central Institute for Regional Studies in Upper Silesia and the Upper Silesia field office of the Reich Commissioner for the Strengthening of Germandom (RKF) in 1940; responsible for expulsions of Poles and Jews; served in the Wehrmacht, 1943–1944; involved in the establishment of the German Red Cross tracing service after the war; classified as a 'follower' (*Mitläufer*) during denazification proceedings in Munich in 1949; later worked in the administrations of various German employers' associations and as deputy chairman of the Franco-German Youth Bureau.

5 See Doc. 27.

6 See the Regulation on the Prohibition of Ritual Slaughter: *VOBl-GG* 1939, no. 1, 26 Oct. 1939, p. 6.

7 See the Regulation on the Abolition of the Tax Exemption and Tax Concessions of Jewish Corporations: *VOBl-GG* 1939, no. 8, 30 Nov. 1939, p. 60.

8 See the Regulation on the Labelling of Shops in the General Government: *VOBl-GG* 1939, no. 8, 30 Nov. 1939, pp. 61–62. According to the regulation, Jewish shops were to be 'visibly identified with the Star of Zion'.

9 See the Regulation on the Visible Identification of Jews and Jewesses in the General Government, 23 Nov. 1939: *VOBl-GG* 1939, no. 8, 30 Nov. 1939, p. 61.

10 See Doc. 46.

11 See Doc. 55.

12 See Doc. 58.

years' duration and is extended only in exceptional cases and as a correctional measure. Where possible, deployment is undertaken on the basis of vocational skills and with housing in a camp. Anyone who avoids registration or impedes the performance of forced labour can be punished with up to 10 years of penal servitude.

Furthermore, it was made a requirement that all Jewish assets must be registered, and the status of the assets on the effective date of this regulation is to be taken as the basis for registration. The following are deemed to be owners of Jewish assets: Jews who held Polish citizenship on 1 January 1939 or have acquired it since that time; stateless Jews; non-Jewish spouses of Jews; partnerships in which more than half of the partners are Jews; limited partnerships in which more than half of the personally liable partners are Jews; corporations in which more than 25 per cent of the shareholders are Jews. Assets that are not registered will be seized.[13]

Use of the railways was prohibited to Jews.[14]

A directive in *Verordnungsblatt GG* no. 4, dated 2 March 1940, stipulates the establishment of an independent section for Jewish affairs in the Office of the Governor General, Interior Administration Department – Population and Welfare – and within the corresponding offices at the lower levels of the administration. The tasks of these sections for Jewish affairs include the following: the registration of Jews and the decision as to whether someone is a Jew, the establishment of councils of Jewish elders, regulations pertaining to Jews, and the handling of general matters arising relating to the Jews, with the exception of welfare.

The establishment of these sections for Jewish affairs in all administrative offices has made it possible to handle all Jewish affairs consistently and effectively.

A regulation of May 1940 prohibits the employment of non-Jewish female individuals under the age of 45 in Jewish households across the board.[15] The use of motor vehicles by Jews is to be permitted only in urgent, exceptional cases.

A draft regulation was prepared in May 1940 concerning the definition of the term 'Jew'. This stipulates that the term 'Jew' is defined in the General Government by applying the provisions under Reich law.[16]

The Governor General has ordered the resettlement of the Jews from Cracow, noting that such a large Jewish population is not acceptable for a city that is the seat of government.[17] The Jewish Council has made the requisite arrangements for this resettlement. Within the first few days, even before the order to resettle was formally issued, 1,200 Jews

13 See Doc. 81.

14 See the Regulation on the Use of the Railway by Jews in the General Government of 26 Jan. 1940: *VOBl-GG* 1940, no. 10, 6 February 1940, p. 45.

15 The Regulation on the Curtailing of the Employment of Female Non-Jewish Domestic Workers in Jewish Households was not issued until 19 Sept. 1940: *VOBl-GG* 1940, no. 57, 27 Sept. 1940, p. 309.

16 See the Regulation on the Definition of the Term 'Jew' in the General Government of 24 July 1940; *VOBl-GG* 1940, no. 48, 1 August 1940, pp. 231–232.

17 See Doc. 104. Stadthauptmann Schmidt, at the meeting of the GG government on 10 June 1940, had spoken of initially forcing 20,000 Jews to leave Cracow. Then, on 15 July, there was talk of expelling all 60,000–70,000 Jews from Cracow: Präg and Jacobmeyer (eds.), *Diensttagebuch des deutschen Generalgouverneurs*, pp. 240, 255.

have already been resettled, and 1,000 more received passes and tickets on 24 June for their departure from Cracow.

[…][18]

DOC. 131
On 5 July 1940 Propaganda Minister Goebbels notes that Governor General Frank now considers the Jewish question insoluble[1]

Diary of Joseph Goebbels, entry for 5 July 1940

5 July 1940 (Friday)
Yesterday: a stormy and eventful day. In brief.

English fleet attacks French fleet in the port of Oran.[2] French offer resistance. Heavy losses. Churchill's most rabid cynicism. Pétain[3] delivers a statement that is scathing in the extreme. The Führer tells the French that they are permitted to scuttle their ships if in danger. The impact on the world is tremendous. We hurl everything into the fray. In the evening Churchill's speech in the House of Commons. He sets out the entire case with unparalleled cynicism. Denies all rumours of peace. One hopes he sticks to it. Otherwise the English will never give us a moment's rest.

They bombed German cities again. With heavy civilian casualties for us. But we are attacking England. But when will it really get going? At the moment it is impossible to keep the press even halfway in line. And even more so the people. They are positively thirsting for war with England.

Hungary has come over all friendly towards Germany. Those hypocrites! All winter long they reckoned our chances were nil. And now they are back on top with us again. But they can't dupe us any longer.

Pan-Slavism is spreading all over the Balkans. Russia is seizing the moment. Perhaps we will have to take on the Soviets at some point after all.

Arranged the reception of the Führer in Berlin in every detail. Will be splendid.

Discussed press issues with Rienhardt.[4] German newspaper in Belgium has been set up.[5] That will have to be done in Paris too.

18 The report goes on to deal with the Section for Voluntary Welfare Organizations.

1 Diaries of Joseph Goebbels, from 16 May 1940 to 20 Nov. 1940: RGVA, 1477. Published in *Die Tagebücher von Joseph Goebbels*, part 1: *Aufzeichnungen 1923–1941*, vol. 8: *April–November 1940*, ed. Elke Fröhlich (Munich: Saur, 1998), pp. 205–206. This document has been translated from German.

2 To prevent the French navy from falling into Hitler's hands, the Royal Navy destroyed several French warships off the Algerian coast on 3 July 1940, as a result of which nearly 1,300 French sailors lost their lives.

3 Philippe Pétain (1856–1951), career officer and politician; Marshal of France in the First World War; minister of war in 1934; ambassador to Spain in 1939; head of state of the Vichy regime, 1940–1945; imprisoned from 1945.

4 Rolf Rienhardt (1903–1975), lawyer; joined the NSDAP in 1923; head of the NSDAP Main Press Office from 1934.

5 The *Brüsseler Zeitung*, the official newspaper of the German occupiers in Belgium, was published from 1 July 1940 until 1944.

Dr Frank reports to me on situation in General Government. Poles are kowtowing and working busily. They respect us. Must learn to see us as a master race. Scarcely possible now to solve the Jewish question. Russians at the border growing increasingly insolent. We must never give up the East again.

Du Prel[6] is being replaced in Cracow. In his place, Schmidt-Hamburg.[7]

A great many film questions decided. New problems crop up daily there.

D'Alquen[8] makes his farewells. He is going to Bizerte. Nice, intelligent boy. Naumann is taking his place again.[9]

More documents published from secret French sources. What confusion, what dilettantism, and what lack of direction on the opposing side. And how the English have left France in the lurch! It would be hard to bear if they are not put in the dock for this.

The Oran naval battle is the big sensation. Pétain gives orders to fire on and capture English merchant vessels. The Franco-English coalition looks set to turn into a Franco-English war. Churchill's speech is so insulting to France that an explosion must come soon. We add fuel, stir things up. Report from our confidential informants about the effects of our radio broadcasts to France during the war: cannot be praised highly enough. We played a large part in ensuring that France collapsed so quickly and so completely.

New Romanian government under Gigurtu.[10] Very much on our side. Manoilescu will be foreign minister.[11]

6 Dr Maximilian Baron du Prel (1904–1945); lawyer; took part in the Beer Hall Putsch in 1923; joined the NSDAP in 1932 and the SS in 1940; editor for the *VB* and head of the press office of the League of National Socialist German Lawyers in 1933; chief press officer for the General Government in the Office of the Governor General, then worked in the NSDAP Reich Press Office, Oct. 1939 – July 1940; co-founder and secretary general of the Union of Nationalist Journalists' Associations in 1941.

7 Erich Schmidt (1900–1981), office worker; joined the NSDAP in 1931 and the SS in 1942; worked in the police force and in the National Socialist press in Hamburg; with the Reich Chamber of Culture in Berlin in 1939; head of the Propaganda Department in the General Government, July 1940 – Jan. 1941; in the Reich Commissariat in Oslo until the end of 1941; thereafter head of the 'Planten un Blomen' exhibition halls in Hamburg; lived in Hamburg and Dettingen a.d. Erms after the war.

8 Gunter d'Alquen (1910–1998), journalist; joined the SA in 1926, the NSDAP in 1927, and the SS in 1931; *VB* political correspondent from 1932; editor-in-chief of the SS newspaper *Das Schwarze Korps* from 1935; SS war correspondent from Sept. 1939; worked in Goebbels's ministerial office for several weeks in 1939 and 1940; in British captivity, 1945–1948; later sentenced to fines in two court proceedings; co-owner of a weaving mill in Mönchengladbach.

9 Dr Werner Naumann (1909–1982), economist; joined the NSDAP in 1928 and the SS in 1933; Goebbels's personal assistant and office manager from 1938; served in the war in 1939–1940, during which time d'Alquen acted in his place; state secretary in the Reich Ministry of Public Enlightenment and Propaganda (RMfVuP) in 1944; in hiding, 1945–1949; active in radical right-wing politics in the 1950s; later director of a metal factory in Lüdenscheid.

10 Ion Gigurtu (1886–1959), politician; prime minister of Romania, July–Sept. 1940; accepted members of the far-right Iron Guard into the government for the first time and tried to pass anti-Jewish legislation modelled on the Nuremberg Laws; arrested several times from 1944; sentenced to 15 years in prison in 1956; died in prison.

11 Mihail Manoilescu (1891–1950), foreign minister in Gigurtu's government.

London spreads rumour in Kiel of an impending large-scale bombing raid by intruding on Hamburger Welle's signal. This results in something of a panic in the city. I'm having the case thoroughly investigated. But we will […][12] the English gentlemen.

Home late, and tired. Still dictated appeal for the Führer's return to Berlin. It will be grand and ceremonious. Long talk with Naumann. Organization of the office. And then a few hours of sleep.

DOC. 132
On 12 July 1940 Governor General Frank reports on Hitler's intention to deport the European Jews to Madagascar[1]

Minutes of the meeting of department heads of the government of the GG in Cracow, dated 12 July 1940

[…][2]
Also very important is the Führer's decision, made at my request, that there will be no further transports of Jews into the General Government. In relation to the broader political picture, I can tell you that there is a plan to transport the entire Jewish tribe, within the shortest conceivable time after the conclusion of peace, from the German Reich, the General Government, and the Protectorate to an African or American colony. The current thinking focuses on Madagascar,[3] which is to be relinquished by France for this purpose. Here, in an area of 500,000 square kilometres, there will be plenty of space for a few million Jews. I sought to have the Jews in the General Government also share in this benefit of building a new life for themselves on new soil. That idea was accepted, and the result will be a colossal easing of the burden in the foreseeable future.
[…][4]

12 One word missing in the original.

1 AIPN, GK 95, vol. 2. Copy in IfZ-Archives, Fb 105, vol. 7, fols. 1645–1658, here p. 1648. Published in Präg and Jacobmeyer (eds.), *Diensttagebuch des deutschen Generalgouverneurs*, p. 252. This document has been translated from German.

2 Frank was reporting on his conversation with Hitler on 8 July 1940, in which the latter had stated that he viewed the General Government as a 'component part' of the Reich and had praised Frank for having 'succeeded' in 'keeping the Poles quiet' with only a small number of personnel.

3 See Doc. 145.

4 In what follows, Frank reported, among other things, that Hitler endorsed the repressive measures against the Poles in the General Government.

DOC. 133

On 15 July 1940 the official in charge of Jewish affairs for the SS and Police Leader in Lublin requests a supply of 30,000 Jewish forced labourers[1]

Letter from the official in charge of Jewish affairs for the SS and Police Leader in District Lublin, Dr Karl Hofbauer, to the head of the Labour Department, District Lublin, for the attention of Oberregierungsrat Jache, dated 15 July 1940[2]

Re: supply of Jewish forced labourers
To speed up the expansion of the border fortifications[3] between the Bug and the San, we require substantial numbers of Jewish forced labourers in the near future.

I request that you supply 3,000 men to Belzec[4] by Wednesday 17 July 1940.

I request that you make preparations for providing 5,000 more Jews by the beginning of next week.

To be able to complete the trench in the time ordered, a total of 30,000 men must be at work by the beginning of August. I therefore request that everything be set in motion at the employment offices immediately so that they will be able to provide the required numbers of forced labourers.

We will undertake guarding the transports.

DOC. 134

On 17 and 18 July 1940 the physician Zygmunt Klukowski describes the first deportation of Jews from Szczebrzeszyn in District Lublin to a labour camp[1]

Handwritten diary of Zygmunt Klukowski,[2] entries for 17 and 18 July 1940

17 July
Today was a very difficult day for the Jews. They have had relative peace for several months. They only had to provide several dozen people for labour in Zamość each day, for the farm in Bodaczów, and for the local barracks. Other than that, they remained

1 APL, 498/748, fol. 5. This document has been translated from German.
2 At the bottom of the letter there are official stamps and handwritten notes dated 2 August 1940, signature He [Hecht].
3 See Docs. 15 and 82.
4 In 1940 Bełżec was the site of a large forced labour camp for Jews.

1 Zygmunt Klukowski, Dziennik, no. 3, fols. 5RS–7RS; Library of the Catholic University of Lublin, manuscript division 813. Published in Zygmunt Klukowski, *Zamojszczyzna*, vol. 1: *1918–1943*, ed. Agnieszka Knyt (Warsaw: KARTA, 2007), pp. 175–176. The diary is available in English translation: *Diary from the Years of Occupation, 1939–1944*, ed. Andrew Klukowski and Helen Klukowski May, trans. George Klukowski (Urbana, IL: University of Illinois Press, 1993). This document has been translated from Polish.
2 Dr Zygmunt Klukowski (1885–1959), physician; studied medicine in Moscow and Cracow; director of the hospital in Szczebrzeszyn, 1920–1946; served in the war in eastern Poland in Sept. 1939; briefly detained on multiple occasions; in the Polish underground, 1941–1944; persecuted by the Polish state security service after the war; sentenced to two years in prison (released after one year) in 1951. He began writing the diary quoted here in June 1939.

completely untouched, and that a Jew got a beating from a gendarme or a police officer every now and then does not count. They were already beginning to regain their former self-assurance, which could be seen from the way they behaved on the street. However, a few days ago a notification arrived unexpectedly that 500 Jews from Szczebrzeszyn were to be sent to a labour camp.[3] Wild panic and frenzied activity set in among them. Jews besieged physicians to obtain medical certificates, tried to get themselves admitted to a hospital for the most trivial of ailments, sent delegations to the starostwo[4] in Biłgoraj and Zamość, to the employment office, etc. Eventually, after energetic efforts, they succeeded in having this number reduced to 130.

This roundup of Jews actually took place this very morning. The 'Judenrat'[5] selected 130 young men, handing each one their summons, but only 98 turned up. The rest escaped or hid. Gestapo men arrived from Zamość. They were reinforced by 20 soldiers on horseback. The hunt for Jews began. The mothers, sisters, and fathers who tried to be as close as possible to the frightened Jewish youth gathered on the market square – they gave them things, talked to them, bid them farewell – were driven away. Several received a blow to the back with a rod. Soldiers were sent off in all directions to look for the fugitives. They tore along the pavements on beautiful Polish horses. Some fugitives were found, while parents were taken in place of others. Members of the Judenrat also got their share. The deputy chairman was beaten with truncheons and told to lie flat on the square for an hour. Finally, the market square and the adjacent streets were cleared of most Jews, who were grouped into threes in a single column, in the direction of the railway station. They were surrounded on all sides by soldiers on horseback. This procession was accompanied by the weeping and wailing of Jewish women hiding in gateways and side streets.

A big part of the Polish population observed this roundup. Not even the slightest sign of empathy was to be seen on many faces; on the contrary, there were laughter and jokes. The remark of a citizen who used to be in the Legion[6] was typical: 'I do not feel sorry for them because I saw how they disarmed the Polish soldiers.'

After the first batch had left, reprisals were announced because not everyone had shown up. Jewish shops were closed all day. There were very few Jews on the streets.

In the afternoon, an announcement was put up on walls from the incumbent mayor, Borucki,[7] who by order of the German authorities is calling on citizens to strictly observe the curfew and not 'wander' around town after 10 p.m. Should breaches of this ban continue, curfew hours will change again, and one will be allowed out only until 8 p.m., just as before.

3 The author may be referring to one of the large camps in the south of District Lublin (Bełżec, Cieszanów). Those seized in Szczebrzeszyn were initially forced to work daily in Zamość, in the vicinity of which forced labourers had to work on river regulation. Klukowski visited one of these camps after an outbreak of typhus. On 23 July 1940 he described the dreadful conditions: Klukowski, *Zamojszczyzna*, p. 177.

4 Polish: 'regional authority'.

5 German in the original here and below: 'Jewish Council'.

6 Allusion to the Polish Legions commanded by Piłsudski during the First World War.

7 Jan Borucki was from the Poznań area; initially supervisor of sanitation in Szczebrzeszyn; then deputy mayor of Szczebrzeszyn from Oct. 1939 and subsequently mayor after the arrest of the incumbent mayor in June 1940; shot dead by the Germans in Sept. 1941.

18 July
Great unrest among the Jews. They expect that many more will be taken to the labour camp. A regulation from the mayor was issued and, in a custom dating back to the old days, it was posted up on walls: all Jews aged 16 to 50 must report to the Judenrat every day. No Jew is permitted to go beyond the town boundary without a special permit issued by the Judenrat. Anyone caught outside the town without a permit will be severely punished and sent to a labour camp.

DOC. 135
On 21 July 1940 the Order Service in the Litzmannstadt (Lodz) ghetto lists people shot dead at the perimeter fence in the space of a few days[1]

Report by the Jewish elder in Litzmannstadt, Order Service, unsigned, dated 21 July 1940 (carbon copy)[2]

Report on the persons shot before curfew in the past week.

1. Emanuel Fischman, born on 13 November 1924, son of Chaim and Ryfka, née Samulewicz, address 53 Bierstr., shot *on 16 July 1940* at 3 p.m., 1 m from the wire fence near 42/44 Hamburgerstr. Witness: Ester Lewartowska, address 42 Hamburgerstr.
2. Perec Familier, born on 22 August 1878, son of Abram Gerszon and Laja Liba, address 2 Hanseatenstr., shot *on 19 July 1940* at 2.15 p.m. near 39 Wirkerstr., 1 m from the wire fence.
3. Menasze Rotszyld, born on 16 January 1910, address 26 Alexanderhofstr., shot *on 20 July 1940* at 6 p.m. near 3 Waldstr., 1 m from the wire fence.
4. Hinda Holzman, born on 12 September 1922, daughter of Ide Laib and Malka, née Salumowicz, address 2 Baluter Ring, A[partment] 32, shot *on 21 July 1940* at 9 a.m. near 77 Holzstr., 1 m from the wire fence.
5. Sura Goldband, born in 1923 in Izbica/Kujaw.,[3] daughter of Szlojma and Chinda, née Brzezinska, address 7 Hirtenweg/A[partment] 12, shot *on 21 July 1940* at 9 a.m. near 77 Holzstr., 1 m from the wire fence.
6. Eljasz Rosenfarb, born on 15 December 1919 in Lodz, son of Icek and Laja, née Ajzen, address 13 Hanseatenstr., shot *on 21 July 1940* at 9.30 a.m. near 101 Holzstr., around 80 m from the wire fence.[4] Witnesses: Abram Szyldwach, 26 Inselstr., Dwojra Kalmanowicz, 101 Holzstr.
7. Herman Rosenblum, 20 years old, born in Frankfurt am Main, son of Chil Majer and Sura, née Pasternak, address 26 Inselstr., shot *on 21 July 1940* at 9.30 a.m., near 101 Holzstr., around 80 m from the wire fence. Witnesses: Abram Szyldwach, 26 Inselstr., Dwojra Kalmanowicz, 101 Holzstr.

1 APŁ, 221/31866b, fol. 139. Copy in USHMM, RG 05 008M, reel 6. Published as a facsimile in Michal Unger (ed.), *The Last Ghetto: Life in the Lodz Ghetto, 1940–1944* (Jerusalem: Yad Vashem, 1995), p. 63. This document has been translated from German.
2 The original contains handwritten notes.
3 Izbica Kujawska.
4 Many of those shot later had also not even gone near the fence.

DOC. 136

Warschauer Zeitung, 21/22 July 1940: report on a lecture given by an academic at the Institute for German Eastern Research[1]

The Poles made Warsaw a Jewish metropolis. After New York, the largest Jewish city in the world. The Jewish problem in the General Government. In many cities, more than half of the inhabitants are Jews. Of the Jews in former Poland, 23 per cent were unable to support themselves.

Cracow, 20 July

We have already reported, on various occasions, on the Jewish problem in the former Polish territory. Today we use a talk given by the lecturer Dr Seraphim[2] of the Institute for German Eastern Research[3] as the occasion to present a revealing overview of the whole problem.

Germany today, including the Protectorate of Bohemia and Moravia and the General Government, is home to approximately 2.7 million Jews. Germany thus ranks as the third-largest Jewish state in the world, behind the United States of America and the Soviet Union. The problem of the Jews today, however, is not one of infiltration or assimilation and of curbing the Jews' sphere of political and economic influence. Rather, it is now a problem of the racial composition of the population. East European Jewry is shaped by its history to a much greater extent than Jewry in other regions. Of course the Jews in Central and Western Europe also have a historical past, but for the most part they only migrated from the Jewish heartland of Eastern Europe from the eighteenth century onwards, with the influx most notable in the nineteenth and twentieth centuries. Things are different in Eastern Europe.

The Jews bringing up the rear

The Jews in this territory are almost exclusively the offspring of the Jews who migrated into the *Ostraum* from the southern and western parts of Europe between the thirteenth and the seventeenth centuries. They followed in the wake of the Germans' advance eastwards, but only after the completion of each stage of colonization. The Jews themselves never headed eastwards as colonial pioneers. Up to a point, their migration eastwards was a consequence of the privileges granted to Jews: these made the Jews into a class with special personal and economic advantages. But these privileges, granted since the mid thirteenth century, were not the decisive factor in the Jews' migration to Eastern Europe. Rather, this migration was above all the result of the change *in the significance of certain trade routes* that began precisely during these centuries. The Tatar invasion of southern Russia caused the trade routes between the Baltic and the Black Sea to atrophy.

1 *Warschauer Zeitung*, no. 171, 21/22 July 1940, pp. 5–6. This document has been translated from German.

2 Dr Peter-Heinz Seraphim (1902–1979), economist; deputy head of the Institute for Eastern European Economics in Königsberg from 1933; published *Das Judentum im osteuropäischen Raum* in 1938; worked at the Institute for German Eastern Research in Cracow, 1939–1940; professor in Greifswald in 1940; editor of the periodical *Weltkampf*, published by the Institute for the Study of the Jewish Question, 1941–1943; director of studies at the Academy of Public Administration in Bochum after the war.

3 The institute, founded by Hans Frank in Cracow in April 1940, was supposed to provide scientific advice to the government of the GG; it was headed by the lawyer Dr Wilhelm Coblitz.

The dissolution of the Byzantine Empire and the shift of the European centre of gravity to the area made up of northern Italy, central Germany, and western France resulted in a relocation of the trade routes. The southern trade route with the Levant became less important. The northern Hanseatic sea route was under the control of the German cities, but the land routes, which ran north and south of the Carpathian range from eastern Germany to the coast of the Black Sea, were open to trade and increasingly gained in importance. At the points where *they* intersected or branched, the Jews established themselves, later flooding into the rural areas as well.

After the influence of royal power declined, especially in the Polish-Lithuanian state, the Jews placed themselves under the protection of the magnate class, and later of the nobility. From the seventeenth century onwards, the position of the Jews begins to change. They increasingly spill into every pore of economic life. Thus in the countryside they come face to face with the broadest social class, from whom they had previously been geographically separated as a result of their residing in the cities en masse. The peasantry, sucked dry, fought back, but the Jews' innate toughness enabled them to withstand such resistance as well as the internal struggles of disintegrating Poland and the storms of the Nordic War, although their dominant position in the economy was shattered. When the focus of world traffic shifted again, to the Atlantic Ocean, following the discovery of the New World, the heartland of East European Jewry sank into poverty as a result. On the whole, the Jews were proletarianized or turned to craft trades for their livelihood.

Nevertheless, until the last part of the eighteenth century, the Jews of Eastern Europe managed to maintain their cohesion as a group within the firm confines of their religious faith. But from the middle of the nineteenth century onwards, the development of Jewry in Eastern Europe ceased to take a homogeneous course. While the Jews in Austria, Hungary, and Prussia were granted full freedom of movement and even equal rights in some cases, in Russia the policy pertaining to the Jews took a different direction. During the second half of the nineteenth century, governments tried to limit the Jews' influence to the area in which they had been located since time immemorial, without attempting a real solution to the Jewish problem. However, in the longer term, neither the laws and decrees nor the periodic pogroms achieved anything. With masterful dexterity, the Jews knew how to circumvent all the directives or bribe the civil servants. With the beginning of industrialization in the second half of the nineteenth century, the Jews in Russia and Congress Poland once again gained an *economically dominant position.* They infiltrated the entire sector of foreign trade and completely took over the running of the economy, as financiers, as publishers, as factory owners, as owners of the transport and distribution system and of import and export businesses, and as wholesalers and retailers. The influence exerted by Jewry developed along these lines up to the present day.

Linguistic homogeneity

From the *historically determined nature of the East European Jews*, as shown here, there result fundamental principles that explain the distinctive quality of eastern Jewry in racial, religious, linguistic, ethnopolitical, and social terms. Rabbinical Orthodoxy, it is true, no longer possesses the dominant influence it once had, but it nonetheless remains the outer ring that binds this ethnic group together. In linguistic terms, too, the Jews of Eastern Europe remain united, while assimilation has largely come to prevail in the western part of the continent. 'Yiddish' – a mixture of Middle High German, Hebrew, and

Slavonic – is still the vernacular used by four-fifths of the Ostjuden. With regard to ethnopolitics, in the majority of the Jews in the East we find a pronounced affirmation of their nationhood, with Herzl's Zionism having had a particularly strong influence on this in the second half of the previous century. While we thus observe great uniformity in religious, linguistic, and ethnic terms among the Jews of Eastern Europe, and correspondingly also among the Jews of the General Government, the exact opposite is true with respect to their racial composition. There is no distinct, well-defined Jewish type to be found here. Besides the general racial mixture of Jews overall, determined over the centuries, eastern Jewry also exhibits an admixture of approximately 50 per cent Near Eastern blood, with Oriental, Mediterranean, Eastern Baltic, Nordic, and Dinaric racial components as well.

The social classification of the Ostjuden by occupation is decidedly lopsided. In Galicia, 80 per cent of the Jews live in urban communities, as do 83 per cent of the Jews in Congress Poland; 40 per cent of all Jews are engaged in trade and commerce; 38 per cent work in manufacturing and crafts; and 23 per cent of the Jews in former Poland were unable to support themselves. The social tensions within Jewry were exacerbated by the rise of socialist ideologies.

Jewish calculations dating from 1935 shed significant light on the Jews' domination of economic life in former Poland. According to this information, there were 202,000 Jewish commercial enterprises and 123,000 non-Jewish ones in Poland (excluding the Corridor[4] and the western territories that were once torn from Germany), and consequently 63 per cent of trade was controlled by the Jews. And these statistics do not even include public limited companies. If they are taken into account, the figure for the degree of Jewification of Polish commerce would probably rise to 75 or 80 per cent. According to a survey conducted in 216 Polish cities in 1933, 13,322 (86 per cent) of the 15,482 retail businesses were Jewish. The share of Jewish craft enterprises in 1933 was, for example, 57 per cent in *Warsaw* and 52 per cent in *Lublin*. Similar figures appear for all the other branches of the economy.

Annual population growth of 8.7 per cent

The percentage of Jews in the General Government population is extremely difficult to determine. A large proportion of the Jews, despite their affiliation with the Mosaic faith, put themselves down as Poles in previous Polish censuses. But the counts based on affiliation with the Mosaic faith nonetheless remained the most reliable, because the process of assimilation and religious conversion was significantly *less advanced* in the relatively closed world of *eastern Jewry* than among the Jews of Central and Western Europe. In 1931 the total number of Jews living in what is now the General Government was approximately 1,300,000. With an average annual growth rate of 8.7 per cent (115,000 per year), and taking into account an emigration figure of 45,000 Jews, the population for 1939 can be estimated at 1,370,000. The flight of countless Jews to now Russian eastern Poland in that year due to the war, and the subsequent influx from the Reich, if set against one another, result in a surplus of approximately 100,000 Jews migrating into the territory, so that the total number of Jews in the population is now estimated at approximately 1,470,000. Of this multitude, around four-fifths live in

4 The Polish Corridor was a region granted to Poland after the First World War to enable Polish access to the coast. It created a 'corridor' that separated East Prussia from the rest of Germany.

cities, most of which have no single dominant majority population. *Warsaw* – next to New York, the largest Jewish metropolis in the world – has the largest Jewish population. It is followed by *Cracow* and *Lublin*. On average, the Jews constitute about 30 per cent of the population in the cities. Here and there, there are cities with 40 per cent and 50 per cent Jews, and in a few small towns the Jews are even in the majority.

Constructive solution essential

In conclusion, it must be said that, in the East and likewise in the territory of the General Government, as a result of the Jews' historical past and the characteristic quality of their dealings in every sphere of life, the character of Jewry has *taken on an unusual, peculiar form*. The inherent difficulties of a solution to the Jewish problem in this territory are further aggravated by this circumstance. It is obvious that this problem can be solved neither quickly nor easily. In the process, one must keep in mind the fundamental insight that placing restrictions on the Jews *is not sufficient* on its own. In place of limiting the Jews' influence and isolating them, one must rather find a *constructive solution* that effectively supplements the measures just noted. Previous actions taken in this sphere are already indicative of the rudiments of a solution to this question in a quite specific direction. *There can be no doubt that Germany will one day find a constructive solution in the National Socialist sense.*[5]

DOC. 137

On 22 July 1940 the commander of the 18th Army bans officers and soldiers from criticizing the persecution of Poles and Jews[1]

Order (marked 'secret') issued by the commander of the 18th Army (Ic no. 2489/40, secret), General Georg von Küchler,[2] army headquarters, dated 22 July 1940 (copy)[3]

1) On the basis of the order issued by the commander of the army, reference AOK 18 Abt. Ic no. 2477/40, secret, dated 22 July 1940, with respect to the German–Russian relationship,[4] I ask the commanding generals to oppose vigorously all rumours about the German–Russian relationship by instructing the officer corps and notifying the troops in a suitable manner.

The following are to be made known to the troops as *the reasons for shifting the 18th Army Command*, with its subordinate troops, from the West *towards the East*:

5 The article is illustrated with photos, which include a shot taken by the photographer Sieredzki, with the caption 'Grimy dealers sell Jewish "treats" in the Lublin ghetto', and portrait shots taken by the photographer Gerspach, with the caption 'An array of particularly expressive Jewish types, such as can be seen at every turn in the General Government'.

1 Copy in IfZ-Archives, NOKW-1531. This document has been translated from German.

2 Georg von Küchler (1881–1968), career officer; commander of the 3rd Army during the invasion of Poland in 1939, then of the 18th Army; commander of Army Group North in the war against the Soviet Union, 1942–1944; sentenced to 20 years in prison at the High Command Trial in 1948; released in 1953.

3 Contained in a letter from the Oberquartiermeister (a senior officer on the general staff), signed Schlieper, dated 25 July 1940, asking the higher authorities 'to inform the officers and officials about the content of the commander's order as soon as possible after their arrival in the East'.

4 This could not be found.

Securing the newly gained *Lebensraum* in the East.
Demonstrating our military strength to the Poles.
Preparing for the peacetime quartering of army units in the eastern territory.

2) I further ask that you ensure that every soldier in the army, particularly every officer, refrains from criticizing the ethnic struggle being carried out in the General Government, like the treatment of the Polish minorities, the Jews, and church matters. The ethnic struggle that has been raging along the eastern border for centuries requires unique, drastic measures if a definitive ethnopolitical solution is to be found.

   Certain Party and state organizations have been given the task of waging this ethnic struggle.

   The soldier must therefore keep out of these other organizations' tasks. He must also not interfere in these tasks by offering criticism. Instruction on these questions must begin immediately, particularly for the soldiers now transferred from the West to the East, as they may hear rumours and misrepresentations concerning the purpose and meaning of the ethnic struggle.

DOC. 138

On 22, 23, and 24 July 1940 members of the SS Cavalry in Kielce report conflicts with non-commissioned Wehrmacht officers who were defending Jews[1]

Reports by members of the SS Cavalry, signed Georg Dech,[2] Oleg Brakel,[3] Jakob Hermann, and Josef Lang,[4] to the 2nd Squadron of the SS Death's-Head Cavalry Regiment in Kielce, dated 22, 23, and 24 July 1940

Report

When I met a Jew in Petrikauerstraße who did not step aside to make way for me, I punched the man in the face, whereupon two non-commissioned Wehrmacht officers rushed up to help the Jew, and one of them took hold of my uniform and struck out at me. These two NCOs were quite deliberately helping the Jew stay on his feet, and this in the presence of several other Jews who had come up to us in the meantime.

I am quite astonished at this behaviour on the part of the NCOs and feel obliged to report it.

I should add that one thing these two NCOs said was that they wondered what I was doing punching the Jew because, after all, Jews were people too. Unfortunately, I was unable to establish what unit these two NCOs served in.

I regard the actions taken against me by these two NCOs as absolutely harmful to Germandom, and, as a member of the SS, I think that even if one on some occasion punches a Jew without cause, under no circumstances should the Jew be helped in this

1 Copy in BArch, RS 4/334: see also Doc. 123. This document has been translated from German.
2 Presumably Georg Dech (b. 1923), farmer; acquired citizenship in Łódź as an ethnic German in 1940.
3 Oleg Brakel (b. 1920), SS-Sturmmann and candidate for non-commissioned rank.
4 Joseph Lang (b. 1918); acquired citizenship in Łódź as an ethnic German in 1940.

manner. The whole thing is made worse because the incident occurred in the presence of a substantial number of Jews.

Report

SS cavalrymen Oleg Brakel and Jakob Hermann have the following encounter with members of the Wehrmacht to report:

On 22 July 1940 at 8.15 p.m., the two of us were taking a walk in the area of Radomerstraße and found ourselves at a dead end. To get back on the right route, we looked for a way out through a courtyard, and suddenly we saw a sergeant major, a corporal, and four enlisted men in front of us. The sergeant major then started to say that we probably had nothing better to do than beat up Jews. He said we were roving about in the streets like thugs. SS Cavalryman Brakel said that we had not been beating up any Jews just now, and in reply he was told that he was lying. When the sergeant major asked whether the men were on duty, the reply was that SS men were always on duty. As identification, SS Cavalryman Brakel then produced his pay-book.

Then the sergeant major asked what had become of the Jewish girls arrested yesterday. They were innocent, he said, and were employed in the kitchen that served the barracks. In general, he said, the Jewish question was no business of the SS at all.

The two SS men now wanted to learn which barracks the sergeant major and his men were associated with, and followed them to Bocendinskastraße[5] and up as far as the city barracks. Then a regimental sergeant major arrived and scolded the SS cavalryman for having followed the sergeant major. SS Cavalryman Brakel replied that the intention was to determine where the sergeant major was barracked. Several NCOs and enlisted men who had also appeared insulted the two SS men in a vile manner and demanded that they leave the area immediately. When SS Cavalryman Brakel then asked to be allowed to speak to the sergeant major, a private jumped out and punched SS Cavalryman Brakel. Both SS cavalrymen then retreated while being subjected to further kicks.

Report

I was taking a walk with SS Cavalryman Lang (we are both ethnic Germans) in Bocendinskastraße. Walking ahead of us were several Jews, and behind us were several Wehrmacht NCOs. A Jew walking ahead of us told his fellow Jews who were approaching not to greet the SS, [and added that] the Wehrmacht would take care that nothing happened to us [to the Jews]. Two Polish women crossed the street and said to us in Polish that we should beware and not lay a finger on the Jews, because the whole thing was a done deal between the Wehrmacht and the Jews.

As a result, we took no action of any kind.

5 Correctly: Bodzentyńska.

DOC. 139

On 23 July 1940 the employment office in Lublin reports on an unauthorized roundup conducted by the SS in Lublin[1]

Memorandum (marked 'for information') from the employment office in Lublin, signed Hecht, for the head of the Labour Department in District Lublin, Oberregierungsrat Jache, dated 23 July 1940

Memorandum

The Lublin Employment Office (Department of Jewish Deployment) – Mr *Wagner* – rang this morning and informed me that during the night of 22/23 July, approximately 300 Jews had been brought to the Lublin airfield[2] as a result of an SS roundup. The Lublin Employment Office has received no information about this measure. On the basis of this telephone call, I immediately drove to the Lublin airfield with Mr Wagner of the Lublin Employment Office to make enquiries there about the 300 Jews. At the Lublin airfield, I then had discussions with Dr *Hofbauer* and Unterscharführer *Riedel*[3] about this matter. It emerged that

1) the roundup took place during the night of 22/23 July; it was carried out by the SS under the command of Unterscharführer Riedel on orders from above;

2) in this roundup, approximately 300 Jews were captured and transported to the Lublin airfield;

3) the 300 Jews are to be utilized for the local airfield.

I pointed out to Dr Hofbauer that such a measure should be undertaken only in consultation with the Lublin Employment Office, and that all other measures concerning labour deployment are prohibited. [SS]-Unterscharführer Riedel stated that, for the time being, he would not make the 300 Jews available to the employment office. It was then agreed with Unterscharführer Riedel that these 300 Jews must be properly recorded in the Lublin Employment Office's card index, and that on Wednesday afternoon, at 4 p.m., members of the Jewish Council will record the names of the Jews who were rounded up. Commenting on the roundup, Dr Hofbauer further stated that it had probably been arranged between SS-Brigadeführer Globocnik[4] and Oberregierungsrat Jache. I replied that I had no knowledge of these measures. Other than that, Dr Hofbauer says that the employment office and the Labour Department should largely hold off regarding Jewish labour deployment, as changes are to be expected in the near future.

Unterscharführer Riedel went on to say that the SS will take Jews from the ghetto in Lublin by means of roundups whenever the need arises.

1 APL, 498/748, fols. 7 –8. This document has been translated from German.
2 The location of a forced labour camp.
3 Horst Riedel (b. 1910), retailer; joined the NSDAP in 1933 and the SS in 1941; head of the workshops in Lublin that employed Jewish forced labourers in 1940; head of the SS enterprise Deutsche Ausrüstungswerke in Lublin.
4 Odilo Globocnik (1904–1945), engineer and building contractor; joined the NSDAP in Austria in 1931 and the SS in 1934; deputy Gauleiter of Vienna in 1933; Gauleiter of Vienna in 1938; relieved of his post due to financial irregularities and transferred to Reichsführer-SS Himmler's personal staff in Feb. 1939; SS and Police Leader in Lublin, Nov. 1939–Sept. 1943; in charge of Operation Reinhard and simultaneously managing director of Ostindustrie GmbH in Lublin in 1943; Higher SS and Police Leader for the Operational Zone of the Adriatic Coast, 1943–1945; committed suicide after being captured.

DOC. 140

Gazeta Żydowska, 23 July 1940: report on the situation of the Jewish population in Warsaw since September 1939[1]

From days of horror in Warsaw

Of all the cities currently in the territory of the General Government, Warsaw has encountered the greatest misfortune. The storm of war passed over other places, but Warsaw remained in its flames for several weeks. The storm's violence is illustrated by the fact that even today, ten months later, entire districts lie in rubble despite the clean-up operation. In addition to the communication arteries in the city centre, Jewish quarters suffered the most. In normal times the quarters north and north-west of the Saxon Gardens[2] were already a sad picture of misery and neglect, which was the result of the city administration's policies – which were, by the way, pursued quite openly. After the siege of Warsaw, any remaining possibilities for a human existence have vanished. The following snapshots from Warsaw's Jewish quarter are intended only for readers in the provinces, for a Varsovian will see them as irrelevant, as no words can describe what he's been through …

Erev Rosh Hashanah[3] – the day passed very calmly; people have almost become used to the air raids by now. Life in the Jewish quarter is all the livelier between one siren alarm and the next. The markets on Nalewki, Leszno, and Bagno are packed; only with difficulty can one push one's way through Nowolipki and Karmelicka. Despite the barricades, the falling rubble and exploding bombs, this is Erev Rosh Hashanah. The sky is suffused with a beautiful blue; the sun is starting to set in the west. Then it begins! …

Night has fallen, but it's not dark. The sky is blood red; tongues of fire shoot up into the sky. There is still water and a fire brigade; it rushes north. Nalewki is burning, Gęsia is burning, Nowolipki is burning!

Here and there, holiday candles are lit behind blacked-out windows; there are still some around. They pale pitifully in comparison to the huge blaze which rises up from the Jewish quarter into the sky. Rosh Hashanah 5790.

Yom Kippur.[4] 500 cannons aimed at Warsaw thunder day and night, hundreds of aeroplanes ceaselessly drop their bombs. There is no longer any defence, there is nothing to eat, life on the streets has ceased. Not only the Jews are fasting on this Yom Kippur. This Yom Kippur will not last one day or one night, but also the following day, and it will last many more days.

Sukkot[5] *– Simchat Torah.*[6] The cannons are silent. The war in Warsaw is over. The great synagogue on Leszno is standing,[7] the Community centre on Grzybowska is standing, nothing but rubble all around.

1 *Gazeta Żydowska*, no. 1, 23 July 1940, pp. 4–5. This document has been translated from Polish. *Gazeta Żydowska* was the only legal newspaper for the Jewish population in occupied Poland. It was published from 23 July 1940 to 30 August 1942 by the German propaganda authorities in Cracow with the help of Jewish journalists, and appeared every two or three days.

2 Polish: Ogród Saski.

3 In the year 5790, i.e. 1939, the evening before the Jewish New Year fell on 13 Sept.

4 In 1939 the Day of Atonement fell on 23 Sept.

5 A Jewish holiday also known as the Feast of Booths.

6 A Jewish holiday celebrating public Torah readings.

Plac Żelaznej Bramy.[8] A fragment of ancient Rome. The ruins of the Colosseum rise against the grey sky to the north-west. The great market rotunda – the centre of Jewish trade in this area – once stood here. The scorched window frames of whatever remains of the surrounding houses look out hopelessly onto this strange image of Rome. People stare aghast – their property either lies buried beneath the rubble or has gone up in flames.

Opposite is the market hall. It was once surrounded by hundreds of big and small shops. One now looks for a morsel of bread or a drop of water, but in vain. Hunger claws, thirst burns. Supplies of herring and pickles are dug up from the debris of undamaged cellars. Grasp at them quickly – they are the first fresh shoots of a growing street trade. They are enough for a while. Later, hunger returns with double the force.

Every useful piece of wood is removed from smoking rubble, from ramparts and trench ditches, and is sawn up. People search for planks to burn, planks to make primitive beds, and planks that can be used as stretchers for the wounded and the dead. They are carried through torn streets still stained in blood. Crowds of terror-stricken people gather. Parents look for their children, sisters for their brothers. If they are not there, they turn away in resignation. Hunger once more stifles fear. Once again, one looks for something to eat.

Water is lugged from the Vistula; old wells are opened up in courtyards. Hundreds of people queue for a few litres of yellow, putrid water. Even if one trades everything that could be salvaged from the disaster, *a drop of water cannot be bought at any price.* In times of greatest poverty, not even the cleverest trader will sell this greatest of treasures.

A house front has collapsed; only a part of the second floor of the rear building has miraculously survived. But how is one to get there? There is nothing left of the stairs. The owners of the destroyed apartments sit crouched on the rubble in the courtyard and weep. They have escaped with nothing more than their lives, but there, on the second floor, one might perhaps still find useful household items. An emaciated figure, one of the fathers, stands up. He rolls up his coat and begins his backbreaking labour. With death-defying courage, he climbs up the rubble higher and higher; bricks crumble beneath his hands – he looks for a new handhold – the rubble gives way beneath his feet – he finds new support. He has spent his entire life poring over books and has never been active – now he moves confidently as if in a trance. Women and children hold their breath, dead silence, only their eyes, wide with terror, express what they feel. Now he is on top, one more turn and the figure disappears through a window. Several moments of tense anticipation pass – then things fall down. A chipped pot, linen covered in soot, and – what luck – one miraculously saved cushion. The remnants of petty bourgeois prosperity. But one is happy and will share.

Who can understand what it means to stand for many hours in the street, in the cold rain, in the sharpest winter frost? There is not a single shop on Królewska, Graniczna, and Krochmalna. Śliska and Zielna are in ruins. On Grzybowski Square, in the Saxon Gardens and in Bagno former shop owners stand in rows one or two deep. From what

7 The author is referring to the main synagogue in Warsaw, located on Tłomackie Street. It was damaged during a German air raid in Sept. 1939.

8 A square near the Saxon Gardens, not far from Mirowski Square. From 1940 both squares were situated on the 'Aryan side' and adjoined the ghetto walls.

is left of their supplies, they offer a pair of stockings, a pair of shoes, an undergarment, fruit drops, poppy-seed cakes. From the market hall on Mirowski Square to the border of the Jewish quarter, life continues only in the streets. The temperature is 25 degrees below zero. In one home, 20 people huddle inside a bathroom spared by the bombs. There is no coal, there is no water, there is no gas.

But there is *typhus*. New barricades are set up, this time against the epidemic. The sanitation authorities clamp down on this enemy with trenches and barbed wire. In the spring, these are turned into walls that surround the containment areas. The Jewish quarter can be reached only via a roundabout route. Warning signs hang everywhere on the closed gates of quarters stricken or suspected of being stricken with the epidemic. Everyone steers clear of these houses. From windows and balconies, baskets and bags are lowered on ropes so that food can be pulled up. Pale faces lean over the balustrades when these baskets go up.

In this city, the words of the prophets are being borne out in full. All the horsemen of the Apocalypse – *War, Hunger, Disease, Death* – loom over the Jewish quarter in Warsaw.

E.G.[9]

DOC. 141

On 24 July 1940 the Selbstschutz in Lublin cautions the Jewish population against gatherings and demonstrations[1]

Announcement by the SS and Selbstschutz in Lublin, SS-Obersturmführer, signature illegible, dated 24 July 1940[2]

Warning

Recently both the Jewish Religious Community and its departments have [become] the setting of unlawful gatherings, attended mainly by women. In light of this, warning is hereby given that any gatherings in front of the Jewish Religious Community's building are strictly prohibited.

Any demonstrations whatsoever against the Jewish Religious Community will be nipped in the bud, and those who provoke these incidents or incite others to do so will be arrested and severely punished.

Owners of the adjacent buildings and apartments who give sanctuary to the demonstrators [will] likewise [be] held strictly accountable.

9 Probably Elza Grosman (Else Grossmann).

1 APL, 891/2, fol. 3. Announcement in German and Polish. This document has been translated from German.

2 Official stamp: SS and Selbstschutz Lublin transit camp.

DOC. 142

On 25 July 1940 the Labour Department of the General Government issues instructions for the deployment of Jewish forced labourers from Cracow[1]

Letter from the Office of the Governor General for the Occupied Polish Territories, Labour Department, Cracow (G.Z.: II 5317/40), Circular Decree no. 105/40, draft signed Dr Gschließer,[2] to the heads of the labour departments of the district governments and of the employment offices in the General Government, dated 25 July 1940 (copy)

Re: labour deployment of Jews; *here:* resettlement from Cracow
Case file:

Circular Decree no.	86/40	of	12 June 1940	–	4,212[3]
Circular Decree no.	100/40	of	5 July 1940	–	5,312[4]
Circular Decree no.	103/40	of	23 July 1940	–	5,317[5]
Circular Decree no.	104/40	of	25 July 1940	–	4,032.[6]

In the near future, the Jews residing in the city of Cracow will receive the order to leave the city limits from the Governor General. For economic reasons, a relatively small number of craftsmen and persons in retail/wholesale occupations and the free professions who cannot be immediately replaced will remain in the city for the time being. The total number of Jews living in Cracow is presently assumed to be 67,000.

The Jews were offered the opportunity of voluntary resettlement by a given deadline (15 August 1940), including permission to take all movable property with them. Very few took advantage of this opportunity. The forced relocation will therefore be on a very significant scale and must be expedited by every possible means. Appropriate preparations for this measure must be carried out immediately.

The referral of the Jews to new places of residence is to proceed systematically, in such a way that the Jews' manpower is harnessed and the Jews' capacity to support themselves[7] is largely preserved. A productive deployment of these Jewish workers is indispensable in any case, given the existing labour shortage in some regions and for some projects. In planning the deployment, it will have to be assumed on the one hand that the scope for housing in camps with communal meals will be quite limited, and on the other that the

1 APL, 498/745, fols. 34–37. This document has been translated from German.
2 Dr Ernst Gschließer (1898–1964), lawyer; in the Austrian Fatherland Front, 1934–1938; deputy head then chief of the Vienna Regional Employment Office in 1936; joined the NSDAP in 1938; labour deployment specialist for the Ostmark in the Reich Ministry of Labour, Sept. 1938; in charge of labour deployment and refugee affairs for the chief of the civil administration (CdZ) in Cracow from Sept. 1939; head of the section for labour deployment within the Labour Department of the General Government from July 1940; after the war practised law in Innsbruck.
3 The Labour Department's Circular Decree no. 86/40 of 12 June 1940 established the procedures for registering Jewish forced labourers. It is not included in the file. However, the file does contain Circular Decree no. 104/40, which makes reference to it: APL, 498/745, fols. 46–49.
4 Regarding Circular Decree no. 100/40, see Doc. 154, fn. 4.
5 In the Labour Department's Circular Decree no. 103/40, dated 23 July 1940, Gschließer added to the provisions of his decree of 5 July 1940 and ordered that Polish and Jewish forced labourers must always be housed separately: BArch, R 52 II/251, fol. 33r–v.
6 The Labour Department's Circular Decree no. 104/40, dated 25 July 1940, specified the registration procedures for the individual occupational groups: APL, 498/745, fols. 46–49.
7 Underlined by hand in the original.

resettlement will involve, in addition to deployable Jews, a significantly higher number of non-deployable children and family members. Therefore, proceed as follows:

1) *Unmarried* male Jews suitable for outdoor work in gangs are to be admitted to the existing camps that are still able to absorb them (particularly such camps as are available near water projects) or to the camps that are to be built. In the process, a few skilled tradesmen (tailors, cobblers, carpenters, cooks, barbers, and others) are to be assigned to each gang to maintain footwear and clothing, add to the camp's equipment, and carry out cleaning and other tasks. A physician is also to be assigned to larger groups.
2) The bulk of the resettled *Jewish families* are in the main to be sent to places – including smaller places – in the immediate vicinity of which there are construction projects with substantial manpower requirements (hydraulic structures, repair work for the Eastern Railway, road construction, afforestation, etc.). In these places, (non-camp) housing is the concern of the Council of Elders of the Jews. Families will furthermore have to provide their own food. Their capacity to support themselves will be ensured by deployment in groups at the nearby work projects, to which they will be brought, if required, by rail or in the vehicles of the construction firms, and by the wages associated with this. In many regions where labour resources are currently in short supply, this systematic deployment of the resettled Jews will ensure that the manpower needs of future tasks there are met.
3) The large number of women affected by the resettlement makes it necessary – as does the intensification of Jewish labour deployment generally – to seek out special deployment possibilities for Jewish women. In particular, the scope for group deployment of Jewish women and girls in industrial firms for tasks that can be learned quickly, for use in afforestation, etc. should be explored. I request that tasks which are not suited to women because they are too arduous be excluded from consideration from the outset.
4) An attempt must be made to create new job opportunities for the deployment of Jews. In particular, I request that it be determined, in consultation with the municipal administrations, whether demolition work on buildings that were damaged in the course of the war cannot be carried out on a larger scale, with at least a portion of the costs covered by the utilization or sale of the bricks and the scrap iron.

I ask that the heads of the employment offices immediately make contact with the organizations requiring labour, particularly the Eastern Railway, the road construction agencies, the forest administrations, and also of course the Kreishauptmannschaften, in order to identify all the deployment possibilities for Jews. In this way, the basis can be laid for the intensification of Jewish labour deployment and, beyond that, for a constructive solution to the evacuation of the Jews from Cracow. In the negotiations, it can be pointed out that taking in the Jews resettled from Cracow, the General Government's seat of government, is a duty incumbent upon the General Government as a whole.

I ask that the heads of the employment offices report to the heads of the labour departments in the districts no later than 5 August 1940, providing information separately for the four categories above. These department heads are to forward the reports to me with their comments, after any necessary consultations with other relevant district government departments, by 11 August of this year.[8]

8 These reports are not included in the file.

DOC. 143

On 25 July 1940 the National Socialist People's Welfare Organization in Schroda describes the confiscation of goods from Jewish shops to benefit ethnic Germans in September 1939[1]

Letter from NSDAP Gau Wartheland, Kreis Schroda, Office of People's Welfare (file reference: St/S), head of Kreis office, signature illegible, to the Kreis representative of the Posen Trustee Office, Party Comrade Paul Gärtig, Schroda, dated 25 July 1940

Re: takeover of goods from Jewish shops

Immediately after the troops occupied the German eastern territories,[2] the NSV embarked on welfare measures. For this purpose, all the goods in stock in the Jewish shops in the individual localities were confiscated and placed at the NSV's disposal. The lack of staff or other helpers meant that no lists were compiled detailing the nature and extent of the stocks. Nor do I know the names of the Jewish shops located here in the Kreis, because my predecessor, the special representative and Party Comrade Salm, did not pass on any such records to me. Confiscation of the inventory held in the Jewish shops was carried out not only in Kreis Schroda, but also, to my knowledge, across the entire Gau territory.

The confiscated supplies were stored by the NSV and distributed to the ethnic Germans. Distribution was based on need, as far as the available staff could assess this. This one-off relief effort was an urgent priority, since most of the ethnic Germans, insofar as they were unable to take their possessions with them,[3] had their entire stock of clothing and household linen stolen or destroyed by the Poles. The goods were therefore handed out free of charge.

If your office has an interest in ascertaining the extent of the stocks of goods, this can only be done by using the card indexes kept here of the persons who receive support. However, I should point out that these card indexes present an unclear picture, especially since items were distributed not only from the confiscated supplies, but also from supplies received from the Gau warehouse in Posen in November and December, as well as thereafter.

Heil Hitler![4]

1 APP, 759/17. This document has been translated from German.

2 This refers to the conquered territories in western Poland.

3 This presumably refers to members of the resident ethnic German minority who fled or were forcibly displaced during the Wehrmacht invasion of Poland.

4 The Kreis representative of the Posen Trustee Office forwarded the letter on 30 July (incorrectly 'August' in the document) 1940 to the Posen Trustee Office, which sent it to Berlin on 1 August 1940. The Berlin headquarters responded on 10 August 1940 that it did not agree with the Kreis representative's 'declared intention to discontinue the further recovery of receivables' from the confiscations; rather, the 'stocks of goods were to be ascertained in full': APP, 759/17.

DOC. 144

On 28 July 1940 Jewish representatives report to the American embassy in Berlin on the persecution of Jews in western Poland[1]

Memorandum (marked 'strictly confidential') from Polish-Jewish representatives to the American embassy in Berlin[2]

Jews in Kutno and other towns annexed to the Reich
The territory incorporated into the Reich is still inhabited by over half a million Jews, including about 220,000–250,000 in Lodz alone.[3] The Jews have been put under a tremendous terror and go in daily fear for their lives. With cool calculation and inhuman method the physical and moral crushing of these people is gotten at with the ultimate aim of their complete wiping out in the wake. The yellow patches adorning the Jewish breasts and backs were only the commencement of a well thought-out plan that is now being consequently and ruthlessly put into operation. In the economical respect the Jews have been annihilated during a few short weeks. The small number of better-off Jews was deprived of the immovable and movable property: the Jewish shops have been either closed down or given away to Germans. The artisans lost their workshops; the cabdrivers and carters their horses and vehicles; even the Jewish homes have been rifled of the whole furniture and other necessities. No one but he that could visit the towns and places incorporated in the Reich might gain a notion of the dejection that filled the Jewish streets and see the downcast, stigmatized Jewish population stealing wide-eyed with horror through the streets of their home towns and only he may fully size up the disaster that befell those scared and maltreated people.

But the destructive process has not yet been carried to its close. At the present time two actions are in progress; one aimed at isolating the Jews in so-called ghettos, or rather concentration camps where they are hermetically shut up and deprived of all contact with the outer world (Lodz) and another – the deportation action.

In those towns where no ghettos are established and a few scores of Jewish families have been left behind after the deportations they are starved out and inhumanly tortured by means of compulsory labour. In Wielun Jews are not permitted to walk on the sidewalk or speedway only in the gutter. In Plock one day the pensionaries of the local aged-home have been sent away and it is believed that they are dead.[4] From Uniejów we are informed that the whole Jewish population of either sex over 16 years of age has to report each day for compulsory unpaid labour and the Jewish council must care for their food.

1 NARA, US State Department, Internal Affairs Poland – Race Problems, Decimal Files 860c.4016/620.

2 Enclosure no. 2, dispatched to the senior officer of the American embassy, Alexander Kirk, on 15 August 1940, concerned the situation of the Jewish population in the General Government. The memo is based on information Landreth M. Harrison of the US embassy in Berlin received from Jewish representatives in Warsaw and Cracow during a trip to Warsaw. Enclosure no. 1 dealt with the 'Jewish refugee problem', and Enclosure no. 3 with the 'Deportation of the Jewish population from Cracow'. In the original, select passages have been underlined by hand.

3 Nearly 160,000 people lived in the ghetto at the time it was sealed off in late April 1940.

4 The author may be referring to the murder of 36 disabled people from a home for the elderly run by Catholic nuns, which took place on 7 Jan. 1940 in a forest near Płock.

Since, however, the latter has no means at its disposal the labourers succumb to hunger and exhaustion. In Kutno a ghetto has been established on the outskirts of the town. The Jewish population, numbering over 8,000 persons, has been given five ruined buildings of an old factory with 111 rooms and no installations like kitchens, etc. Only a part of the Jews could be accommodated (priority was given to women and children) in these half ruined dwellings and the other [*sic*] are encamped till now in the open field or in improvised huts that could not be finished (the permission for supplying timber has been withdrawn when the work was still in progress). The spot on which these five buildings with their 8,000 Jewish inhabitants are standing has been fenced in with barbed wire. When a young boy who fled from the ghetto in Lodz tried to slip through the fence and was shot [*sic*]. The ghetto has only one well at which there is all day long a queue standing to get some water. Food is being supplied in a state unfit for consumption. The people are swelling with hunger and the mortality reaches unprecedented dimensions, owing to the lack of the most indispensable drugs. In the last days we received a letter with the urgent request to send obstetrician's instruments, of which there are none in the ghetto. Similar ghettos are in existence in Zychlin, in Brzeziny, etc. We are hearing the desperate cries for help of those hopeless people, but it is rarely that we can come to their aid.

From Zagórów (distr. Konin) we learn, that on July 18th all Jews from Kleczew, Golina and Wilczyn 1,600 in all have been rounded up and sent with only small bundles to carry, to Zagórów where 145 Jewish families were already carrying on a wretched existence.

From Konin alone over 10,000 Jews have been removed to a small and poor village (Grójce) where they must needs [*sic*] stay in the open for lack of housing accommodation. These are only a few of the very numerous facts that have come to our knowledge until up to date.

July 28, 1940

The Jewish ghetto of Lodz.

The area which is now covered by the ghetto of Lodz and carries between 220 and 250,000 persons was inhabited before the war by 70,000 people and was already then considered as overpopulated. The houses of this suburb of Lodz (Baluty) are old and deprived of all comfort, not even sewerage is installed, and only 10 % of the dwellings have got water-closets. The streets are mostly narrow and dark. One who knew this suburb before the war will easily imagine the conditions of living to which nearly a quarter of a million people have been committed. The ghetto is fenced in by fences of barbed wire guarded heavily by the German police on the out- and the Jewish police on the inside. Before the gates of the ghetto a 'neutral zone' has been established where the head of the Jewish Community[5] negotiates daily for the provisions that are being daily supplied to the ghetto. The provisions consist of flour, grits onions, rapeseed-oil (very small quantity) sometimes sugar and milk (600 liters for 250,000 persons, in this at least 40,000 children). The provisions are distributed in some 40 breadlines where long queues are waiting all day long for their rations (curfew-time begins at 8 o'clock in the evening). There is no other supply of food, as the gates of the ghetto are hermetically

5 The Jewish elder was Mordechai Chaim Rumkowski.

shut and approach is forbidden under pain of death. Several braves [*sic*] have been already shot in trying to get through the fences. Thus it is that the ghetto has no meat, no cereal except grits and no fuel. The inhabitants are now building their fires with parts of the furniture and the approaching winter is viewed with apprehension. The artisans have not got their working gear or either no material, and even should they have both here is nobody whom they could sell their produce, as there is no egress from the ghetto. For the same reason there is no trade possible. No wonder therefore that the people of the ghetto dream of its being open, if only for the space of two hours a day.

About 85 % of the Jews shut up in the ghetto have already spent all their means and are solely dependent on the aid of the ghetto. But the resources of the community are dwindling too by reason of the expenditure borne for the purchase of provisions and the time is drawing near when it will be entirely out of money for feeding the population of the ghetto. They are trying to save the situation by introducing a ghetto currency (Judenmark),[6] this is, however, resented by the population, which sees the last lender [*sic*] link with the outer world gone.

Chronical underfeeding and the distressing conditions have driven up the mortality, especially among the infants and children. The medical assistance is hampered by the lack of drugs, accommodation, and beds for the patients. Hand-luggage could only be taken by the Jews moving into the ghetto. No furniture could be moved under pain of death.

The worst plight is that of the deportees from the towns around Lodz (Zgierz, Aleksandrów, Pabianice) whose distress surpasses all imagination. To sum up, the Jews of Lodz have been shut up in a huge concentration camp and unless they are speedily delivered from it they will be soon carried off by the dreadful condition in which they live.

DOC. 145
On 31 July 1940 Reichsstatthalter Greiser discusses the resettlement of the Jewish population with the GG government in Cracow[1]

Minutes of the meeting in Cracow between Governor General Frank, Higher SS and Police Leaders Krüger and Koppe, Reichsstatthalter Greiser, the Senior Commander of the Security Police and SD in the General Government Streckenbach, and the head of administration in the Warthegau, Mehlhorn, dated 31 July 1940

[...][2]
First of all, he [Greiser] saw a *discussion of the Jewish problem* as essential. Things have indeed changed somewhat here recently, in that a different position has now been taken on the question of evacuating the Jews. On the basis of a conversation with the Reichs-

6 German in the original. After 8 July 1940 this coupon, nicknamed 'rumki' after Rumkowski, became the only legal currency in the ghetto, but had no value outside the ghetto's walls.

1 AIPN, GK 95, vol. 5. Copy in IfZ-Archives, Fb 105, vol. 7, fols. 1754–1765, here 1754–1762. Published in Präg and Jacobmeyer (eds.), *Diensttagebuch des deutschen Generalgouverneurs*, pp. 261–264. This document has been translated from German.

führer-SS,[3] he had been able to ascertain that the plan is henceforth to deport the Jews to certain territories overseas.[4] During this conversation, he stated that he must and will acquiesce in such a decision, of course, but that the Jewish problem, to the extent that it impinges on his Gau, must somehow be resolved before the onset of winter. Naturally this depended on the duration of the war. Should the war be of longer duration, an interim solution would have to be found.

He stated that the question of the *drawing of the shared boundary*[5] would probably not be completely resolved today; however, it must once again be subjected to a thorough examination with the relevant Reich offices in Berlin, so that certain differences of opinion could be cleared up once and for all.

Reichsstatthalter Greiser then elaborated on the *Jewish problem* in greater detail and emphasized the fact that, in Lietzmannstadt[6] and the surrounding area, a certain concentration of Jews en masse can be observed. In Lietzmannstadt itself, the Jews have been put into a ghetto. The operation per se has been completed, but it is merely provisional in nature. There are approximately 250,000 Jews in this ghetto.[7] These 250,000 Jews, whose number may increase to 260,000, must leave the Warthegau at some point. The plan was to transport them to the General Government in a suitable manner, and the intention was to clarify the mode of this transfer today as well. The new decision has come in the meantime, and he [Greiser] places the greatest emphasis on clarifying the possibility of transfer, because it would be an impossible state of affairs for the Warthegau to keep these Jews crowded together in the ghetto throughout the winter, for reasons of both food policy and especially disease control. An interim solution that offers an opportunity to deport these Jews to another territory must therefore be found at all costs.

The *Governor General* remarked that Reichsführer-SS Himmler had officially informed him in Berlin that, by order of the Führer, he was not going to undertake any deportations of Jews.[8] As to the General Government, he has decreed the evacuation of 45,000 to 50,000 Jews from Cracow to begin with.

SS-Obergruppenführer *Krüger* disclosed that the question of *resettling all Jews from the General Government* was presently being addressed. Position papers on this topic have already been written, discussing the means by which the operation to send Jews overseas will be carried out.[9] As for resettlement, he recommended that Lietzmannstadt be given primary consideration.

2 In the course of this discussion, Frank announced that the 'Office of the Governor General' would officially be known in future as the 'Government of the Governor General'. He then welcomed Greiser, who set out his position regarding issues affecting both the Warthegau and the General Government.

3 The conversation between Greiser and Himmler is thought to have taken place on 26 July 1940.

4 This refers to the Madagascar project: see Doc. 132.

5 This refers to drawing the boundary between the Warthegau and the General Government; in autumn 1939 Frank had attempted to have the Łódź region attached to the General Government.

6 Here and in what follows: as in the original. Correctly: Litzmannstadt (Łódź).

7 In fact, when the ghetto was sealed off at the end of April 1940, it had just under 160,000 inhabitants.

8 The meeting with Himmler had taken place in Berlin on 8 July 1940, during Frank's visit to Germany.

9 The head of the section for Jewish affairs in the Reich Foreign Office, Franz Rademacher, had submitted the revised version of his Madagascar plan on 3 July 1940. See PMJ 3/92.

SS-Brigadeführer *Streckenbach* emphasized that it is not yet possible to say anything definite about the entire operation. So far, the only certainty is that his office has been instructed to ascertain how many Jews there are in the entire area currently occupied by Germany. According to the current plan, the Jews are to be sent to *Madagascar.* When and how the deportation is to proceed is a question for the peace agreement.[10] Whether Madagascar is where they will go has also not yet been finally decided.

SS-Obergruppenführer *Krüger* pointed out that he also touched on the *question of the Gypsies* in a recent conversation with Reichsführer-SS Himmler. All the Gypsies are to be taken to the General Government. It is probably a question of 30,000 Gypsies in total, from the Old Reich and other territories. But details about this entire operation cannot be provided yet because the question of the Gypsies' citizenship still needs to be sorted out.

The Higher SS and Police Leader of the Warthegau, Gruppenführer *Köppe*,[11] pointed out that the situation with regard to the *Jews in the Warthegau* is getting worse every day. The ghetto in Lietzmannstadt was actually created solely on the understanding that the deportation of the Jews would begin this year, by mid year at the latest. Apart from that, he observed, now that the Führer has given the name Lietzmannstadt to the former city of Lodsch, everyone is convinced that this city will ultimately become part of the Warthegau and remain so.

The *Governor General* had no objections to this but could not concur with the view that consequently Lietzmannstadt is already a German city today. This process of Germanization will take perhaps fifteen years. He was very keen to emphasize that the General Government is undoubtedly in a far more difficult position than the Warthegau, also when it comes to the Jewish question. The question of resettlement within the General Government is becoming more difficult each day, not least given the plan to construct new military training grounds. If carried out in practice, this plan to create military training grounds will require the resettlement of around 180,000 Poles.[12]

SS-Gruppenführer *Köppe* then provided more detailed information on the implementation of the *settlement measures in Warthegau territory.* The settlement plan drawn up in the Warthegau envisages the settlement of between 60,000 and 70,000 ethnic Germans. In addition, 10,000 Jews[13] will arrive from Bessarabia soon, and arrangements must also be made to house them. There are currently 588,000 Germans living in the Warthegau, compared with 1.6 million Poles. In total, 8 million Poles still live outside the General Government.

Counter to this, the *Governor General* pointed to the great difficulties standing in the way of taking in Polish populations, for example from Hungary, Lithuania, Romania, and other countries. The difficult conditions that would inevitably result are indicated by the fact that, at present, the General Government already has a population density of up to 180 persons per square kilometre in places. The average settlement density in the General Government is far higher than in the Reich. Under such circumstances, and with an increased influx of Poles into the General Government, he could hardly accept

10 The peace agreement with France, the colonial power in Madagascar, was never concluded.
11 Correctly: Koppe.
12 See Docs. 82 and 83.
13 The writer presumably means: Bessarabian Germans.

responsibility for ensuring that epidemics and other types of catastrophes, such as famines, do not occur. This is, he said, an extraordinarily serious problem, one that can be solved only in cooperation with all the agencies concerned.

SS-Brigadeführer *Streckenbach* pointed out that, in addition to the demands made by the Warthegau, very substantial demands to take in Poles are being made by East and West Prussia and Silesia as well. At present, the resettlement of 120,000 Poles *from the Warthegau* is under way; they are to make room for the Germans coming from Volhynia. Of these 120,000 Poles, 58,000 have arrived in the General Government to date, which still leaves 62,000. This operation should have been concluded as early as the beginning of July, but it has been delayed by the transport problems. Furthermore, there is the possibility of resettling 20,000 to 30,000 ethnic Germans from Lithuania, as well as removing 41,000 Poles from Gotenhafen.[14] The General Government had a population density of 102 persons per square kilometre at the time of the takeover, but today it has already reached an average of 136 persons. This figure is now increasing because enormous stretches of land must be freed up for the construction of military training grounds, bridgeheads, etc. After this work is done, a population density of 145 persons per square kilometre in the General Government must be expected. In peacetime, that is, before the outbreak of the Polish war, the territory of the General Government was a shortfall area in terms of food supply. Cracow used to purchase an additional 245,000 tonnes of cereals annually.

Given this state of affairs, Reichsstatthalter *Greiser* took the view that it was impossible for the General Government to take in the 250,000 Jews, even as an interim measure.

The *Governor General* fully endorsed this opinion and accordingly concluded that this situation warrants a clarification of the relationship between the Warthegau and the General Government. The situation is becoming catastrophic for both regions. Therefore, the question must also be brought to a definite conclusion. He considered himself obliged to give the Warthegau absolute priority in terms of keeping the territory German. Nor could he harbour the ambition to make the General Government into a German territory. At any rate, the time for that has not yet come. But if the resettlement is to proceed in such a way that the General Government would have to admit these masses of people, then the conditions must be clear from the start. The conditions must be set in such a way that they can be fulfilled in the general German interest. Should this mass of Poles come into the General Government, the necessary food supplies would have to be secured entirely at the Reich's expense. This is necessary for the very reason that the General Government has an important task to carry out on behalf of the German Reich.

Regierungspräsident[15] *Mehlhorn* emphasized that over time, the city of *Lietzmannstadt* has indeed for the most part successfully been turned into a German city. Anyone who was in this city in November and goes back there today will readily be able to ascertain that the place has completely changed and that the Germans are in control across the board. Further evidence of this is the fact that there have been no further fatal assaults on policemen or members of the Wehrmacht since then. The city's external appearance is also thoroughly German. In addition to the strong ethnic German element

14 Gdingen.

15 Herbert Mehlhorn was not at this point a Regierungspräsident but the head of the administration in the Reichsstatthalter government in the Warthegau: see Doc. 43, fn. 4.

among the resident population, numbering approximately 60,000 to 80,000, a large number of Reich Germans are now there with their families and have found work in the city. The ghetto was set up precisely because there was a desire to protect the ethnic Germans and Reich Germans from epidemic disease. The city, with its 700,000 inhabitants, has no normal water supply system, no sewer system. The Reich Health Leader has made every conceivable effort to improve the hygiene conditions. Of course, the Jews and Poles, and to some extent the ethnic Germans, too, would have a certain immunity to typhus if they survived this disease in their youth. For the Reich Germans, of course, the situation is different. He said he felt compelled to point out that 30 per cent of the German civil servants and employees in his government had fallen ill with dysentery this summer and were therefore unable to work. This is an impossible state of affairs for a German city in the long term. Should the war last any longer, he considered it out of the question for the Jews to remain in Lietzmannstadt. Reich German men and women cannot possibly be exposed to the danger of epidemic disease. The Jewish question must therefore be resolved in one way or another.

The Governor General fully acknowledged the difficulty of the Jewish problem, especially for Lietzmannstadt, but once again stated his opinion that the General Government can help only once all the food policy and economic questions have been resolved. […][16]

DOC. 146

On 1 August 1940 the personnel office in District Cracow warns Reich German employees against using the services of Jewish artisans[1]

Circular from the personnel office, District Cracow (file ref.: 105 420-Pers/40), signed Hönigl,[2] to all department heads, dated 1 August 1940

Re: work done by Jewish artisans
Reich German public officials and employees have repeatedly had work done by Jewish artisans, particularly tailors and seamstresses. I wish to point out that this is incompatible with the stance that Reich Germans must adopt here. I therefore ask that, from now on, Reich German civil servants and Reich employees will have no more private work done for them by Jewish artisans.

16 Frank then concluded the meeting.

1 AIPN, GK 110/2, fol. 3. Copy in USHMM, RG 15 024M. This document has been translated from German.

2 Paul Hönigl (b. 1895), lawyer; joined the NSDAP in Austria in 1932; joined the SS in 1937; worked in Special Department IVd-8 ('Jewish assets') of the Reichsstatthalter of Gau Niederdonau in 1938; employed in the Interior Administration Department in District Cracow, Oct. 1939 – Oct. 1940; then worked again in the administration of Gau Niederdonau; in prison, 1945–1947; thereafter employed as a labourer in Vienna.

DOC. 147

Szaniec, 1 August 1940: a Polish underground newspaper comments on German policies towards the Jews[1]

Always the same people

From the very beginning Nazi propaganda has declared world Jewry, along with its overt and covert influence, to be the principal enemy. However, this has not prevented Hitler from opportunistically entering into an agreement with Bolshevism, the strongest domain of Jewish influence – regarded by Hitler as enemy no. 1.

This agreement, officially concerned with Poland's partition, must presumably have contained additional clauses on Jewry in the territory taken from Poland.

Supposedly, all citizens of the Polish state are equally persecuted by the German authorities and individual Germans. The reality is different. Hitler's main goal is to rid Europe of Jews. In the initial phase, the Jews were to be deprived of their larger assets, cut off from sources of income, and locked away in ghettos. The first point of the programme has basically been realized, although it has been partially compromised by Jews bribing German officials from whom many Jews have been able to buy their freedom, thereby rescuing, for a relatively small sum, assets of incomparably greater value. This system of plunder had to be successful as it is too rooted in German psychology. However, it has affected Poles to an equal degree and this statement is very crucial for our further deliberations.

The Germans have not cut off the Jewish masses from their sources of income and trade, other than as a consequence of plunder. The fact that Jews have often been tasked with supplying the army is deeply puzzling (apart from the star – [they wear] a green armband as well). Small Jewish shops and stalls are flourishing. Pedlars, now more numerous than ever, trade in junk without any restrictions. They have thus acquired the skills to get by, which in many cases cannot be said for the Poles.

The ghetto also remains nothing more than a mere announcement. It has only been set up in places where the more ruthless measure would have been expulsion; it has not been set up anywhere else.

Thus, up until now, it has not been evident that the Germans aim to solve the Jewish question here.

The Gestapo as well, i.e. everything that is commonly known by that name, is strangely restrained towards Polish Jews, insofar as that gang of ruffians is at all capable of being restrained. Unlike the mass executions of Poles, the murder of Jews remains an exception and takes place only insofar as is necessary to clarify mutual relations. Arrests are a similar matter. Maltreatment is not ordained by the system, but is the independent action of individuals – German sadists.

One can't help but assume that this restrained approach is the Gestapo's payment for the massive involvement of Jews as police informers.

Jews are no longer being rounded up and taken to Germany. Their forced labour at home is arduous, but it is not a blow to their national existence, whereas for us perhaps the worst thing is our youth being taken away to the Reich.

1 *Szaniec*, no. 29/30, pp. 2–3; Biblioteka Narodowa, MF 48 691. This document has been translated from Polish.

Thus, despite appearances, it must be conclusively stated and with absolute objectivity that the fates of Jews and Poles are not identical; for them: harassment, plunder, and a police system whose benevolence makes life difficult even for the Germans; and for us – total annihilation.

The alleged community of fate means that many Poles forget the real nature of Jewry, have empathy for individual victims of violence among the Jews, and generalize this empathy. These Poles are prepared to condemn even the slightest hint of antisemitism, which they perceive as the destruction of a common anti-German front, the sowing of discord in a unified society, as a renewal of the conflict[2] – they even see it as grist to the German mill. We advise these Poles to look to the East, where the Bolsheviks have raked in a chunk of Poland and where the Jews have gained total power. There they have been able to show what they really feel and of what they are capable. The very same Jews who, before September, made so much noise about defending Poland the Fatherland are now competing with the GPU[3] in exterminating the Poles. The random border along the Bug[4] has shown us two different sides of Jewry. Which one is real? Is it the one under the Germans, which arouses our empathy? Or is it the one that is drunk on red power and serves as an outlet for long-suppressed hatred of us? There is too much proof of anti-Polish acts of terror by Soviet Jews and the Jews under German rule are waiting too impatiently for the invasion of the Bolsheviks to leave any doubt. There is only one side to Jewry – the one east of the Bug, where it can show its true colours. We should draw full consequences from this. Times are unsettled, battles lie ahead, and perhaps even a short-lived revolution once the German state falls. Let's not allow sentimental humanitarianism to close our eyes to the basic truth: a Jew can be bought or forcibly tamed, but it is impossible to reach an agreement with him from a position of weakness.

DOC. 148

On 2 August 1940 an anonymous informer alleges that the Jewish Council in Lublin gives preferential treatment to the well-to-do[1]

Letter, signed Anonymous, to the section for Jewish affairs in Lublin,[2] dated 2 August 1940[3]

Translation

1. I hereby inform the German authorities that all 24 members of the Jewish Council are using their position solely for private ends. Every one of them has given jobs or official posts to their sons, daughters, or relatives. These people do nothing at all –

2 This is a reference to the Polish–Jewish tensions of the pre-war period.

3 Official designation of the Soviet secret police until 1934 (also OGPU). It was later also used to refer to the NKVD.

4 The demarcation line between the German and the Soviet zones of occupation in accordance with the Boundary and Friendship Treaty of 28 Sept. 1939.

1 YVA, O-6/393. This document has been translated from German.

2 Dr Karl Hofbauer was the official in charge of Jewish affairs for the SS and Police Leader (SSPF) in District Lublin.

3 Handwritten. Original in Polish, with official typed translation into German (signed Ku.).

they just shirk their obligation to work. Positions where one person would suffice are occupied by 15 to 20 people who come from the richest families, such as the Kohen, Rajz, Goldsabel, Spironurmann, Tennenbaum, Davidsohn, Goldsztern, Hochgemein, Kerschenblum, Lerner, and Lewinzon [families]. They are all hiding 'in the Jewish Council'.

2. The truly rich people, such as Zylber, Kenigsberg, Wurman, Izraelit, Mincmann, Rongold, Wolmann, Horowicz, and the owners of the biggest buildings, don't pay the taxes that have been imposed and don't give anything from their hoards and assets to the Community either; they just pay the members of the Jewish Council so they won't set the taxes too high for them. The Jewish Council crushes the impoverished and ruined Jews with overly high taxes, which they extort by threatening arrest. Last week, Dr *Hofbauer* summoned a few rich Jews and demanded a certain sum from them. The people would have easily been able to provide the sum themselves, but did not do so. Instead, they called all of Lublin together and, by making threats of arrest, extorted the last pennies from poor folks.
3. It often happens that the Jewish Council arrests someone at midnight. But those arrested are always just poor people, not a single rich one. It is a fact that the average taxpayer pays 15 to 20 times more taxes, while the rich taxpayer pays taxes that are only two to three times higher.
4. If the authorities need 100 to 150 people for Tyszowiec or Belcec,[4] the Jewish Council sends the summons to 1,000 Jews. From each one of these people who are called up, the Jewish Council collects 200, 300, 400 zl.[5] for its members and counts them as fees for exempting someone from labour.

These are the facts of the Jewish Council's reign over the Lublin population, who have been deprived of their rights.

Comment: I will still have occasion to describe the Jewish Council's activity in relation to the boycott of German goods.[6]

4 The place names are misspelled in the German translation. The SS operated large labour camps for Jews in Tyszowce (between Tomaszów Lubelski and Hrubieszów) and in Bełżec (a few kilometres south of Tomaszów Lubelski).

5 Here the official typed German translation deviates from the Polish original, which contains the following: '200, 300, 400, and 500 zł.'.

6 This refers to the campaign by Polish Jews to boycott German goods, which began in 1933: see PMJ 1/43.

DOC. 149
Dror, August 1940: Tuwia Borzykowski sets out an agenda for Jewish youth work[1]

R. Domski[2]
Today's youth in this time

The age in which we currently live can certainly be described as one of the saddest in human history. All foundations of life until now have been shattered. Nothing new has yet been created. The younger generation that has to live and breathe in this transitional time has not found a source from which to draw spiritual nourishment. A spiritual crisis has thus arisen that is leading to degeneration and dangerous anarchy in all the ways that these youth think and feel.

Youth, who from a psychological perspective form a particular group within society, differ from their elders in that they are impetuous in nature and their emotions are more intense. The feelings of the young are like an accumulator that collects all the impressions of their surroundings. This is how strong impulses are generated among youth, whether negative or positive, depending on the place and time in which the youth live. That is why it is indeed no coincidence that the youth have always played a significant role in sociopolitical life and that all social and progressive national ideals have been spread by youth.

By now, the historical role of youth has changed somewhat. With the support of state and cultural institutions, bourgeois educators have had the opportunity to direct the youth's energy in the wrong direction. They have steered the youthful passion for creating something new towards the formation of a new order, a fascist one. The rebelliousness of youth has been used to destroy rather than to build. Young people have been harnessed to serve all kinds of misdeeds, producing barbarism and devastation, moral depravity, and medieval despotism. This atmosphere corrodes and poisons the minds of the young generation.

We, the Jewish youth, cannot free ourselves from the influence exerted by the overall situation of youth in general. In addition, there is also the specific Jewish situation of not having a country of our own and the particular hatred that we young people are subjected to. The main reasons for the tragedy of our Jewish youth are the war and the occupation by the National Socialists.

We have been cast into the role of pariahs, insulted and spat on, branded with symbols of shame and ridicule. The Jewish youth are being robbed of their character both physically and mentally in the Nazi labour camps. Jewish children have been cut off from access to schools and education. All are threatened by poverty and unemployment, which have taken the lives and livelihoods of thousands. This has prematurely aged the

1 *Dror*, no. 3, Tamuz 5700 (7 July–4 August 1940), pp. 11–12, AŻIH, Ring I/1029 (705). This document has been translated from Yiddish. *Dror* was an underground newspaper of the Dror Zionist youth league, which was closely associated with the Poale Zion-Right party.

2 Pseudonym of Tuwia Borzykowski (1911–1959); grew up in Radomsko; active in the Dror youth league and the Poale Zion party; in Warsaw from mid 1940; editor with the underground press; instructor at a Zionist agricultural training facility in the Warsaw neighbourhood of Czerniaków in the second half of 1942; fought with the ŻOB in the armed resistance in 1943; in 1949 moved to Israel, where he was one of the founders of the Ghetto Fighters' House (Beit Lohamei Hagetaot).

young Jewish generation and created people who are worn out, apathetic, and distrustful, lacking confidence and any means for changing their lives.

What do we need to do in this situation? Where do we have to direct our attention? Of course, there is no one single answer for all Jewish youth. The cure must be as diverse as the sickness. For one, there is the situation of young people living on the streets and in courtyards, not attending school, without supervision, in whom all the negative traits of the adult world are reflected. They practise itinerant trade. And then, the situation is quite different for young people who have had the opportunity to get an education. However, they keep their distance and do not want to stoop to the level of the Jewish masses.

First, the former must be provided with a basic level of education. Reading and writing classes, Yiddish, Hebrew, maths classes, etc. must be set up.[3] Young people must be brought in off the streets into a warm, friendly environment, and we must plant in them a sense of solidarity and responsibility as much as possible. Through song and play we can create an atmosphere that is suitable for young people, for those who had to grow up too soon. And the latter group of young people must be infused with the consciousness that they are part of a community of shared destiny involving all of the Jewish masses. They must be brought down from their Mount Olympus, and a feeling of national belonging must be awakened in them. A socialist consciousness must be instilled in them. They must be made socially active in all aspects of Jewish life. They need to be shown all the spiritual values the Jewish people have created over its history. And finally we must gather the better part of the Jewish youth, which has already been brought up in our groups, and form from it a powerful avant-garde of Jewish youth.

We are probably the only ones in all of Jewry to have adopted the concept of 'going to the people', and we are following this path despite all difficulties and dangers. We bring confidence to the dark corners of Jewish life, where dejection rules.

We have always admired those generations of fighters who were pioneers of freedom through their underground work. The work of the Paris Commune, the Russian revolutionaries, the Hashomer and Haganah,[4] and many other freedom movements have always been symbols of our youth work. However, fate demands of us that we not only learn from others, but that we ourselves also wage an underground war for the renewal of Jewish life and human life in general.

3 Until summer 1941, when the Warsaw Jewish Council opened its own schools, CENTOS secretly organized courses in the JSS's public soup kitchens, which were located in former school buildings; the teachers were disguised as cooks. The illegal school organization was headed by a governing body that included representatives of various political viewpoints.

4 Zionist paramilitary organization in Palestine during the British mandate (1920–1948). Hashomer, founded in 1909, was its predecessor organization.

DOC. 150

Between 2 and 5 August 1940 the chairman of the Warsaw Jewish Council describes the increasing restrictions on the Jewish population[1]

Handwritten diary of Adam Czerniaków, entries for 2 to 5 August 1940

2 August 1940 – +12°C. Asked to the Treuhandaußenstelle[2] for Wednesday morning about housing. Ujazdów Avenue closed to Jews. Jewish residents are forbidden to enter. Attempts to move the signboard up to Pius Street. Of the 641,000 złoty for bread ration cards, only approximately 30,000 złoty remain. The administrator of the Community building on Śliska demanded rent from the refugees. Discussion with the tax office on Daniłowiczowska. A property tax will be introduced for the benefit of the Community. A 50 per cent surcharge from businesses. Refugees from Cracow on the steps of the Community [building].

3 August 1940 – +14°C. Chilly. Off to the community at 7.30 a.m. The housing matter remains unclear. Tempel's situation is bad.[3] The Arbeitsamt[4] will contact all those refusing to work.[5] According to certain sources, Jews will be expelled from all the streets that cross Ujazdów Avenue (Lindenallee). In the provinces there have been orders to hand over shops, along with their inventories, to various Polish men and women for a few złoty.

4 August 1940 – +18°C. Off to the Community in the morning. A meeting was to take place regarding the Cracow refugees.[6] Supposedly an easing of tensions. The meeting has been postponed until Tuesday. At 1.30 p.m. I went to Otwock for a few hours. At the 'Brijus' sanatorium I met a woman veterinarian for the first time in my life, a certain Miss Neufeld. A madman escaped from Zofiówka.[7] He was run over by a train. The police brought in the corpse. On the way back to Warsaw at 8 p.m. Half an hour by car.

1 YVA, O-33/1090. Published in Czerniaków, *Dziennik getta warszawskiego*, pp. 135–136. This document has been translated from Polish.
2 German in the original: 'trustee branch office'.
3 Aleksander Tempel, lawyer, member of Warsaw's Jewish Council, fled to the Soviet Union in early Nov. 1939 and returned to Warsaw a few months later. Czerniaków campaigned with the German authorities for his release, evidently unsuccessfully.
4 German in the original: 'employment office'.
5 On 30 July 1940 Czerniaków had made a note that Inspector Peemöller from the employment office was threatening the property managers with sanctions if the number of those reporting for work continued to be so low: *Dziennik getta warszawskiego*, p. 134.
6 In summer 1940 thousands of Jews who had to leave Cracow went to Warsaw: see Docs. 104 and 156.
7 'Brijus' (Yiddish pronunciation of bri'ut, Hebrew for 'health') was a sanatorium of the Jewish Anti-tuberculosis Society; Zofiówka was a home for the mentally ill and was under the supervision of the Society for the Welfare of Mentally Ill Jews. The Social Welfare Section of the Warsaw Jewish Council supported the institutions financially, and influential individuals from the Warsaw ghetto could go there to convalesce. The institution's patients and residents were murdered during the destruction of the Otwock ghetto on 19 August 1942. Lebensborn Ostland took over the building in 1943.

5 August 1940 – +18°C. Community in the morning. A part of the riverbank will be de-Jewified (Wiejska, Książęca, Rozbrat, etc.). After lunch, a meeting about the JSS[8] (memo to the authorities about a share in tax revenue, trams, gas, electricity, and poll tax).

DOC. 151
Between 5 and 12 August 1940 the physician Zygmunt Klukowski describes the persecution of the Jews in Szczebrzeszyn[1]

Handwritten diary of Zygmunt Klukowski, entries for 5 to 12 August 1940

Monday, 5 August
Mayor Borucki has proposed converting the burned-out Jewish synagogue into a municipal cinema. He sent to Zamość for Klimek, a civil engineer, who prepared the necessary measurements and sketches in two days. Upon hearing of this, the terrified Jews immediately sent to me a delegation composed of the three most important members of the Kahal,[2] asking for advice on how to prevent this. What could I have advised them, given how things are today?! I told them to go to Borucki. Great commotion among the Jews again since this morning, but for a different reason this time. Many gendarmes arrived here unexpectedly, who along with the local police surrounded Jewish shops and began confiscating goods. Apparently, they are to give them to Christian cooperatives.

Thursday, 8 August
This afternoon Gestapo men arrived at the home of the hospital's closest neighbour, Michał Bryłowski, wanting to arrest him. Michał Bryłowski was a career officer who, along with his wife, is currently living with his father. He was not home, so they took his wife and younger brother Zygmunt, a pupil at a grammar school, as hostages and sent them to a prison in Zamość. Weeping and wailing among the Jews again. Three hundred men have to go to a labour camp. They've already been summoned. They are all to report on Monday, 12 August. The second reason for the commotion is news that the Germans plan to remove all Jews from the apartments on Zamojska and from the market square. Where they should go and whether they will find anywhere to stay – that doesn't concern anyone.

Sunday, 11 August
Great commotion and unrest among the Jews before tomorrow's roundup. The Jews themselves told me in confidence that many of those who have been summoned have escaped, and as a result everyone is now afraid that they will go after whoever they can. It appears that they fear violence not just from the Germans, but especially because of

8 Żydowska Samapomoc Społeczna (Jewish Social Self-Help, JSS). A Jewish social welfare committee set up in Warsaw to provide social assistance to Jews.

1 Zygmunt Klukowski, Dziennik, no. 3, fols. 16–21r; Library of the Catholic University of Lublin, manuscript division, 813. Published in Klukowski, *Zamojszczyzna*, vol. 1, pp. 181–183. This document has been translated from Polish.

2 Hebrew: 'Community'.

the several incidents that have already taken place here. Yesterday evening, eleven-year-old Izrael Grojser was hit on the head with a stone and killed. This evening a Jewish woman was brought to the hospital, also with a fractured skull. Many Jews report to the hospital begging to be admitted or hidden if only for tonight and the following day. Of course, I refused, as there is a categorical ban on admitting Jews to hospitals. I've admitted only one Jew, who had written approval for this from the Ortskommandant.[3] Today my wife and I went to Zwierzyniec. En route, we saw an unusual number of Jews leaving town. I have never seen such great commotion among them.

Monday, 12 August
Jews have been secretly leaving the city all night. I stood at the window for a few hours in the night and at dawn and observed everything through my binoculars. It was not only those summoned who escaped or hid, but nearly every male Jew! Consequently, instead of 300 Jews, only 50 were rounded up today. That is why there was a raid in the town and nearby villages. Headed by Mayor Borucki, apart from the police and two militiamen, quite a number of the town's residents voluntarily took part. However, the raid was unsuccessful because only a dozen or so Jews were caught. The elderly were kept in custody, the rest were herded to the railway station. Only Jewish women and children are now seen on the streets. The mood among them is terrible. Depression and despair have engulfed them completely. At noon, with a drum roll, the German authorities announced that every Jew who had been summoned but had failed to turn up would be shot as soon as he is found. It is unknown what will happen next. Only one thing is certain, the Germans will not carry on as usual and will think of something to show that their orders are to be obeyed.
[…][4]

DOC. 152
Gazeta Żydowska, 6 August 1940: article on the situation of the Jewish Community in Oświęcim[1]

From Auschwitz (Oświęcim)

When one speaks of the 'Ältestenrat'[2] of the Jewish Community in Oświęcim, one cannot but mention the work of its chairman, Mr Józef Gross,[3] who, since assuming leadership of the Community, has succeeded in improving relationships inside the Community's administration in quite a short time. In particular, he has employed young, capable intellectuals in the administration. He has solved the problem of obligatory physical

3 German in the original: 'local military commander'.
4 The final part of the diary entry for 12 August 1940 concerns a discussion between Klukowski and a Catholic priest about the former church building of the Greek Catholic community in Szczebrzeszyn.

1 *Gazeta Żydowska*, no. 5, 6 August 1940, p. 4. This document has been translated from Polish.
2 German in the original: 'Council of Elders'.
3 Józef Gross was the chairman of the Jewish Council in Oświęcim from Jan. 1940. In spring 1941 the 5,500 Jews who remained in the city were deported to Sosnowiec and Będzin. See Doc. 269.

labour of Oświęcim's Jewish population.[4] Mr Gross's work extends far beyond the confines of the Jewish Community in Oświęcim, because he *has enabled the stay of over 100 refugees from Bielsko-Biała in Oświęcim*, providing them with a roof over their heads and warm food. One should note that Oświęcim, which is incorporated into the Reich, is one of the towns with the largest concentration of Jews in the Reich, in addition to which it accommodates a rather high number of Jewish refugees from Upper Silesia and the Cieszyn region, and this number is growing every day. Recently a further transport of Jews arrived in Oświęcim from Żywiec, Bielsko, Biała, Andrychów, Kęty, Dziedzice, Czechowice, Brzeszcz, Jawiszowice and the surrounding area. Despite its favourable location, Oświęcim is not an industrial town, nor are its surroundings particularly rich in agriculture. Before the war, virtually 90 per cent of Oświęcim's Jews lived from peddling in nearby Upper Silesia. Today these masses, unprepared for physical labour and not knowing any trade or other profession, are condemned to starvation. Thus, the Jewish Council in Oświęcim faces the difficult task of creating opportunities for any kind of meagre existence for the dense Jewish settlement in Oświęcim.

The energetic work and hitherto fruitful activity of the Jewish Council in Oświęcim allow us to believe that this task will be fulfilled in the nearest future.

DOC. 153

On 8 August 1940 the employment office in Neu-Sandez (Nowy Sącz) in the General Government orders the Jewish Council in Mszana Dolna to set up a forced labour camp[1]

Letter from the head of the employment office in Neu-Sandez (G.Z. 5318), signed L. S.,[2] to the Jewish Council in Mszana Dolna, dated 8 August 1940 (copy)

Official Order

By order of the Higher SS and Police Leader in the General Government for the Occupied Polish Territories, I hereby delegate to you all responsibility for managing the forced labour camp for Jewish workers to support the establishment of the *Poręba Wielka* state game preserve. Your tasks include:

1) *Proper selection and timely provision of forced labourers in the requisite numbers.*

In general, the order applies only to unmarried male Jews between the ages of 18 and 30. Exceptions are permissible but require the approval of the head of the branch office in Limanowa. The number of workers to be provided in each case will be made known to you by special order. At present, the number is 25.

2) *Preparing the accommodation and keeping the premises clean.*

The premises should be fitted out to include bedsteads, food bowls, washing facilities, etc.

4 The Jewish Council had to call up 300 young male adults and teenagers, who were deployed as forced labour by the SS in the construction of Auschwitz concentration camp.

1 YVA, O-21/14, fol. 24. This document has been translated from German.

2 Presumably Leon Stern, who was acting head of the employment office in 1941/42. The copy also contains the note 'signature illegible'.

3) *Enforcing strict camp rules.*
The forced labourers must be ordered to keep themselves clean, to adhere to the strictest punctuality, and particularly not to leave the camp outside working hours unless the Polish architect performing supervisory duties has given his permission in each individual case. As with all other matters, a request for time off must not be presented by individual forced labourers, but instead by the forced labourers' elder, who incidentally will be appointed by the head of the branch office in Limanowa.
4) *Feeding the forced labourers, including preparation of meals in accordance with the rules.*
Food is to be procured by the Jewish Council on its own responsibility and transported to the forced labour camp on schedule.

Any difficulties that might endanger the proper performance of your duties must be reported immediately to the Neu-Sandez employment office by telephone, specifically to the head of the employment office. Delays in making such a report will be regarded as a violation of this official order.

The Higher SS and Police Leader in the General Government for the Occupied Polish Territories reserves the right to impose a fine of 500 zloty on the Jewish Council in Mszana Dolna for any violation of this official order that comes to our attention.[3]

DOC. 154

On 9 August 1940 the Chełm employment office calls for all Jewish forced labourers to be paid[1]

Report from the Chelm employment office (G.Z. II B 2. 5317/40), signed Meier, to the head of the Labour Department of the Governor of District Lublin,[2] dated 9 August 1940 (copy)[3]

Re: labour deployment of the Jewish population
Case file: Order of 5 July 1940 G.Z. II 5317/40[4] Circular Decree 100/40
To gain an overview of the male Jews deployed as free workers I asked the companies to submit lists of the names of Jews they currently employed.[5] Likewise, I asked the heads of the labour camps to send in similar lists of the Jews currently performing forced

3 JSS Chairman Weichert sent this copy to the government of the GG, Interior Administration Department, Population and Welfare Division (BuF) on 11 Sept. 1940 'with the request to kindly organize the necessary measures': YVA, O-21/14, fol. 24.

1 APL, 498/746, fols. 75–76. This document has been translated from German.
2 Oberregierungsrat Jache.
3 The original contains handwritten annotations and underlining.
4 Circular Decree 100/40 issued by the Labour Department in the government of the GG dealt with the deployment of Jewish labour. It required that Jews must be registered in a card index, regulated the implementation of the forced labour scheme as well as the distribution and compensation of forced labourers, and decreed that forced labourers should be supervised by the SS and the police: Pospieszalski (ed.), *Documenta Occupationis*, vol. 6, part 2, pp. 568–572.
5 This refers to Jewish workers who had not been forcibly recruited by the SS or the civil labour administration and who were employed by firms on the basis of regular work contracts.

labour. I requested that those newly assigned to jobs as free workers be properly remunerated, and I also pointed out that the Jews must be registered for social insurance.

The Jewish Council in Chelm is trying to complete all the tasks assigned to it, something that cannot be said of the Jewish councils in Hrubieschow, Wlodawa, and the other rural localities.

The requests for Jewish workers come to me directly from individual users. So far no difficulties have arisen in this regard. What is remarkable is that I receive requests from every conceivable agency in my office every day, asking for Jews to be exempted from forced labour or for Jews deployed in forced labour to be subject to exchange. These are Jewish craftsmen who worked for the various agencies *in exchange for a small payment*. Now, of course, these offices are trying to maintain a cheap workforce. In individual cases, and after an exhaustive review, I have undertaken some reallocation. The *SS offices refuse to employ Jews in exchange for payment as a matter of principle*. At present, the SS offices are using 170 Jews as construction workers and 70 Jews as agricultural workers. Other agencies (such as the *municipal administration* and the *customs border guards*) also refuse to compensate the Jews, but, on the other hand, neither do they want to relinquish the Jewish workers so that the employment office can deploy them elsewhere. Paragraph (7) of Circular Decree 100/40 specifies that a change in the terms of work on the basis of this decree should *not* occur for schemes already in place. In accordance with Circular Decree 100/40 no compensation can be demanded in these cases, on the face of it because all the schemes in question involving the SS offices, municipal administrations, customs offices, etc. have been in place for some time. However, this results in other users also becoming unwilling to pay the Jewish workers and they invoke those agencies' employment of Jews without pay. Moreover, there could be cases in which both Jews who have been deployed for some time, i.e. without payment, and newly assigned Jews, i.e. with payment, are working alongside one another at the same workplace. This could cause great difficulties unless one could assign other Jews to schemes already in place without insisting that they be remunerated.

I request clarification on this question. In addition, for the reasons cited above, I request that I am granted the authority to assign Jewish workers to or let them remain in schemes that want to make use of their labour only if they are compensated in accordance with the rules.

As for medical care for the camp inmates, I ordered the available Jewish physician to visit the individual camps weekly and to report to me on the inmates' health status, so that sick workers can be replaced immediately if disease were to break out.

With regard to the registration of all Jews, including the […],[6] negotiations are currently still being conducted with the Kreishauptmannschaft. The creation of a tracing file for the card index of Jews has proved urgently necessary.[7]

6 One word is illegible (possibly: 'children').

7 The Labour Department in District Lublin sent a copy of the report to the Labour Department of the General Government. The head of this office, Max Frauendorfer, decided on 4 Sept. 1940 that it was necessary to adhere to the provisions in Circular Decree no. 100/40, dated 5 July 1940, according to which 'the pay for Jews, as a matter of principle, amounts to 80 per cent of the pay for Poles'. If at all possible, Jews were to be employed as pieceworkers; wherever that was not possible, a lower wage could be decided upon 'with the consent of the employment office': APL, 498/745, fol. 73.

DOC. 155

On 12 August 1940 the head of the Main Trustee Office East decrees how confiscated and temporarily administered assets should be exploited[1]

Circular decree on the sale of confiscated and temporarily administered assets

Minister President Reich Marshal Göring, as Plenipotentiary for the Four-Year Plan, in § 2, items a–f of his directive on the Main Trustee Office East of 12 June 1940 (*Deutscher Reichsanzeiger* and *Preußischer Staatsanzeiger* no. 139/40), has delegated the power to make permanent transfers of rights, i.e. to sell confiscated or temporarily administered assets. In his accompanying decree for this purpose, he has instructed me to sell, for now, at most 10 per cent of the individual groups of confiscated assets; this has been done, particularly with respect to maintaining the interests of the soldiers currently serving in the armed forces.

For implementation, I stipulate as follows:

1. *Scope of realization*

The permissible quota to be sold, 10 per cent, is calculated for each Trustee Office district on the basis of the sum total of properties subject to confiscation in the individual groups, in accordance with § 2 a and b and § 3 of the directive of 12 June 1940 issued by Reich Marshal Göring.

The following are to be regarded as groups:

1. banks and insurance companies
2. industry
3. trade
4. crafts
5. other professions (including enterprises in the cultural sector, liberal professions)
6. ownership of buildings and land.

The provisions concerning the following will remain unchanged:

a) sale of enterprises in the trade and crafts sectors up to 20,000 Reichsmarks (including land that falls within the value limit, circular dated 8 December 1939, no. 2/39; *Materialsammlung*, p. 41,[2] *Mitteilungsblatt*, no. 1, p. 22);

b) sale for the benefit of those confirmed as resettlers, in accordance with the guidelines and the administrative circular of 29 April 1940 (*Mitteilungsblatt*, no. 2, p. 32).[3]

1 *Mitteilungsblatt der Haupttreuhandstelle Ost*, no. 5, 27 August 1940, pp. 154–156. This document has been translated from German.

2 Minister President Field Marshal Göring, Plenipotentiary for the Four-Year Plan, Chairman of the Ministerial Council for the Defence of the Reich (ed.), *Haupttreuhandstelle Ost: Materialsammlung zum inneren Dienstgebrauch* (1940 [no place or publisher given]), pp. 41–42.

3 The order concerned the sale of commercial businesses and plots of land to resettlers or to the German Resettlement Trustee Office GmbH (Deutsche Umsiedlungs-Treuhand-GmbH, DUT), determining the existing assets and the purchase price. As early as 20 Feb. 1940, the Main Trustee Office East (HTO) and the DUT had established joint guidelines for 'permanently allowing' German resettlers to take possession of commercial undertakings and plots of land: source as in fn. 1, pp. 31–32. German resettlers were persons from the Baltic republics, Volhynia, Galicia, and the Narev region, as well as Reich Germans and ethnic Germans who had lived abroad and had lost their livelihoods and returned to Reich territory as a result of the war.

In addition, the assets released to resettlers in accordance with (b), even if their value exceeds 20,000 Reichsmarks but does not amount to 50,000 Reichsmarks, will not be counted against the 10 per cent quota that is to be approved for sale in all groups and categories.

2. *Scope of assets subject to sale*

Only those assets which are subject to confiscation and temporary administration by the Main Trustee Office East may be sold, i.e. only those belonging to citizens of the former Polish state who are of Polish or Jewish ethnicity.

Where the precondition named in (1) exists, it must be included in the record and be documented by written confirmation from the office in charge, according to the provisions in force in each case as applicable to the citizenship and ethnicity of the person who hitherto had the right of disposal. In all cases where there may be doubts concerning ethnicity, the case file must be sent to the General Section Head for the Strengthening of Germandom (GV SS), Main Trustee Office East, for the purpose of obtaining a final decision by the Reich Commissioner for the Strengthening of Germandom.[4]

3. *Applicants*

Applicants must be examined to determine their reliability and objective suitability and must give reason to expect a strengthening of Germandom in the incorporated eastern territories.

The circular decree issued by the Reichsführer-SS Reich Commissioner for the Strengthening of Germandom on Compliance with the Ranking for the Installation of Trustees or Owners for Businesses and Enterprises of Every Kind in the Incorporated Eastern Territories of 22 April 1940 O 79 (3 February 1940) Dr F. / K. (*Mitteilungsblatt*, no. 2, p. 31) is the basis on which the applicants will be ranked.[5] This decree must be applied to residential property as well. The right to grant exceptions for certain regions with the approval of the Reich Commissioner for the Strengthening of Germandom will be reserved. To ensure the legitimate claims of soldiers serving in the armed forces, properties should be transferred to Reich German applicants only if the applicant has been discharged from the army.

If there are any concerns related to the wartime economy and national economy that permit no delay, exceptions to this can be made in individual cases, with the consent of the Main Trustee Office East.

4. *Examination of applicants*

The office in charge of the sale (cf. 6) will initiate the examination of the applicant's objective suitability. Political reliability will be examined by the Reich Security Main

4 Until early April 1941 the General Section Head for the Strengthening of Germandom at the HTO and the liaison between the SS leadership and the HTO central office was Bruno Galke (b. 1905), economist; joined the NSDAP in 1932 and the SS in 1933; worked full time in the supervisory and governing bodies of various SS companies from 1933; Special Plenipotentiary for Heritage (Ahnenerbe) of the RFSS, 1935–1938; in American captivity in 1947.

5 The circular decree established the ranking of the applicants: 1. native ethnic Germans who resided in Poland on 31 Dec. 1938; 2. German resettlers living abroad; 3. returning migrants who had given up their residence in the territory after 1 Oct. 1918; 4. other Reich Germans as well as legal persons with purely German capital. Germans evacuated from the West could only be temporary administrators.

Office, Berlin. Otherwise, proceed in accordance with the implementing regulation (enclosed).[6]

5. Terms of transfer

(a) Conclusion of contract

Sale contracts, until otherwise provided by law, must be concluded between the temporary administrator and the buyer. If the sale is made to the temporary administrator, he must be dismissed, and a new temporary administrator must be appointed to carry out the sale. The effectiveness of the contracts must be made contingent upon the approval of the Trustee Office. The approval must be noted on the sale contract. One copy must be placed in the files. The written approval must be dated, signed, and supplied with an official stamp.

(b) Purchase price

The purchase price must be appropriate. The purchase price must be established on the basis of painstaking investigations. In every case, a valuation must be obtained. For larger properties (over 50,000 Reichsmarks), two valuers must be consulted as a general rule. In establishing the purchase price, an immaterial value – the so-called goodwill that exists at the time of the sale – must be taken into account if the purchaser would as a consequence be enriched to a substantial and unjustified degree. In the case of small retail or craft businesses (up to a sale price of 20,000 Reichsmarks), the immaterial value is in principle not taken into account. Any assessments made in this respect during the disposition negotiations must be included in the record with the aim of subsequently proving that non-consideration of goodwill could not be expected to lead to results that, in economic terms, were obviously unjustifiable.

An appropriate down payment of at least 20 per cent and an appropriate amortization of the remaining purchase-price balance must be required as a general rule. In view of the administrative costs saved as a result, an appropriate discount for cash payment can be granted for a partial payment of more than 75 per cent. For purchase-price balances, it is necessary to work towards securing repayment, depending on the circumstances of the individual case, through creation of a mortgage or land charge, assignment as security, provision of a guarantee, etc., but with due regard for ethnopolitical concerns. Purchase-price balances that come due more than one year after the contract has been concluded are to be charged an interest rate of 3 per cent; shorter-term purchase-price balances are not subject to the interest requirement. The request for payment of legal interest on arrears is unaffected by this.

In the disposition of craft and retail trade businesses in cities that still have a heavily preponderant Polish or Jewish population, the assignment of the business can take place without payment if no German craftsmen or retailers can be placed there in any other way. In addition, subsidies can be granted in these cases by the head of the Trustee Office, in accordance with special guidelines.

6 The enclosure ('Implementing Regulation and Course of Processing for Purchase Applications from Ethnic Germans, Resettlers, and Eastern Applicants') stated that consideration must be given to the fact that some of the applicants had taken part in the war: *Mitteilungsblatt der Haupttreuhandstelle Ost*, no. 5, 27 August 1940, p. 156.

(c) Drawing up the contract
The detailed wording of the contract will have to take into account the value and size of the property to be conveyed. It is important to note that the transfers of rights must be made under the care of a prudent trustee and, where required, personal responsibility for them must be taken.

For simpler transactions, the applicable guidelines are those concerning the conclusion of sales contracts for confiscated or temporarily administered companies, as well as a sample sales contract dated 7 March 1940 A 3–1512 (*Mitteilungsblatt*, no. 1, p. 22).

(d) Assumption of liabilities and receivables
The buyer assumes the receivables and debts substantiated during the period of temporary administration (new receivables and debts) as well as those receivables and debts from the period preceding the temporary administration (old receivables and debts) for which the liable parties and creditors are Germans or foreigners. Any claims against Poles or old debts to Poles will not be assumed.

The old debts that the buyer must assume hereinafter are to be listed in the sales contract, wherever possible.

The buyer assumes the encumbrances that have been entered in the land register or in the mortgage record, with the exception of encumbrances entered for Polish creditors. If the cancellation of the encumbrances entered for Polish creditors cannot be performed immediately (appointment of a temporary administrator for the creditor and granting of consent for cancellation by this administrator), the seller assumes the obligation to release the buyer.

Once the legal arrangements concerning debts, now in preparation, have been enacted, it will be possible to simplify this provision.

(e) Strengthening of Germandom
The transfers are intended to promote the strengthening of Germandom. The obligation to bring about a sale on the most advantageous terms must be subordinated to that aim as well.

The buyer must be informed that, in accordance with the legal regulations, he needs official permission for the resale of a company that he has acquired, and that he can expect issuance of such a permit for a sale that takes place less than five years after the transaction only if he can prove the existence of circumstances for which he is not responsible. The same applies to shutdowns, the acceptance of partners, and the selling of stakes in corporations.

In the sale of plots of land, pending further notice, the entry of a priority notice in the land register must be arranged to ensure that the German Reich (Main Trustee Office East) has the right to repurchase at the purchase price in the event of sale within five years of the transaction, but not at a price exceeding the fair market value. Once a final legal regulation has made it mandatory to obtain a permit for all asset transfers in the incorporated eastern territories, the intention is to have the priority notice deleted.

(f) Auxiliary conditions
The buyer must carefully preserve the books, receipts, and business papers found on the company premises. He is required to provide information to the Main Trustee Office East at all times, about all business transactions, including those from the period prior to the conclusion of the sale, if possible.

Should the political clearance certificate not be on hand when the contract is concluded, it must be agreed that the seller can withdraw from the contract on instructions from the Main Trustee Office East or its authorized Trustee Office if it subsequently emerges – on the basis of certification by the Reich Security Main Office, Berlin – that there are substantial political objections to the applicant.

6. *Responsibility and procedures*

Pending further notice, I reserve the right to realization of properties with a sales price in excess of 500,000 Reichsmarks for myself.

I will make use of a special staff dealing with sales, for which I will make detailed provisions later. In all cases, the GV SS, the department in charge, and the Legal Department are to be involved; for all arms factories, the liaison officer for the Wehrmacht High Command (OKW) must be included. The Trustee Office in charge must be informed on an ongoing basis.

In addition, the Trustee Offices (including the branch in Litzmannstadt) will organize sales. Permission for contracts concerning properties with a sales price in excess of 100,000 Reichsmarks may be issued by the Trustee Office only after the approval of the Main Trustee Office East has been obtained. For contracts which may be concluded without the approval of the Main Trustee Office East, a copy must be forwarded.

Every sales contract, prior to conclusion, must be co-signed by the Legal Department. If it concerns arms factories, the prior consent of the OKW must be obtained through the OKW's liaison officer for the Main Trustee Office East. When such sales contracts are submitted, a written opinion issued by the relevant regional armaments inspectorate or the local armaments inspectorate must be included.

In all cases, the following must be included in the files:

a) a written statement showing that the purchase price is adequate, backed up by figures, to be dated by the official in charge and signed with his full name, on the basis of an expert estimate – for larger properties, two expert assessments;
b) an inventory sheet for the property coming up for sale, provided with the temporary administrator's assurance that the inventory is accurate and complete;
c) in addition, for business enterprises of all kinds whose purchase price exceeds 50,000 Reichsmarks, an interim financial statement as of the cut-off date.

Dr Winkler[7]
Berlin, 12 August 1940

7 Max Winkler (1875–1961), Reich Postal Service official; briefly mayor of Graudenz in 1919; member of the Prussian Landtag for the German Democratic Party; in Berlin as Reich trustee for the territories ceded after the First World War, 1920–1933; received an honorary doctorate from the Danzig Institute of Technology in 1929; joined the NSDAP in 1937; Reich Plenipotentiary for the German Film Industry from 1937; also head of the Main Trustee Office East from 1939; interned in 1945; classified as 'exonerated' (*entlastet*) in denazification proceedings in 1949; then worked in the film industry and was involved in the break-up of the Ufa Film GmbH conglomerate on behalf of the West German government.

DOC. 156

On 12 August 1940 the chairman of the Polish Central Welfare Council criticizes the circumstances under which Jews are expelled from Cracow[1]

Letter from the chairman of the Polish Central Welfare Council,[2] Cracow Central Office (no. 1570/40), signed Count Adam Ronikier,[3] to the Stadthauptmann of Cracow,[4] dated 12 August 1940 (copy)[5]

The pressure of the forcible evacuation of the Jews from Cracow, ordered to begin on 16 August, and of the confiscation of the assets they left behind, has resulted in such a panicked flight of Jews from Cracow, almost unparalleled in the history of mass migrations, such a squandering and destruction of their economic assets, that I, as chairman of the Central Welfare Council for the Occupied Polish Territories, feel compelled to speak up in the public interest of the entire population of this country, and to state the following:

1. It is not in the interest of the entire population of this country to bring about a mass removal of the Jews from Cracow. The long-established close connections and interlinking in all areas of economic and social life between the Jewish and the non-Jewish population cannot be dislodged in a mechanical and violent manner without causing irreparable harm to public life across the entire country.

2. As is apparent from a map presented to the various offices which shows the distribution of epidemic disease and overpopulation, the localities in every part of the territory of the General Government are so oversaturated with refugees that any further mass resettlement would undoubtedly risk unleashing a total and economically catastrophic human deluge as well as the spread of disease.

3. Even though it was announced that Jews who moved voluntarily would be free to settle anywhere in the territory of the General Government, newly arriving Jews are not allowed in; enormous registration fees are demanded of them; their registration forms are not accepted; and such obstacles are placed in their way that voluntary resettlement

1 YVA, O-6/298, fols. 9–11. Copy made by the Cracow Department of the Jewish Historical Institute, produced in the immediate post-war period. This document has been translated from German.

2 Social welfare in the General Government was regulated according to racist criteria. From May 1940 the Polish Central Welfare Council (RGO) was the central welfare organization for the Polish (non-Jewish) population in the General Government, with its central office in Cracow. The Jewish Social Self-Help (JSS) was responsible for the Jewish population, and the Ukrainian Central Welfare Council for the Ukrainian population. All three organizations operated under the umbrella of the Chief Social Welfare Council (NRO).

3 Adam Ronikier (1881–1952), architect; National Democratic Party politician; Polish Regency Council envoy in Berlin in 1918; chairman of the RGO and the NRO, 1940–1943; briefly under arrest in 1944; fled Poland in 1945; emigrated to the USA.

4 Carl Gottlob Schmid (1889–1966), lawyer; worked in the Württemberg administration from 1915; joined the NSDAP in 1933; deputy Stadthauptmann of Cracow from Sept. 1939 and acting Stadthauptmann of Cracow, Feb. 1940–March 1941; special representative for the reorganization of the municipal administration in Prague, Nov. 1941–June 1942; then head of the local administration division in the Interior Administration Department of the General Government; civil servant in the Baden-Württemberg state administration, 1948–1957.

5 Notes in the original made by Schmid: '12 August 1940. (1) personally delivered and discussed, (2) to be filed'.

is made extremely difficult, indeed impossible. I can name a whole range of localities in this connection: Myślenice, Gdów, Wieliczka, Zembrzyce, Harbutowice, etc.

4. It also often happens that the assets of the voluntary resettlers who have brought their belongings with them are confiscated *along the way*. This explains why a substantial portion of Cracow's Jews who were determined to leave Cracow voluntarily are delaying their resettlement, as these Jews are not able to undertake the relocation easily and safely. A sufficient extension of the deadline for voluntary resettlement would make relocation possible on a far greater scale and thereby avoid unnecessary hardship.

5. It is a vital necessity for public life in this country that approximately 30,000 Jews remain in Cracow.[6]

6. To ensure that the Jews who resettle voluntarily will have the freedom to migrate and can freely choose their new place of residence, all local administrations in the General Government for the Occupied Polish Territories must be instructed emphatically once again not to place obstacles of any sort in the way of Jews leaving Cracow.

7. Those who have volunteered to be resettled must be provided with adequate financial means so that they do not go hungry in their new place of residence and can engage in economic activity in some way.

8. The names of the localities where the forcibly resettled Jews and their families will find their new residences will have to be made known so that the Jewish relief committees can provide help and advice to them promptly and in an organized fashion.

9. All forms of relief and benefits will have to be paid as before to the greatest possible extent to all Jews who have decided to voluntarily resettle and have been unable to act on this decision by the scheduled deadline, owing to all sorts of difficulties.

Only under the conditions listed above could the evacuation of the Jews from Cracow, which the German authorities have deemed necessary, be carried out in a humane, considerate, and compassionate fashion.

These last requirements are based not only on humane and emotional considerations, but also – and primarily – on concerns for the public interest of the entire population.

Under these sad circumstances, when the distress of the unfortunates is so great and public order is threatened in such a significant way, I take the liberty, in my capacity as chairman of the Chief Social Welfare Council for the Occupied Polish Territories, to most respectfully request the Stadthauptmann of Cracow to take the aforementioned circumstances into account and to issue or set in motion the corresponding directives.

6 Note in the original, in Polish: 'Next to this sentence, Schmid added a handwritten question mark.'

DOC. 157
On 12 August 1940 the Jewish elder in the Litzmannstadt (Lodz) ghetto calls for public peace and order to be maintained[1]

Announcement no. 104 from the Jewish elder in the Litzmannstadt (Lodz) ghetto, Chaim Rumkowski,[2] dated 12 August 1940

Jews!
The recent events were caused by irresponsible elements who want to bring disarray to our lives.[3] They have only their own benefit in mind and are hindering the implementation of a constructive *relief effort* for the population.

Within the short time since the establishment of the ghetto, and after great effort, we have managed to procure work from outside for some of the tailors, carpenters, cobblers, decorators,[4] needleworkers, and quite soon also for other craftsmen, as well as handloom weavers.

The Community's budget is overstretched. Care for sick children and the elderly always takes priority. *Nonetheless*, new *kitchens* for people of all ages are being set up.

In addition to the large soup kitchen for workers and the unemployed, which will serve 10,000 lunches each day, and in addition to kitchens for various sections of the population (including for religious Jews), residential blocks will be provided for as well.[5]

This is the constructive plan that has been prepared. It is no easy task.

I therefore appeal to you: be *calm*. Do not let yourselves be misled by irresponsible people who want to disrupt the work done so far and the plans for the future.

Jews, be *calm*.

I will do everything possible and will always endeavour to carry out my duties as conscientiously as possible.

1 YIVO, 241/228. This document has been translated from German.
2 Mordechai Chaim Rumkowski (1877–1944), businessman; Zionist member of the Jewish Community's executive committee in Łódź before 1939; appointed Jewish elder in Łódź in Oct. 1939; head of the Jewish administration in the Litzmannstadt (Lodz) ghetto, 1940–1944; expanded production for the Wehrmacht and for German companies with the intention of ensuring the survival of at least some of the ghetto inhabitants; deported in August 1944 to Auschwitz, where he was murdered.
3 In August 1940 people asking for bread and work had organized demonstrations in the ghetto.
4 Rumkowski meant upholsterers but used the wrong German word.
5 This refers to the so-called building committees that had been formed, initially at the population's urging, and from late March 1940 under Rumkowski's direction. They were in charge of individual buildings, and their tasks included food distribution. They ran communal kitchens that provided hot meals for the inhabitants of individual buildings. The committees were disbanded by late 1940, and Rumkowski's administration took over their tasks.

DOC. 158

On 13 August 1940 a physician describes how the Gestapo robbed Jews in Warsaw in the winter of 1939/1940[1]

Record of the witness testimony of Z. Sz. or Sch.[2] given before the Joint Aid Committee for Polish Jews[3] in Jerusalem, dated 13 August 1940

Germans in Warsaw.
Good-natured Gestapo men.
Doctor Z… Sz… from Warsaw, currently living in Jerusalem, testifies as follows: in addition to my husband's statement of 29 May 1940,[4] I can provide examples of 4 'amusing' episodes from life in Warsaw last winter, that is, during the period from December 1939 to March 1940.

One day, in the daytime, a grey police (military) car pulled up in front of the house on Królewska Street and out of it climbed a German military physician in a Gestapo uniform, but with a physician's badge, as well as an ordinary Gestapo man. They inquired about the apartment of the absent physician Dr K. As his apartment had been destroyed in the bombing, they sought out his wife, a subtenant in another apartment. They demanded the husband's medical instruments and office equipment. As they did not find these items during the search, because they were not there, they took … bed linen, a fountain pen, some soap, and a small jewellery scale (a keepsake) instead. When Mrs K. complained to them that they had taken almost everything from her, they retorted that what was left was sufficient for another two households, and when she asked them to give back the scale as a memento of her father, the physician replied: 'Für Sie ist das ein Andenken und ich brauche das.'[5] Afterwards, in another room that was part of the landlord's apartment, they noticed a fireproof safe; they ordered it to be opened and found an old gold watch and a table lamp. They took the lamp straightaway but hesitated about the watch, so they locked the safe and took the key, saying they would be back the next day at a given time. They came back the next day, but the landlord was away. Because they were unable to open the safe without him, they fell into a rage, stamped their feet, and threatened everyone present. In the meantime, they collected various other items, which they loaded into the car and drove off, announcing a further visit. This time the landlord was there, they opened the safe and took the watch, instructing him to report to the Gestapo office at 25 Szucha Avenue for a receipt. When the landlord went to Szucha Avenue the next day, he did not meet the Gestapo men at the gate as had been arranged, and inside no one knew about any such physician. However, the caretaker advised him to go to the building at 16 Szucha Avenue, where the Gestapo officers lived. He went there and found the apartment where that German physician was staying, and went inside. The physician was visibly uneasy that he had been found, and

1 YVA, O-55/70, fols. 4–6. This document has been translated from Polish.
2 At the beginning of the document 'Z… Sz…' and at the end 'Z… Sch…'.
3 Joint Aid Committee for Polish Jews (Zjednoczony Komitet Pomocy dla Żydów Polskich): this designation is presumably another term for the Committee of Four. See Doc. 13, fn. 2.
4 Her husband's statement was not found in the file.
5 German in the original: 'For you it's only a keepsake and I need it.'

when asked for the receipt he telephoned for the Gestapo man with whom he had committed the robbery. He then sent the Gestapo man with the owner of the watch to the Gestapo; there they went from one clerk to the next, but no one considered themselves responsible. At last, the Gestapo man showed one of the clerks the stolen watch and said: 'Bei diesem Juden haben wir diese Uhr gefunden.'[6] At this, the clerk asked the owner of the watch: 'Haben Sie mehr solche?',[7] and when he received a no in reply, that this was just a memento, he replied that the matter did not belong to his area of responsibility. However, the Gestapo man put the watch back in his pocket and said to the owner: 'Sie sind frei, können nach Hause gehen.'[8] The next day, the same German physician and Gestapo man came to Mrs K. again to carry out a search. They ran into the landlord on the steps. They greeted him politely and the Gestapo man, who was following behind the physician, discreetly removed the watch from his pocket and returned it to its owner, evidently keeping this a secret from the physician. Thus ends the story of the watch, stolen by the physician, a Gestapo officer, and secretly returned by a Gestapo man.

Another 'amusing' episode concerned a physician, Dr L. Dr L. is a young physician, a bachelor, but has an older brother, also a physician, who is well known in Warsaw and has a large practice and considerable wealth. This brother is currently in Soviet captivity. Dr L. simply had 'bad luck'. The Germans had already seized him in the street several times and, disregarding his physician's armband, had ordered him to remove heavy objects from looted apartments. This time, when he returned home to his parents, with whom he lived, he encountered Gestapo men carrying out a search of the house, looking for gold and valuables. When he entered, the Gestapo men demanded that he give them these items. Dr L. replied truthfully that he possessed nothing of that kind. The Gestapo men became indignant at that, as they knew that he was a wealthy man, owned property and jewellery. They even knew that he had received a large dowry. Dr L. replied that this was a misunderstanding, that they had mistaken him for someone else, and that he was a bachelor and therefore had never received a dowry, but the Gestapo men declared he could not deceive them and, enraged, began the search. During the search, in a table drawer, they found revolver bullets about which Dr L. knew nothing – the Gestapo men themselves had evidently planted the bullets. They arrested Dr L. and his father and beat up the mother. For 4 weeks, no one knew where they were being held, but thanks to the efforts of Dr L.'s sister-in-law, an Aryan – probably of German descent – they were released. Dr L. returned in a good mood. He said that he had been held at Pawiak[9] in first-class company, had learned to play bridge there, and the head of the cell had been some count whom the prison staff, consisting of Poles, respected, and that he had it easy in prison as there had been neither Gestapo men nor house searches there. The very same Gestapo men who had arrested him visited him a few days after his release. They were very polite and tried to convince him that he must pay them something. 'Sir,' they said, 'all this has cost you nothing, you know well enough that one pays a lot in such cases, and you paid the lawyer only 600 zł., so we could not get much from that. You should put yourself in our position, we cannot incur losses in your case.' Dr L. countered that

6 German in the original: 'We found this watch at this Jew's place.'
7 German in the original: 'Have you more of the same?'
8 German in the original: 'You are free; you can go home.'
9 Prison at 24/26 Dzielna Street in Warsaw.

he had no money, at which the Gestapo men became upset and left, saying that they would return and that maybe in the meantime he would earn something. They returned a few more times. They also encountered Dr L. in the street. They were always very polite and always asked him to make good their loss. Dr L. explained to them that he was a young physician and had few patients; if they wanted, they could send him patients and then he would give them their cut. This did not suit the Gestapo men and they suggested to Dr L. that should he want to leave, they would arrange that for him at a relatively low price. For a relatively low fee, they also offered him documents certifying that he was of Aryan descent. They even offered to supply him with evidence that he belonged to the 'hohen Adel'[10] and assured him that all the documents would be 'authentic'. In short, one could see that the Gestapo men desperately wanted to make money and were genuinely upset by the fact that none of the 'deals' were working out. I do not know how this whole episode ended.

My acquaintance lawyer G. was walking without a Jewish armband on her upper arm through the courtyard of the building in which she lived. A Polish policeman happened to be in the courtyard. He stopped her, checked her papers, and demanded 20 zł. for not wearing an armband. Mrs G. explained that she was not out on the street but at home – but it didn't help. She then offered the policemen 6 zł. because that was all she had on her. The policeman replied that he could not agree to that, as he would make a loss, for the Germans pay him 20 zł. per person in such cases. Mrs G. responded that he could perhaps take less from his 'own kind'. However, the policeman disagreed and Mrs G. had to go to a shop and borrow the missing 14 zł., and gave the policeman the full amount.

During a house search of a certain gentleman, a Jew, twenty shirts were found in a wardrobe. The Germans took these shirts but generously returned two of them to the owner, put the rest aside and went to search the next room. Taking advantage of the Germans' temporary absence, the owner exchanged these two shirts for better ones. When the Germans came back, one of them noticed this and said threateningly: 'Wissen Sie, dass man bei uns für Diebstahl zwei Jahre Zuchthaus bekommt?'[11] These words bear witness to the strong sense of justice among today's Germans.

DOC. 159

On 14 August 1940 the teacher Chaim Kaplan describes the gruelling situation of Jews in Warsaw[1]

Handwritten diary of Chaim Kaplan, entry for 14 August 1940

In my apartment today there was a gathering of friends who visited me unexpectedly. All were weighed down by worries, their faces haggard and sunken, because they have all been discharged from their posts. L. has lost 15 kilos; he is hunched over and despondent,

10 German in the original: 'high nobility'.

11 German in the original: 'Do you know that here you get two years of penal servitude for theft?'

1 AŻIH, 302/218, fols. 31–35. This document has been translated from Yiddish. Published in Kaplan, *Megillat yissurin*, pp. 298–300. An incomplete English translation can be found in Kaplan, *Scroll of Agony*, pp. 161–163.

despairing beyond all measure: For how long? When will it end? A whole year without an income. He lives on miracles. Where will help come from? Last summer he was in Druskieniki[2] with his wife, from there she travelled to Truskavets.[3] And now? They go a whole week without a bite of meat to eat.

Or take P. He is a shrewd and learned merchant who has read a lot, studied a lot, and seen a lot. He was a senior employee with signing power at a German firm in Warsaw; his livelihood was secure. He lived in abundance. Soon after the city had been captured, he was laid off without notice and received three months' severance. He risked his life and fled to Russia. There he wandered around without staying anywhere, and once he grew tired of wandering, he again risked his life by returning. His severance pay has already been exhausted. As a result, he, too, lives on miracles. He is waiting for the Bolsheviks as if for the spring rains. If they don't come, it would be tantamount to his disgrace. His last groszy are melting away …

The next one is my good and dear friend K. In the past, i.e. last year, he was a wealthy merchant. A magnificent apartment on Niecała Street, four luxuriously furnished rooms. He was an official partner in one business and a silent one in another. Quadruple income, a trip to spa towns every year, an admirer and lover of Yiddish authors. And now? The occupiers took a fancy to his apartment, of all places, and they took it away from him by brute force. He had to vacate it within three hours and leave behind his furniture. His two businesses are gone. All earnings have run dry. Fortunately, he had a bit of money. He lives in a small room with his sister and lives off his cash reserves, which are dwindling by the day. He eats without any pleasure because he is worried about the future. He counts his money every day, which pierces him in the heart: how long will it last? His face is sunken and he loses weight every day. Can you still call this a life? He has a married daughter; the couple fled to Russia while he stayed behind, alone and forlorn. His eyes are also turned eastwards. He is waiting for 'them' as if for the Messiah … What do you think? Will they come?

The fourth is my dear friend F., formerly the head of the export agency of a Danzig [-based] company that has been liquidated because its owners were Jewish. As a wealthy merchant – educated, smart, shrewd, and worldly-wise – he lived in prosperity and lacked none of the finer things in life. Two years ago he got a nice six-room apartment on Senatorska. Friends and acquaintances who had a respected name in the business world, in public life, and in the Zionist movement visited him regularly – he was living well. And now? As the bombs fell and Warsaw was shelled, half of his apartment was destroyed when it was hit by a shell, creating a ruin. He used to be someone in business, but who remembers him now? Everything is wrecked. He lives off the cash that he saved up.

He had confirmation of a certificate[4] and was already prepared for the journey, but the 'Gestapo' stopped him and other members of the Central Committee.[5] Now he walks around all day looking for a new business [opportunity] – to no avail. There are no

2 Popular resort in Poland during the interwar period.

3 Truskavets (Polish Truskawiec): a resort town in present-day Ukraine famed for its mineral springs.

4 Certificate entitling the bearer to enter Palestine as an immigrant.

5 Most likely a reference to the Central Committee of the Zionist Organization.

longer any businesses allowed to Jews. Everything is forbidden. All sources have dried up. In addition, people are afraid to request a permit and thereby be registered with the 'murderer', even if the permit is granted. Ultimately the goods will end up in a different place. Wherever you turn, everything is locked up and sealed. Everywhere you go to do business, another danger lurks. You are chained without shackles.

So his money will run out as well. And where does that lead? How long will all this go on? A clever and talented man is excluded from society. An almost superfluous person! And yesterday he had the privilege of receiving 'guests' whose reputation leaves the heart of every Jew trembling. One cannot call them 'guests'; they are thieves. They broke in and stole two expensive rugs and other valuables from him. But that is not the main issue – such things happen every hour. Every Jew is prepared for this. The two carpets can go to hell with their new owners! The main question is: Do I know when this ghastliness called war will end? Do I have any advice on how we might be saved from this ordeal?

And the last one, who also comes last in life, is the Hebrew teacher M., one of the best Hebrew teachers in Warsaw. Well known, respected, educated, although not blessed with riches in the past. His income was meagre, but he managed. Free in what he did, with a secure income, he followed the course he had set himself: Hebrew cultural work in the Tarbut school where he worked.[6] He never made much, but it was enough for his needs. His surroundings and his work fulfilled him financially and spiritually.

After the city was occupied the schools were closed and he lost his position. Hunger loomed. CENTOS began its work and set up public soup kitchens for children in need, among whom were also several of his pupils. He was appointed inspector and was to oversee a hundred children during mealtimes. Punishing work! A nerve-wracking job! But he has no other option. He receives a free meal every day and 100 złoty a month. And he is happy.

So you can live on 100 złoty per month if you really want to. Wartime is different! You have to make do with less!!

But this small salary was also lost because CENTOS is supported by the Joint [JDC], which no longer has any money to pay for his position. All institutions, including CENTOS, which were supported by the Joint have fallen silent, as there is no money any more. He has not been paid his salary for three months. He is plagued by hunger pangs. In his case, too, I can only ask: How will it end for him?

And I lower my head as if to say: my own fate is unknown to me – how should I know that of other people?

This gathering was a microcosm of Warsaw. There are thousands upon thousands of them. And really, what will our fate be?! Who is wise enough to clear this up for me?!

6 Tarbut (Hebrew: 'culture'), Zionist cultural organization founded in 1922 and supported by the American Jewish Joint Distribution Committee (JDC). Tarbut was a network of secular educational facilities with Modern Hebrew as the language of instruction. It was active particularly in Poland, Romania, and Lithuania. In 1939 the organization maintained 270 schools, attended by 45,000 students; this number represented around 9 per cent of the Jewish pupils and university students in Poland.

DOC. 160

On 20 August 1940 the Kreishauptmann of Krakau-Land introduces restrictions on Jews' freedom of movement within the Kreis[1]

The Kreishauptmann of Kreis Krakau-Land[2]
Directive on Restrictions on the Movement of Jews, 20 August 1940.

With reference to § 2 of the Regulation on the Introduction of Forced Labour for the Jewish Population in the General Government of 26 October 1939, and § 4 of the First Implementing Regulation thereto of 11 December 1939,[3] I order the following for the area under the authority of the Kreishauptmann of Krakau-Land:

§ 1. I forbid all Jews living in the Kreis Krakau-Land, initially until 15 October 1940, to go beyond the boundaries of their place of residence, either permanently or temporarily.

'Place of residence' is defined as the municipality or village in which the Jew has his residence or his permanent lodging.

§ 2. This ban does not apply:

a) to Jews who are used for special tasks by the German administration. These Jews must establish their identity by presenting valid papers issued by a German authority and bearing an official stamp, which expressly confirm that they are working for the German administration.

b) to Jews who are on their way to undertake forced labour. These Jews must establish their identity by presenting valid papers bearing a date and an official stamp and issued by the Landkommissar or Stadtkommissar or by the institution where they are deployed for forced labour.

c) in exceptional cases involving public or private emergencies. In such cases, Jews must establish their identity by presenting papers bearing a date and an official stamp and issued by the town or village mayor. In particular, the papers must contain the Jew's name, place of residence, and occupation, as well as the purpose, destination, and probable duration of his journey.

§ 3. I reserve the right to issue exceptional permissions for special reasons, upon written request. Simultaneously, under the same conditions, I hereby give the Landkommissare and Stadtkommissare the authority to grant exceptions in their jurisdictions.

§ 4. Contraventions of this directive will be punished with imprisonment for up to 8 weeks or fines of up to 10,000 zloty, or both, unless a harsher penalty is provided for under other relevant regulations.

1 AAN, 1335/214/II-5, fol. 2. Copy in USHMM, RG 15 008M, reel 4. Poster in German and Polish. This document has been translated from German.

2 Dr Egon Höller (1907–1991), lawyer; joined the NSDAP in Austria in 1932, the SA in 1933, and the SS in 1938; took part in the attempt to overthrow Austrian Chancellor Dollfuss in 1934; dismissed from the civil service and imprisoned for 14 months in 1935; fled to Germany in 1936; worked for the Reichsstatthalter in Vienna in 1938; Kreishauptmann of Krakau-Land and then Stadthauptmann of Lemberg, Oct. 1939–Feb. 1942; in Allied captivity in 1945; businessman in Munich after the war.

3 See Docs. 27 and 55.

§ 5. This directive comes into force on the day it is displayed on the noticeboard of the local administration.

The Kreishauptmann
Dr Höller

DOC. 161

On 27 August 1940 an anonymous informer denounces a Jewish company owner in Warsaw[1]

Letter to the Security Police in Warsaw, dated 27 August 1940

I hereby inform you of the following:

In Wola, on Obozowa Street there is a factory called 'Tytan' and nearby, on Św. Stanisława Street, a factory called 'Cyklop', which forms a single financial entity with 'Tytan'.

The official owner of the business is a Jew, Landau, who has appointed frontmen to represent him in order to disguise the Jewish nature of the business.

Landau himself appears to be in hiding.

There is no doubt that his representative and right-hand man, Aleksander Szkopek, manager of the factory, knows his whereabouts.

Aleksander Szkopek is a meche.[2]

He was baptized in 1935 solely to become an officer. Taking advantage of the fact that his appearance does not betray his Jewish origins, not only does he not wear an armband, but he also claims to be a Pole.

To conceal his origins (he was sought several times by the Jewish Community and finally bought himself out) and his membership in the former Polish army – Szkopek was not registered anywhere after the war, nor did he appear for the registration ordered at the time.[3]

Recently, given the threat of the death penalty, he now intends to register, and he might possibly take this opportunity to also register at his place of residence. He has lived at the factory for a long time, but now lives in Bielany,[4] across from the CIWF.[5] I do not have the exact address.

Even if he does register, he will no doubt remain in hiding out of fear of being sent to Germany for labour.

His telephone number is 2.31.01.

I state all the above facts for ideological reasons, as I hate the Jews, especially meches who flaunt their nationality and religion.

Warsaw, 27 August 1940

Should this notification result in any consequences, I shall inform you, gentlemen, of other, more important matters.

1 AIPN, GK 106/161 (703/31, CA MSW 684), vol. 1, fol. 42. This document has been translated from Polish. The anonymous letter, which was sent by post, appears to have been intercepted by the Polish underground organization Muszkieterowie (Musketeers) before the Security Police broke up the group and took possession of the notification.

2 'Baptized Jew', here used as a derogatory term.

3 Former officers of the Polish army had to register in autumn 1939.

4 District in Warsaw.

5 Centralny Instytut Wychowania Fizycznego: Central Institute of Physical Education.

DOC. 162

A report written in July/August 1940 outlines the economic harm caused by the persecution of the Jews in Poland[1]

Report, unsigned, July/August 1940[2]

The destruction of Jewish economic assets in Poland

Introduction

The military operations and their consequences have shaken Poland's economic life in general and have completely ruined Jewish economic life.

Here, we will speak only of the General Government, that small part of the former Polish Republic where almost 50 per cent of all the Jews previously living in the former Polish Republic are now crowded together. There can be no talk of a private economic structure at all in the part of Poland under Soviet occupation (more than 53 per cent of the territory), because it is under communist rule. The situation is similar, though in quite a different manner, in the remaining parts of Poland, which were incorporated into the Third Reich. The economic conditions are completely different there too, and the term 'economic ruin' would be inappropriate for the local Jewish population, as the majority of the municipalities there have been emptied of Jews, and wherever this has not yet occurred, the Jewish population is mostly locked up in cramped ghettos.

In the following, I will seek to demonstrate that the war, having done no more than cause a profound tremor in economic life in the General Government, has brought about the complete destruction of Jewish economic activity.

The total area of General Government territory is 96,600 square kilometres. According to official statistics, this territory has more than 12,500,000 inhabitants, including 9,940,000 Poles, more than 1,500,000 Jews, 700,000 Ukrainians, 90,000 Germans, and almost 350,000 Gorals.[3] This means there are 129 inhabitants per [square] kilometre, with the three districts Warsaw, Cracow, and Radom, where the soil is far less fertile than elsewhere in Poland, being the most densely populated.

The aforementioned population density and the fact that the territory of the General Government has been cut off from the former main centres of Polish industry in Silesia, the Dąbrowa Basin, Lodz, and Eastern Galicia (the petroleum region) alone constitute sufficient proof that the General Government's overall economy has been shaken. In addition, thousands of factories, workshops, warehouses, commercial enterprises, and private assets were partly or completely destroyed during the bombing raids and the conflagrations. Even after the end of hostilities, hundreds of large and small enterprises

1 AŻIH, Ring II/3 (126). This document has been translated from German.

2 Handwritten note at the top right, indicating the month: VII–VIII 1940. The memorandum was most likely meant for the Jewish councils in the General Government, so that they could take suggestions from it to ease their plight. The paper was written in German, which meant that it was also prepared for the occupying authorities – at least for their information. It may be the work of Michał Weichert and is certainly based on JSS reports from Warsaw.

3 Polish inhabitants of the Beskids whom the German occupying power declared to be a separate ethnic group.

of various kinds had to be liquidated or put on a completely different footing as a result of the new official economic and quota systems.

These detrimental shocks, which were felt in the economy overall, were partially countermanded for the non-Jewish population by the establishment of new non-Jewish companies of considerable size in place of the liquidated Jewish ones (in Warsaw, 23 large non-Jewish companies were established in the first few months after the end of hostilities; each of them employs more than 20 persons). In addition, the vast majority of the Polish population in the General Government, people who worked in agriculture before the war, remained on their land, which they cultivate and which feeds them. Also, the Polish workers and the great majority of government officials continue to hold their previous jobs in the factories or in their offices. The situation is different with respect to the Jewish economy, which was completely ruined, first by the severe damage suffered during the hostilities, and later by the legal regulations systematically directed against the Jewish economy.

The previous professional structure of the Jewish population in Poland

Let us look at what the normal state of the Jewish economy in the country was previously, for we are convinced that familiarity with the social and professional structures of Polish Jewry in the pre-war period will provide proof that Polish Jewry includes many elements which can be usefully employed both to rebuild the ruined country efficiently and to support the subsequent emigration of the Jewish population.

First and foremost, the numbers from the 1931 census give us an objective picture of the tasks the Jews performed in the economic life of former Poland.[4] These numbers contradict the deeply rooted but thoroughly incorrect belief that the bulk of the Jews depend exclusively on commerce. It turns out that, in total, 38 per cent of the economically active Jews were involved in the commercial sector, but 43 per cent worked in the sector of industry and craft trades. The dominance of the industry sector is even more pronounced among the Jews in the General Government. Some 240,000, or 46 per cent of the more than half a million economically active Jews, were employed in the industry sector, mainly as skilled craftsmen, while barely 200,000 Jews, or 38 per cent of all economically active Jews, worked in the commercial sector there.

In the last decade before the war, the process of industrialization made even more headway among the Jews, as is confirmed by the census conducted by the Jewish Community in Warsaw on 28 October 1939, at the behest of the German authorities. In that census, 156,000 (43.3 per cent) of the 356,000 Jewish residents of Warsaw were deemed to be economically active, and 81,422 of them worked in the sector of industry and craft trades.

At the time of the registration for forced labour, 117,000 men between the ages of 12 and 60 lived in Warsaw, and 53,000 of them were skilled craftsmen and workers with skilled training. The registration shows that those who were not directly involved in the labour process constitute quite a small minority. In the entire territory of the General Government, we have a round number of 36,000 (6.9 per cent) independent Jewish business owners who employ paid workers. The vast majority, however – 93 per cent of

4 *Drugi powszechny spis ludności z dn. 9.XII.1931 r: Formularze i instrukcje spisowe. Deuxième recensement général de la population du 9. XII, 1931: Formulaires et instructions* (Warsaw: Główny Urząd Statystyczny, 1932).

the Jewish population – make up a mass of working people whose members depend exclusively on their own effort and labour, working as independent businessmen, craftsmen, handymen, or labourers.

Apart from the significant predominance of the artisan categories in the territory of the General Government, the Jewish working class also occupies a very important place there, accounting for 46.8 per cent of all economically active Jews. The group of workers itself totals 42.6 per cent; in most branches of industry, workers constitute more than half, and in the textile industry, they amount to 72.5 per cent. If one also takes into account that the Jewish industrial population is concentrated mainly in small-scale industrial and craft production, it must be acknowledged that this proportion is quite significant.

The distribution across branches is different for Jews compared to non-Jews. Of the total number of Jews working in industrial production and the skilled crafts and trades, 43.9 per cent are in the garment industry, 14.2 per cent in food-related industries, 7.9 per cent in textile production, 7.6 per cent in the timber industry, and 6.6 per cent in the metal industry.

Within the garment industry, the number of Jewish tailors represented 47.8 per cent, in the Lublin voivodeship as much as 66.9 per cent, and in the Kielce voivodeship 63.4 per cent.

Among those in the underwear and linen sector, the Jews account for half of all those employed.

In the shoemaking trade, 35 out of every 100 shoemakers or cobblers are Jews. In the Lublin and Kielce voivodeships, the proportion of Jews is as high as 57 per cent and 45 per cent.

In the cap-making industry, the Jewish share is 73 per cent; 61.5 per cent of furriers are Jews; in the leather industry, the share of Jews is 45 per cent; and 73 per cent of hatters and milliners are Jews.

In the sectors of the metal industry, Jews account for 50 per cent in plumbing, 65.6 per cent in jewellery and watchmaking, and 11.2 per cent in the metalworking industry.

In the building trades, the number of Jews is especially large among roofers and glaziers (80 per cent), though they constitute a smaller share of masons and carpenters (20 per cent on average, but 35 per cent in the Lublin voivodeship and 28 per cent in the Kielce voivodeship).

While the share of Jews in larger-scale textile manufacturing is low (16 per cent), they account for 42 per cent of workers in the smaller-scale cottage industry within the textile sector.

In the timber sector, Jews hold a significant position only in woodworking and furniture manufacturing (20 per cent).

The share of Jews in commerce is naturally far larger than in industry. In the central voivodeships, where the economic structure generally corresponded to that of the present General Government territory, Jews accounted for 55.9 per cent overall, though only 47.8 per cent in wholesale.

The proportion of Jews in agriculture is small. In all of Poland 125,000 Jews, or 4 per cent, made a living in agriculture. It was precisely in the territory of the General Government that agriculture was most poorly represented. The number of Jews in this sector could probably be estimated at 28,000 there.

The first heavy blows

In the very first days of the war, in early September, when the outbreak of war engulfed the whole country simultaneously from three sides, north, west, and south, the entire edifice of the Jewish economic structure in Poland began to collapse. Many thousands of Jewish manufacturers, retailers, craftsmen, and labourers left their workplaces and their homes to go to the larger cities, primarily Warsaw. During the first weeks of the war, the number of Jewish refugees in Warsaw already totalled approximately 100,000. Around 50,000 to 60,000 Jews from Lodz alone sought refuge in Warsaw. Whole streets and neighbourhoods there were incinerated as a result of the bombing; large bazaars, commercial centres, factories, and workshops were destroyed in a matter of minutes; and economic life as a whole came to a sudden standstill. After military operations ended and Warsaw capitulated, i.e. at the end of September, the following picture of Jewish economic life in ruins presented itself:

According to the Warsaw municipal administration, around 75 per cent[5] of all the buildings in Warsaw were destroyed or completely ruined. The Jewish neighbourhoods suffered the most: more than 50 per cent of the shops in the streets of the two most important commercial centres in Warsaw (Nalewki and Grzybow) were consumed by fire. Around 20 per cent of the Jewish shops which were not destroyed were robbed during the unrest, liquidated, or closed, and around 1,500 Jewish apartment buildings and factory buildings were burned or destroyed. Seven large bazaars with approximately 3,000 Jewish shops fell victim to the flames, and approximately 30,000 Jewish homes in various neighbourhoods were destroyed by bombs or consumed by fire. More than 6,000 Jews were killed during the bombings, and twice that number were seriously injured (in all of Poland, the number of Jews killed in the bombings exceeded 20,000). In Warsaw, around 20,000 Jewish enterprises of various kinds were destroyed or made subject to liquidation as a result of hostilities. In addition, Warsaw's devastated Jewish population had to provide housing and the most urgent help for the enormous mass of refugees and people whose homes had been burned down.

In the countryside, things looked no better. In more than 100 cities and small towns, almost all the Jewish trade bazaars and centres of employment had gone up in smoke. In several towns, only a tiny percentage of Jewish buildings had been saved.

Moreover, the Jewish population faced another misfortune: the [working] classes, who had their savings with PKO[6] or other savings institutions, lost their hard-earned pennies when all of these institutions were shut down in the very first days of the war. In this respect as well, the Jews' situation was far more dismal than that of the non-Jewish population, because when war broke out, the officials who worked for the government or the municipal institutions were given several months' pay in advance for the evacuation, while Jews who were in need were literally left without the means to get by.

The consequences of the anti-Jewish legal provisions

After the cessation of hostilities, the Jewish population in Poland tried to adjust to the newly created conditions and to organize economic life on a new basis. Gradually the

5 The author presumably means 25 per cent. According to modern-day estimates, approximately 12 per cent of the buildings in Warsaw were destroyed by the effects of the war in Sept. 1939.

6 Polska Kasa Oszczędności (Polish Savings Bank).

Jewish workshops and shops were opened, and the Jewish population proved its complete readiness to take an active role in rebuilding the country's economic life. However, the Jews encountered tremendous difficulties that made this impossible.

As soon as the new order in Poland was in its early phase, a number of regulations were issued that harmed the Jewish economy. In early October this year, i.e. shortly after hostilities in Poland ceased, a regulation concerning cash turnover was promulgated and dated 18 September. This regulation contains the following heavy restrictions on Jews' economic activity in the country: (1) a maximum of 500 złoty can be disbursed to a Jew, the remainder must be deposited in a blocked account with a financial institution; (2) banks are permitted to pay out a maximum of 250 zł. per week to a Jew from his accounts, or to credit the same amount to his accounts; (3) a Jewish family is allowed to possess a maximum of 2,000 złoty outside the financial institutions.[7]

These 3 provisions were made even more severe by the Governor General's Foreign Currency Department circular,[8] dated 20 November 1939. It decrees that a Jew can receive a maximum payment of 500 zł. per month, while the remainder must be paid into his blocked account with a financial institution.[9]

The above provisions have made it impossible for Jews to conclude any commercial transaction or to process an order, because the retailer must have a substantial sum of money available when purchasing goods or processing sizeable orders, especially now, when credit transactions have completely vanished from the scene. How can a Jewish retailer or craftsman, who is allowed to have only 2,000 zł. and to collect only 500 zł. from his receivables each month, purchase the necessary goods or raw materials if he has to pay cash for the goods and then often wait several months before he sells the goods? Hundreds of Jewish firms therefore had to be liquidated immediately once the aforementioned regulations were issued.

Small-scale Jewish industry and retail never took loans from the large banking houses, so these groups are not in line for the easing of cheque transactions contained in the aforementioned Regulation of 18 September 1939.

The economic information bulletin of 31 January this year published a regulation of District Warsaw which stated that when new companies are entered into the commercial register, special permission for their entry must be obtained from the District Governor. However, such permission is granted only if the Aryan origin of the person establishing the company has been proven.[10] This regulation thus makes it impossible for Jews to

7 The Chief of the Civil Administration for the 14th Army (Army Command 14), War Economy Department, ordered these restrictions for Jews in § 6 and § 8 of his Directive on Payments and Monetary Transactions: APKr, 33, SMKr/62.

8 This is a reference to Governor General Frank.

9 Directive no. 4 of the Head of the Foreign Currency Department in the Office of the Governor General on General Measures for the Securing of Jewish Assets: *VOBl-GG* 1939, no. 7, 20 Nov. 1939, pp. 57–58.

10 *Wirtschaftsmitteilungen: Amtliches Informationsbulletin der Industrie- und Handelskammer in Warschau*, no. 13, 31 Jan. 1940, p. 7: approval for founding new registered companies. An application to obtain the approval of the District Governor had to be filed (in German) with the Economic Affairs Department in the district office and had to be accompanied by 'a statement concerning the Aryan descent of the founders of the company'.

establish new companies or to transform existing companies into new ones, as Polish law requires all larger companies to be entered in the commercial register.

The above regulation is also particularly significant because a shortage of capital often forces retailers and craftsmen to band together in cooperatives, and as such they must be entered in the commercial register, even if they are not among the 'large companies'.

Significant difficulties for the Jewish economy were also caused by the as yet unpublished regulation issued by the financial authorities which states that tax refunds for Jews are out of the question, and that Jewish taxpayers are not permitted to benefit from legal tax shields either. The refusal to recognize legal concessions even for earlier years,[11] although these concessions have been taken into account in the company's calculations until now, has meant complete ruin for many Jewish companies.

The regulation of 29 September 1939 provides for the appointment of temporary administrators only if the person previously authorized to manage the company is out of the country, or if efficient company management is impossible for specific reasons.[12] In reality, however, administrators have been installed at many Jewish firms where the owners are present and are beyond all reproach with regard to company management.

In a large number of Jewish businesses, the temporary administrators and trustees have primarily brought about the removal of Jewish workers and employees. In some cases, this happened at the request of the supply centres which provide raw materials and refused to supply the necessary materials as long as Jews were employed by the companies in question. This happened at a large number of pharmacies, where the Jewish pharmacists were removed and the pharmacies passed into the hands of non-Jews, who dismissed the Jewish workers and employees first of all. As a result, there has been a huge increase in unemployment among Jews, both in clerical and in manual work.

Jewish craftsmen have been hit hard by the restrictions to which they are subjected when seeking to change the locations of their workshops, as well as by the prohibition that makes it impossible for craftsmen who have to perform forced labour to either sell the tools of their trade or have them at their disposal. Under the provisions of the Polish Law on Industry, every craftsman could easily change the location of his workshop in Warsaw. At present, because many workshops have been destroyed by the hostilities and craftsmen are forced to change their locations as a result, the formalities for changing the workshop sites ought to be made easier. In fact, however, a Jewish craftsman's request to change the address of his workshop has been rejected with the explanation that this would be a new workshop, and that Jews are not permitted to open them. Likewise, all requests made by the craftsmen who were expelled from their previous home towns and have come to Warsaw are being denied, although they were working legally in their previous home towns, on the basis of their craftsman's cards.

Paragraph 6 of the Regulation on the Introduction of Forced Labour for Jews of 12 December 1939[13] forbids all Jews who are subject to forced labour from selling or

11 See the Regulation on the Abolition of the Tax Exemption and Tax Concessions of Jewish Corporations: *VOBl-GG* 1939, no. 8, 30 Nov. 1939, p. 60.

12 Regulation of the Commander of the Army on the Appointment of Temporary Administrators for Companies, Businesses, and Plots of Land in the Occupied Formerly Polish Territories: Göring (ed.), *Haupttreuhandstelle Ost*, pp. 41–42.

13 See Doc. 58.

having at their disposal the tools of their trade or their machines, without written permission from the German authorities. This restriction affects all Jewish craftsmen and makes their situation particularly difficult, as it is now often necessary to liquidate the ruined workshops, to create cooperatives, and to sell the workshops of craftsmen who have died or emigrated.

As a consequence of the profound convulsions in economic life, Warsaw and several other cities have lost their previous sales market and their previous supply sources for goods and raw materials. To adapt to the new conditions, personal negotiations with companies in other cities must be conducted. For Jewish retailers and craftsmen, however, communication with other cities has been made almost impossible, as they are forbidden to travel by rail, and travel permits are only rarely issued to them.[14]

In addition, Jews are not permitted to be out and about between 9 p.m. and 5 a.m. Furthermore, according to the regulation of 11 December of last year, Jews are not allowed to move from one municipality to another without special permission from the authorities.[15] Jewish factory owners, retailers, and craftsmen therefore have no way of establishing contact with retailers in other cities.

Jewish lawyers have been expelled from the legal profession, a development that deprived a great many Jewish intellectuals of the opportunity to earn a living and denied the Jewish population a means of obtaining legal assistance. The request to appoint even a small number of Jewish lawyers was denied on the grounds that Jews could seek advice from Polish lawyers. It was not taken into account that a large percentage of Jews have a very poor command of the Polish language, and that the Polish lawyers are not familiar with the conditions of Jewish life.

Retired Jewish civil servants, and later also disabled persons, widows, and family members of Jews who were covered by social insurance were stripped of their right to a pension and to social insurance benefits, which increased the number of Jews who have lost any chance of gaining a livelihood.

The Regulation on the Prohibition of Street Trading, issued by the mayor of Warsaw[16] on 15 January this year, provides that Jews may trade only in certain streets and at certain places.[17] These streets correspond more [or] less to the layout of the ghetto, which was to be introduced in November of last year.[18] As a result, rumours concerning the ghetto intensified, which constrained all economic initiative among the Jewish population.

Also, the Regulation on the Introduction of Forced Labour for the Population of the General Government of 26 October of last year[19] and the risk it created that the person concerned could be summoned for forced labour at any time inhibits all initiative among the Jewish population.

14 According to the Regulation of 26 Jan. 1940, Jewish travellers were not allowed to use the railways and had to obtain an exemption permit for any rail travel: see the Regulation on the Use of the Railway by Jews in the General Government of 26 Jan. 1940: *VOBl-GG* 1940, no. 10, 6 February 1940, p. 45.

15 See Doc. 55.

16 The German Stadtpräsident of Warsaw was Oskar Dengel.

17 Directive on the Prohibition of Street Trading of 5 Jan. 1940, issued by the Stadtpräsident of Warsaw: *Amtsblatt des Chefs des Distrikts Warschau*, 1940, no. 2, 14 Feb. 1940, pp. 32–34.

18 See Doc. 39.

19 See Doc. 27.

A few weeks ago, a few new regulations were announced concerning the appointment of temporary administrators for all Jewish buildings, the dismissal of all Jewish property managers,[20] and the cancellation of all the licences for tobacco trading that were held by disabled Jews.

At the beginning of the year, an announcement concerning the reorganization of the Warsaw municipal administration departments appeared in the Warsaw District Office's official publication. From this we learned that Department II is supposed to carry out the Aryanization of Jewish buildings and properties.[21] Implementation of this plan began in June. More than 5,000 property managers have been dismissed; Jewish house owners, close to 25,000 persons, no longer control their property; and the new temporary administrators are even beginning to dismiss the Jews previously employed in the buildings, such as metalworkers and plumbers. Altogether, an additional 70,000–80,000 Jewish families have become unemployed as a result.

The regulations mentioned above by no means constitute an exhaustive list of the legal measures directed against the Jewish economy. They encompass, as we have shown, almost every branch of the economy, and they are enough to paint a picture of the dismal economic situation of the Jewish population.

Resettlements, construction, ghettos, and requisitions.
To complete the gloomy picture of the Jewish economic situation at present, we will touch on a number of other phenomena that have severely affected the Jews in the General Government:

1) The mass expulsions of Jews from more than one hundred large and small towns that have been incorporated into Reich territory and from a great many densely populated Jewish settlements in the General Government.
2) The establishment of complete or partial ghettos for Jews in several cities within the General Government.
3) The arrests of Jews for forced labour, in the streets and in their homes.
4) The seizure of Jewish assets.

To this day, resettlements have affected more than half a million Jews, who are now staying in approximately 300 large and small towns and villages in the General Government and have no prospect at all of leading a normal economic life again. The majority of these unfortunates have been housed in various refugee shelters under terrible conditions. They were forced to leave the tools and machines of their trade behind in their former home towns or to sell them extremely cheaply, if they were permitted to do so at all.

There is no need to describe how detrimental it is to the Jews' economic situation to be locked in a ghetto. It is also superfluous to describe how badly it affects the Jews' daily economic activity when the fear of being suddenly seized for labour prevents them

20 On 11 July 1940 the JSS informed the Population and Welfare Division of the government of the GG that this would 'result in unemployment for around 10,000 Jewish property management employees': YVA, O-21/16.

21 On 15 Jan. 1940 the Stadtpräsident of Warsaw announced the new distribution of duties: Department II, headed by Dr Laschtowiczka, was in charge of monitoring the Polish administration; of Polish personnel, assets, and property; of forestry and hunting; and of the economic control of businesses: *Amtsblatt des Chefs des Distrikts Warschau*, 1940, no. 2, 14 Feb. 1940, pp. 35–37.

from moving freely about the city, although the Jewish councils of elders have repeatedly asked the authorities that the question of labour deployment be resolved by means of regulating the provision of an appropriate number of Jewish workers.

In addition, there are the repeated requisitions of Jewish assets. The regulations of 16 November 1939[22] and 24 January 1940[23] provided that private assets may be confiscated only if they are needed for the authorities' public use, and a certain procedure for this was also stipulated. In fact, these regulations are ignored in relation to Jewish residents. In many cases, requisitions of goods and money are carried out in Jewish shops and workshops without any record being made of the number and value of the assets requisitioned, and also without any confirmation from the agents or representatives who carry out the requisition. Often furniture, clothing, food, and the like are taken from private Jewish homes, even from the homes of the very poor.

All of this, in combination with the regulations mentioned previously, systematically leads to the destruction of Jewish economic life and renders impossible any honest attempt on the part of the Jews to contribute to rebuilding the grievously ruined economy of this country or to secure a modest livelihood for themselves.

The result

At present, the destruction of the economic life of the Jews in the General Government is complete. What could still be salvaged from the hostilities has been destroyed by the events described here. Large-scale Jewish trade and industry no longer exist; Jewish capital has been frozen and blocked in the banks; Jewish real estate (buildings and plots of land) has been almost completely expropriated; Jews have been completely eliminated from banking, insurance, and transport, as from all other large businesses; all the management and supervisory boards of public limited companies are free of Jews; all the liberal professions, with the exception of physicians and dentists, are closed to Jews; Jewish craftsmen are encumbered with debt; and the percentage of Jewish workers in every branch of the economy has plummeted. For example, in the garment industry, where the share of Jews was at 43 per cent before the war and therefore quite significant, their proportion has now decreased to 3 per cent. It is surely no exaggeration to assert that more than 90 per cent of the Jewish population in the General Government is on the verge of economic ruin, threatened by hunger, cold, disease, and all the sad phenomena that are attendant upon hunger.

Conclusion

Under the current circumstances, it is futile to suggest ways in which the Jewish masses might be retrained and which components of the Jewish population might be employed to benefit the entire country. But we want to try to call attention to a few suggestions that should be made in individual localities, if not everywhere, in order to prompt the local authority to employ large numbers of Jews as a paid workforce in various branches of the economy.

22 Presumably the Regulation on the Confiscation of the Assets of the Former Polish State within the General Government of 15 Nov. 1939: *VOBl-GG* 1939, no. 6, 20 Nov. 1939, p. 37.

23 Regulation on the Duty to Register Jewish Assets in the General Government issued by the Governor General for the Occupied Polish Territories: see Doc. 81.

As we have seen previously, a great many trained Jewish workers are now being lost, workers who could be utilized to great advantage, even within the narrow confines of the present-day wartime economy. The fact that Jewish craftsmen in the General Government are well qualified was recently acknowledged by the German authorities in a circular from the Labour Department in the Office of the General Government, which was sent to the heads of the labour departments of the district governments several weeks ago.[24]

Even if we assume that, owing to the great shortage of raw materials and to low consumption, the volume of artisanal production cannot reach more than 30–40 per cent of the pre-war level at this time, the need for manpower is nonetheless increased by the present shortage of machines and tools. Therefore, if one takes the pre-war circumstances as a starting point, it can be expected that an additional 100,000 to 120,000 Jewish artisans could find employment in various branches of the skilled crafts and trades even at this time.

Depending on the local conditions and their previous relations with the authorities, the Jewish councils of elders should present specific suggestions on how work might be found for certain categories of trained Jewish workers, such as carpenters, metalworkers, furriers, etc. Also on how collective workshops might be set up, workshops that could make their services available not only to the population, but also to the authorities. In several cities, there would even be hope of obtaining raw materials from the authorities if the Jewish councils were to undertake a proper, well-motivated initiative to find employment for skilled Jewish workers.

More could also be accomplished in agriculture. Jews have a great many well-qualified workers in the dairy industry and in market gardening. There are more than 10 sizeable Jewish properties in the countryside which are under temporary administration and on which, with proper effort, around 5,000 young Jewish farmworkers could find employment. Admittedly, the majority of Jewish farmworkers are on the other side of the demarcation line, as the majority of Jewish agricultural settlements were in Eastern Galicia and Volhynia. However, it would not be an exaggeration to assume that in the territory of the General Government there are approximately 10,000 to 15,000 Jews who are suited for agricultural work.

The question of unskilled workers could be more difficult, but here certain efforts would have to be made to retrain the young Jewish workers as well. Naturally, this question would have to be handled with the greatest care, and the physical strength, age, health, and previous occupation of the retrained individuals would have to be taken into account. One would have to distinguish between physically strong workers accustomed to physical labour and persons whose job chiefly involves intellectual work. Undoubtedly, if the selection of manpower is efficient, an appropriate number of workers for so-called public works will be found among the large masses of the unemployed. Naturally, one must try hard to ensure that these workers are also properly remunerated.

24 In a circular letter dated 5 July 1940, Max Frauendorfer, the head of the Labour Department in the government of the GG, took the view that Jewish manpower should be urgently exploited, especially as there were also skilled workers and craftsmen among the Jews who were subject to forced labour in the General Government, in contrast to the situation in the Reich: Berenstein et al. (eds.), *Faschismus – Getto – Massenmord*, pp. 210–212, here p. 211.

Among those who do intellectual work, a sizeable number of persons who could be considered for teaching to retrain and prepare the youth for productive occupations could be found. In addition, those now working in trade could find employment in productive labour, if properly retrained.

We cannot present a concrete, thoroughly developed plan here, because the implementation of such a plan and the return of Jewish workers to multiple branches of the economy does not depend on us. We also recognize that considerable capital and interest-free loans would be needed to realize even the smaller plans for employing the Jews mentioned above, and machines, tools, and raw materials in particular would have to be purchased. All of this should not deter us from urging the Jewish councils to act with proper initiative, as experience so far has proven that efforts to provide work for hundreds of Jewish workers have been successful where such initiative was shown. However, this initiative must take into account the local circumstances everywhere, as the general tendency in these matters is unfavourable. We therefore leave it to the Jewish councils concerned to make the appropriate suggestions.

DOC. 163
On 1 September 1940 Irena Glück describes events in Cracow on the first anniversary of the start of the war[1]

Handwritten diary of Irena Glück,[2] entry for 1 September 1940

Sunday, 1 September 1940
Today is the anniversary of the start of the German-Polish war. This torture and suffering, which have affected nearly the entire population of Europe and shaken the world, have lasted one year already. For the world does not remember such destruction and barbarity as that spread by the germans.[3] Today these scoundrels have a holiday. On the square in Cracow they have hung up magnificent flags adorned with a gold fringe. As of today, the square is to be called 'Hitlerplatz'.[4] Frank is to speak on this square and the entire ceremony is also to be held there. That scoundrel Gebels,[5] the most fierce enemy of the Jews, is also to come to Cracow. Flags flutter from every German window. I would really like for at least a couple of English planes to come to Cracow on this day but – well, the English are slow. It rained yesterday, but today, despite being cloudy, it's not raining. Apparently a Polish secret organization distributed leaflets instructing that neither Poles nor Jews appear in the city or take the trams on this day; only physicians may leave the house and only on urgent matters.

1 AŻIH, 302/270, typewritten copy of a handwritten diary entry, pp. 29–30. The handwritten original has not survived. This document has been translated from Polish.
2 Irena Glück (1924–1942?), daughter of a physician; kept a diary from May 1940 to August 1942 in which she described her life in Cracow and, following the expulsion, in Niepołomice near Cracow; resettled in August 1942 to Wieliczka, then deported to Belzec, where she was murdered.
3 The word is consciously written here with lower case as an expression of contempt.
4 Rynek Główny, the main market square in Cracow's old town.
5 The author means Joseph Goebbels, who took part in the celebrations in Cracow.

Big fuss made over that flag at Mrs Cuzerowa's. For Strzyżewski[6] ordered a flag and sent it to the chemist, and Mr Dordcheimer hung it up. Later Mr S. was angry that it had been hung up. Yesterday we noticed that the flag was tangled up and Muszka Strzyżewska came and kicked up a row about why it was not hanging straight.

Andzia wrote that Zygmuś is healthy and looks well now. Mummy was very worried about Andzia's furniture, which she wanted to remove from her apartment where the expellees are. She had already obtained all the necessary papers, but in the meantime, that scoundrel in Dębniki,[7] the clerk you had to go with, constantly caused difficulties. The horses returned 4 times with nothing. Only recently did she manage to fetch the furniture from the bedroom, which has been placed in Mrs Cyzerowa's apartment, as well as from the living room-kitchen, with half the wardrobe. It is at the Strzyżewkis', but I hope that through S. a few more things can be fetched. Resettled Jews are not allowed to show themselves in Cracow, just like others cannot come back once they have left Cracow. Papa has a residence card.[8] Many people who submitted applications have received such cards. However, many applications have been rejected. In any case, these people have six days for departure. I have fixed myself up with a room between the consultation room and the waiting room, in that cubbyhole behind the curtain. It is very tight, but I would still have room for my dearest gorgeous Cesiunia and Janka. I miss them terribly, even madly. Today I will write a letter to Cesia.

I got a letter from my good friend Hanka H. She is in Otwock.

DOC. 164

On 5 September 1940 the Jewish Social Self-Help's executive committee in Cracow meets for the first time[1]

Minutes of the Jewish Social Self-Help (no. 110/T/Sp.), executive committee in Cracow, dated 5 September 1940

Minutes

[of the] first meeting of the Jewish Social Self-Help's executive committee on 5 September 1940.

In attendance: Prof Bieberstein, Dr Hilfstein, Director Jaszuński, Dr Tisch, Dr Weichert, and Dr Wielikowski.

Mr Zabłudowski apologized for his absence, explaining that he was visiting the Jewish labour camps in District Lublin on behalf of the Warsaw Jewish Council.

The chairman of the Central Welfare Council, Count Adam Ronikier, was present as a guest.

6 Aleksy Strzyżewski was the trustee of the pharmacy that belonged to the Jewish Cyzer family; he lived in the same house as the Glück family (75 Dietlring). See Halina Nelken, *Pamiętnik z getta w Krakowie*, ed. Stanisław Wcisło (Toronto: Polski Fundusz Wydawniczy w Kanadzie, 1987), p. 103.

7 District in Cracow.

8 'Karta pozostania': Jewish residents who wanted to continue living in Cracow had to apply to the German authorities for a residence permit.

1 YVA, O-21/18, fols. 1–4. This document has been translated from German.

Agenda:

(1) Election of a provisional chairman and provisional allocation of work
(2) Financial matters
(3) Jewish relief committees
(4) Appointment of advisors to the district governors
(5) Organization and personnel matters
(6) Food aid
(7) Winter relief
(8) Associations and foundations
(9) Miscellaneous

Dr Weichert opened the meeting and welcomed the guest.

Count Ronikier expressed his appreciation.

Dr Weichert asked Dr Tisch to take the minutes and, with the members of the executive committee now having been confirmed, proposed that agenda item (1) be amended by deleting the word 'provisional' and also by adding the words 'for the 1940/1941 fiscal year'. In addition, he proposed combining agenda items (3) and (5), as well as items (6) and (7).

The motions were unanimously adopted.

Item 1. Election of the chairman and allocation of work for the 1940/1941 fiscal year

Nominated by Dr Tisch, Dr Weichert was unanimously elected to serve as chairman.

Dr Weichert moved to elect Mr Jaszuński as deputy chairman. The motion was passed unanimously.

Dr Weichert suggested the following allocation of work:

Bookkeeping – Prof. Bieberstein
Health services – Dr Hilfstein
Work and economic assistance – Director Jaszuński
Food aid – Dr Wielikowski
Organization and personnel matters – Dr Tisch
Child welfare, especially care of orphans – Zabłudowski

The motion was unanimously adopted.

Item 2. Financial matters

After Mr Jaszuński's[2] report the following resolutions concerning his motion were unanimously adopted:

I. The executive committee notes that, given the growing impoverishment of the Jewish population and the large-scale exclusion of Jews from every area of economic life, the number of Jews availing themselves of social welfare is constantly growing. As a result, the Jewish Social Self-Help will only be able to fulfil its social welfare duties if the organization systematically receives ample allocations of public funds. In particular, it is absolutely essential for the Jewish welfare

2 Józef Jaszuński (1881–1943), engineer and socialist from St Petersburg, affiliated with the Bund; in Grodno after 1917; from 1928 in Warsaw, where he was director of ORT in Poland; member of the local council of the Warsaw Jewish Community in the 1930s; member of the Warsaw Jewish Council, 1939–1943, first as chairman of the Emigration Commission, then as head of the Occupational Training and Schools Section; simultaneously served as deputy chairman of the Jewish Social Self-Help (JSS) executive committee, 1940–1942; in Jan. 1943 taken with his wife Zofia, their son Michael, and their daughter-in-law Bronia to Treblinka and murdered there.

establishments and institutions to receive corresponding allocations from the revenue of the residents' tax that is currently collected. This also applies to revenues from special taxes and payments that are introduced in individual cities and communities for the benefit of social welfare.

II. The Jewish Social Self-Help [JSS] executive committee expresses the opinion that the Jewish councils, when drawing up the budgets of the Jewish communities, have to include in their preliminary estimates regular, sizeable subsidies in aid of the social welfare establishments and institutions. At the same time, the executive committee notes that the above requirement cannot be met until the Jewish councils are relieved of the duty to perform various tasks unrelated to their work and their budgets are balanced.

III. The JSS executive committee fervently appeals to the Jewish population, despite their desperate financial situation, to make generous donations and gifts in aid of social welfare, taking into account the use of the sums coming in over the next few months for the Jewish Winter Relief Agency.

IV. The JSS executive committee requests the Central Welfare Council to continue its efforts to obtain official permission to set up a lottery, the proceeds of which are to be divided accordingly among the Polish, Ukrainian, and Jewish central organizations for social welfare.

Item 3. (Items 3 and 5 of the previous agenda) Organization and personnel matters

Dr Tisch[3] reported on the preliminary work towards creating the Jewish relief committees[4] and proposed the following resolutions, which were adopted unanimously:

I. In the very near future, Jewish relief committees are to be set up at the main offices of all the General Government Kreis- and Stadthauptleute.

II. In view of the fact that, in many places, the Kreishauptleute have called upon the Jewish councils to nominate members of the Jewish relief committees and have appointed the relief committees on the basis of these nominations, the executive committee resolves to submit a request to the Population and Welfare Division of the government of the GG that it issue a circular calling the attention of the Kreis- and Stadthauptleute to the wording of § 12 of the Jewish Social Self-Help's statute.[5]

Item 4. Appointment of advisors to the district governors

Based on Dr Weichert's motion, the following advisors to the district governors were unanimously appointed:

3 Dr Eliasz (Elijahu, Eliyahu) Tisch (1889–1956), lawyer and politician; Zionist activist in Eastern Galicia since his youth; member of the executive committee and managing director of the Jewish Social Self-Help, 1940–1942; imprisoned in the Plaszow forced labour and concentration camp, 1943–1944; simultaneously worked in the Jewish Aid Office; survived the German occupation (probably thanks to the industrialist Oskar Schindler, who saved many Jews from this camp) and emigrated to Palestine.

4 In accordance with § 12 (2) of the JSS statute, the relief committees discharged 'in their [respective] areas the tasks incumbent upon the Jewish Social Self-Help as prescribed by its statute': Fritz Arlt (ed.), *Die Ordnung der Fürsorge und Wohlfahrt im Generalgouvernement* (Beuthen: Ostdeutsche Morgenpost, 1940), p. 116.

5 In accordance with § 12 (1), the power to nominate the five members in charge of the Jewish relief committees belonged to the JSS and not to the Jewish councils located at the administrative seats of the Kreis- and Stadthauptleute: ibid.

For District		Cracow	Dr Zimmermann, Juda; address: Cracow, 6 Stanisława.
»	»	Warsaw	Dr Wielikowski, Gamsej; member of the executive committee of the Jewish Social Self-Help; address: Warsaw, 3 Skorupki.
»	»	Radom	Diament, Józef; chairman of the Jewish Council in Radom and chairman of the Council of Elders of the Jewish population in District Radom;[6] address: Radom, 8 Kilińskiego.
»	»	Lublin	Dr Alten, Marek; deputy chairman of the Jewish Council in Lublin; address: 6 P.O.W. [Str.].

Item 5. (Items 6 and 7 of the previous agenda) Food aid and winter relief

After Dr Wielikowski's[7] report, the following motions were unanimously adopted:

I. The executive committee will approach the relevant authority [in order to ensure]:
   1) that ration cards for food are issued to the Jewish population in all localities of the General Government,
   2) that the quality of food for the Jewish population is consistent with that of the non-Jewish population,
   3) that foodstuffs are allocated from the quotas in sufficient quantities, at the set prices, to the Jewish relief committees for purposes of Jewish welfare,
   4) that the authorities afford sufficient meals to Jewish workers placed in public work assignments and labour camps,
   5) that support and additional food from the Jewish Social Self-Help for the deployed Jewish labourers may be provided by its representatives on site.

II. A committee of two persons will be set up to organize the Winter Relief for the Jewish poor.

Dr Hilfstein[8] and Dr Wielikowski were assigned to the committee.

Item 6. (Item 8 of the previous agenda) Associations and foundations

Dr Weichert reported on this issue and proposed the following:

The Jewish Social Self-Help executive committee resolves:

I. to request the supervisory authority to expedite the issuance of an implementing regulation to the Regulation on Associations of 23 July 1940[9] in line with the

6 This is a reference to the Ober-Ältestenrat der jüdischen Bevölkerung des Distrikts Radom. In the other three General Government districts that existed at this time – Cracow, Warsaw, and Lublin (District Galicia was created the following year, in 1941) – Councils of Elders were to be established in each Jewish Community. District Radom was unique in having a 'united' Council of Elders to represent the entire Jewish population within its borders.

7 Dr Gustaw (also known as Gamsej/Gamzej/Gamschei) Wielikowski (1889–1943), lawyer; studied in Munich, where he earned his doctoral degree with the thesis 'Die Neukantianer in der Rechtsphilosophie' ['The neo-Kantians in the philosophy of law']; active in left-wing Zionist groups until the end of the First World War; member of the JSS executive committee, 1940–1942; head of the social services section of the Warsaw Jewish Council from 1941; deputy chairman of the latter, 1942–1943; shot and killed during the Warsaw Ghetto Uprising in April 1943.

8 Dr Chaim Hilfstein (1876–1950), physician; president of the Hebrew Secondary School in Cracow; member of the JSS executive committee and the Chief Social Welfare Council (NRO) from 1940; in Plaszow concentration camp in 1944; among those saved by Oskar Schindler; lived in Prague in 1945; emigrated to Palestine in 1946; died in Tel Aviv.

9 The Regulation on Associations of 23 July 1940 ordered the dissolution of all military, political, and academic clubs and societies. Assets and files were to be seized on behalf of the General Government, the establishment of new associations was forbidden, and further association activities were subject to punishment: *VOBl-GG* I 1940, no. 48, 1 August 1940, pp. 225–228.

principles developed by the Central Welfare Council and authorized by the Population and Welfare Division.

II. to address a circular to the Jewish relief committees and Jewish councils and to request that, in accordance with the Regulation on the Rights of Foundations in the General Government of 1 August 1940, they undertake the registration required by § 1 of said regulation.[10]

The motions were unanimously adopted.

Item 7. (Item 9 of the previous agenda) Miscellaneous

A. Supporting members

Dr Weichert proposed a motion to state that the Jewish Central Welfare organizations, which declared their affiliation with the Jewish Social Self-Help immediately after confirmation of the statutes by the Office of the Governor General, will henceforth be accepted as supporting members of the Jewish Social Self-Help within the meaning of § 5 (2) of the statute.

They include:

1) the Society for Safeguarding the Health of the Jewish Population, 'TOZ';
2) the Jewish Central Association for the Care of Orphans, 'CENTOS';
3) the Association for the Promotion of Skilled Trades and Agriculture among Jews, 'ORT';
4) the Central Association for the Support of Interest-Free Loans and the Promotion of Productive Labour among the Jewish Population, 'CeKaBe' [CKB];
5) the Jewish Central Emigration Society, 'JEAS'.

The motion was unanimously adopted.

B. Distribution of care packages

Dr Tisch announced that the Polish Central Committee had allocated foodstuffs to the Jewish Social Self-Help.

Dr Wielikowski nominated Prof Bieberstein[11] and Dr Tisch to be tasked with handling the distribution [of food].

As no other motions were put forward, Dr Weichert closed the meeting.

10 The Regulation on the Rights of Foundations in the General Government stipulated that foundations either had to be registered by 30 Sept. 1940 or dissolved by that date if they were not deemed to be in the public interest. The continued operation of unauthorized organizations was subject to fines and imprisonment: *VOBl-GG* I 1940, no. 50, 14 August 1940, pp. 244–246.

11 Dr Marek Bieberstein (1891 or 1892–1944), Jewish religious educator; chairman of the Jewish Council in Cracow from Sept. 1939; charged with currency offences in 1940 and sentenced to one and a half years in prison; first held in Cracow, then confined in Tarnów; released while suffering from a serious heart condition in summer 1942 and forcibly relocated to the Cracow ghetto; taken to Plaszow concentration camp with his family when the ghetto was liquidated and murdered there in May 1944.

DOC. 165

On 7 September 1940 police officer Borsutzky reports from Wadowitz (Wadowice) that several arrests have been made on 'suspicion of race defilement'[1]

Report by the police officer in charge of the Wadowitz Urban Police department, signed Borsutzky, dated 7 September 1940 (received on 8 September 1940)[2]

Incident report for the period 1–7 September 1940
1. Arrest of one member of the Wehrmacht and three Jewish women
(on suspicion of race defilement)
Around 10 p.m. on 31 August 1940, I discovered that a member of the Wehrmacht was present in the building at 16 Horst-Wesselstraße, in which only Jews live. I searched the building and found Lance Corporal Westphal from the 3rd Company of Regional Defence Battalion 413[3] in the apartment of the Jewish family Rosner. Present in the apartment were Mrs Rosner and her daughters, Helene and Lotte. The Jew Rosner himself is currently serving a prison sentence. The suspicion arose quite some time ago that the daughters were engaging in prostitution. Members of the Wehrmacht have frequently been seen entering the building. Lance Corporal Westphal had removed his tunic, belt, and cap in the apartment, which is to say that he had made himself comfortable there. That he had had sexual intercourse with one of the daughters was something I could not prove; [he] also denied having done so. He was aware that association of any kind with Jews is prohibited. I had already caught Westphal leaving the building on a previous occasion and warned him, so he was not there for the first time; rather, it is likely that he visited the Jews on a regular basis. Westphal was handed over to the post commander, First Lieutenant Vogler, and Mrs Rosner and her daughters [were] arrested and held in the police prison. A charge was filed with the senior public prosecutor and with the Secret State Police in Bielitz.

DOC. 166

Gazeta Żydowska, 13 September 1940: article on the situation of the Jewish Community in Działoszyce[1]

Działoszyce

Before the war, it is unlikely that many people had heard of the small town of Działoszyce. [It is] a small provincial town somewhere in the Kielce region, with few residents and no outsiders that disturb their peace, while they [the residents], given their own

1 AŻIH, 233/105, fol. 1. Copy in USHMM, RG 15 008M, reel 6. This document has been translated from German.
2 The original contains partially illegible handwritten alterations that change the first person to the third person singular. It also contains the following handwritten insertions: 'include!' and 'Included in the incident report. Pi'.
3 This is a reference to the Landesschützen-Bataillon.

1 *Gazeta Żydowska*, no. 16, 13 Sept. 1940, p. 4. This document has been translated from Polish. Published in Marian Fuks, 'Małe Judenraty w świetle "Gazety Żydowskiej" 1940–1942', *BŻIH*, nos. 126 and 127 (1983), pp. 169–199, here pp. 190–191.

worries, had little time to deal with so-called 'social work'. Then suddenly everything changed! There is hustle and bustle in the town. New people, new faces arrive from every direction.[2] New problems arise: housing must be found for all these people to somehow make their stay possible.

The situation is very difficult, as there is little room and the influx of people is enormous. The Jewish Community now becomes active. It goes from house to house and, where possible, acquires vacant rooms. The situation then rapidly escalates once the influx from Cracow sets in. The Community does not ponder for long. As there are some synagogues standing empty, the people will be housed there. Temporary housing has been found for 200 of them.

In one synagogue a room was renovated, large cooking pots were set into a brick wall, and it now has a kitchen, just like that! At first 50 meals were served per day, last week 400 meals were served, and today tear-off coupons for 520 meals have already been sold.

The committee is now forced to turn to various organizations for help, but its efforts thus far have not been particularly successful.

DOC. 167

Westdeutscher Beobachter, 15 September 1940: Herbert Wiegand's article on Germany's historic mission in occupied Poland[1]

Amid ghettos and miserable hovels. German progress in the General Government. The fulfilment of a historical mission.

By Dr Herbert Wiegand[2]

A few days ago, we were walking through the ghetto situated on the outskirts of the old German city of Cracow. A crowd of Jews was moving around on the cobblestones of the run-down streets like a swarm of filthy grey insects. As with larvae that look to faeces for sustenance, they also did their little deals. Things that would otherwise only be found on rubbish dumps were still in demand there. Occasionally, the goods being traded would have met the standards of a junk dealer. Thousands of Jews, the sons of Ahasuerus,[3] who are beating a retreat from Europe, are liquidating the last remnants of their parasitic existence there.

2 The comparatively peaceful situation in Działoszyce in District Radom in the General Government, where the population was predominantly Jewish, attracted large numbers of refugees. By 1941 the population had doubled to almost 12,000 residents.

1 *Westdeutscher Beobachter*, Cologne, no. 470, 15 Sep. 1940. The *Westdeutscher Beobachter* was founded in 1925 as an NSDAP weekly newspaper. It began daily publication in 1930 and was the main National Socialist daily in Gau Cologne-Aachen. This document has been translated from German.

2 Dr Herbert Wiegand (b. 1909), lawyer; joined the NSDAP in 1932 and again in 1937; after his studies in 1936, trained to become a journalist in the political section of the *Westdeutscher Beobachter* in Cologne.

3 Ahasuerus: synonym for the 'Wandering Jew' who, according to Christian legend, taunted Jesus on the way to his crucifixion and is therefore cursed to roam the earth until the expected second coming of Christ.

A young lad wearing the trousers and jacket of the former Polish army stood in a circle of wheelers and dealers.[4] On one arm, he held aloft a shirt that he was offering for sale. We do not know whether it was his last one or his own, or possibly even a stolen one. We were also unable to see anything tragic in this unremarkable event. If this specific experience may be used to gain general insight into the situation, then it is certainly to be found in the guilty verdict against the leaders of the rapacious Polish state, who have taken to their heels.

Anarchy and disintegration

Polish history, insofar that one can speak of such a thing, has been marked by sell-out and a way of life that squandered the resources that were there. The assets that Poland possessed were never put to use. The enrichment provided by a foreign, specifically German, ethnic heritage compensated for the country's inability to create and develop its own assets. The three partitions of Poland towards the end of the eighteenth century, carried out by Prussia, Austria, and Russia, are history's bill for the anarchy and disintegration of a body politic that was never able to generate its own momentum.

One year has now passed since Poland was forced to pay for the cardinal error of its policies with the loss, virtually overnight, of its statehood. A reallocation of land in what used to be Polish territory was undertaken on a grand scale, resulting in the creation of Germany's new eastern Gaue, the Warthegau and Danzig-West Prussia, together with the General Government. In the two new eastern Gaue, the political and state administration of the Reich has been introduced as the organizing principle. These two Gaue are elements of the Reich, like every other Gau. The General Government is also a part of the Reich, but because of its special ethnopolitical and economic problems, it is governed in accordance with distinctive administrative principles. It is an entirely new kind of administrative unit in the Greater German sphere of influence.

The General Government encompasses, roughly speaking, the lower and central Vistula region and is divided into the districts of Cracow, Radom, Lublin, and Warsaw. Each district is subdivided into ten Kreise. Cracow is the administrative centre for these eastern territories.

Two million Jews

The German men who are on outpost duty in the Vistula region and do the most difficult pioneering tasks for the Reich constantly face an extraordinary variety of problems in their daily work. It requires untold effort to bring order to the utterly chaotic Polish and Jewish living conditions. Crucial development work was already performed there in the East during the war. While all eyes looked to the West over the past months, German hands worked hard to get a ruined country running normally and productively again. One can take a degree of pleasure in observing these processes. The launch of the resettlement of ethnic Germans took place largely via the territory of the General Government – a territory in constant flux and where the Jewish question alone is a seemingly insoluble arithmetical exercise. There are almost 2 million Jews among the 14 million

4 The author has used the pejorative term 'Mauschelnde' in the original, rendered here as wheelers and dealers. This adjectival noun is created from a verb in German with antisemitic roots. *Mauscheln* means to secure certain advantages for oneself or to make deals in an opaque, deceitful, corrupt, or underhand way. The original meaning of the term, derived from the Yiddish form of the Jewish name Moses, was 'to do business like a Jewish merchant', understood negatively.

inhabitants in an area of 100,000 km^2, which is to say 2 million representatives of a dissolute race unaccustomed to taking a natural interest in work and in economic life. Added to this destructive element is the host of Poles, whose energies were squandered in the past because of the lack of proper organization of labour and the economy. The situation becomes clearer when one travels for hours by train through this land, consisting of vast fields, pastures, forests, and marshes. Throughout history, it has always been the decisive contribution of German people that made a productive exploitation of this rich land possible. Left to its own devices, Poland has lived solely off the wasteful consumption of the available resources and moreover has given vent to its political tendencies in a chauvinism put on show by the Frenchified Polish intelligentsia. The country's leaders were so out of touch with the political and economic realities that the military and economic collapse in September last year was merely the logical consequence.

Conversation with Dr Frank

For a year now, a disciplined German hand has been turning the legacy left behind by the Pied Pipers who have fled the country into a new and fruitful chapter. We recently had the opportunity to speak with the Governor General, Reich Minister Dr Frank, about the first phase of work in the General Government. This interview gave us insight into the vast scope and historical roots of the pioneering work by Germans in the Vistula region – work guided exclusively today by the unconditional German claim to leadership.

Owing to the exceptional scope of his authority, the Governor General is in a position to engage in administrative activities on a scale scarcely possible in any other territory of the Reich, thanks to his independent discretionary powers. The Governor General unites in his person the authorities of all the Reich ministries. At the same time, he is also the General Plenipotentiary for the Four-Year Plan. Legislative power rests with him.

The Governor General talked with us primarily about how the German claim to leadership is being fulfilled. It is clear that the German leaders are continuing a mission in the Vistula region today that Germans began centuries ago by tackling the barbaric and primordial condition this land was in. The example of the British Empire should serve as a cautionary tale for us and prevent us from behaving like colonial exploiters and dividend profiteers. The work in the Vistula region requires self-confident people, perhaps more than in any other place in the Reich. At the same time, it is vital, here as everywhere, to carry out one's duties unassumingly. It is not in keeping with the German creative force to become caught up in arrogance and self-absorption.

Dr Frank explained to us that today the General Government can fully rely on its own financial resources and does not need any support from the Reich. The new territory must become predominantly self-sufficient. It no longer has the production capability of the old Polish state, as important regions of agricultural production and industry now lie outside the borders of the General Government. However, this has already been compensated by increasing agricultural and industrial productivity. The supply situation in the General Government is very substantially improved compared to the previous winter, and, notwithstanding a degree of rationing, a shortage of the most important necessities is hardly noticeable.

A land in pieces

Travelling through the General Government gives one a vivid picture of where serious work will still need to be done in the future. The Polish farmers do not even live in cottages, but rather in veritable shacks. Cultivation of the land is as antiquated as the 'dwellings'. Under German guidance and instruction, agricultural productivity has increased as compared to earlier times, but it has naturally not been possible to eradicate the fundamental problems of Polish land cultivation so quickly. One might say that the countryside has truly been torn to shreds in some places by the absurd fragmentation of acreage through inheritance. Fields that are kilometres long and around 20 metres wide, the so-called ribbon or strip fields, are a common sight, especially in Western Galicia and the Carpathian foothills. The farmers repeatedly divided the acreage among their sons and ended up creating these inefficient stretches of land.

The stark contrast between the rich and the poor is probably nowhere as great as it is in what was formerly Poland. There is no so-called middle class to serve as a connecting link in the communal structure. Even today, splendid manor houses rise above the wretched settlements of the smallholders, devoid of the smallest sign of culture. Count Potocki's estate amounts to 200,000 acres. A man surrounded by 50 to 60 servants in a vast, magnificent palace and who called nearly the entire town of Lancut, with around 5,000 inhabitants, his own. On the fringes of this opulence, Polish farmers live in hovels that in the Reich would not be deemed fit to house even livestock.

Fruitful harvest

This territory, in which the signs of social and economic disorganization will gradually disappear, will now remain forever German. The German leadership has begun to rectify the state of the economy, which was already chronically deficient in what was formerly Poland. The fundamental evils – Polish corruption and the lax handling of administrative duties – have been successfully addressed in the past year, and the stimulus provided by Germans has sparked the initiative that was missing across Poland. The increased food contingents provided by Polish farmers after the recent harvest reflect a remarkable rise in agricultural production.

The reform of economic life required excluding the Jews, as demonstrated by the fact that there are many municipalities in which Jews account for up to nearly 100 per cent of residents. Banks, industrial enterprises, and the property market were largely under Jewish influence. We naturally clamped down on this with the necessary thoroughness. The compulsory registration of Jewish assets and the visible identification of Jewish shops resolved this state of affairs. Forced labour for a period of two years has also been introduced across the board for Jews, who are consequently assigned to forced labour groups. The unfamiliar sight of Jewish labour squads can often be seen on a walk through the streets of the General Government today. The Jews of what was formerly Poland have now been given an opportunity to finally make themselves useful.

Polish labour conscription

Poles between the ages of 18 and 60 are also subject to public labour conscription.[5] Even though this labour conscription for Poles also entails forced labour, it is not a matter of obtaining and exploiting a cheap workforce. The introduction of extensive social

5 On 26 Oct. 1939 Governor General Frank issued the Regulation on the Introduction of Compulsory Labour for the Polish Population of the General Government. After that date, Poles between the ages of 18 and 60 were subject 'to compulsory public labour, with immediate effect': *VOBl-GG* 1939, no. 1, 26 Oct. 1939, pp. 5–6.

legislation proves that the German administration is willing to give the Poles a share of the profits that they earn through their service. The previous, inadequately developed system of social welfare and pension provision has already been superseded through an improvement in social welfare provision.

The German claim to leadership in the Vistula region, which can be asserted once more today thanks to our Wehrmacht's glorious feats, is historically justified. All the essential features present in what was formerly Poland are German in origin. One characteristic sign of the more recent development is that there is no factory in the entire General Government without machines of the latest standard that were manufactured in Germany. However, German achievements also date back to earlier times. The Vistula region first became part of the German Lebensraum in the Neolithic period. Indo-Germanic farming peoples made their way from northern Germany into the primordial landscape, until then inhabited solely by hunters and nomads. With their mattocks and ploughs, they made the land cultivable and fruitful. Over the centuries, pioneers and colonists repeatedly moved to the eastern territories and brought order to the Vistula region. There was a particular surge in development when the electors of Saxony gained the Polish royal crown. The Polish state undoubtedly owed its golden age to the cultural development work of German burghers and farmers.

Today there are myriad stone witnesses to this fact. The prolific construction work on properties owned by the state and the nobility in Warsaw and the central Vistula region was carried out by German and Italian master builders. Cracow rose up in the fourteenth and fifteenth centuries at the hands of German builders, and Warsaw owed its development into a metropolis to the work of German architects in the seventeenth and eighteenth centuries. The exhibition 'German Achievements in the Vistula Region', which opened in Cracow on 1 September, illustrates the historic work of Germans as masters and mentors in rural and urban life.

The German will to culture

Poland has once and for all forfeited the right to self-determination. As Dr Frank said in his address on 1 September, the National Socialists have come to this land as enforcers of the will of many generations who have given this land its distinctive character and created masterpieces of incomparable radiance and beauty.[6] The opening of the German State Theatre in Cracow on 1 September was a surprising and marvellous example of the new German will to culture in the General Government. The production of Hebbel's drama *Agnes Bernauer* was marked by attention to detail and high standards of acting. The company of this State Theatre will soon be engaged for regular guest performances in Radom, Warsaw, Lublin, and Deutsch-Przemysl. German cultural life has made a painstaking and promising start down overgrown paths.

It is certainly not easy to bring light to this bloodied land. A walk through the streets of Warsaw best demonstrates that the actual reconstruction and revival of spirits will be a slow process. On the battlefields, Poland has experienced the fragility and collapse of its power in an event of Dantean force. To survive in this world order, the outward forms of the life of a people must amount to more than attractive dancing

6 See Hans Frank's diary in IfZ-Archives, Fb 105, vol. 8, fols. 1785–1791, here fol. 1788.

and melancholy music. The workday must be full and get the blood flowing, which is why German hands now hold sway over a land that had abandoned itself to lethargy and frivolous play.[7]

DOC. 168

On 19 September 1940 the Commander of the Security Police and the SD in District Lublin orders the confiscation of all Jewish registers of births, deaths, and marriages[1]

Letter from the Commander of the Security Police and the SD for District Lublin, Department III A 3 B (no. 1984/40), signed Schmer,[2] to the Kreishauptleute in Lublin (received on 23 September 1941),[3] Janów,[4] and Puławy,[5] dated 19 September 1940[6]

Re: confiscation of the Jewish registers of births, deaths, and marriages, and church registers

Case file: none

In accordance with an order of the Governor General and the Reich Security Main Office, and a requisition from the Reich Office for Kinship Research, the Jewish registers of births, deaths, and marriages, and any other books that are kept in lieu of registers of

7 The article was illustrated with five photos bearing the following captions: (1) 'Four of two million. The Jews in the General Government have now been mostly grouped into forced-labour gangs. They must now wear an armband with the Star of Zion. There is no longer much opportunity for wheeling and dealing.' (2) 'A village of Polish origin in the General Government. The peasants' dwellings are usually even more wretched. Large families live in veritable wooden sheds.' (3) 'St Mary's Church in Cracow, in which the largest altarpiece in medieval Europe was created by the renowned German sculptor Veit Stoß of Nuremberg.' (4) 'Front of the old Cloth Hall on Adolf-Hitler-Platz in Cracow. The German master builder Martin Lindintolde constructed this edifice around 1360. It is where the German patricians had their commercial warehouses and sales tables, and the master craftsmen displayed the fruits of their labour. A great many stalls and shops are still located in the Cloth Hall today.' (5) 'The outstanding accomplishments of the German State Theatre, which opened in Cracow on 1 September, place it at the apex of German cultural activities in the General Government. A stage set from the production of Hebbel's drama *Agnes Bernauer*.' The photographs were supplied by Paul Brandner and the photo news agencies Weltbild and Scherl.

1 APL, 501/75, fol. 33. Published in Berenstein et al. (eds.), *Faschismus – Getto – Massenmord*, p. 101. This document has been translated from German.

2 Johann Schmer (1891–1970), cobbler; on the police force from 1921; joined the NSDAP in 1933 and the SS in 1940; Gestapo chief under the Commander of the Security Police in Lublin, Nov. 1939–Dec. 1941, simultaneously acting Commander of the Security Police in Lublin, August–Dec. 1941; then Gestapo chief for the Senior Commander of the Security Police in the General Government until Jan. 1944.

3 The Kreishauptmann of Lublin-Land was Emil Ziegenmeyer.

4 Henning von Winterfeld (1901–1945?), administrative civil servant; joined the NSDAP and the SA in 1932; Regierungsrat in 1933; Landrat in Wolmirstedt, 1934/1935–1936; Landrat in Graslitz, Sudetenland, then with the government in Breslau, 1938–1939; Kreishauptmann in Radzyń, Oct. 1939–August 1940, then in Janów Lubelski until Oct. 1940 and in Krasnystaw until Jan. 1941; Landrat in Graslitz, 1942; served in the war from Sept. 1944; went missing in action in April 1945.

5 Alfred Brandt (1895–1945), farmer; in the Freikorps Diebitsch and the Border Force East after 1918; member of the German Völkisch Freedom Party (DVFP) until 1924; joined the NSDAP and the SA in 1930; from 1931 Kreisleiter and Kreisbauernführer (Kreis farmers' leader) in Rummelsburg, Pomerania, where he was also Landrat, 1933–1934; worked in the NSDAP's agricultural policy organization until 1939; Kreishauptmann in Puławy, 1940–1944; shot and killed by Soviet units near Stolp in 1945.

6 The original contains handwritten underlining.

vital records, should be sent to the 'Central Office for Jewish Registers of Births, Deaths, and Marriages, Berlin N 4, at 28 Oranienburger Str.'[7]

I therefore request that all Jewish registers of births, deaths, and marriages be collected with the assistance of the Jewish councils within the local Kreis and immediately forwarded to the office named above. The Jewish councils shall bear the costs of packaging and transport. Should this not be possible, the 'Central Office for Jewish Registers of Births, Deaths, and Marriages in Berlin' will reimburse the costs. A letter detailing the specific registers and the town and Kreis of origin must accompany the crates addressed to Berlin. A copy of the enclosed letter is to be sent to the local office.

I request to be notified within six weeks of receipt of my letter whether all the registers of births, deaths, and marriages from the local Kreis have been sent to Berlin.

DOC. 169

On 20 September 1940 the Jewish elder in the Litzmannstadt (Lodz) ghetto reports on the extremely cramped living conditions[1]

Letter (no. 1529/br/40) from the Jewish elder in the Litzmannstadt ghetto, Chaim Rumkowski, to Senior Public Health Officer Dr Merkert,[2] Ghetto Food and Supply Office,[3] dated 20 September 1940[4]

Re: living quarters in the ghetto
With reference to the personal conversation with your Mr *Biebow*,[5] I hereby inform you of the number of living quarters available in the ghetto.

In total, the ghetto has
2,330 buildings,
48,000 rooms, including kitchens,

7 The Jewish Community's library, located at 28 Oranienburger Straße, was sequestrated by the Gestapo in 1938; the 'Central Office for Jewish Registers of Births, Deaths, and Marriages' was opened at the same address on 6 April 1939 under the head of the Reich Office for Kinship Research, Dr Kurt Mayer (1903–1945).

1 APŁ, 221/31866b, fol. 203. Copy in USHMM, RG 05 008M, reel 6. This document has been translated from German.
2 Dr Alexander Merkert (b. 1881), physician; joined the SS in 1933 and the NSDAP in 1937; deputy medical officer in the Iserlohn region; deputy medical officer in Litzmannstadt from Nov. 1939; retired in late 1941; subsequently worked in Litzmannstadt as a general practitioner, company medical officer, and panel physician for the police.
3 The Ghetto Food and Supply Office (known as the Ghetto Administration from Oct. 1940), comprising approximately 250 persons, was the German administrative organization for the Litzmannstadt ghetto in 1940.
4 The original contains underlining and a handwritten note in the upper margin: 'Senior Public Health Officer Dr Merkert'; beneath the letter: '38:15 = 2.53. 150000:38000 4.-. Average 4 pers. per room. To be filed. Ghetto 18/10.40' (initials illegible).
5 Hans Biebow (1902–1947), merchant; joined the NSDAP in 1937; head of the German administration of the Litzmannstadt ghetto, May 1940–1944; organized the economic exploitation of the ghetto and the labour of ghetto inhabitants for the German war economy; played a key role in the deportations of ghetto inhabitants to Kulmhof (Chelmno) extermination camp and to Auschwitz-Birkenau in 1942 and 1944; sentenced to death and executed in Łódź in 1947.

of which approximately 5,000 *rooms* are used for economic purposes (factory premises, etc.) and approximately 5,000 *rooms* for my institutions, such as hospitals, children's homes, orphanages, homes for the elderly, schools, the [Jewish] Order Service, offices, etc., etc. That leaves *38,000 rooms*, including kitchens.

An average of 4–6 persons live in each of these rooms, although I wish to note that many rooms, especially the kitchens, here in the ghetto (Old Town) are very small, and they can only house two persons.

By contrast, 4–6 persons and more live in medium-sized rooms.

Sincerely,

DOC. 170

On 20 September 1940 the Jewish Social Self-Help's executive committee instructs local aid committees on their tasks[1]

Circular no. 7, from the Jewish Social Self-Help's executive committee (Wt/Sch.),[2] Cracow, to the Kreis and municipal aid committees, dated 20 September 1940 (draft)[3]

Re: Jewish Kreis and municipal aid committees launch their activities

As we have already announced in circular no. 4, the Jewish Social Self-Help's executive committee is currently setting up Jewish aid committees in all Kreis seats and independent municipalities within the General Government.[4] Once committee members have been recommended and the delegate has familiarized himself with the local conditions, the executive committee will submit the list of committee members to the Stadt- or Kreishauptmann for approval.

A committee may be officially constituted – that is, the chairman and vice chairman elected and the tasks divided among individual members in accordance with the statutes and regulations[5] – only once the Kreishauptmann has granted approval. Nevertheless, a committee may begin preparatory work immediately. In particular, it must gather all the material on welfare related to the Jewish population in a given town or Kreis and forward this to us. This primarily concerns residential care facilities in each town, such as hospitals, homes for the elderly, and orphanages, with details of their capacity and the number of people under their care in recent months, as well as the source of their funding (the Jewish council, association, etc.). In addition, the number of refugees and local residents in need of welfare in each town must be specified, along with any type of aid provided to them, such as soup kitchens, supplementary nutrition for children, the allocation of

1 AŻIH, 211/114, fols. 41–42. This document has been translated from Polish.
2 The abbreviation 'Wt' stands for Michał Weichert.
3 The original contains handwritten additions and deletions. 'W' (Weichert) is written in the upper margin.
4 With circular no. 4 on the 'formation of Jewish aid committees', the executive committee of the Jewish Social Self-Help (JSS) initiated the staffing of these institutions in the Kreis seats and the independent municipalities: YVA, O-21/20.
5 Arlt (ed.), *Die Ordnung der Fürsorge und Wohlfahrt im Generalgouvernement*, pp. 114–116 (statutes) and pp. 123–126 (regulations).

non-perishable food, financial assistance, housing aid, clothes, medical treatment, material aid, etc.[6]

According to the statute and regulations, the aid committees are autonomous institutions, and they are independent of the Jewish councils. In cases where Jewish councils have been providing welfare, the aid committees should be recognized step by step and in consultation with the Jewish Social Self-Help's executive committee in Cracow. According to the regulations, an aid committee comprises five members.[7]

The aid committees in Kreis seats should have letterheads with the following headers:

Jüdische Soziale Selbsthilfe	Jewish Social Self-Help
Jüdisches Hilfskomitee Kreis Rzeszów	Jewish Aid Committee in Kreis Rzeszów

In independent municipalities (Cracow, Warsaw, Radom, Lublin, Częstochowa, Chełm), the municipal committees should have letterheads with the following headers:

Jüdische Soziale Selbsthilfe	Jewish Social Self-Help
Jüdisches Hilfskomitee Krakau Stadt	Jewish Aid Committee in Cracow City

The Kreis committees should have the following headers:

Jüdische Soziale Selbsthilfe	Jewish Social Self-Help
Jüdisches Hilfskomitee Krakau Land	Jewish Aid Committee Krakau Land

The aid committees should use a rectangular stamp for correspondence and a round stamp for certificates and documents. Correspondence in German should be stamped with a German stamp, and correspondence in Polish with a Polish stamp.

In accordance with the regulations part II, rule § 1(2),[8] an aid committee should send copies of all outgoing letters to the Stadt- or Kreishauptmann and should strictly observe all the provisions of the statute and the regulations parts I and II, which we have sent you. If in doubt, you are to contact us for clarification.

One must remember that the purpose of the aid committees and the entire Jewish Social Self-Help organization is to provide assistance to as many Jews as possible. The aid committees should therefore keep their administrative expenditures to a minimum. To this end, you should arrange for rent-free premises, if possible, and all work should be done on a voluntary basis. It is permitted in exceptional cases only and with the approval of the Jewish Social Self-Help's executive committee in Cracow to employ – aside from manual labourers – clerical workers on a contractual basis for a set period of time; we will send you a template of this contract upon request.

Yours respectfully,

6 This paragraph has been added by hand in the original: 'Insofar as reports, lists, photographs, etc. relating to the earlier period have already been collected, either for the central authorities, for the local administrations, or for Jewish welfare institutions such as the AJDC, I request that these be sent to us, in duplicate if possible.'

7 This paragraph is crossed out in the original.

8 Part II of the regulations stipulated that the German administrative authorities would supervise the JSS: Arlt (ed.), *Die Ordnung der Fürsorge und Wohlfahrt im Generalgouvernement*, p. 126.

DOC. 171

On 20 September 1940 the Stadthauptmann of Tschenstochau (Częstochowa) complains about conditions in the SS labour camp for Jews in Cieszanów[1]

Letter from the Stadthauptmann[2] of Tschenstochau, unsigned, to the Governor of District Radom, Interior Administration Department,[3] dated 20 September 1940 (copy)

Re: camp for Jews in Cieszanow/Lublin[4]

The Jewish Council in Tschenstochau informed me of the following:

A large number of unmarried Jewish workers have been transferred to Kreis Lublin from Tschenstochau. While both the work and the treatment have been appropriate at all sites, the conditions in Cieszanow labour camp are reportedly untenable. Workers who went to answer the call of nature with the guard's permission have been shot in the back and killed. The available beds are not hygienic; there is only mouldy straw, which carries germs and increases the risk of epidemics. Meals are also insufficient. The sick are not separated from the healthy, nothing is done to prevent lice, food sent by relatives is not delivered, etc.

Camp inmates from Tschenstochau are apparently writing alarming letters to their relatives, leading them to bombard the Jewish Council with calls to intervene in the situation. This clamour has now grown to such proportions that I have been forced to have the German police protect the local Jewish Council from daily attacks by the relatives of these forced labourers.

I am writing to inform you of the situation, and I leave any further initiatives up to you.[5]

1 APL, 498/746, fol. 226. This document has been translated from German.

2 Richard Wendler (1898–1972), lawyer; joined the NSDAP and the SA in 1928, and the SS in 1933; mayor of Hof from 1933; Stadtkommissar in Kielce from 1939; Stadthauptmann of Tschenstochau from Nov. 1939; governor of District Cracow, 1942–1943; governor of District Lublin, 1943–1944; lived under a false name, 1945–1948; sentenced to three years in a labour camp in 1948; released early in 1950; lawyer in Munich from 1955.

3 The department was headed by Hans Kujath (1907–1963), lawyer; joined the NSDAP in 1932 and the SS in 1933; legal clerk in Eberswalde; head of the Interior Administration Department in District Radom from Jan. 1940; Stadthauptmann of Radom from June 1940; Stadthauptmann of Lemberg from August 1941; Kreishauptmann of Czortków, April 1942–Feb. 1944; in the Waffen-SS from Sept. 1944; interned, 1945–1947; classified as a 'follower' (*Mitläufer*) in 1952 in the Lüneburg denazification proceedings; subsequently worked as a lawyer.

4 The labour camp for Jews in Cieszanów on the German–Soviet border existed from mid May to late autumn 1940. Approximately 5,000 people were imprisoned in the camp and forced to build border fortifications.

5 On 31 Oct. 1940 the Labour Department of District Lublin (Section II: 5318) noted that it could not do anything about the situation 'because this camp is run exclusively by the SS': APL, 498/746, fol. 228.

DOC. 172

In summer 1940 an unidentified Jewish forced labourer describes the daily routine in a labour camp[1]

Handwritten report for the underground archive of the Warsaw ghetto, undated, summer 1940

Our day at the camp

'Wake up, wake up, get up!' the group leader's voice rang out. I sprang from my bunk and quickly began to get dressed. We sleep in a large brick stable, on straw, under blankets. Some people brought pillows from home, but most just put their trousers or a shirt under their heads. All the gaunt and sunburned figures are now rising from their bunks. They put on their tattered, torn, and mostly dirty undergarments, and more torn clothes on top. Once we've washed ourselves, the group leader's stern voice summons us to roll call. We stand in three rows and obey the commands. After the roll call, we line up at the pots for coffee. I take 200 grams of bread out of my rucksack, cut myself a mouldy piece, eat it quickly, and wash it down with bitter black coffee. Our commandant ate even quicker, for he is already calling us to get to work. The work is hard now during the harvest. We help the farmers in the fields. We bind sheaves, rake hay, weed potato fields, drain marshes, carry stones and planks, fell trees in the woods and remove them with carts. There is no shortage of work. While we work, neither the group leader nor the farmers spare us from remarks such as: 'Why are you moving like a slowcoach? Faster. Show some energy. You're just standing around and gawking again', etc. You can't rest for a moment, even though your hands are often dropping off from exhaustion. Suddenly a fellow inmate signals that an officer is approaching. He is a young man of medium height, with broad shoulders, blond hair, and green eyes. I don't know if he stares specifically at Jews in a way that makes it difficult to withstand his gaze, or whether he simply has such a penetrating stare. He gets easily irritated with the most trivial matters, but he also forgets quickly. Ever since he's been given responsibility for the camp, his only concern is that the Jews work well and hard; he doesn't care whether they eat well, whether they have shoes or a comfortable place to sleep.

As soon as we hear he is coming, we find new strength, heaven knows from where. We forget our hunger and our wet shoes. We work energetically without a second's rest. He stops, speaks to the group leader, and leaves again. We sigh with relief and work slower. Lunch at noon. We each get a bowl of soup. We search for potatoes with the spoon, and argue, and complain that there are so few. Everyone peeks into the bowl of their fellow inmate to see if he has more. There's one hour of rest after lunch, and then work starts again [and lasts] until 7 p.m. For supper: 200 grams of bread and a cup of black coffee. Then we chat and sing, and then the group leader's voice once again summons us to go to sleep. I lie tired under the blanket and try to fall asleep, but my fellow inmates' loud conversations keep me from sleeping. Lights out!!! Dead silence. Now everyone falls asleep, only to wake up again tomorrow at 5.30 for work.[2]

1 AŻIH, Ring I/1206 (622). This document has been translated from Polish.

2 Enclosed with the report is a pencil drawing of forced labourers felling trees in the foreground and uniformed guards in the background.

DOC. 173

In summer 1940 a German university student reports on her work to help resettled ethnic Germans and on her impressions of Jews in Leslau (Włocławek)[1]

Report by Irene Körner, summer 1940[2]

Women students' assignment
Reichsgau Warthe 1940
Report on my work at a kindergarten in Kreis Leslau, Warthegau
My fellow students and I were overjoyed when we heard that we will be posted to the East. With great excitement and enthusiasm for the work ahead, we travelled to the assembly point in Grotniki, where we attended various training courses and lectures to prepare for our mission. We waited impatiently for the practical part of our assignment to begin.

I was assigned along with three fellow students from the University of Heidelberg to work at a kindergarten in Kreis Leslau. We set off filled with anticipation. We had been told, 'You're headed for an utterly desolate region. You're going to the steppe.' However, we were pleasantly surprised when we arrived in Leslau.

Our first positive impression was the Adolf-Hitler-Platz: wide, spacious, and planted with attractive greenery. Above the square a clear blue sky, against which the two tall red towers of the cathedral stood out. Horst-Wessel-Straße, the broad main street, looked tempting because we had been told it led down to the Vistula. Lots of German shops had been opened and had surprisingly good window displays. At other shops people were hard at work putting them in order. The town was working so hard at its German appearance that it was a joy to behold. Particularly novel for us four from the Old Reich was the treatment of the Jews. Whereas in Litzmannstadt and Kutno we had looked with a certain revulsion at the ghettos where the members of this crooked-nosed race were gathered, it struck us here in Leslau that the Jews could walk freely in all the streets, though not on the pavement but only on the thoroughfare, and each wears a yellow triangle on their back. We often came across a Jewess waddling along the road with her female Polish friend walking beside her on the pavement. But when we reached the Vistula, we forgot all about Jews and Poles and enjoyed the wonderful view that lay before us: the broad flowing Vistula, behind us the town with the cathedral and the beautiful park, in front of us the Vistula hills. Only the destroyed bridge (which was already being rebuilt, however) was a reminder that there had been a war here less than a year ago. So Leslau even had 'hills'! That meant that life was tolerable here, because only a landscape with hills, forests, and water can make me feel truly at home in my surroundings. – The office of the Kreis leadership of the National Socialist People's

1 BArch, R 49/3051, 'Berichte der Teilnehmerinnen am Studentinnen-Einsatz bei der Umsiedlungsaktion im Reichsgau Wartheland' ['Reports by participants in the women students' assignment as part of the resettlement operation in the Reichsgau Wartheland']. This document has been translated from German.

2 In 1940 many young female university students were recruited to take part in temporary assignments to help families from Eastern Europe who were being resettled in the annexed territories of western Poland.

Welfare Organization in Leslau is located on Adolf-Hitler-Platz. Here, too, people were hard at work. Jewish workmen were in the process of giving the corridor an attractive coat of paint.

We were received very kindly. Mr Sandelmann, head of the Kreis office, was eager to find the best possible placement for us. He had learned of our mission only that morning and was now in some consternation as to where he could deploy us so quickly.

Nothing seemed to him to be good enough for us, but when he saw that we had no illusions about the work we had to do and were all the keener to tackle it, he was very relieved. And now we could set about planning. It was clear to Mr Sandelmann that we should embark on each assignment in pairs; he thought it would be too much to cope with for someone on her own. So we divided up into pairs, and I partnered with Wilma Rosenkranz from Rheydt.[3]

There were two possible locations for our assignment. Sarnovo near Lubranek, a very prosperous village where Volhynians[4] had been settled. A building for the harvest kindergarten[5] was already available there: the fire engine house. Our two fellow students, Heidi Immendörfer[6] and Irmgard Notwang,[7] quickly opted for Sarnovo. That left Wilma and me with Krzywa Gora, meaning 'crooked mountain', which was still part of Landkreis Leslau and was located 7 km from town. Nothing at all had been prepared there, but that was precisely what we liked so much about it. We were looking forward to setting up something completely from scratch.

That very afternoon the two of us drove with the head of the Kreis office and the leader of the local NSDAP branch to the site of our future efforts in order to find suitable premises.

We first took a closer look at the rectory. Construction had begun several years ago, but, just like the church next to it, it was only half completed. All the same, both buildings were being used – that's Poland for you! For now, the house could not serve our purpose, but there are plans to expand it by next year to provide space for a permanent kindergarten with modern equipment and a district nurse's station. Next, several Polish homes were subjected to a closer look. The inhabitants stood trembling on the threshold and watched us anxiously as we roamed with a critical eye through the rooms. They were utterly convinced that they would be [forcibly] evacuated in the next few days, but everything was too small and too infested with vermin. Then the leader of the local NSDAP branch made a suggestion: there was a fairly large building with a lovely gable roof at the fork in the Leslau–Thorn road in Hohensalza. It had previously been a Russian inn. At a right angle to it, leaving a wide gateway free, stood a fine, long, and very solidly built stable. The plan was to turn it into premises for the Hitler Youth, with further plans to expand the building to house the NSDAP. The local NSDAP leader was willing to make this property available to us for the summer. We were thrilled and in-

3 Wilma Rosenkranz (b. 1919), medical student in Heidelberg in 1940.

4 This is a reference to the so-called Volhynian Germans, who were resettled in the Warthegau in 1940 based on the agreement concluded between the German Reich and the USSR on 28 Sept. 1939.

5 The Erntekindergarten offered seasonal child day-care for populations in rural areas, typically during the summer and autumn months when mothers worked full-time in agricultural production. This special type of kindergarten was widespread during National Socialism.

6 Heidi Immendörfer (b. 1920), medical student in Heidelberg in 1940.

7 Correctly: Irmgard Nothwang (b. 1920), medical student in Heidelberg in 1940.

spected everything closely. When viewed from the road, the building resembled a Sleeping Beauty castle, concealed as it was behind the dense brambles and bushes that had run riot here over the years. The large central entrance was no longer accessible at all. Behind the building was a yard with an open well, 15 metres deep. A broad orchard stretched out beyond that, planted with young trees, most of which had suffered frost in the winter. A forest of young pines enclosed this perfect playground from all sides. Was there sand anywhere on our grounds? In our view, a sandpit was practically the most important feature of the whole kindergarten set-up, but we were reassured that all this would be provided. We then had to look at our building from the inside too, of course. To the right and left of the entrance corridor were two big rooms with tall windows that let in lots of light. The room on the right would serve as the day room and dining room, and the other would be used for our children's afternoon naps. In addition to this, there was also a small, empty kitchen, and another little room where the two of us would live. We would have liked to start setting up the very next day in order to get to our actual work as soon as possible, but the walls and ceiling first needed to be whitewashed, simple tables and benches for our little ones still had to be made, etc. It would probably take a few more days. During that time, we could make ourselves quite useful at the kindergarten run by the National Socialist People's Welfare Organization in town and also see how a kindergarten functioned that served lunch. The building there had been opened just four weeks earlier and set a high standard with its attractive and practical facilities. It was the pride of the Kreis office head.

Our day was busy with the work in the municipal kindergarten, which we really enjoyed. Even so, we yearned to finally be able to do things in and for 'our' kindergarten. One week later, the Jewish craftsmen had at last successfully completed their work.

Now we could start thinking about our interior furnishings and the tableware, which were very simple to get hold of. The National Socialist People's Welfare Organization had a very large warehouse with all of these things, which came mainly from rich Jewish and Polish homes. There was porcelain galore. We could simply take our pick. That was fun. Fifty sets of dishes for 'our children' had already been prepared for us. But among all the tasteless clutter, there were also some things we could put to good use: a few pretty vases here, some lovely glasses there, and even cups made of Rosenthal[8] porcelain for our guests. We found a nice polished table and two brand-new wicker chairs, a copper-red divan cover, a practical little kitchen cupboard, and many other useful things.

We felt very rich when we moved into 'our new home'. Things had become very civilized since our last visit. 'Our industrious Jews' had painted the walls a lovely yellow, and the Polish woman who lived with her family in two of the building's rooms had made everything very tidy and clean. Now, on with the work aprons and down to work! For the children's nap room, we had brought along a dozen Polish recliners made for children.

In the day room, we now had two long, low tables with little benches at the sides. We placed them at a right angle to one another: one table along the wall opposite the door, the other along the wall with windows. In the corner next to the large tiled stove, we created a nice play area for our older children using two high, short benches that made

8 Rosenthal is a renowned German porcelain manufacturer, established in 1879.

a serviceable table. Along the left wall, we placed the long, high table that we had found and put a bench in front of it. We wanted to use it as a sideboard. The twelve drawers additionally provided an enormous amount of storage space.

We also found three cupboards there. The small, low one was to become our linen cupboard, so it went into our room. With the help of a wooden rod and a few nails, we turned the tall one into a respectable wardrobe for our clothes. However, when the local NSDAP leader gave us a lovely wardrobe that was like new, we converted our old one back into a toy cupboard. Then there was one more piece, a very posh one: a wide cupboard with glass doors. Admittedly, one door was off its hinges and slightly damaged, so the piece of furniture looked more like a wreck at first, but some deft handiwork put that right. But what could we do about the dreadful condition of the cupboard's interior? On the spur of the moment, we took some white paper and used it to line the cupboard, covering every little spot. How smart it suddenly looked! Afterwards we arranged our tableware very nicely in the cupboard, making sure to show off our pretty, brightly coloured china coffee pots. This way, we avoided the expense of curtains for the glass doors, and everyone could be envious of our luxurious china cabinet.

Unfortunately, we were not very lucky with wall decorations. We had managed to get hold of a fine, large portrait of the Führer at the National Socialist People's Welfare Organization. It dominated the wall opposite the door. I had also brought with me a number of pretty, colourful charts for children, which we were able to use to create a nice frieze on the wall with windows. A pretty calendar hung above our stove corner, and we also needed to put some flowers in the space at once. We had brought lovely brown earthenware jugs for that purpose. When we looked at our 'kindergarten' now, we were extremely satisfied.

The next thing to tackle was the corridor. A large, heavy oak table with thick, carved legs stood there, making a somewhat solemn impression. But it could serve us quite well as a sturdy surface on which to place a big bunch of flowers that we had picked. Wooden planks with pegs had been attached low on the walls; surely they had come from a kitchen at some point. They were nicely painted and already looked as if they had never known any purpose other than holding little children's coats.

The Jews had already beaten a path through the wilderness in front of the building to the road. We then turned our attention to the kitchen, and before long we were done there as well. Our little kitchen cupboard was mounted onto the wall opposite the cooker, and above it a wooden shelf for pots. Both were quickly painted white. The white table that we had brought with us went under the window, and to the right of it we put a white bench with a double shelf to serve as our water station. On the other side, we put a washstand with two basins and quickly found spots for our pots and bowls and pails too.

I already had a clear idea of how we should arrange our little room. Our nice polished table went beneath the window, with the desk chair in front of it. Our couch went next to it, against the wall opposite the door. Yes, it is astonishing how genteel we were! We had stuffed two straw mattresses for ourselves. We faced an uphill battle in fending off our well-intentioned supervisors and all the bedsteads we were constantly offered. During the day, we laid these mattresses on top of each other and used several woollen blankets to make a bolster. Then we put our splendid divan cover over the whole thing. Its copper-red colour lent some warmth to the room. Next to it was an attractive, short brown bench that served us well as a little reading table and looked very nice with a bouquet of flowers beneath the map of Germany. There was space for our little linen cupboard against the wall next to it. We placed our wicker chairs on either side of the tiled stove. They were quite inviting with their wonderful seat cushions, which I had made by folding two tapestries together. There was still room next to the table for a little bench.

The local NSDAP branch leader had given us a pretty woodcut for the empty wall above our couch that all our visitors admired.

Our house was already furnished and ready that evening, so the next morning I was able to begin looking for a market gardener and for a farmer who would deliver milk to us. The latter was easy to find, but the market gardener was a Pole. Even with the help of young Müller, an ethnic German, it was very hard to get what we wanted. It was often the case that I got cauliflower instead of kohlrabi etc., leading to some amusing mix-ups. At the beginning we didn't know a word of Polish, and the Poles couldn't communicate in German. But I suppose that's what hands are for.

In the afternoon, the entire SA had reported for duty at our place to clear the 'jungle'. A short time later, our forecourt facing the road was immaculate. We treated the men to coffee and seized the opportunity to drum up interest in our kindergarten. We were elated that the German people here were so endlessly grateful that their children would once more 'learn' something, that they would know 'German discipline' and learn to speak German again. They only had this one condition: 'Be strict. The children need the rod.' But we were optimistic and hoped to manage without the need to resort to smacking.

The ethnic German men made a very good impression on all of us. Most of them were lean and haggard, with stern, serious faces. You could tell by looking at them that they had suffered a great deal in recent years because of their Germanness. Many of them had been displaced and mistreated by the Poles when the German troops were advancing, so they knew what they owed to the Führer. But there were also some among them who had been swept along by the others and had not clearly realized until now that they were Germans.

On Monday morning, we made everything very pretty; after all, we were expecting our little ones. At 8 a.m., not one had come yet. Our spirits were slowly sinking, but then, in the distance, we saw them approaching. The mothers were coming too! Dressed in their Sunday best and holding the hands of their children, who were clean and also in Sunday attire. We had not expected it to be so festive, but we were happy that the ethnic German women had insisted on seeing where and how their children would be placed. When they saw how much the children enjoyed the cocoa-coffee (made by a company in Leslau) that was served after we had recorded their personal information, the mothers left satisfied.

By the second day, we had already added 60 children to our list. That was quite a crowd. We ended up having to order more cups and spoons from Leslau. We were very pleasantly surprised by our little charges. After the time we had spent working in the town kindergarten, we did not have high hopes concerning cleanliness, but the children were very clean and nicely dressed, almost without exception. Nearly all the older girls wore a black satin pinafore with sleeves and a white collar. Most of the children were blond and looked very healthy. In some, however, we could see the hardship they had suffered all the more clearly: at the age of 12, they were still as slightly built as 7-year-olds.

That's why I wanted to make a real effort with the cooking. I had also taken on the running of the household, and every day I made lunch and the morning and afternoon coffee. The Polish woman saw to cleaning the vegetables and to the washing-up. All this to make sure that these children of sorrow would soon have round, rosy cheeks.

And now to our daily routine: the day started at 8 a.m., although we rose a good bit earlier, of course, and tidied our room. Meanwhile, our Polish woman drew water from the well and made a fire at my request. I had already learned enough Polish to teach her how to do it, so that I could put on the water for coffee. A few children had already arrived by then, in dribs and drabs. Some were even rattling at the big door at 7.30. Until the whole 'flock' had gathered, they were allowed to engage in free play and busy themselves as they wished. That was not so easy at the outset, because we had no play-things at all. Fortunately, the weather was often fine, and the littlest ones were always happiest in the sandpit.

Then it was time for gymnastics. That was fun, and it is hard to say who enjoyed it more: the children or me. They were all still terribly stiff and awkward in the beginning, but every day we saw a little progress. It was too cute when they all so earnestly imitated the high-knee exercises, or when they all wanted to win first place in the leapfrog competition and some rolled over head first in the process. My, how they enjoyed breakfast then! I had to refill pot after pot, so great was their thirst for coffee. If at all possible, they went back out to the playground afterwards for fun running games with Auntie Wilma. The older girls helped me peel and cut onions in the kitchen, or they peeled potatoes with the Polish woman or cleaned vegetables. How eagerly they did so! They were proper little house-mothers, my big girls.

While the meal was cooking, I had a bit of time again for our little ones. I could always steal away now and then to peek into the kitchen. Wilma was then able to bring in the big children and 'hold school'. We also had a blackboard, you see, and a terrific amount of chalk. It was a joy to see how eagerly they did sums and read or even did dictation exercises. The children all worked cheerfully, and it turned out that most of them were very gifted. That meant I sat down with our 'real' kindergarten children and engaged in activities with them which varied depending on the weather. Often I played circle games and finger games with them or told them a fairy tale. Whenever it was raining outside, our 'newspaper heap' had to fill in (we had had people give us lots of newspapers, as we had no toys in the beginning) and I had to make paper-doll chains with my scissors, etc. It was so much fun to see how they all held hands and could march along in a long row. Then, if you glued together the two at the ends, they could play 'ring-a-ring o' roses' while we sang so nicely in accompaniment. At other times, my charges were allowed to 'paint'. Once they showed me how their home and their garden looked, another time the subject was a train, etc.

And then, of course, we sang lots of songs for little children, and before we knew it, 12 o'clock had come.

Our 'giant bowl' was quickly set up on the bench in front of the building, and the bars of soap, the hand brushes, and some towels were set beside it. The older children scooped water from the well into the bowl, and then the group crowded round to wash their hands. At first, we had to inspect many a little hand rather closely to see whether it was really clean, but in general our older children made sure that everyone went to the table with clean hands. I finished preparing the meal in the meantime, and while

Wilma checked off the attendance list inside, I was able to arrange everything and take food over to the Polish woman and her two boys. (In exchange for helping us, each day the woman received 1 RM and lunch). Then, when I came in with the big bowl, the whole 'gang' became lively, with 'oohs' and 'aahs' coming from all around. But as soon as I had stepped up to a little table to join them, they joined hands and waited quietly. They knew that Auntie Irene was going to say some words now to begin the meal, and they all wanted to listen closely, because it was a different saying or quotation each time. Then they set to and ate heartily. I took great pleasure every time in seeing how eagerly they all cleaned their plates, often taking several helpings. And I was very proud that I had guessed the correct amount on the very first day.

After the meal, the little ones were bundled onto the recliners and covered with woollen blankets. One of us, usually Wilma, kept watch so that they could all sleep soundly and undisturbed. The big girls quickly cleared away the plates, cleaned the tables, and swept the room. The Polish woman washed the dishes, and I tidied the kitchen. I then took charge of the older children. We were outdoors in fine weather, of course, playing and singing. This midday singing lesson was especially important to me, because the children did not know any songs, apart from a few old battle songs. 'The world's brittle bones are trembling…'[9] was their favourite. So I sang a lot of jolly children's songs with them, and I was amazed at how quickly the children picked them up, whereas any Hitler Youth songs, which usually have difficult lyrics, took rather a long time.

Everyone was especially fond of 'Under the roof, yippee …'[10] and 'A cuckoo sat on a tree'.[11] Whenever I asked, 'What do you want to sing?', the answer was sure to be 'Auntie, kokaki ka ki ka koko' and 'simsela dim bam basela dusela dim'.[12]

Other special favourites were 'The hunter walked along the pond'[13] and 'The frogs in the lake are having a party today'.[14]

The little ones all had ruddy cheeks after sleeping and were very thirsty for coffee.

After coffee, it was time for free play again, and then we all sang and played together for another hour or hour and a half. When it rained, we made pretty things by folding paper – helmets, little ships, houses, little baskets, and many other lovely items, which was fun. The children often drew something nice. Other times, one of the aunties told an especially nice story, and of course we didn't forget the singing either. Then, at 6 p.m., when it was time to call it a day, the group let out a general howl of discontent. We would quickly form a circle, sing a song, and brusquely salute each other with 'Heil Hitler' before the whole bunch headed home, charging and tottering and stumbling off in all

9 German title: 'Es zittern die morschen Knochen…'. This song was composed by Hans Baumann (1914–1988) and became a standard among many NSDAP organizations, including the Hitler Youth, the German Labour Front, and the SA. It has since been deemed a National Socialist symbol, the contemporary use of which is outlawed by and deemed an offence under § 86a ('Use of Symbols of Unconstitutional Organizations') of the German Criminal Code.

10 German title: 'Unter'm Dach, juchhe…'.

11 German title: 'Auf einem Baum ein Kuckuck saß'.

12 These two strings of non-lexical vocables form the refrains of the respective children's songs that the author mentions in the previous sentence.

13 German title: 'Der Jäger längs dem Weiher ging'.

14 German title: 'Heut ist ein Fest bei den Fröschen im See'.

directions. Afterwards, the two of us tidied up, swept, and dusted. Then our work was done for the day. We would sit down in our cosy little room and think about the next day's schedule and meal planning. Then I still had to do my food accounts and write out my order lists before making entries in the kindergarten log. The log contained various columns for each day: menu, personal-hygiene activities, other activities, observations about the children, parental contact, etc. It was fun to answer these questions and simultaneously to hold ourselves accountable for everything. The two of us frequently found ourselves discussing this or that child, sharing our observations and opinions with each other. When our work ended, Wilma summarized all the assessments of the individual children in a notebook.

We enjoyed the work so much, and with each passing day we realized more and more just how we had grown inwardly attached to it. Near the end, it was a very strange feeling for us whenever we thought: only seven more days, only six more days … We would have preferred to forget about everything at home and keep on with our work, because here we could see what we were doing, and we knew and sensed that this work was important.

After all, we could see progress in 'our little children' every day. We paid particular attention to how the children talked, how they spoke. We had some children in the group who didn't speak a single word of German and only understood it poorly in the beginning. After some time, they could understand more or less everything that was said to them, and towards the end we even heard a German word come out of their mouths now and then. That elated us, because it was a start, and if the children now remained under German tutelage, they would soon be able speak German properly. But even with the children who could speak German well, we had to be extremely vigilant to ensure that they did not speak Polish among themselves. The temptation to do so was always great, of course. Polish rolled so easily and naturally off the tongue; it simply bubbled forth.

After we had properly intervened a few times in the beginning, the children themselves started paying attention and kept a close watch to ensure that none of their schoolmates dared to speak Polish. I enjoyed observing how they all ran to us at first to tell on each other, but when we vigorously reprimanded them for doing so, they soon took to handling it themselves, and often things even got rough. But that was the best way to do it.

We still had to rouse a certain sense of honour, especially in the boys. In the beginning, every boy, even the older ones, burst out crying and came running to one of the 'aunties' whenever a schoolmate had shoved him.

But once they understood that such behaviour is unworthy of a German boy, it quickly stopped. Then they simply returned the favour and were good friends again.

The last day in Krzywa Gora drew near. Our replacements, two female students from Göttingen, had arrived, and we had finished packing our suitcases.

But now it was time to savour the last few hours. Rain had unfortunately been coming down in sheets since early morning, but it could not stop us from sharing one final happy day together. For the first time, I was able to devote myself completely to the children without having to think about cooking or about the market gardener and the shopkeeper. Before the two 'new' aunties brought the coffee, we formed a circle and sang a lovely morning song to start the day, followed by some amusing songs about rain. One cup of coffee was all the children wanted that day, because soon they were saying, 'Auntie, carry on, don't stop!'

Next we pushed all the benches, tables, and chairs into a corner so that we would have plenty of room. The big boy Heinrich opened the windows wide, and then we were ready to do gymnastics. It was fun. 'Auntie, keeping going', they said. 'Auntie, more jumping jacks!' And so I had to keep extending the gymnastics lesson again and again. What a din there was; what a happy racket!

It was a good thing that our trusty old building was so solidly built, for who knows – it might otherwise have collapsed in the end, what with the jumping up and down of more than 100 legs that stormed none too gracefully through the room. Eventually, however, even the nicest gymnastics lesson had to end. My voice had almost given out, because it was no small thing to make myself heard over this joyful noise. And then the little flock began to cling to my apron strings again: 'Auntie, [sing] "Geesey, geesey, goosey",[15] please!' 'No, Auntie, be so kind [and sing] "The little pointed cap"!'[16] 'Oh, Auntie, [let's sing] "The bumpkin is going around" instead!'[17] Those were my big boys, of course. The auntie was 'so kind' as to play all three and many more games with the cheerful, lively throng. And what enthusiasm and devotion each one of them showed. We clearly sensed that they all wanted to make the most of the last hours with us and be with us longer. Not a single one was unruly or naughty that day. Even the older boys joined in games that were usually 'too childish' for them. None of the little ones wanted to take a nap, either. They all were afraid that the aunties would slip out unnoticed.

When the car really did drive up, it was a difficult farewell. The children's many tears did not make leaving any easier for us. Even the face of our 14-year-old Heinrich looked strangely forlorn. I did not dare to say another word to him, or else the tears that he so heroically held back would have welled up in his eyes, and I did not want to do that to the big lad. So I just gave his hand a firm squeeze. And then the flower-laden car took us farther and farther away from our dear white building and the children waving farewell.

Those five weeks in the East were so rich in new and powerful impressions, in experiences, and in pleasurable work that they will always count among my loveliest and most eventful holidays. I would gladly return to the Vistula next year to see what has been built and created in this land looking optimistically to the future.

How wonderful it must be whenever one is able to put all one's energy into the service of this new German country, to have a hand in creating its German visage.

15 German title: 'Wulle, wulle Gänschen'.

16 German title: 'Die kleine Zipfelmütze'.

17 German title: 'Der Plumpsack geht um'. These are three song-based circle games for children. The first two involve dancing or gesturing based on what is described in the lyrics, and the third is a type of drop-the-handkerchief game.

DOC. 174

Between 20 and 22 September 1940 the chairman of the Warsaw Jewish Council describes his efforts to prevent the construction of the Warsaw ghetto[1]

Handwritten diary of Adam Czerniaków, entries for 20 to 22 September 1940

20 September 1940 – At the Community in the morning I was informed that Leist[2] wanted to see me. During the meeting, L. introduced me to a high-ranking District official. He requested that the workers from the battalion not pass through the avenue or the square. The official then suggested that I provide 3,000 men from the Order Service. L. explained that the entire Polish police force had only 3,000 men, so 1,000 would suffice us. He added that we would have 'selbständige Autonomie'.[3] The official asked why our headquarters are on Grzybowska, and whether Elektoralna or Leszno might not be better. That suggests that this is about the establishment of a ghetto in the Sperrgebiet.[4]

After lunch I was summoned to Dr Klein,[5] Schubert,[6] etc. at Brühl Palace. We discussed the Jewish question. In response to the remark that the Jews must be allowed to work in peace, they replied that everything is related to the question of the ghetto. I gave a detailed account of the situation and handed them a written list of grievances concerning the various restrictions. They contacted the Deputy Governor[7] so that he could receive me in their presence. He replied that, for the time being, he would receive only them. I am to come to the Brühl Palace on Monday or Tuesday, so Leist announced a meeting next week and said I would receive certain instructions.

He will sign the regulations for the Order Service.

No transport to the camp today. Not enough people. Horrifying rumours about me [are circulating] among the Jews, namely that I've been arrested or that I've committed suicide. At home at 58 Wspólna,[8] it was announced that Jewish tenants have no right to take anything with them.

1 YVA, O-33/190. Published in Czerniaków, *Dziennik getta warszawskiego*, pp. 152–153. This document has been translated from Polish.

2 Ludwig Leist (1891–1967), customs officer; employed in the Reich customs administration, 1921–1934; joined the NSDAP and the SA in 1930; worked for the SA in Würzburg, 1935–1939; worked in Warsaw's city administration, 1939; representative of Warsaw's district governor from March 1940; Stadthauptmann, late 1940–1944; sentenced to eight years in prison in Warsaw in 1947; released in 1954.

3 German in the original: 'independent autonomy'.

4 German in the original: 'restricted area'. This refers to the so-called epidemic containment zone established in the northern part of Warsaw city centre in autumn 1939.

5 Dr Hans Klein (1907–1981), lawyer; joined the NSDAP in 1933; employed at the Central Social Insurance Office in Nuremberg, 1934–1935; worked for the government administration in Ansbach, then the Bezirk office in Schabach, 1934–1936; Kreishauptmann in Garwolin, Oct. 1939–1941; simultaneously deputy head of the Interior Administration Department in District Warsaw until March 1943; subsequently served in the war; Oberregierungsrat in the administration of the Upper Palatinate in Regensburg after the war.

6 Probably Richard Schubert; worked in the Interior Administration Department in District Warsaw.

7 Dr Heinrich Barth (b. 1900), lawyer; joined the NSDAP and the SA in 1933; head of the Political and Legal Department of the NSDAP Legal Office from 1935; chief of staff and deputy district governor of Warsaw, Oct. 1939–Dec. 1940; department head at the Reich Legal Office, 1941–1942; Gerichtsdirektor (judge and local court director) in Munich, 1942–1945.

21 September 1940 – + 14 °C. At the Community in the morning. At 11 a.m. to Supinger[9] about the ghetto. On Monday there will be a meeting about this matter in the District. Meanwhile, in response to requests from the people affected, he wants to reduce the size of the restricted zone by excluding Świętojańska and Świętojerska. Otherwise, the boundary will run along Zielna, not Marszałkowska. The residents of a building on Wspólna have been informed that Jews are not permitted to take their things with them. The tenant Czernecki has been thrown out of his apartment. He was not permitted to take his belongings.

22 September 1940 – At the Community in the morning. I am preparing a memo on our situation for tomorrow. Tomorrow will certainly be a day of action. Meanwhile I don't know where we will live in a few days' time or whether they will take everything from us. All we have are furniture and clothes.

My car was stopped on Jerozolimskie Avenue. The things I had to listen to, [ranged| from 'Jüdische Schweine', 'Wie lange werdet ihr herumspazieren?', to 'So etwas',[10] and similar.

DOC. 175

On 26 September 1940 the chief of police in Kattowitz (Katowice) orders the expulsion of Jews who have moved there from the General Government[1]

Letter from the chief of police in Kattowitz,[2] Department II 90.00, signed Weber, to the chief of police in Sosnowitz[3] (received on 1 October 1940), to the Königshütte police office, and to the police stations in the jurisdiction of Special Section Commando I–IV, dated 26 September 1940

Treatment of the Jews

In accordance with the instructions of the Secret State Police – the State Police office – in Kattowitz, the police registry offices must ensure that Jews from the General Government do not, under any circumstances, succeed in registering with the police.[4] In the event that such cases are identified or become known, arrest these Jews immediately and take them to the State Police office, which will arrange for their immediate deportation to the General Government.

8 Czerniaków still lived outside the so-called epidemic containment zone.
9 Correctly: Erwin Suppinger (1886–1955), civil engineer; joined the NSDAP in 1933 and the SA in 1934; head of the Civil Engineering Office in Würzburg in the 1930s; head of the Civil Engineering Department in Warsaw from Jan. 1940; head of the Building Administration Department until April 1940; senior construction consultant in Würzburg after the war.
10 German in the original: 'Jewish pigs', 'How much longer are you going to wander around?', 'Just look at that!'

1 APK, 807/318, fol. 3. This document has been translated from German.
2 Wilhelm Metz (1893–1943), farmer; with the border force in Upper Silesia, 1919–1921; joined the NSDAP and the SA in 1930; chief of police in Oppeln in 1933; chief of police in Troppau (Opava), 1938–1939; chief of police in Katowice, 1940–1943; in charge of the police organization in the annexed eastern strip, with headquarters in Sosnowiec until 1940.
3 Until early Oct. 1940 the deputy chief of police in Katowice was concurrently the chief of police in Sosnowiec.
4 Circular no. 8 from II B – Special Unit to Police Stations, NSDAP Kreisleitungen, and the Landrat in Zawiercie and Blachownia: APK, 807/318, fols. 1–2.

In the urban Kreise of Kattowitz and Königshütte, where local registry offices have not yet been set up at the police stations, the residence registration offices at police headquarters in Kattowitz and at the police office in Königshütte will be watching out for Jews possibly moving in from the General Government. However, the police stations in these urban Kreise must also focus on ensuring that Jews who have returned from the General Government and are residing in the police precinct without having registered are taken to the State Police office.

DOC. 176

On 26 September 1940 the Polish resistance activist Kazimierz Gorzkowski reports on the situation of the Jewish population[1]

Daily chronicle[2] of Kazimierz Gorzkowski,[3] entry for 26 September 1940

A. No. 124. W.Z.[4] *26 September 1940*
1. On the 20th, 21st, and 22nd of this month Jewish women were rounded up in Warsaw. On the 23rd approximately 3,000 of the women who had been detained were sent to District Lublin for the potato harvest. A similar recruitment of a further 7,000 women is to take place soon.
2. On the 21st and the 22nd of the month, the Gestapo and the German police searched all the Jewish-owned bakeries in Warsaw. The search included bakeries that had been allocated white flour. Substantial quantities of flour were requisitioned, thus immobilizing nearly all the Jewish-owned bakeries. Several dozen employees and bakery owners were severely beaten during the search.
3. On the 21st of this month, between 5 and 8 p.m., on Aleje Jerozolimskie and Nowy Świat,[5] German soldiers and Gestapo men stopped Jewish passers-by and forced them to bow to them. Anyone who was slow to do so was beaten until they bled. Even those who bowed were beaten and shouted at: 'Are you my comrade that you bow to me?' On the same day, soldiers and Gestapo men pushed Jewish passengers out of trams, injuring several of them.
4. Last week 240 Jews who had assembled on Napoleon Square for forced labour were arrested. Those who were arrested were taken to Pawiak prison,[6] where they were or-

1 Kazimierz Gorzkowski, 'Andrzej's Chronicles', A. No. 124, pp. 1–2; AAN, 1349/231/VII. This document has been translated from Polish. Published in Kazimierz Gorzkowski, *Kroniki Andrzeja: Zapiski z podziemia 1939–1941*, ed. Tomasz Szarota (Warsaw: Państwowe Wydawnictwo Naukowe, 1989), pp. 264–267.

2 In his chronicle of everyday life under occupation, Gorzkowski regularly recorded news about the Jewish population. This served as a collection of material for the underground press and would form the basis of future research on the history of occupied Poland. Only parts of the chronicle have survived.

3 Kazimierz Gorzkowski (1899–1983), bank employee; Polish nationalist activist in Lublin; NCO in the Polish Military Organization (Polska Organizacja Wojskowa) in 1917; in the scout movement in Warsaw during the 1920s; in the ZWZ-AK resistance movement, 1939–1945; arrested in 1946; sentenced to 15 years in prison in 1948; released in 1956 and subsequently rehabilitated; thereafter worked at the National Museum in Warsaw and for a trade union federation.

4 Wiadomości Żydowskie.

5 Polish for 'New World', the most popular shopping street in Warsaw city centre at the time.

dered to undress. Thereafter 80 people were selected and ordered to pick out the best items from the mountain of clothes and undergarments, while the rest were released. The next day, those who had been arrested were taken to a place near Raszyn, where they were put to work constructing a road junction leading to the SS building. The work lasts 10 days and is unpaid. The workers return to the prison for the night.
5. There are rumours that the Jewish party Bund is resuming its political activity.
6. Warsaw's municipal administration has ordered the closure of Jewish writing rooms.
7. A bloody event took place in Otwock. The germans[7] organized a roundup, because not many people reported for forced labour. During the roundup anyone attempting to escape was shot at, and seventeen Jews were killed.
8. In the last weeks of August, in the factory towns of Ostrowiec, Wierzbnik, Starachowice, and the surrounding villages, all Jews between the ages of 18 and 45 were ordered to place themselves at the disposal of the German authorities within 48 hours. On the day of the roundup, groups of those who had been summoned and persons accompanying them gathered before the respective offices, which gave the military escort the opportunity to treat the entire crowd with unrestrained brutality. As a result, several dozen people were taken to see a physician. Seventy people were transported from Wierzbnik alone. Only those employed in businesses considered 'most useful' were exempt.
9. Out of a population of 200,000 Jews, only half remain in Łódź today, squeezed into a cramped ghetto in conditions of abject misery and hunger.[8] The inhabitants are prohibited from moving beyond the ghetto walls. As there is no question of supplying these masses with a normal or even a humane amount of food, death and disease take their toll. There is a notable decrease in the number of suicides among the Jews. This is supposedly a sign of the great psychological resilience of this race and its desire to see the day when it will be able to exact revenge.
10. According to *Gazeta Żydowska*, the combined deficit of all the Jewish welfare facilities in the General Government amounts to at least 8 to 10 million złoty per month.
11. In connection with the Governor General's most recent regulation on the Jewish school system,[9] a conference with representatives of all types of former Jewish secondary schools took place at the Jewish Community Centre in Warsaw. The consensus is that all Jewish children of school age should be allowed to attend school. Yiddish[10] and Hebrew are to be the languages of instruction, and lessons are to be taught in the national-religious Jewish spirit.
12. In Grodzisk Maz[owiecki], approximately 100 men were sent to a forced labour camp in Bełżec, near Lublin. Around 30 Jewish girls are working in Laski, a village near Grodzisk. They rotate out every four weeks. As in all forced labour camps, the treatment is inhumane.

6 Notorious prison dating from tsarist times.
7 The word is intentionally written in lower case as an expression of contempt.
8 In fact there were nearly 160,000 ghetto residents after the ghetto was sealed in late April 1940.
9 According to the Regulation on the Jewish School System in the General Government, 31 August 1940 (*VOBl-GG* I 1940, no. 51, 11 Sept. 1940, p. 258), the Jewish councils had to arrange for primary, vocational, and technical schools, which were henceforth considered private institutions. Despite this general regulation for the General Government, the German authorities prohibited students from attending school in the Warsaw ghetto until Sept. 1941.
10 The word used for Yiddish here is the pejorative term 'żargon' (literally 'jargon').

13. Rypin's residents have noted a series of facts illustrating the occupiers' exceptional sadism towards the Jewish and Polish populations. The Gestapo locked one of the Jewish residents, a 56-year-old woman, in a closet, which was then boarded up. It was only after a few days that a neighbour heard the moans of the woman, who was exhausted by fear and hunger, and rescued her. The poor woman had gone half insane by the time she was rescued from her torment.
14. A Jewish Order Service has been set up in Tarnów. It serves the Jewish quarter by patrolling the main streets. It helps the police control traffic at the city's busiest points.
15. *Gazeta Żydowska*, which is published in Cracow, ran a very telling article about the new directive on Jewish education, which states, among other things: 'In today's times, a Jewish school, and not just within the General Government, but in most European countries, has the task of helping to raise the young generation in a strictly Jewish spirit. In contrast to past understandings of the concept, "strictly Jewish" should be understood as neither a solely religious upbringing nor an upbringing based exclusively on Jewish national principles, but one that combines the basic principles of these two types of schools and guarantees the maximum degree of general education.' Furthermore, 'Jewish youth, even those educated in Jewish schools, have previously been overly influenced by the culture of their own environment. This has thus led to a partly conscious and partly subconscious assimilation', whereas 'a Jew must learn to tread his own path and look neither to the left nor the right.'[11]
16. Under the provisions of a decree issued by the Landrat[12] of Kreis Bielsko, all Jewish and Polish houses in Bielsko will be administered by the 'Grundstücksgesellschaft der Haupttreuhandstelle Ost m.b.H Berlin'.[13]
17. We receive reports of the increasing misery among the so-called work battalions, which are rife with tuberculosis and scurvy. The help provided by the Jewish Religious Community, which consists of collecting donations from the families of those sent to the work battalions, is inevitably minimal. As a result of the US's refusal to agree to a dollar exchange rate of 5.75 [złoty], financial support from the American Joint [JDC], which had been generous thus far, has now ceased entirely.
18. In the drive to combat usury and illegal trade, the most radical measures are being applied. This particularly concerns Jews who still have goods and can sell them on the black market. That is why they will be subject to strict compulsory labour. They will be placed in special concentration camps once the season ends (German Nutrition Plan for 1940/1941, part 4, § 1).[14]

11 Elza Grosman, 'Dzieci do szkoły' ['Children to school'], *Gazeta Żydowska*, no. 16, 13 Sept. 1940, p. 1.
12 German in the original. Siegfried Schmidt (1905–1944), lawyer; joined the NSDAP in 1933; worked in the Office of the Oberpräsident in Königsberg (now Kaliningrad), 1933; subsequently in the Landrat office in Bergisch-Gladbach; SD employee; at the Reich Ministry of the Interior, 1937–1939; Landrat in Bielsko, Nov. 1939–1942; subsequently served in the war; killed in action.
13 German in the original: 'Real Estate Private Limited Company of the Main Trustee Office East, Berlin'. The Real Estate Company in Berlin was founded on 27 May 1940 by the Plenipotentiary for the Four-Year Plan, the Main Trustee Office East (HTO), and the Reich Commissioner for the Strengthening of Germandom. It organized the administration, management, and sale of expropriated property. On 17 Feb. 1941 the real estate administration split from the HTO, and on 24 Sept. 1942 it was converted into four autonomous Gau real estate companies (with offices in Gdynia, Katowice, Cracow, Poznań, and Ciechanów).
14 The German Nutrition Plan for 1940/1941 could not be found.

DOC. 177

On 7 October 1940 the Interior Administration Department in the General Government orders that no pensions are to be paid out to Jews deported from the Reich[1]

Letter from the head of the Interior Administration Department in the Office of the Governor General (no. 5776/40), signed Kundt, to the district governors and the Stadt- and Kreishauptleute (carbon copy of a copy), dated 7 October 1940

Re: pension payments to the Jews evacuated from the Reich
In view of recent events, I announce the following:

In accordance with a directive issued by the Reich Minister of Labour,[2] social insurance institutions in the German Reich will resume pension payments to Jews evacuated from the Reich to the General Government if the Office of the Governor General or an agency authorized by him declares that there are no objections to the payments 'for political reasons'. This also applies to Jews who hold German citizenship.

Such clearance certificates will be issued neither by the Office of the Governor General nor by any other General Government agency. This means that no pension payments whatsoever will be made to Jews by the social insurance institutions of the Reich.

DOC. 178

On 11 October 1940 the Jewish elder of the Litzmannstadt (Lodz) ghetto declares Saturday a day of rest[1]

Announcement no. 134 from the Jewish elder of Litzmannstadt ghetto, Chaim Rumkowski, to ghetto residents, dated 11 October 1940 (poster)

Announcement no. 134
Residents of the ghetto!

Saturday is a *rest day!*

I therefore call on all business owners to close their businesses and shops (budki)[2] on *Saturday.*

I also prohibit all street trading on Saturdays.

Only the health office and its departments, the main ration depot, the milk shops for children and invalids, and all manner of kitchens may be open on Saturday.

All ghetto residents must heed this announcement.

1 YVA, O-21/31, fol. 116. Published in Berenstein et al. (eds.), *Faschismus – Getto – Massenmord*, p. 186. This document has been translated from German.
2 This could not be found.

1 YVA, O-34, fol. 142. Published as a facsimile in Unger (ed.), *The Last Ghetto*, p. 147. The poster is written in German, Polish, and Yiddish. This document has been newly translated from German.
2 Polish in the German section of the original: 'stalls'. The word does not appear in the Yiddish text on the poster.

DOC. 179

On 15 October 1940 a prisoner functionary in a forced labour camp for Jews in Obidowa asks the American Jewish Joint Distribution Committee for food aid[1]

Letter from Mgr. Emanuel Warenhaupt,[2] Chabówka, to the American Jewish Joint Distribution Committee in Cracow (copy), dated 15 October 1940

With reference to my conversation with Dr Rosenberg, with whom I had the opportunity to speak during his visit to Maków, I would like to turn to the Committee and request as much assistance as the Committee is able to provide us with within the framework of its resources and possibilities.

Although I had the opportunity to speak with Dr Rosenberg several weeks ago, I am writing to you only today because even though we expected the arrival of a larger number of Jewish workers then, it is only today that approximately 150 of them have arrived.

At present, there are 250 Jews here in total.

We are employed by the STUAG Strassen und Tiefbau AG[3] company to reconstruct the Cracow–Zakopane motorway, and specifically an 18 km long stretch of the Chabówka–Nowy Targ road.

We work 10 hours a day, from 7 to 12 p.m. and from 1 to 6 p.m. We take our meals during the one-hour break from 12 to 1 p.m.

The Jews are involved solely in excavation work, although there are specialist workers among us who are qualified for other jobs.

Our pay is 20 per cent lower than that of the Aryans [and it is] based on the pay scale with which you are probably familiar.

Jews from Maków, Jordanów, Chabówka, Rabka, and the surrounding villages have been employed in the aforementioned work thus far. They are all very poor people who have been ruined by war; some of them are expellees who had been deported from areas incorporated into the Reich and whose entire wealth consisted of one torn set of clothing and a worn out pair of shoes. Today they look ragged, like skeletons or other apparitions.

For 10 weeks, we lived in a barracks intended as summer accommodation. I want to point out that it was located at the top of a hill, where the cold and the frequent rain hit us hard.

As for food, it has been catastrophic in every respect since our very first days here. We have been working here since 27 August of this year.

The company is not interested in supplying us with food. It does not provide us with anything other than bread rations.

We have always purchased our own food and still do; however, as we are unable to get anything with food coupons, we pay exorbitant prices on all food items. So, for example, we pay 40 gr. for 1 kg of potatoes, but to get them we have to go from village to village and outright beg people to sell them to us.

As the bread rations are so minuscule, we sometimes prepare three meals a day by cooking potatoes in various ways – either soup with potatoes or potatoes with soup.

1 YVA, M-28/5, fol. 12r–v. This document has been translated from Polish.

2 Emanuel Warenhaupt was a member of the Judenrat in Maków. Mgr. is short for Magister (holder of a master's degree), then commonly used as part of a title.

3 A road construction company established in Vienna in 1928.

It is troublesome that these meals cost so much, as each worker eats at least 1 kg of potatoes at every meal, and 3 kg a day costs 1.30 złoty to which one must add the cost of preparing the soup. As a result, each worker's pay barely covers the cost of his food. We have no flour to prepare the soup, and for the roux we need flour, which we also have to buy at exorbitant prices. The people from whom we have received small offerings cannot be considered as regular benefactors, since they may refuse to help us the next day. It goes without saying that throughout this entire time we have not had any barley, grain, peas, beans, or groats of any kind in the pot, and indeed, we no longer remember them as so much time has passed that we have forgotten what they are.

Another matter I wish to point out is that it is not only our company which does not makes an effort to provide for us; our Judenraty[4] are taking the same approach. Not a single Judenrat has visited us or cared to ask whether we need help, and it is high time we received help from someone.

The undersigned is the so-called Lagerführer,[5] who is responsible for all matters related to supplying and purchasing food. He settles all the issues that arise between the Jewish workers and the company. The undersigned is therefore the confidant of all the Jews employed here.

Finally, I do not want to paint too vivid a picture of this tragedy, because you gentlemen must be familiar with it already. I only wish to stress once again that help is essential to us, and we are counting on it from the American Joint Distribution Committee.

I look forward to your reply.

Kind regards,

DOC. 180

Warschauer Zeitung, 16 October 1940: article on the establishment of a neighbourhood for Germans and a ghetto for Jews[1]

A German quarter in Warsaw in the south-eastern corner of the city. A sealed-off residential district in the north for the Jews. Definitive ruling from the District Governor establishes clear parameters.

Report by the Krakauer Zeitung and the Warschauer Zeitung
gff.[2] *Warsaw*, 16 October.
By order of the Governor of District Warsaw, SA-Brigadeführer Dr Fischer, a residential district for Germans will be established in the city of Warsaw to create clean, wholesome, and sufficient living space for the Germans who live and work here. At the same time, the

4 Polish plural form of Judenräte: 'Jewish councils'.
5 German in the original: 'camp supervisor'.

1 *Warschauer Zeitung*, no. 245, 16 Oct. 1940, p. 5. This document has been translated from German.
2 Robert [J.] Greiff (1915–1967), journalist; trainee at various newspapers in Lower Silesia in the 1930s, and simultaneously attended university in Breslau; correspondent for the *Krakauer Zeitung* in Warsaw in 1940 and in Cracow in 1942; later served in the war; journalist in West Germany after the war; head of the Germany and International Affairs desk at the news magazine *Der Spiegel*, 1959–1965; thereafter worked freelance.

Jewish part of Warsaw's population is going to be concentrated in a sealed-off residential district, providing the clean separation necessary to prevent the spread of diseases from the Jewish residential districts – which are well-known breeding grounds for epidemic disease – to the rest of the population. The District Governor's new arrangement will be implemented swiftly and establishes clear parameters once and for all.

Warsaw's German quarter, comprising the south-eastern part of the city and bordering on the Vistula, will serve as a place of residence for all Germans living in Warsaw, who – unless they already live in this area – must move there. The Governor has not yet set the final deadline for the completion of the resettlement process. The District Governor furthermore reserves the right to impose residence bans and restrictions for Poles in the German residential district. Germans who currently live outside the German quarter will be assigned housing within the German residential district by the Resettlement Department in the Office of the District Governor.[3] Exemptions from the requirement to relocate to the German quarter are permitted for reasons of official business but must be approved by the District Governor's representative for the City of Warsaw.[4]

The sealed-off Jewish residential district includes the northern part of the city (see the map for the precise perimeters[5]), and by 31 October all Jews still living outside the Jewish residential district must move into that neighbourhood, where living spaces will be assigned to them by the Jewish elder. Poles living within the Jewish residential district must leave their homes by 31 October.[6] If they voluntarily vacate their residences by this date, they retain the right to choose a new residence freely. After this date, however, they will be forcibly evacuated, and the Polish Municipal Housing Office will assign them new housing. Poles are prohibited from settling in the German residential district, and those who are forcibly evacuated are not permitted to take furnishings with them. They may only take along hand luggage, bed linen, and keepsakes.

Additional implementing regulations to this order from the District Governor[7] will be issued by the District Governor's representative for the City of Warsaw.[8] Violations

3 This office was responsible for the ethnic segregation of the inhabitants, in particular for the forced relocation of Jews from the area surrounding Warsaw into the Warsaw ghetto. From Jan. 1940 to March 1941 it was run by Waldemar Schön (1904–1969), lawyer; joined the SA and the NSDAP in 1930; held several Party offices including deputy Kreisleiter from 1933 and Reichsredner (Reich orator) from 1938; head of the Resettlement Department in District Warsaw from Jan. 1940; head of the Interior Administration Department from 1941; with the NSDAP Reichsleitung from 1940; clerical worker and later lawyer in Bavaria after the war.

4 Ludwig Leist.

5 A map accompanied the article.

6 With his Second Directive on the Establishment of the Jewish Residential District of 31 Oct. 1940, the District Governor of Warsaw extended the deadline for 'voluntary resettlement' until 15 Nov. 1940: *Amtsblatt des Gouverneurs des Distrikts Warschau*, no. 10, 11 Nov. 1940, pp. 147–148.

7 Directive issued by the District Governor of Warsaw, Fischer, on the Establishment of a Jewish Residential District in the City of Warsaw, 2 Oct. 1940: *Amtsblatt des Gouverneurs des Distrikts Warschau*, no. 10, 11 Nov. 1940, pp. 145–147.

8 Announcement by Leist, dated 16 Oct. 1940, on the establishment of a Jewish residential district in the city of Warsaw. Published in Pospieszalski (ed.), *Documenta Occupationis*, vol. 6, part 2, pp. 544–545 (from *Krakauer Zeitung*, 18 Oct. 1940). Leist changed the perimeters of the ghetto again with his directive of 14 Jan. 1941: *Mitteilungsblatt der Stadt Warschau*, no. 3, 18 Jan. 1941, pp. 1–5.

of this order will be punished using all available means.[9] The extensive preparations that the German authorities have made will ensure the smooth implementation of these measures.

DOC. 181

On 18 October 1940 the Lublin employment office records the mass escape of Jews from a forced labour camp[1]

Memorandum by a civil servant in the Lublin employment office, signed Hecht, dated 18 October 1940[2]

1) *Memorandum*:
The head of the Department of Road Construction, Baurat[3] Muth, just telephoned and informed me that approximately 400 Jews arrived on 17 October 1940 for [work at] his construction site in Krasnik. Three Selbstschutz men guard these Jews in Krasnik camp. Today Baurat Muth found out that approximately 300 Jews had escaped from Krasnik camp during the night of 17–18 October 1940 and that the remaining ones, approximately 100 of them, will probably escape today over the course of the day. I told Baurat Muth that I unfortunately no longer have anything to do with the matter, as the transport of 400 Jews was duly delivered to Krasnik camp. I furthermore informed Building Officer Muth that he himself must ensure that Krasnik camp is adequately guarded. In reply, Baurat Muth informed me that he had contacted SS- and Brigadeführer Globocnik[4] about the guard detail in Krasnik camp, and that Globocnik said he was unable to provide any guards. Baurat Muth went on to say that the Jews from the Belzec camp are completely unfit for work and that it takes every last bit of strength for them just to stay on their feet. Baurat Muth intends to send a telegram before the day is out to inform his superiors in Cracow of this whole incident.
2) To Oberregierungsrat *Jache*, for information.
3) To be filed.

9 Under the Regulation on Administrative Penalty Proceedings in the General Government of 13 Sept. 1940, penalties of up to 1,000 złoty or jail terms of three months could be imposed: *VOBl-GG* I 1940, no. 56, 23 Sept. 1940, pp. 300–301.

1 APL, 498/748, fol. 111. This document has been translated from German.
2 The original contains handwritten underlining and the initial 'J[ache]'.
3 Baurat was a title indicating seniority held by construction specialists employed in public service.
4 Correctly: SS-Brigadeführer Globocnik.

DOC. 182

On 19 October 1940 Ruth Goldbarth writes to her friend Edith Blau about her anxiety and despair prior to her move to the Warsaw ghetto[1]

Handwritten letter from Ruth Goldbarth in Warsaw to her friend Edith Blau in Minden (Westphalia), dated 19 October 1940

Dearest Edith,

Thank you for your kind letter. We unfortunately hoped in vain that we would 'be spared'. We have to move by the 31st! Edith, it's terrible! I am simply unable to describe it to you, and you couldn't possibly imagine it! Since 13 October we have all been running around from morning till night – today is already the sixth day – and we still haven't found anything. I'm unable to write much to you about all that; I can't even think about what will happen. But one thing I do know: the despair that fills me now is as great as my previous efforts have been to keep a stiff upper lip and not to lose faith and hope. Unless a miracle happens, it's over, Edith, completely over! My God, why is there no end to these tribulations at long last, why does it keep getting worse?!! Believe me, I'm already half mad. I can't think any more, can't cry any more, though I am haunted night and day by the images from Maryś's home. When I walk up and down the streets looking for a place to live, I often think I would just as soon drown myself in the Vistula as live here. At the same time, I am well aware that that is all nonsense, that we will get used to the streets, the apartments, even if there are four to six of us living in one room. But everything else! If we are cut off from the world! Hear nothing more from you all! If we can't get any food, any coal! If disease breaks out! If, if … oh, what do I know! I have just got back from the city; 'our' part has been reduced in size again, by a couple of streets, and this happens every other day. Some people have already moved three or four times. Granted, it doesn't involve so much work, since we're only allowed to take along hand luggage anyway, but the space is already so very, very tiny as it is. I don't know what's going to happen, Dita! Sweetie, why are you so far away? Why am I so alone in all this chaos and confusion! I just can't go on any longer!! Nonsense, so many people are having an even worse time, and they have to get through it too! But it is enough to … to, to just make you feel like hanging yourself! I have a request: Ditli, try to find out from the Relief Association or elsewhere what possibilities there are for emigration, what sort of papers a person can get, and under what conditions. That information might be important for us.

And write back at once!

As always,

Ruth

Lutek[2] wrote a few days ago. There's news from Nusia[3] too, somewhere in Central Asia; the Szcz. wrote something. O-Beni was not here, just wrote a completely crazy letter again, and I can't make any sense of it. There was news from Aga and Sorrel as well. Ruth v. W. supposedly has a very good job in a Berlin photo lab!

1 USHMM, RG 10 250*02, WA 025. This document has been translated from German.

2 Lucjan (Lutek) Orenbach.

3 Their mutual friend Danuta had fled to the part of Poland annexed by the Soviets, from where she was deported to Central Asia.

DOC. 183
On 21 October 1940 the Jewish Social Self-Help issues a memorandum on events surrounding resettlement into the Warsaw ghetto[1]

JSS memorandum, dated 21 October 1940 (carbon copy)

Re: resettlement into the Jewish residential district in Warsaw
I. The official section of the *Warschauer Zeitung* dated the 18th of this month and placards put up the same day promulgated a 'Public notice regarding the formation of a Jewish residential district'. In this notice, signed by the District Governor's representative, Dr Leist,[2] the perimeters of the Jewish residential district were officially established.[3] On the 19th of this month at 2 p.m., there was a radio announcement that a number of streets have been excluded from the ghetto, from Żelazna (Eisengrubenstraße)[4] to Okopowa. A similar notice also appeared in the 20–21 October 1940 edition of the *Warschauer Zeitung*, in the brief announcements from the General Government.

On the morning of 21 October 1940, the chairman of the Jewish Council, the engineer Czerniakow, went to the District Governor's representative, Dr Leist, where he was received by the adjutant,[5] who was not aware of either the radio announcement or the notice in the *Warschauer Zeitung*. He placed a telephone call to the Office of the District Governor and told the chairman of the Jewish Council that an order of this sort probably exists, and that the chairman should convey it to his fellow Jews. In reply, the chairman said that he did not feel qualified to alter the orders of the District Governor's representative.[6]

The Trustee Office[7] issued a circular dated the 19th to the temporary administrators of Jewish buildings. It [stated] that the employees of the property management offices and the caretakers must remain in the Jewish residential district. The Polish newspaper *Nowy Kurjer Warszawski* has published a report that the caretakers must leave the Jewish properties, while the civil servants and workers for the larger enterprises are allowed to remain in their homes.[8]

At the same time, runaway rumours have begun to spread that other streets will also be excluded from the Jewish residential district. This state of affairs has led to complete

1 YVA, O-21/14, fols. 64–65. This document has been translated from German.
2 Leist did not hold a doctorate.
3 Leist's announcement on the establishment of a Jewish residential district in the city of Warsaw is dated 16 Oct. 1940: see Doc. 180, fn. 8.
4 This is a reference to Eisenstraße (Żelazna). Eisengrubenstraße was the German name for Chłodna.
5 Leist's aide Emil Braun (1904–1943), administrative assistant; joined the SA in 1934 and the NSDAP in 1937; in the Warsaw municipal administration from 1940 as head of the Housing Office and in other positions; died as the result of an attempt on his life by Polish resistance fighters.
6 Czerniaków describes the conversation with Emil Braun on 21 Oct. 1940 in his diary: *The Warsaw Diary of Adam Czerniakow*, p. 209.
7 Under the German occupation, Jewish-owned land and buildings were confiscated and put under the control of trustees. Frank ordered the formation of an administrative office for the General Government in Cracow, known as the Trustee Office, on 15 Nov. 1939. Its branch office in Warsaw took charge of the confiscated Jewish properties in District Warsaw: see Doc. 194.
8 Correctly: *Nowy Kurier Warszawski*. In mid October 1940 the newspaper reported almost daily on the implementation of Governor Fischer's decision to create the ghetto. The report mentioned here appears in issue no. 248, dated 21 Oct. 1940, p. 3.

confusion, and according to information we have received from Warsaw, only very few people are swapping their apartments, because those who are supposed to relocate have no idea where they are permitted to move to. As was pointed out in Memorandum I, the residential district for Jews established in the official public notice of 16 October 1940 is significantly smaller than what had been accepted until that time as the residential district for Jews, the so-called epidemic containment zone. If the streets listed in the radio announcement were to be added to the Polish residential district, then according to the information provided by the Jewish Council, the number of Aryans required to leave the Jewish quarter would total 75,000, while 140,000 Jews would be resettled in the Jewish area. In addition, if the Aryan caretakers and the employees of the property management offices were to remain in the Jewish residential district, the number of Poles to be moved out would then decrease by another 10,000.

The Jewish Council in Warsaw reports that the latest changes to the perimeters are based on outdated and therefore erroneous calculations. For example, the percentage of residents living in Żelaznastraße (Eisengrubenstraße) who are Jews amounted to 46 per cent in the first half of this year, 52 per cent on 1 October, and [is] 65 per cent at present. The situation is similar for Chłodnastraße, where four months ago 47 per cent to 48 per cent of residents were Jews, and now that number stands at more than 60 per cent.

II. On the 14th of this month the Jewish Council was instructed to tear down some of the walls that had been built some time ago. After the Jewish Council had set about doing this on the 15th of this month, it was given a new order that called for a halt to some of the demolitions already under way, while ordering that others commence.

The provision of the 15th of this month that Poles are permitted to live on both sides of the streets bordering [the] Jewish residential district resulted in property managers and caretakers acting on their own authority to brick up existing gateways and to create others in order to connect the buildings to the Polish residential district.

While the authorities invite representatives of the Polish population to all the meetings, the representatives of the Jewish population are not received by the District Governor's authorities overseeing resettlement and are unable to present the wishes of the Jewish population to officials.

In light of the circumstances described above, we respectfully take the liberty of putting forward the following proposals for your kind consideration:

1. It would be desirable to have authoritative clarification that the perimeters established in the official notice of the 16th of this month [are] binding, with permission granted for Jews to live on the side of the street that borders the Jewish residential district.

2. It would be desirable for representatives of the Jewish population to be given a hearing before the final decision is taken. We venture to name the following individuals, who have already gained the authorities' trust in the course of their work:

1) Adam Czerniaków, engineer, chairman of the Jewish Council in Warsaw;
2) Josef Jaszuński, deputy chairman of the executive committee of the Jewish Social Self-Help, member of the Jewish Council;
3) Dr Gamsej Wielikowski, member of the JSS executive committee;
4) Abraham Sztolcman, engineer, member of the Jewish Council, director of the Jewish Relief Committee in Warsaw.

DOC. 184

On 23 October 1940 the ghetto guard force in Litzmannstadt (Lodz) reports on the unauthorized photographing of the ghetto[1]

Report from the ghetto guard force[2] in Litzmannstadt (log no. 224/40; K. II/5. 622/40), police precinct officer in charge, signature illegible, dated 23 October 1940[3]

Re: confiscation of film

Around 11.25 a.m. on Wednesday, 23 October 1940, police officer trainee Eugen *Franz* noticed that the married housewife Hildegard *Jankowski*, born 18 June 1917 in Danzig, address Danzig-Langfuhr, 2 Ernst-Hausen-Str., was travelling in a horse-drawn cab (cab no. 89) along the Bal[uter] Ring [Bałucki Rynek] and taking photographs. Mrs Jankowski was taken to the ghetto guardhouse, where her film was taken away from her.

Jankowski stated that she did not know that taking photographs of the ghetto is prohibited.

Mrs Jankowski will be in Litzmannstadt for approximately ten more days, at 7 Brückenstraße, in the home of Werner *Arke*.

The film, along with the daylight loading cartridge, is enclosed with the report.[4]

DOC. 185

Warschauer Zeitung, 23 October 1940: article about a training lecture given by the head of the Resettlement Department in District Warsaw[1]

Why a Jewish residential district in Warsaw? Reichsamtsleiter Schön[2] gave a talk as part of guidance for troops.

Report by the Krakauer Zeitung and Warschauer Zeitung

gff.[3] Warsaw, 23 October.

As part of the efforts to offer instruction and guidance to the troops, the head of the Resettlement Department in the Office of the District Governor, Reichsamtsleiter *Schön*, addressed the men of an army battalion on the subject of the Jewish question. This event, as the battalion commander emphasized in his introductory remarks, also marked the start of a series of guest lectures and social events to boost troop morale and provide

1 APŁ, 203/24, fol. 108. Copy: USHMM, RG 05 008M, reel 9. This document has been translated from German.

2 The perimeter of the Litzmannstadt ghetto was guarded and patrolled on the exterior by two Order Police battalions, which were responsible for ensuring that there was no contact between the Jewish inhabitants of the ghetto and the outside world. These battalions were militarized units of the uniformed German Order Police.

3 Handwritten notes appear in the upper margin.

4 This is not included in the file. On 29 Oct. 1940 Jankowski told the police that she merely wanted to take a few photos: APŁ, 203/24, fol. 109. The police took no further action.

1 *Warschauer Zeitung*, no. 251, 23 Oct. 1940, p. 6. This document has been translated from German.

2 Waldemar Schön.

3 Robert J. Greiff.

guidance. These events will be held over the course of the winter in cooperation with the Troop Instruction and Guidance Section of the Department of Public Enlightenment and Propaganda in the Office of the District Governor. Greetings from the head of the Department of Public Enlightenment and Propaganda, Regierungsrat Ohlenbusch,[4] were conveyed by Party Comrade *Huhn*.[5]

Reichsamtsleiter Schön spoke next, introducing his talk with an overview of the historical development of Jewry in the remotest parts of the East in order to emphasize that the Jewish question per se is not a new one, although the manner of handling it is. For the first time, he explained, racial principles were now being applied in tackling the Jewish question, whereas religious or economic considerations had previously been decisive. After characterizing Jewry and its predominant features, the Reichsamtsleiter turned his attention to the establishment of the Jewish residential district in Warsaw. This was necessary, first, for reasons of public health, as the Jew carries the germs of dangerous epidemics that do less harm to him than to the rest of the population, whose members must be protected at all costs from the spread of infectious diseases. Second, economic considerations mean that it is necessary to eradicate the Jewish influence from the economy once and for all. This influence manifests itself above all in illicit trading and profiteering. Only once this has been accomplished, he explained, will it be possible to rigorously secure the food supply, which is first and foremost in the interests of the Polish population.

Reichsamtsleiter Schön then sketched out details of how this closed-off residential district will be established administratively. It will be managed by a Jewish Council, invested with appropriate powers, including the authority to set up its own Jewish Order Service with a strength of 1,000 men. In addition, the Jewish Council will have to use its own resources to provide sanitary facilities within the Jewish residential district.

4 Wilhelm Ohlenbusch (b. 1899, d. after 1991), primary school teacher; joined the NSDAP and the SA in 1930; district propaganda chief, 1931–1933, then Kreisleiter in Oldenburg; Regierungsrat, head of propaganda for the NSDAP in the General Government, and head of the Department of Public Enlightenment and Propaganda in District Warsaw, 1939; head of the Propaganda Main Office in the government of the GG from Feb. 1941; imprisoned in Brandenburg an der Havel after the war; in Oldenburg from 1956, and later in Spain.

5 Presumably Erich Huhn (b. 1903); joined the NSDAP in 1933; section head in the Department of Public Enlightenment and Propaganda in District Warsaw, head of the propaganda department in Radom from Dec. 1941.

DOC. 186

On 25 October 1940 a German Jewish refugee criticizes the conscription of Jews for Polish military service in Britain[1]

Letter from Izak Rothman[2] to the *Jewish Chronicle*, London, 25 October 1940

Conscription of Poles in Britain
A Typical Case of Hardship

We print below, exactly as it reached us, a letter from a refugee, Mr. Izak Rothman, of 10 Talbot Square, W.2. In publishing this letter in its original inaccurate and awkward English, we feel that the sincere sentiments of the author are expressed with far greater truth than if his words were 'translated' into more ordinary idiom. His case is typical of a sufficient number of Jewish refugees of Polish nationality in this country to merit the space devoted to it.

Allow me to refer to the article in *The Jewish Chronicle* of September 27, 1940, page 11, under the headline 'Conscription of Poles in Britain' and 'Polish Jews' Insufferable Position,' and excuse please my bad English.

I am a refugee from Nazi oppression, 29 years of age, who lived in Germany (Cologne) since 1913. I come over to England through Bloomsbury House,[3] 14 months ago, with a view of further re-emigration to the United States. I would now be on the turn to get my visa, but I cannot get the Exit Permit from the Home Office because the Polish Consulate is not willing to give me the necessary letter freeing me from military service with the Polish Army, because I happen to have a Polish passport.

Six years long I lived a life of serfdom in Germany, and more than one year one of distress in this country, waiting suffering but patiently, because full of hope, for the day when I could go into a place, where I could again start to live a life like a human being. But now the Polish authorities are preventing me from doing so. I have no connection with Poland whatever. I have never eaten from their soil there, never earned my living there. When I was born there in 1911 it was part of the Austrian Empire. I have never been in Poland for more than 4 weeks. I cannot speak 10 words of their language and I know nearly nothing of their history.

The only contact I had with Polish authorities was, when my brother as early as 1933 was thrown into a concentration camp in Germany, and I asked thereupon the Polish Consulate in Duesseldorf to intervene. I was shouted at by the official that they are not there to help Jewish Communists (which, of course, he was not a bit).

The second time in my life it was in October, 1938, when my mother,[4] like nearly all Jews in Germany with Polish passports, was expelled overnight by the Nazis to Poland, where she was held by the Polish authorities for more than half a year in a

1 *Jewish Chronicle*, 25 Oct. 1940, p. 6. The *Jewish Chronicle* is a London-based weekly newspaper founded in 1841.

2 Izak Rothman, also Rothmann (b. 1911); from 1915 lived in Cologne with his parents, who were from Galicia; fled to Britain via the Netherlands in 1939.

3 From 1938, Woburn House in London's Bloomsbury district served as a seat for many British aid organizations for Jewish refugees from Germany and the German-occupied territories.

4 Presumably Chana or Anna Rothmann, née Flaumenhaft (b. 1886); murdered in Auschwitz.

concentration camp, in safe distance from the 'fatherland,' namely in no man's land, on the Polish side of the frontier,[5] living, like all of them, on the charity of the Jewish American Joint Committee. At last she got a visa for Belgium, where to she went, and from where I haven't heard anything since the invasion of her.

Now I have never reproached the Poles for not having helped my family, not outwardly and not inwardly, because I admit never having had, physically or spiritually, the slightest relation with them – not because of any hatred but out of sheer indifference towards them, I want to stress. But, I do not know why, as they never helped me, they should be able to hinder me to re-emigrate from England to the USA. If I was not good enough to work and live from them, then I should not be good enough to fight for them and to be held back here, only because of the fact that owing to some artificial post-war manipulation I was bestowed with a Polish passport.

I have no permission to take up work in this country. As my guarantor in Holland, who helped me to come over here, is unable to lend me any help now, I am living on 20s a week, which I get from the Bloomsbury House, and for which I am ever so thankful.

My sorrow of the possibility of being bombed is a mere tiny one, compared with the sorrow of whether I will have enough money or not to buy my bread and milk to-morrow. This is what I owe to the Polish authorities. Far from ever having helped me, be it from getting out of Germany or in any other way (which, as mentioned I never expected them to do) they are asking me now to serve with their Army, thus compelling me to commit a treachery towards my family which has suffered so much through them, in various ways, which I do not want to point out here further, as I want to forget it.

My family of five is now dispersed in all corners of the world. I do not know of the whereabouts of my mother and my brother who are in by Nazis occupied territories, and, unable to do anything from here. It is my duty to emigrate to trace them and help them.

(signed) *Izak Rothman.*

P.S. Please overlook if I have used some harsh words. I do not want to offend Poland, now, in this unfortunate hour of hers. In truth, I feel deep sympathy with a nation in need, with such a fine record of genuine patriotism, as the Polish. What I intended, was to point out the facts concerning myself in relation to Poland.

5 See Doc. 95, fn. 5.

DOC. 187

Berliner Börsen-Zeitung, 27 October 1940: article about shops being closed down in East Upper Silesia[1]

Restructuring in East Upper Silesia. Overcrowding in the retail sector is being eliminated.

From our economics correspondent
Breslau, 25 October. Before Upper Silesia was torn apart after the World War, intense overcrowding was already making its presence felt in trade, specifically in retail trade, in this industrial region. During the Polish era the situation in East Upper Silesia deteriorated further. For every German shop forced to close in the first few years as a result of boycotts and terror, three new Polish ones opened up. In the grocery business and in footwear and clothing, very small shops proliferated to such an extent that medium-sized businesses were put at risk. The whole basis for the distribution of goods had become unstable. Almost all the Jews were engaged in trade, not only in shops but also in their apartments and basements. The business practices of the Jewish retailers contributed to a further decline in the population's already low standard of living. The Polish retailers suffered from the Jewish infestation of trade even more than the Germans did; they soon realized that pushing out the German retailers did not solve their problems. After a few years, Poles lost their appetite for the retail business and left this activity to ethnic German shops, which steered clear of Jewish practices and were able to gain a solid customer base among Poles as well.

When East Upper Silesia became part of the Reich again, one of the most difficult tasks for the economic administration was to restructure trade and cleanse it of corrupt elements. For this purpose, the Trustee Office East and the Retail Economic Group created 'Handelsaufbau Ost',[2] which set up offices in *Kattowitz*, *Posen*, *Litzmannstadt*, and *Danzig*. In the new territories incorporated into Upper Silesia, there are in total 12,500 retail shops and 450 wholesale businesses. Of that number, around 10,000 retail shops and 250 wholesalers are in East Upper Silesia. When the German administration moved in, approximately 270 shops were closed immediately. Although the process of taking inventory and checking the businesses for their viability and their owners for their suitability has not yet been completed, we can assume that around 7,000 retail shops in East Upper Silesia are in ethnic German hands. Of the remaining 3,000 shops, almost all must be closed in order to eliminate the overcrowding that is hampering the distribution of goods. Almost without exception, these are enterprises that cannot provide a subsistence level income. Elimination of these businesses makes room for the establishment of approximately 1,000 new retail firms. Because around 700 more businesses are in trusteeship – to date 22 firms have transitioned into orderly circumstances through being sold – there would thus be 1,700 firms that could be considered for ethnic Germans, frontline soldiers, and resettlers.

1 *Berliner Börsen-Zeitung*, no. 508/509, 27 Oct. 1940, supplement to the business section. This document has been translated from German.

2 Handelsaufbau Ost dealt with the Germanization of commercial and retail businesses: see also Doc. 129.

A complete restructuring is envisaged in other parts of East Upper Silesia. Almost all retail shops there are in Jewish or Polish hands. Overcrowding in this sector is particularly severe, so at least 1,000 of the 2,500 shops will have to be closed. Ethnic German trustees currently run around 200 companies in that region; the other companies are still run by the old owners. The reorganization in this part of East Upper Silesia is particularly difficult because of a shortage of [local] ethnic Germans who want to acquire a shop. Additional recruits will be found from among frontline soldiers, ethnic German resettlers, and Reich Germans. In the territories newly incorporated into Upper Silesia, too, the transfer to sound ownership of those companies that are to be preserved is proceeding gradually; *the financial terms for suitable German applicants are favourable.* The transformation of the retail sector is therefore not being tackled at excessive speed. Bringing in a competent, hard-working class of shopkeeper is understood to be the most important prerequisite for sound conditions; until that has been achieved, the medium-sized and larger businesses will continue to be managed by trustees. That is necessary not least because there will be many frontline soldiers who meet the requirements for running a retail business in every respect and are willing to build a life for themselves as independent entrepreneurs in the eastern territories.

Things are less straightforward when it comes to reorganizing the wholesale sector. Up to now, only one-tenth of all wholesale companies have had trustees assigned to them, and the others necessarily continue to be managed by the old owners, naturally under the oversight of the Trustee Office East and the Wholesale Economic Group. The pool of German applicants is determined by the amount of capital required. Successful attempts to pair up German wholesale companies with ethnic Germans who are reliable and suitable but lack capital appear to offer a promising route to reorganizing the wholesale sector in East Upper Silesia as well.

DOC. 188

Between 25 and 31 October 1940 Emanuel Ringelblum describes conditions in the Warsaw ghetto before it was sealed off[1]

Handwritten diary of Emanuel Ringelblum, entries for 25 to 31 October 1940

My dearest,

The matter of the ghetto creates great complexities and difficulties for Jewish enterprises operating under Christian names. [A Jewish proprietor] has the chance to control [his business] and can remain [its] owner as long as [his] business stays in the ghetto. But the moment the business moves elsewhere, the Jewish owner basically loses all of his property. 'You Jewish swindler', said a soldier to a Jew who had concealed from him

1 Ringelblum, Notatki 1939–1941, AŻIH, Ring I/449 (507/1). This document has been translated from Yiddish. Published in Ringelblum, *Ksovim fun geto*, vol. 1: *Togbukh fun varshever geto*, pp. 166–169. As the second page of the manuscript is illegible in many places, it was translated based on the transcription that appears in *Ksovim fun geto*. Any phrases that did not make sense were checked against the manuscript.

that he was carrying money. A tale of the two sides to the Sodom question: turn things inside out and you have Sodom on your hands.[2]

Jews spent today, 25 October, [the festival of] simkhes toyre,[3] as they do every year. An acquaintance of mine saw a group of Jews in silk caftans dancing and singing in the street on their way home from synagogue. In short, they were celebrating the holiday!

There was a Polish–Jewish conference yesterday with Count Ronikier, who spoke out against the tendency among some Poles to claim more and more streets in the ghetto for themselves. In his view, a joint struggle must be waged against the ghetto, not a war between the two peoples. I heard about a respected Pole who expressed his delight that, after centuries, the dream of a ghetto had come true. Fresh notices from Leist[4] are posted every day concerning the ghetto's perimeter, which includes Żelazna and other streets. They say this is in response to the Gestapo's efforts to shrink the ghetto. Leist says he will not be terrorized by the Polish population. On Łucka, there have been cases of Poles who moved out in the morning, only to return in the afternoon based on loudspeaker announcements and drive Jews out of their apartments, stealing their belongings in the process. Rabble-rousing against the Jews yesterday over the loudspeaker: 'They are a plague that must be eradicated'. Instances of people being beaten for failing to offer greetings [by doffing their hats] are steadily rising, so people are performing these greetings more and more often. It is impossible to go out nowadays without some kind of hat or head covering, as previously.

There was a gathering somewhere. Following the gathering, an automobile was standing there and people were rounded up for labour. One man took the lead, lined up the crowd in four rows, and led them safely out of danger. Heard the following true story: 200 Jews were captured for labour. Each one received a number and was ordered to wait at the railway station. Two hundred families [from] Germany arrived there. Each family had a number. [Each] Jew led his group to a specified address, and there they found a heated apartment with supper on the table. News from the countryside about ghettos being formed there. The Jews from Sokołów have been resettled in Węgrów. Groups of several hundred Jews are constantly being driven out of Tomaszów. Wherever Jews work, there are two groups of Jews: locals who are treated well and new arrivals who are beaten (Jews under special protection).

Today, 26 October, there were rumours again that part of Żelazna will be returned to the ghetto to create a connection between the two ghettos. When a car ran out of petrol, a group of Jews was ordered to pull it. A soldier standing around ordered everyone to doff their hats. He berated a Jew who passed through with a handcart, wanting to know why he hadn't doffed his cap. A Jew was asked where he was going. The Jew had lost his

2 The Sodom story in Genesis contains few details regarding the city's transgressions that spurred God to destroy it. However, the Talmud (Sanhedrin 109a and 109b) provides more information. One vignette relates the topsy-turvy justice meted out by a judge in Sodom who orders a man who has been unjustifiably beaten by two soldiers to compensate the soldiers for their trouble. The reference to Sodom in Ringelblum's entry presumably refers to the twisted justice or ethos of Sodom, whereby the Jewish man in Ringelblum's anecdote is accused of swindling for having concealed his own money from the soldier.

3 Yiddish pronunciation of the Jewish holiday Simchat Torah, which marks the end of the yearly cycle of Torah readings and the beginning of a new cycle that starts anew with Genesis.

4 Ludwig Leist, head of the German city administration.

entire family of nine during the war. He was taken 15 kilometres outside the city and left there amid peals of laughter.

Various items are being purchased en masse for Łódź, with Jews acting as brokers. When a Jew asked to keep some of his things, he was told, 'If England wins, you'll get everything back'. In many buildings, people erected sukkahs on the roofs, on the balconies, in the courtyards, etc.[5] All it took was slipping the policeman 10 złoty. Everywhere, people danced and sang as if there were no war. Thirty men were seized from the study house for labour. It is said that some converts to Christianity remain outside the ghetto. They cannot bring themselves to move here. A few individual Jews have bought themselves the right to live outside the ghetto until 1 January. There was a major commotion today after a priest gave a sermon in church and ordered the Christians from Leszno not to budge so as to keep it for the Christians. He is also said to have distributed leaflets to this effect. Naturally, the Jewish population is feeling very uneasy, since they still do not know where they can move to. Every day, old Nergep[6] goes to the office [of his company, which is] worth millions, even though he has nothing to do there. He aims to protest against the seizure of his property. The mere fact of his going there is enough to underscore his silent protest. He doesn't enter from the front, however, because he is liable to get a beating from them [the Germans] there, so he goes in through the back door. Even so, the Polish employees bid him 'good morning'.

Today, 27 October, Polish policemen were on patrol in Praga[7] and announced that any Jews still in Praga after 31 October would be shot. This caused blind panic in the city. I heard from someone who had come from Częstochowa that Jews there were arrested at work and negotiations were held concerning the amount of the bribe (300,000 zł.) they [the Germans] demanded.

Today, 28 October, a new story cropped up: part of Ciepła, where there is a police building, is to be left out of the ghetto. This has increased uncertainty, of course. It became clear today that the resettlement operation would be extended until 15 November. Doffing the hat has become a truly inescapable obligation. Anyone who fails to do so properly is ordered to march past and doff their hat. A rumour circulated today that it will be necessary to have a permit to leave the ghetto.

Today, 31 October, another piece of news: the establishment of the ghetto has officially been extended until 15 November. The following streets have also been added: Leszno, Wronia, Żelazna, Grzybowska.

A soldier came to the Community administration: he does not want to requisition the apartment until he receives an apartment for the Jewish dentist whose home he is taking. I have heard many stories about how Poles have fought with the Jews over apartments and, in addition to paying the difference in rent, have demanded compensation for moving their belongings, for renovation, etc. It appears that 70,000–80,000 Jews

5 Sukkahs are temporary tabernacles featuring natural materials traditionally erected for the Jewish Feast of Tabernacles, known as Sukkot (Yiddish: sukes).

6 This is a reference to Abraham Gepner (1872–1943), businessman; Warsaw city councillor and chairman of the Jewish Merchants' Association prior to Sept. 1939; head of the Supply Office of the Warsaw Jewish Council, 1939–1943; supported the resistance led by Jewish youth organizations, 1942–1943; murdered during the Ghetto Uprising.

7 Praga is the district of Warsaw located east of the Vistula.

have moved into the ghetto. The haste is due to what happened in Łódź last year.[8] A terrible article appeared in the *Litzmannstädter Zeitung* two days ago: 'The Jews in Łódź have thieved; we will not let them go until they return everything that they have taken. They will build the Frankfurt [an der Oder]–Łódź motorway.[9] All men, not only adult ones, but all males. And not in May, but in January. Women will also be employed in this.'

A decree was issued today that Jews who want to ride the tram must buy a permit for 5 złoty. It turns out that Leist, the District, and the Gestapo were against the ghetto in Warsaw. The Party was in favour of it and won.

Jews are forbidden to purchase new series of stamps intended for stamp collectors.

DOC. 189

On 31 October 1940 the Gestapo in Kattowitz (Katowice) requests information about the deployment of the Jewish labour force[1]

Circular no. 9 (marked 'confidential! very urgent!') from the Gestapo, State Police Head Office in Kattowitz (II B – 4126–40), signed Dr Riedel,[2] dated 31 October 1940 (copy)[3]

Re: labour deployment of the Jews in Upper Silesia.
Case file: *none*.
The Reichsführer-SS and Chief of the German Police in the Reich Ministry of the Interior has appointed SS-Oberführer and Chief of Police Schmelt[4] to register and direct the deployment of foreign labour in Upper Silesia. Under the decree to this effect,[5] sole responsibility for utilizing Jewish manpower has been assigned to the Special Commissioner of the Reichsführer-SS for the Deployment of Foreign Labour in Upper Silesia,

8 Presumably: this year. The German occupation authorities in Łódź had accelerated the ghettoization process for the Jewish population with brute force in Feb. and March 1940. Numerous people were shot or beaten to death in the process.

9 This was reported in the *Litzmannstädter Zeitung*, no. 299, 28 Oct. 1940, in an article about a speech given by Wilhelm Maul (b. 1903), the head of propaganda in the Warthegau.

1 AŻIH, 212/6, fol. 149. Copy in USHMM, RG 15 060M, reel 1. Published in *Verzeichnis der Haftstätten unter dem Reichsführer-SS (1933–1945): Konzentrationslager und deren Außenkommandos sowie andere Haftstätten unter dem Reichsführer-SS in Deutschland und deutsch besetzten Gebieten* (Arolsen: ITS, 1979), p. lvii. This document has been translated from German.

2 Dr Kurt Riedel (b. 1903), lawyer; with the State Police in Oppeln from 1936; Kriminalrat, 1937; joined the NSDAP in 1937 and the SS in 1938; deputy chief of the Gestapo head office in Katowice, August 1940 – July 1941; Kriminaldirektor at the Gestapo head office in Stettin, 1942; head of Department IV (Gestapo) under the commander of the Security Police in Warsaw, 1944; pronounced dead after the war.

3 This is a typed copy from the Jewish Representative Body in Będzin.

4 Albrecht Schmelt (1899–1945), farmer; joined the NSDAP in 1930 and the SS in 1939; chief of police in Breslau, 1934–1942; Special Commissioner of the SS for the Deployment of Foreign Labour in Upper Silesia from Oct. 1940 to March 1944; simultaneously Regierungspräsident in Oppeln from May 1941. As head of Organization Schmelt, which arranged for the deployment of Jews as forced labour in road construction and arms factories, he had at his disposal more than 50,000 workers in 177 camps; investigated for corruption in 1944.

5 This has not been found.

with offices in Sosnowitz at 6 Rathausstr. All offices and authorities are instructed to use all available means to assist with the systematic implementation of the Special Commissioner's assignment.

To obtain a quick overview of the deployment of the Jewish workforce to date, I am calling on every company that is still employing a number of male or female Jews by the hour, by the day, or on a full-time basis to send a list in triplicate to Department J of the Special Commissioner of the Reichsführer-SS for the Deployment of Foreign Labour in Upper Silesia. This list, which must be sent without delay and by 10 November 1940 at the latest, must provide the following information:

a) name and exact location of the company,
b) name, exact address of the enterprise or the trustee or the temporary administrator,
c) total number of all salaried employees and labourers (sum of ethnic German, Polish, and Jewish workers),
d) of these, the number of Jews,
e) remuneration of the Jews so far; for labourers in terms of an hourly wage, for salaried employees in terms of a monthly salary.
f) whether the remuneration has been paid directly to the Jews; if not, who received it.
g) whether the wage tax and other legal deductions have been paid for the Jewish workforce, and
h) which tax office they were paid to.
i) why no request has been made to the relevant employment office for the assignment of ethnic Germans or, if necessary, Polish workers.

The companies concerned must be informed in the strongest terms that the required reports must be complete, accurate, and submitted on time.

DOC. 190
On 1 November 1940 the Chief of the Security Police and the SD drops his earlier objections to the use of Jews for motorway construction[1]

Express letter from the Chief of the Security Police and the SD (IV A 5 b – 2136/40 g.), signed Müller, to the inspector general for German roadways,[2] Berlin, 3 Pariser Platz (received 4 November 1940), dated 1 November 1940[3]

Re: deployment of Jewish labourers on the construction of the Reich autobahn between Frankfurt a. d. Oder and the former Reich border.
Reference: your correspondence dated 7/9/11/17 October 1940 – no. 6520–326.26a – and my letter of 17 October 1940 – IV A 5 b – 2136/40 g –.[4]
After reviewing the matter once more, I have now dropped my objections to the deployment of Jews from the Warthegau for work on the Reich autobahn section between

1 BArch, R 4602/285, fol. 323. Published as a facsimile in Erhard Schütz and Eckhard Gruber, *Mythos Reichsautobahn: Bau und Inszenierung der 'Straßen des Führers' 1933–1941* (Berlin: Ch. Links, 2000), p. 85. This document has been translated from German.

Frankfurt an der Oder and the former Reich border, provided these Jews are kept separate from the other workers with regard to both their housing and their work site and provided their return to the Warthegau is guaranteed once the work is complete. I have informed the Reichsstatthalter in Reichsgau Wartheland in Posen[5] accordingly. I request that you contact him immediately concerning the allocation of the Jewish workers.

The question of the labour deployment of Jews on the other sections of the Reich autobahn currently under construction is unaffected by this.

DOC. 191

Gazeta Żydowska, 1 November 1940: article on the situation of the Jewish Community in Ostrowiec Świętokrzyski[1]

Ostrowiec Świętokrzyski[2]

A Council of Elders was formed in September 1939. The activity report for the past year includes the following information:

The *Social Welfare Section* invited to its office Jews who have volunteered to be taxed to support the Winter Relief for the poor. The proceeds from this operation amount to 66,095 złoty. Shortly thereafter, in November 1939, coal and potatoes were purchased and distributed, and financial aid was paid out. Clothing was distributed in January 1940. A lot of work went into providing the expellees who arrived in December with food and aid. During the period under review, financial aid totalling 18,209.69 złoty was paid out. The total expenditure of all social welfare sections amounts to 205,616.58 złoty.

The *Housing Section* operates very effectively, which is why a large number of resettled people have come to Ostrowiec. The section experienced considerable problems, because the authorities have demolished homes in the Jewish quarter to make room for a motorway. There are 400 homeless people, which includes 60 families. Nevertheless, the section has intensified its efforts, and the homeless have all been housed relatively well.

On 16 January of this year a big soup kitchen with six large cooking vats was set up. It serves 1,600 meals a day. A total of 215,740 meals were served during the period under review. A campaign to provide supplementary food for children was launched on 27 January of this year. Every day 360 breakfasts are served. A total of 10,055 breakfasts were served during this period.

2 Fritz Todt (1891–1942), civil engineer; joined the NSDAP in 1922 and the SA in 1931; inspector general for German roadways from 1933; Reich minister of armaments and munitions from 1940; killed in a plane crash.
3 The original contains handwritten underlining and notes, portions of which are illegible. Handwritten addition at left: 'Oberregierungsrat Dr Birkenholz. Nt 4/11.'
4 These are not included in the file.
5 Arthur Greiser.

1 *Gazeta Żydowska*, 1 Nov. 1940, p. 4. This document has been translated from Polish.
2 Ostrowiec Świętokrzyski was located south of Radom in District Radom in the General Government.

In February of this year, Ostrowiec was hit by a typhus and typhoid fever epidemic. On the instructions of the authorities, the Jewish Council opened a Hospital for Epidemic Diseases located in the synagogue building, which had been converted for this purpose. There are 4 wards for infectious diseases: typhus, typhoid fever, dysentery, and smallpox. There is also a ward for internal medicine and a maternity ward. An electrotherapy ward was set up in August of this year. The hospital has 100 beds. The number of beds was increased during the epidemic. The full-time staff includes 3 physicians, headed by the director, and 6 nurses. The total costs of maintaining and running the hospital during the period under review amounted to 80,974.67 złoty. Due to the outbreak of infectious diseases in Ostrowiec, a sanitation unit made up of 60 people was created. As of 1 October, the total costs of maintaining sanitary hygiene amount to 36,492.24 złoty.

It is worth mentioning that in a letter dated 16 May, the commissioner of Ostrowiec praised the Judenrat[3] for its efforts in combating the epidemic and expressed special recognition to the sanitation unit.

The Jewish Council has also devoted considerable energy to the question of food supplies for the Jewish population.

The Council is also involved in providing the authorities with a workforce. A total of 89,321 Jews have been sent to work during the period under review.

The broad scope of social welfare, medical care, sanitation, etc. has led to the introduction of levies. These levies are charged each quarter in advance. A system has been introduced by which the amounts levied are negotiated in advance with those scheduled to pay, and appeals are considered. During the period under review, proceeds from the levies have amounted to 182,195.40 złoty and subsidies from the Joint [JDC] to 57,500 złoty.

The Jewish Council organized a major campaign to *help Jewish workers in labour camps*. Two delegates are permanently stationed wherever camps are located, and they supply the inmates with clothes, footwear, food, and other essential aid.

DOC. 192

On 3 November 1940 the Polish government in exile's minister for social affairs promises the Jews equal status after the war[1]

Address given by the Polish government's minister for labour and social affairs, Jan Stańczyk,[2] at an event held by the Academy of Polish Jewry, London, dated 3 November 1940

Gentlemen! You have gathered here in London, far from the homeland, under extraordinary circumstances, to declare the profound attachment felt by Polish citizens of Jewish nationality to Poland, our mutual and presently very unfortunate fatherland. I

3 German in the original: 'Jewish Council'.

1 AIP, A.5/21. This document has been translated from Polish.

2 Jan Stańczyk (1886–1953), coalminer; Sejm delegate for the Polish Socialist Party (PPS), 1922–1930; secretary general of the Central Trade Union of Miners, 1925–1939; minister for labour and social affairs in the Polish government in exile, Oct. 1939 – Nov. 1944; held the same office in the communist-dominated Polish government in Warsaw, June 1945 – July 1946.

have the honour of addressing you on behalf of the Polish government. There is no doubt that all of us, regardless of nationality, creed, or political and social views, have but one desire at this time – to defeat the enemies who have invaded our country and destroyed not only the liberty, but also the prosperity of its citizens,[3] and who torment them in a barbaric manner previously unknown in the history of mankind. We all took with us from Poland images of burning cities and villages, of murdered children, women, and elderly people. We are all picturing a tortured Poland, a nation persecuted across all religious and social classes. The patches that distinguish Jews from Poles to diminish them in the eyes of the Nazi tyrants symbolize the invaders' hatred of Poland and its citizens. To us, these patches are a badge of honour. To us, they mean that we are fighting and suffering together for the ideals that are and shall remain the most noble in the hearts and minds of mankind. There is also no doubt that the root of this devastating war is totalitarianism, with its barbaric ideology of national and racial hatred. Mankind shall know no peace and enslaved nations shall not be liberated until the perpetrators of this barbaric ideology have been crushed. By fighting this ideology and its supporters, we are fighting not only for the liberation of our own fatherland, but also for the freedom of all tormented peoples and nations. In this festive moment, I do not wish to gloss over the fact that there were people in Poland as well who let themselves be seduced by the harmful slogans of totalitarianism, racism, and antisemitism. However, I wish to stress with pride that these slogans have not become the slogans of Polish society in general. They have always been alien to the Polish character. The current government strongly opposes these slogans in line with this national character and in keeping with all its declarations to date. The Polish nation has remained faithful to its most precious traditions of freedom, as conveyed by the words: 'For our freedom and yours'. We do not know how long the war will last, but I do know that a long road of bitter experience lies ahead of us, and that our people there in the homeland and the entire Polish population have experienced a period of even crueller persecution. We shall endure this ordeal, and our unfortunate nation will remain steadfast in the struggle for liberation; it will overcome any suffering inflicted upon us by our merciless enemy. I know that the enemy will be defeated and that Poland will be free. In several declarations, the president of the republic,[4] the prime minister, and the commander-in-chief, General Sikorski, have expressed the ideals which underlie the struggle for our country's liberation, as well as the principles by which we want to organize the political and social life of a liberated Poland. On behalf of the government of the republic, I wish to assure you once again, ladies and gentlemen, that nothing shall distract us from the democratic principles that guarantee equal civil, political, and social rights to every citizen of the future Poland. As Polish citizens in a liberated Poland, the Jews will have the same rights and duties as all of Polish society. They shall be able to practise their culture, religion, and traditions without hindrance. This will be guaranteed not only by the laws of the state, but also by the joint sacrifices made for its liberation and by the joint suffering endured during this most tragic period of oppression. By fighting in the Polish army alongside their Polish

3 This is a reference to the patches made of yellow cloth that Jews had to wear in parts of occupied Poland.

4 Władysław Raczkiewicz (1885–1947), president of the Polish government in exile, 1939–1947.

comrades-in-arms, the Jews – Polish citizens – have gained the inalienable right to prosperity, to happiness, and to work in peace in a liberated fatherland, which we seek through our sacrifices and suffering, and which we shall certainly attain.

DOC. 193
On 5 November 1940 the Polish underground periodical *Wiadomości Polskie* reports on the ghetto in Warsaw[1]

In our homeland. General Government.
Warsaw resettlements. The long list of many forms of German harassment that have been inflicted on a significant portion of Warsaw's population includes the issue of the ghetto. Although its establishment was announced a long time ago, the decision was repeatedly postponed, and even quite recently, on 11 October,[2] the chairman of the Jewish Community was officially informed that the matter was no longer under consideration for the time being. Hence the surprise was all the greater when, the day after this announcement, Governor Fischer's directive to establish the Warsaw ghetto was announced over the megaphones on 2 October. The Polish and Jewish populations affected by the order had only 19 days to resettle. The regulation stipulated that Jews were to vacate their apartments with only hand luggage,[3] whereas Poles were given until 31 October to move to new premises with all of their furniture. After this date, evacuations would be carried out by force. Shops and businesses were given 6 months to relocate. During the construction of the ghetto, the occupiers simultaneously established the boundaries of a 'German district' in Warsaw, from which they have not removed Poles for the time being, although they have prohibited Polish nationals who have been evicted from the Jewish quarter from moving in.

Without passing judgement on the issue of the ghetto itself, we can state that its construction at the present moment must have been planned as part of the vicious harassment of a large number of the capital's residents. The regulation affected nearly a quarter of a million people (according to official statistics, 140,000 Poles living within the boundaries of the planned ghetto and 104,000 Jews dispersed across various parts of the city),[4] forcing them to move in late autumn when everyone had already stocked up on food and heating fuel, which they were usually unable to take with them due to transport costs and difficulties. Those impoverished Poles whose access to the German district has been blocked and who are unable to find a roof over their heads anywhere else are in a particularly tragic situation. The city council's interests have also been seriously jeopardized, as it is now facing the liquidation or relocation of several businesses located within the ghetto. This is why despair spread through the affected districts when

1 *Wiadomości Polskie*, no. 32, 5 Nov. 1940, pp. 7–8. Biblioteka Narodowa, MF 47 326. This document has been translated from Polish. The news bulletin *Wiadomości Polskie* was an influential mouthpiece of the underground organization Service for Poland's Victory (SZP), which was reorganized as the Union of Armed Struggle (ZWZ) and subsequently as the Home Army (ZWZ-AK): see Doc. 72. It appeared monthly from 1939 and then biweekly between Sept. 1942 and 1944.
2 The date 11 October appears to be an error.
3 See Doc. 180, fn. 7.
4 In fact, approximately 30,000 Poles and 100,000 Jews were subject to forced resettlement.

the future boundaries of the ghetto were announced in the press on 14 October.[5] Numerous delegations travelled to Cracow to seek a revision of the boundaries or at least a postponement of the ghetto's construction until the spring. Simultaneously several people with personal influence among the occupiers undertook efforts of their own in Warsaw to exclude their property from the Jewish quarter. These did indeed lead to a few minor adjustments of the boundaries, but major changes were not expected until the delegations had returned from Cracow. Meanwhile, on 16 October the offices of the occupying authorities issued an implementing regulation to the Governor's directive which greatly exacerbated the issue of resettlement. According to this regulation, all persons who were to be resettled, both Poles and Jews, were to vacate their apartments 'like refugees', that is, with only hand luggage.[6] They were to leave the remainder of their belongings at the authorities' disposal. Even though this regulation was not publicly announced, it spread through the city like wildfire, causing downright panic among those concerned. Over a period of four days, from 16 to 19 October, the streets of the affected districts in Warsaw were clogged with all kinds of vehicles transporting furniture in all directions. Both Poles and Jews did this, despite the clear prohibition. In most cases those resettling encountered no objections from the police. On 19 October, once most of the resettlement had already been completed, the population was informed over the megaphones about a change to the ghetto's boundaries, which were reduced by nearly 30 per cent. This new regulation forces those Poles who had previously moved out of streets that have now been excluded from the ghetto to move again, and it is a particularly tragic situation for those Jews who had moved into these vacated buildings and who now, in light of the overcrowded ghetto, cannot find a roof over their heads.

Public opinion rightly sees these regulations issued by the occupying authorities, supposedly unplanned and then suddenly revised, as an attempt to temporarily distract the majority of Warsaw's population from public affairs and to preoccupy people to the point that the only thing they can think about is getting a roof over their heads. However, this is a double-edged sword, because the wave of hatred for the occupier who torments us all is simultaneously on the rise.

5 On page 1 of issue 242, 14 Oct. 1941, the Polish-language daily newspaper *Nowy Kurier Warszawski* published two further announcements made by the governor of District Warsaw, Ludwig Fischer, regarding the establishment of the ghetto and its outer perimeter.

6 The stipulation mentioned here cannot be found in Leist's 16 Oct. 1940 announcement of the establishment of a Jewish residential district in the city of Warsaw: see Doc. 180, fn. 8. The directive issued by the Governor of District Warsaw two weeks earlier had stated that Jews who were to be relocated were only permitted 'to take refugee luggage and bedding'. The deportees generally failed to adhere to this rule and instead took their home furnishings with them. In some cases Germans confiscated the furniture, or Polish landlords prevented it from being removed.

DOC. 194

On 8 November 1940 the Trustee Office for District Warsaw gives an overview of land and properties owned by the Jewish population now under compulsory administration[1]

Report from the Trustee Field Office, signature illegible,[2] seen by Schlosser,[3] for the Interior Administration Department[4] (Dr Z., received 23 November 1940), dated 8 November 1940 (carbon copy)

Activity report of the Trustee Field Office for the period 1–31 October 1940
I.
The Trustee Field Office's report for the month of October 1940 will be restricted to presenting a purely factual report, based on fixed groups of figures obtained through statistical evaluation.

At the end of the month, a total of 393 businesses were administered by a total of 296 trustees, which indicates an increase of 37 businesses and 7 trustees compared to the previous month. This number does not include the 43 mills confiscated in the course of mill registration. These are administered by a common trustee.

Of the total number of 393 businesses administered by trustees, 36 underwent mandatory audits in the reporting period. Assignments for audits of 89 businesses have been given to the auditing firms and auditors working in the General Government, while the remaining total of 268 businesses have not been audited yet. This large number of unaudited businesses is made up to a significant extent of small and very small businesses with little capital which cannot be expected to incur the expenses of an audit at present.

The following figures resulted from 32 of the total of 36 audited businesses:

The total assets amounted to 107,381,000 zloty, including (a) current assets of 37,058,000 and (b) non-current assets of 70,323,000 zloty. Added together, the balance sheet totals of these 32 businesses amount to 132,713,000 zloty.

The audit reports show that at the closing date for the last audit 15 businesses had a combined net profit of 601,366.00 zloty, while the remaining 17 businesses had a net loss of 1,660,470.00 zloty. The capital of the 32 audited firms totalled zl. 22,124,874.43. This was offset by an overall debt in the amount of zl. 17,119,282.83.

The sum of the pre-war tax debts was zl. 2,740,709.00, which was offset by post-war tax obligations amounting to zl. 71,196.00.

We are intentionally refraining from providing a critical appraisal of the figures presented above. The tasks of future reporting will be to continue to follow those companies

1 AIZ, Doc. I-151/14, fol. 52–58. Copy in YVA, MF JM 814. This document has been translated from German.

2 The head of the Trustee Field Office in District Warsaw in 1940 was the lawyer Dr Hans Ballreich.

3 Heinrich Schlosser (1876–1953), lawyer; managing director of the Linz Electricity and Tram Company, 1919–1935; head of the Department for Economic Affairs in District Warsaw from March 1940 to 1943; lived in Munich after the war.

4 The head of the Interior Administration Department in District Warsaw from Nov. 1939 to Jan. 1941 was Dr Otto Gauweiler (1910–1969), lawyer; at the local court in Neustadt an der Weinstrasse from 1926; joined the NSDAP in 1929; worked in the NSDAP administration from 1934; head of the NSDAP Reich Office from 1937; wounded on active duty in 1941; Regierungsrat in the office of the chief public prosecutor in Hamburg in April 1942; in the Munich district administration in 1944; practised law in Munich after the war.

whose balance sheet figures were the subject of special evaluation in this report, to present additional supplementary reporting results and to draw critical conclusions from them.

II.

The registration of Jewish-owned real estate has continued to make good progress. This means that important, indispensable groundwork has been done for the legal resolution of this subject, which can be anticipated to occur soon. Without this work, a swift and successful implementation of the expected legal measures would scarcely be possible given the amount of real estate owned by Jews.

In a mandatory trustee meeting on 18 October, the opportunity arose[5] to report on the necessity of our registration measures and on the problems resulting from the administration of such large assets.

The transfer of Jewish real estate to the administration of the Trustee Field Office must not be limited to mere management and utilization; rather, it automatically entails the need to address the difficult problems of the ownership of land and buildings in District Warsaw. These problems include both the extremely difficult task of reconstruction and the social significance of property ownership – especially in the city of Warsaw itself. The Trustee Field Office, which holds in trust the largest and most valuable share of the urban real estate in District Warsaw, must automatically assume a leading role in this.

When it comes to economic opportunities, it is crucially important to process the statistical data from the administration of more than 4,000 buildings. The figures for two and a half months (mid July – end of September) are now available. Even though it is still too soon to draw final conclusions from this material, which covers a relatively short period of time, it is nonetheless very enlightening in many respects.

For *September*, the figures are as follows:

the peacetime target rent amount of zl. 7,064,877
compared with revenues amounting to zl. 5,453,800,

or 77 per cent of the contractually stipulated rent. This result must be seen as altogether favourable considering current earning capacity, especially as it means an increase of 11 per cent in comparison with the month of August. Even though the result is satisfactory *at the moment*, a deficit of 23 per cent over the long term represents a serious threat to the profitability of the real estate administered by the Trustee Field Office, which we must not fail to point out. Further improvement can be expected only when the general economic situation takes a turn for the better. It is unlikely that the income balance from rent payments will be more favourable during the winter months.

The level of rent arrears, which amounted to zl. 29,216,500 as of 30 September 1940, is particularly indicative of the true economic status of the recorded real estate.

A part of these arrears was offset over the month under report by payments made by the tenants for the rental property (zl. 299,300.00), and another part was waived in view of the debtors' financial situation, provided that current obligations were met or that a reasonable remainder was paid in instalments (zl. 132,600.00). Finally, zl. 92,000 were initially written off as a loss because the sum was completely unrecoverable. This amount will increase significantly, however, once an audit of all the cases has been conducted.

In total, the rent arrears represent a sum equivalent to four months' rent; therefore, to all intents and purposes, *one-third* of the total annual rent has not been paid since the

5 Deleted here: 'for the undersigned'.

war began. It is likely that the majority of these arrears can no longer be recovered. This is all the more regrettable as there is simultaneously a *short-term debt* amounting to zl. 20,190,000. The increase in comparison with the previous month only seems like an increase, because it can be attributed to the further registration of Jewish assets.

Considering the anticipated legal arrangements, which will also address the regulation of these liabilities, instructions were given not to pay debts now that are about to be secured (with the exception of tax obligations).

It was also in the interest of preserving the value and earning capacity of the registered properties to carry out *urgently needed maintenance work* before the onset of winter. The resultant adverse consequences for certain categories of creditor had to be accepted in order to avoid the risk of considerable damage occurring or expanding if necessary repairs were not undertaken. From gross receipts amounting to 5,453,800 zloty, the following costs were paid:

1.	Salaries of property managers	zl.	778,300	i.e. 12.5 %	of total revenue
2.	Social security payments	»	69,200	» 1.1 %	»
3.	Taxes and charges	»	898,400	» 14.4 %	»
4.	Electricity, gas, water	»	590,800	» 9.5 %	»
5.	Waste water, chimney cleaning and rubbish collection	»	219,700	» 3.5 %	»
6.	Fire insurance and other insurance	»	39,200	» 0.63 %	»
7.	Mortgage interest	»	78,100	» 1.25 %	»
8.	Minor maintenance work	»	961,300	» 15.45 %	»
9.	Major maintenance work	»	399,600	» 6.45 %	»
10.	Legal expenses	»	19,500	» 0.35 %	»
11.	Other expenses	»	250,300	» 4.15 %	»
12.	Heating fuel	»	12,100	» 0.25 %	»
13.	Repayment of mortgage capital	»	54,700	» 0.85 %	»
14.	Advance payments to Aryan co-owners	»	39,000	» 0.62 %	»
In all:		»	4,410,200		

The *net income* of *zl. 1,810,025* was used as follows:

a)	the ‘temporary administrators of seized properties’ received the amount of	zl.	966,355.28
b)	a cash reserve (around zł 275 per property) was held back for the individual property managers	zl.	843,672
Together		zl.	1,810,025.82.[6]

In the month under report, as can be seen from the breakdown above, a total amount of *1,360,900 zl.* (635,900 zl. in the previous month) was disbursed for maintenance work, i.e. an average of 427 zl. (253) per property.

6 The figures given here and in the following breakdowns do not add up to the stated amounts because they are illegible in some places.

Without exception, these disbursements were paid from current receipts and exceeded the scope of normal maintenance work. One particular problem is that a great many properties yield no profit at all or such small sums, so maintenance, especially repairs of damage caused by the war, cannot be paid for from this source. Finally, there are also numerous unfinished buildings under our administration, structures that could be put in order with relatively little expenditure. A sum of *200,000 zl.* was initially earmarked within the scope of the temporary administration as a so-called compensation fund, for maintenance work and the completion of unfinished structures in order to halt the destruction of major economic assets. This amount is naturally far from sufficient for the task that falls to the Trustee Field Office, namely the preservation of valuable assets.

In many cases, only relatively small expenditures are required to make a property habitable once again, or – if the structure is incomplete – to bring it to completion.

Ways and means must absolutely be found to make the net profits from the administration of abandoned and Jewish property available for the tasks of reconstruction. The destruction of significant economic assets is to be anticipated if these efforts fail. The intention is to carry out a development programme for these properties in the foreseeable future, focusing on those in urgent need of maintenance work or completion. The properties in question are, of course, primarily those that will yield enough to repay the necessary loans within a reasonable time. This period should not exceed 2 years.

To avoid giving a false picture, however, it must be pointed out that the current surplus must be regarded as a so-called fictitious profit because the targeted net proceeds must be described as quite modest in view of the amount of the peacetime target rent and the capital value of the registered properties. Nonetheless, it will be possible to bring about a substantial improvement on the basis of these surpluses and thus an increase in profits for the registered properties if only these funds remain for this purpose.

III. *Overview*

of the position of the asset administration by trustees as of 31 October 1940.

Debit

I.	*Cash assets*	5,311.95 zl.
II.	*Bank balance*	
1.	*Emissionsbank in Polen,*[7] *Warsaw*	
a)	Account: Utilization proceeds from Jewish leather goods and footwear	215,221.13 zl.
b)	Account: Utilization proceeds from Kaftan Leather Trading Office, subsequent accounting entry	386,899.32 zl.
c)	Account: Utilization proceeds from Jewish textile warehouses	614,381.29 zl.
d)	Account: Special	3,715.18 zl.
e)	Account: Utilization proceeds from hides and pelts	44,941.58 zl.
2.	*Municipal Savings Bank, Warsaw*	
a)	Account: Proceeds from confiscated Jewish property	1,053,097.72 zl.
b)	Account: Miscellaneous	103,909.65 zl.

7 Central bank created for the General Government in 1941.

c) Account: Proceeds from management of Jewish and abandoned property	351,603.11 zl.
d) Account: Cash in transit – siphoned-off operating surpluses	52,000.00 zl.
3. *Allgemeine Kreditbank A.G., Warsaw*	
Current account: Proceeds from utilized machinery of Jewish owners	14,196.23 zl.
III. Hides Centre, Kropp	4,512.28 zl.
IV. Expense accounts	
1. Account: Bank charges	41.10 zl.
2. Account: Administration expenses	
a) for processing and finishing of leather and leather goods	12,393.95 zl.
b) for payment to textile trading company	9,611.00 zl.
c) Administrative costs	1,848.40 zl.
3. Reimbursable cash advances	9,774.40 zl.
In all	2,883,427.39 zl.

Credit

Utilization proceeds from Jewish inventories

1. Blocked accounts of Jewish leather companies (Kaftan)	zl.	231,220.62
2. Proceeds from confiscated Jewish real estate	zl.	1,134,098.97
3. Abandoned real estate	zl.	575,136.61
4. Proceeds from abandoned property	zl.	364,741.93
5. Creditors from utilized textile and footwear inventories	zl.	705,801.76
6. Creditors from utilized confiscated machinery	zl.	14,196.25
7. Miscellaneous	zl.	2,572.10
8. "	zl.	45,890.27
9. Earmarked donations and deposited bribes	zl.	7,420.00
10. Reimbursement of expenses for services	zl.	4,348.90
In all	zl.	2,883,427.39

A comparison of the closing figures as of 31 October 1940 with those for 30 September 1940 indicates an increase in capital inflow of around 1,000,000 zloty. At the same time, it must be noted that the payments into the account 'Proceeds from confiscated Jewish real estate' lag far behind the payments received from the proceeds of abandoned property. This contradicts the final report on temporary property administration to a certain extent. However, it is only an apparent contradiction, as an additional transfer in the amount of zl. 400,000 was made to the account 'Proceeds from confiscated Jewish real estate' at the beginning of this month.

Payments into the account 'Proceeds from abandoned property' resulted from the clearing of extensive inventory that was unclaimed or abandoned.

In the meantime, a sum of zl. 600,000 has been placed with the municipal savings bank in a fixed deposit account for a term of 6 months at an interest rate of 13 per cent, and 400,000 zl. for a term of 3 months at an interest rate of 14 per cent.

The bank account balances were checked at the end of October against figures supplied by the banking institutions involved and were found to be in order.

DOC. 195

On 8 November 1940 the mayor of Otwock, near Warsaw, announces the procedure for handing over homes vacated by Jews[1]

Announcement by the mayor of Otwock,[2] signed Jan Gadomski,[3] dated 8 November 1940 (poster)

Announcement

Concerning the Jewish residential district and resort to be established in Otwock in accordance with the directive by the Kreishauptmann and publicly announced on the 7th of this month,[4] I hereby inform you of the following for your careful attention:

1) *The vacated homes of the Jews* who have moved to the Jewish residential district or resort are to be *reported to the municipal administration's registration office within 24 hours.*

   The obligation to register applies to the property owner or his representative. The following information must be provided when registering: street, address, number of apartments being vacated, and number of rooms in each apartment.

2) Within the same period, the same information must be provided to the *Jewish Council (13 Kościuszkistraße)* on apartments in the Jewish residential district or resort that are vacated by Poles, *because the Jewish Council is responsible for housing the Jews in the Jewish areas as per the Kreishauptmann's directive.*

3) The property owners or their representatives must come to the municipal administration office within 24 hours to register or deregister all persons arriving and leaving. *These registrations are not subject to charge. Persons who are not registered will not receive food ration cards.*

4) Rent may be required only for one month in advance, and in accordance with the regulation issued by the Governor General on 12 April 1940 may not exceed the level or the amount as of 31 August 1939. *Violations will be deemed 'rental price-gouging'.*

5) *Unauthorized* occupancy of the vacated apartments is prohibited. The apartments may be rented or exchanged only with the approval of the building's owner.

6) I have appointed a special commission chaired by Deputy Mayor Wacław Czarnecki to implement the directive issued by the Kreishauptmann, to provide all related information, and to settle any disputes that have arisen between landlords and tenants.

1 APW, 486/132, fol. 3. Poster in German and Polish. This document has been translated from German.

2 Before the war Otwock was a popular spa and vacation destination; a large proportion of patients and visitors were Jewish.

3 Jan Gadomski was mayor of Otwock before the war and from the autumn of 1939 until at least 1942.

4 The Kreishauptmann had ordered the establishment of a 'Jewish residential district' in Otwock on 4 Nov. 1940; source as fn. 1, fol. 1. Alongside the 'Jewish residential district' established in the central part of the town, a separate ghetto was created in the former spa district in the north-eastern outskirts of the town. Jewish patients in the clinics, sanatoria, and therapeutic facilities in the former spa district were forced to remain in this 'spa district ghetto'. The Kreishauptmann was Dr Hermann Rupprecht (1905–1985), lawyer; Regierungsrat with the Alzenau Kreis administration, 1933–1939; joined the NSDAP in 1937; Kreishauptmann of Warschau-Land, Oct. 1939–Jan. 1945; captured in 1945; extradited to Poland in Nov. 1946, sentenced to lifelong imprisonment, and released to West Germany; Oberregierungsrat in the administration of the Bavarian district of Swabia after the war.

The commission's office hours are daily (except Sunday) from 2 to 4 p.m.

The commission's offices are located in the Spa Resort Administration (entrance from Hoża-Strasse) Staircase I, Room 9.

Information for the Jews will be issued by the Jewish Council.

DOC. 196
On 9 November 1940 members of the German administration in Litzmannstadt (Łódź) discuss forced labour projects for Jews[1]

Memorandum by the head of the Ghetto Administration Office in Litzmannstadt, Office 027, Senior Clerical Officer Quay,[2] dated 9 November 1940[3]

Major items of note from the meeting held at the government building in Litzmannstadt on 9 Nov. 1940, 11 a.m.
Topic of discussion: labour deployment of the Jews

Regierungsvizepräsident Dr Moser noted at the outset that by all accounts a Reich Plenipotentiary for the Deployment of Foreign Labour is to be appointed in Kattowitz.[4] The Regierungspräsident[5] ordered immediate verification with the mayor of Kattowitz by telephone. It is hoped that the initiative to appoint a new Reich Plenipotentiary will result in an accelerated start to construction work for the Reich autobahn from Litzmannstadt to Frankfurt/O., for which a huge contingent of Jews can be deployed.

According to the Regierungspräsident, the work could not be started before now because the Organization Todt was not yet able to make a sufficient number of barracks available.

Mayor Dr Marder[6] lodged a protest against the tax office's request that tax arrears be paid out of the loan granted for supporting the Jews. The Regierungspräsident shared

1 APŁ, 221/28531a, fols. 166–170. Published as a facsimile in Henry Friedlander and Sybil Milton (eds.), *Archives of the Holocaust: An International Collection of Selected Documents*, vol. 22: *Zentrale Stelle der Landesjustizverwaltungen, Ludwigsburg* (New York: Garland, 1990), pp. 98–102. This document has been translated from German.

2 Wilhelm Quay (1886–1976), administrative official; senior clerical officer in the Düsseldorf Audit Office in the 1930s; seconded to the Regierungspräsident in Kalisch in Feb. 1940; secondment transferred to Litzmannstadt in April 1941 when the seat of the district government changed from Kalisch to Litzmannstadt; returned to the municipal administration in Düsseldorf in Feb. 1945; dismissed by order of the military government in Sept. 1945; returned to office in Jan. 1947; municipal administrator in 1950; retired in 1952.

3 Besides Quay, those present included Regierungspräsident Uebelhoer; his deputy, Dr Moser; Regierungsrat Herder; Oberregierungsrat Hauke, representing the police; Kreisbauernführer (Kreis Farmers' Leader) Plaß, representing the Kreis agricultural administration; Mayor Dr Marder from the municipal administration; and Hans Biebow for the ghetto administration.

4 Himmler had appointed Albrecht Schmelt as his Special Commissioner for the Deployment of Foreign Labour on 15 Oct. 1940: see Doc. 189.

5 Friedrich Uebelhoer.

6 Dr Karl Marder (1902–1945), economist; joined the NSDAP in 1933 and the SS in 1935; Obermagistratsrat (department head) and treasurer in the municipal administration of Frankfurt an der Oder, 1933–1939; mayor of Oppeln, 1939; deputy of the acting mayor of Łódź from Nov. 1939; acting mayor of Łódź from May 1940; in the Waffen-SS from Oct. 1944.

the mayor's view and promised to clarify the matter with the central [tax] authorities in Berlin.

Mr Biebow stated that the current tasks of the Luftwaffe, the Navy, and the Army would draw on all available skilled workers among the ghetto inmates until 1 January 1941, and that no new tasks could be carried out before this date.

For the purpose of maintaining productive capacity, Regierungsvizepräsident Dr Moser suggested asking the Main Trustee Office East to have its administrators identify all machinery available in businesses that have been closed down and restricted (carpenter's benches, sewing machines, shredders, etc.), so that they can be taken to the ghetto workshops for further use. Rust removal, lubrication, assembly, and long-term maintenance of these machines and of all machines yet to be identified and already in use in the ghetto are to be performed only by Jews. The complaint about the sluggish pace of work at the Main Trustee Office East was countered by the Regierungsvizepräsident with the request that all relevant paperwork be submitted to *him personally* for forwarding.

The Jews are essentially to be deployed *only* in large-scale activities, especially as the representatives of the chief of police at the meeting, led by Oberregierungsrat Hauke, claimed that no additional supervisory officials could be made available because there is a severe shortage of personnel. It was therefore decided to establish contact with the commanders of Police Battalions 101 and 113 to reinforce the guards, but above all with the Death's Head units stationed in Litzmannstadt. The mayor and the chief of police are to reach an agreement on this issue on behalf of the district government.

Mayor Dr Marder also proposed that the following work, which has already been planned, be undertaken by the Jews:

a) Demolition of the ghetto as far as the firebreak line (this reduction in the size of the ghetto is needed also because the city hospital, which is located within the ghetto area, is to be converted into a school for midwives and will therefore no longer be available to the Jews anyway).
b) Road repair and construction as well as river regulation work. (Approximately 6,000 Jews are needed. The start of the work depends on the delivery of the barracks which were ordered as a priority a long time ago.)
c) Cleaning of the ghetto, including all repairs to streets, paths, and buildings, with consideration given to whether the demolition of buildings in the ghetto, the stacking of the resulting lumber, bricks, etc. can also be carried out by Jews without the current customary and *expensive* involvement of construction firms.
d) New construction of three pairs of semi-detached houses inside the ghetto at a total cost of 200,000 Reichsmarks.
e) Installation of perimeter lighting in the ghetto and new construction of observation towers with floodlights.

Under no circumstances are Jews to be made available to private companies. Jewish workers may be loaned only to urban municipalities and Kreis administrations to perform large-scale tasks. Mayor Dr Marder was asked to discuss with the Landräte whether it would be more expedient to concentrate the Jews from our district who have been called up for special work (in processing cloth and wood) in Litzmannstadt or to leave them in their current residences. There was unanimous agreement that the assignments for all the towns and Kreise should be run *only* through the ghetto administration in

Litzmannstadt. It was suggested to try to obtain large-scale orders for colonial uniforms as well from 1 January 1941.

Mayor Dr Marder pointed out that ethnic Germans who own buildings in the ghetto have received no mortgage interest. The view was advanced that these creditors be paid from the ghetto's funds – i.e. from the Jews' assets. The buildings' real value, not the net value, must be used as a basis when determining the compensation. This concerns around 300 cases, a list of which is to be prepared and presented *immediately* to the Main Trustee Office East by the Regierungsvizepräsident.

Mayor Dr Marder further stated that when calculating the compensation for the Jews (payment), at least 30 per cent ought to be paid to the city administration (ghetto administration) for overhead expenses (for housing the Jews, insurance, fumigation, transport, etc.). In the course of the discussion, agreement was reached on a ratio of 60:40 per cent.

With reference to the outcome of the meeting held on 24 October 1940,[7] it was emphasized again that the Jews are under 'compulsory economic management', and private companies should be entirely excluded, to protect the interests of the Reich. The Berlin company Günther Schwarz must not form an exception in this regard either. Therefore, it was suggested that the authorities in question (Luftwaffe, navy, Wehrmacht, etc.) should be requested in future to award no more contracts to private companies as long as the work can be carried out by interned Jewish workers who are a burden on the Reich.

The Regierungspräsident called for final notice to be given to the Jews, on pain of death, to hand over concealed valuables and personal effects of all kinds and also to give up Jewish assets which have been placed with ethnic Germans for safekeeping.

Additional savings and food rationing within the ghetto are to be achieved by setting up community kitchens and by feeding the Jews on a mass basis. The food is to be aligned with prison food in such a way that the working Jew receives the best type of food while the idle Jew receives the poorest type. Mayor Dr Marder was asked to have a food plan prepared immediately. This plan is to set out the various types of prison food and should be based on a medical opinion on minimum food requirements.

Mr Biebow suggested that those doing the heaviest labour should be granted extra food to keep them at full working capacity and to ensure that the three contracts are completed on schedule. The Regierungspräsident agreed to this suggestion, with the qualification that the bonus would have to be handed out and consumed at the workplace in order to prevent any abuse (passing on food to family members etc.)

The expedited introduction of the community kitchen will also save a considerable amount of coal. At the suggestion of Mayor Dr Marder, these cost-saving measures are to include removing gas pipes and light fixtures from their mountings, as these items are in short supply in the inner city, and introducing a ban on gas and electric light at certain times. It was suggested that a police regulation be issued setting 8 p.m. as the hour at which lights and heat must be turned off in the buildings in the ghetto.

7 At the urging of the deputy Regierungspräsident, it was decided at the meeting on 24 Oct. 1940 that food rations for the ghetto inmates should be significantly smaller than for average consumers, with higher rates envisaged for Jews who were working than for those who were not working: APŁ, 221/117, fols. 204–205.

To oversee the Jewish chimney sweeps, who have greatly neglected their duties so far, the services of the Polish chimney-sweep guild-master are to be enlisted. He will live in the ghetto and will be granted leave once a week to visit his family, with due regard for the sanitary regulations.

In conclusion, the Regierungspräsident appealed to those present to keep in mind the need for extreme frugality in the handling and management of the ghetto to ensure that the Reich is not burdened with any unnecessary expenses arising from the economic control and regulation of the Jews. This approach must be adopted not only by the authorities in charge but also by all contracting companies, which in the public interest should settle for simply having their general expenses reimbursed. The Regierungspräsident suggested, therefore, that contracts for the supply of the ghetto be limited to a few large companies, namely those which are willing to forego a *profit*. Any surpluses generated by Jewish labour deployment must not be used by the authorities (city and Kreis administrations) for their own purposes, but must be credited to a special account. The funds in this account will later be used for developing the Warthegau and will thus automatically benefit all administrative offices involved in handling the Jews.

DOC. 197

On 13 November 1940 the director of the Main Trustee Office East gives the Litzmannstadt (Łódź) Trustee Office permission to pay informers from the ghetto[1]

Letter from the director of the Main Trustee Office East (Wg./Schr.), signed Winkler, to the Litzmannstadt Trustee Office, 8 Strasse der 8. Armee, to Deputy I and II, lawyer Wagner[2] and Departments I and II for filing, dated 13 November 1940 (carbon copy)

Re: granting of bribes

As the lawyer Mr Wagner has informed me, Jews from the ghetto have recently been going to the police and revealing assets that have been bricked in, buried or concealed in some other way in the municipal area of Litzmannstadt outside the ghetto in exchange for bribe money. I have no objections to bribes being made available from trust property at the request of the chief of police or the head of the local criminal police for the purposes mentioned above, provided the assets uncovered in this way are taken to the Trustee Office.[3]

I have sent a copy of this letter to the chief of police.

1 BArch, R 144/345. This document has been translated from German.

2 Willi Wagner (1907–1945), commercial employee; worked for a trading company in Africa, 1929–1939; joined the NSDAP in 1934; interned by the British in Sept. 1939; extradited to Germany in Jan. 1940; worked in Department A 1 of the Litzmannstadt Trustee Office on the registration of Polish and Jewish companies, April 1940 – Jan. 1943; later served in the war; died near Poznań.

3 Following an audit of the Litzmannstadt mayor's Food and Supply Office carried out between 23 Jan. and 2 Feb. 1941, an official from the Reich Audit Office confirmed that these payments came out of the account for the ghetto's food supply and handling. See Susanne Heim and Götz Aly (eds.), *Bevölkerungsstruktur und Massenmord: Neue Dokumente zur deutschen Politik der Jahre 1938–1945* (Berlin: Rotbuch, 1991), pp. 44–73, here p. 52.

DOC. 198

On 15 November 1940 the SS special commissioner for foreign labour in Upper Silesia orders the Jewish councils to register all Jewish employees[1]

Letter from the SS special commissioner for foreign labour (log no. 111/Pr.[J.]), signed Schmelt, Sosnowitz, 6 Rathausstraße, to the head of the Councils of Elders of the Jewish Religious Communities in East Upper Silesia, Merin,[2] Sosnowitz, dated 15 November 1940 (copy)[3]

Re:
In accordance with a state police regulation, all businesses in East Upper Silesia were required to report all Jewish employees who work for them by the hour, by the day, or on a permanent basis by 10 November. From the names reported here it is evident that only some of the Jewish employees have been reported.

I am therefore imposing the following requirement on all local councils of elders through the head of the Councils of Elders of the Jewish Religious Communities in Sosnowitz:

Every council of elders must demonstrably request by 24 November 1940 that all male and female Jews living in its area who are fit for work inform it in writing by *30 Nov. 1940* whether they are employed by a commercial enterprise by the hour, by the day, or on a permanent basis. Furthermore, all Jews fit for work must be required with immediate effect to report any change in employment from one enterprise to another, any new job, and termination as a result of dismissal to the relevant council of elders within 24 hours. This registration of whether and where Jews who are fit for work are employed is to be made on a form at the local council of elders. The requisite forms are to be produced by the councils of elders. They must contain the following information:

Surname, first name, occupation (e.g. tailor, metalworker, commercial employee, etc.), date of birth, city/town, and street address of the Jew,
Name, city, and street of the enterprise in which the Jew is employed,
Nature of the employment,
Terms of employment (by the hour, by the day, or permanently),
Remarks:

The local councils of elders must first sort the report forms they receive according to the businesses in which the reporting Jews are employed. Then they must compare them with the lists that my office will give them with the names of those businesses which reported the Jews they employed as instructed. The Jewish men or women whose names appear on these lists have no further reporting requirement; instead, they will be registered with the local council of elders in a card index or on lists.

1 APK, 119/2757, fols. 12–14. This document has been translated from German.

2 Moshe Merin, also known as Moszek or Moniek Meryn (1906–1943), retailer; member of the Zionist Organization in Sosnowiec; represented the organization on the council of the Jewish Community from Jan. 1939; appointed chairman of the Jewish Council by the German occupiers in Sept. 1939; head of the Councils of Elders of the Jewish Religious Communities of East Upper Silesia in Jan. 1940; on 21 June 1943 deported to Auschwitz, where he perished.

3 The special commissioner sent the copy to Regierungspräsident Springorum in Katowice with the request that the police be deployed if Jews attempted to avoid registration. Those arrested were to be taken to the holding camp for Jews in the New Jewish School on Gleiwitzer Strasse in Sosnowiec; see Doc. 199.

All the forms for Jews whose names are not on the company lists sent by my office must be promptly taken to my office by the head of the Councils of Elders of the Jewish Religious Communities in Sosnowitz. Before delivery, these forms should be sorted according to the businesses where the Jews are employed.

Jews who are fit for work but fail to submit a reporting form as requested by the council of elders in charge must be reported to the local police. When the forms are handed out to the Jews who are fit for work, they must be informed by the local council of elders that they can expect to be arrested and taken to a penal camp if they fail to submit a form or do not submit it on time.

I am making the local councils of elders responsible for the complete registration of all male and female Jews fit for work who are employed by enterprises as set out in the regulation above, and for immediately notifying the local police of any Jews who fail to comply with the registration requirement. From 1 December 1940, councils of elders in whose regions Jews who are fit to work have been found to be employed in businesses without having registered in accordance with this directive will be dissolved and their members taken to labour camps. From 1 December 1940, the precise implementation of this directive will be overseen by representatives of my office, who will monitor the enterprises and inspect the premises of the councils of elders.

DOC. 199

On 21 November 1940 the Regierungspräsident in Kattowitz (Katowice) orders the police to enforce the registration of Jews who are fit for work[1]

Directive from the Regierungspräsident in Kattowitz (I P 1), signed Springorum,[2] to the Landräte and police chiefs, dated 21 November 1940

Regarding: deployment of foreign labour in Upper Silesia.
Reference: no case file.
In an order dated 15 November 1940, the Reichsführer-SS and Chief of the German Police's special commissioner for the deployment of foreign labour in Upper Silesia (Sosnowitz, 6 Rathausstraße, telephone 61 450)[3] required the Councils of Elders of the Jewish Religious Communities in East Upper Silesia to provide him with the names of all male and female Jews who are fit for work and employed in a business by the hour, by the day, or on a permanent basis. As per this order, the councils of elders will, by 24 November 1940 at the latest, direct all Jews who are fit for work and who live in their region to state in writing by 30 November 1940 whether they are employed by a company. In addition, all Jews able to work will be instructed by the councils of elders with immediate effect to report any change of workplace and any new or terminated employment to the council

1 APK, 119/2757, fol. 15. This document has been translated from German.
2 Walter Springorum (1892–1973), lawyer; joined the NSDAP in 1933 and the SS in 1934; Ministerialrat in the Prussian Interior Administration; Regierungspräsident in Kattowitz from Oct. 1939 to 1944; deputy Oberpräsident from August 1944; on the supervisory board of West German steel corporation Hoesch after the war.
3 The special commissioner was Albrecht Schmelt.

of elders in charge within 24 hours. In addition, the councils of elders have been instructed to report to the local police station any Jews capable of work who in spite of this demand fail to fill out and submit the reporting forms.

The implementation of this regulation issued by the Reichsführer-SS and Chief of the German Police's special commissioner requires the constant and vigorous cooperation of all local police stations.[4] In this process, I particularly request that all Jews who are reported by the councils of elders for violation of the reporting requirements be taken into custody. The Reichsführer-SS and Chief of the German Police's special commissioner is currently establishing a camp for Jews in Sosnowitz, where all Jews in violation of the reporting requirement will be taken. I request that all Jews who are arrested for violating the applicable directives from the local Jewish councils be transferred to this camp and that the special commissioner is simultaneously informed of this. The camp in Sosnowitz is located in the new Jewish school on Gleiwitzer Straße.

Based on previous experience, one must anticipate that the members of the local Jewish Councils may possibly come into conflict with the Jewish population when trying to implement the tasks assigned to them by the Reichsführer-SS and Chief of the German Police's special commissioner. I therefore request that appropriate police measures be taken to ensure that the members of the Jewish Councils, who are personally responsible for implementing the instructions given to them, are in no way hindered in their work by actions of the Jewish population.

DOC. 200

On 23 November 1940 the Jewish elder in the Litzmannstadt (Lodz) ghetto informs the Municipal Health Office about developments in the ghetto[1]

Memorandum by the Jewish elder in the Litzmannstadt ghetto (no. 2692/br/40), Rumkowski, for the Municipal Health Office, Litzmannstadt, 113 Adolf-Hitler-Straße, dated 23 November 1940

I hereby venture to submit to you in the enclosed a brief memorandum on how the ghetto has been organized until now and politely request that you kindly examine it.
Most respectfully

Memorandum

Even before the ghetto was sealed off, I imagined that it would be a cohesive single entity which would have to support itself by its own efforts and would have to conduct all its internal affairs with its own funds.

I therefore wrote a letter to the mayor in Litzmannstadt[2] in good time, namely on 5 April 1940, in which I put forward my plan for how to ensure that life could go on in the ghetto and stated that I have enough good and skilled workers from every sector at my disposal. I asked for an opportunity to organize labour in the ghetto so that the

4 See Doc. 198.

1 APŁ, 221/31866a, fols. 7–11. Copy in USHMM, RG 05 008M, reel 6. This document has been translated from German.

2 YIVO, RG 241/44; the Stadtkommissar (later mayor) in 1939/40 was Franz Schiffer.

ghetto community might be put to productive use for the authorities and the city, simultaneously ensuring the livelihood of the ghetto population. This plan was endorsed by the authorities, and I proceeded at once to regulate all aspects of life in the ghetto and to implement the labour programme. As early as 13 May 1940, immediately after the ghetto was sealed off, I informed the mayor of the number of registered tailors and needleworkers and their capabilities.[3]

Over time, despite the greatest difficulties and a lack of tools and materials, I succeeded in putting a good number of workshops and factories into operation. I would like to note that in some cases the previous owners had left these facilities in a completely ruined state and I repaired them, mostly with resources raised in the ghetto. To date I have got the enterprises listed below up and running, ensuring in that process both that they are clean and that the work is carried out in a diligent and neat manner. I placed particular value on ensuring that the army contracts are fulfilled meticulously and cleanly, and I assigned the best workers to these tasks.

The following enterprises are currently in operation:

10 tailors' workshops,
1 sewing room,
1 textile manufacturing division,
1 knitting factory,
1 hosiery department,
2 shoemakers' workshops,
1 felt-footwear division,
1 blanket production division,
1 decorators' division,
1 rubber coat factory,
1 fur processing division,
1 hat-making division,
1 tannery,
2 carpenters' divisions,
1 metalworking division,
1 scrap collection point.

In addition, the following are in preparation:

3 additional sewing rooms,
1 dye works,
1 down and feather division,
1 goldsmiths' workshop.

I am also opening several additional facilities for supplying the army. Although these companies continue to increase their production, the proceeds they generate have so far not been enough to pay for the needs of the ghetto population.

The officially authorized introduction of mark receipts enabled me to take the Reichsmarks out of circulation.

I am also continuing to appropriate raw materials, goods of all kinds, and valuables in the ghetto from those who do not offer up these items voluntarily. I have reworked them so that they can be used as a whole to cover my bills for food.

3 Message from Rumkowski dated 13 May 1940; YVA, MF JM 1159.

At the same time, I have set up a purchasing centre in my bank, where gold, silver, precious stones, furs, and other valuables are purchased without constraint. I transfer these items to the ghetto's Food and Supply Office as well.

Another source of income for me is the so-called indirect tax, which I take out of the income when my foodstuffs are sold.

With these resources, I managed to survive until October 1940 through my own efforts without any subsidies from outside. I am also trying hard to repay the loan granted to me as soon as possible. For now, I have used only part of it.

In addition to these measures I have been busy continuing my efforts to ensure public order in the ghetto and to stop the smuggling that has arisen.

Through my announcements, I have organized the internal life of the ghetto in such a way that the regulations of the authorities were implemented while, on the other hand, my labour and payment programme could be realized unhindered.

I have also put special emphasis on the preservation of public health. Various diseases, especially the dysentery epidemic, caused me great difficulties. Despite the primitive means at my disposal, I set up the hospitals, out-patient clinics, emergency response teams, etc. within a short time, and as a result of this work and my strict directives, I succeeded in getting the epidemic under control with only the relatively small number of physicians I had.

As a result of this constructive and systematic arrangement of internal affairs in the ghetto, it was possible for me to provide for those still unemployed and also for children, the sick, and the elderly.

As indicated by the enclosed announcements dealing with financial assistance, all those truly in need now receive the minimum sustenance. Last week I also started the winter drive, by which I intend to supply the whole population with the most necessary foodstuffs for the winter months (enclosure no. 3).[4]

All this and my constant efforts on behalf of my workshops and factories allowed me to raise the productivity of those enterprises substantially. Some are already working in two shifts, and now two shifts will be introduced in almost all of them.

The quality of the work and the cleanliness of the workshops have been judged flawless by all the commissions that have made inspection visits.

Production has increased week by week, and it would increase even more if the last two measures regarding food and lighting in the ghetto had not been introduced.[5] I fear that part of the productivity achieved so far might be impaired as a result.

The daily delivery of bread from the city brings in a good deal of bread that can make people ill. The officials from the warehouse administration of the ghetto's Food and Supply Office, the Gestapo, and the Municipal Health Office have also noticed this. This has led to a great many cases of gastrointestinal disease.

In addition, in some cases the bread delivered weighs less than the declared weight.

Shutting down the bakeries in the ghetto put around 1,000 people out of work, which means that approximately 4,000 people have become completely destitute as a result. That creates an additional load on my welfare budget of around 40,000 marks per

4 This is not included in the file.

5 See Doc. 196.

month. At the same time, my budget has been reduced by around 200,000 marks per month, the income from selling flour to the bakers and from baking bread.

The consequences of the reduction of bread and fat rations are even more serious.

A worker who does not get enough bread and fat is incapable of doing his work properly, and this causes production to suffer.

Even if he gets the ration allocated to him as a heavy labourer, he takes a small part of it for himself and sets aside most of it, naturally, for his family. So he stays hungry.

Given the general undernourishment, people are weakened and they are very susceptible to infectious diseases. Therefore, I most politely request that *flour* rather than bread be delivered to me, so that I can have the bread baked in the ghetto again. In addition, I politely request an increased allocation of flour and fat. With regard to lighting, I would like to request most politely that I be allowed to have the lights burning in the homes even after 8 p.m.

If this were to be granted, I would decree that electricity consumption be limited as far as possible, so that overall consumption of electricity in people's homes would increase only minimally.

DOC. 201

On 23 November 1940 the Regierungspräsident in Kattowitz (Katowice) places further restrictions on economic relations between Jews and non-Jews[1]

Police Regulation on Economic Dealings with Jews

On the basis of the Regulation by the Head of the Civil Administration in Kattowitz of 24 October 1939 on the Use of Police Force (VOBl. no. 21, 24 October 1939), the following police regulation is hereby issued for the Kreise of Bendzin, Chrzanow, and Olkusch and the town of Sosnowitz:

§ 1

I) Owners of German and Polish shops are not permitted to sell any food, alcohol, or tobacco to Jews.
II) The purchase of food, alcohol, and tobacco from Jewish shops is prohibited for persons of German ethnicity and for Poles.
III) Jews may not buy food, alcohol, or tobacco from German or Polish shops, nor may the owners of a Jewish shop provide these goods to persons of German ethnicity and Poles.

§ 2

The provisions of § 1 apply equally to wholesalers, but with the stipulation that the Jewish Wholesalers' Office for Foodstuffs and Horticultural Products for the Jewish Population in East Upper Silesia in Sosnowitz[2] is permitted to make purchases from

1 *Amts-Blatt des Regierungspräsidenten in Kattowitz*, no. 43, 30 Nov. 1940, p. 236. This document has been translated from German.

2 This organization exclusively supplied Jewish retailers and played a central role in providing food for the Jewish population. Springorum authorized it in July 1940 at the request of Moshe Merin.

all wholesalers located in the area between the police boundary and the customs boundary.[3]

§ 3

Jewish shops are to be made clearly recognizable as such from the outside.

§ 4

A fine of up to 150 Reichsmarks can be imposed for violations of these provisions. In individual cases and in the event the fine cannot be collected, coercive detention of up to six weeks can be imposed, unless a more severe penalty is permissible under other provisions.

§ 5

This regulation comes into force on 1 December 1940.
The Regierungspräsident,
signed Springorum.

DOC. 202
On 28 November 1940 the Jewish Council in Tschenstochau (Częstochowa) appeals to the Jewish population for donations[1]

Call for donations by the winter relief committee at the Council of Elders of the Jews in Tschenstochau,[2] 22 Marienallee, unsigned, dated 28 November 1940 (copy)

Appeal to the Jewish population!
Winter is just around the corner – nonetheless, thousands of Jews cannot afford a hot meal and have no appropriate clothing. Hunger and cold await us!

In view of this exceptional misery, the Jews cannot callously ignore the situation. The entire Jewish community must now make every possible effort to relieve the distress of the starving masses threatened by the cold.

A winter relief committee has been formed at the Council of Elders to assist those unfortunates. Its task must be to collect money and clothing from all Jewish citizens as quickly as possible. In the coming days, collectors delegated by the winter relief committee will be sent out into the town. They will visit the Jewish citizens and appeal to their kind hearts.

As these collectors are working in a voluntary capacity, the winter relief committee asks the Jewish inhabitants to give their visitors a friendly welcome and donate money and clothing. Every donor should remember that every penny and every article of clothing can alleviate the difficult situation of someone who has been arbitrarily afflicted!

3 The police boundary ran approximately along the border of the German Reich that had existed until 1919, while the customs boundary was further east, along the border with the General Government that had been fixed in late 1939.

1 AŻIH, 213/3, fol. 397. Copy in USHMM, RG 15 061M, reel 1. The German version was presumably prepared for the German supervisory bodies. This document has been translated from German.
2 The chairman of the Jewish Council from 16 Sept. 1939 was Leon Kopiński (1890–1943), businessman.

No sacrifice is too great! Remember that the donor is more fortunate than the one who benefits from the donation!

Help is essential! We hope this appeal will reach your hearts!

Let us translate the slogan 'Winter relief as quickly as possible' into action!

DOC. 203

On 30 November 1940 the Transfer Bureau in Warsaw informs German officials of the future organization of the ghetto's food supply[1]

Letter from the head of the Resettlement Department, signed Mohns,[2] to the District Governor's representative for the City of Warsaw, Food Supply Department (received on 4 December 1940), dated 30 November 1940[3]

Re: E 508 resettlement log no. 635/40/M/Ha.

The Transfer Bureau at the Resettlement Department for the Jewish Residential District will begin its work on 1 December 1940.[4] From that date onwards, coal and potatoes for the entire Jewish residential district will be distributed from there. The Department of Food and Agriculture will be represented at the Transfer Bureau. The chairman of the Jewish Council told me today, however, that he will not be able to set up the whole administrative apparatus for the other food ration cards including the bread ration cards by 1 December 1940. I have therefore granted him an extension of the deadline to 31 December.[5] Until then, the distribution of food for the Jewish residential district, with the exception of coal and potatoes, will remain your responsibility.

At the same time I am requesting that you send me a list of the amounts of food that can be allocated to the Jews per capita on a monthly basis. I need this information to set up the Transfer Bureau and to prepare for food delivery to the Jewish residential district from 1 January 1940 onwards.

Heil Hitler!

1 APW, 485/17, fol. 8. This document has been translated from German.

2 Otto Mohns (1895–1965), businessman; joined the NSDAP in 1937; deputy head of the Resettlement Department at the Office of the Governor of District Warsaw from 1940 to March 1941, then the office's acting head until May; simultaneously head of District Warsaw's Interior Administration Department from April; Landkommissar in Radzymin from Oct. 1941; lived in the Lauenburg district in northern West Germany after the war.

3 The original contains handwritten underlining and official stamps: 'Stadthauptmann Warsaw, no. 019 666'.

4 The Transfer Bureau regulated and controlled official economic transactions between the Warsaw ghetto and the outside world; see Doc. 252.

5 Czerniaków noted on 29 Nov. 1940: 'I went to see Mohns. The [validity of the] bread ration cards [was] extended to December.' Cited in *The Warsaw Diary of Adam Czerniakow*, p. 221.

DOC. 204
On 30 November 1940 the Polish underground paper *Placówka* calls for trade to be placed in Polish hands[1]

Let's take care of trade
Trade in our country has mainly been in foreign hands. Since time immemorial, farmers have produced grain, bred pigs and cattle, produced milk and eggs, etc., but trade in these goods has been almost completely dominated by Jews. The number of Poles engaged in trade could be counted on the fingers of one hand, and that only in recent times. Most importantly, farmers often had to sell their produce at prices below their production costs. Except for brief intervals, this has been the case for over twenty years and has taken its toll – especially under the Sanacja governments, when Jews amassed fortunes by trading in grain, poultry, dairy products, animals for slaughter, etc.

We worked and produced the goods, but foreigners got rich from them. Since no nation has ever lost anything from trade and many have only become rich thanks to it, it is unsurprising that we lost one of the most important pillars of wealth by letting trade slip from our hands. As is generally known, we are not a wealthy nation, and it is very difficult to obtain capital. The lack of free capital makes it very difficult or impossible to access credit, which is why it is very expensive. A farmer obviously cannot afford to pay high interest rates because the land produces relatively low yields. However, credit is essential to farming because irrigation, buying better machinery, or constructing solid buildings requires larger sums of ready money than a farmer will be able to get anywhere.

It is high time to put an end to this. It is high time to take care of trade, to remove it from foreign hands and take it into our own hands. We Poles produce, and therefore we should also trade in the goods we produce, regardless of whether the goods in question came from a farm or were manufactured in a factory by one of our workers. Only we are masters of our lands and our cities, not the Jewish migrants, and only we can decide how things should and will be.

Due to the lack of substantial capital, we cannot take over wholesale trade right away, but many of us can easily go into retail trade. Let's begin with market stalls, which should be completely in our hands. The cost of such a stall and its goods is considerably lower than that of a one-hectare farm. On such a farm, a farmer and his family will suffer from hunger, whereas a stall can provide its owner with a decent livelihood. With certain skills, hard work, and thrift, one can transition from a market stall to a shop, and later trade on a larger scale. In this way, we can gradually gain control of wholesale trade.

If we want our country to be wealthy, we should not forego the opportunities trade offers us. There are countries such as Switzerland that do not even have a single gold mine of their own, no petroleum, and no coal, but they are wealthy nevertheless. They owe this mostly to trade. We should also take this path. This current war might be to our advantage. Despite considerable difficulties, great opportunities in trade as well as in crafts and other small enterprises are opening up to us. There is no time to lose. Let's not allow this opportunity to pass us by. Practice makes perfect!

1 *Placówka: Organ wsi polskiej*, no. 9, 30 Nov. 1940, p. 4. Biblioteka Narodowa, MF 50 773. This article has been translated from Polish. *Placówka: Organ wsi polskiej* was a publication of the right-wing radical group Szaniec. It was published from July 1940 until at least 1 Jan. 1944 and had a circulation of 3,000 to 10,000 copies.

DOC. 205

On 3 December 1940 the head of the Councils of Elders of the Jewish Communities in East Upper Silesia asks a relief organization in Geneva for financial aid[1]

Letter from the head of the Councils of Elders of the Jewish Religious Communities in East Upper Silesia,[2] signed Czarna,[3] Sosnowitz, to the Relief Committee for the War-Stricken Jewish Population in Geneva,[4] attention of Dr A. Silberschein,[5] 247 rue de Paquis, dated 3 December 1940

In connection with your telegram regarding the needs of the Jewish population in the formerly Polish territories, we hereby inform you of the following:

The Central Office of the Jewish Religious Communities in East Upper Silesia, based in Sosnowitz, deals with the care of the Jewish population in East Upper Silesia and the Warthegau and conducts a wide range of welfare activities in that region.[6]

East Upper Silesia comprises 96 localities with a Jewish population of approximately 112,000 persons; the Warthegau comprises 66 localities and 140,000 persons.

The situation of both regions is extremely serious, and we are unable to meet the ever-growing needs of the Jewish population from our own resources.

We therefore take the liberty of most politely requesting that you kindly allocate monthly aid in the amount of 30,000 Reichsmarks for East Upper Silesia and the Warthegau.

We hope our request will meet with complete understanding on your part, and we would be extremely grateful to you for dealing with this to our benefit.

If you wish, we will be happy to provide you with detailed information about our welfare activities and our broad sanitary and preventive efforts.

Awaiting your news with great interest, we remain
with the highest esteem

1 YVA, M-20/86, fols. 145–146. This document has been translated from German.

2 Moshe Merin.

3 Fanny Czarna (1907–1943), Moshe Merin's secretary, representative, and partner; perished in Auschwitz.

4 RELICO, the Relief Committee for the War-Stricken Jewish Population, was founded in Geneva in 1939 under the leadership of Abraham Silberschein. The organization was supported by the World Jewish Congress. It arranged for the delivery of money, food, and medicine to the Jewish population in German-occupied Poland and was very active in refugee relief work.

5 Dr Abraham (also Adolf Henryk) Silberschein (1882–1951), lawyer; leading politician of the Poale Zion-Hitachduth Party in Eastern Galicia in the 1920s; member of the Sejm, 1922–1927; later co-founded the World Jewish Congress; delegate to the 21st Zionist Congress in August 1939, then founder and head of the relief organization RELICO in Geneva; published the multi-volume documentary report *Die Judenausrottung in Polen* ('The Destruction of the Jews in Poland') in Geneva in 1944/45.

6 In 1940, as the representative of the American Jewish Joint Distribution Committee (JDC), Merin also brokered funds for the Jewish communities in the Warthegau, with the exception of the Lodz ghetto.

DOC. 206

An opposition group in the Litzmannstadt (Lodz) ghetto calls on ghetto residents to join a food protest on 4 December 1940[1]

Handwritten leaflet, dated late November/early December 1940

To all who are starving:

Our unelected representatives[2] want to starve us, and we have the following proof: (1) Hundreds of people have not yet received their benefits for the 12th m[onth], which should have been paid out between 1 November and today; (2) *the potato coupons,*[3] *which could have protected us from hunger have been withdrawn.* Rations have been issued in place of coupons. This is how they squeeze the last pennies out of us so that we have nothing with which to buy bread. Potatoes will be issued when they are no longer edible. This is why we call on you to come out to the junction of Brzezińska and Młynarska on 4 December at 11 a.m. and show that we *would rather die by the sword rather than of hunger.* We urge you, especially former soldiers, to show up and join this decisive struggle. At the same time, we turn to those who were starving yesterday and are policemen today: keep in mind that the struggle forced upon us will be bloody. We will not let ourselves be starved to death. We will not let ourselves be lulled into registering for work, as nothing will come of it, and even if it does, our families will still die of hunger.

Committee for the protection of Jews from starvation

Remember that it is better to die by the sword than of hunger.

Enough of the empty promises.

DOC. 207

Warschauer Zeitung, 4 December 1940: article about the Warsaw ghetto[1]

Warsaw Jews completely left to their own devices. A drive through the Jewish residential district. Jewish Order Service introduced. Sharp practices spreading among the Jews themselves.

Report by the Krakauer and Warschauer Zeitung

gff.[2] Warsaw, 4 December

For a few days now, the Warsaw Jews are living on their own among themselves. The process of resettlement into the closed-off Jewish residential district, which can be entered only with special identity cards, has been completed. Apart from the employees

1 AŻIH, 230/143, fol. 43 (11). Copy in USHMM, RG 15 070M, reel 5. This document has been translated from Polish.

2 This is a reference to the Jewish administration.

3 Ration coupons.

1 *Warschauer Zeitung*, no. 286, 4 Dec. 1940, pp. 5–6. This document has been translated from German.

2 Robert [J.] Greiff.

and workers at the non-Jewish companies still located within the Jewish residential district, no one else enters the part of the city reserved for the Jews, where several hundred thousand Israelites now dwell. Traffic between the Jewish quarter and the other parts of the city on public transport has been specially regulated.

Jews left to themselves: anyone who has ever peeped into the Jews' streets in some godforsaken small Polish town and has taken a sniff will have no trouble imagining what things are like in Warsaw now. The drab streets are filled with teeming life, surging to and fro and giving the appearance of lively activity, so that one might assume that something substantial and significant is going on here. They run and push with packages and bundles, they shuffle, bent low, under the weight of grimy sacks, shove handcarts along, laden with unsightly rubbish, they bargain and haggle with spluttering persuasiveness in the dark doorways and along the streets in tiny, narrow shops. But behind it all is merely the much-loved 'little deal'. With one major difference now, of course: Warsaw's Jews are no longer able to cheat the goyim,[3] especially the gullible Polish small farmers, with an oily smile; they can no longer buy up goods that are in short supply and then drive up the prices to dizzying heights or do crooked black-market deals. Now they try their luck with other members of their race, only to notice before long that not much is to be gained there. But the best business seems to be the trade in armbands, to which several street vendors, embracing the boom, have applied themselves for quite some time. The armbands are available in two versions, of course, one the standard version made of fabric with the Star of Zion sewn onto it, and the other a durable version made of celluloid for those who are better off, which is washable like a rubber collar. Or is it the woman there in a hallway, exerting considerable vocal effort to tout her hairpins, buttonholes, and ribbons and, like a snake charmer, making her wares dance before her, who sells the most? That life is still sweet for the Jews even today is proven by the grimy man with a whiskery grin, holding a vendor's tray and selling candied fruits with his unwashed hands.

The Jewish Council is responsible for keeping order in the Jewish residential district. It is a sort of self-governing body for the Jewish community, and it is now forming and training its own Jewish Order Service with a strength of 1,000 men. The members of this Order Service are identified by an armband and a special cap, and as a sign of their power they carry a rubber truncheon, which they doubtless know how to use on other members of their race. They are also involved in the checks at the entry points for the Jewish residential district that are performed by German and Polish police. The Jewish Council, which naturally carries out its work under the oversight of the German authorities, will also be responsible for ensuring specific hygienic conditions in the Jewish residential district, because one of the decisive reasons for the spatial separation of the Jewish and the non-Jewish populations was the fact that the Jews, by way of the countless vermin with which they are infested, had indirectly become the carriers of dangerous contagious diseases, particularly typhus. They themselves have a certain degree of immunity to these diseases, but the danger for the rest of the population is all the greater. In addition, the Jewish Council must attend to welfare tasks, and it is allowed to impose taxes on the members of its community in order to perform them.

3 Hebrew: 'non-Jews' (*goy*, pl. *goyim*).

Also working in the field of welfare is the Jewish Social Self-Help, which is funded exclusively from Jewish assets and covers around 150,000 Jews. Its operations are also supervised by the Germans.

The favourable effect of creating the closed-off Jewish residential district can certainly be sensed by anyone who has noted, with a sigh of relief, the absence of late of the hook-nosed armband-wearers in Warsaw's streets, which were far more reminiscent of Central European standards as a result. Similar measures will be introduced everywhere in the district, as Governor Dr *Fischer* recently announced. Separate Jewish residential districts already exist in some Kreise such as Lowitsch.[4] In economic terms, the advantages will be seen only after a while, once the difficulties necessarily associated with the removal of the Jewish businesses from the Jewish residential district have been duly resolved. Then it will be possible over time to completely suppress illicit trade and price gouging, which has been the Jews' pre-eminent 'field of work' until now. This is especially significant for the implementation of the necessary measures in the food sector. Until now, these measures have been negatively affected by the economically destructive activities of the Jews. Only the thorough eradication of Jewish influence, which was especially great in District Warsaw owing to the great number of Jews converged in this city of over a million inhabitants, will clear the way for an organized, smoothly run economy.[5]

DOC. 208

On 7 December 1940 Ignacy Schwarzbart, the Jewish representative in the Polish government in exile in London, describes his discussion with the engineer Józef Podoski[1]

Diary of Ignacy Schwarzbart,[2] entry for 7 December 1940

Saturday, 7 December 1940
At work since 6 a.m. Correspondence.

At 9.30 I dictated news to Goldschmid for Ita[3] and Cajt.[4]

4 In Łowicz, the Kreis seat, Kreishauptmann Schwender set up two ghettos for Jews in the spring of 1940, isolating them from the rest of the town by erecting walls and fences. He ordered the 7,000 ghetto inmates to be deported to the Warsaw ghetto from Feb. 1941.

5 The original contains photographs by 'Bil', Mieczysław Bilażewski, photographer and actor; made documentary films about Danzig before the war; worked for the firm publishing *Warschauer und Krakauer Zeitung* from 1939; owner of Bil Photos, Warsaw, from 1941. The photographs have the following captions: (1) 'A member of the Jewish Order Service with armband, cap, and rubber truncheon.' (2) 'From left to right, our photomontage shows a Jewish coachman. Next to him, the official identifying symbol, the Star of Zion, is being sold off to fellow Jews. At the entrances to Warsaw's Jewish residential district, a check is under way. Below left, members of the Jewish Order Service assert themselves over other members of the chosen people. In the centre, the typical gesture of the woman haggling shows that business is still very good in the Jewish residential district. On the right, a column of the Jewish Order Service on the march.'

1 Ignacy Schwarzbart's diary from 1 Oct. to 27 Dec. 1940, fols. 149–151; YVA, M-2/746. This document has been translated from Polish.

From 11.30 to 1.45 meeting at the Cumberland[5] with the engineer Józef Podoski (Junosza),[6] who left Warsaw in late September. A man of average intelligence, it seems. When I asked him what party he belonged to, he replied that he was not affiliated with any party, that he had always acted humanely when it came to social matters, and that he employed Jews in his office, but he was sympathetic to nationalist ideology. I met with him on Minister Kot's suggestion so that he could inform me about the circumstances of Jews in Poland and I could brief Podoski, who is leaving for America, about the situation of Jews in America. Podoski's information generally tallied with the reports he had written for the government and with which I am familiar. I asked what he thinks Jewish–Polish relations will look like in a future Poland and whether antisemitism can be expected to disappear. To this he replied (verbatim):

> Many Poles from the intelligentsia, the bourgeoisie, and even the workers have taken over the economic positions held by Jews, as Jews have had to resign as a result of legislation or Nazi pressure. Thus, despite Polish hatred of Nazism and of the Germans as occupiers, Polish politics has achieved one of its goals – namely, a strengthened Polish bourgeoisie. Should the Jews later try to regain these positions, there will naturally be antagonism – a competition. The Polish social classes concerned are quietly pleased with this turn of events. I believe we can expect a rise in antisemitism. I think that even the left-wing parties, if they want to be applauded by their supporters, will have to adopt certain antisemitic tones, particularly given this web of economic interests.

In response to my question as to whether the Jewish population has been responsible for any incidents that would politically justify a surge in antisemitism, Mr Podoski replied:

> Not as far as the German occupation is concerned. By the way, despite their current suffering, the Jews are actually privileged vis-à-vis the Poles in certain respects. Jewish communities registered Jewish assets while the Polish assets were registered by the Germans, and more recently, secretly by the Poles themselves. As a result, the Jews will have the most detailed lists of losses and confiscations later on, while the

2 Dr Ignacy Schwarzbart (1888–1961), lawyer; chairman of the Zionist student fraternity Haschachar in Cracow in 1911; officer and military judge in the Austro-Hungarian Army during the First World War; editor-in-chief of Cracow's *Nowy Dziennik*, 1921–1925; activist for the General Zionists; Sejm delegate, 1938/1939; fled in 1939; member of the National Assembly (the parliament in exile) of the Polish Republic in London, 1940–1945; in New York from 1946; subsequently head of the organizational department of the World Jewish Congress.

3 The author is referring to the Jewish Telegraphic Agency. This news organization was founded in 1917 by Jacob Landau as the Jewish Correspondence Bureau and has borne the name Jewish Telegraphic Agency since 1919. In the 1930s it had branches in many places including Berlin, Warsaw, Jerusalem, and New York.

4 The author is referring to *Di Tsayt*, a Yiddish-language daily newspaper published by Morris Myer in London between 1913 and 1950.

5 The Cumberland was one of the hotels in London in which the Polish government in exile resided.

6 Józef Podoski (1904–1998), engineer; served in the war in Sept. 1939; subsequently fled from Soviet captivity to France and later to Britain, where he was adjutant to the commander-in-chief of the Polish Army's chief of staff; served in the war, 1944/1945; returned to Poland in 1947; sentenced to eight years in prison in 1949; rehabilitated in 1954; subsequently worked as a professor at the Warsaw University of Technology.

> Poles will not. The second privilege is that Jews are now no longer rounded up in the streets while Poles are. Jews are not deported for labour in Germany, Poles are. The ghettos were largely fiction, at least until late September.[7] The ghetto gates bore the following sign: 'Seuchengefahr',[8] so the reasons given were not racist. Only in Łódź is the ghettoization stricter. The evacuation from Cracow was insignificant, as whoever wanted to leave left. The Jews seem to have bought their freedom. The Lublin Reservation has gone quiet, from what I've heard.

In answer to my next question as to whether the experience of shared suffering will eliminate antisemitism, Mr Podoski replied: 'It certainly is doing that in individual cases.' Another question addressed whether the Jews had taken any positive steps regarding the Polish issue. Mr Podoski explained that Jews, whose businesses were to be taken over by a trustee, have on their own initiative repeatedly assured Poles that they would prefer that they [the Poles] occupy these positions, as they do not wish to complicate matters to the Poles' disadvantage. In answer to my question as to whether the Jews are part of or have been involved in the resistance, Mr Podoski replied that he does not know. When I remarked that this would be essential to the common cause, Mr Podoski declared that it would indeed be very necessary, as it would work in the Jews' favour politically.

As for the Russian occupation, Mr Podoski noted that many Poles who had returned from the Russian to the German occupation zone reported that the Jews there had happily welcomed the Bolsheviks. When I said that Poles had done the same, and that in the German zone there are people and cliques that sympathize with the Germans, Mr Podoski replied that undoubtedly there are such individuals, such as Messrs Twardowski in Cracow[9] and Bartel in Lwów,[10] and that particularly in Cracow certain Polish circles associate and even socialize with the Germans. I mentioned Zakopane's Gorals[11] and asked whether he believes that a principle of collective responsibility should be introduced, as it would also have to apply to the Poles. 'Of course,' declared Mr Podoski.

To my question about which political trend and which party enjoys the greatest support among Polish society – the Endecja, the peasants, or the PPS[12] – Mr Podoski replied that it was difficult to say, but there was no doubt that the mood was becoming somewhat more radical despite the current momentum of nationalism. According to Mr Podoski the mood among the Polish population is intriguing. The older generation is bro-

7 Most ghettos were not sealed until late Sept. 1940.

8 German in the original: 'danger of epidemic'.

9 Probably the priest Jan Twardowski, a leading member of the Polish Central Welfare Council (RGO) in Cracow.

10 Kazimierz Bartel (1882–1941), mathematician; Sejm delegate, 1922–1930; repeatedly prime minister of the various Sanacja governments, 1926–1930; vice chancellor of Lwów Polytechnic National University from 1930; senator from 1937; professor at Lwów Technical University, 1939–1941; refused to join the Supreme Soviet of the Soviet Union in 1940; shot dead by the German police in July 1941.

11 Schwarzbart is referring to the fact that parts of the Goral ethnic group from Poland's mountainous southern border region collaborated with the Germans.

12 Polish Socialist Party (PPS).

ken in spirit, but the young generation is determined. Should the right moment arrive, most likely not a single German will be left standing.

To my question as to whether the antagonism is directed against the Germans to the same degree as it is against the Russians, Mr Podoski replied that among the young generation it certainly is, although in his opinion all the animosity should be directed at the Germans.

Mr Podoski spoke of corrupt Germans, of the fact that their plans span many years, and said that urban planning and the electrification of the country had been planned on a large scale, but the implementation of these plans was quite chaotic. Despite the ban, any amount can be withdrawn from the PKO (Polish Savings Bank) as long as a bribe of 25 per cent is paid.

Overall, Mr Podoski painted a gloomy picture as far as the Jews are concerned, and it already seems necessary to petition the government to implement appropriate measures.

I discussed many other issues with Mr Podoski: the Ukrainian question and Poland's stance towards the government, in response to which Mr Podoski clearly stressed Sosnkowski's authority[13] over Sikorski's. In general, Mr Podoski related the information very calmly and factually, without betraying his own stance or proclivities. In any case, the informant's average intelligence did not appeal to me enough to want his opinion. Nevertheless, the examples of 'privileged Jews' sufficiently illustrated the degree to which the political lens of an average Pole has twisted reality. The way in which Mr Podoski predicted a rise in antisemitism indicated that there is a degree of satisfaction in Poland that something has been achieved, at least in matters pertaining to the Jewish question, in the course of this terrible catastrophe. In the end Mr Podoski asked me for letters of recommendation addressed to Jewish individuals in America, where he wants to hold talks with all the groups.[14] If Mr Podoski's is a typical example of the mood, then it seems that the Polish psyche – in terms of attitudes towards the Jews – has not changed much.

So, will not my task therefore be a Sisyphean one?

I walked through the streets of war-torn London, brightened by the winter sun and bustling with pre-Christmas activity, and returned home in low spirits.[15]

13 Kazimierz Sosnkowski (1885–1969), diplomat and military commander; joined the PPS in 1904; studied at Lwów Polytechnic from 1907; chief of staff of the 1st Brigade of the Polish Legions during the First World War; arrested and imprisoned in Magdeburg, 1917–1918; minister of defence from August 1918; minister of military affairs, 1920–1923; Polish representative to the League of Nations in 1925; commander of the VII Corps District from 1925; successor of the Polish president in exile, 1939; resigned from the Polish government in exile, 1941; commander-in-chief of the Polish Home Army, 1943–1944; after the war emigrated to Canada, where he lived until his death.

14 On 11 Dec. 1940 Schwarzbart gave letters of recommendation addressed to Arieh Tartakower, Jakub Appenszlak, and Chaim (Henryk) Szoszkies to Podoski: see Ignacy Schwarzbart's diary from 1 Oct. to 27 Dec. 1940, fol. 154; YVA, M-2/746.

15 Schwarzbart subsequently described discussions he had on the same day with other Polish-Jewish interlocutors.

DOC. 209

On 10 December 1940 a welfare official in Busko reports on the arrival in Chmielnik Kielecki of Jews expelled from Radom[1]

Report by Busko[2] welfare official Stefan Sobociński, dated 10 December 1940

Report on the arrival and distribution of the transports of Jews from Radom.[3]

1) By order of Department III of the Kreishauptmann's office in Busko, I went to Chmielnik on 4 December 1940. After my arrival, I inspected the places used for meals and housing. I found everything prepared.

   The kitchen is clean and properly equipped. Three large cauldrons have been installed, with a smaller cooking range, a storeroom for the food, a room for washing dishes, a dining room, and an office. The hot meal was adequately prepared and 200 grams of bread provided per capita.

   The arrivals were lodged in 20 dormitory buildings, which have been provided with plenty of straw. The various dormitories held between 10 and 40 persons. There were 60, 70, 100, and 125 persons housed in 4 larger rooms.

2) At 7.15 p.m. the first train arrived on the siding by the new school. The gendarmerie and the police were on hand. The carts for baggage transport were made available by the town of Chmielnik. The Council of Elders in Chmielnik assembled the Jewish youth, who were given numbers and then escorted to their allocated quarters in their assigned groups. Children and the infirm were taken on carts. The train was unloaded in around 45 minutes and pulled back. In the meantime, the second train arrived. After the people still remaining from the first train had been taken away, the second train was cleared in the same order, and the people were taken to their assigned places.

   Meals were served, some in the kitchen and others in the lodgings.

3) The transport to the designated villages took place on 5 December 1940. At 8 a.m. the carts arrived at the little market in Chmielnik. Loading and transport began at 10.30 a.m. and lasted until around 3 p.m.

   On 5 December of this year, the following villages were scheduled to take charge of the persons concerned: Wiślica, 150 persons; Szydłów, 100; Kurozwęki, 50; and Nowy Korczyn, 250.

   Because six of the families scheduled for Nowy Korczyn were kept back for various reasons, and because everyone lay low just so that they could stay in Chmielnik, it was not possible to add to the group, and only 223 persons departed for Nowy Korczyn.

   The Council of Elders in Chmielnik[4] was instructed that when those remaining behind were rounded up, the missing persons had to be sent on without fail to the villages as scheduled.

1 AIPN, GK 639/37a, fol. 23r–v. Copy in USHMM, RG 15 022M, reel 9. This document has been translated from German.

2 Busko was in the south of District Radom in the General Government.

3 In late autumn 1940 the German authorities in Radom had forced 2,000 local Jews out of the city: *Gazeta Żydowska*, no. 42, 13 Dec. 1940, p. 4.

4) The second transport was delayed en route on 5 December 1940 and could not be sent on from Kielce until 5.36 p.m., so it did not arrive in Chmielnik until 12 a.m. (midnight). Unloading the train and housing the people proceeded quickly and without incident.

The 150 persons scheduled to go to the village of Pacanów, who were supposed to continue on without getting off the train in Chmielnik, had to remain in Chmielnik, and the dormitories were more crowded as a result.

The official in charge of the convoy said he had been ordered to take the entire transport to Chmielnik, and nothing could be done about that.

After I informed the Kreishauptmann's office in Busko of this incident, the municipality of Pacanów was charged with sending carts to fetch the group on 7 December of this year, early in the morning.

As I learned from a long-distance call with the Council of Elders in Chmielnik, only 78 persons, rather than 150, were transported to Pacanów. I was able to see that here for myself when a meal was provided for the transport by the Jewish Religious Community in Busko. The transports to Wiślica, Nowy Korczyn, Stopnica, and Oleśnica were also provided with food on their way through Busko.

5) In general, the handover and distribution of the transports was carried out smoothly and without incident. This was greatly helped along by the Council of Elders in Chmielnik, which carried out the measures and instructions of the Kreishauptmann's office and organized everything in an exemplary manner. Apart from minor illnesses, attributable to the long journey and the weather, there is nothing in particular to mention.

6) The one thing that might be worth noting is the impression made by the evacuees inflicted on the Kreis. There is an element consisting of the destitute and the wretched, criminals and street prostitutes, dirty and in rags and tatters. It would not be too much to say that they are scum, and that one could hardly find much worse. From what was experienced and observed on the spot, it can be very clearly foreseen that this element, distributed among the population of the Kreis, will be a great obstacle to the efforts of the administration to improve public safety and the health care system.

It would therefore be in the interest of the general public to prevent such events from being repeated in the future. Because if an epidemic breaks out, which must be feared, the whole population of the Kreis, including the Germans, is at risk.

Addendum: It has subsequently been reported from Chmielnik that a pregnant woman has been transferred to the hospital in Stopnica.[5]

4 The chairman of the Jewish Council from a few weeks after the German invasion was Abraham Langwald.

5 The whole report by the Busko welfare officer was probably the basis for a report in *Gazeta Żydowska* (no. 4, 14 Jan. 1941, p. 7) on the Jewish Community in Chmielnik Kielecki.

DOC. 210

On 11 December 1940 rabbis in Cracow ask the Governor of District Cracow to relax the rules for the deportation of the Jews[1]

Letter from the rabbinate in Cracow to the Governor of District Cracow, Dr Wächter, signed Sch. Rappaport,[2] Fraenkel,[3] and Kornitzer,[4] dated 11 December 1940 (copy)

To the Honourable Governor of District Cracow, Dr Wächter,
Re: resettlement of Jews from Cracow
Permit us to submit the following respectful and most humble request in the matter of the resettlement of the Jews from Cracow, which is currently being implemented:

A directive was issued in May of this year which requires a considerable part of the Jews residing in Cracow to leave the city. The Jews who left Cracow by 15 August 1940 were allowed to choose their future place of residence for themselves and to take their personal belongings with them. At the same time, the authorities in charge told the Jews who wanted to remain in Cracow and were prepared to comply with certain directives that they might submit written requests to this effect, detailing the reasons for staying behind. An office for the resettlement of Jews was set up at the office of the General Government's Population and Welfare Division to evaluate the aforementioned requests.

The Jews have complied with the directive mentioned above: a large part left the city of Cracow, and the rest submitted applications to the aforementioned office seeking exemption from the compulsory resettlement. Most of these applications were dealt with favourably by the Governor General's Office, Interior Administration Department, Jewish Resettlement Section, in that most of the petitioners received identity cards exempting them from resettlement. In some cases, these applications were denied, with instructions given to leave Cracow by a certain date. The individuals in question abided by these instructions fully and completely.

Now a directive has been issued in the matter of the resettlement of the Jews from Cracow that requires that the documents granting exemption from resettlement are reviewed. For this purpose, questionnaires along with supplements were handed in. On the basis of these reconsiderations, thousands of Jews received resettlement orders, but with this difference: they are no longer allowed to choose their future place of residence themselves, and the worldly goods they are allowed to take are limited to 25 kg of hand baggage per person. Among those affected by this resettlement mandate are, naturally, small children, infants, pregnant women, the sick, the elderly, indeed 80-year-olds and some even more advanced in age. And now, in the midst of winter. We hardly need to

1 YVA, O-6/298, fols. 2–4. Copy from the Cracow department of the Jewish Historical Institute, dating from the immediate post-war period. This document has been translated from German.
2 Szabtaj (Schabtaj, Szabse) Rappaport (1884–1941/42), rabbi in Cracow; murdered in Auschwitz.
3 Simcha Alter Fraenkel-Teumim (1870–1942), chief rabbi in Krakau-Podgórze and Skawina; worked at the Cracow Jewish Community in a relief organization for displaced persons; died of an illness in Nov. 1942.
4 Schmelke Kornitzer (1905–1942?), rabbi; in Cracow from 1925; on the Jewish Community's executive body from 1933 and became its chairman in 1935; fled to Lublin and Warsaw in 1939; returned to Cracow in 1940; arrested with Rabbi Rappaport and deported to Auschwitz, where he is thought to have been murdered in 1942.

emphasize how gravely these people were affected. It is not enough that they have to leave their home, in most cases their birthplace; in addition, there is no way for them to choose their own place of residence for the future, perhaps with relatives or acquaintances. The hand baggage limit of 25 kg per person is far from sufficient. Children, invalids, pregnant women, and the elderly urgently need something to sleep on. Household goods, such as cooking utensils and laundry supplies, are absolutely essential for a family. These items are *indispensable for reasons of hygiene alone.* Even these most urgently needed items weigh more than 25 kg per person. The same importance must be attached to bedding, without which our children are at risk of freezing to death in the low temperatures prevailing in this country.

Furthermore, those affected are not aware of any contravention of the directive of the worthy authorities. These people have satisfied the directive with respect to submission of a request to remain. They acted in good faith, believing that they were complying with instructions from higher authorities, and when they were put in the fortunate position of possessing a document signed by the Cracow Stadthauptmann[5] entitling them to remain in Cracow, they were all firmly convinced that the fact of their remaining in Cracow – with the identity cards in their pockets – could not be seen by anyone as disloyal behaviour.

We as the religious leaders of the Jewish Community in Cracow, to whom the spiritual well-being of the Jews in Cracow was entrusted, can only entreat you most humbly, Noble Sir, to be gracious enough to give consideration to the misery of the Jews affected by resettlement. We know, Noble Sir, that your attention is too engaged by the multitude of official duties to have time left to give consideration to us as well. But this has to do with human lives, the lives of thousands.

We venture to request most humbly and respectfully, Noble Sir, that you will be gracious enough to arrange for those subject to resettlement to be given an extended deadline, as more time is needed to liquidate their present businesses. Further, we ask you to arrange for them to be allowed to take with them all the items they need, including household goods and, for craftsmen, tools and machines, and to be issued passes authorizing them to travel by train, so that they can choose their future place of residence themselves and go to relatives and acquaintances living far from Cracow who will make their hard lot an easier one.

It would do us the greatest honour, Noble Sir, if you would be gracious enough to grant us a personal audience.

With the greatest esteem!

5 Carl Gottlob Schmid.

DOC. 211

On 12 December 1940 the Governor of District Warsaw calls for the death penalty for leaving the ghetto without permission[1]

Letter from the Governor of District Warsaw, signed Dr Fischer, to Governor General Frank, Cracow (received by the office of the Governor General on 16 December 1940 and by the Interior Administration Department on 17 December 1940), dated 12 December 1940[2]

Re: penal provisions for the Regulation on Restrictions of Movement
The formation of the ghetto in Warsaw has made it absolutely essential to create adequate penal provisions for violations of the ghetto rules. Under the current rules, punishment is permissible only on the basis of individual directives, which can involve penalties only in accordance with administrative proceedings, i.e. only fines of up to 1,000 zloty and up to 3 months in prison if the fine cannot be collected.[3] These penalties can by no means meet the need to point out most emphatically to the Jews and especially to those in the Warsaw ghetto that the rules must be obeyed. Only the harshest punishments, including the death penalty in particular, guarantee success in this respect.

In order to prevent any movement by Jews outside the Jewish residential district without authorization now and in the future, I request that a first implementing regulation for the Regulation on Restrictions of Movement in the General Government of 13 September 1940 is issued in line with the enclosed draft.

Heil Hitler!

2 enclosures[4]

Enclosure I
First Implementing Regulation for the Regulation of the Governor General on Restrictions of Movement in the General Government of 13 September 1940 (VBl. GG. I, p. 288)[5]

§ 1

Jews who act in contravention of §§ 1 and 2 of the Regulation on Restrictions of Movement in the General Government will be sentenced to penal servitude or in especially serious cases to death.

§ 2

This regulation comes into force on 1 January 1941.[6]

1 BArch, R 52 II/251, fols. 48–49. This document has been translated from German.
2 The original contains handwritten annotations and underlining.
3 See Doc. 180, fn. 9.
4 The second enclosure contains a short explanatory statement in which the essentials of the proposal letter are repeated.
5 *VOBl-GG* 1940 I, no. 55, 20 Sept. 1940, p. 288.
6 The request for harsher punishments was subsequently repeated several times and then implemented in the form of the Third Regulation on Restrictions of Movement of 15 Oct. 1941. It threatened 'Jews who leave their assigned residential district without authorization' with the death penalty: *VOBl-GG* 1941, no. 99, 25 Oct. 1941, p. 595. See PMJ 9/13.

DOC. 212

In the autumn of 1940 a baptized woman of Jewish descent living in Warsaw is denounced[1]

Anonymous letter to the German occupying authorities, autumn 1940

Very Important!
Felicja Schwarcberg, Jewess, together with sister applicant, living at 31 Koszykowa str., apt. 5, had themselves baptized 3 weeks ago and forged paper that baptism was before 1 June 1939 for 600 zl. Recently they also made adjustment in the record books.

In their possession they have a typewriter working together with a secret organization that operates wrong policy against the Greater Reich Germany, publishing false printed news, spreading to their confidants. As loyal citizen, I inform Supreme Power, for investigation of this above and stopping this activity.

The above-named are harmful for society.

Felicja, after baptism Aleksandra, always went without shameband,[2] for better working in the Polish organization. Three weeks ago 'Aleksandra' paid 525 zl in Gestapo for not wearing shameband.

For better going unnoticed the sister has rented room to a Reich German for office, so that activity runs in best order.

I also noted that the same have already rented a second apartment at 59a Złota Street, and already transferred some small things, for example coal etc. All the remarks are stated in full correctness.

DOC. 213

On 29 December 1940 the underground newspaper *Barykada Wolności* publishes two reports on conditions in the Warsaw ghetto[1]

On the other side of the walls (Two reports from the 'ghetto')

Life in the district which the Germans call the Jewish quarter and the people of Warsaw call the ghetto – a name originating from the darkest Middle Ages – is characterized by a historically unprecedented barbarity. Our comrades in the ghetto have sent us two reports depicting the appalling living conditions of the Jewish population, particularly of those most impoverished.

1 AIPN, GK 106/161 (703/31, CA MSW 684), vol. 1, fol. 83. On the process by which this and other denunciations were initially intercepted by the Polish underground and only subsequently came into the hands of the Security Police, see Doc. 161, fn. 1. This document has been translated from the faulty German of the original.

2 Armband with a Star of David.

1 *Barykada Wolności*, 29 Dec. 1940, p. 4; Biblioteka Narodowa, MF 57 715. This article has been translated from Polish. *Barykada Wolności* was an underground newspaper that appeared in Warsaw from April 1940. It was published by a left-wing socialist group of the same name, which had broken away from the social democratic majority of the Polish Socialist Party (PPS) in autumn 1939 and joined forces with other circles to form the Polish Socialists in Sept. 1941. In May 1942 the newspaper was incorporated into the fortnightly periodical *Robotnik: Dwutygodnik Polityczny Polskich Socjalistów.*

First Report

Population density: Approximately 450,000 people currently live in the Jewish quarter. There are approximately 80,000 rooms used as habitation. The average density is almost 6 people to a room.

Ghetto without bread: The Jewish quarter was not supplied with bread rations for a few days. The Germans prevented the flour allocation from being delivered by denying Jewish carriage drivers permission to enter the quarter. Permits were only issued a week later, but this did not change the fact that the Jewish population had to go without bread for a week.

Closure of pharmacies: The pharmacies in the Jewish quarter were closed for several days because their Aryan employees (there are no Jewish employees) were denied entry to the Jewish quarter.

Evacuation of Czyste hospital:[2] The occupiers have ordered that the Jewish hospital be transferred to the Jewish quarter. The hospital will be divided into two parts. One part will be housed at the school for the Merchants' Association, and the other part at the Tax Officials' Hospital.[3] Only the latter has the proper facilities; the school building does not meet hospital standards at all.

Looting continues in the Jewish quarter: Leszno and Ogrodowa streets were looted most recently. Furniture, warm clothing, and even food was stolen from apartments. Moreover, despite the ban on entering the ghetto, many German 'knights' are carrying out 'confiscations' on their own initiative.

In addition to the above, the despicable attitude of the Jewish and Polish bourgeoisie towards 'ghetto' affairs is also worth mentioning.

On one side of the wall, the Jewish Community, led by the so-called 'intelligentsia', has become a place for haggling over 'positions' and 'petty deals', while on the other side, efforts are still being made to whittle down the size of the 'Jewish quarter' even further.

Father Godlewski,[4] for example, keeps trying to exclude Grzybowski Square, as well as Próżna and Bagno streets. Recently the owner of the bakery at 31 Sienna Street, Bernatowicz, 'threatened' the entire section of Sienna from Sosnowa to Wielka.

Second Report

At the guard posts at the entrance to the ghetto, three people – two men and one woman – were shot dead trying to smuggle in bread from the Aryan side. The woman was killed in the following way: she was permitted to go past the guard post and was shot dead only once she had walked a few dozen metres further.

2 In 1939 Dr Kurt Schrempf, who headed the German municipal health office in Warsaw, had designated Czyste Hospital at 17 Dworska Street as the only hospital for the Jewish Community.

3 The Tax Officials' Hospital (Szpital Skarbowców) was one of the makeshift hospitals founded immediately after the war broke out. The name refers to its location in the building at 1 Leszno Street, which belonged to the tax authorities. It later housed the Czyste hospital surgical ward and was then used for typhoid patients.

4 Marceli Godlewski (1865–1945); served as a priest for Catholic ghetto residents at the church on Grzybowski Square in the ghetto until 1943; politically aligned with the National Democracy (Endecja) movement.

Elsewhere, the guards allowed a group of women and children to pass through to Kercelak Square[5] only to brutally beat them when they were on their way back with the bread and potatoes they had bought.

At the Jewish cemetery, the gendarmes caught two men smuggling bread and ordered the Jewish policemen who were on duty there to bury them up to their necks in soil. They asked them if they were still alive, and when they replied in the affirmative – they ordered that they be buried up to their nostrils. They were only dug out when one of them started bleeding from the nose.

It is reprehensible that Polish boys gather around some of the guard posts and ask the Germans to rob Jewish pedestrians of their groceries. They then share the stolen bread and meat among themselves. The older Polish generation should keep a watchful eye on these children for is this not the treacherous seed of Nazi education, which seeks to enlist unattended Polish children into its pernicious service?

Prices have risen by 20–30 per cent on average, as foodstuffs are not allowed into the ghetto. Meat and bread prices have risen by 60–80 per cent. Of course, this hits the poor hardest.

The housing situation remains desperate. Thanks to special protection, big apartments stand almost empty (after all, they belong to wealthy people). The smaller apartments are alarmingly overcrowded – up to 20 people per room.

Labour camps are being dissolved and successive groups of workers who have been released are sent here. The 'healthy' ones come on foot, in rags, while the sick come in carts, almost naked. According to preliminary estimates, the death rate in the labour camps amounted to 10 per cent; 4 per cent were shot dead, and the rest died of contagious diseases. There were eight deaths from frostbite.

In the wake of all this sombre news, picture the cynicism of the following scene: at the corner of Leszno and Żelazna, the German gendarmerie arranged some amusement for themselves. Jewish male and female passers-by were ordered to dance to music played by a street band. They were surrounded by the Jewish Order Service as well as the Polish and German police. The whole scene was filmed to document the cheerful mood prevailing in the ghetto. This happened on 7 December.[6]

5 See Doc. 90, fn. 9.
6 See Doc. 232.

DOC. 214

On 31 December 1940 the Jewish Social Self-Help comments on the exclusion of the Jewish population from social insurance[1]

Letter from the JSS executive committee (no. 1589 T/B.), unsigned, to the government of the GG, Interior Administration Department, Population and Welfare Division, dated 31 December 1940

Re: social insurance and pension recipients

I.

In accordance with the provisions of Polish law, which with some changes remains applicable in the territory of the General Government, workers must be signed up for social insurance by their employers. Social insurance provides three types of insurance, specifically:

(a) retirement insurance and unemployment insurance,
(b) health insurance,
(c) accident insurance.

The insurance premiums are calculated separately for each type of insurance listed above, and the insurance payments for the insured workers are also regulated separately for each insurance under (a), (b), and (c). Insofar as Jewish workers are concerned, the Second Regulation on Social Insurance in the General Government of 7 March 1940 (GG P 1940 I., p. 92)[2] has created an exceptional situation. The regulation cited has left in force the requirement for the Jews to pay all insurance contributions, without exception, from now on. At the same time, however, it has deprived them of the right to claim payments, with the exception of specific types of medical treatment. Recently, however, the majority of the Jews have even lost access to the medical benefits paid for by the social insurance funds. That is because non-Jewish physicians have been prohibited from treating Jews, while the vast majority of the social insurance funds employ no Jewish physicians, who are the only ones authorized to provide medical care to Jews. In particular, the Jews were excluded from obtaining unemployment assistance under the Regulation on the Guarantee of Unemployment Assistance of 16 December 1939 (GG P I, p. 226),[3] and the corresponding provision was retained in the currently applicable Regulation on the Guarantee of Unemployment Assistance of 9 November 1940 (GG P I, p. 329).[4]

Given this state of affairs, social insurance for the Jews has lost the essential features of insurance and has been transformed into additional taxation of the Jews, which weighs especially heavily on the working classes among the Jewish population.

The Jewish workers affected, who have lost all benefits provided by the social insurance funds, are appealing in huge numbers to the Jewish welfare and social service institutions, which lodged complaints in this matter with the Interior Administration Department's Population and Welfare Division during the first few months of this year.

1 YVA, O-21/16/2, fols. 72–73. This document has been translated from German.
2 *VOBl-GG* 1940 I, no. 18, 13 March 1940, pp. 92–95. The legal entitlement to social insurance benefits was hereby abolished. On the basis of § 8, medical treatment and assistance was all that could still be provided to the Jewish population.
3 *VOBl-GG* 1939, no. 13, 21 Dec. 1939, pp. 226–228.
4 *VOBl-GG* 1940 I, no. 64, 20 Nov. 1940, pp. 329–337.

In this connection, the Governor General's Office, Interior Administration Department, Population and Welfare Division, in a letter dated 2 April 1940, no. 2243/40,[5] has informed the head of the Jewish Social Self-Help in Warsaw that payments of social insurance benefits to Jews cannot be made at this time. Should there be a substantial improvement in the financial situation of the social insurance funds in the near future, resumption of payments of social insurance benefits to Jews can be anticipated. A letter containing the same information, reference no. 2244/40, was sent to the chairman of the Jewish Community in Warsaw on the same day.[6]

It is only the Jews who have so far not had their right to receive financial benefits from the social insurance funds restored, while the cited regulation of 9 November 1940 has again established the exclusion of the Jews from these benefits.

II.

Special treatment is required in the matter of those Jews who acquired rights to retirement pay and pensions from the social insurance funds before 1 September 1939. These are persons either who were awarded pensions and retirement pay because they had reached the age of 65 or lost the ability to work, or who were widows and orphans of deceased insured workers. Most of these people have no other livelihood or are incapable of working. The fact that they have been deprived of pensions and retirement pay has left them in a situation with no way out. Therefore, the Jewish Social Self-Help's executive committee ventures to approach the esteemed authorities of the General Government with the polite request that the right of all Jews to annuities and retirement pay that they acquired before the outbreak of war be reinstated in accordance with the same principles now applicable to the Poles.

Apart from persons awarded the right to pensions or retirement pay by the social insurance funds before the war, there are a number of Jews in the territory of the General Government who actually acquired the right to pensions and retirement pay before the war but did not receive any notification to that effect from the social insurance funds, as their cases had not been processed before the war began. All these cases involving Jews were suspended and those affected were informed that they should turn to the Jewish social service institutions in case of need. These institutions, however, struggle constantly with financial difficulties and are unable to meet the needs of pensioners or the needs of workers who are unable to work.

The same is true of the Jews who have lost their pensions and retirement pay due to the Regulation on the Provisional Arrangement of Benefit Payments to Pension Recipients of the Former Polish State and the Polish Self-Governing Bodies of 9 December 1939 (GG P I, p. 206)[7] and the Regulation on Benefits for Military Pension Recipients of the Former Polish State and Their Families of 20 December 1939 (GG P 1940 I, p. 1).[8]

Exactly like the retirees and pension recipients mentioned above, these are mostly people who are unable to work because of infirmity or advanced age, and it would only

5 This is not included in the file.
6 This is not included in the file.
7 *VOBl-GG* 1939, no. 12, 21 Dec. 1939, pp. 206–208. § 1 (4) states: 'Jews do not receive these benefits.'
8 *VOBl-GG* 1940 I, no. 1, 15 Jan. 1940, pp. 1–3. Under § 5, the Jewish population was also excluded from receiving these benefits.

be right and proper as well as a great benefit to them if their right to draw pensions and retirement pay were restored.

We have put together a list of the various recipients and applicants for retirement pay, pensions, and annuities based on enquiries made with the Jewish Communities in the General Government, and we venture to enclose this compilation.[9] We can provide original letters confirming this information at any time.

DOC. 215
Polish neighbours denounce Mr and Mrs Kowalewski as Jews[1]

Anonymous letter to the Criminal Police in Warsaw from late 1940 or early 1941

Are you aware that the owners of the building at 6 Czarneckiego Street,[2] the Kowalewskis, are not Aryans, and yet they are still not living in the ghetto? Mrs Luba Kowalewska is most definitely a Jew, we know her from Russia, and there is no explanation for this. Not only has she not joined her fellow Jews, but she lives here in the city and, like her husband, curses everything German. For example, they said that they would beat up Hitler and rip him to shreds, and murder any Germans they encounter. They call all the Gestapo men thieves, yet they have forgotten with whose money they got rich and thanks to whose money they now own houses. Isn't this perhaps also the result of theft, and from whom?

The poorest of the poor have been robbed by the Kowalewskis and their accomplices. They arrived from Russia with nothing, so where did these sudden riches come from? Their larders are currently so stocked with provisions that it would be worth to divide them up and give them to those who were robbed. Such thieves and swine should hang.

The neighbours

DOC. 216
In early 1941 the Jewish Council in Włoszczowa reports on the social welfare it provided in 1940[1]

Report by the Jewish Council in Włoszczowa,[2] Aid Committee for Refugees and the Poor, drawn up by Aleksander Fargel, early 1941

Social welfare activities in 1940

In October 1939, at a time when the war had inflicted the greatest chaos and disruption on the Jewish population and when all state institutions and self-governing authorities

9 This is not included in the file.

1 AIPN, GK 106/161 (703/31, CA MSW 684), file 3, fol. 63. This document has been translated from Polish.

2 Stefan Czarniecki Street, in the Żoliborz neighbourhood.

1 AŻIH, 223/1, fols. 3–12. Copy in USHMM, RG 15 073M, reel 1. This document has been translated from Polish.

had been completely dismantled, a Council of Elders (Aeltestenrat)[3] made up of seven members of the Jewish population was appointed as the representative body of the Jewish population. It was responsible for carrying out all the orders issued by the authorities to the Jewish population. The now dispersed Jewish population could no longer be described as an organized whole, and was suddenly faced with the necessity of creating its own authoritative body, which from that moment on was to manage every aspect of life, and above all to carry out those executive functions which had until then been the sole remit of the state. This hardly seemed feasible to the members of the Council of Elders, nor indeed to the rest of the Jewish population, who lacked discipline and thus unfortunately could not adapt to these new circumstances. The work facing the Council of Elders was therefore extremely difficult. On the one hand, it was directly responsible to the authorities, and on the other hand, it was responsible to the population, whom it had to defend and protect, and at the same time rapidly educate and attune to the new living conditions. From then on, the Council of Elders – which later became the 12-member Jewish Council – would have to overcome enormous and ever-changing obstacles in order to carry out its difficult tasks.

When the war broke out, Włoszczowa had 6,500 permanent residents, of whom 2,700 were Jews – that is, 42 per cent. In the first few days of October 1939, as a result of military operations and the destruction of the neighbouring towns of Szczekociny and Przedbórz, a considerable number of fire victims and refugees who were resettled by order of the authorities arrived in Włoszczowa. Meanwhile a number of refugees also arrived from other Polish towns, which made it necessary to carry out an accurate census of the Jewish population. This was the first important task carried out by the Jewish Council. The census revealed that Włoszczowa's Jewish population numbered 3,000 souls – that is, 300 more than before the war – and that the new arrivals were mostly poor people and fire victims who had lost all of their belongings in the upheavals of war. Thus they all inevitably became a burden on the local population and were completely dependent on the aid provided by permanent residents. The war led to the significant impoverishment of the local population and considerably swelled the ranks of the poor, so that the order of the day was to provide sustainable social welfare.

The Jewish Council immediately set up a Social Welfare Section made up of several members who promptly [set to work] providing aid; they collected donations for this purpose and distributed food, medicine, and clothing among the most impoverished people. This operation met with significant obstacles, because at that time a war levy of 80,000 złoty had been imposed on the Jewish population. This sum was paid in full, but such a drastic strain on financial resources seriously affected the Jewish Council's income, and consequently the social welfare operation as well.

On 13 December 1939 a group of 217 Jews who had been forcibly resettled from the Poznań region arrived in Włoszczowa. The transport consisted mainly of elderly people and included a large number of women.

The people of Włoszczowa warmly welcomed these unfortunates. A special welcoming committee was organized for the expellees and awaited them at the railway station

2 Włoszczowa was in the south-west of District Radom in the General Government.
3 German in the original: 'Council of Elders'.

where they were given their first warm meal. In the meantime, the town took care of preparing accommodation, which was a considerable problem due to the already overcrowded housing conditions. The designated collection point was the Beth-Hamidrash,[4] where throughout the day, on their own initiative, the people of Włoszczowa brought food for the new arrivals. From there, individual families were directed to their accommodation, a process which lasted several days. The expellees had arrived with virtually no money, and so the most important task after arranging accommodation was to provide them with food. A soup kitchen was immediately set up for the refugees. Unfortunately, a shortage of the necessary funds and the Jewish Community's increasing financial difficulties prevented this operation from being continued long-term. A plan was devised to apply to the American Joint Distribution Committee for help. A delegation comprising Dr Chaim Fargel[5] and Josef Kochen[6] was immediately appointed and went to Warsaw to obtain funds for providing social welfare. They returned on 7 January 1940 with an initial grant of 2,500 zł. and quite a respectable quantity of clothing and medicine from the TOZ.

The social welfare operation, which had hitherto been conducted chaotically and haphazardly by a few groups of volunteers, now had to be organized in such a way as to yield the greatest possible return, given its financial resources.

To this end, on 10 January 1940 the United Aid Committee for Refugees and the Poor began operating under the authority of the Jewish Council in Włoszczowa and thereafter took on the heavy and onerous responsibility of caring for the displaced and the poor.

Work on expanding the soup kitchen and distributing the donated clothing began immediately. A large number of refugees were also provided with beds. During this period a number of refugees from Łódź streamed into Włoszczowa. Several hundred people arrived and had to be provided with food and medical care. It therefore became necessary to set up a second soup kitchen, the construction of which began immediately. The lack of food and fuel rations, the harsh winter, and the resulting supply shortages made the work so difficult that at times it seemed altogether impossible. To make matters worse, a typhus epidemic broke out, and the German authorities ordered the Jewish Council to set up an epidemiological hospital within two days and to run it at the Council's own expense, or risk a levy being imposed on the town. Thanks to superhuman efforts, the hospital was able to open on 27 January, within the specified time frame, albeit without any medical equipment or medication. Within 48 hours the entire building that had been designated as the hospital was thoroughly renovated, and within one day 25 beds were put up, 25 quilts were sewn, and several hundred pieces of bed linen and underwear were collected. The amount of work and effort involved was so immense and the time frame so brief that it can only be fully appreciated in retrospect.

In view of the increasing impoverishment of the Jewish population and the lack of funds, the committee was unable to fulfil all of its tasks, especially when one considers

4 Jewish house of study, where teaching focused on the study of the Torah and Talmud.

5 Dr Chaim Fargel was probably the chairman of the Jewish Council; shot dead by a gendarme during the liquidation of the Włoszczowa ghetto on 18 Sept. 1942.

6 Josef Kochen (b. 1906), businessman; the only available information on his subsequent fate is that he was murdered.

that the monthly expenses rose to 15,000 zł. during this period. A delegation from the committee once again went to Warsaw and this time received 5,000 zł. in aid from the AJDC[7] and an additional 1,000 zł. from the TOZ. Unfortunately, expenses increase out of all proportion to income. The second soup kitchen, which had been operational since 21 January, had to increase the number of meals it served daily, while the financial situation of those who ate there was such that requesting a payment of even a few pennies was out of the question. The typhus epidemic continued to spread and primarily afflicted the poorest, whose hospital treatment had to be covered in full by the Social Welfare Section. Despite these seemingly insurmountable difficulties, the social welfare operation continued without the slightest interruption. In January and February, a fuel drive was conducted for 250 families comprising 735 people in total. A total of 150,000 kg of coal was distributed free of charge.

A new wave of forced resettlement placed a heavy burden on the town. On 18 February, after two days of waiting, a transport of 440 people who had been resettled from Włocławek arrived at the train station. The arrivals' condition was appalling in every respect. [They were] penniless, completely exhausted, and many were sick. Due to the lack of housing, they could not all be housed in Włoszczowa, and so they were directed to the three neighbouring rural local authorities of Kurzelów, Kluczewsko, and Dobromierz. Only a few families were able to stay in the town itself; the rest were lodged with local farmers. Only the Kurzelów group, numbering around 275 people, remained together. The rest were housed in a dozen villages within the areas of the rural local authorities mentioned above, up to 20 km from Włoszczowa. These people were faced with utterly desperate conditions. They lived with farmers in villages that were many kilometres apart, they suffered from hunger, and blizzards and temperatures of minus 30 degrees made communication with the town impossible. Despite these difficulties, however, the day after the transport arrived, two committees accompanied by a physician went through all the villages to inspect the accommodation, to record the number of expellees, and to get an idea of what aid was most urgently required. According to the committees' reports, the most important matter was to set up a soup kitchen in Kurzelów, to organize accommodation sensibly, and to gather the remaining expellees in one place and provide them with beds, because almost all of them had to sleep on the floor. Furthermore, medicine would have to be ordered and delivered immediately, because the arrivals were in a very poor state of health. Thanks to financial aid provided by the AJDC, this operation made brisk progress. Unfortunately, despite the best efforts, concentrating the expellees housed in the area of the rural local authorities of Dobromierz and Kluczewsko proved impossible. Thanks to the authorities' assistance, however, the entire group assigned to Kurzelów was housed, despite widespread resistance on the part of the locals. Work on the soup kitchen in Kurzelów commenced at the same time, and by 10 March 300 free meals were being served daily. However, supplying the three functioning soup kitchens became increasingly difficult because prices were rising daily and funds were scarce. As the local population became increasingly impoverished, income from local sources steadily decreased, while the number of people receiving social welfare simultaneously increased dramatically. The soup kitchens in

7 An abbreviation for the American Jewish Joint Distribution Committee.

Włoszczowa had to constantly increase the number of meals they provided, yet such was the financial situation of those in need of help that it was impossible to charge even 10 gr. for a meal. In order to cut costs, the two kitchens in Włoszczowa were merged on 1 April, and from then on a single kitchen served more than 700 meals a day. The typhus epidemic continued to spread and of course primarily affected the poorest people, whose treatment costs were shouldered by the social welfare system. With the number of patients constantly increasing, the hospital administration repeatedly requested new equipment, which consumed large sums of money. For example, in March 1940 over 4,500 zł. was spent on hospital upkeep, and the number of patients increased to 50.

As early as 12 March, the committee began supplying the refugees in the villages located within the area of the rural local authorities of Dobromierz and Kluczewsko with dry goods, which were distributed in weekly deliveries. This involved significant costs and delivery problems. By way of illustration, from 12 March to late 1940 the following quantities of dry goods were distributed to the refugees in the areas covered by the local authorities of Dobromierz and Kluczewsko:

3,052.50 kg of bread,
15,600 kg of potatoes,
1,721.40 kg of rye flour,
523.90 kg of wheat flour,
835.70 kg of groats,

as well as other goods.

During this period, after strenuous effort, the committee was also able to purchase wood with which to make beds for the refugees. This work was entrusted to the carpenters among the refugees, and 75 two- or three-person beds were made and distributed free of charge, thereby supplying all the arrivals from Włocławek.

On the instructions of the AJDC, the committee carried out a detailed census of all the refugees, which reflects the situation as of 25 March 1940. The census was conducted in Włoszczowa as well as all the surrounding villages and resulted in 1,455 registered refugees, that is about 28 per cent of the total Jewish population. Of these, 75 per cent were receiving social welfare. If we add in the poor people among the local residents, then we have a full picture of the enormous burden placed on the committee.

Unfortunately, the funds received from the AJDC and the TOZ decreased, and it became increasingly necessary to resort to local funds. The population's material situation, which was deteriorating by the day, now made it impossible to collect voluntary offerings and donations. In order to avoid restricting the scope of the relief effort, a permanent tax was imposed on the local population to pay for social welfare. Collecting this tax was often very difficult, because a considerable portion of the population was not and is not aware of the obligations that weigh on every single Jew today.

To maintain the whole enormous apparatus required to help the poor, it was often necessary to resort to coercive measures. Despite the huge expense of maintaining the hospital, running the soup kitchens, and feeding the refugees, the committee resolved to undertake a wide-ranging campaign for Passover. For this purpose it mobilized all of its financial resources and quickly set to work, with commendable results. Thanks to the matzos received from the AJDC and the funds collected locally (the 8,000 zł. grant from the AJDC arrived on 19 April, after the foodstuffs had been purchased), 595 families comprising 2,225 people were provided for, and the following goods were distributed at a total cost of 8,500 zł:

2,579.5 kg of matzos,
11,182 kg of potatoes,
1,483 kg of beetroots,
909 kg of onions,
5,416 eggs,
360 kg of salt,
50 kg of meat,
21 kg of soap.

The Passover campaign was a complete success, especially considering that the majority of the refugees at the time were even provided with kitchen utensils.

The committee's financial situation deteriorated more and more, and this in turn affected those who received social welfare. Due to the lack of funds there were increasingly frequent disruptions in the supply of dry goods to the refugees housed in the surrounding villages. The soup kitchens reduced the number of meals they served as well as the portion sizes. In this difficult situation, they once again turned to the AJDC for help. Thanks to the funds obtained by the committee, the foodstuffs, and large quantities of clothing, the situation temporarily improved, which primarily enabled the continued operation of both the soup kitchens and the medical services, the latter of which consumed considerable sums of money due to the ongoing typhus epidemic. However, the external funds were relatively small in comparison to the sums received from local sources. The soup kitchens were threatened with closure, and it was only thanks to the most strenuous effort and sacrifice that this did not come to pass.

On 10 July 1940, the establishment of the ghetto dealt the Jewish population of Włoszczowa a heavy blow. Over 4,000 people were squeezed into about a dozen alleys, with over a dozen crammed into each small room. Shopkeepers and craftsmen were deprived of their workplaces and thus their only means of livelihood, and they were suddenly thrust into the ranks of those to whom they had hitherto provided considerable assistance. The situation was catastrophic because the committee was suddenly receiving no income whatsoever. The deliveries of dry goods to the refugees therefore ended, and the remaining funds were used to help the poor with their relocation. Unfortunately, our appeals and calls to outside institutions for help were not very successful, as the financial situation of the Joint [JDC] had also deteriorated considerably by that time. Despite everything, in an effort to keep the soup kitchens running, small charges for meals were introduced, which led to a rapid decline in the number of people using the kitchens. This was a visible expression of the prevailing poverty. The introduction of these charges only kept the kitchens going for a very short time. As the existing debts had already grown to 7,000 zł, further loans were refused. In the end, we were forced to close the soup kitchen in Włoszczowa on 1 September.

The conscription and dispatch of young Jews to the labour camp in Cieszanowa caused such enormous distress, especially among the families concerned, that aid was redirected to helping those in the labour camp. Most of those who were sent, also including refugees, found themselves working under extremely harsh conditions without proper food, clothing, or footwear. A collection was therefore quickly organized in the town, and within two days 9 sacks and 1 crate of clothes and food were sent to the camp. In addition, on average 15 to 20 food parcels containing bread, sugar, jam, etc. were sent by mail every day. The relief campaign on behalf of the workers in the camp consumed more than 10,000 zł. within six weeks.

Naturally this had an impact on the local operation and ultimately led to the closure of the soup kitchen in Kurzelów, which was still running at that time. This was a heavy blow for the refugees, but the lack of the necessary funds made it impossible to keep the kitchen running. Income from local sources decreased considerably and collecting contributions proved very difficult, as nearly the entire population was shouldering the costs of maintaining those in the camp. The attention of the population and of the committee was entirely focused on these workers, which is why social welfare in the town during this period was limited solely to supplying extra food to the refugees by distributing dry goods on a very limited scale, as well as providing aid in cash on an ad hoc basis. In view of the committee's extremely difficult situation, a delegate was once again sent to Warsaw to appeal for help from the AJDC, the TOZ, and other institutions. The financial situation of these institutions was no better than ours, and to make matters worse, the establishment of the Warsaw ghetto had directed the attention of these institutions solely to providing aid in Warsaw. Apart from a small quantity of medicine from the TOZ, we received no assistance whatsoever.

In the meantime, the long-awaited return of the workers from the labour camp took place, unfortunately accompanied by the sad news of the deaths of seven young men. With the return of the workers, a great burden was lifted from the Social Welfare Section. Although the cost of providing medical care rose immediately because the arrivals were in very poor health, nonetheless their return made it possible to resume a more extensive relief operation in the surrounding area. The lack of outside help once again forced us to obtain funds from the local population.

The allocated quota of potatoes had to be collected quickly because it was already quite late in the year and the first frosts had set in. The refugees and the poor were quickly supplied with potatoes. Although the suspension of potato deliveries made it impossible to complete this operation, nevertheless all the refugees in Włoszczowa, Kurzelów, and other surrounding villages, as well as almost all the local poor people, received a free per capita allocation of 100 kg of potatoes.

In November, thanks to donations from Switzerland, the AJDC sent 1,000 kg of wheat flour and a certain amount of other foodstuffs, which were distributed among all the social welfare recipients and children. However, all of this was of little help to the refugees and the poor, whose poverty continued to increase. In view of the risk of a typhus epidemic, a pre-emptive vaccination campaign was carried out in November and December 1940, and 2,000 people were vaccinated free of charge. The cramped living conditions and lack of fuel have naturally had an impact on hygiene, which we are constantly struggling to uphold. The committee arranged for special information signboards calling for the maintenance of cleanliness to be hung in shops and doorways, and several thousand leaflets instructing how to combat infectious diseases have also been distributed.

Repeated campaigns to distribute articles of clothing have benefited around 550 people who have received over 1,300 items of clothing, some 400 of which were collected in the town alone.

A year of work of the Jewish Council's Aid Committee for Refugees and the Poor, a year of hard and intensive work, has above all been marked by the self-sacrificing attitude of all the staff as well as the local population, which has played a crucial role in funding the entire social welfare operation. If the assistance we were able to provide was not always what we would have wished, and if it was inadequate both in our view and in the view of those in need, this was not our fault. Many a plan failed due to the lack of adequate funds.

With the advantage of a whole year's experience, we have embarked on our work in the new year under even more difficult conditions, but with the same motto: Help by joining forces!

DOC. 217

On 3 January 1941 Jewish property owners in Chełm ask the Jewish Social Self-Help executive committee to intercede with the occupation authorities on their behalf[1]

Handwritten letter from Jewish property owners in Chełm to the JSS executive committee in Cracow (received on 13 January 1941), dated 3 January 1941

The undersigned Jewish property owners in the town of Chełm-Lubelski
Request
As of 1 December 1939 all property owned by Jews in the town of Chełm is under the temporary administration of the Treuhandstelle.[2]

There are approximately 500 properties owned by Jews in Chełm, and gross revenue amounts to approximately 75,000 złoty per month.

Almost 90 per cent of these property owners have no sources of income other than their property, and this property has been their one and only source of livelihood.

In response to individual applications and the efforts of the local Jewish Council, the Treuhänder[3] initially granted pensions to several property owners based on this revenue, while others received rent reductions for apartments in their buildings. However, all of these reductions were eventually withdrawn. In other words, not a single property owner has received a pension for over *6 months*, and yet everyone has been paying rent for apartments in their own buildings as of December 1939.

It is evident that we property owners are heavily affected by the current situation. As I have already mentioned above, we have no sources of income other than our buildings, and we have no savings because the pre-war urbanization mandated by the Polish government depleted all our funds.[4] Thus, with our property now under the Trustee Office's administration, we are left with no sources of income whatsoever – all the more so because most of us are of advanced age and unfit for work, in addition to having to care for numerous family members.

1 AŻIH, 211/285, fols. 8–10. This document has been translated from Polish.
2 German in the original: 'Trustee Office'.
3 German in the original: 'trustee'.
4 This is a reference to the cost of urban improvements, to which landlords had to contribute.

The local Jewish Council has frequently interceded with the local authorities to ask that they once again reduce our rent for the apartments in our own buildings and reinstate our pensions from the revenue, but all these efforts have been in vain.

Because our *rent reductions have been withdrawn*, many of us are overdue with our rent payments, and the Treuhänder is threatening to evict us from our apartments.

To guarantee us a minimum subsistence level and a roof over our heads in such a difficult time as this, we warmly and humbly ask the honourable JSS[5] executive committee to apply to the *relevant central authorities*, requesting that:

a) any of our properties with a monthly revenue under 200 złoty be exempted from trustee administration;

b) we be granted pensions from a portion of the income derived from our properties that generate a monthly revenue exceeding 200 złoty;

c) we be granted rent relief for apartments in our own buildings in the form of an outright exemption from rent for these dwellings.

Please send a reply to Chaskiel Szylkrot,[6] Chełm Lub.[elski], at 1 Mały Rynek Street.

Hoping for a favourable response to our request,

Respectfully,[7]

DOC. 218

The head of the General Government's Interior Administration Department reports on a meeting held on 8 January 1941 at the Reich Security Main Office concerning the resettlement of around one million persons[1]

Report on a meeting on questions concerning the settlement of Poles and Jews in the General Government, signed Westerkamp (W/Pi.),[2] Cracow, dated 13 January 1941[3]

Report

on the meeting at the Reich Security Main Office in Berlin about the *resettlement of Poles and Jews* to the General Government held on 8 January 1941

I.

In addition to the representatives of the General Government (SS-Obergruppenführer Krüger, Oberregierungsrat Dr Schepers,[4] Spatial Planning, and the undersigned Main

5 Jewish Social Self-Help.

6 The only fact known about Chaskiel Szylkrot is that he was murdered.

7 The text is followed by 21 mostly illegible signatures, including: H. Zylbercwajg; P[inchas] Orensztejn (1890–1942), businessman; L[ipe] Herc, businessman; E. Lewin; Nusyn Dawid Mandler; J[icchak/Icchak] Cukierman (1884–1941), businessman; and Sz[apse] Rozenblit.

1 AIPN, GK 95, vol. 15. Copy in IfZ-Archives, Fb 105, vol. 11, fols. 2498–2502. This document has been translated from German.

2 Eberhard Westerkamp (1903–1980), lawyer; Regierungsrat in the Prussian Ministry of State, 1932; joined the NSDAP in 1937; Landrat in Osnabrück until 1939; head of the Interior Administration Main Department in the government of the GG from Oct. 1940 to Jan. 1942; served in the war; farmer, 1945–1948; employed in the West German public administration, 1949–1956; state secretary in the Lower Saxony Ministry of the Interior, 1956–1959; worked as a lawyer from 1960.

3 The original contains handwritten additions.

Department Head Westerkamp with Dr Föhl,[5] Interior Administration), all other offices involved in this question were represented at this meeting: the Reich Commissioner for the Strengthening of Germandom, the Wehrmacht High Command, the Army High Command, the Reich Ministry of Transport, the Reich Ministry of Economics, the Reich Ministry of the Interior, the inspectors of the Security Police of the Eastern Territories, the Gau representative from Vienna. The meeting was chaired by SS-Gruppenführer Heydrich.

The following points were agreed:

1. The General Government will negotiate questions of resettlement exclusively with the Reich Security Main Office, which is in turn in contact with all relevant offices in the Reich. This will preclude subordinate authorities in the incorporated eastern territories undertaking any individual initiatives of their own in relation to the General Government.
2. In 1941, a total of 831,000 persons from the Reich's eastern territories are to be resettled in the General Government; in addition, around 180,000 persons will be resettled within the General Government specifically for Wehrmacht purposes.[6]

   The representatives of the General Government have raised no fundamental objection to these planned resettlements because taking in people from the Reich was set as the most urgent task of the General Government in 1941 on behalf of the Reich both by the Führer's general directive and the earlier general statements from the Governor General.
3. The number of 831,000 results from
   a) the necessity of making space for the ethnic Germans returning to the Reich,
   b) the establishment of military training areas,
   c) the resettlement of Jews.

The following overview gives a detailed breakdown:

For ethnic Germans who are to be resettled

to the area of

Danzig-West Prussia	100,000
Warthegau	148,000
East Upper Silesia	150,000
East Posen	46,000
	444,000

4 Dr Hansjulius Schepers (1909–1991), economist; joined the NSDAP and the SS in 1933; assistant lecturer at the University of Göttingen, 1933–1935; from 1935 worked on counter-intelligence matters for Hanns Kerrl, head of the Reich Office for Spatial Planning; Oberregierungsrat and head of the Office for Spatial Planning in the General Government from Oct. 1939; Hans Frank's deputy as Reich defence commissioner in 1940.

5 Dr Walther Föhl (1908–1975), historian; advisor in the NSDAP's Office for Genealogical Research from 1931/1932; joined the SA in 1933 and the SS in 1935; deputy head of the General Government's Population and Welfare Division, Dec. 1939–summer 1940, then head of this division until the end of May 1941; served in the war, June–Dec. 1941; again deputy head of the Population and Welfare Division, 1942–Jan. 1943; served in the war again; district archivist in Kempen after the war.

6 This referred to forced removals of people from tracts of land in the General Government confiscated in order to be turned into Wehrmacht training grounds for manoeuvres etc.

To enhance the position of ethnic Germans already resettled	50,000
Auschwitz concentration camp[7]	20,000
Housing for families of public servants	50,000
Poles who fled before evacuation	5,000
	569,000
Wehrmacht projects	
Konin-Pleschen	80,000
Sieradz	40,000
Warthelager (Oberneg)	20,000
Air Force North (Ryppin)[8]	22,000
Army North (Mlava)	25,000
Bizia near Beuthen	10,000
Thorn	5,000
	202,000
Resettlement of Viennese Jews	60,000
	831,000

4. For now, the impending resettlements have been scheduled for the period from 1 February to 30 April 1941 as follows:

	Evacuation to benefit ethnic Germans	Evacuation for military training areas
East Prussia	30,000	8,500
Silesia	24,000	10,000
Danzig-West Prussia	40,000	27,000
Warthegau	90,000	19,000
	184,000	64,500
Vienna	*Jews*	
	10,000	

In summary (1 February to 30 April 1941)	
Evacuation to benefit ethnic Germans	184,000
Evacuation for military training areas	64,500
Jews from Vienna	10,000
	258,500
From which are to be deducted 2,000 workers for the military training areas with their families	10,000
remainder	248,500

5. The representatives of the General Government have been promised that the people to be resettled will be furnished as well as possible with clothing and food for the first two weeks.

7 This concerns the resettlement of people to make way for the expansion of Auschwitz concentration camp.

8 Correctly: Rypin.

6. The question of funds in General Government currency per capita to be given to the people being resettled is yet to be resolved. The per capita amount should be at least 60 zloty.
7. In addition, it was agreed that the transports would operate according to schedules on which the General Government agencies can rely; a messaging system will be worked out which will enable the agencies of the Reich Security Main Office and the Eastern Railway to notify the authorities of the General Government (Interior Administration) of the arrival of each train in good time, so that all the necessary preparations can be made.
8. To make their position clear, the representatives of the General Government emphasized the difficulties which this impending task will cause for the General Government. The Reich Security Main Office objected and argued that the population density in the General Government was hardly going to exceed the average population density in the Reich even with the coming resettlements. It goes without saying that this comparison is misleading, because the area of the General Government will be so greatly reduced by providing 2,500 sq. km for Wehrmacht facilities and by the need to free up the entire military protection zone along the Narev, Vistula, and San rivers, amounting to an estimated 12,000 sq. km, that one can assume a population density of 170 for the remainder of the General Government. In addition, the General Government lacks all the natural prerequisites for taking in such masses of people; the necessary conditions are more likely to be found in the Reich. A comparison of population density must therefore inevitably lead to false conclusions.

II.

Initial joint response to the above from the Interior Administration Department and the Spatial Planning Department:

1. Under the current circumstances, registration of the masses flocking in and control of their final whereabouts cannot be guaranteed. Even now it is being reported, for instance from District Radom, that people who have been resettled keep migrating back from the east towards the west. This is confirmed by information received at the Reich Security Main Office indicating that approximately 50,000 of those evacuated so far have already reappeared in the Warthegau. While housing them in barrack camps and the like is not an option at this time, it will nonetheless be necessary to dispense with registration.
2. To avoid catastrophes, which would certainly be disadvantageous for the Reich, the Kreishauptleute and Stadthauptleute must provide *housing* for the evacuees coming into their Kreise. According to the reports on hand, there are currently no vacant shelter facilities. According to a statement by the representative of the Wehrmacht High Command, an increased influx into the General Government must be anticipated, which would exacerbate these problems. Shelter will have to be provided chiefly by parcelling out the new arrivals to the already overcrowded quarters occupied by local families.
3. For the same reasons, it must be ensured at all costs that the new arrivals can be provided with the necessary *food*.
4. Evacuees who are fit for work must be put to *work* immediately. During the winter, the work projects in question will involve primarily clearing snow and doing some preparatory work for construction projects. In addition, churches and monasteries would have

to be made available for housing the homeless, ideally on the basis of an independent decision by the church authorities. The political concerns this might raise (easier for the hostile clergy to exert influence) would have to be tolerated. The work schemes carried out solely for the purpose of keeping the evacuees busy, which in many cases are of questionable productive value, cannot be paid for mainly by the General Government and the local authorities. *Assistance from the Reich* must be sought for this.[9]

DOC. 219
On 8 January 1941 the chairman of the Warsaw Jewish Council reports on its financial situation[1]

Report by the chairman of the Jewish Council and president of the Council of Elders of the Jewish Religious Community in Warsaw (no. Tr 64/362), Czerniaków, to the office of the District Governor of Warsaw, Resettlement Department, Transfer Bureau,[2] Palais Brühl, dated 8 January 1941[3]

Compelled by the circumstances, I have described the Jewish Council's very poor financial situation to the authorities on various occasions and asked for these circumstances to be investigated. I have also asked persistently for conditions to be created under which the Jewish Council could balance its expenditures with its income and in general operate on the basis of an actual preliminary budget, which would be achievable in spite of the difficulties that are piling up. I would not be doing my duty if I failed to state that the present financial situation far exceeds all the previous difficulties with which the Jewish Council had to contend.

By way of illustration, I venture to cite the following figures:

The cash balance on 6 January 1941 was 132 zloty.

The cash balance on 7 January 1941 was 517 zloty.

This occurred at a time when the Jewish Council's expenditures normally amount to between 40,000 and 50,000 zloty per day, while the income runs on average to between 10,000 and 20,000 zloty per day.

Foreseeing this state of affairs, as well as in connection with the difficult tasks and directives given to the Jewish Council and in regard to its obligations to the 400,000 persons whom it must look after, I have reported on the state of affairs at hand many times, as mentioned above. Moreover, I have presented radical schemes to remedy the Community's poor financial state and a minimal programme that would make it possible to manage the budget efficiently and systematically, at least to some extent.

9 These resettlements were carried out only in part because Germany was preparing to invade the Soviet Union. When the resettlements were stopped on 15 March 1941, deportations had been carried out only from the Warthegau. In total, they affected 19,226 persons, including 2,140 Jews.

1 APW, 485/340, fols. 10–16. This document has been translated from German.

2 The head of the Transfer Bureau was Alexander Palfinger (1894–1961); deputy head of the ghetto administration in Lodz from spring 1940; made head of the Transfer Bureau for the Warsaw ghetto in late 1940 after differences of opinion with Hans Biebow, the head of the Lodz ghetto administration; in Warsaw until May 1941; in charge of Jewish affairs at the Kreishauptmann's office in Tarnopol from the summer of 1941.

3 The original contains handwritten underlining and annotations.

Without touching on the maximal programme for the Community's financial rehabilitation here, which – as I understand – is also being contemplated by the authorities and for which I am now preparing the applications – I will confine myself now to a piecemeal approach to this matter. Below I will therefore give you a short summary of the schemes for rehabilitating the Community's finances that I outlined to the authorities.

First, towards the end of May 1940, I applied for approval of taxation on behalf of the Jewish Council in Warsaw, primarily with regard to the continuous tax that is collected when food ration cards are distributed through a surcharge in the amount of, for example, 1 zloty per month. Second, on 24 June 1940 I submitted the scheme for charging an extra amount for the local trade tax cards, in the amount of 100 per cent of the tax basis in each case. And third, on 24 June 1940 I also submitted the plan for taxation of real estate owned by Jews in the amount of 4 per cent of the tax basis.[4]

Fourth, in view of the lamentable financial situation of the Jewish welfare institutions, I submitted a scheme according to which subsidies would be given to the Jewish Council out of the amounts raised by the city administration to support social welfare, specifically out of the surcharge for tram tickets, electricity, and gas as well as the residence tax.[5]

Fifth and finally, I appealed to the authorities to allow me to take out a loan from a Warsaw bank in the amount of at least 300,000 zloty to ease the transitional difficulties of the Jewish Council.

Of these schemes, the first taxation plan was approved. This will raise a sum in the amount of more than 300,000 zloty per month for the Jewish Council's coffers, collected when the food ration cards are distributed. This relatively substantial sum has enabled me to keep the budget at a corresponding level. As a result, the Jewish Council's chronic deficit was considerably reduced. This deficit results from the fact that so far the Jewish Council's income has never covered the expenditures, because every month the expenditures foreseen in the preliminary budget were substantially increased by completely unexpected expenditures which were brought about by unanticipated directives that are issued almost daily.

Last month, the sum also came in from this source but could not be used to meet the Jewish Council's normal needs because very large sums had to be spent on erecting the walls and fences and on setting up the Transfer Bureau. The amount spent on this totals almost 300,000 zloty. This expenditure left a gap in the Jewish Council's financial situation and increased its debts to suppliers, employees, workers, etc. These debts in total now amount to around 2,000,000 zloty.

The second scheme of an additional fee in the amount of 100 per cent of the local trade tax cards was authorized by your directive of 5 December 1940.[6] It has not been implemented, however, and to the best of my knowledge this is because the city administration has not received instructions to that effect from the District Governor's representative for the City of Warsaw. As the trade tax is paid during the current month and no additional payments for the Jewish Council are being demanded of the Jews paying the local trade tax, it must be feared that it will be very difficult to collect the fees for the benefit of the Jewish Council after the trade tax cards have been paid.

4 APW, 485/341, fols. 3–9; also in this file is a poster dated 2 July 1940, with text in German, Polish, and Yiddish, which announces the taxation of food ration cards in the ghetto (fols. 36–37).

5 A handwritten note saying 'no! h.' appears in the left margin here.

6 Not in the file.

The third scheme, concerning a charge on Jewish real estate, has not been approved so far. It is indeed the case that in the meantime we have obtained control of the Jewish properties within the Jewish residential district. But the conditions, which incidentally have nothing to do with the aforementioned tax scheme but are related to the management of the properties, are such that no income of any sort can be expected, and they more likely represent a superfluous burden with various expenditures.

The fourth plan, concerning subsidies to support social welfare, has indeed been well received by influential figures in social welfare, but has not been formally implemented with regard to Jews so far.

Thus, Jewish social welfare has to contend with tremendous difficulties. I could not reconcile it with my conscience, and would not be fulfilling the duties delegated to me by the authorities, if I failed to point out here the alarming state of the welfare institutions. Every day, reports and inspections of orphanages, shelters, etc., the thousands of poor at the gates of the Community, its facilities and welfare institutions bear witness to how absolutely necessary it is to find resources to ease the situation that has arisen. Realistically, I have always sought and continue to seek sources of income within the Jewish community. All my proposals have burdened this population alone. For the sake of justice, I have striven and strive to burden the affluent population more than the poor. The second and third of the schemes listed above have a similar aim. To mitigate the effects of the first plan concerning food ration cards, I ordered around 70,000 Jews to be relieved of the obligation to pay the surcharge on the food ration cards.

To sum up the above, I request that you kindly consider issuing directives in the following matters to prevent the impending financial collapse of the Jewish Council and to enable it to cover the most necessary expenditures:

1) Establishing the principle that the Jewish Council must operate in accordance with a fixed budget, i.e. that expenditures must be offset by income.
2) The matter of surcharges for the local trade tax cards in the amount of 100 per cent, for the benefit of the Jewish Council. I request that you approach the District Governor's representative for the City of Warsaw in this matter so that the city administration is given instructions to that effect. As I have tried to make clear above, this matter is very urgent.
3) Approval of the terms for adding an additional charge in the amount of 4 per cent of gross income to the property tax for the benefit of the Jewish Council.
4) Awarding the necessary percentage of the residents' tax collected by the city administration to the Jewish Council for social welfare purposes, as well as increasing the prices of tram tickets and the charges for electricity and gas.
5) Taking out a bank loan in the amount of 300,000 zloty. I most courteously request that you contact the Office of Bank Supervision so that it will approve taking this loan from Warsaw banks.

In connection with the above I have the privilege of pointing out once again that in the search for other income sources, I ordered that fees in the amount of 0.50 zloty or 1 zloty are collected for the signs that must be posted on the doors of Jewish residences. I also ordered that 0.50 zloty are collected monthly per housing unit for the needs of our Health Department, i.e. for controlling epidemic diseases. In addition, the introduction of Jewish identity cards is envisaged following a suggestion from the authorities. More affluent persons could be charged a fee for being issued such a document. This might allow us to collect an amount with which some of the Jewish Council's current needs and some of the debts could be covered. So far, however, I have not received any directive to that effect.

Finally, after the Jewish Council takes charge of the postal service in the Jewish residential district, income could be obtained from the sale of special postage stamps (also to stamp collectors). As a matter of form, I venture to point out that the postal administration, as before, does not take a favourable view of this idea.

In conclusion, I take the liberty to add that it is most desirable that relations between the Jewish Council and the Temporary Administration of Jewish Properties are regulated. Following your letter of 26 November 1940, I justifiably assumed that the great efforts invested in this area of activity by the Jewish Council would be appropriately honoured. Previous practice and the scale of charges proposed by the Temporary Administration clash with your directive of 26 November 1940[7] and promise no corresponding income of any sort for the Jewish Council.

DOC. 220

On 9 January 1941 the chairman of the Warsaw Jewish Council requests improvement in the supply of allocated items[1]

Letter from the chairman of the Jewish Council and president of the Council of Elders of the Jewish Religious Community in Warsaw (no. Tr 64/369), Czerniaków, to the office of the District Governor of Warsaw, Resettlement Department, Transfer Bureau,[2] dated 9 January 1941

Raising the necessary capital for the Jewish residential district's economic turnover brings great difficulties. First, the Jewish Council itself has no funds of any sort available and constantly has to struggle with a large deficit; second, the Jewish residential district's food supply has come to almost a complete standstill, which makes it impossible to mobilize the retailers' modest monetary reserves. In addition, it must be taken into consideration that the labour market has been extraordinarily diminished since the Jewish residential district was sealed off and that unemployment has already reached alarming proportions.

To alter this state of affairs it would be necessary to put to work our medium-sized business and crafts sectors, whose potential is considerable, and to provide the Jewish residential district with allocated and non-allocated items that have been approved for unregulated trade. To better explain the difficulties in obtaining money from the distribution organization[3] in order to stimulate transactions with the Transfer Bureau, I would like to point out that the population of the Jewish residential district received only a quantity of 3½ kg of flour per inhabitant for baking ration-card bread in December 1940; that to this day, that is, up to 9 January of this year, we have not succeeded in bringing into the Jewish residential district the flour allotted in December for the last 4 coupons of the food ration cards (coupons 9, 10, 11, and 12); that the population of the Jewish residential

7 This presumably refers to the transfer of control over food ration cards to the Jewish Community: see *The Warsaw Diary of Adam Czerniakow*, p. 220.

1 APW, 485/340, fols. 17–18. This document has been translated from German.
2 The head of the Transfer Bureau was Alexander Palfinger.
3 This is a reference to the Jewish Council's Supply Office (Zakład Zaopatrzenie, Zakład Zaopatrywania): see Doc. 285, fn. 5.

district did not receive any soap, sugar, jam, heating fuel, etc., etc. in December; and that the matter of granting the Jewish Council the exclusive right for sales of monopoly items has not yet been dealt with.

Given this situation, I have the honour of requesting most courteously that you might most kindly arrange for the allocation to the Jewish residential district by means of ration-card distribution in addition to the bread flour (I venture to repeat my request for an increase in the bread rations – cf. my letter no. Tr. 15/23112 of 27 December 1940) other allocated items such as soap, sugar, potatoes, coal, firewood, jam, macaroni, etc.

Finally, I take the liberty of emphasizing that it is absolutely necessary to facilitate contact between the heads of the Jewish Council's Provisioning Section[4] and the respective sections at the Transfer Bureau, so that they can discuss the Jewish residential district's manufacturing capabilities for the outside world. In addition, the question of purchasing opportunities for items approved for unregulated trade, such as vegetables, fish, certain raw materials, etc., would have to be discussed, and the Jewish Council might be able to indicate supply sources. My economic experts are of the opinion that this is the only way to stimulate sales in the Jewish residential district and keep the population from starving.

DOC. 221

On 10 January 1941 the branch of the Jewish Central Association for the Care of Orphans (CENTOS) in Cracow asks the Stadthauptmann to allocate food to them[1]

Letter from the Jewish Social Self-Help in Cracow, Jewish Relief Committee for the city of Cracow, Central Association for the Care of Orphans, CENTOS (no. 27/41), signed Rachela Mahler[2] and Dr Gizela Thon,[3] to the Stadthauptmann of Cracow, Department of Food and Economic Affairs, dated 10 January 1941 (copy)

Re: the request by the board of the orphanage at 21 Dajworstraße in Cracow[4] and the day nurseries at 1 Meiselsgasse[5] for food allocation in exchange for ration coupons

The Jewish Social Self-Help, Jewish Relief Committee for the city of Cracow, has established a Department for the Care of Orphans (CENTOS), which runs an orphanage at

4 The Provisioning Section was responsible for the distribution of items of daily use.

1 YVA, O-21/14/1, fol. 4. This document has been translated from German.
2 Rachela Mahler (d. 1942) worked in Jewish poor relief; chairwoman of the Cracow group of the Women's International Zionist Organization (WIZO); deported from the Cracow ghetto to Belzec in 1942. Her son Zygmunt was a member of the Cracow branch of the Jewish Combat Organization (ŻOB).
3 Dr Gizela Thon (b. 1904), secondary school teacher; as general secretary of CENTOS headed the branches in District Cracow and represented child welfare on the board of the Jewish Social Self-Help (JSS) in Cracow.
4 The orphanage at 21 Dajwór Street in Kazimierz, Cracow's Jewish quarter, was opened in late 1940. In May 1941 it was moved to 8 Krakusa Street, in the ghetto.
5 This is probably a reference to the day nurseries listed below. After the onset of the war, CENTOS set up two orphanages, which were transferred to three other buildings in late Dec. 1940, including those at 1 Podbrzezie Street and 17 Meiselsgasse. The children spent the night with foster parents and went to the nursery during the day. They were deported from Cracow with their foster parents or taken to the ghetto in March 1941.

21 Dajworstraße. Twenty-three children between the ages of 2 and 12, including many foundlings, are looked after and given all their meals there. (The number of persons fed, including two childcare workers, is twenty-five.)

In addition, the CENTOS Department runs two day nurseries, at 17 Meiselsgasse and 1 Podbrzeziegasse, where around 200 children receive a two-course lunch. (The number of children fluctuates because of the harsh winter and the lack of warm clothing and shoes. A great many children fell ill as a result of the wretched living conditions.)

Because the children come from the poorest strata of the population and are undernourished and because the CENTOS Department is in an unfavourable financial situation, we implore you to kindly allocate the provisions listed below in exchange for ration coupons, namely:

flour, beans, sugar, hulled and pearl barley, milk, jam, washing powder, soap, and cooking fat.

DOC. 222

On 12 January 1941 writers and journalists begin producing the 'Daily Chronicle of the Lodz Ghetto'[1]

'Daily Chronicle Bulletin of the Lodz Ghetto',[2] no. 1, dated 12 January 1941

Archive Department
Daily Chronicle Bulletin, no. 1
12 January 1941
Weather. 10 degrees below zero. No wind, sunny.
The chairman inspects the Registration Department. In the morning, Mr *Rumkowski*, chairman of the Jewish Council, inspected the Population Records Office at 4 Miodowa Street. During the visit he showed a keen interest in the work of officials in the individual departments, including the Registration Office, the Civil Registry, the Statistics Department, and the Archives. After his inspection he had a lengthy discussion with the lawyer Mr Neftalin, who is head of the Registration Department.[3]

1 APŁ, 278/1079, fols. 1–7. Published in English translation in Lucjan Dobroszycki (ed.), *The Chronicle of the Łódź Ghetto, 1941–1944*, trans. Richard Lourie et al. (New Haven, CT, and London: Yale University Press, 1984), pp. 3–8. Unabridged edition: Julian Baranowski et al. (eds.), *Kronika getta łódzkiego/Litzmannstadt Getto 1941–1944*, 5 vols. (Łódź: Wydawnictwo Uniwersytetu Łódzkiego, 2009). This document has been newly translated from the original Polish.

2 Under the leadership of Julian Cukier (1904–1943), the Lodz ghetto archives chronicled events for future generations. The daily entries largely followed a fixed pattern and were supplemented by articles on specific topics. Initially the chronicle was written in Polish. When German-speaking authors also joined the archives following the deportation to the ghetto of approximately 20,000 Jews from Western Europe, the chronicle was written in both Polish and German from Sept. until late 1942, and thereafter exclusively in German. The chronicle was produced until July 1944.

3 Henryk Neftalin (1908–1945), lawyer; head of the Registration Department in the Lodz ghetto, which registered the inhabitants and assigned them accommodation; deported to Auschwitz in August 1944; perished in Dachau concentration camp.

Births and deaths. Fifty-two people died in the ghetto today. The primary causes of death were: (1) heart disease, (2) exhaustion from hunger and cold, (3) tuberculosis. Fourteen births were registered (seven boys and seven girls).

Demands made by members of the [Jewish] Order Service. Today a staff delegation presented a petition at the Order Service headquarters calling for better conditions, namely the reintroduction of supplementary food and fuel and a wage increase. The authorities[4] rejected the petition because the aim of distributing food among the overall population as equitably as possible rules out the possibility of granting preferential treatment to any group of people, even those who have public service responsibilities. However, in order to ease the burden on the Order Service, the commander[5] promised to do his best to expand the police canteens so that they can also cater for the families of police officers. To this end, the canteens will provide three meals a day to over 2,000 people.

Crime. According to reports from the Order Service duty posts, twelve thefts and six other offences were recorded today.

Attempted suicide. Eighteen-year-old Abram Nożycki (21 Zgierska) threw himself from a window on the third-floor staircase at 2 Marynarska Street.[6] The emergency physician who was called to the scene noted a series of injuries, and after administering first aid, he transported the patient, who was in a critical condition, to Hospital No. 1.

From the Provisioning Section.[7] The Provisioning Section is currently in the midst of a reorganization process, which involves decentralizing individual departments, such as those responsible for the sale of colonial goods,[8] bread, fuel, vegetables, dairy products, etc. The reorganization, which commenced on the first of this month, will be completed by the end of the month. It will undoubtedly make the distribution of food more efficient.

A second food ration allocation. A notice from the Jewish elder announcing a second food ration available with a ration card was posted on [the ghetto] walls today. Sales will begin on the 14th[9] of this month. This ration is more generous than the first because a range of vegetables has been allocated. It is also possible (until further notice) to purchase food with coupons from the first ration card, which is very convenient. The public reacted very favourably to the announcement.

4 The author is referring to the German ghetto administration.

5 The commander of the Jewish Order Service was Leon Rozenblat (1892/1894–1944), bank manager and member of the Banking Council and the Central Bureau of Labour Departments, Trade and Control Unit; commander of the Jewish police force in the Lodz ghetto from 1940; appointed deputy to the Jewish elder, Chaim Rumkowski, in September 1940; head of the evacuation commission responsible for compiling lists of people to be deported out of the ghetto; in 1944 deported on the final transport to Auschwitz, where he was murdered, possibly at the hands of another inmate.

6 Abram Nożycki (1922–1942), tailor; perished in the ghetto.

7 The Provisioning Section was responsible for the distribution of daily essentials.

8 In the original 'artykuły kolonialne', literally 'colonial goods', originally referred to imported goods such as tea and coffee, but in the context of the ghetto the term came to mean groceries more generally.

9 This has been corrected by hand; it originally read '29th'.

The market prices of basic commodities. In private trade today, bread was sold at 6.50 RM[10] per kg, potatoes at 2.50, groats at 12, coal dust at 0.60, coal at 1–2 (depending on the type), wood at 0.70, matches at 0.20 (per box), tobacco at 2.90 (50 gr.).[11]
Supply problems. One of the most serious supply problems this week was a missing delivery of groats. It is worth mentioning that this foodstuff, which is the most important staple after bread and potatoes, has so far been supplied in relatively large quantities, and this week is the first time a consignment has failed to arrive. The weekly demand for groats is 50,000 kg, which provides every ghetto resident with 50 gr. of this item. The private market has already reacted by increasing prices to 12 RM per kg, with sugar costing 9 RM, whereas previously these amounts were the other way round.
Increase in the bread ration? Rumours on this subject persist. This issue preoccupies ghetto residents greatly and everyone is talking about it.
Chronicle of the Rescue Service. The Rescue Service was called out fifty-nine times today. Physicians pronounced five people dead and provided first aid to the remaining fifty-four. Three of the deaths were caused by exhaustion. Thirty-five cases of internal disease were recorded, as well as seventeen injuries, one attack of insanity, and one suicide.
Street demonstrations. Yesterday's demonstrations by crowds demanding an increase in food and fuel rations continued this morning. It is worth noting that since the events of September,[12] the ghetto has not witnessed a single breach of the peace. It has been established beyond doubt that this action was organized by irresponsible individuals intent on disrupting the law and order established by the concerted efforts of the ghetto authorities, who are responsible for the peace, security, and welfare of its residents. What is striking is that the individuals who incited the crowd were recruited from among the workers who benefited from the additional food rations they received by reselling these rations at exorbitant prices. The demonstrations took place in front of the hospital building on Łagiewnicka Street and at several places along Brzezińska Street. Several times the crowds tried to steal food from wagons. Thanks to the strenuous efforts of the Order Service, these attempts were thwarted. Frequent police patrols monitored the streets of the ghetto throughout the day. Peace was fully restored in the afternoon.
A sad display of savagery. A crowd of several hundred people demolished a wooden shed at the property on 66 Brzezińska Street. While the wood was being stolen, the roof of the shed collapsed, crushing several people under its weight. Despite their desperate cries of pain, no one came to their aid, and the looting continued. Thirty-six-year-old Frania Szabnek[13] succumbed to her injuries, and two other people were seriously injured. This deplorable display of moral depravity, which is the direct result of disgraceful agitation by criminal elements, clearly illustrates the need to radically combat the parasitism of the underworld.

10 When referring to currency, the Chronicle used RM (abbreviation for Reichsmark), but this meant in practice ghetto marks, which had no value outside the ghetto.
11 The rationed items were distributed among shops under the supervision of the Jewish elder. The free market, which was considerably more expensive, existed alongside these shops.
12 The author is referring to the food protests of August and Sept. 1940, which were violently suppressed by the German police. See also Doc. 206 on a food protest called for Dec. 1940, and Doc. 247, fn. 5, on Rumkowski's formation of a special assault unit in Sept. 1940 to suppress protests and demonstrations.
13 Frania Szabnek (1905–1941), office worker.

Paradoxes of ghetto life. An 8-year-old informant. An 8-year-old boy came to one of the Order Police stations to denounce his own parents for not giving him his allocated bread ration. The boy demanded an investigation and punishment for the culprits. No comment …

They stole the staircase. The inhabitants of one building found themselves in a very unsettling situation. They awoke to discover that during the night, unknown perpetrators had stolen … the stairs, including the banisters.

The purchase of furs. The deadline for registering furs expired the day before yesterday. Now that this operation, which has enjoyed keen interest among thousands of ghetto residents, has ended, it is worth reviewing the whole process and what it has achieved. The requirement to register all types of furs for purchase was communicated to the inhabitants by the chairman in Announcement no. 179, dated 17 December of last year.[14] The original deadline was 1 January this year, but due to the high number of responses it was extended until the 10th of this month, whereby according to the order, after this deadline 'any furs still in the possession of private individuals will be confiscated'.[15] The Jewish Elder's Bank,[16] situated on Ciesielskia Street, was entrusted with purchasing the furs. By the 10th of this month, the bank had paid out 350,000 RM for the furs it had purchased, and there were (approximately) 3,500 sellers. On the 9th of this month, cash payments were partially suspended, and in order to intensify the operation, the bank limited itself solely to accepting declarations and paying out advances. Only smaller items were purchased. A characteristic feature of this operation is that the more expensive furs were declared in the initial phase, whereas towards the end the items were mostly of poor quality. Fur coat linings, collars, and ladies' fur accessories were the items most frequently submitted for purchase. On the busiest days, over 5,000 fur items passed through the experts' hands. On average, appraisals exceeded pre-war prices by 25 per cent (at a ratio of 1 RM to 2 złoty). Concerning the quality of the furs that were sold, almost 50 per cent were very poor, 30 per cent were fair, and barely 20 per cent were good. The number of brand-new furs offered for sale was negligible. Experts carried out the appraisals, and the furs were then passed on to a commission, which determined the amounts to be paid out. Depending on the information available to the commission, it would often consider the petitioner's situation when setting the appraisal price, and sometimes it increased the purchase price significantly. Consequently, the whole operation, which was carried out in line with the chairman's guidelines, served to provide material assistance to those who had been compelled to give up their furs. Although the operation was carried out by order of the [German] authorities, it is fair to say that it was of great benefit to the population concerned. This is because the chairman managed to obtain permission to carry out purchases on his own authority. With regard to the population's needs, another favourable development is that those who work in public service and require particularly warm clothing are exempt from the obligation to sell their furs. This applies to physicians, nurses, police officers, and caretakers. Additionally, by virtue of the powers vested in him, the chairman has also exempted a number of sick and elderly people from this obligation. Finally, it is worth noting that furs of little value

14 YIVO, RG 241/301.

15 Announcement no. 188, 31 Dec. 1940: YIVO, RG 241/309.

16 The Bank for Purchase of Valuable Objects and Clothing was opened in August 1940.

were also exempted from the obligation to be sold. In all of these cases, those concerned received the relevant documentation, and their furs were provided with an official seal.

The fact that it was possible to process the cases of several thousand people concerned in such a short time can be attributed to the exceptionally efficient technical organization, the hard work, and dedication of the entire staff, who were well aware of their responsibilities. To sum up the results of this operation now that it has been completed, it is quite clear that the work was without a doubt carried out in the spirit of meeting the needs of those concerned to the greatest possible extent and with a full understanding of their social position. Unfortunately, one is struck by the fact that, in a large number of cases, many of those concerned failed to appreciate these good intentions; they were under the false impression that the purchase of the furs was a standard, profit-oriented commercial transaction. Firstly, the chairman personally initiated the operation and worked with the commissions on the first day. Then he inspected the bank several times and gave detailed instructions to the members of the commissions. The tasks were divided up as follows: management remained in the hands of Mr J. Szkólnik[17] and Mr J. Izraelski.[18] Two commissions were in operation, and on the busiest days there were three. These were composed of the bank's board members, represented by the director, H. Szyfer;[19] the board members P. Blaugrund[20] and H. Fajner;[21] and A. Englard,[22] a member of the appraisal committee. Mr Opatowski[23] and Mr S. Brajtsztajn[24] served as experts.

Necessity is the mother of invention
Mr Wosk's[25] *sensational ideas*

The unbelievably difficult living conditions in the ghetto provide an extraordinary opportunity for human ingenuity, including the chance to develop innovations to solve the wide variety of problems caused by the shortage of so many basic necessities. The Community authorities received a visit from Mr Henryk Wosk, the well-known inventor and holder of numerous patents, who proposed the formation of a Department for Ideas and Innovations, modelled on the former Patent Office. Mr Wosk proposes that ghetto residents submit purposeful ideas to this department in return for reimbursement of any costs incurred. For their part, the ghetto authorities will inform the department of unresolved issues, which should then be communicated to the public. The department will award prizes to those who devise the best solutions to these issues. In addition, inventors will be given the opportunity to work on putting their ideas into practice. This

17 Jakub Szkólnik (b. 1893), bank employee; head of the Jewish Elder's Bank; member of the Chief Audit Office; later head of the Hat Department; deported to Auschwitz in 1944.
18 Jehuda Nisen Izraelski (b. 1908), retailer; on the management board of the Jewish Elder's Bank; deported to Auschwitz in 1944.
19 Herman Szyfer (b. 1884), public official; chairman of the management board of the Jewish Elder's Bank; later head of the Tobacco Department.
20 Perec Blaugrund (b. 1892), businessman, bank official; head of the Fur Department.
21 Correctly: Hersz (Henryk) Majer Fajner (1907–1944), businessman and bank councillor; head of the Benefits Section, which was responsible for social welfare in the ghetto; in July 1944 deported to Chełmno, where he was murdered.
22 Aron Józef Englard (1881–1944); perished in the ghetto.
23 Josef Opatowski (b. 1884), furrier in Łódź before the war.
24 Correctly: Szoel Rywen Brejtsztejn (b. 1889), retailer in Łódź before the war.
25 Henryk Wosk (b. 1908), master locksmith and galvanizer.

will bring about a series of advantages, such as the chance to provide work to individuals who are currently unemployed but are fit for work, and it will encourage ideas that when realized will help to improve the lives of the residents. Regarding Mr Wosk's most recent ideas, the following are worth mentioning: (1) discovering uses for frozen or rotten potatoes; (2) utilizing coal dust completely; (3) feasible methods of manufacturing dry ice cheaply under the present circumstances; (4) replacing glass, which is currently in short supply, with other suitable materials. Mr Wosk's proposals have aroused considerable interest among influential circles in the ghetto.

The implementation of Mr Wosk's initiative will undoubtedly prompt further productive ideas at a time when the only flourishing form of ingenuity in the ghetto relates to a single specific, commercial aim – producing goods of no value whatsoever to consumers, purely to sell them for a profit. We have in mind examples such as the mass production of 'confectionery', which is either worthless or even potentially harmful, and the manufacture of all kinds of counterfeit goods, ranging from gold to fuel.

DOC. 223
On 15 January 1941 the government of the GG discusses resettling hundreds of thousands more Poles and Jews in the General Government[1]

Minutes of the government meeting in Cracow on 15 January 1941[2]

In his introductory remarks the Governor General stated that the purpose of this meeting was to hold a detailed discussion of questions associated with the resettlement of Poles and Jews in the General Government.

At a time when the General Government was experiencing the most unusual and most difficult economic, transportation, general political, and military conditions, it would be an almost unbearable additional burden to admit hundreds of thousands of people with foreign ethnic and racial backgrounds into the territory of the General Government. These people are expropriated in Germany and come here dispossessed, to an area where they can see absolutely no opportunity for rebuilding their lives in any way. But, he said, the only standpoint from which the entire matter should be considered is that of Reich policy. Any criticism of such measures based on lingering remnants of human concern or considerations of expediency must be completely ruled out. The resettlement has to take place and the General Government must take in these people, because this is one of the great tasks that the Führer has set for the General Government.

The Governor General said the task now was to discuss how it might be possible to fulfil this request from the Reich and to draw the necessary conclusions regarding the administrative measures required. Another important question to address was what the

1 AIPN, GK 95, vol. 10. Copy in IfZ-Archives, Fb 105, vol. 14, fols. 2480–2497. This document has been translated from German.
2 The following officials attended the meeting: Hans Frank, Josef Bühler, Friedrich-Wilhelm Krüger, Otto Wächter, Paul Riege, Bruno Streckenbach, Eberhard Westerkamp, Alfred Spindler, Walter Emmerich, Hellmut Körner, Max Frauendorfer, Hansjulius Schepers, Herbert von Streit, and Walther Föhl.

Reich must do to help the Governor General meet the Reich's demands. Both on 4 November and at a later meeting in December, the Führer had explained to the Governor General that resettling Poles in the General Government was part of his policy and that the measures necessary for carrying out this resettlement must be implemented during the war, because after the war they would result in international difficulties. The Führer had given assurances that he would do everything possible to provide the General Government with what it needs in the way of food and other support.

Obergruppenführer Krüger reported on the meeting held in Berlin on 8 January 1941 at the Reich Security Main Office.[3] For the General Government, Obergruppenführer Krüger, Main Department Head Westerkamp, Oberregierungsrat Dr Schepers, and Dr Föhl had attended the meeting.

Krüger reported that Gruppenführer Heydrich, who chaired the meeting, had said it was necessary for the Reich to remove the Poles and Jews from the eastern territories as quickly as possible so that the resettlement of ethnic Germans from Volhynia, Lithuania, etc. could finally be carried out. According to figures cited by Gruppenführer Heydrich, the total number of people to be evacuated is 831,000. Moreover, it is necessary to resettle about 200,000 people within the General Government on account of military training areas that are to be built, which amounts to a total of one million people being resettled in the space of one year. The situation is difficult inasmuch as the Wehrmacht unexpectedly announced that troops in the General Government are to be further reinforced and that the date set for the evacuation of the military training areas will be brought forward from 1 May to 1 April. Efforts to have this date postponed on grounds of weather, poor road conditions, transportation difficulties, etc. have unfortunately been unsuccessful. The Wehrmacht has refused to postpone, citing military reasons.

In practice, the resettlement of a million people means that two trains per day, each carrying a thousand people, have to arrive in the General Government. During the above meeting, all parties questioned whether the Reich Ministry of Transport would be able to satisfy these extraordinary demands. The representative of the Reich Ministry of Transport did not give a binding promise, but believed overall that the project could be carried out as long as there are no disruptions caused by special requests by the Wehrmacht.[4]

Specifically it was determined that the following numbers of people are to be evacuated by 1 May this year: 30,000 from East Prussia, 24,000 from Silesia, 40,000 from Danzig-West Prussia, and 90,000 from the Warthegau, i.e. a total of 184,000 people. The following numbers of people are to be resettled in the context of the evacuation of the military training areas for the Wehrmacht: 8,500 people from East Prussia, 10,000 from Silesia, 27,000 from Danzig-West Prussia, and 19,000 from the Warthegau, i.e. a total of 64,500. Of these, the Wehrmacht intends to retain 2,000 workers and their families, 10,000 people in all, for work at the military training areas. Thus, 184,000 + 54,500, or 238,500 people in total, will have to be evacuated by 1 May 1941 within the framework of the so-called 3rd Short-Range Plan. In addition, 10,000 Jews will be resettled from Vienna.

3 See Doc. 218.

4 The name of the representative of the Reich Ministry of Transport who took part in the meeting of 8 Jan. 1941 is not known.

During the above meeting it was pointed out that, in light of the experience of the previous year, the planned form of resettlement could not be sustained by the General Government. Above all, it must be deemed important that the resettled families are adequately clothed and have sufficient food for an initial period. It was agreed that the intention is to provide the people with food for a fortnight.

The question of the resettled people taking money with them was also discussed. This point, however, was deemed hardly the most important, since there are certainly no objections on the part of the General Government to a few more zloty coming in. It is much more important that the General Government is not burdened in other respects, as it was last year.

Obergruppenführer Krüger said that both he and Main Department Head Westerkamp were asked in Berlin to establish plans for the entire year, and to do so in such detail that the district governors and the Kreishauptleute charged with implementing the operation know exactly what is to happen, because once the transports have crossed the Reich border, the Reich will no longer be involved. There are plans to set up reporting centres and reporting points at the border in collaboration with the Reich Railway, so that the central offices can be immediately notified when trains arrive, thereby making sure unscheduled transports are prevented.

Main Department Head Westerkamp declared that he had nothing to add to the report given by Obergruppenführer Krüger. He said that it was emphasized during the negotiations in Berlin that it must be guaranteed that the resettlement operation is implemented uniformly.

Dr Föhl started by making several announcements about technical details which were discussed concerning the handling of the transport trains in Berlin, and then reported on the negotiations concerning the money that people may take with them. Initially, a figure of 100 zloty was discussed. Given the currency situation at the time, however, there was no interest on the part of the General Government in bringing in as much money as possible, and the amount was therefore set at 20 zloty. Today, however, there is no reason not to allow as much money as possible to be brought in. The amount could easily be set at 80 or 100 zloty. That would really be the least that the Reich could do, since it is receiving not only the land previously owned by the Poles, but also certain assets of the ethnic Germans who are being settled there.

The Governor General thanked the gentlemen, especially Obergruppenführer Krüger, for their remarks and for representing the General Government's stance when they were in Berlin. He said that the General Government has a stance that is absolutely loyal to the Reich, but it is in the interests of the Reich that the General Government should not collapse. The General Government is not refusing to take on the task it has been given. Matters in the East cannot be resolved at all otherwise, and it is still doubtful whether they can be resolved even in this way.

The Governor General then enquired in detail how the transfer of the resettled persons was proceeding and what arrangements were being made to this end.

Dr Föhl responded that first of all the number, timing, and destination stations for the transport trains would be determined during a scheduling meeting. In total, there are 248 destination stations. Certain standard quantities of food have been established for the transport, with each train to receive the respective amount. As for sanitary matters, it is planned for the people first to be grouped in assembly camps in order to prevent epidemics. Housing them more permanently is naturally a difficult matter.

Main Department Head Westerkamp mentioned that he took part in a meeting in Lublin where the housing conditions of those already resettled was discussed. A dismal picture of the housing conditions emerged. If the same is true everywhere, it will be very difficult to house the new transports in an orderly fashion. There has been talk of 50,000 evacuees having reappeared in the Warthegau by way of uncontrolled return migration and of a constant stream of people migrating back and forth.

Obergruppenführer Krüger remarked that such unplanned return migration leads to further difficulties by its very nature, since the local authorities on the other side naturally detain the people and send them back again. One location shifts the blame to the other.

Brigadeführer Streckenbach voiced doubts as to whether it was even possible to tackle return migration effectively. He said that there is no hermetically sealed border, and occupying the road does not guarantee that the border is not crossed at a distance from the road. Returnees are typically captured not in the Warthegau, but in the Old Reich. Since they do not feel safe enough in the Warthegau, they move further away, into Reich territory. This naturally presents the risk of epidemics being spread.

The Governor General enquired about the attitude of the Kreishauptleute towards the resettlement.

Main Department Head Dr Westerkamp replied that the situation is naturally very difficult for the Kreishauptleute. One need only imagine the situation at the moment a transport arrives. It is important not to leave the Kreishauptleute without help and advice. The Kreishauptleute, for their part, then need to instruct the wojts[5] on how the stream of resettled people can be housed.

The Governor General considered it necessary to issue general guidelines to the district governors. These guidelines should indicate the intended programme for handling the entire operation, the method of resettlement, and which offices are responsible.

Main Department Head Westerkamp was of the opinion that the details should be left up to the resourcefulness of the Kreishauptmänner, but that fundamental questions – e.g. whether or not to erect barracks – must be clarified in the guidelines. The Kreishauptleute will be told that the wojts must take care of housing in such a way that one or two additional people are housed in each dwelling. It will of course be impossible to avoid families being forcibly separated in this process.

The Governor General asked whether it would be expedient to distribute the incomers by district and to allow the governors to impose differing burdens on the Kreise under their authority.

Dr Föhl stated that this has already been done.

Governor Dr Wächter explained with the help of a map that there is an area comprising more than one-third of District Cracow which cannot possibly receive resettled persons. The area concerned comprises the border zone along the San river, the border zone with

5 Correctly: wójtowie (Polish local administrative officials).

Slovakia, the Wehrmacht training areas, and the oilfields.[6] The influx of evacuees to any of these areas cannot be permitted. Moreover, there must be no Jews sent to Cracow.

It goes without saying, he said, that the Kreishauptleute are up in arms. He, the Governor, had seen for himself the difficulties with housing in the Kreise. The conditions are appalling. Even if people can be brought to the destination stations, he could hardly imagine how they are to be kept there.

The population quickly resorts to physical force in order to stop people who are traditionally disliked in the area from being settled there. The difficulties will naturally increase as the number of settlers increases.

The Governor General enquired about the need for workers that the Reich has announced.

Main Department Head Dr Frauendorfer stated that the Reich would need 120,000–150,000 additional agricultural workers.

Governor Dr Wächter pointed out that the experience has been that those who are resettled have generally included only those in need of care, persons who are sick, weak, or the very elderly.

Main Department Head Dr Frauendorfer proposed that the 120,000 to 150,000 be deducted from the total number of evacuees.

The *Governor General* took the view that the total number should be let in and then the 120,000–150,000 should be sent back on special transports. The Labour Department would have to intervene in good time to determine how many persons fit for work there are on each transport.

Obergruppenführer Krüger said it would be extremely difficult to establish such information under the given circumstances. Another question to be considered was the extent to which the distinctly Ukrainian areas should be burdened with the resettlement.[7]

The Governor General stated on this point that individual Kreise could not be treated differently. Preferential treatment of Ukrainian Kreise would destroy the unity of the General Government.

Brigadeführer *Streckenbach* said it was illusory to deliberate about the issue of border zones and Ukrainian areas. In practice, any influence on the evacuees ceases the moment the people leave the train. If a Polish Kreis is heavily burdened with evacuees, it is clear that the people crowded into this Kreis will begin to migrate to an adjacent, less burdened Ukrainian Kreis.

Governor Dr Wächter complained that the Reich Security Main Office was telling the evacuees semi-officially or officially that they would be compensated in the General Government. The people come to the Kreishauptleute and tell them that they have been promised compensation.

Brigadeführer Streckenbach denied that the Reich Security Main Office had officially promised the people compensation. The only possible explanation was that some subordinate offices which had to deal with the desperate evacuees had given people this hope of compensation in order to get rid of them.

6 This is a reference to the Kreise Krosno and Jasło in the Carpathian foothills, where oil had been produced since the mid nineteenth century.

7 A large Ukrainian minority lived in Kreis Chełm (District Lublin) and Kreis Przemyśl (District Cracow).

The *Governor General* wanted to know exactly who had made these promises of compensation.

As far as influence on the evacuees was concerned, direct influence on the people naturally ceased in the moment they left the train. The influence of the police, however, could make itself felt in the ensuing few days when the people were loitering in the streets without work. There was also the influence of the municipal administration, which is responsible for issuing food coupons.

In general, he said, it can doubtlessly be said that the resettlement is a very unusual, immense, and unique task. It is an enormous task, which the German men here in the General Government are being asked to carry out.

State Secretary Dr Bühler[8] said he thought it would be impossible to distribute one million people as planned within the territory of the General Government. In terms of security, disease prevention, and nutrition, the burdens were so great that it would be impossible to get by without unrest. He proposed that large-scale work projects be set up and that the evacuees be housed in labour camps.

The *Governor General* replied that the strongest possible measures would be taken against unrest. The Reich would need to help in the event of difficulties with food provision. He said he would address the issue of work projects at a later stage.

The district governors will be sent the government's guidelines, and it will be up to them to take care of matters. It will be necessary to include extraordinary funds in the budget. It is, he said, imperative that the district governors be helped in every way possible.

Dr Föhl proposed that the Church be required to create space in monasteries and churches for the purpose of housing evacuees.

The *Governor General* instructed *Dr Föhl* to discuss this matter with Archbishop Sapieha.[9] However, there are concerns that housing evacuees in churches would attract too much attention and would probably fail as these spaces are difficult to heat.

Governor Dr Wächter talked about the construction of barracks. In general, it will probably be inexpedient to construct barracks, but in individual cases, namely where work projects are being carried out, the construction of barracks could be considered.

The *Governor General* stated that this question would be discussed separately.

Main Department Head Dr Emmerich addressed the issue of compensation, stating that the Main Trustee Office East was of the opinion that those who have been resettled must be compensated. He said it had been indicated that with regard to such compensation the General Government must at least assist by making the payment in zloty.

8 Dr Josef Bühler (1904–1948), lawyer; worked in Hans Frank's law firm, 1930–1932; joined the NSDAP in 1933; became a local court judge in 1933 and chief public prosecutor at the Higher Regional Court in Munich in 1935; head of Frank's ministerial office from 1938; chief of staff, state secretary, and deputy to Frank after the latter's appointment as governor general, 1939/1940–1945; attended the Wannsee Conference in 1942; convicted and executed in Poland in 1948.

9 Adam Stefan Sapieha (1867–1951), priest; studied in Vienna and Cracow; bishop of Cracow from 1911; archbishop of Cracow from 1925; member of the Polish Senate, 1922–1923; highest Catholic dignitary remaining in Poland from 1939; supported the Polish Central Welfare Council (RGO) and intervened several times with Governor General Frank in protest against violence and terror and on behalf of Jews in the General Government who had converted to Christianity; cardinal in 1946.

The *Governor General* noted that the head of the Main Trustee Office East[10] had written to the Governor General demanding that the General Government take on payment of the compensation. This request had been rejected, whereupon the Main Trustee Office East wrote that its request had been completely misunderstood, that the General Government should merely be the paying agent, and that the Reich would pay the compensation. The General Government had agreed to this; nothing more on this matter had been heard, however, from the Main Trustee Office East.

Regarding the question of compensation, *Main Department Head Dr Schepers* saw a danger of political disagreement within individual Kreise. The Wehrmacht has namely agreed to compensate those evacuated both from the military training areas in the Reich and the areas in the General Government. As a result, evacuees who receive compensation and those who do not could be resettled next to each other in a single location, which could naturally lead to difficulties.

The *Governor General* said these concerns were of no importance.

The important question now was what the General Government must demand of the Reich in order to be able to carry out the operation. He explicitly emphasized that it would be impossible for the General Government to take on such a burden without the Reich offering something in exchange.

First of all, it must be determined what needs to be done to provide housing locally for the Poles who are to be resettled. Should barrack camps be erected?

Main Department Head Westerkamp reported that, during the Berlin discussions, Gruppenführer Heydrich had declared barrack camps to be unfeasible, believing that such housing would entail too much maintenance. Gruppenführer Heydrich had therefore strongly advised against the construction of barracks. He said the matter could be handled in such a way that the new arrivals would be assigned to families one by one. This system, however, can probably no longer be adopted, as it has already been used to house people from earlier transports.

The *Governor General* cited the example of the town of Reichshof,[11] which at present has about 20,000 inhabitants and will perhaps have to house an equal number, as evidence that constructing barrack camps is by no means a Polish-friendly option or one motivated by compassion, but merely a measure in keeping with the growth of the town. If a city grows slowly over time, it deals with this growth by putting up new buildings accordingly. There is therefore no reason to explain why buildings should not also be built when the growth happens quickly, suddenly, or, to use an expression from the world of film, is 'speeded up'. Building barracks should at least be considered for the exceptional emergency needs of the sick, the infirm, and those believed to be infected by an epidemic disease, as well as for children and those unable to work. Of course, it will be impossible to house all 800,000 people in barracks. The construction of barracks will have to be divided into two phases: (a) barracks for immediate emergency needs; (b) barracks to permanently house those who cannot be housed elsewhere. The barracks system would naturally involve very high costs.

The *Governor General* then instructed the representative of the Forestry Department, who had arrived in the meantime, to provide timber for 100 barracks with a capacity of

10 Max Winkler.

11 Rzeszów.

500 persons each and if necessary to deduct the required amount of timber from the Wehrmacht's quota. This course of action is entirely in keeping with the instructions from the Führer, who in the Reich Chancellery on 4 November, in the presence of the Governor General and General Jodl, issued an order which stated that such resettlement needs would take precedence over the interests of the Wehrmacht.

[The Governor General stated that] apart from housing, the most important problem is food. Those fit for work, who will be readily recognized as such, are to be recorded immediately in a form of special register and will be overseen by the employment office, from which they will then receive their food cards. Matters are more difficult with the remaining people, who are not fit for work.

Main Department Head Körner[12] pointed out that the people would initially have their transport rations, but that they would use them up within a few days of arrival. Temporarily, rations provided from field kitchens could be contemplated.

The *Governor General* said it would be worth considering whether the Department of Food and Agriculture should make a warehouse available to each Kreishauptmann for the purpose of feeding the resettlers. The Führer had given a firm pledge that he would intervene to help should food provision prove difficult. What was the position of the Reich Ministry of Food and Agriculture on this?

Main Department Head Körner stated that he had not yet negotiated with the Reich Ministry of Food and Agriculture, but such negotiations needed to be initiated. The Department of Food and Agriculture was not in a position to scrap its entire food plan. He had asked the Governor General to prepare a letter to this effect to the Reich Minister of Food and Agriculture.

The *Governor General* agreed; he would also inform the Führer through Reichsleiter Bormann and inform the Reich Marshal through State Secretary Körner.

On the question of housing, *Main Department Head Westerkamp* also noted that it was still being considered whether the necessary space would be freed up by forcing the Jews closer together into ghettos.

On this issue, *Obergruppenführer Krüger* referred to the plan developed by Brigadeführer Globocznik,[13] which, however, only pertains to Lublin. It should be considered whether this could be extended to the entire General Government.[14]

Main Department Head Westerkamp noted that the Chief of Staff of District Warsaw[15] had spoken to him in great earnest about the conditions in the Warsaw ghetto. The reports on the conditions in the ghetto are contradictory, however, in that one side claims that all food deliveries have ceased, while according to other reports there is still sufficient food available.

12 Hellmut Körner (1904–1966), farmer; joined the NSDAP in 1930, and became regional farmers' leader in Saxony; head of the Main Department of Food and Agriculture in the General Government; active in Reich Commissariat Ukraine from 1941; in the Race and Settlement Main Office from late 1944; company manager in Hamburg after the war.

13 Correctly: Globocnik.

14 This is probably a reference to the plans for a ghetto in Lublin: see Doc. 257.

15 Dr Herbert Hummel (1907–1944), lawyer; joined the NSDAP in 1932 and the SA in 1933; public prosecutor in Munich from 1933; head of the Reich Main Office in the Reich Legal Office from 1935; head of administration at the Office of the Governor of District Warsaw; deputy governor of District Warsaw, 1943–1944; killed during the Warsaw Uprising.

The *Governor General* said he intended to make the decision whether the Warsaw ghetto should be maintained or dissolved dependent on the outcome of his forthcoming visit there.[16] Under no circumstances could he allow a city like Warsaw to be completely contaminated.

Then the Governor General turned to the large-scale project to regulate the Vistula river. This concerns a length of 900 km, including parts where no work has ever been done and parts where no work has been done in about fifty years. The regulation of the Vistula offers the possibility of employing an enormous number of workers in a productive way for a long time to come. In particular, it could partly solve the problem of employing the growing numbers of Polish youth. Otherwise there is a danger that the main contingent of the Polish resistance movement will be recruited from among the ranks of these young people.

Brigadeführer Streckenbach noted that the resistance movement is making itself felt very strongly and is appearing in even greater numbers than a year ago. This also applies to the eastern territories incorporated into the Reich. The resistance movement's activity has so far been limited mostly to gathering like-minded people and propaganda. However, some cases of concrete action have been recorded, such as in Lublin.[17]

The *Governor General* urgently warned against taking the dangers in this too lightly. It should not be forgotten that the Poles are the sworn enemies of Germandom. It would be completely wrong to be deceived by the objective and loyal attitude of individual Poles, because these loyal Poles merely provide the protective screen behind which the resistance movement carries out its dangerous work. It was a mistake to be misled by the accommodating manner or loyal behaviour of some Poles, as this can lead one to underestimate the real danger.

Brigadeführer Streckenbach pointed out that significantly it has been mostly Poles who are working for the Germans who are found to be the pillars of the resistance organization. As soon as one of these people is arrested, the German department head arrives and asks why one of his best people has been arrested. This course of events is familiar from the efforts to combat the illegal communist movement in the Reich.

The *Governor General* asked the head of the Finance Department, Main Department Head Spindler, how the resettlement was affecting the General Government's budget.

Main Department Head Spindler replied that a certain increase would be seen in public welfare expenditure. However, exact figures cannot be given. The welfare costs are borne by the local authorities and the Kreise. The budgetary situation of some local authorities has improved considerably in the recent past, but many are still under great pressure.

The Governor General ordered that issues concerning resettlement must not be pursued half-heartedly. This matter is an absolute necessity for the Reich. The Kreise and local authorities must be given support.

At the request of the Governor General, *Brigadeführer Streckenbach* explained the reasons for the resettlement operation as follows:

The resettlement of the Poles and Jews from the Germanized eastern territories is predicated on the return of the ethnic Germans from Lithuania, Volhynia, etc. to the eastern territories incorporated into the Reich and also on the necessity of creating mili-

16 Frank was in Warsaw from 17 to 20 Jan. 1941.

17 These have not been identified.

tary training areas. The construction of large military training areas in the East is an inevitable measure resulting from the development of military technology. Resettlement itself is a matter that has already been discussed many times. The question often arises as to why such short deadlines are set in resettlement agreements, and why the operation is scheduled at such an inconvenient time of year. Resettlement agreements must be concluded because the fate of the ethnic Germans in the areas from which they are to be resettled depends on the speed of the resettlement. Certainly, the Reich has a treaty of friendship and also formally good relations with Soviet Russia, but in practice, ethnic Germans in the areas occupied by the Russians have been treated extraordinarily badly. The same applies to Germans in Romania and also in Hungary, where, however, Germans are going to be left for specific reasons. As of now, evacuated ethnic Germans have been living as unused German manpower in camps scattered all over the Reich for months, waiting to be resettled. Understandably, the mood among these people is not very good; their original faith and confidence are in danger of being shaken if they cannot be resettled soon. The original plan, which involved gradual resettlement, i.e. evacuating a Polish farm and then placing a German there, has proven unfeasible. Some of the farms are too small and need to be rounded out in order to reach the desired size for the creation of a new class of German farmers in the East. As the Governor General has already explained, it is also necessary to carry out the operation during the war, because during the war there is still the opportunity to carry out relatively rigorous measures without regard to international public opinion. It should also be remembered that the resettlement of the Poles from the eastern territories – as well as, incidentally, the evacuations from Alsace-Lorraine[18] – is being carried out in compliance with the conditions stipulated for the Germans in both territories in 1918/19.[19] Some of the Germans who were resettled from the territories separated from Germany at that time were treated worse than the Poles are now.

The *Governor General* said the comparison was not entirely accurate, since the Polish republic which could be made responsible for the resettled Poles no longer exists. Hundreds of thousands of German soldiers and members of the civil administration live in the area of the General Government, and it is not a matter of indifference if epidemics or unrest were to break out here.

Main Department Head Schepers proposed that all construction projects be prepared and pursued according to plan, especially those in which many manual workers as well as women and children can be employed. The most suitable work for this is in forestry, where large numbers of children and female labourers could be used for reforestation tasks.

The *Governor General* concluded by asking whether there was any prospect of successfully implementing the resettlement operation.

Main Department Head Westerkamp thought it might be possible to succeed with the first few trains, albeit with great difficulty. But later it would become necessary to stop the influx temporarily and pause the programme for a few months.

18 After the end of the First World War, some of the German population was expelled from areas that came under Polish or French rule.

19 After the defeat of France in 1940, the Reich annexed Alsace-Lorraine, and the occupying authorities expelled to unoccupied France those elements of the French population deemed undesirable.

The *Governor General* expressed misgivings about this; if a programme was started and then suddenly halted, difficulties would naturally result. In any case, everything possible must be done, for only then can it be demonstrated that implementation is impossible.

The Governor General thanked all officials entrusted with this difficult task and ordered that another meeting be held after the Warsaw trip.

The meeting closed at 13:15.

DOC. 224
On 19 January 1941 the Polish underground newspaper *Barykada Wolności* calls on Jews and Poles to wage a joint struggle for freedom[1]

Behind ghetto walls and walls of misunderstanding

(Sent from the ghetto)
In the ghetto, which Nazi Germans shamefully refer to as the Jewish residential district, the population receives a weekly ration of 250 gr. of bread and is robbed by the marauding occupiers day after day of its food supplies, clothing, and money; it is oppressed and mistreated.

Isolated in the ghetto, the Jewish population is dependent on gossip and rumours, which seep in from the rest of Warsaw in distorted form. The ghetto's population feels imprisoned and is slipping into a prison psychosis.

Fed communist and Zionist propaganda, which here falls on the fertile soil of bitterness and despair, it [the ghetto population] resents the Polish population for not coming to its aid, for shying away, for leaving it at the mercy of Nazi violence. In this atmosphere of resentment, the Jewish population forgets that it is also a part of the Polish population.

Polish–Jewish racial misunderstandings did not originate with the German occupation. Polish nationalists from OZON,[2] Endecja,[3] and Falanga[4] have stirred up racial hatred among the Polish population which is similar to the racial hatred the Nazis stirred up in the German population. German propaganda has found worthy fascist champions among the representatives of OZON and Falanga – but the Polish nationalists do not constitute the entire Polish population.

1 *Barykada Wolności*, no. 30, 19 Jan. 1941, p. 4. This document has been translated from Polish.

2 OZON/OZN (Obóz Zjednoczenia Narodowego), Camp of National Unity: a right-wing movement founded in 1937 under the authoritarian Sanacja governments with the aim of uniting the nation after Joseph Piłsudski's death. It ruled Poland until the outbreak of the Second World War. In 1942 it became the Camp of Fighting Poland (Obóz Polski Walczącej, OPW) and was part of the Polish resistance until 1944.

3 Designation for the National Democracy movement based on the initial letters of the Polish abbreviation ND (Narodowa Demokracja).

4 Right-wing extremists from a splinter subgroup of the National Radical Camp (ONR), which broke away from the National Democracy movement; banned from the mid 1930s but continued to operate illegally.

Polish Jews must remember that, together with the Polish people, they were the first to resist Nazi violence in this war, they fired the first shots in the fight against fascism, which is both their enemy and the enemy of the Polish people.

If it now turns away from the Polish cause and believes that the Polish population has forgotten the people behind the ghetto walls, then the Jewish population facilitates the work of German propaganda, which aims to drive a wedge between Poles and Polish Jews.

We have no illusions, and we do not wish to deceive anyone. The Polish bourgeoisie will not take up the struggle for the Jewish cause. But the Polish proletariat is struggling against the ghetto, and the moment it drives the occupiers from our country, it will also tear down the shameful ghetto walls.

Warsaw's workers can't remain indifferent to the fact that the Jewish worker is dying of hunger, oppressed, and beaten, any more than they can remain indifferent to the fate of any proletarian. Beyond the ghetto walls, beyond the walls of indifference and hostility, the Polish worker offers us his fraternal helping hand.

The struggle of the Polish and the Jewish people is the common struggle for freedom.

DOC. 225

On 21 January 1941 the Kreishauptmann in Grójec orders Polish village officials to resettle the rural Jewish population in six small towns[1]

Letter from the head of the Population and Welfare Division, Ernst Maurer,[2] at the office of the Kreishauptmann in Grójec,[3] to the Jewish Council in Grójec[4], dated 21 January 1941

All Jews living outside the towns of Blendow, Tarczyn, Mogielnica, Góra Kalwaria, Warka, and Grójec must immediately relocate to the town closest to them. The village officials are personally responsible to me for ensuring that no more Jews are living in their administrative area by 27 January 1941. The Jews must be immediately informed of this by the village officials and must be sent to the nearest town under the village official's personal supervision. They must be given instructions to take with them for the mayor

1 AŻIH, Ring I/760 (881). Published in Polish in Zdzisław Szeląg (ed.), *Żydzi w Grójeckiem: Słownik – historia, kultura, gospodarka* (Grójec: Towarzystwo Literackie im. Adama Mickiewicza, 2007), appendix. This document has been translated from German.

2 Ernst Maurer (1912–1989), businessman; joined the NSDAP in 1938; head of the Population and Welfare Division for Kreis Grójec from May 1940; Landkommissar in Buczacz from Sept. 1941, then in Zaleszczyki from Nov. 1941 and in Borszczów from early 1942; served in the war from June 1942; head of the Department for Economic Affairs in Kreis Grójec, then Landkommissar in Głowno; managing director of a heating company in Freiburg im Breisgau after the war.

3 Werner Zimmermann (1900–1994), lawyer; worked for the Reich tax authorities in Hamburg from 1925; Regierungsrat in 1929; joined the NSDAP in 1932; Landrat in Meppen, 1934–1939; deputy Landrat in Kattowitz in 1939; Kreishauptmann in Grójec, March 1940 – Jan. 1945; lived in Koblenz after the war.

4 The Jewish Council in Grójec was established on 24 Jan. 1940. It had 12 members, most of whom were former employees of the Jewish Community. In late Nov. 1940 the German authorities established the ghetto for the town's nearly 6,000 Jewish inhabitants. The Grójec ghetto was not surrounded by a wall, but its perimeter was under constant guard.

in charge of the respective town. By 27 January 1941 the village official must report to me the names of the Jews who have been relocated and where they have been resettled. In addition, the mayors of the respective towns must provide me with a list of names of the Jews who registered with them by 29 January 1941. It is strictly forbidden to send Jews to a town other than the one that was designated by the village official from whose community the Jews came.[5]

This measure has become necessary because the Jews in the countryside evade any kind of health check and have on various occasions caused diseases to spread.

At the same time, as of 27 January 1941 I ban all Jews from moving anywhere outside the community where they reside, in this case outside the places listed above, without a permit, which can only be issued by me. After this date, any Jew found outside his residential community without a valid permit may be shot immediately. The Jewish Councils will immediately make these orders public and will be personally responsible to me for any failure to comply with them.

DOC. 226
At an NSDAP rally in Lublin on 22 January 1941, Governor General Hans Frank calls for ruthlessness towards the Jews[1]

Transcript of the speech given by Hans Frank at the NSDAP rally in Lublin on 22 January 1941

[...][2]

Now we are confronted with the small remainder of people who still say: My God, the National Socialists are so harsh to the Poles and the Jews here! To these people I say: we will govern harshly but justly and ensure that the word 'German' is uttered with awe, and that the mass murder which the Polish people have committed, to their own shame and to the shame of their history, will never be repeated. We will never forget the infamous acts this people as a whole and its individual representatives have committed against our nation. Sixty thousand graves of ethnic Germans who were murdered, tortured to death here in the Vistula region, are an indictment of these acts.[3]

5 The Germans concentrated the Jews from the rural areas in the six towns listed in the document before they deported them to the Warsaw ghetto in late February 1941.

1 AIPN, GK 95, vol. 10. Copy in IfZ-Archives, Fb 105, vol. 11, fols. 2549–2559, here 2558–2559. Published in Präg and Jacobmeyer (eds.), *Diensttagebuch des deutschen Generalgouverneurs*, pp. 330–331. This document has been translated from German.

2 Before this passage, Frank talked about the NSDAP's history and about the necessary unity within the German *Volksgemeinschaft*.

3 In early 1939 the Reich Ministry of Public Enlightenment and Propaganda launched a campaign which detailed alleged Polish atrocities committed against the German minority in Poland. This campaign was intensified after the invasion and continued throughout 1940 in the German press as well as in films and books. The crimes described were either fabrications or hugely exaggerated. The number of around 58,000 ethnic Germans killed by Poles in autumn 1939 was invented and launched in a pamphlet entitled *The Polish Atrocities against the German Minority in Poland*, published on behalf of the Reich Foreign Office and compiled by Hans Schadewald (Berlin: Volk und Reich, 1940).

I will not talk about the Jews; they are no longer of interest. Whether they go to Madagascar[4] or somewhere else, all that is of no interest to us. It is clear to us that this mishmash of Asiatic progeny had best traipse back to Asia, where it came from. (Laughter)

As long as the Jews are here, they must work, but not in the way the Jews worked before. In this matter, I want to appeal to your resolve. We still have a small minority of daydreamers with humanitarian ideas and people who, out of sheer genuine German good-naturedness, are prone to let world history pass them by. We who have stood with the Führer in this struggle for twenty years cannot be asked to make any more allowances at all for the Jews. It is the express order that the General Government is to be the home of the Poles. As for the way we treat the Poles, may a look back at their own history be a serious reminder for them of how much better, more justly, and more equitably they are being treated by the National Socialist leadership of this territory. If the Jews today are looking for sympathy throughout the world, it leaves us cold. Our only concern is to ensure that what German blood was sacrificed for remains protected by the dignified, unified, far-sighted attitude of the National Socialist leadership.

[...][5]

DOC. 227

On 23 January 1941 the Stadthauptmann of Kielce plans ghettos in Kielce and Chęciny[1]

Letter (marked 'confidential') from the Stadthauptmann of Kielce[2] to the Kreishauptmann of Kielce-Land[3] (received on 25 January 1941), dated 23 January 1941[4]

I would like to set up the ghetto in Kielce as soon as the weather permits. I have 45,000 square metres of living space at my disposal in the ghetto district in Kielce, which breaks down into around 2,000 rooms. If I use this space to its maximum capacity, I can

4 After the fall of France in June 1940, officials at the Reich Security Main Office (RSHA) and the Reich Foreign Office drew up a plan to deport four million European Jews to the island of Madagascar, then a French colony. The plan was later abandoned. See PMJ 3/91, 92, 94, 99, and 101.

5 In what followed, Frank thanked SS and Police Leader Odilo Globocnik and Governor Ernst Zörner for their work and called for obedience and eternal loyalty to Hitler.

1 AIPN, GK 652/129, fols. 1–2. Copy in USHMM, RG 15 031M, reel 13. This document has been translated from German.

2 Hans Drechsel (1904–1946), commercial employee; member of the right-wing paramilitary Viking League, 1924–1926: joined the NSDAP and SA in 1930; worked at various companies; mayor of Markranstädt, then mayor of Meißen, 1934–1935; Stadtkommissar in Piotrków from Sept. 1939; Stadthauptmann of Kielce from 1941, also Kreishauptmann there from mid 1941; imprisoned at the beginning of 1945 following disciplinary proceedings; died in an internment camp in 1946.

3 Eduard Jedamzik (1901–1966), retailer and lawyer; member of a Freikorps in Upper Silesia, 1919–1921; joined the NSDAP in 1932 and the SS in 1933; worked in various Gestapo offices, 1935–1939; Kreishauptmann of Kielce-Land, Nov. 1939 – August 1941; in Drohobycz until June 1942; head of Einsatzgruppe D's Einsatzkommando 10b in southern Russia, Dec. 1942 – Feb. 1943, then head of the Gestapo in Chemnitz; in Section III of the Reich Security Main Office (RSHA), Nov. 1943–1945; interned, June 1945 – Oct. 1948; thereafter lawyer in Nuremberg.

4 The original contains handwritten underlining and annotations.

therefore house around 20,000 persons in the Kielce ghetto. This would leave 5,000 Jews in Kielce who would have to be housed elsewhere.

I ask that you have someone look into whether these 5,000 Jews might be housed in Checiny if the same residential concentration is used. I am of course prepared to accept a corresponding number of Poles from Checiny in the city of Kielce in exchange. As Poles cannot be housed in such cramped conditions and because I still have to take into account around 5,000 evacuees who will be funnelled into my city, I ask that you set the number of Poles to be moved from Checiny to Kielce at no more than 2,500.

I would be grateful if your office could undertake the appropriate preliminary work so that we can soon proceed with the establishment of the ghetto.

Heil Hitler![5]

DOC. 228
On 29 January 1941 the Jewish Community's secretary in Chlewiska describes developments since 1 November 1939[1]

Handwritten letter (marked 'very urgent') from the Jewish Community's secretary in Chlewiska, Jakub Tenenbaum, to the executive committee of the Jewish Social Self-Help (JSS) in Cracow (received on 3 February 1941), dated 29 January 1941

Most esteemed gentlemen,

On 29 January 1941 we received your letter dated 25 January 1941 about providing us with assistance.[2] It is in our interests that you receive a detailed summary of the circumstances facing the Jews living in the town of Chlewiska. Before we turn to the actual description, however, we would like to make the following correction: Herszek Broniewski is the chairman[3] of the Jewish residents in the town of Chlewiska and not J. Tenenbaum, to whom your letter was addressed. Jakub Tenenbaum is in fact his secretary. The error arose because the acting secretary, J. Tenenbaum, signed his name in place of Chairman Broniewski, who is illiterate. In future, we ask that you address your cor-

5 Further correspondence about the establishment of the ghetto up to August 1941 followed. On 31 March 1941 Stadthauptmann Hans Drechsel issued the Regulation on the Establishment of a Jewish Residential District in the City of Kielce, published in Berenstein et al. (eds.), *Faschismus – Getto – Massenmord*, pp. 124–125; see also Gustav Andraschko, 'Jüdisches Wohnviertel auch in Kielce', *Krakauer Zeitung*, no. 80, 8 April 1941, p. 6. In Chęciny the Germans confined around 4,000 persons in a ghetto from 10 July 1941.

1 AŻIH, 211/300, fols. 3–5. This document has been translated from Polish.

2 On 25 Jan. 1941 the executive committee of the Jewish Social Self-Help (JSS) had informed Tenenbaum that it did not have the necessary funds to provide regular financial support, but that it would endeavour to convince the central authorities to ensure that Chlewiska received funds from the residents' poverty relief tax. If necessary, these funds could be transferred upon presentation of the original receipts for food purchases: see AŻIH, 211/300, fol. 2.

3 Tenenbaum referred to the chairman of the local Jewish community as 'sołtys', the senior Polish administrative official of the town as 'wójt', and the Kreishauptmann as 'starosta'.

respondence not to Chairman Tenenbaum, but to the secretary for the Jewish residents in the town of Chlewiska. We now turn to a detailed description of the circumstances facing the local Jews:

On 1 November 1939 a German police unit arrived in Chlewiska. In this context, a workforce was required. For this purpose, the Chlewiska local administration appointed Herszek Broniewski as elder and made him responsible for ensuring that Jewish residents showed up for the work they had been assigned. From this date onwards, exclusively Jews, who obeyed every order, performed labour for the German police. These Jewish workers never received any payment or remuneration. There were cases of Jews having to work late into the night. Work increased threefold during the summer [because]: 1) two units of German police arrived in Chlewiska: a mounted and an infantry unit; 2) the superintendent of the local estate needed a workforce for the estate; 3) the local administration also recruited workers for its own purposes. The work became arduous and difficult. Herszek Broniewski, the Jewish workers' representative, found himself facing a difficult task, particularly as he was forced to provide for the Jewish workers at his own expense, as was the Jewish shop, which is owned by Chana Tenenbaum, an impoverished widow with six children to support. Mr Jan Wiener, the superintendent of the local estate, witnessed first-hand the exceptionally hard labour performed by the Jewish workers, whether this was with German police horses or on the estate. The Kreishauptmann of Kreis Końskie, Dr Albrecht, was another witness to this, as he often visited Chlewiska in the course of his inspections. We provide an example of this hard labour below.

In October 1940 the local administration called on Herszek Broniewski to instruct the Jews to load geese for transport to Końskie. There were 800 geese in total. For this work Jews arrived from villages located 8 km from Chlewiska. The work lasted an entire week and was carried out diligently and competently. In this case, the wójt, Mr Stanisław Cios, promised to allocate 200 kg of potatoes per person, as well as sugar and bread ration cards for the aforementioned work. But just as the Jewish workers did not receive a single penny for their work prior to 1 October 1940, there were nothing but empty promises when it came to the work they did with the geese.

Potatoes:

On several occasions, the wójt gave a positive reply on this matter, i.e. he promised a supply of potatoes. However, the secretary of the local administration, Mr Knopiński, gave a negative response. To date, the secretary's stance has prevailed. There have been cases in which local Christian farmers, who had harvested up to 3,000 kg of potatoes, have been allocated a further 700–1,000 kg of potatoes. The Jewish workers, who had no harvest of their own and who were in any event entitled to potatoes for their work for the German police, on the Chlewiska estate, or for the local administration, were not given so much as a single potato.

Sugar:

The representative of the Jews living in the town, Herszek Broniewski, was informed that the sugar allocation had been sent from Końskie for those people who did not have their own crops, livestock, etc. He therefore visited the secretary of the local administration, who comes from the Poznań region. He received the following response verbatim: 'There is no sugar for the Jews.' This is how the state of affairs on the subject of sugar allocations ended to date. Then the next issue arose, namely:

Bread rations:

In November 1940 we were informed that the Chlewiska local administration would issue bread rations. The Jewish elder, who also owns a bakery, went to the local administration to ask the secretary for an allocation of flour in order to bake bread for the town's 120 Jewish residents. He received the following response from the secretary: 'We have been sent 5,000 kg of flour. I cannot set aside a suitable ration for the Jewish population from such an amount. You will be allotted flour once a larger amount has been sent.' In December 1940, 13,000 kg of flour arrived from Końskie. Herszek Broniewski once again went to the local administration expecting a favourable resolution of the matter, as promised by the secretary himself. This time he met with a response along the lines of: 'Get out of the room!' Permission to bake bread (for the entire town) was granted to only one bakery; the owner, a certain Mr Kowalczyk, *also* comes from the Poznań region. This gentleman's attitude and his manner of treating the Jews when distributing bread rations is deplorable. The distribution of daily rations proceeds as follows: some people receive 70, 40, or perhaps 35 g of bread per day, while others receive no bread rations at all. In addition, the distribution of rations has been very erratic and is dependent on Mr Kowalczyk himself. I provide the following example: when Herszek Broniewski tried to claim his daily bread ration, Mr Kowalczyk responded: 'He doesn't need any bread.' To this day Chairman Broniewski has not received any bread. From 1 January to 20 January 1941, Jews received no bread at all. Since 20 January, out of 120 Jews, 3 (three) have each received 40 g per day.

We should also add that, to this day, five Jewish workers have been required to work for the German police every day and have not been paid a single penny. As for fuel – which, in view of the prevailing frost, is particularly important – Herszek Broniewski went to see the superintendent of the local estate and was told: 'Get permission from the Kreishauptmann's office if you want firewood.'

Most esteemed gentlemen,

The Jews living in the town of Chlewiska are in a desperate situation! They have to work constantly and be available to report on demand without receiving a penny from the Polish local administration. This labour has ruined their clothing, damaged their health, and wasted their time. Of the 120 members of the Jewish population, Chairman Herszek Broniewski and the widowed owner of the grocery store, who has six children to support, have had to provide for all the men – 18–20 people. In return, the local administration's 'secretary' has refused trade licences to both shops, i.e. the bakery and the grocery store, so that both families are now struggling with hunger. The aforementioned Broniewski also supports his 82-year-old father and mother. A certain Moszek Broniewski, who is mute and paralysed, has literally nothing to eat. Aron Wassersztajn, who is a patient at the hospital in Radom and whose right leg has been amputated, cannot support himself due to his financial difficulties. We have many similar examples. We have written twice to the Council of Elders in Końskie about these issues, but we have not yet received a reply.

We therefore turn to the Jewish Social Self-Help as an institution which may be in a position to help. Simply put, we have no alternative. Gentlemen, as you can see from the brief description of the situation facing this town's Jewish residents, their fate is pitiful.

On behalf of these twenty-two[4] families in Chlewiska who are in such dire straits, we humbly request your gracious and prompt help with the following matters:

1. To graciously and quickly provide any form of aid, whether food, clothing, or money to purchase such items for Chlewiska's poorest residents;
2. Your gracious and rapid assistance in securing trade licences for the shop selling groceries and rationed goods and the bakery for the year 1941, which would then provide the Jews living in the local Community with vital aid in order to keep them alive;
3. Your gracious financial support in obtaining fuel, which is vital given the prevailing frost. We also ask for your kind support, as far as this is possible, in obtaining fuel permits from the Kreishauptmann's office in Końskie;
4. Your gracious intervention in the matter of securing allocations of potatoes, sugar, bread, etc.

In response to your question about the price of food, we kindly inform you that we can purchase these items on the following terms and in the following quantities:

At least	5,000 kg of potatoes	at a price of	25 zł per 100 kg	= 1,250 zł
»	500 kg of 80 per cent rye flour	»	250 zł per 100 kg	= 1,250 zł
»	25 kg of sugar	»	8.50 zł per kg	= 212.50 zł
»	25 litres of paraffin	»	8.00 zł per litre	= 200.00 zł
				2,912.50 zł

Most esteemed gentlemen,

We trust that you will not leave our request unanswered, and in circumstances known only to God himself,

Gentlemen, we remain, with the greatest respect,

PS. We can provide a list of the 25 families and 120 Jewish residents of Chlewiska upon request.[5]

4 Further on, the document references 25 families.

5 In March the executive committee of the JSS transferred 200 złoty, which was used up immediately. On 14 July 1941 Gidala Broniewski, Herszek Broniewski's successor, made it clear that if no help were provided, they would starve. On 21 July 1941 the executive committee of the JSS replied that it was unfortunately impossible to provide help, as the funds had been allocated primarily to places where public soup kitchens were operating. Moreover, the number of people in need of help in Chlewiska was relatively small. Broniewski was advised to turn to the Jewish Relief Committee in Kreis Końskie: AŻIH, 211/300, fols. 6–24.

DOC. 229

On 30 January 1941 Shloyme Frank describes the strike in the workshops of the tailors and carpenters in the Litzmannstadt (Lodz) ghetto[1]

Diary of Shloyme Frank,[2] entry for 30 January 1941

30 January

The tailor and carpenter strike collapsed completely today.[3] The chairman[4] did not yield, and the workers could not hold out any longer. Their terrible hunger pangs forced them to give in. They came to work in droves, some shaking with hunger. Those who returned made no more demands, nor did they speak a word to anybody. With a bowed head, each one proceeded to his workshop. Hearing that the divisions were filling up with the returning workers, the chairman ordered that everyone be given a double ration of soup that had been thickened up. In the evening, the workers' leaders issued a statement: Fellow workers! Starving Jewish masses! So as not to drop from hunger or cold, we sadly had to concede to the chairman and his accursed lackeys. What did we ask for? Certainly nothing impossible. We demanded:

1) that the wages of workers performing heavy physical labour be raised;
2) that the workers be given food for a part of their wages;
3) that the soup provided at work come with a piece of bread;
4) that workers receive better and more humane treatment.

Those were our demands. Unfortunately, the men in charge rejected our demands and threatened to put us in prison. But we could no longer look on as our children perish from hunger and cold. We had no other alternative or option. Death to the Jewish traitors! Death to their lackeys! They will not escape vengeance.

Signed by all occupational divisions.

1 The original for this entry could not be found (a part of the diary covering Dec. 1941 to Oct. 1942 is held at AŻIH, 302/3). Published in Shloyme Frank, *Togbukh fun lodzher geto* (Buenos Aires: Tsentral-farband fun poylishe yidn in argentine, 1958), p. 28. This document has been translated from Yiddish.

2 Shloyme Frank, formerly Frenkel (1902–1966), journalist; member of the Jewish Order Service in the Lodz ghetto; interned in various camps, 1944–1945; lived in Israel after the war.

3 Between August 1940 and 1944 workers in the Lodz ghetto regularly demonstrated in the streets and held hunger strikes.

4 This refers to Chaim Rumkowski, chairman of the Council of Elders.

DOC. 230

On 31 January 1941 the Kreishauptmann of Kreis Sochaczew-Blonie orders the expulsion of the Jewish population and their relocation to Warsaw[1]

Order from the Kreishauptmann of Kreis Sochaczew-Blonie,[2] signed Reimann, assessor,[3] Sochaczew, dated 31 January 1941 (facsimile)

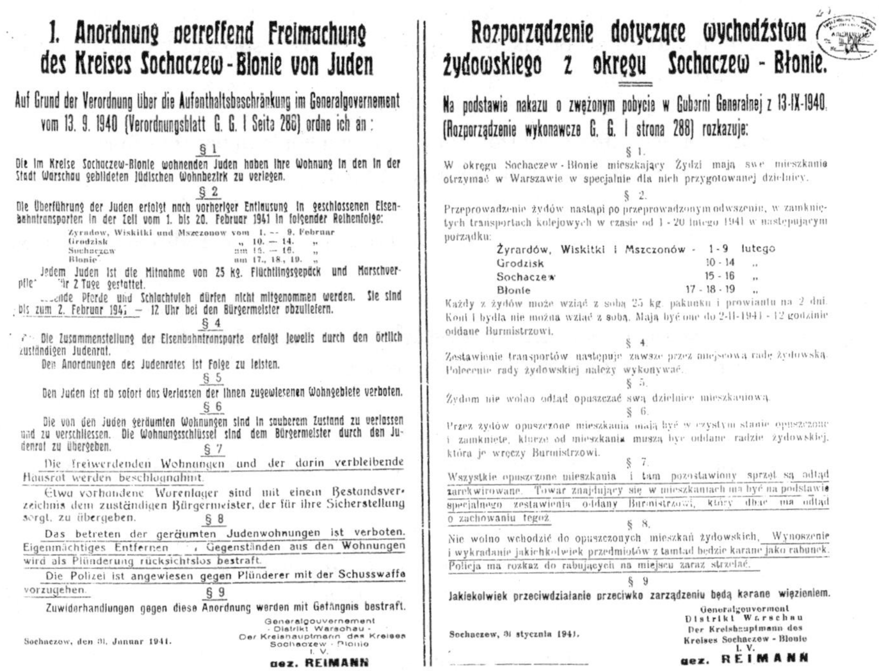

1. Anordnung betreffend Freimachung des Kreises Sochaczew-Blonie von Juden

Auf Grund der Verordnung über die Aufenthaltsbeschränkung im Generalgovernement vom 13. 9. 1940 (Verordnungsblatt G. G. I Seite 288) ordne ich an:

§ 1

Die im Kreise Sochaczew-Blonie wohnenden Juden haben ihre Wohnung in den in der Stadt Warschau gebildeten jüdischen Wohnbezirk zu verlegen.

§ 2

Die Überführung der Juden erfolgt nach vorheriger Entlausung in geschlossenen Eisenbahntransporten in der Zeit vom 1. bis 20. Februar 1941 in folgender Reihenfolge:

Zyradow, Wiskitki und Mszczonow	vom 1. — 9.	Februar
Grodzisk	„ 10. — 14.	„
Sochaczew	am 15. — 16.	„
Blonie	am 17., 18., 19.	„

Jedem Juden ist die Mitnahme von 25 kg. Flüchtlingsgepäck und Marschverpfle[illegible] für 2 Tage gestattet.

[illegible]ende Pferde und Schlachtvieh dürfen nicht mitgenommen werden. Sie sind bis zum 2. Februar 1941 — 12 Uhr bei den Bürgermeister abzuliefern.

§ 4

Die Zusammenstellung der Eisenbahntransporte erfolgt jeweils durch den örtlich zuständigen Judenrat.

Den Anordnungen des Judenrates ist Folge zu leisten.

§ 5

Den Juden ist ab sofort das Verlassen der ihnen zugewiesenen Wohngebiete verboten.

§ 6

Die von den Juden geräumten Wohnungen sind in sauberem Zustand zu verlassen und zu verschliessen. Die Wohnungsschlüssel sind dem Bürgermeister durch den Judenrat zu übergeben.

§ 7

Die freiwerdenden Wohnungen und der darin verbleibende Hausrat werden beschlagnahmt.

Etwa vorhandene Warenlager sind mit einem Bestandsverzeichnis dem zuständigen Bürgermeister, der für ihre Sicherstellung sorgt, zu übergeben.

§ 8

Das betreten der geräumten Judenwohnungen ist verboten. Eigenmächtiges Entfernen [illegible], Gegenständen aus den Wohnungen wird als Plünderung rücksichtslos bestraft.

Die Polizei ist angewiesen gegen Plünderer mit der Schusswaffe vorzugehen.

§ 9

Zuwiderhandlungen gegen diese Anordnung werden mit Gefängnis bestraft.

Sochaczew, den 31. Januar 1941.

Generalgouvernement
- Distrikt Warschau -
Der Kreishauptmann des Kreises
Sochaczew - Blonie
I. V.
gez. REIMANN

Rozporządzenie dotyczące wychodźstwa żydowskiego z okręgu Sochaczew - Błonie.

Na podstawie nakazu o zwężonym pobycie w Guberni Generalnej z 13-IX-1940. (Rozporządzenie wykonawcze G. G. I strona 288) rozkazuje:

§ 1.

W okręgu Sochaczew - Błonie mieszkający Żydzi mają swe mieszkanie otrzymać w Warszawie w specjalnie dla nich przygotowanej dzielnicy.

§ 2.

Przeprowadzenie żydów nastąpi po przeprowadzonym odwszenie, w zamkniętych transportach kolejowych w czasie od 1 - 20 lutego 1941 w następującym porządku:

Żyrardów, Wiskitki i Mszczonów -	1 - 9	lutego
Grodzisk	10 - 14	„
Sochaczew	15 - 16	„
Błonie	17 - 18 - 19	„

Każdy z żydów może wziąć z sobą 25 kg. pakunku i prowiantu na 2 dni. Koni i bydła nie można wziać z sobą. Mają być one do 2-II-1941 - 12 godzinie oddane Burmistrzowi.

§ 4.

Zestawienie transportów następuje zawsze przez miejscowa radę żydowską. Polecenie rady żydowskiej należy wykonywać.

§ 5.

Żydom nie wolno odtąd opuszczać swą dzielnice mieszkaniową.

§ 6.

Przez żydów opuszczone mieszkania mają być w czystym stanie opuszczone i zamknięte, klucze od mieszkania muszą być oddane radzie żydowskiej, która je wręczy Burmistrzowi.

§ 7.

Wszystkie opuszczone mieszkania i tam pozostawiony sprzęt są odtąd zarekwirowane. Towar znajdujący się w mieszkaniach ma być na podstawie specjalnego zestawienia oddany Burmistrzowi, który dbać ma odtąd o zachowaniu tegoż.

§ 8.

Nie wolno wchodzić do opuszczonych mieszkań żydowskich. Wynoszenie i wykradanie jakichkolwiek przedmiotów z tamtąd będzie karane jako rabunek. Policja ma rozkaz do rabujących na miejscu zaraz strzelać.

§ 9

Jakiekolwiek przeciwdziałanie przeciwko zarządzeniu będą karane więzieniem.

Sochaczew, 31 stycznia 1941.

Generalgouverment
Distrikt Warschau
Der Kreishauptmann des
Kreises Sochaczew - Blonie
I. V.
gez. REIMANN

1. [1st] Order on Freeing Kreis Sochaczew-Blonie of Jews

Based on the Regulation on Restrictions of Movement in the General Government of 13 September 1940 (*Verordnungsblatt G.G.* I, page 288), I hereby order:

§ 1

The Jews living in Kreis Sochaczew-Blonie must transfer their residence to the Jewish residential district that has been established in the city of Warsaw.

1 AAN, 1335/214/V-14, fol. 25. This document has been translated from German. The text is from a poster in German and Polish (reproduced here).

2 Karl Adolf Pott; Sochaczew was in District Warsaw.

3 'Assessor' typically referred to a civil servant with probationary status.

§ 2

The Jews must undergo delousing prior to their transports on sealed trains between 1 and 20 February 1941. These transports will take place in the following order:

Zyradow, Wiskitki, and Masczonow:	1–9 February
Grodzisk:	10–14 February
Sochaczew:	15–16 February
Blonie:	17, 18, 19 February

Each Jew will be permitted to take 25 kg of luggage and provisions for two days.

No horses or livestock may be taken along. These must be surrendered to the mayor by noon *on 2 February 1941.*

§ 4

The local Jewish councils are responsible for assigning people to the transports.

All orders from the Jewish councils must be obeyed.

§ 5

With immediate effect, Jews are not allowed to leave the residential districts that have been assigned to them.

§ 6

The Jews must leave their residences in a clean state and lock them. The keys must be handed over to the mayor through the Jewish Council.

§ 7

The vacated apartments complete with all remaining furnishings will be confiscated.

Any stores of goods must be inventoried and surrendered to the mayor, who will secure them.

§ 8

Access to the vacated Jewish apartments is forbidden. Any unauthorized removal of items from these apartments will be considered looting and will incur punishment to the full extent of the law.

The police have been ordered to fire at looters.

§ 9

Any violation of this order will incur imprisonment.

DOC. 231

In January 1941 the Jewish underground newspaper *Nasze Hasła* calls on Jewish youth to participate in the imminent revolution[1]

Jewish youth!

The war between two capitalist–imperialist blocs that has now lasted for seventeen months has wrought havoc. The degenerate fascist governments, their cruel terror and bestial lawlessness, sow death and destruction everywhere. When we examine the list of losses societies have suffered, we find an unbroken chain of social atrophy and barbarization in every sphere of life. Economic ruin, the appalling impoverishment of broad

1 *Nasze Hasła*, January 1941, pp. 1–2; AŻIH, Ring I/1319 (699). *Nasze Hasła* was published monthly in Warsaw between 1940 and 1941 as the official bulletin of the Poale Zion-Left. This document has been translated from Polish.

segments of the population, the unending, systematic torture of Jews – this is life today. With its brute force and violence as well as its entire social and ideological disposition, the Nazi system aims to degrade and completely ostracize the individual. Nazism has directed its deadliest weapon against its most dangerous enemy – freedom and progress, the world of knowledge and science, scholars and students.

Young Jews in education are at a crossroads. Having been deprived of schools, education, and teachers, they are frittering away life's opportunities.

Clear signs of mental vacuity, a complete lack of ambition, and spiritual nihilism characterize the majority of these young people. Appalled by the horrors of today, they either want to 'live and enjoy life' or have succumbed to apathy and pessimism. Let us remember that this is a harmful psychosis which does not befit today's sombre times. Let us remember that the day will come when the sea of blood spilled by the warring capitalist–imperialist blocs will be replaced by a 'new October for Europe and the entire world'.[2]

Jewish youth! In this bulletin, we turn to you who have long understood us to help us bring back those who have temporarily strayed from the right path. This is your sacred duty – we will help you. Be vigilant so that you hear and grasp the signs of impending events. Jewish youth, you will participate in a great social transformation, a definitive solution once and for all to a series of social questions, among which the Jewish question will no doubt play a prominent role. It is also up to you to achieve the noble aims of the international working class, to heal our economic structure, and to create a strategic basis for the Jewish proletariat and its socialist objectives in workers' Palestine.

Only enthusiasm for great ideals can draw young people away from mundane hedonism. Only joy in creating a better life and a new social order from the ruins of a fragile capitalist system can truly bring you – the youth – satisfaction. Be prepared.

DOC. 232

In early 1941 a ghetto inmate describes the progressive isolation of the Jewish population in Warsaw since summer 1940[1]

Handwritten report by 'Tilem'[2] for the underground archive of the Warsaw ghetto, reported after January 1941 (copy)[3]

Sealing the ghetto

In summer 1940 the situation deteriorated for the Jews as a result of the ban on using certain streets, e.g. Ujazdowskie Avenue, or entering Napoleon Square, and then the regulations on separate trams for Jews and districts where Jews are to register [with the

2 This is a reference to the October Revolution in Russia.

1 AŻIH, Ring I/485 (I/361). This document has been translated from Polish.
2 Probably Nechemia Titelman, also Tytelman; member of the Poale Zion-Left; founder of the Shtern sports club; fled to the Soviet Union in Sept. 1939; returned to Warsaw in May 1940; contributed to the underground archive of the Warsaw ghetto; murdered in 1943.
3 This is the second and more legible of the two versions.

police]. However, none of these restrictions gave any indication that a sealed ghetto would be created, which soon did happen. The first rumours about Jews being evicted from selected buildings began to circulate in early October. Hence, on 2 October we received news that all the residents at 8 Żelazna Brama Square would have to vacate the building within a few hours. A considerable commotion set in. The residents left their apartments hurriedly and moved in with relatives or friends. Panic then gripped all the neighbouring buildings. People began to pack their belongings in a hurry. However, the following day it became clear that the entire issue of the building at 8 Żelazna Brama Square was instigated by a Volksdeutsche,[4] who was allegedly later arrested, whereupon the people moved back in. A few days later there was a similar incident at 13 Graniczna Street. In the morning, several Germans barged into the house and started to beat everyone and demand that they move out. However, as this incident also proved harmless, people began to calm down.

The Jewish New Year passed peacefully.[5] It wasn't until Yom Kippur,[6] at around 2 p.m., that it was announced via megaphone that separate Polish, German, and Jewish residential districts would be established. The boundaries of the Jewish and German districts were announced. The boundary of the Jewish quarter was to run from the east along Graniczna Street, Żabia Street, Bankowy Square, Rymarska Street, etc. We were convinced that we would remain where we were (at 8 Żelazna Brama Square), and this consoled us to a certain degree. Rumours began to spread and caused ever-greater panic. The Jews who were to relocate to the Jewish quarter would allegedly not be permitted to take any belongings with them. Nonetheless, the Jews remained calm during the holiday. I observed that the announcement about the ghetto did not interrupt prayer services in houses of worship. The announcements about creating a Jewish quarter were repeated over the following days, and the regulation on taking along items turned out not to be a rumour after all.[7] The boundaries were not fixed, they were fluid, and no one really knew whether they would have to vacate their home. Indeed, there was constant talk that the ghetto would be abolished and that the whole affair was only about extorting ransoms from the Jewish population. Nevertheless, those in danger of losing their belongings began to pack and to give their belongings to their Christian acquaintances for safekeeping. In some buildings the caretakers did not permit Jews to leave with suitcases or belongings. A few days later, the daily *Kurier Warszawski* published a plan of the Jewish residential district.[8] The plan differed significantly from the original announcement. In particular, it did not include all of Żelazna Brama Square or Przechodnia Street. Jews had to relocate to the Jewish district by 30 October. During this time, and even thereafter, when the deadline for resettlement was extended until 15 November, changes were made to the district's boundaries. For example, Chłodna Street up to Okopowa Street was initially included in the ghetto. Later on all of Chłodna Street was included, and eventually it was only partially included. The case was similar with Grzybowska Street from Żelazna Street onwards, among other cases. At the same time, the voluntary

4 German in the original: 'ethnic German'.
5 The Jewish New Year fell on 3 Oct. 1940.
6 Yom Kippur fell on 12 Oct. 1940.
7 See Docs. 180 and 193.
8 *Nowy Kurier Warszawski*, 15 Oct. 1941, p. 4.

exchange of apartments provided for in the regulation began. Due to the constant changes to the boundaries of the residential district, several people had to move two or three times. Ultimately the district was to be created on 15 November, but no one believed that the ghetto would be sealed. On 15 November many were surprised that the German gendarmerie was posted at the exits of the Jewish residential district. I say many, as the regulation to create the Jewish district was essentially unambiguous in this regard. The regulation mentioned a 'geschlossenen Wohnbezirk'.[9] In any case, the Jewish residential district was not so strictly sealed. Firstly, Poles could enter virtually without difficulty, and the gendarmerie allowed Jews and others to pass, particularly members of the Jewish Order Service, who often went to Długa Street or to the market to purchase various items. At some of the exits, however, particularly at the junction of Żelazna and Chłodna streets, horrific scenes unfolded.[10] The German gendarmerie specifically demanded that all the Jews passing by should bow. They would stop Jews whom they ordered to exercise while holding bricks, to climb walls, or to lie in the mud, etc. One time, at the corner of Żelazna and Chłodna streets, the gendarmerie stopped a street band and ordered it to play music. Then, under the threat of a beating, an elderly woman and a Jew with a white beard were forced to dance. These scenes were photographed.[11] At crossings, especially at this exit, Jews had to run, but despite hurrying across, they could not avoid blows. None of these types of harassment deterred Jews from taking advantage of the gendarmerie's distraction to cross to the other side. After all, they could purchase food there at lower prices. This was particularly true for groups of children and the poor. However, the situation took a turn for the worse when the gendarmerie began to shoot. In December and January, and even later, every few days or sometimes even daily, there were cases of people shot dead by the gendarmerie. Sometimes only one person was shot, sometimes a few people at a time. Jews began smuggling on a massive scale, either as a means of self-defence or perhaps just to earn some money. Smuggling took place through the exits, through walls and fences, over piles of rubble, and through certain connecting buildings (which were later excluded from the ghetto). These people repeatedly risked their lives transporting food to the Jewish side, thereby probably saving thousands from death. Berenson,[12] a lawyer, said on several occasions – and he wasn't joking – that one of the first monuments that should be erected after the war is [a monument to the unknown] smuggler.

In late January the Jewish residential district was sealed completely. However, in various ways, particularly through the courthouse[13] and over walls, Jews managed to cross over to the so-called Aryan side.

9 German in the original: 'closed-off residential district'.

10 The junction between the larger north end and the smaller south end of the ghetto was on Chłodna Street.

11 See Doc. 213.

12 Leon Berenson (1882–1941), lawyer; defended Polish socialists in political criminal proceedings before the war; perished in the Warsaw ghetto in April 1941.

13 The court building was accessible from both the ghetto and the 'Aryan side'.

DOC. 233

On 5 February 1941 the Jewish Social Self-Help Committee for Kielce reports on the reorganization of welfare activities and on its upcoming tasks[1]

Monthly report for January 1941 of the JSS, Kielce branch (no. 510/41), the chairman of the Jewish Social Welfare Committee, Herman Lewi,[2] for the JSS central office (received on 16 February 1941), dated 5 February 1941[3]

Activity report of the Jewish Social Welfare Committee in Kielce for January 1941
As of 1 January 1941, the Jewish Social Self-Help Committee for the city of Kielce took over the previous tasks of the welfare section of the Council of Elders of the Jews in Kielce.

The tasks of the Jewish Social Welfare Committee are as follows:

(1) Providing midday meals for the Jewish poor in the form of cooked food and, in part, raw produce.

(2) Disbursing one-time financial aid,
" aid for travel expenses to refugees passing through,
" regular monthly support payments,
" subsidies for the orphanage and home for the elderly, as well as distributing food, among other things, to the aforementioned institutions.

(3) Providing medical assistance

(4) Distributing shoes and clothing.

With regard to (1), the Jewish Social Welfare Committee operates a soup kitchen that caters for 1,500 persons daily. Due to the technical impossibility of further expanding the kitchen and to the shortage of fuel, the Committee was forced to distribute 'raw produce'. In the month under review, the number of persons receiving 'raw produce' increased by 350 persons, which means that 1,100 families, or 5,500 persons, are currently being provided for. The Jewish Social Welfare Committee is therefore helping approximately 7,000 persons daily.

The cooked midday meals and 'raw produce' are distributed in the following manner: The petitioner submits a request. A decision is then taken systematically at the board meetings of the Jewish Social Welfare Committee. Based on the decision of the members of the Jewish Social Welfare Committee, the petitioner is informed by the office, is registered, and receives relevant credentials. The 'raw produce' is issued at the soup kitchen's storehouse four days a week.

Beneficiaries receive bread and flour or bread and hulled barley.

With regard to (2a), the disbursement of one-time financial aid is individual in nature.

(2b) Refugees who are passing through are granted aid to cover travel costs, enabling them to get to the next town and the nearest Council of Elders.

1 YVA, O-21/36, fols. 288–289. This document has been translated from German.

2 Herman Lewi (1880–1942), entrepreneur; founder and co-owner of a furniture factory in Kielce; chairman of the Jewish Community and city council member; chairman of the Jewish Relief Committee for the City of Kielce, 1940–1942; simultaneously chairman of the Jewish Council, Dec. 1940 – August 1942; shot dead in Dec. 1942.

3 The original contains handwritten underlining.

(2c) The payment of regular monthly support is based on a decision by the board.

(2d) The Jewish Social Self-Help Committee disburses regular monthly subsidies to the orphanage and home for the elderly and distributes food, firewood, articles of clothing, etc.

With regard to (3), the Jewish Social Self-Help provides the Jewish poor with medical assistance. The Committee directs the sick to the outpatient clinic of the Council of Elders, where they receive medical attention. All medical interventions are performed in the outpatient clinic itself, and if patients are bedridden, the physician makes a house call. Medicines are provided free of charge or at low cost from the JSS pharmacy. The seriously ill are also directed to the hospital.

With regard to (4), the Jewish Social Self-Help Committee also distributes articles of clothing to the poorest members of the Jewish population.

The Committee is currently setting up for the first time a centre where children can receive a supplementary meal. To this end, a special venue is being designated where the children will be given breakfast every day as of 6 February of this year. A detailed registration process was carried out, and the children most in need from among several hundred applications have been selected to receive breakfast – consisting of bread and coffee – every day. Although 7,000 persons were already benefiting from the support of the Jewish Social Welfare Committee as of 1 February of this year, the number of those applying for aid continues to grow. The Committee is therefore trying to expand its activities. Last month, the Committee appealed to the Stadthauptmann[4] with a request for the allocation of food, which would enable the Committee to carry out the relief operation to help members of the Jewish population who are most in need.

DOC. 234

Between 6 and 8 February 1941 Hersh Vaser describes how the inhabitants of the Warsaw ghetto are being terrorized[1]

Handwritten daily entries by Hersh Vaser[2] for 6–8 February 1941

Thursday, 6 February 1941

A new regulation for the city of Warsaw: offices may be open from 8.30 a.m. to 5 p.m., and public premises and shops until 6 p.m.[3] Jews interpret this as the gradual introduction of a state of siege. The regulation applies to the whole of Warsaw.

I registered yesterday for work in labour camps.

4 Hans Drechsel.

1 AŻIH, Ring I/467 (302), fols. 41–43. The entries written by Vaser cover the period from 1 Dec. 1940 to 30 May 1942. Published in English translation in Hersh Wasser, 'Daily Entries of Hersh Wasser', ed. Joseph Kermish, *Yad Vashem Studies*, no. 15 (1983), pp. 201–282, here pp. 258–260. This document has been newly translated from Yiddish.

2 Hersh Vaser, also Hersh/Hersz Wasser (1912–1980), economist; party member of Poale Zion-Left; head of the Central Refugee Committee from 1940; secretary of the underground archive of the Warsaw ghetto; lived in Israel from 1950.

3 The regulation of 6 Feb. 1941 shortened opening hours: *Gazeta Żydowska*, no. 13, 6 Feb. 1941, p. 2.

Mr R.'s home was searched today. The incessant searches in the Jewish residential district are a general plague. German and P[olish] agents (all acting on their own account) show up based mostly on Jewish denunciations. Twenty-two 'lokshn'[4] were confiscated from R., which he had bought from looters for 800 [zł.].

CKU[5] members will be insured through the health insurance fund. There is a story going around that a woman among the expellees from Karczew was forced to drag herself and her three-day-old baby son to Warsaw only three days after giving birth. She went to her former employer and was received warmly. A festive circumcision ceremony was organized, during which the attending physician – an obstetrician – stated that mother and child were the healthiest in all of Poland. If that's the case, then I am convinced that we will all survive these trials and tribulations.

Antisemitism is raging among the masses on the other side [of the ghetto walls]. You would have imagined that the forced separation of the two peoples would work in their [the Poles'] favour. In reality, they [the Poles] claim that the Jews – confined behind walls – enjoy the utmost freedom and lead a good life, whereas they, the Poles, perish in prisons or are sent to the most remote corners of Germany to perform forced labour. We Jews have it easy! They think we have reason to be in good spirits!

In the course of 15 minutes, as I stood on the corner of Orla and Leszno, seven people from different social strata approached me for alms.

A group from Kalisz [was] detained.

The transfer plan [via the Transfer Bureau] is not yet working in practice. The bread supply is still in the hands of the municipal authorities. The Committee for Labour and Production has shifted into high gear, as the authorities have ordered it to set up tailors' workshops for 1,800 people and large cobbler workbenches, causing a stampede of interested financiers, craftsmen, and workers. Licences for the first instalment of business have already been assigned.

As an aside, paying bribes is a repellent Jewish business practice. The head of the Committee, -n,[6] told me that he could easily make 25,000 złoty within a few days if he were even slightly 'for the taking'. It is therefore easy to imagine what is going on in the actual community, where there is next to no moral integrity. Of course, the percentage of refugees among the craftsmen and workers must and will be guaranteed.

Friday, 7 February 1941

Today was filled with incidents of Jews being beaten and taken to undertake various jobs. Falenty: moving bricks and the like.[7] People were still being beaten and arrested at 8 p.m. Forces began entering several houses on Dzielna Street as early as 7 a.m., dragging the inhabitants violently off to work. My acquaintance N., who had received violent blows to the back, told me that it could have been even worse, because others received blows to the

4 Yiddish in the original: 'noodles', here used as slang for US dollars.

5 Centralna Komisja Uchodźców (CKU): Central Refugee Committee, which looked after the resettled persons and refugees in the Warsaw ghetto on behalf of the Jewish Aid Committee.

6 Probably Chil Rozen (d. 1942), engineer and merchant; teacher and co-owner of Loar secondary school; head of the labour battalion in 1940, then of the Labour Section of the Jewish Council; shot dead in the Warsaw ghetto in Sept. 1942.

7 The Security Police had an estate in the municipality of Falenty, which was south-west of Warsaw.

face, head, and stomach. Upon my life, it would be good to know what the others had done to merit being hit on the head and in the face. Oy, Jewish patience and faith!

There is a story going around that a guard is constantly followed by a horde of children. He is their guardian and protector. He lets them cross the ghetto perimeter, and he is fond of them in his own way.

A soldier entered a Jewish shop at 4 Muranowska Street and politely said that he was hungry. The Jew[ish owner] obsequiously brought him one cake and then another. When [the soldier] had finished eating, he reached for his wallet, but found no money; he thanked [the shopkeeper] and left.

The tramways were not forgotten in today's roundups. On Leszno Street, four vehicles were loaded up with nothing but tram passengers.

At night, the streets are so dark (the regulation that shops may be open [only] until 6 is largely to blame) that they inadvertently have an infernal look. Just add piles of snow, slippery conditions, and throngs of people to complete the picture. Good thing that spring is coming.

Today I got 400 [zł.] as compensation for Blumtshe's stolen overcoat.[8]

Saturday, 8 February 1941

People are saying that a state of siege is being prepared in Warsaw. Perhaps there is something to it.

One street vendor's idea: Don't be left scratching your head – buy a comb from me for 30 groszy.[9]

A gendarmerie patrol went to 'Melody Palace'[10] at 12 Rymarska Street yesterday with plans to arrest a number of guests. A call to 13 Leszno Street helped.[11]

Today, I saw with my own eyes the cruel game of capturing and beating Jews. The Jews' panic and confusion perfectly illustrated how utterly frayed their nerves are. The image of a rampaging German with a long whip in his hand and a group of Jews running back and forth, scared to death, teaches us a lesson about what constitutes a monster – [evoking] terror and indulging one's basest instincts and desires.

A Jew lives on Gęsia Street whose income consists of collecting on overdue bills of exchange. What is interesting is the way he 'works'. In front of his victim's door, he suddenly becomes a 'Volksdeutscher'[12] with a swastika, who in perfect German (as a German refugee) uses every intimidation method in the book against the uncooperative debtor.

Oyneg Shabes.[13]

8 Presumably Bluma, the wife of Hersh Vaser.

9 A play on words. A literal translation of the original phrase 'lozt zikh nisht krikhn oyfn kop' means not to let (something) crawl on one's head. The phrase is also used idiomatically in Yiddish and means 'do not let someone scoff at/mock you'.

10 A revue theatre in the Warsaw ghetto. It belonged to Regina Judt, who had good relations with the German administration: see *The Warsaw Diary of Adam Czerniakow*, p. 178.

11 The Office for Combating Illicit Trade and Price Gouging (Urząd do Walki z Lichwą i Spekulacją) was located at 13 Leszno Street. It was under the control of the Gestapo and was meant to be a counterweight to the Jewish Council. It was headed by Avrom Gantsvaykh (also known as Abraham Gancwajch) and Dovid Shternfeld (also known as Dawid Szternfeld) until its dissolution on 17 July 1941. Ghetto inhabitants turned to this office whenever they wanted to contact German agencies.

12 German in the original: 'ethnic German'.

13 Meeting of the Oyneg Shabes (also: Oneg Shabbat – literally 'joy of the Sabbath') group responsible for the underground archive, whose members always met on Saturdays.

DOC. 235
On 8 February 1941 the 'Daily Chronicle of the Lodz Ghetto' records the expansion of economic production[1]

'Daily Chronicle Bulletin of the Lodz Ghetto', no. 29, dated 8 February 1941

Archive Department
Daily Chronicle Bulletin, no. 29
Thursday, 8 February 1941

The impressive development of labour divisions
The ghetto is a major industrial and manufacturing centre
Exactly one year ago today, the chief of police for the city of Litzmannstadt signed a regulation to establish a ghetto and to surround it with barbed wire.[2] At that time, no one could have foreseen – not even in their dreams – that within one year, an industrial centre on such a universal scale would be thriving in the ghetto, or that despite the enormous difficulties encountered at every turn, it would be possible to create workshops employing up to 10,000 workers.

The establishment of these work centres has also been of enormous psychological significance, in that it has prevented the complete demoralization of thousands of people by allowing them to return to their previous occupations and [thereby] become productive individuals, useful to the community as a whole and serving the public good.

When creating these workshops, it was necessary to start literally from scratch. There were no factories, no machines, no suitable premises, no facilities, no raw materials, and – most importantly – no orders.

There was nothing in these places where today a 6,000-strong army of tailors and a host of skilled workers from every branch of manufacturing ply their trades, including weavers, spinners, knitters, chain makers, shoemakers, upholsterers, carpenters, furriers, glove makers, milliners, hosiers, slipper manufacturers, electricians, metalworkers, tanners …

Of course this is not all. The figures provided above will continue to increase because, as we learned from the chairman's speech on the first of this month, wide-ranging development plans have been drawn up to create and implement new branches of production as well as to considerably expand the existing workshops.[3] The establishment of these ghetto work centres generally dates back to 30 April 1940, the day before the ghetto was sealed. It was then that Chairman Rumkowski decided to concentrate his efforts on creating the ghetto's own workshops. He launched this initiative straight away and deployed all the resources at his disposal to realize this great undertaking. Now that this work, which rests on solid foundations and is yielding returns, has been completed, it is

1 APŁ, 278/1079, fols. 41–42. This document has been translated from Polish.
2 Police Regulation on the Jews' Rights of Housing and Residence and the subsequent implementing regulations of 8 Feb. 1940: *Lodscher Zeitung*, 9 Feb. 1940.
3 In his speech 'Work and Rest – The Steadfast Motto of Chairman Rumkowski's Activities', Rumkowski had announced the employment of a higher number of workers and young people: Julian Baranowski et al. (eds.), *Kronika getta łódzkiego/Litzmannstadt Getto 1941–1944*, vol. 1: *1941* (Łódź: Wydawnictwo Uniwersytetu Łódzkiego, 2009), pp. 88–95, here p. 94.

worth adding that all the effort and energy have paid off, because the output of the workshops has become the chief source of income by which the inhabitants of the ghetto are supplied with food.

The brains behind and the hub for the planning and essential organization of all the various departments is the Central Office of Labour Divisions, which has its headquarters on Bałucki Square. Its director, Mr Aron Jakubowicz, was appointed to lead the work centres as soon as the plans came into effect.[4] His tireless efforts and his innovative vision found particular recognition in the speech the chairman addressed to him.[5]

When we consider the overall output of the labour divisions, the most significant aspect to note is that 70 per cent of the total output can be attributed to the Central Office's initiative, and the remaining 30 per cent to other orders received.

The first step to creating these industrial centres was the scrupulous registration of all the skilled workers living in the ghetto. At the same time, negotiations were initiated with the authorities regarding potential orders.

At first there were very few orders: merely a handful of orders which trickled in from civilians. However, as the workshops expanded, larger orders for military supplies began to come in. The first to be expanded were the tailors' workshops, followed by the workshops for shoemakers, carpenters, house- and felt-slipper manufacturers, tanners, milliners, hosiers, and metalworkers (whose output is predominantly earmarked for the ghetto's internal requirements).

The tasks of the Central Office include maintaining contact with the authorities, in their capacity as clients; collecting raw materials and delivering them to the appropriate division for processing; collecting the finished goods and forwarding them to customers; and finally resolving all the problems which arise from such a large-scale operation and under what are, at the very least, abnormal working conditions.

The greatest obstacle to production and to aspirations for production on a larger scale is the limited number of orders. If a greater number of orders were received, production in the most important division – namely the tailoring division – could be tripled. Currently the tailoring division employs 6,050 people, whereas if semi-skilled tailors were to be included, the number of employees could reach 12,000. The situation is similar in other divisions.

Customers are evidently satisfied with the work of these centres, the best proof of which is the fact that some customers order the same item several times. In some sectors it has been noted that certain items are of better quality than before the war – this is especially true of civilian clothing.

The reason for this is that many exceptional craftsmen who previously ran their own small businesses now pass on their experience and knowledge to thousands of workers, who benefit from it.

This is all the more remarkable when we consider the workers' poor working and living conditions.

4 Aron Jakubowicz (1910–1981), retailer; deputy to the Jewish elder and head of the Central Office of Labour Divisions in the Lodz ghetto; initially deported to Auschwitz in 1944, then to Sachsenhausen and Königs Wusterhausen; lived in Israel after the war.

5 In his speech Rumkowski praised the head of the Labour Division 'for his proactive work, creativity, and perseverance': Baranowski et al. (eds.), *Kronika getta łódzkiego*, vol. 1, p. 94.

In recent weeks, for the first time, an order was received from one of the largest fashion houses in Berlin for superior quality women's and children's clothing (dresses for women and girls, pyjamas, children's clothing). If this trial proves successful, such orders will keep coming in.

The best measure of decent and sound workmanship is very few returns (out of several hundred thousand military shirts, barely 700 have been returned). It must be added here that the commissions that receive the returned goods inspect them very thoroughly.

An even more persuasive indication of our workers' professionalism is the fact that in relation to a number of orders for civilian clothing, 5 to 10 per cent more items have been produced from the material delivered than the customer had anticipated when placing the order.

As far as remuneration for the work is concerned, then the wages [of the workers] in the ghetto are higher than in the small towns in the surrounding area, for which particular credit is due to Chairman Rumkowski.

The scale of the work carried out by the individual divisions is best demonstrated by the impressive production figures for January.

There are 16 labour divisions in total. In January they produced a total of 170,000 items, namely: the tailoring division [made] 104,000 items, i.e. ready-made civilian and military clothing of all kinds; the textile factory produced 2,700 kg of yarn; the weaving mill produced 5,000 m of assorted fabrics, etc. The rubber coat factory produced 3,300 items; the hosiery factory, 43,000 pieces; the felt-shoe factory, almost 7,000 pairs [of shoes]; the quilt factory, 170 quilts; the upholstery factory, 97 items; the furriers' workshop, 143 fur coats and 68 pairs of fur footwear; the hat factory, almost 4,500 items; the shoemakers' workshops, over 6,500 pairs of shoes; the knitwear workshops, almost 9,000 pieces; the carpenters' workshops, 133 sets of furniture; the linen workshop, 3,200 items; the tannery, 221 leather pieces; and the glove factory, almost 2,500 dozen [pairs].

In total the factories have produced 170,000 assorted items weighing 10,500 kg. Bearing in mind the conditions under which these factories were established and continue to operate, their achievements should be recognized as record-breaking.

DOC. 236

On 10 February 1941 the Governor of District Warsaw reports on the forced resettlement of 72,000 Jews to the Warsaw ghetto[1]

Situation report by Governor Ludwig Fischer for January 1941, Warsaw, dated 10 February 1941

[…][2]

VII. Resettlement

1. Regarding the *resettlement of ethnic Germans*, it remains apparent that many ethnic Germans want to be exempted from resettlement. Such requests are only granted when the indispensability of the petitioner has been firmly established, which happens in consultation with the resettlement unit of the Ethnic German Liaison Office.[3]

   Many ethnic Germans have not yet even registered for resettlement. To remedy this situation, food ration cards will only be issued to ethnic Germans in future upon presentation of the certificate of registration from the Ethnic German Liaison Office.
2. Another 62,000 evacuees[4] have been assigned to the district, even though the housing and food situation in District Warsaw is not very good. To free up more space, Jews living in the western part of the district must leave their places of residence and move to the Jewish neighbourhood in Warsaw. According to current estimates, this will result in the resettlement of 72,000 Jews, creating room for around 62,000 Poles. The resettlement is already well under way. Nearly every day, 1,000 Jews arrive in Warsaw and are first taken to a quarantine area. The evacuees from the territory of Posen and Danzig include some politically questionable elements, meaning that constant monitoring by the Security Police is necessary.
3. Work is currently under way to reinforce the security of the borders of the *Jewish residential district*. Most of the initial defects have already been eliminated. Changes to the Jewish residential district's borders will continue to be necessary in the interest of Aryan enterprises. The relocation of Aryan enterprises currently situated in the Jewish residential district is also still in progress.

   The configuration of the entry and exit points will be improved as well. Pedestrian traffic will be regulated by a turnstile entrance, vehicle traffic by a moveable barrier.

1 AIPN, GK 196/280 (NTN 280), fols. 233–249, excerpt from fols. 245–246. Copy in IfZ-Archives, Fb 95/60. This document has been translated from German. Published in Polish translation in Krzysztof Dunin-Wąsowicz et al. (eds.), *Raporty Ludwiga Fischera Gubernatora Dystryktu Warszawskiego 1939–1944* (Warsaw: Książka i Wiedza, 1987), pp. 249–263, here pp. 259–260.

2 The monthly report is 17 pages long. Fischer reported first on Frank's visit to Warsaw from 17–20 Jan. 1941, on the political and economic situation, and on individual departments within the district's administration.

3 The Ethnic German Liaison Office (Volksdeutsche Mittelstelle, VoMi) was set up in 1935 to coordinate Nazi policies towards German-speaking minority groups abroad; from 1939 it was integrated into the SS and was involved in the resettlement to the Reich of ethnic German minorities from the Baltic region, Soviet-occupied eastern Poland, and Romania. Between summer 1940 and 1941 it was also involved in the resettlement of ethnic Germans from the General Government to the annexed Polish territories.

4 Poles from the annexed territories who had been expelled to make homes and farms available for incoming German settlers.

A large goods-handling site in the northern part of the Jewish residential district is nearing completion. Fumigation chambers will also be built so that finished products can be exported in future in perfect condition from the Jewish residential district.[5] The number of permits for individuals has been limited to 15,000 for Aryans and to 400 for Jews.

4. Apartments in the *German residential area* are being allocated to Germans on an ongoing basis. A revocable residence permit will be granted temporarily to Poles for apartments within the German residential area which are unsuitable for Germans due to the condition of the premises.

[…][6]

DOC. 237
On 11 February 1941 the Kreishauptmann in Janów Lubelski requests permission to expel Jews from Kraśnik[1]

Letter from the Kreishauptmann in Kreis Janów Lubelski, signed Asbach,[2] to the Office of the Governor of District Lublin, Interior Administration Department, Population and Welfare Division (received on 14 February 1941),[3] dated 11 February 1941[4]

Re: partial resettlement of Jews

I request authorization for the partial resettlement of Jews from Krasnik[5] to Radomyśl, Kosin, and Trzydnik.

This resettlement is urgently needed in order (1) to improve the sanitary conditions in Krasnik, which is heavily occupied by members of the Wehrmacht, and (2) to create housing for the Wehrmacht and other public officials.

5 These fumigation chambers were used to kill any lice and other insects and larvae in textiles by means of hydrogen cyanide (Zyklon B). The process had been developed during the First World War. For the history of this gassing technique, which the Germans began using in 1941 to murder people, see Hermann Breymesser and Erich Bernfus, *Blausäuregaskammern zur Fleckfieberabwehr: Grundlagen, Planung, Betrieb* (Berlin: Special publication of the *Reichsarbeitsblatt*, 1943).

6 The text that follows discusses health care, schooling, the judicial system, and the activity of the Department of Public Enlightenment and Propaganda.

1 APL, 498/892, fols. 99–100. This document has been translated from German.

2 Hans-Adolf Asbach (1904–1976), lawyer; joined the NSDAP in 1932; in the Gau administration of the German Labour Front in Stettin, 1934–1939; group leader in the Interior Administration Department of the General Government from Jan. 1940; Kreishauptmann in Janów Lubelski, Oct. 1940 – August 1941, then in Brzeżany; served in the war from Feb. 1943; co-founder of the League of Expellees and Persons Deprived of Rights (BHE) in 1950; member of the Landtag and minister of social affairs in Schleswig-Holstein, 1950–1957.

3 The division was headed by Richard Türk (1903–1984), farmer; joined the NSDAP in 1925; mayor of Schreiberhau, 1934–1936; head of the Population and Welfare Division in District Lublin, Jan. 1940–April 1942; coordinated the deportations of Jews from Lublin to Belzec, then deputy head of the Population and Welfare Division of the government of the GG; regional director of the Rhineland-Palatinate League of Expellees after the war.

4 The original contains handwritten notes: 'II R. ha[ndling] with all previous orders on resettlement of Jews, T[ürk].'

It is common knowledge that the Jew, due to his uncleanliness, is a carrier of epidemic typhus as well as typhoid. However, the Jews have ignored and sabotaged all the safety measures taken. The resettlement is now meant to be a punishment, designed to lend greater force to the orders that have been issued.

It will also free up a number of much-needed apartments. The dwellings known to be breeding grounds for vermin will be eliminated. An additional group of apartments will be needed for the Wehrmacht, which currently occupies a large share of the office space of the Krasnik municipal administration, making it impossible for the administration to function properly.

Furthermore, housing is needed for Germans from the Reich who are part of the postal service, the police, the Kreis cooperative, and others.

Members of the Polish police and the Criminal Police are also searching for places to live. Not allocating apartments to these employees means that they have to be paid substantial separation allowances.

To resolve all these complaints, a partial resettlement of Jews from Krasnik was absolutely necessary. After consultation with the mayor in Radomyśl, housing for the resettled Jews has been found there, albeit under pressure. It is also easy to understand that the Jews from Krasnik are seeking to evade resettlement, because relocation will also pull the rug out from under any shady wheeling and dealing.

In addition, I would like to point out that the Governor,[6] at the last meeting of the Kreishauptleute, expressly authorized them to concentrate the Jews more and more.

DOC. 238

On 13 February 1941 the District Governor's representative for the City of Warsaw prohibits the exchange of goods with Jews outside the ghetto[1]

Order on Supplying Goods to Jews Outside the Jewish Residential District Within the City of Warsaw

Based on §§ 1–4 of the Regulation of the Governor General on Restrictions of Movement in the General Government of 13 September 1940 (*Verordnungsblatt GG* I, p. 288), §§ 4–6 of the First Implementing Regulation to the Regulation of the Governor General of 26 October 1939 on the Introduction of Forced Labour for the Jewish Population of the General Government of 11 December 1939 (*Verordnungsblatt GG* 1939 I, pp. 231 et seq.),[2] the Regulation of the Governor General on Price Setting in the General Government of 12 April 1940 (*Verordnungsblatt GGP* I, p. 131), and the Regulation of the Governor General on Administrative Penalty Proceedings of 13 September 1940

5 In addition to Janów, where the Kreis administration was based until 1942, Kraśnik was the only township in this largely rural Kreis.

6 Ernst Zörner.

1 *Mitteilungsblatt der Stadt Warschau*, no. 8, 25 Feb. 1941, pp. 1–2, in German and Polish. This document has been translated from German.

2 See Doc. 55.

(*Verordnungsblatt* GGP I, pp. 300 et seq.),[3] I hereby order the following for the City of Warsaw:

1. It is prohibited to sell, give away, or otherwise provide goods of any kind to Jews outside the Jewish residential district of the City of Warsaw.
2. In each instance, both parties – that is, both the party who provides the item and the party who accepts the item – are liable to prosecution.
3. Whoever violates this order will be penalized with a fine of up to 1,000 zloty or, if the fine cannot be collected, with imprisonment of up to three months, unless other penal provisions stipulate a greater punishment.
4. Juveniles from the ages of 14 to 21 may be penalized with forced-labour conscription.
5. In cases where violations are committed by juveniles under the age of 14, punishment will be imposed on their legal guardians.
6. This order shall come into force on the day of its promulgation.

Warsaw, 13 February 1941.
The District Governor's Representative for the City of Warsaw
The Police Administrator (signed) Leist

DOC. 239
After 16 February 1941 Łaja Efrajmowicz describes her forced resettlement to the Warsaw ghetto[1]

School essay by Łaja Efrajmowicz,[2] dated after 16 February 1941[3]

What resettlement looked like here:
Resettlement is terrible. Initially, they resettled us in the ghetto. Everyone had to give up their apartment and squeeze in elsewhere. Tough luck. We soon came to accept this. But it did not last long. We were only there for two weeks when people began to murmur that there would be resettlements to Warsaw. We refused to believe this. Soon thereafter, however, there were notices in the streets that the city was to be cleared of Jews by 16 February and that you could take only 25 kg with them. This news hit us hard. People ran around like mad, asking: what will happen? What should they take first? Whoever still had any money got hold of a cart and rode off, and whoever had no money went on foot and left everything behind. I will remember our resettlement for as long as I live.

3 See Doc. 180, fn. 9.

1 AŻIH, Ring I/860 (305). Published in Ruta Sakowska (ed.), *Archiwum Ringelbluma*, vol. 2: *Dzieci – tajne nauczanie w getcie warszawskim* (Warsaw: Wydawnictwo Naukowe PWN, 2000), p. 117. This document has been translated from Polish.

2 Łaja Efrajmowicz attended school at 68 Nowolipki Street. Izrael Lichtensztejn, an employee at the school, forwarded this essay to the underground archive.

3 The document was filed undated in the underground archive of the Warsaw ghetto. The date stems from the content: between Feb. and April 1941 the German administration expelled the Jewish population from the western part of District Warsaw into the already overcrowded ghetto: see Docs. 236 and 252.

DOC. 240

On 17 February 1941 Józef Winer from the Jewish Social Self-Help reports on his inspection of Radoszyce[1]

Report by the Jewish Social Self-Help inspector Józef Winer[2] on his impressions of Radoszyce[3] on 15 February 1941,[4] dated 17 February 1941

In accordance with Chairman Diament's[5] instructions and in connection with the letter from the JSS executive committee in Cracow, dated 11 February of this year, no. 1042/41,[6] on 14 February I went to Radoszyce via Końskie, with Dr M. Sawicki[7] from Końskie. Having familiarized myself with the local situation, I report the following:

We have visited nearly all the apartments that house people suffering from typhus, and note the following:

1. Young men who once worked at a forced labour camp have brought the disease into town. It is mainly family members of these young men, or their relatives and nearest neighbours, who were or are ill with the disease.
2. There have been fifty cases of the disease, including seven deaths thus far.
3. There are approximately twenty people currently suffering from the disease, five of whom are in a provisional clinic that is not yet fully equipped and has been set up on the initiative of the local Council of Elders, under instructions from the Kreis physician in Końskie. The rest of those who are sick are in their apartments.
4. As there is no quarantine facility, the patients and their relatives are sharing private apartments.

Following our assessment of the state of affairs described above, we visited the local physician, Dr Fidler, who is selflessly engaged in fighting typhus among Radoszyce's Jewish population. We both concluded that the epidemic could be brought under control without major difficulties if Dr Fidler were provided with a specially equipped hospital consisting of 15–20 beds and a quarantine facility for the patients' families. I should add that, during our discussion, Dr Fidler stressed that the epidemic could reach alarming proportions and subsequently turn catastrophic for the entire town should these conditions not be met.

I then also held a series of talks with representatives of the local Jewish population and convened a plenary session of the Council of Elders. Upon hearing various opinions, I appointed a special commission to combat the epidemic and to set up a hospital and a

1 AŻIH, 211/159, fols. 26–27. This document has been translated from Polish.
2 Józef Winer, thought to have been a qualified engineer; Józef Diament's colleague, 1940–1941.
3 Radoszyce was in District Radom in the General Government, south-west of Radom.
4 The original contains a stamp: 'No. 1127a'.
5 Józef Diament (b. 1894), bookkeeper; came from the assimilated Jewish community in Radom; co-owner of an iron foundry; from late Sept. 1939 chairman of the Jewish Committee for Social Self-Help in Radom, which became the 'Supreme Council of Elders for the Jewish Population in District Radom' under the German occupation; also Jewish social welfare advisor to the District Governor of Radom and head of the Jewish Social Self-Help (JSS) municipal committee in Radom; arrested in late April 1942 and deported to Auschwitz.
6 This letter is not in the file.
7 Dr Michał Sawicki, physician at a Jewish outpatient clinic; member of a welfare committee in Końskie, 1939–1940; thereafter a member of the JSS aid committee.

quarantine facility, with help from the citizens. The members of this commission include:

From the Council of Elders: Mr Rutkowski, Mordka – Council Chairman; Mr Finkler, Icek – Council Secretary.

Not from the Council: Mr Opatowski, Wolf; Mr Okowit, Lejzor.

In light of the fact that, as I learned while I was there, the local Council of Elders neither enjoys great moral standing among the population nor has sufficient experience in social work, I deemed it appropriate to appoint as the committee chairman Mr Sz. Edelist[8] – a member of the Jewish Aid Committee in Końskie and a proven social activist with significant experience in combating epidemics. Mr Edelist accepted this appointment and immediately contacted the committee in Radoszyce.

The first task I set the committee was to find suitable premises for an epidemic hospital that would house separate wards for men and women, as well as offices; to find premises for a quarantine facility; and to form a sanitary police unit from the ranks of young Jews in Radoszyce, which would be tasked with inspecting Jewish apartments where sanitary conditions leave much to be desired and in many cases fail to meet the most basic standards. The sanitary police will receive special instructions and guidelines from Dr Fidler, who, incidentally, has taken the lead on this entire sanitation operation.

I consider it essential to immediately provide aid in cash and in kind to facilitate all of these indispensable directives. For the time being, cash assistance should amount to 3,000 (three thousand) złoty and be payable to the Jewish Aid Committee in Końskie, care of Mr Edelist.[9] In addition to the above, I propose the allocation of at least 100 (one hundred) yards of linen to Radoszyce for bed sheets, gowns, caps, etc., as well as 15 blankets. I stress once again that this aid is needed as soon as possible, and that only swift and immediate action can contribute to eliminating the epidemic.

8 Szabsia Edelist (b. 1888), craftsman; responsible for the economic affairs of the JSS municipal aid committee in Końskie, 1940–1941.

9 On 19 Feb. 1941 the JSS head office in Cracow reported that it would initially transfer 1,500 złoty to Mr Edelist and would send a second instalment upon receiving proof of how the money was spent: AŻIH, 211/159, fol. 28.

DOC. 241
On 18 February 1941 a Jew from Łuków is denounced for making anti-German statements in public[1]

Anonymous handwritten letter from Łuków[2] to the Kreishauptmann in Radzyń,[3] dated 18 February 1941

Please be so kind as to note the following:
The Jew Lejbman Icek, who lives in Łuków, discusses politics in the street every day, and it is all aimed against the German government; that is to say, he discusses the bombing in Germany, the food shortage, etc.

DOC. 242
On 18 February 1941 Lucjan Orenbach describes his desperate living conditions in Tomaszów Mazowiecki[1]

Handwritten letter from Lucjan (Lutek) Orenbach in Tomaszów Mazowiecki to his girlfriend, Edith Blau, in Minden (Westphalia), dated 18 February 1941

5.[2]
My dearest Edith,

Your lovely letter arrived yesterday. I've missed your letters so much recently. All the memories have returned so vividly, for I met your friend from Danzig, Mrs Mira Ryczke.[3] She has lived here for a year, and it is only now that we got to know each other. I recently met her at Roma's[4] and … we started chatting. Everything came back.[5] We talked about you, about everyone, and we couldn't stop. I brought her some photographs. She was touched to see them. That's a surprise for you, isn't it?

1 AIPN, GK 106/161 (703/31, CA MSW 684), file 2, fol. 7. This document has been translated from Polish. For more on the letter, see Doc. 161, fn. 1.
2 Łuków was in Kreis Radzyń in District Lublin in the General Government. The denunciation was made three months before the open ghetto in Łuków was established.
3 Dr Fritz Schmige (1880–1974), lawyer; Landrat in East Prussia, 1920; joined the NSDAP in 1933; Landrat in Liegnitz, 1933–1939; head of the Interior Administration Department in District Lublin, 1939; simultaneously chief of staff from Feb. 1940; Kreishauptmann in Radzyń, June 1940 – Oct. 1941; Landrat in Braunau (Sudetenland) until 1945; from 1945 in Wiesbaden, where he worked for several years in the Ministry of Finance in the West German state of Hesse.

1 USHMM, RG 10 250*08, TM 060. This document has been translated from Polish.
2 Orenbach numbered his letters to Edith Blau. Added in the top left-hand corner: 'Who is this Heinz? Thank you very much for the photograph! Very nice.'
3 Mira Kimmelman, née Ryczke (b. 1923); grew up in Danzig; lived in Tomaszów when the German occupation began; after 1941 prisoner in Majdanek, Auschwitz, and Bergen-Belsen; lived in the USA after the war. She published her memoirs under the title *Echoes from the Holocaust: A Memoir* (Knoxville: University of Tennessee Press, 1997).
4 Probably Roma Michlewicz (1923–1945); grew up in Tomaszów; later in Bliżyn camp and Auschwitz, where she was murdered.
5 This sentence refers to the summer they spent together in Bydgoszcz in 1939.

Other than that, everything is the same. I've been ill. In any case, everyone is ill. The first signs of spring are here. Water everywhere on the streets. The snow is melting, and so is my heart. Memories … memories …

All of us here are alive and yet not alive. Sometimes I no longer know whether I'm alive or not. Is it *me* or is it not me? Sometimes you have to repeat to yourself a hundred times: I'm alive, you're alive, he's alive. You forget that you *exist*.

There's the Community. The abominable and abhorrent Community. You work mechanically, joke around a little, but without really being present. Then you go home for lunch. You read a book and don't understand anything. Then the Community again. At 6 o'clock, after work, we go to Mrs Sz.'s for rehearsal. The music bounces off your ears and only brings back distant, sad memories of *having once been alive*. And this is how it is all day, from morning until evening. I don't know: Is it me or is it not me? Am I alive or am I dead? Only once you're in bed at night do you search your conscience. Who am I? What do I want? What am I doing?!

The answer is: I'm a miserable slacker, a drunk, a dreamer.

What do I want? I want to live, but to really *live*, I want to be *someone*. I want to be able to do something. I want to love and be loved.

What do I do? Nothing. Absolutely nothing. I while away time. I waste time. I wander around the Community. I recite verses. I drink vodka. Vodka, liqueur, wine, cognac, caraway liqueur … I smoke a lot of cigarettes. I cough. A terrible cough. I whistle ('Umarł Maciek, umarł …'[6]). I dream, I dream a lot, but I don't think about anything. I wait and wait, but expect nothing. I grow, I'm getting older and turning into an even bigger idiot. I love … I love someone who is not here; someone who is heaven-knows-where and has a short little nose and a funny, crooked tooth.

Sometimes I write letters. I waste paper. There are many kisses, but few thoughts. And that's all.

Sometimes I listen to people praising me. All of Tomaszów says that I am talented, that I can do this and that. But people always judge others either too harshly or too lightly. Everyone is pleased with me, except me. Time flies. I am getting older. Time is running out. What will become of me? What will I achieve in life?

Now there's nothing. Now I'm dead. I'm gone. There's a place called Tomaszów. There's a stupid *dream* of Tomaszów. But what will happen *once I wake up*? Where will I go? What will I do? Who will I be? That's important. 'Today' is not important. 'Today' is a bad, silly dream. But 'tomorrow'.

These are my thoughts. But let's leave it be. Idle talk. Soon it will be spring. You'll have to raise your head and take a deep breath. After all, we love. After all, [I] still have many youthful years ahead [of me].

I wrote to Ruth[7] a long time ago, but haven't heard back yet. As to Auschwitz, you can get accurate information from the Mehls; they live nearby (*Adolf Mehl, Chelmek, Kreis Chrzanów, Oberschlesien*).[8] We haven't heard anything new about how things are in Auschwitz for a long time.

6 'Maciek has died, he's died'; the title of a popular song in the Second Polish Republic.
7 Ruth Goldbarth.
8 German in the original: 'Kreis Chrzanów, Upper Silesia'.

And now, stay healthy. Write back immediately! Warm greetings to your mama from all of us. The warmest kisses from me, always.

Lutek

Fredek sends his greetings. He'll write more in the next letter.

DOC. 243
On 22 February 1941 the Jewish Social Self-Help executive committee requests a special grant from the Chief Social Welfare Council[1]

Letter from the Jewish Social Self-Help executive committee (no. 1426/41), signed Weichert, to the Chief Social Welfare Council, dated 22 February 1941 (carbon copy)

Re: special grant for the Jewish Municipal Welfare Committee in Warsaw
With reference to our chairman's[2] discussion with Chairman Count Ronikier on the 20th of this month, we humbly turn to the Chief Social Welfare Council with the following matter:

The decision taken by the Polish Central Welfare Council, based on negotiations with the Jewish Social Self-Help, to reduce the share of funds and donations that the JSS receives from the Chief Social Welfare Council to 17 per cent also provides for the possibility of offering the JSS a one-time grant in certain cases that merit special consideration.

One such case has arisen in Warsaw. For some time now, Jewish social welfare institutions, particularly children's homes and public soup kitchens, have been struggling with insurmountable financial difficulties. Income from their own sources and from foreign aid is dwindling with each passing day. Despite continuous efforts, to this day we have failed to obtain even a single cent from the municipal grant fund, from which the kitchens run by the SKSS[3] receive support.[4] Moreover, since October 1939 we have not received any payments from the partially released funds given to the SKSS for *the entire population* of the city of Warsaw. Public soup kitchens have had to suspend their operations on several occasions. They were recently closed for three weeks and were only able to reopen thanks to a transaction arranged with the SKSS in which ham was exchanged for potatoes. They are currently once again threatened with closure.

As the Central Welfare Council is aware, the authorities have ordered the resettlement of more than 70,000 Jews to Warsaw over the next few weeks. This operation is currently under way.[5] Emergency assistance for the resettled persons, which was once

1 YVA, O-21/17, fol. 100. This document has been translated from Polish.
2 Michał Weichert.
3 The SKSS (Stołeczny Komitet Samopomocy Społecznej), the Social Self-Help Committee for the capital, was an aid committee established in Sept. 1939. It collected money and other donations from the Polish population for social causes. It ran soup kitchens, several of which were staffed by nuns.
4 Since 1940 Weichert had been trying to obtain funds for the Jewish Social Self-Help (JSS) from the revenue from the municipal residents' tax. Czerniaków also undertook such efforts: see Doc. 219.
5 Jews living in towns in the western part of District Warsaw were expelled to the Warsaw ghetto: see Docs. 236 and 252.

sufficient to provide them with a warm meal once a day and a roof over their heads, requires enormous expenditure in the short term. The Jewish Social Self-Help executive committee has allocated 100,000 złoty for this purpose from funds earmarked for the Winter Relief. The local authorities have pledged 200,000 złoty on the basis of the support granted to the JSS by the General Government's Division of Bevölkerungswesen und Fürsorge[6] in Cracow. Measured against the need, however, these are paltry sums.

At such a difficult time as this, we turn to the Chief Social Welfare Council [with the request], in accordance with the aforementioned decision, to grant a larger one-off sum for the purpose of supporting the resettled persons. We are confident that the Chief Social Welfare Council will not refuse our request.[7]

Respectfully

DOC. 244

On 23 February 1941 the writer Jarosław Iwaszkiewicz describes a tram journey through the Warsaw ghetto[1]

Notes by Jarosław Iwaszkiewicz,[2] dated 23 February 1941

Warsaw, 23 February 1941

I thought the day I spent in Warsaw yesterday would make for an excellent story or report titled 'Twenty-four hours in occupied Warsaw'. That day – Marysia's fifteenth birthday[3] – was very special, like a summary of our entire life, with all of its dreadfulness and quasi-temptations. It only lacked an erotic motif, which would have to be worked in, for I am decidedly old-fashioned and cannot imagine a story, let alone a report, without an erotic plot. I spent last night in Warsaw[4] to be closer to the hospital and to Marysia, who has now been there for three months. Julek Krzyżewski[5] came by in the morning. He is currently working at the Bata factory in Krenau, Oberschlesien[6] – in other

6 German in the original: 'Population and Welfare Division'.

7 The Chief Social Welfare Council (NRO) granted this request: see Doc. 264, point 6.

1 The handwritten original has not survived. Published in *Jarosław Iwaszkiewicz: Notatki 1939–1945*, ed. Andrzej Zawada (Wrocław: Wydawnictwo Dolnośląskie, 1991), pp. 46–50. This edition is based on a typewritten copy of the notes prepared in the mid 1940s, with the author's handwritten corrections and additions. This document has been translated from Polish.

2 Jarosław Iwaszkiewicz (1894–1980), writer; grew up in Ukraine; artistically linked to the Skamander poetry group from 1920; newspaper editor; worked at the Ministry of Foreign Affairs until 1939; editor-in-chief for various literary magazines after the war; chairman of the Polish Writers' Union; Sejm delegate from 1952; awarded the State Prize on several occasions.

3 It was actually her seventeenth birthday. This was probably an intentional mistake to protect the author's daughter from being recruited for forced labour: see Doc. 167, fn. 5.

4 Iwaszkiewicz lived primarily on the Stawisko estate in Podkowa Leśna, approximately 20 km from Warsaw.

5 Juliusz Krzyżewski (1916–1944), poet; made his debut in 1935; served in the war in Sept. 1939; lived in Chełmek as a factory worker from 1939; soldier in the Home Army; perished during the Warsaw Uprising in 1944.

6 German in the original: 'Upper Silesia'.

words, Chrzanów[7] – and he told me about his life in that dingy backwater. Nothing but horrors, of course – they are threatened with eviction any day now and will have to resettle somewhere here. At least there they have a house that belongs to his wife's mother. I couldn't listen to him for long because I had to attend a funeral. Little Henio K.[8] died. His mother was overwhelmed with despair, and it was very sad for us as well. A tragic funeral. Not many people, but a lot of flowers, which froze in yesterday's severe frost, and amidst this tragedy the teacher's awful speech, brimming with more platitudes than you could imagine. 'Dear Henry, you're looking down on us, and we … the fatherland … the fatherland.' Every other word – fatherland. Henio's young friends seemed to look at her with hatred and surprise: 'Why is she going on about the fatherland?' It's terrible to misuse such a painful word on such an occasion; it was like revealing one's most intimate thoughts in a public place. The funeral left me distressed. From there I had to head straight to the Land Registry to sell a building plot on Leszno to some bailiff working for the court. The Land Registry always leaves a terrible impression on me. It lacks the discreet atmosphere of safe deposit box rooms at banks, where people are so embarrassed when they meet, as if they were meeting in a brothel. But you also see people there whom you wouldn't encounter anywhere else. It is extremely busy at the Land Registry, where people like my bailiff make money and 'secure' their capital by buying property. The German authorities have just introduced into the deeds a clause on 'pure Aryan' descent. The notaries read this clause on concealing the actual purchase and sale price like any other new clause – with a certain irony in their voices, perfunctorily. Our notary explains to both parties that these are newly introduced clauses. He says this in a tone that seems to indicate that it is of no significance. He allegedly spent some time in Pawiak for drawing up a deed in which the parties did not entirely meet the requirements of the Aryan clause. At least that is what you hear. Once the deed has been drawn up – a surprise. My bailiff invites me over for lunch. He does this in such a way that, in spite of all my efforts, I can't refuse. I have to accompany him, and he lives all the way out in Koło.[9] It's not very convenient for me, but what am I to do? We go. It is the first time I've been on a tram that passes through the ghetto. It stops on this side of the wall, then goes all the way down Leszno and doesn't stop until it has passed the other wall. The bailiff and I stand on the front platform of the tram and I observe the scene before me with a heavy heart. What strike me most are the streets packed with dark, dense crowds. These crowds look exotic, not at all like what you see on Nalewki.[10] Numerous shops, street peddling. I notice beggars with pale, ghastly faces lying in the street and on the pavements. Several are covered with newspapers: those are corpses. I see a man with a rickshaw – a hearse cart. He pushes a big black box in front of him. I don't know whether there is already a corpse inside, or whether it's empty. There are several beautiful coffee houses on Leszno. The tram driver has a few parcels. Whenever he slows down for a bend, he throws them to people only he recognizes. Eager, greedy hands grab the parcels, and they disappear into the dark throng. Shivers run down my

7 The city, which the occupiers renamed Krenau, was home to a shoe factory owned by the Bata company.
8 Pseudonym of Eryk Piątkowski, the son of an Iwaszkiewicz family friend.
9 Part of the Wola neighbourhood in western Warsaw.
10 A street in Warsaw's Muranów neighbourhood inhabited by numerous Jews.

spine at the thought of my friends and their parents living here. I get news from them, but it's as if it is written from a different world. I can't shake off this impression. I find it difficult to eat at the bailiff's, even though it's delicious: herring as an appetizer to go with the vodka, then borscht with pierogi, roast turkey, and compote. Black coffee eo ipso, which is a rarity now. I haven't had black coffee at home for a long time. After lunch in a tiny, neat, comfortable room, I quickly take my leave and again make my way back through the ghetto, which is now settling down for the night. They have an earlier curfew. I am now on my way to Marysia at the hospital. I haven't been there since yesterday. I'm very anxious. At the hospital, everything is the same: blue linoleum, green plants, blue embroidered napkins on the tables on every floor, and calm, smiling nurses. Unfortunately, Marysia's state remains unchanged. The physician treating both Henio and her told her that Henio's death made a deep impact on her. She lies emaciated and pale; her big eyes have rings under them. She looks at me the way she did on that Christmas Eve when she hummed Christmas carols in her faint, affectionate voice while looking at the little Christmas tree I had bought her. But this is her birthday. Miraculously I got hold of an orange for her. She was very happy. However, as these journeys through Koło and Leszno were extremely time-consuming, I can't stay long at the hospital. In any case, I absolutely abhor hospitals and always leave as fast as I can. Besides, a certain charming actress has invited me to quite an early dinner. She is not performing on stage currently; she is taking singing lessons instead. She will sing for us. So, I bid my child farewell and rush to the other end of Warsaw, to this confounded dinner, but it turns out to be very pleasant. There are a few friendly, intelligent people, including Lulek Schiller.[11] The menu is exquisite: herring to go along with the vodka for starters, then borscht with little patties, turkey, and then compote. Black coffee eo ipso. I find the similarity between lunch and dinner on two such separate occasions very amusing. We drink quite a lot, and when it's time to leave, I realize that from so far away, I won't make it back home on Trębacka before the curfew. So I accompany one of the guests to his place nearby. We are very drunk. We drink more wine as we walk to his apartment. It is getting very late. Suddenly my host's tenant appears, a *german*,[12] also drunk, and he starts a thorough discussion on matters of principle. He discusses basic issues such as law, ethics, and Germany's right to rule the world. In principle, I don't like such discussions, and certainly not with a drunk german, so I escape upstairs, where I find my host's magnificent bedroom. I put on his pyjamas and lie down under a satin quilt. At this point, a woman should be introduced into the story – for example, an encounter with the host's wife, who would turn out to be the woman with whom I had hopelessly fallen in love fifteen years ago. Back then I would have given half of my life for what's happening today. But today this is of absolutely no importance to me. It would have been a good plot twist. Unfortunately, however, there was no woman. I fell asleep calmly and woke up early. I got dressed and left. It was frosty but pleasant. I walked down Ujazdów Avenue from Belvedere. Hoar frost on all the tree branches. Bright, seemingly foggy sky and crunchy snow underfoot. Warsaw seemed so beautiful, so calm, this Sunday morning. I entered the Church of St Alexander and attended mass, standing behind a pillar some-

11 Leon Schiller (1887–1954), theatre director, drama critic, and composer.

12 Here and below the word is intentionally written in lower case as an expression of contempt.

where. One of our most distinguished writers stood in the middle of the church and ostentatiously prayed from a big prayer book. He looked at me with certain disdain. I knew he was a prominent member of the underground. I was seized with remorse that I had spent yesterday the way I did, and felt like beating my breast like a tax collector.[13] Lord, forgive me for yesterday.

As I was leaving, the old verger stood at the main entrance and turned back the men. 'There's a lorry out in front. Heaven knows what that could mean,' he said. 'Gentlemen, you can leave through the side exit, straight onto Wspólna.'

DOC. 245

On 27 February 1941 the head of the Municipal Health Office in Litzmannstadt (Łódź) criticizes the shortcomings of efforts to prevent epidemic diseases in the ghetto[1]

Letter from the head of the Municipal Health Office in Litzmannstadt (500 Dr.N./F.), Public Health Officer Nieberding,[2] to the chief of police in Litzmannstadt,[3] dated 27 February 1941

Re: ghetto

For several months now, I have been trying to induce the Jewish elder to make liberal use of chlorinated lime. Since early January he has had orders from me to apply chlorinated lime *in abundant quantities several times a day* to every lavatory, every privy, every cesspit, and every gutter. I have explicitly ordered that this be done during periods of frost as well, so that large amounts of chlorinated lime are present in the necessary locations as soon as the thaw sets in. Each time, my inspections revealed that the Jewish elder is either not meeting his obligations at all or is doing so only very inadequately. As dysentery and typhoid are still rampant in the ghetto despite the cold weather, we should expect a tremendous increase in these epidemics by this summer if he does not immediately carry out every one of the measures to keep them under control. It might not matter to us how many Jews die of these epidemics, but unfortunately the pathogens do not stop at the ghetto fence. Therefore, by ignoring my instructions, the Jew is putting the rest of the city in danger.

13 This is a reference to the New Testament, Luke 18:13: 'And the tax collector, standing afar off, would not so much as raise his eyes to heaven, but beat his breast, saying "God, be merciful to me a sinner!"' (New KJV).

1 APŁ, 221/31866a, fol. 20. Copy in USHMM, RG 05 008M, reel 6. This document has been translated from German.

2 Dr Karl Nieberding (1888–1966), physician; public health officer in Varel in 1919; head of an NSDAP Kreis office for public health in the city of Oldenburg from 1937; acting public health officer in Włocławek, Jan.–Sept. 1940; public health officer and head of the Municipal Health Office in Łódź until August 1942, then in Bernburg an der Saale and in Dessau; held in US captivity, 1945–1946; later a physician in private practice in Varel.

3 Karl-Wilhelm Albert (1898–1960), electrical engineer; in Freikorps Epp, 1919–1921; production engineer in Würzburg and later in Frankfurt am Main; joined the NSDAP and the SS in 1932; SD employee from 1933; in the SD Main Office, 1937–1939; chief of police in Oppeln, 1939–1940, and then in Łódź, July 1940–1944; simultaneously head of the SS Litzmannstadt Section, Oct. 1940–July 1941; held in an internment camp, 1945–1947; later lived in Erndtebrück.

I must therefore ask you to exercise your full authority and to force the Jew to rigorously and faithfully carry out my orders or those of my officials (Dr Misdorf[4] and Public Health Supervisor Benthin) to the letter.

DOC. 246
On 27 February 1941 the Jewish Social Self-Help head office records a telephone conversation about the arrival of Viennese Jews in Kielce[1]

Record (St./Sch.) of a telephone conversation between the chairman of the Jewish Social Self-Help, Weichert, and the chairman of the Jewish Municipal Welfare Committee in Kielce, Herman Lewi,[2] dated 27 February 1941

Re: resettlers from Vienna

Mr Levi reports that the 1,000 people who have been resettled from Vienna have arrived in Kielce without luggage or bed linen. Some of them had only a few undergarments and pieces of clothing with them.[3] Most of them are in a deplorable condition. Approximately 70 per cent of them are elderly and sick, and Mr Levi also reports that there are 80 mentally ill people and 30 geriatrics among them.

Dr Weichert requested the details in writing.[4]

The people who have been resettled have been housed in private accommodation, as there are no other vacant premises.

In response to Dr Weichert's question as to whether those who have been resettled brought any food provisions with them, Mr Levi replied that these provisions would be sufficient for a few days at most. Mr Levi will send a detailed list of the provisions they brought with them to Cracow by express mail tomorrow.

Mr Levi announced that he had discussed the matter with the Stadthauptmann,[5] and that this discussion will continue tomorrow.

Dr Weichert informed Mr Levi that, on the basis of our circular letter, he should request[6] that food rations as well as money be allocated for the sustenance of the resettled people, and that he should report to us on this conversation by telephone. Dr Weichert explained that the allocated quotas are not meant to be free of charge and must be paid for, and that the Stadthauptmann must provide cash for this purpose, independent of the quotas. Dr Weichert mentioned Warsaw as an example.

4 Dr Helmut Misdorf (1902–1943), physician; senior public health officer and acting head of the Department of Hygiene and of Health Safety in the Municipal Health Office in Łódź from 1940 until autumn 1941; thereafter served in the war; killed in action in the Soviet Union.

1 YVA, O-21/36, fol. 277. This document has been translated from Polish.
2 Spelling in the document: Levi.
3 The transport left Vienna on 19 Feb. 1941 carrying 1,004 Jewish men, women, and children. It arrived in Kielce on 20 Feb.
4 This sentence was inserted by hand.
5 German in the original. The Stadthauptmann of Kielce was Hans Drechsel.
6 Here the word 'demand' (*zażądał*) has been crossed out and replaced with the handwritten word 'request' (*prosił*).

Moreover, Dr Weichert said it will be necessary to ask the Stadthauptmann not only for food aid, but also for funds for these purposes as well as to combat epidemics, and finally for medical care. The quota allocations are to be made at the [standard] quota prices.

Dr Weichert explained that we[7] would try to provide them with financial assistance as far as our resources allow, and that the ZKOM[8] and the Jewish Council, for their part, must also make every effort to support the resettled people.

Mr Levi explained that he would send us all the above details in writing, and it was also agreed over the telephone that on Sunday, the 2nd of this month,[9] Mr Levi will report by telephone on his conversation with the Stadthauptmann and on the general state of affairs.[10]

DOC. 247

On 28 February 1941 the commander of the Jewish Order Service marks the first anniversary of the Jewish police in the Lodz ghetto[1]

Order of the day no. 35, from the commander of the Jewish Order Service,[2] dated 28 February 1941, annex to the 'Daily Chronicle Bulletin' of the Lodz ghetto, no. 49, dated 1 March 1941 (carbon copy)

Order of the day no. 35

On 25 February 1940 I was summoned to see the chairman of the Jewish Council of Elders, who at that time still had his office in the city at 19 Południowa.

When I arrived, I was informed that the chairman was ill. Despite this, he received me. I found the chairman on his sickbed, having just received injections.

I understood the gravity of what he had been through and the burden of his duties, the result of which was that even though he did not want to be in bed, agitation and fatigue had run him off his feet.

Immediately upon my arrival, the chairman got down to business, *explaining to me that the German authorities had ordered that a Jewish police force be established within two days, i.e. on 27 and 28 February.*

He asked whether I would take on this task.

After a moment's consideration I agreed.

And so, on 1 March 1940, the entity came into being – the so-called police.

Today marks the first anniversary of the establishment of the Order Service, which has already earned the right to be called police.

7 The JSS head office in Cracow.

8 Żydowski Komitet Opiekuńczy Miejski: Jewish Municipal Welfare Committee.

9 This is a reference to 2 March.

10 On 5 March 1941 the Stadthauptmann promised Lewi a grant of 6,000 złoty and held out the prospect of a further 1,000–1,500 złoty, but also informed him that he was unable to provide foodstuffs because he had no allocations at his disposal: YVA, O-21/36, fol. 274.

1 APŁ, 278/1079, fols. 47–48. This document has been translated from Polish.

2 Leon Rozenblat.

Under the crushing profusion of duties, unaware of the social relationships and local conditions in the Community, I often turned to the venerable chairman for his enlightening advice.

The early days of building up the Order Service will surely live in everyone's memory for a long time, given the particular circumstances surrounding our living and working conditions.

The building that houses our organization was constructed in a very modest manner. The modest space, coupled with the flood of duties and tasks that confronted us then, [initially] made it impossible to provide the militia with the appropriate organizational framework.

Gradually, however, as we overcame the immense number of difficulties that piled up, the Order Service began to grow and expand its remit.[3]

After assessing the territorial requirements of the ghetto in connection with the expansion of its boundaries, I created four precincts and assigned each one a suitable headquarters.

I founded '*HIOD*'[4] for guard services.

At the same time, *the following were created to perform special tasks*: the *Commandant's Office*, the *Investigation Office* as the sole judicial authority (until the court was established), the *Price Monitoring Department*, and the *Hygiene Department*, as well as the *Reserve Department attached to the Commandant's Office*.

In the autumn an emergency response unit was formed, known as the '*Überfall-Kommando*'[5] (what is today the Bałucki Rynek precinct).

Due to the long distances between the guard posts, especially in winter, '*HIOD*' was disbanded.

At the same time, in the separate area of Marysin II, which constitutes a type of cultural and educational centre,[6] precinct V was formed.[7]

When we think back to the unforgettable days and nights the Jewish population experienced during their resettlement from the city to the ghetto, we remember the tremendous burden of responsibility that was placed on our shoulders; the militiamen and their commanders displayed significant self-sacrifice and self-denial as they performed their difficult and very dangerous duties in 24- or even 48-hour shifts.

In these exceptional times, which required of us an enormous amount of willpower, the only incentive we had was the thought of the relief we were providing to our brothers and sisters, who had been deprived of a livelihood.[8]

3 From late 1940 the Order Service, commonly known as the Jewish ghetto police, numbered 700 men.

4 The Auxiliary Order Service existed from May to Nov. 1940. It was tasked with preventing the demolition of wooden houses and fences as well as thefts from shops and kitchens.

5 German in the original: 'assault squad'. In mid Sept. 1940 Rumkowski ordered the formation of a special unit tasked with suppressing protests and demonstrations.

6 This north-eastern and sparsely built-up part of the ghetto had children's settlements and several collectives, above all the Zionist youth associations.

7 The following paragraph is taken from the collection of papers containing supplementary texts and fragments that deviate from the ghetto chronicle: annex no. 49 of the 'Daily Chronicle', APŁ, 278/1080, fols. 30–31.

8 This is a reference to the forcible resettlement of the Jewish population from their homes, which began in Feb. 1940, and in which the Jewish Order Service was forced to participate on behalf of the German authorities.

Another noteworthy moment was the creation of the 'police cordon' to cut off the city from the ghetto.[9]

It won't be out of place when I mention that our working conditions *were and still are completely different and incomparably more difficult than those of any other police force.*

We had our hands full combating smuggling, escorting food delivery vehicles, [managing] the permanent queues of people awaiting their turn in front of shops and soup kitchens, dismantling various wooden buildings – and all this at a time when there were difficulties with supplying food for 160,000 people: these were tasks that demanded a great deal of our strength and energy.

To make matters worse, *troublemakers sought to create the greatest possible antagonism between the population and the police.*

Despite our best intentions, on many occasions these circumstances forced us to oppose our brothers who, in their naivety, *have let themselves be carried away by the pernicious slogans spread by vile agitators* recruited mainly from among the long-standing residents of the Bałuty neighbourhood,[10] which is known for its criminal tradition.

Summing up our year of activity, *I am pleased to say that we have overcome all the difficulties with our strength and our resources that were limited by the circumstances.*

It is difficult for me to foresee the future. I hope, however, that you will continue to carry out your duties *for the common good, by remaining steadfast in your positions of responsibility.*

In view of the difficult overall situation, we must forego even the most modest celebrations. I must therefore limit myself to expressing my heartfelt thanks in this way *to all the officers, non-commissioned officers, and enlisted men for their dedicated service.*

I wish everyone good health and continued success in their work.

In conclusion, I turn to those whom a merciless death has torn from our ranks, honouring their blessed memory. For this reason, I ask you to observe a minute of silence.

9 From the outset, monitoring the ghetto perimeters was one of the Jewish Order Service's main tasks.

10 This poor neighbourhood in the northern part of Łódź city centre comprised the core of the ghetto.

DOC. 248
On 3 March 1941 the Kreishauptmann of Sokolow-Wengrow (Sokołów-Węgrów) reports on the establishment of ghettos[1]

Report by the Kreishauptmann of Sokolow-Wengrow, signed Gramß,[2] accuracy verified by Deputy Kreishauptmann Beau,[3] to the Interior Administration Department (received on 6 March 1941), dated 3 March 1941 (carbon copy)

Situation report on Kreis Sokolow-Wengrow for February 1941
I. General remarks
A. In the month under review, all available resources were concentrated on carrying out three important special assignments:
1) the Otto Programme;[4]
2) establishing Jewish residential districts;
3) recording quotas by the Department of Food and Agriculture.

These measures will be key in determining the administrative work for the next three months.

a) The Otto Programme
The road-construction programme is now in full swing. Various road builders from the German Reich are working on the individual construction phases, and three Wehrmacht road-construction battalions will soon be deployed. The greatest concern is housing the German personnel from the Reich. As noted in earlier reports, Sokolow itself is absolutely brimming with various Wehrmacht units. The Wehrmacht has already been using the vast majority of serviceable buildings for months now. Two months ago the housing situation was constricted even further, to the point of unsustainability, when a field commander's office and its large staff was transferred to the town. The ideal occupancy limit has long since been exceeded, and as things stand now, there is not a single room to be found in Sokolow that would be fit to lodge a Reich German. Most of the buildings not being used by the Wehrmacht or by the German authorities are completely run down, so that even if steps were taken to continue clearing these buildings of Poles, a considerable amount of money, time, and materials would be necessary to repair them in even a makeshift fashion. From the perspective of a properly thought-out long-term housing policy, and considering the sudden need for housing and billeting that must be met

1 AIZ, I-151/27, fols. 47–61. Copy in YVA, MF JM 814. This document has been translated from German.
2 Ernst Gramß (1899–1946?), agronomist; took part in the Beer Hall Putsch in 1923; joined the NSDAP in 1923, the SA in 1928, and the SS in 1934; worked in various offices in the Reich Food Estate (Reichsnährstand), 1933–1938; Reichslandwirtschaftsrat (official in the Reich Food Estate) in 1938; head of the Department of Food and Agriculture in District Warsaw, 1939–1940; Kreishauptmann in Sokołów, June 1940–July 1944; subsequently served in the war; officially declared dead in 1956.
3 Emil Beau (1910–1971), printer; joined the NSDAP in 1932; attended the NSDAP training academy Ordensburg Vogelsang, 1936–1940; deputy Kreishauptmann in Sokołów, 1940–1941; Stadtkommissar in Stanisławów, 1941–1942; department head under the Kreishauptmann in Stryj, 1942–1943; thereafter head of the police division under the Stadtkommissar in Reval; worked in the NSDAP Main Office for Organization, 1944; lived under a false name for some time after the war.
4 The 'Otto Programme' was the code name for a project to construct 1,700 km of roads; it commenced in late July 1940.

immediately, provisional repair measures are neither feasible nor justifiable. A major factor here is the fact that I must categorically reject any further concentration of Poles due to the danger of epidemics that such a step would entail. Conditions in Wengrow are similar to those in Sokolow. In addition to Kaluczin, Wengrow is also the most dangerous place in District Warsaw in terms of the risk of typhus infection.

Since three Wehrmacht road-construction battalions are going to be deployed very soon, I emphatically pointed out the billeting difficulties to the relevant Wehrmacht authorities during preliminary talks.

Billeting the numerous staff officers as well as the rank and file will only be possible if the Wehrmacht provides the necessary barracks, since the Wehrmacht already occupies even the larger estates in my Kreis. If, as the Wehrmacht has indicated, the barracks are not available, at least not on the scale required, I will have to decide to use churches as makeshift quarters. The season allows for such housing solutions at this time.

It has frequently been my experience that excessively rosy reports from on high gloss over the reality of the situation. Orders and arrangements are then made based on inaccurate assumptions, and in part prove impossible to carry out. Or, at the very least, they lead to major hindrances that turn into serious problems, each with its own wide range of potential consequences that are impossible to predict. For example, the road builders deployed in my Kreis were told in an official meeting that the housing issue had been splendidly resolved.

If the people coming here to work for these companies must now resign themselves to living in the most wretched makeshift housing for weeks on end, it will ultimately be at the expense of their performance and willingness to work; it does not serve the project as a whole. I have also informed the relevant road-construction authorities of these grievances in detail. I was assured that suitable barracks would be procured.

Timber is needed to put up site huts and sheds for storing equipment. However, the quota allocated to me cannot cover this need, since I am forced to use this relatively small amount of construction timber to repair building shells that were not completed due to damage caused by the war. An additional allotment of timber must therefore be made available by all means for the Otto Programme.

The delivery of rocks has begun in earnest. Transporting them will inevitably put a great strain on the drivers concerned.

Road construction is also currently being impeded by the fact that the roads have to be cleared of piled-up snow to a width of 6 metres. The large-scale deployment of workers has begun, but it is not proceeding at the desired pace due to a notable lack of appropriate tools and equipment.

b) The Jewish question

The Jews have been completely denied freedom of movement within the Kreis as well – a measure justified by the need to put a stop to illicit trade. The Jews are concentrated in six localities in the Kreis, namely:

Sokolow,
Wengrow,
Sterdyn,
Kosow,
Stoczek,
and Lochow.

The establishment of Jewish residential districts in the aforementioned towns will soon be completed, and the few Jews still living in villages in the Kreis will be moved to one of these six towns. I have prohibited Jews who are not Kreis residents from entering Kreis Sokolow-Wengrow under threat of punishment, which means that all traffic within the Kreis will soon be free of Jews.

Every Jew residing in the Kreis was registered on 15 February of this year. Residence permits have been issued to some 20,000 Jews, pending further notice. Once the weather allows, the Jewish residential districts will be sealed off. In consultation with the Employment Office, arrangements have been made for the Jews' labour deployment.

The task of self-administration within the Jewish residential area has been transferred to the Jewish Council, and orders to set up sanitary facilities, quarantine centres, and prisons have been given and will be carried out soon.

c) Securing foodstuffs subject to quotas

The Kreis's own grain requirements are gradually being secured with the help of the Sonderdienst.[5] However, these measures are proving extremely difficult to carry out, since the number of available law enforcement authorities is not yet sufficient. For the same reason, illicit slaughtering, which is occurring on a considerable scale, cannot be prevented to the necessary extent. To further restrict illicit trade, I have prohibited meat dishes of any kind from being served in restaurants. Only a few establishments are authorized to supply Reich Germans, and this is done via [ration] cards.

B. Bauernschenke[6]

As part of a fitting event held on 8 February 1941, I officially opened the first German tavern in Kreis Sokolow-Wengrow – the Deutsche Bauernschenke. It was meant as a gift from the Kreishauptmann to the Wehrmacht and all the Reich Germans who are working in the Kreis. The design and interior decoration match our people's characteristic style and can without exaggeration be called a great success. All the guests feel very comfortable in the inviting, comfortable rooms, and the place is extremely popular. Since this would make a good opportunity for a Reich German to earn a living, the plan is to lease the tavern to a capable professional. The opening of the Deutsche Bauernschenke represents an important cornerstone of Party work, which can only now start up according to its customary pattern. This establishment has become the centre of cultural and political life for Germans living in the Kreis.

[...][7]

5 The Sonderdienst (Special Service) was an auxiliary police force in the General Government which consisted of ethnic Germans. It was directly subordinate to the GG government, in contrast to the regular police force under the command of the Higher SS and Police Leader.

6 The name translates roughly as 'The Farmers' Tavern'.

7 In what follows, the report deals with personnel matters; the mood among Germans from the Reich and the Polish population; developments in the departments responsible for food and agriculture, public health, and veterinary services; economic problems; and the efforts of the Population and Welfare Division on behalf of ethnic Germans' welfare.

DOC. 249

On 4 March 1941 the Jewish Council in Lublin requests that the curfew be shortened in order to contain the risk of epidemic disease[1]

Letter from the Jewish Council at the Jewish Religious Community in Lublin (no. 1195/41), Chairman,[2] p.p. Dr Alten,[3] to the Stadthauptmann of Lublin,[4] dated 4 March 1941

Re: *curfew regulation for Jews*
By order of the District Governor of Lublin on 4 June 1940, the curfew for Jews was set at 7 p.m.

§ 4 of the First Implementing Regulation of 11 December 1939 to the Regulation on the Introduction of Forced Labour for the Jewish Population of the General Government of 26 October 1939 states: 'Jews in the Gen[eral] Gov[ernment] are forbidden to enter and use paths, streets, and open public spaces between 9 p.m. and 5 a.m. without permission. Directives from local German authorities that contain further restrictions on movement are unaffected by this.'[5]

The Jewish Council in Lublin politely requests that the curfew for Jews be set at 9 p.m. when it is fixed for the spring and summer.

The Jewish population was previously distributed across all of the city's residential districts, whereas now it is concentrated in cramped quarters in the Jewish neighbourhood designated by the authorities. In late 1939 and early 1940, the Jewish Council additionally had to take in several thousand resettled Jews, so that the population density at present is incomparably higher than it was before.

In its concern for the health of the Jewish population and as part of its spirited efforts to do everything that might prevent the emergence of infectious diseases, the Jewish Council considers it desirable that the Jewish population should be given the opportunity, mainly in the spring and summer, not to have to return in the early evening hours to their rather scanty living quarters, which, given the high density of closely packed buildings, often lack an adequate supply of light and air. Our request will seem all the more reasonable if one takes into account the fact that most of the Jewish quarter lacks

1 APL, 891/2, fols. 13–14. This document has been translated from German.
2 Henryk Bekker (1886–1942); studied civil engineering in Munich; active in the Jewish People's Party; city councillor in Lublin from 1929; chairman of the Lublin Jewish Community from 1936; chairman of the Jewish Council, 1939–1942; in late March 1942 deported to Belzec, where he was murdered.
3 Dr Marek Alten (1885–1942), lawyer; officer in the Austro-Hungarian Army during the First World War; activist in the Zionist Organization in Lublin until 1939; deputy chairman of the Jewish Council in Lublin and head of the JSS in District Lublin, 1939–1942; succeeded Bekker as Jewish Council chairman in late March 1942, after Bekker's deportation; shot dead in Nov. 1942.
4 Friedrich August (Fritz) Saurmann (1893–1973), journalist; joined the NSDAP in 1932; deputy mayor of the city of Mainz, 1933–1935; chairman of the Mainz Carnival Association (Mainzer Carneval-Verein) in 1934; excluded from the Party for 'separatism' and 'philosemitism' in 1935 (rehabilitated in 1936); Stadthauptmann of Lublin from June 1940; suspended for corruption in 1942; Kreishauptmann in Biała Podlaska, 1943–1944; chief executive of the German Chemical Industry Trade and Employers' Association (Fach- und Arbeitgeberverband der Chemischen Industrie) after the war.
5 For the wording of this Implementing Regulation, see Doc. 55.

sewers and working Jews only finish up for the day at 7 p.m., which means that their only opportunity to rest outside the cramped and stuffy living quarters and to air their apartments is after 7 p.m.

The health and hygiene factors cited above make it our duty to submit this request, especially since the previously mentioned provisions of the Regulation of 26 October 1939 permit Jews to be on the streets and in open public spaces until 9 p.m., strictly speaking, thus enabling the authorities in charge to set the curfew at 9 p.m.[6]

DOC. 250

On 6 March 1941 Polish underground organizations call on Poles to refuse to serve as guards in camps for Jews[1]

Biuletyn Informacyjny,[2] 6 March 1941

On 1 March of this year, a summons appeared on the walls of the capital and other Polish cities calling upon Poles with military training to join an auxiliary *volunteer* service to guard the Jewish barracks.

However, since:

1. the *voluntary* service of Poles under German command is tantamount to *treason*;
2. auxiliary service for the police (gendarmerie) may force Poles to perform acts that dishonour their good name;
3. there is no guarantee that anyone who volunteers for this service will not be *deported* to Germany or to another country, which would deprive Poland of people with military training who will be crucial when Poland steps up the fight against the occupying power;
4. every Pole who enters into German service frees up one German to fight on the front against our allies, thereby delaying our victory and the restoration of our Independence;[3]
5. last year the Polish government in exile issued an order to refrain from even the appearance of cooperation with the anti-Jewish campaign organized by the Germans;[4]
6. our German enemy will take advantage of this auxiliary service to show the whole world that we are cooperating in the extermination of the Jews and will attempt to discredit us in the eyes of the world;

6 On 1 May 1941 the curfew in the Lublin ghetto was set at 9 p.m. See also Doc. 293.

1 *Biuletyn Informacyjny*, 6 March 1941, p. 1; Biblioteka Narodowa, microfilm 45 816. Published as a facsimile in Andrzej Krzysztof Kunert (ed.), *Polacy – Żydzi. Polen – Juden. Poles – Jews, 1939–1945: Wybór źródeł. Quellenauswahl. Selection of documents* (Warsaw: Oficyna Wydawnicza RYTM, 2001), pp. 188–189. This document has been translated from Polish.

2 *Biuletyn Informacyjny* was the underground weekly of the Union of Armed Struggle (ZWZ), which later reorganized into the Home Army (ZWZ-AK). The publication appeared in Warsaw from late 1939 and over time became the most influential underground newspaper with the highest circulation (over 40,000 copies in 1944); its last issue appeared in Jan. 1945.

3 Capitalized in the original.

4 This order could not be found. This might be a reference to secret instructions that the Polish government issued to leading figures in the underground.

the organizational and military forces operating within Poland on behalf of the Polish government in exile call upon all Poles to categorically reject any thought of joining the ranks of the auxiliary service under the command of the German police (gendarmerie).

The editors of Polish underground newspapers and journals are requested to print this appeal.

DOC. 251
On 6 March 1941 Salomea Cytryń describes daily life in the Warsaw ghetto to her husband[1]

Handwritten letter from Salomea Cytryń[2] in Warsaw to Nusyń (Natan) Cytryń[3] in Murnau, dated 6 March 1941[4]

Dearest Nateniek,

I received your letter from the 15th along with the transfer of 65 zł. just a moment ago. Why did you send me money when you need it for parcels? Here the sending of all parcels has been suspended. I've been to the post office with the shirts a few times, and I can't send them. I receive all your letters. I can't send the enclosed letters to your parents or to Heniek, because I'm only allowed to write postcards. I have not received any letters from your parents or from Emilia, but I have received two food parcels from Heniek, and one is still on the way; we have also received 200 zł. from Tosia. You can imagine what a relief this has been to us! Pork, goose fat, groats, flour dumplings, tea! In spite of all this, I was happiest about your parcel from Heniek. Today I'll write to your parents and to Heniek. […][5] I'll tell you now what's been keeping me busy. The Order Service has granted licences for seven snack bars to 21 women, and I am one of them. I own a snack bar at 15 Twarda with two other women. We sell biscuits, tea, etc. I have to get up at 5 a.m. to brew the tea in time, and I am busy there until 4 p.m. But my work does not end there, because later I go from one shop to the next with cooking oil. I thank God for that. I would be happy if you were with us. I work hard! I am no longer a woman in search of a living! Marysia, Daniek's fiancée, invited me to her performance at the theatre (for free). Despite my exhaustion, I had to accept her invitation. […][6] Marysia is the jewel of the theatre, a future celebrity; her acting is wonderful! I close this letter with a kiss, dearly beloved, Kos.[7]

We hope to see you again as soon as possible. Mother and Father.[8]

Beloved and adored Papa! Your wedding anniversary is not far off. I hope you will be with us by then. I miss you. Janek.[9]

1 YVA, O-6/553, fol. 1. This document has been translated from Polish.
2 Salomea Cytryń, née Kazimierska (1902–1942), from Włocławek; forcibly resettled to Warsaw, where she lived at 28/53 Twarda Street from 1939. The last letter her husband received from her was sent on 18 June 1942.
3 Nusyń Cytryń, lieutenant in the Polish army; prisoner of war in Oflag VII A (Block B IV, prisoner no. 186) in Murnau (Upper Bavaria); lived in Canada after the war.
4 The original contains handwritten notes and underlining.
5 One word is illegible.
6 Two words are illegible.
7 Salomea Cytryń.
8 Salomea Cytryń's parents.
9 Salomea and Nusyń Cytryń's son. The last four sentences are written in different handwriting.

DOC. 252
On 10 March 1941 Governor Fischer reports on the forced labour of Jews and their expulsion from District Warsaw[1]

Situation report from Governor Ludwig Fischer for the month of February 1941, Warsaw, dated 10 March 1941

[…][2]
IV. Labour Department
[…][3]
3. *Recruitment of agricultural workers for deployment in the Reich*
The preliminary work of recruiting agricultural workers for deployment in the Reich is virtually complete. The total quota of agricultural workers from the General Government amounts to 220,000. District Warsaw must supply 17 per cent = 37,400 of these workers, most of whom will be sent to Pomerania and Lorraine. To guarantee that the quota is met, 250 recruitment bases have been set up in the district. […][4]
4. *Labour deployment of Jews*
In the month of February the deployment of Jews for labour was again modest in scale. German agencies made use of only around 1,800 Jews, which was mainly due to the poor weather conditions at the start of the month. District Lublin requested 10,000 Jews for land-improvement work for early March and another 15,000 Jews for a later date. In District Warsaw, another 25,000 Jews have been earmarked for dyke and land-improvement work, meaning that the large-scale deployment of some 50,000 Jewish labourers in total can be expected. Many of these Jews will be taken from the Jewish residential district in Warsaw, which should noticeably alleviate the situation there.
[…][5]

VIII. Resettlement Department
1. From now on, the *naturalization process* for ethnic Germans identified by the Ethnic German Liaison Office will be handled by the Central Immigration Office.
2. A lack of barracks led to extraordinary difficulties with the admission of the *evacuees* who arrived on seven train transports. It will only be possible to admit the 62,000 evacuees who are expected to arrive in the near future by pulling all the Jews out of the parts of District Warsaw that lie to the west of the Vistula so that the evacuees from Reich territory can take over the vacated dwellings.[6]

1 AIZ, Doc. I-151/27, fols. 62–83, quotes fols. 72–73 and 77–79. Copy in IfZ-Archives, MA 158/3. This document has been translated from German. Published in Polish translation in Dunin-Wąsowicz et al. (eds.), *Raporty Ludwiga Fischera*, pp. 264–283, quotes pp. 272–273 and 277–279.
2 The monthly report is 22 pages long. Fischer first reported on the political and economic situation in the district, then on developments in the Kreise, and finally on individual departments.
3 Fischer first addressed wage development in Warsaw and then the employment situation.
4 The subsequent text goes into further detail on the recruitment of agricultural workers for Reich territory.
5 The subsequent text addresses social security, housing, and developments in the Food and Agriculture, Forestry, and Internal Affairs departments.

3. Resettlement requests from Poles who want to move from the eastern territories of the Reich[7] to the General Government have become more and more common. Such requests are normally rejected unless the applicants are relatives of Poles who are either in the service of the German administration or who have already been evacuated from the eastern territories to the General Government.
4. A perimeter-regulation commission has made additional improvements to the perimeters of the *Jewish residential district* to further curb the illicit trading and smuggling that takes place at the perimeters. In connection with this, the committee reviewed whether it would be possible to omit from the district various large Aryan enterprises currently located either on the periphery of the Jewish residential district or within it, and facilitated the necessary perimeter adjustments.[8]

   The posting of parcels from the Jewish residential district has been suspended with effect from 24 February 1941.[9]
5. The *Transfer Bureau* primarily handled the entire process of providing the Jewish community with the necessary supplies. Based on a purchase note that must be submitted by the Jewish Council, and after prepayment of an amount roughly equivalent to the value of the quantities requested by the Jewish Council, the goods in question are purchased from capable suppliers on the Transfer Bureau's account.

   In total, 5,000 tailors, 3,700 cap makers, and 1,000 shoemakers can be immediately deployed in large workshops to produce goods for the major orders that are expected. The Wehrmacht High Command's Procurement Office in Berlin has already announced orders for the Wehrmacht to this effect.

   Preparations have also been made to deploy some 30,000 Jewish textile workers.

   The labour deployment of Jews outside the Jewish residential district consists of work details of around 2,000 people who perform a variety of menial tasks for the various agencies and offices each day, as well as labourers quartered in barracks for external deployment. The latter's deployment is currently still being arranged. In consultation with the Employment Office, some 40,000 Jews are being mustered at the moment and will be transported to different parts of the General Government for land-improvement work and other tasks at the end of the month.

   Commercial dealings between the Jewish residential district and its Aryan surroundings, which are also regulated by the Transfer Bureau, take place at the goods transfer point. We have noticed that procurement requests from the Aryan business world do not always correspond to actual needs, but are instead often motivated by a desire to engage in speculative behaviour. Among the numerous deals, the purchase of a large number of tools for the local armaments inspectorate, amounting to 100,000 złoty, is particularly noteworthy.

   The level of epidemics and infectious diseases in the Jewish residential district is relatively low. In February 1941, only 110 cases of epidemic typhus, 26 suspected cases

6 See Doc. 236.

7 This refers to the territories of Poland annexed to the Reich.

8 This meant that these large enterprises were located outside the ghetto perimeter from this point forward.

9 This was only a provisional regulation. It was not until Nov. 1941 that Dr Lauxmann, head of the Postal Department in the government of the GG, definitively prohibited the posting of parcels from the Warsaw ghetto.

of epidemic typhus, and one case of typhoid fever were identified.[10] Six health stations where Jewish physicians are permanently on duty have been set up in the Jewish residential district.

6. In the *German residential district*, work is still ongoing to create shared accommodation.

[...][11]

DOC. 253

Krakauer Zeitung, 13 March 1941: article about a presentation on ethnic policies in District Warsaw given by Reichsamtsleiter Schön[1]

The ethnopolitical order in District Warsaw. Driving the Jew out of commerce and crafts. Promoting a Polish middle class. Insights from the fourth lecture evening at the Warsaw People's Education Centre.

From our own correspondent
Warsaw, 13 March
The fourth and once again well-attended lecture evening organized by the German People's Education Centre in Warsaw was held in the concert hall at Brühl Palace. The evening was devoted to the subject of the ethnopolitical order in District Warsaw, and the topic was presented by Reichsamtsleiter *Schön*, who oversees the Resettlement Department in the Warsaw District Governor's Office.

The speaker began by discussing the grand German development project in the East. This project, he noted, proves that the Germans have once again come to this area as bearers of culture, just as they did centuries ago. The area's final order is now in the process of being established. Reichsamtsleiter Schön cautioned, however, that this will only be possible if the efforts to build the state and its economy go hand in hand with a sound and coherent ethnopolitical order which, in turn, can only be based on the laws of blood.

The speaker also situated the ethnopolitical order of District Warsaw within this broader context, mentioning the resettlement of the ethnic Germans who live there.[2] He said that these measures are unavoidable as a means to establish clear ethnic boundaries and to preserve valuable German blood for the German people. He then added that a definitive solution to the Jewish question is also being prepared as part of the future ethnopolitical order. Reichsamtsleiter Schön, who at this point provided an interesting look back at the history and development of Jewry in Poland, said that it is absolutely

10 In the winter of 1940–1941, typhus was the deadliest infectious disease. Many cases were not reported, however, which means that the actual infection rates were much higher than Fischer indicated here.

11 The subsequent text discusses healthcare, schooling, the judicial system, and the activities of the personnel and propaganda departments.

1 *Krakauer Zeitung*, 13 March 1941, p. 5. This document has been translated from German.

2 This refers to measures which had been under way since summer 1940 to resettle ethnic Germans from the General Government to the annexed Polish territories. Further such measures were envisaged but did not take place.

necessary to break the yoke of Jewish influence in order to prevent the whole development project from being jeopardized in the long run.

He described the political, hygiene-related, and economic reasons for establishing the Jewish residential districts in District Warsaw. He emphasized that the exclusion of Jewry from the economic sphere, in which Jews in Poland have established themselves particularly in commerce and the craft trades, would be conducive to the emergence of a sounder economic structure within the Polish population. Up to this point, a Polish middle class has never existed, because the sources of income for this section of the population were in Jewish hands. For example, the 4,000 to 5,000 retail and craft businesses that have already been given to Poles in Warsaw mark an important step towards the creation of a Polish middle class. To conclude, Reichsamtsleiter Schön placed all of these individual processes within the larger historical context of the new order in Europe which the Führer is seeking to establish.

DOC. 254

On 14 March 1941 the acting mayor of Staszów instructs the Jewish Council on bathing and delousing procedures to combat epidemics[1]

Directive (no. 19/41) issued by the acting mayor of Staszów, Józef Suchan, to the Jewish Council in Staszów[2] (received on 14 March 1941),[3] dated 14 March 1941

In order to combat typhus in Staszów more efficiently, I order the following, effective immediately:

1. a) Bathing hours at the Jewish bathhouse are extended to 6 p.m.
   b) Bathing hours for men are from 8 a.m. to 1 p.m., and for women from 1 p.m. to 6 p.m.

   During men's bathing hours, women will clean apartments and utensils, and boil linen.

   Prior to bathing, all men should be shaved with a straight razor rather than clippers, but their heads should be shaved clean with clippers.

   c) As the high number of Jewish employees at the bathhouse disrupts normal bathing, the number of staff should be reduced to the minimum required to operate the bathtubs and boilers, as too many people crammed together in a tight space will create conditions conducive to lice and infections.

   As far as bathing protocol (not administration and general management) is concerned, I entrust the management of the bathhouse to Mr Wiktor Sawicki, who is currently employed there.

   d) Since the capacity of the sterilization stoves is not conducive to quick sanitizing and bathing, the hospital's sterilization stove must be operated simultaneously.

1 AŻIH, 222/1, fol. 2. Copy in USHMM, RG 15 073M, reel 1. This document has been translated from Polish.
2 Staszów was south-east of Kielce in District Radom in the General Government.
3 The directive was sent for the attention of Dr Lamieszewsk of the Polish police, Michał Jasiński from the sanitation inspectorate, and Wiktor Sawicki.

2. In cases where typhus is suspected, apartments must be systematically disinfected with sulphur.
3. Quarantine building no. 2 (at the Jewish cemetery) has been designated for isolating people with typhus, while building no. 1 (Górno Rytwiańska) is for quarantine and those suspected of having a contagious disease and awaiting a diagnosis.

DOC. 255
On 15 March 1941 the Jewish Welfare Committee in Kielce reports on the circumstances of Jews forcibly resettled to Nowa Słupia[1]

Report by the Jewish Welfare Committee in Kielce, signed Leon Sachnowicz,[2] for the Jewish social welfare advisor to the Governor of District Radom, Józef Diament (received on 17 March 1941), dated 15 March 1941 (carbon copy)[3]

On the basis of instructions received via telephone and the authorization given by the chairman[4] on 13 March 1941, I travelled to Słupia Nowa[5] on 14 March 1941 to inspect the living conditions of the people resettled from Hohenburg (Wyszogród)[6] and other localities, and I determined the following:

1. *Arrival and housing*

At Kielce railway station, the transport comprised 1,002 people. Of these, 13 sick people were transported to the hospital in Kielce. The rest travelled on horse-drawn carts. One person died suddenly en route, and 988 people arrived in the town. Some arrived with their entire families, but most were on their own, as the rest of their families had not been resettled for the time being. There were a considerable number of children among the arrivals. A detailed list of the families will be presented in the next few days.

Housing them involves insurmountable difficulties. The small town is situated behind Święty Krzyż[7] and is very difficult to access. It has approximately 2,000 residents, half of whom are Jews. Even before the war the Jews there lived in very cramped conditions, up to seven people to a single room. There are approximately 200 Jewish families. It is almost impossible to house all the resettlers in these 200 apartments. On the first day, up to a dozen people were housed in each room. I visited these apartments and saw that several cramped, damp rooms held up to 25 people, including the locals. The sanitary conditions in these rooms are downright catastrophic. The resettlers lie next to each other on straw on the floor. There is not a single straw mattress. They do not undress at

1 YVA, O-21/37, fols. 202–203. This document has been translated from Polish.
2 Leon Sachnowicz was a member of the Jewish Welfare Committee in Kielce from late 1940.
3 The original contains handwritten underlining.
4 This is a reference to the chairman of the Jewish Social Self-Help (JSS), Michał Weichert.
5 An old designation for the municipality of Nowa Słupia. Nowa Słupia was east of Kielce in District Radom in the General Government.
6 Wyszogród (renamed Hohenburg) was in the annexed Polish territory of Ciechanów that was incorporated into East Prussia as Regierungsbezirk Zichenau.
7 'Holy Cross'; the second highest mountain in the Świętokrzyskie mountain range, also known as Łysa Góra ('Bald Mountain').

all. The town's more merciful residents offer their beds to women and children, while they themselves lie on the floor. I visited apartments in which up to 40 people were housed. There was not enough room for everyone, and approximately 400 resettlers were put up in the synagogue, where plank beds were set up. The sanitary conditions for those housed at the synagogue are even worse.

2. *Sanitary conditions*

The resettled people are living in appalling sanitary conditions, as are local residents. People do not undress when they go to bed. They stay in damp, unventilated rooms. Some of the arrivals have lice, and there is no way to delouse or bathe them. I visited the bathhouse. It is a mikveh[8] made up of a single room. People undress there. Steps lead down to a pool that can barely hold eight to ten people at a time. There are no showers at all. The water in the mikveh is dirty. It is changed very rarely, three to four times a year. There is a general lack of water in the town. It is brought from a stream that flows down the slopes of Święty Krzyż. This water is even used for drinking. The Council of Elders has neither soap nor medication. Medication is purchased at the pharmacy at normal prices. The town has one physician, a Christian, and there are two medical orderlies among the resettlers. There are also sick people among the resettlers, but there is no place where they can be isolated. At the synagogue, for example, a seriously ill person with open tuberculosis lies in the same plank bed as healthy children.

3. *Food supply*

Along with the transport from Kielce, 900 loaves of bread weighing a kilo each, 675 kg of groats, 690 kg of flour, and 300 kg of pearl barley arrived. In addition, on the day the transport arrived, the Kreis Relief Committee received the following allocation of foodstuffs for the resettlers: 100 kg of groats, 100 kg of pearl barley, 250 kg of flour, 100 kg of marmalade, and 10 kg of sugar. The Council of Elders in Słupia received money from me for this allocation for which it paid 816 złoty. The Council of Elders is setting up a kitchen for 1,000 people at the synagogue; it will be ready in a few days. For the time being, all the foodstuffs have been distributed among the resettlers, who cook for themselves in their quarters. I note that along with the resettlers a wagon full of potatoes arrived, which was shipped to Słupia during my stay. They have not yet been weighed. I estimate there is about 1,000 kg, although we must ultimately expect far less, as some have surely gone bad. Nowa Słupia is not normally allocated foodstuffs; in particular it does not receive any flour for baking bread. Given this state of affairs, a shortage of bread for the resettlers is expected as early as Monday, the 17th of this month. There are absolutely no fats either, which is why it remains doubtful that the kitchen can be put into operation.

4. *The Council of Elders in Słupia Nowa*

The Council of Elders is in a very poor financial situation. They have a monthly budget of approximately 2,000 złoty and end each month with a deficit of 600–700 złoty. Part of this budget goes towards social welfare. It is impossible for them to care for nearly 1,000 new arrivals out of their own funds. With few exceptions, the town's residents are very poor. They mainly earn their living from door-to-door peddling. I have heard that 80 per cent of the population should be receiving social welfare, but only 10 per cent

8 Jewish ritual bath.

actually do because there are no funds. Personally I have no confidence in the Council of Elders. Chil Zylberman,[9] a miller who was appointed head of the committee formed in connection with the aid operation for the resettlers, made a very good impression on me. I asked him to take the matter of supplying provisions into his own hands. Employing the new arrivals in their own professions is out of the question. For example, there is only one Jewish barber in the town, who earns money only once a week, on Fridays, and cannot live on that. I mention this because I tried to find work for one of the resettlers, a barber, but failed. It is the same with other craftsmen. I do not expect any of them to find work. One hundred and twenty Jews are employed at a nearby mine, and they each earn 1.60 złoty per day.

Conclusions

1. Immediate action is required to provide foodstuffs for the resettlers. Otherwise the kitchen cannot open.
2. They need to be provided with several hundred straw mattresses, beds, and medication.
3. Immediate financial support is required. Up to 5,000 złoty should be provided for the time being.
4. A more serious effort should be made to resettle at least 800 people from Słupia to neighbouring towns, i.e. to Łagów (9 km), Raków (18 km), and Chęciny near Kielce.

Respectfully,

DOC. 256
On 20 March 1941 the Piaski gendarmerie post reports on arrests of forcibly resettled Jews[1]

Letter from the gendarmerie post in Piaski (log no. 336/41), gendarmerie officer and deputy post commander Strugat (?), to the gendarmerie platoon in Lublin, dated 20 March 1941

Re: return of evacuated Jews
Concerning: radiogram from the Lublin Kreishauptmann, dated 17 March 1941[2]
As directed, patrols were conducted to search for the evacuated Jews who were on the way from Krasnystaw to Lublin. A total of 136 Jews were picked up and transported back to their starting point by Police Battalion 306-Lublin. The sum of 2,523 zloty was found on the Jews in cash. This sum was transferred to the Kreishauptmann in Lublin on 20 March 1941.

Seven horses which the Jews had used for transport were secured. Three of these horses have already been sold to farmers by the representative of the Kreis agricultural officer – Section Head *Dittert*[3] – while four are being looked after at a farm.

Police Battalion 306 arrived here at 2.45 p.m. on 17 March 1941, and travelled back again to its base at 11.00 p.m.

9 Chil Zylberman (1909–1941), murdered in Auschwitz.

1 APL, 501/141, fol. 25. This document has been translated from German.
2 Not found. The Kreishauptmann was Emil Ziegenmeyer.
3 Paul Dittert (b. 1897).

DOC. 257
On 20 March 1941 the Governor of District Lublin announces the establishment of the ghetto in Lublin[1]

Announcement concerning the establishment of a closed-off Jewish residential district in the city of Lublin

Public interests dictate that a closed-off Jewish residential district (ghetto) be established in the city of Lublin with immediate effect. I hereby issue the following directives for the implementation of this measure:

1. The following streets demarcate the ghetto of the city of Lublin: corner of Kowalska via Kowalska, Krawiecka along the block of apartment buildings shown in the sketch,[2] across the open plot, crossing Sienna to Kalinowszczyzna up to the corner with Franciszkanska, Franciszkanska up to the corner with Lubartowska, Lubartowska as far as the corner with Kowalska.
2. All Jews resident in the city of Lublin have to live in this Jewish residential district. Jews are prohibited from residing permanently outside the ghetto.
3. The non-Jews living within the Jewish residential district have until 31 March 1941 to move to places of residence outside the ghetto. Information about available housing will be provided by the Municipal Housing Office, Resettlement Department (Market Square, Tribunal).[3]

   Non-Jews who have not left their residences in the Jewish residential district by 31 March 1941 will be forcibly resettled. They will only be allowed to take luggage up to a maximum weight of 25 kg per person with them during forcible resettlement. Bulky items will be confiscated.
4. The Jews still living outside the ghetto have to move into the Jewish residential district by 5 April 1941.

   The Jews living in the Kalinowszczyzna and Sierakowszczyzna areas of the city have to clear their residences by 20 April 1941 and relocate to the ghetto.

   Housing in the ghetto will be allocated by the Jewish Housing Office at 10 Lubartowska. Jews who resettle may take furniture, items intended for personal use, and shop fittings and properly acquired stocks of goods with them.

   Where furniture and other goods cannot be stored at the new accommodation in the Jewish residential district, they must be offered to the Trustee Office branch in Lublin. They may only be sold on the open market once permission has been given by the branch office.

   Furniture and items intended for personal use in Jewish apartments that have been left and are used by other tenants must be reported to the Trustee Office branch in Lublin. More detailed instructions concerning the manner of their sale or the use of these objects for other purposes will be given by the Trustee Office branch.
5. Jews who have not moved from their places of residence into the Jewish residential district within the deadlines that have been set will be forcibly resettled from the city

1 APL, 498/892, fols. 312–315. This document has been translated from German.
2 A map showing the location of the ghetto area was attached to the announcement.
3 The Crown Tribunal: a former city hall and court building.

of Lublin. During forcible resettlement, they may only take luggage up to a maximum weight of 25 kg per person. Jews who voluntarily move out of Lublin within the deadlines may take all their possessions with them. The Jewish Council will be notified of the localities in District Lublin that can be considered for resettlement.

Applications for resettlement must be submitted to the Municipal Housing Office in Lublin via the Jewish Council.

6. Shops, workshops, and other enterprises owned by Jews that are located outside the ghetto will remain provisionally exempt from resettlement; they must be registered with the Municipal Housing Office in writing immediately, and must not be used as living quarters on any account.
7. Non-Jewish offices, workshops, and enterprises located within the ghetto must be moved to other parts of the city by 20 April 1941. Applications for exemptions must be submitted to the Stadthauptmann in Lublin.
8. Non-Jews are prohibited from residing in and visiting the ghetto without authorization. Non-Jews must not give shelter to Jews. Non-Jews who violate this order will have their apartments seized.
9. I hereby charge thc Stadthauptmann in Lublin[4] with implementing the measures for establishing the ghetto.[5]
10. The Jewish Council of the city of Lublin must ensure the orderly establishment of the Jewish residential district, the preservation of order, and the maintenance of sanitary and welfare facilities. The Jewish Council is answerable to the Stadthauptmann for the smooth implementation of the measures.
11. Anyone who fails to comply with these directives and implementing provisions, as well as further directives and implementing provisions issued in the course of the resettlement operation, will be prosecuted and punished severely. Assets will be seized.

Lublin, 20 March 1941
The Governor of District Lublin
Signed Zörner
Governor

4 Fritz Saurmann.
5 A bypass first had to be constructed because a heavily used arterial road cut through the quarter.

DOC. 258

On 20 March 1941 the underground newspaper *Morgn-Fray* calls on Jewish youth to show solidarity with the Polish population[1]

We swear!

In silence and with heads bared, we have received the terrible news of another mass murder. The last groans of the more than 100,000 people murdered so far can still be heard, the blood of those victims who had the misfortune of falling into the executioners' hands – tens of thousands of bodies shot up and riddled with bulletholes – is still fresh, and already new graves have joined the thousands of others holding our brothers ... Our hands clench into fists, our teeth gnash, and in our hearts a hope flares up ... We swear, we swear.

When we call on the Jewish masses to show solidarity, to protect the general interests of workers, we are met with animosity. Did the Polish workers speak out when we were marked with armbands, when we were forced into sealed ghettos? Did one of them tear down the shameful posters – 'Jews and lice' – recently posted in the streets?[2] On the contrary, the Poles who come into contact with Jews show their contempt and hatred for Jews – and especially for Jewish workers – at every turn.

Needless to say, the only ones who actually think this way are the so-called nationalist-minded circles, who are looking for an excuse to justify their dirty work helping the occupiers, either directly or indirectly. We particularly wish to emphasize that the rabble-rousers, bands of smugglers, and street gangs that have recently appeared, and that support and are supported by the occupiers, have never been, nor are they now, a reflection of the Polish people. *The Polish masses are not traitors*; the Polish working masses have written 'Liberty, Equality, Fraternity' in golden letters on their flag. That is why we are not indifferent to their joy or sorrow, as their fate is closely linked to ours. It is not the dirty riff-raff who are slain or languish in prison, but the *noble* and *honourable*, the Polish heroes and martyrs, those who fight for human rights and liberation.

We now await an immense new and tragic wave of people being snatched up the same way they were last year. Just like a year ago, hundreds of thousands of farmers and workers will be torn from their cottages and houses and sent as slaves to Germany, and who knows whether they will ever return. Tens of thousands of young Jewish workers will also be torn from their homes and will either be tortured to death in the 'camps' or return forever crippled.

Like dangerous gangsters, the Community leaders and their helpers from *Gazeta Żydowska* have taken advantage of this and released the vile 'hakhshore'[3] plan – to

1 *Morgn-Fray*, no. 2, 20 March 1941, p. 1; AŻIH, Ring I/1317 (692). This document has been translated from Yiddish. *Morgn-Fray* was the underground newspaper of the communist organization Sierp i młot (Sickle and Hammer) and Robotniczo-Chłopska Organizacja Bojowa (Combat Organization of the Workers and Farmers). It was published in Warsaw between March and Dec. 1941.

2 A German propaganda poster at that time featured the skull-shaped head of a Jew with an oversized louse crawling across his beard. The poster bore the inscription 'Żydzi – wszy – tyfus plamisty' ('Jews – lice – typhus'). Published in Paul Weindling, *Epidemics and Genocide in Eastern Europe, 1890–1945* (Oxford: Oxford University Press, 2000), p. 2.

3 Yiddish pronunciation of the Hebrew word 'hachsharah': training, preparation. As part of so-called hakhshore classes, Zionist youth in particular prepared Jews for emigration to Palestine in the 1920s and 1930s by teaching them agricultural skills and crafts, as well as Hebrew.

voluntarily replace the displaced farmers and workers with Jewish manpower. Under the guise of 'resettlement', this gang seeks to commit the vilest of villainous acts and thus to help our bloodiest enemies drive a wedge between the Polish and the Jewish masses. Doing so will facilitate the [German] plan to tear Polish farmers away from their native soil.

We call upon all Jewish youth: do not betray the interests of the Jewish and Polish masses in their joint battle against a common enemy.

The plans of the careerist Community leaders, whose own physical well-being comes at the expense of the welfare of the masses, amount to licking the occupiers' boots. Jewish youth who cherish the hope of living in a free and liberated Poland must throw such plans back in the Community leaders' faces in disgust.

We want to warn them[4] here and now: the game is almost up – we are going to make you pay for absolutely everything.

DOC. 259

On 20 and 25 March 1941 seventeen-year-old Halina Nelken describes her observations and feelings after moving to the Cracow ghetto[1]

Handwritten diary of Halina Nelken,[2] entries for 20 and 25 March 1941

20 March 1941[3]
The entry from two days ago describes how 'confused' I was on the day I moved to the ghetto.[4] I fought back sadness and tears at the same time as I enjoyed some gallows humour with Felek[5] at the sight of this 'mass migration'.[6] Lorries and removal vans overloaded with junk moved in one direction, and from the opposite direction came the Poles, because the people from this part of Podgórze had to vacate their apartments for us. Kaźmierz[7] is suddenly going to be full of 'Aryans'! The chaos surrounding the move caused Felek and me to break into fits of laughter. In the afternoon I had to go to the pharmacy,[8] but on my way back in the evening I instinctively headed home, towards

4 The Community leaders.

1 The diary was written between 1938 and 1942 and is in the Nelken family's possession. Published with revisions in Nelken, *Pamiętnik*, pp. 115–117; English edition: Halina Nelken, *And Yet, I Am Here!*, trans. Halina Nelken with Alicia Nitecki (Amherst, MA: University of Massachusetts Press, 1999), pp. 73–74. This document has been newly translated from Polish.

2 Halina Nelken (1923–2009); grew up in Cracow; lived in various camps, 1942–1945; continued her education after the war, studying art history and philosophy; emigrated to the USA in 1959.

3 On 3 March 1941 the Governor of District Cracow ordered that Cracow's Jewish population be forcibly relocated to the Podgórze neighbourhood by 20 March 1941. Podgórze had been designated as the ghetto.

4 On 18 March Halina Nelken wrote, 'My mental state today is a perfect mixture of all moods': Nelken, *Pamiętnik*, p. 115.

5 Halina Nelken's older brother, Felicjan.

6 The reference here is to the migration period in late antiquity.

7 A part of Cracow, also spelled Kazimierz, that was inhabited predominantly by Jews until March 1941.

8 Halina Nelken found employment at a pharmacy.

Długosz Street. As I looked back and saw the arch of Piłsudski Bridge emerge in the evening mist and the group of trees in our Planty Park, my eyes filled up with tears of sadness. I didn't want to see the new apartment, still without our furniture, just as I won't go to the former house now bereft of it. We could not take all the furniture with us anyway, because we have only one room and a kitchen in the ghetto. Besides, the glass cupboard and mahoganies from Grandma's room were sold long ago, and all the silver and porcelain is at Józka's.[9] The only consolation is that our piano was returned to us, as the hospital was transferred to the ghetto.

They will seal the ghetto today. I don't know if I'll be able to continue working unless I get a permit. If not, I will have wasted a year. I play Chopin's 'Dream' with one finger, and I fight back the tears.

25 March 1941

No! I don't want my empty stomach to rumble, for the room to be so cold, for my father to be so appallingly thin and exhausted after these last days that his skin hangs from him like from a skeleton. I don't want mother to be so haggard. I don't want us to always be hungry, cold, bitter, and disheartened. God, what can I do to help? There's no way out. There's really no way out of our situation. We have no money, no provisions, and no hope of getting decently paid work. How can my meagre 60 złoty help? It barely covers my odds and ends. How can this meagre little wage help in the face of the mountain of small debts and the fact of … having to live?

For the time being Mother is shielding Felek from these problems, but I think that is wrong. Felek is an egotist. Why shouldn't he know what's going on? Why should only I bear the burden of sharing responsibility, just like our parents, and struggle to find a way out of this horrible situation – from which, unfortunately, there is no way out? What to do, oh, what to do? How to help? It's enough to drive you mad!

This evening my heart was bleeding at the sight of the haggard, exhausted faces of my parents, who aren't even old yet. On a sudden impulse, I wanted to hug my father's poor, greying head. I wanted to hold my mother's overworked, discoloured hands, which were once so smooth. Instead, I threw harsh, mean words at them, although I was choking back tears, and deep down I was angry with myself. I am mean. I am helpless. The only excuse I have is that the war has made me like this.

9 The Nelken family gave their nanny, Józefa, some household items to prevent them from being confiscated.

DOC. 260
On 25 March 1941 Governor General Frank announces Hitler's commitment to remove the Jewish population from the General Government first[1]

Minutes of the government meeting in Cracow on 25 March 1941[2]

[...][3]
Agenda item 2: *resettlement issues*
On this matter, the Higher SS and Police Leader, SS-Obergruppenführer *Krüger*, stated that the *resettlement of Poles and Jews* to the General Government has been halted for the time being. Resettlement within the General Government for the purpose of clearing areas for military training is progressing.

Governor General and Reich Minister Dr *Frank* announced that the Führer had told him at their meeting on 17 March that, in future, *resettlement* to the General Government would be made dependent on this territory's capacities. Furthermore, the Führer made a commitment that, in recognition of its achievements, the General Government would be the first territory to be made *free of Jews*. Incidentally, it should be noted that the heavy demands made of the General Government concerning resettlement were not due to any ill will on the part of the authorities involved, but resulted from the unavoidable necessity of repatriating Germans from the East.
[...][4]

DOC. 261
On 20 and 28 March 1941 a nurse describes the conditions in a children's hospital in the Warsaw ghetto[1]

Handwritten reports for the underground archive of the Warsaw ghetto (copy), dated 20 and 28 March 1941[2]

20 March 1941
Scenes from a children's hospital
My shift is from 3 to 11. When I arrive at my ward, it's sheer hell. Children with measles are lying two or three to a bed, all with the measles rash. Crimson red, watery eyes, and

1 AIPN, GK 95, vol. 16. Copy in IfZ-Archives, Fb 105, vol. 12, fols. 2704–2745, here fols. 2716–2717. This document has been translated from German.
2 This meeting was attended by Hans Frank, Josef Bühler, Friedrich-Wilhelm Krüger, the district governors, the Governor General's representative, and the department heads.
3 Frank began by passing on Hitler's thanks and appreciation to those present for the work they had done, and then dealt with the administration in the General Government.
4 The subsequent discussion focused on transport problems in the General Government. In an internal address given the same day, Frank had already noted Hitler's plans for the future of the General Government and said that, in addition to the Jews, the Poles would also have to leave the General Government. In Frank's words, Hitler was determined to 'make the territory a purely German land in the course of 15 to 20 years': Präg and Jacobmeyer (eds.), *Diensttagebuch des deutschen Generalgouverneurs*, p. 335.

1 AŻIH, Ring I/490 (989). This document has been translated from Yiddish. Published as a facsimile and in Polish translation in Sakowska (ed.), *Archiwum Ringelbluma*, vol. 2, pp. 130–139.

little shaved heads covered with scabs from which lice are creeping. 'Careful – lice,'[3] my colleague says, warning me not to get too close to the children. Along with a helper, I have 50 children to look after. All this work is enough to drive us mad. What first? Distribute the medicine, administer injections, serve food, [or] redo dressings[4] on the heads to treat the lice? The telephone rings. 'Hello!' – 'There are ten children waiting at reception. You need to send someone down to fetch them.' I wring my hands in exasperation. I have no beds, no linen, no blankets, no covers. I call up the head nurse. What am I to do with the children waiting down at reception? Where am I supposed to put them, and what will I dress them in? Her reply is short: put a third child in any bed currently shared by two, and done. Very simple! I send the young woman helper down to fetch the children. She hauls up a new transport for me. I look at the charts – already a third 'point'[5] with measles, Kałuszyn. All are naked, and we have nothing to put on them. The laundress isn't working. There is no coal. The rooms are terribly cold. The children huddle under the blankets and shiver with fever. Tired and hungry, blue with the chill, they fall asleep. Reluctantly, I must wake them. The creatures look at me with astonished faces, wondering why I am not letting them sleep. They see the needle, an injection,[6] and scream at the top of their lungs. One cries, 'I want to go home!' 'Where is your home?' 'Far away from here.' 'Where are you from?' 'From Kałuszyn.[7] They drove us out.' Another one: 'I want my clothes. I want to get dressed. I don't want to be naked. I am ashamed.' From the other room comes a cry, 'Miss, I am going to go home!' 'Now, where is your home?' 'My home is there.' 'Okay, once you've had a good night's rest, you can go home.'[8] I pass from bed to bed, checking that they are clean and getting them ready for bedtime. When I pick up the blanket from a bed shared by three two-year-olds, I feel sick. I hold my nose – [the stench is] suffocating. The bed is full of excrement. All three are crying, and there is no knowing which of them did it. Such cases are quite common.

In the hallway there is a five-year-old boy, bloated from hunger. He is dying of hunger. He came to the hospital yesterday on account of [his] swollen eyes. His hands and feet are the size of pumpkins. Many different tests are performed – could be the kidneys, could be the heart. But no, it isn't the kidneys or the heart. The child still moves his lips, begging for a piece of bread. I try to feed him something; perhaps he will be able to get something down. Alas, the throat is swollen shut; nothing goes down. It's too late. The physician asks him, 'Did you get anything to eat at home?' 'No!' 'Do you want to eat now?' 'Yes!' A few minutes later, he coughs up his final piece of bread, and with this expression on his lips, he sinks into sleep. Dead for a piece of bread.

2 The author, Dora Wajnerman, had fled from Łódź and worked as a nurse in the children's hospital in the ghetto in 1941.
3 This sentence in the original is in Polish but written in the Yiddish alphabet; the same also applies to other parts of the text that are in Polish.
4 This word is in Polish in the original.
5 Here and in what follows, 'point' refers to a makeshift shelter for people expelled to the Warsaw ghetto.
6 This word is in Polish in the original.
7 On 5 and 6 March 1941, approximately 500 Jews from Kałuszyn in Kreis Mińsk Mazowiecki were expelled to the Warsaw ghetto.
8 This exchange is in Polish in the original.

The ten-year-old refugee from Piaseczno[9] admitted to the hospital [was] filthy, neglected, and suffering from [bone] tuberculosis in his ankles. Having been bathed, he now lies in a ward in clean garments, in a clean bed, with 15 other children suffering from the same disease. I relieve a previous shift and take over [nursing] duty. We go from bed to bed, and they tell me about each child's condition. I find myself already standing at the Piaseczno refugee's bedside. It is Tsigler Avromek, who has contracted gonitis tuberculosis.[10] He has come from a 'point' for refugees from Piaseczno. I want to see his face – impossible. The blanket is drawn over his head. I pull away the blanket and want to ask him something. He starts screaming and crying as if I were trying to kill him. 'What happened to you?' 'I have nothing to live for,' he says. 'I want to die.' 'Why?' 'My father is at a point where there is nothing to eat, so I would rather starve too, as long as I am with my parents.' Some days pass [and I ask him], 'Well, silly, do you want to go to the point, to your father? Do you have it so bad [here]?' 'Oh no,' he says. 'I just feel sorry for my father and my mother because they have nothing to eat. And I eat five times a day! Maybe you could take some of my food to my mother?' The day comes when Avromek has to be discharged from the hospital. I say to him: 'Well, Avromek, tomorrow you will go [back] to your father.' He doesn't react and his face clouds over, as if it gives him no pleasure at all that he must return to bitter hardship. On the day Avromek is supposed to leave the hospital, we notice on his temperature chart that he has developed a fever. Everything was fine when his temperature was taken. It turns out that Avromek himself raised the temperature on the chart by two whole degrees, from 37 to 39, so as not to be discharged from the hospital so soon. It was no use, however. With a sad look on his face, Avromek had to say goodbye to the hospital.

Scenes from a children's hospital
(continued)
At reception
The physician on duty who admits the children to the hospital is terribly upset. A mother is sitting there with her child, whose minutes [on this earth] are numbered. She nurses a last hope that the hospital can save its life. 'You must pay 15 złoty in burial costs, because the child is gravely ill and the hospital has no funds for burials.' The mother is a deportee. She now lives at a point and does not have a single grosz to her name. 'Your child cannot be admitted to the hospital if you cannot pay 15 złoty.' The tearful mother jumps up in rage and takes out on the physician all the anger and pain that has been building up inside her since the beginning of the war. 'You're no physician – you are a murderer! You are murdering my child! You have no heart, no feeling, no humanity, if my child has to die because of 15 złoty. My child and I have already been displaced four times. Where am I to supposed to get even a single grosz?' The mother's heart dissolves into tears. The child lies blue[-faced] on the table, wheezing, gasping, taking its last breath. The physician cannot stand to watch the scene and runs out of the room. The mother, left alone with her dying child, wails helplessly until the building's caretaker comes in and tells her to leave. Cursing bitterly, she takes her child and goes. 'This hospi-

9 The Jewish population of Piaseczno in Kreis Warschau-Land was expelled to the Warsaw ghetto between 22 and 27 Jan. 1941.

10 These two words are in roman script in the original.

tal should burn! Heartless physicians, murderers, fiends!' Scenes like this occur very frequently.

28 March 1941
I am on duty on the spotted fever (typhus) [ward]. It is 8 o'clock in the evening. It seems to me that I can breathe a sigh of relief: my sixty children, having eaten dinner and satisfied their hunger, have calmed down somewhat. As they begin to doze off, the rooms grow quiet. Alas, the telephone rings. 'Hello! What is it?' I have to prepare eight beds for eight children from the point [located] at [the corner of] Niska and Stawki. The epidemic is spreading. I already have enough on my hands. Children who come to us with typhus get a bath and a delousing in the room [where patients are] admitted and then [go through the procedure] a second time when they arrive on the ward. The eight children are already on the ward, and I am busy preparing to bathe them again. 'Hello!' The physician is calling me: 'Nurse, please be careful when bathing the children, they have a lot of lice.' I grit my teeth and get to work. The first little patient is five-year-old Avromek. I take him gingerly and place him in the tub, thinking: just one bite from a louse and I'll get typhus too. I don't have to search long. His whole head is covered with a carapace [of scabs], and from under it crawl the lice that infect so many people with the dreaded disease. [He's now been] bathed again and dressed in clean clothes. But I still have to wash and clean his head. Using the clippers, I cut around his scabs. He writhes in pain, but I have to remain indifferent because I have instructions to get rid of the gunk where the lice proliferate. By now his little head is all bloody, and the carapace has been removed. Then I make the proper bandages[11] with Sebacil for him and put my little patient to bed. I do the same for the others. After that I start registering them and filling out the appropriate charts for each child. While I do this, each child tells me where he or she comes from. 'We have already been expelled five times. From Łódź to Konstantynów, from Konstantynów to Łowicz, from Łowicz to Głowno, from Głowno to Skierniewice, and from Skierniewice to Warsaw.[12] Each time they took some of our things. And on the way, the Germans beat my father so badly that he had to be taken to hospital and is not yet well. And on the way from Skierniewice to Warsaw, my little sister fell off the wagon and was killed. Now we have been living at a "point" for a couple of days. We have no bed to sleep in, and we eat a small piece of bread with black coffee, and my mother can't cook anything for lunch.'

I feed them, their little hands shaking [as they reach] for the bowl of soup. 'I want some more.' But I'm afraid I have nothing left. The hospital is not in a position to sate the hunger of all the displaced children who have not eaten their fill for many long months. The moment they see the bread and the soup pot, dozens of little hands reach up to me, and their tiny bodies quiver, as if gripped by fever, at the sight of food.

11 This word is in Polish in the original.

12 The expulsion likely proceeded via the following stations: from Łódź to Konstantynów in Dec. 1939; from Konstantynów to Głowno (District Warsaw) in Jan. 1940; from Głowno to Łowicz and back; then from Głowno to Skierniewice; and finally from Skierniewice to Warsaw in Feb. or March 1941.

DOC. 262
In March 1941 the underground newspaper *Za Naszą i Waszą Wolność* challenges German antisemitic propaganda[1]

Antisemitism – a German propaganda tool

We have always maintained that antisemitism is a tool of German propaganda. The Nazis wanted to use antisemitism to divert the attention of the Polish masses from the danger Nazi Germany posed to Poland. It is an open secret that the Nazis have spent huge sums of money on strengthening and subsidizing antisemitic parties in Poland. Father Trzeciak could say a thing or two about this.[2] The most vocal antisemites before the war, those who claimed that the Jews were Poland's greatest enemy and that the most important matter was to combat the 'Jewish onslaught', turned out to be mostly German spies. Today they are faithfully serving the germans[3] and the Gestapo, have declared themselves Volksdeutsche,[4] and at every turn betray Poland, whose most ardent patriots they once claimed to be. Antisemitism was harmful not only because it distracted the Polish masses from the real enemy, not only because it disarmed them spiritually and morally, but also because it deprived Poland of the sympathies of those very countries whose support and help was of prime importance. The same thing is happening now. We read in *Głos Polski*[5] (22 Feb. [19]41):

> There is no deceit or slander that the Germans have not yet employed in their propaganda with the intent to disparage and undermine Poland. The most cynical deceit of this kind consists in accusing the Polish population under the German occupation of active and barbaric antisemitism. According to this propaganda, the Germans are supposedly the best guardians of the Jewish population because they protect it from Polish pogroms, while the Poles are supposedly the Jews' greatest enemies, which England and America should know. They have fallen back on earlier patterns of playing off Jewish affairs against Poland in the years 1918–1926, unabashed by contemporary Germany's actual attitude towards Jewry. Typical of this cynical and mendacious German propaganda is a book by Erich Seifert,[6] published by the NSDAP in Berlin, entitled *The Jew on the Eastern Frontier,* in which he argues that the Poles wanted to exact revenge on the Jews for the collapse of the Polish state. The terrible pogroms and raids inflicted on the Jewish population by the Germans are well

1 *Za Naszą i Waszą Wolność*, no. 2, March 1941, pp. 7–9; AŻIH, Ring I/1340 (700). This document has been translated from Polish. *Za naszą i waszą wolność* was one of the Bund's monthly journals and appeared in Polish from 1941 to 1942.

2 Dr Stanisław Trzeciak (1873–1944), Catholic priest; professor at the St Petersburg Theological Academy, 1907–1918; in Poland from 1918; priest in Przemyśl and then in Warsaw, 1923–1928; also on the staff of the Instytut Wschodni ('Eastern Institute'), which conducted research on the Soviet system, 1926–1939; one of the leading intellectual representatives of antisemitism in Poland during the 1930s.

3 The word is intentionally written in lower case here as an expression of contempt.

4 German in the original: 'ethnic Germans'.

5 'Z kraju. […] Wyrafinowane oszustwa propagandowe niemieckie', *Głos Polski*, no. 3 (30), 22 Feb. 1941, p. 4; AAN, 1583, 256/2. The underground newspaper *Głos Polski*, which appeared fortnightly between 1939 and 1944, was closely associated with the news and propaganda apparatus of ZWZ-AK and was distributed within the General Government and in Łódź.

> known. In Seifert's book these pogroms are attributed solely to the Poles, whose thirst for revenge was allegedly curbed by the German authorities, who 'succeeded in introducing law and order everywhere'. This was supposedly met with the warmest gratitude on the part of the Jews. Reading these lies, one is reminded of the sinister scenes staged by the Germans in Warsaw in spring 1940, when small groups of hired guttersnipes attacked Jews while Germans soldiers defended them, which in turn was filmed as a fake corpus delicti.[7] One must expect that the Germans will intensify their activities, that more such 'documents' will be produced with the intent of harming Poland in the eyes of England and America, which are sensitive to the Jewish cause. With time we might even hear the accusation that the establishment of the Warsaw ghetto was the result of a Polish initiative slyly attributed to the German authorities, those best and most sincere … defenders of the Jewish people.

We deliberately quote this passage from *Głos Polski* at length. *Głos Polski* is one of the most serious newspapers among the Polish underground press. It is not the mouthpiece of a 'fringe' party. We fully agree with the passage from *Głos Polski*. During those ghastly days in spring 1940, when crowds – by no means only guttersnipes – attacked Jews and plundered Jewish shops in Warsaw, we immediately clarified the true nature of these despicable attacks and revealed that they were the work of the Germans. No one in America and England will believe the rubbish in Seifert's book. Representatives of Jewish workers in Poland are duly showing everything that the German occupier is using against the Jewish masses in Poland. Not even films 'irrefutably' documenting German soldiers defending Jews against Poles or showing what a good life the Jews have in the ghetto, how the Germans have provided them with employment opportunities, how they ensure that they are fed, etc., are of any help. But one has to face the truth – the whole truth. It goes without saying that the Nazis' cynical lies – that they were the ones who defended the Jews against the Poles, and that the Jews were grateful for it – can at best convince only covert Nazis in America and England. But it is not this nonsense that poses a danger to Poland. The danger of Poland being disparaged and undermined lies elsewhere, namely, in the fact that the Germans will refer to *Polish documents and Polish sources*. We have before us a pamphlet titled *The Great Ideology of the Polish People*, published by the 'Origins of a Great Poland' (Warsaw, 1940),[8] in which we read: 'Poland's internal ideal is to create a geographical base – a Polish heartland – in the western and central parts of the Polish Republic. All alien national elements must be eradicated from this area, especially the Jews, whose resettlement beyond this area should be the first step in solving the Jewish question.' We know that this is the ONR's view.[9] We could say more about the ONR's other recommendations for the 'day after' the war. But it is not

6 Correctly: Hermann Erich Seifert (b. 1902), journalist; reporter for *Der Angriff*, the Gau newspaper of the Berlin branch of the NSDAP; published the propagandistic *Der Jude an der Ostgrenze* in Berlin in 1940 (Schriftenreihe der NSDAP, Gruppe VII: *Der Osten Europas*, vol. 3); the book had evidently been written in Lublin.

7 See Doc. 98.

8 The 23-page pamphlet *Wielka Ideologia Narodu Polskiego* was written by Bolesław Piasecki (1915–1979), who went by the pseudonym Leon Całka and was the leader of the radical right-wing group Falanga National Radical Camp (ONR-Falanga); this underground publication was brought out by Szczerbiec publishing house.

9 See Doc. 98, fn. 6.

only the ONR that continues to zealously foment antisemitism in Poland. It is also spread in the Polish press that is published by the Germans. It is endemic in the underground press, in countless circulars published by various economic associations, chambers of commerce and industry, and guilds, as well as among both large and small groups of citizens who appeal to the German authorities so that, with the occupier's blessing, they can inherit the Jewish property and assets liquidated by the Nazis. The Germans are certainly already in the process of documenting this very material with which to denigrate and undermine the future Poland. It is the duty of every genuine Polish patriot, everyone who works and strives for a future Free Poland, so that it has the conditions, as far as possible, for full and unhindered economic and political development – it is everyone's duty to prevent the Nazi occupiers from using this poisoned weapon. Not just because England and America are 'sensitive to the Jewish cause', as *Głos Polski* claims. In fact, England and America are probably even more sensitive to the Polish cause. They keep providing evidence of this. Sensitivity is not the issue here. At the end of 1939, General Sikorski declared: '… in this struggle, relentlessly waged between two camps, Poland is on the side of the light, alongside the nations fighting for universal justice, for the rebirth of mankind, and this is our great strength.' Whoever fights for such ideals, for such a Europe, cannot be an antisemite, cannot employ the tools of Nazi propaganda, and cannot believe in Nazi ideals. And that is why 'Polish' antisemitism constitutes *treason against Poland*, because it places weapons in the hands of Poland's enemies, and it allows the Nazis to disparage, undermine, and harm the future Free and Just Poland.

DOC. 263
On 3 April 1941 leading German occupation officials discuss the isolation and economic exploitation of the Warsaw ghetto's inhabitants[1]

Minutes of a meeting on 3 April 1941[2]

Main Department Head Dr *Emmerich* presented the Governor General with a report from the *Reich Board for Economic Efficiency*, General Government branch,[3] concerning the economic performance of the Jewish residential district in Warsaw.[4]

Governor *Fischer* highlighted the three reasons that had prompted the establishment of a sealed Jewish residential district, which were political, economic, and hygienic in

1 AIPN, GK 95, vol. 10. Copy in IfZ-Archives, Fb 105, vol. 12, pp. 2812–2818. Published in Präg and Jacobmeyer (eds.), *Diensttagebuch des deutschen Generalgouverneurs*, pp. 342–346. This document has been translated from German.

2 This meeting, which was held on the occasion of an inspection of the Department of Food and Agriculture in District Warsaw, was attended by Walter Emmerich, Ludwig Fischer, Hans Frank, Rudolf Gater, Herbert Hummel, Ludwig Leist, Paul Moder, Hansjulius Schepers, and Waldemar Schön.

3 From 1940 to 1944 the branch office in the General Government was headed by Dr Rudolf Gater (1905–1989), economist; obtained a doctorate in Zurich in 1931; worked for the Reich Board for Economic Efficiency from 1935, initially in Saarbrücken and then from 1938 in the Austria Office, where he was one of the officials responsible for winding up and Aryanizing Jewish businesses; later worked for the Board for the Rationalization of German Industry (RKW) in West Germany.

nature. Politically it was a matter of eliminating the Jews' influence on the Polish population, which had always been directed against the Germans and had undermined all the measures taken by German authorities. For instance, effective price-control measures with a chance of success had not been feasible because the Jews made them impossible. On an economic level, it would only be possible to establish a well-ordered economy once the Jewish element had been completely eliminated. For [public] health reasons, the isolation of the Jewish portion of the population was crucial to effective disease control because there would always be the danger of typhus spreading as long as the Jews were moving about freely. It has proved to be the case that the number of people who have fallen ill with typhus has decreased considerably since the ghetto was sealed off. Appropriate measures have been taken to ensure that no major epidemics could ever spread in the ghetto. The Jewish physicians in the ghetto have been organized and tasked with keeping the ghetto clean and taking all other necessary precautions.

After initial difficulties, the establishment of the ghetto went better than expected. The Jews still have significant funds at their disposal, as shown by the prompt payment of rents. There are still sufficient quantities of food in the ghetto, which means there is no danger of famine in the next few months.[5] Apart from this, the provision of supplies to the Jewish population has been properly secured.

Every day 25,000 Jews are deployed for land-improvement works, and another 15,000 are put to work at various enterprises in the city. Trade and commerce are still taking place in the ghetto itself. Polish businesses continue to work with Jewish businesses through the mediation of the Transfer Bureau, and Polish firms continue to employ Jewish craftsmen in large numbers.

Economic exchange between the ghetto and the outside world is carried out by the aforementioned Transfer Bureau. This agency is not an independent entity, but rather a purely technical instrument designed to serve as an intermediary that receives and forwards orders and instructions from the relevant departments.

For Main Department Head Dr *Emmerich*, the crucial question was whether the transactions that the Transfer Bureau has been tasked with managing might be organized in such a way that the external trade balance offsets the deficit in the ghetto's

4 This economic report had been drawn up by Dr Gater and his aide, Meder, on behalf of the Economic Affairs Main Department (Dr Emmerich). It was 53 pages long and concluded that the approximately 450,000 people in the Warsaw ghetto would require an annual state subsidy of about 100 million złoty in order to satisfy their minimum needs. If the German occupation administration wished to 'avoid or at least reduce this subsidy', there were three conceivable alternatives, which could be combined with one another: 1. 'Undersupply … without considering the resulting consequences'; 2. more efficiently 'exploit the Jewish labour force' in order to boost revenues; 3. partially unseal the ghetto so that some Jewish craftsmen could secure orders and thereby contribute to supporting the ghetto's residents economically. Gater and Meder accordingly discussed the food supply for the ghettoized population. At first they calculated the costs for a 'more or less sufficient diet' for all the 'inhabitants and/or particularly favoured sections [of the population]', and then they mentioned the possibility of regarding the ghetto 'as a means' of 'liquidating Jewry' ('das jüdische Volkstum zu liquidieren'). Published in Heim and Aly (eds.), *Bevölkerungsstruktur und Massenmord*, pp. 84–138, quotations taken from pp. 87–88, 113, 138.

5 By this point hunger was already rampant among a large segment of the Jewish population in the General Government, especially in the sealed ghettos. The dramatic rise in food prices meant that existing financial reserves were rapidly depleted. See also Doc. 261.

balance of payments. The notion guiding all economic measures related to the ghetto has been maintaining Jewry's ability to survive. The question is whether it would be possible to solve this problem in a productive way, i.e. to bring enough work into the ghetto and/or extract enough of the ghetto's output to ensure equilibrium in the balance of payments.

[Main Department Head Dr *Emmerich* noted that] in all economic considerations concerning the ghetto, it is necessary to disregard the fact that things are still going well in the ghetto at present and that enough provisions are still available there. The ghetto is not something that can be wound up in a year; rather, it is being established for a longer period of time, and economic plans therefore also have to be drawn up for a commensurable time frame.

Main Department Head Dr *Emmerich* then commented in detail on the report he had presented. As regards the Transfer Bureau, he remarked that the question of personalities had of course also played a major role in its creation, as had the question of how the government was to cooperate with this body.[6] There is a danger that the Transfer Bureau's autonomy might prove so far-reaching that it could lead to constant conflicts between the government's departments and the Transfer Bureau. The allocation of raw materials to the ghetto is also a difficult problem. The question arises as to whether factories in the ghetto should receive preferential treatment in the allocation of raw materials, even at the risk of workers in non-Jewish factories becoming unemployed as a result.

[Main Department Head Dr *Emmerich* continued by saying that] it was also difficult to find an arrangement to deal with the debts Jews owe to Aryan individuals and institutions. If the Jews are sealed off and forced to deplete their capital, then they will no longer be able to fulfil their obligations to the outside Aryan world, and creditors may be harmed in the process.

Dr *Gate*[7] from the Reich Board for Economic Efficiency, General Government branch, reported on his work, which principally deals with questions of economic planning and streamlining business operations. He said that the key problem of the Jewish residential district was the issue of its economic performance, noting that the ghetto is an economic area in its own right, but one that has to be connected to the outside world; raw materials have to be taken into the ghetto and finished goods brought out. He said that efforts had been made to quantify the ghetto's demand side by calculating a Jew's minimum needs. This calculation was based not on the method for calculating subsistence levels, but rather on a method of calculation that only takes the value in terms of the external trade balance into account. These calculations arrived at a daily requirement of 93 groszy per Jew. The Jews have to earn this amount to be able to pay for the assets that go in from outside. The daily total therefore works out at some 500,000 zloty. The question of what the Jews who are deployed outside the ghetto contribute to the ghetto's maintenance must also be examined. Such contributions would depend on the levels of pay in the labour camps; on average, it would be possible to reckon with 10 zloty per week. Taking into consideration the fact that an individual Jew could only be deployed

6 The head of the Transfer Bureau was Alexander Palfinger, who was dismissed in May 1941 due to political differences.

7 Correctly: Gater.

outside the ghetto for seven to eight months per year, the calculation showed that three Jews would have to be deployed on labour details outside the ghetto to match the external trade balance value of one Jew inside the ghetto. If more favourable pay levels in the camps were taken as the basis, this ratio would perhaps improve to 2:1. There is no real experience yet as to the output of a Jew's labour in the Jewish residential district. According to estimates, enterprises in the ghetto should expect overhead expenses of 80 per cent on top of wages. Assuming daily productivity of 5 zloty per capita, then 60[,000] to 65,000 Jews would have to be employed in production in order to compensate for the deficit in the balance of payments to the necessary extent. The numerous Jews who do domestic outwork for Polish companies have been factored into these figures.

The Economic Affairs Department has continued to examine the question of which workers are available in the Jewish residential district. Based on statistics from the Labour Department, it arrived at a figure of approximately 30,000 craftsmen who could be used to address the external trade balance. No such statistics are available for female workers. Calculations put the ratio of men to women [workers] at approximately 60:40. It is likely safe to assume that the necessary skilled workers are available in the Jewish residential district. On a side note, the Jewish Council has set up certain [vocational] schools that will produce a new pool of workers.

The employment of Jews is essentially an organizational problem, but opinions still differ on how to solve it. Main Department Head Emmerich has proposed bringing in German wholesalers, because these wholesalers have well-established structures in place and are in a position to collect orders and funnel them into the Jewish residential district. This approach would likely result in a productive outcome. The companies would have to be granted a certain amount of influence on the organization of Jewish labour in order to guarantee that all requirements concerning quality, delivery dates, etc. would be met in the Jewish residential district.

The matter of obtaining loans also raises difficult organizational questions. It will not be possible to spark economic activity in the ghetto without a major credit commitment. According to calculations, approximately 30–40 million zloty would need to be borrowed. This figure is based on a manufacturing turnover, excluding materials, of 135 million zloty per annum and a turnover, including materials, of approximately 400 million zloty per year. It is evident from these figures that the businesses in the ghetto would be very large manufacturing enterprises.

In summary, it would be in the interests of all the authorities involved to find ways of getting 65[,000] to 70,000 Jews in the ghetto into productive work. If this proves possible, then the establishment of the Jewish residential district may be regarded as a success.

The *Governor General* referred to the reservations that had been expressed to him by the head of the Finance Department,[8] which amount to the concern that things in the Warsaw ghetto would take a course similar to that of the Jewish residential district in Litzmannstadt, where the Reich is having to sustain the Jews. Providing permanent welfare of this nature would pose a significant budgetary strain. Given the importance of

8 Dr Alfred Spindler.

this question, it is to be recommended that a representative from the Finance Department be involved in the discussion of such detailed problems in future.

SS-Gruppenführer *Moder*[9] reported on questions related to the police guarding the Jewish residential district. One Polish and one German guard stand sentry day and night at each of the 15 entrances to the ghetto. Seventy-five German and 400 Polish policemen are deployed on patrols in the ghetto every day. Maintaining order within the Jewish residential district itself is the task of the Jewish Order Service, which reports to the Polish police.

From a policing perspective, the ghetto is considered a necessity in eliminating Jewish influence on the Polish population and combating the risk of epidemics. The Polish population has certainly welcomed the establishment of the Jewish residential district.

SA-Oberführer *Leist* likewise advocated the retention of the Jewish residential district and described it as a great relief to the city, especially in terms of personnel. All the services that the city had previously needed to provide have now been handed over to the Jewish Community. The city's interests are now merely focused on ensuring that the fees for gas, water, and electricity are duly received. At the moment, thought is being given to whether it would be possible to charge a flat rate for these fees. The idea is that the Jewish Council would be tasked with collecting these fees while receiving an appropriate share of the total collected. Having such a stake would offer an incentive for the Jewish Council to collect the money.

Reichsamtsleiter *Schön* regarded Dr Gate's analyses as too theoretical. In particular, Dr Gate had failed to recognize that the living conditions for the ghetto's inhabitants are determined not only through labour deployment, but above all by maintaining trade relations. A thorough examination revealed that trade relations have been maintained, in particular because the Jews still possess raw materials and finished goods that are important for the armaments industry.

An extensive discussion then followed of how orders between the Jewish residential district and outside companies should be processed, and in what way the Jewish Council, the Transfer Bureau, and a special board of trustees still to be formed should be involved in this. No agreement could be reached on this issue. The *Governor General* gave instructions to make this issue the subject of thorough deliberations. In his concluding remarks, the Governor General noted that it is necessary to find a way forward that avoids any setbacks wherever possible. He recommended that during the initial period, as the Jewish residential district's economic relations are being established, the head of the Economic Affairs Department and the Governor of District Warsaw should personally take charge of the matter. He noted that the government is assuming tremendous responsibility with the establishment of the Jewish residential district for 500,000 people, and that any failure will always be held against the government of the GG. Litzmannstadt should serve as a

9 Paul Moder (1896–1942), commercial employee; active as a Freikorps commander after 1918; joined the NSDAP in 1922 and the SS in 1931; official in charge of policing and security in Altona in 1933; leader of SS Main District East (later SS Main District Spree) in Berlin, 1934–1939; SS and Police Leader in District Warsaw from Nov. 1939; served in the war in France in June 1940; dismissed from his post and demoted by Himmler on 19 July 1941, because Moder had travelled to see his family in Berlin at the time of the attack on the Soviet Union; subsequently sent to the front and killed in action in the Soviet Union.

serious warning in this regard. Currently, the thorniest issues still include the matter of transfers, defining remits, procuring raw materials, striking a balance between the private sector and ghetto operations, and above all setting up order-placement arrangements between enterprises in the ghetto and clients outside the ghetto. It is to be hoped that the efforts of the authorities involved will succeed in reaching a satisfactory solution to these issues.

DOC. 264
On 5 April 1941 the Jewish Social Self-Help executive committee reports on aid for expelled Jews[1]

Letter from the JSS executive committee (no. 2691/41 Sch.) to the GG government in Cracow, Interior Administration Department, Population and Welfare Division, dated 5 April 1941 (copy)[2]

Activity report by the Jewish Social Self-Help executive committee for March 1941

2.[3] *Aid for resettled persons*
In the past month we have had to shift the main focus of our attention to aid for resettled persons. To our knowledge, more than 4,000 resettled persons from Vienna and some 9[,000] to 10,000 Jews from the territories annexed to the Reich, particularly Płock and the surrounding area, have arrived in the General Government. In addition to this, 9,000 Jews were suddenly resettled from Lublin, the resettlement of Jews out of Cracow was nearly completed, and the resettlement of approximately 45,000 Jews from District Warsaw to the Jewish residential area in the city of Warsaw continued. While those persons coming from Vienna were allowed to take some of their linen and clothing with them and were also provided with food, those resettled from Płock and the surrounding area arrived – according to the reports – in a pitiful state. […]

Despite this, in order to organize appropriate aid activities, we intended to send our delegates to those places where the resettled persons had arrived. Unfortunately, it was [only] possible to do so on a very small scale, because we did not succeed in obtaining travel documents for our delegates.

According to reports, [the people in] some of the transports had to leave the original destination after their arrival and be housed elsewhere. In many cases the resettled persons were assigned to overpopulated places, where sanitary conditions did not meet even the most primitive standards. The aid that we had arranged to be provided for the resettled persons consisted primarily of food. In some places resettled persons were directed to the existing soup kitchens; in others new soup kitchens were set up; and here and there, they were given foodstuffs. Unfortunately, the lack of funds and the soup kitchens' limited capacities did not permit all the resettled persons to be served at least one warm bowl of soup per day. We transferred 200,000 złoty in aid for resettled persons to Warsaw, 77,000 złoty to Lublin, and 60,000 złoty to Radom, and

1 YVA, O-21/19, fols. 4–5 and 7. This document has been translated from German.
2 Weichert, who chaired the JSS, forwarded two copies of the report.
3 The first item is missing from this copy, as are the parts of the text indicated by ellipses below.

we earmarked 10,000 złoty to be distributed in Cracow. In addition, the city of Warsaw received 200,000 złoty from the Population and Welfare Division, arranged by the Governor of District Warsaw's representative. This sum has been paid to the Transfer Bureau. [...]

Apart from the monetary aid intended for food, we were able to deliver 1,700 paper mattresses stuffed with straw for distribution; 3,400 paper mattresses have been purchased and will be distributed among the resettled persons next month. Unfortunately, we were unable to fulfil the relief committees' and delegations' repeated requests to supply medicine, bandages, blankets, linen, and clothing. The 990 blankets [and] linen we purchased have been distributed, but we did not have any of the other items. [...]

4. Aid in the form of clothing

We have not had much success to report in this regard either. Our efforts, bolstered by the Chief Social Welfare Council's[4] support, to obtain an allocation of leather from the responsible agency in order to have domestic outworkers in Warsaw manufacture shoes with wooden soles – calculated to be 50 per cent cheaper than the price paid by the Chief Social Welfare Council – remained fruitless. At present, the Chief Social Welfare Council plans to purchase a large number of wooden-soled shoes. The occasional collection of linen for resettled persons has yielded only very modest results.

5. Health services

Nothing of note has occurred in the past month in this regard either, and this is connected to the fact – as already mentioned in the activity reports for January and February – that the remits of the Health Department and the Population and Welfare Division have not been clearly defined. In particular, no steps could be taken to combat the epidemics breaking out in various places. As isolated measures, we made aid payments of 3,000 złoty to a hospital for contagious diseases in Radoszyce[5] and 5,000 złoty to a delousing station to be set up in Cracow, while we spent more than 7,000 złoty purchasing medicine for our drug distribution centre. Of the soap powder purchased by the Chief Social Welfare Council, we received 1,700 kg as our share, which we distributed in the following way: 650 kg for District Cracow, 800 kg for District Warsaw, 200 kg for District Radom, and 250 kg for District Lublin, with 300 kg remaining as reserves.

6. Income

During the month under review, we received 200,000 złoty from the Chief Social Welfare Council as part of the special grant of 500,000 złoty[6] that was approved at our request during the Chief Social Welfare Council meeting on 4 March 1941, with the authorities' permission.[7] [...]

Of the support intended for the Warsaw City Jewish Aid Committee, only 100,000 złoty could be transferred; further sums could not be disbursed for the time being, pursuant to a Population and Welfare Division directive of 27 March 1941, and it is likely that this will be done in the first few days of April. [...]

4 Chief Social Welfare Council: see Doc. 156, fn. 2.
5 See Doc. 240.
6 Handwritten correction from 600,000.
7 See Doc. 243.

7. Meetings and correspondence
Apart from the monthly executive committee meeting (on 10 March) and that of the Chief Social Welfare Council (on 4 March), ten meetings were held at the Population and Welfare Division during the month under review, including one in the presence of Mr Meder[8] and Dr Gepner[9] on matters relating to the employment of craftsmen residing in Warsaw's Jewish residential area and one [convened] jointly with the American Joint Distribution Committee. Three meetings were with the Governor of District Cracow's Resettlement Office, three with the Chief Social Welfare Council, and two with the American Joint Distribution Committee. [...]

9. Plans for the immediate future
In the next month the executive committee will have to look more closely at the problem of aid for resettled persons. This aid must not be limited to bowls of soup; rather, we must think about recruiting capable individuals for work, and we need to find resources for welfare efforts to support those who are fit to perform this work. This issue will be addressed at the executive committee's April meeting.

The transition from rudimentary aid to structural aid will also be an agenda item for the April meeting. The increasing exclusion of Jews from the economic and labour process fills the JSS with anxiety and apprehension. [...]

In addition, it will be necessary to tap into new sources of income for the JSS, particularly Jewish assets, i.e. blocked accounts and enterprises administered in trust. Preliminary talks with the Population and Welfare Division to this effect have already been held on several occasions. The executive committee's efforts to achieve something tangible will now be continued.

Foreign aid, particularly aid from relatives, is to be organized more effectively and standardized as far as possible.

The question of municipal subsidies for the Jewish aid committees also remains to be clarified. Alongside offering voluntary welfare services, they have been tasked with handling welfare services that were paid out of state and municipal funds until the war broke out. [...]

8 Meder, commercial employee; deputy head of the General Government branch of the Reich Board for Economic Efficiency.
9 Presumably Abraham Gepner, who did not hold a doctorate.

DOC. 265

On 7 April 1941 the Reich Minister of Labour rescinds his recently issued circular decree enabling Jewish forced labourers from Poland to be deployed on Reich territory[1]

Express letter from the Reich Minister of Labour[2] (V a 5431/73), signed p.p. Dr Syrup,[3] to the heads of the regional employment offices, with the exception of the Reichsstatthalter in Posen, dated 7 April 1941[4]

Re: labour deployment of Jews
Case file: my circular decree of 14 March 1941-V a 5431/43[5]
According to my circular decree of 14 March 1941, the Jews in the Warthegau were to be immediately assigned to suitable work in Reich territory in order to free up other workers for more urgent projects.

The Führer has now decided that Jews from the General Government and the Warthegau are *not* to be deployed in Reich territory. I therefore rescind my decree of 14 March 1941 with immediate effect.

DOC. 266

Between 10 and 15 April 1941 Ruth Goldbarth writes to her friend Edith Blau about living conditions in the Warsaw ghetto[1]

Handwritten letter from Ruth Goldbarth in Warsaw to her friend Edith Blau in Minden (Westphalia), dated 15 April 1941

My dearest,

I have an awful lot of time to write to you. The building is locked up, my parents have just gone for a lie-down, the sun is shining, and there is a terrible din in the courtyard. The people below have just noticed me at the window and indicated that I should

1 BArch, R 43 II/548a. This document has been translated from German.
2 Franz Seldte (1882–1947), chemist; member of the German National People's Party (DNVP); co-founder of the Stahlhelm (Steel Helmet) First World War veterans' organization, which also served as the paramilitary wing of the DNVP; joined the NSDAP and the SA in 1933; Reich minister of labour from 1933; interned in 1945.
3 Dr Friedrich Syrup (1881–1945), engineer and lawyer; president of the Reich Office for Labour Placement, 1920–1927, and of the Reich Office for Labour Placement and Unemployment Insurance, 1927–1939; briefly served in the Schleicher cabinet in 1932/1933 as Reich minister of labour; member of the Labour Deployment Group in the Four-Year Plan authority from 1936; state secretary in the Reich Ministry of Labour from 1939; joined the NSDAP in 1937; for health reasons hardly worked after 1941; died in Soviet Special Camp Sachsenhausen.
4 Handwritten notes: 'Dr Hölk (?)' at the top right, and 'Section I (?) b 4' at the bottom left.
5 With the circular decree of 14 March 1941 're: labour deployment of Jews', the regional employment offices had been called upon to find opportunities within Reich territory to deploy 42,187 male and 30,936 female Jewish workers from the Warthegau: BArch, R 41/193, fols. 98v–99v.

1 USHMM, RG 10 250*03, WA 057. This document has been translated from German.

come down too, but je m'en fiche pas mal.[2] I want to give you a detailed account today, even if I don't yet know when I will be able to post this letter. – I feel very weird; in fact, I don't know whether to laugh or to cry. The mood here is awfully depressed. It's terrible, my dear, what Uncle[3] has allowed himself to do again. Where's it going to end?! At one point, it almost looked as if Bertha would turn out to be right after all, and now he is behaving like this again and dashing all of our hopes in one fell swoop. We can't bear to think about it! What's more, we have insane inflation as well! Prices are rising by the hour. There have been no deliveries for a couple of days, and food is growing scarcer and more expensive by the minute. The cost of bread today already stands at 9.50 złoty per kilo, with white bread even going for 11 złoty; potatoes cost 3.50. Is that even humanly possible? We still don't have the potatoes we were supposed to be getting with [ration] cards since early March, and bread is also very hard to come by, available only sporadically and in small amounts. It is unspeakable! When you go out onto the street, every hundred steps you see a person lying there, unable to move any further because of hunger. Our doorbell never stops ringing due to a steady stream of beggars. They say the shops have already been looted today! And there is no hope that things will get better in the foreseeable future. Things aren't much better for Jurek.[4] We are in total despair. What can we do?! And the many thousands of poor people who have nothing!! – If it carries on like this, we will truly have just a few weeks left!

Really, when you hear this, you would think we were all sitting around and lamenting! But you should just see us in the courtyard, chatting and laughing as if everything were going swimmingly. And until half an hour ago, I was standing down there with them and fooling around. The 'parówka'[5] has been quite an amusing saga so far. Uncle Paru[6] has done his bit of course, so it's actually not so bad. It was announced yesterday at noon that the building would be locked up, and when I wanted to go round just quickly to see some acquaintances next door shortly before 9 o'clock, I couldn't get out any more. One commission after another showed up today, starting in the early morning. The first one appeared at half past seven – they burst into our room without knocking, just as I was taking off my pyjamas. They inspected the beds, linen, etc., found everything in order, and said that we did not need to be disinfected. They left after barely five minutes. Later we were also exempted from bathing, so we are simply under house arrest. And that is still quite fun for the time being. Just as long as it doesn't go on for a long time! We became chummy with all the guards (Boria's[7] colleagues) straight away, and I deal with any patients through the front gate.[8] Fortunately it is a wrought-iron one with gaps in it, so it is easy to converse with 'the outside'. However, I haven't had any time off. We were treating patients from the building all morning. I don't know yet what it will be like in the afternoon. It's bearable, at any rate!

2 French in the original: 'I really don't care'.
3 Code word for the Germans or more specifically the Wehrmacht, which attacked Yugoslavia on 6 April 1941.
4 Code word for the Poles on the other side of the ghetto walls.
5 Polish in the original: 'steam bath'; used here in the sense of a delousing procedure.
6 Code word for bribery.
7 A Goldbarth family friend who worked in the Jewish Order Service.
8 Ruth Goldbarth assisted her father in his dental practice.

Now I have to tell you about another adventure. Last Sunday I went out with Dorli[9] and various acquaintances to a concert café where performances are held. A very nice little show was supposed to take place there, namely a grotesque [piece] drawn from our life here, which was both very witty and on the mark. It was really very agreeable. The place is quite large, and it has a gallery in addition to the main room. And now just imagine: a chair suddenly comes soaring down from the gallery into the midst of the audience. The music stops, people scream, dishes clatter, and there's a great commotion, which dies down immediately. The show continues until a second chair comes flying down five minutes later, immediately followed by a third and a fourth, one after another, always going in a different direction. The pandemonium was indescribable. Everyone began to run and shout, knocking over tables and chairs and sending dishes crashing to the ground in the process. Utter chaos, in short, and immediately panic set in, as always. And the cause of all the commotion? Two of Adi's[10] friends – totally drunk. Suddenly they appear in the hall; all at once – God knows why – there is dead silence. They walk through the establishment, and everyone breathes a sigh of relief because it looks like the two are going to leave, when all of a sudden one of them gets into an altercation with somebody, thrashes about to the right and the left like a savage, and just for a change the second one starts throwing chairs again. No one could get out because they were standing in front of the exit. In short, the situation was now becoming seriously dangerous, so we retreated into the kitchen to wait there for the matter to take its course. Fortunately the gendarmerie[11] finally appeared and took the two of them away. But it was really very upsetting.

The Saturday before that, my parents had to go on a visit, which meant the assistant also had time off, so I went 'na szaleństwa'[12] with Alinka. The third person to join us was Romek, Nusia D.'s boyfriend from Orłowo, who she was with later in Ciechocinek. Really a friendly chap, smart and funny, and above all what you'd call a nice boy. It's a shame he has lost touch with Nusia. He is the kind of person Nusia needs, and he also speaks very warmly of her. He promised to write to her straight away. I think she'll be very happy about that.

Oh yes, I also wanted to tell you about the gentleman who was at Edith Ch.'s place that time. Like Bubi,[13] he was no longer working for Uncle[14] and had come to tell her that her husband was working as a physician at a sanatorium[15] near Słupsk in Pomerania; he had one and a half rooms to himself and was doing well. The gentleman had taken him there himself. He didn't know whether the others were there too. I don't know what to make of it. It seemed suspicious back then, when he was there for the first time. I'm sure you'll remember that. But ultimately what reason did he have for coming the second

9 Ruth Goldbarth's younger sister Dorothea.
10 Code word for SS men.
11 Probably urban policemen.
12 Polish in the original: 'went out to have a wild time'.
13 Edith's uncle Hermann (known as Bubi) Bradtmüller (1897–1965) was stationed in the General Government as a soldier for a time in 1940: see Ruth's letter to Edith, dated 8 Sept. 1940, in Edith Brandon, 'Ein Mindener Bürger: Hermann Bradtmüller und Familie', published as a booklet, 1994, pp. 12–14: USHMM, 1996. A.0070.1 (Edith Brandon papers).
14 He was no longer serving in the Wehrmacht.
15 Code word for camp or prison.

time? There was nothing to be got out of it, and he must have known that too. Maybe there really is something to it. That fool Edith (I am always annoyed that someone like her has the same name as you) has only just told me about this. What is your take on the matter? Tell me, have you really not been able to find out anything yet from your maid's brother-in-law and the second gentleman?

11 April
We are still locked in. It was only supposed to last 24 hours, but now it's already been 48, and who knows if we'll be stuck over the holiday.[16] Someone or other has been messing about with the cards from the bathing and disinfection (i.e. delousing) centre, and now the commission doesn't want to give the building the all-clear. Sixteen people who have to be bathed were still missing. I also volunteered (after all, it can't do any harm), but it was all to no avail, and there's a great uproar here today. Uncle Paru will have to step in once again to help out. Personally I'm not really bothered by this situation. Daddy often makes urgent house calls, and his assistant goes with him from time to time as well – and Adi has been behaving so badly on the street again lately that it's no fun to go out. The whole building gathers down in the courtyard to discuss the latest goings-on and the prices (just don't think about them). It's quite merry in general. But the practice is losing a lot of business, of course. – Boria was here today and consoled us, and from time to time acquaintances come to the gate and ring for us to go down (the bells lead into all the apartments from the staircase), so it isn't boring. Still, it would be very nice if they let us out for the holiday. I have actually been expecting mail from you for a long time. None will be delivered for the next two days, so I will only be able to get news again on Monday. This letter can't be posted before that, either. Things look really sad here today – no sign of a festive mood, not even matzo or [matzo] flour (you just can't spend 20 złoty on it). I have been invited over for wine and Easter cake, but I don't feel like going. At my grandparents' house in Szamotuły, I used to … oh, forget it, there's no point!

12 April
Hooray, we're free! We have just ceremoniously removed the sign 'Typhus, no entry' from the front door and said goodbye to the last guard. And now I am slightly tipsy! But that doesn't really matter. The occasion had to be celebrated, after all. And I will go for a stroll in a moment. It's already quite warm (it has been bloody cold until now), and I sat on the balcony in the sun this morning – it was so lovely. Maybe spring is finally going to arrive! – First I have to set the coffee table, because Georgie's parents are coming over, and tomorrow we are invited to their place.

15 April
Hooray! I'm so terribly excited! I just received the parcel notification and your letter with the one from Krzemieniec! I just want to confirm this for you quickly, because your letter has been on its way since 4 April, thank goodness, and you are certainly already eagerly awaiting a reply. Thank you so much!!! I will write again very soon! I have already

16 A reference to Passover, which fell on 12–19 April in 1941.

sent someone from the [assembly] point to the post office; once the parcel is here, you will hear all about it, because then I will write to you and Lolo in detail. Today I will just send you a very, very fond kiss.

Yours,
Ruth

The letter with the belt has not arrived. Too bad! Trudno!!![17] My dear, you should see me – with a centre parting and a chignon, quite without curls or a roll. The older generation are delighted, but the younger generation find it too serious and too grown-up. I'm happy, because combing goes much faster!

DOC. 267

On 12 April 1941 the military physician in Międzyrzec issues a warning about an imminent typhus epidemic due to the influx of forcibly resettled Jews[1]

Letter from the base physician at Miedzyrzec, signature illegible, to the Security Police, Radzyń branch office (received on 16 April 1941), dated 12 April 1941[2]

Concerning: telephone consultation on 8 April 1941
Re: danger of typhus due to influx of Jews
After the arrival of more than 1,000 Jews in Miedzyrzec once again over the last six weeks, with several hundred of them coming in the last eight days alone,[3] we urgently request that the influx of Jews be stopped, as otherwise a typhus epidemic is to be expected.

There are currently 28 positive typhus cases at the Jewish and Polish hospital, and one case of typhus has already occurred in the Wehrmacht as well.

Everything possible has been done to prevent the transmission of the disease, both by the town physician and by the military, but the locals – i.e. the Jews – are living on top of one another in such crowded conditions, and keeping the troops strictly separated from the town's inhabitants is not possible either.

The commander therefore *most urgently* requests that any further influx of Jews be halted.

17 Polish in the original: 'Too bad'.

1 APL, 498/273, fol. 13. This document has been translated from German.
2 A carbon copy was forwarded to the mayor of Międzyrzec (Kreis Radzyń in the northern part of District Lublin) for his information: APL, 498/892, fol. 359.
3 In 1940 the Jewish community in Międzyrzec had to take in several large transports from western and central Poland, namely from Nasielsk, Pułtusk, Serock, Łódź, and Gdynia. In addition to this, another 740 forcibly resettled people from Cracow and 1,400 from Mława arrived in early 1941.

DOC. 268

On 14 April 1941 a sergeant in the Wehrmacht writes about his impressions of the eastern region of the General Government[1]

Letter from Kurt Meisel,[2] dated 14 April 1940, sent by military mail

We have been encamped in a small, desolate town close to the Russian border[3] for about three weeks. Of the 24,000 inhabitants in this dump, 22,000 belong to the Jewish race. A large number of them have been expelled from Germany or have emigrated from the Warthegau. But here, their days of doing deals are well and truly over. We have been helping the German mayor to get them registered and dragging the layabouts from their dilapidated digs in order to put them to regular work, especially building roads, levelling the ground, etc. The conditions in the Jewish houses are indescribable – so much squalor, filth, and vermin. Subhumanity in the truest sense of the word! As such, the fate of this pervasive scourge will not exactly be rosy.

DOC. 269

Gazeta Żydowska, 18 April 1941: article on the expulsion of the Jewish Community from Oświęcim to Sosnowiec and Będzin[1]

The resettlement of Oświęcim's Jews
In the week leading up to Passover,[2] the disciplined Jewish population of Oświęcim and the surrounding areas, in accordance with the will of the German authorities, left Oświęcim. They travelled by train, by car, by cart, and on foot to the Dąbrowa Basin to settle there with their families.

The most prominent leaders of the Central Committee of the Jewish Community's Councils of Elders in Sosnowiec[3] came to Oświęcim to carry out the resettlement effort. An army of over 1,000 Jewish workers from all the surrounding communities in the Dąbrowa Basin was mobilized. Using several hundred goods wagons supplied by the town authorities and the resettlement police, they came to Oświęcim to transport Jewish property, furnishings, household appliances, and dismantled workshops to the train station in Brzezińska, near Oświęcim, from where the goods were transported in goods wagons to Sosnowiec.

1 Published in *Der Arbeitskamerad: Werkzeitschrift für die Betriebsgemeinschaft Commerz- und Privatbank*, vol. 8, no. 6 (June 1941), p. 51 (heading: 'Aus Feldpostbriefen'); HAC-S3/A102/1–6. This document has been translated from German.
2 Kurt Meisel (1905–2000), bank clerk; worked for Commerzbank in Berlin; served in the war; worked for Commerzbank in Düsseldorf after the war.
3 Possibly Chełm.

1 *Gazeta Żydowska*, 18 April 1941, p. 5. This document has been translated from Polish. Published in Marian Fuks, 'Małe Judenraty w świetle "Gazety Żydowskiej" 1940–1942', *BŻIH*, nos. 126 and 127 (1983), pp. 179–180.
2 The week prior to 12 April 1941.
3 Official designation: Central Office of the Councils of Elders of the Jewish Religious Communities in East Upper Silesia.

A resettlement committee was organized and, together with the so-called block commanders, worked day and night for seven days to transport – in one huge, continuous, and quite extraordinary effort – the belongings of more than 5,000 Jews.

Moreover, local transport companies from Bielsko, Cieszyn, Katowice, Wrocław, and Sosnowiec worked constantly to transport the household appliances and furnishings of Oświęcim's Jewish population on lorries and in huge furniture vans.

Sosnowiec's Jewish police[4] maintained order and came to Oświęcim for this very purpose.

Within a few days, the Jewish Community's Council of Elders closed all Jewish social institutions, workplaces, businesses, homes for the elderly, soup kitchens, etc. in Oświęcim. The critically ill were transported to hospitals in nearby communities, particularly to Sosnowiec.

The Council of Elders and the kahal officials[5] were the last to leave the town.

Oświęcim's Jews arrived in Sosnowiec and Będzin mainly by train, in organized transports, in comfortable passenger carriages, and under medical and sanitary supervision. Their hand luggage was taken from them at the train station in Oświęcim and then handed back to them once they reached their destination.

The Dąbrowa Basin, particularly the towns of Sosnowiec and Będzin, welcomed those resettled from Oświęcim with exceptional hospitality and kindness.

Thanks to the efforts of the Central Committee of the Jewish Community's Councils of Elders, five resettlement camps were set up in Sosnowiec: in the school buildings at 6 Mährischestr[aße], 18 Modrowstr[aße], and 15 Parkstr[aße]; in the 'Rialto' cinema at 18 Warschauerstr[aße]; and at 13 Bömischestr[aße]. In these camps the resettled people underwent thorough medical examinations and were given free food and proper care until they received an apartment.

A special Housing Department at 22 Modrowstr[aße] was in charge of allocating apartments.

In addition to the people being resettled, hundreds of goods wagons carrying the furnishings and household appliances of Oświęcim's [Jews] arrived in Sosnowiec. All the able-bodied men in Sosnowiec were summoned to help unload the goods wagons and store the items in four huge furniture warehouses. The fact that the weather alternated between frost and rain significantly hampered the devoted work of Sosnowiec's Jewish youth. In Sosnowiec, just as in Oświęcim, the German administration and authorities did everything in their power to facilitate the resettlement effort. In addition, the opportunity arose to familiarize oneself with the exceptionally efficient organization, diligence, punctuality, and selfless work of officials from the headquarters as well as of hundreds of Jewish volunteers, both male and female, who worked tirelessly to aid the resettlement effort.

The Central Committee of the Jewish Community's Councils of Elders in Sosnowiec, and indeed the entire Jewish population of the Dąbrowa Basin, carried out their task to the great satisfaction of Oświęcim's Jewish population.

For this, those resettled thank them with a hearty 'God bless you'.[6]

4 This is a reference to the Jewish Order Service.

5 Officials of the Jewish Council.

6 The Jews expelled from Oświęcim to Będzin and Sosnowiec in 1941 were deported to extermination camps during the summer and autumn of 1942, together with the Jews from the same towns.

DOC. 270

On 19 April 1941 the government of the GG and top officials from District Warsaw meet in Cracow to discuss the economic situation in the Warsaw ghetto[1]

Minutes of the meeting of the government of the GG, Cracow, dated 19 April 1941[2]

Meeting: deliberations on the regulation on economic transactions with the Warsaw ghetto

Undersecretary *Kundt* initially gave an overview of *how the regulation was drawn up*. As Undersecretary Kundt explained, the original draft had needed to be revised because it had given Governor Fischer special authorization for District Warsaw that deviated from other administrative practice. Governor Fischer was now raising an *objection* to the version of § 1 according to which the District Governor was only to be authorized to pass measures for the Warsaw ghetto within the framework of the general guidelines laid down by the government. In the case under discussion, however, the relevant main department of the government must have the power to promulgate fundamental guidelines where necessary.[3]

The second *objection* was raised by Banking Commissioner *Paersch*[4] based on fundamental fiscal policy considerations. This was also why the Governor General had delayed signing the regulation.

Governor *Fischer* pointed out that the original version of § 1 had been discussed with State Secretary Bühler and Undersecretary Kundt. At the time, the restriction 'within the framework of the general guidelines laid down by the government' had not been included in that version of § 1. This draft regulation had already been signed by the Governor General. There was no avoiding the fact that a particular agency would have to take on responsibility for the ghetto. On the strength of this, he had made appropriate preparations and had himself given authorization based on § 1. It should go without saying, and he could also guarantee, that when it came to establishing the ghetto, as [District] Governor he had not intended to do anything that was against the interests of the General Government and/or its government. If authorization were granted but every individual government main department was also able to issue parallel directives for the ghetto on its own initiative, then it would be impossible for him to carry out his work successfully.

1 AIPN, GK 95, vol. 15. Copy in IfZ-Archives, Fb 105, vol. 12, fols. 2901–2913. This document has been translated from German.

2 The meeting was attended by Hans Frank, Ernst Kundt, Ludwig Fischer, Otto Wächter, Alfred Spindler, Walter Emmerich, Fritz Paersch, Oskar Plodeck, Eberhard Westerkamp, Albert Weh, Rudolf Pavlu, Rudolf Gater, and Oberregierungsrat Reetz (Labour Main Department).

3 Fischer's objection was not accepted. Paragraph 1 of the regulation of 19 April 1941 authorized the Governor of District Warsaw to 'issue the requisite directives and take the necessary measures to ensure order in the Jewish residential district in Warsaw within the framework of the guidelines issued by the GG government'. *VOBl-GG* 1941, no. 35, 28 April 1941, p. 211.

4 Dr Fritz Paersch (1893–1974), lawyer; became a Reichsbank official in 1925; appointed to the Reichsbank's board of directors in 1934; director of the Emissionsbank (central bank created for the General Government) and head of the Banking Supervision Agency in the General Government, 1940–1945; worked for the municipal authorities in Berlin in 1945; dismissed in 1946; appointed chairman of the Currency Commission in the western sectors of Berlin in 1948; on the executive board of the Central Bank of the state of Hesse from 1952.

Banking Commissioner *Paersch* felt it was also necessary to appraise the situation from a fiscal policy perspective. The ghetto established in Warsaw was modelled on the Lodsch ghetto. Unlike the Warsaw ghetto, the Lodsch ghetto is run by the city.[5] The Lodsch ghetto holds 150,000 people, while the city has a total population of approximately 600,000. The difficulties in Warsaw have become even greater since a closed-off ghetto was established. In Lodsch it was assumed that it would be possible to remove the Poles and the Jews from the city immediately once the eastern territories were incorporated. Conditions in the Lodsch ghetto are easier to assess in terms of economic and fiscal policy because it was established at an earlier date. In Lodsch attempts were made to organize potential labour for the ghetto residents expediently, through both general labour deployment and employment on commission. Employment on commission was primarily used in the textile business and in carpentry. However, the Lodsch ghetto still required a monthly subsidy of 1 million Reichsmarks. In Lodsch every effort was correspondingly made to put the Jews to work in appropriate ways. Warsaw will also face the problem of having to cover these costs one day, once the old stocks have been used up. The memorandum by the Reich Board for Economics[6] argued that approximately 20,000 ghetto residents could be put to work. One conclusion that could be drawn from this is that it would lower the daily expenditure to 100,000 zloty. The experiences in Lodsch will have to be assessed again, particularly to ensure that the large food stocks, which were built up before the ghetto was established, are not exhausted. In addition, Paersch said he agreed with the broad outlines of the regulation in terms of content, even though some of the information necessary for an adequate appraisal of the problem was still missing. However, it was still necessary to establish the quantity of stock that was present and/or had been found in the Warsaw ghetto, as well as which orders the ghetto had been able to obtain and bill for to date, and finally what production facilities had by now been set up in Warsaw.

The *Governor General* agreed to the establishment of the ghetto in Warsaw and expressed the opinion that there was nothing else that could have been done. The choice was between a closed-off residential district or a closed-off ghetto. If a closed-off residential district had been created and adapted to the Lodsch model by stages, then the economic relationships between the Jews and the other inhabitants would not have been disrupted. Each individual would have been responsible for paying his own way and would therefore not have been a burden on the general public, as will now be the case if all economic ties with the ghetto are cut. By establishing a closed-off ghetto, the individual's responsibility for making a living is shifted to the general public.

Governor *Fischer* pointed out that efforts had been made to learn from the experience gained in Lodsch. Conditions there were studied for months on end, and he had regularly sent officials there to observe the overall development of the Lodsch ghetto. The Lodsch ghetto was confronted with a difficult situation because all the stock and production equipment were removed from it right at the start. This was not the path followed in Warsaw; what has been extracted since November last year is of no import-

5 The Łódź ghetto administration, led by Hans Biebow, was part of the city administration.
6 Correctly: Reich Board for Economic Efficiency. See Doc. 263.

ance whatsoever economically. This comprises foreign currency, gold, and similar assets. Very few textiles were seized. What comes out of the Warsaw ghetto goes to the Trustee Office immediately and is then sold by the Transfer Bureau. According to a statement from the employment office, there are 115,000 male and 60,000 female Jews in the Warsaw ghetto who are fit to work. At present, about 12,000 Jews are employed in the city of Warsaw on an ongoing basis. [A total of] 25,000 Jews were recruited for land improvement works, and District Lublin also ordered 25,000 Jews, most of whom have probably been dispatched by now. Overall, therefore, there are not many men now left in the ghetto who still have to be put to work. Workshops are also beginning to operate, with an initial workforce of 6,000 to 7,000 workers. Taking all of this into consideration, he has no concerns in this regard about the Warsaw ghetto. If a closed-off residential district were established and at the same time the Jews were allowed to move about freely, the danger would be much greater, because then the Jews would take everything they could get hold of outside into the ghetto and hoard it there. Then one could just as well let the Jews live outside a closed-off residential district. He felt, however, that a fundamental agreement had already been achieved in Warsaw. The economic aspects in particular have been examined quite thoroughly, and the objections raised by some parties were discussed long ago. The necessary precautions have been taken to ensure that the whole ghetto question is dealt with in full accordance with the guidelines issued by the Economic Affairs Department.

Banking Commissioner *Paersch* saw these details as a significant clarification of the situation, but said he still lacked information about whether and to what extent supplies were removed after the ghetto was sealed on 25 November 1940.

Governor *Fischer* was unable to provide statistical information about this, but felt able to give assurances that the amounts taken out were not very significant.

Banking Commissioner *Paersch* pointed out that there was a great shortage of workers in the Reich, while there were sufficient workers available here. The problem of securing workers in sufficient numbers posed certain difficulties. This was also why it had not been possible to run the Lodsch ghetto without monthly subsidies of 1 million Reichsmarks.

Governor *Fischer* said that in many instances people were starting from false premises. From the very beginning, great importance had been placed on not severing the Jews' business relations with the Poles. Even today brisk business is being done.

Head of the Finance Main Department *Spindler* initially had reservations about the regulation because reports indicated that an annual subsidy of 100 million zloty would be required on an ongoing basis.[7] This would be intolerable for the tax authorities. However, he dropped his reservations after Ministerialdirigent Emmerich explained that such a sum would be out of the question. He wanted to know how much certainty there was that an annual grant of 72 million would not be necessary.

Governor *Fischer* was unable to specify a particular sum, but stressed that business relations between the inhabitants of the ghetto and the outside world would not be severed. On the contrary, they would be cultivated. To this end, a German consortium had been set up in Warsaw. It should also be kept in mind that the Wehrmacht had

7 See Doc. 263, fn. 4.

already placed large orders with the ghetto. In contrast to the way things are done in Warsaw, everything that could in any way be turned into money was extracted from the ghetto in Lodsch, so that the Jews did not have the slightest opportunity to work in any way. The time had been used to build up the ghetto [in Warsaw] economically. For the time being, nothing more could be done. He saw no danger to the ghetto on the whole, even if only 115,000 Jewish workers were employed, and there would soon be a shortage of workers there as well.

Ministerialdirigent *Emmerich* saw the establishment of the Warsaw ghetto not as a purely municipal problem, but, with all its implications, as a problem for the whole economy. Whether the issue is the procurement of raw materials or of orders from the Reich, the central authorities need to address the question and seek a balance between broad economic interests and the particular interests of the ghetto. The way in which the ghetto is permitted to have dealings with the outside world is an organizational question. In the process of determining how extensive such contacts need to be, there could be a move in the direction of isolating the Jewish residential district, but this must always be contingent upon appropriate measures being in place to overcome in practice the obstacles to these contacts. He was not completely convinced that economic issues had always been taken into consideration. Evidently people's ideas about the problem had not been entirely clear from the beginning.

Governor *Fischer* contradicted him, saying there had been a clear idea from the very beginning. He gave the urgent order to examine how trade could be maintained between the ghetto and the rest of the city and said his representative Schön had worked on the same issues.

In response, Ministerialdirigent *Emmerich* pointed out that the officials in charge had evidently thought of the Transfer Bureau as a business organization. Had the authorities adhered to the initial approach of cutting telephone lines, etc., etc., the result would have been an unparalleled bureaucratic machinery which would have had to get involved whenever someone simply wanted to visit the ghetto. Admittedly the Transfer Bureau did plan to maintain trade, but had initially chosen the wrong tactics when it came to organizational conditions. This was why he had taken an interest in the whole question in the first place, and it was also what had prompted the intervention by Dr Gater, who took stock of the individual complexes from a general economic point of view. He had set aside his reservations after it was made clear that the Transfer Bureau would not be the agency liable for recovery claims made by the Wehrmacht, for example. Indeed, the Transfer Bureau could not take on such risks in the first place. During the extensive discussions in Warsaw, it had become apparent that the authorities had to deal with private business competitors. The tailors, for example, had formed cooperatives, and on the other hand they dealt with German companies that had a contractual relationship with the Transfer Bureau. Capitalist methods would have to be used in the ghetto, but care should be taken not to put an official agency into a position where it would not be able to honour its commitments. At this point there was no longer any difference of opinion between Governor Fischer and the Economic Affairs Department.

Governor *Fischer* reminded everyone that he had spent three weeks setting up the details of the Transfer Bureau, and that he had been surprised by the agency's achievements. He found that its work was certainly grounded in business principles.

Ministerialdirigent *Emmerich* was above all interested in the turnover figures and believed that the final figures would be very modest, given that the ghetto had already been in existence for five months. The Economic Affairs Department, he said, is very interested in helping the Warsaw authorities.

In the further course of the discussion, participants commented on the *Transfer Bureau's* tasks. Head of the Finance Main Department *Spindler* stressed that the Transfer Bureau must not be burdened with risks it could not withstand. Banking Commissioner *Paersch* wanted to see it as an agency that would monitor the performance of public-sector contracts.

Main Department Head *Westerkamp* felt that supervision of the ghetto should be separated administratively from that of the city. The representative for the City of Warsaw would then have to be put in charge of these matters. He could appoint a commissioner with a certain degree of independence. At the same time, it should be borne in mind that certain interrelations could not simply be made to disappear.

Governor *Fischer* reminded everyone that the city administration could not take on this task alone. In addition, the District's Economic Affairs Department was also working on questions related to the overall economy on behalf of the city. Administrative procedures would be significantly simplified if some coherence were created in these matters. Indeed, a large number of the tasks performed on behalf of the city were carried out by the District in any case. This was purely a question of expediency.

The *Governor General* felt it should be possible to secure an arrangement under which measures would be taken in consultation with the District Governor's representative.

Governor *Fischer* stressed that, in the interests of the city administration, numerous posts for clerical workers and labourers could be cut under the current arrangement.

Main Department Head *Westerkamp* was still of the opinion that Leist, as the District's representative, had to shoulder overall responsibility. In addition, the ghetto was practically a foreign city.

Governor *Fischer* reminded everyone that the establishment of the ghettos was a new phenomenon to which general administrative principles could not easily be applied. For five months, measures concerning the ghetto had been taken by the District in consultation with, and never in opposition to, the city administration.

Undersecretary *Kundt* explained that he had been persuaded of the expediency of undertaking this division, although from the point of view of general administrative principles the establishment of the ghetto should remain an absolute exception.

The Transfer Bureau's remit was to promote and monitor trade, but it had nothing to do with individual business transactions, and it was therefore not a business. The fundamental question of whether the ghetto would cost money over time could be argued later. The main objective was to manage the ghetto's economic life in such a way that it cost the state almost nothing.

Head of the Finance Main Department *Spindler* said he was willing to accept that a certain financial risk had to be taken.

Banking Commissioner *Paersch* did not feel his reservations had been dispelled by what Governor Fischer said. After all, the facts of the matter were clearly that a ghetto had existed for several months, and now the accounts showed that it had to be subsidized with 1 million Reichsmarks every month. However, this subsidy was being funded by the Main Trustee Office East.

Ministerialrat *Plodeck*[8] wanted to know whether a deficit would potentially have to be covered by funds from his administration. Current indications led him to fear that this was the case.

The *Governor General* felt that, if no ghetto for the Jews were established in Warsaw to deal with the difficulties at least to some degree, then it would have to be accepted that the economy would be completely uncontrollable, given that the Jews would be able to do business without restraint. In this matter, the lesser evil would probably have to be chosen. Everyone was sure to agree, he added, that it was impossible to dissolve the ghetto and allow the Jews to work freely. Furthermore, the Führer had assured him that the General Government would be the first territory completely free of Jews. It was therefore not a permanent burden, but a typical wartime phenomenon, maybe even a measure in defence of the Reich.[9] Even if this measure were to incur costs, it was comforting for him to know that half a million Jews were under control. He agreed with Governor Fischer that this was a completely new measure. At the same time, he urged him to think of this whole question of the Warsaw ghetto as a matter for the General Government, and not merely as one for the District. If any difficulties were to occur, even with regard to a single measure, Governor Fischer must always get in touch with the government immediately. Before taking any measures, Governor Fischer must give the relevant government department heads the opportunity to contribute. By the same token, the government had to provide Governor Fischer with all the support possible. In such negotiations, Governor Fischer would not be allowed to instruct a section head to represent him, but would have to attend in person.

Undersecretary *Kundt* wanted it to go on record that the establishment of the ghetto in Warsaw was a one-off measure and would not be emulated in the other districts.

The *Governor General* ordered that this be put on record.

Following the deliberations, the *District representative* for the City of Cracow[10] reported on the establishment of the *Jewish residential district in Cracow*. This was a residential district where approximately 15,000 Jews were to be housed.[11] In other respects the conditions in Cracow were not comparable to those in the city of Warsaw.

Main Department Head *Westerkamp* argued for tough enforcement of the provisions concerning restriction of movement for Jews. Action had to be taken against contraventions of the prohibition to leave the ghetto, including the most severe punishments, potentially including the death penalty.

The *regulation* was then signed.

8 Oskar Friedrich Plodeck (b. 1890); head of the Trustee Office Department in the Office of the Governor General from Dec. 1939; Ministerialrat and head of the Economic Affairs Department from 1939/1940; head of Department S (Trustee Administration and Special Tasks of the General Government's Economic Affairs Department) from 1942.

9 Hitler appointed Frank as Reich defence commissioner for the General Government in Dec. 1939.

10 Rudolf Pavlu (1902–1949), accountant; joined the NSDAP in 1931 and the SS in 1938; chief of staff to State Commissioner Wächter in the Reichsstatthalter's Office in Vienna in 1938; appointed head of the Labour Department in District Cracow in 1940; Stadthauptmann of Cracow, 1941–1943; interned after the war; escaped from detention; committed suicide in fear of being extradited to Poland.

11 The ghetto in Cracow was established in March 1941. In spring 1941 it had between 16,000 and 22,000 inhabitants.

Governor *Fischer* then also announced an intended *reduction of rents* in Warsaw, against which no objections were raised by the Price Setting Department.

Head of the Finance Main Department *Spindler* remarked that he was in favour of this measure in principle, provided the Interior Administration Main Department agreed to it.[12]

Governor *Fischer* presented the Governor General with a *map of the city of Warsaw* with the ghetto boundaries drawn on it.

DOC. 271
On 20 April 1941 an onlooker describes children on the verge of starvation compelled to beg in the Warsaw ghetto[1]

Handwritten note for the underground archive of the Warsaw ghetto, dated 20 April 1941

Snapshots from the Warsaw ghetto
1941

1. An emaciated boy walks down Grzybowska Street. He bends over, smears his hand with dirt, and puts it into his mouth. Mixed in with the filth are grain coffee grounds. He walks on, picks something up off the ground, and puts that into his mouth as well. He does not cry out or beg, just keeps going. With his head bowed, he looks for whatever the ground will give him.
2. On Karmelicka Street, a child about 18 months old sits on a cushion. It is sitting still. A girl stands at a distance. It looks as if she is watching over the child. Women and men walk past, and no one notices, no one takes an interest in the youngest beggar in Warsaw. A little beggar girl walks past with a bit of fish in her hand (it is still possible to obtain these 'smelt'[2]). She stops in front of the child, breaks off a piece of fish, and sticks it into the child's mouth. The child snaps it up greedily.
3. Going from Orla Street to Zamenhofa Street, I encounter corpses covered with paper: one on Orla, the other on Karmelicka.
4. The following notice from the youth group has been posted in Polish in the gateway at 38 Sienna Street: The youth group's managing committee calls on all of its members to cooperate fully with the anti-beggar campaign. Any member of the group who encounters a beggar at the gate or on the stairs is requested to inform him that alms are distributed only on Fridays, and that going from door to door is unnecessary. This request is also addressed to the youth group.
   20 April 1941
   Chairman

12 Nothing is known about the implementation of this proposal.

1 AŻIH, Ring I/492 (1017). This document has been translated from Yiddish.
2 Small silvery fish similar to sardines.

DOC. 272

On 25 April 1941 the Stadthauptmann of Tschenstochau (Częstochowa) calls on the local military commander to ban German soldiers from entering the ghetto[1]

Letter from Stadthauptmann Dr Wendler (log no. Dr. W./Br, 13.3./41) to the Stadtkommandant's office in Tschenstochau (carbon copy), dated 8 April 1941

Re: closed-off Jewish residential area
I know from both police reports and from personal experience that soldiers from all the units posted here entertain themselves by looking around the ghetto and going for strolls there in droves. The Jewish residential area was created to ensure the Jews are separated from the Aryans, and above all to minimize the risk of infection, particularly typhus. However, as a result of the German soldiers' behaviour, exactly the opposite is now happening. There is now a greater chance of becoming infected in the closed-off residential area than previously, and I therefore request that the German Wehrmacht, who have no business there, be banned from entering the Jewish residential area by means of a garrison order. You will be familiar with the boundaries because I had my order forwarded to you at the same time as the decree.[2] Signs to this effect will also be put up in the near future; they have simply not been procured yet. But it is absolutely essential to make it clear immediately that wandering around in the ghetto out of pure curiosity is not only undignified, but also dangerous, and is therefore prohibited.

I would be grateful if you were to forward an order to this effect.[3]

DOC. 273

On 25 April 1941 the German ghetto administration in Litzmannstadt (Lodz) passes on to the Jewish elder the complaints made by the commander of a forced labour camp[1]

Letter from the mayor of Litzmannstadt,[2] ghetto administration, letter no. 2815 (027/1/B/A), B[enthin], to the Jewish elder in the Litzmannstadt ghetto, dated 25 April 1941[3]

Re: inspection of the camps for Jews along the Reich autobahn, Frankfurt/Oder-Schwiebus section
The camp administrator has raised the following complaints:

1 APCz, 4/0/3, fol. 29. Copy in YVA, MF JM 1489. This document has been translated from German.
2 Enclosed with the letter was a copy of an announcement Wendler had made on 8 April 1941, according to which the Jews were to be resettled in a closed-off quarter between 9 and 17 April 1941, and members of the Wehrmacht were to be made aware of this, 'so that the military does not cause any difficulties for those moving house': APCz, 4/0/3, fols. 22–28.
3 On 29 April 1941 (log no. 453) the Wehrmacht's Ortskommandantur I/522 informed Wendler about 'the order from the commandant's office which prohibits [Wehrmacht] presence in the ghetto': YVA, O-6/430, fol. 36.

1 APŁ, 221/31866a, fols. 37–38. Copy in USHMM, RG 05 008M, reel 6. This document has been translated from German.

1) The identity cards to which you have attached photographs will all have to be re-issued, and the Jews must on no account be given further papers with old photographs and text printed in Polish on them. Some of the construction workers have up-to-date identity cards, and some have quite outdated ones.
2) You provide the transport chief in charge with so-called transport lists. They merely provide information about names, etc. The really important information is missing, i.e. the occupation of the individual workers. You can imagine that, when Jews are deployed, some individuals are always chosen to manage the camp, while others are needed to carry out tailoring work, and then inquiries first have to be made at the camp to find out who is suitable for these tasks. Of course everyone then volunteers in the hope of being exempted from work that involves digging and earthworks.
3) Money transfers from relatives and acquaintances living outside the ghetto, so-called donations, as well as support from ghetto inhabitants, are not permitted. Payments of this kind may only be made to workers deployed outside the ghetto with the permission of the ghetto administration. Furthermore, a whole series of camp inmates receive charity parcels, which are completely unnecessary because adequate food is provided. The undersigned knows from experience that goods have been sent which go off easily, and the recipients risk illness from consuming spoiled food.
4) A whole series of workers suffering from infectious diseases have been dispatched to the autobahn. The infections were not identified during the German authorities' examinations or during your checks because their conditions had abated, but they have recurred now that these workers were deployed to the camp. Such workers must not leave the ghetto. You must therefore pay strict attention to ensure that the workers state straight away, before they are examined, whether they have previously suffered from an infectious condition.
5) Before the workers are dispatched, regardless of where they are being taken, proper clothing should be a priority, because it is not acceptable for Jews to arrive wearing completely ragged clothes and useless footwear, which is what happened when workers were deployed to the autobahn.

Stringent compliance with the points set out above is important for you, especially as wages will otherwise be docked to pay for special measures taken by the management on site, which will in turn have a negative effect on the food available to the workers' relatives who remain behind in the ghetto.

2 Werner Ventzki (1906–2004), lawyer; joined the NSDAP in 1931; head of the Gau office of the National Socialist People's Welfare Organization in Pomerania, 1934–1939; member of Stettin City Council until 1936; head of the welfare department at the office of the Oberpräsident of Pomerania; head of welfare for the ethnic German population in Posen (Warthegau) from 1939/1940; mayor of Litzmannstadt, April 1941–mid 1943; subsequently served in the Waffen-SS; West Berlin representative of the Federal Ministry for Expellees, Refugees, and Disabled Veterans; later Oberregierungsrat in the West German federal administration in Bonn.

3 A copy went to the Municipal Health Office, Department 500/Medical Officer, for information (received on 26 April 1941). At the end of the document there is a handwritten note: 'to be filed ghetto (medical officer)'.

DOC. 274
In late April 1941 Jan Kapczan reports on 'racial policy research' carried out in Łódź and the reception of expelled Jews in the Warsaw ghetto[1]

Handwritten report by Jan Kapczan[2] from late April 1941 (transcript in two copies by Mordechaj Szwarcbard[3])

Material on the financial management of the Jewish communities in the occupied territory during the war

The financial management of the Jewish communities under G[erman] occupation will one day be the subject of very interesting research. While historians investigate the reasons for the fall of Nazism, economists and statisticians will enthusiastically examine the budgets of the Jewish self-governing bodies within the boundaries of the Jewish quarters – de facto territorial entities – encircled by walls or barbed wire.

It is a well-known fact that the expenses of the Jewish communities are immense, while revenues are constantly diminishing due to the general impoverishment of the Jewish population. Securing money is the hardest part of the work the Jewish communities do. No wonder the search for new sources of revenue has come to dominate, inducing these communities to profit from every misfortune that befalls the Jews, from every persecution or prohibition.

There is undoubtedly much truth in the general accusations. The Jewish 'governments' and certain machinations of the communities are all too vexing.

Everyone is familiar with a number of such facts – such scandals – from personal experience, and no one will be unfamiliar with the greatest scandal currently unfolding: the labour camps in Warsaw (April 1941).[4]

To prove this claim, I will present two cases from different areas and times.

I. Łódź, January and February 1940

Among the large number of orders the Jewish elder in Łódź received from the various offices almost daily, there was one from the Nazi Party Office of Racial Policy to provide a certain number of clean, deloused Jews for racial research every day until further notice.[5] Since this order (like all the others) came into force immediately, 20 men who had registered for Jewish forced labour were sent there the following day. At the Office of Racial Policy, some 'physicians' in white smocks (under which, as in Pawecki's excellent pictures, one caught sight of filled-out brown trousers and SA military boots) measured the Jews' heads and noses with some kind of gauge, paying particular attention to their

1 AŻIH, Ring I/65 (34). The document has been translated from Yiddish.
2 Jan Kapczan wrote this report for the underground archive of the Warsaw ghetto. Nothing more is known about the author.
3 Mordechaj Szwarcbard (1896–1942?); member of the Poale Zion-Left party; worked at the soup kitchen for refugees from Łódź and contributed to the underground archive in the Warsaw ghetto; thought to have been murdered in Treblinka.
4 The author is alluding to corruption and the abuse of authority with regard to the organization of forced labour in the Warsaw ghetto.
5 This could not be found.

noses. After the measurements had been taken, they were photographed. There was no lack of harassment as all of this transpired. Some had a clump of hair shorn from their heads with clippers, while others had all or even just half of their beards cut off.[6] On their way out, the men were tripped up and subjected to other similar harassments. Of course the 'researchers' got a real kick out of this kind of research, but for those being researched it was awful, even unbearable. Among the Jews it was said that terrible things happened in the administrative building where the Office of Racial Policy was located. Apart from the men being beaten and having their heads shorn and their beards cut off, rumour had it that the Germans would paint or even brand a Star of David on the men's foreheads. People were afraid of the building.

Meanwhile, the 'physicians' left after a week or ten days without leaving a message to stop providing Jews, so the Community kept sending them at first, and then stopped after a few days. At the same time, the Community's tax-collection department made a large number of duplicates of official summonses for examination at the Office of Racial Policy. These summonses threatened harsh penalties for failure to report and also contained a special stamp: 'Your name and address have been forwarded to the German authorities.' These summonses were sent to those who had stopped paying Community taxes.

The delinquent taxpayers got scared and went to the Community office straight away. There, as a deterrent, they were put through a comedy that affected them like an Aeschylean[7] tragedy: they cleared their debts and … were excused from being examined.

It should be pointed out that – as became known later – in the two months after the travelling office of racial research departed, the Łódź Community collected a tremendous amount of overdue taxes. In this case by using racism …!

II. End of January 1941 [Warsaw]

Jews expelled from the smaller towns in the area are arriving in Warsaw, including 1,200 people from Pruszków. They endured terrible experiences that cannot be related here and will be detailed separately in the report on the deportation from Pruszków. The refugees arrived by train. They were sent from [Warsaw's] Danzig train station[8] directly to the municipal disinfection centre on Spokojna, where they had to endure a whole slew of harassments that had nothing whatsoever to do with the sanitary operation. Later that night, in temperatures as low as minus 25 degrees, they were placed in quarantine at 109 Leszno.[9] Their arrival was awful. The large building used as the quarantine facility had not been heated the entire winter. The pipes for both the water and the sewage lines were frozen. The latrines overflowed with excrement. All the hallways and rooms were crowded with refugees from other towns, and there was nowhere to stand or to sit. It was noisy and stuffy. The cries of children and the groans of the old and the crippled were lost in the general din. Everyone somehow managed to make a place for themselves to spend the night until morning, when it would be possible to go

6 Removing half of the beard constituted a particular denigration of the victim.

7 A reference to Aeschylus (525/524 BC–456/455), dramatist in ancient Greece, often known as the 'father of tragedy'.

8 In the original 'dantsiker banhoyf'; in Polish referred to as Dworzec Gdański (Gdańsk station).

9 See Doc. 298.

out into the city, to family or friends. The children were unable to sleep a wink. The noise did not let up for a moment and grew much louder with the start of the day. People began moving about, stretched, and got ready to leave. But that was impossible, not even to get some water, because the quarantine facility was situated in the Aryan quarter. This meant that you had to pay 20 groszy for a glass of water.

Minutes turned into hours, and the hours dragged on. Nobody had heard anything about being let out. There was no one to ask. The person in charge of the quarantine facility was nowhere to be found. It was noon, and we had the feeling he was deliberately hiding from us, probably in order to wear down the people being held there and weaken their ability to resist.

Some suspicious characters then appeared and tried to coax us with obsequious deference to settle the matter with the person in charge more quickly, because people could sit here for a long time otherwise. We fall into conversation with people from Piaseczno, who tell us the same thing happened to them. They first had to pay up before they were let out. We now sensed and knew for sure that we were in a fix. We spread out across the building and waited. Our instinct was to fight back! A while later we got hold of the man in charge, Halber.[10] We selected a delegation and agreed on a course of action. Mr Halber explained that he could not release anyone because an order from the German authorities obliged him to keep us for 14 days and to observe our state of health. The negotiations dragged on. The early January dusk was already approaching, and with it the thought of spending another night here, as terrible as the last … They demanded 10,000 złoty from us! We were seized by a terrible rage, and we were unable to think straight. Why should we have to pay? We explained how we had been expelled; we told of our destruction. We asked for the release of our women and children, our old and infirm. We young men would remain as hostages. It was no use.

We saw that nothing would be taken into consideration. The only thing we could do was to pay. We gathered all the refugees and squeezed their last groszy out of them. We collected 1,000 złoty, which we paid as a first instalment.

They let us out, keeping our suitcases and some of our bedding and clothes as collateral. After we left the quarantine facility, the relevant YGO[11] bodies took an interest in our situation. There we found much compassion and understanding. Members of the YGO executive committee intervened with the Community on our behalf, and after protracted efforts they managed to reach a deal that we would only have to pay an additional 4,000 złoty.

The collection of this 'ransom' took longer than ten days, and for more than two weeks the refugees from Pruszków had neither bedding nor a change of clothes. Once the money was paid, they began releasing our luggage.

I have documented two cases here, each of which evokes different feelings. Whereas the former leaves a bad taste in the mouth, the latter evokes disgust and contempt.

10 Maurycy Halber; deputy head of the Labour Battalion for the Warsaw Jewish Council and employee of the Security Police in 1940; head of the quarantine facility located at 109–111 Leszno Street in 1941.

11 The Yidishe Gemeynde-Organizatsye (Jewish Community Organization) was an administrative entity subordinate to the Jewish Council.

DOC. 275
Contemporary Jewish Record: article on the situation of Jewish refugees in eastern Poland up to April 1941[1]

In Soviet Poland and Lithuania[2]
By David Grodner[3]

Rigid censorship and the absence of accredited news correspondents have made it impossible for American readers to learn what is really happening to Jews in Soviet Poland and Lithuania. The impression that Polish refugees have found a friendly home in these areas is fostered largely by Communistic propaganda, which has publicized the letters of those elated by their escape from Nazi Poland or those who had the good fortune to make a fair adjustment under the new conditions. Having spent at least six months in Soviet Poland and more than that time in Lithuania, including the period of its occupation, I feel it my duty to tell what I have seen happen to the religious, communal and cultural life of Jews under their new Soviet masters. In particular, more ought to be known about the fate of at least one hundred thousand Polish Jewish refugees who sought a haven from the Nazi invaders only to be driven mercilessly to the frozen tundras of Siberia.[4]

Newspapers in the United States have exaggerated the number of Jews in Soviet Poland. Altogether, there are about 1,200,000 Jews in Western Ukraine (former Galicia) and Western Byelorosya (White Russia). In addition, approximately 500,000 Jews fled there from Nazi Poland.[5] About 60 per cent of these refugees, it must be noted, arrived before the Red Army entered the country.

On the night of September 6, 1939, the propaganda chief of the Polish Army announced over the radio that Warsaw was to be evacuated and ordered all inhabitants of military age to leave the city. (Later, it was rumored that this official was a German spy carrying out Nazi orders.) About 200,000 persons left Warsaw that night and headed for the Bug River, where the Polish Army was planning to make a last stand. There is no

1 *Contemporary Jewish Record*, no. 4/2, April 1941, pp. 136–147. The periodical *Contemporary Jewish Record: Review of Events and Digest of Opinion* was published bimonthly in New York by the American Jewish Committee (AJC) between 1938 and 1945. Proofs of this article can be found on file at the State Department. On 17 Feb. 1941 the AJC wrote to the State Department to ask whether the article's critical tone with regard to the Soviet Union might prevent its publication. Ray Atherton, Acting Chief, Division of European Affairs, raised no objection: see NARA, RG Decimal File 860c.4016/630.

2 While eastern Poland was annexed by the Soviet Union on 17 Sept. 1939, Lithuania was not annexed until 15 June 1940.

3 Pseudonym of Israel Stolarski (1900–1965), teacher; editor of the *Haynt* and *Lodzher Folksblat* newspapers from 1925; trade unionist; member of the Marxist-Zionist Poale Zion party, 1926–1939; delegate to the World Zionist Congress in Geneva in August 1939; returned to Warsaw and fled to the USA via the Soviet Union and Japan; lived in New York, where he worked as a tailor and a writer from 1940.

4 Almost all of the 65,799 Jewish refugees and displaced persons from German-occupied Poland who had registered with Soviet offices by early 1940 were deported to the interior of the Soviet Union in June 1940.

5 This figure is a considerable overestimate. The number of Jewish refugees who fled or were displaced to Soviet-occupied eastern Poland is estimated today at 200,000 to 300,000.

doubt that the Germans would have met with great resistance along this strategic line, had the Poles not been attacked by the Red Army from the rear.

While a number of refugees managed to escape before the Nazi hordes occupied their towns, most of them, including many Czech and Austrian Jews, were rounded up by the Gestapo and driven to the frontier.[6] There they streamed across the Soviet boundaries at three points: Zaremb Koscielny,[7] a village near Bialystok; Drohyczyn, a village bordering on the Bug River near Semiatycze;[8] and Przemysl, the point of entry for Jews from Galicia and those deported from Czechoslovakia. It was at Zaremb Koscielny and Drohyczyn that the most poignant incidents took place. Those I witnessed at Zaremb Koscielny, I shall never forget.

During the first few weeks of this mass exodus, the Red Army guards permitted everyone to cross the border and frequently showed a sympathetic attitude. Around 15 October, however, the borders were suddenly shut tight. The sentries were no longer friendly, and frequently towns and villages near the border were searched for refugees who had somehow got across. The hunt extended as far as the railroad station of Czyzew, a town ninety *versts*[9] from the border. Those caught were shipped back to Nazi Poland. Soviet border guards shot at anyone trying to cross the border. Nazi guards, in turn, fired at anyone trying to get back. The unfortunate refugees, caught between two lines of fire, had no choice but to remain in a no-man's land along the border.

Meanwhile, the weather had grown bitterly cold and many froze to death. Only after great difficulties could Jews living in the border towns receive permission from the Soviet authorities to bury the dead and the murdered. I myself witnessed the tragic burial of a seventy-year-old man, a young mother, and her three-months-old baby, all of whom died of exposure.

Thousands eventually gathered in these no-man's lands. Nazi guards would have 'fun' with them, and their cries would be heard on both sides of the boundary. The actress, Ida Kaminsky,[10] was forced to clean open latrines with her hands. The actor, Zisha Katz, was beaten so badly by the Nazis that he was incapacitated for days. Later he committed suicide in the 'happy' and 'liberated' Bialystok.[11] It is impossible to describe the appearance of these refugees, hungry, starved, ill, and dressed in rags. Local Jews did their utmost to help them, frequently sharing with them their crowded quarters and their last piece of bread. On the other side, the Red soldiers stood grimly and silently holding their guns ready. When finally the refugees had reached a point of desperation, they stampeded past the Soviet guards. Several were shot, but most of

6 This is a reference to the forced deportations organized by Eichmann: see Doc. 18.

7 Correctly: Zaręby Kościelne.

8 Correctly: Siemiatycze.

9 Correctly: 19 versts (equivalent to about 20 km).

10 Correctly: Ida Kamińska (1899–1980), actress and director in Yiddish theatre and film; fled to eastern Poland in 1939; director of the Yiddish state theatre in Lwów; fled to Kyrgyzstan in June 1941; returned to Poland in 1947; director of the Yiddish theatre in Warsaw, which gave many guest performances abroad; emigrated to Israel in 1968, and subsequently to the USA; published *My Life, My Theater* in 1973.

11 Zisha Katz, actor and comedian on Yiddish-language stages in Poland; performed in various theatres and travelling troupes; gave guest performances in France and North America, 1938–1939; in Sept. 1939 fled with his two sons to Białystok, where he performed until March 1940; failed to return to his wife in Warsaw; took his own life in July 1940.

them got across after overpowering the sentries by sheer weight of numbers. Sometimes Red soldiers who sympathized with these unfortunates disregarded the orders of their superiors.

Another way to cross was devised by a Jewish waiter from Warsaw. After eight days of hunger and cold in no-man's-land together with thousands of others, he made a red flag out of a piece of cloth, and led a march of refugees toward the border, all singing 'International' at the top of their lungs. The Soviet guards, confused by this unusual scene, lowered their guns and allowed most of the people to enter the country.

The situation was much worse at Drohyczyn. Here, the refugees had to cross the Bug River in rowboats, frequently under a hail of bullets from both Nazis and Soviets. Bodies of the unlucky ones were usually found on the banks of the river a few days later. It was in this way that the Labor Zionist leader, Tarczyc,[12] former City Councillor of Pulawy, found his eternal rest together with his family of five.

It was not long before the larger cities of the newly-occupied eastern provinces were crowded with refugees. Their condition was unbelievable. Refugee relief was organized on a systematic scale with the aid of the Joint Distribution Committee only in Bialystok, Wilno and Kowel. In other places, the refugees were left to their own meager resources, and relatively few of them could find permanent quarters or sufficient food. At first, they slept in the fields and woods. Later, they found temporary shelter in railroad stations, empty goods waggons, *batei midrashim* (houses of study), synagogues, school buildings and the collective quarters of the Holutzim (pioneers training for settlement in Palestine). Here they lived for months, herded together like cattle, hungry and unwashed.

Most fortunate were those who found quarters in the Halutz shelters, where it was clean and possible to get warm food. In Kowel, for instance, more free meals were handed out by the Halutz co-operative than by the official Soviet kitchens for refugees. The manager of the *kibutz* (co-operative), a young energetic member of the Hashomer Hatzair, had an uncanny faculty for producing food almost by magic. And the motto of his group everywhere was the formula pronounced at the Passover *seder*:[13] 'All who are hungered – let them come and eat!'

Despite their unbearable living conditions and anxiety over the fate of their families across the border, the refugees considered themselves fortunate in having escaped Nazi hell. They considered their difficulties temporary and felt certain that the Soviet authorities would give them full opportunity to become adjusted. Former merchants, middle-class people and artisans were willing to become workers, and determined to ignore politics if only they could earn their daily bread. The Soviet authorities, however, made a sharp distinction between local residents and refugees, treating the latter as lepers and excluding them from the right to work. The more stabilized local condition[s] became, the worse grew the situation of the refugees.

The problem created by these unfortunates could have been solved in a decent and humane manner had the government so desired. The authorities, however, rejected

12 Presumably Icchak Tarczyc.

13 Hebrew: literally 'order', the term indicating the meal on the first evening of Pesach (Passover), which takes place according to a specific order indicated in the Mishna (the first part of the Talmud) and also involves reciting the Haggadah text.

every proposal presented by the Joint Distribution Committee and, with few exceptions, refused to do anything themselves. The result was that about half a million refugees were left to shift for themselves as best they could. Only in Kowel, Bialystok, Lwow, Rouno and Luck did the authorities establish free kitchens for them, and then half-heartedly. In Bialystok, for the 33,000 refugees officially registered in November 1939, and for the hundreds who arrived with each day, only one kitchen was set. It was located in a Talmud Torah on Piekna Street, and the destitute had to stand in line for hours in order to get a bowl of watery soup and a piece of black bread.

Government regulations, which followed each other in rapid succession, added to their troubles. Local residents in comfortable circumstances were frequently driven out together with the refugees whom they had sheltered and their apartments [were] 're-distributed,' usually among army officers and the Soviet officials who had flocked to the occupied regions. Even those unfortunates who had found shelter in public halls and offices of sympathetic organizations were in constant fear of being thrown out. Several hundred refugees who lived in the headquarters of the Merchants Association in Bialystok were driven out in the middle of the night when the authorities suddenly decided to use the offices for a new tailors' co-operative.

During the first weeks of the Soviet occupation of Poland, few economic changes were perceptible. Factory owners were ordered to double the salaries of their workers but were promised no further interference. Stores remained open, but speculation was rampant, and complaints to the authorities about the rapid rise of prices were of no avail. Russian soldiers and officials, who were well supplied with rubles and did not have to wait on line, soon bought out all the available supplies. Some merchants were wise enough to exchange their rubles for dollars via the Black Bourse – an institution still very much alive in the USSR – and then leave for Lithuania. When I left, the value of the dollar on the Black Bourse ranged between 170 and 190 rubles.

Speedy nationalization of all economic life was ordered at the end of this brief period. Declassed merchants and artisans were left without means of earning a living, while those working in factories lost the pay increases the Soviets had originally given them. Dissatisfaction was prevalent and riots broke out in the factories in Bialystok late in December 1939, and in other towns.

Special employment offices, called 'labor departments' in Western Byelorosya and 'labor bourses' in the Western Ukraine, were opened and soon crowded with refugees seeking work. Officials, however, refused to register them. Instead, efforts were made to persuade them to leave for the interior of Russia. Representatives of factories in the Donbas and other regions offered them jobs, promising them good working conditions and an advance of fifty rubles. The response was immediate; people stood in line for days and nights to register for these jobs. In Bialystok alone, 20,000 registered in one week; in Brest-Litovsk, 10,000. Many of them were accepted, given special passports and rushed to the interior on goods trains.

At first, they sent back glowing reports of their new circumstances, but shortly thereafter they began to return in large numbers. Most of them, it was learned, had been employed as unskilled laborers, quartered in wooden barracks and paid only five rubles a day despite the fact that a modest meal cost eight rubles. Local residents in these towns were sympathetic and helped them to run away. Nevertheless, those who remained, particularly the professionals, made relatively good adjustments.

Nationalization of industry brought with it a flurry of illegal trading. In every town and village there suddenly arose illegal markets, called 'Toltchok,'[14] where people gathered to buy and sell. (Such places still exist throughout the Soviet Union, twenty-three years after the November revolution.[15]) Some refugees managed to eke out a precarious existence through the illegal sale of necessities, but after a short time many of them in desperation began to return to Nazi Poland. The abrupt devaluation of the zloty in December 1939 gave added impetus to the movement.[16] It is unbelievable but true that the first to steal back to Nazi Poland were the workers who had formerly been most radical. Men who had been jailed in Poland for communist activities, including a former member of the Central Committee of the Communist Party of Poland, returned to face an uncertain future in the Generalgouvernement. They were joined by others who for one reason or another lost all hope of a decent life under Soviet rule. In some weeks, the number going back reached thousands.

The refugees, however, were not the only ones to suffer from the rapid transition to Soviet economy. The native residents – particularly the urban Jewish population – who automatically received Soviet citizenship, were also severely hit. The declassed and those unable to get jobs in the new state-owned establishments either lived on the earnings of their relatives or sold their personal belongings. Even those fortunate enough to obtain jobs had to lower their standard of living radically because of the low wages and high prices. For instance, a weaver in Bialystok earning 250 rubles a month as a Stakhanovite,[17] could never lift himself above the level of mere sustenance. Bread was sold at the official price of one ruble a kilogram; meat, eight rubles; and butter, twenty rubles. Clothing was too expensive for the average worker to buy. A small wagonload of firewood sold at the official price of sixty to seventy rubles.

Following the Soviet-Nazi agreement of April 1940 for an exchange of populations, but excluding Jews, Soviet authorities began a grim resolution of the refugee problem. Those who refused to go to Siberia and Kazakstan or rejected an offer of Soviet citizenship, either because it meant permanent separation from their families or the end of their hopes for emigration, were rounded up by the N.K.V.D. (secret police, formerly the OGPU). Raids were made night after night, and those caught were packed on goods trains and shipped to Siberia, Kazakstan, the Arkhangelsk region, and even far-off Kamchatka. No distinction was made between young and old, women and children. Frequently families were separated in the rush, since refugees were given only two hours to pack forty kilograms of their belongings.

In one case, during the temporary absence of a prominent Labor Zionist who had all his papers ready to leave for Palestine, his wife and thirteen-year-old son were seized in

14 Russian in the original: 'push'; literally: 'impulse'.

15 This is a reference to the October Revolution, which began on 6/7 Nov. 1917 according to the Gregorian calendar.

16 On 21 Dec. 1939 Soviet officials withdrew the złoty from circulation, and all bank deposits over 300 złoty were seized. The złoty's exchange rate with the rouble sank to as low as 50 per cent of its former value.

17 The Stakhanovite movement, named after the miner Aleksey Stakhanov, was a propaganda campaign launched by the Soviet Union in 1935 to increase workers' productivity. It encouraged workers to exceed production targets, and the best workers were rewarded with benefits and extra provisions.

Bialystok at one o'clock in the morning and shipped to a labor camp in Siberia, 150 kilometers from the nearest railroad. Although the Labor Zionist leader – who must remain anonymous for obvious reasons – made strenuous efforts to have them freed, he finally had to leave without them. The wife and children of an outstanding scholar at present residing in New York, are inmates of another Siberian labor camp. Ironically enough, none of the Jewish deportees were settled in Biro-Bidjan, the supposed autonomous Jewish region of the Soviet Union. It is estimated that the number of Polish-Jews exiled to Siberia and similar regions is well above 100,000.

The high-handed methods of Soviet authorities aroused resentment even among local residents who had welcomed the entry of the Red Army. No discussions were permitted at meetings of factory or Communist Party cells. In the campaign preceding the elections to the National Assemblies,[18] speeches delivered by local Jewish and Polish Communists usually were disregarded by the Russian leaders. It took time for the native Communists to learn the real Moscow line, and frequently the process of learning was painful.

I witnessed an illustrative incident held in the market place of Zaremb Koscielny, where 90 % of those gathered were Jews and the chairman was a captain in the Red Army. A Polish Jewish Communist, evidently unaware that it was forbidden to speak against fascism, delivered a speech bitterly attacking the Nazis and comparing their persecution of Jews to the new freedom from racism under Soviet rule. The chairman, after several vain attempts to check him, finally drove him unceremoniously off the platform.

Another incident was even more pointed. A Jew from Wloclawek, a Polish town now incorporated into the Reich, brought a yellow badge, which the Nazis were forcing the Jews to wear, to the editorial offices of the Yiddish daily, *Bialystoker Shtern*.[19] The editors listened carefully to his story and expressed their sympathy. The refugee, however, told them: 'I didn't come to listen to your sighs. I want you to write about this barbarism in your paper.' The editor sighed again and said: 'Sorry, but we can't print this. It's forbidden.'

For a while, a revival of Yiddish cultural activities was attempted in the occupied territories. White Russian, Ukrainian and Yiddish writers came from the interior to visit their 'liberated' colleagues. Bialystok was honored by a visit from the famous poets, It[z]ik Fefer[20] and I[t]zik Platner.[21] At a meeting of Yiddish writers, Fefer exclaimed: 'Back to the past! We are celebrating at present the eight hundredth anniversary of Judah Halevi.[22] Judah the Maccabean and the Hasmoneans are national heroes and revolutionaries.'[23]

18 This is a reference to the manipulated elections to the Western Byelorussian and Western Ukrainian national assemblies, which were organized by the Soviet occupation authorities and held on 22 Oct. 1939.

19 Following the Red Army's occupation of Białystok in Sept. 1939, many Yiddish-speaking writers from western and central Poland fled the city. Some of them worked for the *Bialystoker Shtern*, which appeared from Sept. 1939 to June 1941.

20 Itzik Fefer, also Feffer (1900–1952), Yiddish poet in the Soviet Union; war correspondent and acting chair of the Jewish Antifascist Committee from 1941; travelled to the USA on behalf of the committee, and continued on to Canada and Mexico in 1943; NKVD informant; accused of high treason in 1948, in the course of Stalin's antisemitic purges; executed in 1952.

21 Itzik, also Ayzek, Platner (1895–1961), Polish-born Yiddish poet; lived in Kaunas (Lithuania) from 1920 and in the USA, 1927–1932; editor of the *Oktyabr* newspaper in Minsk (Soviet Union); lived in Saransk from 1941, and thereafter again in Minsk; arrested in 1948 and interned in a labour camp until 1956.

Those in the audience accepted his statements as proof that Soviet policy on Jewish national life was undergoing a profound change. Many among them, including Moses Brodersohn,[24] the former editor of a Lodz paper, and Ephraim Kaganovsky[25] of the Warsaw *Hajnt*[26] atoned publicly for their reactionary past and promised to be good Soviet writers. Their hopes, however, were soon shattered. The prominent Soviet writer, David Hoffstein,[27] speaking [at] a mass meeting of Yiddish journalists in Lwow (Lemberg) told a group headed by the Communist, Alter Katsizne,[28] who had asked for permission to publish a Yiddish paper: 'You ought to be thankful that the great Stalin permits you to live. There is no need for a Yiddish paper in Lemberg and no such paper will be published.' Later, the *Bialystoker Shtern*, which never enjoyed a circulation of more than one thousand, suspended publication. At present, only three Yiddish papers are published: the *Emes*[29] in Wilno, the *Folksblat*[30] in Kaunas, and one in Latvia.[31]
[...][32]

22 This is a reference to the 800th anniversary of the death of Judah Halevi (*c.*1075–1141), a Spanish-Jewish philosopher and the most important Jewish poet of the European Middle Ages.

23 Judas Maccabeus (Hebrew: Jehuda haMakabi, d. 160 BCE), of the Hasmonean dynasty; leader of a Jewish revolt against Seleucid rule in 165 BCE, which resulted in the capture of Jerusalem and ended with the rebels' defeat in 160 BCE.

24 Moses Brodersohn, also Moyshe Broderzon (1890–1956), Yiddish poet and playwright; lived in Russia during the First World War; co-founder of the Łódź-based avant-garde literary and artistic group Yung-Idish (Yung-Yidish); fled to Białystok in 1939; lived in central Asia, 1941–1943, and thereafter in Moscow; arrested in 1950 and sentenced to ten years in a labour camp; rehabilitated in 1955; moved to Poland in 1956.

25 Efroim Kaganowski (1893–1958), Yiddish writer; lived in Russia during the First World War; returned to Poland in 1921; worked for the Yiddish daily press (*Haynt, Der Moment*, and others); lived in the Soviet Union during the Second World War; returned to Poland in 1946; lived in Paris from 1949.

26 *Haynt* was published in Warsaw from 1908 to 1939. It was considered the most important Yiddish-language daily newspaper in Poland, with a circulation of over 100,000 copies before the First World War and about 50,000 afterwards. The newspaper was Zionist-leaning from 1920, while under the leadership of the political editor Icchak Gruenbaum and the editor-in-chief Abraham Goldberg.

27 David Hoffstein (1889–1952), Yiddish and Hebrew writer from Ukraine; moved from the Soviet Union to Germany in 1924; moved to Palestine in 1925; lived in Kyiv from 1926; member of the Jewish Antifascist Committee in the Soviet Union from 1941; executed in 1952.

28 Alter Katsizne, also Kacyzne (1885–1941), Yiddish writer and photographer; lived in Warsaw from 1910; active in the literary scene; owned a photo studio; worked as a photographer for the New York daily newspaper *The Jewish Daily Forward* in Poland, for which he was sent on trips to Palestine and South Africa; fled to Lwów 1939; fled to Tarnopol in 1941; murdered by Ukrainian collaborators.

29 The *Vilner Emes* was a Soviet daily newspaper in Yiddish that appeared from August 1940 to June 1941. It was almost exclusively made up of translations of articles from *Pravda* and other central Soviet daily newspapers. The newspaper was edited by Dovid Umru (1910–1941), Yiddish writer from Lithuania; director of the Yiddish state theatre in Vilna, 1940–1941; murdered by the Gestapo in July 1941.

30 In the 1930s, the *Folksblat* served as the official publication of the Folkspartei, a political party influenced by Simon Dubnow's ideas. During the Soviet occupation it became a propaganda vehicle for communist officials.

31 This is a reference to the periodical *Oyfboy*, which was published in Riga, Oct. 1940 – June 1941.

32 Not included in the proofs sent to the State Department is a section on the self-censorship of Jewish newspapers in the Baltic states and the liquidation of Baltic relief organizations: see fn. 1.

The Yiddish Scientific Institute in Wilno, formerly a center of scholarly activity, is silent.[33] One of its leaders, Zalman Reizen,[34] has been under arrest since September 1939. Others, like Kalmanovitch,[35] were dismissed. The present head, Moses Lehrer, is a former clerk in the institution, and once vociferously cursed Stalin in public. He bought his immunity and advancement by spying on writers and other groups. Another renegade, Noa[c]h Prylutski,[36] received an appointment as professor of Yiddish at Wilno University. His anti-Zionist record was of help.

Since Communists consider Hebrew a counter-revolutionary language, all Hebrew schools, both secular and religious, were closed, and Yiddish-language schools opened in their place. At the same time, however, efforts were made to direct Jewish children into the Russian schools. Teachers were forbidden to urge Jewish parents to send their children to Yiddish schools. And when one of them criticized this order at a teachers conference, he was decried in the press as a Trotzkyite, a nationalist and a 'diversionist,' and ha[u]led before the N.K.V.D. Had it not been for the intervention of an important Communist, he might have found himself on the way to Siberia.

In Lithuania, in particular, Soviet national policy was conducted at the expense of the Poles and Jews. In Kaunas, instead of the six Hebrew *gymnasia* (secondary schools) which existed before the Soviet occupation, only three Yiddish institutions were opened. The number of Yiddish elementary schools is also less in comparison with the numerous Hebrew Tarbuth[37] and other schools which previously existed, and many Hebrew and Yiddish teachers are unemployed.

In Wilno, the results of one day's registration for school revealed that 60 % of the parents preferred Polish schools for their children, 30 % Yiddish, and only 3.5 % Lithuanian. Angered by these results, the authorities immediately discontinued the registration. The Commissariat of Education opened sixty-five elementary schools, of which thirty-six were Polish; twenty, Yiddish; three, Russian; one, White Russian; and five, Lithuanian. The teaching of Lithuanian, a language unknown in Wilno, was made obligatory in the first year of all schools, and the language of instruction in the trade schools and in the University of Wilno, where most of the students are Jews and Poles. Of course, no Jewish history is taught in the Yiddish schools.

There is little doubt that the Jewish religion, too, will meet the same fate it has suffered in the U.S.S.R. The *yeshivoth*[38] ceased to exist in Soviet occupied Poland immedi-

33 YIVO (Yidisher Visnshaftlekher Institut, 'Yiddish Scientific Institute') was founded in Vilna in 1925 for the purpose of researching Yiddish language, literature, and culture, as well as the history of Jews in Eastern Europe.

34 Zalman Reizen, also Zalmen Reyzen (1887–1941), Yiddish linguist; worked at YIVO in Vilna; edited the daily newspaper *Vilner Tog*; arrested by Soviet forces in 1939 after the Soviet invasion; subsequently shot.

35 Dr Zelig Kalmanovič (1885–1944), Yiddish linguist and translator; studied in Berlin and Königsberg; received his doctorate from St Petersburg University; lived in Lithuania and Latvia, 1922–1928, and thereafter in Vilna, where he co-founded and worked for YIVO; kept a diary while in the Vilna ghetto; deported to Estonia in Sept. 1943; murdered in Narva forced labour camp in 1944.

36 Noach Pryłucki (1882–1941), linguist and folklorist; member of the Sejm for the Jewish Folkspartei, 1922–1929; co-founder of the party and the Warsaw Yiddish-language daily newspaper *Der Moment*; collected folksongs and proverbs; professor of Yiddish in Vilna in 1939; murdered by the Gestapo in August 1941.

37 See Doc. 159, fn. 6.

ately upon the entry of the Red Army. Prayer is permitted in synagogues and houses of study, although their walls are decorated with pictures of Lenin, Stalin and Molotoff. While Lithuania was still independent, about 2,000 Polish *yeshivah* teachers and students, aided by the 'green railroad line,'[39] smuggled themselves across the Soviet and Nazi borders into Wilno,[40] where the Joint Distribution Committee provided them with shelters, food and clothing. After the Soviet occupation, students continued their studies, but as individuals in the houses of prayer. Rabbis, beadles, teachers of religion and cantors have lost their occupations. Kosher meat is accepted by the co-operatives, and therefore *shohetim* (ritual slaughterers) can still find employment.[41]

Together with the liquidation of Jewish communal institutions, there was begun a purge of Jewish leaders. The first victim was Professor Moses Schorr of Warsaw, a former Polish Senator and a leader in the struggle against anti-Semitism, who was arrested in Ostrog near the Russo-Polish frontier and later sentenced to fifteen years in prison. Dr. Joshua Gottlieb,[42] a former Sejm Deputy and a valiant fighter for Jewish rights in Poland, was given the right to live in Pinsk, his native town, after signing a pledge of loyalty to the Soviet regime, but was later arrested and exiled to Siberia. Another former Sejm Deputy, Dr. Emil Sommerstein,[43] was taken into custody in Lwow. His wife, who was deported to Siberia with her child, was reported by eyewitnesses to have committed suicide after her guards had brutally violated her.[44]

It is impossible to list all the known names of Jewish communal leaders who were arrested. Among them were the lawyer Gorfinkel, head of the Lithuanian Keren Hayesod;[45] Itzkowitz, the leader of Agudas Yisroel;[46] Wachstein, a prominent Zionist, who was arrested in Lemberg; Shmoish of Kolomyja, and Chmielnik of Bialystok, both active Poale Zion heads; and a number of Poale Zion municipal deputies. Also taken into custody were the Revisionist leaders Biegun and Krol, and the former Polish Consul in Honduras, Sheskin.

38 Plural of *yeshivah*; traditional Jewish school devoted chiefly to the study of rabbinic texts and the Talmud.

39 A reference to the so-called 'grüne Grenze', an unmarked border.

40 This is a reference to the organized illegal network that helped to smuggle individuals over the unmarked border to Lithuania; the Soviet government handed over the Vilna region to Lithuania in Oct. 1939.

41 The following four paragraphs, starting 'Together with the liquidation' and ending with 'escaped Soviet justice', did not appear in the proofs sent to the State Department: see fn. 1.

42 Dr Joshua Gottlieb (1882–1940 or 1941), journalist; studied law in Berlin; worked for the newspapers *Hajnt* and *Der Moment*; Sejm deputy, 1936–1938; acting chair of the Jewish Association in Warsaw; fled to Pińsk in Byelorussia in Sept. 1939.

43 Dr Emil Sommerstein (1883–1957), lawyer; defence counsel at the Polish constitutional court; Zionist Sejm deputy; founder of a credit union for small businesses in Lwów; imprisoned in the Soviet Union, 1939–1941; subsequently active in pro-Soviet committees; member of Poland's first communist government (known as the Lublin Committee) in 1944; chairman of the Central Committee of Jews in Poland; lived in the USA from 1946; worked for the World Jewish Congress.

44 Ida Sommerstein (née Durstenfeld) was deported to Kazakhstan in April 1940. Contrary to what the article states, she did not commit suicide, but was released in late 1941, after the Soviet Union granted amnesty to Polish citizens on 12 August 1941. Along with other Polish prisoner-of-war recruits to the Anders Army, in April 1942 she was evacuated to Iran, from where she managed to get to Jerusalem.

45 Organization founded in 1920 to fund the World Zionist Organization.

46 Agudas Yisroel was founded by Orthodox Jews in Kattowitz (Katowice) in 1912 as a conservative political party independent of the Zionist movement. As the largest religiously oriented Jewish party, it played a key role in representing the interests of a significant portion of the Jewish population during the Second Polish Republic.

Newspaper editors arrested include R. Rubinstein of the Kaunas *Yiddishe Shtimme*,[47] and Hescheless of the *Lwow Chwila*,[48] a Polish Jewish paper. The editors of *Nasz Przeglad*, a Warsaw Polish Jewish daily,[49] were deported to the Ural region, where they are doing forced labor in a sugar refinery. The editor of *Dos Wort*,[50] a Kaunas Labor Zionist paper, was released from prison only after he became dangerously ill. In addition, there were mass arrests and sometimes executions of Jewish merchants and industrialists, particularly in the Bialystok area. Their families were deported to Siberia.

The brunt of the persecutions, however, was borne by the leaders of the Bund (General Alliance of Jewish Workers), a member of the Second International, which had been continually hounded by the Polish Government. Victor Alter[51] was arrested in Kowle a few days after the entry of the Red Army while on his way to submit a declaration of loyalty to the Soviet Government. Henryk Ehrlich[52] was arrested in Brest Litovsk by a Warsaw carpenter, a Communist. Anna Rosenthal,[53] elderly leader of the Wilno Bund and once a prisoner in Tsarist jails, was accused of accepting bribes from industrialists to betray striking workers in spite of the fact that she had never been active in the trade unions. She is still in jail. Other Bund leaders arrested in Wilno were Zhelezniakov, Dr. Lipshitz, Leon Older, Perez Guterman and others. The leader of the Polish clothing workers, Heshel Himelfarb,[54] was arrested in Wilno in the winter of 1939, while the Bundist Shoel Goldman and the Polish Socialist Kapitulka[55] were later sentenced to death in Bialystok. Less than a handful of the trade union leaders escaped Soviet justice.

A heroic example of devotion to Jewish ideals is the story of the Halutzim, about 2,000 of whom smuggled their way into Lithuania from the Nazi and Soviet-occupied areas of Poland. Many of them crossed Poland by foot from places as far off as Posen in the west and the Rumanian border in the south, seeking to escape both the Nazis and

47 Ruvn Rubinstein, also Rubinshteyn (1891–1967), lawyer and journalist; studied in St Petersburg; secretary of the Central Committee of the Zionist Organization in Russia in 1917; interned in a Soviet prison in 1920; thereafter lived in Kaunas, where he edited the General Zionist newspaper *Yidishe Shtime*, 1925–1940; arrested by the Soviet authorities in 1940; granted amnesty in 1943; moved to Poland in 1945; lived in Munich, 1946–1948; thereafter lived in Israel.

48 Henryk Hescheles (1886–1942), journalist; studied in Vienna; member of Lwów City Council; editor-in-chief of the newspaper *Chwila*, published in Lwów from 1919 to 1939; murdered by the Germans in Lwów in 1942.

49 The newspaper *Nasz Przegląd* represented the views of General Zionists and was published from 1923 to 1939, with a circulation of about 20,000 copies.

50 The editor of *Dos Vort* was Berl Cohen.

51 Victor Alter (1890–1943), engineer; political leader of the Bund; served on Warsaw City Council; member of the Socialist International executive committee; arrested by the NKVD in Sept. 1939; released in Oct. 1941, as a result of the July 1941 Polish–Soviet treaty (Sikorski–Mayski Agreement) and the subsequent amnesty for Polish citizens; arrested again on 4 Dec. 1941; executed by a Soviet firing squad without a trial in Feb. 1943.

52 Henryk Ehrlich or Erlich (1882–1942); political leader of the Bund; editor of the Yiddish daily newspaper *Folks-Tsaytung*; member of Warsaw City Council; member of the Socialist International executive committee; arrested by the NKVD in Sept. 1939; released in August 1941, after the Polish–Soviet treaty of July 1941; arrested again in October 1941; took his own life in a Soviet prison.

53 Anna Rosenthal, née Heller (1872–1940), dentist; teacher with the Jewish school organization CISzO in Vilna; worked for YIVO; represented the Bund at the Socialist International Congress in 1931; arrested in Soviet-occupied Vilna in 1940; died in a Soviet prison.

54 Hershel Himelfarb (1889–1964), trade unionist.

55 Presumably Tomasz Kapitułka (1893–1939), communist politician.

the Communists. They were the first initiators of the systematic underground railroad, the 'green railroad line.'

In Poland, immediately after the Soviet occupation, the authorities permitted the Halutzim to maintain their collective training farms, but six weeks later the Hehalutz movement was liquidated. Its offices, assembly halls, and shelters were confiscated. The movement, however, continues to function underground. It publishes secret mimeographed bulletins and even sends special emissaries to re-establish contact with the old existing members in the interior of Russia.

In Lithuania, however, the Halutz training farms continued to exist as late as October 1940. Soviet commissars tried to convert their members to communism and to have them reorganize as *sovkhozes* (state farms).[56] The Halutzim refused.

In general, all labor Zionist groups are still secretly very active. The general Zionists, the orthodox, and Socialists (Bund) are politically more apathetic, but the Lithuanian Revisionists are reported to be maintaining a rather closely co-ordinated underground movement. It should be added that refugee communal leaders are permitted to leave the USSR. Some have gone to the United States; others to Palestine. However, only refugees may emigrate; Soviet citizens cannot leave the land of socialism.

DOC. 276

On 1 May 1941 the Polish underground newspaper *Wolność* polemicizes against an article in the *Krakauer Zeitung*[1]

The Jews, the Germans, and typhus

On 23 April 1941 the *Krakauer Zeitung* ran a propaganda article intended to combat typhus in Poland. This propaganda boils down to calling on Poland's population to avoid all contact with Jews, who – according to National Socialist theory – are carriers of typhus germs.[2] This nonsense is spread with the aid of suitable posters,[3] with talks in schools, on the radio, and in films.

The German nation has produced many learned scientists, outstanding physicians, and bacteriologists. Those Germans who have not succumbed to racial mania must be terribly ashamed that their official representatives are now spreading blatant lies for political purposes, without any opposition from their own medical community.

Typhus spreads where there is poverty, for where there is poverty, there are dirt and lice. But lice do not know what racism is and do not distinguish between Aryan and non-Aryan dirt. By resettling and systematically robbing the population, confiscating

56 Collective state farms worked by wage labourers.

1 *Wolność*, 1 May 1941, p. 5: AAN 1583/1165/1. This document has been translated from Polish. *Wolność* was an underground newspaper published by a group of Polish social democrats in Cracow.

2 See Robert Greiff's article on District Warsaw, 'Propaganda-Aktion gegen das Fleckfieber: Die lebensbedrohliche Fleckfieberinfektion wird von Läusen übertragen. Erreger sind Mikroorganismen, genannt Rickettsien' ['Propaganda campaign against typhus: The life-threatening typhus disease is transmitted by lice. The pathogens are microorganisms called rickettsias'], *Krakauer Zeitung*, 23 April 1941, p. 6.

3 See Doc. 258, fn. 2.

apartments, and cramming people into cramped spaces, the German authorities are fuelling the epidemic with great speed and efficiency.

Sealed ghettos in cities and towns – with their appalling living conditions and poverty, exacerbated by the ban on normal means of earning a living as well as the continuous persecution and theft – can easily become breeding grounds for all manner of diseases. The occupiers are solely to blame for this state of affairs.

In peacetime, there were only sporadic cases of typhus among both the Aryan and the Jewish populations in Poland. The deep divide between Jews and Poles has been created solely for political purposes.

The occupiers' aim in all the countries they have conquered is to weaken and break up societies – antisemitism is the only means that leads to that result.

DOC. 277
On 5 May 1941 the Jewish Social Self-Help executive committee reports on the appalling conditions in forced labour camps for Jews[1]

Letter from the JSS executive committee (no. 3779/41 WT/Sch.)[2] to the government of the GG, Interior Administration Department, Population and Welfare Division,[3] Cracow, dated 5 May 1941

Re: labour camps

As the head of the Interior Administration Department's Population and Welfare Division requested continuous updates about the situation in the labour camps for the Jewish population, we venture to inform you of the following:

In a letter from Warsaw dated 28 April 1941, no. 124, our deputy chairman J. Jaszuński informed us of the following:

> The members of the camp guard, whose task is to watch over the camp inmates, behave aggressively towards those who have been conscripted, causing the inmates to panic. In one case, the inspector from the German employment office reported three members of the camp guard to the authorities; in another case, which had taken place a few days earlier, the German gendarmerie disarmed and arrested members of the camp guard on the street. Reports from the camps about the maltreatment of camp inmates by the camp guards have now reached Warsaw and are causing understandable distress. Furthermore, reports have reached us from the camps that the food provided is not adequate to the working conditions. People carry out heavy work while standing in water and they receive 150–200 grams of bread a day, half a litre of watery soup, and black coffee twice a day. The appearance of those who are sent back from the camps because they are sick is horrifying. In addition, we have had reports of deaths. At Łęki, for instance, nine people died in the course of one day.[4] In view of these incidents, the Jewish population is becoming convinced that going to the labour camps is associated with dangers not merely to their health, but also to their lives. It is therefore obvious that this completely undermines the whole

1 YVA, O-21/15, fols. 46–47. This document has been translated from German.
2 The initials WT stand for Michał Weichert.
3 The head of the Population and Welfare Division was Dr Walther Föhl.

> approach taken by the Jewish Council. At the same time, the representatives of the Labour Section (i.e. of the Jewish Council), who are in touch directly with those who have been called up, explained to me that if tolerable conditions were to prevail in the labour camps and the food provided were adapted to the requirements of heavy physical labour, any demand for Jewish workers would be satisfied immediately and overwhelmingly by volunteers.

In a letter dated 29 April, no. 35, Dr Wielikowski also informed us that, in a meeting on 29 April 1941, the commissioner for the Jewish residential district, Mr Mohns, had ordered that a Jewish camp guard be formed immediately at Dąbrowice camp near Skierniewice,[5] where the complaints about the treatment of workers had originated, to ensure that further incidents are prevented. At the same time, he ordered the Jewish Council to second ten men from the Order Service there. This measure was to be seen as a trial, and if it were to prove successful, the Polish and Ukrainian camp guards would be replaced with Jewish ones at other camps as well.

In addition, Dr Wielikowski informed us by telephone on 4 May that 35 people who had been released after spending ten days at the Wilga camp near Garwolin[6] were questioned on the orders of the Oberinspekteur at the employment office in Warsaw, Mr Ziegler.[7] They unanimously stated that the workers performing heavy labour received 100–200 g of bread and one bowl of thin soup per day as food. They stated that deaths had occurred. The Ukrainian camp guards had mistreated the workers. A German commission visited the site and found that the food was insufficient, while the camp guard had set up a camp canteen where – according to these statements – 1 kg of bread had been sold for 12 zloty, and other foodstuffs at significantly inflated prices.

Dr Wielikowski requests that the Population and Welfare Division contact Oberinspekteur Ziegler from the employment office by telephone and obtain precise information from him.

By bringing the above communications from members of the JSS executive committee to your attention, we take the liberty of humbly requesting that the Population and Welfare Division arrange for sufficient food to be provided to Jews in the labour camps, and that the performance of policing duties be transferred to the Jewish Order Service instead of the Polish and Ukrainian camp guards.

4 A labour camp for Jews holding approximately 350 prisoners was located in the village of Łęki in the eastern part of District Warsaw from 1941 to 1943. In total, around 1,000 persons passed through the camp. The prisoners had to carry out river regulation work. Forty-eight of them died as a consequence of a typhoid fever epidemic.

5 Between 1941 and 1944 there was a labour camp for Jews in the village of Dąbrowice (District Warsaw). The approximately 300 inmates had to carry out dyke construction work.

6 A labour camp for Jews was located in the village of Wilga (District Warsaw) from April 1941 to 1944. The number of inmates, who had to carry out river regulation work, remained constant at approximately 900.

7 Friedrich Ziegler (1891–1978), civil servant; worked at Warsaw employment office as head of the section for the labour deployment of Jews from 1940, then at the employment office in the Warsaw ghetto (77 Leszno Street) with 300 to 400 Jewish staff; appointed Regierungsinspekteur in 1942; lived in Mannheim after the war.

DOC. 278

On 6 May 1941 an unidentified person reports on the expulsion of Jews from Drobin[1]

Handwritten report for the underground archive of the Warsaw ghetto (copy by Bluma Vaser[2]), dated 6 May 1941

Details of the experiences of the Jews in Drobin[3] from the outbreak of the war until their partial exodus from the shtetl.

Before the war, there were 300 families in Drobin. Later, during the war, another 400 refugee families from various towns joined them.

The shtetl was bombed on 2 September 1939. The bombs killed a number of Christians and damaged parts of the church and adjacent government buildings. On 5 September the German army entered Drobin. German soldiers attacked Jewish businesses and threw the merchandise outside, where it was immediately looted by Poles. A few days before Rosh Hashanah,[4] 300 Christians and 300 Jewish men were arrested and sent to a camp in Sierpc. They were released four days later. On Yom Kippur, German soldiers rounded up all the Jewish men aged 18 and above and tortured them cruelly for four whole hours. They beat them, made them do various exercises, cut their beards, etc. They pulled Jews wearing prayer shawls and holding Torah scrolls out of the synagogue and forced them to dance on top of the Torah scrolls in the middle of the street. The scrolls were then ripped apart. Soon after Yom Kippur,[5] the Jewish population was forced to pay several thousand złoty. Then the authorities confiscated Jewish shops, taking away their merchandise. Furniture, money, linen, clothing, bedding, and kitchenware were also taken from private residences. With permission from the authorities, Polish shops opened on the premises of the former Jewish businesses. The Polish population's attitude towards the Jews deteriorated sharply at that point, and the Poles approached the authorities with a plan to expel the Jews from the shtetl, following the example of other towns. In response, members of the Polish intelligentsia were sent to camps.[6] Soon after Yom Kippur, rumours spread that the synagogue and houses of study would be set on fire. Yet because they adjoined Polish houses, the Poles intervened, and the synagogue and houses of study were torn down [instead]. The old cemetery was also ploughed under and converted into a garden. The Polish people had a hand in this, too. Even before the war, they had demanded that a path be cut through the cemetery. At the same time, a concentration camp was created at the fire station, where Jews and Christians were con-

1 AŻIH, Ring I/725 (801). This document has been translated from Yiddish.

2 Bluma Vaser (1912–1990); contributed to the underground archive of the Warsaw ghetto; Hersh Vaser's wife: see Doc. 234, fn. 2.

3 In the interwar period Drobin was part of the county of Płock in the voivodeship of Warsaw. Following the Nazi occupation, the area was annexed and incorporated into East Prussia as Regierungsbezirk Zichenau (Ciechanów). On the eve of the Second World War, 1,300 Jews lived in Drobin.

4 Meaning prior to 14 Sept. 1939.

5 Yom Kippur fell on 23 Sept. 1939.

6 During the so-called Intelligenzaktion (Operation Intelligentsia) between autumn 1939 and early 1940, local Polish leaders and members of the intelligentsia were arrested and shot dead, either individually or in groups.

fined for various offences, such as keeping merchandise in private residences, engaging in trade (for Jews), etc. Since trade was prohibited and punishable by death, Jews were greatly cheated by their Christian business partners. By order of the [German] authorities, a Jewish Council was established in Drobin, which consisted of new representatives (the old Community leaders had refused to be part of the Jewish Council). The Jewish Council set up a soup kitchen and imposed a levy on the population for this purpose. It also received financial support from the Joint [JDC], in addition to undergarments and clothing. At the behest of the authorities, the Jewish Council provided a few hundred workers every day (to build roads, to cut stone, etc.). Women and children over the age of seven were also sent to work in the fields. The authorities paid 1 mark and 40 pfennigs per day for work, from which the Jewish Council deducted 40 pfennigs for its institutions. Meanwhile Jews were being snatched off the streets – even members of the Jewish Council – and sent to a neighbouring labour camp, where they worked for seven weeks. There were also cases of Gestapo officials from towns in the area attacking and torturing the Jewish population. The members [of the Jewish Council] intervened, and these assaults stopped. In the month of July, many Jews living in the business district were evicted from their homes, which were then taken over by ethnic Germans and Poles. Four months later these Poles were also evicted. On 7 March the Jewish Council received an order to draw up a list of 50 per cent of the Jewish inhabitants, who were to be deported from the town. The sick, the elderly, and the poor were sent to Działdowo,[7] where they were badly tortured over the course of eight days (the men). From there they were sent to Piątków,[8] and the next morning the Jews were driven out of town, to where the poorest strata of the Polish population live. There they moved into small, cramped quarters, four to five families per dwelling, whereas the Christians moved into the Jewish homes. Cases of Poles looting Jewish homes in those days have come to light.

7 A transit camp for Polish prisoners of war and civilian detainees was established in Działdowo (Soldau) in late Sept. 1939; it was used as a transit camp for deportees from Regierungsbezirk Zichenau from Feb. to May 1940; in May and June 1940 the SS murdered more than 2,000 disabled people in gas vans at this camp.

8 The correct location is Piotrków Trybunalski, often simply referred to as Piotrków.

DOC. 279
On 11 May 1941 the Zionist activist Rywka Glanc writes to Natan Szwalb from the training camp in Hrubieszów[1]

Handwritten letter from Rywka Glanc,[2] Hrubieszów, to Natan Szwalb,[3] Geneva, dated 11 May 1941[4]

Dear Natan,

I've finally received your long-awaited letter, and it turns out that my previous letters from Lublin never reached you. Not much is happening here. Our family Galilu[5] is doing well and has a wonderful way of raising their wonderful little son Itonka,[6] who makes us very happy. He brightens up our lives in these hard times. We have your parcels, which we occasionally receive, to thank for this, as they enable us to feed and raise him appropriately.[7] I often take him along to Aunt Bikusz,[8] who is very happy to see us. We remind her of former times, when we could all be together. How I miss those days!

In the coming days I'm going with the Szloszim[9] family to a farm near Hrubieszów for agricultural work. Although I don't expect adequate food there, this is the only work opportunity available right now.

You ask why the Community doesn't help us. It's difficult to explain the reasons behind their stance towards us. Perhaps you could write to them and exert your influence on that clique, as all my efforts have been in vain. I only managed to obtain work for our entire family by forcing it out of them.

We are worried about Cyla[10] and her family in Warsaw. It's difficult for her to feed such a large family[11] under the current circumstances. Many of them have left for Czer-

1 The Pinhas Lavon Institute for Labour Movement Research, Israel, Nathan Schwalb's collection, III–37A-1–18, fol. 3r–v. This document has been translated from Polish. Published in Hebrew translation in Ruth Zariz (ed.), *Mikhteve halutsim mi-Polin ha-kevushah, 1940–1944* (Ramat Ef'al: Bet lohame ha-getaot, 1994), pp. 81–82.

2 Rywka Glanc, also Rivka Glanz (1915–1943); activist in the Hehalutz youth movement; member of the Dror youth movement; lived in Lublin and the surrounding area in 1941; in Warsaw in 1942; sent to Częstochowa (Tschenstochau), where she died as a fighter in the Jewish Combat Organization (ŻOB).

3 Natan Szwalb, also Nathan Schwalb (1908–2004), trade unionist; member of Zionist youth movements; studied law in Lwów; emigrated to Palestine in 1929; worked for Hehalutz in Prague and Vienna, 1938–1939; subsequently helped to establish the global headquarters of Hehalutz in Geneva, where he undertook aid and rescue efforts together with the American Jewish Joint Distribution Committee (JDC) and the Swiss Red Cross; returned to Palestine in 1945; worked for the Histadrut trade union from 1946.

4 Bracha Kamm's address is given as that of the sender; Rywka Glanc was staying with her at the time. Kamm (b. 1923 or 1924) was an activist in the Dror youth movement in Hrubieszów; attended training courses in Warsaw in 1941; murdered during the German occupation.

5 The author uses code names: here the reference to 'galil' (Hebrew for 'district') probably means 'in the district'.

6 'Iton' (Hebrew): 'newspaper'; with the Slavic diminutive '-ka': 'small newspaper'.

7 The parcels enabled work on the underground newspaper.

8 Hebrew for 'visit'.

9 Hebrew in the original: 'thirty'. This means she travelled with thirty activists.

10 Probably Cywia Lubetkin, who also went by the Polish first name Celina. Cyla is a shortened form.

11 The author is referring to her comrades from the youth movement in Warsaw.

niaków near Warsaw,[12] others for Sokołów,[13] also for work, and the rest have stayed with Cyla in Warsaw. She's complained that she hasn't heard from you in a long time.

We've received the parcels you've sent.

We don't have many opportunities to visit Cegielnik, as the journey is expensive and we can't afford it now. Only a few of our family members have accepted his hospitality.[14]

I often meet with Chedwa. I've met Gordon's[15] family in Lublin.

What's new with Bendery?[16] Write to us frequently and in detail about him, as we all miss him.

It would really help our family if you could try to send us parcels containing clothes, especially now that we are working and everything is completely worn out.

Please, Natan, write to us often. You can't imagine how happy your letters make us.

Shalom

DOC. 280

On 15 May 1941 an employee at the Reich Ministry of Finance advocates relieving the Main Trustee Office East of its responsibility for making welfare payments to Jews[1]

Letter from the Reich Ministry of Finance, Berlin, Augustin Section (LG 4080–12 I A), signed Augustin,[2] to the Reich Minister of the Interior,[3] Berlin, dated 15 May 1941 (copy)

Re: welfare payments to Poles and Jews in the annexed eastern territories

The Main Trustee Office East has hitherto made welfare payments to Poles and Jews whose real estate has been confiscated and who are in need. It no longer intends to do

12 There was an estate in the Czerniaków suburb of Warsaw where Jewish youth from the Warsaw ghetto did agricultural work.

13 There were several estates near Sokołów where seasonal work was done as part of Zionist agricultural training.

14 Cegielnik probably stands for contacts in Slovakia. Szlomo Cegielnik (1916?–1942); head of the Dror youth movement in Białystok at the beginning of the war; in Warsaw from spring 1940; on 15 Nov. 1940 sent to Slovakia to organize escape routes; arrested by the Slovak police in spring 1942 and deported to the General Government; murdered in Belzec extermination camp.

15 This is probably a reference to the Gordonia youth movement.

16 This is probably a code name for Palestine.

1 BArch, R 2/56140, fol. 127. This document has been translated from German.

2 Karl Augustin (1877–1966), public administrator; member of the German People's Party (DVP); mayor of Berlin-Charlottenburg, 1924–1936; subsequently held leading functions in the Reich Ministry of Finance; promoted to Ministerialdirigent in 1941; as head of Section 17 dealt with matters related to revenue sharing between municipalities; interned in 1945; classified as 'exonerated' (*entlastet*) during denazification proceedings in Wiesbaden in 1946; subsequently worked in the Ministry of Finance of the West German state of Hesse; awarded the Order of Merit of the Federal Republic of Germany in 1952.

3 Dr Wilhelm Frick (1877–1946), lawyer; head of the Political Police, 1919–1921; head of the Munich Criminal Police in 1923; took part in the Beer Hall Putsch in Nov. 1923; subsequently detained, dismissed from the police service, and reinstated in late 1924; joined the NSDAP in 1925; state minister of the interior and national education in Thuringia, 1930–1931; Reich Minister of the Interior, 1933–1943; Reich Protector of Bohemia and Moravia, 1943–1945; sentenced to death at the Nuremberg Trials and executed in 1946.

this in future (see the letter from the Main Trustee Office East of 7 April 1941, I 5 A 22 333).[4]

I concur with the comments made by the Main Trustee Office East. The benefit payments to Poles in need must be taken from the financial allocations intended for this purpose. The Jews must fund the welfare payments to their racial comrades in need themselves (see below).

The Main Trustee Office East's task is to administer and renovate confiscated real estate so that it can be taken over by Germans. Having to make these welfare payments is hindering it in the fulfilment of its task.

I request that you approve the revocation of the directive issued by the Main Trustee Office East on 4 May 1940.[5]

In the Warthegau, 65 per cent of the pay for Jewish employees is deducted and paid into reconstruction accounts held by the NSDAP and the Landräte (see my letter of 6 February 1941, LG 4006–254 I A[6]). I request consideration of whether these sums could be used to support impoverished Jews while this matter is being addressed. Please reply promptly to my letter of 6 February 1941, mentioned above.[7]

DOC. 281

On 17 and 22 May 1941 the head of the public health section of the German ghetto administration in Lodz (Łódź) demands that the inhabitants dispose of their sewage within the ghetto boundaries[1]

Report by Section Head Misdorf (City Administration 500/1/4), Lodz, dated 17 and 22 May 1941

We have thoroughly inspected the area mentioned by Police Station 6 G.[2] The complaints are only too justified. Sewage of various kinds comes through concrete-lined sewers from the centre of the ghetto and flows into an open stream with regulated banks

4 On 7 April 1941 the Main Trustee Office East recommended that responsibility for welfare for the Jewish population be transferred to the Jewish communities; the decision to this effect by the Reich Ministry of Finance was adopted on 8 Nov. 1941: BArch, R 2/56140, fols. 125 and 134.

5 According to a decision adopted by the Main Trustee Office East (Berlin) on 4 May 1940, welfare payments to Poles and Jews whose assets had been confiscated could only be approved if their assets covered the costs for such payments. From that point on, welfare for Poles and Jews could be granted up to the full rate of public welfare: *Mitteilungsblatt der Haupttreuhandstelle Ost*, no. 6, 15 Oct. 1940, pp. 215–216.

6 Not in the file. In Sept. 1940 Reichsstatthalter Greiser decreed that 65 per cent of the hourly pay for Jewish forced labourers agreed with third-party companies was to be deducted and transferred to a special account with Deutsche Bank in Posen under the name 'The Gauleiter, NSDAP Reconstruction Account'. If the forced labourers were ghetto inmates, the same proportion was to be deducted and paid to the Landrat in charge; 35 per cent was to be credited to the Jewish forced labourers and their relatives.

7 The Reich Ministry of the Interior only conceded and agreed to this step in the spring of 1942, and the Main Trustee Office East stopped making benefit payments on 1 April 1942: APŁ, 176/649, fols. 121–122.

1 APŁ, 221/31866a, fols. 43–45. Copy in USHMM, RG 05 008M, reel 6. This document has been translated from German.

at the corner of Telegrafenstraße and Schlüsselbundstraße. While this sewage may not smell pleasant, this in itself is probably no reason for greater concern thus far. At the corner in question, however, the Jew lets the contents of his septic cart flow into this sewage through an improvised contraption (photographs will be taken), resulting in an utterly unbelievable stench. The ratio of waste water from the concrete pipes to the sewage from the septic cart is approximately 5:1. Just under a kilometre downstream from this point, the ditch passes onto non-Jewish territory, flows along the boundary between the two territories for a while, creates a nuisance for the guards there, and flows yet further down into the Lutka.[3] The Lutka joins with the Balutka approximately 1 km further downstream, and then flows in a westerly direction to Konstantinow and Lutomiersk. However, it is so contaminated with sewage and so polluted that there is absolutely no sign of any kind of self-purification, for example on Mörserstraße (the last stop on Line 4). No purification can be seen until Lutomiersk, i.e. approximately 16 km downstream. Therefore it must be expected that the stream flows through non-Jewish territory for at least quite a few kilometres, and that it not only carries the wholesome components of completely untreated Jewish sewage, but also carries much more dangerous pathogens that cause intestinal diseases, such as typhoid fever and dysentery. It is only when water's self-purification process has dropped below a certain minimum level of putrefaction that microorganisms in the water can kill off pathogens such as typhoid fever and dysentery. Then they do it at quite a rapid rate. However, the water that passes from the ghetto into non-Jewish territory is raw, only very slightly diluted sewage.

On no account can these conditions be tolerated any longer. If we do so, we are likely to have many times the number of people contracting dysentery etc. in non-Jewish territory as we did last year. Adding chlorinated lime or the like is completely out of the question. This can only be done by means of a fluid that consists mostly of water, and even then the quantities are huge, even for heavily diluted sewage. But the Jew does have some nice pieces of open land within the ghetto territory. In addition to other places, there is a large area with gravel pits and ponds located on a site that is roughly enclosed by M-Straße, Rüdigerstraße, König-Marke-Straße, and Bleigasse. There used to be a brickworks there, and several deep excavations of various sizes are still there today. However, if the Jew were to deploy a great many workers, without special equipment or particular help from us, he could excavate pits of approximately 100 m in length, just under 50 m in width, and 6–8 m in depth (the depth would depend on the level of the groundwater). This ditch could then be covered with a lot of wood, which can still be found in the ghetto despite everything – I am thinking of the many garden fences and various other superfluous wooden structures in the ghetto. The wood would then have to be treated with carbolineum, so that we do not end up with a general plague of flies. The Jew would then deposit his sewage at a more or less precisely specified point until one ditch was completely filled, although this would take several months.

There are of course reservations about this, as there are about everything. Firstly, the Jew will perform the excavation and other work only very reluctantly. It would be a

2 A police officer at Police Station 6 (G) [G for ghetto] had written to Urban Police Section Command North on 5 May 1941 that sentries who kept watch at an open sewer were being exposed to potentially harmful fumes, and he asked for immediate assistance: APŁ, 221/31866a, fol. 42.

3 Correctly: the Łódka, a river that flows through Łódź.

matter for the ghetto administration to force him to work a little quicker. Secondly, he will claim he has no wood. But that is not true. At the most, a few single, solid tree trunks and thick planks would have to be delivered to him. Thirdly, he probably will not have any carbolineum. We would certainly have to supply him with it. But he could also treat the wood with a thick coating of chlorinated lime. Furthermore, the area mentioned is unfortunately quite close to the eastern boundary of the ghetto. However, since it is probably only Poles who live to the east of this, and they are also very scattered, they can see for themselves how to deal with it. They would certainly have to be forbidden from using any unboiled water, because the groundwater would be in quite a nasty hygienic condition within a radius of at least 300 m, even though it would probably not be contaminated with germs. Fourthly, the Jew with his sewage cart might not be able to get from his so-called District II across Hohensteinerstraße into the eastern part of his ghetto. This would mean he would simply have to install a smaller ditch in his western District II.

Most of all, time is of the essence in this matter.

Lodz, 22 May 1941

Supplement to the report dated 17 May 1941

In the meantime, the options for Jews to dispose of their sewage have been further investigated. The Jews now want to build biological sewage works in the three areas of the ghetto that are separated from one another, and they are hoping to be finished with these structures in six weeks. They then want to release the discharge from the sewage works into the Balutka, and at one point into the Ludka as well. Biological sewage works are of course in themselves a significantly better solution than simple cesspits. However, they may only be put into operation once our investigation (the discharge from the works will be tested for putrefaction etc.) has concluded that these inflows are acceptable for the Ludka and the Balutka. Until then *the Jews will absolutely have to* excavate the proposed cesspits and put them into operation, *and do so immediately.* However, I request that the gasworks be instructed to supply the Jews with approximately 150 to 300 litres of a cheap raw tar product (distillate) every day, which can be spread thinly and rapidly over an aqueous surface, and which seals it hermetically while giving off the most penetrating odour possible, and for the Jews to spread this distillate over their cesspit daily to prevent a plague of flies.

DOC. 282

Krakauer Zeitung, 18 May 1941: an article by Bruno Hans Hirche argues for ghettoization in the General Government and points to historical parallels[1]

A life of their own within walls. Recent observations in the Warsaw Jewish residential district. Alongside the grimy kaftan, the respectable paletot. The Cracow Jewish residential district has now been completed as well.

1 *Krakauer Zeitung*, 18/19 May 1941, pp. 5–6. This document has been translated from German.

From our own correspondent
B. H. H.[2] *Warsaw*, 18 May
Heavens, what a teeming throng! It pushes and shoves, halts, jolts, begins to move again, floods up and down the streets, and extends as an endless ribbon along the grey walls of the buildings. It does not matter what time of day it is. Whether you come early in the morning, at midday, or in the evening, the same picture of swirling, seething animation always presents itself. This is Warsaw's Jewish residential district, which, in its compactness, currently conveys what is probably the most complete picture of the Jewish way of life, apart from the Lublin ghetto.

We have already highlighted on various occasions that loafing is the most notable characteristic among the Jews. That uncleanliness, dirt, and lice form the most characteristic elements in which they live is also something we have involuntarily had to witness often enough. And the many experiences in which we saw that haggling and black marketeering are their favourite occupations were one reason for the necessary establishment of the segregated living areas. These traits of griminess, sloth, and illegal wheeling and dealing are extremely familiar to us. But the rather more sophisticated manifestation of life in the Warsaw Jewish residential district has, one might say, only recently been revealed to us. Here, a respectable paletot over a clean suit cut in the latest style, or a stylish suit jacket and colourfully fluttering little dress, above which a jaunty little hat bobs up and down on a raven-black head: all this appears alongside the dirty kaftan – like day and night side by side. Among the gaunt, yellowish faces with unkempt, greasy beards suddenly appear powdered, bright red painted half-hatched beauties, though of course whether ostentatious, thickly applied lipstick etc. really constitutes beauty is open to debate. But along with the dirty, moist, glistening haggler's hand with its fingernails caked in dirt, the fleshy, well-nourished, better-groomed little hand of a more elegant being gesticulates here in similar agitation, its carefully varnished nails glittering in the sunshine.

Yes, there is even a hotel here just for their own race, with a cosmopolitan bar and a spacious cabaret that is filled evening after evening with glittering, fashionable life.

This observation once again confirms the generosity of the German administration, which allows the Jews to live a life unique to their kind, within their own residential area. And they enjoy it to the utmost. Now that it is no longer the German and the Pole who fall victim to their innate swindling, their fellow Jews will just have to do. Business is business! The main thing is the money in their coffers! It does not bother their hypocritical minds that it is their own flesh and blood they are now cheating, and that they are now ruining some of their own relatives! Even within their own confines, their rapacity knows *no* bounds. If one of their own is writhing in pain on the street, it leaves the Jews completely cold. No one attends to him; let him gasp his final breath swiftly. They assiduously avoid this bundle of distress. The streaming flood then surges past to the left and the right, as if around an island. This crowd is unscrupulous. Not a trace of social feeling. This becomes only too evident in their own households.

2 Bruno Hans Hirche (b. 1911), journalist; joined the NSDAP in 1932; left the SS in 1935; worked in Weimar as a local news reporter and press photographer for *Der Nationalsozialist*, the official Party paper for Gau Thuringia in the 1930s; chief reporter for the *Krakauer Zeitung* from Nov. 1939; left Cracow in Nov. 1942; author of *Erlebtes Generalgouvernement* (Cracow: Buchverlag Deutscher Osten, 1941).

And how much more unscrupulously did they exploit the Poles, and above all the Germans of this region! Permit us to let a Pole himself testify. In a polemic written in 1618, the Cracow astronomer Sebastian Miczynski[3] castigates the Jews as parasites in another's land and as thieves of others' property (published by Burgverlag Krakau GmbH, the publishing house of the Institute for German Eastern Research, in an edition[4] edited and translated by J. Sommerfeldt[5]). Using the example of the clothiers, he perceptively uncovers Jewish machinations. This example is particularly close to our hearts at the moment, because we only recently spent time with the Governor General, Dr *Frank*, meeting the Tomaszów German clothiers, and were able to see for ourselves their industriousness and diligence through the generations and the centuries. They told us how they had also been exploited by the Jews in the most ruthless fashion. Miczynski wrote about this back in 1618:

> This is how the disgraceful Jews have taken the traders' and merchants' businesses from the towns and destroyed the artisan trades, particularly the more highly developed ones, on which the cities' livelihoods overwhelmingly depend. I will discuss the clothiers briefly here. They face great obstacles across their whole industry due to the insolent Jews, and for the following reasons, namely: 1. The Jews import various kinds of cloth, e.g. Dutch, English, Spanish, and others from overseas, both by the piece and by the roll, contrary to all treaties concluded with the cities, and contrary to the privileges of the kings. They do not display the cloth for sale in the city, but export it to Hungary, Moravia, and Silesia. 2. They have also bought up the Moravian cloth, which is the best in general, and, even worse, they have the Silesian cloth, which is not as good and is ten cubits shorter than the Moravian, reworked 'in the Moravian style', and sell it as Moravian cloth. In this way they defraud the citizens of Poland and contravene holy King Stefan's edict (1582).[6] 3. They carry the cloth around the market in lengths of two, three, or four cubits. If this is then seen by one of the nobility or someone who needs the cloth, he buys it from the Jew straight away; and if he needs more, they take him to the other Jewish shops. 4. They also carry finished garments around in the marketplace and sell them in the arcades. They manufacture these garments themselves with the help of journeymen tailors, whom they employ to do this. 5. They keep a keen lookout, and if a nobleman, or a stranger, or a shopkeeper from a small town comes to Cracow to buy cloth, or if they meet him outside the city or at the city gate and learn that he needs cloth, they entice him to the Jewish cloth shops by promising him a good, honest purchase. Everyone can see from this that the Jews do a great deal of harm to clothiers everywhere, but particularly in Cracow.[7]

3 In 1618 Sebastian Miczyński, a professor at Jagiellonian University in Cracow, published the anti-Jewish pamphlet *Zwierciadło Korony Polskej* ('The mirror of the Polish crown'), which was partly responsible for sparking anti-Jewish riots in Cracow. The Germans used quotations from this text on anti-Jewish propaganda posters: YVA, M-54/56.

4 Josef Sommerfeldt (ed. and trans.), *Hie Bürger hie Jude: Eine Krakauer Kampfschrift aus dem Jahre 1618* (Cracow: Bürgerverlag Krakau, 1941). The German title translates as 'The citizen here, the Jew there: A Cracow polemic from the year 1618.'

5 Dr Josef Sommerfeldt (1914–1992), historian; joined the SA in 1933 and the NSDAP in 1937; employed in the Legislation Department of the General Government in 1939; worked at the Institute for German Eastern Research in the Race and Nationality Research Section as head of the Jewish Research Section; worked for the Johann Gottfried Herder Research Council from 1950; journalist in the Lower Bavarian town of Straubing from 1953.

6 Stefan Batory (1533–1586), king of Poland from 1576.

Well, steps have now been taken to establish a Jewish residential district in Cracow as well. Walls are being put up around it. Police posts control the traffic that passes through. In the chapter entitled 'The Jews in Cracow' in the compilation from the aforementioned polemic, J. Sommerfeldt, who is in charge of Jewish research at the Institute for German Eastern Research, has proven that, apart from Warsaw, it was Cracow above all that suffered most severely from the Jewish culture of exploitation, even at that time.

> The Jews' economic expansion had a particularly devastating effect on the German Hanseatic City of Cracow. This is why Cracow was the first city in Poland to take up the fight against the Polish Jews with determination towards the end of the 15th century. In 1485 a treaty was concluded between the citizens of Cracow and the Jewish community in which the Jews were only allowed to trade in unredeemed pawned items, as well as peddling clothes and collars which were made by Jews. This agreement shook the foundations of Polish Jewry's livelihoods and was bound to provoke the most intense resistance among them, especially as Polish Jewry was being replenished and reinforced at this time by a constant influx of the shrewdest and most experienced businesspeople from Western Europe. In Cracow, however, the citizens appear to have had some initial success in having their demands accepted. In 1495 the Cracow Jews were driven out to Kasimir,[8] which was still an independent town at the time. But in 1521 the citizens of Cracow had to complain to the king that the Jews were not abiding by the treaty of 1485. Another complaint followed in 1533. In the 1530s and 1540s, the Cracow patriciate, the voivode, and the bishop waged joint campaigns against the Jews because they had set up warehouses in Cracow in spite of the agreements. Even the Synod at Piotrków Trybunalski demanded in 1542 that the number of Jews be reduced and the number of Jewish warehouses in Cracow be cut to six.
>
> However, the citizens' resistance to the Jews was futile. Although the citizens of Cracow had obtained an edict from the king in 1566, according to which Jews were to be forbidden to acquire new premises, in 1576 Stefan Batory gave the Jews in Cracow the right to rent shops and storerooms in the city without hindrance and to visit the market with their goods. He also treated them the same as Christians in terms of taxes. With this, the hundred-year struggle for the city of Cracow's economy was decided in favour of the Jews. The privileges of 1609, 1615, and 1619 only confirmed the victory of Cracow's Jewry.
>
> Where now are the citizens who once magnificently entertained and lavished gifts upon Emperor Charles, the kings Casimir the Great of Poland, Louis of Hungary, and Peter of Cyprus, and the princes Otto of Bavaria, Siemowit of Masovia, Boleslaus of Świdnica, Ladislaus of Opole, and Boguslaus of Szczecin? Where are the citizens who made large sums of money available to their lords in times of need? Where are those who built the churches, founded the monasteries and the hospitals, and supported the monks? All of your goods, my Cracow, and your great riches have passed via villainous cunning into the hands of the Jews. The wretched remainder of the merchants have moved to Nuremberg, to Danzig, and to various other cities. One finds hardly any buildings in Cracow, if any at all, that are free of 'repurchase'.[9]

7 This slightly abridged excerpt is taken from Sommerfeldt (ed. and trans.), *Hie Bürger hie Jude*, pp. 41–42.

8 Correctly: Kazimierz, the Jewish settlement located outside Cracow's walls that was later incorporated into the city.

9 Sale for repurchase: a form of purchase agreement that granted the seller the right to buy back the goods sold.

Complete desolation, may God preserve you, must therefore be expected in Cracow shortly.

There is no cause for this other than the Jews. They have deprived Cracow of its status as the greatest warehouse of the state and are now selling all kinds of goods to other cities. They trade in all types of goods by buying them up on the roads and at the customs offices, and in doing so will not abide by the treaties they have concluded with the city, not even the privileges granted to this city by the holy Polish kings in days gone by. In addition, they drive up prices by exporting all kinds of goods and articles to Hungary, Moravia, Silesia, and elsewhere. They trade in spices, in grains of all kinds, in honey, sugar, milk, and whatever else is necessary for sustenance. In a word: there is nothing too expensive and nothing too cheap for them to trade in this city (as in others).

And it is not enough for them to sit in the shops and conduct trade; some of them go around the market as well as the houses and courtyards of Kasimir, Kleparz, Garbarz, Biskupie, and Zwierzyniec,[10] carrying goods around and selling them. When people need something else, they entice them into the Jewish shops by promising them good, cheap merchandise.

Consequently, a poor shop-owner can neither buy nor sell anything of quality because of these damned Jews. I would like to give some details of this. One of the Jews living in Cracow goes by the name of Bocian. Apart from his various other businesses, and apart from his transport enterprise to Danzig, he also has seven shops here and agents almost everywhere in Poland. He has turnover of 300,000–400,000 zloty, for there is no article that he does not buy or sell. And then there is a Jew called Moses who imports various goods from Frankfurt, Leipzig, and the Netherlands. The citizens of Cracow used to get goods from these places under better conditions than they do now from this scoundrel. Then there are the two Israels, two brothers. They travel to Lemberg, where various goods come from Turkey, in particular approx. 2,000 Persian lynx. They seized almost all the furs there. Swietlik Moses has almost all the sable furs in his hands. He sends his agents to the fairs in Moravia, Vienna, Hungary, and Prague. They buy up goods and sell them to the careworn merchants in Poland for twice the price. Faivel cheated the Danzig and Elbingen retailers, and earned about 300,000 zloty by doing so. He too buys up nearly all types of goods.

In this way these stinking rascals, along with yet others whom I have not mentioned here, have taken all the trade and every opportunity to buy goods away from Cracow's citizens, and made the city poor.

But it is not enough for these villainous Jews to get their hands on all the tenancies, all business, all trade, all craft products and goods, and therefore on all the staples; they also harm the Christians by buying up food. There is a decree (1588) issued by our then King Sigismund III that the Jews must not buy up goods and food by intercepting these goods outside the cities. This, however, like other provisions, is not being implemented due to the citizens' negligence. For the Jews buy up the very best goods and food not only in the cities, particularly at the market in Cracow, but even venture outside the gates of the cities for this purpose. There the Jews acquire the very best animals, such as ducks, geese, chickens, grouse, calves, pike, carp, and so forth. There they seize the carts with the best vegetables, and the Christians are left to fight over what falls out of the Jews' beards. They have to gather the scraps the Jews leave like crumbs from their lords' tables. If someone wanted to say something to a Jew or scare

10 Villages near Cracow at the time, which are today part of the city.

him off from buying something now, then that would be a terrible injustice, and the Jew would soon find an opportunity to take revenge for it.[11]

Things are different now, of course. What the Polish state was not capable of accomplishing over many decades, the energetic German administration has achieved within the short period of a year: keeping a close eye on the doings of the Jewish clique and, where necessary, rapping their knuckles as well. The Jewish residential districts are one step on the way to a clean break from Israelite filth and profiteering. They put back in its place a people which, in its innate impertinence, has attempted to ignore that place, as well as the whole world's legal, commercial, and social conventions, over and over again. This can no longer be easily done in the same way over the high walls of the Jewish residential districts in the General Government, and the guards of a hard but just order now stand at their brick gateways.

DOC. 283
On 21 May 1941 the Education Department in District Radom bans vocational courses for Jews[1]

Letter from the head of District Radom's Science and Education Department (Nr. 9/B/IV 215/9) to the Interior Administration Department, Population and Welfare Division,[2] Radom District Governor's office, dated 21 May 1941

Re: introduction of vocational courses for Jews – file ref. I D 2 - D - 6 - 41
The introduction of vocational courses for Jews in Kreis Tomaschow[3] is not desirable. The German administration has to prepare young Polish people for economic life in the General Government and the Greater German Reich. In accordance with our National Socialist world view, the Jewish population must be removed from the economic life of Germans. Although Jews are still needed as craftsmen in our General Government at the moment, this is a transitional phenomenon. For the future, we Germans must liberate ourselves from Jewish craftsmen. This is why the introduction of short vocational courses for Jews must be prohibited, as it will never be possible for a Jew to be 'assigned to productive labour deployment'.

The Jews will not receive any licence from the Science and Education Department to hold such vocational courses.[4]

11 This excerpt is taken from Sommerfeldt (ed. and trans.), *Hie Bürger hie Jude*, pp. 32–36.

1 APR, 209/1008, fol. 6. Published in Georg Hansen (ed.), *Schulpolitik als Volkstumspolitik: Quellen zur Schulpolitik der Besatzer in Polen 1939–1945* (Münster: Waxmann, 1994), p. 307. This document has been translated from German.

2 The Population and Welfare Division for District Radom was headed by Dr Hans Gutt (1884–1967), lawyer; attended Munich University; legal officer of the German-Saxon People's Council in Transylvania; moved to Germany in 1936; Regierungsrat in Radom from 1940; lived in Munich after the war.

3 Tomaszów Mazowiecki.

4 The letter is followed by two handwritten notes: 'File' and 'One enclosure' (not in the file), and the initials 'Jd'.

DOC. 284

On 21 May 1941 a tax inspector in Busko comments on rising food prices[1]

Letter (marked 'personal') from the Regierungsrat in Busko-Zdroj, Dr Geigenmüller,[2] to the head of the Finance Department for the GG government in Cracow, Spindler, dated 21 May 1941

Re: pricing, food supply, spreading rumours, etc.

Over the last eight to ten days, prices on the so-called black market for food and other items have risen noticeably, some of them by far more than 100 per cent.

	8–10 days ago	Now
1 kg flour	2–3 zloty	10–11 zloty
1 quintal[3] potatoes	25–30 zloty	-200 zloty
1 kg haricot beans	3 zloty	7 zloty
1 kg bacon	10–12 zloty	16–17 zloty
1 kg butter	13–15 zloty	24–25 zloty
1 quintal wheat	250–400 zloty	1,000–1,200 zloty
1 quintal rye	150–200 zloty	700 zloty
2 kg bread	4 zloty	10 or more zloty
1 kg meat		3–4 zloty
a) veal		4 zloty
b) beef		Supposedly not available
c) pork		9–11 zloty
1 egg	20–25 groszy	35–50 groszy
1 kg sugar	5–6 zloty	10–12 zloty
1 litre milk	80 groszy	1 zloty

The prices of which we have been informed by diverse parties, including Polish sources, apply to Kreis Busko. What is noticeable is that the same rise has now occurred even in the most remote villages, and that prices are increasing so rapidly everywhere that they can no longer be tracked because they change several times a day.

In Kielce 2 kg of bread is said to cost 15 zloty and 1 quintal of potatoes 150 zloty; in Warsaw potatoes are said to cost 400 zloty. Potato peelings have apparently even been sold there for 1.50 zloty per kg. An egg is said to cost 1.50 zloty there.

At the same time as this sudden rise in prices, shopkeepers are withholding their goods, which means it has become impossible to get anything for money any more, not even with ration coupons. It is said people now only want to barter in kind. The farmers demand cloth, soap, and the like in exchange for their produce. The mood among the population is said to be worse than ever as food rations are far too meagre, especially in Warsaw, where people have already collapsed on the street because of hunger.

In Polish circles, there is talk of a downright state of panic attributed to the following:

1 AAN, 111/1020/3, fols. 333–336. This document has been translated from German.

2 Dr Otto Geigenmüller (1906–1969), lawyer; joined the NSDAP in 1933 and the SS in 1934; head of the State Police office in Halle an der Saale, 1934–1935, and in Frankfurt am Main, 1935–1936; then worked for the tax authorities in Würzburg and Hamburg; obtained a doctorate in 1937 on 'political protective custody in National Socialist Germany'; worked for the Security Service, 1939–1941; became a tax inspector in District Radom in 1941; in Lublin from 1943; lived in Quickborn in north-western Germany after the war; then worked at the Cologne-Land tax office.

3 That is, 100 kg.

For one thing, the Wehrmacht is buying up so much produce[4] without observing the maximum prices. For instance, soldiers have long been paying 35 groszy for an egg without hesitation. Apart from this, too much has been siphoned off by the quotas.[5] A great many purchasers are still coming to the district from Warsaw and Cracow, the latter on the light railway. And then the Jews have been buying up conspicuous amounts recently. Some suspect they are creating stocks in case they are sent away to a ghetto or forced to go somewhere else. Others believe they have received instructions to do this from the USSR, where they have the best connections and with which they are in constant contact, in order to stir up unrest. At any rate, people are surprised at where they have suddenly got so much money, and they are linking it to the production of counterfeit money. For instance, a Jewish counterfeiter's workshop that mainly produced 50- and 10-zloty notes is said to have been raided recently in Kielce. I have not received any reports about counterfeit money. I have, however, had cashier's offices and bailiffs instructed to examine incoming tender particularly attentively. In addition, there are claims that in all the larger towns the Jews are making use of existing 'black exchanges'[6] for their machinations.

In the main, however, this state of panic is attributed to the case of Rudolf Hess,[7] which came as a complete surprise and has shaken the population's confidence in the stability of the German regime and, therefore, the currency. Some conclude that Germany's situation must be very unfavourable if the Reich's third man has flown to England. Either there were serious differences of opinion among the leading men in Germany on account of their various assessments of the overall situation, or it was a 'trick' by the government, which has actually sent Hess to England for negotiations. In the beginning, a huge variety of fantastical rumours circulated: revolution in Germany, Göring had poisoned himself, the Russians had invaded the General Government, Rudolf Hess had spoken to the German people on English radio and warned them against following the Führer and the government into the abyss, etc.

Right-minded Poles are said to have thought little of these rumours from the outset, but they do share the opinion of the less circumspect elements that the Hess affair would inevitably have the effect of prolonging the war. In the meantime, the excitement and the initial impulse to rashness have faded away, especially as things have evidently stayed calm in Germany and the Hess affair has to be regarded as a one-off. It is worth mentioning in this regard that, in the last few days, the following phrases could be seen in German and Polish on the sign for Gebrüder Bieling, a German company in Busko (Centre): Heil Hess! Long live Poland!

Assessments differ of the relationship with the USSR. Some still think a war likely because Germany needs to secure Ukraine for food-supply reasons. In addition, it is said, Germany would have to wage this war pre-emptively because it could not wait for a stronger Russia to attack a Germany weakened by the further course of the war. As has

4 In spring 1941 more and more troops were transferred to the General Government for the planned attack on the Soviet Union.

5 These were quotas for agricultural products that farmers had to supply to the occupation authorities at set prices.

6 This is a reference to the black market.

7 This is a reference to the flight of Hitler's deputy, Rudolf Hess (1894–1987), to Scotland on 10 May 1941.

been said, Germany would have to deal with the constant threat of a Jewish regime which is constantly seeking revenge for strategic, but also for ideological, reasons.

Others claim the Führer has changed his plans in view of the fact that Hess knew everything or at least a very great deal. They say he intends to content himself with the cession of Ukraine, the leasing of the oil areas of Baku and Batumi for 25 years, and the concession of the Baltic states' fleet bases (others speak of the cession of the Baltic states). The Russian is said to have an unsurpassed fear of the Germans and will meet all these demands as the price of peace, to which, as an important factor, the right for German troops to pass through Russian territory in the direction of Turkey–Iraq would also be added. Nobody doubts that the passage of German forces through its territory would represent a great risk for the USSR. They say Russia has sealed itself off hermetically over the years, and the Russians would then come together with foreigners in large numbers for the first time, and not only that, but with well-equipped, disciplined, contented German soldiers who would be able to open the Russian people's eyes, above all those of the young generation, to their absolutely wretched economic and social situation. In addition to this, there is general agreement that the Russian would not be a match for the German armies in the slightest. – People are pretty much groping in the dark as far as Turkey's attitude is concerned.

With regard to supplies for the big cities, one may note that the railway ban[8] has heavily decimated the army of black-market traders. It was to be expected that the food situation for the population would become critical. Indeed, the panic that is now setting in has come early and is likely attributable to the agitation of the Jews, who are said to have got a strong fillip from the Hess affair, as well as other unreliable elements. There is no denying that the Jews have had close ties to the USSR from the beginning. In connection with manifestations of unrest among the working population, I can report that today a deputation of workers from Busko State Baths[9] outlined the bleakness of the food situation to me, and asked me for help. More and more complaints are also coming in from the officials in the tax offices. One office has excused its workforce's poor performance as being due to malnourishment.

I have seen for myself that the black-market prices are rising at a frightening rate.

DOC. 285

On 21 May 1941 the chairman of the Jewish Council in Warsaw describes his discussion with leading German officials[1]

Handwritten diary of Adam Czerniaków, entry for 21 May 1941

21 May 1941 – At the Community in the morning. A call from Rozen. They visited Łękno(?)[2] and one other camp. Appalling conditions. No one will last a month. The companies are stealing food. The beatings will stop. The results of the work, which – one may add – is very arduous, are limited.

8 A temporary ban on civilians using the railways.

9 Busko was a spa town.

1 YVA, O-33/1090. Published in Czerniaków, *Dziennik getta warszawskiego*, pp. 184–185. This document has been translated from Polish.

At 9.30 a.m. Wielikowski and I went to see Auerswald.[3] Governor Fischer received us. He began by saying that his aim is not to starve the Jews to death. Food rations might be increased, and there will be work or assignments for the workers. He pointed out that the corpses on the streets make a bad impression. There are indeed corpses lying around (their faces are covered with newspapers and bricks). He said the corpses must be quickly removed. He thinks there might be additional rations for the police and the officials.

The Governor is a relatively young man in civilian clothes and boots with spurs. His manner was polite. In the end, he said that he expects compliance, or else …

When asked whether it would be possible to obtain a loan before the budget is approved, he said 'yes'.

At 3 p.m. Dr Auerswald and Bischof[4] visited me at the Community. They inquired about food supplies and production. Reading between the lines, I sensed their displeasure with the Transfer Bureau and perhaps also with the ghetto boundaries. I raised the issue of the ghetto. In Cracow, a significant portion of the population has permits and shops outside the ghetto. Auerswald replied that Cracow was not Warsaw, and that regulations must be followed. He disliked the proposed layout of the ghetto. I asked whether we could suggest our own. He replied that we could, as every change to the boundaries has to be submitted to him.

Bischof agrees that the Council should be independent of the Supply Office.[5] A merchants' association will be created outside the ghetto to supply the ghetto with goods. He inquired whether we have any financial experts on the Council.

They want to give us 500 tonnes of oats for oatmeal.[6] Unfortunately we don't have any mills. There is a mill outside the ghetto, on Białostocka in Praga. The yield from 1 kg of oats is 60 per cent. That gives 14 servings.

Some people from the Propaganda [Department] came by and said that Cracow[7] does not want the Community to publish a newspaper. Dr Auerswald supports this.

2 Probably Łęki: see Doc. 277, fn. 4.

3 Heinz Auerswald (1908–1970), lawyer; joined the SS in 1933 and the NSDAP in 1939; legal officer for the SS from 1934 and for the Berlin Court of Justice from 1938; officer in the Urban Police in Poland, Sept. 1939; thereafter head of the Population and Welfare Division in District Warsaw; commissioner for the Jewish residential district in Warsaw from 15 May 1941; Kreishauptmann in Ostrów, Nov. 1942 – Jan. 1943; subsequently served in the war; lawyer in Düsseldorf after the war.

4 Max Bischof (1898–1985), banker; member of the Fatherland Front aligned with Engelbert Dollfuss; employed at the Österreichische Länderbank from 1920; based in Warsaw, 1929–1935; employed at the Länderbank in Vienna, 1935–1939; coordinator of Polish banks in the General Government from 1939; also representative for the supervision of public and private banks in the General Government, 1940–1945; head of the Transfer Bureau in the Warsaw ghetto, May 1941–1943; personnel manager at the Länderbank in Vienna after the war. Bischof was married to a Jewish woman and enjoyed Hans Frank's special protection.

5 The Jewish Council's Supply Office had the task of distributing the foodstuffs legally supplied to the ghetto. The Production Section, which was later converted into the private limited company Jüdische Produktion GmbH with the use of private funds, was responsible for producing goods and selling them to German and Polish buyers.

6 On 28 May 1941 Czerniaków noted that the ghetto would receive only 250 tonnes of oats and 125 tonnes of flour: Czerniaków, *Dziennik getta warszawskiego*, p. 187.

7 This is a reference to the government of the GG.

DOC. 286

On 23 May 1941 the underground newspaper *Biuletyn Informacyjny* describes the living conditions of the Jewish population under German occupation[1]

The Jews

The Germans have resolved the Jewish question at home by means of the so-called Nuremberg Laws, the main purpose of which was to prevent any Jewish influence on German culture; the economic consequences were less important. It is different in Poland. In the words of one German writer, it is not for nothing that the General Government is 'one of the most magnificent testing grounds of German creative power', and here the Germans' creative urge is completely unhindered. Therefore they have not only tackled this question differently here than at home, but they have also gone much further in resolving it.

Thus far we can identify two phases in the Germans' handling of Jewish affairs in Poland – the disenfranchisement phase and the segregation phase.

It began with the disenfranchisement of the Jews, primarily economic disenfranchisement. For this purpose, all Jewish property (factories, workshops, warehouses, banks) was taken over by trustees or commissioners, Jews' bank accounts were frozen, Jews were forbidden to travel by train, etc. At the same time, goods were confiscated on an enormous scale, and Jewish white-collar workers in non-Jewish sectors were dismissed. Eventually all Jewish schools were closed, and Jews were banned from libraries, theatres, cinemas, and cafés. The Jewish communities were burdened with the task of financially maintaining hospitals, asylums, and orphanages for which the municipalities had previously paid. To starve the Jews, the bread and sugar quotas allocated on ration cards were reduced. These directives reached a new pitch with the visible identification [of the Jews] and [their] conspicuous humiliation: armbands, separate tram and railway carriages, the ban on entering green spaces, the requirement to make way for Germans and bow to them.

Apart from the very detailed official directives (only a fraction of which we have mentioned), there were daily raids on Jewish homes, which went unpunished; blatant robbery; and various forms of public torment, mainly beatings. However, all of this was merely a prelude to the Jews' total segregation by locking them up in ghettos. The ghettos were introduced gradually: first in Łódź (in April of last year), then in Warsaw (November), and finally in Cracow, Lublin, Radom (March–April of this year), and smaller cities. There are three types of ghettos: completely sealed (Łódź), semi-sealed (e.g. Warsaw, where people can enter and exit with permits), and open ghettos (in a few smaller cities).

Jewish quarters were set up in great haste. In Warsaw 80,000 Poles had to move out of the ghetto and 110,000 Jews had to move in within a single month.[2] Elsewhere a mere two weeks were allotted for this two-way migration.

The segregation of the Jews had many consequences, particularly economic ones. The ghetto residents were condemned to trade only with their fellow Jews, most of whom were poor and a large percentage even utterly destitute. This isolation from the

1 *Biuletyn Informacyjny*, 23 May 1941, pp. 5–7; Biblioteka Narodowa, MF 45 816. This document has been translated from Polish.

2 In fact, it was approximately 30,000 Poles and 100,000 Jews who had to move.

outside world has prevented food from being delivered and made smuggling more difficult than ever. This has inevitably exacerbated the already rapidly growing poverty. The Jews were crammed into what was usually the most run-down neighbourhood, and this has had disastrous consequences in terms of health. As an example, we shall cite a few details from the Warsaw ghetto:

The ghetto was set up in an exceptionally densely built-up part of the city. The area was mapped out in such a way that it did not contain a single park, did not border the Vistula, and the only space where trees could be found was the cemetery. The overcrowding is appalling. On average there are 6 people to a room, and sometimes even up to 20. According to the calculations of the Population Statistics Department, there are 70 people per hectare in the whole of Warsaw, whereas in the ghetto there are 1,110 per hectare.

This isolation from the outside world has deprived a considerable number of Jews of their livelihood. In the ghetto, only 10–20 per cent are employed in shops and workshops. All legal trade in goods and currency takes place via an intermediary body (Transferstelle).[3] The aim is to extort from the wealthiest Jews all the goods, gold, and diamonds still in their possession. In addition, Jewish possessions and goods leak out through smuggling. The ghetto – reliant exclusively on internal trade – is in the process of liquidation, because this is the only way it can obtain money to survive. Since no more goods or raw materials come in, reserves are increasingly dwindling. Liquidation leads to even greater impoverishment. The prices of goods in the ghetto are not much higher than before the war, but food prices, already alarmingly high all across Warsaw, are even higher in the ghetto. The full horror of the conditions faced by this population group becomes clear when we consider that Jews only receive 750 g of bread per week with their ration cards, and that they are completely without fuel in the winter.

From January [1941], Jews were brought from small cities and towns in District Warsaw to this already overcrowded and starving Warsaw ghetto. The population increased to almost 500,000. This increased density has caused indescribable sanitary conditions, terrible hunger, and deprivation. Masses of pale, emaciated people, mostly unemployed, wander aimlessly through the crowded streets; beggars sit and lie on the walls; people collapsing from hunger is a common sight. The number of abandoned infants in the orphanage increases by more than a dozen every day. Several people die of hunger in the streets every day. Infectious diseases, especially tuberculosis, are spreading.

At the same time, the Germans continue to rob the wealthiest Jews of their property. Their treatment of the Jews continues to be exceptionally inhumane. Torment and wild, bestial antics are endemic.

The labour camps set up last autumn are a separate chapter on Jewish suffering. The conditions there have been terrible. Meagre food, inadequate housing, hard labour, and poor hygiene conditions have led to a soaring mortality rate. This was exacerbated by the camp guards' cruel treatment and murder of the Jews. In one camp alone – Bełżec – approximately 100 Jews were shot.

It is not worth dwelling on the legal aspect of the regulations and directives issued by the occupier – they correspond neither to Poland's basic laws nor to international

3 German in the original: 'Transfer Bureau'.

law, and even less to divine or positive law. The Germans' treatment of Jews is evidence of a truly outrageous savage degeneracy and barbarism.

The political, social, economic, cultural, and religious consequences of the situation presently facing the Jews in Poland are far-reaching. There is no room to discuss them in detail here. We merely wish to draw conclusions.

By ruining the Jews and Jewish commerce, the Germans have destroyed commerce throughout the entire country to an enormous extent. It would therefore be naive to assume that they will allow the Poles to take Jews' places. On the contrary, the vacant premises are already being taken over by German retail firms, and especially by wholesalers who have a monopoly on both buying and selling food in the countryside. The Poles have only been left with market stalls formerly owned by Jews and some of the humbler shops. The 'solution' to the Jewish question in the economic sphere is to replace the Jewish industrialist, wholesaler, or even retailer with a German industrialist, wholesaler, or retailer.

And what will the solution to the Jewish question in Poland look like more generally? What next? There is no answer to this question. The Germans themselves claim that the General Government is still awaiting a final solution to the Jewish question. We must conclude that the Jewish question here has reached a dead end from which there is no way out. Or rather, there is only one way out: gradual extermination through poverty, hunger, and infectious diseases. This will be the third act of the Jewish tragedy on Polish soil.

DOC. 287

On 28 May 1941 teenager Khaym Gluzshteyn reports on the gala honouring the writer Y. L. Perets in the Warsaw ghetto[1]

Handwritten report by Khaym Gluzshteyn, dated 28 May 1941

3.[2] *The Perets*[3] *commemoration on Shabes*[4]

The Perets commemoration took place on Shabes at 5 Tłomackie.[5] When I entered the hall, it was already packed with people. First on stage was the children's choir,[6] which

1 AŻIH, Ring I/673 (1064). This document has been translated from Yiddish. Published as a facsimile and in Polish translation in Sakowska (ed.), *Archiwum Ringelbluma*, vol. 2, pp. 83–84, 86.

2 Preceding Khaym Gluzshteyn's report are two accounts of the same event by other authors filed under the same archival reference number.

3 Also Isaac Leib Peretz, Polish: Icchok Lejb Perec (1852–1915), lawyer; one of the pioneers of modern Yiddish literature in Poland; also wrote in Hebrew. The gala was held on the occasion of Perets's birthday on 18 May. It was organized by the cultural association IKOR, which was led by members of the Poale Zion-Left party.

4 Shabes (Shabbos) is the Yiddish pronunciation of the word Shabbat (Sabbath). The date in question was Saturday, 24 May 1941.

5 This was the location of the Main Judaic Library (Główna Biblioteka Judaistyczna), home to much of the cultural life in the Warsaw ghetto. The books had been removed by the Germans in late 1939.

6 A children's choir from the school at 68 Nowolipki Street overseen by the school organization CISzO.

sang one of Perets's songs. Comrade[7] Zagan[8] then gave a talk. He described who Perets was, what he accomplished, and what he did on behalf of Jewish children, before leaving the audience with the hopeful message that we will survive the war. Comrade Linder[9] spoke after Comrade Zagan. He also talked a lot about Perets, but said that he is not as certain as Comrade Zagan that we will make it through the war. Following Comrade Linder, the teacher Comrade Likhtensteyn[10] recited many stories written by Perets. He, too, spoke about who Perets was and what he did for the Jewish people. After all the presentations, the people [in the audience] were in great spirits and felt freed of their worries. They had forgotten their woes completely. A few dances were then performed, followed by a famous Jewish singer,[11] who sang a song by Perets. A few minutes later, the great Jewish artist Comrade Samberg[12] came out onto the stage. He recited a very beautiful story written by Perets and received a huge round of applause. Afterwards, Comrade Sorele[13] sang some Yiddish songs. The celebration concluded with more singing by the children's choir. The people were very pleased with the event.

7 The use of the title 'Comrade' indicates membership in the Poale Zion movement.

8 Shakhne Froym Zagan, also Szachne Efroim Sagan (1892–1942); active in the 1930s as a leader in Poale Zion-Left and CISzO; member of the political underground in the Warsaw ghetto and of Oyneg Shabes; organized schools with Yiddish as the language of instruction; member of the Jewish Social Self-Help (JSS) and IKOR; murdered in Treblinka in early August 1942.

9 Menakhem, also Menachem, Linder (1911–1942), economist; member of the YIVO Institute for Jewish Research during the 1930s; member of the political underground in the Warsaw ghetto and of Oyneg Shabes; organized soup kitchens; co-founder of IKOR in Dec. 1941; murdered during the night of 17 to 18 April 1942.

10 Yisroel Likhtenshteyn, also Israel Lichtenstein (1904–1943), teacher; party member of Poale Zion-Left during the 1930s; editor of the Yiddish weekly *Literarishe bleter*; worker in the children's soup kitchen in the school building at 68 Nowolipki Street in the Warsaw ghetto; member of IKOR; member and archivist of the underground archive of the Warsaw ghetto; died shortly before or during the Ghetto Uprising in 1943.

11 Sabina Szyfman, soprano singer. The event programme had announced Diana Blumenfeld, actor and singer of Yiddish songs and wife of famous actor Jonas Turkow. She survived, along with her husband and daughter, on the 'Aryan side' with the help of the Council to Aid Jews and in particular with the help of Irena Sendlerowa. After the war, she emigrated to the USA: Sakowska (ed.), *Archiwum Ringelbluma*, vol. 2, p. 270. With the support of the London-based Polish government in exile, the Council to Aid Jews (codename Żegota), a cross-party organization founded by socialists and Catholics and with Jews among its initiators, came into being in late 1942 with the aim of assisting assimilated Jews in particular. One of its leading members was Irena Sendlerowa, also Sendler (1910–2008), who had a Polish studies background; member of the Polish Socialist Party (PPS); social worker from 1939 and head of the children's section of the Council to Aid Jews from autumn 1942. She rescued Jewish children from the Warsaw ghetto and placed them with Polish families. She was arrested by the Gestapo in 1943; co-founded children's homes and homes for the elderly after the war; honoured as Righteous Among the Nations by the State of Israel in 1965.

12 Ajzyk Samberg (1889–1943), actor; renowned and popular actor of the Yiddish stage in Poland; worked for the Jewish Central Association for the Care of Orphans (CENTOS) and the artists' soup kitchen in the Warsaw ghetto; performed at Nowy Azazel theatre; murdered as part of Operation Harvest Festival (Aktion Erntefest) in District Lublin in Nov. 1943.

13 Presumably Sore, also Sara, Grinberg, student at one of the CISzO schools. She participated in numerous IKOR musical and literary events in the ghetto.

DOC. 288

On May 1941 the Jewish Council in Bendzin (Będzin) announces that a 'Jew exclusion order' has been imposed on parts of the city centre[1]

Proclamation issued by the acting head of the executive committee of the Jewish Representative Body in Bendzin, unsigned, dated 30 May 1941[2]

I herewith give notice of a letter from the Chief of Police in Sosnowitz[3] to the Central Committee dated 28 May 1941 with the request that it be adhered to most strictly.

To the Central Office of Jewish Religious Communities in Upper Silesia
Sosnowitz
Re: Jew exclusion order in Bendzin
I hereby impose a Jew exclusion order on Kattowitzerstraße, Gartenstraße, and Hallenstraße – from Kattowitzerstraße to Marktstraße and the Main Square – in Bendzin as of 1 June 1941. Outside the hours of business reserved for Jews at the authorities *(8–10 a.m.)*, the aforementioned streets may only be used by Jews to visit the authorities:

1) with an official summons to an authority or
2) with a certificate issued by myself.

The prohibition on the use of the streets covered by the Jew exclusion order must be announced immediately to all community members. Strict compliance with this directive must be ensured.
In an acting capacity

DOC. 289

On 30 May 1941 the Polish government in exile's representative in occupied Poland reports on the Jewish residential district in Warsaw[1]

Report by the representative in the occupied country, Cyryl Ratajski,[2] for the Polish government in London (no. O.VI.2471/41), dated 30 May 1941 (carbon copy)

The Jewish residential district in Warsaw
The separate, sealed Jewish residential district in Warsaw, established in November 1940, has only recently been given a legal foundation. According to the regulations, it is by law an independent municipal administrative unit under the authority of a special German

1 AŻIH, 212/1, fol. 3. Copy in USHMM, RG 15 060M, reel 1. This document has been translated from German.
2 The original features the stamp of the executive committee of the Jewish Representative Body in Będzin.
3 From Oct. 1940 the acting chief of police in Sosnowitz (Sosnowiec) was Alexander von Woedtke (b. 1889), career officer; joined the NSDAP in 1930 and the SS in 1931; inspector of the SS Main District North from 1936; chief of staff in Bydgoszcz from 1939; subsequently posted to Breslau; acting chief of police in Erfurt from March 1940; chief of police in Sosnowitz, July 1941–1944; supervised the policing of the Jewish communities.

1 SPP, 3.1.1.13A. This document has been translated from Polish.

commissioner invested with the powers of a municipal starosta[3] and, in matters of municipal management, under the authority of the chairman of the Jewish Council, who has been granted the powers of a mayor. The Office of the Jewish Council is divided into several administrative departments and includes the Order Service (the so-called Jewish police) and a special supply unit,[4] which is currently being set up and is meant to become a limited liability company. Moreover, the residential districts also have a tax office, which collects state taxes, and a municipal executive body, which for the time being continues to forward all municipal tax revenues to the Warsaw City Council's finance office. This situation will supposedly change, but for the time being the Jewish Council, which has taken over municipal administrative duties, has not received any tax revenue. The Council covers its budgetary needs with a per capita tax, which is the same for all residents; with a compensatory tax, the amount of which depends on the wealth of the individual payer; and with one-off contributions that are collected sporadically. All of these revenues do not suffice to cover the Jewish Community's substantial needs. The population in the Jewish residential district currently numbers between 510,000 and 520,000, of whom 240,000 have been categorized as impoverished and in need of support from social welfare funds. Not all of them receive aid, however, because the very modest food rations allow the Community to only distribute approximately 120,000 bowls of soup per day – that is only enough for half of the residents in need. The individual food allocations on the ration cards are entirely inadequate. They provide only 2,500 g of bread and 180 g of sugar per month. The population must purchase all other foodstuffs on the open market, which is supplied only via smuggling, because importing food, fuel, etc. into the Jewish residential district is officially forbidden. Under these conditions the food prices in the Jewish residential district are outrageously high compared to those in the Aryan district. In late May 1941 bread cost 32 złoty per kg, potatoes 8.50 złoty per kg, butter (in tiny quantities) 100 złoty per kg, lard 90 złoty per kg, etc. The prices of other foodstuffs have not soared quite so much, and since the biggest wholesalers in various sectors can be found in the Jewish residential district, these goods find eager buyers in the Aryan part of the city. Of course all trade with the Aryan district is conducted illegally, i.e. by means of smuggling, because legal trade between the ghetto and the outside world (i.e. 'trade across the wall', so called because of the walls encircling this district) may only be conducted through the mediation of a special German authority, the so-called

2 Cyryl Ratajski (1875–1942), lawyer; studied in Berlin; legal clerk in Torgau and then lawyer in Ratibor; member of the Polish National Committee at the Paris Peace Conference in 1919; mayor of Poznań for many years; interior minister, 1924–1925; joined the Christian Democratic Labour Party (SP) in 1937; briefly arrested in 1940; from Dec. 1940 in Warsaw, where he was the representative of the Polish government in exile for the General Government, and from 1941 to August 1942 for the whole of occupied Poland; died from an illness.

3 The Regulation on the Jewish Residential District in Warsaw (19 April 1941) provided for the appointment of a commissioner: *VOBl-GG* 1941, no. 35, 28 April 1941, pp. 211–212. The Governor officially appointed the commissioner with a directive issued on 14 May 1941: *Amtsblatt des Chefs des Distrikts Warschau*, no. 5, 20 May 1941. The commissioner received his instructions directly from the District Governor, and was at the same time responsible for 'general Jewish affairs' in the district. A further directive issued by Fischer on 15 May 1941 transferred 'the functions and powers of a mayor' in the Jewish residential district to the chairman of the Jewish Council in Warsaw: ibid., p. 52; see also *Krakauer Zeitung*, 18 May 1941, p. 6.

4 The author is referring to the Supply Office: see Doc. 285, fn. 5.

'Transferstelle'.[5] This clearing bureau was set up with the sole purpose of mediating the purchase of goods for the Jewish population and the sale of goods from the Jewish residential district. For this it takes 10–25 per cent [commission], and the sums collected for the benefit of the Jews are not paid out to them individually. Moreover, this apparatus is by its very nature totally unsuitable for trade purposes. This is why it is not only Jews and Poles who avoid this mediation, but even the Germans themselves, and above all the military authorities, who place orders and make purchases directly in the ghetto, paying the sellers in cash, even though this is forbidden by law.

The Jewish population is in an extremely precarious financial situation because only approximately 4,000 craftsmen and workers are employed in the collective workshops run by the Jewish Community, where they fulfil orders placed by the German authorities (they are mainly tailors, hat makers, and sometimes cobblers). The same number of people also work for the army. Approximately 50,000 people make a living from illegal trade, i.e. smuggling. The rest are involved in various dealings, such as retail, speculation in foreign currency and securities, etc., but for the most part they are unemployed. The wealthier people sell any jewellery and valuables they have left, but such people are few and far between, while the poor simply die of hunger and infectious diseases (mainly those affecting the heart and lungs). Both the catastrophic state of nutrition and the disastrous housing and sanitary conditions result in an extremely high mortality rate, which increases from month to month and claimed up to 5,000 lives in May. Calculated annually, this yields an average of 120 deaths per 1,000 people, which is twelve times as many as before the war. Since the birth rate has dropped to a minimum, not only is there no natural population growth, there is even a decline. Nevertheless, the number of inhabitants is constantly increasing due to the arrival of Jews who are being forcibly resettled from small provincial towns where there is no intention of creating separate Jewish residential districts. Only approximately 8,000 people have been deported for forced labour (mainly land reclamation work). The reason for this small number is that among the Jews there is a lack of suitable resources to perform such heavy physical labour. The corpses of people who died while at work (approximately 20 per day) are brought in daily, as are seriously ill people in need of convalescence. The working conditions during such operations, especially the housing in barracks and the food, are disastrous. The camp guards, who are mainly Ukrainians, also treat [the forced labourers] very badly.

Polish police serve in the Jewish residential district, but the police force consists of units that were put together especially for this purpose – mainly individuals from Poznań and Pomerania. The Jewish Order Service is not involved in solving crimes, but hands over such matters to the Polish police. The uniformed German police do not operate in the Jewish residential district (they only patrol its perimeters). However, the Gestapo does operate in this district by means of secret Jewish agents and an undercover special unit created to combat illicit trade.[6] It is also obvious that the German authorities are striving to isolate the Jewish residential district politically as well. For instance, there are plans to take away the Jews' identity cards, which document their Polish citizenship, and to replace

5 German in the original: 'Transfer Bureau'.

6 The author is referring to the Office for Combating Illicit Trade and Price Gouging (Urząd do Walki z Lichwą i Spekulacją).

them with Jewish passports, as well as to introduce a special currency for the ghetto.[7] The apparent explanation for this is that the Warsaw ghetto is an experiment which will serve as a model for shaping Jewish affairs across Europe in the future, upon the introduction of 'the new National Socialist order'. It is noteworthy that nowhere else in the General Government have any sealed Jewish residential districts been established, with the exception of Warsaw. Where such districts have been created at all, they established merely zones in which Jews are allowed to settle, but Aryans are not prohibited from entering, as is the case in Warsaw. Moreover, the Jews may move about the city freely, or at least are allowed to leave the confines of the ghetto with a permit. Even in the areas annexed to the Reich, Jews in some places live under far better conditions than in Warsaw.

This is why 400 to 500 people per day secretly leave the Warsaw ghetto and attempt to return to the provinces or even to get beyond the cordon,[8] to reach the places from which they were once expelled or where they have relatives, etc. The only other sealed Jewish residential district apart from Warsaw is the Łódź ghetto. It has existed considerably longer than the one in Warsaw, which is why the conditions in which the Jews live and the effects of those conditions are felt more keenly. This is illustrated by the fact that in the first three weeks of May 1941, as many as 1,080 Jews (out of a population of 150,000) died in Łódź, while there were eight births. Such a high mortality rate is the result of exhaustion and the consequent lack of resistance to disease; no one dies of hunger in Łódź because the entire Jewish population there is fed in communal kitchens. Following this example, the commissioner of the Jewish residential district in Warsaw has also suggested setting up similar communal kitchens and dissolving individual family households.

DOC. 290

The chroniclers of the Lodz ghetto describe daily events from 14 to 31 May 1941[1]

'Daily Chronicle Bulletin of the Lodz Ghetto', nos. 110–114, dated 14 to 31 May 1941

Archive Department
Daily Chronicle Bulletin, no. 110
Wednesday, 14 May 1941
Weather: Cloudy, warm.
Arrests: Today 8 people were arrested for theft and 25 for various other offences.
Deaths: 32 people died in the ghetto today.
Suicide attempts: At 2 o'clock in the afternoon, 51-year-old Ides Śmietanka[2] jumped out of the window of her apartment on the second floor at 48 Limanowskiego Street. She

7 The Nazis had previously introduced a monetary system specifically for the Lodz ghetto in summer 1940. Ghetto currency was only valid within the ghetto itself. See also Doc. 144.
8 This is presumably a reference to measures repeatedly taken by German and Polish police from 1941 in order to combat smuggling and black-market trade. These measures included controls, raids, and closing off certain areas.

1 APŁ, 278/1079, fols. 94–98. Abridged version published in English translation in Dobroszycki (ed.), *The Chronicle of the Łódź Ghetto*, pp. 54–58. This document has been newly translated from Polish.
2 Idesa (Ides) Śmietanka (1894–1941), housewife; perished in the ghetto on 15 May 1941.

broke her leg and suffered head injuries. The seriously injured woman was taken to Hospital No. 1.

Orders placed by the military: The tailoring division has received considerable orders from the military. Most of the orders placed were for field uniforms[3] and trousers. The undergarments department received orders for 50,000 military shirts. In addition, orders were placed for several thousand women's dresses and for women's undergarments. The skilled tailoring workshop is engaged in the production of gloves. Large orders for alterations to military uniforms are expected soon. However, there are very few orders for civilian men's suits. Due to a lack of material and orders, the rubber raincoat workshop remains closed.

Archive Department
Daily Chronicle Bulletin, no. 111
Thursday, 15 May 1941
Weather: Cloudy and warm.
Arrests: 14 people were arrested for theft, 1 for resistance to authority, and 16 for various other offences.
Deaths and births: 21 people died in the ghetto today; there was 1 stillbirth.
Suicide: At 8 o'clock in the evening, 21-year-old Pesa Trop,[4] suffering from mental illness, threw herself from the third floor of the building at 12 Zydowska Street. She was taken to Hospital No. 1 and died at midnight.

Air raid precautions: The chief of police has sent the Jewish elder instructions concerning air raid precautions. According to these instructions, a large container with 100–150 litres of water and a box of sand are to be placed on the top landing of each staircase. There must be a bucket of water and 3 bags containing 5–10 kg of sand in front of every door. In front of the entrance to each air raid shelter there should be: 1 handheld fire hose, 1 fire hook, 1 firemen's rope, 1 ladder, 1 first-aid kit, several buckets, small sand shovels, 1 large shovel, and 1 axe. The air-raid wardens are to be equipped with yellow armbands bearing the inscription 'L.S.-Wart'.[5] To implement these instructions, meetings are being held under the chairmanship of the Order Service commander. It should be noted in passing that – apart from the lack of a number of the required items in the ghetto – the houses in Bałuty have no air-raid shelters.

Archive Department
Daily Chronicle Bulletin, no. 112
From 16 to 20 May 1941
Weather: Over the course of the above-mentioned five days, the warm and mostly sunny weather persisted.
Arrests: 50 people were arrested for theft, 20 for resistance to authority, and 100 for various other offences.

Deaths and births: Over the course of the above-mentioned five days, 194 people died in the ghetto; 5 births were registered, of which 4 were boys and 1 was a girl.

3 These were simple service uniforms such as those worn during military training.
4 Pesa Trop (1920–1941), worker.
5 German in the original: 'Luftschutzwart', 'air-raid warden'.

Shot dead: On 17 May, at 4.15 p.m., 49-year-old Mordka Moszkowicz[6] dropped dead from a bullet fired by a guard. The incident took place at the wire fence on the corner of Smugowa and Franciszkańska Streets.

Suicide attempts: On 16 May, 22-year-old Łaja Ruchla Turko,[7] 15 Stary Rynek, poisoned herself with hydrochloric acid. She died in Hospital No. 1 on the same day. On the 19th, at 7 o'clock in the evening, Mr and Mrs Gliksman attempted to take their own lives by swallowing sublimate.[8] They are a young married couple. The husband, an electrical engineer by trade, is only 23 years old, and his 20-year-old wife, Sara, is a seamstress. They were taken to Hospital No. 1 in a critical condition.

Fire: At 4 o'clock in the morning on 18 May, the floor of the tailoring division building at 16 Jakóba Street caught fire. Before the fire brigade arrived, the night watchmen guarding the vegetable warehouse in the immediate vicinity extinguished the fire. The damage is negligible.

Arrivals: In the period from 30 April to 15 May, 10 people registered for permanent residence in the ghetto, 8 of whom had been released from prisons; 3 ghetto residents went to Warsaw with special permits.

Archive Department
Daily Chronicle Bulletin, no. 113
From 21 to 26 May 1941
Weather: Considerably warmer, with temperatures already reaching 25 degrees; mostly sunny, on Sunday a brief thunderstorm with a heavy downpour.
Arrests: Over the course of the above-mentioned 6 days, 38 people were arrested for theft, 12 for resistance to authority, and 71 for various other offences.

Deaths and births: Over the course of the above-mentioned 6 days, 200 people died in the ghetto; 1 baby girl was born.

The chairman's return: On 20 May Mr Rumkowski, the chairman of the Council of Elders of the Jews, returned to the ghetto after an 8-day stay in Warsaw. During his stay in Warsaw he signed contracts with 13 medical specialists who will soon come to the ghetto. The arrival of these 13 physicians in the ghetto will be extremely important for the public health service.[9]

Suicides: On 20 May the bridge at Plac Kościelny was once again the scene of a desperate jump. The incident occurred just before curfew ended. The 30-year-old tailor Icek Wajnblum committed the desperate act.[10] He was taken to Prison No. 1[11] in a critical condition.

At 5.30 in the morning on the 25th, a young woman threw herself from a window on the first floor of the building at 12 Smugowa Street. The desperate woman was rescued.

6 Mordka Moszkowicz (1892–1941), weaver.
7 Łaja Ruchla Turko (1918–1941), housewife.
8 This is a reference to mercury chloride, a highly toxic disinfectant.
9 Rumkowski stayed in the Warsaw ghetto from 13 to 20 May 1941 to recruit medical specialists for the Lodz ghetto. He had several discussions with representatives of the American Jewish Joint Distribution Committee (JDC) and the Jewish Community. He ultimately managed to persuade 12 physicians to relocate to Lodz.
10 Icek Wajnblum (1911–1941), tailor; perished in the ghetto on 28 August 1941.
11 This is probably a reference to Hospital No. 1.

Suspension of the deputy prison director: Mr Szternberg, the deputy prison director, has been suspended from duty. The suspension is related to an investigation into his activities before he took up his position at the prison.

Shot dead in the street in broad daylight: On 22 May a tragic event took place in the centre of the ghetto, far from the wire fences. As we well know, ghetto residents are most often shot at the checkpoints, usually after curfew. The perpetrators are always guards on duty around the Jewish district. The scene of Thursday's harrowing incident was one of the busiest intersections, at Franciszkańska Street and Zawiszy Street. At around 1.30 in the afternoon, two men without patches[12] passed by near the intersection and proceeded along the side of Franciszkańska Street with even-numbered addresses, from the higher house numbers, in the direction of Zawiszy Street. At the corner, one of them drew a revolver from his coat pocket and fired two shots, apparently blindly. The first shot lightly wounded a certain Mordka Brygiel (25 Kielm Street) in the hand,[13] while the second shot mowed down 55-year-old Tauchen Bigeleisen, who was standing on the opposite side of Franciszkańska Street.[14] The man who was killed lived nearby, at 35 Zawiszy Street. After the shot was fired, indescribable panic broke out in the street, and the perpetrators were able to walk quickly away unhindered, [proceeding] along Zawiszy Street in the direction of Bałuty Market. Immediately afterwards, a larger squad of Order Service guards, led by the senior officer of the first precinct, Mr Berkowicz,[15] arrived at the scene of the crime. The body was lying in the gutter on the street corner. The bullet had pierced the victim's temple, causing instant death. The body was lying in a huge pool of blood. The Order Service stopped the traffic, cordoned off the crime scene for several dozen metres from where the body was, and did not allow anyone through the cordon that had been set up, except representatives of the responsible authorities. Meanwhile the injured Brygiel was taken to hospital by ambulance. The relevant German authorities were immediately notified of the incident, and the chief of the German Criminal Police stationed in the ghetto[16] arrived promptly, with two investigators and a police dog. They initiated a detailed investigation at the crime scene: they interrogated the eyewitnesses, took measurements, recorded the personal details of the person killed, and so on. The chief of the Criminal Police told one of the members of the Order Service that the militiamen were obliged to identify the perpetrators even at the expense of their own lives.

12 In other words, not wearing the yellow star. On 11 Dec. 1939 the District Governor in Kalisz, Friedrich Uebelhoer, who was responsible for the city of Łodź, had ordered that the Jewish population must wear a 10 cm yellow star at chest level and on the back of their clothing: *Dokumenty i materiały*, vol. 3: *Getto Łódzkie*, p. 23.

13 Mordka Brygiel (1904–1942), baker; in Feb. 1942 deported to Kulmhof (Chelmno), where he was murdered.

14 Tauchen Bigeleisen, also Bigelajzen (1886–1941), night watchman.

15 Samuel Berkowicz (b. 1900), retailer; senior officer and deputy commander of the Order Service in the Lodz ghetto.

16 Dr Walter Zirpins (1901–1976), banker and lawyer; active in a Freikorps in Upper Silesia after 1918; Kriminalkommissar in 1928; joined the SS in 1939; worked in Section IV (Gestapo) of the Reich Security Main Office (RSHA) in 1939; staff officer at the Security Police's Officer Training School; chief of the Criminal Police in the Lodz ghetto, 1940 to late 1941; section head for the Criminal Police in the Ministry of the Interior of Lower Saxony in 1951; head of the Criminal Police in Hanover from 1956; one of West Germany's leading experts on economic crime.

According to the description given by one of the eyewitnesses, a member of the Order Service, one of the perpetrators was wearing a light-coloured coat and hat and had a walking stick; the other man, smaller in stature than his companion, was said to be wearing a grey coat. No sooner had the representatives of the German authorities finished their investigations than a hearse carried away the man who had been killed, the bloodstained pavement was cleaned up, and normal traffic was restored at the scene of the tragedy. This incident had a devastating impact on the ghetto.

Citizens from Pabianice in the ghetto: On 23 May a transport of 200 men from Pabianice arrived in the ghetto; they were sent to Germany for forced labour. They were housed in the local prison on Czarnieckiego Street until the day of their departure.

Prisons: In the period from the 17th to the 22nd, 3 people returned to the ghetto from the prisons.

Fires: On the 23rd, at around 9 o'clock in the evening, the floor of the single-storey house at 20 Pieprzowa Street caught fire. The cause of the fire was the faulty chimney construction. The local fire brigade put out the fire. On the 24th, at around 10 o'clock in the evening, soot in the chimney at 21 Rybna Street caught fire. The fire brigade promptly removed the source of the fire.

Trade in community commodities prohibited: Today the Jewish elder's announcement no. 273 was posted, introducing a ban on trade in foodstuffs originating from community ration quotas.[17] The mainstay of the food trade was the sale of items from the quotas. This applied to street and market trading as well as to shops. With the ban in place, legal trade will now only be possible with items from parcels sent from abroad. Announcement no. 272, posted on the same day, regulates food rations for the period up to and including 4 June.[18]

The day after announcement no. 273 appeared, the Order Service officers were instructed to put a stop to any food trading that violated [the ban]. Against this background, from the early hours of Monday morning men from the Order Service confiscated food in the streets, market squares, and shops. Scales and weights were also confiscated. In the course of a single day, this rigorous operation succeeded in bringing the otherwise flourishing food trade to a complete standstill.

In turn, illicit trading began immediately and was marked by a steep price increase. For example, after legal trade was abolished, the price paid for bread sold under the counter shot up from 10 to 12 marks per loaf, and the price of swedes from 0.90 to 1.20 marks. Similarly, all other foodstuffs also became more expensive.

Emergency measures taken by the Order Service: On the 26th the Order Service took emergency measures to stop the increasing number of curfew violations. At exactly 9 p.m., the Order Service commenced frequent patrols on every street in the ghetto; they herded the population into their homes, and any pedestrians who dawdled were taken to the precincts, where they were fined or received prison sentences for being out on the street after 9 p.m.

The citizens from Pabianice: On 26 May, after 3 days in prison, the citizens from Pabianice were handed over to the German authorities to be sent away for labour.

17 Announcement no. 273, 25 May 1941: YIVO, RG 241/389.

18 YIVO, RG 241/388.

Archive Department
Daily Chronicle Bulletin, no. 114
From 27 to 31 May 1941
Weather: The last few days of May were marked by beautiful, sunny, and warm weather.
Arrests:
Deaths and births:[19]
Food procurement in the ghetto: According to information provided by the delivery office at Bałuty Market, supply deliveries to the ghetto correspond to the registered demand. Recently the first spring vegetables arrived, consisting of rhubarb and chives. There will soon be a demand for a larger amount of spring vegetables. A large quantity of beetroots and swedes has arrived to supplement an earlier, incomplete order. The potato supply is inadequate and does not exceed 80,000 kg per day. Instead of groats, the ghetto receives barley flakes. Coal is supplied as part of the quota recently allocated by the ghetto administration. The milk supply has increased considerably and is up to 7,000 litres per day in various forms. The butter and margarine supply is insufficient. The ghetto will no longer receive methylated spirit. Methylated spirit is only supplied for technical use. Recently a large consignment of all kinds of medicines was delivered as had been ordered. The matchstick crisis was overcome once a large consignment of matches arrived, consisting of 50 crates of 5,000 boxes of matches each.

Orders for the labour divisions: The divisions have received large new orders for the production of all types of undergarments, women's dresses, and men's civilian clothing. The considerable influx of orders has brought about an increase in the output of the tailoring workshops. On 29 May a consignment of 2,500 pairs of military shoes, which had previously been returned due to identified defects, was handed over to the German authorities. The hat workshop was running full steam in order to process orders from the military. The rubber raincoat workshop remains closed. A new department has been put into operation in response to orders from the German authorities – the brush workshop – which produces brooms and paintbrushes. To supply this workshop, a new department focusing on finishing bristles has been put into operation at the tannery.
Shortage of building materials: As basic building materials, primarily cement and tar, have been completely exhausted, most of the construction work carried out by the local construction department has been suspended. The most important construction projects nearing completion include the refurbishment of the premises of the following departments: hosiery at 50 Brzezińska Street, hats at 47 Brzezińska, undergarments at 14 Dworska, and shoemaking at 79 Franciszkańska.

Which physicians are coming from Warsaw? As the 'Daily Chronicle' has already reported, during his stay in Warsaw the chairman recruited 12 physicians (most of them from Łódź) to work in the ghetto.[20] The list of these physicians is as follows: Dr Michał Eliasberg[21] and Dr Arno Kleszczelski,[22] surgeons; Abram Mazur,[23] ENT specialist; Salomon Rubinstein, radiologist; Janina Hartglas[24] and Benedykt Moszkowicz,[25] paediatri-

19 There is no text after the subheadings 'Arrests' and 'Deaths and births'.
20 Daily Chronicle Bulletin no. 113 mentions 13 physicians.
21 Dr Michał Eliasberg (1891–1973).
22 Arno Kleszczelski (b. 1899).
23 Dr Albert Abram Mazur (1893–1976); emigrated to Sweden in 1945.

cians; Józef Goldwasser,[26] Alfred Lewi,[27] Izak Ser,[28] Nekrycz,[29] Alicja Czarnożyłówna,[30] and Izrael Geist,[31] specialists in internal medicine.

Arrest of the chairman of the summary court: The arrest of Bronowski,[32] chairman of the summary court[33] (the former court clerk), on direct orders from the presiding judge caused a sensation in the ghetto. He was arrested on the night of 12 to 13 May in his apartment, which was subjected to a thorough search. It is alleged that he was in possession of approximately 1,000 marks, a very substantial sum compared to his salary. Bronowski was placed in a detention cell at the Order Service precinct. He is under suspicion of having accepted bribes from defendants. As is well known, Bronowski presided over the majority of the summary court sessions, and thus would have been able to influence the verdicts significantly. The arrest was reported in issue 11–12 of the *Geto-Cajtung*,[34] which appeared on 30 May. The chairman of the Council of Elders of the Jews will personally decide the detainee's fate once the case has been investigated in detail.

The presiding judge will personally hand down sentences in cases of abuse of office, fraud, or theft that harms the community. As is well known, these powers have fallen to the summary court until now.

Announcement no. 275, which was posted everywhere on 30 May,[35] states that the chairman of the Council of Elders of the Jews has entrusted the lawyer Henryk Neftalin with the task of investigating all reports, statements, and complaints concerning abuse of office or theft committed in official premises, institutions, and business enterprises. His reports will constitute the basis for the presiding judge's verdicts. This will be carried out according to the procedure mentioned in the previous news item.

Combating trade in foodstuffs: Due to the ban on trading in foodstuffs from the community ration quotas, 80 Order Service officials have been assigned to a special inspection division. As reported in the latest issue of the *Geto-Cajtung*, the above-mentioned trade was abolished because parasitic behaviour was rampant among those traders who prey on the misery of the consumers who offload their food rations at ridiculously low prices, while the traders resell these products at steep prices.[36]

24 Dr Janina Hartglas (1888–1943).
25 Benedykt Moszkowicz (b. 1893), from Warsaw.
26 Dr Józef Goldwasser (b. 1886); deported to Auschwitz in 1944.
27 Dr Alfred Lewi (b. 1899).
28 Dr Izak Ser (b. 1908).
29 Dr Izak Majer Nekrycz (b. 1908).
30 Dr Alicja Paulina Czarnożył (b. 1912).
31 Dr Izrael Geist, also Gaist (b. 1892).
32 Samuel Bronowski (b. 1907), office worker; chairman of the summary court, March–May 1941.
33 In August 1940 Rumkowski had ordered the establishment of a court, which was in operation from Sept. On 15 March 1941 he also set up a summary court to prosecute abuse of office, fraud, and theft.
34 The Yiddish-language *Geto-Cajtung*, or *Geto-tsaytung*, was the official newspaper of the Council of Elders of the Jews and appeared weekly from 7 March to 21 Sept. 1941 (APŁ, PSŻ 278/1075). The articles, including this news item, were translated into German for the German authorities: *Getto-Zeitung für Informationen, Verordnungen und Bekanntmachungen*, nos. 11–12, 30 May 1941, p. 6, APŁ, 278/1076, fol. 156.
35 YIVO, RG 241/390.
36 *Getto-Zeitung für Informationen, Verordnungen und Bekanntmachungen*, nos. 11–12, 30 May 1941, pp. 4–5, APŁ, 278/1076, fols. 154–155.

Vocational training: The vocational training campaign continues to expand. The result of this campaign will be the occupational restructuring of a large section of the middle-aged population, whose strengths will be utilized for the appropriate tasks. The intention of this campaign is for all those who are fit to work to become useful members of the ghetto community.

Whit Sunday:[37] To mark this holiday, which falls on the first two days of June, the population has received additional food rations. With regard to the current procurement issues, mention must be made of the shortage of potatoes caused by recent disruptions to railway traffic.

Revue premiere: The House of Culture staged a revue on Saturday, 31 May. It consisted of sketches, current affairs pieces,[38] monologues, and dance performances. Considering the conditions in the ghetto, first and foremost the lack of professional performers, the revue exceeded all expectations. Without qualification, the event reached the level of good pre-war theatre. The revue owes its success to the artistic director, Mr Puławer,[39] who is the author of many successful texts, and to Mr Janowski,[40] as well as to the masterful set design by the painter, Mr Szwarc.[41] The revue was performed entirely in Jewish [Yiddish]. The audience at Saturday's premiere demanded encores for a range of numbers with thunderous applause.

After the performance, Chairman Rumkowski delivered a long speech in which he shared with the audience his impressions of his recent trip to Warsaw. In the Warsaw ghetto, he said, one is struck by the disparity between the tragic poverty of the overwhelming majority of the population and the prosperity of a handful of still wealthy Jews who can afford all the restaurants, confectioners, and shops, even with their staggering prices. Alongside this false glamour and the sight of a few well-fed, fortunate people dressed in the latest fashions, one sees endless crowds of unemployed people whose appearance is downright horrifying. The Warsaw ghetto is characterized by utter disorganization and chaos. The leader of the ghetto devoted the final passage of his speech to the relentless struggle he is pursuing against the hydra of crime and corruption, which disrupts harmony at work.

37 This is a reference to the Jewish festival of Shavuoth (Pentecost or the Feast of Weeks), which is celebrated seven weeks after Passover. It commemorates the receipt of the Ten Commandments on Mount Sinai.

38 These were presumably re-enacted 'typical' scenes from everyday life in the ghetto.

39 Mojżesz Puławer (b. 1903), actor and director; director of the Avantgarde drama troupe in the Lodz ghetto; deported to Auschwitz in August 1944; lived in Israel after the war.

40 Szymon Janowski (1912–1944), writer and dramaturg; hospital caretaker in the Lodz ghetto; in August 1944 deported to Auschwitz, where he was murdered.

41 Alter Pinchas Szwarc, later Pinchas Schaar (1923–1996), painter and sculptor; lived in Israel, Munich, and New York after the war.

DOC. 291
In May 1941 the Commission for Polish Jewry reports on the situation in German-occupied Poland[1]

Report (marked 'only for interior circulation') for the US Department of State by the Commission for Polish Jewry[2] in Jerusalem, dated May 1941

Dear sir,

We are sending you herewith some material which throws light on the sufferings of the Jewish Population under German and Russian occupation. The material is based on the recorded evidence of persons who have arrived here from Poland.

In view of the historical importance of this material, and in order to preserve it for future use, we are endeavouring to collect all the available data.

In the event of your desiring to make use of this material, you are kindly requested to mention the source.

Yours faithfully,
Commission for Polish Jewry

The Situation in German Occupied Poland.
(A Report presented in February 1941)

The attitude of the German Authorities to the Jews in the area of the 'Government General' can generally speaking be compared with their attitude to the Polish population in those areas of Poland which have been incorporated in Germany proper. The Jews in the 'Government General' and the Poles in the annexed areas are forced for example, to leave their homes within half an hour and are cooped up in special quarters. As against this it may be said that the attitude towards the Jewish population is, by comparison with the attitude towards the Polish population, based on the view that the Jews constitute an inferior group to the Poles. The Germans are always careful not to use the same methods in their persecution of Jews and Poles. As a result, both the Jews and the Poles have the impression that the others are better treated than themselves. The Poles argue at times that the position of the Jews is better than their own because only Polish[3] youth has so far been sent in masses for forced labour in Germany itself. They also argue that the number of arrests and political murders among the Jews is smaller than among the Poles. As against this, however, the attitude towards the Poles is better from an economic point of view. The Poles are regarded as legal citizens and their private life is practically not interfered with. Naturally, their economic position is difficult as a result of the general factors operating in Poland in the economic sphere. None-the-less the Poles have an opportunity of getting jobs and of earning a livelihood. It is only in the most recent German Ordinances which were responsible for the establishment of the Jewish ghetto that measures were taken to equate the position of the Jews and the Poles. These measures it may be said have resulted in the establishment of closer bonds between Jews and Poles.

1 NARA, RG 59, Decimal File 860c.4016/635. The original document is in English.
2 See Doc. 13, fn. 2.
3 In the original, erroneously, 'Jewish'.

The attitude of the Poles to the Jews differs in different strata of the population. The Polish intelligentsia, for example, has been more hard hit than others, both morally and materially.

To many professions they are altogether denied entry. For example, the position of professors, teachers, and Government officials is very bad. Psychologically also their position is difficult. The way they have stood up to conditions is, however, magnificent. They are possessed of a strong faith in the final victory of Britain and they show great courage in withstanding the most difficult of circumstances. These are the people who are at the head of the underground Polish national movement which is growing from day to day. Generally speaking, the attitude of the Polish intelligentsia to the Jews is fair and decent. Polish friends help the Jews in all places and take every opportunity of expressing their sympathy towards the Jews. They hide Jewish property in their homes, even though this is bound up with considerable danger. Similarly, they help the Jews in these professions which the Jews are not allowed to occupy. This enables a large proportion of the Jewish intelligentsia to earn a livelihood. The [chief representative] of the Lawyers' Association, Novodovski,[4] a well-known National Democrat and leader of the anti-semitic movement, refused as head of the Bar Council to sign a Decree enacting an Aryan Clause against Jewish lawyers and was sentenced to a few months imprisonment (this information is not accurate – the Editor).[5] The younger lawyers are an exception to what we have said. Most of them have been appointed administrators of Jewish property and their anti-semitism is open and extreme. Most of them are members of the Naara,[6] the extreme antisemitic Polish Party. The Polish police has been purged of all its better elements for all the policemen have been forced to take an oath of loyalty to the German Government. The police today comprises many criminal elements who constitute a large proportion of the informers and of the Agent provocateure.

The Polish workers are for the most part strong enemies of Germany and as a consequence their attitude towards the Jews is sympathetic.

The tram drivers are outstanding in their patriotism and democratic spirit. For the most part they belong to the Polish Socialist Party. When searches and police enquiries were being conducted in the streets they were of great assistance to Jews and Poles alike. When the Jewish tram service[7] was instituted they gave a great deal of help to the Jews in overcoming their difficulties. The peasants too whose economic position is better than that of other sections of the population have taken up an anti-German stand and from all accounts are playing a great part in the underground national movement.

4 Correctly: Leon Nowodworski (1889–1941), lawyer; dean of the Warsaw Lawyers' Association, member of the executive committee of the National Party (SN), 1928–1930; co-organized the civil defence of Warsaw in Sept. 1939; later member of the Main Council for National Defence (Rada Główna Obrony Narodowej) and co-founder of the SZP underground organization; head of the legal department of the SZP's government delegation in 1940/41.

5 Nowodworski had been arrested by the German occupying forces in Nov. 1939 and released one month later. He died of a heart attack in Warsaw in Dec. 1941.

6 This is probably a reference to Obóz Narodowo-Radykalny (National Radical Camp, ONR), a far-right movement formed in April 1934 as a breakaway faction from the National Democratic milieu. It was banned by the Polish government in 1935 but continued its activities underground.

7 See the section *The Economic Position of the Jews* below.

The only sections in the population whose attitude towards the Germans has been guided by opportunistic principles and who have adopted an inimical attitude towards the Jews are the members of the middle class and the lumpen proletariat. These elements quickly came under the influence of German propaganda and it was they who were responsible for the anti-Jewish disturbances during Passover.[8]

[...][9]

Migration. The one longing of the Jews and of many of the Polish intelligentsia is to leave the country. Since the spring, however, there has been no way of leaving. Only a few individuals are able because of their connections or by heavy bribery to leave the country. Even travelling inside the Reich is fraught with many difficulties.

The Economic Position of the Jews. Jews are no longer citizens of the country. A Jew cannot buy houses or lands. He may sell only by special permit and only if the purchase price is deposited in a frozen account on which he can draw to a maximum of 500 zlotys a month. Most of the houses in the large towns are run by administrators, for the most part Polish lawyers, Volksdeutsche[10] or Ukrainians. The Chief Administrator of Houses is a Ukrainian. Administrators have also been appointed to run Jewish-owned commercial concerns and factories. House owners in Cracow receive a very small monthly sum, while in Warsaw they receive nothing. Some of the large factory owners receive a small monthly allowance. Jewish managers and workmen are systematically dismissed. It is extremely rare to find a Jew employed in industry or commerce. Jewish lawyers are forbidden to engage in their profession. Recently Jewish dentists were obliged to fill in a questionnaire, which is an indication is due to be aryanised.[11] A few Jewish engineers have succeeded in obtaining employment. Doctors get employment only because of the small number of doctors available in the country. Small shopkeepers are still earning something, and relatively speaking, are doing well. Street hawking is flourishing both among Jews and Poles. A decree has been issued obliging Jewish shopkeepers to sell out all their stocks. In practice most Jewish shops have been looted by the Germans (Jewish shops are marked by the Shield of David sign and bear signs in Yiddish and Polish: the signs in Polish shops are written in Polish and German). A whole range of goods are no longer available.

Artisans are treated very well, but they earn very little as a result of the general position. The only people doing really well are the porters, for people are constantly on the move (among the Poles the transport companies are similarly doing very well). The restriction of the movement of Jews in the cities and the introduction of the regulations on special Jewish arm-bands have had the effect of worsening the economic position still further. Jews live on air. How they manage to live at all is a riddle! The position of the intelligentsia is, of course, worst of all. Jews are allowed to possess not more than 2000 zlotys in cash.[12] The value of 2000 zlotys today is that of 400 zlotys before the war. Banks are allowed to pay out to Jews not more than 500 zlotys a month. The accounts of

8 Anti-Jewish riots had occurred in March 1940: see Doc. 98.

9 The paragraphs that follow concern the destruction of Polish cultural life, the forced labour of Poles, the persecution of Poles in the territories annexed by the German Reich, and the economic situation of the Polish population.

10 German in the original: 'ethnic Germans'.

11 As in original: presumably 'an indication they are due to be aryanised'.

12 See Doc. 13, fn. 6, and Doc. 40.

Jews in the banks are frozen. Naturally, ways are found of getting round these restrictions because otherwise people could not live at all.

Jews cannot travel by rail without a special permit which is not easily obtainable (it often takes as long as several weeks to get).[13] Two months ago a special Jewish tram service was initiated. There are 3–4 Polish trams in service and one Jewish tram marked by a yellow sign. Trams run at half hourly intervals. Apart from these trams there are mixed trams marked with a white and yellow sign. In the mixed trams the first compartment is reserved for Germans and Poles. The Germans enter the trams through the front doorway and a few rows of seats are reserved for them. The Poles enter through the rear door. The second compartment is reserved for Jews. It often happens that the first compartment is overcrowded while the second is empty. The Poles however are not allowed to use the second compartment and this often leads to trouble. Once a Polish priest entered the Jewish compartment saying that he had always travelled with Jews and that he intended to do so in future. Nobody dared to do anything to him.

At first, curfew was fixed for the entire population at 5 o'clock in the afternoon (in Warsaw curfew began at 7 – the Editor). Subsequently, curfew was postponed till 7 o'clock and finally till 9 o'clock. Now, curfew begins for Poles at 10 o'clock and for Jews at 9 o'clock. Recently, Poles have been allowed to be on the streets until 11 o'clock. Jews are allowed to be on the streets outside the ghetto till 7 o'clock and inside the ghetto till 9 o'clock.[14] As a result of difficulties of communication Jews are now forced to be inside the ghetto at six o'clock, and the punishment for a breach of the law is very severe. In the railways special compartments have been set aside for Jews and Jews must secure a special permit for each journey. The cost of the permit is very high and it is valid only for short periods. Jewish merchants are therefore forced to bribe ticket inspectors or to leave the carriage at every station and to hide from the inspectors. In October 1940 Jews were forbidden to cross the Uyadovski Boulevard which is now called Victory Boulevard. Jews are also forbidden to cross the Hitler Square (formerly Pilsudski Square). It has been announced that similar restriction will be applied to other places.

In many trams there are no Jewish compartments and consequently communications with many parts of the city are difficult. Since the beginning of winter Jews have been forced to wear special arm bands,[15] and this makes it easy to ascertain whether Jews are observing the regulations. Jews are forbidden to enter the better cafes. The sale of Jewish arm bands is forbidden in many shops. Jews are forbidden to buy books or other publications. Since Jews are clearly identified by their arm bands they can be picked out by German and Polish antisemites in search of victims for their sport. In the autumn a Decree was published directing all Jews to bow to all Germans in uniform and to give way to them in the pavements. Often Jews are forced to raise their hats to German soldiers. This Decree has already been in force for some time in Lodz and other cities and as a result Jews in these cities did not wear hats throughout the summer. When a Jew

13 Provisions on rail travel for Jews were set out in the Regulation on the Use of the Railway by Jews in the General Government of 26 Jan. 1940: *VOBl-GG* 1940, no. 10, 6 February 1940, p. 45.

14 From Dec. 1939 a general curfew for Jews between 9 p.m. and 5 a.m. was enacted pursuant to a regulation of 11 Dec. 1939. Other regional and local regulations were permitted. See Doc. 55.

15 From 1 Dec. 1939 the Jewish population of the General Government was required to wear visible identification: *VOBl-GG* 1939, no. 8, 30 Nov. 1939, p. 61. See also Doc. 49.

greets a German the latter stops him and asks: 'Do you know me, Jew?' – and smacks his face.[16] The penalty for not wearing an arm band is [a] fine and imprisonment together. At first it was possible to get out of wearing an arm band by bribing the German or Polish police, but today, the punishment is very heavy – as much as nine months' imprisonment and a fine running into thousands of zlotys. Persons who have been Christians from birth have been punished for not wearing arm bands.[17]

Postal communications. Postal communications with foreign countries have been made as difficult as possible since the publication of the Decree of April 1940.[18] Everyone who wants to post a letter must wait for hours in a queue in front of the Post Office. Regulations have been issued governing the size and contents of the letters. The sender's address is always checked up by reference to his Passport. In practice, it is impossible for Jews to send letters abroad, except through the medium of Polish friends or of persons whom they pay for the purpose. Many persons have been arrested in connection with the contents of letters which they have received or sent. Jews are allowed to send telegrams abroad only through the Jewish Community. Each telegram must receive the stamp of the Gestapo. This latter provision applies to the whole population.

Jews are forbidden to attend schools. In the autumn the first attempt was made to organise elementary schools. Jewish cultural life is at a complete standstill. One Jewish paper appears in the Polish language. This is the 'Gazette Jidovska'[19] which appears in Cracow. The paper is naturally under German control and every week is forced to publish articles showing how good the situation of the Jews is under German rule.

The Ghetto. Worse than all the actual persecution is the fact that the Jew is not safe even in his own house. In Lodz and in many of the cities in the areas annexed to Germany special quarters were set aside for Jews some time ago. In some places Jews have been living for months in the open in camps fenced in by barbed wire. These Jews are driven from place to place. In Litzmannstadt (Lodz) the Jews are living in a ghetto where the sanitary conditions are frightful. It is forbidden to provide medical attention to children below three and to people above 50.[20] During the summer there were a large number of deaths from dysentery and other diseases.

16 The obligation of Jewish men to greet Germans or Germans in uniform had been introduced in various instances locally in 1940. The Higher SS and Police Leader (HSSPF) East revoked these orders on 5 Dec. 1940 for members of the Waffen-SS after reaching an agreement with the Wehrmacht: Daily Order no. 4, Cracow, 9 Dec. 1940, BArch, MF 41 503. Soon afterwards the Interior Administration Department of the General Government ordered the district governors to take measures in any remaining instances where male Jews were being ordered to greet Germans: circular from Westerkamp (I 5754/40), signed Westerkamp, 15 Jan. 1941, BArch, R 52/II/252, fol. 8.

17 The Regulation on the Visible Identification of Jews (23 Nov. 1939) did not specify the group of people affected; this was set out in the Regulation on the Definition of the Term 'Jew' in the General Government (24 July 1940). The regulation ruled that a person had to wear visible identification if he or she had at least two grandparents who belonged or had belonged to the Jewish community: *VOBl-GG* I 1940, no. 48, 1 August 1940, pp. 231–232.

18 According to the Regulation on Information Exchange (2 April 1940), the Wehrmacht High Command was to decide which countries were to be regarded as 'non-hostile foreign countries': *Reichsgesetzblatt* I, 1940, p. 823.

19 Correctly: *Gazeta Żydowska.*

20 There was no official ban. Elderly people were treated in the hospitals in the Lodz ghetto. Orphanages and homes for the elderly also provided medical care, at least until the deportations in Sept. 1942.

The ghetto is now being systematically introduced in all the cities in the Gouvernement Generale. In Warsaw some 150,000 Poles and 100,000 Jews are affected.[21] The city is being divided into three districts: German,[22] Polish, and Jewish. A number of Poles have been allowed to stay on in the German district, presumably as a sort of guarantee against air raids. The Germans have taken over the best houses. The Poles have been forced to leave the Jewish district. They were given a limited period in which to move their belongings. Likewise the Jews were forced to leave the Polish district but were not allowed to move their furniture. On the day of the publication of these Decrees Poles and Jews wept openly in the streets. The ghetto laws disrupted the economic existence of Poles and Jews alike, and was a great blow at their morale. Their stoic moral resistance of the Jews and the Poles was shaken and there were many cases of suicide. Jews and Poles showed a fine spirit of solidarity and helped each other as much as they could. They exchanged flats, promising to look after each other's furniture and property. The laws particularly affected the economic position of the Poles who not only lost their means of livelihood but were also forced to pay very high rents in the better districts. The economic foundations of Jewish life were completely shaken. Most of the Jewish intelligentsia had lived by renting out rooms and catering to private boarders, and had sometimes been given a helping hand by their Polish neighbours. But the economic results of the new Laws cannot be compared in sadistic cruelty to the moral results. The Jews were hounded with brutal thoroughness. It is said that one of the Professors at the University of Heidelberg received a special mark of distinction for working out a scientific plan for breaking the morale of the population in German-occupied territory.

Who is a 'Jew'. A distinction is made between three categories of Jews: a) Jews whose Jewish ancestry goes back at least three generations; b) Jews whose parents are Jewish; c) Jews of the Mosaic persuasion. The first category is subject to certain restrictions, and the other two categories to different restrictions.

Arrest and persecution of Jewish Youth. We have said the arrests and persecutions of Poles are more numerous than of Jews. However, thousands of Jews, especially Jewish intellectuals, have been arrested as hostages or on various charges, and very few of them have been released. Some have been in prison for a full year. In January a secret radio station was discovered, and then some hundreds of members of the free professions, most of whom were Jews, were arrested; they have not since been heard of. After numerous efforts the most that the Jewish Community Council can do is to get lists of those who have 'died'. Nor can one be certain that these lists are correct. Often, in their sadism the Germans announce that people are dead when they are still alive. The Jewish youth is forced to work at various jobs in the cities. At first they were set to work at the most degrading jobs, but now the situation has improved. The richer Jews release themselves from forced labour by a monthly payment, 60 zlotys to the Jewish Community Council. This money is used for the benefit of those impressed for forced labour. In the summer the Germans began to transfer Jewish youth for forced labour outside the cities. They were sent from Warsaw to a labour camp near Lublin. Conditions in the camp are ter-

21 In fact, approximately 30,000 Poles and 100,000 Jews were forced to relocate to the ghetto.
22 A neighbourhood for Germans had been planned but, due to security concerns, was only partly realized towards the end of the occupation: see Doc. 180.

rible.[23] They are forced to work [for] days at an end standing in water in their ordinary clothes. They sleep on rotten straw. The death rate has reached 10 %. The labour camps are in [the] charge of Nazis trained in the sadistic school of the concentration camp.

DOC. 292
Biuletin, May 1941: article in a Jewish underground newspaper on the Polish National Democracy movement's post-war anti-Jewish plans[1]

Spectres

It would have been reasonable to think the terrible fate that has befallen Poland would sober everyone up, or at least the main Polish parties, let's say. That they would recognize the folly and the terrible damage they have done to Poland with their wild, antisemitic propaganda. But it turns out everything has remained the same. Time and terrible experiences have taught the Polish reactionaries nothing at all.

We have before us an illegal pamphlet, issued by the National Democratic Party,[2] concerning the future of Poland.

We will not go into all the details of the pamphlet now, and instead focus only on how the National Democrats[3] want to solve the Jewish question in the future Poland. For starters, they state that 'German policy concerning the Jews is baffling, to say the least. Today, the Germans are treating the Jews better than they do the Poles, at any rate.' How vile and cynical does someone have to be to make such a claim? From the very first moment, the Germans have made it their aim to destroy the two million Polish Jews who had the misfortune of falling into their clutches.

Only a person who has sold their soul can speak of Jews receiving 'better' treatment from the Germans. We refuse to weigh the sorrows of the Polish people against the sufferings of the Jewish masses under the Nazi occupation to see which side is heavier. We'll leave that to the small-minded National Democrats. We need only mention one word – 'ghetto' – to sufficiently characterize the 'better' treatment the Jews receive at German hands.

So how do the National Democrats want to solve the Jewish question in the new Poland they hope to build? 'Only the national government will solve the Jewish question.

23 Numerous forced labour camps for Jews were in existence in District Lublin in summer and autumn 1940. Conditions were appalling in most of them. A total of 5,253 young Jewish men were deported from Warsaw to those camps.

1 *Biuletin*, no. 6 (16), May 1941, pp. 4–5; AŻIH, Ring I/1300 (682). This document has been translated from Yiddish. *Biuletin* was the Bund's underground newspaper and was published in Warsaw in 1940 and 1941.

2 Correctly: National Party (SN).

3 In the original, the term 'endekish' is used for National Democratic, while 'endekes' is used for National Democrats. Both terms derive from the Polish abbreviation ND, or Endecja, for National Democratic or National Democrats. These terms were already being used pejoratively during the interwar period. The pamphlet mentioned here is probably a text by L. Podolski titled *Quo vadis*: see 'Dyktatura grupy narodowej' ['Dictatorship of the nationalists'], *Wolność: WRN* [= Wolność, Równość, Niepodległość], no. 15, Oct. 1941, pp. 7–8. AAN, 1583/1164/2. *Wolność: WRN* was the journal of the underground Polish Socialist Party (PPS).

Anyone who belonged to the Mosaic faith after 1 January 1941 will be considered a Jew. Jews who converted to Christianity before 1 January 1941 will be recognized as Poles. However, if it can be demonstrated that a converted Pole has done something to harm the interests of the nation or the state, then this Pole will be considered a Jew and will be excommunicated.'

All of this means that we are dealing with an exact copy of Hitler's Nuremberg Laws. The only difference is that this proposal is a bit more tolerant and does not require an 'Aryan' grandmother. Apart from that, however, everything is the same as it is in Hitler's laws.

But let's leave aside the converts to Christianity who are allowed to be Poles and look at what is planned for the Jews. Jews' lives 'will be circumscribed by a special legal statute designed in such a way that even living [under this statute] will compel (the Jews) to emigrate' (p. 62). The author does not elaborate on this 'legal statute', but the pamphlet does give us a foretaste of how the author envisages it in his fantasies.

'It is necessary to cut all regular ties between Jews and non-Jews, and not only in economic life, but also with regard to cultural and personal exchanges. The Jews will have to live in complete isolation for as long as they refuse to emigrate.'

'Marriage between Jews and non-Jews will be strictly forbidden.'

'Fully aware of the importance of Jewish emigration, the Polish national movement and the Polish national government will ensure that the Jews emigrate from Poland to Palestine, Syria, or Abyssinia' (p. 66).

Here we have the National Democratic programme concerning the Jewish question laid bare for all to see; it matches what the ONR demanded in the old Poland and includes upgrades based on Hitler's current system in Poland, i.e. ultimately the 'ghetto'. The National Democrats still show a little compunction in calling it 'complete isolation'.

It is a good thing that this pamphlet has come out. The National Democrats' mask has slipped, and everyone has seen their ugly Hitlerian mug. The effect is such that the National Democrats got scared, stopped circulating the pamphlet, and retracted it. But the cat is out of the bag, and now we know what the National Democrats intend to do in the future Poland. We will not engage in polemics with them; it isn't worth the trouble. But there is one thing we want to say to these dedicated servants of Hitler, who lick his boots while those selfsame boots trample their own fatherland: It is not you, National Democrats, who will build the new Poland. That Poland you dream of is lost forever. It was a Poland of capitalists and landowners, a Poland of oppression and misery, of wealth and privilege for a small group and of suffering and want for the majority of the Polish population. That Poland is already gone. Others will build the country anew, and you will have no say at all in this new socialist Poland.

The Jewish masses in Poland will endure and will survive Hitler, just as they will survive all the impotent desires and spectres of the past, of the National Democrats, and of the ONR.

DOC. 293
On 3 June 1941 the chief of staff in District Lublin makes plans to isolate the Jewish population behind a high wall[1]

Memorandum by the Chief of Staff in District Lublin, signed Losacker,[2] for SS and Police Leader Globocnik, Landrat Kipke,[3] Department Head Türk, Dr Becher,[4] Department Head Schöller,[5] Stadthauptmann Saurmann, and Regierungsrat Dr Bausenhardt,[6] dated 3 June 1941[7]

Re: ghetto in Lublin[8]
Despite the prohibition on [them] using Krakauerstraße,[9] Jews are seen very frequently on Krakauerstraße. It is proving an ever more urgent necessity to confine the Jews in Lublin to the ghetto and seal them off from the rest of the city. This will only be possible if the ghetto is surrounded with a wall that is at least 3 metres high. There must be no more than four exits [from the ghetto] into the city. These gates, which must be locked at night, will have to be guarded. The Jewish Order Service is to be primarily deployed for patrolling purposes, but it will have to be monitored closely by police officers. The Jews still living outside the ghetto will have to gradually move into the ghetto. It will only be possible to leave the Jewish residential district with an identity card issued by

1 APL, 498/892, fols. 493–494. This document has been translated from German.
2 Dr Ludwig Losacker (1907–1994), lawyer; joined the NSDAP in 1931 and the SS in 1933; worked in the SD, 1936–1937; subsequently held posts in the Reich Ministry of the Interior and various companies; Kreishauptmann in Jasło, 1939–1940; chief of staff in District Lublin, Jan.–July 1941; then in Galicia; head of the Interior Administration Department of the General Government from Jan. 1943; governor of District Cracow, May–Oct. 1943; subsequently served in the Waffen-SS; representative of the Chemical Industry Employers' Association and director of the German Industrial Institute in Cologne after the war.
3 Dr Alfred Kipke (1898–1953), lawyer; member of the German People's Party (DVP); joined the NSDAP in 1933; Landrat in Wolmirstedt from 1936; Landkommissar in Thorn (West Prussia) in 1939; head of the Interior Administration Department in District Lublin, June 1940–Sept. 1941; then worked in the Interior Administration Department of the General Government; Kreishauptmann in Tarnów from 1942.
4 Probably Dr Hans Becher (b. 1908), lawyer; joined the NSDAP in 1929; awarded a doctorate (on tax law) from the University of Leipzig in 1931; worked at the Main Department of Justice of the General Government in 1943.
5 Fritz Schöller (1909–1973), teacher; joined the NSDAP and the SA in 1928; later served in the SS; worked for the Reich Ministry of Public Enlightenment and Propaganda; from 1936 head of a Nazi Party regional office (Gauamt), Gau head of training in Franconia, and councilman in Nuremberg; worked for the Propaganda Department in District Warsaw, Oberregierungsrat, 1939–1941; head of the Propaganda Department in District Lublin from May 1941 until at least late 1943; teacher in Central Franconia after the war.
6 Correctly: Dr Walter Bausenhart (1907–1994), lawyer; joined the NSDAP in 1933; worked in the Municipal Department of the Württemberg Ministry of the Interior from 1937; Regierungsrat in the Municipal Department of the Reich Ministry of the Interior from 1939; chief of police in Warsaw, June 1940 – Aug. 1941; later served in the war; taken captive; after his release worked in the civil service of the West German state of Schleswig-Holstein; deputy chief of staff and head of the Department for Expellees, Refugees, and Disabled Veterans in the Schleswig-Holstein Ministry of Labour, Social Affairs, and Expellees, 1963–1971.
7 The original contains handwritten annotations.
8 On the establishment of the ghetto in Lublin, see Doc. 257.
9 Lublin's main street before the war, Krakowskie Przedmieście.

the Stadthauptmann/Chief of Police. Such identity cards will only be issued to Jews who pursue employment that mainly serves German interests. Individual agencies' convenience or their bad practice of employing Jewish staff must be given no consideration. The Jews will have to be back in the ghetto at 7 p.m. In special, exceptional cases, Jews will be allowed to return to the ghetto as late as 9 p.m., the time at which Jews within the ghetto have to leave the streets as well.

The process of transferring ownership of those shops located outside the ghetto that are still in Jewish hands to Aryan ownership must be accelerated. However, this is essentially to be undertaken in such a way that the Jew in question can open a shop of the same type and equivalent value in the ghetto. Transferring the stocks of goods from such Jewish shops located outside the ghetto to the Jewish residential district is to be generally permitted, provided these are not goods that Jews are not allowed to purchase (e.g. textiles that require a purchase permit).

Production facilities will have to be set up in the ghetto to ensure the Jews have the means necessary to make a living. The Economic Affairs Department will fit out such Jewish workshops with the help of the Stadthauptmann, and will also provide opportunities for domestic outwork for Jews.

For reasons of expediency, the Jews will have to construct the walls around the ghetto themselves.

DOC. 294

On 8 June 1941 Bernhard Deutsch asks the World Council of Churches refugee committee for help after his deportation to Kielce[1]

Letter from Bernhard Deutsch,[2] Kielce, 3 I. Aleja Świętego Wojciecha, District Radom, General Government of Poland, to the Secretary of the Committee for Ecumenical Aid to Refugees[3] of the World Council of Churches[4] in Geneva, dated 8 June 1941

Dear Sir,

The undersigned hereby take the liberty of requesting your help, Esteemed Secretary, for the following reasons: although we are Protestants, we were brought here on a transport

1 Archives of the International Committee of the Red Cross (AICRC), G59/2/106–16, Relief to Poland, 26 June 1941–10 Dec. 1946. Copy in USHMM, RG 19 045M, reel 2, frames 1772–1773. This document has been translated from German.

2 Bernhard Deutsch (1881–1942?) was deported from Vienna to Kielce on 19 Feb. 1941.

3 In May 1939 the Provisional Committee of the World Council of Churches, which was being set up at that time in Geneva, cooperated with aid organizations to establish a Committee for Ecumenical Aid to Refugees at Bloomsbury House in London. The committee was relocated to Geneva in Sept. 1939. One of its main tasks was to help Christian refugees leave territories under Nazi rule.

4 The director of the Committee for Ecumenical Aid to Refugees was Dr Adolf Freudenberg (1894–1977), lawyer and pastor of the Confessing Church; legation counsellor at the Foreign Office until 1935, when he left on account of his wife's Jewish origins; studied at the theological colleges in Bethel and Berlin-Dahlem; briefly detained in June 1937 and barred from university; subsequently lived in Basel; returned to Germany in 1947. Apart from Freudenberg, Dr Adolf Keller (1872–1963) was working in Geneva as the secretary general of the European Central Office for Ecclesiastical Aid, which was sponsored by the Federation of Swiss Protestant Churches.

from Vienna and have been housed in a 'sealed Jewish residential quarter'. We have been stripped of all funds, we had to leave everything behind in Vienna, and there are no opportunities of any kind to work and earn money here. Once a day, the Jewish Religious Community here gives us soup with 60 g of bread. Apart from this, we are completely reliant on our friends' charity, on parcels that are sent to us. Misery, hunger, and death are increasing daily. As mail posted from Switzerland is permitted, while all mail from Vienna is prohibited, we take the liberty of asking you most sincerely to assist us, be it with food parcels or be it with consignments of old clothes (gentlemen's and ladies'), quite regardless of their condition, as we have good opportunities to reuse them here. Please do not be offended by our candid language. Our misery compels us to use it.

In the hope that our plea for help will be heard, we thank you most sincerely in advance and remain humbly yours in gratitude,

Bernhard Deutsch and family (wife and son)

Alfrida Spitzer[5]

DOC. 295
On 8 June 1941 Fela Kamelgarn asks the Jewish elder of the Lodz ghetto to find her work[1]

Handwritten letter from Fela Kamelgarn,[2] 23 Sulzfelderstraße, Apartment 23, to Rumkowski, the chairman of the Jewish Council of Elders in the Lodz ghetto (received by the secretary's office at 1 Dworskastraße[3] on 9 June 1941), dated 8 June 1941

Petition

As my request to return to my parents' house in Pabianice has been denied, I am once again forced to turn to you, Honourable Chairman, to ask that I be considered for any available work.

As fate would have it, I have already spent over a year in the ghetto, relying on the generosity of my relatives. However, my relatives have now denied me any support, as they themselves are in an extremely dire financial situation. To date I have not received and do not receive any unemployment benefits. I therefore have no livelihood. I am without parental care and entirely alone in a foreign town. Yet I am still young and fit for any work. I do not want to be a burden on my relatives or to live off unemployment benefits. I have only just turned 17 years old. I have completed a one-year bookkeeping course with I. Mantinband[4] in Litzmannstadt, as well as a two-year internship, and [have had] an office job (retail) in Pabianice.

5 Alfrida Spitzer (1883–1942) came from Bucharest and lived in Vienna before the war; he was deported from Vienna to Kielce on 19 Feb. 1941 and murdered in Auschwitz.

1 YVA, O-34/568. This document has been translated from Polish.
2 Probably Fajga Kamelgarn (b. 1923), bookkeeper from Pabianice who lived in the Lodz ghetto; perished during the German occupation.
3 The secretary's office, to which ghetto residents could address petitions and letters of complaint.
4 Probably Israel Mantinband (1864?–1942), teacher in Łódź; deported to the Warsaw ghetto, where he perished.

In consideration of the fact that I am a minor, of my critical emotional and financial situation, and of my ardent desire to work, I believe that you, Honourable Chairman, whose ingenuity supports all those who are unfortunate, will respond favourably to my request and promptly assign me work. For that I thank you in advance. I promise to work diligently and to the satisfaction of my supervisors.

DOC. 296
Miriam Chaszczewacka describes her experiences in Radomsko between 21 April and 12 June 1941[1]

Handwritten diary of Miriam Chaszczewacka,[2] entries for 21 April to 12 June 1941

Monday, 21 April 1941
I've made up with everyone. It's only Irka I'm still quite angry with, even though we live across from each other, but I have completely forgotten about that, and no wonder, as I've been preoccupied with so many other things.

One blow after another. (1) They didn't let us perform. (2) We prepared Passover Seder,[3] but it didn't work out, even though we put so much effort into it. As to (3) – not so fast.

We decided to set to work. We published two issues of our gazette and packed it with hope and slogans, such as 'Cheer up' and 'We'll pull through'. This wasn't enough for us. We looked for teaching materials, we split into two groups, and most importantly – I. and I were to teach the others Hebrew. We were very happy. We didn't mind that the ghetto had been reduced in size and that we had been completely cut off from the countryside. We didn't care about politics, or that the Germans are taking Yugoslavia[4] – nothing. We were happy despite the terrible conditions, if one may say so. And then the third and worst blow struck us. The meetings became too conspicuous, and third parties began to warn us discreetly. Today, when we should have been giving our first Hebrew lesson, we instead dissolved the organization entirely.

Things are so difficult for us, although we promised ourselves that we would always think about it, study as much as possible on our own, and work. Although we reprise the powerful texts of Hebrew songs, things are really terrible.

I promised Różka, Frania, and Fela that I'll teach them nonetheless.

It's good that I'll be busy; it will give me extra strength. In the coming days we will have lessons at Miss N.'s place. I'm knitting myself a jumper, and now I remember the classes that I had completely forgotten, because the exam is on 10 May, so I have to study.

We did not sing during that sad meeting. Instead I. quietly translated the words of the song 'Yamim Bochim'. The heavens weep. I keep repeating to myself: 'Ve af al pi chen, ve lamrot hakol Eretz Israel.'[5] Eretz Israel, despite everything.

1 YVA, O-3/3382, handwritten original, fols. 3–10; typewritten copy, fols. 10–16. This document has been translated from Polish.
2 Miriam Chaszczewacka (1924–1942) was a member of the Zionist youth movement.
3 See Doc. 275, fn. 13.
4 The Wehrmacht's invasion of Yugoslavia began on 6 April 1941. On 17 April the Yugoslavian commanders signed an unconditional surrender.

Tuesday, 29 April 1941
What ghastly weather; feels like November. You lose heart due to the constant rain and mud.

Estusia, Marek, and I have lessons with Miss H. As if out of spite, she's ill and we don't have any lessons, only more boredom.

We've fallen out with the girls Bronka, Klara, Ala, and Irka again, because they continue to organize dances and ignore us, and then pretend nothing's happened. Klara was close to us as long as we had our meetings, but now it's as if she doesn't know us. Estusia, Frania, Różka, and I have completely distanced ourselves from them. I wouldn't even mind a confrontation, but hardly anyone goes out in this weather. We study for our classes, even though they already bore me and I don't know if it makes any sense at all.

And to make matters worse, there's no bread or potatoes. There's commotion in town, and famine might break out.

I'm starting to believe – in fact, I've known for a long time now – that youth is a treasure, even if it is passing by under such miserable conditions. Does anyone else still really believe in tomorrow and keep assiduously repeating that it will get better? We've just learned the German [poem] 'Habe Sonne in Herzen',[6] which ends like this:

Hab' ein Lied auf den Lippen
verlier nie den Mut
Hab Sonne im Herzen
und alles wird gut.[7]

On Friday, I made the whole house laugh by saying: 'I'm 16 years old and "He"[8] is 50 or even older, so I'll outlive him.'

It is easily said, but in reality – the main thing is not to worry.

Tuesday, 13 May 1941
Exams are over. We passed with flying colours. All of us have a very good overall grade, except for the three who have a 'satisfactory', and Estusia who has a 'good'. We will receive our certificates on Saturday.

I will teach Hebrew to Frania, Rózia, and Fela. They insist on paying me, so I said they can give me the amount I need for Miss H., perhaps a bit more.

The bread situation is terrible again. Father is barely eating. Potatoes are expensive and scarce. Food in general is terribly expensive. Moreover, a great many parcels are being sent to other towns every day. Dreadful letters are arriving from all over. Warsaw is full of corpses every day.[9] The abyss is getting deeper and deeper.

Only today is the weather nicer, a proper May. Only our hearts are not in a May mood.

5 Hebrew: 'Despite everything, we yearn for Eretz Israel.'
6 German in the original: 'Keep the sunshine in your heart'.
7 German in the original: 'Keep a song on your lips / Don't let your courage fall / Keep the sunshine in your heart / And fine will be all'. These are the last four lines of the poem 'Hab Sonne im Herzen' by Cäsar Flaischlen (1864–1920), a lyricist and poet from Stuttgart who wrote in dialect and was well known in the early twentieth century.
8 The author is referring to Hitler.
9 During this period several thousand people perished every day in the Warsaw ghetto.

Thursday, 22 May 1941
Yesterday Mama ran the kindergarten in Mrs B.'s new apartment, and as if out of spite, Mrs B.'s little son fell ill. I don't know what will happen now.

We still don't have our certificates, but they don't mean anything anyway.

Ala will learn tailoring at Wanda G.'s place. She says she had really dreamed of something else, but what else can she do? Her older sister is getting married, her parents are elderly, and someone has to earn money.

I'm so worried about the kindergarten that I can't gather my thoughts.

I should write more often to include a bit of politics.

So, Hess has escaped to England, which the Polish press explains by saying he was not in his right mind;[10] and now the latest news: they themselves[11] have announced that war with America is inevitable. America is demanding that France not hand over its bases in Syria to them.

Food is now in plentiful supply, but it's all so terribly expensive.

Thursday, 12 June 1941
In retrospect, I always regret having written so little, as I never feel like describing so many events at once. A clear view of all these events will only be possible after the war.

Well, as far I can recall the Germans have won on Crete and England has occupied Syria, France's colony. As for Russia, things are quiet, but a lot of mechanized transport is headed in that direction.

The high prices were terrible. (I write 'were terrible' as if it were already over, because some things have become cheaper now, but for how long?) The mark was terribly expensive, and black bread used to cost 30 złoty. A kg of potatoes used to cost 3 złoty, and today it costs 2.80 or even less. Bread is portioned out like exquisite cake, and sometimes Father did not want to eat at all. In the morning we cook millet or barley groats (for a time they used to cost 20–21 złoty per kg), and in the evening watery soup, or vice versa. For lunch [we have] whole potatoes with kefir or white borscht, as we get 1.5 litres of milk every day.

I'm very busy these days, since I help my mother at the Fröbel kindergarten[12] in the mornings. That's why I've moved my lesson with Heniek to 5 o'clock, after my lesson at Miss Hela's.

Różka, Frania, and I are now an inseparable trio, and although we have little time, we see each other every day, if only for half an hour. Together with Felek and Lolek, we also read Jewish novels from the jubilee edition of *Hajnt*.[13] This is meant as extracurricular work.

Last week, Father wrote to his sister in Russia. I really wish she would write back soon.

10 Hitler's deputy, Rudolf Hess (1894–1987), fled to Scotland on 10 May 1941.

11 A reference to the Germans.

12 Friedrich Fröbel (1782–1852) was the founder of kindergartens and influential in the field of educational reform.

13 Probably *Haynt, yoyvl bukh*, which was published in 1938 under Abraham Goldberg's editorship in honour of the thirtieth anniversary of the newspaper's founding.

DOC. 297

On 14 June 1941 the senior administrative official from the Kreishauptmann's office in Lublin-Land reports attempted bribery by Jews[1]

File note from the senior administrative official of Department VIII, Krumbiegel (?), to Department IV,[2] dated 14 June 1941

1. During an inspection in Piaski on 9 June 1941, I was told by the driver Guja that a member of the local Jewish Community had approached him with the suggestion that the undersigned should name any sum to the Jewish Council, which the Council would pay if the construction of the ghetto in Piaski could be delayed for several months. As is my duty, I hereby report this attempted bribery.
2. To Department IV for further action under criminal law.[3]

DOC. 298

In mid June 1941 an employee of the Society for the Promotion of Agriculture among Jews describes the ordeal of forced labour[1]

Handwritten report by the ToPoRol[2] employee Stefan Cukierman[3] for the underground archive of the Warsaw ghetto, mid June 1941 or later

Impressions from a labour camp

I walked down Nalewki on 14 May 1941. As the day was unsettled – so-called roundups for the labour camps were taking place – I withdrew into a doorway. I waited in the doorway for half an hour. When I stepped out, a man from the Jewish Order Service came up to me and demanded to see my identity card. Since I worked for the 'Toporol' agricultural society, I felt safe, so I showed him my identity card. He told me to accompany him to the Commissariat, where they would surely release me after checking my

1 APL, 501/139, fol. 38. This document has been translated from German.
2 Department IV was the Police Department.
3 On 16 June 1941 Kreishauptmann Emil Ziegenmeyer served the Jewish Council in Piaski with a penalty notice for 2,000 złoty. The chairman of the Jewish Council, businessman Mendel Polisecki (1895–1942), denied having anything to do with the attempted bribery, referred to his 'extremely precarious financial situation', and asked to have 'the penalty that has been set remitted by means of clemency': APL, 501/139, fol. 37.

1 APL, 501/139, fol. 38. This document has been translated from German.
2 ToPoRol (Towarzystwo Popierania Rolnictwa wśród Żydów), the Society for the Promotion of Agriculture among Jews, was an organization founded by the American Jewish Joint Distribution Committee (JDC) in 1933. In the Warsaw ghetto, under the direction of Israel Sudewicz, it cultivated land and grew vegetables. The Jewish Social Self-Help (JSS) and the building committees were supposed to leave the harvest for the poorest people. In collaboration with the welfare association CENTOS, approximately 20 agronomists tended the small allotments, which also served as children's playgrounds.
3 Stefan Cukierman was arrested in Warsaw on 15 May 1941 and deported to Frysztak camp (north-east of Jasło) in District Cracow, where he remained until early June 1941. Upon returning to Warsaw he wrote a report, which he passed on to the underground archive.

card. At the Commissariat I waited for my identity card to be checked. This took quite a long time, and eventually I realized that I'd been tricked. I turned to everyone and explained that as a 'Toporol' student,[4] I was indispensable, but to no avail. I had no other choice but to give up, but I simultaneously requested permission to send a message home and inform my parents. Unfortunately the Order Service men would not even hear of it. In reply to my persistent pleas, one of them said that I would be able to write not just a message, but an entire letter from the camp. At 5.30 p.m. they came for us and placed us under quarantine at 109 Leszno.[5] In the car, after much persuasion and for a fee, I managed to give a policeman a note to take home for me. I later discovered that my parents never received it. After we arrived at the quarantine [building], we queued up to see a physician. The medical examination was quick. After the examination, a bath, and then a bit of soup (it was already 1.30 in the morning). We slept two to a bunk. We woke up terribly hungry the next morning. We began to demand food, until finally, at 3 p.m., we each got one quarter of a loaf of bread. We left for Gdańsk railway station at 5 p.m. that day.[6] We were each given one quarter of a loaf of bread for the journey. The train set off at 8 p.m. We had already eaten our quarter of bread by then. The supervisors calculated that we would reach our destination, i.e. Frysztak,[7] at 9 a.m., yet the trip took two days and two nights, without food or drink, in goods wagons. We reached the camp two days later at around 4, so hungry and tired that we could barely stand. The people of Frysztak, all Jews, gave us a warm welcome (they served us tea). At 6 o'clock we were given supper and breakfast together, consisting of 600 g of bread, 30 g of butter, 50 g of Emmental cheese, and 0.5 litres of soup with meat. This was intended to last us until noon the next day. The next day we got up at 4 a.m. We were given coffee, and at 5 o'clock we set off for work. The work was not hard on the first day. We were assisted by a foreman, a paramedic, and a Jewish policeman. At noon we were given a very greasy soup with meat and 150 g of bread. We finished work at 6 p.m. and then returned to the camp. We were given supper at 7. We spent the night on a synagogue floor that was covered with straw. It was very dirty there. Unbelievably huge lice were crawling all over the place during the night. I discovered that I and another 150 people had been transferred to a different firm.

The wake-up call was an hour earlier than the day before. We walked 8 km to work. We would return from work at 9 p.m., and sometimes even at 10. The work was very hard. We often returned to the camp too tired to eat supper. We simply collapsed onto the bunks and fell asleep straight away. I had an accident after three weeks of work. An iron rail fell on my arm and broke my collarbone. The physicians discharged me from work. I left with a group of nearly 80 patients. The army gave us 60 g of bread, cheese, butter, and soup for the journey. The return journey was much worse than the journey there. We travelled for two days and three nights. We didn't receive anything to eat

4 As in the original.

5 The quarantine building was located outside the ghetto.

6 A large railway station north of Warsaw and in the direct vicinity of the Warsaw ghetto. The goods depot of this station served as the *Umschlagplatz* (literally 'reloading point', in practice the holding area for deportees) prior to deportation.

7 Frysztak forced labour camp, which existed until Nov. 1941, held approximately 2,000 inmates, who were housed in two synagogues and had to perform construction work on roads, tunnels, and quarries.

during the journey. We reached Warsaw at 6 a.m. Three people died during the journey, partly from starvation and partly from exhaustion. We were all dazed and only semi-conscious. While in quarantine, we were not given any bread, only some borscht and beetroots at 4 p.m. The behaviour of the quarantine personnel was shocking. They refused to answer our questions and shouted at us as if we were convicts rather than camp inmates. Eventually, after two days of this torment, starved and emaciated, we were released and escorted to the Jewish residential district.

DOC. 299
Schoolboy Dawid Rubinowicz describes the events that took place in Krajno from 16 to 22 June 1941[1]

Diary of Dawid Rubinowicz,[2] entries for 16 to 22 June 1941

16 June: Papa went to see the gendarmerie in the morning. Mama went with him. We were all very sad when Papa left the house. I stared out the window for hours, thinking they might return. But as the hours passed, there was still no sign of them. I had all sorts of thoughts. Had they been arrested? Did the gendarmerie even exist? I no longer knew what to think. I took my wooden sandals to the cobbler so that he could fit them with straps. While I was waiting at the cobbler's for my straps, a boy from Bieliny ran in to the cobbler's because he didn't know where we lived. He said that Uncle should go and tell the gendarmerie whose grain it was, because they had temporarily arrested Papa.[3] We ran home immediately with this very unpleasant news. Everyone was horrified by the news. Uncle went to the gendarmerie right away. Auntie went with him. We children stayed at home with Grandma. We did not eat any supper. I went to bed at midnight.

17 June: Zelman came to us from Południowa. We were very curious as to why he had come. He said that someone had cycled over from Bieliny and we should hide our more valuable undergarments and clothes because the gendarmerie would be here soon. We hid all of our valuable belongings while he was still here. I went out a few times to see if they were coming, but they were nowhere in sight. Terrible panic gripped the village, as if bandits were about to advance. Then they arrived; first they searched a farmer's house, and then they left. When they were near, my heart was pounding so fast that I thought it would explode. Thank God the gendarmerie did not come to us, although they were

1 The original diary was found in Bodzentyn in the Kielce voivodeship in the late 1950s and acquired by the journalist Maria Jarochowska, who published the diary in Warsaw in 1960 and in a German translation in Berlin in 1961. The original has since been lost. Reproduced in Dawid Rubinowicz, *Pamiętnik Dawida Rubinowicza*, ed. Adam Rutkowski (Warsaw: Książka i Wiedza, 1960), pp. 15–19. The diary has also been published in English translation as *The Diary of Dawid Rubinowicz*, trans. Derek Bowman (Edinburgh: William Blackwood, 1981). This document has been newly translated from Polish.

2 Dawid Rubinowicz (1927–1942) lived in Krajno, a village near Kielce; the occupying authorities transferred him, his parents, and his siblings to the ghetto in Bodzentyn in March 1942; the family is thought to have been deported to Treblinka six months later and murdered there.

3 The Jewish population was forbidden to stockpile food supplies.

probably meant to. I said they would come on their way back. We were so terrified that we didn't know what was happening to us. The gendarmerie didn't come on their way back either. I immediately followed them to see where they would go. They went to wherever they had been in the morning. I can't say whether they confiscated anything because I don't know. I immediately went to my cousin's so that he could cycle over to Bieliny and bring them some food, because they hadn't eaten for such a long time. Then I brought him a package, and he left immediately. When I got back home I had something to eat, and my brother took the cow out to pasture. My brother couldn't bring himself to eat anything. I went to my brother so that he could come and eat. While I was watching over the cow, my sister ran up to me and said they were all on their way back. I was very happy when she told me that. My cousin was already back because he had met them en route. I immediately ran home to see if they had arrived. They arrived after about half an hour. You can imagine how happy we all were to see them. Papa told us what it was like for them in custody and who had brought them food. He told us everything in detail.

18 June: Yesterday I forgot to write that when Zelman visited us, he said that everyone had been arrested, but they returned – thank God! I've cheered up a bit since yesterday's events.

I lost so much strength during those two days that I doubt I will recover it in three months.

20 June: We went to the forest to look for wood. It was nice in the forest. I found three mushrooms, and we each took home a bundle of wood.

22 June: It was still dark when Papa woke us up and told us to listen to the awful noise coming from the north-east. It was so loud that the earth shook. We could hear it the entire day. Around evening we met some Jews on their way from Kielce. They said that Soviet Russia had declared war on Germany. Only then did I understand what that noise was.

DOC. 300

On 20 June 1941 the National Democratic underground newspaper *Walka* incites hatred against the Jews in the ghetto[1]

The ghetto and Auschwitz

Jewish propaganda, which is always perfect, has intensified considerably in recent days, and the effects are immediately apparent. Horrific descriptions of suffering among the ghetto residents, reports of piles of corpses lying in the streets there every day, and expressions of polite sympathy can be heard at every turn across broad swathes of our society.

1 *Walka*, 20 June 1941, p. 6. This document has been translated from Polish.

The Jews are undoubtedly severely persecuted. Nazi Germany has declared a merciless war on them by devising a policy of completely isolating them until it acquires territories to which they can be expelled, as if they were an alien, harmful element in the national body politic.

Meanwhile this provisional territory has been found – Poland's occupied provinces, where new transports from Germany arrive day and night. Here the policy of persecution and isolation continues. Initially the Jews were 'branded' with armbands displaying the Star of David, one of their most sacred symbols. Then they were prohibited from going to cinemas, theatres, cafés, and even parks. They were subjected to petty humiliation on a daily basis, since this policy was essential to domestic propaganda and was pursued flagrantly. Eventually the Jews were locked up in a ghetto created specifically for this purpose. Of course, life there is no fun at all. Terribly cramped living conditions, confinement in a small area that you are not permitted to leave, and ultimately hunger caused by all of these restrictions, difficulties with supply deliveries, and the lack of humanity on the part of the Jewish Community, which remains unconcerned with the dreary masses, the poor kaftan Jews. Death from epidemic typhus is increasingly frequent.

And yet one should not forget that German plans clearly describe the Jews' current circumstances as temporary. They are to be removed from Germany's entire 'living space', which includes the 'General Government'. They have been ostracized and are used for different kinds of labour, but they have been isolated to the point that they are therefore no longer exposed to the humiliations, great and small, on the part of the Germans, who do not interfere with the Jews' self-governance. Since the Jews controlled Poland's economic life before the war, the Germans now find it difficult to do without them, and this is why Jewish deliveries[2] and manufacturing for the military are prospering and generating enormous profits for entrepreneurs. Their considerable influence on the country's financial life has led to the accumulation of enormous capital in the ghetto. Every day carts full of food enter the ghetto under the watchful eye of a German policeman, who enriches himself through this humanitarian activity. Prices in the ghetto are no higher than 20–30 per cent [of prices outside the ghetto], and there is a whole array of products that are even cheaper.

Auschwitz, Oranienburg, Mauthausen; roundups, torturing innocent people to extract confessions from those without any knowledge of 'political activity' – all of these horrific words are known in the ghetto only by hearsay.

However, one should remember that it is not the Jews, but rather we who are Germany's 'no. 1 enemy'. As a young, healthy, dynamic nation, we stand in the way of expanding 'lebensraum',[3] and consequently we are to be removed. It is difficult to resettle us, however, since Poland is our fatherland. According to the German saying, we are to be 'uprooted'.

The policy of exterminating our people is being enacted with the greatest cruelty and ruthlessness – qualities that distinguish Germany from the rest of the world. Although we have not been 'degraded' with armbands bearing the white eagle, which we would

2 Presumably a reference to deliveries of supplies to the Wehrmacht from the workshops in the ghetto.

3 German in the original; correctly: 'Lebensraum' ('living space').

have worn with less pain than the Jews wear their Stars of David, signs reading 'Nur für Deutsche'[4] are nevertheless becoming more widespread, and the example of Cracow illustrates where this development may lead.[5] We are not degraded by propaganda as much as the Jews, but sexual relations between Poles and Germans are perceived as 'racial defilement' and are therefore punishable by death in the Reich. Our humiliation is not insignificant; it is fundamental, and thousands of our comrades, with or without bundles containing their belongings, are leaving this 'ancient Germanic land' where they've resided since time immemorial.

There is perhaps no need to mention the persecution, the roundups, the arrests, and the shootings of 'hostages'; the deaths of hundreds of children in the resettlement camps; the urns inscribed with 'Heil Hitler' which contain the ashes of fathers, brothers, and sons; Oflag[6] officers dying of tuberculosis; our comrades dying of exhaustion while at 'work' or as a result of English bombs; or farmers being tortured for failing to meet a 'quota'.

And the ghetto? Without much ado it closes in on us unnoticed, particularly since railway transport has been suspended and we are only able to move about the country with the same permits with which hundreds of Jews continuc to wander around Warsaw. We have no money to buy food and are gradually being thrown out of the better apartments and pushed to the outskirts. Poles who have just moved to Cracow are only permitted to live in Kazimierz.[7]

However, those who are shocked at the sight of a Jew lying on a street in the ghetto are advised to go to Annopol[8] and ask the RGO for the mortality rates of poor Poles who have died of epidemic typhus, or the number of deaths from tuberculosis, which kills hundreds of children and young people every month.

Finally, let us take a look not just at the 'General Government', but also at Poland as a whole. Should the author of these words succeed – even if only in the name of fighting a common enemy and in the name of shared suffering – in forgetting that moment in September 1939 when he was accosted by Jews, it nevertheless remains a fact that the Jews are privileged while Poles are being 'uprooted' beyond the Bug river,[9] just as they are here.

It is not a matter of determining whose suffering is greater or who is more persecuted. It is a matter of saving and preserving one's nation. We are subject not only to Jewish but also to German propaganda, which does not conceal the persecution of the Jews, even while it protects and cares for us by 'arranging' our economic existence and ensuring cheap food, while thousands of us are dying as a result of regulations cleverly devised by the authorities especially for this purpose.

4 German in the original: 'Only for Germans'.
5 As the capital of the General Government, Cracow was at the centre of German efforts at Germanization, which affected the appearance of the city as well as cultural life.
6 'Offizierslager': German for 'camp for officers'; German prisoner-of-war camps in which only officers were imprisoned.
7 In March 1941 the Jewish population had been expelled from Kazimierz, the traditionally Jewish district of Cracow, to the neighbourhood of Podgórze, where a ghetto was created.
8 This probably refers to Warsaw's outer neighbourhood, which has since been incorporated into the city.
9 The author is referring to the Soviet occupation zone in eastern Poland.

The ghetto and Auschwitz. Does it not suffice to juxtapose these two words, which embody the occupiers' stance towards Jews and Poles?

One should have compassion for the persecuted Jews. It is a Christian virtue. *To forget the persecution of our comrades, however, is a crime.*

DOC. 301

Krakauer Zeitung, 21 June 1941: report about new restrictions on the Jewish population in District Warsaw[1]

Movement restricted for Jews. District Governor of Warsaw appeals to population to safeguard public health.

Warsaw, 21 June

In a directive that came into force on 17 June, the Governor of District Warsaw has banned Jews[2] from the Grojec, Lowitsch, and Sochaczew-Blonie Kreise, as well as the part of Kreis Warsaw-Land located to the west of the Vistula. Furthermore, Jews are forbidden from leaving the municipality where they have their residence or habitual abode and/or the Jewish residential district assigned to them. The Kreishauptmann in charge may grant exceptions. In conjunction with this directive, it is forbidden to provide Jews in contravention of these provisions with accommodation, food, drink, or other forms of support.

In an appeal to the population of District Warsaw published at the same time, the District Governor pointed out that the establishment of Jewish residential districts had led to a dramatic decline in the number of typhus cases in the District. However, there have recently been several new typhus cases outside the Jewish residential districts that were demonstrably caused by Jews roaming about. This was the reason why the regulation was promulgated. Anyone who violates the regulation faces imprisonment or a fine of up to 10,000 zloty, in serious cases even penal servitude. In his appeal, the District Governor further expressed the expectation that the District's population will support these measures, which were ordered in the interest of their own health, and will hand over to the police any Jews found roaming outside their Jewish residential district without permission. Only in this way will it be possible to effectively protect the District's German and Polish populations from the dangers to their health that any contact with the Jews represents.

1 *Krakauer Zeitung*, 21 June 1941, p. 5. Published in Pospieszalski (ed.), *Documenta Occupationis*, vol. 6, no. 2, pp. 546–547. This document has been translated from German.

2 Fischer's regulation of 17 June 1941 was published in Polish as a directive issued by Dr Schönhals on 24 June 1941 in *Gazeta Żydowska*, no. 51, 27 June 1941, p. 7. Dr Heinrich Schönhals (1901–1981), lawyer; joined the NSDAP in 1933; mayor of Offenbach, 1933–1934; Landrat in Alsfeld in 1937; worked in the Interior Administration Department of the General Government from April 1941 as head of Department III (Police Affairs), and from May 1942 as head of Department Ia (Civil Service and Organizations).

DOC. 302
On 25 June 1941 the German mayor of Poddębice describes the situation of the Jewish population[1]

Diary of the mayor of Poddębice, Franz Heinrich Bock,[2] entry for 25 June 1941[3]

Wednesday, 25 June 1941
Feeding the 3,000 Jews is now causing more serious difficulties. These poor people do not receive food ration cards, only occasional allocations of low-quality flour, bran, turnips, and horsemeat. These allocations are delivered quite irregularly by the Landrat's office, depending on when rejected goods come in. The per capita quotas that the Jewish elder is able to distribute are hardly sufficient to keep people from starving to death.

It now pays off for a Jew to have made friends with a Pole, because then he also gets extra food. As I have repeatedly experienced, the Poles help the Jews very noticeably. But certainly not as a general rule. A large proportion of the Jews previously made themselves thoroughly unpopular. The Poles are not favourably disposed towards Jews. On the contrary, their basic attitude is definitely antisemitic. I have always noticed that there are no mixed marriages between Jews and Poles in my town, and that the Poles are pretty much indifferent to the fate of the Jews forced into the ghetto. That's the way it is. Only the Jews who made friends when they were still living in freedom can hope for help from outside. The Poles are now getting even with the others for all the times they were ripped off. What they grabbed before, the Jews now have to give back to the Polish suppliers. Black-market prices are said to be mercilessly high.

'What are the Jews supposed to live on?' I asked Landrat Dumpf[4] when he was here today. 'They will have to stew in their own juices,' he answered. 'You don't have to concern yourself with them.'

His own questions centred on the butcher's shops here, but he did not reveal the reason. He does not like to be asked questions. – There is usually nothing good behind such displays of interest. Well, we will see.

1 IfZ-Archives, Ms 95/2, fols. 208–209. This is a typewritten copy that dates from the late 1940s and, according to the author, was produced on the basis of the original shorthand diary entries (which were subsequently burned); published in Alexander Hohenstein, *Wartheländisches Tagebuch aus den Jahren 1941/42* (Stuttgart: DVA, 1961), pp. 152–153. This document has been translated from German.
2 Franz Heinrich Bock (1901–1964), employment officer; joined the NSDAP in 1934; mayor of Poddębice (in the eastern Warthegau) from Jan. 1941; subjected to disciplinary measures in 1942 for his tolerant behaviour towards Jews and Poles, following which he resigned from office and was expelled from the Party; served in the war in 1944; captured by US forces in 1945; after the war worked as a letting agent in Braunschweig; his diary of his years in occupied Poland was published under the pseudonym Alexander Hohenstein.
3 The original contains handwritten and typewritten corrections.
4 When the diary was published in 1961, the names of the people and places mentioned were changed, and the new names stuck over the old ones in the typescript. According to the key to these names in IfZ-Archives, Ms 95/3, Dumpf was Willi Madré (1908–2002), butcher; joined the NSDAP in 1926; mayor of Eberstadt (Hesse), 1934–1936; attended a one-year training course for future Party leaders at the NSDAP training academy Ordensburg Vogelsang; Stammführer (group leader) at the Krössinsee training centre for future Party leaders; acting Landrat of Kreis Lentschütz from May 1940; initially lived in Italy after the war, then near the West German towns of Detmold and Bad Nauheim.

When Dumpf turned up, I at first had him told I was not there, left the building through Steinemann's[5] office, and hurried over to my prisoners in protective custody. I informed them briefly, and had all the cells locked and barred behind them. Then I came back. Woe betide me if the Landrat had found the cells open and the men outside![6]

However, he did not ask about the Russians at all, looked at the accounts ledger, and drove off.

DOC. 303
On 30 June 1941 the politician Ignacy Schwarzbart calls on Polish Jews to do everything in their power to reinforce the Polish army[1]

An appeal by Ignacy Schwarzbart, London, dated 30 June 1941[2]

To the Polish[3] Jews:
Poland has been fighting relentlessly for its independence and freedom for 22 months now. It has not capitulated for even a moment. In France, at Narvik, and in the Middle East, as well as with its volunteer service in Britain, the Polish army – which, together with the government, embodies the Republic of Poland – has once again demonstrated, in full view of the world, its unwavering determination to continue the struggle for victory alongside Britain and its allies. Polish Jews have participated and continue to participate in all of Poland's armed conflicts and battles, thereby fulfilling their self-evident patriotic and civic duty.

Our government and the High Command are currently planning to increase the number of Polish combat troops fighting outside Britain's borders. There is no doubt that Polish citizens, irrespective of their faith or nationality, will appreciate the importance of these efforts, and that Polish Jews, wherever they may be, in word and deed reinforce their shared concern and responsibility for the fate and future of the Polish Republic, in which they shall be full and equal citizens.[4]

All Jewry is on the side of the embattled democracies. Its future destiny is one element in the gigantic war these democracies are currently waging against a flood of barbarism and violence. Poland's struggle for freedom is also our fight – the struggle of Polish Jews.

5 Steinemann was Waldemar Ziegelmann, an ethnic German who served as the mayor's assistant; captured by US forces in North Africa in 1943; returned to West Germany in 1951.
6 Under an order dated 21 June 1941, Bock had to detain all Soviet citizens in the town. Because they had promised the mayor they would not run away, their cell doors were not locked.

1 YVA, M-2/123, fol. 39. This document has been translated from Polish.
2 The original contains handwritten corrections. Schwarzbart drafted the appeal on 19 June 1941 and revised it eleven days later. His words were also addressed to Jews in North America, who were critical of the Polish government in exile but demonstrated their support for General Bronisław Duch's mission to organize a Polish army in Canada. Sikorski, the commander-in-chief of the Polish army, thanked Schwarzbart for his 'exceedingly patriotic appeal' on 3 July 1941: YVA, M-2/123, fols. 40 and 38.
3 In the original, 'Polish' is capitalized as a mark of respect, even though Polish orthography dictates lower case.
4 See Doc. 192.

Common destiny, common hope, and a common future for all are forged through shared suffering.

War is waged in the service of a great cause. Our future is forged through joint action.

As the deputy for Polish Jews on the National Council of the Republic of Poland, I turn to You,[5] Polish Jews, with this appeal, wherever You may be, in the strong belief that You will lend Your genuine, heartfelt support to all the activities undertaken by the High Command in its efforts to expand and strengthen Poland's armed forces, so that we may secure our common victory.

DOC. 304
In mid 1941 the German health authorities warn against contact with Jews and the homeless[1]

Public notice, dated mid 1941

Beware of typhus

Typhus is a disease caused by uncleanliness and dirt.

The louse is the sole carrier of typhus.

The louse first infects itself by sucking the blood of someone with typhus and then passes on typhus bacteria to a healthy person.

The battle against typhus is a battle against lice.

1. Avoid lice-ridden people and those who are in contact with anyone suffering from typhus.
2. Do not provide beggars, vagabonds, or other lice-ridden people with overnight accommodation.
3. Maintain the maximum level of personal hygiene.
4. Eradicate lice on your body, clothes, and undergarments.
5. Immediately inform a physician of any unexplained illness accompanied by fever.
6. Avoid the Jews, because they are the most lice-ridden. Jews constitute 90 per cent of typhus patients.

Combat lice and you will be protecting yourself against typhus.[2]

5 As a sign of respect, the second person plural pronoun 'you' is capitalized in the original Polish.

1 AAN, 1335/214/I-17, fol. 36. Copy in USHMM, RG 15 008M, reel 2. This document has been translated from Polish.

2 The poster, which includes simple hand-drawn illustrations, was probably disseminated by the Department of Health in District Warsaw. In villages, official announcements were posted on notice boards. While typhus cases had previously increased during the winter months, the epidemic in the Warsaw ghetto reached its peak in mid 1941 and abated only in the autumn.

DOC. 305

Gazeta Żydowska, 2 July 1941: the chairman of the Warsaw Jewish Council calls for obedience and discipline among the Jewish population[1]

Appeal from the chairman of the Jewish Council[2]
Mr Czerniaków, chairman of the Warsaw Jewish Council, has issued the following appeal to the Jewish population:

The times we now live in demand self-restraint, calm, and emotional control. In the face of current events, we must not lose our heads and we must prove that we understand the gravity of this historic moment, and that we are able to adapt to it fully. Everyone is expected to comply with all decrees issued by the authorities and the Jewish Order Service and to strictly obey orders. The entire population must follow instructions immediately in order to avoid being subjected to coercive measures. Everyone must understand that they not only bear personal responsibility, but that their recklessness or failure to observe the rules and regulations threatens the population as a whole. This applies to *air raid protection* in particular. There must be absolute obedience, without exception, since its purpose is to ensure the welfare of the population.

The Jewish *business community* is expected to refrain from exploiting these difficulties for its own gain. Any such behaviour, which harms the population's most fundamental interests, is a crime that will be condemned and prosecuted with the utmost severity. Any hoarding of goods and any unwarranted price increases will be punished. Anyone acting in this way casts himself out from the community.

I demand obedience and discipline from the entire Jewish population. From the business community, I demand conduct that befits the economic necessities and does not exacerbate the current difficulties.

1 *Gazeta Żydowska*, 2 July 1941, p. 3. This document has been translated from Polish.
2 This response was prompted by the outbreak of war with the Soviet Union and its repercussions on the situation in Warsaw.

DOC. 306
On 3 July 1941 Wanda Lubelska describes her life in the Warsaw ghetto[1]

Handwritten letter from Wanda Lubelska[2] to her friend Halina Grabowska,[3] dated 3 July 1941[4]

Dear Zeta,

I've been waiting for the news you promised, but since I haven't received it, I'm writing to you, as the matter is urgent.

In one of your letters you wrote about our library, and that you would try to sell it as soon as you can. Dear Zeta, forgive me for writing to you about this, but unfortunately the library has become a very important issue for us.[5] Our lives are more and more dominated by the war. We are becoming quite helpless in the face of mounting difficulties at every turn. The idea of living off one's own work here is a complete utopia. People are dying one by one. There have been seven deaths in our building since Dad died. We've already sold nearly everything; only the most essential items remain, but even those will soon have to go. Rysio[6] no longer drives rickshaws because he has an abscess on his leg from the many hours of friction. Lessons have ceased for nearly all children. I'm only teaching two lessons now. The posters have been taken down, the competition is huge, and unfortunately my competitors are more experienced and have skills that I don't. Days go by, each worse and more hopeless than the last. When war broke out with Russia, we thought that things would change any day. We thought they would release us from the world's most terrible prison, in which a person in the street throws himself upon another who is eating bread, where 400 more people are buried in the cemetery each day, where little children do not know the taste of milk. Typhus is spreading here. Every other house has been locked up for this reason.[7] The price of every food rises by 100 per cent five minutes after every radio announcement stating that the situation on the front has changed. In this heaving turmoil of profiteers, merchants, and our policemen, our trio[8] is aimlessly adrift like a ship without a helmsman, a ship dam-

1 Biblioteka Narodowa, Zakład Rękopisów, Akc. 8261. This document has been translated from Polish. Published as a facsimile in Wanda Lubelska, *Listy z getta* (Warsaw: Biblioteka Narodowa, 2000), pp. 52–54.

2 Wanda Lubelska (1923–1942), member of the scouting movement; her mother was a violinist and her father a company manager; attended classes run by the underground movement from 1939 and simultaneously worked as a private tutor; lived in the Warsaw ghetto from Nov. 1940; received financial support from non-Jewish former classmates; deported on the first transport to Treblinka in July 1942 with her mother and brother; perished there.

3 Halina Grabowska, known as Zeta (1923–1944), member of the scouting movement; studied at a technical college run by the underground movement in 1939; tried to help the Lubelska family with some of her friends; active in the Polish resistance; arrested after a failed attack on Higher SS and Police Leader Wilhelm Koppe in the General Government in June 1944; shot dead by the Gestapo in late July.

4 The original contains handwritten deletions.

5 The Lubelska family had left their library behind on the 'Aryan side' of Warsaw.

6 Ryszard, the author's brother.

7 Buildings affected by epidemics were locked up and frequently placed under strict quarantine.

8 The author, her brother, and her mother.

aged by more than one storm and completely wrecked by the last hurricane, which left it without a helmsman.

Dear Zeta! Sell those books if you possibly can. I'm sorry to burden you with this. You've suggested it yourself. However, I hesitated before deciding to ask you to do so because I'm ashamed to be asking for anything at all, especially from you, as you've already done so much for me. Please forgive me for all this.

I'd very much like to write something about myself, but I can't get down to anything like that. I rush about all day, but in the end, I'm not really doing anything at all. I feel unwell. Unfortunately, sometimes I lose my strength. Now I live only for the hope that one day all will be well with the world again, just as it was before the war, that one will no longer have to see these macabre streets every day, that I will once again stroll through our wonderful Zolibórż,[9] and that I will be able to study. Unfortunately, one of us four[10] will not live to see that day.

Dear Zeta! Once again, please forgive me, give a kiss to all the dear girls taking the high school leaving exams. I'm very sorry that I have not replied to Zosia Cz.[11] I'll do so as soon as I can. I saw Elszka[12] on the tram; she hasn't changed one bit. Sometimes someone walks past my window, but I've forgotten their name, their surname ... Eight months of prison! I'm sending you hugs and kisses. Greetings from Mum and Rysiek.

Your Wandzia

DOC. 307

On 7 July 1941 the Lublin Jewish Council discusses how to combat the typhus epidemic[1]

Minutes of a general meeting of the Jewish Council in Lublin, signed H. Bekker, dated 7 July 1941[2]

Minutes no. 36 (97)

Chairman Bekker gave a report on combating the typhus epidemic, which is spreading throughout the Jewish quarter. The operation has been coordinated with the public hygiene authorities. Stricter quarantine measures will be introduced for isolation facilities. A public health division comprising 400 people will be created. The Health Section will lead the entire operation. The question of supplying the isolation facilities with food and

9 A neighbourhood in the northern part of Warsaw with a modern residential complex.
10 One word has been deleted here (possibly: 'father').
11 Presumably Zofia Czechowska, one of Wanda Lubelska's former schoolmates.
12 Elźbieta Maykowska, one of Wanda Lubelska's former schoolmates.

1 APL, 891/3, Bl. 169. This document has been translated from Polish. Facsimile published in Nachman Blumental (ed.), *Documents from Lublin Ghetto: Judenrat without Direction (Te'udot mi-geto Lublin – Judenrat lelo Derech)* (Jerusalem: Yad Vashem, 1967 [Hebrew]), p. 176.
2 Present at the meeting were the chairman of the Council, Bekker; his deputy, Alten; Council members Kestenberg, Halberszstadt, Schlaf, Kerszenblum, Lerner, Hochgemein, Kerszman, Lewinsohn, Siegfried, Bursztyn, Hufnagiel, Rechtman, Tenenbaum, Kelner, Lewi, Kantor, Dawidsohn, Edelsztajn, Cymerman, Goldsztern, and Kacenelenbogen, a lay judge who worked for the Lublin municipal administration. Absent were Council members Goldsobel and Wajselisz. The minutes were recorded by the Council secretary, lawyer Dawid Hochgemein.

the necessary funds remains to be discussed. The provisioning office has promised to allocate 15,000 kg of potatoes and 1,800 kg of meat. Council Member Tenenbaum suggested imposing a levy on the population. The Council decided as follows: the Jewish population will be required to pay a one-off levy to combat the epidemic. This levy will amount to 8–20 złoty per family. The issue of payments and their practical implementation is a matter for the Health Section.

For the time being, it has been decided to allocate 3,000 złoty to the Health Commission from the Community's budget.

DOC. 308
Ostdeutscher Beobachter, 7 July 1941: article on policies towards Jews in the General Government[1]

The solution to a major problem: the administrative regulation of the Jewish question in the [General] Government

For both hygiene-related and political reasons, a distinct separation of the Jewish elements from the rest of the population was required in the General Government. The German administration has resolved this problem in a very interesting fashion.

Isolation has been imposed in such a way that the Jews in the cities are gathered together in their own residential districts, intended just for them. This has so far been done in the most significant Jewish cities, such as Warsaw, Cracow, Radom, Kielce, etc. Without special permission, no Jews are allowed to leave their residential district permanently or even just temporarily; conversely, non-Jews also only have access to the Jewish districts on the basis of special identity cards issued by the relevant German agencies. In Warsaw, segregation extends to tram services as well. Tramcars that have to go through a non-Jewish district when travelling from one part of the Jewish residential district to another have to pass through these parts of the city without stopping.[2] The Jews are completely among their own kind in the districts assigned to them. Their relations with the outside world are centralized as much as possible. In Warsaw, for example, order and supervision in the Jewish residential district are incumbent upon a commissioner[3] appointed by the German District Governor, who avails himself of the Warsaw Transfer Bureau and the chairman of the Warsaw Jewish Council to perform his functions. The Transfer Bureau arranges supplies of food and the sale of the industrial products manufactured in the Jewish residential district, while the Jewish chairman, who is elected by the inhabitants of the Jewish residential district, forms the highest authority of the Jewish self-administration.[4] A Jewish Order Service identified by its special armbands and caps, and armed with rubber truncheons, ensures law and order are upheld in the Jewish residential district.

1 *Ostdeutscher Beobachter*, 7 July 1941, p. 2. This document has been translated from German.
2 For some time trams travelled through the Warsaw ghetto and were not allowed to stop there: see Doc. 244. There was also a tram line marked with the Star of David for journeys within the ghetto.
3 Heinz Auerswald.

These Jewish residential districts have their own hospitals and isolation wards, as well as social facilities such as soup kitchens, homes for the elderly, and children's homes. Jewish physicians are not in short supply in former Poland either. Raising funds for the Jewish district's public and social expenditure is a matter for the Jewish Council, which is able to levy the requisite taxes and charges. Jewish children are required to attend school in accordance with the general provisions.[5] In view of the wealth of the larger Jewish districts and the Jewish intelligentsia, which had a significant presence in former Poland, there is no lack of educational institutions, libraries, and theatres there.[6] Now the Jews are no longer able to engage in the exploitation of the non-Jewish population, they are forced to do productive work. The Jewish self-administration institutions are very anxious to urge the other members of their race to undertake this work. Currently 30,000 Jews are also deployed on regulation works along the Vistula, and are being paid for this.[7]

DOC. 309

On 9 July 1941 a report by the Population and Welfare Division in District Lublin describes conditions in the camp at Trawniki[1]

Report from the Population and Welfare Division,[2] signature illegible, to the Interior Administration Department in District Lublin, Dr Kipke, Lublin, dated 14 July 1941 (copy)[3]

Report on the inspection of the reception camp in *Trawnicki*[4]
The reception camp for refugees and suspicious persons detained by the Wehrmacht is located in Trawnicki on a publicly owned estate. The camp itself is secluded and closed off. The overwhelming majority of the camp inmates are Jews, including Russian political commissars and agitators, for whom a special area cordoned off by barbed wire has been set aside.

In the rest of the camp there are Russians, Poles, and also approx. 140 Ukrainians, again separated from one another. At present there are 676 camp inmates in total.

4 At the end of Sept. 1939, after the previous office holder, Maurycy Meisel (1872–1941/42), had fled, Adam Czerniaków was appointed chairman of the Jewish Community by the Stadtpräsident of Warsaw, Stefan Starzyński. See also Doc. 39, fn 2.
5 Children in the Warsaw ghetto were only allowed to attend school again from Sept. 1941.
6 The ghettos had in fact been set up in the poorest quarters, and the prestigious streets had been incorporated into the residential areas that were reserved for the German occupiers.
7 Jews had to carry out land improvement and river regulation works on numerous forced labour projects and at a large number of camps.

1 APL, 498/892, fol. 554. Published in Nachman Blumental (ed.), *Dokumenty i materiały z czasów okupacji niemieckiej w Polsce*, vol. 1: *Obozy* (Łódź: Centralna Żydowska Komisja Historyczna, 1946), p. 259. This document has been translated from German.
2 The head of the Population and Welfare Division in District Lublin was Richard Türk.
3 The original contains lines added by hand.
4 In the autumn of 1939 the Wehrmacht set up a reception camp for Polish prisoners of war in the village of Trawniki (incorrectly spelled in the document), south-east of Lublin; Soviet prisoners of war were interned there in the summer of 1941. Later it was used as a labour camp for Jews and as a training camp for non-German auxiliary forces, whom the Germans also used for murder operations.

The camp is run by the SS, and police officers have been detailed to guard it. The interrogations that must be conducted immediately on the spot are led by the Gestapo. Kazakhs (eastern Siberians) who have been selected by the camp inmates are used to guard the Jews.

The Jews in the camp make a frightful, almost bestial impression, and are completely degenerate.

The Ukrainians are treated particularly solicitously, among them a cavalry captain who has been in prison for 18 months. The man is ill and will be handed over to the Ukrainian Aid Committee forthwith once his interrogation has been carried out.

The camp administration is in the process of installing large cooking vessels and separating the rooms for the individual groups of inmates. At present food is provided from a field kitchen.

At this point it is not possible to make any precise statements about the camp's future size, not even as estimates, as this will depend on whether transport is available. Over the next few days, however, an intake is expected of approx. 1,500 new inmates, who are currently still at Zamość.

Food costs are estimated at 80–90 groszy per head per day, and approx. 1.20 zloty for the Ukrainians; some potatoes and groats have been brought in and, apart from bread, these form the main staples.

There is a quite urgent need for medication, which is not available at all. A Pole who was freed from the prison in Lemberg acts as the camp physician here. He reported the first case of dysentery today.

DOC. 310

On 14 July 1941 the chairman of the Jewish Council in Chęciny asks the Kreishauptmann in Kielce for support against insurgents[1]

Handwritten letter from the chairman of the Council of Elders of the Jewish population in Chęciny, J. W. Rajz,[2] to the District Governor in Kielce[3] (received on 16 July 1941), dated 14 July 1941[4]

In accordance with Paragraph 6 of the Regulation of the District Governor of 5 July 1941,[5] we hereby respectfully inform you of the following:

The Jew Jankiel Gnat, resident here at 25b Bóżnicznastraße, who, along with his wife, has long been known as an insurgent and disruptor of peace and order and as an agitator against the directives of the Council of Elders, was once again responsible for a severe breach of the peace at 1.30 p.m. on the 12th of this month.

1 AIPN, GK 652/129, fol. 58r–v. This document has been translated from German.
2 Joel Wolf Rajz, also spelled Reiz.
3 Hans Drechsel.
4 The original contains underlining and the handwritten note: 'I Fr (to be filed)'.
5 On 3 July 1941 the Kreishauptmann in Kielce had ordered the Polish mayor of Chęciny to establish a Jewish residential district. The directives issued by the mayor and the Jewish Council were classified as 'absolutely binding', and anybody found in contravention had to be reported: AIPN, GK 652/129, fol. 52r–v. See also Doc. 227.

In the mayor's office (in disregard of office hours), he and also his wife accused J. W. Rajz, Chairman of the Council of Elders, of accepting from the Jews

Jankiel Naifeld	the	sum	of	500	zloty,
Josek Liberman	"	"	"	500	" ,
and Chil Gertler	"	"	"	200	" .

These sums were collected as taxes from the aforementioned persons in the presence of officials from the Council of Elders in exchange for numbered receipts, and have served to cover the expense connected with the establishment of the Jewish residential district (e.g. fencing, resettlement, installation of the kitchen, and so forth). The incident was witnessed by the commander of the Polish police post, Jasinski, as well as the members of the Council of Elders Chil Manela and H. Gotlib (head of the Order Service in Chęciny).

Given that these are persons of the most disreputable character, whose activities are highly dangerous to the order within the residential district, the Council of Elders and particularly its chairman J. W. Rajz ask for[6] the *most severe* and immediate punishment of the two persons in question. *If possible, we request* their immediate evacuation from Chęciny.[7]

Respectfully

DOC. 311
The Jewish Social Self-Help executive committee reports on its work in May and June 1941[1]

Report by the JSS executive committee (Wt/Sch.),[2] unsigned, dated 15 July 1941[3]

Report by the executive committee of the Jewish Social Self-Help on its work in May and June 1941

The period under review covers the months of May and June. During this period the organization was further expanded. At present there are 34 Jewish aid committees in the Kreis seats, six in independent municipalities, and 222 delegations. There are ten Kreis aid committees in both District Cracow and District Lublin, nine in District Radom, and five in District Warsaw; there are 68 delegations in District Cracow, 65 in District Radom, 81 in District Lublin, and eight in District Warsaw. In addition, the JSS executive committee is in contact with the Jewish councils in 53 towns that have neither an aid committee nor a delegation. The questionnaires approved by the Population and Welfare Division have been sent out to all these towns. Responses have already been received from 125 towns.[4] With the correspondence that has come in from another 190 places,

6 The original includes the abbreviation 'gesch.' here. The meaning of the abbreviation has not been established.

7 Handwritten note: 'Excellent!'

1 YVA, O-21/32, fols. 958–961. This document has been translated from German.

2 The abbreviation Wt stands for Michał Weichert's last name.

3 This report on the JSS's work was most likely drawn up for the Population and Welfare Division.

4 These are preserved in the JSS's archived papers: AŻIH, 211.

they provide a rough picture of the situation of the Jewish population in the General Government and the massive mismatch between the Jewish Social Self-Help's capacities and the actual needs.

As is evident from the reports, the impoverishment of the Jewish population is advancing relentlessly. The elimination of the Jews from economic life that has been going on since the end of 1939 is almost complete. The establishment of closed-off Jewish residential districts has almost completely halted the exchange of goods and services with the non-Jewish population and has made it almost impossible for Jews to work. Measured against the price of food, the remuneration for the few employed Jewish craftsmen and workers is so low that it is not even enough to feed the employees, let alone their families.

It is therefore no wonder that the number of people in need of assistance is growing at a frightening rate. So far we have received 50 reports from District Cracow, 35 from District Radom, and 38 from District Lublin. According to these reports, 29,507 (that is, 38.9 per cent) of the 75,967 Jewish residents in District Cracow are in need of assistance, 26,701 (that is, 46.4 per cent) of the 57,703 in District Lublin, and 48,611 (47.7 per cent) of the 101,830 in District Radom.

In this respect only those Jews who are either reliant on being fed exclusively at soup kitchens or on housing in mass shelters are currently regarded as being in need of assistance. In addition to this, broad sections are unable to earn a living and are reliant on support from the social welfare institutions. The mass shelters are overwhelmingly fitted out in a makeshift fashion in former prayer houses or dilapidated dwellings, while plank beds, blankets, and sacks of straw are in short supply. The soup kitchens are only able to serve bowls of thin soup once a day. Due to a shortage of financial resources and food rations, the kitchens have had to be closed in several places over the last two months, and the welfare recipients have lost the bowl of soup that was often their only daily nourishment (Białaczew, Biłgoraj, Gielniów, Kamionka, Koluszki, Legionowo, Odrzywół, Przygłow-Włodzimierzów, Radomyśl, Tomaszów Mazowiecki, Tschenstochau, Zarnów, etc.). The general food ration for the Jews is significantly smaller than for the Polish population. While the Poles receive bread, flour, sugar, meat, lard, eggs, and jam, the Jews only get around 100 grams of bread a day, occasionally around 200 grams of sugar for a month, and only very rarely a little jam. There are many places where the Jews do not receive ration cards at all.

The establishment of the Jewish residential districts has resulted in a dangerous deterioration of living conditions. Because these districts' borders were so tightly drawn, thousands of local Jews and Jews who had arrived during the war were forced to leave their residences without other homes being allocated to them, while some were resettled for the second or third, and even the fourth and fifth, time. Some of the remaining Jewish population have been housed in cramped apartments without sewers which lack any hygienic facility whatsoever and where, in the best case, three to four persons are housed in one small room. There are places where ten to twenty people have been allotted a single room.

The people's diminished resistance due to malnourishment and the poor living conditions in the cramped rooms and mass shelters were bound to give rise to the threat of contagious diseases, particularly as the normal demand for linen and clothes cannot be met at all, and the cleaning and mending of completely worn-out garments and pieces of linen come up against almost insurmountable difficulties. Reports are constantly coming in from various places about the outbreak and spread of contagious diseases, typhus in particular. The necessary measures, conducted with all rigour by the authorities, specifically the establishment of epidemic hospitals and delousing stations and the isolation of persons suspected of suffering from diseases, entail enormous expenses that the Jews are unable to cover. In some places their isolation goes so far that no food is being delivered to the population, and not even mail or remittances. The mortality rate is rising drastically. There are no precise figures from the individual towns; statistical data is only available from Warsaw. The number of deaths there was 445 in November 1940, 3,811 in May 1941, and 4,290 in June; in May 366 people contracted typhus there, and 837 in June. Of the 402 deaths recorded in May at the 55 shelters for resettled persons with their 6,000 residents, 278 were due to starvation: 62 in the first ten days of the month, 95 in the second ten days, and 121 in the third ten days, to be precise.

The situation for children is particularly sad. As a consequence of the shortages of milk, flour-based products, and vitamin-rich food, their malnourishment is shocking. At an orphanage in Otwock, for instance, 60 per cent of the children were found to have suffered significant weight loss, and 20 per cent minor weight loss, while 70 per cent were found to have skin conditions due to vitamin deficiencies.

The normal functioning of the Jewish hospitals and sanatoriums is becoming more difficult by the day. With the establishment of the Jewish residential districts, many institutions have had to leave their well-equipped facilities, and it has only been possible for them to be placed provisionally in private houses. Even in towns where there are no Jewish residential districts, the premises of Jewish hospitals have in some cases been used for other purposes. Before the war the Jewish hospitals were, with some minor exceptions, integrated into the network of municipal welfare institutions; now they have to be maintained by the Jews themselves. The ever-increasing shortages of medicine, dressings, and bandages, and the scarcity of food, often make treatment at a hospital completely impossible.

The conditions described above have confronted the JSS with tasks that it is by no means equal to, given its limited resources, particularly as it is having to provide not only voluntary welfare services, but also welfare services that used to be incumbent on the state and the municipal institutions before the war. If, based on the available studies and according to Prof. Seraphim, the number of Jews in the General Government stands at 1,700,000[5] and the proportion of welfare recipients amounts to 45 per cent, that is to say 765,000, and taking into account the inflation prevailing on the open market, we were to set the expenditure for one welfare recipient at just 1 złoty per day for food, housing, and medical assistance, we would arrive at a sum of 22,950,000 złoty a month. That sum would have to be spent just to give the hungry a bowl of soup and a cup of coffee, to give the homeless a roof over their heads, and to help the sick through the very worst. This amount is offset by only relatively small sums. For instance, the JSS received 450,000 złoty from the American Joint Distribution Committee in May, and 520,000 złoty in June; the subsidies from the Population and Welfare

5 In the brochure *Die Wirtschaftsstruktur des Generalgouvernements* (p. 27), published in March 1941, Peter Heinz Seraphim stated that 'the number of Jews' in the General Government was about 1.7 million on 1 July 1940.

Division, which were still 221,000 złoty in April and 225,000 złoty in May, fell to 45,900 in June, and exactly the same sum has been promised for July. We have therefore been forced to fall back on our reserves in order to distribute 969,000 złoty in May and 798,024 złoty in June. We have now exhausted all our resources.

We have urged our aid committees and delegations to encourage the Jewish population to make the greatest possible sacrifices. Voluntary collections of money and donations in kind have been held, and various levies have been introduced for welfare purposes with the approval of the authorities. In comparison to the levels of need, however, the amounts raised have been ridiculously small. More proof of how very much the Jewish population has declined economically.

It has to be said that the Population and Welfare Division has been apprised of most of the facts described here on different occasions in petitions, position papers, and memoranda, as well as at meetings, and that they were met with complete understanding. Measures to remedy the very greatest ills have been promised by the authorities and sometimes also taken. The efforts of the Population and Welfare Division have succeeded in bringing about a significant improvement in housing and the sanitary conditions in the labour camps compared to last year. Pursuant to its orders, some Kreishauptmänner have made some funds available to the Jewish aid committees from the revenues collected from the residents' tax, from the fund for assistance to relocated persons, and also from special funds. It is also thanks to the Population and Welfare Division's involvement that the Economic Affairs Department of the GG government has been paying particular attention to employing Jewish craftsmen in the Jewish residential districts, that the commissioner for the Jewish residential district in Warsaw has instituted a generous scheme to provide meals in the soup kitchens, under which more than 117,000 midday meals are now being served every day, and finally that an increase in the food rations for the Jewish population has been promised in certain towns. Some Kreishauptmänner (Biała Podlaska, Busko, Dębica, Kielce, Końskie, Lublin, Miechów, Neu-Sandez, Opatów, Radom, Radzyń, Reichshof) allocated rationed foods to the Jewish aid committees, and some even ration coupons (Busko, Dębica, Krasnistaw, Miechów, Opatów, Radom, Radzyń, Reichshof). The financial aid and the quantities of food allocated are far too small to be able to remedy the great need. The charitable donations from abroad that the JSS has received in the last two months are certainly welcome, but the 16,728 kg of bacon, the 8,864 kg of lard, and the proportion of the clothing consignment assigned to the Jews are no more than a drop in the ocean of misery and need.

Only the continued benevolent support of the Population and Welfare Division could enable us to fulfil our tasks even to a small extent. First of all, a significant increase in the main subsidies would have to be considered; furthermore, the Kreishauptmänner would have to be instructed to disburse the share of the residents' tax allotted to the Jewish aid committees, and to collect the religion taxes levied on those businesses administered in trust. We would have to move closer to getting dormant Jewish accounts released and to tapping into new sources of revenue for the purpose of providing welfare services.

First and foremost, however, it would be important to favourably consider relaxing the entry and exit policies concerning the Jewish residential districts and to accelerate the recruitment of Jewish workers who are standing idle and their integration into the economic process. This seems the most pressing concern to us at the moment. The changes promised to us by the GG government's Economic Affairs Department[6] have prompted us to raise this as one of the most important issues of today's deliberations. With the active support of the Population and Welfare Division, we hope we will be able to take a further decisive step in reducing the burden on the welfare services, on the one hand, and in providing assistance for the most destitute Jews, on the other, in the very near future.

In May 1,211 letters were received and 1,153 sent out, including five circulars; in June 1,343 letters were received and 1,350 sent out, including six circulars.

The balance sheet is attached.

One enclosure[7]

DOC. 312

On 15 July 1941 the Jewish Social Self-Help executive committee meets representatives of the GG government[1]

Minutes of the eighth meeting of the JSS executive committee in Cracow on 15 July 1941, forwarded on 25 July 1941 by the executive committee (no. 7580/41 – I. 1 Sch.), unsigned, to the GG's Population and Welfare Division, Cracow (carbon copy)[2]

Minutes
of the eighth meeting of the executive committee of the Jewish Social Self-Help on 15 July 1941

1. Report on the JSS's work
Dr Weichert read out the enclosed report on the JSS's work in May and June 1941[3] and drew attention to the fact that barely 130,000 złoty from the revenues raised by the residents' tax had been received to date.[4] The sum that had been paid in from the religion tax levied on businesses under trusteeship in just one city (Tarnów) – 16,200 złoty – showed what substantial amounts would be available for social welfare if the sums we have indicated were actually received from this source of income.

Assessor Heinrich requested a list of the sums received from the revenues of the residents' tax and asked for the reasons for any refusals to be stated.

Dr Alten remarked that, in Lublin, the JSS had been refused its share of the residents' tax on the grounds that the Stadthauptmann[5] did not have any funds at his disposal.

6 The GG government's Economic Affairs Department had suggested easing the ghettos' isolation in order to integrate them more effectively into the production process: see Doc. 263.
7 Not in the file.

1 YVA, O-21/18, fols. 23–26. This document has been translated from German.
2 The meeting was attended by Lothar Weirauch, Herbert Heinrich, and Hexel from the GG government; Michał Weichert, Józef Jaszuński, Chaim Hilfstein, Eliasz Tisch, Marek Alten, Gustaw Wielikowski, and Benjamin Zabłudowski from the JSS executive committee; and the advisor to the Radom District Governor, Józef Diament.
3 See Doc. 311.
4 On the residents' tax, see Doc. 164.
5 Fritz Saurmann.

Dr Wielikowski added that the religious tax levied on businesses under trusteeship in Warsaw had been calculated at 330,000 złoty and that, as far as the residents' tax was concerned, the commissioner for the Jewish residential district[6] took the view that a special arrangement would be reached for the city of Warsaw and the residents' tax would be incorporated directly into the budget of the Jewish residential district.

2. *Economic assistance*
Director Jaszuński noted that the process of eliminating Jews from economic life had been brought to an end.

Currently Jews are only deployed for labour in small numbers. For a start, it is necessary to consider the use of Jews for labour outside their residential districts in the labour camps, which represents a liability in the budgets of the Jewish residential districts. The workers' situation was described at the previous meeting; the camp inmates were not getting sufficient food and remuneration, meaning that the Jewish communities had to help support them and their families.

In response to the question by Oberverwaltungsrat Weirauch[7] about who had ordered the Jewish communities to support the labour camps, Jaszuński replied that no such orders had been given, but that the starving workers had to be helped anyway.

In response to another question from Oberverwaltungsrat Weirauch about the current situation in the labour camps, Dr Wielikowski explained that all the labour camps in District Warsaw had been closed down, but that two new model labour camps consisting entirely of volunteers had been established at the instructions of the Governor,[8] and another two had been promised.

Jaszuński continued his comments on labour deployment in the Jewish residential districts, which fall into two categories. The first category comprises the closed-off Jewish residential districts where the closing off is handled liberally, such as in Cracow, Radom, and Tschenstochau. There, perhaps 20–25 per cent of the Jewish population is employed outside the Jewish residential districts. The second category comprises the hermetically sealed Jewish residential districts, such as in Warsaw. It is necessary to distinguish between two periods when looking at the experiments in this particular residential district: the first period, when the Transfer Bureau was not yet an independent institution, and the second period, after the Transfer Bureau had become independent. During the first period, the authorities took a bureaucratic approach. For instance, an order was issued in January 1941 to mobilize thousands of Jewish tailors, cobblers, and hosiers, and the workshops were fitted out, but no orders came in and no work was performed. This was a great waste of money, for some workers had previously been in employment, which they left because they were convinced they had now found the right thing. Only at the end of March and in April did the first orders come in, and the raw

6 Heinz Auerswald.

7 Lothar Weirauch (1908–1983), lawyer; joined the SA in 1930 and the NSDAP in 1932; deputy Kampfgruppenführer (group leader) in the National Socialist German Students' League; head of the Main Career Guidance Department in the Gau Silesia National Socialist Association of Legal Professionals, 1934–1940; deputy head of the Population and Welfare Division in the General Government from Sept. 1940, and from May 1941 its head; Free Democratic Party (FDP) politician, undersecretary in various federal ministries, and Stasi informant in West Germany after the war.

8 Ludwig Fischer.

materials arrived after that. It then turned out that the workshops were not well equipped, because no one knew what was going to be produced. The hosiery workshops have still not received any orders. The big change occurred in May. Department Head Emmerich explained to our chairman that the Transfer Bureau's previous policy would have to be changed and that the time had come to promote private initiative. In June the Transfer Bureau was given a new head, Director Bischof, who established a Jewish Economic Council.[9] At a meeting between Director Bischof and this Economic Council on 18 June, which was also attended by the speaker, it was announced that confiscations would no longer be carried out, and that every Jew who was willing to work could expect an easing of conditions. However, the confiscations in the Jewish residential district continued all the same. Individual sections of the Jewish Council registered four cases of confiscation and removal of goods in the Jewish residential district on 30 June, 1 July, and 3 July 1941, which affected licensed retailers and goods that had been entered in their ledgers. It cannot be ruled out that other confiscations have taken place without coming to the attention of the Jewish Council.

The sums earned in the workshops have been far too small to cover the labour costs and do not meet the needs of the Jewish residential district by a long way, especially as there are 100,000 Jewish men and women in gainful employment in Warsaw. However, the fact that there is no direct contact with the employers causes difficulties. The following factors have also constrained economic life: that no directive against confiscation of machines and goods has been issued, and that restrictions on Jews taking part in cash transactions have not been revoked, regardless of the fact that these restrictions became irrelevant following the elimination of the Jews from economic life. Furthermore, the resettlements and relocations of Jews continue to be of great consequence in this respect, as they inhibit a feeling of security and stability.

According to precise calculations, which are set out in detail in the memorandum[10] presented, a worker requires a sum of 865 złoty a month to cover only the most basic needs. It is therefore clear that a worker who only earns 6 złoty a day and whose family is starving would not be able to calmly devote himself to his work. There are two ways out here: the workers either have to get additional food rations for their families, or they have to receive a level of remuneration that would allow them to afford the most primitive level of subsistence.

Dr Weichert also added that he had recently been called in by the Population and Welfare Division for a meeting in the Economic Affairs Department, which was attended by Main Department Head Emmerich, Dr Gater, Director Bischof, and Dr Schlosser. Director Bischof informed him that he was making efforts to have increased food rations allocated to the Jewish workers, just like the ones for the armaments workers.

Dr Wielikowski remarked he has reason to believe that the resettlement of Jews in District Warsaw from smaller places to larger towns, as well as the sealing of all Jewish residential districts, is imminent.

9 The Economic Council for the Jewish Residential District was intended to coordinate economic activities in the ghetto with the German authorities pursuant to the instructions of the Transfer Bureau; its members included the chairmen of the Association of Craftsmen and the Association of Retailers.

10 Not in the file.

Assessor Heinrich explained that agricultural skills courses as described in our Circular No. 16[11] can no longer be organized, because every piece of land has to be used to the full in view of the food situation. When Jaszuński mentioned that agricultural workers are even being sought, Assessor Heinrich replied that there are no objections to be made to the employment of Jews in agriculture. Jaszuński emphasized that the agricultural courses in Warsaw are being run with great success, in response to which Assessor Heinrich explained that the courses already running would be allowed to continue; merely new ones may not be organized.

3. Miscellaneous

a) Combating disease

Dr Hilfstein commented:

In the countries known to be breeding grounds for contagious diseases, such as Serbia, Montenegro, etc., [infection rates for] these diseases tend to wane in May of each year. In the territory of the current General Government, diseases have also disappeared at around the same time in the past. By contrast, there are currently still cases of typhus in July of this year. This is due to the reduced resistance caused by malnourishment, the poor housing conditions, the shortages of soap and linen, and the fact that whole apartment buildings, blocks of buildings, or streets are cordoned off when a contagious disease is detected. This means that food cannot be delivered, which in turn causes malnourishment and thereby reduces the resistance of the healthy isolated population, leading to new victims.

Many localities have received instructions to set up hospitals and bathing stations. These towns and villages, of which there are more than a few, have also received funds from us for these purposes. Under the current conditions, these facilities would swallow up large sums, which the Jews are not capable of raising.

Dr Hilfstein further emphasized that we are threatened by a new series of epidemic diseases such as typhoid fever, dysentery, and cholera. In order to fulfil our tasks, we would need to have sufficient quantities of medicine and appropriate funds at our disposal. He therefore finished by requesting the Population and Welfare Division to provide us with more money for sanitary services and for combating contagious diseases.

Diament from Radom reported that there are no Jewish pharmacies in the Jewish residential district.

b) Food

Dr Alten outlined the food situation in District Lublin, where neither the Jewish heavy workers nor the rest of the Jewish population are allocated anything more than bread and 200 grams of sugar per capita each month. In some places, resettled people are not even getting ration cards. He further mentioned that it would make our work easier if it were permitted to raise money through collections. He therefore asked for the food situation to be remedied, and to arrange for permission to collect money on the JSS's behalf in Lublin.

11 The Polish version of the circular of 28 Jan. 1940 is preserved in YVA, O-21/14-1, fol. 20.

c) Permits to run craft workshops
Dr Alten reported that in Lublin many craftsmen who carry out orders for the Germans have not been given commercial permits. This is why the cobblers, for example, have not received any leather supplies for repairs. In addition, these craftsmen are at risk of being punished at any time. He therefore asked for this matter to be resolved.

DOC. 313
Jewish News Bulletin, 15 July 1941: the Council of Polish Orthodox Jews comments on the current situation in Poland[1]

The Polish Agudas Yisroel
History is and has been witness to various changes. The significance of many ideals and problems, to say nothing of names, has fundamentally changed over the course of decades and centuries.

The Polish Agudas Yisroel: Who does not know the meaning of this name? If we are permitted to compare World Agudas Yisroel to a crown, then we would undoubtedly view the Polish Agudas Yisroel as the biggest jewel in that crown. There is no need to describe the suffering of the Orthodox masses, both men and women, gathered behind the banner, the real banner, of Agudas Yisroel in Poland. There is also no need to describe the Nazi regime's tens of thousands of Jewish victims: victims who have fallen in the current struggle between evil and the defenders of freedom. What is the significance of the Polish Agudas Yisroel now, when seven million of our brothers find themselves in the heat of battle?

Around eight months ago, a Polish Agudas Yisroel Representative Council was founded on British soil, with the aim of representing and speaking on behalf of Agudas Yisroel's Polish members, who are scattered under the German and Russian occupations and across Great Britain.

This Agudas Yisroel is clearly only a miniature version of the Agudas Yisroel in Poland, but it must be stressed that its zeal and ideals have not changed.

Once more, Agudas Yisroel is fighting for its aims along with other organizations formed on this island. This publication, the official bulletin of the newly formed Agudas Yisroel in Poland, begins its activity in exile in the spirit of the Agudas Yisroel motto:

Any problems that arise in daily Jewish life must be resolved in the spirit of the Torah.

1 *Jewish News Bulletin*, 15 July 1941, p. 7 (Column: The Council of Polish Agudits Speaks), YVA, O-55, box 24. This document has been translated from Polish. The *Jewish News Bulletin* appeared from July 1941 and was the official publication of the Council of Polish Orthodox Jews in London.

DOC. 314

On 16 July 1941 the head of the Central Resettlement Office in Posen (Poznań), Rolf-Heinz Höppner, reports that murdering Jews unfit for work with 'a fast-acting means' is being considered[1]

Memorandum by the head of the Central Resettlement Office in Posen (L Hö/S), signed SS-Sturmbannführer Höppner,[2] for RSHA Section IV B 4, Eichmann, 16 July 1941 (carbon copy)[3]

Dear Comrade *Eichmann*,

Enclosed is a file note that summarizes various discussions in the Reichsstatthalter's office here. I would be grateful if you could comment on them when the opportunity arises. Some of the suggestions sound fantastical, but in my opinion could certainly be implemented.

One enclosure

File note

Re: solution to the Jewish question

The solution to the Jewish question in Reichsgau Wartheland has been touched upon by various agencies during meetings at the Reichsstatthalter's office. The following solution has been proposed:

1. All the Jews in the Warthegau would be taken to a camp made up of barracks for 300,000 Jews that would be constructed as close as possible to the coal trunk line[4] and would include barracks for production facilities, tailors' workshops, cobblers' workshops, etc.
2. All the Jews in the Warthegau would be taken to this camp. Jews who are fit for work could be combined into work details as required and taken out of the camp.

1 AIPN, GK 196/36 (NTN 36), fol. 567. Published as a facsimile in Datner et al., 'Wysiedlanie ludności', pp. 27F–29F. This document has been translated from German.

2 Rolf-Heinz Höppner (1910–1998), lawyer; joined the NSDAP in 1930, the SA in 1931, and the SS in 1934; head of the Ethnic Policy Section in the Posen (Poznań) Reichsstatthalter's office from 1939; simultaneously head of the Posen SD Main District and the Posen Central Resettlement Office, 1940–1944; head of the Gau Office for Ethnic Policy Questions from mid 1942; appointed chief of staff in the Reichsstatthalter's office in July 1944; imprisoned by the British, 1945–1947; extradited to Poland; sentenced to life imprisonment in Poznań in 1949; released in 1957; subsequently Oberregierungsrat in the West German Federal Ministry for Housing.

3 Handwritten note in the upper margin: 'V/3'. The carbon copy comes from the papers of Hermann Krumey (1905–1981), the head of the Litzmannstadt Central Resettlement Office. Krumey was a non-dispensing pharmacist; joined the Sudeten German Party (SdP) in 1935, and the NSDAP and the SS in 1938; on the evacuation staff attached to Higher SS and Police Leader Koppe in Posen from Nov. 1939; head of the Litzmannstadt Central Resettlement Office from spring 1940; with Eichmann in Budapest in 1944 oversaw the deportation of Hungarian Jews to Auschwitz; ran a non-dispensing pharmacy in the West German town of Korbach, near Kassel, after the war; Kreis councillor for the League of Expellees and Persons Deprived of Rights (BHE); sentenced to five years in prison by the Frankfurt am Main Regional Court in 1965; sentenced to life imprisonment in 1969 on appeal.

4 The coal trunk line was the railway line that ran from the Upper Silesian coal-mining field through the Warthegau to Gdynia. It crossed the Warsaw–Posen line to the east of Koło. In Nov. 1941 Kulmhof (Chelmno) extermination camp was established near this junction.

3. According to SS-Brigadeführer *Albert*, a camp of this kind could be guarded with significantly fewer police personnel than is now the case. In addition, the danger of contagious diseases that the surrounding population faces again and again in Litzmannstadt and other ghettos would be kept to a minimum.
4. This coming winter there is a danger that it will no longer be possible to feed all the Jews. It should be seriously considered whether the most humane solution would be to use some fast-acting means to finish off the Jews who are not fit for work. That at any rate would be more agreeable than letting them starve to death.
5. It has further been proposed that all female Jews who might still be expected to bear children should be sterilized at this camp so that the Jewish problem could actually be solved entirely within this generation's lifetime.
6. The Reichsstatthalter[5] has not yet commented on this matter. People have the impression that Regierungspräsident *Uebelhoer* does not want the Litzmannstadt ghetto to disappear, since he seems to be doing rather well from it. As an example of how money can be made with Jews, I was informed that the Reich Ministry of Labour pays 6 Reichsmarks from a special fund for every Jew deployed for labour, but the Jew only costs 80 pfennigs.

DOC. 315

Gazeta Żydowska, 21 July 1941: article on the efforts of the Warsaw Jewish Council to increase the ghetto's commercial productivity[1]

The Jewish residential district's balance of trade
H.S., Warsaw, 19 July 1941
The question of the economic existence of Warsaw's Jewish residential district has recently come to the *fore*. It is the most pressing problem at the moment and is extremely difficult to solve by any means.

The Jewish residential district in Warsaw has neither raw materials nor sufficient capital, nor any industry in the broad sense of the term. All it has is labour: the labour of skilled and unskilled workers. This labour, if exploited, may become the only *export* commodity that can even out imports, at least to a certain degree.

An average of 12,600,000 złoty per month is needed to supply the entire population of the Jewish residential district with food. How can the residential district raise such a sum if it has no capital reserves? Only by *importing work*. To even out the residential district's balance of trade only partially, no fewer than 63,000 *workers* must be employed at an average daily wage of 8 złoty, assuming 25 working days per month. This is the only way to raise the aforementioned sum of 12,600,000 złoty per month necessary to feed the Jewish population.

The chairman of the Warsaw Jewish Council, aware of the gravity of the situation, is sparing no effort to create *employment* opportunities, first for artisans and skilled workers, and then for unskilled workers. Many collective *workshops* have been created, despite difficulties with finding work premises. So far, only a relatively small number of

5 Arthur Greiser.

1 *Gazeta Żydowska*, 21 July 1941, p. 3. This document has been translated from Polish.

tradesmen have found employment in these workshops. Only around 10 per cent of the labour force designated to cover the import of food has been employed. Nevertheless, there is hope that the number of people in employment will gradually increase until it reaches the level necessary to supply the residential district with food.

Meanwhile the problem of supplying the residential district with food is becoming more *urgent* and demands concentrated effort and planned action on the part of the entire population. In addition, ŻTOS[2] must not settle for the working methods it has employed so far. ŻTOS should leave the well-trodden path and adapt to the current circumstances, which demand extraordinary efforts.

Occasionally one has the impression that those employed by aid organizations are drowning in the piles of documents, plans, memoranda, and resolutions, and that the flood of meetings, consultations, conferences, and inspections drain all of their strength and attention, and blind them to *reality.* Routines and habits have caused these people to get stuck in their old ways and suppressed the exceptional fervour and burst of energy which the gravity of the situation requires.

We must face reality! Aid must be adapted to the current circumstances.

Enough with the consultations – it is now time to *act*! All endeavours and resources must be mobilized for the great relief effort!

DOC. 316

On 22 July 1941 Governor General Frank informs high-ranking German officials of Hitler's announcement that the Jews will be removed as quickly as possible from the General Government[1]

Minutes of the GG government's meeting on economic policy in Cracow on 22 July 1941

[…][2]

During a meeting that I was able to have with him at the Reich Chancellery three days before the invasion,[3] the Führer told me, among other things, that it will be from the General Government that the Jews are first removed. In the next few days I will give the order to prepare for clearing the Warsaw ghetto. We must ensure under all circumstances that we remove the Jews from the General Government as rapidly as possible, because in the future the General Government will no longer be a reception site, but exclusively a transit camp, as the Führer himself said. We have the honour to be so singled out for distinction by the Führer that we now constitute the bridge between the gigantic eastern

2 Żydowskie Towarzystwo Opieki Społecznej (Jewish Social Welfare Association); its activities were incorporated into the structures of the Jewish Social Self-Help at the instruction of the occupying authorities.

1 AIPN, GK 95, vol. 15. Copy in IfZ-Archives, Fb 105, vol. 14, fols. 3369–3462, here fols. 3372–3373. This document has been translated from German.

2 Frank began by welcoming the incorporation of Eastern Galicia into the General Government. He remarked that Hitler had expressed his appreciation of the policies pursued in the General Government, and informed him that the General Government's new status within the National Socialist world empire would reduce the burden on Warsaw and other cities.

3 A reference to the attack on the Soviet Union on 22 June 1941.

space that is opening up and our people's self-contained Reich. And with the ongoing victories of our glorious Wehrmacht in the East, at a time of great bravery and the most outstanding demonstration of the virtues of the German soldier, comes the lofty duty for us to think only of this great task.
[...][4]

DOC. 317
In July 1941 the Jewish Social Self-Help and the American Jewish Joint Distribution Committee adopt resolutions on welfare[1]

Minutes of a joint meeting of the JDC and the JSS executive committee in Cracow, dated 30 July 1941

Agenda items:	Resolutions:
1. A financial plan for the funds allocated to the JSS on 1 July 1941	The accounts department was instructed to draw up such a financial plan.
2. The matter of receipts for welfare payments issued to date	Instructions were given to send the missing receipts for welfare payments issued to date to the JDC within two days.
3. The latest allocation of welfare payments	The JDC requested that in future welfare payments should not be allocated and paid out without prior consent from the JDC's representative, as was the case last time. This request was acknowledged.
4. The budget and the JSS's administrative expenses	Dr Weichert suggested the following: 1. The JDC should bear the JSS's administrative costs as of 1 February 1941. 2. The JDC should cover 50 per cent of the JSS's administrative expenses. The JSS's administrative budget amounts to approximately 12,000 złoty per month. 3. The JDC to pay 30 per cent rent for its premises (approximately 800 złoty per month).

4 Frank went on to paint a rosy future for the General Government and welcomed the fact that Hitler had reaffirmed its status as an independent administrative unit. After this, there was a discussion of the Food and Cultivation Plan for the year 1941/42.

1 YVA, M-28/2, fols. 102–104. This document has been translated from Polish.

4. The JSS will provide the JDC with financial reports each month.
5. Dr Weichert requested reserve funds sufficient to cover one month's administrative expenses.

The JDC's representatives declared that they would discuss the above requests with the JDC's management and reach a decision in the next few days.

5. Biannual reports for 1941

The JDC's head office requested a statistical report for the first half of 1941. As basic paperwork is missing, forms for the biannual reports have to be sent to the relevant committees.

Dr Weichert said the JDC may already have these papers. If not, the means of distributing the special forms will have to be discussed. The matter is to be clarified in the next few days.

6. District meetings with JSS, JDC, and 'KOP'[2] representatives, with the following agenda:
    a) Food supplies
    b) Controlling epidemics and health situation
    c) Constructive aid (cash funds, vocational schooling)
    d) Local self-help
    e) Einwohnerabgabe[3] and other revenue
    f) Blocked and frozen accounts

Dr Weichert agreed to these suggestions and has scheduled the first meeting on these topics for the second half of August.

7. The founding of a Central Purchasing Department:
    a) The JSS purchases (on the free market)
    b) Purchasing rationed goods (foodstuffs)
    c) Obtaining a coal allocation for GG welfare facilities

Dr Weichert agreed in principle to the plan to set up a Central Purchasing Department, but said he would have to consult with Mr Jaszuński on this matter. He asked that we also come to an understanding with Mr Jaszuński personally in Warsaw. We shall return to this topic in a few days.

2 Kreis aid committees (Komitety Opiekuńcze Powiatowe).
3 Here and below, German in the original: 'residents' tax'.

d) Joint purchases with the NRO e) The problem of obtaining raw materials	
8. Creating a quarterly budget for the Jewish Social Self-Help in the GG to cover: a) Regular subsidies (NRO, the JDC) b) Occasional subsidies (special funds) c) Possible loans from blocked (frozen) accounts d) Local collections e) Welfare payments from Jewish communities f) Einwohnerabgabe g) Subsidies from the Kreischefs[4] h) Funds for Viennese refugees from the Jewish Community in Vienna	Basically, such a plan should be devised, initially for internal purposes.
9. The JSS monthly bulletin	This matter is in progress, and the first issue will probably appear in August.
10. The composition of local KOP branches	This involves including delegates from smaller towns in the respective KOPs. It was decided that this matter should be addressed on an individual basis.
11. A circular decree on interest-free loan funds	A circular decree on the possibility of opening interest-free loan offices will be sent out within the next few days, if the local communities are to launch such an initiative.
12. Farms	Once the relevant paperwork has been prepared, the authorities will be asked to permit Jews to operate a few farms, according to the JSS's needs.

4 German in the original: 'Kreis leaders', i.e. Kreishauptleute.

13. First-aid kits for small outpatient clinics	In agreement with Dr Hilfstein, distribution of first-aid kits for small towns will be taken into consideration.
14. Kielce – Chęciny, in connection with the resettlement of Jews from Kielce to Chęciny[5]	Designated JSS representatives are to be sent to Chęciny in the next few days to organize help locally.
15. The plan for inspection tours (Palk, Reinberg,[6] Tisch, etc.)	Dr Tisch must be consulted about planning the inspection trips in August. The aim is to visit several dozen localities.
16. Dr Hilfstein's plan to gather materials	Mr Bornstein[7] is to devise a plan for gathering materials and to implement it in consultation with Dr Hilfstein.
17. Loans for Viennese refugees	In one of the towns which houses refugees from Vienna, 2,000 złoty will be set aside to provide special loans to these refugees on a trial basis.
18. The JDC's welfare payments to ORT	ORT is to be informed of the exact sums that have been allocated and paid out.
19. Other JDC welfare funds for […][8]	According to the news we have received from Berlin, Prague, and Vienna, approximately 700,000 złoty can be expected to be sent in the first days of August.
20. Organizing aid in the form of shipments of medicine and clothing from various overseas countries	It was pointed out that a JSS representative needs to be sent to Vienna and Prague to discuss and organize shipments, especially for the Viennese refugees in the General Government. Dr Weichert agreed to discuss this matter with the authorities.

5 See Doc. 227.
6 A. Reinberg, civil engineer; inspector in Kielce in 1941 on behalf of the JSS executive committee.
7 Icchak (Isaak) Bornstein, head of the American Jewish Joint Distribution Committee (JDC) delegation in Warsaw; escaped from the Warsaw ghetto in late April 1942; murdered in Będzin.
8 One word is illegible.

DOC. 318

On 31 July 1941 the Polish underground paper *Placówka* warns against the Jews' return after the war[1]

The Jews

Thanks to a campaign that went on for several years, awareness of the Jewish menace had become increasingly widespread within the Nation[2] even before the war. The Poles gained an ever-greater understanding of the pernicious influence that Jewish activity and the Jews' Talmudic immorality has on them. Acting in legitimate self-defence and well-founded national interest, we began to exclude the Jews from Polish economic life. We were unable to oust them from the topmost positions, we were unable to force them from power, we were unable to de-Jewify the legal and medical professions, but we took more and more trade out of their hands in the towns and in the countryside, cutting their power and influence off at the roots, so to speak. For Jewry, the stall belonging to a peasant's son represented a greater threat than the removal of a few officials, the so-called Shabbos goyim[3] (Jewish stooges).

The Germans have hit Jewry extraordinarily hard. However, as we wrote in *Placówka* several times before, we cannot feel the slightest gratitude to them for this, because their entire anti-Jewish offensive amounts to common robbery, which is crippling our national wealth. Moreover, this unsolicited assistance is paid for with the terrible suffering of servitude, which is crueller than anything the Jews are suffering at the hands of the Germans.

Today the Jews are weak and have no influence. However, once Poland is liberated, they will immediately want to tear down the ghetto walls, take back the factories and the houses that they obtained through exploitation, take back the shops that Polish merchants built up from nothing, and force their way in everywhere, spreading disease, fraud, and usury. They will want to rebuild their financial empire and resume their march to power over Poland, the world, and the despised goyim. We cannot allow this to happen and we have to remove them from Poland. In order to achieve this, special laws (we can even do without them) or ghettos will not suffice pogroms are not necessary. On the contrary, what we need is the [Polish] People's firm resolve – an economic boycott. Do not trade with the Jews! All those who currently engage in trade should remain active, and new traders should join their ranks, so that the Jew is unable to buy or sell anything at all. This is the prerequisite for our victory. In any event, the Jews will use all of their cunning and deploy all of their influence, and they will not shrink from fraud, bribery, and crime to avoid defeat, anything to win.

The Jews are a powerful and dangerous adversary – powerful because they have profoundly infiltrated our Nation, and dangerous because they act insidiously and deceptively. Therefore it is best to identify the sources of their strength right away.

The power of the Jews rests on two foundations: money and organization.

1 *Placówka*, no. 12 (22), 31 July 1941, pp. 1–2. Biblioteka Narodowa, MF 50 774. This document has been translated from Polish.

2 Capitalized in the original, here and below, as a means of emphasis.

3 Plural of (Yiddish) *Shabbos goy*: a non-Jew hired on the Sabbath to perform tasks that Jews were forbidden to do on that day.

By skilfully corrupting Aryan nations, the Jews have sought to use their money to buy not only goods, but also people – their help, their consciences, and their souls. The Shabbos goyim they had won over earlier supported the Jews in whatever ways they could, paved the way for them, facilitated and camouflaged their interests – to the detriment of their own Nation. It will take generations to root out the fatal seeds sown by Jewish degenerates. Let's not deceive ourselves and think that the Jews will then be too poor to once again buy the help of those who are traitors to their own Nation. They were so wealthy that even several years of German plunder will not manage to ruin them. They will always have enough to bribe Poles, after which they will secure a rich stream of new income for themselves. This is precisely what we must prevent them from doing in the long run, even if the gold owned by international Jewry should come to their aid. We have already set out effective battle tactics above.

The second pillar of Jewish power has always been thought to be their excellent internal organization based on their extraordinary national solidarity, their ability to exercise substantial power behind the scenes, and their ruthless methods of governance. Furthermore, not only have the Jews never denied this, but – as is evident today – they have even deliberately sought to convince us of the unique advantages of their dangerous and clandestine organization. Meanwhile, as we see more and more clearly when we observe the Jewish ghetto, Jewish solidarity was just another lie disseminated by these strange people, who are incapable of all that is healthy, natural, or innate in normal societies. The Jewish elders based their power on appalling ruthlessness and terror, to which the general Jewish population surrendered solely out of fear. There could be no talk of any sort of solidarity. Under the harsh conditions of isolation, when hunger held every single Jew in its clutches, a wild battle for bread broke out among them, a battle that knew no bounds, no moral rules, and no human feelings. The Jewish elders steal and cheat without the slightest scruple when food rations are distributed, and the deceived masses despise their leaders, curse them, and take every opportunity to denounce them (in secret, of course) to the German police. The Jewish Order Service, the instrument of the Council of Elders, easily surpasses any police service in the world in terms of its ruthlessness, with the possible exception of the Soviet police, which is also comprised of Jews. These observations allow us to look confidently to the future, when our solidarity and that of the Jews will face each other in battle. In this respect, we need not worry about the outcome.

There is one more valuable lesson to be learned from a close look behind the ghetto walls. The Jews behave towards the Germans in an extraordinarily humble, submissive, and loyal manner. They practically kiss the boot that kicks them. They direct the hatred they feel for their confinement in the ghetto not at the Germans, but exclusively at us, and vow to take bloody revenge on us for their current suffering. This phenomenon can be only be attributed to the Jews' spiritual deformity, which makes them show respect, loyalty, and even love for the strong, but when they come across anyone who is weak or whom they perceive to be weak, their arrogance knows no bounds.

Let's remember this well, and let's be strong!

DOC. 319

In summer 1941 a representative of the Roman Catholic Church in Poland stresses the urgent need for a 'solution to the Jewish question'[1]

Report by a representative of the Roman Catholic Church in Poland, undated, written after mid July 1941[2]

Ecclesiastical report from Poland for the period from June to mid July 1941

The stance of the occupying authorities towards the church and religion is strikingly inconsistent and ambivalent. On the one hand, the Germans would like to be seen as defenders of Christianity, especially in view of the war with Bolshevik Russia. They have declared themselves as the new Crusaders both on the radio and in posters and newspapers. On the other hand, however, they have as a matter of principle no real intention of changing their practice of suppressing all that is Catholic and ecclesiastical. Two of their insidious attempts to win over the upper echelons of the clergy in particular are worth mentioning. First, one of the bishops was persuaded to write a pastoral letter denouncing the Bolsheviks, thereby lending the Church's authority to German activities in the East. Then, quite recently, a well-known 'person of trust' in ecclesiastical matters, the Franciscan Father Odillo,[3] was sent to the episcopate to propose that the bishops assume a type of regency in the General Government, not only in clerical matters, but also in the civil and public spheres. This latter, admittedly not very credible, information originates from Father Odillo himself, who recently made this very suggestion to one of the bishops, claiming that he had been instructed to suggest such an idea to the senior clergy on behalf of the German authorities. If there is even a grain of truth in this entire affair, then the proposed role of the episcopate would nevertheless surely have been limited to establishing a modus vivendi with the occupation authorities in a subjugated Poland – not for the benefit of the Poles, of course, but for that of the Germans. Since neither a Darlan[4] nor a Kissling[5] could be

1 SPP, Interior Ministry, file 46, no. 8/Church, fols. 1–10 [fol. 4 is missing]. This document has been translated from Polish. Published as a facsimile in Krzysztof Jasiewicz, *Pierwsi po diable: Elity sowieckie w okupowanej Polsce 1939–1941* (Warsaw: Instytut Studiów Politycznych PAN – Oficyna Wydawnicza Rytm, 2001), pp. 1195–1203.

2 The author's name is unknown. The date is based on the heading. The report was included in the materials sent regularly from occupied Poland to the government in exile.

3 Odilo (baptized: Joseph) Gerhard (1902–1978), Franciscan friar from Salmünster and Fulda; lived in Wieluń, Poland, to learn Polish, 1931–1932; German parish priest in Cracow, 1935–1938; interned in a camp on suspicion of being a German spy in 1938; later released by the German occupiers; again active in Cracow as a priest to the German congregation from Feb. 1940; thought by the Poles to be an informer; arrested by the Gestapo for illegal trade and sent to Dachau concentration camp in 1942; active in the Catholic home mission in Ulm and elsewhere after the war.

4 François Darlan (1881–1942), French naval officer; deputy head and later head of the Ministry of Naval Affairs, 1926–1934; commander of the navy from 1937; appointed admiral, 1939; minister of the navy, 1940–1942; deputy prime minister, Feb. 1941–April 1942; ordered an armistice on 8 Nov. 1942 after the Allied landing in North Africa; high commissioner of France in Africa with US support after the Allied landing in North Africa; murdered in Algiers in Dec. 1942.

5 Correctly: Vidkun Quisling (1887–1945), Norwegian career officer; minister of defence, 1931–1933; founded Nasjonal Samling in 1933, supported the German occupation of Norway, and then proclaimed himself head of government, although the German occupation authorities did not initially recognize him as such; prime minister of the Norwegian collaborationist government from Feb. 1942; sentenced to death after the war by a Norwegian court and executed on 24 Oct. 1945.

found among Poland's secular public figures who would openly collaborate with the occupiers, they may have sounded out the clergy with a view to exploiting the nation's fervent Catholicism. I still do not know whether Father Odillo actually presented this plan to other members of the episcopate. The bishop to whom he spoke responded tersely that we already have enough misfortunes and difficulties to deal with in the clerical sphere without taking on the extra burden of such activities in the civil and public spheres, with which we are unfamiliar.

One example of the ceaseless pressure on the Church is a new threat: in the coming academic year, first-year courses at the seminaries will be prohibited. In addition, there have been a number of new and unfortunate arrests of priests and clergy. These sporadic arrests, made at various locations – most recently in Cracow – have been taken to the extreme in Warsaw. The entire Capuchin monastery (22 people) was arrested and imprisoned, with the exception of two friars who managed to escape. Prior to this, several Pallottines from Ołtarzew had already been arrested.[6] Elsewhere thorough searches have been carried out, and further arrests have been threatened. The reasons were supposedly of a political nature, such as reading and distributing underground newspapers, disseminating news unfavourable to the Germans, supporting secret organizations, etc. However, no clear line can be drawn between what is religious and what might be considered national activity. The Germans, who react at every turn to any whiff of *einen politischen Katholizismus*[7] at every turn, would like to confine the clergy to a sphere of some kind of absolute religious abstraction. Meanwhile a priest living among his own terribly oppressed people cannot fail to be sensitive to the issues that are causing pain and outrage among the faithful, nor can he fail to help those who are sacrificing themselves or suffering in defence of the nation. This is why in Catholic regions – such as Alsace, Belgium, the Catholic provinces of the Netherlands, and above all Poland – national and religious oppression are always closely intertwined.

In addition to the arrests, we should note that members of religious orders have been thrown out of their own houses for military purposes. For example, the Jesuits in Cracow were dispossessed of the remaining part of their large seminary building on Kopernik Street, without the slightest concern over where the evicted clerics would go. There have been dozens of similar cases in other places. The storerooms of Jesuit publishing houses in Cracow were also ransacked, and various purely religious publications were destroyed, notably those that were devoted to St Andrzej Bobola[8] or those that contained even the slightest reference to Our Lady, the Mother of God, as Queen of the Kingdom of Poland.

There are tidings of Job from the Poznań area, Pomerelia, and from the areas annexed to the Reich in general. Masses are only held in a small number of churches; the last vestiges of monastic life are being eliminated, including convents where the nuns dedicate themselves to tending the sick. The destruction of the Catholic religion, which is

6 The Pallottines are a religious community within the Roman Catholic Church, founded by Vincenzo Pallotti (1795–1850) in Rome in 1835. They have run a seminary in Ołtarzew, near Ożarów Mazowiecki, in the Mazovia region, since 1927.

7 German in the original: 'a political Catholicism'.

8 Andrzej Bobola (1591–1657), Catholic priest and Jesuit; descended from a noble family in eastern Poland; murdered by the Cossacks during the Chmielnicki uprising and consequently regarded as a Polish martyr.

still somewhat concealed in the General Government, is revealed here in all its overt brutality. Moreover, the occupation authorities carry out all of these acts of persecution in strict secrecy, so that it is difficult to learn the truth. The death of Archbishop Nowowiejski[9] and the fate of his suffragan, Bishop Wetmański,[10] for example, were kept secret for a long time. In another similar case, it appears that for 22 months now there has been no word of the 15 Jesuits whom war caught unprepared in Gdynia and Grudziądz. They were presumably shot dead or imprisoned.

Let us now turn to the positive side. We are pleased to note that an ever-increasing number of important organizations – which are already preparing for military, political, or ideological service in a future, reborn Fatherland – have adopted a decisive Catholic stance and come together on the basis of this common platform. There is good reason to hope that the new Poland, which will emerge out of the chaos of war following Germany's defeat, will be truly and fundamentally Catholic. Substantial difficulties are to be expected during the initial period of rebirth due to the differences in opinions and approaches that have not yet been completely resolved between the pro-independence organizations, and due to possible clashes between the country and the government in London.[11] Nevertheless, certain measures are being taken to ensure that, as soon as Germany falls, a wise and energetic person who is also a prominent Catholic will lead Poland. When the time comes, the ecclesiastical authorities would render a great service to both the Catholic and the Polish cause by giving this person their utmost support.

Looking to the future, as various important groups of people are doing at this very moment by developing public work programmes in – by God's grace! – a reborn Poland, [...][12]

inconsistent and improper. The teachers, most of whom belonged to left-wing organizations, exerted a rather sinister influence. The large landowners were more or less indifferent to the concerns of the rural population and were preoccupied solely with their own affairs. Although the government adopted various measures over the 20-year period of independence, these measures were either poorly planned and unsystematic, or – in most cases – totally devoid of any sound Catholic social thinking. Finally, it must also be said that our people did not have enough good shepherds. Among the priests, the share of those who were thoroughly bad or corrupt was small, but the share of sincere, capable, and conscientious priests was even smaller. The vast majority of them were effectively craftsmen in their trade, performing their duties without vocation, without devotion, and without any genuine love for God or the souls entrusted to them. Remarkably often, they alienated the faithful with a certain materialistic attitude to their clerical responsibilities and with a lack of kindness and sincere goodwill towards their parishioners. Even members of religious orders, who occasionally worked in a missionary capacity in the villages, too often reverted to their old ways (drunkenness, uncleanliness, theft)

9 Antoni Julian Nowowiejski (1858–1941), bishop of Płock; arrested in Feb. 1940; perished in Soldau camp in May 1941.

10 Leon Wetmański (1886–1941), suffragan bishop in the Płock diocese; arrested in Feb. 1940; perished in Soldau camp in Oct. 1941.

11 This is a reference to the Polish government in exile in London.

12 The next page is missing in the original. The report continues with an overview of developments in the interwar period in Poland.

and spent too little time building up a genuine spiritual culture. As a result, during the occupation the perfidious practice of mutual denunciation to the German authorities became commonplace among the rural population, not so much out of malice as from a lack of intelligence and character.

For all of these interrelated reasons, even before the war, our good, impoverished people began to prick up their ears to listen to communist or quasi-communist slogans, or at any rate to radically leftist slogans – and they continue to do so today. They began to form associations in an attempt to find a way to improve their lot and to attain the social advancement they craved, without the intelligentsia's participation. Despite their deep attachment to the Church and to their faith, they began to view their shepherds with resentment, and unfortunately their rejection extended even to the head of Christendom, about whom absurd slander was spread in the villages. These popular movements are not yet deeply entrenched or widespread, and the damage they have caused could be repaired without major difficulties. However, a few things are required to achieve this.

First of all, there is a need for a sensible and genuinely Catholic government that would truly meet the needs of the people and enact the necessary economic and educational reforms, not for the sake of short-term partisan or demagogic purposes, but for the actual good of the country. Furthermore, significant work needs to be done to improve the calibre of the clergy. We need many more priests by vocation who truly seek only the kingdom of God. Thirdly, there is an urgent need to find a solution to the Jewish question, which is nowhere else in the world as acute as it is in Poland, where some 4 million of this highly pernicious and in every respect dangerous element live among or rather leech off us.

Let us add a few important remarks to the last two points.

The clergy in Poland is not rich in absolute terms, but it is relatively wealthy in comparison to the rural poor or the urban proletariat. On the one hand, this constitutes a thorn in the side of the poor, and on the other, it means that the overwhelming majority of candidates for the priesthood basically attend the seminaries with material rather than spiritual aims in mind. For both of these reasons, therefore, it would perhaps be a good idea if the Polish Church were to hand over some of its land to the state for the use of smallholders – obviously in return for appropriate and guaranteed compensation. After all, sizeable areas of land have hitherto been in the possession of certain Roman Catholic and Ruthenian dioceses,[13] cathedral chapters, monasteries, convents, and countless parishes, of which some have benefices of 100, 200, 300, 500, or more hectares, especially in the regions of Poznań, Pomerania, and eastern Małopolska.[14] Of course, the land made available in this way would not in itself solve the whole agricultural question (sensible people are also considering other solutions), but it would contribute to alleviating the problem and would also eliminate a substantial source of the misunderstanding and

13 Particularly in former eastern Poland, there were Roman Catholic bishoprics, on the one hand, and Uniate dioceses of the Greek Catholic Church, on the other hand, whose members originated from the Ruthenian population of Eastern Galicia. These dioceses practised the Orthodox liturgy under the Polish-Lithuanian Commonwealth, but had been brought under the pope's authority with the signing of the Union of Brest (1596).

14 This is a reference to Eastern Galicia.

envy between the rural population and their shepherds. I think it would suffice for the Church to retain one outlying estate per episcopal see and one per seminary. The cathedral chapters could finance themselves with townhouses or well-invested capital. The parish priests would then be left – as is predominantly the case under the former Russian partition – with 6 acres, i.e. 3 hectares each. If well managed, this would provide the priests with an adequate living, in conjunction with their salaries and the *iura stolae*.[15] Perhaps there would then be fewer 'landlords' and more 'shepherds' in the parishes, and people would have fewer occasions for resentment and jealousy.

As far as the Jewish question is concerned, it should be seen as a peculiar dispensation of Divine Providence[16] that the Germans – apart from the many wrongs they have inflicted and continue to inflict on our country – have made a good start in this one respect, by indicating a way of ridding Polish society of the Jewish plague and by showing us the path that must be followed – with less cruelty and less brutality, of course, but nonetheless with resolve. It was clearly God's will that the occupiers took the solution to this burning question into their own hands, because the Polish people are too soft and too unsystematic and would never have decided to take the active steps that are required in this matter. It is clear that this is a burning issue, for the Jews are causing incalculable damage to our religious and national life. Not only do they suck the nation dry economically; prevent Polish trade from developing and block access to trade for a portion of the rural population; and strip our towns and cities of their Catholic character, but they also demoralize the entire society in a multitude of ways. They propagate corruption and bribery. They pervert our public life through their covert influence on the levers of government and administration. It is they above all who run brothels and traffic in persons and pornographic literature. They seduce the people into drunkenness, corrupt the youth, and undermine literature, art, and public opinion with immoral and un-Catholic views. Finally, they always ally themselves with everything that has the potential to harm, weaken, and degrade both the Church and Poland. It is strange that even today, when the Germans so ruthlessly persecute them, some peculiar psychological response nevertheless induces them to hate the Poles more than the Germans and to vow to take revenge on the Poles for the injustice they have suffered.

According to the opinion of the most important people in the country, the Jewish question must be formulated differently in a resurrected Poland. Another objective that must also be pursued consistently on the international stage is the emigration of the Jews to some overseas state of their own. However, until this can be achieved, it will be necessary to a considerable extent to exclude the Jews from our society. They must leave the villages and small towns altogether, and in the larger cities they must have their own enclosed settlements. They must have their own religious primary and secondary schools, and in universities and colleges their numbers must be regulated by a strict *numerus clausus*. They must be banned from the army, from public office, and – with Catholic young people in mind – from the teaching profession as well. Finally, through various means, their participation in the legislature, their engagement in the liberal professions in matters concerning Christians, and their involvement in certain branches of

15 Revenue from the fees charged for performing the holy sacraments (such as baptism and marriage).
16 Capitalized in the original as a means of emphasis.

trade and industry must be reduced. All of this will be very difficult and will certainly lead to friction between the government in exile, which is subjected to quite strong Masonic and Jewish influences, and the country that is already in the process of organizing itself today, but these are matters on which the health of the – by God's grace – resurrected Fatherland will depend.

Finally, the last issue of great importance is the relationship between Polish society and the Little Russian[17] and Byelorussian minorities living within the country's borders.

This whole question is extremely involved and complex. Moreover, it ultimately depends on the outcome of the present war and cannot be fully unpacked here. We only wish to touch on its religious aspect. The country's leading figures are aware that Poland's mission is to propagate nearer and further East the Catholic culture that it received from Rome a thousand years ago as its most valuable religious and national treasure. Moreover, our country does not have a shortage of spiritual and secular figures who are willing to dedicate themselves to this noble cause. However, there is one sore point that has already led to certain misunderstandings and will probably lead to more in the future. Particularly in the first phase of the Uniate movement, in an effort to win over followers of the Eastern Church for Rome after the Great Schism, some priests of foreign origins, unfamiliar with this whole complicated issue, were willing to recognize the Ruthenian population's already exaggerated ethnographic and geographical claims. Moreover, with the same objective of drawing the Eastern Church towards Rome, they exaggerated the significance and success of missionary work through the Eastern rite, to the detriment of the Latin rite. These same Uniate activists have sometimes accused the Poles of being fundamentally incapable of converting the Ruthenian populations and of displaying narrow-minded and nationally driven chauvinistic tendencies.

Beginning with the latter accusation, it is perhaps clear that the Poles – in view of ethnic and linguistic bonds, in view of their detailed and centuries-old knowledge of the area, and in the light of their achievements in this respect, both in the distant and the recent past – are called above all others and are also better suited to spreading Catholic culture among the Eastern Slavs than anyone else. It would be deeply unjust to claim that in such a profoundly Catholic population there are no people sufficiently free of national prejudice and antipathy who could embark on such an impartial and purely Catholic undertaking. Of course it is out of the question to demand that Poles should sacrifice their well-founded, age-old national claims for the sake of converting Ruthenia.[18] Nor can Poland, which has been faithful to the Church for a thousand years, be seen as a *quantité négligeable* with regard to this conversion, at the expense of which the Ruthenians or the Russians could be won over. It is clear that the conversion of Ruthenia is a major undertaking for the Eastern Rite, but one cannot close one's eyes to the fact – confirmed a thousand times over – that the Latin rite is facing at least as great a task. The best time in the history of the Uniate was when it was under the strong Latin influence and was imbued with the Latin spirit. However, when the Uniate turned away from these Latin influences, it either became an instrument of nationalist struggle and hatred,

17 The term 'Little Russian' is a reference to the Ukrainian minority.

18 This is a reference to members of the Greek Orthodox Church in the parts of Poland inhabited by Byelorussians and Ukrainians.

as is the case with a large portion of the so-called Ukrainians in eastern Małopolska, or it achieved insignificant and superficial successes, as is the case with the recent activities of the current Uniate campaign. As for the Russians in particular, knowledgeable experts on the subject of the East and on the distinctive Eastern psyche maintain that the Russian will only truly convert when he adopts the Latin rite. The accuracy of this assertion is confirmed by the fact that among the Russians, even among the clergy who were converted to the Uniate church, quite a number have returned to the Schism. It therefore seems appropriate not to entrust the great work of winning the East for Christ solely to the Uniate church, but also to grant the Latin rite a significant role.

DOC. 320

Yunge Gvardie, July 1941: article commenting on the wartime situation of the Jews[1]

The war and the Jews

Every war triggers major upheavals across a country's entire political, economic, and cultural spectrum. Apart from calamity, immense damage, and a sea of spilt blood, various epidemics break out, and the impoverishment of the working class takes on the most tragic proportions.

We know that, in capitalist societies, wars are natural outgrowths of the social order. Truly every generation has its own stories to tell about enslavement and oppression, murder and extermination. Those who write the official accounts of history might shine a spotlight on monarchs and military heroes, celebrating each of them as a divine being sent to earth, but in fact the same ordeal that millions are enduring today is concealed behind these narratives.

We knew many years ago that the current war would be far more terrible than anything that came before. Everything the human mind has devised for the good of the world has been placed at the Devil's disposal.

Hitlerism is a natural outgrowth of capitalism. It is nothing new; it is simply cruel in its brutality and novel in its shape and dynamism. Today, as all of Europe languishes under the boot of Hitler's Germany, it is no longer a question of one country or one people fighting for liberation; it is a global issue.

The shape of Jewish bourgeois society, hemmed in by ghetto walls, may have changed, but much remains of the old ways. Hitlerism has hit the well-to-do Jews hard, because they are being punished as Jews. Otherwise they would have been able to serve the movement, as they served former reactionary movements. They would have sold out, just as some of the Polish reactionaries are doing.

Throughout all the difficult times the Jewish community has faced whenever the reactionaries make assaults – accompanied by antisemitism – on the freedom of the workers' movement, Jewish nationalism has sprouted and sown mistrust in an effort to

1 *Yunge Gvardie*, July 1941, pp. 12–14; AŻIH, Ring I/1311 (687). This document has been translated from Yiddish. *Yunge Gvardie* ('Young Guard') was the Yiddish underground newspaper published by the Bund's youth organization, Tsukunft ('Future'). Only one issue has survived.

curb the fighting spirit of the Jewish masses who joined the general struggle against reactionaries – for freedom. Jewish nationalism claims that we are in exile and will suffer as long as this situation continues. What Jewish nationalists refuse to see is that we Jews are not the only ones in exile – today, all the nations under Hitler's control are in exile. The Austrians and the Czechs, the Poles and the Dutch are persecuted and oppressed. Although they have their own countries, none of them have been spared a fate similar to that of the Jews. The illegal socialist press includes horrific descriptions of the revenge exacted by fascism.

With the evil intention of deepening ethnic hatred, the antisemites tell the world that the Jews are united. The Jewish bourgeoisie liked the compliment [of national unity], felt flattered, and soon 'national' hacks seized upon it.

In this terrible Hitlerian prison, there is no equality among the victims of racial theory. The Jewish bourgeoisie have no opportunity to engage freely in economic activity. But within the deformed framework imposed by the occupiers, they follow their class interests with the most ruthless egoism, whether through clandestine, illegal trade and partnerships or by exploiting protections and connections. With the occupiers' blessing, the Jewish bourgeoisie control the institutions and defend their interests at the expense of the health and lives of the masses.

Bourgeois Jewish young people are facing a deep crisis, which is both material and ideological in nature. Before the war, the interests of the Jewish masses were alien and hostile to the bourgeois young people, who strove with all of their might to secure careers. And when the reactionaries and antisemitism raged and engaged in wild orgies, these young people replied: 'Let's go away from here to a country of our own. There we will be among our own; there we will be the equals of others.' In the meantime, life has dealt them a blow, and most young people are experiencing disappointment. They are moving closer to the life of the Jewish masses and placing their hopes in the ideals of the socialist-minded working class.

A considerable number among them has not made – nor does it want to make – peace with the colossal changes in communal life. They are not honest with themselves and are morally confused. Against their will, these young people must now come into contact with the suffering and downtrodden Jewish masses. Until now, Yiddish culture, literature, and language were alien to them. They had no relationship to the life of the Jewish masses, striking an attitude of hardened indifference. Today they go on about learning Yiddish in order to speak the language of the Jewish masses, but this is nothing more than hollow words, which they do not mean and which amount to nothing. They continue to remain deaf and dumb. They fill their empty days with private English lessons. They dream of fleeing, of emigrating, or they live for the moment, playing cards, flirting, and engaging in cheap philanthropy. They remain deaf, however, to the battle cry of the Jewish and Polish masses. They lack the will and the faith to take up the fight for a new, humane life – here, in Poland, together with millions of their enslaved and persecuted brothers. However, those young Jews who had already tasted hardship before the war will not allow themselves to be numbed. Life is too difficult and too harsh. These young people, on the brink of ruin, struggling for a piece of bread, believe in the great tomorrow that awaits us all in a liberated world. They share the suffering, the hopes, and the struggles of the working class and the oppressed European peoples who are fighting against Hitlerism for a socialist order in Europe.

Indeed, Jewish nationalism is no different from any other nationalism. Today the 'Jewish people' are betting on the English card. Let Churchill win, and he will give us a great land. The Jewish socialist youth lives under no such illusions.

At the end of this war, there will be freedom and equal rights for all in a socialist Europe – this Messiah will also ransom the Jews.

DOC. 321

Representatives in Warsaw of the Polish government in exile describe the attitude of the German occupation authorities to the Jewish population since September 1939[1]

Report by the Polish government's representatives in occupied Poland on the German occupation authorities' policy on ethnic minorities, Warsaw, dated December 1941[2]

[…][3]

V. Relation to the Jewish population

I.

The relation of the German occupation authorities to the Jewish population is essentially determined by the same political egotism as that which determines their relation to other ethnic groups in the conquered territories, but it differs considerably in terms of its goals and methods.

With regard to Aryan ethnic groups, in this case the Slavs (Poles, Ukrainians, Byelorussians, and even the so-called Goralenvolk,[4] or the Masurians and Kashubs),[5] the Germans ultimately intend to regulate the territorial position, roles, and responsibilities of these groups *within Europe*. Even when they resettle the Polish population en masse from the western territories to the Vistula basin, the Germans do not question the fact that Poland is (indisputably, by the way!) an intrinsic part of Europe. Any ideas about resettling the Poles outside Europe seem to come up merely for propagandistic purposes. The German agenda envisages these peoples adapting to the new situation and integrating themselves into the new European order, based on the hegemony of the Germanic race. They are to recognize the primacy of the Germanic order, but remain in Europe,

1 AAN, 1325/202/I-45, fols. 793–885, here fols. 855–872. This document has been translated from Polish.

2 The original document contains handwritten underlining, as well as changes and deletions. The original title, 'The Nationalities Question' (Zagadnienie narodowościowe), is crossed out and replaced with: '38. The German Occupier's Nationalities Policy' (38. Polityka narodowościowa okupanta niem.).

3 Polish government representatives (Delegatura Rządu R.P. na Kraj) who were active in the underground collected news from the occupied territory and regularly compiled reports, which were then delivered by couriers. The authors were former high officials, politicians, and academics. Whether this 93-page report reached the Polish government in London is unknown. The excerpt presented here is preceded by an introduction and several sections: I. The new legal framework in Polish territories; II. The relationship to the German population; III. The Ukrainian question; IV. Contrived national groups (1. German theories of nationality, 2. The real aim of German policy, 3. Kashubs, 4. Masurians, 5. Upper Silesians).

4 German in the original: 'Gorals'.

5 See Doc. 82.

as part of the family of European peoples. In their relation to the Jews, on the other hand, the Germans proceed on the basis of the fundamental thesis that this ethnic group constitutes an entirely alien, superfluous, and destructive entity in Europe, from which the fundamental political maxim follows: *to remove the Jews from Europe* – the complete elimination of this political, cultural, and economic element from the Aryan environment. This guiding principle has been expressed many times in statements made by the most prominent and influential representatives of National Socialism: among others, Hitler has advocated this on several occasions since the start of the war, e.g. in his speech in Berlin in January 1941,[6] and Governor Frank did the same in a speech in August 1940.[7] According to the Germans, Europe, or at least the German sphere of influence, should be completely cleansed of any Semitic elements, which, after victory in the war, should be accomplished by means of a massive resettlement of Jewry to an area beyond the European continent – the details of which, by the way, have not been specified – or even by exterminating the Jews altogether.

This is not the place to explain or to analyse the ideological foundations of this concept. It is undoubtedly based on both a direct racial antipathy towards Semites and also the National Socialists' political experiences, especially during wartime, and manifests itself in the belief that the war against resurgent Germany was instigated and accelerated by international Jewry and is currently being funded and politically spearheaded by Jewish finance – an anonymous power. Hitler has made this point ever more forcefully in his latest pronouncements (since autumn 1940), which shed an exceptionally clear light on both the war's sociological background and its ultimate goals. This is also why the emotionally charged stance of National Socialism (especially the Party, the press, and the administration) regarding Jewish affairs is always very radical and ostentatious. It is in this domain that National Socialism rages with all its force; it is here that its ruthless, brutal radicalism, in terms of both goals and methods, is continuously unleashed.

The radical nature of the methods used in relation to the Jews in the occupied territories of the Polish Republic also has local roots, the first of which is the high Jewish population density and the prominence of the Jews particularly in the economic life of these territories. The young German National Socialist administration in the occupied territories was confronted with a Jewish question on such a scale that it was bound to act. There were approximately 2,000,000 Jews living in the German-occupied territories, of whom, for example, more than 400,000 lived in Warsaw alone. The occupiers saw with their own eyes, quite concretely, the unparalleled Jewification of Polish cities in general, and in particular of the legal and medical professions, trade, skilled crafts, banking, industry, even literature, etc. They realized that attempting to incorporate this element into the regimented, totalitarian economic system that the occupation had in-

6 On 30 Jan. 1941, in a speech at the Sportpalast in Berlin, Hitler had reminded the audience of his threat, which he said was originally made on 1 Sept. 1939: should the world once again be plunged into war, this would lead to the extermination of the Jewish population in Europe. In fact, Hitler had first made the public threat of extermination in his speech to the Reichstag on 30 Jan. 1939: see PMJ 2/248.

7 This presumably refers to Frank's speech to representatives of District Lublin on 25 July 1940, in which he announced a mass deportation of Jews overseas: Präg and Jacobmeyer (eds.), *Diensttagebuch des deutschen Generalgouverneurs*, p. 258.

troduced to these areas would pose major difficulties. Notions upheld by the Germans such as price stability, controlled trade, the abolition of uncontrolled currency exchange and foreign exchange rates, the disclosure of commodity stocks, discipline in production and exchange – all fictitious ideas, which the German administration nevertheless categorically pursued – were not compatible with the marked Jewish predominance in Polish economic life. This alone could have justified a struggle against Jewry in order to curtail its role in economic life and to restrict its contacts with the rest of the population in the occupied territories and with the German administration. At the same time, however, there were other motives at play: the desire to appropriate substantial Jewish property – banks, factories, and shops, as well as real estate and even household goods – and the intention, at least to a certain extent, to channel the Polish population's attention along the lines of an *anti-Jewish front* that posed no threat to the Germans. Here German propaganda left no stone unturned in manipulating the Polish population's interests and emotions. Polish government policies were thus analysed accordingly (the Jewification of the administration, the mixed marriages of Polish dignitaries, the Masonic–Jewish influences on Polish life, and the growth of Jewish financial power in Poland to the detriment of the Polish population); Jewry's corrupting influence on Poland's culture and its young people was shown; and the benefits for Poles of an employment sector free from Jews were pointed out, etc. In general, the German administration was well aware of the fact that large sections of society (in skilled crafts and small-scale trade, among schoolchildren and university students, the rural population, the civil service, and even in working-class circles) made fertile ground for the seeds of antisemitism, due to the high concentration of Jewry on Polish territory. The conditions were favourable enough for the occupation authorities to stir up such sentiments and to enable certain Polish circles to become politically active, while in other areas they were expected to remain silent and resign themselves [to the situation]. As early as the beginning of spring 1940, cryptic notices, written in poor Polish and containing suspicious symbols (Topo-Krzyż – Beilkreuz),[8] began to appear in the windows of Christian shops in Warsaw, intended to identify them as 'Aryan shops' (arische Geschaefte).[9] These notices, written in two languages – German and Polish – were of course distributed according to German directives and were part of an organized anti-Jewish propaganda campaign.[10] This, incidentally, was subsequently abandoned and replaced by direct action on the part of the German authorities, which promised better, more immediate results. During this period (spring 1940) – at a time when the police were acting with conspicuous restraint – gangs of youths attempted to loot Jewish shops in Warsaw, in the vicinity of Żelazna-Brama, Leszno, and Elektoralna. Public opinion explicitly associated these excesses with German incitement and unanimously condemned the occupation for such political acts. In Polish industrial enterprises, the Germans insistently distributed the Jew-baiting periodical *Der Stürmer* for circulation among both manual labourers and clerical workers. However, these efforts on the part

8 Polish and German in the original: 'hatchet cross'. For further details on this symbol, see Doc. 98, fn. 4.
9 German in the original: 'Aryan businesses'.
10 The group behind these antisemitic campaigns was known as Atak ('Attack') and was linked to the eponymous Warsaw publishing house: see Doc. 98, fn. 4.

of the occupation institutions to engage Polish groups in anti-Jewish campaigns were not entirely successful. The Warsaw Bar Association opposed the exclusion of Jews from the legal profession, for which, incidentally, some leading Christian lawyers faced serious repercussions on an individual level on many occasions.[11] The Polish population protected Jewish property from theft, e.g. during evictions, and it denounced the barbaric decrees of the occupation authorities, including the ban on dispensing medicine to children under three years of age or to elderly people over 60 years of age, etc.[12] Indeed the general attitude of the Polish public on this subject did not change, even when more concrete information reached the German-occupied areas about the conduct of the Jewish population in Soviet-occupied territory, where the Jews had readily succumbed to Bolshevism and had adopted an unfriendly attitude towards the Polish population and the Polish state.

II.

The plight of the Jewish population in the occupied territories, from the first September days to the present, consists of one long sequence of degradation, persecution, violence, and expropriation. This includes both the systematic use of exceptional legislation enacted by the authorities at various levels of the hierarchy and de facto, unchecked, unpunished abuses on the part of the administration, the Gestapo, the German population itself, and also the army. *The Jews are subjected to exceptional laws de jure, but are outside the law de facto with regard to a whole range of matters.* This is largely similar to the situation of the Polish population in the so-called territories annexed to the Reich. Jewish property, the Jews' personal dignity, their freedom of movement, the right to have a roof over their heads, the fulfilment of their basic human needs, religion, education, employment, social security, and finally the personal security of the Jewish population – all this (just as is the case for the Polish population there) is dependent on the will of the administration, on the whim of individual officials or Volksdeutsche,[13] and on laws and regulations which are casually prescribed and rigorously applied.

German propaganda tries to present the systemic violence, expropriation, and restrictions imposed on the Jewish population as an attempt to introduce proper German order into Jewish life in order to realize the principle of Jewish national and religious autonomy. Thus Dr Dietrich Redeker wrote (*Warschauer Zeitung*, 13 March 1940)[14] – in a tone that repeatedly colours German pronouncements – that the ghettos serve only to implement the principle of '*Juden für sich*'.[15] They thus constitute the technical framework for Jewish autonomy. Redeker clearly had no idea of the actual methods used to realize this 'autonomy', that Jewish property was looted openly in the streets, that Jews were beaten with whips and rifle butts, or that even Jewish women were slapped in the face. He had the audacity to claim that the Germans, in carrying out their plans with respect to the Jews, do not commit acts of violence in the streets, do not torture or abuse them, do not instigate pogroms or commit robberies, as had been the case for the Jews

11 See Doc. 291.
12 Proof of such an official prohibition could not be found; see also Doc. 291, fn. 20.
13 Here and below, German in the original: 'ethnic Germans'.
14 See Doc. 94.
15 German in the original: 'Jews for themselves'.

under ... Polish rule. This, then, is how the Germans are allegedly striving to realize the autonomy of the Jewish population within the appropriate framework. As far as the essence of German policy is concerned, however, this autonomy is of course merely intended as a transitional phase, preceding and paving the way for the extermination of Jewry in Europe altogether. However, even in its present form, in this transitional period, Jewish autonomy is merely a pipe dream. It is an administrative measure intended to bring about the complete impoverishment of the Jewish population, to facilitate the expropriation of its property, to eliminate its economic expansion, and to confine it to a mass prison, threatened by starvation, epidemics, cultural backwardness, and the direct aggression of the occupation authorities. The religious communities are burdened with extensive and significantly expanded administrative, economic, and welfare duties. Simultaneously, however, they are deprived of the ability to raise the necessary funds, or their access to such funds has become unreliable as it is dependent on various circumstances over which the communities have no influence whatsoever (e.g. social security loan allocations from the GG budget, shares of local taxes, shares of social insurance funds, etc.).

The fundamental goal – regardless of any possibilities that might arise after the war – is *to tear the Jews from mainstream life, to set them apart and to sow discord between them and the Polish population, and to poison the Jews with the ineluctable germ of psychological isolation.*

This strategy is already producing tangible results. Among the Jewish population – objectively unjustly, but subjectively quite understandably – recriminations against the Polish population are beginning to grow. The Jews complain about the lack of a more decisive Polish response to their oppression; a psychosis of isolation is beginning to develop; a mutual rivalry often emerges over who has suffered the most, etc. The barbed wire surrounding Jewish residential districts makes communication difficult. Moreover, the Germans take advantage of every opportunity to deepen the resentment (e.g. in February 1941 they solicited volunteers among the Polish population to serve as guards in the camps for Jews, which they were about to set up at various locations across the General Government.[16] In March 1941 notices were posted equating the Jews with lice and typhus.[17] The ghettoization of the Jews in Warsaw was justified on the grounds that it was necessary to eliminate the competing Jewish demand for food and provisions, etc.). Thus *there is an increasing risk of a significant escalation of Polish–Jewish conflicts*, which, in the course of the present war, could be exploited by the Germans to confuse British and American public opinion about the future fate of the Polish territories.

In relation to the non-Semitic population, the occupation authorities constantly repeat and emphasize the principle of 'Keine Berührung mit den Juden!'[18] This maxim has been applied throughout the occupied territories by requiring Jews to use separate train or tram compartments or carriages; by prohibiting them from entering cafés, cinemas, and restaurants; by forbidding [non-Jews] to receive treatment from Jewish physicians and dentists; by forcing Jews to wear armbands; and finally by creating separate Jewish residential districts (the so-called ghettos), or barrack camps for the Jewish popu-

16 See Doc. 250.
17 See Doc. 258, fn. 2.
18 German in the original: 'No contact with the Jews!'

lation. Measures aimed at cutting direct ties between the Polish and Jewish populations are evident at every turn. On 1 February 1941, after the Jewish residential district had been sealed, a special office (an agency of the General Government in Warsaw), the so-called *Transferstelle*,[19] was created in Warsaw and given the task of bringing all aspects of Aryan–Jewish relations under German control. It got to the point that even the claims of laundresses, building caretakers, craftsmen, etc. (which often amounted to more than 10 zł) could no longer be collected directly from Polish creditors who were denied entry passes to the ghetto. Instead, they had to take the official route through the apparatus of the Transferstelle (predominantly staffed by Reichsdeutsche[20] brought from the Reich specifically for this purpose). A clear example of this attempt to eliminate any 'Beruehrung'[21] between the Aryan element and the Jewish population was the notices (which bore no clear reference to any legal decree or issuing authority) that were posted in Warsaw, albeit in only a handful of locations (e.g. in municipal clinics, hospitals, etc.), forbidding Jewish women from engaging in … prostitution, and imposing fines for sexual intercourse between Aryans and Jewish women.[22] In autumn 1941 an official announcement was made in Warsaw that leaving the ghetto illegally would be punishable by death,[23] and eight people were killed as a result.

The German authorities spared no effort to justify these directives, which were intended to prevent contact between the Aryan population and Jewry. Arguments based on health and hygiene were in the foreground. The German press, official announcements, etc. persistently sought to prove that the Jews were carriers of bacteria and especially typhus, which, while harmless to the Jews themselves, risked causing an epidemic among the Aryans.[24] This was, for example, the justification for the establishment of the Warsaw ghetto put forward by none other than the head of the Warsaw District Office, Schoen. As a corollary to such declarations, a form of oppression developed that was particularly burdensome for the Jewish population: the compulsory isolation of infected buildings and the compulsory bathing of entire communities of tenants under conditions that made a mockery of hygiene. Sometimes there were mass resettlements (e.g. in Kałuszyn).[25] *Economic arguments* were also put forth. Allegations of so-called Schleichhandel[26] appeared regularly in the *Warschauer* [*Zeitung*] and the *Krakauer Zeitung*. The establishment of the Warsaw ghetto was justified on the grounds '*da es sich als notwendig erweist, den jüdischen Einfluss, der sich zumeist im Schleichhandel und Preistreiberei ausreicht, ein für allemal aus der Wirtschaft auszumerzen, weil nur dann, was je vor allem im Interesse der polnischen Bevölkerung liegt, eine durchgreifende Sicherung der Ernährung möglich ist*'[27] (*Warschauer Zeitung*, no. 251, 23 January 1940, comments by the above-

19 Here and below, German in the original: 'Transfer Bureau'.
20 Here and below, German in the original: 'Reich Germans'.
21 German in the original: 'contact'.
22 See Doc. 37.
23 Third Regulation on Restrictions of Movement in the General Government (15 Oct. 1941), *VOBl-GG* 1941, no. 99, 25 Oct. 1941, p. 595; see also Doc. 211.
24 On the transmission of typhus, see Doc. 276, fn. 2.
25 See Doc. 33.
26 German in the original: 'illicit trade'.
27 This quotation is in German in the original: 'that it proves necessary, and is certainly in the interest of the Polish population, to eradicate Jewish influence – which is mainly apparent in illicit trade

mentioned Reichsamtsleiter Schoen[28]). This argument was false and disingenuous, of course. The struggle against Jewry did not improve the situation of the Christian population in any way and the one issue had nothing to do with the other. After the Jewish residential district in Warsaw was sealed off, bread rations for the population were reduced (March 1941). The prices of lard, meat, flour, etc. on the free market rose continuously, and trade was unable to adapt to the German price policies due to the constant requisitioning and plundering of stock. To the outside world, however, German propaganda maintained that the anti-Jewish terror was intended to protect the interests of the Aryan consumer. The Polish public was quite aware of these tactics as part of the occupation authorities' propaganda efforts.

III.

The hostility of the German authorities towards the Jewish population became apparent within a few days of the German troops' invasion of Polish territory. The Jews (just like the Poles, incidentally) immediately became the target of various forms of harassment, restrictions, and persecution. Typical of this period were constant street terror and raids on homes, which usually involved the looting of property (furs, valuables, the more expensive furniture, bed linen, and even soap, food supplies, cash, and similar other things). This looting of homes in particular has reached epidemic proportions: the Jew is no longer the master of his own possessions. Sometimes the Germans burst in repeatedly and confiscate whatever they like, even now that the Jews have been resettled in separate residential districts: there too the looters break in and shamelessly take everything of value. It has been completely arbitrary from the very beginning. The Jewish population was terrorized *ex improviso*,[29] so to speak, and had to endure slaps in the face, beatings, insults, and the crudest forms of robbery. They have no right to defend themselves and no authority protects them. Cash is taken right out of their pockets, furs and coats from Jewish women's shoulders, household goods and bed linen from their homes. Jews are seized in the streets for work, and Jewish women, for example, are ordered to scrub the floors in the barracks using their own clothes and coats as rags for scouring and cleaning. Jews are taken to haul coal, to remove items from Jewish homes, to clear the streets and squares of snow, etc. No one knows on whose authority people are being recruited for these tasks. Every uniformed German exercises the right to confiscate things and to force people to perform certain tasks as he sees fit. Young or elderly Jewish men are generally seized for such work; women and girls are seized more rarely. This 'work' is enlivened by harassment and ridicule: mandatory dancing, humiliating exercises, kicks, insults, and mockery. The duration of such work is completely arbitrary, with food given only on a whim and, of course, no payment at all. Occasionally better treatment is encountered (from older NCOs, Austrian soldiers, etc.): warm food, humane conduct.

and price gouging – from the economy once and for all, because only then will it be possible to thoroughly safeguard the food supply'. The word 'ausreicht' (meaning 'to be sufficient') in the original should correctly be 'auswirkt' ('to be apparent in').

28 This article is entitled: 'Warum Judenwohnbezirk in Warschau?' ('Why a Jewish residential district in Warsaw?'): see Doc. 185.

29 Latin in the original: 'unexpectedly', 'out of the blue'.

However, the requisitioning of property from shops, warehouses, factories, etc. was a particularly bitter pill to swallow.[30] As a rule, these requisitions were simply common robberies. Various authorities issued orders concerning confiscation or requisition, but quite often German policemen, soldiers, Volksdeutsche, or Reichsdeutsche took the goods on their own initiative. These requisitions took place in the most brutal and lawless manner: neither inventories of the items taken nor any receipts were drawn up. The goods were either seized and removed or secured on the spot. Occasionally it was possible to save many of the items by means of bribes. In Warsaw and Łódź there were cases in which the owners were given the opportunity to buy or to ransom their confiscated items. Those who had confiscated the goods would sometimes sell them on and thereby line their own pockets. The aggrieved Jews (or indeed Poles in similar circumstances) rarely dared to check whether the confiscation had in fact been authorized, because any such enquiry, especially one involving accusations of theft, would end in beatings or arrests. The Jewish population was affected by these thefts even more than by the theft of furniture or furs, etc., because the damage they caused was often substantial and sometimes ruined even very wealthy merchants, who were only able to protect themselves from these losses to a limited extent by hiding their goods, pretending to sell them to Aryans, or sending servile and venal Volksdeutsche[31] to represent them, etc.

This plunder and mistreatment was widespread. The Jewish population quickly realized that they were completely defenceless and tried to protect themselves either by not leaving their homes, or by going out into the streets without money or valuables, or by storing valuable items in Aryan homes for safekeeping. In many cases the Poles provided considerable help in this respect, although they risked severe punishment and reprisals.

From the very beginning there has been a significant difference between the treatment of Jews and the treatment of the Aryan population, especially the Polish population. *On the whole, the persecution of the Jewish population does not involve bloodshed; they are not the target of the most draconian persecution.* The Jews do not engage in intense political activity, they have not established a clandestine press,[32] and they do not organize political conspiracies. With few exceptions, the Gestapo finds no reason for extensive interference in Jewish circles. There are no large-scale arrests of Jews, they are not sent to concentration camps, one hears nothing of the mass slaughter of the Jewish population, and Jews are not sent to the Reich for forced labour. As set out above, the persecution is limited to looting, harassment in the streets, humiliation, and exploitation through forced labour, but no Jewish blood is shed, and the Jewish intelligentsia is not exterminated en masse (as is the case, for example, with the Polish lawyers, priests, political activists, and large landowners in the Poznań region, etc.). *The Jewish population by and large remained on the sidelines of the Polish tragedy of September*: the shock of defeat and its immediate aftermath concerned the Jews on a different level than it did the Poles. The Jewish population became only concerned with tackling their own problems, anxious to ensure their own survival independently of the wider concern for the Polish nation. Political unrest among them was minimal and when present then it often took the form of longing … for the Bolsheviks' intervention;[33] there was no widespread co-

30 Change of tense in the original.

31 Here and below, German in the original: 'ethnic Germans'.

32 In fact, Jewish underground newspapers had been appearing in Warsaw since March 1940.

33 Ellipsis in the original.

operation with Polish groups. That is why there were no Jews among the victims in Pawiak, Oświęcim, Dachau, or blood-soaked Palmiry (the execution site of Poles in the Kampinos forest).[34] Although there were [Jewish] victims (Nalewki in Warsaw, the hostages taken after Kot's[35] escape, the massacre of Jews in Ostrów Mazowiecka after the warehouses were burned down),[36] these were rather random and exceptional incidents. Compared to the Poles, the Jews were only subjected to direct assaults: kicks, slaps, compulsory dancing in the streets, the theft of furs, goods, jewellery, and cash, restrictions on movement in the streets, being barred from parks and cafés, ostentatious public contempt, local forced labour (even in forced labour camps), limited food supplies, and a number of legal restrictions aimed mainly at expropriation. It is worth noting that in the territories annexed to the Reich,[37] the Jewish population was subjected neither to systematic mass expulsion nor strict ghettoization (except in Łódź and a few other places) until spring 1941. Although the German press claimed that by autumn 1940 there was not a single Jew left in Pomerania, for example, the fact is, firstly, that Pomerania had the smallest Jewish population overall (with the exception of Gdynia). Secondly, even as late as 1941 there were still no strictly sealed Jewish residential districts in the Dąbrowa Basin,[38] for example, and certainly no mass resettlements of Jews. Except in Łódź, where anti-Jewish repression reached extensive proportions ([the] ghetto), Jews in the territory of the so-called Neureich,[39] assuming they remained in their places of residence, did not experience anything similar to the persecution suffered by the Polish population there. This may have been due to the relatively small number of Jews and their political passivity in those regions. Moreover, most of the Jews from the so-called western territories left as soon as military operations ceased, and in many cases even before the war broke out (Poznań, Bydgoszcz, Toruń, Gdynia,[40] Gdańsk, etc.).

The first measures taken by the German occupation authorities with respect to Jewish affairs were of a somewhat technical and preparatory nature. Apart from the arbitrary assaults, acts of violence, and humiliations described above, it should be noted that the first regulation introduced was the requirement for Jews to *wear an armband on their right arm* (a white armband with the Star of David), which came into force on 1 December 1939.[41] In some areas of the so-called Neureich, Jews had to wear yellow patches on their chests and backs.[42] The obligation to wear an armband applies to both men and

34 One of the first mass shootings took place near Palmiry, west of Warsaw, on 27 Dec. 1939. A total of 106 Warsaw residents were killed. Subsequently both Christian and Jewish prisoners were executed at this site until July 1941.

35 See Doc. 39.

36 On 11 Nov. 1939, in the small town of Ostrów Mazowiecka in the eastern part of District Warsaw, German police reservists murdered the entire Jewish population, a total of 159 men and 196 women and children. Members of Reserve Police Battalions 11 and 91 took part in the crimes; the police detail was under the command of Karl Brenner (1895–1954), a colonel in the Urban Police and SS-Standartenführer.

37 German in the original.

38 Part of the 'eastern strip' of East Upper Silesia, which had been annexed to Reich territory.

39 Here and below, German in the original: 'New Reich', a reference to the Polish territories that had been annexed to Reich territory.

40 See Doc. 30.

41 See Doc. 130, fn. 9.

42 See Doc. 35, fn. 5.

women (above the age of 12). Jewish establishments (shops, businesses, factories, but not private residences) were required to display a small sign with the Star of David on it. Significantly, this order provided a somewhat cursory definition of who is considered a Jew: in fact, this matter was not fully settled until August 1940, that is, eight months later, in an order issued by Governor Frank.[43]

The next regulation issued by the occupation authorities, which was also preparatory in nature, was the order of 1 February 1940 concerning the obligation to register Jewish property.[44] The declaration had to be made by the end of February 1940. Prior to this order, in autumn 1939, Jewish bank accounts had been blocked (albeit without issuing a general decree) and all banknotes issued by the Bank of Poland had to be handed in for safekeeping or exchanged. The obligation to register property covered all possible types of assets: bank accounts, promissory claims from invoices, etc., inheritance rights, real estate holdings, stocks, shares, mortgage rights, pensions and annuities, industrial enterprises, stock-in-trade, means of transport, cash, jewellery, household goods, and even clothes and bed linen, furs, paintings and carpets, gifts, etc. – regardless of where the asset is located or whether a legal claim applies (whether abroad or at home, in one's own possession or only in trust, as security, with a forwarding agent, etc.). This registration, which incidentally failed – especially with regard to cash, property, etc. – was preceded by an order stipulating that a Jewish family could not hold more than 2,000 złoty in cash or collect payments in excess of 500 złoty,[45] as well as an order prohibiting Jews from selling, leasing, mortgaging, or exchanging any assets in their possession.[46]

The aforementioned regulations had a severe effect on the material aspects of Jewish business interests, particularly the obligation to register property and the ban on transfers of ownership, which created the basis for the establishment of trusteeships, expropriations, the dismissal of Jewish employees, etc. The Jewish population resisted their implementation with great ingenuity: fictitious appropriations; German stooges, primarily Volksdeutsche, were appointed to management and supervisory boards; goods and supplies were concealed; bank accounts were signed over to Christians. These are just a few examples of how Jews tried to defend themselves against the economic onslaught mounted by the occupation authorities. In some respects, these efforts were successful: certain Jewish assets, naturally mainly those that were relatively easy to conceal (so not real estate, for example), were saved, and they secured their owners' existence for months. Even after the ghettos were sealed, more affluent Jews continued to have considerable funds at their disposal and found ways to close their bank accounts, sell hidden goods, and the like. Jews living in the ghetto or in the suburbs continued to run their factories and businesses, even though these had ostensibly already been Aryanized.

IV.

There are countless German orders aimed at restricting, excluding, or humiliating the Jewish population in various ways. All of these deny and trample upon the fundamental

43 See Doc. 130, fn. 17.

44 Correctly: 24 Jan. 1940; see Doc. 81.

45 See Doc. 40.

46 These restrictions had been ordered in Sept. 1939 by the head of the civil administration for the military commander.

principles of the Polish constitution and of European civilization regarding the equality of civil rights, especially in the sphere of private law. In many cases they are not generally applicable regulations valid throughout the occupied territories, but local ordinances which are sometimes valid only in a single town, based on the initiative or the whim of a single person, [such as] the local police chief, the Kreishauptmann, or a Party member. In this respect as well, the plight of the Jews is very similar to that of the Poles in the western territories.

For example, as of December 1939 the payment of disability pensions and unemployment benefits to Jews was stopped, and they were advised to turn to Jewish charitable institutions or the Jewish religious communities for help.[47] However, these bodies did not receive a single penny from national social insurance funds, even though Jewish workers had contributed to these funds for many years. The social insurance funds continued to provide medical assistance to Jews for a certain period of time, but this was discontinued in Warsaw, for example, when the ghetto was established in autumn 1940. This denial of social insurance claims is in essence a direct confiscation of beneficial entitlements

Pawnbrokers in Warsaw have been instructed to restrict transactions with Jews. One restriction was that a Jew could redeem his own pawned belongings only with the consent of the foreign exchange authorities, allegedly due to trading in gold, which was forbidden to Jews. Jews are forbidden to engage in bookselling or publishing. The Jewish population are not allowed to use public reference or lending libraries. Works by Jewish authors (scholarly works and literature, both Polish and foreign works) were removed from bookshops and reference as well as lending libraries, although this purge was not carried out consistently.

Jewish physicians and dentists are unofficially forbidden to treat Aryan patients (this was the case even before the Jews were locked up in their own residential districts). Apartments belonging to Jewish physicians and dentists have to be marked as such with the Star of Zion. Aryan physicians are not permitted to treat Jews. Jews are not allowed to run pharmacies. Dispensing medicines to Jews in pharmacies is subject to various restrictions (for example, there was a ban – albeit never officially announced – on dispensing medicines to Jewish children under the age of three and to elderly people over the age of sixty).

Jews are barred from the legal and judicial professions entirely; from journalism, teaching, acting, and the arts insofar as they cater to the needs of the Aryan population. Jews are of course barred from all posts in the state administration, local government, and public institutions, and even from private Aryan fiduciary enterprises. Under these circumstances, numerous dismissals took place as early as 1939 and increased at the beginning of 1940, whereby not only were rights to earned pensions forfeited, but notice periods were not observed, nor were any severance payments made. From autumn 1940, anyone who worked for or was employed by a public institution had to prove their Aryan ancestry, which entailed enormous technical difficulties as well as substantial costs and, in the case of mixed marriages, gave rise to complex moral predicaments. Another typical measure was the campaign to stop Jews employing Aryan domestic staff.[48]

47 See Doc. 214, fn. 8.
48 See Doc. 130, fn. 16.

The aforementioned attacks on Jews' personal rights inevitably made it necessary to define who is a Jew. This was done in Governor Frank's aforementioned order of 1 August 1940, according to which the deciding factor is not religion, but race, although membership in the faith community is nevertheless considered a criterion of Semitism:

(a) If three out of four [of a person's] grandparents were Jews, i.e. they were members of Jewish religious communities (even if they were later baptized), *the person concerned is a Jew.*

(b) If two grandparents were Jews in the above sense, *the person concerned is considered a Jew.*

(c) If, in the case of (b), the person in question was a member of a Jewish community on 1 September 1939, or was married to a Jew, *then he is a Jew.*

(d) If, however, the person with two Jewish grandparents was himself a Christian before 1 September 1939, *then he is of mixed blood.*

The Jews and all those who are considered Jews are subject to all the discrimination resulting from the anti-Jewish regulations. Those of mixed blood are treated more leniently, e.g. they do not have to wear armbands or live in the ghettos, but they are still forbidden to work in the public sector, in the legal profession, etc. Keeping one's Jewish descent or one's identity as a member of the Semitic race a secret is severely punished, as is any violation of the regulations concerning visibly displayed insignia (armbands, signs). As a result, the Jewish population is subject to various forms of persecution and harassment. Both officially appointed and unappointed people are constantly on the lookout for any concealment or denial of Semitic ancestry. Denunciations and attempts at coercion or blackmail are becoming more frequent. Many people did not move to Jewish residential districts: they are blackmailed, disguise themselves by changing their names and addresses. Korczak, the renowned author and educator, was arrested because he refused to wear an armband etc.[49]

The German local government agencies are putting a lot of effort into even sometimes quite petty harassment of and discrimination against the Jewish population, and because [these measures] are unpredictable, vicious, and chaotically implemented, everyday life for the Jewish population has become extremely difficult. Regulations restricting the right to own a telephone, for example, prohibitions on walking in certain streets or squares, bans on using benches along avenues and in parks, the obligation to bow to uniformed Germans and to uncover their heads when passing German institutions. In summer 1940, an order was issued in Warsaw requiring Jews to make way for any German they encounter on the street and to step into the road if requested to do so. It got to the point that, for a certain period of time (August–September 1940), many Warsaw Jews stopped wearing hats in the streets altogether in order to avoid being reprimanded and persecuted, which in turn led to assaults and persecution. In the beginning (autumn 1939), before separate quota allocation shops for Jews had been set up, the Germans would force Jews out of queues or make them go to the end of the line. At the

49 Janusz Korczak, pseudonym of Henryk Goldszmit (1878/79–1942), paediatrician and educator; spent a year studying and training in Berlin; director of a Jewish orphanage in Warsaw from 1911; served as a physician in the Russian army during the First World War; wrote numerous children's books as well as publications about his pedagogical experiences and ideas; travelled to Palestine in 1934 and again in 1936; in August 1942, along with the children from his orphanage, deported to Treblinka and murdered there.

Warsaw post office there were separate queues for Jews until the ghetto was established. The caterers' and confectioners' associations were forced to put up signs reading 'Juden Eintritt verboten'[50] or 'Nicht für Juden'.[51] Separate carriages or compartments were set aside for Jews on trains and trams, and certain tram lines (such as the no. 9 in Warsaw) were forbidden to Jews. However, even in the compartments designated for them, Jews were not safe from persecution. If there was no space, soldiers or the gendarmes would unscrupulously remove the Jews (incidentally, this also happened to the Polish population). Since 1 January 1940 Jews have been subject to a general ban on train travel, issued by Governor Frank; in exceptional circumstances they could obtain permits for train travel,[52] but hardly anyone bothered to do so, not least because the district administrators had confidential instructions not to issue such permits. Such prohibitions did not exist in the so-called Neureich. In Cracow, Jews were even forbidden to use horse-drawn carriages. After the ghetto was established in Łódź, all horses were removed from the Jewish residential district, not to mention motor vehicles. There were insufficient means to transport goods.

The discrimination against the Jewish population in relation to food supplies (quota allocation) was outrageously oppressive. The Polish population was also treated despicably in this respect (limited and insufficient rations, irregular supply and distribution, poor quality, and finally some considerable gaps in the list of goods [allegedly] supplied). The Jewish population was treated even worse. The bread ration – the only commodity which was in fact distributed regularly to some extent – was only half the size of the Polish ration (for example, in autumn 1940 the Jewish bread ration was 250 grams every other day, but since then it has been reduced to 100 grams a day). Many other items that were allocated to the Polish population in very small quantities (e.g. meat, sugar, noodles, and similar) were entirely inaccessible to Jews. Jewish restaurants never received any meat allocations. The Jewish population had to pay high administrative fees for ration cards (up to 2 złoty per person). Jews had only a few designated (Jewish) shops sparsely scattered around the city, which made shopping difficult.

The Jews were severely discriminated against in relation to the so-called curfew. Since summer 1940, the curfew for Jews in Warsaw, for example, usually began earlier than for Poles. For Jews the so-called Polizeistunde[53] basically began at 9 p.m.,[54] while for Poles it began at 11 p.m. (and for Germans at midnight, or not at all). After the ghetto was established, but before it was sealed (October 1940), Jews were allowed to remain outside the ghetto only until 7 p.m. There were also other restrictions. For instance, on the anniversary of the founding of the General Government (October 1940), an order was issued in Cracow that on the days of the anniversary celebrations (25–27 October 1940), Jews were only allowed to be on the streets between 5 a.m. and 9 a.m. (Saturday, 26 October 1940), or between 5 a.m. and 10 a.m. (Sunday, 27 October 1940). Violations carried a fine of up to 1,000 złoty or 3 months' imprisonment.[55]

50 German in the original: 'Entry forbidden to Jews'.
51 German in the original: 'Not for Jews'.
52 The ban was imposed on 26 Jan. 1940: see Doc. 130, fn. 15.
53 German in the original: 'curfew'.
54 See Doc. 55.
55 See also Doc. 108.

A significant and, for the Jews, particularly troublesome restriction (incidentally, one which has never been published) is the ban on gathering for communal prayer, as prescribed in the Jewish religion. The houses of prayer have been closed, and prayer is conducted in secret.[56] The ritual bathhouses are closed, and there are incidents of synagogues being burned down (Częstochowa,[57] Ciechanów, etc.) or converted into power stations (e.g. in Przemyśl), warehouses, garages, etc. Jews are rounded up for labour on the Jewish high holidays.

V.

A particularly severe way of tormenting the Jewish population, one which is now widespread, is the establishment of separate, usually *sealed residential districts for Jews (the so-called ghettos)* in designated cities. This is the effective culmination of the process of isolating the Jews from mainstream social life, of confining and subjugating the Jewish population economically, politically, and socially. The perfidy of the occupation policy is particularly blatantly expressed in the fact that, in their public pronouncements, the occupation authorities portray this enslavement of the Jews as the realization of … Jewish autonomy.

At present, separate Jewish residential districts already exist in most cities in the occupied territories. The first ghetto was established in Łódź (early 1940); the subsequent ghettos were established in Łowicz, Warsaw (November 1940), Cracow (March 1941), Lublin (late March 1941), Radom, Kielce, Częstochowa, etc., [and were] often preceded by chaotic evictions and relocations of Jews from one street or district to another. In Cracow the complete evacuation of all Jews from the city was initially ordered (August 1940), along with a ban on their resettlement in certain areas (including Zakopane and the surrounding area). More than 35,000 people were expelled from Cracow as part of this operation. A sealed ghetto was later established in Cracow (early March 1941). In early December 1940, for example, approximately 2,000 Jews in Radom, who had not lived there before the war, were expelled. They were dispersed across the province (near Sandomierz, Busko, etc.) without being provided with any assistance or employment. In addition to the separate Jewish residential districts in larger cities, the question arose of how to isolate those Jews who lived scattered in various villages and small towns. On the one hand, the German press announced the construction of barrack camps 'behind barbed wire' in every district, and in February 1941 there was even an announcement regarding the recruitment of Poles, Ukrainians, and others to guard these camps for Jews.[58] On the other hand, Jews were resettled en masse from certain areas in selected districts to the existing Jewish residential districts in the cities (thus, for example, several thousand Jews from Piaseczno, Kałuszyn, Grójec, Mszczonów, Karczew,[59] etc. were forcibly resettled in the already overcrowded Warsaw ghetto, where hunger and contagious diseases were rampant). They were stripped of all their belongings, apart from small bundles, and they swelled the number of the unemployed in the Warsaw ghetto.

56 The occupation authorities did not allow the Jewish Council to open synagogues in Warsaw until April 1941, when they were permitted to open three: *Gazeta Żydowska*, no. 34, 29 April 1941.

57 See Doc. 67.

58 See Doc. 250.

59 These were small towns around Warsaw from which the Jewish population was expelled in 1941.

It is difficult to estimate the exact number of Jews who are now (December 1941) forced to live in isolated, sealed Jewish residential districts. In Warsaw alone this number exceeds 400,000, in Łódź it reaches 200,000, and in Cracow (following the initial expulsions) it is not less than 50,000. At present, one can assume that approximately 1.5 million Jews are confined 'behind the walls', which amounts to approximately 75 per cent of the total Jewish population in the German occupied territories. These numbers speak for themselves.

The methods by which this 'house arrest' for large masses of people is organized are similar in every city. Since the greatest number of people who have been affected are in Warsaw, it is enough to at least briefly describe the process of ghettoization of the Warsaw Jews.

As early as November 1939 the German authorities informed the Warsaw Religious Community that the Jewish population would have to move out of the city centre and a number of other districts in Warsaw, and that they intended to take hostages to ensure the implementation of this order.[60] Upon hearing this news, many Jews, especially members of the intelligentsia and young people, fled Warsaw (including to the Soviet side). Due to opposition from the military and from the German public health authorities, the plan was abandoned at that time and was only implemented a year later, in autumn 1940. For the whole of that year, Warsaw's Jewish population lived under the threat of the ghetto. In early spring 1940 the marking out of the so-called epidemic containment zone (Seuchensperrgebiet)[61] began, the borders of which largely corresponded to those of the future ghetto, and demarcated the area with walls and warning signs. In July 1940 the Germans issued an order according to which Jews were forbidden to settle outside this 'Seuchensperrgebiet' and the Aryan population was forbidden to settle within its borders when changing apartments. During evictions (e.g. from modern buildings, from buildings on certain streets, etc.) – these occurred on a daily basis – Jews were only allowed to move to an area located behind the so-called 'little walls'[62] (which, incidentally, had been built and constantly modified at the Jewish Community's expense). As a rule, they forfeited all of their belongings, as they were allowed to take almost nothing from the apartments.

In this way the Jewish population was made 'ripe' for the ghetto. Anyone who was able to do so hid their furniture, moved their supplies, and rented or at least secured an apartment in the future ghetto. On 12 October 1940 the definitive order on the establishment of a separate Jewish residential district was issued. Thirteen days were initially given for the move [to the ghetto], but under the pressure of the prevailing circumstances, the deadline was later extended by a further two weeks.[63] The order triggered an enormous, unparalleled mass displacement of people. Approximately 100,000 Jews and 90,000 Poles or Aryans were forced to move.[64] Over 50,000 apartments changed

60 Published in Czerniaków, *Dziennik getta warszawskiego*, pp. 62–63.

61 Polish and German in the original.

62 Until mid 1940 the mandatory residential district for Jews was separated from the rest of the city by approximately 50 individual sections of wall.

63 Directive by Warsaw District Governor Fischer on the Establishment of a Jewish Residential District in Warsaw (2 Oct. 1940) and Second Directive on the Establishment of the Jewish Residential District (31 Oct. 1940), *Amtsblatt des Gouverneurs des Distrikts Warschau*, no. 10, 11 Nov. 1940, pp. 145–148; see also Doc. 180, fn. 6 and 7.

64 In fact, 30,000 Poles were forced to move.

tenants, sometimes two or three times. The housing market; speculation in means of transport; the hunt for food and fuel supplies, which was motivated by concerns that the ghetto might be sealed; and finally the dissolution of various credit and trade relations, etc., as well as the looting of movable property – all assumed enormous proportions. In addition, the ghetto perimeters – even though they had been in preparation for a year – were changed three times during the relocation phase, which resulted in repeated resettlements, additional costs, and confusion. Due to these changes, almost one third of the originally intended area was excluded from the ghetto. The entire administrative apparatus failed: the housing agency, the regulation of transport costs – all of this existed only on paper. Those who were more affluent, more resourceful, or more ruthless came out on top. The poor were sometimes completely ruined and became homeless or moved into cellars, stairwells, attics, kitchens, etc. The cost of this relocation alone (not counting other losses) can be estimated at 10 million złoty.

In the end, Warsaw acquired a ghetto that makes a mockery of civilization. Almost 400,000 people have been crammed into a district that was severely damaged during the September 1939 siege, that has neither modern buildings nor gardens or green spaces, and on top of all this, people have been deprived of work and livelihoods. Of this number, more than 200,000 are direct or indirect victims of the war. They include those resettled from other places (more than 100,000 people), people who have been dispossessed and robbed, people who have lost their jobs, etc., etc. More than 250,000 people found themselves in the ghetto without any financial resources or means of subsistence and have become a burden on the welfare organizations. The housing density – which was already considerable even before the ghetto was established – currently averages 5–6 people to a room. Among the less affluent social classes, more than ten people live in one room, including families who are strangers to each other – children alongside the elderly, the healthy alongside the sick. The sanitary conditions in the ghetto are appalling. Refuse has not been removed from the Warsaw ghetto for months, hospitals are either makeshift or non-existent, and medical supplies are limited. The exact mortality rate in the ghetto is not available, but there is no doubt that it is likely to be high (disease, hunger). There are also reports of suicides precipitated by psychological shock and financial ruin. The pre-harvest drought in 1941 led to further food supply shortages, and has had dramatic consequences. In April 1941, for example, 2,060 people were buried in the Jewish cemetery, of whom 1,998 were buried free of charge (the homeless from shelters, the dead on the street, etc.). In May more than 3,800 people died, in June 4,300, and in autumn over 5,000 people died per month, which leads to the enormously high mortality rate of 15 per cent annually. In some houses, for example at 12 Lubecki Street, entire families perished. At 3 Krochmalna Street one third of the residents died within three months. There is practically no opportunity to leave the ghetto. Even Aryans can obtain an entry permit only with great difficulty and only in exceptional circumstances. As for the Jews, only Jewish Community employees and members of the Jewish militia (Order Service) receive permits, and infrequently a few others. Recently rumours have been circulating that the mail for the ghetto is to be specially censored at the Transferstelle. The Transferstelle is becoming the sole legal intermediary for contact with the sealed Jewish residential district. Although illegal communication is flourishing, it is extremely risky because the ghetto perimeters are constantly patrolled by the police: the German Ordnungspolizei[65] (brutal and ruthless), the Polish police (powerless), and the

Jewish police (timid and overzealous). These police forces are corrupt, demoralized, and loathed by the entire population.

In economic terms the ghetto is dead. The existing reserves of goods and raw materials have either been confiscated and taken away or are being traded illegally, which is becoming increasingly difficult to detect. New raw materials and heating fuel are not legally allowed in. The market for goods (e.g. the countryside and other cities) is accessible only through the German inspection and Transfer Bureau (the so-called Transferstelle), and is therefore de facto irrelevant, as the imposed price regulations have killed any potential trade initiatives. Moreover, the Transferstelle simply plunders the goods exported from the ghetto: for example, the officials of this institution buy up the goods transported to transit warehouses (at minimal prices) and sell them on at a huge profit. Machines and tools are not repaired and many of them have been confiscated. The credit market has come to a standstill because a number of restrictions have been imposed, and banking transactions have been completely suspended. The Transferstelle is completely dominated by Reichsdeutsche (Party members, the SA), who proceed according to the maxim that the ghetto must make every payment, but may not collect any debts. In addition to trade and industry, which – as far as it was in Jewish hands – has been completely liquidated, skilled crafts and domestic outwork have also suffered greatly. For example, Jewish shoemakers don't receive any leather, the trustees who oversee Jewish buildings do not employ any Jewish plumbers, stove fitters, joiners, etc. According to Jewish statistics, more than 50 per cent of Jewish businesses have gone bankrupt in the course of setting up the ghetto, and the number of employees has sunk to around 10 per cent of pre-war levels overall. The situation continues to deteriorate. The general difficulties brought about by the ongoing war have had an even more profound impact on the ghetto (coal shortages, transport problems, the lack of bank loans, the impact of economic regulation, etc.). The more affluent Jews liquidate their assets, partly by 'smuggling' them over to the Aryan side, but there is no real economic activity. A few new cafés and small variety theatres have sprung up in the ghetto. Although a few trading companies relocated from Aryan neighbourhoods have been revived, the fear of requisitions and economic terror paralyses any more extensive activity. Efforts are being made to open a Jewish bank, and craftsmen are forming cooperatives, primarily to acquire food. The Jewish Community has set up a commission charged with distributing orders and negotiating larger supply deliveries.

Food supply is the primary concern of the Jews in the ghetto. The allocated quotas (the so-called ration cards) – especially on the scale currently delivered – do not cover even one quarter of the bare minimum of the human body's calorific requirements. After all, the current allocation is de facto 100 grams of poor-quality bread per day, and at times even these quantities of bread have not been delivered to the ghetto (disputes over entry permits for the cart drivers!).[66] In mid 1941, for example, the nutritional value of the provisions legally supplied to the ghetto was about 400 calories per person per day, or about 10–15 per cent of the necessary daily requirement. All the rest – especially lard, meat, sugar, potatoes, coal, dairy products, and vegetables – had to be obtained on the free market. For example, 100 per cent of the lard in the ghetto was smuggled in.

65 German in the original: 'Order Police'.

66 See Doc. 213.

Today the free market is in fact a black market, and so the ghetto faces a twofold problem: transportation [of the goods] to Warsaw and their delivery to the ghetto. The occupation authorities make no effort to solve this problem. Apart from the question of rationed goods, the issue of supplying the people in the ghetto with food simply does not exist as far as they are concerned, any more than it does in relation to the remaining urban population (except for the Volksdeutsche). The Germans, however, are aware that the ghetto is supplied with smuggled goods. Many Germans make excellent money from this, which involves both enormous bribes and huge quantities of goods transported by German suppliers using German vehicles. Some articles (mainly vegetables) enter the ghetto more or less legally, while the rest get in only through smuggling, which has become a type of black market in Poland. The German police do prosecute this trade. Scenes straight out of Dante's Inferno are played out at the ghetto perimeters, in which young smugglers, usually Christians, are beaten, there are chaotic pursuits during which gunfire is exchanged, etc. According to Jewish sources, in the first few weeks after the sealing of the ghetto, approximately 30 food smugglers were killed, most of them Poles. Prices in the Jewish residential district surge and fluctuate. For example, a tonne of coal reached around 1,000–1,500 złoty, and a kilogram of bread up to 25 złoty, which in individual cases meant a price difference of 25–30 per cent, to the ghetto's disadvantage. The Polish population rails against the smugglers and accuses the ghetto of demanding excessive supplies of food. In view of this situation, the Jewish Community is trying to take the procurement of food and the operation of soup kitchens for the population (one per house or per block) into its own hands. This campaign has come a long way and has been met with the approval of the ghetto's poor population, but it has been hobbled because the Germans refuse to provide any food for the soup kitchens. The Community has suggested planting allotments, breeding goats and rabbits, setting up communal kitchens, etc. This paints a picture of the dire food situation in the ghetto. The number of deaths from starvation is a proof of this. In August 1941, for example, there were more than 1,500 deaths. Only the affluent circles in the ghetto were still able to reach a satisfactory level of nutrition by late 1941.

VI.

One of the most troublesome methods by which the occupation authorities oppress the Jews is the introduction and organization of so-called forced labour.

Since the very first days of the German invasion of Polish territory, unpaid or poorly paid Jewish labour was exploited for the purposes of the army and the civil administration. This happened by systematically and randomly hunting for people on city streets, regardless of their age, profession, occupation, state of health, etc. Since this labour was unpaid, it was a tempting prospect for businesses, made all the easier by no one being able to effectively defend themselves or object. All German agencies and authorities were deaf and unresponsive in this respect. The Jewish labour force was exploited in many different ways: from road work and repairing railway lines to clearing rubble after bombardment or snow from the streets, to carrying personal suitcases or furniture out of looted Jewish apartments.

In addition to this random 'mobilization' of manpower off the street, there was a rapid shift to a more systematic exploitation of the Jewish labour pool. The German authorities and agencies demanded that the Jewish communities provide contingents of workers on a daily basis (or for other specified periods). In Warsaw, for example, this demand amounted to approximately 12,000 people per day, which was a very substantial number. Significantly, after the employment offices (in agreement with the Jewish Community) introduced remuneration for Jewish workers in September 1940, the demand fell to 500–600 people per day. Instead, a new method of supplying labour emerged: the Gestapo arrested Jews under false pretences, either on the streets or at home, and only released them after they had been forced to work (for free, of course) to clear their debt. This also ceased towards the end of 1940, especially in Cracow.

At the same time, the so-called *Arbeitszwang* practice began to develop.[67] It is based on Governor Frank's order of 20 November 1939, according to which Jews between the ages of 14 and 60 were obliged to spend at least two years in special work camps, which were intended to accustom them to manual labour.[68] This educational objective was to be achieved under the direction of the SS and the police. Implementing regulations were issued in December 1939, requiring the male Jewish population to register (with the religious communities) and forbidding Jews from moving house without permission from the German authorities.[69] Panic ensued, and mass emigration to the Soviet side followed. For the time being, however, no labour camps were actually set up – except for the so-called work battalions, which provided manpower for local projects (e.g. for roadworks, military construction, etc.). Only in late spring and summer 1940 did Jews begin to be called up in certain places (Warsaw, Łowicz, Międzyrzec, Lublin, etc.) to work outside the cities, mainly in the Lublin area. The work was either agricultural or involved special construction projects (roads, military buildings, river regulation, etc.). Not much is known about the extent of these conscriptions, but they do not seem to have been very significant, perhaps because of their experimental character. Approximately 4,000 people were drafted from Warsaw (out of a total of over 115,000 people who registered). The Jewish communities decided who was to be subject to conscription, whereby they managed to defuse the situation to some extent, for example by exempting the main breadwinners of families, the sick, and skilled craftsmen. Some people, especially wealthy Jews, bought themselves out of enlistment. In some places the conscription process was utterly chaotic (in Otwock, for example, those who tried to escape were shot at), but again these were not large contingents.

Housing, food, and the work itself were found to be of a very poor standard. Those who were drafted had to provide their own equipment (clothing, blankets, certain tools), although to some extent the Jewish communities took on this task by collecting public donations [for this purpose]. The conscripts were billeted in barns, dilapidated houses, and abandoned factory buildings. In such conditions, dirt and lice prevailed. There were no bathing facilities, [so] dysentery and other diseases were rampant. Food was scarce and of poor quality. The Jewish communities either organized additional food supplies or took on full responsibility for supplying these pseudo-camps with food. Diseases spread, and the number of people discharged or found to be unfit [for work] was high. Desertion was rare – due to the severe punishments. The Jews regarded these camps – wrongly, of course – as a variation on Oświęcim or Mauthausen.

67 German in the original: 'forced labour'.
68 Correctly: 26 Oct. 1939; see Doc. 27.
69 See Doc. 55.

This whole camp operation is not very extensive thus far. It is difficult to foresee whether it will expand. In spring 1941 it began to take on somewhat larger proportions. The German press reported that, in District Warsaw alone, 25,000 Jews were to be assembled in forced labour camps and employed in agricultural and land-improvement work,[70] road construction, and large-scale regulation work on the Vistula. This would suggest that Zwangsarbeit[71] was to be realized on a larger scale. Rumours even circulated in Jewish circles that the conscription of Jews to undertake employment in the public sector was to be greatly expanded in the General Government in 1941, while the entire Polish workforce would be relocated for labour in the Reich. At the same time, however, some labour camps (e.g. in Józefów near Lublin) were liquidated. In theory, approximately 500,000 people of Jewish nationality could be subject to forced labour. However, this exceeds both the German administration's capacities and its demands. That is why the operation seems to be relatively limited. Jews are thus exempted from working in the Reich, bribes can be paid, and some brutalities are mitigated (e.g. by exempting the main family breadwinners). It is clear that the so-called educational value of the entire operation, so emphatically proclaimed in the occupiers' pronouncements, is non-existent. Those who are conscripted for work – or rather, those who are actually working – are primarily the poor, day labourers, the Jewish lumpenproletariat, those who have never been strangers to physical, often very difficult and poorly paid work. The more affluent elements, the children of Jewish plutocrats, etc. generally know how to get out of it, usually by paying bribes or providing a proxy. Although the failure to appear for work carries severe penalties (up to 10 years in prison), in some cases this threat of punishment is only nominal. The organization and practice of forced labour bear all the hallmarks of torture and persecution but none of the features necessary for training or educational purposes. It is typical of the occupation authorities' approach that, apart from an idea or an initial impulse, there is no systematic implementation, no plan, and no clear objective.

VII.

Jewish cultural and intellectual life (similarly to the Polish case) has been destroyed by the terror of the occupation. Destruction and denial are the guiding principles of the occupation policy in this domain.

In the very first months, the Jewish school system, including even primary schools, was completely annihilated. When the Polish schools (primary and vocational) were reopened, Jewish children were not admitted. Teachers of Jewish descent were also dismissed.[72] The rabbinical schools were closed. In September 1940 the Germans tasked the religious communities with setting up primary and vocational schools, which produced some tangible results. In Warsaw several vocational courses were launched (for locksmiths and mechanics, photographers, electricians, and bookbinders; for girls: tailoring, knitting, making ornamental flowers for clothing, etc.). The primary schools initially operated only to a limited extent (shortage of premises and textbooks), because in the meantime the German authorities withdrew their permission on the grounds that there was a risk of epidemics.

70 See Doc. 263.
71 German in the original: 'forced labour'.
72 See Doc. 56.

It was not until April 1941 that Germans allowed primary schools for about 5,000 Jewish children (with Hebrew as the language of instruction) to open.

Jewish theatre does not exist, and actors of Jewish descent are not permitted to perform for an Aryan audience. Light entertainment performers make their debuts in cafés and bars in the Jewish residential districts of Warsaw, Łódź, Cracow, etc. Polish artists are not allowed to perform any Jewish works (music, poetry, or drama).

The only Jewish publication was the *Gazeta Żydowska*,[73] published in Warsaw (in Polish) under the supervision of the Abteilung für Volksaufklärung und Propaganda.[74] This paper (which, incidentally, is generally better edited than the *Nowy Kurier Warszawski* for the Poles) has a poor reputation and has failed to earn either trust or recognition. Apart from that, nothing else is published for the Jews. Jewish books and books by Jewish authors (even if written in or translated into Polish) were banned, regardless of their content or intellectual orientation. In bookshops and lending libraries, these works were struck from the catalogues and either removed or impounded on the spot. The great Judaic library in Warsaw was confiscated and taken away; the rich holdings of the Berson Museum[75] (ancient Jewish artefacts, antiques, and manuscripts) were also looted and taken away.

The Jews' social life is shattered and paralysed. All political organizations, such as the Association of Jewish War Veterans,[76] the Association of Jewish Independence Fighters,[77] the Jewish Student Organization, political parties, Zionist organizations, etc. are wasting away underground. Economic associations are in the hands of Treuhänder.[78] There are only a few charitable and welfare organizations, and even this work is beset with significant and increasing difficulties.

The Jewish intelligentsia shares the tragic fate of the Polish intelligentsia, but with the essential difference that victims of violence among the Jews are the exception. Jewish lawyers, engineers, and even physicians have been dismissed and removed from their posts, but Jewish lawyers, for example, have not experienced even a fraction of the great catastrophe that befell the Polish legal profession. Jews are not permitted to hold public office. The presence of Jews on the management and supervisory boards of industrial concerns, banks, and the like is now unthinkable: they were removed from those positions in early 1940. After the ghetto was established, the vast majority of the Jewish intelligentsia, alienated not only from the Mosaic faith, but also from Jewish culture, found themselves crammed into the ghetto under conditions which are both unpleasant and demoralizing. They find no sphere of activity there, and they encounter mistrust and rejection at every turn. Thus the Jewish intelligentsia, which, as such, have displayed little resilience of spirit, are living in a state of turmoil and are in the throes of a profound moral and ideological transformation. Bitterness, political agitation, and antipathy

73 The *Gazeta Żydowska* was actually published in Cracow.

74 The name of the department is in German in the original: 'Department of Public Enlightenment and Propaganda'.

75 The Mathias Berson Museum of Jewish Antiquity in Warsaw was founded in 1905 and existed until 1939. After the war its holdings were stored in Lower Silesia, and from there they ended up in museums in Israel, the USA, and elsewhere.

76 Polish: Związek Kombatantów Żydów.

77 Polish: Związek Żydów Niepodległościowców.

78 German in the original: 'trustees'.

towards Poles and Polishness are spreading among them, and they frequently exhibit a longing for communism.

Underground activity, which always begins with the work of the intelligentsia, was and remains weak in Jewish circles. Jewish activists fear provocation and denunciation, and point out that the Gestapo maintains an elaborate network of informants among the Jews. After the ghetto was established, young Jews rushed to join the Order Service[79] and are now revelling in their imaginary power, eagerly cooperating with the German police. The Jewish population as a whole is very hostile to its own militia, and especially accusing it of corruption, egoism, and a lack of national spirit.

A characteristic feature of Jewish cultural life – and one closely associated with the ghetto's existence – is the increasing influence of the rabbinate, which cooperates closely with the communities, as well as the encroachment of Yiddish within the ghetto.[80] The Jewish Community in Warsaw organized a mandatory Yiddish language course for its employees. Candidates for the Order Service are required to know this pseudo-language. There is a trend towards introducing Yiddish as the official internal language of the ghetto and using it on signs. There have been proposals to establish an institution for the entire General Government, with the participation of Jewish scholars and the consent of the occupation authorities, to promote the Hebrew language and to research Jewish issues. Rabbis have been granted wide-ranging powers to supervise family and domestic life. The Community supports them in this, as it is anxious to bring the prevailing public mood under its control and to stifle the widespread criticism levelled against it. The Community, affluent Jewish circles, and the rabbinate are the three factual pillars of Jewish autonomy. They work together closely and deliberately. This block stands in opposition to the proletarian masses and the enclave of Christian Jews who have found themselves in the ghetto. The plight of the latter is unfortunate. The Community does not recognize them and stirs up public feeling against the assimilationists, while the sealing of the ghetto and the rigorous application of the 'Aryan paragraph' make it impossible for them to return to the Polish milieu. Thus they live on the margins, as it were, threatened with complete isolation from the labour market and from social welfare. Despondency and resentment are rife in these circles and are exacerbated by the numerous tragedies which occurred when mixed marriages were torn apart due to the requirement to move to the ghetto. Even before the Jews were ghettoized, the German authorities contrived (sometimes very persistently) to effect separation or divorce in mixed marriages, for example in the case of Polish civil servants married to Jewish women. In Warsaw there are numerous known cases of partners in mixed marriages separating voluntarily and the spouses of Semitic descent going into hiding to escape persecution or humiliation. Intellectuals are the group most affected by this and have had to endure such painful experiences.

On the other hand, many people of Jewish descent have in effect gone underground: they did not move to the ghetto; they are hiding in the countryside, disguising themselves by using Polish names, etc. They sometimes fall victim to intrigue and blackmail, have to buy off police informers, and live in a state of constant nervous tension. [...][81]

79 The Jewish Order Service in the Warsaw ghetto had 2,000 members at most.
80 In this passage, Yiddish is referred to using the pejorative term 'żargon' (literally 'jargon').
81 The following section is the conclusion of the report: 'VIII. Conditions in eastern Poland.'

Glossary

American Jewish Joint Distribution Committee (AJDC, JDC, Joint)
Committee founded in the United States in 1914 to coordinate the relief efforts of American Jewish aid organizations. It provided funding and aid to Jews and Jewish organizations, especially in Eastern Europe. Following the outbreak of the Second World War, its efforts extended to Nazi-occupied and Nazi-controlled territories, including the ghettos, where it supported schools, orphanages, cultural institutions, and other important areas of Jewish life.

Aryan (*Arier*)
Term used in nineteenth-century European racist thought to describe peoples supposedly descended from the Indo-Europeans. It was used in Nazi Germany to support the idea of the inequality of human races and the superiority of 'Aryans', particularly of those with 'German and related blood', over 'non-Aryan races', above all Jews.

Aryanization (*Arisierung*)
Nazi term for the process of robbing Jews of their property and belongings, and excluding them from a 'racially purified' economy. It involved the confiscation or liquidation of Jewish property, assets, and businesses and the forced transfer of these to non-Jews or to the Reich.

Bezirk
An administrative subdivision within a geographical region. In the annexed Polish territories, the term was used as shorthand for Regierungsbezirk, an administrative area that consisted of a number of Kreise.

Blocked account (*Sperrkonto*)
An account from which the holder cannot freely make withdrawals without permission from a third party. The Nazis forced Jews to open blocked accounts as a means of gaining control over their assets.

Bund (short for Algemeyner Yidisher Arbeter-bund in Lite, Poyln un Rusland; General Jewish Labour Bund in Lithuania, Poland, and Russia)
Jewish socialist party formed in 1897 in the Russian Empire. Its Polish section was active until the German invasion in 1939, when it went underground. Members were referred to as Bundists.

Central Resettlement Office (Umwandererzentralstelle, UWZ)
Office founded in November 1939 under the name Office for Resettling Poles and Jews. It was renamed in March 1940 and had its headquarters in Posen (Poznań), with branch offices in Litzmannstadt (Łódź) and Kattowitz (Katowice). It was staffed by members of the Security Police and formed part of the apparatus set up under Himmler as Reich Commissioner for the Strengthening of Germandom. The office was charged with organizing the displacement and deportation of Jews and Poles from the annexed territories to the General Government.

Central Welfare Council (Rada Główna Opiekuńcza, RGO)
Polish welfare organization active in the General Government from 1940 to 1944. The RGO had its headquarters in Warsaw and local offices in all districts. It operated soup kitchens, provided clothing and health services, and supplied aid to orphans and displaced persons. The RGO was under German supervision, but it was in

contact with the Polish underground and cooperated with Jewish relief organizations, including the Jewish Social Self-Help (JSS).

Chief Social Welfare Council (Naczelna Rada Opiekuńcza, NRO)
Umbrella organization consisting of the welfare organizations for the Polish population ([Polish] Central Welfare Council, RGO), the Ukrainian population (Ukrainian Central Welfare Council), and the Jewish population (Jewish Social Self-Help, JSS).

Criminal Police (Kriminalpolizei)
Criminal investigation force that, together with the Gestapo, constituted the Security Police (Sipo).

District (of the General Government)
Administrative region in the General Government which comprised several smaller administrative subdivisions from the Second Polish Republic. There were initially four such districts (*Distrikte*): District Warsaw, District Radom, District Cracow, and District Lublin. A fifth district, District Galicia, was added after the German invasion of the Soviet Union in summer 1941.

District Governor (Gouverneur des Distrikts or Distriktchef)
Head of a district in the General Government.

Einsatzgruppe
Special task force of the Security Police first deployed during the occupation of Austria and the Sudetenland in 1938. They were instructed to monitor political activity and to identify and arrest political opponents and other targeted groups. Following the invasion of Poland (1939) and the Soviet Union (1941), they were tasked with eliminating 'racial and political enemies', and operated as mobile killing units as the German armed forces advanced into Eastern Europe. Additional Einsatzgruppen were formed and deployed as the Germans occupied more countries.

Einsatzkommando
A subunit of an Einsatzgruppe deployed locally in parts of occupied Europe.

Endecja (contracted form of ND for Narodowa Demokracja; National Democracy)
A right-wing nationalist and antisemitic political movement founded by Roman Dmowski in 1897 and active during the Second Polish Republic. In the 1930s, its aims were mostly represented by the National Party (Stronnictwo Narodowe, SN). The movement ceased to exist in 1947.

Freikorps
Nationalist and anti-revolutionary paramilitary groups formed in the wake of Germany's defeat in the First World War. The Freikorps were used by the Reich government to suppress domestic left-wing revolts and patrol the Reich's eastern borders. In 1919 approximately 200,000 men were members of a Freikorps. Many prominent representatives of the Nazi state came from the Freikorps ranks.

Gau (Nazi Party term for 'region')
The largest NSDAP territorial subdivision below the level of the Reich. After the Nazis came to power in 1933, the Gaue increasingly replaced the individual states (Länder) as the regional administrative unit of the Third Reich.

Gauleiter ('Gau leader')
Head of an NSDAP Gau.

Gendarmerie

German rural police force in charge of keeping order in rural areas and smaller municipalities. The gendarmerie was part of the Order Police (Ordnungspolizei).

General Government

German administrative region in occupied central and southern Poland. The General Government was initially divided into four districts: Cracow, Warsaw, Lublin, and Radom. A fifth district, District Galicia, was added in August 1941 after the German invasion of the Soviet Union. The position of governor general was held by Hans Frank from October 1939 to January 1945.

Gestapo (contracted form of Geheime Staatspolizei; Secret State Police)

Secret State Police established by Hermann Göring in 1933 with the aim of combating internal 'enemies of the state'. From 1934 it was led by Heinrich Himmler and in 1936 it became part of Reinhard Heydrich's Security Police. In 1939 the Security Police merged with the SD to form the Reich Security Main Office (RSHA). Thereafter it became known as RSHA Amt IV (Office IV) and was headed by Heinrich Müller. It was divided into five departments: (a) Political Opponents, (b) Sects and Churches, (c) Administration and Party Affairs, (d) Occupied Territories, and (e) Security and Counter-intelligence.

Ghetto

A common term for a poor, densely populated Jewish neighbourhood; originally the name of the restricted Jewish quarter of sixteenth-century Venice. After the German invasion of Poland in 1939, it was used for sections of towns and cities in Nazi-dominated Europe where the Jewish population was concentrated and segregated prior to their deportation. The German administration officially referred to them as 'Jewish residential districts' and imposed a Jewish self-administration run by a Jewish Council or Jewish Council of Elders and headed by a Jewish elder.

Higher SS and Police Leaders (Höhere SS- und Polizeiführer, HSSPF)

Officials appointed by Himmler from 1937 to act as his deputies, responsible for ensuring police control and coordinating the activities of the Security Police, the SD, and the Order Police in all occupied territories and, to a more limited extent, in the Reich.

Home Army (Armia Krajowa, AK)

Polish underground army under the control of the Polish government in exile in London. It was formed in February 1942 from its precursor organization, the Union of Armed Struggle (Związek Walki Zbrojnej, ZWZ), and absorbed most other Polish armed resistance groups. The Polish Home Army was one of the most significant resistance organizations in German-occupied Europe during the Second World War.

Jewish Combat Organization (Żydowska Organizacja Bojowa, ŻOB; Yidishe Kamf Organizatsye)

Jewish armed underground resistance group formed in the Warsaw ghetto on 28 July 1942 with cells in several other ghettos. The ŻOB recruited its members mostly from among the younger left-wing inhabitants of the ghettos. It was one of the driving forces behind the Warsaw Ghetto Uprising in spring 1943.

Jewish Community
Body representing the Jewish inhabitants of a municipality.

Jewish Council (Judenrat) / Jewish Council of Elders (Jüdischer Ältestenrat)
Administrative agency established on German orders in Jewish communities in Nazi-occupied Europe. The first councils were set up in Poland only days after the German invasion in early September 1939. Their tasks were defined on 21 September in instructions from Heydrich to the commanders of the Einsatzgruppen. The councils' main function was to ensure the implementation of anti-Jewish orders and regulations. They were also in charge of providing services to the Jewish population inside and outside the ghettos (housing, medical supplies, food distribution) and organized cultural events. From 1940 they were ordered to provide workers for forced labour and they were later also required to prepare lists with names of Jews to be deported to extermination camps.

Jewish elder (Judenältester)
A Jewish representative appointed by the German authorities in the Jewish communities of the occupied territories.

Jewish Order Service (Jüdischer Ordnungsdienst)
Public order service made up of Jews and formed by the Jewish councils in autumn 1940 on German orders. Its units were deployed by the Jewish councils inside the ghettos and residential districts in occupied Poland and charged with maintaining order as well as enforcing the councils' orders. The service was officially subordinate to the Jewish Council, but in fact it was also under the control of the German police authorities. It was colloquially referred to as the 'ghetto police'.

Jewish Social Self-Help (Żydowska Samopomoc Społeczna, JSS; Yidishe Sotsyale Aleynhilf)
Jewish relief organization founded shortly after the German invasion of Poland under the chairmanship of Michał Weichert. It had its headquarters in Cracow and local branches in a number of ghettos. The JSS was supported by the American Jewish Joint Distribution Committee and coordinated the efforts of welfare organizations across Poland to provide material relief to Jews. It was initially independent of the Jewish councils and under strict German control. On 20 Jan. 1942 the German authorities put the Jewish councils in charge of the local JSS committees. Following mass deportations of ghetto inhabitants as part of Operation Reinhard, the work of the JSS ended in summer 1942. It was replaced by the Jewish Aid Office (Jüdische Unterstützungsstelle, JUS). The JUS continued parts of the JSS's work until it was dissolved in 1943.

Kreis
German administrative subdivision above the local/municipal level; also used to refer to the subdivision of a Nazi Party Gau.

Kreishauptmann (plural: Kreishauptmänner, Kreishauptleute)
Head of a German Kreis administration in the General Government. The Kreishauptleute were in charge of rural administrative subdivisions, while the Stadthauptleute were in charge of larger towns and cities.

Kreishauptmannschaft
German Kreis administration in the General Government.

Kreisleiter

Head of an NSDAP Kreis, a Nazi Party regional subdivision.

Kreisleitung

Leadership of an NSDAP Kreis.

Landkommissar

Official appointed in a rural area at the level below the Kreis in the General Government, subordinate to the Kreishauptmann.

Landrat (plural: Landräte)

Head of a Kreis administration within the German Reich and the annexed territories.

Main Trustee Office East (Haupttreuhandstelle Ost)

German administrative office established by Hermann Göring on 1 November 1939 in Berlin and charged with transferring the assets and property of the Polish state and Polish citizens (both Poles and Jews) in the annexed territories and the Reich to German ownership. A separate Trustee Office was set up for the General Government.

Militärbezirk

Provisional German military administrative unit established after the invasion of Poland in September 1939. In the annexed territories, the two Militärbezirke of West Prussia and Posen were incorporated into the Reichsgaue Danzig-West Prussia and Posen (the latter subsequently renamed Reichsgau Wartheland) respectively in October 1939.

Ministerialdirektor

Senior civil servant in the administration of the German Reich, typically within a ministry.

Ministerialdirigent

High-ranking civil servant in the Reich administration, typically within a ministry. The rank of Ministerialdirigent was above Ministerialrat and below Ministerialdirektor.

Ministerialrat

High-ranking civil servant in the Reich administration, typically within a ministry.

Mischling (person of 'mixed blood')

Classification under Nazi racial law to describe an individual of combined Aryan and non-Aryan, particularly Jewish, descent. The First Regulation on the Reich Citizenship Law (14 November 1935), one of the Nuremberg Laws of 1935, categorized *Mischlinge* according to the number of Jewish grandparents: *Mischlinge* of the first degree ('half Jewish' – one Jewish parent or two Jewish grandparents) and *Mischlinge* of the second degree ('quarter Jewish' – one Jewish grandparent). Marriages were effectively prohibited between Aryans and '*Mischlinge* of the first degree' (those with two Jewish grandparents).

National Party (Stronnictwo Narodowe, SN)

Conservative-nationalist and antisemitic party founded in 1928 during the Second Polish Republic. It constituted the main right-wing opposition to Józef Piłsudski's Sanacja regime. The SN was dissolved in 1947.

Oberfeldkommandantur (OFK)

Headquarters of the German military administration for larger regions.

Oberpräsidium
The highest administrative office in a province of Prussia, headed by an Oberpräsident.

Oberregierungsrat
Civil service rank in a German ministry or other government agency, senior to Regierungsrat.

Old Reich (Altreich)
Germany within its 1937 borders, prior to the annexation of Austria in March 1938 and of the Sudetenland in October 1938.

Operation Reinhard (Aktion Reinhard/Reinhardt)
Code name for the deportation of Jews from the General Government and Bezirk Białystok, as well as other German-occupied regions, and their murder in the Belzec, Sobibor, and Treblinka extermination camps between spring 1942 and summer/autumn 1943. The operation was overseen by Odilo Globocnik and was named after Reinhard Heydrich, Chief of the Security Police and the SD. Heydrich had died on 4 June 1942 of injuries sustained during an assassination attempt in Prague.

Order Police (Ordnungspolizei, Orpo)
German uniformed police force. From 1936 it constituted one of the two branches of the German police, the other one being the Security Police, and it was made up of the Urban Police (Schutzpolizei), Municipal Police (Gemeindepolizei), the gendarmerie (Rural Police), and their respective subdivisions. The Order Police was incorporated into the SS and police apparatus in 1936. During the war, its tasks extended to policing the civilian population in Nazi-occupied territories, and it was also directly involved in killing operations.

Ortskommandantur
Local (town-level) headquarters of the German military administration in the occupied territories.

Regierungspräsident
German civil service official in charge of a Regierungsbezirk (an administrative area in the annexed Polish territories). A deputy Regierungspräsident was known as Regierungsvizepräsident.

Regierungsrat
Senior civil service rank in a German ministry or other government agency, subordinate to an Oberregierungsrat.

Reich Commissariat for the Strengthening of Germandom (Reichskommissariat für die Festigung deutschen Volkstums)
Office created by a decree issued by Hitler on 7 October 1939 which put Himmler in charge of the Reich's overall Germanization policy. Himmler's agenda involved 'retrieving' those allegedly of 'German blood' from among the resident population of the occupied territories, displacing and deporting persons classified as 'of alien race' from the annexed eastern territories, and resettling ethnic Germans from different parts of Eastern Europe there. Beyond these immediate resettlement operations, the Reich Commissariat drew up extensive plans and strategies for 'ethnically reordering' the territories occupied by the Reich.

Reich Germans (Reichsdeutsche)

Designation commonly used by the Nazi regime to distinguish Reich citizens who lived inside the German Reich from Reich citizens who were resident abroad (Auslandsdeutsche) and from foreign citizens with German ethnicity (Volksdeutsche, ethnic Germans). After the annexation of Austria in March 1938, Austrian citizens also acquired the status of Reichsdeutsche.

Reich Security Main Office (Reichssicherheitshauptamt, RSHA)

Office headed by Reinhard Heydrich and created by Heinrich Himmler on 27 September 1939 by merging the SD and the Security Police. This meant combining institutions of the Nazi Party and of the state within a single organization. The RSHA played an important role in the Nazi regime's policies of persecution and extermination. It was tasked with intelligence gathering and criminal investigation. Through the work of Section IV D 4 (later IV B 4), run by Adolf Eichmann, the RSHA was instrumental in the implementation of the 'final solution'.

Reichsamtsleiter

High-ranking Nazi Party official, head of an NSDAP office or section at Reich level.

Reichsgau

Administrative subdivision in some of the territories annexed to the German Reich between 1938 and 1945, including Austria and western and northern Poland.

Reichsgesetzblatt (Reich Law Gazette, *RGBl*)

Official gazette in the German Reich that published laws and regulations between 1871 and 1945.

Reichsleiter (Reich leader)

The most senior political rank in the NSDAP, second only to the Führer. Hitler appointed these individuals to oversee a range of portfolios (i.e. propaganda, law, finance, foreign policy). The different Reichsleiter were collectively designated as the Reichsleitung ('Reich leadership').

Reichsstatthalter (Reich governor)

Officials appointed to head the German states (Länder) and implement Hitler's political orders. The Gauleiter frequently also held the post of Reichsstatthalter. After the German invasion of Poland in September 1939, two new Reichsstatthalter posts were created for the Reichsgaue Posen (later Wartheland) and Danzig-West Prussia.

Sanacja ('healing')

Authoritarian-centrist political movement concerned with 'national healing' in interwar Poland. Its name has become synonymous with the authoritarian regime in power between 1926 and the German invasion in 1939. The movement was led by Józef Piłsudski, who remained the driving force behind the regime until his death in 1935. Marshall Edward Rydz-Śmigły succeeded him as the movement's leader.

SD (abbreviation for Sicherheitsdienst; SS Security Service)

The intelligence service of the SS and NSDAP, founded in 1931 by Heinrich Himmler and headed by Reinhard Heydrich. Its tasks included the detection and surveillance of those classed as political and ideological enemies, especially Jews, communists, Social Democrats, and Freemasons. In 1939 the SD was incorporated into the Reich Security Main Office (RSHA) along with the Security Police (Gestapo and Criminal Police). The SD played an instrumental role in the planning and implementation of the 'final solution'.

Security Police (Sicherheitspolizei, Sipo)
One of the two police branches created by Himmler's reorganization of the entire German police apparatus in 1936 (the other being the Order Police or Orpo). The Security Police was headed by Reinhard Heydrich between 1936 and 1942 and was made up of the Gestapo and the Criminal Police. It was incorporated into the Reich Security Main Office in 1939.

Sejm
The Polish parliament: the lower of the two houses in the two-chamber parliamentary system.

Selbstschutz ('self-protection')
Term used for several ethnic German militias formed with the support of the Nazi regime in the late 1930s in areas of Central and Eastern Europe which had a sizeable ethnic German population, particularly Czechoslovakia, Poland, and Ukraine. Selbstschutz units were involved in many crimes against Poles and Jews in Poland. The units were dissolved in 1940 and many of their members joined the Sonderdienst auxiliary units, the SS, and police forces.

SS (abbreviation for Schutzstaffel; 'protection squadron')
Paramilitary force established in 1925 by the NSDAP and led by Heinrich Himmler from 1929. From 1934 the SS ran the concentration camps. Other branches of the SS included the Waffen-SS and the Allgemeine-SS (membership organization).

Stadthauptmann (plural: Stadthauptmänner, Stadthauptleute)
Head of a German municipal Kreis in the General Government, analogous to Kreishauptmann.

Stadtkommandant
Head of the military administration for a city (Stadtkommandantur).

Stadtkommissar
Official appointed in an urban area at the level below the Kreis in the General Government, subordinate to the Kreishauptmann.

Stadtpräsident
Term used for the German head of the city administration in occupied Warsaw.

Starosta (plural: starostwo)
Head of a Polish regional authority.

Transfer Bureau (Transferstelle)
German administrative office responsible for controlling the flow of goods and services in and out of the Warsaw ghetto from December 1940. Effectively, the Transfer Bureau became the German agency in charge of the official ghetto economy.

Underground archive of the Warsaw ghetto (Oyneg Shabes / Oneg Shabbat or Ringelblum archive)
Secret collection of accounts, notes, and documents compiled by the Oyneg Shabes ('Joy of the Sabbath') group led by historian Dr Emanuel Ringelblum, which used to meet on the Sabbath. The archive was intended to document conditions in the ghetto and form the basis of future books about it. Its collection was buried in 1943, and most of it has been rediscovered. The surviving roughly 25,000 sheets today form one of the most important resources for first-hand accounts of the Holocaust in occupied Poland from a Jewish perspective.

Verordnungsblatt (*VOBl*)
Gazette that published legislation, regulations, and decrees, including anti-Jewish ones, issued by the German authorities in the different occupied territories.

Waffen-SS
Military branch of the SS, established in 1939.

Wehrmacht
Collective term for the German armed forces – army (Heer), air force (Luftwaffe), and navy (Kriegsmarine) – from 1935 to 1945. The Wehrmacht was the successor organization to the Reichswehr (1919–1935). The Wehrmacht High Command (Oberkommando der Wehrmacht, OKW) under Wilhelm Keitel coordinated military activities, while each of the three military branches had its respective high command: OKH (army), OKM (navy), and OKL (air force).

Wójt (plural: wójtowie)
Polish local administrative official.

World Jewish Congress (WJC)
International organization founded in Geneva in August 1936 with the backing of the American Jewish Congress (AJC). Its aim was to represent Jews around the world, promote Jewish unity, support the establishment of a Jewish national home in Palestine, campaign for political and economic equality for Jews across Europe, and combat Nazism and antisemitism. The organization is still active today.

Zionism
Jewish nationalist movement that originated in Central and Eastern Europe in the late nineteenth century and advocated the re-establishment of a Jewish state in Eretz-Israel (Land of Israel – Palestine).

Approximate Rank and Hierarchy Equivalents

NSDAP and Civil Service

NSDAP	Civil Service
Reichsleiter	Staatssekretär
–	Oberpräsident (only in Prussia)
Gauleiter	Unterstaatssekretär
Hauptbefehlsleiter	Ministerialdirektor
Oberbefehlsleiter	Regierungspräsident
Befehlsleiter	–
Hauptdienstleiter	Ministerialdirigent
Oberdienstleiter	–
Hauptbereichsleiter	Ministerialrat
Kreisleiter	
Oberbereichsleiter	Regierungsdirektor
Bereichsleiter	–
Hauptgemeinschaftsleiter	Amtsrat
Ortsgruppenleiter	
Obergemeinschaftsleiter	Oberinspektor
Gemeinschaftsleiter	Inspektor
Haupteinsatzleiter	–
Einsatzleiter	–
Hauptbereitschaftsleiter	Obersekretär
Oberbereitschaftsleiter	Sekretär
–	Verwaltungsassistent
Bereitschaftsleiter	–
–	Assistent
Hauptarbeitsleiter	Assistent
Oberarbeitsleiter	Amtsgehilfe
Arbeitsleiter	–
Oberhelfer	–
Helfer	–
Polit. Leiter-Anwärter	–

Source: Michael Buddrus, *Totale Erziehung für den totalen Krieg: Hitlerjugend und nationalsozialistische Jugendpolitik* (Munich: De Gruyter, 2003).

SS, Wehrmacht, British Army, US Army

SS	Wehrmacht	British Army	US Army
–	Reichsmarschall	–	–
Reichsführer-SS	Generalfeldmarschall	Field Marshal	General of the Army
SS-Oberstgruppenführer	Generaloberst	–	General
SS-Obergruppenführer	General der Waffengattung (Infanterie, Artillerie, etc.)	General	Lieutenant General
SS-Gruppenführer	Generalleutnant	Lieutenant General	Major General
SS-Brigadeführer	Generalmajor	Major General	Brigadier General
SS-Oberführer	–	Brigadier	–
SS-Standartenführer	Oberst	Colonel	Colonel
SS-Obersturmbannführer	Oberstleutnant	Lieutenant Colonel	Lieutenant Colonel
SS-Sturmbannführer	Major	Major	Major
SS-Hauptsturmführer	Hauptmann	Captain	Captain
SS-Obersturmführer	Oberleutnant	First Lieutenant	First Lieutenant
SS-Untersturmführer	Leutnant	Second Lieutenant	Second Lieutenant
SS-Sturmscharführer	Stabsoberfeldwebel	Regimental Sergeant Major (Warrant Officer Class 1)	Sergeant Major
–	Oberfähnrich	–	Senior Officer Candidate
SS-Hauptscharführer	Oberfeldwebel	Staff Sergeant Major (Warrant Officer Class 1)	Master Sergeant
SS-Oberscharführer	Feldwebel	Warrant Officer Class 2	Technical Sergeant
–	Fähnrich	Ensign	Officer Candidate
SS-Scharführer	Unterfeldwebel	Staff Sergeant	Staff Sergeant
SS-Unterscharführer	Unteroffizier	Sergeant	Sergeant
–	Stabsgefreiter	Corporal (senior)	–
–	Obergefreiter	Corporal	Corporal

SS, Wehrmacht, British Army, US Army

SS	Wehrmacht	British Army	US Army
SS-Rottenführer	Gefreiter	Lance Corporal	Acting Corporal
SS-Sturmmann	Obersoldat	Private (senior)	Private First Class
SS-Mann	Soldat	Private	Private
SS-Anwärter	–	–	–

Sources: SS/Wehrmacht ranks: Heinz Antzt, *Mörder in Uniform: Organisationen, die zu Vollstreckern nationalsozialistischer Verbrechen wurden* (Munich: Kindler, 1979). Wehrmacht/US army ranks: Tim Ripley, *The German Army in World War II, 1939–1945* (Hoboken: Taylor and Francis, 2014). Wehrmacht/British army ranks: Ben H. Shepherd, *Hitler's Soldiers: The German Army in the Third Reich* (New Haven: Yale University Press, 2017).

Security Police (SIPO)
Sicherheitspolizei (SIPO)
Chef der deutschen Polizei / Chief of the German Police Chef der SIPO / Chief of the SIPO Kriminaldirigent Reichskriminaldirektor Regierungs- und Kriminaldirektor Oberregierungs- und Kriminalrat Regierungs- und Kriminalrat Kriminaldirektor Kriminalrat / detective chief superintendent Kriminalkommissar / detective superintendent Kriminalinspektor / detective inspector Kriminalobersekretär / detective chief sergeant Kriminalsekretär / detective sergeant Kriminaloberassistent / detective chief constable Kriminalassistent / detective constable Kriminalassistentenanwärter / detective constable candidate

Source: Hans-Christian Harten, *Die weltanschauliche Schulung der Polizei im Nationalsozialismus* (Paderborn: Ferdinand Schöningh, 2018).

Abbreviations

§	section (of a German law, code, or regulation)
§§	sections (of a German law, code, or regulation)
AA	Auswärtiges Amt (German Foreign Office)
AAN	Archiwum Akt Nowych (Central Archives of Modern Records), Warsaw
AG	Aktiengesellschaft (public limited company)
AIP	Archiwum Instytutu Polskiego (Archives of the Polish Institute), London
AIPN	Instytut Pamięci Narodowej (Archive of the Institute of National Remembrance), Warsaw
AIZ	Archiwum Instytutu Zachodniego (Archives of the Institute for Western Affairs), Poznań
AJDC	American Jewish Joint Distribution Committee
AOK	Armeeoberkommando (Army Command)
AP	Associated Press
APCz	Archiwum Państwowe w Częstochowie (State Archive in Częstochowa)
APK	Archiwum Państwowe w Katowicach (State Archive in Katowice)
APKr	Archiwum Państwowe w Krakowie (State Archive in Cracow)
APŁ	Archiwum Państwowe w Łodzi (State Archive in Łódź)
APL	Archiwum Państwowe w Lublinie (State Archive in Lublin)
APP	Archiwum Państwowe w Poznaniu (State Archive in Poznań)
APR	Archiwum Państwowe w Radomiu (State Archive in Radom)
APW	Archiwum Państwowe w Warszawie (State Archive in Warsaw)
Art.	article (of a German law, code, or regulation)
AZHRL	Archiwum Zakładu Historii Ruchu Ludowego w Warszawie (Archive of the Institute for the Peasant Movement), Warsaw
AŻIH	Archiwum Żydowskiego Instytutu Historycznego (Archives of the Jewish Historical Institute), Warsaw
BA-MA	Bundesarchiv-Militärarchiv (German Federal Archives, Military Archives Department), Freiburg im Breisgau
BArch	Bundesarchiv (German Federal Archives)
BCE	Before the Common Era
Bd.	Band (volume)
BuF	Bevölkerung und Fürsorge (Population and Welfare Division, Interior Administration Department)
BŻIH	*Biuletyn Żydowskiego Instytutu Historycznego* (Bulletin of the Jewish Historical Institute, Warsaw)
CdZ	Chef der Zivilverwaltung (chief of the civil administration)
CE	Common Era
CENTOS	Centralne Towarzystwo Opieki nad Sierotami i Dziećmi Opuszczonymi (Jewish Central Association for the Care of Orphans)
CISzO	(also Tsysho) Tsentrale Yidishe Shul Organizatsye (Central Yiddish School Organization)
CKU	Centralna Komisja Uchodźców (Central Refugee Committee)
CPSU	Communist Party of the Soviet Union

CSU	Christlich-Soziale Union (Christian Social Union)
CZA	Central Zionist Archives
DÖW	Dokumentationsarchiv des österreichischen Widerstands (Documentation Centre of Austrian Resistance), Vienna
DNVP	Deutschnationale Volkspartei (German National People's Party)
DUT	Deutsche Umsiedlungs-Treuhand-GmbH (German Resettlement Trustee Office)
DVFP	Deutschvölkische Freiheitspartei (German Völkisch Freedom Party)
DVP	Deutsche Volkspartei (German People's Party)
EWZ	Einwandererzentralstelle (Central Immigration Office)
FDP	Freie Demokratische Partei (Free Democratic Party)
fol.	folio (of an archival source)
FSB	Federal'naya sluzhba bezopasnosti Rossiyskoy Federatsii (Federal Security Service of the Russian Federation)
GARF	Gosudarstvennyy Arkhiv Rossiyskoy Federatsii (State Archive of the Russian Federation), Moscow
GG	General Government
GG P	Generalgouvernement Polen (General Government, Poland)
GmbH	Gesellschaft mit beschränkter Haftung (private limited company)
GPU	Gosudarstvennoe politicheskoe upravlenie (State Political Directorate, also translated as the State Political Administration)
GStAPK	Geheimes Staatsarchiv Preußischer Kulturbesitz (Secret State Archives Prussian Cultural Heritage Foundation), Berlin
HAFIP	Hilfsaktion für notleidende Juden in Polen (Relief Effort for Jews in Need in Poland)
HIA	Hoover Institution Archives, Stanford, CA
HSSPF	Höherer SS- und Polizeiführer (Higher SS and Police Leader)
HTO	Haupttreuhandstelle Ost (Main Trustee Office East)
IfZ-Archives	Archiv des Instituts für Zeitgeschichte München – Berlin (Archives of the Leibniz Institute for Contemporary History), Munich
IKOR	Yidishe Kultur Organizatsye (Organization for Yiddish Culture)
IMT	International Military Tribunal, Nuremberg
JDC	*see* AJDC
JPS	Jewish Publication Society
JSS, also ŻSS	Żydowska Samopomoc Społeczna (Jewish Social Self-Help)
JUS	Jüdische Unterstützungsstelle (Jewish Aid Office)
Kc.	koruna česká (Czech koruna or crown)
KJV	King James Version (Bible)
LHA	Landeshauptarchiv (Regional Main Archive)
MRR	Muzeum Okręgowe w Rzeszowie (Regional Museum in Rzeszów)
MVSN	Milizia Volontaria per la Sicurezza Nazionale (Voluntary Militia for National Security)
NAP	Národní archiv (National Archives of the Czech Republic), Prague
NARA	National Archives and Records Administration, College Park, MD
NCO	non-commissioned officer
ND ('Endecja')	Narodowa Demokracja (National Democracy)
NKVD	Narodnyy komissariat vnutrennikh del (People's Commissariat for Internal Affairs)

NRO	Naczelna Rada Opiekuńcza (Chief Social Welfare Council)
NSDAP	Nationalsozialistische Deutsche Arbeiterpartei (National Socialist German Workers' Party)
NSKK	Nationalsozialistisches Kraftfahrerkorps (National Socialist Motor Corps)
NSV	Nationalsozialistische Volkswohlfahrt (National Socialist People's Welfare Organization)
Oflag	Offizierslager (prisoner-of-war camp for officers)
OGPU	Ob'edinennoe gosudarstvennoe politicheskoe upravlenie, *see* GPU
OKH	Oberkommando des Heeres (Army High Command)
ONR	Obóz Narodowo-Radykalny (National Radical Camp)
OPW	Obóz Polski Walczącej (Camp of Fighting Poland)
ORT	Russian acronym for the 'Society for Trades and Agricultural Labour'
OZON/OZN	Obóz Zjednoczenia Narodowego (Camp of National Unity)
PMJ	*The Persecution and Murder of the European Jews by Nazi Germany, 1933–1945*
PNF	Partito Nazionale Fascista (National Fascist Party of Italy)
p.p.	*per procurationem* (by proxy)
PPS	Polska Partia Socjalistyczna (Polish Socialist Party)
r–v	recto and verso (front and reverse side of a page)
RELICO	Relief Committee for the War-Stricken Jewish Population
RF	Reichsführer
RFSS	Reichsführer-SS
RGO	Rada Główna Opiekuńcza (Polish Central Welfare Council)
RGVA	Rossiyskiy gosudarstvennyy voennyy arkhiv (Russian State Military Archives)
RKF	Reichskommissar für die Festigung deutschen Volkstums (Reich Commissioner for the Strengthening of Germandom)
RM	Reichsmark
RMdI	Reichsministerium des Innern (Reich Ministry of the Interior)
RMfVuP	Reichsministerium für Volksaufklärung und Propaganda (Reich Ministry of Public Enlightenment and Propaganda)
RSHA	Reichssicherheitshauptamt (Reich Security Main Office)
SA	Sturmabteilung (Storm Troopers)
S.A.	Spółka Akcyjna (term for a joint stock company in Poland)
SD	Sicherheitsdienst (SS Security Service)
SKSS	Stołeczny Komitet Samopomocy Społecznej (Social Self-Help Committee for the Capital)
SN	Stronnictwo Narodowe (National Party)
SPP	Studium Polski Podziemnej (Polish Underground Movement Study Trust), London
SS	Schutzstaffel (Protection Squadron)
SSPF	SS- und Polizeiführer (SS and Police Leader)
SSR	Soviet Socialist Republic
Str.	Straße (street)
StS	Staatssekretär (State Secretary)
SZP	Służba Zwycięstwu Polski (Service for Poland's Victory)
TASS	Telegraph Agency of the Soviet Union (Soviet news agency)
ToPoRol	Towarzystwo Popierania Rolnictwa wśród Żydów (Society for the Promotion of Agriculture among Jews)

TOZ	Towarzystwo Ochrony Zdrowia Ludności Żydowskiej (Society for the Protection of the Health of the Jewish Population in Poland)
TsDAVOV	Tsentral'nyy derzhavnyy arkhiv vyshchykh orhaniv vlady ta upravlinnya Ukrayiny (Central State Archive of the Highest Organs of Government and Administration of Ukraine), Kyiv
USHMM	United States Holocaust Memorial Museum, Washington, DC
UWZ	Umwandererzentralstelle (Central Resettlement Office)
v	verso (reverse side of a page)
VB	*Völkischer Beobachter*
VEJ	*Die Verfolgung und Ermordung der europäischen Juden durch das nationalsozialistische Deutschland 1933–1945*
VOBl	*Verordnungsblatt* (law gazette)
VOBl-GG	*Verordnungsblatt für das Generalgouvernement* (law gazette for the General Government)
YIVO	Yidisher Visnshaftlekher Institut (Yiddish Research Institute, Jewish Research Institute)
YVA	Yad Vashem Archives, Jerusalem
ŻOB	Żydowska Organizacja Bojowa (Jewish Combat Organization)
ZWZ	Związek Walki Zbrojnej (Union of Armed Struggle)
ZWZ-AK	Związek Walki Zbrojnej-Armia Krajowa (Home Army)

List of Archives, Sources, and Literature Cited

Archives

Archiv des Instituts für Zeitgeschichte München – Berlin (IfZ-Archives, Archives of the Leibniz Institute for Contemporary History), Munich
Archives of the International Committee of the Red Cross (AICRC), Geneva
Archiwum Akt Nowych (AAN, Central Archives of Modern Records), Warsaw
Archiwum Instytutu Pamięci Narodowej (AIPN, Archive of the Institute of National Remembrance), Warsaw
Archiwum Instytutu Polskiego (AIP, Archives of the Polish Institute), London
Archiwum Instytutu Zachodniego (AIZ, Archives of the Institute for Western Affairs), Poznań
Archiwum Państwowe w Częstochowie (APCz, State Archive in Częstochowa)
Archiwum Państwowe w Katowicach (APK, State Archive in Katowice)
Archiwum Państwowe w Krakowie (APKr, State Archive in Cracow)
Archiwum Państwowe w Łodzi (APŁ, State Archive in Łódź)
Archiwum Państwowe w Lublinie (APL, State Archive in Lublin)
Archiwum Państwowe w Poznaniu (APP, State Archive in Poznań)
Archiwum Państwowe w Radomiu (APR, State Archive in Radom)
Archiwum Państwowe w Warszawie (APW, State Archive in Warsaw)
Archiwum Żydowskiego Instytutu Historycznego (AŻIH, Archives of the Jewish Historical Institute), Warsaw
Arkhiv vneshney politiki Rossiyskoy Federatsii (AVP RF, Foreign Policy Archive of the Russian Federation), Moscow
Archiwum Zakładu Historii Ruchu Ludowego w Warszawie (Archive of the Institute for the Peasant Movement), Warsaw
Biblioteka Narodowa (National Library), Warsaw
Biblioteka Uniwersytecka Katolickiego Uniwersytetu Lubelskiego (Library of the Catholic University of Lublin)
Bundesarchiv (BArch, German Federal Archives), Berlin
Central Zionist Archives (CZA), Jerusalem
Dokumentationsarchiv des österreichischen Widerstands (DÖW, Documentation Centre of Austrian Resistance), Vienna
Geheimes Staatsarchiv Preußischer Kulturbesitz (GStAPK, Secret State Archives Prussian Cultural Heritage Foundation), Berlin
Gosudarstvennyy Arkhiv Rossiyskoy Federatsii (GARF, State Archive of the Russian Federation), Moscow
Hoover Institution Archives (HIA), Stanford, CA
Lavon Institute for Labour Research, Tel Aviv
Moreshet Mordechai Anielevich Memorial Holocaust Study and Research Center, Givat Haviva
Muzeum Okręgowe w Rzeszowie (MRR, Regional Museum in Rzeszów)
Národní archiv (NAP, National Archives of the Czech Republic), Prague
Rossiyskiy gosudarstvennyy voennyy arkhiv (RGVA, Russian State Military Archives), Moscow
Studium Polski Podziemnej (SPP, Polish Underground Movement Study Trust), London
Tsentral'nyy arkhiv Federal'noy sluzhba bezopasnosti Rossiyskoy Federatsii (FSB, Central Archive of the Federal Security Service of the Russian Federation), Moscow
Tsentral'nyy derzhavnyy arkhiv vyshchykh orhaniv vlady ta upravlinnya Ukrayiny (TsDAVOV, Central State Archive of the Highest Organs of Government and Administration of Ukraine), Kyiv

United States Holocaust Memorial Museum (USHMM), Washington, DC
US National Archives and Records Administration (NARA), College Park, MD
Vatican Apostolic Archive
Yad Vashem Archives (YVA), Jerusalem
YIVO Institute for Jewish Research (YIVO), New York

Newspapers, Magazines, and Official Bulletins

Amts-Blatt des Regierungspräsidenten in Kattowitz
Amtsblatt des Chefs des Distrikts Lublin
Amtsblatt des Chefs des Distrikts Warschau
Barykada Wolności
Berliner Börsen-Zeitung
Biuletin
Biuletyn Informacyjny
Contemporary Jewish Record: Review of Events and Digest of Opinion
Daily Herald
Der Arbeitskamerad: Werkzeitschrift für die Betriebsgemeinschaft Commerz- und Privat-Bank
Deutscher Reichsanzeiger
Filmwelt
Gazeta Żydowska
Goniec Krakowski
Illustrierter Beobachter
Jewish News Bulletin
Lodscher Zeitung (from 1941: *Litzmannstädter Zeitung*)
Manchester Guardian
Mitteilungsblatt der Haupttreuhandstelle Ost
Mitteilungsblatt der Stadt Warschau
Morgn-Fray
Nasze Hasła
Neue Zürcher Zeitung
New York Times
Nowe Życie
Nowy Kurier Warszawski
Ostdeutscher Beobachter
Placówka: Organ wsi Polskiej
Reichsgesetzblatt
Soldatenzeitung
Szaniec
Verordnungsblatt des Chefs der Zivilverwaltung Krakau (VOBl-CdZ Krakau)
Verordnungsblatt des Generalgouvernements (VOBl-GG)
Verordnungsblatt (VOBl) des Reichsstatthalters im Reichsgau Wartheland
Walka
Warschauer Zeitung
Wiadomości Polskie
Wirtschaftsmitteilungen: Amtliches Informationsbulletin der Industrie- und Handelskammern in Warschau
Wolność
Yunge Gvardie
Za Naszą i Waszą Wolność

Diaries and Memoirs

Alter Shnur,'"Min Hametzar" – The Diary of Alter Shnur', *Dapim Leheker Hashoah Vehamered*, vol. 1 (April 1951 [Hebrew]).
Biberstein, Aleksander, *Zagłada Żydów w Krakowie* (Cracow: Wydawnictwo Literackie, 1985).
Birenbaum, Halina, *Hope Is the Last to Die: A Personal Documentation of Nazi Terror*, trans. David Welsh (New York: Twayne, 1971 [Polish edn, 1967]).
Czerniaków, Adam, *Adama Czerniakowa dziennik getta warszawskiego, 6 IX 1939–23 VII 1942*, ed. Marian Fuks (Warsaw: Państwowe Wydawnictwo Naukowe, 1983).
Czerniaków, Adam, *The Warsaw Diary of Adam Czerniakow: Prelude to Doom*, ed. Raul Hilberg, Stanislaw Staron, and Josef Kermisz, trans. Stanislaw Staron and the Staff of Yad Vashem (Chicago: Ivan R. Dee, 1999).
Frank, Shloyme, *Togbukh fun lodzher geto* (Buenos Aires: Tsenṭral-farband fun poylishe yidn in argentine, 1958).
Goebbels, Joseph, *Die Tagebücher von Joseph Goebbels*, part 1: *Aufzeichnungen 1923–1941*, vol. 7: *Juli 1939–März 1940*, ed. Elke Fröhlich (Munich: Saur, 1998).
Goebbels, Joseph, *Die Tagebücher von Joseph Goebbels*, part 1: *Aufzeichnungen 1923–1941*, vol. 8: *April–November 1940*, ed. Elke Fröhlich (Munich: Saur, 1998)

Goebbels, Joseph, *Die Tagebücher von Joseph Goebbels*, part 1: *Aufzeichnungen 1923–1941*, vol. 9: *Dezember 1940–Juli 1941*, ed. Elke Fröhlich (Munich: Saur, 1998).

Halder, Franz, *Kriegstagebuch: Tägliche Aufzeichnungen des Chefs des Generalstabes des Heeres 1939–1942*, vol. 2: *Von der geplanten Landung in England bis zum Beginn des Ostfeldzuges (1.7.1940–21.6.1941)*, ed. Hans-Adolf Jacobsen and Alfred Philippi (Stuttgart: W. Kohlhammer, 1963).

Hassell, Ulrich von, *The Ulrich von Hassell Diaries, 1938–1944: The Story of the Forces against Hitler inside Germany*, trans. Geoffrey Brooks (London: Frontline Books, 2011 [German edn, 1946/1988]).

Hohenstein, Alexander, *Wartheländisches Tagebuch aus den Jahren 1941/42* (Stuttgart: DVA, 1961).

Hosenfeld, Wilm, *'Ich versuche jeden zu retten': Das Leben eines deutschen Offiziers in Briefen und Tagebüchern*, ed. Thomas Vogel (Munich: DVA, 2004).

Huberband, Shimon, *Kiddush Hashem: Jewish Religious and Cultural Life in Poland during the Holocaust*, ed. Jeffrey S. Gurock and Robert S. Hirt, trans. David E. Fishman (Hoboken, NJ: Ktav, 1987).

Iwaszkiewicz, Jarosław, *Jarosław Iwaszkiewicz: Notatki 1939–1945*, ed. Andrzej Zawada (Wrocław: Wydawnictwo Dolnośląskie, 1991).

Kaplan, Chaim, *Megillat yissurin: Yoman getto varshah* (Tel Aviv: Am Oved, 1966).

Kaplan, Chaim, *Scroll of Agony: The Warsaw Diary of Chaim A. Kaplan*, ed. and trans. Abraham I. Katsh (London: Hamilton, 1966; New York: Macmillan, 1965).

Klukowski, Zygmunt, *Diary from the Years of Occupation, 1939–1944*, ed. Andrew Klukowski and Helen Klukowski May, trans. George Klukowski (Urbana, IL: University of Illinois Press, 1993).

Klukowski, Zygmunt, *Zamojszczyzna*, vol. 1: *1918–1943*, ed. Agnieszka Knyt (Warsaw: Ośrodek KARTA, 2007).

Lask, I. M. (ed.), *The Kalish Book* (Tel Aviv: Societies of Former Residents of Kalish and the Vicinity in Israel and U.S.A., 1968).

Nelken, Halina, *And Yet, I Am Here!*, trans. Halina Nelken with Alicia Nitecki (Amherst, MA: University of Massachusetts Press, 1999 [Polish edn, 1987]).

Nelken, Halina, *Pamiętnik z getta w Krakowie*, ed. Stanisław Wcisło (Toronto: Polski Fundusz Wydawniczy w Kanadzie, 1987).

Perechodnik, Calel, *Am I a Murderer? Testament of a Jewish Ghetto Policeman*, ed. and trans. Frank Fox (Boulder, CO: Westview, 1996).

Perechodnik, Calel (Calek), *Spowiedź*, ed. David Engel (Warsaw: Ośrodek KARTA, Żydowski Instytut Historyczny, 2016).

Poznański, Jakub, *Pamiętnik z getta łódzkiego*, ed. Horacy Safrin (Łódź: Wydawnictwo Łódzkie, 1960).

Reich-Ranicki, Marcel, *The Author of Himself: The Life of Marcel Reich-Ranicki*, trans. Ewald Osers (London: Phoenix, 2002 [German edn, 1999]).

Reizer, Franciszka, *Dzienniki 1939–1944* (Warsaw: Ludowa Spółdzielnia Wydawnicza, 1984).

Ringelblum, Emanuel, *Ksovim fun geto*, vol. 1: *Togbukh fun varshever geto, 1939–1942*, ed. Artur Eisenbach, Tatiana Berenstein, Bernard Mark, and Adam Rutkowski (Warsaw: Yidish bukh, 1961).

Ringelblum, Emanuel, *Polish-Jewish Relations during the Second World War*, ed. Joseph Kermish and Shmuel Krakowski, trans. Dafna Allon, Danuta Dabrowska, and Dana Keren (New York: Howard Fertig, 1976 [Polish edn, 1958–1959]).

Rosenberg, Alfred, *The Political Diary of Alfred Rosenberg and the Onset of the Holocaust*, ed. Jürgen Matthäus and Frank Bajohr, trans. Kathleen Luft and Jan Lambertz (Lanham: Rowman and Littlefield, 2015 [German edn, 2015]).

Rubinowicz, Dawid, *The Diary of Dawid Rubinowicz*, trans. Derek Bowman (Edinburgh: William Blackwood, 1981 [Polish edn, 1960]).

Rubinowicz, Dawid, *Pamiętnik Dawida Rubinowicza*, ed. Adam Rutkowski (Warsaw: Książka i Wiedza, 1960).

Sierakowiak, Dawid, *The Diary of Dawid Sierakowiak: Five Notebooks from the Łódź Ghetto*, ed. Alan Adelson, trans. Kamil Turowski (New York and Oxford: Oxford University Press, 1996 [Polish edn, 1960]).

Wasser, Hersh, 'Daily Entries of Hersh Wasser', ed. Joseph Kermish, *Yad Vashem Studies*, no. 15 (1983).

Weichert, Michał, *Yidishe aleynhilf 1939–1945* (Tel Aviv: Menoyre, 1962).

Zapruder, Alexandra (ed.), *Salvaged Pages: Young Writers' Diaries of the Holocaust* (New Haven, CT: Yale University Press, 2002).

Zelman, Leon, *After Survival: One Man's Mission in the Cause of Memory* (New York: Holmes & Meier, 1998).

Works Published before 1945

Agnon, Shmuel J., 'Polen – die Legende von der Ankunft', in S. J. Agnon and Ahron Eliasberg (eds.), *Das Buch von den polnischen Juden* (Berlin: Jüdischer Verlag, 1916).

Al masu'ot polin (Merhavya: Hakibutz Ha'artzi Hashomer Hatzair, 1940).

Döblin, Alfred, *Reise in Polen* (Berlin: S. Fischer, 1926).

Dubnow, S. M., *History of the Jews in Russia and Poland from the Earliest Times until the Present Day*, trans. I. Friedlaender (Philadelphia, PA: Jewish Publication Society of America, 1916).

Główny Urząd Statystyczny Rzeczypospolitej Polskiej, *Mały rocznik statystyczny Polski, wrzesień 1939 – czerwiec 1941* (Warsaw: Zakład Wydawnictw Statystycznych, 1990 [English edn, 1941]).

Mintz, Benjamin, and Israel Klausner (eds.), *Sefer hazeva'ot: Te'udot eduyot vedinim veḥeshbonot al sho'at hayehudim bemilḥemet ha'olam hasheniya* (Jerusalem: R. Mas, 1945).

Polish Ministry of Information [in Exile], *The German New Order in Poland*, part 3: *The Persecution of the Jews and the Ghettoes* (London: Hutchinson, 1942).

Roth, Joseph, *The Wandering Jews*, trans. Michael Hofmann (London: Granta Books, 2001 [German edn, 1927]).

Ruppin, Arthur, *Die Juden der Gegenwart: Eine sozialwissenschaftliche Studie*, 3rd edn (Berlin: Jüdischer Verlag, 1920).

Seraphim, Peter-Heinz, *Das Judentum im osteuropäischen Raum* (Essen: Essener Verlagsanstalt, 1938).

Sommerfeldt, Josef (ed. and trans.), *Hie Bürger, hie Jude: Eine Krakauer Kampfschrift aus dem Jahre 1618* (Cracow: Burgverlag Krakau, 1941 [Polish edn, 1618]).

Verhandlungen des Reichstags: IV. Wahlperiode 1939, vol. 460 (Berlin: Verlag der Reichsdruckerei, 1939).

Primary Source Collections

Akten zur deutschen auswärtigen Politik 1918–1945, series D: *1937–1945*, vol. 8/1: *Die Kriegsjahre: 4. September 1939 bis 18. März 1940* (Baden-Baden: Imprimerie Nationale, 1961).

Arkhiv vneshney politiki Rossiyskoy Federatsii, *Dokumenty vneshney politiki*, vol. 22/2 (Moscow: Mezhdunarodnyye otnosheniya, 1992).

Bańkowska, Aleksandra, and Maria Ferenc Piotrowska, *Archiwum Ringelbluma: Konspiracyjne archiwum getta warszawy*, vol. 27: *Żydowska Samopomoc Społeczna w Warszawie (1939–1943)* (Warsaw: Wydawnictwo Naukowe PWN, 2017).

Baranowski, Julian, et al. (eds.), *Kronika getta łódzkiego/Litzmannstadt Getto 1941–1944*, 5 vols. (Łódź: Wydawnictwo Uniwersytetu Łódzkiego, 2009).

Baranowski, Julian, et al. (eds.), *Kronika getta łódzkiego/Litzmannstadt Getto 1941–1944*, vol. 1: *1941* (Łódź: Wydawnictwo Uniwersytetu Łódzkiego, 2009).

Berenstein, Tatiana, Artur Eisenbach, and Adam Rutkowski (eds.), *Eksterminacja Żydów na ziemiach polskich w okresie okupacji hitlerowskiej: Zbiór dokumentów* (Warsaw: Żydowski Instytut Historyczny, 1957).

Berenstein, Tatiana, Artur Eisenbach, Bernard Mark, and Adam Rutkowski (eds.), *Faschismus – Getto – Massenmord:*

Dokumentation über Ausrottung und Widerstand der Juden in Polen während des Zweiten Weltkrieges ([East] Berlin: Rütten & Loening, 1960).

Blet, Pierre, Robert A. Graham, Angelo Martini, and Burkhart Schneider (eds.), *Actes et documents du Saint Siège relatifs à la Seconde Guerre mondiale*, vol. 3: *Le Saint Siège et la situation religieuse en Pologne et dans les pays baltes 1939–1945*, part 1: *1939–1941* (Città del Vaticano: Libreria Editrice Vaticana, 1967).

Blumental, Nachman (ed.), *Te'udot mi-geto lublin – yudenrat le-lo derekh / Documents from Lublin Ghetto: Judenrat without Direction* (Jerusalem: Yad Vashem, 1967 [Hebrew, with preface and introduction in English]).

Borwicz, Michał M., Nella Rost, and Józef Wulf (eds.), *Dokumenty zbrodni i męczeństwa* (Cracow: Wojewódzka Żydowska Komisja Historyczna w Krakowie, 1945).

Czarnocka, Halina, et al. (eds.), *Armia Krajowa w dokumentach 1939–1945*, vol. 1: *Wrzesień 1939 – czerwiec 1941* (London: Studium Polski Podziemnej, 1970).

Datner, Szymon (ed.), 'Działalność warszawskiej "Gminy Wyznaniowej Żydowskiej" w dokumentach podziemnego archiwum getta warszawskiego ("Ring II")', *BŻIH*, no. 73, (1970), pp. 101–132.

Datner, Szymon, Janusz Gumkowski, and Kazimierz Leszczyński, 'Wysiedlanie ludności z ziem polskich wcielonych do Rzeszy', *Biuletyn Głównej Komisji Badania Zbrodni Hitlerowskich w Polsce*, vol. 12 (1960).

Dobroszycki, Lucjan, *The Chronicle of the Łódź Ghetto, 1941–1944*, trans. Richard Lourie, et al. (New Haven, CT, and London: Yale University Press, 1984).

Dunin-Wąsowicz, Krzysztof, Marek Getter, Józef Kazimierski, and Janina Kaźmierska (eds.), *Raporty Ludwiga Fischera Gubernatora Dystryktu Warszawskiego 1939–1944* (Warsaw: Książka i Wiedza, 1987).

Eisenbach, Artur (ed.), *Dokumenty i materiały do dziejów okupacji niemieckiej w Polsce*, vol. 3: *Getto łódzkie* (Warsaw: Centralna Żydowska Komisja Historyczna w Polsce, 1946).

Fatal-Knaani, Tikva (ed.), *The Jewish Underground Press in Warsaw*, vols. 1–3, trans. Shulamit Berman, Sandy Bloom, Moshe Devere, and Naftali Greenwood (Jerusalem: Yad Vashem, 2017–2020).

Friedlander, Henry, and Sybil Milton (eds.), *Archives of the Holocaust: An International Collection of Selected Documents*, vol. 22: *Zentrale Stelle der Landesjustizverwaltungen, Ludwigsburg* (New York: Garland, 1990).

Hansen, Georg (ed.), *Schulpolitik als Volkstumspolitik: Quellen zur Schulpolitik der Besatzer in Polen 1939–1945* (Münster: Waxmann, 1994).

Heim, Susanne, and Götz Aly (eds.), *Bevölkerungsstruktur und Massenmord: Neue Dokumente zur deutschen Politik der Jahre 1938–1945* (Berlin: Rotbuch, 1991).

Kermish, Joseph, (ed.), *To Live with Honor and Die with Honor! Selected Documents from the Warsaw Ghetto Underground Archives 'O.S.' (Oneg Shabbath)*, trans. M. Z. Prives et al. (Jerusalem: Yad Vashem, 1986).

Kermish, Joseph, et al. (eds.), *Ittonut ha-mahteret ha-yehudut be-Warsha*, 6 vols. (Jerusalem: Yad Vashem, 1979–1997).

Kunert, Andrzej Krzysztof (ed.), *Polacy – Żydzi / Polen – Juden / Poles – Jews, 1939–1945: Wybór źródeł / Quellenauswahl / Selection of Documents*, trans. Krystyna Piórkowska and Siegfried Schmidt (Warsaw: Oficyna Wydawnicza RYTM, 2001).

Landau, Ludwik, *Kronika lat wojny i okupacji*, vol. 1: *Wrzesień 1939 – listopad 1940*, ed. Zbigniew Landau and Jerzy Tomaszewski (Warsaw: Państwowe Wydawnictwo Naukowe, 1962).

Lubelska, Wanda, *Listy z getta* (Warsaw: Biblioteka Narodowa, 2000).

Łuczak, Czesław (ed.), *Documenta Occupationis*, vol. 8: *Wysiedlenia ludności polskiej na tzw. ziemiach wcielonych do Rzeszy 1939–1945* (Poznań: Wydawnictwo Instytutu Zachodniego, 1969).

Noakes, Jeremy, and Geoffrey Pridham (eds.), *Nazism 1919–1945*, vol. 3: *Foreign Policy, War and Racial Extermination: A Documentary*

Reader (Liverpool: Liverpool University Press, 2001).

Pospieszalski, Karol Marian (ed.), *Documenta Occupationis*, vol. 4: *Niemiecka lista narodowa w 'Kraju Warty': Wybór dokumentów* (Poznań: Wydawnictwo Instytutu Zachodniego, 1949).

Pospieszalski, Karol Marian (ed.), *Documenta Occupationis*, vol. 5: *Hitlerowskie 'prawo' okupacyjne w Polsce: Wybór dokumentów*, part 1: *Ziemie 'wcielone'* (Poznań: Wydawnictwo Instytutu Zachodniego, 1952).

Pospieszalski, Karol Marian (ed.), *Documenta Occupationis*, vol. 6: *Hitlerowskie 'prawo' okupacyjne w Polsce*, part 2: *Generalna Gubernia: Wybór dokumentów i próba syntezy* (Poznań: Wydawnictwo Instytutu Zachodniego, 1958).

Präg, Werner, and Wolfgang Jacobmeyer (eds.), *Das Diensttagebuch des deutschen Generalgouverneurs in Polen 1939–1945* (Stuttgart: DVA, 1975).

Sakowska, Ruta (ed.), *Archiwum Ringelbluma: Konspiracyjne archiwum getta warszawy*, vol. 2: *Dzieci – tajne nauczanie w getcie warszawskim* (Warsaw: Wydawnictwo Naukowe PWN, 2000).

Sakowska, Ruta, et al. (eds.), *Archiwum Ringelbluma: Konspiracyjne archiwum getta warszawy* (Warsaw: Wydawnictwo Naukowe PWN, 1997–).

Trial of the Major War Criminals before the International Military Tribunal, vol. 26 (Nuremberg: Secretariat of the Tribunal, 1947).

Trial of the Major War Criminals before the International Military Tribunal, vol. 35 (Nuremberg: Secretariat of the Tribunal, 1949).

Trial of the Major War Criminals before the International Military Tribunal, vol. 36 (Nuremberg: Secretariat of the Tribunal, 1949).

Unger, Michal (ed.), *The Last Ghetto: Life in the Lodz Ghetto, 1940–1944* (Jerusalem: Yad Vashem, 1995).

Verzeichnis der Haftstätten unter dem Reichsführer-SS (1933–1945): Konzentrationslager und deren Außenkommandos sowie andere Haftstätten unter dem Reichsführer-SS in Deutschland und deutsch besetzten Gebieten (Arolsen: International Tracing Service, 1979).

Zariz, Ruth (ed.), *Mikhteve halutsim mi-Polin ha-kevushah, 1940–1944* (Ramat Ef'al: Bet lohame ha-getaot, 1994).

Secondary Literature

Adler-Rudel, Salomon, *Ostjuden in Deutschland 1880–1940: Zugleich eine Geschichte der Organisationen, die sie betreuten* (Tübingen: Mohr, 1959).

Alberti, Michael, *Die Verfolgung und Vernichtung der Juden im Reichsgau Wartheland 1939–1945* (Wiesbaden: Harrassowitz, 2006).

Alroey, Gur, 'Jewish Migration, 19th Century to Present', in Immanuel Ness (ed.), *The Encyclopedia of Global Human Migration* (London: Wiley, 2013).

Aly, Götz, *'Final Solution': Nazi Population Policy and the Murder of the European Jews*, trans. Belinda Cooper and Allison Brown (London: Arnold; New York: Oxford University Press, 1999 [German edn, 1995]).

Aly, Götz, and Susanne Heim, *Architects of Annihilation: Auschwitz and the Logic of Destruction*, trans. Allan Blunden (London: Phoenix, 2003 [German edn, 1991]).

Avrutin, Eugene M., Jonathan Dekel-Chen, and Robert Weinberg (eds.), *Ritual Murder in Russia, Eastern Europe, and Beyond: New Histories of an Old Accusation* (Bloomington, IN: Indiana University Press, 2017).

Bacon, Gershon C., 'Poland from 1795 to 1939', in Gershon David Hundert (ed.), *The YIVO Encyclopedia of Jews in Eastern Europe*, vol. 2 (New Haven, CT: Yale University Press, 2008), pp. 1390–1403.

Bacon, Gershon C., *The Politics of Tradition: Agudat Yisrael in Poland, 1916–1939* (Jerusalem: Hebrew University Magnes Press, 1996).

Baron, Salo W., *The Russian Jew under Tsars and Soviets* (New York: Macmillan, 1964).

Bauer, Yehuda, *American Jewry and the Holocaust: The American Jewish Joint Distribution Committee, 1939–1945* (Jerusalem: The Institute of Contemporary Jewry, The Hebrew University; Detroit, MI: Wayne State University Press, 1981).

Baumgart, Winfried, 'Zur Ansprache Hitlers vor den Führern der Wehrmacht am 22. August 1939: Eine quellenkritische Untersuchung', *Vierteljahrshefte für Zeitgeschichte*, vol. 16, no. 2 (1968), pp. 120–149.

Ben-Sasson, Havi, '"Chcemy wierzyć w inną Polskę": Stosunki żydowsko-polskie w podziemnej prasie żydowskiej getta warszawskiego', *Zagłada Żydów: Studia i Materiały*, no. 1 (2005), pp. 96–113.

Bender, Sara, 'Die Juden von Chmielnik unter deutscher Besatzung (1939–1943)', in Christoph Dieckmann and Babette Quinkert (eds.), *Im Ghetto 1939–1945: Neue Forschungen zu Alltag und Umfeld* (Göttingen: Wallstein, 2009), pp. 74–96.

Berenstein, Tatiana, and Adam Rutkowski, 'Prześladowania ludności żydowskiej w okresie hitlerowskiej administracji wojskowej na okupowanych ziemiach polskich (1.IX.1939–25.X.1939)', *Biuletyn Żydowskiego Instytutu Historycznego*, no. 38 (1961), pp. 3–38, and no. 39 (1961), pp. 63–87.

Bering, Dietz, *The Stigma of Names: Antisemitism in German Daily Life, 1812–1933* (Ann Arbor: University of Michigan Press, 1992 [German edn, 1987]).

Beyrau, Dietrich, 'Antisemitismus und Judentum in Polen, 1918–1939', *Geschichte und Gesellschaft*, vol. 8, no. 2 (1982), pp. 205–232.

Birn, Ruth Bettina, *Die Höheren SS- und Polizeiführer: Himmlers Vertreter im Reich und in den besetzten Gebieten* (Düsseldorf: Droste, 1986).

Blatman, Daniel, *En direct du ghetto: La presse clandestine juive dans le ghetto de Varsovie 1940–1945*, trans. Nelly Hansson (Paris: Cerf, 2005 [Hebrew edn, 2002]).

Blatman, Daniel, *For Our Freedom and Yours: The Jewish Labour Bund in Poland, 1939–1949*, trans. Naftali Greenwood (London: Vallentine Mitchell, 2003 [Hebrew edn, 1996]).

Blatt, Thomas T., *From the Ashes of Sobibor: A Story of Survival* (Evanston, IL: Northwestern University Press, 1997).

Böhler, Jochen, *Auftakt zum Vernichtungskrieg: Die Wehrmacht in Polen 1939* (Frankfurt am Main: Fischer, 2006).

Böhler, Jochen, *Der Überfall: Deutschlands Krieg gegen Polen* (Frankfurt am Main: Eichborn, 2009).

Bömelburg, Hans-Jürgen, 'Der Kollaborationsvorwurf in der polnischen und jüdischen Öffentlichkeit nach 1945 – das Beispiel Michał Weichert', in Joachim Tauber (ed.), *'Kollaboration' in Nordosteuropa: Erscheinungsformen und Deutungen im 20. Jahrhundert* (Wiesbaden: Harrassowitz, 2006), pp. 250–288.

Bömelburg, Hans-Jürgen, and Bogdan Musiał, 'Die deutsche Besatzungspolitik in Polen 1939–1945', in Włodzimierz Borodziej and Klaus Ziemer (eds.), *Deutsch-polnische Beziehungen 1939–1945–1949: Eine Einführung* (Osnabrück: fibre, 2000), pp. 43–111.

Bonusiak, Włodzimierz, *Polska podczas II wojny światowej* (Rzeszów: Wydawn. Wyższej Szkoły Pedagogicznej, 1995).

Brechtken, Magnus, *'Madagaskar für die Juden': Antisemitische Idee und politische Praxis 1885–1945* (Munich: R. Oldenbourg, 1997).

Breitman, Richard, and Allan J. Lichtman, *FDR and the Jews* (Cambridge, MA, and London: The Belknap Press of Harvard University Press, 2013).

Broszat, Martin, *Nationalsozialistische Polenpolitik 1939–1945* (Stuttgart: DVA, 1961).

Browning, Christopher R., *The Final Solution and the German Foreign Office: A Study of Referat D III of Abteilung Deutschland, 1940–43* (New York: Holmes & Meier, 1978).

Browning, Christopher R., *Nazi Policy, Jewish Workers, German Killers* (Cambridge and New York: Cambridge University Press, 2000).

Browning, Christopher R., *The Origins of the Final Solution: The Evolution of Nazi Jewish Policy, September 1939 – March 1942* (Lincoln, NE: University of Nebraska Press; Jerusalem: Yad Vashem, 2004).

Brustin-Berenstein, Tatiana, 'Jüdische Soziale Selbsthilfe', in Götz Aly (ed.), *Arbeitsmarkt und Sondererlaß: Menschenverwertung, Rassenpolitik und Arbeitsamt* (Berlin: Rotbuch, 1990), pp. 156–174.

Budnitskiy, O. V. (ed.), *Evreyskaya emigratsiya iz Rossii 1881–2005* (Moscow: Rosspen, 2008).

Burleigh, Michael, *Germany Turns Eastwards: A Study of Ostforschung in the Third Reich* (New York: Cambridge University Press, 1988).

Chinciński, Tomasz, and Paweł Machcewicz (eds.), *Bydgoszcz 3–4 września 1939: Studia i dokumenty, Einsatzgruppen* (Warsaw: Instytut Pamięci Narodowej, 2008).

Cohen, Raya, 'The Lost Honour of the Bystanders? The Case of Jewish Emissaries in Switzerland', in David Cesarani and Paul A. Levine (eds.), *'Bystanders' to the Holocaust: A Re-evaluation* (London: Taylor & Francis, 2002), pp. 146–170.

Cohen, Raya, *The Story of Witnesses to Destruction: Jewish Emissaries in Switzerland, 1939–1942* (Tel Aviv: Am Oved, 1999 [Hebrew]).

Corni, Gustavo, *Hitler's Ghettos: Voices from a Beleaguered Society, 1939–1944*, trans. Nicola Rudge Iannelli (London: Arnold, 2002 [Italian edn, 2001]).

Cüppers, Martin, *Wegbereiter der Shoah: Die Waffen-SS, der Kommandostab Reichsführer-SS und die Judenvernichtung 1939–1945* (Darmstadt: WBG, 2005).

Cygański, Mirosław, 'Z akt szefa zarządu cywilnego przy dowództwie 8 armii niemieckiej, październik 1939 r.', *Najnowsze Dzieje Polski*, vol. 3 (Warsaw: Państwowe Wydawnictwo Naukowe, 1959), pp. 224–230.

Datner, Szymon, Janusz Gumkowski, and Kazimierz Leszczyński, 'Wysiedlanie ludności z ziem polskich wcielonych do Rzeszy', *Biuletyn Głównej Komisji Badania Zbrodni Hitlerowskich w Polsce*, vol. 12 (1960), pp. 3–180, 3F–184F.

Dean, Martin, and Mel Hecker (eds.), *United States Holocaust Memorial Museum Encyclopedia of Camps and Ghettos, 1933–1945*, vol. 2: *Ghettos in German-Occupied Eastern Europe* (Bloomington, IN: Indiana University Press, 2012).

Dieckmann, Christoph, and Babette Quinkert, 'Einleitung', in Christoph Dieckmann and Babette Quinkert (eds.), *Im Ghetto 1939–1945: Neue Forschungen zu Alltag und Umfeld* (Göttingen: Wallstein, 2009), pp. 9–29.

Diner, Dan, *Beyond the Conceivable: Studies on Germany, Nazism, and the Holocaust* (Berkeley, CA: University of California Press, 2000).

Dingell, Jeanne, *Zur Tätigkeit der Haupttreuhandstelle Ost, Treuhandstelle Posen 1939–1945* (Frankfurt am Main: Peter Lang, 2003).

Dmitrzak, Andrzej, *Hitlerowskie kontrybucje w okupowanej Polsce 1939–1945* (Poznań: Wydawnictwo Naukowe UAM, 1983).

Dreifuss (Ben-Sasson), Havi, *Relations between Jews and Poles during the Holocaust: The Jewish Perspective*, trans. Ora Cummings (Jerusalem: Yad Vashem, 2017 [Hebrew edn, 2009]).

Dreifuss, Havi, '"The Work of My Hands is Drowning in the Sea, and You Would Offer Me Song?!": Orthodox Behavior and Leadership in Warsaw during the Holocaust', in Glenn Dynner and François Guesnet (eds.), *Warsaw: The Jewish Metropolis: Essays in Honor of the 75th Birthday of Professor Antony Polonsky* (Leiden and Boston, 2015), pp. 467–495.

Ebbinghaus, Angelika, and Karl Heinz Roth, 'Vorläufer des "Generalplans Ost": Eine Dokumentation über Theodor Schieders Polendenkschrift vom 7. Oktober 1939', *1999: Zeitschrift für Sozialgeschichte des 20. und 21. Jahrhunderts*, vol. 7, no. 1 (1992), pp. 62–94.

Eisenbach, Artur, *The Emancipation of the Jews in Poland, 1780–1870*, trans. Janina Dorosz (Oxford: Blackwell, 1991 [Polish edn, 1988]).

Eisenbach, Artur, 'Jewish Historiography in Interwar Poland', in Yisrael Gutman, Ezra Mendelsohn, Jehuda Reinharz, and Chone Shmeruk (eds.), *The Jews of Poland Between Two World Wars* (Hanover, NH: University Press of New England, 1989), pp. 453–493.

Eisenbach, Artur (ed.), 'Raport Jana Karskiego o sytuacji Żydów na okupowanych ziemiach polskich na początku 1940 r.', *Dzieje Najnowsze*, vol. 21, no. 2 (1989), pp. 179–199.

Engel, David (ed.), 'An Early Account of Polish Jewry under Nazi and Soviet Occupation Presented to the Polish Government-in-Exile, February 1940', *Jewish Social Studies*, vol. 45, no. 1 (1983), pp. 1–16.

Engel, David, *In the Shadow of Auschwitz: The Polish Government-in-Exile and the Jews, 1939–1942* (Chapel Hill, NC: University of North Carolina Press, 1987).

Engelking, Barbara, and Jacek Leociak, *The Warsaw Ghetto: A Guide to the Perished City*, trans. Emma Harris (New Haven, CT, and London: Yale University Press, 2009 [Polish edn, 2001]).

Engelking, Barbara, Jacek Leociak, and Dariusz Libionka (eds.), *Prowincja noc: Życie i zagłada Żydów w dystrykcie warszawskim* (Warsaw: Wydawnictwo Instytutu Filozofii i Socjologii PAN, 2007).

Epstein, Catherine, *Model Nazi: Arthur Greiser and the Occupation of Western Poland* (Oxford: Oxford University Press, 2010).

Evans, Richard, *The Third Reich at War: How the Nazis Led Germany from Conquest to Disaster* (London: Penguin, 2009).

Fahlbusch, Michael, *Wissenschaft im Dienst der nationalsozialistischen Politik? Die 'Volksdeutschen Forschungsgemeinschaften' von 1931–1945* (Baden-Baden: Nomos, 1999).

Fink, Carole, *Defending the Rights of Others: The Great Powers, the Jews, and International Minority Protection, 1878–1938* (Cambridge: Cambridge University Press, 2004).

Förster, Jürgen, 'Wehrmacht, Krieg und Holocaust', in Rolf-Dieter Müller and Hans-Erich Volkmann (eds.), *Die Wehrmacht: Mythos und Realität* (Munich: Oldenbourg, 1999), pp. 948–963.

Friedlander, Henry, *The Origins of Nazi Genocide: From Euthanasia to the Final Solution* (Chapel Hill, NC: University of North Carolina Press, 1995).

Friedrich, Klaus-Peter, *Der nationalsozialistische Judenmord und das polnisch-jüdische Verhältnis im Diskurs der polnischen Untergrundpresse (1942–1944)* (Marburg: Herder-Institut, 2006).

Friedrich, Klaus-Peter, 'Juden und jüdisch-polnische Beziehungen in der Zweiten Polnischen Republik (1918–1939)', *Zeitschrift für Ostmitteleuropa-Forschung*, vol. 46, no. 4 (1997), pp. 535–560.

Friedrich, Klaus-Peter, 'Rassistische Seuchenprävention als Voraussetzung nationalsozialistischer Vernichtungspolitik: Vom Warschauer "Seuchensperrgebiet" zu den "Getto"-Mauern (1939/40)', *Zeitschrift für Geschichtswissenschaft*, vol. 53, no. 7 (2005), pp. 609–636.

Fuks, Marian, 'Małe Judenraty w świetle "Gazety Żydowskiej" 1940–1942', *Biuletyn Żydowskiego Instytutu Historycznego*, nos. 126 and 127 (1983).

Fulbrook, Mary, *A Small Town Near Auschwitz: Ordinary Nazis and the Holocaust* (Oxford: Oxford University Press, 2012).

Gerrits, André W. M., *The Myth of Jewish Communism: A Historical Interpretation* (New York: Peter Lang, 2009).

Gitelman, Zvi, 'Native Land, Promised Land, Golden Land: Jewish Emigration from Russia and Ukraine', *Harvard Ukrainian Studies*, vol. 22 (1998), pp. 137–163.

Głowacki, Albin, *Sowieci wobec Polaków na ziemiach wschodnich II Rzeczypospolitej 1939–1941* (Łódź: Wydawnictwo Uniwersytetu Łódzkiego, 1998).

Golczewski, Frank, *Polnisch-jüdische Beziehungen 1881–1922: Eine Studie zur Geschichte des Antisemitismus in Osteuropa* (Wiesbaden: Steiner, 1981).

Goshen, Seev, 'Eichmann und die Nisko-Aktion im Oktober 1939: Eine Fallstudie zur NS-Judenpolitik in der letzten Etappe vor der "Endlösung"', *Vierteljahrshefte für Zeitgeschichte*, vol. 29, no. 1 (1981), pp. 74–96.

Gottwaldt, Alfred, and Diana Schulle, *Die 'Judendeportationen' aus dem Deutschen Reich 1941–1945: Eine kommentierte Chronologie* (Wiesbaden: Marix, 2005).

Grabowski, Jan, 'German Anti-Jewish Propaganda in the Generalgouvernement,

1939–1945: Inciting Hate through Posters, Films, and Exhibitions', *Holocaust and Genocide Studies* vol. 23, no. 3 (2009), pp. 381–412.

Grabowski, Jan, *Na posterunku: Udział polskiej policji granatowej i kryminalnej w zagładzie Żydów* (Wołowiec: Czarne, 2020).

Grabowski, Jan, and Dariusz Libionka (eds.), *Klucze i kasa: O mieniu żydowskim w Polsce pod okupacją niemiecką i we wczesnych latach powojennych 1939–1950* (Warsaw: Stowarzyszenie Centrum Badań nad Zagładą Żydów, 2014).

Grelka, Frank, 'Rural Hubs of Early Destruction: The Waterworks' Camps in the Lublin District, 1940–1942', *Yad Vashem Studies*, vol. 45, no. 2, 2017, pp. 39–67.

Gross, Jan T., *Fear: Anti-Semitism in Poland after Auschwitz. An Essay in Historical Interpretation* (New York: Random House, 2007).

Gruner, Wolf, *Jewish Forced Labor Under the Nazis: Economic Needs and Racial Aims, 1938–1944*, trans. Kathleen M. Dell'Orto (Cambridge: Cambridge University Press, 2006).

Gruner, Wolf, 'Von der Kollektivausweisung zur Deportation der Juden aus Deutschland (1938–1945): Neue Perspektiven und Dokumente', in Birthe Kundrus and Beate Meyer (eds.), *Die Deportation der Juden aus Deutschland: Pläne – Praxis – Reaktionen 1938–1945* (Göttingen: Wallstein, 2004), pp. 21–62.

Gruner, Wolf, and Jörg Osterloh (eds.), *The Greater German Reich and the Jews: Nazi Persecution Policies in the Annexed Territories, 1935–1945*, trans. Bernard Heise (New York and Oxford: Berghahn, 2015 [German edn, 2010]).

Guesnet, François, *Polnische Juden im 19. Jahrhundert: Lebensbedingungen, Rechtsnormen und Organisation im Wandel* (Cologne: Böhlau, 1998).

Gutman, Yisrael (ed.), *Emanuel Ringelblum: The Man and the Historian* (Jerusalem: Yad Vashem, 2010).

Gutman, Yisrael, *The Jews of Warsaw, 1939–1943: Ghetto, Underground, Revolt*, trans. Ina Friedman (Bloomington, IN: Indiana University Press, 1982 [Hebrew edn, 1977]).

Gutman, Yisrael, and Shmuel Krakowski, *Unequal Victims: Poles and Jews during World War II*, trans. from Hebrew and Polish by Ted Gorelick and Witold Jedlicki (New York: Holocaust Library, 1987).

Haar, Ingo, *Historiker im Nationalsozialismus: Die deutsche Geschichtswissenschaft und der 'Volkstumskampf' im Osten* (Göttingen: Vandenhoeck & Ruprecht, 2000).

Hagen, William W., *Anti-Jewish Violence in Poland, 1914–1920* (Cambridge: Cambridge University Press, 2018).

Haumann, Heiko, *Geschichte der Ostjuden* (Munich: Deutscher Taschenbuch-Verlag, 1998).

Haumann, Heiko, 'Juden in der ländlichen Gesellschaft Galiziens am Ende des 19. und zu Beginn des 20. Jahrhunderts', in Andrea Löw, Kerstin Robusch, and Stefanie Walter (eds.), *Deutsche – Juden – Polen: Geschichte einer wechselvollen Beziehung im 20. Jahrhundert* (Frankfurt am Main: Campus, 2004), pp. 35–58.

Heinemann, Isabel, *'Rasse, Siedlung, deutsches Blut': Das Rasse- und Siedlungshauptamt der SS und die rassenpolitische Neuordnung Europas* (Göttingen: Wallstein, 2003).

Herbert, Ulrich, *Best: Biographische Studien über Radikalismus, Weltanschauung und Vernunft 1903–1989* (Munich: C. H. Beck, 2016).

Hilberg, Raul, *The Destruction of the European Jews*, vol. 1 (New Haven, CT: Yale University Press, 2003).

Hoffman, Eva, *Shtetl: The Life and Death of a Small Town and the World of Polish Jews* (Boston: Houghton Mifflin, 1997).

Horwitz, Gordon J., *Ghettostadt: Łódź and the Making of a Nazi City* (Cambridge, MA: Belknap Press of Harvard University Press, 2008).

Huener, Jonathan, *The Polish Catholic Church under German Occupation: The Reichsgau*

Wartheland, 1939–1945 (Bloomington, IN: Indiana University Press, 2021).

Jacobs, Jack (ed.), *Jewish Politics in Eastern Europe: The Bund at 100* (Basingstoke: Palgrave, 2001).

Jansen, Christian, and Arno Weckbecker, *Der 'Volksdeutsche Selbstschutz' in Polen 1939/40* (Munich: Oldenbourg, 1992).

Jaroszewski, Zdzisław (ed.), *Zagłada chorych psychicznie w Polsce 1939–1945 / Die Ermordung der Geisteskranken in Polen 1939–1945* (Warsaw: PWN, 1993).

Jasiewicz, Krzysztof, *Pierwsi po diable: Elity sowieckie w okupowanej Polsce 1939–1941* (Warsaw: Instytut Studiów Politycznych PAN – Oficyna Wydawnicza Rytm, 2001).

Jastrzębski, Włodzimierz, and Jan Sziling, *Okupacja hitlerowska na Pomorzu Gdańskim w latach 1939–1945* (Gdańsk: Wydawnictwo Morskie, 1979).

Jockheck, Lars, *Propaganda im Generalgouvernement: Die NS-Besatzungspresse für Deutsche und Polen 1939–1945* (Osnabrück: fibre, 2006).

Kaczmarek, Ryszard, *Górny Śląsk podczas II wojny światowej: Między utopią niemieckiej wspólnoty narodowej a rzeczywistością okupacji na terenach wcielonych do Trzeciej Rzeszy* (Katowice: Wydawnictwo Uniwersytetu Śląskiego, 2006).

Kalbarczyk, Sławomir, 'Żydzi polscy wśród ofiar zbrodni sowieckich w latach 1939–1941', *Pamięć i Sprawiedliwość*, vol. 40 (1997/98), pp. 173–194.

Kassow, Samuel D., *Who Will Write Our History? Rediscovering a Hidden Archive from the Warsaw Ghetto* (New York: Vintage Books, 2009).

Katz, Dovid, 'Yiddish', in Gershon David Hundert (ed.), *The YIVO Encyclopedia of Jews in Eastern Europe*, vol. 2 (New Haven, CT: Yale University Press, 2008), pp. 979–987.

Katz, Steven T. (ed.), *The Shtetl: New Evaluations* (New York: New York University Press, 2007).

Kershaw, Ian, *Hitler, 1936–1945: Nemesis* (London: Penguin, 2000).

Kłańska, Maria, 'Juden in Krakau und Kazimierz', in Maria Kłańska (ed.), *Jüdisches Städtebild Krakau* (Frankfurt am Main: Jüdischer Verlag, 1994), pp. 7–39.

Klein, Peter, *Die 'Gettoverwaltung Litzmannstadt' 1940–1944: Eine Dienststelle im Spannungsfeld von Kommunalbürokratie und staatlicher Verfolgungspolitik* (Hamburg: Hamburger Edition, 2009).

Klier, John D., and Shlomo Lambroza (eds.), *Pogroms: Anti-Jewish Violence in Modern Russian History* (Cambridge: Cambridge University Press, 1992).

Kligsberg, Moyshe, 'Di yidishe yugnt-bavegung in Poyln tsvishn beyde velt-milkhomes (a sotsyologishe shtudye)', in Joshua A. Fishman (ed.), *Studies on Polish Jewry, 1919–1939: The Interplay of Social, Economic and Political Factors in the Struggle of a Minority for Its Existence* (New York: YIVO Institute for Jewish Research, 1974), pp. 137–228.

Kligsberg, Moyshe, 'Die jüdische Jugendbewegung in Polen zwischen den Weltkriegen: Eine soziologische Studie', *Osteuropa*, vol. 58, nos. 8–10 (2008), pp. 131–146.

Koehl, Robert Lewis, *RKFDV: German Resettlement and Population Policy, 1939–1945. A History of the Reich Commission for the Strengthening of Germandom* (Cambridge, MA: Harvard University Press, 1957).

Komogorow, Wiktor, et al. (eds.), *Deportacje obywateli polskich z Zachodniej Ukrainy i Zachodniej Białorusi w 1940 roku* (Warsaw: Instytut Pamięci Narodowej, 2003).

Konieczny, Alfred, 'Die Zwangsarbeit der Juden in Schlesien im Rahmen der "Organisation Schmelt"', in Götz Aly, Susanne Heim, and Miroslav Kárný (eds.), *Sozialpolitik und Judenvernichtung: Gibt es eine Ökonomie der Endlösung?* (Berlin: Rotbuch, 1987), pp. 91–110.

Kosmala, Beate, 'Der deutsche Überfall auf Polen: Vorgeschichte und Kampfhandlungen', in Włodzimierz Borodziej and Klaus Ziemer (eds.), *Deutsch-polnische Beziehungen 1939–1945–1949: Eine Einführung* (Osnabrück: fibre, 2000), pp. 19–41.

Kotowski, Albert S., *Hitlers Bewegung im Urteil der polnischen Nationaldemokratie* (Wiesbaden: Harrassowitz, 2000).

Krakowski, Shmuel, 'The Fate of Jewish POWs of the Soviet and Polish Armies', in Asher Cohen, Yehoyakim Cochavi, and Yoav Gelber (eds.), *The Shoah and the War* (New York: Lang, 1992), pp. 233–244.

Krausnick, Helmut, and Hans-Heinrich Wilhelm, *Die Truppe des Weltanschauungskrieges: Die Einsatzgruppen der Sicherheitspolizei und des SD 1938–1942* (Stuttgart: DVA, 1981).

Krzywiec, Grzegorz, 'The Balance of Polish Political Antisemitism: Between "National Revolution", Economic Crisis, and the Transformation of the Polish Public Sphere in the 1930s', in Frank Bajohr and Dieter Pohl (eds.), *Right-Wing Politics and the Rise of Antisemitism in Europe, 1935–1941* (Göttingen: Wallstein, 2019), pp. 61–80.

Kuznitz, Cecile Esther, *YIVO and the Making of Modern Jewish Culture: Scholarship for the Yiddish Nation* (Cambridge: Cambridge University Press, 2014).

Lehnstaedt, Stephan, *Okkupation im Osten: Besatzeralltag in Warschau und Minsk 1939–1944* (Munich: Oldenbourg, 2010).

Leszczyński, Anatol, *Sejm Żydów Korony 1623–1764* (Warsaw: Żydowski Instytut Historyczny, 1994).

Levin, Itamar, *Walls Around: The Plunder of Warsaw Jewry during World War II and Its Aftermath*, trans. Rachel Neiman (Westport, CT: Praeger, 2004 [Hebrew edn, 2003]).

Libionka, Dariusz, 'Antisemitism, Anti-Judaism and the Polish Catholic Clergy during the Second World War, 1939–1945', in Robert Blobaum (ed.), *Antisemitism and Its Opponents in Modern Poland* (Ithaca, NY: Cornell University Press, 2005), pp. 233–264.

Libionka, Dariusz, 'ZWZ-AK i Delegatura Rządu RP wobec eksterminacji Żydów polskich', in Andrzej Żbikowski (ed.), *Polacy i Żydzi pod okupacją niemiecką 1939–1945: Studia i materiały* (Warsaw: Instytut Pamięci Narodowej, 2006), pp. 15–207.

Lipstadt, Deborah E., *Beyond Belief: The American Press and the Coming of the Holocaust, 1933–1945* (New York: Free Press, 1986).

Longerich, Peter, *Heinrich Himmler: A Life*, trans. Jeremy Noakes and Leslie Sharpe (Oxford: Oxford University Press, 2012 [German edn, 2008]).

Loose, Ingo, 'Eksterminacja chorych w Kraju Warty: Stan badań i kontrowersje', in Michał Musielak and Katarzyna B. Głodowska (eds.), *Medycyna w cieniu nazizmu / Medicine in the Shadow of Nazism* (Poznań: Wydawnictwo Naukowe Uniwersytetu Medycznego im. Karola Marcinkowskiego w Poznaniu, 2015), pp. 155–167.

Loose, Ingo, *Kredite für NS-Verbrechen: Die deutschen Kreditinstitute in Polen und die Ausraubung der polnischen und jüdischen Bevölkerung 1939–1945* (Munich: Oldenbourg, 2007).

Loose, Ingo, '"Thus ends … the golden age of Jewry in Germany": The Reactions to the November Pogrom in the Jewish Press in Poland in 1938/39', in Andreas Nachama, Uwe Neumärker, and Hermann Simon (eds.), *Fire! Anti-Jewish Terror on 'Kristallnacht' in November 1938* trans. Adam Blauhut et al. (Berlin: Topography of Terror, 2008 [German edn, 2008]), pp. 128–135.

Löw, Andrea, 'Arbeit, Lohn, Essen: Überlebensbedingungen im Ghetto', in Jürgen Zarusky (ed.), *Ghettorenten: Entschädigungspolitik, Rechtsprechung und historische Forschung* (Munich: Oldenbourg, 2010), pp. 65–78.

Löw, Andrea, *Juden im Getto Litzmannstadt: Lebensbedingungen, Selbstwahrnehmung, Verhalten* (Göttingen: Wallstein, 2006).

Löw, Andrea, 'Ordnungsdienst im Getto Litzmannstadt', in Paweł Samuś and Wiesław Puś (eds.), *Fenomen getta łódzkiego 1940–1944* (Łódź: Wydawnictwo Uniwersytetu Łódzkiego, 2006), pp. 155–167.

Löw, Andrea, 'Zwischen Untergang und Selbsthilfe: Juden im Kreis Radzyń während des Zweiten Weltkrieges', *Zeitschrift für*

Geschichtswissenschaft, vol. 53, no. 8 (2005), pp. 716–735.
Löw, Andrea, and Markus Roth, *Juden in Krakau unter deutscher Besatzung 1939–1945* (Göttingen: Wallstein, 2011).
Łuczak, Czesław, *Pod niemieckim jarzmem (Kraj Warty 1939–1945)* (Poznań: PSO, 1996).
Łuczak, Czesław, *Polityka ludnościowa i ekonomiczna hitlerowskich Niemiec w okupowanej Polsce* (Poznań: Wydawnictwo Poznańskie, 1979).
Madajczyk, Czesław, *Polityka III Rzeszy w okupowanej Polsce* (Warsaw: Państwowe Wydawnictwo Naukowe, 1970).
Marcus, Joseph, *Social and Political History of the Jews in Poland, 1919–1939* (Berlin: De Gruyter, 1983).
Marszałek, Józef, *Obozy pracy w Generalnym Gubernatorstwie w latach 1939–1945* (Lublin: Państwowe Muzeum na Majdanku, 1998).
Matthäus, Jürgen, Jochen Böhler, and Klaus-Michael Mallmann (eds.), *War, Pacification, and Mass Murder, 1939: The Einsatzgruppen in Poland*, trans. Kathleen Luft et al. (Lanham, MD: Rowman & Littlefield, 2014 [German edn, 2008]).
Maurer, Trude, 'The Background for Kristallnacht: The Expulsion of Polish Jews', in Walter Pehle (ed.), *November 1938: From 'Reichskristallnacht' to Genocide*, trans. William Templer (New York: Berg, 1990 [German edn, 1988]), pp. 44–72.
Maurer, Trude, *Ostjuden in Deutschland 1918–1933* (Hamburg: H. Christians, 1986).
Meindl, Ralf, *Ostpreußens Gauleiter: Erich Koch - eine politische Biographie* (Osnabrück: fibre, 2007).
Mendelsohn, Ezra, *The Jews of East Central Europe between the World Wars* (Bloomington, IN: Indiana University Press, 1987).
Mendelsohn, Ezra, *Zionism in Poland: The Formative Years, 1915–1926* (New Haven, CT: Yale University Press, 1981).
Michman, Dan, *The Emergence of Jewish Ghettos during the Holocaust*, trans. Lenn J. Schramm (Cambridge: Cambridge University Press, 2011).
Michman, Dan, *Holocaust Historiography: A Jewish Perspective. Conceptualizations, Terminology, Approaches and Fundamental Issues* (London: Vallentine Mitchell, 2003).
Michman, Dan, 'O okolicznościach ustanowienia warszawskiego Judenratu: Nowy punkt widzenia', *Kwartalnik Historii Żydow / Jewish History Quarterly*, vol. 221, no. 1 (2007), pp. 33–41.
Michman, Dan, 'Reevaluating the Emergence, Function, and Form of the Jewish Councils Phenomenon', in *Ghettos, 1939–1945: New Research and Perspectives on Definition, Daily Life, and Survival. Symposium Presentations* (Washington, DC: The United States Holocaust Memorial Museum Center for Advanced Holocaust Studies, 2005), pp. 67–84.
Michman, Dan, 'Why Did Heydrich Write the Schnellbrief? A Remark on the Reason and on Its Significance', *Yad Vashem Studies*, vol. 32 (2004), pp. 433–447.
Milton, Sybil, 'The Expulsion of Polish Jews from Germany, October 1938 to July 1939', *Leo Baeck Yearbook*, vol. 29, no. 1 (1984), pp. 169–199.
Miron, Guy, and Shlomit Shulhani (eds.), *The Yad Vashem Encyclopedia of the Ghettos during the Holocaust* (Jerusalem: Yad Vashem, 2009).
Młynarczyk, Jacek Andrzej, *Judenmord in Zentralpolen: Der Distrikt Radom im Generalgouvernement 1939–1945* (Darmstadt: WBG, 2007).
Młynarczyk, Jacek Andrzej (ed.), *Polen unter deutscher und sowjetischer Besatzung 1939–1945* (Osnabrück: fibre, 2009).
Modras, Ronald, *The Catholic Church and Antisemitism: Poland, 1933–1939* (Chur: Harwood Academic Publishers, 1994).
Moser, Jonny, *Nisko: Die ersten Judendeportationen* (Vienna: Steinbauer, 2012).
Moser, Jonny, 'Nisko: The First Experiment in Deportation', *Simon Wiesenthal Center Annual*, vol. 2 (1985), pp. 1–30.
Mühle, Eduard, *Für Volk und deutschen Osten: Der Historiker Hermann Aubin und die*

deutsche Ostforschung (Düsseldorf: Droste, 2005).

Müller, Klaus-Jürgen, *Das Heer und Hitler: Armee und nationalsozialistisches Regime 1933–1940* (Stuttgart: DVA, 1969).

Müller, Rolf-Dieter, *Der Zweite Weltkrieg 1939–1945* (Stuttgart: Klett-Cotta, 2004).

Müller, Rolf-Dieter, *Hitlers Ostkrieg und die deutsche Siedlungspolitik: Die Zusammenarbeit von Wehrmacht, Wirtschaft und SS* (Frankfurt am Main: Fischer, 1991).

Musiał, Bogdan, *Deutsche Zivilverwaltung und Judenverfolgung im Generalgouvernement: Eine Fallstudie zum Distrikt Lublin 1939–1944* (Wiesbaden: Harrassowitz, 1999).

Musielak, Michał, *Nazizm w interpretacjach polskiej myśli politycznej okresu międzywojennego* (Poznań: Wydawnictwo Poznańskie, 1997).

Namysło, Aleksandra, 'Wpływ kierownictwa Centrali Żydowskich Rad Starszych Wschodniego Górnego Śląska na postawy i zachowania Żydów wobec rzeczywistości okupacyjnej', in Aleksandra Namysło (ed.), *Zagłada Żydów na polskich terenach wcielonych do Rzeszy* (Warsaw: Instytut Pamięci Narodowej, 2008), pp. 176–185.

Namysło, Aleksandra (ed.), *Zagłada Żydów zagłębiowskich* (Będzin: Instytut Pamięci Narodowej, 2004).

Natkowska, Monika, *Numerus clausus, getto ławkowe, numerus nullus, 'paragraf aryjski': Antysemityzm na Uniwersytecie Warszawskim 1931–1939* (Warsaw: Żydowski Instytut Historyczny, 1999).

Offer, Miriam, *White Coats in the Ghetto: Jewish Medicine in Poland during the Holocaust*, trans. Naftali Greenwood (Jerusalem: Yad Vashem, 2020 [Hebrew edn, 2015]).

Östreich, Cornelia, *'Des rauhen Winters ungeachtet ...': Die Auswanderung Posener Juden nach Amerika im 19. Jahrhundert* (Hamburg: Dölling & Galitz, 1997).

Pätzold, Kurt (ed.), *Verfolgung, Vertreibung, Vernichtung: Dokumente des faschistischen Antisemitismus 1933 bis 1942* (Frankfurt am Main: Rödenberg, 1984).

Petersen, Hans-Christian, *Bevölkerungsökonomie, Ostforschung, Politik: Eine biographische Studie zu Peter-Heinz Seraphim (1902–1979)* (Osnabrück: fibre, 2007).

Pickhan, Gertrud, *'Gegen den Strom': Der Allgemeine Jüdische Arbeiterbund 'Bund' in Polen 1918–1939* (Stuttgart: DVA, 2001).

Pickhan, Gertrud, 'Polen', in Wolfgang Benz (ed.), *Handbuch des Antisemitismus: Judenfeindschaft in Geschichte und Gegenwart*, vol. 1: *Länder und Regionen* (Munich: De Gruyter Saur, 2008), pp. 276–283.

Pilichowski, Czesław (ed.), *Obozy hitlerowskie na ziemiach polskich 1939–1945: Informator encyklopedyczny* (Warsaw: Państwowe Wydawnictwo Naukowe, 1979).

Podolska, Aldona, *Służba Porządkowa w getcie warszawskim w latach 1940–1943* (Warsaw: Wydawnictwo Fundacji 'Historia pro Futuro', 1996).

Pohl, Dieter, 'Die Reichsgaue Danzig-Westpreußen und Wartheland: Koloniale Verwaltung oder Modell für die zukünftige Gauverwaltung?', in Jürgen John, Horst Möller, and Thomas Schaarschmidt (eds.), *Die NS-Gaue: Regionale Mittelinstanzen im zentralistischen 'Führerstaat'* (Munich: Oldenbourg, 2007), pp. 395–405.

Pohl, Dieter, 'Ghettos im Holocaust: Zum Stand der historischen Forschung', in Jürgen Zarusky (ed.), *Ghettorenten: Entschädigungspolitik, Rechtsprechung und historische Forschung* (Munich: Oldenbourg, 2010), pp. 39–50.

Polit, Monika, *Mordechaj Chaim Rumkowski – Wahrheit und Legende: 'Meine jüdische Seele fürchtet den Tag des Gerichts nicht'*, trans. Jürgen Hensel, Heidemarie Petersen, and Małgorzata Sparenberg (Osnabrück: fibre, 2017 [Polish edn, 2012]).

Pollmann, Viktoria, *Untermieter im christlichen Haus: Die Kirche und die 'jüdische Frage' in Polen anhand der Bistumspresse der Metropolie Krakau 1926–1939* (Wiesbaden: Harrassowitz, 2001).

Polonsky, Antony, *The Jews in Poland and Russia*, vol. 1: *1350–1881* (Oxford: Littman Library, 2009).

Polonsky, Antony, 'Przytyk Pogrom', in Gershon David Hundert (ed.), *The YIVO Encyclopedia of Jews in Eastern Europe*, vol. 2 (New Haven, CT: Yale University Press, 2008), pp. 1482–1483.

Prais, Lea, *Displaced Persons at Home: Refugees in the Fabric of Jewish Life in Warsaw, September 1939–July 1942*, trans. Naftali Greenwood (Jerusalem: Yad Vashem, 2015).

Pufelska, Agnieszka, *Die 'Judäo-Kommune': Ein Feindbild in Polen. Das polnische Selbstverständnis im Schatten des Antisemitismus 1939–1948* (Paderborn: Ferdinand Schöningh, 2007).

Radziwończyk, Kazimierz, '"Akcja Tannenberg" grup operacyjnych *Sipo* i *SD* w Polsce jesienią 1939 r.', *Przegląd Zachodni*, vol. 22, no. 5 (1966), pp. 94–118.

Reder, Eva, *Antijüdische Pogrome in Polen im 20. Jahrhundert: Gewaltausbrüche im Schatten der Staatsbildung 1918–1920 und 1945–1946* (Marburg: Herder-Institut, 2019).

Rice, Monika, 'Envisioning Poles: Polish-Jewish Relations at the Beginning of the German Occupation', *Yad Vashem Studies*, vol. 46, no. 1 (2018), pp. 11–40.

Rieß, Volker, *Die Anfänge der Vernichtung 'lebensunwerten Lebens' in den Reichsgauen Danzig-Westpreußen und Wartheland 1939/40* (Frankfurt am Main: Peter Lang, 1995).

Rohde, Horst, 'Hitlers erster "Blitzkrieg" und seine Auswirkungen auf Nordosteuropa', in Klaus A. Maier, Horst Rohde, Bernd Stegemann, and Hans Umbreit, *Das Deutsche Reich und der Zweite Weltkrieg*, vol. 2: *Die Errichtung der Hegemonie auf dem europäischen Kontinent* (Stuttgart: DVA, 1979), pp. 79–158.

Röhr, Werner, Elke Heckert, and Wolfgang Schumann (eds.), *Nacht über Europa*, vol. 2: *Die faschistische Okkupationspolitik in Polen (1939–1945)* (Cologne: Pahl-Rugenstein, 1989).

Roschke, Carsten, *Der umworbene 'Urfeind': Polen in der nationalsozialistischen Propaganda 1934–1939* (Marburg: Tectum, 2000).

Rosenkötter, Bernhard, *Treuhandpolitik: Die 'Haupttreuhandstelle Ost' und der Raub polnischer Vermögen 1939–1945* (Essen: Klartext, 2003).

Rosman, Moshe, 'Poland before 1795', in Gershon David Hundert (ed.), *The YIVO Encyclopedia of Jews in Eastern Europe*, vol. 2 (New Haven, CT: Yale University Press, 2008), pp. 1381–1389.

Rossino, Alexander B., *Hitler Strikes Poland: Blitzkrieg, Ideology, and Atrocity* (Lawrence, KS: University Press of Kansas, 2003).

Roth, Markus, *Herrenmenschen: Die deutschen Kreishauptleute im besetzten Polen – Karrierewege, Herrschaftspraxis und Nachgeschichte* (Göttingen: Wallstein, 2009).

Rubin, Icchak (Henryk), *Żydzi w Łodzi pod niemiecką okupacją 1939–1945* (London: Kontra, 1988).

Rudnicki, Szymon, 'From "Numerus Clausus" to "Numerus Nullus"', in Antony Polonsky (ed.), *From* Shtetl *to Socialism: Studies from Polin* (London: Littman Library of Jewish Civilization, 1993), pp. 359–381.

Rudorff, Andrea, 'Arbeit und Vernichtung *reconsidered*: Die Lager der Organisation Schmelt für polnische Jüdinnen und Juden aus dem annektierten Teil Oberschlesiens', *Sozial.Geschichte Online*, no. 7 (2012), pp. 10–39.

Rutherford, Phillip T., *Prelude to the Final Solution: The Nazi Program for Deporting Ethnic Poles, 1939–1941* (Lawrence, KS: University Press of Kansas, 2007).

Rutowska, Maria, *Wysiedlenia ludności polskiej z Kraju Warty do Generalnego Gubernatorstwa 1939–1941* (Poznań: Instytut Zachodni, 2003).

Sakowska, Ruta, *Die zweite Etappe ist der Tod: NS-Ausrottungspolitik gegen die polnischen Juden, gesehen mit den Augen der Opfer*, trans. Jochen August (Berlin: Hentrich, 1993 [Polish edn, 1986]).

Sakowska, Ruta, 'Instytucje pomocy społecznej w getcie warszawskim: Struktura organizacyjna 1940–1942', in Krzysztof Dunin-Wąsowicz, Janina Kaźmierska, and

Barbara Winnicka (eds.), *Warszawa lat wojny i okupacji 1939–1944*, vol. 2 (Warsaw: Państwowe Wydawnictwo Naukowe, 1972), pp. 119–137.

Sakowska, Ruta, *Ludzie z dzielnicy zamkniętej: Z dziejów Żydów w Warszawie w latach okupacji hitlerowskiej październik 1939–marzec 1943*, 2nd edn (Warsaw: Wydawnictwo Naukowe PWN, 1993).

Schütz, Erhard, and Eckhard Gruber, *Mythos Reichsautobahn: Bau und Inszenierung der 'Straßen des Führers' 1933–1941* (Berlin: Ch. Links, 2000).

Seidel, Robert, *Deutsche Besatzungspolitik in Polen: Der Distrikt Radom 1939–1945* (Paderborn: Schöningh, 2006).

Serwański, Edward, *Wielkopolska w cieniu swastyki* (Warsaw: Pax, 1970).

Shapiro, Robert Moses, *The Polish Kehile Elections of 1936: A Revolution Re-examined* (New York: Holocaust Studies Program, Yeshiva University, 1988).

Shore, Marci, *Caviar and Ashes: A Warsaw Generation's Life and Death in Marxism, 1918–1968* (New Haven, CT: Yale University Press, 2006).

Silberklang, David, *Gates of Tears: The Holocaust in the Lublin District* (Jerusalem: Yad Vashem, 2013).

Sroka, Irena, *Górny Śląsk i Zagłębie Dąbrowskie pod okupacyjnym zarządem wojskowym* (Katowice: Śląski Instytut Naukowy, 1975).

Steffen, Katrin, *Jüdische Polonität: Ethnizität und Nation im Spiegel der polnischsprachigen jüdischen Presse 1918–1939* (Göttingen: Vandenhoeck & Ruprecht, 2004).

Steinbacher, Sybille, 'East Upper Silesia', in Wolf Gruner and Jörg Osterloh (eds.), *The Greater German Reich and the Jews: Nazi Persecution Policies in the Annexed Territories, 1935–1945*, trans. Bernard Heise (New York and Oxford: Berghahn, 2015 [German edn, 2010]), pp. 239–266.

Steinbacher, Sybille, *'Musterstadt' Auschwitz: Germanisierungspolitik und Judenmord in Ostoberschlesien* (Munich: Saur, 2000).

Steinweis, Alan, *Studying the Jew: Scholarly Antisemitism in Nazi Germany* (Cambridge, MA: Harvard University Press, 2006).

Stiller, Alexa, 'Reichskommissar für die Festigung deutschen Volkstums', in Ingo Haar and Michael Fahlbusch (eds.), *Handbuch der völkischen Wissenschaften* (Munich: Saur, 2008), pp. 531–540.

Stiller, Alexa, *Völkische Politik: Praktiken der Exklusion und Inklusion in polnischen, französischen und slowenischen Annexionsgebieten 1939–1945* (Göttingen: Wallstein, 2021).

Stola, Dariusz, *Nadzieja i zagłada: Ignacy Schwarzbart – Żydowski przedstawiciel w Radzie Narodowej RP (1940–1945)* (Warsaw: Oficyna Naukowa, 1995).

Strippel, Andreas, *NS-Volkstumspolitik und die Neuordnung Europas: Rassenpolitische Selektion der Einwandererzentralstelle des Chefs der Sicherheitspolizei und des SD 1939–1945* (Paderborn: Schöningh, 2011).

Szarota, Tomasz, *On the Threshold of the Holocaust: Anti-Jewish Riots and Pogroms in Occupied Europe. Warsaw – Paris – The Hague – Amsterdam – Antwerp – Kaunas*, trans. Tristan Korecki (Frankfurt am Main: Peter Lang, 2015 [Polish edn, 2000]).

Szeląg, Zdzisław (ed.), *Żydzi w Grójeckiem: Słownik – historia, kultura, gospodarka* (Grójec: Towarzystwo Literackie im. Adama Mickiewicza, 2007).

Tomaszewski, Jerzy, *Preludium zagłady: Wygnanie Żydów polskich z Niemiec w 1938 r.* (Warsaw: Wydawnictwo Naukowe PWN, 1998).

Trunk, Isaiah, *Judenrat: The Jewish Councils in Eastern Europe under Nazi Occupation* (New York: Macmillan, 1972).

Trunk, Isaiah, *Łódź Ghetto: A History*, ed. and trans. Robert Moses Shapiro (Bloomington, IN: Indiana University Press, 2006 [Yiddish edn, 1962]).

Umbreit, Hans, *Deutsche Militärverwaltungen 1938/39: Die militärische Besetzung der Tschechoslowakei und Polens* (Stuttgart: DVA, 1977).

Unger, Michal, *Lodz: Aharon ha-getaot be-polin* (Jerusalem: Yad Vashem, 2005).

Unger, Michal, *Reassessment of the Image of Mordechai Chaim Rumkowski*, trans. Naftali Greenwood (Jerusalem: Yad Vashem, 2008).

Urbanek, Joanna, *Everyday Life in the Shadow of Terror: German Occupation in Poland, 1939–1945*, trans. Katarzyna Gucio (Gdańsk: Muzeum II Wojny Światowej, 2015 [Polish edn, 2014]).

Urynowicz, Marcin, *Adam Czerniaków 1880–1942: Prezes getta warszawskiego* (Warsaw: Instytut Pamięci Narodowej, 2009).

Veidlinger, Jeffrey, *In the Midst of Civilized Europe: The Pogroms of 1918–1921 and the Onset of the Holocaust* (New York: Metropolitan Books, 2021).

Volkmer, Gerhard F., 'Die deutsche Forschung zu Osteuropa und zum osteuropäischen Judentum in den Jahren 1933–1945', *Forschungen zur osteuropäischen Geschichte*, vol 42 (1989), pp. 109–214.

Walter, Dirk, *Antisemitische Kriminalität und Gewalt: Judenfeindschaft in der Weimarer Republik* (Bonn: Dietz, 1999).

Wasserstein, Bernard, *Britain and the Jews of Europe, 1939–1945* (London: Institute of Jewish Affairs, 1979).

Weinberg, Gerhard L., *A World at Arms: A Global History of World War II*, 2nd edn (New York: Cambridge University Press, 2005).

Weindling, Paul, *Epidemics and Genocide in Eastern Europe, 1890–1945* (Oxford: Oxford University Press, 2000).

Weiss, Aharon, 'Jewish Leadership in Occupied Poland – Postures and Attitudes', *Yad Vashem Studies*, vol. 12 (1977), pp. 335–365.

Weitbrecht, Dorothee, *Der Exekutionsauftrag der Einsatzgruppen in Polen* (Filderstadt: Markstein, 2001).

Wierzbicki, Marek, *Polacy i Żydzi w zaborze sowieckim: Stosunki polsko-żydowskie na ziemiach północno-wschodnich II RP pod okupacją sowiecką (1939–1941)* (Warsaw: Stowarzyszenie Kulturalne 'Fronda', 2001).

Wildt, Michael, *An Uncompromising Generation: The Nazi Leadership of the Reich Security Main Office*, trans. Tom Lampert (Madison, WI: University of Wisconsin Press, 2009 [German edn, 2003]).

Winstone, Martin, *The Dark Heart of Hitler's Europe: Nazi Rule in Poland under the General Government* (London: Tauris, 2015).

Wojciechowski, Marian, *Die polnisch-deutschen Beziehungen, 1933–1938*, trans. Norbert Damerau (Leiden: Brill, 1971 [Polish edn, 1965]).

Wyman, David S., *The Abandonment of the Jews: America and the Holocaust, 1941–1945* (New York: Pantheon, 1984).

Zalewska, Gabriela, *Ludność żydowska w Warszawie w okresie międzywojennym* (Warsaw: Wydawnictwo Naukowe PWN, 1996).

Żbikowski, Andrzej (ed.), *Polacy i Żydzi pod okupacją niemiecką 1939–1945: Studia i materiały* (Warsaw: Instytut Pamięci Narodowej, 2006).

Żbikowski, Andrzej, *U genezy Jedwabnego: Żydzi na Kresach Północno-Wschodnich II Rzeczypospolitej, wrzesień 1939–lipiec 1941* (Warsaw: Żydowski Instytut Historyczny, 2006).

Zimmerman, Joshua D. (ed.), *Contested Memories: Poles and Jews during the Holocaust and Its Aftermath* (New Brunswick, NJ: Rutgers University Press, 2003).

Zimmerman, Joshua D., *Poles, Jews, and the Politics of Nationality: The Bund and the Polish Socialist Party in Late Tsarist Russia, 1892–1914* (Madison, WI: University of Wisconsin Press, 2004).

Ziółkowska, Anna, *Obozy pracy przymusowej dla Żydów w Wielkopolsce w latach okupacji hitlerowskiej (1941–1943)* (Poznań: Wydawnictwo Poznańskie, 2005).

Żyndul, Jolanta, *Państwo w państwie? Autonomia narodowo-kulturalna w Europie Środkowowschodniej w XX wieku* (Warsaw: DiG, 2000).

Żyndul, Jolanta, *Zajścia antyżydowskie w Polsce w latach 1935–1937* (Warsaw: Fundacja im. K. Kelles-Krauza, 1994).

Index

Newspapers and periodicals are included in the index only if the text contains information about them (e.g. publication period, editors), and not if they are merely mentioned or cited as a source.

C

N

S